Edward Gibbon

The History of
the Decline and Fall of
the Roman Empire

28 SELECTED CHAPTERS

*Edited and annotated, with an Introduction
by Antony Lentin and Brian Norman*

**WORDSWORTH CLASSICS
OF WORLD LITERATURE**

For my husband
ANTHONY JOHN RANSON
with love from your wife, the publisher.
Eternally grateful for your unconditional love,
not just for me but for our children,
Simon, Andrew and Nichola Trayler

10

Readers who are interested in other titles from
Wordsworth Editions are invited to visit our website at
www.wordsworth-editions.com

For our latest list and a full mail-order service contact
Bibliophile Books, 5 Thomas Road, London E14 7BN
TEL: +44 (0)20 7515 9222 FAX: +44 (0)20 7538 4115
E-MAIL: orders@bibliophilebooks.com

This edition published 1998 by Wordsworth Editions Limited
Cumberland House, Crib Street, Ware, Hertfordshire SG12 9ET

ISBN 978-1-85326-499-3

Text © Wordsworth Editions Limited 1998
Introduction © Antony Lentin and Brian Norman

Wordsworth® is a registered trademark of
Wordsworth Editions Limited,
the company founded by Michael Trayler in 1987

Typeset by Antony Gray
Printed and bound in Great Britain by
Clays Ltd, St Ives plc

CONTENTS

INTRODUCTION

Gibbon's *The History of the Decline and Fall of the Roman Empire*, published between 1776 and 1788, is generally acknowledged to be the undisputed masterpiece of English historical writing. Its length alone is a measure of its monumental quality: seventy-one chapters, of which twenty-eight, or two fifths, appear in full in this edition. In its chronological range across thirteen centuries, covering the history of Europe from the second century AD to the fall of Constantinople in 1453, and in the sustained distinction and eloquence of its style, it was immediately recognised as a triumphant realisation of eighteenth-century ideas on how history should be written and as a classic work of literature 'which can only perish with the language itself.'

Edward Gibbon was born at Putney in 1737, the son of a well-to-do but wayward Tory squire. His mother died when he was ten, and his sickly childhood was cheered by a kindly maternal aunt. His formal education was irregular. For two years he attended Westminster School and was also put in the charge of private tutors. Gibbon, however, was essentially self-taught, an omnivorous and precocious bookworm. In his *Memoirs*, he tells of a visit to Stourhead in Wiltshire at the age of 14, where he 'was immersed in the passage of the Goths over the Danube when the summons of the dinner-bell reluctantly dragged me from my intellectual feast.' In 1752, when his health had improved, his father sent him to Magdalen College, Oxford. Neglected by the dons and carried away by his own study of religious books, he converted to Roman Catholicism, a piece of 'childish revolt', as he later wrote, which, though sincere, would have automatically disqualified him from any public career in Protestant Britain. Five years at Lausanne (1753–58) in the care of a Calvinist minister, who taught Latin and ancient history at the Academy there, had a crucial effect on his development. He returned to England cured, he wrote, of his 'religious folly'. He was an accomplished Latinist, had a perfect command of French, and combined a passion for French literature with an interest in the new school of 'philosophical' history headed by Voltaire (who settled outside Geneva in 1755). In 1761 he published his first work, in French, *Essai sur l'étude de la littérature (Essay on the Study of*

Literature). At Lausanne he also formed a lasting friendship with a young Swiss scholar, Georges Deyverdun, and became engaged to Suzanne Curchod, the daughter of a minister. She had no dowry to offer, however, and Gibbon broke off the engagement when his father would not agree to the marriage. 'I sighed as a lover,' he recalled, 'I obeyed as a son.' Suzanne Curchod later married Jacques Necker, the future finance minister of Louis XVI of France, and remained a friend of Gibbon for the rest of his life. He never married.

From 1758 to 1763 Gibbon continued his wide reading, ensconced in the library at the family manor house at Buriton, Hampshire. His studies were interrupted by military duties as a captain in the Hampshire Militia during the Seven Years' War. After the war, he travelled from 1763 to 1765 on the continent on the 'Grand Tour', the normal prerequisite to an official career. At Paris he met the celebrated *philosophes* d'Alembert, Diderot, Helvétius and d'Holbach, before proceeding, via Lausanne, to Italy. 'It was at Rome,' he states in a famous passage in his *Memoirs*, 'on the fifteenth of October 1764, as I sat musing amidst the ruins of the Capitol while the barefooted friars were singing vespers in the Temple of Jupiter, that the idea of writing the decline and fall of the city first started to my mind.' Before settling on the final choice for his life's work, however, he made several false starts, including a *History of the Liberty of the Swiss*, which he never completed.

Returning to England in 1765, he found his father in physical and psychological decline, and the family finances in chaos. Gibbon set about straightening them on his father's death in 1770, a task which he accomplished with the help of his friend, Holroyd, whom he had met at Lausanne during his Grand Tour. He could now enjoy what he called 'the first of earthly blessings – independence': freedom from an overbearing father, freedom from serious financial worries, freedom to lead a social and literary life of his own choice. He moved to London, became known as a man of fashion, joining 'The Club' patronised by Dr Samuel Johnson, the painter Sir Joshua Reynolds, the politician Edmund Burke and the economist Adam Smith. He cut a foppish and 'out of the ordinary' figure as a frenchified would-be man of the world, snuffbox in hand, with his large head and pug face, short, pot-bellied body and spindly legs – 'Monsieur Pomme de Terre', as some people called him. In 1774 he also became a Member of Parliament, supporting the policy of Lord North with his vote during the war of American independence, though without ever venturing on a maiden speech.

From 1773 he was hard at work on *The History of the Decline and Fall of the Roman Empire*. In his *Memoirs* he recounts his initial difficulties: 'At the outset all was dark and doubtful; even the title of the work, the true era of the Decline and Fall of the Empire, the limits of the introduction, the division of the chapters, and the order of the narrative; and I was often tempted to cast away the labour of seven years.' He also laboured to find his own style: 'Many experiments were made before I could hit the middle tone between a dull chronicle and a rhetorical declamation.' He rewrote chapter 1 three times, and chapters 2 and 3 twice. The first volume appeared in 1776 and was an instant success, acclaimed by David Hume and William Robertson, the two leading British historians. Chapters 15 and 16, however, in which he discussed the rise of Christianity, provoked a furore in the Church of England and a barrage of hostile pamphlets. His purpose, complained one excitable clerical opponent, was 'to bring about the decline and fall of the Christian religion.' Unruffled, Gibbon pushed on with his work, pausing only to dash off his *Vindication* in 1779 – a brilliant defence of his scholarship against his clerical critics. His financial security was enhanced in the same year by the award of a sinecure at the Board of Trade. In return he penned an able defence of Lord North's attempts to put down the American Revolution.

In 1781 he published the second and third volumes of *The Decline and Fall*, bringing his account down to the end of the Western empire. In 1783, however, after the fall of Lord North's ministry (and with it Gibbon's sinecure), he left England for the sake of economy, returning to Lausanne, where he set up house with his old friend Deyverdun. Here, in a property overlooking Lake Geneva and the Alps, he completed his last three volumes, returning briefly to England in 1788 to oversee their publication and enjoy their reception. Back in Lausanne, he wrote his *Memoirs*, itself a masterpiece of eighteenth-century autobiography. His last years were clouded by the death of Deyverdun, the outbreak of the French Revolution (which he deplored and which threatened to spill over into Switzerland) and his own declining health, caused by a gigantic 'hydrocele' or swelling in the scrotum. He returned to London in 1793 to comfort his friend Holroyd (now Lord Sheffield) on the death of his wife, and died there in January 1794, aged 56. He was buried in the Sheffield family vault in the parish church at Fletching, Sussex. It was Sheffield who published Gibbon's *Memoirs* and *Miscellaneous Works*, including his minor essays and letters.

In Victorian Britain *The Decline and Fall* continued to be accepted as a classic of historical writing despite its controversial attitude to religion. In his carefully annotated edition of 1838, Milman, Dean of St Paul's, sought to arm Christian readers against Gibbon's infidelity; but John Henry Newman, the future Roman Catholic cardinal, himself paid tribute to Gibbon's accuracy when he ruefully admitted in 1845 that 'the chief, perhaps the only English writer who has any claim to be considered an ecclesiastical historian, is the unbeliever Gibbon.' In his great edition of 1896–1900, J. B. Bury likewise acknowledged that while nineteenth-century scholarship generally had chipped away at Gibbon's façade, it had not undermined the basic edifice. *The Decline and Fall* was also admired as a massive literary structure and for the meticulous artistry which supported, conveyed and embellished its sustained narrative flow and prodigious wealth of learning. 'Gibbon is a kind of bridge,' wrote Carlyle, 'that connects the ancient with the modern ages. And how gorgeously does it swing across the gloomy and tumultuous chasm of these barbarous centuries.' Among its admirers was Winston Churchill, who took to it instantly as a young subaltern in India. 'I devoured Gibbon,' he wrote. 'I rode triumphantly through it from end to end and enjoyed it all.' He sided with Gibbon 'against the disparagements of his pompous-pious editor [Dean Milman]'. Gibbon's prose, of which he learned whole chunks by heart, was to have a lasting impact on his own writings and speeches. In our own day, while *The Decline and Fall* is seldom studied in its entirety, reading Gibbon has been recommended as an educational experience in itself. As Regius Professor of Modern History at Oxford 1957–80, Hugh Trevor-Roper (Lord Dacre) encouraged his undergraduates to read Gibbon in order to broaden their perspectives 'and so fortify themselves against . . . narrow specialisation.' Gibbon took the same bracing view of his chosen discipline. 'The experience of history,' he wrote, 'exalts and enlarges the horizon of our intellectual view' (chapter 48).

Few modern historians could venture on an enterprise of the scale of *The Decline and Fall* without risking the derision of specialists. In Gibbon's time it was still just possible to take on thirteen centuries. Our understanding of these centuries has obviously developed in the last two hundred years, so that Gibbon cannot now be considered the last word on the subject; and he was notoriously dismissive of the history of the eastern, Byzantine empire – 'a tedious and uniform tale of weakness and misery' (chapter 48). Even so, in his overall coverage he is peerless and likely to remain so. The breadth and depth of his learning are amazing: and he still remains remarkably reliable. He made himself master of all available primary sources. He cites over 8000 sources, including collections of maps, coins, medals and inscriptions as well as conventional written evidence, which he not only digested but approached critically, as his footnotes make clear. Later advances enable modern scholars to fault his accuracy; his contemporaries could not. He was true to the historian's first duty: to get his facts right. He was also able to convey them with an overwhelming narrative sweep, always lively and compelling.

For Gibbon, however, history was much more than accurate chronicle or lucid narrative, though he gives us both. Rome's decline and fall was not merely intrinsically interesting: it had meaning and importance for contemporary society. In explaining both in broad outline and in telling detail the story of Rome's decline, he also suggested to 'the philosophic reader of the present age' reflections about the decay of societies generally. Did history repeat itself? *The Decline and Fall* was written during the American revolution and the Pugachov rebellion in Russia. Did the loss of America portend the decline of the British empire? Could a mass revolt of Asiatic tribes in Russia presage a new wave of barbarian invasions in the west? Gibbon knew that he had chosen a subject of pervading interest to an age which idolised the classics and which, priding itself on its own lofty standards of civilisation, was ready to let itself be interested in the decline of classical civilisation. How did Gibbon account for that decline? Looking back in his final chapter, he wrote: 'I have described the triumph of barbarism and religion' (chapter 71). There spoke the authentic voice of the Enlightenment, a writer steeped in classical learning and infatuated by Rome, its history, its architectural remains, its literature and the values which had long dominated Western Europe, the Near East and North Africa. The Empire comprised 'the most numerous society that has ever been united under the same system of government' (chapter 2) – and he lamented the decline which he so scrupulously investigated.

He also knew that he had written something epic in its scale and grandeur which might rival the ancient classics themselves (and such modern works as Fielding's *Tom Jones*, which Gibbon hailed as an immortal masterpiece). He enjoyed the celebrity which *The Decline and Fall* gave him as 'the historian of the Roman empire' and the lasting reputation which he believed would attach to his name. In another memorable passage in his *Memoirs*, he dramatically reinvokes the completion of his great work:

> I have presumed to mark the moment of conception: I shall now commemorate the hour of my final deliverance. It was on the day, or rather night, of the 27th of June 1787, between the hours of eleven and twelve, that I wrote the last lines of the last page, in a summerhouse in my garden. After laying down my pen I took several turns in a *berceau*, or covered walk of acacias, which commands a prospect of the country, the lake and the mountains. The air was temperate, the sky was serene, the silver orb of the moon was reflected from the waters, and all nature was silent. I will not dissemble the first emotions of joy on the recovery of my freedom, and, perhaps, the establishment of my fame. But my pride was soon humbled, and a sobre melancholy was spread over my mind, by the idea that I had taken an everlasting leave of an old and agreeable companion, and that, whatsoever might be the future date of my *History*, the life of the historian must be short and precarious.

For Gibbon, as for his admired classical authors, writing was always a work of conscious artistry. He drew in *The Decline and Fall* on Roman models, such as Cicero and Tacitus, on traditions of formal rhetoric, on modern literary sensibility and even on theatrical convention. He described the theme of *The Decline and Fall* as 'the greatest, perhaps, and most awful *scene* in the history of mankind' (chapter 71), and he wrote with a mind to the eye, the ear, the intellect and the emotions of the reader. In what C. S. Lewis called his 'aqueductive sentences', he carefully shaped and finished his prose in his mind before committing it to paper. It was his invariable practice, he tells us in his *Memoirs*, 'to cast a long paragraph in a single mould, to try it by my ear, to deposit it in my memory, but to suspend the action of the pen till I had given the last polish to my work.' His writing supposes a like-minded audience, sophisticated and fastidious; and the ends of his carefully patterned paragraphs almost invite applause. 'The style of an author should be the image of his mind,' he insisted; and he quickly establishes a kind of genteel intimacy with the reader through his distinctive authorial voice, reflective and ruminative, but confident, authoritative, rational and 'philosophical'. Always in absolute control of his material, he guides the reader with unruffled assurance through many centuries and many lands and peoples, explaining what is worthy of attention, dismissing what is unworthy, bringing the new insights of the Enlightenment to bear on the events of the past and injecting history with fresh meaning for the present. We read *The Decline and Fall* above all to enter into the peculiar cast of Gibbon's mind and to share his unique perspectives. He is, as Trevor Roper calls him, 'the greatest of the historians of the Enlightenment.'

One of the delights of reading Gibbon is his irony. This involves first of all a sense of fun, an amused and amusing way of looking at his subject-matter. In chapter 7, describing the Emperor Gordian, he writes as follows, in a characteristic Gibbonian sentence, leisurely, polished, elegantly balanced and pointed, with a mild sting in the tail:

> Twenty-two acknowledged concubines, and a library of sixty-two thousand volumes, attested the variety of his inclinations; and from the productions which he left behind him, it appears that the former as well as the latter were designed for use rather than ostentation.

Gibbon seems figuratively to roll his tongue around the phrases (which need to be read aloud to produce their full flavour); and his unexpected application of the same metaphor ('productions') to two disparate objects (books and bastards) provokes a smile, especially when the joke is revealed at the end of the sentence. This piece of irony is a good example of Gibbon's tone of voice, the urbane sense of humour which engages the reader in a collusive relationship of knowing detachment. We find the same humour in many of his footnotes, where he pokes fun at credulous or slipshod editors, or purveys salacious details of emperors and empresses 'veiled in the obscurity of a learned language' (chapter 40).

Elsewhere he uses irony with a more serious, more subversive aim. Nowhere more so than in his frequent discussions of religion and Christianity. Gibbon's irony involves neither taking him literally, nor necessarily assuming that he means the exact opposite of what he says; it does mean asking what he means us to think. It means joining him in taking a critical look at things. His intention once caught from his tone, the effect is both highly entertaining and highly revealing. It tells us much about Gibbon and the attitudes of the age of the Enlightenment, and the standards from which its leading thinkers looked (often looked down) on certain aspects of the past. His views are those of what he frequently refers to as a 'philosopher', which in his time indicated a *philosophe* or one who shared the Enlightenment outlook, rational, utilitarian and humane.

Take another example. In chapter 15, discussing the claims of the early Christians about the resurrection of the dead, and a challenge to those claims by 'a noble Grecian', he wrote:

> . . . it seems difficult to account for the scepticism of those philosophers who still rejected and derided the doctrine of the resurrection. A noble Grecian had rested on this important ground the whole controversy, and promised Theophilus, bishop of Antioch, that, if he could be gratified with the sight of a single person who had been actually raised from the dead, he would immediately embrace the Christian religion. It is somewhat remarkable that the prelate of the first eastern church, however anxious for the conversion of his friend, thought proper to decline this fair and reasonable challenge.

Gibbon's mock-seriousness ('it seems difficult to account', 'it is somewhat remarkable') once more raises a central point for which he was much criticised in his time and later. His attacks on Christianity, however subtle and covert, were after all only thinly camouflaged by his ironic phraseology. They were clear enough to the perceptive reader and deeply offensive to the devout. 'Who', complained one of his eminent ecclesiastical critics, Archdeacon Paley, 'can refute a sneer?' So far as we can tell, Gibbon was not an atheist. His comments on Islam in chapter 50, for example, suggest that he was probably a deist of sorts and a believer in a universal system of morals. He expressed admiration for the ethical tenets of the New Testament. As a historian, he was far from underestimating the important role of religion in history. He was extremely knowledgeable about various religions, including Islam. At the same time he was immensely sceptical about religious fervour (or 'enthusiasm', as he called it), which he thought irrational and often harmful. He believed that the civic values of the Roman republic, which he admired and which survived for a time into the empire, were partly undermined by the rise of Christianity, and that 'the last remains of the military spirit were buried in the cloister.' (chapter 38). It was true that religions, including Christianity, had often proved socially and politically useful at particular moments in history, and that astute rulers had successfully harnessed mass 'enthusiasm' to particular ends. He devotes three chapters to analysing the rise of Christianity and its eventual instatement as the official religion of the Roman empire by the Emperor Constantine in the fourth century AD. But he did not regard any religion as 'true'; he was ironical at the expense both of the wordliness and the unworldliness of institutionalised Christianity, and he had a clear distaste for many of the attitudes which popular religion encouraged. He was impatient of the hairsplitting metaphysical speculation which monopolised the attention and divided the loyalties of the Christian world; he was ironically contemptuous of the Christian heresies and indignant at their bloody suppression; and he disdained the so-called monastic virtues, which he described, revealingly, as 'painful to the individual and useless to mankind' (chapter 20). Miracles and visions, relics, monks, hermits and their often outlandish mortifications, the proliferation of martyred saints, are the frequent objects of his wit. Richard Porson, another of his learned critics, complained that 'his humanity seldom sleeps, save where virgins are ravished or Christians martyred.'

Gibbon also has much to say about the 'barbarian' invaders who overran the empire in successive waves across the centuries, the German tribes, the Goths, the Huns, the Vandals, the Arabs, the Seljuk Turks, etc. Indeed it is remarkable how by close study of the variety of human ethnography, he succeeds in avoiding repetitiveness. Another key quality, both of his style and his historical approach, is balance. Just as he weighs his primary sources, so he carefully sifts and evaluates historical factors in presenting his measured conclusions. He brings out in his nuanced prose the complexities and contradictions inherent in Rome's experience of the 'barbarians'. With his classical predilections, he presents a set of stereotypes of tribal societies as backward, cruel, unlettered and superstitious; and he does not conceal his antipathy. He had no sympathy for Rousseau or the myth of the 'noble savage.' At the same time he is remarkably fair and objective in drawing out the counterbalancing contributions of 'primitive' societies, in particular their natural vigour, their instinctive love of independence and their sense of tribal honour. These he contrasts with the passivity, the lack of creative energy and originality which he saw as characteristic of imperial Roman society even in its Antonine heyday, 'the period in the history of the world during which the condition of the human race was most happy and prosperous' (chapter 3). For despite this emphatic assertion of the material blessings of peace, law and civilisation, it was in the Antonine age, Gibbon believed, that Roman society fatally reconciled itself to loss of political freedom and 'having attained its full strength and maturity, began to verge towards its decline' (Preface to volume 1 of the first quarto edition). 'The Roman world was indeed peopled by a race of pygmies,' he declares, sounding a note of contempt for the citizens of the empire, followed by an unmistakeable acclamation of the German invaders: 'when the fierce giants of the north broke in and mended the puny breed. They restored a manly spirit of freedom; and, after the revolution of ten centuries, freedom became the happy parent of taste and science' (chapter 2). Political freedom was a possession of absolute significance to Gibbon; and its resurgence, as he noted, came with the 'barbarians'. The infusion of 'barbarian' vigour became the life-blood of modern Europe Their tribal rivalries founded the independent, competitive states, coexisting in creative rivalry; and from the primal instinct of the 'barbarians' for liberty originated the freedom, political and intellectual, which Gibbon prized so highly in the British civilisation of his day.

ANTONY LENTIN
BRIAN NORMAN
The Open University

THE PRESENT EDITION

The twenty-eight complete chapters selected for this edition cover most of the topics which Gibbon considered to be connected with Rome's decline and fall and which he describes in his concluding chapter as featuring 'many of the events most interesting in human annals: the artful policy of the Caesars, who long maintained the name and image of a free republic [1–3], the disorders of military despotism [4–7, 13]; the rise, establishment, and sects of Christianity [15–16, 20–21, 23, 28, 37]; the invasion and settlements of the barbarians of Germany and Scythia [9, 30, 34–36]; the institutions of the civil law; the character and religion of Mohammed [50]; the temporal sovereignty of the popes; the restoration and decay of the Western empire of Charlemagne; the crusades of the Latins in the East [58–59]; the conquests of the Saracens and Turks [57]; the ruin of the Greek empire [68]; the state and revolutions of Rome in the middle age [71].' To these are added chapters 8 and 24 on Persia and the emperor Julian's attempt to conquer it. An editorial précis of the chapters not included in this edition is inserted where the omissions occur.

The text in this edition is based on the text edited by J. B. Bury in seven volumes, Methuen & Co., 1909–14. It incorporates emendations from the edition by David Womersley, Allen Lane, Penguin Press, 1994. Gibbon's footnotes are retained, but Bury's critical additions to them are omitted. The present editors supply brief footnotes of their own in square brackets to explain particular words or expressions or to give important historical information. Words commonly found in Gibbon but no longer in common use, or whose meaning has changed, are also listed in a short glossary. Foreign words and passages in Gibbon's footnotes (in Latin, Greek, French and Italian) are reproduced in this edition and are also translated (the English appearing in square brackets) unless already translated or substantially paraphrased by Gibbon in the body of his text.

FURTHER READING

Recent complete editions of Gibbon's *The History of the Decline and Fall of the Roman Empire* are the Everyman edition (1980) and the edition of David Womersley, Allen Lane, The Penguin Press (1994). Readers anxious to check Gibbon's accuracy should consult the annotated edition by J. B. Bury, Methuen (1909–14). Gibbon's *Memoirs of My Life*, edited by Betty Radice, is published by Penguin (1984). There is also a bicentenary edition by S. Constantine and O. A. J. Cockshutt, Ryburn, 1994. The standard studies by D. M. Low, *Edward Gibbon*, Chatto and Windus (1937) and G. M. Young, *Gibbon*, Rupert Hart-Davis (1948) may be supplemented by Patricia Craddock's two-volume biography, *Young Edward Gibbon: Gentleman of Letters*, Johns Hopkins University Press (1982) and *Edward Gibbon, Luminous Historian 1772–1794*, Johns Hopkins University Press (1989), and by L. Gossman, *The Empire Unpossess'd: An Essay on Gibbon's Decline and Fall*, Cambridge University Press (1981) and Roy Porter, *Edward Gibbon: Making History*, Weidenfeld and Nicolson (1988). An excellent short introduction is J. W. Burrow, *Gibbon*, Oxford University Press (1985). H. L. Bond, *The Literary Art of Edward Gibbon*, Oxford University Press (1960) considers *The Decline and Fall* as 'epic'. G. W. Bowersock and S. R. Graubard (eds.), *Edward Gibbon and The Decline and Fall of the Roman Empire*, Harvard University Press (1977) is an important collection of essays, now supplemented by Rosamund McKitterick and R. Quinault (eds), *Edward Gibbon and Empire*, Cambridge University Press (1996). Selected chapters of *The Decline and Fall* are analysed in two Open University courses, entitled *The Enlightenment:* A204, units 10–12, The Open University (1979, reprinted 1991), and A206, *The Enlightenment. Studies I*, ed. M. Bartholomew, D. Hall and A. Lentin, The Open University (1992), pp. 289–324.

GLOSSARY

A list of words used sometimes by Gibbon with the following meanings:

accuse	demonstrate, criticise
ages	centuries
artificial	skilful, effected with artistry, fabricated
devote	condemn, sacrifice, give up
discover	reveal
discriminate	distinguish, differentiate
enthusiasm	religious zeal, fanaticism
expect	await
fabulous	fictitious, imaginary
grateful	welcome, pleasing
(h)aruspices	priests who inspected the entrails of sacrificial animals, soothsayers
insensibly	gradually, imperceptibly
intestine	internal
in the room of	instead of, in place of
limits	frontiers
magazine	store, warehouse
partial	biased, partisan
prevent	anticipate, pre-empt
specious	attractive, plausible
temporal	worldly

LIST OF MAPS

CHRONOLOGICAL LIST OF ROMAN EMPERORS

The English forms of names are given when they are in general use.

1 FROM 27 BC TO THE FALL OF THE EMPIRE IN THE WEST

Augustus, 27 BC–AD 14
Tiberius, 14–37
Gaius (Caligula), 37–41
Claudius, 41–54
Nero, 54–68
Galba, 68–69
Otho, 69
Vitellius, 69
Vespasian, 69–79
Titus, 79–81
Domitian, 81–96
Nerva, 96–98
Trajan, 98–117
Hadrian, 117–38
Antoninus Pius, 138–61
Marcus Aurelius, 161–80
Commodus, 180–92
Pertinax, 193
Didius Julianus, 193
Septimius Severus, 193–211
Caracalla, 211–17,
    with Geta, 211–12
Macrinus with
    Diadumenianus, 217–18
Elagabalus, 218–22
Alexander Severus, 222–35
Maximin, 235–38
Gordian I with Gordian II, 238
Maximus with Balbinus, 238
Gordian III, 238–44
Philip, 244–49
Decius, 249–51
Gallus, 251–53
Aemelian, 253
Valerian with Gallienus, 253–60
Gallienus, 260–68

Claudius II, 268–70
Aurelian, 270–75
Tacitus, 275–76
Florianus, 276
Probus, 276–82
Carus, 282–83
Carinus with Numerian,
    283–84
Diocletian, 284–305
    with Maximian 286–305
Galerius, 305–11
    with Constantius I, 305–06
    with Constantine I, 306–11
    with Maxentius, 306–11
    with Licinius, 307–11
    with Maximin, 308–11
Constantine I, 311–37
    with Maxentius, 311–12
    with Licinius, 311–24
Constantine II
    with Constantius II and
    Constans, 337–40
Constantius II, 340–61
    with Constans, 340–50
Julian, 361–63
Jovian, 363–64
Valentinian I with Valens, 364–75
    with Gratian, 367–75
Valens with Gratian and
    Valentinian II, 375–78
Theodosius, 379–95
    with Gratian, 379–83
    with Valentinian II, 379–92
    with Arcadius, 383–95
    with Honorius, 392–95

The following Emperors after 395 ruled only in the West

Honorius, 395–423
Valentinian III, 425–55
Maximus, 455
Avitus, 455–56
Majorian, 457–61
Libius Severus, 461–65

Anthemius, 467–72
Olybrius, 472
Glycerius, 473–74
Julius Nepos, 474–75
Romulus Augustulus, 475–76

2 THE ROMAN EMPERORS IN THE EAST 395–1453

Arcadius, 395–408
Theodosius II, 408–50
Marcian, 450–57
Leo I, 457–74
Leo II, 474
Zeno, 474–91
Anastasius I, 491–518
Justin I, 518–27
Justinian I, 527–65
Justin II, 565–78
Tiberius II, 578–82
Maurice, 582–602
Phocas, 602–10
Heraclius, 610–41
Constantine III, 641
Constans II, 641–668
Constantine IV, 668–85
Justinian II, 685–95 (banished)
Leontius, 695–98
Tiberius III, 698–705
Justinian II, 705–11 (restored)
Philippicus, 711–13
Anastasius II, 713–16
Theodosius III, 716–17
Leo III, 717–41
Constantine V, 741–75
Leo IV, 775–80
Constantine VI, 780–97
Irene, 797–802
Nicephorus I, 802–11
Stauracius, 811
Michael I, 811–13
Leo V, 813–20
Michael II, 820–29

Theophilus, 829–42
Michael III, 842–67
Basil I, 867–86
Leo VI with Alexander, 886–912
Constantine VII, 912–59
    with Alexander, 912–13
    with Romanus I, 919–44
Romanus II, 959–63
Basil II and Constantine VIII,
    963–1025
    with Nicephorus II, 963–69
    with John I, 969–76
Constantine VIII, 1025–28
Romanus III, 1028–34
Michael IV, 1034–41
Michael V, 1041–42
Constantine IX, 1042–54
Theodora, 1054–56
Michael VI, 1056–57
Isaac I, 1057–59
Constantine X, 1059–67
Romanus IV, 1067–71
Michael VII, 1071–78
Nicephorus III, 1078–81
Alexius I, 1081–1118
John II, 1118–43
Manuel I, 1143–80
Alexius II, 1180–83
Andronicus I, 1183–85
Isaac II, 1185–95 (dethroned)
Alexius III, 1195–1203
Isaac II, 1203–04 (restored)
    with Alexius IV, 1203–04
Alexius V, 1204

Latin Emperors of the East

Baldwin I, 1204–05
Henry, 1206–16
Peter of Courtenay, 1217
Robert, 1221–28
Baldwin II, 1228–61
  with John of Brienne, 1228–37

Eastern Emperors in Nicaea

Theodorus I, 1204–22
John III, 1222–54
Theodorus II, 1254–58
John IV, 1258–61
  with Michael VIII, 1259–61

Restored Eastern Emperors in Constantinople

Michael VIII, 1261–82
Andronicus II, 1282–1328
  with Michael IX,
    1295–1320
Andronicus III, 1328–41
John V, 1341–91
  with John VI Cantacuzene, 1341–55
  with Andronicus IV, 1379–81
Manuel II, 1391–1425
  with John VII, 1399–1402
John VIII, 1425–48
Constantine XI, 1448–53

The enumeration of the later Constantines and Johns in these lists is in accordance with current practice rather than Gibbon's.

LIST OF CHAPTER TITLES

CHAPTER 1

The extent and military force of the Empire in the age of the Antonines

IN THE SECOND CENTURY OF THE CHRISTIAN ERA, the empire of Rome comprehended the fairest part of the earth, and the most civilised portion of mankind. The frontiers of that extensive monarchy were guarded by ancient renown and disciplined valour. The gentle, but powerful, influence of laws and manners had gradually cemented the union of the provinces. Their peaceful inhabitants enjoyed and abused the advantages of wealth and luxury. The image of a free constitution was preserved with decent reverence. The Roman senate appeared to possess the sovereign authority, and devolved on the emperors all the executive powers of government. During a happy period of more than fourscore years, the public administration was conducted by the virtue and abilities of Nerva, Trajan, Hadrian, and the two Antonines. It is the design of this and of the two succeeding chapters, to describe the prosperous condition of their empire; and afterwards, from the death of Marcus Antoninus, to deduce the most important circumstances of its decline and fall: a revolution which will ever be remembered, and is still felt by the nations of the earth.

The principal conquests of the Romans were achieved under the republic; and the emperors, for the most part, were satisfied with preserving those dominions which had been acquired by the policy of the senate, the active emulation of the consuls, and the martial enthusiasm of the people. The seven first centuries* were filled with a rapid succession of triumphs; but it was reserved for Augustus to relinquish the ambitious design of subduing the whole earth, and to introduce a spirit of moderation into the public councils. Inclined to peace by his temper and situation, it was easy for him to discover that Rome, in her present exalted situation, had much less to hope than to fear from the chance of arms; and that, in the prosecution of remote wars, the undertaking became every day more difficult, the event more doubtful, and the possession more precarious and less beneficial. The experience of Augustus added weight to these salutary reflections, and effectually convinced him that, by the prudent vigour of his counsels, it would be easy to secure every concession which the safety or the dignity of Rome might require from the most formidable barbarians. Instead of exposing his person and his legions to the arrows of the Parthians, he obtained, by an honourable treaty, the restitution of the standards and prisoners which had been taken in the defeat of Crassus.[1]

His generals, in the early part of his reign, attempted the reduction of Ethiopia and Arabia Felix. They marched near a thousand miles to the south of the tropic; but the heat of the climate soon repelled the invaders and protected the unwarlike natives of those sequestered regions.[2] The northern countries of Europe scarcely deserved the expense and labour of conquest. The forests and morasses of Germany were filled with a hardy race of barbarians, who despised life when it was separated from freedom; and though, on the first attack, they seemed to yield to the weight of the Roman power, they soon, by a signal act of despair, regained their independence, and reminded Augustus of the vicissitude of fortune.[3] On the death of that emperor his testament was publicly read in the senate. He bequeathed, as a valuable legacy to his successors, the advice of confining the empire within those limits which nature seemed to have placed as its permanent bulwarks and boundaries: on the west the Atlantic ocean; the Rhine and Danube on the north; the Euphrates on the east; and towards the south the sandy deserts of Arabia and Africa.[4]

Happily for the repose of mankind, the moderate system recommended by the wisdom of Augustus was adopted by the fears and vices of his immediate successors. Engaged in the pursuit of pleasure or in the exercise of tyranny, the first Caesars seldom showed themselves to the armies, or to the provinces; nor were they disposed to suffer that those triumphs which *their* indolence neglected should be usurped by the conduct and valour of their lieutenants. The military fame of a subject was considered as an insolent invasion of the Imperial prerogative; and it became the duty, as well as interest, of every Roman general, to guard the frontiers intrusted to his care, without aspiring to conquests which might have proved no less fatal to himself than to the vanquished barbarians.[5]

The only accession which the Roman empire received during the first century of the Christian era was the province of Britain. In this single instance the successors of Caesar and Augustus were persuaded to follow the example of the former, rather than the precept of the latter. The proximity of its situation to the coast of Gaul seemed to invite their arms; the pleasing, though doubtful, intelligence of a pearl fishery attracted their avarice;[6] and as Britain was viewed in the light of a distinct and insulated world, the conquest scarcely formed any exception to the general system of continental measures. After a war of about forty years, undertaken by the most stupid,[7] maintained by the most dissolute, and terminated by the most timid of all the emperors, the far greater part of the island submitted to the Roman yoke.[8] The various tribes of Britons possessed valour without conduct, and the love of freedom without the spirit of union. They took up arms with savage fierceness, they laid them down, or turned them against each other, with wild inconstancy; and while they fought singly, they were successively subdued. Neither the fortitude of Caractacus, nor the despair of Boadicea, nor the fanaticism of the Druids, could avert the slavery of their country, or resist the steady

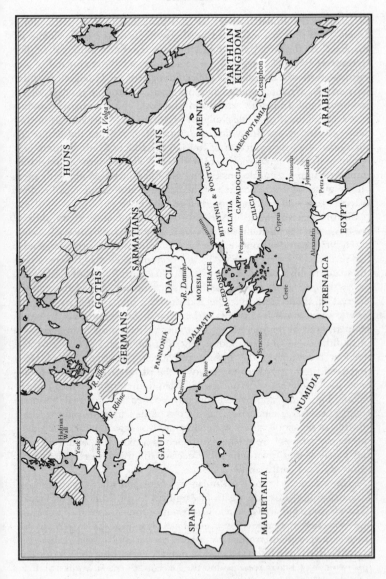

The Roman empire at its greatest extent in the time of Trajan, AD *c.*100

progress of the Imperial generals, who maintained the national glory, when the throne was disgraced by the weakest or the most vicious of mankind. At the very time when Domitian, confined to his palace, felt the terrors which he inspired, his legions, under the command of the virtuous Agricola, defeated the collected force of the Caledonians at the foot of the Grampian hills; and his fleets, venturing to explore an unknown and dangerous navigation, displayed the Roman arms round every part of the island. The conquest of Britain was considered as already achieved; and it was the design of Agricola to complete and ensure his success by the easy reduction of Ireland, for which, in his opinion, one legion and a few auxiliaries were sufficient.[9] The western isle might be improved into a valuable possession, and the Britons would wear their chains with the less reluctance, if the prospect and example of freedom was on every side removed from before their eyes.

But the superior merit of Agricola soon occasioned his removal from the government of Britain; and for ever disappointed this rational, though extensive, scheme of conquest. Before his departure the prudent general had provided for security as well as for dominion. He had observed that the island is almost divided into two unequal parts by the opposite gulfs or, as they are now called, the Friths of Scotland. Across the narrow interval of about forty miles he had drawn a line of military stations, which was afterwards fortified, in the reign of Antoninus Pius, by a turf rampart, erected on foundations of stone.[10] This wall of Antoninus, at a small distance beyond the modern cities of Edinburgh and Glasgow, was fixed as the limit of the Roman province. The native Caledonians preserved, in the northern extremity of the island, their wild independence, for which they were not less indebted to their poverty than to their valour. Their incursions were frequently repelled and chastised; but their country was never subdued.[11] The masters of the fairest and most wealthy climates of the globe turned with contempt from gloomy hills assailed by the winter tempest, from lakes concealed in a blue mist, and from cold and lonely heaths, over which the deer of the forest were chased by a troop of naked barbarians.[12]

Such was the state of the Roman frontiers, and such the maxims of Imperial policy, from the death of Augustus to the accession of Trajan. That virtuous and active prince had received the education of a soldier, and possessed the talents of a general.[13] The peaceful system of his predecessors was interrupted by scenes of war and conquest; and the legions, after a long interval, beheld a military emperor at their head. The first exploits of Trajan were against the Dacians, the most warlike of men, who dwelt beyond the Danube, and who, during the reign of Domitian, had insulted, with impunity, the majesty of Rome.[14] To the strength and fierceness of barbarians they added a contempt for life, which was derived from a warm persuasion of the immortality and transmigration of the soul.[15] Decebalus, the Dacian king, approved himself a rival not unworthy of Trajan; nor did he despair of his own and the public fortune, till, by the confession of his enemies, he had exhausted every resource both of valour and policy.[16] This memorable war, with a very short suspension of hostilities, lasted five years; and as the emperor could exert, without control, the whole force of the state, it was terminated by the absolute submission of the barbarians.[17] The new province of Dacia, which formed a second exception to the precept of Augustus, was about thirteen hundred miles in circumference. Its natural boundaries were the Dniester, the Theiss or Tibiscus, the Lower Danube, and the Euxine Sea. The vestiges of a military road may still be traced from the banks of the Danube to the neighbourhood of Bender, a place famous in modern history, and the actual frontier of the Turkish and Russian Empires.[18]

Trajan was ambitious of fame; and as long as mankind shall continue to bestow more liberal applause on their destroyers than on their benefactors, the thirst of military glory will ever be the vice of the most exalted characters. The praises of Alexander,* transmitted by a succession of poets and historians, had kindled a dangerous emulation in the mind of Trajan. Like him, the Roman emperor undertook an expedition against the nations of the east, but he lamented with a sigh that his advanced age scarcely left him any hopes of equalling the renown of the son of Philip.†[19] Yet the success of Trajan, however transient, was rapid and specious. The degenerate Parthians, broken by intestine discord, fled before his arms. He descended the river Tigris in triumph, from the mountains of Armenia to the Persian gulf. He enjoyed the honour of being the first, as he was the last, of the Roman generals who ever navigated that remote sea. His fleets ravished the coasts of Arabia; and Trajan vainly flattered himself that he was approaching towards the confines of India.[20] Every day the astonished senate received the intelligence of new names and new nations that acknowledged his sway. They were informed that the kings of Bosphorus, Colchos, Iberia, Albania, Osrhoene, and even the Parthian monarch himself, had accepted their diadems from the hands of the emperor; that the independent tribes of the Median and Carduchian hills had implored his protection; and that the rich countries of Armenia, Mesopotamia, and Assyria, were reduced into the state of provinces.[21] But the death of Trajan soon clouded the splendid prospect; and it was justly to be dreaded that so many distant nations would throw off the unaccustomed yoke, when they were no longer restrained by the powerful hand which had imposed it.

It was an ancient tradition that, when the Capitol was founded by one of the Roman kings, the god Terminus (who presided over boundaries, and was represented according to the fashion of that age by a large stone) alone, among all the inferior deities, refused to yield his place to Jupiter himself. A favourable inference was drawn from his obstinacy, which was interpreted by the augurs as a sure presage that the boundaries of the Roman power would never recede.[22] During many ages, the prediction, as it is usual, contributed to its own accomplishment. But though Terminus had resisted the majesty of Jupiter, he submitted to the authority of the emperor Hadrian.[23] The resignation of all the eastern conquests of Trajan was the first measure of his reign. He restored to the Parthians the election of an independent sovereign; withdrew the Roman garrisons from the provinces of Armenia, Mesopotamia, and Assyria; and, in compliance with the precepts of Augustus, once more established the Euphrates as the frontier of the empire.[24] Censure, which arraigns the public actions and the private motives of princes, has ascribed to envy a conduct which might be attributed to the prudence and moderation of Hadrian. The various character of that emperor, capable, by turns, of the meanest and the most generous sentiments, may afford some colour to the suspicion. It was, however, scarcely in his power to place the superiority of his predecessor in a more conspicuous light than by thus confessing himself unequal to the task of defending the conquests of Trajan.

The martial and ambitious spirit of Trajan formed a very singular contrast with the moderation of his successor. The restless activity of Hadrian was not less remarkable when compared with the gentle repose of Antoninus Pius. The life of the former was almost a perpetual journey; and as he possessed the various talents of the soldier, the statesman, and the scholar, he gratified his curiosity in the discharge of his duty. Careless of the difference of seasons and of climates, he marched on foot, and bareheaded, over the snows of Caledonia, and the sultry plains of the Upper Egypt; nor was there a province of the empire which, in the course of his reign, was not honoured with the presence of the monarch.[25] But the tranquil life of Antoninus Pius was spent in the bosom of Italy; and, during the twenty-three years that he directed the public administration, the longest journeys of that amiable prince extended no farther than from his palace in Rome to the retirement of his Lanuvian villa.[26]

Notwithstanding this difference in their personal conduct, the general system of Augustus was equally adopted and uniformly pursued by Hadrian and by the two Antonines. They persisted in the design of maintaining the dignity of the empire, without attempting to enlarge its limits. By every honourable expedient they invited the friendship of the barbarians; and endeavoured to convince mankind that the Roman power, raised above the temptation of conquest, was actuated only by the love of order and justice. During a long period of forty-three years their virtuous labours were crowned with success; and, if we except a few slight hostilities that served to exercise the legions of the frontier, the reigns of Hadrian and Antoninus Pius offer the fair prospect of universal peace.[27] The Roman name was revered among the most remote nations of the earth. The fiercest barbarians frequently submitted their differences to the arbitration of the emperor; and we are informed by a contemporary historian that he had seen ambassadors who were refused the honour which they came to solicit, of being admitted into the rank of subjects.[28]

The terror of the Roman arms added weight and dignity to the moderation of the emperors. They preserved peace by a constant preparation for war; and, while justice regulated their conduct, they announced to the nations on their confines that they were as little disposed to endure as to offer an injury. The military strength, which it had been sufficient for Hadrian and the elder Antoninus to display, was exerted against the Parthians and the Germans by the emperor Marcus. The hostilities of the barbarians provoked the resentment of that philosophic monarch, and, in the prosecution of a just defence, Marcus and his generals obtained many signal victories, both on the Euphrates and on the Danube.[29] The military establishment of the Roman empire, which thus assured either its tranquillity or success, will now become the proper and important object of our attention.

In the purer ages of the commonwealth* the use of arms was reserved for those ranks of citizens who had a country to love, a property to defend, and some share in enacting those laws which it was their interest, as well as duty, to maintain. But in proportion as the public freedom was lost in extent of conquest, war was gradually improved into an art, and degraded into a trade.[30] The legions themselves, even at the time when they were recruited in the most distant provinces, were supposed to consist of Roman citizens. That distinction was generally considered either as a legal qualification or as a proper recompense for the soldier; but a more serious regard was paid to the essential merit of age, strength, and military stature.[31] In all levies, a just preference was given to the climates of the north over those of the south; the race of men born to the exercise of arms was sought for in the country rather than in cities, and it was very reasonably presumed that the hardy occupations of smiths, carpenters, and huntsmen would supply more vigour and resolution than the sedentary trades which are employed in the service of luxury.[32] After every qualification of property had been laid aside, the armies of the Roman emperors were still commanded, for the most part, by officers of a liberal birth and education; but the common soldiers, like the mercenary troops of modern Europe, were drawn from the meanest, and very frequently from the most profligate, of mankind.

That public virtue, which among the ancients was denominated patriotism, is derived from a strong sense of our own interest in the preservation and prosperity of the free government of which we are members. Such a sentiment, which had rendered the legions of the republic almost invincible, could make but a very feeble impression on the mercenary servants of a despotic prince; and it became necessary to supply that defect by other motives, of a different, but not less forcible nature – honour and religion. The peasant, or mechanic, imbibed the useful prejudice that he was advanced to the more dignified profession of arms, in which his rank and reputation would depend on his own valour; and that, although the prowess of a private soldier must often escape the notice of fame, his own behaviour might sometimes confer glory or disgrace on the company, the legion, or even the army, to whose honours he was associated. On his first entrance into the service, an oath was administered to him with every circumstance of solemnity. He promised never to desert his standard, to submit his own will to the commands of his leaders, and to sacrifice his life for the safety of the emperor and the empire.[33] The attachment of the Roman troops to their standards was inspired by the united influence of religion and of honour. The golden eagle, which glittered in the front of the legion, was the object of their fondest devotion; nor was it esteemed less impious than it was ignominious, to abandon that sacred ensign in the hour of danger.[34] These motives, which derived their strength from the imagination, were enforced by fears and hopes of a more substantial kind. Regular pay, occasional donatives, and a stated recompense, after the appointed term of service, alleviated the hardships of the military life,[35] whilst, on the other hand, it was impossible for cowardice or disobedience to escape the severest punishment. The centurions were authorised to chastise with blows, the generals had a right to punish with death; and it was an inflexible maxim of Roman discipline that a good soldier should dread his officers far more than the enemy. From such laudable arts did the valour of the Imperial troops receive a degree of firmness and docility, unattainable by the impetuous and irregular passions of barbarians.

And yet so sensible were the Romans of the imperfection of valour without skill and practice, that, in their language, the name of an army was borrowed from the word which signified exercise.[36] Military exercises were the important and unremitted object of their discipline. The recruits and young soldiers were constantly trained, both in the morning and in the evening, nor was age or knowledge allowed to excuse the veterans from the daily repetition of what they had completely learnt. Large sheds were erected in the winter-quarters of the troops, that their useful labours might not receive any interruption from the most tempestuous weather; and it was carefully observed that the arms destined to this imitation of war should be of double the weight which was required in real action.[37] It is not the purpose of this work to enter into any minute description of the Roman exercises. We shall only remark that they comprehended whatever could add strength to the body, activity to the limbs, or grace to the motions. The soldiers were diligently instructed to march, to run, to leap, to swim, to carry heavy burdens, to handle every species of arms that was used either for offence or for defence, either in distant engagement or in a closer onset; to form a variety of evolutions; and to move to the sound of flutes in the Pyrrhic or martial dance.[38] In the midst of peace, the Roman troops familiarised themselves with the practice of war; and it is prettily remarked by an ancient historian who had fought against them, that the effusion of blood was the only circumstance which distinguished a field of battle from a field of exercise.[39] It was the policy of the ablest generals, and even of the emperors themselves, to encourage these military studies by their presence and example; and we are informed that Hadrian, as well as Trajan, frequently condescended to instruct the inexperienced soldiers, to reward the diligent, and sometimes to dispute with them the prize of superior strength or dexterity.[40] Under the reigns of those princes, the science of tactics was cultivated with success; and as long as the empire retained any vigour, their military instructions were respected as the most perfect model of Roman discipline.

Nine centuries of war had gradually introduced into the service many alterations and improvements. The legions, as they are described by Polybius,*[41] in the time of the Punic wars,† differed very materially from those which achieved the victories of Caesar, or defended the monarchy of Hadrian and the Antonines. The constitution of the Imperial legion may be described in a few words.[42] The heavy-armed infantry, which composed its principal strength,[43] was divided into ten cohorts, and fifty-five companies, under the orders of a correspondent number of tribunes and centurions. The first cohort, which always claimed the post of honour and the custody of the eagle, was formed of eleven hundred and five soldiers, the most approved for valour and fidelity. The remaining nine cohorts consisted each of five hundred and fifty-five; and the whole body of legionary infantry amounted to six thousand one hundred men. Their arms were uniform, and admirably adapted to the nature of their service: an open helmet, with a lofty crest; a breastplate, or coat of mail; greaves on their legs, and an ample buckler on their left arm. The buckler was of an oblong and concave figure, four feet in length, and two and a half in breadth, framed of a light wood, covered with a bull's hide, and strongly guarded with plates of brass. Besides a lighter spear, the legionary soldier grasped in his right hand the formidable *pilum*, a ponderous javelin, whose utmost length was about six feet, and which was terminated by a massy triangular point of steel of eighteen inches.[44] This instrument was indeed much inferior to our modern firearms; since it was exhausted by a single discharge, at the distance of only ten or twelve paces. Yet, when it was launched by a firm and skilful hand, there was not any cavalry that durst venture within its reach, nor any shield or corslet that could sustain the impetuosity of its weight. As soon as the Roman had darted his *pilum*, he drew his sword, and rushed forwards to close with the enemy. It was a short well-tempered Spanish blade, that carried a double edge, and was alike suited to the purpose of striking or of pushing; but the soldier was always instructed to prefer the latter use of his weapon, as his own body remained less exposed, whilst he inflicted a more dangerous wound on his adversary.[45] The legion was usually drawn up eight deep; and the regular distance of three feet was left between the files as well as ranks.[46] A body of troops, habituated to preserve this open order, in a long front and a rapid charge, found themselves prepared to execute every disposition which the circumstances of war, or the skill of their leader, might suggest. The soldier possessed a free space for his arms and motions, and sufficient intervals were allowed, through which seasonable reinforcements might be introduced to the relief of the exhausted combatants.[47] The tactics of the Greeks and Macedonians were formed on very different principles. The strength of the phalanx depended on sixteen ranks of long pikes, wedged together in the closest array.[48] But it was soon discovered, by reflection as well as by the event, that the strength of the phalanx was unable to contend with the activity of the legion.[49]

The cavalry, without which the force of the legion would have remained imperfect, was divided into ten troops or squadrons; the first, as the companion of the first cohort, consisted of an hundred and thirty-two men; whilst each of the other nine amounted only to sixty-six. The entire establishment formed a regiment, if we may use the modern expression, of seven hundred and twenty-six horse, naturally connected with its respective legion, but occasionally separated to act in the line, and to compose a part of the wings of the army.[50] The cavalry of the emperors was no longer composed, like that of the ancient republic, of the noblest youths of Rome and Italy, who, by performing their military service on horseback, prepared themselves for the offices of senator and consul; and solicited, by deeds of valour, the future suffrages of their countrymen.[51] Since the alteration of manners and government, the most wealthy of the equestrian order were engaged in the administration of justice, and of the revenue;[52] and whenever they embraced the profession of arms, they were immediately intrusted with a troop of horse, or a cohort of foot.[53] Trajan and Hadrian formed their cavalry from the same provinces, and the same class of their subjects, which recruited the ranks of the legion. The horses were bred, for the most part, in Spain or Cappadocia. The Roman troopers despised the complete armour with which the cavalry of the East was encumbered. *Their* more useful arms consisted in a helmet, an oblong shield, light boots, and a coat of mail. A javelin, and a long broad sword, were their principal weapons of offence. The use of lances and of iron maces they seem to have borrowed from the barbarians.[54]

The safety and honour of the empire was principally intrusted to the legions, but the policy of Rome condescended to adopt every useful instrument of war. Considerable levies were regularly made among the provincials, who had not yet deserved the honourable distinction of Romans. Many dependent princes and communities, dispersed round the frontiers, were permitted, for a while, to hold their freedom and security by the tenure of military service.[55] Even select troops of hostile barbarians were frequently compelled or persuaded to consume their dangerous valour in remote climates, and for the benefit of the state.[56] All these were included under the general name of auxiliaries; and, howsoever they might vary according to the difference of times and circumstances, their numbers were seldom much inferior to those of the legions themselves.[57]

Among the auxiliaries, the bravest and most faithful bands were placed under the command of prefects and centurions, and severely trained in the arts of Roman discipline; but the far greater part retained those arms to which the nature of their country, or their early habits of life, more peculiarly adapted them. By this institution, each legion, to whom a certain proportion of auxiliaries was allotted, contained within itself every species of lighter troops, and of missile weapons; and was capable of encountering every nation with the advantages of its respective arms and discipline.[58] Nor was the legion destitute of what, in modern language, would be styled a train of artillery. It consisted in ten military engines of the largest, and fifty-five of a smaller size; but all of which, either in an oblique or horizontal manner, discharged stones and darts with irresistible violence.[59]

The camp of a Roman legion presented the appearance of a fortified city.[60] As soon as the space was marked out, the pioneers carefully levelled the ground, and removed every impediment that might interrupt its perfect regularity. Its form was an exact quadrangle; and we may calculate that a square of about seven hundred yards was sufficient for the encampment of twenty thousand Romans; though a similar number of our own troops would expose to the enemy a front of more than treble that extent. In the midst of the camp, the praetorium, or general's quarters, rose above the others; the cavalry, the infantry, and the auxiliaries occupied their respective stations; the streets were broad and perfectly straight, and a vacant space of two hundred feet was left on all sides, between the tents and the rampart. The rampart itself was usually twelve feet high, armed with a line of strong and intricate palisades, and defended by a ditch of twelve feet in depth as well as in breadth. This important labour was performed by the hands of the legionaries themselves; to whom the use of the spade and the pickaxe was no less familiar than that of the sword or *pilum*. Active valour may often be the present of nature; but such patient diligence can be the fruit only of habit and discipline.[61]

Whenever the trumpet gave the signal of departure, the camp was almost instantly broken up, and the troops fell into their ranks without delay or confusion. Besides their arms, which the legionaries scarcely considered as an encumbrance, they were laden with their kitchen furniture, the instruments of fortification, and the provision of many days.[62] Under this weight, which would oppress the delicacy of a modern soldier, they were trained by a regular step to advance, in about six hours, near twenty miles.[63] On the appearance of an enemy, they threw aside their baggage, and, by easy and rapid evolutions, converted the column of march into an order of battle.[64] The slingers and archers skirmished in the front; the auxiliaries formed the first line, and were seconded or sustained by the strength of the legions; the cavalry covered the flanks, and the military engines were placed in the rear.

Such were the arts of war, by which the Roman emperors defended their extensive conquests, and preserved a military spirit, at a time when every other virtue was oppressed by luxury and despotism. If, in the consideration of their armies, we pass from their discipline to their numbers, we shall not find it easy to define them with any tolerable accuracy. We may compute, however, that the legion, which was itself a body of six thousand eight hundred and thirty-one Romans, might, with its attendant auxiliaries, amount to about twelve thousand five hundred men. The peace establishment of Hadrian and his successors was composed of no less than thirty of these formidable brigades; and most probably formed a standing force of three hundred and seventy-five thousand men. Instead of being confined within the walls of fortified cities, which the Romans considered as the refuge of weakness or pusillanimity, the legions were encamped on the banks of the great rivers, and along the frontiers of the barbarians. As their stations, for the most part, remained fixed and permanent, we may venture to describe the distribution of the troops. Three legions were sufficient for Britain. The principal strength lay upon the Rhine and Danube, and consisted of sixteen legions, in the following proportions: two in the Lower, and three in the Upper Germany; one in Rhaetia, one in Noricum, four in Pannonia, three in Maesia, and two in Dacia. The defence of the Euphrates was intrusted to eight legions, six of whom were planted in Syria, and the other two in Cappadocia. With regard to Egypt, Africa and Spain, as they were far removed from any important scene of war, a single legion maintained the domestic tranquillity of each of those great provinces. Even Italy was not left destitute of a military force. Above twenty thousand chosen soldiers, distinguished by the titles of City Cohorts and Praetorian Guards, watched over the safety of the monarch and the capital. As the authors of almost every revolution that distracted the empire, the Praetorians will very soon and very loudly demand our attention; but, in their arms and institutions, we cannot find any circumstance which discriminated them from the legions, unless it were a more splendid appearance, and a less rigid discipline.[65]

The navy maintained by the emperors might seem inadequate to their greatness; but it was fully sufficient for every useful purpose of government. The ambition of the Romans was confined to the land; nor was that warlike people ever actuated by the enterprising spirit which had prompted the navigators of Tyre, of Carthage, and even of Marseilles, to enlarge the bounds of the world, and to explore the most remote coasts of the ocean. To the Romans the ocean remained an object of terror rather than of curiosity;[66] the whole extent of the Mediterranean, after the destruction of Carthage and the extirpation of the pirates, was included within their provinces. The policy of the emperors was directed only to preserve the peaceful dominion of that sea, and to protect the commerce of their subjects. With these moderate views, Augustus stationed two permanent fleets in the most convenient ports of Italy, the one at Ravenna, on the Adriatic, the other at Misenum, in the bay of Naples. Experience seems at length to have convinced the ancients that, as soon as their galleys exceeded two, or at the most three ranks of oars, they were suited rather for vain pomp than for real service. Augustus himself, in the victory of Actium,* had seen the superiority of his own light frigates (they were called Liburnians) over the lofty but unwieldy castles of his rival.[67] Of these Liburnians he composed the two fleets of Ravenna and Misenum, destined to command, the one the eastern, the other the western division of the Mediterranean; and to each of the squadrons he attached a body of several thousand marines. Besides these two ports, which may be considered as the principal seats of the Roman navy, a very considerable force was stationed at Frejus, on the coast of Provence, and the Euxine† was guarded by forty ships and three thousand soldiers. To all these we add the fleet which preserved the communication between Gaul and Britain, and a great number of vessels constantly maintained on the Rhine and Danube, to harass the country, or to intercept the passage of the barbarians.[68] If we review this general state of the Imperial forces, of the cavalry as well as infantry, of the legions, the auxiliaries, the guards, and the navy, the most liberal computation will not allow us to fix the entire establishment by sea and by land at more than four hundred and fifty thousand men: a military power which, however formidable it may seem, was equalled by a monarch of the last century, whose kingdom was confined within a single province of the Roman empire.[69]

We have attempted to explain the spirit which moderated, and the strength which supported, the power of Hadrian and the Antonines. We shall now endeavour, with clearness and precision, to describe the provinces once united under their sway, but, at present, divided into so many independent and hostile states.

Spain, the western extremity of the empire, of Europe, and of the ancient world, has, in every age, invariably preserved the same natural limits: the Pyrenean mountains, the Mediterranean, and the Atlantic Ocean. That great peninsula, at present so unequally divided between two sovereigns, was distributed by Augustus into three provinces, Lusitania, Baetica, and Tarraconensis. The kingdom of Portugal now fills the place of the warlike country of the Lusitanians; and the loss sustained by the former, on the side of the East, is compensated by an accession of territory towards the North. The confines of Granada and Andalusia correspond with those of ancient Baetica. The remainder of Spain – Galicia, and the Asturias, Biscay, and Navarre, Leon, and the two Castilles, Murcia, Valencia, Catalonia, and Aragon – all contributed to form the third and most considerable of the Roman governments, which, from the name of its capital, was styled the province of Tarragona.[70] Of the native barbarians, the Celtiberians were the most powerful, as the Cantabrians and Asturians proved the most obstinate. Confident in the strength of their mountains, they were the last who submitted to the arms of Rome, and the first who threw off the yoke of the Arabs.

Ancient Gaul, as it contained the whole country between the Pyrenees, the Alps, the Rhine, and the Ocean, was of greater extent than modern France. To the dominions of that powerful monarchy, with its recent acquisition of Alsace and Lorraine, we must add the duchy of Savoy, the cantons of Switzerland, the four electorates of the Rhine, and the territories of Liège, Luxembourg, Hainault, Flanders and Brabant. When Augustus gave laws to the conquests of his father,* he introduced a division of Gaul equally adapted to the progress of the legions, to the course of the rivers, and to the principal national distinctions, which had comprehended above an hundred independent states.[71] The sea-coast of the Mediterranean, Languedoc, Provence, and Dauphiné, received their provincial appellation from the colony of Narbonne. The government of Aquitaine was extended from the Pyrenees to the Loire. The country between the Loire and the Seine was styled the Celtic Gaul, and soon borrowed a new denomination from the celebrated colony of Lugdunum, or Lyons. The Belgic lay beyond the Seine, and in more ancient times had been bounded only by the Rhine; but a little before the age of Caesar, the Germans, abusing their superiority of valour, had occupied a considerable portion of the Belgic territory. The Roman conquerors very eagerly embraced so flattering a circumstance, and the Gallic frontier of the Rhine, from Basel to Leyden, received the pompous names of the Upper and the Lower Germany.[72] Such, under the reign of the Antonines, were the six provinces of Gaul: the Narbonnese, Aquitaine, the Celtic, or Lyonnese, the Belgic, and the two Germanies.

We have already had occasion to mention the conquest of Britain, and to fix the boundary of the Roman province in this island. It comprehended all England, Wales, and the Lowlands of Scotland, as far as the Friths of Dumbarton and Edinburgh. Before Britain lost her freedom, the country was irregularly divided between thirty tribes of barbarians, of whom the most considerable were the Belgae in the West, the Brigantes in the North, the Silures in South Wales, and the Iceni in Norfolk and Suffolk.[73] As far as we can either trace or credit the resemblance of manners and language, Spain, Gaul and Britain were peopled by the same hardy race of savages. Before they yielded to the Roman arms, they often disputed the field, and often renewed the contest. After their submission they constituted the western division of the European provinces, which extended from the columns of Hercules to the wall of Antoninus and from the mouth of the Tagus to the sources of the Rhine and Danube.

Before the Roman conquest, the country which is now called Lombardy was not considered as a part of Italy. It had been occupied by a powerful colony of Gauls, who, settling themselves along the banks of the Po, from Piedmont to Romagna, carried their arms and diffused their name from the Alps to the Apennine. The Ligurians dwelt on the rocky coast, which now forms the republic of Genoa. Venice was yet unborn; but the territories of that state, which lie to the east of the Adige, were inhabited by the Venetians.[74] The middle part of the peninsula, that now composes the duchy of Tuscany and the ecclesiastical state, was the ancient seat of the Etruscans and Umbrians; to the former of whom Italy was indebted for the first rudiments of a civilised life.[75] The Tiber rolled at the foot of the seven hills of Rome, and the country of the Sabines, the Latins, and the Volsci, from that river to the frontiers of Naples, was the theatre of her infant victories. On that celebrated ground the first consuls deserved triumphs, their successors adorned villas, and *their* posterity have erected convents.[76] Capua and Campania possessed the immediate territory of Naples; the rest of the kingdom was inhabited by many warlike nations, the Marsi, the Samnites, the Apulians, and the Lucanians; and the sea-coasts had been covered by the flourishing colonies of the Greeks. We may remark that, when Augustus divided Italy into eleven regions, the little province of Istria was annexed to that seat of Roman sovereignty.[77]

The European provinces of Rome were protected by the course of the Rhine and the Danube. The latter of those mighty streams, which rises at the distance of only thirty miles from the former, flows above thirteen hundred miles, for the most part to the south-east, collects the tribute of sixty navigable rivers, and is, at length, through six mouths, received into the Euxine, which appears scarcely equal to such an accession of waters.[78] The provinces of the Danube soon acquired the general appellation of Illyricum, or the Illyrian frontier,[79] and were esteemed the most warlike of the empire; but they deserve to be more particularly considered under the names of Rhaetia, Noricum, Pannonia, Dalmatia, Dacia, Maesia, Thrace, Macedonia, and Greece.

The province of Rhaetia, which soon extinguished the name of the Vindelicians, extended from the summit of the Alps to the banks of the Danube; from its source, as far as its conflux with the Inn. The greatest part of the flat country is subject to the elector of Bavaria; the city of Augsburg is protected by the constitution of the German empire; the Grisons* are safe in their mountains; and the country of Tyrol is ranked among the numerous provinces of the house of Austria.

The wide extent of territory which is included between the Inn, the Danube, and the Save – Austria, Styria, Carinthia, Carniola, the Lower Hungary, and Sclavonia – was known to the ancients under the names of Noricum and Pannonia. In their original state of independence, their fierce inhabitants were intimately connected. Under the Roman government they were frequently united, and they still remain the patrimony of a single family. They now contain the residence of a German prince, who styles himself Emperor of the Romans, and form the centre, as well as strength, of the Austrian power. It may not be improper to observe that, if we except Bohemia, Moravia, the northern skirts of Austria, and a part of Hungary, between the Theiss and the Danube, all the other dominions of the house of Austria were comprised within the limits of the Roman empire.

Dalmatia, to which the name of Illyricum more properly belonged, was a long, but narrow tract, between the Save and the Adriatic. The best part of the sea-coast, which still retains its ancient appellation, is a province of the Venetian state, and the seat of the little republic of Ragusa. The inland parts have assumed the Sclavonian names of Croatia and Bosnia; the former obeys an Austrian governor, the latter a Turkish pasha; but the whole country is still infested by tribes of barbarians, whose savage independence irregularly marks the doubtful limit of the Christian and Mahometan power.[80]

After the Danube had received the waters of the Theiss and the Save, it acquired, at least among the Greeks, the name of Ister.[81] It formerly divided Maesia and Dacia, the latter of which, as we have already seen, was a conquest of Trajan, and the only province beyond the river. If we inquire into the present state of those countries, we shall find that, on the left hand of the Danube, Temeswar and Transylvania have been annexed, after many revolutions, to the crown of Hungary; whilst the principalities of Moldavia and Wallachia acknowledge the supremacy of the Ottoman Porte. On the right hand of the Danube, Maesia, which during the middle ages was broken into the barbarian kingdoms of Servia and Bulgaria, is again united in Turkish slavery.

The appellation of Roumelia, which is still bestowed by the Turks on the extensive countries of Thrace, Macedonia, and Greece, preserves the memory of their ancient state under the Roman empire. In the time of the Antonines, the martial regions of Thrace, from the mountains of Haemus and Rhodope to the Bosphorus and the Hellespont, had assumed the form of a province. Notwithstanding the change of masters and of religion, the new city of Rome, founded by Constantine on the banks of the Bosphorus, has ever since remained the capital of a great monarchy. The kingdom of Macedonia, which, under the reign of Alexander, gave laws to Asia, derived more solid advantages from the policy of the two Philips; and, with its dependencies of Epirus and Thessaly, extended from the Aegean to the Ionian sea. When we reflect on the fame of Thebes and Argos, of Sparta and Athens, we can scarcely persuade ourselves that so many immortal republics of ancient Greece were lost in a single province of the Roman empire, which, from the superior influence of the Achaean league, was usually denominated the province of Achaia.

Such was the state of Europe under the Roman emperors. The provinces of Asia, without excepting the transient conquests of Trajan, are all comprehended within the limits of the Turkish power. But, instead of following the arbitrary divisions of despotism and ignorance, it will be safer for us, as well as more agreeable, to observe the indelible characters of nature. The name of Asia Minor is attributed, with some propriety, to the peninsula which, confined between the Euxine and the Mediterranean, advances from the Euphrates towards Europe. The most extensive and flourishing district westward of Mount Taurus and the river Halys, was dignified by the Romans with the exclusive title of Asia. The jurisdiction of that province extended over the ancient monarchies of Troy, Lydia, and Phrygia, the maritime countries of the Pamphylians, Lycians, and Carians, and the Grecian colonies of Ionia, which equalled in arts, though not in arms, the glory of their parent. The kingdoms of Bithynia and Pontus possessed the northern side of the peninsula from Constantinople to Trebizond. On the opposite side, the province of Cilicia was terminated by the mountains of Syria: the inland country, separated from the Roman Asia by the river Halys, and from Armenia by the Euphrates, had once formed the independent kingdom of Cappadocia. In this place we may observe that the northern shores of the Euxine, beyond Trebizond in Asia and beyond the Danube in Europe, acknowledged the sovereignty of the emperors, and received at their hands either tributary princes or Roman garrisons. Budzak, Crim Tartary, Circassia, and Mingrelia are the modern appellations of those savage countries.[82]

Under the successors of Alexander, Syria was the seat of the Seleucidae, who reigned over Upper Asia, till the successful revolt of the Parthians confined their dominions between the Euphrates and the Mediterranean. When Syria became subject to the Romans, it formed the eastern frontier of their empire; nor did that province, in its utmost latitude, know any other bounds than the mountains of Cappadocia to the north, and, towards the south, the confines of Egypt and the Red Sea. Phoenicia and Palestine were sometimes annexed to, and sometimes separated from, the jurisdiction of Syria. The former of these was a narrow and rocky coast; the latter was a territory scarcely superior to Wales, either in fertility or extent. Yet Phoenicia and Palestine will for ever live in the memory of mankind; since America, as well as Europe, has received letters from the one, and religion from the other.[83] A sandy desert, alike destitute of wood and water, skirts along the doubtful confine of Syria, from the Euphrates to the Red Sea. The wandering life of the Arabs was inseparably connected with their independence, and wherever, on some spots less barren than the rest, they ventured to form any settled habitations, they soon became subjects to the Roman empire.[84]

The geographers of antiquity have frequently hesitated to what portion of the globe they should ascribe Egypt.[85] By its situation that celebrated kingdom is included within the immense peninsula of Africa; but it is accessible only on the side of Asia, whose revolutions, in almost every period of history, Egypt has humbly obeyed. A Roman prefect was seated on the splendid throne of the Ptolemies;* and the iron sceptre of the Mamalukes is now in the hands of a Turkish pasha. The Nile flows down the country, about five hundred miles from the tropic of Cancer to the Mediterranean, and marks, on either side, the extent of fertility by the measure of its inundations. Cyrene, situated towards the west and along the sea-coast, was first a Greek colony, afterwards a province of Egypt, and is now lost in the desert of Barca.

From Cyrene to the ocean, the coast of Africa extends above fifteen hundred miles; yet so closely is it pressed between the Mediterranean and the Sahara, or sandy desert, that its breadth seldom exceeds fourscore or an hundred miles. The eastern division was considered by the Romans as the more peculiar and proper province of Africa. Till the arrival of the Phoenician colonies, that fertile country was inhabited by the Libyans, the most savage of mankind. Under the immediate jurisdiction of Carthage it became the centre of commerce and empire; but the republic of Carthage is now degenerated into the feeble and disorderly states of Tripoli and Tunis. The military government of Algiers oppresses the wide extent of Numidia, as it was once united under Masinissa and Jugurtha: but in the time of Augustus the limits of Numidia were contracted; and at least two-thirds of the country acquiesced in the name of Mauritania, with the epithet of Caesariensis. The genuine Mauritania, or country of the Moors, which, from the ancient city of Tingi, or Tangier, was distinguished by the appellation of Tingitana, is represented by the modern kingdom of Fez. Sallè, on the Ocean, so infamous at present for its piratical depredations, was noticed by the Romans, as the extreme object of their power, and almost of their geography. A city of their foundation may still be discovered near Mequinez, the residence of the barbarian whom we condescend to style the Emperor of Morocco; but it does not appear that his more southern dominions, Morocco itself, and Segelmessa, were ever comprehended within the Roman province. The western parts of Africa are intersected by the branches of Mount Atlas, a name so idly celebrated by the fancy of poets;[86] but which is now diffused over the immense ocean that rolls between the ancient and the new continent.[87]

Having now finished the circuit of the Roman empire, we may observe that Africa is divided from Spain by a narrow strait of about twelve miles, through which the Atlantic flows into the Mediterranean. The columns of Hercules, so famous among the ancients, were two mountains which seemed to have been torn asunder by some convulsion of the elements; and at the foot of the European mountain the fortress of Gibraltar is now seated. The whole extent of the Mediterranean Sea, its coasts and its islands, were comprised within the Roman dominion. Of the larger islands, the two Baleares, which derive their names of Majorca and Minorca from their respective size, are subject at present, the former to Spain, the latter to Great Britain. It is easier to deplore the fate than to describe the actual condition of Corsica. Two Italian sovereigns assume a regal title from Sardinia and Sicily.* Crete, or Candia, with Cyprus, and most of the smaller islands of Greece and Asia, have been subdued by the Turkish arms; whilst the little rock of Malta defies their power, and has emerged, under the government of its military Order, into fame and opulence.

This long enumeration of provinces, whose broken fragments have formed so many powerful kingdoms, might almost induce us to forgive the vanity or ignorance of the ancients. Dazzled with the extensive sway, the irresistible strength, and the real or affected moderation of the emperors, they permitted themselves to despise, and sometimes to forget, the outlying countries which had been left in the enjoyment of a barbarous independence; and they gradually assumed the licence of confounding the Roman monarchy with the globe of the earth.[88] But the temper, as well as knowledge, of a modern historian require a more sober and accurate language. He may impress a juster image of the greatness of Rome by observing that the empire was above two thousand miles in breadth, from the wall of Antoninus and the northern limits of Dacia to Mount Atlas and the tropic of Cancer; that it extended in length more than three thousand miles, from the Western Ocean to the Euphrates; that it was situated in the finest part of the Temperate Zone, between the twenty-fourth and fifty-sixth degrees of northern latitude; and that it was supposed to contain above sixteen hundred thousand square miles, for the most part of fertile and well-cultivated land.[89]

NOTES TO CHAPTER 1

* *page 3* [From the founding of Rome in the 8th century bc.]

1 Dion Cassius (liv, 736), with the annotations of Reimar, who has collected all that Roman vanity has left upon the subject. The marble of Ancyra, on which Augustus recorded his own exploits, asserts that *he compelled* the Parthians to restore the ensigns of Crassus.

2 Strabo (xvi, 780), Pliny the elder (*Historia Naturalis*, vi, 32, 35) and Dion Cassius (liii, 723, and liv, 734) have left us very curious details concerning these wars. The Romans made themselves masters of Mariaba, or Merab, a city of Arabia Felix, well known to the Orientals (see Abulfeda and the *Nubian Geography*, p. 52). They were arrived within three days' journey of the Spice country, the rich object of their invasion.

3 By the slaughter of Varus and his three legions [in ad 9]. See the first book of the *Annals* of Tacitus, Suetonius in *Augustus* ch. 23, and Velleius Paterculus, ii, 117, etc. Augustus did not receive the melancholy news with all the temper and firmness that might have been expected from his character.

4 Tacitus, *Annals*, ii, Dion Cassius, lvi, 832, and the speech of Augustus himself, in Julian's *Caesars*. It receives great light from the learned notes of his French translator, M. Spanheim.

5 Germanicus, Suetonius Paulinus, and Agricola were checked and recalled in the course of their victories. Corbulo was put to death. Military merit, as it is admirably expressed by Tacitus, was, in the strictest sense of the word, *imperatoria virtus* [a form of courage reserved for the emperor].

6 Caesar himself conceals that ignoble motive; but it is mentioned by Suetonius, ch. 47. The British pearls proved, however, of little value, on account of their

dark and livid colour. Tacitus observes, with reason (in *Agricola*, ch. 12), that it was an inherent defect. '*Ego facilius crediderim, naturam margaritis deesse quam nobis avaritiam.*' ['I would sooner have believed that it was the quality of the pearls that was lacking, rather than our greed.']

7 Claudius, Nero, and Domitian. A hope is expressed by Pomponius Mela, iii, 6 (he wrote under Claudius), that, by the success of the Roman arms, the island and its savage inhabitants would soon be better known. It is amusing enough to peruse such passages in the midst of London.

8 See the admirable abridgment, given by Tacitus, in the Life of Agricola and copiously, though perhaps not completely, illustrated by our own antiquarians Camden and Horsley. [1551–1623 and 1685–1732.]

9 The Irish writers, jealous of their national honour, are extremely provoked on this occasion, both with Tacitus and with Agricola.

10 See Horsley's *Britannia Romana*, i, 10.

11 The poet Buchanan [1506–82] celebrates, with elegance and spirit (see his *Sylvae*, v), the unviolated independence of his native country. But, if the single testimony of Richard of Cirencester was sufficient to create a Roman province of Vespasiana to the north of the wall, that independence would be reduced within very narrow limits. [Richard of Cirencester: a fictitious chronicler invented by Gibbon's contemporary, Charles Bertram.]

12 See Appian (in *Proem.*) and the uniform imagery of Ossian's poems, which, according to every hypothesis, were composed by a native Caledonian. [The poems of Ossian, a mythical Gaelic bard, though believed by many to be genuine, and extremely popular in the 18th century, were written by James Macpherson.]

13 See Pliny's *Panegyric*, which seems founded on facts.

14 Dion Cassius, lxvii.

15 Herodotus, iv, 94; Julian in the *Caesars*, with Spanheim's observations.

16 Pliny, *Epistles* viii, 9.

17 Dion Cassius, lxviii, 1123, 1131. Julian, *in Caesaribus*, Eutropius, viii, 2, 6, Aurelius Victor in *Epitome*.

18 See a Memoir of M. d'Anville, on the Province of Dacia, in the *Académie des Inscriptions*, xxviii, 444–68.

  * *page 7*   [Alexander the Great.]

  † *page 7*   [Philip of Macedon, father of Alexander the Great.]

19 Trajan's sentiments are represented in a very just and lively manner in the *Caesars* of Julian.

20 Eutropius and Sextus Rufus have endeavoured to perpetuate the illusion. See a very sensible dissertation of M. Freret, in the *Académie des Inscriptions*, xxi, 55.

21 Dion Cassius, lxviii; and the Abbreviators.

22 Ovid, *Fasti*, ii, 667. See Livy and Dionysius of Halicarnassus, under the reign of Tarquin.

23 St Augustine is highly delighted with the proof of the weakness of Terminus, and the vanity of the Augurs. See *de Civitate Dei*, iv, 29.

24 See the *Augustan History*, p. 5, Jerome's Chronicle, and all the Epitomisers. It is somewhat surprising, that this memorable event should be omitted by Dion, or rather by Xiphilin.

25 Dion, lxix, 115; *Hist. August.*, pp. 5, 8. If all our historians were lost, medals, inscriptions, and other monuments, would be sufficient to record the travels of Hadrian.

26 See the *Augustan History* and the *Epitomes*.

27 We must, however, remember that, in the time of Hadrian, a rebellion of the Jews raged with religious fury, though only in a single province. Pausanias (viii, 43), mentions two necessary and successful wars, conducted by the generals of Pius. First, against the wandering Moors, who were driven into the solitudes of Atlas. Second, against the Brigantes of Britain, who had invaded the Roman province. Both these wars (with several other hostilities) are mentioned in the *Augustan History*, p. 19.

28 Appian of Alexandria, in the preface to his *History of the Roman Wars*.

29 Dion, lxxi, *Hist. August.*, *in Marco*. The Parthian victories gave birth to a crowd of contemptible historians, whose memory has been rescued from oblivion, and exposed to ridicule, in a very lively piece of criticism of Lucian.

 * *page 9* [the Roman republic.]

30 The poorest rank of soldiers possessed above forty pounds sterling (Dionysius Halicarn., iv, 17), a very high qualification, at a time when money was so scarce, that an ounce of silver was equivalent to seventy pound weight of brass. The populace, excluded by the ancient constitution, were indiscriminately admitted by Marius. See Sallust, *de Bell. Jugurth.*, ch. 91.

31 Caesar formed his legion Alauda of Gauls and strangers; but it was during the licence of civil war, and after the victory he gave them the freedom of the city for their reward.

32 See Vegetius, *de Re Militari*, i, 2–7.

33 The oath of service and fidelity to the emperor was annually renewed by the troops, on the first of January.

34 Tacitus calls the Roman Eagles, *bellorum deos* [gods of war]. They were placed in a chapel in the camp, and with the other deities received the religious worship of the troops.

35 See Gronovius, *de Pecunia vetere*, iii, 120, etc. The emperor Domitian raised the annual stipend of the legionaries to twelve pieces of gold, which, in his time, was equivalent to about ten of our guineas. This pay, somewhat higher than our own, had been, and was afterwards, gradually increased, according to the progress of wealth and military government. After twenty years' service, the veteran received three thousand denarii (about one hundred pounds sterling), or a proportionable allowance of land. The pay and advantages of the guards were, in general, about double those of the legions.

36 *Exercitus ab exercitando* ['*exercitus* (the Latin for army) comes from exercise'], Varro, *de Lingua Latina*, iv, Cicero, in *Tusculan.*, ii, 37. There is room for a very interesting work, which should lay open the connection between the languages and manners of nations.

37 Vegetius, i, 11, and the rest of his first book.

38 The Pyrrhic Dance is extremely well illustrated by M. le Beau, in the *Académie des Inscriptions*, xxxv, 262, etc. That learned academician, in a series of memoirs, has collected all the passages of the ancients that relate to the Roman legion.

39 Josephus, *de Bello Judaico*, iii, 5. We are indebted to this Jew for some very curious details of Roman discipline.

40 Pliny, *Panegyricus*, ch. 13; Life of Hadrian, in the *Augustan History*.

 * *page 11* [statesman and historian, *c.*200–*c.*118 BC]

41 See an admirable digression on the Roman discipline, in the sixth book of his history.

† *page 11*   [the wars between Rome and Carthage]

42 Vegetius, *de Re Militari*, ii, 5, etc. Considerable part of his very perplexed abridgment was taken from the regulations of Trajan and Hadrian; and the legion, as he describes it, cannot suit any other age of the Roman empire.

43 *Ibid.*, ch. 1. In the purer age of Caesar and Cicero the word *miles* was almost confined to the infantry. Under the Lower Empire, and in the times of chivalry, it was appropriated almost as exclusively to the men at arms, who fought on horseback.

44 In the time of Polybius and Dionysius of Halicarnassus (v, 45) the steel point of the *pilum* seems to have been much longer. In the time of Vegetius it was reduced to a foot or even nine inches. I have chosen a medium.

45 For the legionary arms, see Lipsius, *de Militia Romana*, iii, 2–7.

46 See the beautiful comparison of Virgil, *Georgics* ii, 279.

47 M. Guichard, *Mémoires Militaires*, i, 4, and *Nouveaux Mémoires*, i, 293–311, has treated the subject like a scholar and an officer.

48 See Arrian's *Tactics*. With the true partiality of a Greek, Arrian rather chose to describe the phalanx of which he had read, than the legions which he had commanded.

49 Polybius, xvii.

50 Vegetius, *de Re Militari*, ii, 6. His positive testimony, which might be supported by circumstantial evidence, ought surely to silence those critics who refuse the Imperial legion its proper body of cavalry.

51 See Livy almost throughout, particularly xlii, 61.

52 Pliny, *Historia Naturalis*, xxxiii, 2. The true sense of that very curious passage was first discovered and illustrated by M. de Beaufort, *République Romaine*, ii, 2.

53 As in the instance of Horace and Agricola. This appears to have been a defect in the Roman discipline; which Hadrian endeavoured to remedy by ascertaining the legal age of a tribune.

54 See Arrian's *Tactics*.

55 Such, in particular, was the state of the Batavians: Tacitus, *Germania*, 29.

56 Marcus Antoninus obliged the vanquished Quadi and Marcomanni to supply him with a large body of troops, which he immediately sent into Britain: Dion Cassius, lxxi.

57 Tacitus, *Annals*, iv, 5. Those who fix a regular proportion of as many foot, and twice as many horse, confound the auxiliaries of the emperors with the Italian allies of the republic.

58 Vegetius, ii, 2; Arrian, in his order of march and battle against the Alani.

59 The subject of the ancient machines is treated with great knowledge and ingenuity by the Chevalier Folard (*Polybe*, ii, 233–90). He prefers them in many respects to our modern cannon and mortars. We may observe that the use of them in the field gradually became more prevalent, in proportion as personal valour and military skill declined with the Roman empire. When men were no longer found, their place was supplied by machines. See Vegetius, ii, 25, Arrian.

60 Vegetius finishes his second book, and the description of the legion, with the following emphatic words: '*Universa quae in quoque belli genere necessaria esse creduntur, secum legio debet ubique portare, ut in quovis loco fixerit castra, armatam faciat civitatem.*' ['Whatever is deemed necessary in any kind of war the legion must take with it everywhere, so that wherever it pitches camp, it may make a fortified city.']

61 For the Roman castrametation, see Polybius, vi, with Lipsius, *de Militia Romana*, Josephus, *de Bello Judaico*, iii, 5, Vegetius, i, 21–25 and iii, 9, and *Mémoires* de Guichard, i, 1.

62 Cicero, in *Tusculan.*, ii, 37, Josephus, *de Bello Judaico*, iii, 5, Frontinus, iv, 1.

63 Vegetius, i, 9. See *Mémoires de l'Académie des Inscriptions*, xxv, 187.

64 See those evolutions admirably well explained by M. Guichard, *Nouveaux Mémoires*, i, 141–234.

65 Tacitus (*Annals*, iv, 5) has given us a state of the legions under Tiberius; and Dion Cassius (lv, 794) under Alexander Severus. I have endeavoured to fix on the proper medium between these two periods. See likewise Lipsius, *de Magnitudine Romana*, i, 4, 5.

66 The Romans tried to disguise, by the pretence of religious awe, their ignorance and terror. See Tacitus, *Germania*, 34.

  * *page 15* [in 31 BC, over his last remaining rival, Mark Antony]

67 Plutarch, in *Marc. Anton.* And yet if we may credit Orosius, these monstrous castles were no more than ten feet above the water, vi, 19.

  † *page 15* [the Black Sea]

68 See Lipsius, *de Magnitud. Rom.*, i, 5. The sixteen last chapters of Vegetius relate to naval affairs.

69 Voltaire, *Siècle de Louis XIV*, ch. 29. It must, however, be remembered, that France still feels that extraordinary effort.

70 See Strabo, ii. It is natural enough to suppose, that Aragon is derived from Tarraconensis, and several moderns who have written in Latin use those words as synonymous. It is, however, certain, that the Aragon, a little stream which falls from the Pyrenees into the Ebro, first gave its name to a country, and gradually to a kingdom. See d'Anville, *Géographie du Moyen Age*, p. 181.

  * *page 16* [Julius Caesar, who adopted Augustus]

71 One hundred and fifteen *cities* appear in the *Notitia* of Gaul; and it is well known that this appellation was applied not only to the capital town, but to the whole territory of each state. But Plutarch and Appian increase the number of tribes to three or four hundred.

72 D'Anville, *Notice de l'Ancienne Gaule.*

73 Whitaker's *History of Manchester*, i, ch. 3.

74 The Italian Veneti, though often confounded with the Gauls, were more probably of Illyrian origin. See M. Freret, *Mémoires de l'Académie des Inscriptions*, xviii.

75 See Maffei, *Verona illustrata*, i.

76 The first contrast was observed by the ancients. See Florus, i, 11. The second must strike every modern traveller.

77 Pliny (*Historia Naturalis* iii) follows the division of Italy by Augustus.

78 Tournefort, *Voyages en Grèce et Asie Mineure*, lettre xviii.

79 The name of Illyricum originally belonged to the sea-coast of the Adriatic, and was gradually extended by the Romans from the Alps to the Euxine Sea. See Severini, *Pannonia*, i, 3.

  * *page 17* [name of a canton in the Swiss Alps]

80 A Venetian traveller, the Abbate Fortis, has lately given us some account of those very obscure countries. But the geography and antiquities of the western Illyricum can be expected only from the munificence of the emperor, its sovereign.

81 The Save rises near the confines of Istria, and was considered by the more early Greeks as the principal stream of the Danube.

82 See the *Periplus* of Arrian. He examined the coasts of the Euxine, when he was governor of Cappadocia.

83 The progress of religion is well known. The use of letters was introduced among the savages of Europe about fifteen hundred years before Christ; and the Europeans carried them to America, about fifteen centuries after the Christian era. But in a period of three thousand years, the Phoenician alphabet received considerable alterations, as it passed through the hands of the Greeks and Romans.

84 Dion Cassius, lxviii, 1131.

85 Ptolemy and Strabo, with the modern geographers, fix the Isthmus of Suez as the boundary of Asia and Africa. Dionysius, Mela, Pliny, Sallust, Hirtius, and Solinus, have preferred for that purpose the western branch of the Nile, or even the great Catabathmus, or descent, which last would assign to Asia not only Egypt, but part of Libya.

* *page 19*   [The Ptolemaic kingdom of Egypt ended with the death of Cleopatra in 30 BC.]

86 The long range, moderate height, and gentle declivity of Mount Atlas (see Shaw's *Travels*, p. 5) are very unlike a solitary mountain which rears its head into the clouds, and seems to support the heavens. The peak of Teneriff, on the contrary, rises a league and a half above the surface of the sea, and, as it was frequently visited by the Phoenicians, might engage the notice of the Greek poets. See Buffon, *Histoire Naturelle*, i, 312, *Histoire des Voyages*, ii.

87 M. de Voltaire, xiv, 297, unsupported by either fact or probability, has generously bestowed the Canary Islands on the Roman empire.

* *page 20*   [When Gibbon was writing, the King of Sardinia ruled from Turin and the King of the Two Sicilies from Naples.]

88 Bergier, *Hist. des Grands Chemins*, iii, 1–4: a very useful collection.

89 See Templeman's *Survey of the Globe*; but I distrust both the doctor's learning and his maps.

CHAPTER 2

Of the union and internal prosperity of the Roman Empire in the age of the Antonines

It is not alone by the rapidity or extent of conquest that we should estimate the greatness of Rome. The sovereign of the Russian deserts commands a larger portion of the globe. In the seventh summer after his passage of the Hellespont, Alexander erected the Macedonian trophies on the banks of the Hyphasis.[1] Within less than a century, the irresistible Zingis,* and the Mogul princes of his race, spread their cruel devastations and transient empire from the sea of China to the confines of Egypt and Germany.[2] But the firm edifice of Roman power was raised and preserved by the wisdom of ages. The obedient provinces of Trajan and the Antonines were united by laws and adorned by arts. They might occasionally suffer from the partial abuse of delegated authority; but the general principle of government was wise, simple, and beneficent. They enjoyed the religion of their ancestors, whilst in civil honours and advantages they were exalted, by just degrees, to an equality with their conquerors.

I.   The policy of the emperors and the senate, as far as it concerned religion, was happily seconded by the reflections of the enlightened, and by the habits of the superstitious, part of their subjects. The various modes of worship which prevailed in the Roman world were all considered by the people as equally true; by the philosopher as equally false; and by the magistrate as equally useful. And thus toleration produced not only mutual indulgence, but even religious concord.

The superstition of the people was not embittered by any mixture of theological rancour; nor was it confined by the chains of any speculative system. The devout polytheist, though fondly attached to his national rites, admitted with implicit faith the different religions of the earth.[3] Fear, gratitude, and curiosity, a dream or an omen, a singular disorder, or a distant journey, perpetually disposed him to multiply the articles of his belief, and to enlarge the list of his protectors. The thin texture of the pagan mythology was interwoven with various but not discordant materials. As soon as it was allowed that sages and heroes, who had lived or who had died for the benefit of their country, were exalted to a state of power and immortality, it was universally confessed that they deserved, if not the adoration, at least the reverence of all mankind. The deities of a thousand groves and a thousand streams possessed in peace their local and respective influence; nor could the Roman who deprecated the wrath of

the Tiber deride the Egyptian who presented his offering to the beneficent genius of the Nile. The visible powers of Nature, the planets, and the
elements, were the same throughout the universe. The invisible governors of the moral world were inevitably cast in a similar mould of fiction
and allegory. Every virtue, and even vice, acquired its divine representative; every art and profession its patron, whose attributes in the most
distant ages and countries were uniformly derived from the character of
their peculiar votaries. A republic of gods of such opposite tempers and
interests required, in every system, the moderating hand of a supreme
magistrate, who, by the progress of knowledge and of flattery, was
gradually invested with the sublime perfections of an Eternal Parent and
Omnipotent Monarch.[4] Such was the mild spirit of antiquity, that the
nations were less attentive to the difference than to the resemblance of
their religious worship. The Greek, the Roman, and the barbarian, as they
met before their respective altars, easily persuaded themselves that, under
various names and with various ceremonies, they adored the same deities.
The elegant mythology of Homer gave a beautiful and almost a regular
form to the polytheism of the ancient world.[5]

The philosophers of Greece deduced their morals from the nature of
man rather than from that of God. They meditated, however, on the
Divine Nature as a very curious and important speculation, and in the
profound inquiry they displayed the strength and weakness of the human
understanding.[6] Of the four most celebrated schools, the Stoics and the
Platonists endeavoured to reconcile the jarring interests of reason and
piety. They have left us the most sublime proofs of the existence and
perfections of the first cause; but, as it was impossible for them to
conceive the creation of matter, the workman in the Stoic philosophy
was not sufficiently distinguished from the work; whilst, on the contrary,
the spiritual God of Plato and his disciples resembled an idea rather than
a substance. The opinions of the Academics and Epicureans were of a less
religious cast; but, whilst the modest science of the former induced them
to doubt, the positive ignorance of the latter urged them to deny, the
providence of a Supreme Ruler. The spirit of inquiry, prompted by
emulation and supported by freedom, had divided the public teachers of
philosophy into a variety of contending sects; but the ingenuous youth,
who from every part resorted to Athens and the other seats of learning in
the Roman empire, were alike instructed in every school to reject and to
despise the religion of the multitude. How, indeed, was it possible that a
philosopher should accept as divine truths the idle tales of the poets, and
the incoherent traditions of antiquity; or that he should adore, as gods,
those imperfect beings whom he must have despised, as men! Against
such unworthy adversaries, Cicero condescended to employ the arms of
reason and eloquence; but the satire of Lucian was a much more
adequate as well as more efficacious weapon. We may be well assured
that a writer conversant with the world would never have ventured to

expose the gods of his country to public ridicule, had they not already been the objects of secret contempt among the polished and enlightened orders of society.[7]

Notwithstanding the fashionable irreligion which prevailed in the age of the Antonines, both the interests of the priests and the credulity of the people were sufficiently respected. In their writings and conversation the philosophers of antiquity asserted the independent dignity of reason; but they resigned their actions to the commands of law and of custom. Viewing with a smile of pity and indulgence the various errors of the vulgar, they diligently practised the ceremonies of their fathers, devoutly frequented the temples of the gods; and, sometimes condescending to act a part on the theatre of superstition, they concealed the sentiments of an atheist under the sacerdotal robes. Reasoners of such a temper were scarcely inclined to wrangle about their respective modes of faith or of worship. It was indifferent to them what shape the folly of the multitude might choose to assume; and they approached, with the same inward contempt and the same external reverence, the altars of the Libyan, the Olympian, or the Capitoline Jupiter.[8]

It is not easy to conceive from what motives a spirit of persecution could introduce itself into the Roman councils. The magistrates could not be actuated by a blind though honest bigotry, since the magistrates were themselves philosophers; and the schools of Athens had given laws to the senate. They could not be impelled by ambition or avarice, as the temporal and ecclesiastical powers were united in the same hands. The pontiffs were chosen among the most illustrious of the senators; and the office of Supreme Pontiff was constantly exercised by the emperors themselves. They knew and valued the advantages of religion, as it is connected with civil government. They encouraged the public festivals which humanise the manners of the people. They managed the arts of divination as a convenient instrument of policy; and they respected, as the firmest bond of society, the useful persuasion that, either in this or in a future life, the crime of perjury is most assuredly punished by the avenging gods.[9] But, whilst they acknowledged the general advantages of religion, they were convinced that the various modes of worship contributed alike to the same salutary purposes; and that, in every country, the form of superstition which had received the sanction of time and experience was the best adapted to the climate and to its inhabitants. Avarice and taste very frequently despoiled the vanquished nations of the elegant statues of their gods and the rich ornaments of their temples;[10] but, in the exercise of the religion which they derived from their ancestors, they uniformly experienced the indulgence, and even protection, of the Roman conquerors. The province of Gaul seems, and indeed only seems, an exception to this universal toleration. Under the specious pretext of abolishing human sacrifices, the emperors Tiberius and Claudius suppressed the dangerous power of the Druids;[11] but the priests themselves, their gods, and their altars, subsisted in peaceful obscurity till the final destruction of Paganism.[12]

Rome, the capital of a great monarchy, was incessantly filled with subjects and strangers from every part of the world,[13] who all introduced and enjoyed the favourite superstitions of their native country.[14] Every city in the empire was justified in maintaining the purity of its ancient ceremonies; and the Roman senate, using the common privilege, sometimes interposed to check this inundation of foreign rites. The Egyptian superstition, of all the most contemptible and abject, was frequently prohibited; the temples of Serapis and Isis demolished, and their worshippers banished from Rome and Italy.[15] But the zeal of fanaticism prevailed over the cold and feeble efforts of policy. The exiles returned, the proselytes multiplied, the temples were restored with increasing splendour, and Isis and Serapis at length assumed their place among the Roman deities.[16] Nor was this indulgence a departure from the old maxims of government. In the purest ages of the commonwealth, Cybele and Aesculapius had been invited by solemn embassies;[17] and it was customary to tempt the protectors of besieged cities by the promise of more distinguished honours than they possessed in their native country.[18] Rome gradually became the common temple of her subjects; and the freedom of the city was bestowed on all the gods of mankind.[19]

II. The narrow policy of preserving without any foreign mixture the pure blood of the ancient citizens, had checked the fortune, and hastened the ruin, of Athens and Sparta. The aspiring genius of Rome sacrificed vanity to ambition, and deemed it more prudent, as well as honourable, to adopt virtue and merit for her own wheresoever they were found, among slaves or strangers, enemies or barbarians.[20] During the most flourishing era of the Athenian commonwealth the number of citizens gradually decreased from about thirty[21] to twenty-one thousand.[22] If, on the contrary, we study the growth of the Roman republic, we may discover that, notwithstanding the incessant demands of wars and colonies, the citizens, who, in the first census of Servius Tullius, amounted to no more than eighty-three thousand, were multiplied, before the commencement of the Social War, to the number of four hundred and sixty-three thousand men able to bear arms in the service of their country.[23] When the allies of Rome claimed an equal share of honours and privileges, the senate indeed preferred the chance of arms to an ignominious concession. The Samnites and the Lucanians paid the severe penalty of their rashness; but the rest of the Italian states, as they successively returned to their duty, were admitted into the bosom of the republic,[24] and soon contributed to the ruin of public freedom. Under a democratical government the citizens exercise the powers of sovereignty; and those powers will be first abused, and afterwards lost, if they are committed to an unwieldy multitude. But, when the popular assemblies had been suppressed by the administration of the emperors, the conquerors were distinguished from the vanquished nations only as the first and most honourable order of subjects; and their increase, however rapid, was no longer exposed to the same dangers. Yet the wisest princes who adopted the maxims of Augustus guarded with the strictest care the dignity of the Roman name, and diffused the freedom of the city with a prudent liberality.[25]

Till the privileges of Romans had been progressively extended to all the inhabitants of the empire, an important distinction was preserved between Italy and the provinces. The former was esteemed the centre of public unity, and the firm basis of the constitution. Italy claimed the birth, or at least the residence, of the emperors and the senate.[26] The estates of the Italians were exempt from taxes, their persons from the arbitrary jurisdiction of governors. Their municipal corporations, formed after the perfect model of the capital, were intrusted, under the immediate eye of the supreme power, with the execution of the laws. From the foot of the Alps to the extremity of Calabria, all the natives of Italy were born citizens of Rome. Their partial distinctions were obliterated, and they insensibly coalesced into one great nation, united by language, manners, and civil institutions, and equal to the weight of a powerful empire. The republic gloried in her generous policy, and was frequently rewarded by the merit and services of her adopted sons. Had she always confined the distinction of Romans to the ancient families within the walls of the city, that immortal name would have been deprived of some of its noblest ornaments. Virgil was a native of Mantua; Horace was inclined to doubt whether he should call himself an Apulian or a Lucanian; it was in Padua that an historian* was found worthy to record the majestic series of Roman victories. The patriot family of the Catos emerged from Tusculum; and the little town of Arpinum claimed the double honour of producing Marius and Cicero, the former of whom deserved, after Romulus and Camillus, to be styled the Third Founder of Rome; and the latter, after saving his country from the designs of Catiline, enabled her to contend with Athens for the palm of eloquence.[27]

The provinces of the empire (as they have been described in the preceding chapter) were destitute of any public force or constitutional freedom. In Etruria, in Greece,[28] and in Gaul,[29] it was the first care of the senate to dissolve those dangerous confederacies which taught mankind that, as the Roman arms prevailed by division, they might be resisted by union. Those princes whom the ostentation of gratitude or generosity permitted for a while to hold a precarious sceptre were dismissed from their thrones, as soon as they had performed their appointed task of fashioning to the yoke the vanquished nations. The free states and cities which had embraced the cause of Rome were rewarded with a nominal alliance, and insensibly sunk into real servitude. The public authority was everywhere exercised by the ministers of the senate and of the emperors, and that authority was absolute and without control. But the same salutary maxims of government, which had secured the peace and obedience of Italy, were extended to the most distant conquests. A nation of Romans was gradually formed in the provinces, by the double expedient of introducing colonies, and of admitting the most faithful and deserving of the provincials to the freedom of Rome.

'Wheresoever the Roman conquers, he inhabits,' is a very just observation of Seneca,[30] confirmed by history and experience. The natives of Italy, allured by pleasure or by interest, hastened to enjoy the advantages of victory; and we may remark that, about forty years after the reduction of Asia, eighty thousand Romans were massacred in one day by the cruel orders of Mithridates.[31] These voluntary exiles were engaged for the most part in the occupations of commerce, agriculture, and the farm of the revenue. But after the legions were rendered permanent by the emperors, the provinces were peopled by a race of soldiers; and the veterans, whether they received the reward of their service in land or in money, usually settled with their families in the country where they had honourably spent their youth. Throughout the empire, but more particularly in the western parts, the most fertile districts and the most convenient situations were reserved for the establishment of colonies; some of which were of a civil and others of a military nature. In their manners and internal policy, the colonies formed a perfect representation of their great parent; and as they were soon endeared to the natives by the ties of friendship and alliance, they effectually diffused a reverence for the Roman name, and a desire which was seldom disappointed of sharing, in due time, its honours and advantages.[32] The municipal cities insensibly equalled the rank and splendour of the colonies; and in the reign of Hadrian it was disputed which was the preferable condition, of those societies which had issued from, or those which had been received into, the bosom of Rome.[33] The right of Latium, as it was called, conferred on the cities to which it had been granted a more partial favour. The magistrates only, at the expiration of their office, assumed the quality of Roman citizens; but as those offices were annual, in a few years they circulated round the principal families.[34] Those of the provincials who were permitted to bear arms in the legions;[35] those who exercised any civil employment; all, in a word, who performed any public service, or displayed any personal talents, were rewarded with a present, whose value was continually diminished by the increasing liberality of the emperors. Yet even in the age of the Antonines, when the freedom of the city had been bestowed on the greater number of their subjects, it was still accompanied with very solid advantages. The bulk of the people acquired, with that title, the benefit of the Roman laws, particularly in the interesting articles of marriage, testaments, and inheritances; and the road of fortune was open to those whose pretensions were seconded by favour or merit. The grandsons of the Gauls who had besieged Julius Caesar in Alesia commanded legions, governed provinces, and were admitted into the senate of Rome.[36] Their ambition, instead of disturbing the tranquillity of the state, was intimately connected with its safety and greatness.

So sensible were the Romans of the influence of language over national manners, that it was their most serious care to extend, with the progress of their arms, the use of the Latin tongue.[37] The ancient dialects of Italy, the Sabine, the Etruscan, and the Venetian, sunk into oblivion; but in the provinces, the east was less docile than the west to the voice of its victorious preceptors. This obvious difference marked the two portions of the empire with a distinction of colours, which, though it was in some degree concealed during the meridian splendour of prosperity, became gradually more visible as the shades of night descended upon the Roman world. The western countries were civilised by the same hands which subdued them. As soon as the barbarians were reconciled to obedience, their minds were opened to any new impressions of knowledge and politeness. The language of Virgil and Cicero, though with some inevitable mixture of corruption, was so universally adopted in Africa, Spain, Gaul, Britain, and Pannonia,[38] that the faint traces of the Punic or Celtic idioms were preserved only in the mountains, or among the peasants.[39] Education and study insensibly inspired the natives of those countries with the sentiments of Romans; and Italy gave fashions, as well as laws, to her Latin provincials. They solicited with more ardour, and obtained with more facility, the freedom and honours of the state; supported the national dignity in letters[40] and in arms; and, at length, in the person of Trajan, produced an emperor whom the Scipios would not have disowned for their countryman. The situation of the Greeks was very different from that of the barbarians. The former had been long since civilised and corrupted. They had too much taste to relinquish their language, and too much vanity to adopt any foreign institutions. Still preserving the prejudices, after they had lost the virtues, of their ancestors, they affected to despise the unpolished manners of the Roman conquerors, whilst they were compelled to respect their superior wisdom and power.[41] Nor was the influence of the Grecian language and sentiments confined to the narrow limits of that once celebrated country. Their empire, by the progress of colonies and conquest, had been diffused from the Hadriatic to the Euphrates and the Nile. Asia was covered with Greek cities, and the long reign of the Macedonian kings had introduced a silent revolution into Syria and Egypt. In their pompous courts those princes united the elegance of Athens with the luxury of the East, and the example of the court was imitated, at an humble distance, by the higher ranks of their subjects. Such was the general division of the Roman empire into the Latin and Greek languages. To these we may add a third distinction for the body of the natives in Syria, and especially in Egypt. The use of their ancient dialects, by secluding them from the commerce of mankind, checked the improvements of those barbarians.[42] The slothful effeminacy of the former exposed them to the contempt, the sullen ferociousness of the latter excited the aversion, of the conquerors.[43] Those nations had submitted to the Roman power, but they seldom desired or deserved the freedom of the city; and it was remarked that more than two hundred and thirty years elapsed after the ruin of the Ptolemies, before an Egyptian was admitted into the senate of Rome.[44]

It is a just though trite observation, that victorious Rome was herself subdued by the arts of Greece. Those immortal writers who still command the admiration of modern Europe soon became the favourite object of study and imitation in Italy and the western provinces. But the elegant amusements of the Romans were not suffered to interfere with their sound maxims of policy. Whilst they acknowledged the charms of the Greek, they asserted the dignity of the Latin, tongue, and the exclusive use of the latter was inflexibly maintained in the administration of civil as well as military government.[45] The two languages exercised at the same time their separate jurisdiction throughout the empire: the former, as the natural idiom of science; the latter, as the legal dialect of public transactions. Those who united letters with business were equally conversant with both; and it was almost impossible, in any province, to find a Roman subject, of a liberal education, who was at once a stranger to the Greek and to the Latin language.

It was by such institutions that the nations of the empire insensibly melted away into the Roman name and people. But there still remained, in the centre of every province and of every family, an unhappy condition of men who endured the weight, without sharing the benefits, of society. In the free states of antiquity the domestic slaves were exposed to the wanton rigour of despotism. The perfect settlement of the Roman empire was preceded by ages of violence and rapine. The slaves consisted, for the most part, of barbarian captives, taken in thousands by the chance of war, purchased at a vile price,[46] accustomed to a life of independence, and impatient to break and to revenge their fetters. Against such internal enemies, whose desperate insurrections had more than once reduced the republic to the brink of destruction,[47] the most severe regulations[48] and the most cruel treatment seemed almost justified by the great law of self-preservation. But when the principal nations of Europe, Asia, and Africa were united under the laws of one sovereign, the source of foreign supplies flowed with much less abundance, and the Romans were reduced to the milder but more tedious method of propagation. In their numerous families, and particularly in their country estates, they encouraged the marriage of their slaves. The sentiments of nature, the habits of education, and the possession of a dependent species of property, contributed to alleviate the hardships of servitude.[49] The existence of a slave became an object of greater value, and, though his happiness still depended on the temper and circumstances of the master, the humanity of the latter, instead of being restrained by fear, was encouraged by the sense of his own interest. The progress of manners was accelerated by the virtue or policy of the emperors; and by the edicts of Hadrian and the Antonines the protection of the laws was extended to the most abject part of mankind. The jurisdiction of life and death over the slaves, a power long exercised and often abused, was taken out of private hands, and reserved to the magistrates alone. The subterraneous prisons were abolished; and, upon a just complaint of intolerable treatment, the injured slave obtained either his deliverance or a less cruel master.[50]

Hope, the best comfort of our imperfect condition, was not denied to the Roman slave; and, if he had any opportunity of making himself either useful or agreeable, he might very naturally expect that the diligence and fidelity of a few years would be rewarded with the inestimable gift of freedom. The benevolence of the master was so frequently prompted by the meaner suggestions of vanity and avarice, that the laws found it more necessary to restrain than to encourage a profuse and undistinguishing liberality, which might degenerate into a very dangerous abuse.[51] It was a maxim of ancient jurisprudence that a slave had not any country of his own; he acquired with his liberty an admission into the political society of which his patron was a member. The consequences of this maxim would have prostituted the privileges of the Roman city to a mean and promiscuous multitude. Some seasonable exceptions were therefore provided; and the honourable distinction was confined to such slaves only as, for just causes, and with the approbation of the magistrate, should receive a solemn and legal manumission. Even these chosen freedmen obtained no more than the private rights of citizens, and were rigorously excluded from civil or military honours. Whatever might be the merit or fortune of their sons, *they* likewise were esteemed unworthy of a seat in the senate; nor were the traces of a servile origin allowed to be completely obliterated till the third or fourth generation.[52] Without destroying the distinction of ranks, a distant prospect of freedom and honours was presented, even to those whom pride and prejudice almost disdained to number among the human species.

It was once proposed to discriminate the slaves by a peculiar habit, but it was justly apprehended that there might be some danger in acquainting them with their own numbers.[53] Without interpreting, in their utmost strictness, the liberal appellations of legions and myriads,[54] we may venture to pronounce that the proportion of slaves, who were valued as property, was more considerable than that of servants, who can be computed only as an expense.[55] The youths of a promising genius were instructed in the arts and sciences, and their price was ascertained by the degree of their skill and talents.[56] Almost every profession, either liberal[57] or mechanical, might be found in the household of an opulent senator. The ministers of pomp and sensuality were multiplied beyond the conception of modern luxury.[58] It was more for the interest of the merchant or manufacturer to purchase than to hire his workmen; and in the country slaves were employed as the cheapest and most laborious instruments of agriculture. To confirm the general observation, and to display the multitude of slaves, we might allege a variety of particular instances. It was discovered, on a very melancholy occasion, that four hundred slaves were maintained in a single palace of Rome.[59] The same number of four hundred belonged to an estate, which an African widow, of a very private condition, resigned to her son, whilst she reserved for herself a much larger share of her property.[60] A freedman, under the reign of Augustus, though his fortune had suffered great losses in the civil wars, left behind him three thousand six hundred yoke of oxen, two hundred and fifty thousand head of smaller cattle, and, what was almost included in the description of cattle, four thousand one hundred and sixteen slaves.[61]

The number of subjects who acknowledged the laws of Rome, of citizens, of provincials, and of slaves, cannot now be fixed with such a degree of accuracy as the importance of the object would deserve. We are informed that, when the emperor Claudius exercised the office of censor, he took an account of six millions, nine hundred and forty-five thousand Roman citizens, who, with the proportion of women and children, must have amounted to about twenty millions of souls. The multitude of subjects of an inferior rank was uncertain and fluctuating. But, after weighing with attention every circumstance which could influence the balance, it seems probable that there existed, in the time of Claudius, about twice as many provincials as there were citizens, of either sex and of every age; and that the slaves were at least equal in number to the free inhabitants of the Roman world. The total amount of this imperfect calculation would rise to about one hundred and twenty millions of persons: a degree of population which possibly exceeds that of modern Europe,[62] and forms the most numerous society that has ever been united under the same system of government.

Domestic peace and union were the natural consequences of the moderate and comprehensive policy embraced by the Romans. If we turn our eyes towards the monarchies of Asia, we shall behold despotism in the centre and weakness in the extremities; the collection of the revenue, or the administration of justice, enforced by the presence of an army; hostile barbarians, established in the heart of the country, hereditary satraps usurping the dominion of the provinces, and subjects, inclined to rebellion, though incapable of freedom. But the obedience of the Roman world was uniform, voluntary, and permanent. The vanquished nations, blended into one great people, resigned the hope, nay even the wish, of resuming their independence, and scarcely considered their own existence as distinct from the existence of Rome. The established authority of the emperors pervaded without an effort the wide extent of their dominions, and was exercised with the same facility on the banks of the Thames, or of the Nile, as on those of the Tiber. The legions were destined to serve against the public enemy, and the civil magistrate seldom required the aid of a military force.[63] In this state of general security, the leisure as well as opulence both of the prince and people were devoted to improve and to adorn the Roman empire.

Among the innumerable monuments of architecture constructed by the Romans, how many have escaped the notice of history, how few have resisted the ravages of time and barbarism! And yet even the majestic ruins that are still scattered over Italy and the provinces would be sufficient to prove that those countries were once the seat of a polite and powerful empire. Their greatness alone, or their beauty, might deserve our attention; but they are rendered more interesting by two important circumstances, which connect the agreeable history of the arts with the more useful history of human manners. Many of those works were erected at private expense, and almost all were intended for public benefit.

It is natural to suppose that the greatest number, as well as the most considerable of the Roman edifices, were raised by the emperors, who possessed so unbounded a command both of men and money. Augustus was accustomed to boast that he had found his capital of brick, and that he had left it of marble.[64] The strict economy of Vespasian was the source of his magnificence. The works of Trajan bear the stamp of his genius. The public monuments with which Hadrian adorned every province of the empire were executed not only by his orders, but under his immediate inspection. He was himself an artist; and he loved the arts, as they conduced to the glory of the monarch. They were encouraged by the Antonines, as they contributed to the happiness of the people. But if the emperors were the first, they were not the only architects of their dominions. Their example was universally imitated by their principal subjects, who were not afraid of declaring that they had spirit to conceive, and wealth to accomplish, the noblest undertakings. Scarcely had the proud structure of the Coliseum been dedicated at Rome, before the edifices of a smaller scale indeed, but of the same design and materials, were erected for the use, and at the expense, of the cities of Capua and Verona.[65] The inscription of the stupendous bridge of Alcantara attests that it was thrown over the Tagus by the contribution of a few Lusitanian communities. When Pliny was intrusted with the government of Bithynia and Pontus, provinces by no means the richest or most considerable of the empire, he found the cities within his jurisdiction striving with each other in every useful and ornamental work that might deserve the curiosity of strangers or the gratitude of their citizens. It was the duty of the Proconsul to supply their deficiencies, to direct their taste, and sometimes to moderate their emulation.[66] The opulent senators of Rome and the provinces esteemed it an honour, and almost an obligation, to adorn the splendour of their age and country; and the influence of fashion very frequently supplied the want of taste or generosity. Among a crowd of these private benefactors, we may select Herodes Atticus, an Athenian citizen, who lived in the age of the Antonines. Whatever might be the motive of his conduct, his magnificence would have been worthy of the greatest kings.

The family of Herod, at least after it had been favoured by fortune, was lineally descended from Cimon and Miltiades, Theseus and Cecrops, Aeacus and Jupiter. But the posterity of so many gods and heroes was fallen into the most abject state. His grandfather had suffered by the hands of justice, and Julius Atticus, his father, must have ended his life in poverty and contempt, had he not discovered an immense treasure buried under an old house, the last remains of his patrimony. According to the rigour of law, the emperor might have asserted his claim; and the prudent Atticus prevented, by a frank confession, the officiousness of informers. But the equitable Nerva, who then filled the throne, refused to accept any part of it, and commanded him to use, without scruple, the present of fortune. The cautious Athenian still insisted that the treasure was too considerable for a subject, and that he knew not how to *use it*. *Abuse it then*, replied the monarch, with a good-natured peevishness; for it is your own.[67] Many will be of opinion that Atticus literally obeyed the emperor's last instructions, since he expended the greatest part of his fortune, which was much increased by an advantageous marriage, in the service of the public. He had obtained for his son Herod the prefecture of the free cities of Asia; and the young magistrate, observing that the town of Troas was indifferently supplied with water, obtained from the munificence of Hadrian three hundred myriads of drachms (about a hundred thousand pounds) for the construction of a new aqueduct. But in the execution of the work the charge amounted to more than double the estimate, and the officers of the revenue began to murmur, till the generous Atticus silenced their complaints by requesting that he might be permitted to take upon himself the whole additional expense.[68]

The ablest preceptors of Greece and Asia had been invited by liberal rewards to direct the education of young Herod. Their pupil soon became a celebrated orator according to the useless rhetoric of that age, which, confining itself to the schools, disdained to visit either the Forum or the Senate. He was honoured with the consulship at Rome; but the greatest part of his life was spent in a philosophic retirement at Athens, and his adjacent villas; perpetually surrounded by sophists, who acknowledged, without reluctance, the superiority of a rich and generous rival.[69] The monuments of his genius have perished; some remains still preserve the fame of his taste and munificence: modern travellers have measured the remains of the stadium which he constructed at Athens. It was six hundred feet in length, built entirely of white marble, capable of admitting the whole body of the people, and finished in four years, whilst Herod was president of the Athenian games. To the memory of his wife Regilla he dedicated a theatre, scarcely to be paralleled in the empire: no wood except cedar very curiously carved was employed in any part of the building. The Odeum, designed by Pericles for musical performances and the rehearsal of new tragedies, had been a trophy of the victory of the arts over barbaric greatness; as the timbers employed in the construction consisted chiefly of the masts of the Persian vessels. Notwithstanding the repairs bestowed on that ancient edifice by a king of Cappadocia, it was again fallen to decay. Herod restored its ancient beauty and magnificence. Nor was the liberality of that illustrious citizen confined to the walls of Athens. The most splendid ornaments bestowed on the temple of Neptune in the Isthmus, a theatre at Corinth, a stadium at Delphi, a bath at Thermopylae, and an aqueduct at Canusium in Italy, were insufficient to exhaust his treasures. The people of Epirus, Thessaly, Euboea, Boeotia, and Peloponnesus experienced his favours; and many inscriptions of the cities of Greece and Asia gratefully style Herodes Atticus their patron and benefactor.[70]

In the commonwealths of Athens and Rome, the modest simplicity of private houses announced the equal condition of freedom; whilst the sovereignty of the people was represented in the majestic edifices destined to the public use:[71] nor was this republican spirit totally extinguished by the introduction of wealth and monarchy. It was in works of national honour and benefit that the most virtuous of the emperors affected to display their magnificence. The golden palace of Nero excited a just indignation, but the vast extent of ground which had been usurped by his selfish luxury was more nobly filled under the succeeding reigns by the Coliseum, the baths of Titus, the Claudian portico, and the temples dedicated to the goddess of Peace and to the genius of Rome.[72] These monuments of architecture, the property of the Roman people, were adorned with the most beautiful productions of Grecian painting and sculpture; and in the temple of Peace a very curious library was opened to the curiosity of the learned. At a small distance from thence was situated the Forum of Trajan. It was surrounded with a lofty portico in the form of a quadrangle, into which four triumphal arches opened a noble and spacious entrance: in the centre arose a column of marble, whose height of one hundred and ten feet denoted the elevation of the hill that had been cut away. This column, which still subsists in its ancient beauty, exhibited an exact representation of the Dacian victories of its founder. The veteran soldier contemplated the story of his own campaigns, and, by an easy illusion of national vanity, the peaceful citizen associated himself to the honours of the triumph. All the other quarters of the capital, and all the provinces of the empire, were embellished by the same liberal spirit of public magnificence, and were filled with amphitheatres, theatres, temples, porticos, triumphal arches, baths and aqueducts, all variously conducive to the health, the devotion, and the pleasures of the meanest citizen. The last mentioned of those edifices deserve our peculiar attention. The boldness of the enterprise, the solidity of the execution, and the uses to which they were subservient, rank the aqueducts among the noblest monuments of Roman genius and power. The aqueducts of the capital claim a just pre-eminence; but the curious traveller, who, without the light of history, should examine those of Spoleto, of Metz, or of Segovia, would very naturally conclude that those provincial towns had formerly been the residence of some potent monarch. The solitudes of Asia and Africa were once covered with flourishing cities, whose populousness, and even whose existence, was derived from such artificial supplies of a perennial stream of fresh water.[73]

We have computed the inhabitants, and contemplated the public works, of the Roman empire. The observation of the number and greatness of its cities will serve to confirm the former and to multiply the latter. It may not be unpleasing to collect a few scattered instances relative to that subject, without forgetting, however, that, from the vanity of nations and the poverty of language, the vague appellation of city has been indifferently bestowed on Rome and upon Laurentum.

I. *Ancient* Italy is said to have contained eleven hundred and ninety-seven cities; and, for whatsoever era of antiquity the expression might be intended,[74] there is not any reason to believe the country less populous in the age of the Antonines, than in that of Romulus. The petty states of Latium were contained within the metropolis of the empire, by whose superior influence they had been attracted. Those parts of Italy which have so long languished under the lazy tyranny of priests and viceroys had been afflicted only by the more tolerable calamities of war; and the first symptoms of decay which *they* experienced were amply compensated by the rapid improvements of the Cisalpine Gaul. The splendour of Verona may be traced in its remains: yet Verona was less celebrated than Aquileia or Padua, Milan or Ravenna.

II. The spirit of improvement had passed the Alps, and been felt even in the woods of Britain, which were gradually cleared away to open a free space for convenient and elegant habitations. York was the seat of government; London was already enriched by commerce; and Bath was celebrated for the salutary effects of its medical waters. Gaul could boast of her twelve hundred cities;[75] and, though, in the northern parts, many of them, without excepting Paris itself, were little more than the rude and imperfect townships of a rising people, the southern provinces imitated the wealth and elegance of Italy.[76] Many were the cities of Gaul, Marseilles, Arles, Nismes, Narbonne, Toulouse, Bordeaux, Autun, Vienne, Lyons, Langres, and Treves, whose ancient condition might sustain an equal, and perhaps advantageous, comparison with their present state. With regard to Spain, that country flourished as a province, and has declined as a kingdom. Exhausted by the abuse of her strength, by America, and by superstition, her pride might possibly be confounded, if we required such a list of three hundred and sixty cities as Pliny has exhibited under the reign of Vespasian.[77]

III.   Three hundred African cities had once acknowledged the authority of Carthage,[78] nor is it likely that their numbers diminished under the administration of the emperors: Carthage itself rose with new splendour from its ashes; and that capital, as well as Capua and Corinth, soon recovered all the advantages which can be separated from independent sovereignty.

IV.   The provinces of the east present the contrast of Roman magnificence with Turkish barbarism. The ruins of antiquity, scattered over uncultivated fields, and ascribed by ignorance to the power of magic, scarcely afford a shelter to the oppressed peasant or wandering Arab. Under the reign of the Caesars, the proper Asia alone contained five hundred populous cities,[79] enriched with all the gifts of nature, and adorned with all the refinements of art. Eleven cities of Asia had once disputed the honour of dedicating a temple to Tiberius, and their respective merits were examined by the senate.[80] Four of them were immediately rejected as unequal to the burden; and among these was Laodicea, whose splendour is still displayed in its ruins.[81] Laodicea collected a very considerable revenue from its flocks of sheep, celebrated for the fineness of their wool, and had received, a little before the contest, a legacy of above four hundred thousand pounds by the testament of a generous citizen.[82] If such was the poverty of Laodicea, what must have been the wealth of those cities, whose claim appeared preferable, and particularly of Pergamus, of Smyrna, and of Ephesus, who so long disputed with each other the titular primacy of Asia?[83] The capitals of Syria and Egypt held a still superior rank in the empire: Antioch and Alexandria looked down with disdain on a crowd of dependent cities,[84] and yielded with reluctance to the majesty of Rome itself.

All these cities were connected with each other, and with the capital, by the public highways, which, issuing from the Forum of Rome, traversed Italy, pervaded the provinces, and were terminated only by the frontiers of the empire. If we carefully trace the distance from the wall of Antoninus to Rome, and from thence to Jerusalem, it will be found that the great chain of communication, from the north-west to the south-east point of the empire, was drawn out to the length of four thousand and eighty Roman miles.[85] The public roads were accurately divided by milestones, and ran in a direct line from one city to another, with very little respect for the obstacles either of nature or private property. Mountains were perforated, and bold arches thrown over the broadest and most rapid streams.[86] The middle part of the road was raised into a terrace which commanded the adjacent country, consisted of several strata of sand, gravel, and cement, and was paved with large stones, or, in some places near the capital, with granite.[87] Such was the solid construction of the Roman highways, whose firmness has not entirely yielded to the effort of fifteen centuries. They united the subjects of the most distant provinces by an easy and familiar intercourse; but their primary object had been to facilitate the marches of the legions; nor was any country considered as completely subdued, till it had been rendered, in all its parts, pervious to the arms and authority of the conqueror. The advantage of receiving the earliest intelligence, and of conveying their orders with celerity, induced the emperors to establish, throughout their extensive dominions, the regular institution of posts.[88] Houses were everywhere erected at the distance only of five or six miles; each of them was constantly provided with forty horses, and, by the help of these relays, it was easy to travel an hundred miles in a day along the Roman roads.[89] The use of the posts was allowed to those who claimed it by an Imperial mandate; but, though originally intended for the public service, it was sometimes indulged to the business or conveniency of private citizens.[90] Nor was the communication of the Roman empire less free and open by sea than it was by land. The provinces surrounded and enclosed the Mediterranean; and Italy, in the shape of an immense promontory, advanced into the midst of that great lake. The coasts of Italy are, in general, destitute of safe harbours; but human industry had corrected the deficiencies of nature; and the artificial port of Ostia, in particular, situate at the mouth of the Tiber, and formed by the Emperor Claudius, was an useful monument of Roman greatness.[91] From this port, which was only sixteen miles from the capital, a favourable breeze frequently carried vessels in seven days to the columns of Hercules, and in nine or ten to Alexandria in Egypt.[92]

Whatever evils either reason or declamation have imputed to extensive empire, the power of Rome was attended with some beneficial consequences to mankind; and the same freedom of intercourse which extended the vices, diffused likewise the improvements, of social life. In the more remote ages of antiquity, the world was unequally divided. The east was in the immemorial possession of arts and luxury; whilst the west was inhabited by rude and warlike barbarians, who either disdained agriculture, or to whom it was totally unknown. Under the protection of an established government, the productions of happier climates and the industry of more civilised nations were gradually introduced into the western countries of Europe; and the natives were encouraged, by an open and profitable commerce, to multiply the former as well as to improve the latter. It would be almost impossible to enumerate all the articles, either of the animal or the vegetable reign, which were successively imported into Europe from Asia and Egypt;[93] but it will not be unworthy of the dignity, and much less of the utility, of an historical work, slightly to touch on a few of the principal heads. 1. Almost all the flowers, the herbs, and the fruits that grow in our European gardens are of foreign extraction, which, in many cases, is betrayed even by their names: the apple was a native of Italy, and, when the Romans had tasted the richer flavour of the apricot, the peach, the pomegranate, the citron, and the orange, they contented themselves with applying to all these new fruits the common denomination of apple, discriminating them from each other by the additional epithet of their country. 2. In the time of Homer, the vine grew wild in the island of Sicily and most probably in the adjacent continent; but it was not improved by the skill, nor did it afford a liquor grateful to the taste, of the savage inhabitants.[94] A thousand years afterwards, Italy could boast that, of the fourscore most generous and celebrated wines, more than two-thirds were produced from her soil.[95] The blessing was soon communicated to the Narbonnese province of Gaul; but so intense was the cold to the north of the Cevennes that, in the time of Strabo, it was thought impossible to ripen the grapes in those parts of Gaul.[96] This difficulty, however, was gradually vanquished; and there is some reason to believe that the vineyards of Burgundy are as old as the age of the Antonines.[97] 3. The olive, in the western world, followed the progress of peace, of which it was considered as the symbol. Two centuries after the foundation of Rome, both Italy and Africa were strangers to that useful plant; it was naturalised in those countries; and at length carried into the heart of Spain and Gaul. The timid errors of the ancients, that it required a certain degree of heat, and could only flourish in the neighbourhood of the sea, were insensibly exploded by industry and experience.[98] 4. The cultivation of flax was transported from Egypt to Gaul, and enriched the whole country, however it might impoverish the particular lands on which it was sown.[99] 5. The use of artificial grasses became familiar to the farmers both of Italy and the provinces, particularly the Lucerne, which derived its name and origin from Media.[100] The assured supply of wholesome and plentiful food for the cattle during winter multiplied the number of the flocks and herds, which in their turn contributed to the fertility of the soil. To all these improvements may be added an assiduous attention to mines and fisheries, which, by employing a multitude of laborious hands, serve to increase the pleasures of the rich and the subsistence of the poor. The elegant treatise of Columella describes the advanced state of the Spanish husbandry, under the reign of Tiberius; and it may be observed that those famines which so frequently afflicted the infant republic were seldom or never experienced by the extensive empire of Rome. The accidental scarcity, in any single province, was immediately relieved by the plenty of its more fortunate neighbours.

Agriculture is the foundation of manufactures; since the productions of nature are the materials of art. Under the Roman empire, the labour of an industrious and ingenious people was variously, but incessantly, employed in the service of the rich. In their dress, their table, their houses, and their furniture, the favourites of fortune united every refinement of conveniency, of elegance, and of splendour, whatever could soothe their pride or gratify their sensuality. Such refinements, under the odious name of luxury, have been severely arraigned by the moralists of every age; and it might perhaps be more conducive to the virtue, as well as happiness, of mankind, if all possessed the necessaries, and none the superfluities, of life. But in the present imperfect condition of society, luxury, though it may proceed from vice or folly, seems to be the only means that can correct the unequal distribution of property. The diligent mechanic, and the skilful artist, who have obtained no share in the division of the earth, receive a voluntary tax from the possessors of land; and the latter are prompted, by a sense of interest, to improve those estates, with whose produce they may purchase additional pleasures. This operation, the particular effects of which are felt in every society, acted with much more diffusive energy in the Roman world. The provinces would soon have been exhausted of their wealth, if the manufactures and commerce of luxury had not insensibly restored to the industrious subjects the sums which were exacted from them by the arms and authority of Rome. As long as the circulation was confined within the bounds of the empire, it impressed the political machine with a new degree of activity, and its consequences, sometimes beneficial, could never become pernicious.

But it is no easy task to confine luxury within the limits of an empire. The most remote countries of the ancient world were ransacked to supply the pomp and delicacy of Rome. The forest of Scythia afforded some valuable furs. Amber was brought over land from the shores of the Baltic to the Danube; and the barbarians were astonished at the price which they received in exchange for so useless a commodity.[101] There was a considerable demand for Babylonian carpets, and other manufactures of the East; but the most important and unpopular branch of foreign trade was carried on with Arabia and India. Every year, about the time of the summer solstice, a fleet of an hundred and twenty vessels sailed from Myoshormos, a port of Egypt, on the Red Sea. By the periodical assistance of the monsoons, they traversed the ocean in about forty days. The coast of Malabar, or the island of Ceylon,[102] was the usual term of their navigation, and it was in those markets that the merchants from the more remote countries of Asia expected their arrival. The return of the fleet of Egypt was fixed to the months of December or January; and as soon as their rich cargo had been transported on the backs of camels from the Red Sea to the Nile, and had descended that river as far as Alexandria, it was poured, without delay, into the capital of the empire.[103] The objects of oriental traffic were splendid and trifling: silk, a pound of which was esteemed not inferior in value to a pound of gold;[104] precious stones, among which the pearl claimed the first rank after the diamond;[105] and a variety of aromatics, that were consumed in religious worship and the pomp of funerals. The labour and risk of the voyage was rewarded with almost incredible profit; but the profit was made upon Roman subjects, and a few individuals were enriched at the expense of the public. As the natives of Arabia and India were contented with the productions and manufactures of their own country, silver, on the side of the Romans, was the principal, if not the only, instrument of commerce. It was a complaint worthy of the gravity of the senate, that, in the purchase of female ornaments, the wealth of the states was irrecoverably given away to foreign and hostile nations.[106] The annual loss is computed, by a writer of an inquisitive but censorious temper, at upwards of eight hundred thousand pounds sterling.[107] Such was the style of discontent, brooding over the dark prospect of approaching poverty. And yet, if we compare the proportion between gold and silver, as it stood in the time of Pliny, and as it was fixed in the reign of Constantine, we shall discover within that period a very considerable increase.[108] There is not the least reason to suppose that gold was become more scarce; it is therefore evident that silver was grown more common; that whatever might be the amount of the Indian and Arabian exports, they were far from exhausting the wealth of the Roman world; and that the produce of the mines abundantly supplied the demands of commerce.

Notwithstanding the propensity of mankind to exalt the past, and to depreciate the present, the tranquil and prosperous state of the empire was warmly felt, and honestly confessed, by the provincials as well as Romans. 'They acknowledged that the true principles of social life, laws, agriculture, and science, which had been first invented by the wisdom of Athens, were now firmly established by the power of Rome, under whose auspicious influence the fiercest barbarians were united by an equal government and common language. They affirm that, with the improvement of arts, the human species was visibly multiplied. They celebrate the increasing splendour of the cities, the beautiful face of the country, cultivated and adorned like an immense garden; and the long festival of peace, which was enjoyed by so many nations, forgetful of their ancient animosities, and delivered from the apprehension of future danger.'[109] Whatever suspicions may be suggested by the air of rhetoric and declamation which seems to prevail in these passages, the substance of them is perfectly agreeable to historic truth.

It was scarcely possible that the eyes of contemporaries should discover in the public felicity the latent causes of decay and corruption. This long peace, and the uniform government of the Romans, introduced a slow and secret poison into the vitals of the empire. The minds of men were gradually reduced to the same level, the fire of genius was extinguished, and even the military spirit evaporated. The natives of Europe were brave and robust. Spain, Gaul, Britain, and Illyricum supplied the legions with excellent soldiers, and constituted the real strength of the monarchy. Their personal valour remained, but they no longer possessed that public courage which is nourished by the love of independence, the sense of national honour, the presence of danger, and the habit of command. They received laws and governors from the will of their sovereign, and trusted for their defence to a mercenary army. The posterity of their boldest leaders was contented with the rank of citizens and subjects. The most aspiring spirits resorted to the court or standard of the emperors; and the deserted provinces, deprived of political strength or union, insensibly sunk into the languid indifference of private life.

The love of letters, almost inseparable from peace and refinement, was fashionable among the subjects of Hadrian and the Antonines, who were themselves men of learning and curiosity. It was diffused over the whole extent of their empire; the most northern tribes of Britons had acquired a taste for rhetoric; Homer as well as Virgil were transcribed and studied on the banks of the Rhine and Danube; and the most liberal rewards sought out the faintest glimmerings of literary merit.[110] The sciences of physic and astronomy were successfully cultivated by the Greeks; the observations of Ptolemy and the writings of Galen are studied by those who have improved their discoveries and corrected their errors; but, if we except the inimitable Lucian, this age of indolence passed away without having produced a single writer of original genius or who excelled in the arts of elegant composition. The authority of Plato and Aristotle, of Zeno and Epicurus, still reigned in the schools, and their systems, transmitted with blind deference from one generation of disciples to another, precluded every generous attempt to exercise the powers, or enlarge the limits, of the human mind. The beauties of the poets and orators, instead of kindling a fire like their own, inspired only cold and servile imitations: or, if any ventured to deviate from those models, they deviated at the same time from good sense and propriety. On the revival of letters,* the youthful vigour of the imagination after a long repose, national emulation, a new religion, new languages, and a new world, called forth the genius of Europe. But the provincials of Rome, trained by a uniform artificial foreign education, were engaged in a very unequal competition with those bold ancients, who, by expressing their genuine feelings in their native tongue, had already occupied every place of honour. The name of Poet was almost forgotten; that of Orator was usurped by the sophists. A cloud of critics, of compilers, of commentators, darkened the face of learning, and the decline of genius was soon followed by the corruption of taste.

The sublime Longinus, who in somewhat a later period, and in the court of a Syrian queen, preserved the spirit of ancient Athens, observes and laments this degeneracy of his contemporaries, which debased their sentiments, enervated their courage, and depressed their talents. 'In the same manner,' says he, 'as some children always remain pigmies, whose infant limbs have been too closely confined; thus our tender minds, fettered by the prejudices and habits of a just servitude, are unable to expand themselves, or to attain that well-proportioned greatness which we admire in the ancients, who, living under a popular government, wrote with the same freedom as they acted.'[111] This diminutive stature of mankind, if we pursue the metaphor, was daily sinking below the old standard, and the Roman world was indeed peopled by a race of pigmies, when the fierce giants of the north broke in and mended the puny breed. They restored a manly spirit of freedom; and, after the revolution of ten centuries, freedom became the happy parent of taste and science.

NOTES TO CHAPTER 2

1 They were erected about the midway between Lahor and Delhi. The conquests of Alexander in Hindostan were confined to the Punjab, a country watered by the five great streams of the Indus.

* *page 27* [Jenghis Khan]

2 See M. de Guignes, *Histoire des Huns*, xv, xvi, and xvii.

3 There is not any writer who describes in so lively a manner as Herodotus the true genius of polytheism. The best commentary may be found in Mr Hume's *Natural History of Religion* [David Hume, 1711–76, the philosopher and historian]; and the best contrast in Bossuet's *Universal History*. Some obscure traces of an intolerant spirit appear in the conduct of the Egyptians (see Juvenal, *Satires*, xv); and the Christians as well as Jews, who lived under the Roman empire, formed a very important exception: so important indeed, that the discussion will require a distinct chapter of this work.

4 The rights, power, and pretensions of the sovereign of Olympus are very clearly described in the fifteenth book of the *Iliad*: in the Greek original, I mean; for Mr Pope, without perceiving it, has improved the theology of Homer. [Alexander Pope translated Homer's *Iliad*].

5 See for instance, Caesar, *de Bell. Gall.*, vi, 17. Within a century or two the Gauls themselves applied to their gods the names of Mercury, Mars, Apollo, etc.

6 The admirable work of Cicero, *de Natura Deorum*, is the best clue we have to guide us through the dark and profound abyss. He represents with candour, and confutes with subtlety, the opinions of the philosophers.

7 I do not pretend to assert that, in this irreligious age, the natural terrors of superstition, dreams, omens, apparitions, etc., had lost their efficacy.

8 Socrates, Epicurus, Cicero, and Plutarch, always inculcated a decent reverence for the religion of their own country, and of mankind. The devotion of Epicurus was assiduous and exemplary. Diogen. Laert., x, 10.

9 Polybius, vi, 56. Juvenal, *Satires*, xiii, laments that in his time this apprehension had lost much of its effect.

10 See the fate of Syracuse, Tarentum, Ambracia, Corinth, etc., the conduct of Verres, in Cicero (*Actio* ii, *Orat.* 4), and the usual practice of governors, in the eighth Satire of Juvenal.

11 Suetonius, in *Claud.*, Pliny, *Hist. Nat.*, xxx, i.

12 Pelloutier, *Histoire des Celtes*, vi, 230–52.

13 Seneca, *Consolat. ad Helviam*, p. 74, edit. Lips.

14 Dionysius Halicarn., *Antiquitat. Roman.*, Bk ii.

15 In the year of Rome 701, the temple of Isis and Serapis was demolished by the order of the senate (Dion Cassius, xl, 252), and even by the hands of the consul (Valerius Maximus, i, 3). After the death of Caesar, it was restored at the public expense (Dion, xlvii, 501). When Augustus was in Egypt, he revered the

majesty of Serapis (Dion, li, 647); but in the Pomerium of Rome and a mile round it, he prohibited the worship of the Egyptian gods (Dion, liii, 697; liv, 735). They remained, however, very fashionable under his reign (Ovid, *de Art. Amand.*, Bk i.) and that of his successor, till the justice of Tiberius was provoked to some acts of severity. (See Tacitus, *Annals*, ii, 85, Josephus, *Antiquit.*, xviii, 3.)

16 Tertullian, in *Apologetic.*, 6, 74, edit. Havercamp. I am inclined to attribute their establishment to the devotion of the Flavian family.

17 See Livy, xi and xxix.

18 Macrob., *Saturnalia*, iii, 9. He gives us a form of evocation.

19 Minucius Felix, *in Octavio*, p. 54. Arnobius, vi, 115.

20 Tacitus, *Annals*, xi, 24. The *Orbis Romanus* of the learned Spanheim is a complete history of the progressive admission of Latium, Italy, and the provinces to the freedom of Rome.

21 Herodotus, v, 97. It should seem, however, that he followed a large and popular estimation.

22 Athenaeus, *Deipnosophist.*, vi, 272, edit. Casaubon; Meursius, *de Fortuna Attica*, ch. 4.

23 See a very accurate collection of the numbers of each Lustrum in M. de Beaufort, *République Romaine*, iv, 4.

24 Appian, *de Bell. Civil.*, Bk i, Velleius Paterculus, ii, 15, 16, 17.

25 Maecenas had advised him to declare, by one edict, all his subjects citizens. But we may justly suspect that the historian Dion was the author of a counsel, so much adapted to the practice of his own age, and so little to that of Augustus.

26 The senators were obliged to have one-third of their own landed property in Italy. See Pliny, vi. ep. 19. The qualification was reduced by Marcus to one-fourth. Since the reign of Trajan, Italy had sunk nearer to the level of the provinces.

  * *page 31* [Livy]

27 The first part of the *Verona Illustrata* of the Marquis Maffei gives the clearest and most comprehensive view of the state of Italy under the Caesars.

28 See Pausanias, Bk vii. The Romans condescended to restore the names of those assemblies, when they could no longer be dangerous.

29 They are frequently mentioned by Caesar. The Abbé Dubos attempts, with very little success, to prove that the assemblies of Gaul were continued under the emperors: *Histoire de l'Etablissement de la Monarchie Françoise*, i, 4.

30 Seneca in *Consolat. ad Helviam*, ch. 6.

31 Memnon *apud* Photium, ch. 33. Valer. Maxim., ix, 2. Plutarch and Dion Cassius swell the massacre to 150,000 citizens; but I should esteem the smaller number to be more than sufficient.

32 Twenty-five colonies were settled in Spain (see Pliny, *Hist. Natur.*, iii, 3, 4; iv, 35); and nine in Britain, of which London, Colchester, Lincoln, Chester, Gloucester and Bath, still remain considerable cities (see Richard of Cirencester, p. 36, and Whitaker's *History of Manchester*, i, 3).

33 Aul. Gell., *Noctes Atticae*, xvi, 13. The Emperor Hadrian expressed his surprise that the cities of Utica, Gades, and Italica, which already enjoyed the rights of *municipia*, should solicit the title of *colonies*. Their example, however, became fashionable, and the empire was filled with honorary colonies. See Spanheim, *de Usu Numismatum, Dissertat.* xiii.

34 Spanheim, *Orbis Roman.*, ch. 8, p. 62.

35 Aristides, *in Romae Encomio*, i, 218, edit. Jebb.

36 Tacitus, *Annals*, xi, 23, 24; *Hist.*, iv, 74.

37 See Pliny, *Hist. Natur.*, iii, 5; Augustine, *de Civitate Dei*, xix, 7; Lipsius, *de Pronunciatione Linguae Latinae*, ch. 3.

38 Apuleius and Augustine will answer for Africa; Strabo for Spain and Gaul; Tacitus, in the life of Agricola, for Britain; and Velleius Paterculus for Pannonia. To them we may add the language of the inscriptions.

39 The Celtic was preserved in the mountains of Wales, Cornwall and Armorica. We may observe that Apuleius reproaches an African youth, who lived among the populace, with the use of the Punic; whilst he had almost forgot Greek, and neither could nor would speak Latin. (*Apolog.* p. 596.) The greater part of St Austin's congregations were strangers to the Punic. [St Austin, i.e. St Augustine.]

40 Spain alone produced Columella, the Senecas, Lucan, Martial, and Quintilian.

41 There is not, I believe, from Dionysius to Libanius, a single Greek critic who mentions Virgil or Horace. They seem ignorant that the Romans had any good writers.

42 The curious reader may see in Dupin (*Bibliothèque Ecclésiastique*, xix, 1, 8) how much the use of the Syriac and Egyptian languages was still preserved.

43 See Juvenal, *Satires*, iii and xv; Ammianus Marcellinus, xxii, 16.

44 Dion Cassius, lxxvi, 1275. The first instance happened under the reign of Septimius Severus.

45 See Valerius Maximus, ii, 2, 2. The Emperor Claudius disfranchised an eminent Grecian for not understanding Latin. He was probably in some public office. Suetonius, in *Claudius*, ch. 16.

46 In the camp of Lucullus, an ox sold for a drachma, and a slave for four drachmae, or about three shillings. Plutarch, in *Lucull.*, p. 580.

47 Diodorus Siculus in *Eclog. Hist.*, xxxiv and xxxvi. Florus, iii, 19, 20.

48 See a remarkable instance of severity, in Cicero *in Verrem*, v, 3.

49 See in Gruter, and the other collectors, a great number of inscriptions addressed by slaves to their wives, children, fellow-servants, masters, etc. They are all most probably of the Imperial age.

50 See the *Augustan History*, and a dissertation of M. de Burigny, in the thirty-fifth volume of the *Academy of Inscriptions*, upon the Roman slaves.

51 See another dissertation of M. de Burigny in the thirty-seventh volume, on the Roman freedmen.

52 Spanheim, *Orbis Roman.*, i, 16, p. 124, etc,

53 Seneca, *de Clementia*, i, 24. The original is much stronger, '*Quantum periculum immineret si servi nostri numerare nos coepissent*' ['How great would be the danger if our slaves started to count us.']

54 See Pliny (*Hist. Natur.*, Bk xxxiii) and Athenaeus (*Deipnosophist.*, vi, 272). The latter boldly asserts that he knew very many (πάμπολλοι) Romans who possessed, not for use, but ostentation, ten and even twenty thousand slaves.

55 In Paris there are not more than 43,700 domestics of every sort, and not a twelfth part of the inhabitants. Messange, *Recherches sur la Population*, p. 186.

56 A learned slave sold for many hundred pounds sterling; Atticus always bred and taught them himself: Cornel. Nepos in *Vit.*, ch. 13.

57 Many of the Roman physicians were slaves. See Dr Middleton's Dissertation and Defence.

58 Their ranks and offices are very copiously enumerated by Pignorius, *de Servis*.

59 Tacitus, *Annals*, xiv, 43. They all were executed for not preventing their master's murder.

60 Apuleius in *Apolog.*, p. 548, edit. Delphin.

61 Pliny, *Hist. Natur.*, xxxiii, 47.

62 Compute twenty millions in France, twenty-two in Germany, four in Hungary, ten in Italy with its islands, eight in Great Britain and Ireland, eight in Spain and Portugal, ten or twelve in the European Russia, six in Poland, six in Greece and Turkey, four in Sweden, three in Denmark and Norway, four in the Low Countries. The whole would amount to one hundred and five, or one hundred and seven millions. See Voltaire, *de l'Histoire Générale*.

63 Josephus, *de Bell. Judaico*, ii, 16. The oration of Agrippa, or rather of the historian, is a fine picture of the Roman empire.

64 Suetonius, in *Augustus*, ch. 28. Augustus built in Rome the temple and forum of Mars the Avenger; the Temple of Jupiter Tonans in the Capitol; that of Apollo Palatine, with public libraries; the portico and basilica of Caius and Lucius; the porticoes of Livia and Octavia, and the theatre of Marcellus. The example of the sovereign was imitated by his ministers and generals; and his friend Agrippa left behind him the immortal monument of the Pantheon.

65 See Maffei, *Verona Illustrata*, iv, 68.

66 See the tenth book of Pliny's *Epistles*. He mentions the following works, carried on at the expense of the cities. At Nicomedia, a new forum, an aqueduct, and a canal, left unfinished by a king; at Nice, a gymnasium and a theatre, which had already cost near ninety thousand pounds; baths at Prusa and Claudiopolis; and an aqueduct of sixteen miles in length for the use of Sinope.

67 Hadrian afterwards made a very equitable regulation, which divided all treasure trove between the right of property and that of discovery. *Hist. August.*, p. 9.

68 Philostratus in *Vit. Sophist.*, ii, p. 548.

69 Aulus Gellius, in *Noct. Attic.*, i, 2; ix, 2; xviii, 10; xix, 12. Philostratus, p. 564.

70 See Philostratus, ii, 548, 560; Pausanias, i, and vii, 20; the life of Herodes, in the thirtieth volume of the *Memoirs of the Academy of Inscriptions*.

71 It is particularly remarked of Athens by Dicaearchus, *de Statu Graeciae*, p. 8, *inter Geographos Minores*, edit. Hudson.

72 Donatus, *de Roma Vetere*, iii, 4, 5, 6; Nardini, *Roma Antica*, iii, 11, 12, 13, and a manuscript description of ancient Rome, by Bernardus Oricellarius, or Rucellai, of which I obtained a copy from the library of the Canon Ricardi at Florence. Two celebrated pictures of Timanthes and of Protogenes are mentioned by Pliny as in the Temple of Peace; and the Laocoon was found in the baths of Titus.

73 Montfaucon, *l'Antiquité Expliquée*, iv, 2, i, 9. Fabretti has composed a very learned treatise on the aqueducts of Rome.

74 Aelian, *Hist. Var.*, ix, 16. He lived in the time of Alexander Severus. See Fabricius, *Biblioth. Graeca*, iv, 21.

75 Josephus, *de Bell. Jud.*, ii, 16. The number, however, is mentioned and should be received with a degree of latitude.

76 Pliny, *Hist Natur.*, iii, 5.

77 Pliny, *Hist. Natur.*, iii, 3, 4; iv, 35. The list seems authentic and accurate: the division of the provinces and the different condition of the cities are minutely distinguished.

78 Strabo, *Geograph.*, xvii, 1189.

79 Josephus, *de Bell. Jud.*, ii, 16. Philostratus in *Vit. Sophist.*, ii, 548, edit. Olear.

80 Tacitus, *Annals*, iv, 55. I have taken some pains in consulting and comparing modern travellers, with regard to the fate of those eleven cities of Asia; seven or eight are totally destroyed, Hypaepe, Tralles, Laodicea, Ilium, Halicarnassus, Miletus, Ephesus, and we may add Sardis. Of the remaining three, Pergamus is a straggling village of two or three thousand inhabitants; Magnesia, under the name of Guzel-hissar, a town of some consequence; and Smyrna, a great city, peopled by a hundred thousand souls. But even at Smyrna, while the Franks have maintained commerce, the Turks have ruined the arts.

81 See a very exact and pleasing description of the ruins of Laodicea, in Chandler's *Travels through Asia Minor*, p. 225, etc.

82 Strabo, xii, 866. He had studied at Tralles.

83 See a dissertation of M. de Bose, *Mém. de l'Académie*, tom. xviii. Aristides pronounced an oration which is still extant, to recommend concord to the rival cities.

84 The inhabitants of Egypt, exclusive of Alexandria, amounted to seven millions and a half (Josephus, *de Bell. Jud.*, ii. 16). Under the military government of the Mamalukes, Syria was supposed to contain sixty thousand villages (*Histoire de Timur Bec*, v, 20).

85 The following Itinerary may serve to convey some idea of the direction of the road, and of the distance between the principal towns. I From the wall of Antoninus to York, 222 Roman miles. II London 227. III Rhutupiae or Sandwich 67. IV The navigation to Boulogne 45. V Rheims 174. VI Lyons 330. VII Milan 324. VIII Rome 426. IX Brundusium 360. X The navigation to Dyrrachium 40. XI Byzantium 711. XII Ancyra 283. XIII Tarsus 301. XIV Antioch 141. XV Tyre 252. XVI Jerusalem 168. In all 4080 Roman, or 3740 English miles. See the *Itineraries* published by Wesseling, his annotations; Gale and Stukeley for Britain, and M. d'Anville for Gaul and Italy.

86 Montfaucon (*l'Antiquité Expliquée*, iv, 2, i, 5) has described the bridges of Narni, Alcantara, Nismes, etc.

87 Bergier, *Histoire des grands Chemins de l'Empire Romain*, ii, 1–28.

88 Procopius in *Hist. Arcana*, ch. 30; Bergier, *Hist. des grands Chemins*, Bk iv; Codex Theodosian., viii, v, ii, 506–63, with Godefroy's learned commentary.

89 In the time of Theodosius, Caesarius, a magistrate of high rank, went post from Antioch to Constantinople. He began his journey at night, was in Cappadocia (165 miles from Antioch) the ensuing evening, and arrived at Constantinople the sixth day about noon. The whole distance was 725 Roman, or 665 English miles. See Libanius, *Orat.* xxii, and the *Itineraria*, pp. 572–81.

90 Pliny, though a favourite and a minister, made an apology for granting post horses to his wife on the most urgent business, *Epist.*, x, 121, 122.

91 Bergier, *Hist. des grands Chemins*, iv, 49.

92 Pliny, *Hist. Natur.*, xix, 1.

93 It is not improbable that the Greeks and Phoenicians introduced some new arts and productions into the neighbourhood of Marseilles and Gades.

94 See Homer, *Odyssey*, ix, 358.

95 Pliny, *Hist. Natur.*, Bk xiv.

96 Strabo, *Geograph.*, iv, 223. The intense cold of a Gallic winter was almost proverbial among the ancients.

97 In the beginning of the fourth century, the orator Eumenius (*Panegyric. Veter.*,

viii, 6, edit. Delphin) speaks of the vines in the territory of Autun, which were decayed through age, and the first plantation of which was totally unknown. The Pagus Arebrignus is supposed by M. d'Anville to be the district of Beaune, celebrated, even at present, for one of the first growths of Burgundy.

98 Pliny, *Hist. Natur.*, Bk xv.

99 Pliny, *Hist. Natur.*, Bk xix.

100 See the agreeable Essays on Agriculture by Mr Harte, in which he has collected all that the ancients and moderns have said of lucerne [a clover-like plant used for fodder].

101 Tacitus, *Germania*, ch. 45; Pliny, *Hist. Natur.*, xxxvii, 11. The latter observed, with some humour, that even fashion had not yet found out the use of amber. Nero sent a Roman knight to purchase great quantities on the spot where it was produced; the coast of modern Prussia.

102 Called Taprobana by the Romans, and Serendib by the Arabs. It was discovered under the reign of Claudius, and gradually became the principal mart of the east.

103 Pliny, *Hist. Natur.*, vi; Strabo, Bk xvii.

104 *Hist. August.*, p. 224. A silk garment was considered as an ornament to a woman, but as a disgrace to a man.

105 The two great pearl fisheries were the same as at present, Ormuz and Cape Comorin. As well as we can compare ancient with modern geography, Rome was supplied with diamonds from the mine of Jumelpur, in Bengal, which is described in the *Voyages* de Tavernier, ii, 281.

106 Tacitus, *Annals*, iii, 53, in a speech of Tiberius.

107 Pliny, *Hist. Natur.*, xii, 18. In another place he computes half that sum; *quingenties HS* [i.e. 50 million sestertii] for India exclusive of Arabia.

108 The proportion, which was 1 to 10, and 12½, rose to 14⅖, the legal regulation of Constantine. See Arbuthnot's Table of Ancient Coins, ch. v.

109 Among many other passages, see Pliny (*Hist. Natur.*, iii, 5), Aristides (*de Urbe Roma*) and Tertullian (*de Anima*, ch. 30).

110 Herodes Atticus gave the sophist Polemo above eight thousand pounds for three declamations. See Philostratus, i, 558. The Antonines founded a school at Athens, in which professors of grammar, rhetoric, politics, and the four great sects of philosophy, were maintained at the public expense for the instruction of youth. The salary of a philosopher was ten thousand drachmae, between three and four hundred pounds a year. Similar establishments were formed in the other great cities of the empire. See Lucian in *Eunuch.*, ii, 353, edit. Reitz; Philostratus, ii, 566; *Hist. August.*, p. 21; Dion Cassius, lxxxi, 1195. Juvenal himself, in a morose satire, which in every line betrays his own disappointment and envy, is obliged, however, to say: '*O Iuvenes, circumspicit et agitat vos, Materiamque sibi Ducis indulgentia quaerit.*' *Sat.*, vii, 20. ['Young men, an indulgent ruler is on the look-out to encourage talent for his own advantage.']

* *page 46* [i.e. during the Renaissance of the 15th century]

111 Longin., *de Sublim.*, ch. 43, 229, edit. Toll. Here too we may say of Longinus, 'his own example strengthens all his laws'. [*On the Sublime* was probably a work of the 1st century ad.] Instead of proposing his sentiments with a manly boldness, he insinuates them with the most guarded caution, puts them into the mouth of a friend, and, as far as we can collect from a corrupted text, makes a show of refuting them himself.

CHAPTER 3

Of the constitution of the Roman empire in the age of the Antonines

The obvious definition of a monarchy seems to be that of a state, in which a single person, by whatsoever name he may be distinguished, is intrusted with the execution of the laws, the management of the revenue, and the command of the army. But unless public liberty is protected by intrepid and vigilant guardians, the authority of so formidable a magistrate will soon degenerate into despotism. The influence of the clergy, in an age of superstition, might be usefully employed to assert the rights of mankind; but so intimate is the connection between the throne and the altar, that the banner of the church has very seldom been seen on the side of the people. A martial nobility and stubborn commons, possessed of arms, tenacious of property, and collected into constitutional assemblies, form the only balance capable of preserving a free constitution against enterprises of an aspiring prince.

Every barrier of the Roman constitution had been levelled by the vast ambition of the dictator;* every fence had been extirpated by the cruel hand of the triumvir.† After the victory of Actium, the fate of the Roman world depended on the will of Octavianus, surnamed Caesar by his uncle's adoption, and afterwards Augustus, by the flattery of the senate. The conqueror was at the head of forty-four veteran legions,[1] conscious of their own strength and of the weakness of the constitution, habituated during twenty years' civil war to every act of blood and violence, and passionately devoted to the house of Caesar, from whence alone they had received and expected the most lavish rewards. The provinces, long oppressed by the ministers of the republic, sighed for the government of a single person, who would be the master, not the accomplice, of those petty tyrants. The people of Rome, viewing with a secret pleasure the humiliation of the aristocracy, demanded only bread and public shows, and were supplied with both by the liberal hand of Augustus. The rich and polite Italians, who had almost universally embraced the philosophy of Epicurus, enjoyed the present blessings of ease and tranquillity, and suffered not the pleasing dream to be interrupted by the memory of their old tumultuous freedom. With its power, the senate had lost its dignity; many of the most noble families were extinct. The republicans of spirit and ability had perished in the field of battle, or in the proscription. The door of the assembly had been designedly left open for a mixed multitude of more than a thousand persons, who reflected disgrace upon their rank, instead of deriving honour from it.[2]

The reformation of the senate, was one of the first steps in which Augustus laid aside the tyrant, and professed himself the father of his country. He was elected censor; and, in concert with his faithful Agrippa, he examined the list of the senators, expelled a few members, whose vices or whose obstinacy required a public example, persuaded near two hundred to prevent the shame of an expulsion by a voluntary retreat, raised the qualification of a senator to about ten thousand pounds, created a sufficient number of patrician families, and accepted for himself the honourable title of Prince of the Senate, which had always been bestowed by the censors on the citizen the most eminent for his honours and services.[3] But, whilst he thus restored the dignity, he destroyed the independence, of the senate. The principles of a free constitution are irrecoverably lost, when the legislative power is nominated by the executive.

Before an assembly thus modelled and prepared, Augustus pronounced a studied oration, which displayed his patriotism, and disguised his ambition. 'He lamented, yet excused, his past conduct. Filial piety had required at his hands the revenge of his father's murder; the humanity of his own nature had sometimes given way to the stern laws of necessity, and to a forced connection with two unworthy colleagues: as long as Antony lived, the republic forbad him to abandon her to a degenerate Roman and a barbarian queen. He was now at liberty to satisfy his duty and his inclination. He solemnly restored the senate and people to all their ancient rights; and wished only to mingle with the crowd of his fellow-citizens, and to share the blessings which he had obtained for his country.'[4]

It would require the pen of Tacitus (if Tacitus had assisted at this assembly) to describe the various emotions of the senate; those that were suppressed, and those that were affected. It was dangerous to trust the sincerity of Augustus; to seem to distrust it was still more dangerous. The respective advantages of monarchy and a republic have often divided speculative inquirers; the present greatness of the Roman state, the corruption of manners, and the licence of the soldiers, supplied new arguments to the advocates of monarchy; and these general views of government were again warped by the hopes and fears of each individual. Amidst this confusion of sentiments, the answer of the senate was unanimous and decisive. They refused to accept the resignation of Augustus; they conjured him not to desert the republic which he had saved. After a decent resistance the crafty tyrant submitted to the orders of the senate; and consented to receive the government of the provinces, and the general command of the Roman armies, under the well-known names of Proconsul and Imperator.[5] But he would receive them only for ten years. Even before the expiration of that period, he hoped that the wounds of civil discord would be completely healed, and that the republic, restored to its pristine health and vigour, would no longer require the dangerous interposition of so extraordinary a magistrate. The memory of this comedy, repeated several times during the life of Augustus, was preserved to the last ages of the empire by the peculiar pomp with which the perpetual monarchs of Rome always solemnised the tenth years of their reign.[6]

Without any violation of the principles of the constitution, the general of the Roman armies might receive and exercise an authority almost despotic over the soldiers, the enemies, and the subjects of the republic. With regard to the soldiers, the jealousy of freedom had, even from the earliest ages of Rome, given way to the hopes of conquest and a just sense of military discipline. The dictator, or consul, had a right to command the service of the Roman youth, and to punish an obstinate or cowardly disobedience by the most severe and ignominious penalties, by striking the offender out of the list of citizens, by confiscating his property, and by selling his person into slavery.[7] The most sacred rights of freedom, confirmed by the Porcian and Sempronian laws, were suspended by the military engagement. In his camp the general exercised an absolute power of life and death; his jurisdiction was not confined by any forms of trial or rules of proceeding, and the execution of the sentence was immediate and without appeal.[8] The choice of the enemies of Rome was regularly decided by the legislative authority. The most important resolutions of peace and war were seriously debated in the senate, and solemnly ratified by the people. But when the arms of the legions were carried to a great distance from Italy, the generals assumed the liberty of directing them against whatever people, and in whatever manner, they judged most advantageous for the public service. It was from the success, not from the justice, of their enterprises, that they expected the honours of a triumph. In the use of victory, especially after they were no longer controlled by the commissioners of the senate, they exercised the most unbounded despotism. When Pompey commanded in the East, he rewarded his soldiers and allies, dethroned princes, divided kingdoms, founded colonies, and distributed the treasures of Mithridates. On his return to Rome he obtained, by a single act of the senate and people, the universal ratification of all his proceedings.[9] Such was the power over the soldiers, and over the enemies of Rome, which was either granted to, or assumed by, the generals of the republic. They were, at the same time, the governors, or rather monarchs, of the conquered provinces, united the civil with the military character, administered justice as well as the finances, and exercised both the executive and legislative power of the state.

From what has been already observed in the first chapter of this work, some notion may be formed of the armies and provinces thus intrusted to the ruling hand of Augustus. But, as it was impossible that he could personally command the legions of so many distant frontiers, he was indulged by the senate, as Pompey had already been, in the permission of devolving the execution of his great office on a sufficient number of lieutenants. In rank and authority these officers seemed not inferior to the ancient proconsuls; but their station was dependent and precarious. They received and held their commissions at the will of a superior, to whose *auspicious* influence the merit of their action was legally attributed.[10] They were the representatives of the emperor. The emperor alone was the general of the republic, and his jurisdiction, civil as well as military, extended over all the conquests of Rome. It was some satisfaction, however, to the senate that he always delegated his power to the members of their body. The imperial lieutenants were of consular or praetorian dignity; the legions were commanded by senators, and the prefecture of Egypt was the only important trust committed to a Roman knight.

Within six days after Augustus had been compelled to accept so very liberal a grant, he resolved to gratify the pride of the senate by an easy sacrifice. He represented to them that they had enlarged his powers, even beyond that degree which might be required by the melancholy condition of the times. They had not permitted him to refuse the laborious command of the armies and the frontiers; but he must insist on being allowed to restore the more peaceful and secure provinces to the mild administration of the civil magistrate. In the division of the provinces Augustus provided for his own power and for the dignity of the republic. The proconsuls of the senate, particularly those of Asia, Greece, and Africa, enjoyed a more honourable character than the lieutenants of the emperor, who commanded in Gaul or Syria. The former were attended by lictors, the latter by soldiers. A law was passed that, wherever the emperor was present, his extraordinary commission should supersede the ordinary jurisdiction of the governor; a custom was introduced that the new conquests belonged to the imperial portion; and it was soon discovered that the authority of the *Prince*, the favourite epithet of Augustus, was the same in every part of the empire.

In return for this imaginary concession, Augustus obtained an important privilege, which rendered him master of Rome and Italy. By a dangerous exception to the ancient maxims, he was authorised to preserve his military command, supported by a numerous body of guards, even in time of peace, and in the heart of the capital. His command, indeed, was confined to those citizens who were engaged in the service by the military oath; but such was the propensity of the Romans to servitude, that the oath was voluntarily taken by the magistrates, the senators, and the equestrian order, till the homage of flattery was insensibly converted into an annual and solemn protestation of fidelity.

Although Augustus considered a military force as the firmest foundation, he wisely rejected it as a very odious instrument, of government. It was more agreeable to his temper, as well as to his policy, to reign under the venerable names of ancient magistracy, and artfully to collect in his own person all the scattered rays of civil jurisdiction. With this view, he permitted the senate to confer upon him, for his life, the powers of the consular[11] and tribunitian offices,[12] which were, in the same manner, continued to all his successors. The consuls had succeeded to the kings of Rome, and represented the dignity of the state. They superintended the ceremonies of religion, levied and commanded the legions, gave audience to foreign ambassadors, and presided in the assemblies both of the senate and people. The general control of the finances was intrusted to their care; and, though they seldom had leisure to administer justice in person, they were considered as the supreme guardians of law, equity, and the public peace. Such was their ordinary jurisdiction; but, whenever the senate empowered the first magistrate to consult the safety of the commonwealth, he was raised by that decree above the laws, and exercised, in the defence of liberty, a temporary despotism.[13] The character of the tribunes was, in every respect, different from that of the consuls. The appearance of the former was modest and humble; but their persons were sacred and inviolable. Their force was suited rather for opposition than for action. They were instituted to defend the oppressed, to pardon offences, to arraign the enemies of the people, and, when they judged it necessary, to stop, by a single word, the whole machine of government. As long as the republic subsisted, the dangerous influence which either the consul or the tribune might derive from their respective jurisdiction was diminished by several important restrictions. Their authority expired with the year in which they were elected; the former office was divided between two, the latter among ten, persons; and, as both in their private and public interest they were adverse to each other, their mutual conflicts contributed, for the most part, to strengthen rather than to destroy the balance of the constitution. But when the consular and tribunitian powers were united, when they were vested for life in a single person, when the general of the army was, at the same time, the minister of the senate and the representative of the Roman people, it was impossible to resist the exercise, nor was it easy to define the limits, of his imperial prerogative.

To these accumulated honours the policy of Augustus soon added the splendid as well as important dignities of supreme pontiff, and of censor. By the former he acquired the management of the religion, and by the latter a legal inspection over the manners and fortunes, of the Roman people. If so many distinct and independent powers did not exactly unite with each other, the complaisance of the senate was prepared to supply every deficiency by the most ample and extraordinary concessions. The emperors, as the first ministers of the republic, were exempted from the obligation and penalty of many inconvenient laws: they were authorised to convoke the senate, to make several motions in the same day, to recommend candidates for the honours of the state, to enlarge the bounds of the city, to employ the revenue at their discretion, to declare peace and war, to ratify treaties; and, by a most comprehensive clause, they were empowered to execute whatsoever they should judge advantageous to the empire, and agreeable to the majesty of things private or public, human or divine.[14]

When all the various powers of executive government were committed to the *Imperial magistrate*, the ordinary magistrates of the commonwealth languished in obscurity, without vigour, and almost without business. The names and forms of the ancient administration were preserved by Augustus with the most anxious care. The usual number of consuls, praetors, and tribunes[15] were annually invested with their respective ensigns of office, and continued to discharge some of their least important functions. Those honours still attracted the vain ambition of the Romans; and the emperors themselves, though invested for life with the powers of the consulship, frequently aspired to the title of that annual dignity, which they condescended to share with the most illustrious of their fellow citizens.[16] In the election of these magistrates, the people, during the reign of Augustus, were permitted to expose all the inconveniences of a wild democracy. That artful prince, instead of discovering the least symptom of impatience, humbly solicited their suffrages for himself or his friends, and scrupulously practised all the duties of an ordinary candidate.[17] But we may venture to ascribe to his councils the first measure of the succeeding reign, by which the elections were transferred to the senate.[18] The assemblies of the people were for ever abolished, and the emperors were delivered from a dangerous multitude, who, without restoring liberty, might have disturbed, and perhaps endangered, the established government.

By declaring themselves the protectors of the people, Marius and Caesar had subverted the constitution of their country. But as soon as the senate had been humbled and disarmed, such an assembly, consisting of five or six hundred persons, was found a much more tractable and useful instrument of dominion. It was on the dignity of the senate that Augustus and his successors founded their new empire; and they affected, on every occasion, to adopt the language and principles of Patricians. In the administration of their own powers, they frequently consulted the great national council, and *seemed* to refer to its decision the most important concerns of peace and war. Rome, Italy, and the internal provinces were subject to the immediate jurisdiction of the senate. With regard to civil objects, it was the supreme court of appeal; with regard to criminal matters, a tribunal, constituted for the trial of all offences that were committed by men in any public station, or that affected the peace and majesty of the Roman people. The exercise of the judicial power became the most frequent and serious occupation of the senate; and the important causes that were pleaded before them afforded a last refuge to the spirit of ancient eloquence. As a council of state, and as a court of justice, the senate possessed very considerable prerogatives; but in its legislative capacity, in which it was supposed virtually to represent the people, the rights of sovereignty were acknowledged to reside in that assembly. Every power was derived from their authority, every law was ratified by their sanction. Their regular meetings were held on three stated days in every month, the Calends, the Nones, and the Ides. The debates were conducted with decent freedom; and the emperors themselves, who gloried in the name of senators, sat, voted, and divided with their equals.

To resume, in a few words, the system of the Imperial government, as it was instituted by Augustus, and maintained by those princes who understood their own interest and that of the people, it may be defined an absolute monarchy disguised by the forms of a commonwealth. The masters of the Roman world surrounded their throne with darkness, concealed their irresistible strength, and humbly professed themselves the accountable ministers of the senate, whose supreme decrees they dictated and obeyed.[19]

The face of the court corresponded with the forms of the administration. The emperors, if we except those tyrants whose capricious folly violated every law of nature and decency, disdained that pomp and ceremony which might offend their countrymen, but could add nothing to their real power. In all the offices of life, they affected to confound themselves with their subjects, and maintained with them an equal intercourse of visits and entertainments. Their habit, their palace, their table, were suited only to the rank of an opulent senator. Their family, however numerous or splendid, was composed entirely of their domestic slaves and freedmen.[20] Augustus or Trajan would have blushed at employing the meanest of the Romans in those menial offices which, in the household and bedchamber of a limited monarch, are so eagerly solicited by the proudest nobles of Britain.

The deification of the emperors[21] is the only instance in which they departed from their accustomed prudence and modesty. The Asiatic Greeks were the first inventors, the successors of Alexander the first objects, of this servile and impious mode of adulation. It was easily transferred from the kings to the governors of Asia; and the Roman magistrates very frequently were adored as provincial deities, with the pomp of altars and temples, of festivals and sacrifices.[22] It was natural that the emperors should not refuse what the proconsuls had accepted; and the divine honours which both the one and the other received from the provinces attested rather the despotism than the servitude of Rome. But the conquerors soon imitated the vanquished nations in the arts of flattery; and the imperious spirit of the first Caesar too easily consented to assume, during his life time, a place among the tutelar deities of Rome. The milder temper of his successor* declined so dangerous an ambition, which was never afterwards revived, except by the madness of Caligula and Domitian. Augustus permitted indeed some of the provincial cities to erect temples to his honour, on condition that they should associate the worship of Rome with that of the sovereign; he tolerated private superstition, of which he might be the object;[23] but he contented himself with being revered by the senate and people in his human character, and wisely left to his successor the care of his public deification. A regular custom was introduced that, on the decease of every emperor who had neither lived nor died like a tyrant, the senate by a solemn decree should place him in the number of the gods; and the ceremonies of his apotheosis were blended with those of his funeral. This legal and, as it should seem, injudicious profanation, so abhorrent to our stricter principles, was received with a very faint murmur[24] by the easy nature of polytheism; but it was received as an institution, not of religion, but of policy. We should disgrace the virtues of the Antonines by comparing them with the vices of Hercules or Jupiter. Even the characters of Caesar or Augustus were far superior to those of the popular deities. But it was the misfortune of the former to live in an enlightened age, and their actions were too faithfully recorded to admit of such a mixture of fable and mystery as the devotion of the vulgar requires. As soon as their divinity was established by law, it sunk into oblivion, without contributing either to their own fame or to the dignity of succeeding princes.

In the consideration of the Imperial government, we have frequently mentioned the artful founder, under his well-known title of Augustus, which was not however conferred upon him till the edifice was almost completed. The obscure name of Octavianus he derived from a mean family in the little town of Aricia. It was stained with the blood of the proscription; and he was desirous, had it been possible, to erase all memory of his former life. The illustrious surname of Caesar he had assumed, as the adopted son of the dictator; but he had too much good sense either to hope to be confounded, or to wish to be compared, with that extraordinary man. It was proposed in the senate to dignify their minister with a new appellation; and, after a very serious discussion, that of Augustus was chosen, among several others, as being the most expressive of the character of peace and sanctity which he uniformly affected.[25] *Augustus* was therefore a personal, *Caesar* a family, distinction. The former should naturally have expired with the prince on whom it was bestowed; and, however the latter was diffused by adoption and female alliance, Nero was the last prince who could allege any hereditary claim to the honours of the Julian line. But, at the time of his death, the practice of a century had inseparably connected those appellations with the Imperial dignity, and they have been preserved by a long succession of emperors – Romans, Greeks, Franks, and Germans – from the fall of the republic to the present time. A distinction was, however, soon introduced. The sacred title of Augustus was always reserved for the monarch, whilst the name of Caesar was more freely communicated to his relations; and, from the reign of Hadrian at least, was appropriated to the second person in the state, who was considered as the presumptive heir of the empire.

The tender respect of Augustus for a free constitution which he had destroyed can only be explained by an attentive consideration of the character of that subtle tyrant. A cool head, an unfeeling heart, and a cowardly disposition prompted him at the age of nineteen to assume the mask of hypocrisy, which he never afterwards laid aside. With the same hand, and probably with the same temper, he signed the proscription of Cicero and the pardon of Cinna. His virtues, and even his vices, were artificial; and according to the various dictates of his interest, he was at first the enemy, and at last the father, of the Roman world.[26] When he framed the artful system of the Imperial authority, his moderation was inspired by his fears. He wished to deceive the people by an image of civil liberty, and the armies by an image of civil government.

I.   The death of Caesar was ever before his eyes. He had lavished wealth and honours on his adherents; but the most favoured friends of his uncle were in the number of the conspirators. The fidelity of the legions might defend his authority against open rebellion, but their vigilance could not secure his person from the dagger of a determined republican; and the Romans, who revered the memory of Brutus,[27] would applaud the imitation of his virtue. Caesar had provoked his fate as much by the ostentation of his power as by his power itself. The consul or the tribune might have reigned in peace. The title of king had armed the Romans against his life. Augustus was sensible that mankind is governed by names; nor was he deceived in his expectation that the senate and people would submit to slavery, provided they were respectfully assured that they still enjoyed their ancient freedom. A feeble senate and enervated people cheerfully acquiesced in the pleasing illusion, as long as it was supported by the virtue, or by even the prudence, of the successors of Augustus. It was a motive of self-preservation, not a principle of liberty, that animated the conspirators against Caligula, Nero, and Domitian. They attacked the person of the tyrant, without aiming their blow at the authority of the emperor.

There appears, indeed, *one* memorable occasion, in which the senate, after seventy years of patience, made an ineffectual attempt to reassume its long-forgotten rights. When the throne was vacant by the murder of Caligula, the consuls convoked that assembly in the Capitol, condemned the memory of the Caesars, gave the watchword *liberty* to the few cohorts who faintly adhered to their standard, and during eight and forty hours, acted as the independent chiefs of a free commonwealth. But while they deliberated, the praetorian guards had resolved. The stupid Claudius, brother of Germanicus, was already in their camp, invested with the Imperial purple, and prepared to support his election by arms. The dream of liberty was at an end; and the senate awoke to all the horrors of inevitable servitude. Deserted by the people, and threatened by a military force, that feeble assembly was compelled to ratify the choice of the praetorians, and to embrace the benefit of an amnesty, which Claudius had the prudence to offer, and the generosity to observe.[28]

II.   The insolence of the armies inspired Augustus with fears of a still more alarming nature. The despair of the citizens could only attempt what the power of the soldiers was, at any time, able to execute. How precarious was his own authority over men whom he had taught to violate every social duty! He had heard their seditious clamours; he dreaded their calmer moments of reflection. One revolution had been purchased by immense rewards; but a second revolution might double those rewards. The troops professed the fondest attachment to the house of Caesar; but the attachments of the multitude are capricious and inconstant. Augustus summoned to his aid whatever remained in those fierce minds of Roman prejudices; enforced the rigour of discipline by the sanction of law; and, interposing the majesty of the senate between the emperor and the army, boldly claimed their allegiance as the first magistrate of the republic.[29]

During a long period of two hundred and twenty years, from the establishment of this artful system to the death of Commodus, the dangers inherent to a military government were, in a great measure, suspended. The soldiers were seldom roused to that fatal sense of their own strength, and of the weakness of the civil authority, which was, before and afterwards, productive of such dreadful calamities. Caligula and Domitian were assassinated in their palace by their own domestics; the convulsions which agitated Rome on the death of the former were confined to the walls of the city. But Nero involved the whole empire in his ruin. In the space of eighteen months four princes perished by the sword; and the Roman world was shaken by the fury of the contending armies. Excepting only this short, though violent, eruption of military licence, the two centuries from Augustus to Commodus passed away, unstained with civil blood, and undisturbed by revolutions. The emperor was elected by the *authority of the senate* and *the consent of the soldiers*.[30] The legions respected their oath of fidelity; and it requires a minute inspection of the Roman annals to discover three inconsiderable rebellions, which were all suppressed in a few months, and without even the hazard of a battle.[31]

In elective monarchies, the vacancy of the throne is a moment big with danger and mischief. The Roman emperors, desirous to spare the legions that interval of suspense, and the temptation of an irregular choice, invested their designed successor with so large a share of present power, as should enable him, after their decease, to assume the remainder without suffering the empire to perceive the change of masters. Thus Augustus, after all his fairer prospects had been snatched from him by untimely deaths, rested his last hopes on Tiberius, obtained for his adopted son the censorial and tribunitian powers, and dictated a law, by which the future prince was invested with an authority equal to his own over the provinces and the armies.[32] Thus Vespasian subdued the generous mind of his eldest son. Titus was adored by the eastern legions, which, under his command, had recently achieved the conquest of Judea. His power was dreaded, and, as his virtues were clouded by the intemperance of youth, his designs were suspected. Instead of listening to such unworthy suspicions, the prudent monarch associated Titus to the full powers of the Imperial dignity; and the grateful son ever approved himself the humble and faithful minister of so indulgent a father.[33]

The good sense of Vespasian engaged him indeed to embrace every measure that might confirm his recent and precarious elevation. The military oath, and the fidelity of the troops, had been consecrated, by the habits of an hundred years, to the name and family of the Caesars; and, although that family had been continued only by the fictitious rite of adoption, the Romans still revered, in the person of Nero, the grandson of Germanicus, and the lineal successor of Augustus. It was not without reluctance and remorse that the praetorian guards had been persuaded to abandon the cause of the tyrant.[34] The rapid downfall of Galba, Otho, and Vitellius, taught the armies to consider the emperors as the creatures of *their* will, and the instruments of *their* licence. The birth of Vespasian was mean; his grandfather had been a private soldier, his father a petty officer of the revenue;[35] his own merit had raised him, in an advanced age, to the empire; but his merit was rather useful than shining, and his virtues were disgraced by a strict and even sordid parsimony. Such a prince consulted his true interest by the association of a son whose more splendid and amiable character might turn the public attention from the obscure origin to the future glories of the Flavian house. Under the mild administration of Titus, the Roman world enjoyed a transient felicity, and his beloved memory served to protect, above fifteen years, the vices of his brother Domitian.

Nerva had scarcely accepted the purple from the assassins of Domitian before he discovered that his feeble age was unable to stem the torrent of public disorders which had multiplied under the long tyranny of his predecessor. His mild disposition was respected by the good; but the degenerate Romans required a more vigorous character, whose justice should strike terror into the guilty. Though he had several relations, he fixed his choice on a stranger. He adopted Trajan, then about forty years of age, and who commanded a powerful army in the Lower Germany; and immediately, by a decree of the senate, declared him his colleague and successor in the empire.[36] It is sincerely to be lamented, that, whilst we are fatigued with the disgustful relation of Nero's crimes and follies, we are reduced to collect the actions of Trajan from the glimmerings of an abridgement, or the doubtful light of a panegyric. There remains, however, one panegyric far removed beyond the suspicion of flattery. Above two hundred and fifty years after the death of Trajan, the senate, in pouring out the customary acclamations on the accession of a new emperor, wished that he might surpass the felicity of Augustus, and the virtue of Trajan.[37]

We may readily believe that the father of his country hesitated whether he ought to intrust the various and doubtful character of his kinsman

Hadrian with sovereign power. In his last moments, the arts of the empress Plotina either fixed the irresolution of Trajan, or boldly supposed a fictitious adoption,[38] the truth of which could not be safely disputed; and Hadrian was peaceably acknowledged as his lawful successor. Under his reign, as has been already mentioned, the empire flourished in peace and prosperity. He encouraged the arts, reformed the laws, asserted military discipline, and visited all his provinces in person. His vast and active genius was equally suited to the most enlarged views and the minute details of civil policy. But the ruling passions of his soul were curiosity and vanity. As they prevailed, and as they were attracted by different objects, Hadrian was, by turns, an excellent prince, a ridiculous sophist, and a jealous tyrant. The general tenor of his conduct deserved praise for its equity and moderation. Yet, in the first days of his reign, he put to death four consular senators, his personal enemies, and men who had been judged worthy of empire; and the tediousness of a painful illness rendered him, at last, peevish and cruel. The senate doubted whether they should pronounce him a god or a tyrant; and the honours decreed to his memory were granted to the prayers of the pious Antoninus.[39]

The caprice of Hadrian influenced his choice of a successor. After revolving in his mind several men of distinguished merit, whom he esteemed and hated, he adopted Aelius Verus, a gay and voluptuous nobleman, recommended by uncommon beauty to the lover of Antinous.[40] But, whilst Hadrian was delighting himself with his own applause and the acclamations of the soldiers, whose consent had been secured by an immense donative, the new Caesar[41] was ravished from his embraces by an untimely death. He left only one son. Hadrian commended the boy to the gratitude of the Antonines. He was adopted by Pius; and, on the accession of Marcus, was invested with an equal share of sovereign power. Among the many vices of this younger Verus, he possessed one virtue – a dutiful reverence for his wiser colleague, to whom he willingly abandoned the ruder cares of empire. The philosophic emperor dissembled his follies, lamented his early death, and cast a decent veil over his memory.

As soon as Hadrian's passion was either gratified or disappointed, he resolved to deserve the thanks of posterity by placing the most exalted merit on the Roman throne. His discerning eye easily discovered a senator about fifty years of age, blameless in all the offices of life; and a youth of about seventeen, whose riper years opened the fair prospect of every virtue: the elder of these was declared the son and successor of Hadrian, on condition, however, that he himself should immediately adopt the younger. The two Antonines (for it is of them that we are now speaking) governed the Roman world forty-two years with the same invariable spirit of wisdom and virtue. Although Pius had two sons,[42] he preferred the welfare of Rome to the interest of his family, gave his daughter Faustina in marriage to young Marcus, obtained from the senate the tribunitian and proconsular powers, and, with a noble disdain, or rather ignorance, of jealousy, associated him to all the labours of government. Marcus, on the other hand, revered the character of his benefactor, loved him as a parent, obeyed him as a sovereign,[43] and, after he was no more, regulated his own administration by the example and maxims of his predecessor. Their united reigns are possibly the only period of history in which the happiness of a great people was the sole object of government.

Titus Antoninus Pius has been justly denominated a second Numa.* The same love of religion, justice, and peace, was the distinguishing characteristic of both princes. But the situation of the latter opened a much larger field for the exercise of those virtues. Numa could only prevent a few neighbouring villages from plundering each other's harvests. Antoninus diffused order and tranquillity over the greatest part of the earth. His reign is marked by the rare advantage of furnishing very few materials for history; which is, indeed, little more than the register of the crimes, follies, and misfortunes of mankind. In private life he was an amiable as well as a good man. The native simplicity of his virtue was a stranger to vanity or affectation. He enjoyed with moderation the conveniences of his fortune, and the innocent pleasures of society;[44] and the benevolence of his soul displayed itself in a cheerful serenity of temper.

The virtue of Marcus Aurelius Antoninus was of a severer and more laborious kind.[45] It was the well-earned harvest of many a learned conference, of many a patient lecture, and many a midnight lucubration. At the age of twelve years he embraced the rigid system of the Stoics, which taught him to submit his body to his mind, his passions to his reason; to consider virtue as the only good, vice as the only evil, all things external as things indifferent.[46] His Meditations, composed in the tumult of a camp, are still extant; and he even condescended to give lessons on philosophy, in a more public manner than was perhaps consistent with the modesty of a sage or the dignity of an emperor.[47] But his life was the noblest commentary on the precepts of Zeno.† He was severe to himself, indulgent to the imperfection of others, just and beneficent to all mankind. He regretted that Avidius Cassius, who excited a rebellion in Syria, had disappointed him, by a voluntary death, of the pleasure of converting an enemy into a friend; and he justified the sincerity of that sentiment by moderating the zeal of the senate against the adherents of the traitor.[48] War he detested, as the disgrace and calamity of human nature; but when the necessity of a just defence called upon him to take up arms, he readily exposed his person to eight winter campaigns on the frozen banks of the Danube, the severity of which was at last fatal to the weakness of his constitution. His memory was revered by a grateful posterity, and above a century after his death many persons preserved the image of Marcus Antoninus among those of their household gods.[49]

If a man were called to fix the period in the history of the world during which the condition of the human race was most happy and prosperous, he would, without hesitation, name that which elapsed from the death of Domitian to the accession of Commodus. The vast extent of the Roman empire was governed by absolute power, under the guidance of virtue and wisdom. The armies were restrained by the firm but gentle hand of four successive emperors, whose characters and authority commanded involuntary respect. The forms of the civil administration were carefully preserved by Nerva, Trajan, Hadrian, and the Antonines, who delighted in the image of liberty, and were pleased with considering themselves as the accountable ministers of the laws. Such princes deserved the honour of restoring the republic, had the Romans of their days been capable of enjoying a rational freedom.

The labours of these monarchs were overpaid by the immense reward that inseparably waited on their success; by the honest pride of virtue, and by the exquisite delight of beholding the general happiness of which they were the authors. A just but melancholy reflection embittered, however, the noblest of human enjoyments. They must often have recollected the instability of a happiness which depended on the character of a single man. The fatal moment was perhaps approaching, when some licentious youth, or some jealous tyrant, would abuse, to the destruction, that absolute power which they had exerted for the benefit of their people. The ideal restraints of the senate and the laws might serve to display the virtues, but could never correct the vices, of the emperor. The military force was a blind and irresistible instrument of oppression; and the corruption of Roman manners would always supply flatterers eager to applaud, and ministers prepared to serve, the fear or the avarice, the lust or the cruelty, of their masters.

These gloomy apprehensions had been already justified by the experience of the Romans. The annals of the emperors exhibit a strong and various picture of human nature, which we should vainly seek among the mixed and doubtful characters of modern history. In the conduct of those monarchs we may trace the utmost lines of vice and virtue; the most exalted perfection and the meanest degeneracy of our own species. The golden age of Trajan and the Antonines had been preceded by an age of iron. It is almost superfluous to enumerate the unworthy successors of Augustus. Their unparalleled vices, and the splendid theatre on which they were acted, have saved them from oblivion. The dark unrelenting Tiberius, the furious Caligula, the stupid Claudius, the profligate and cruel Nero, the beastly Vitellius,[50] and the timid inhuman Domitian are condemned to everlasting infamy. During fourscore years (excepting only the short and doubtful respite of Vespasian's reign),[51] Rome groaned beneath an unremitting tyranny, which exterminated the ancient families of the republic, and was fatal to almost every virtue and every talent that arose in that unhappy period.

Under the reign of these monsters, the slavery of the Romans was accompanied with two peculiar circumstances, the one occasioned by their former liberty, the other by their extensive conquests, which rendered their condition more wretched than that of the victims of tyranny in any other age or country. From these causes were derived, 1. The exquisite sensibility of the sufferers; and 2. The impossibility of escaping from the hand of the oppressor.

I. When Persia was governed by the descendants of Sefi, a race of princes whose wanton cruelty often stained their divan, their table, and their bed with the blood of their favourites, there is a saying recorded of a young nobleman, That he never departed from the sultan's presence without satisfying himself whether his head was still on his shoulders. The experience of every day might almost justify the scepticism of Rustan.[52] Yet the fatal sword, suspended above him by a single thread, seems not to have disturbed the slumbers, or interrupted the tranquillity, of the Persian. The monarch's frown, he well knew, could level him with the dust; but the stroke of lightning or apoplexy might be equally fatal; and it was the part of a wise man to forget the inevitable calamities of human life in the enjoyment of the fleeting hour. He was dignified with the appellation of the king's slave; had, perhaps, been purchased from obscure parents, in a country which he had never known; and was trained up from his infancy in the severe discipline of the seraglio.[53] His name, his wealth, his honours, were the gift of a master, who might, without injustice, resume what he had bestowed. Rustan's knowledge, if he possessed any, could only serve to confirm his habits by prejudices. His language afforded not words for any form of government, except absolute monarchy. The history of the East informed him that such had ever been the condition of mankind.[54] The Koran, and the interpreters of that divine book, inculcated to him that the sultan was the descendant of the prophet, and the vice-regent of heaven; that patience was the first virtue of a Mussulman, and unlimited obedience the great duty of a subject.

The minds of the Romans were very differently prepared for slavery. Oppressed beneath the weight of their own corruption and of military violence, they for a long while preserved the sentiments, or at least the ideas, of their freeborn ancestors. The education of Helvidius and Thrasea, of Tacitus and Pliny, was the same as that of Cato and Cicero. From Grecian philosophy they had imbibed the justest and most liberal notions of the dignity of human nature and the origin of civil society. The history of their own country had taught them to revere a free, a virtuous, and a victorious commonwealth; to abhor the successful crimes of Caesar and Augustus; and inwardly to despise those tyrants whom they adored with the most abject flattery. As magistrates and senators, they were admitted into the great council which had once dictated laws to the earth, whose name gave still a sanction to the acts of the monarch, and whose authority was so often prostituted to the vilest purposes of tyranny. Tiberius, and those emperors who adopted his maxims, attempted to disguise their murders by the formalities of justice, and perhaps enjoyed a secret pleasure in rendering the senate their accomplice as well as their victim. By this assembly the last of the Romans were condemned for imaginary crimes and real virtues. Their infamous accusers assumed the language of independent patriots, who arraigned a dangerous citizen before the tribunal of his country; and the public service was rewarded by riches and honours.[55] The servile judges professed to assert the majesty of the commonwealth, violated in the person of its first magistrate,[56] whose clemency they most applauded when they trembled the most at his inexorable and impending cruelty.[57] The tyrant beheld their baseness with just contempt, and encountered their secret sentiments of detestation with sincere and avowed hatred for the whole body of the senate.

II.   The division of Europe into a number of independent states, connected, however, with each other, by the general resemblance of religion, language and manners, is productive of the most beneficial consequences to the liberty of mankind. A modern tyrant, who should find no resistance either in his own breast or in his people, would soon experience a gentle restraint from the example of his equals, the dread of present censure, the advice of his allies, and the apprehension of his enemies. The object of his displeasure, escaping from the narrow limits of his dominions, would easily obtain, in a happier climate, a secure refuge, a new fortune adequate to his merit, the freedom of complaint, and perhaps the means of revenge. But the empire of the Romans filled the world, and, when that empire fell into the hands of a single person, the world became a safe and dreary prison for his enemies. The slave of Imperial despotism, whether he was condemned to drag his gilded chain in Rome and the senate, or to wear out a life of exile on the barren rock of Seriphus or the frozen banks of the Danube, expected his fate in silent despair.[58] To resist was fatal, and it was impossible to fly. On every side he was encompassed with a vast extent of sea and land, which he could never hope to traverse without being discovered, seized, and restored to his irritated master. Beyond the frontiers, his anxious view could discover nothing, except the ocean, inhospitable deserts, hostile tribes of barbarians, of fierce manners and unknown language, or dependent kings, who would gladly purchase the emperor's protection by the sacrifice of an obnoxious fugitive.[59] 'Wherever you are,' said Cicero to the exiled Marcellus, 'remember that you are equally within the power of the conqueror.'[60]

NOTES TO CHAPTER 3

* *page 053* [Julius Caesar]

† *page 53* [Augustus]

1 Orosius, vi, 18.

2 Julius Caesar introduced soldiers, strangers and half-barbarians, into the senate. (Suetonius in *Caesar*, ch. 80.) The abuse became still more scandalous after his death.

3 Dion Cassius, iii, 693, Suetonius in *Augustus*, ch. 35.

4 Dion, iii, 698, gives us a prolix and bombastic speech on this great occasion. I have borrowed from Suetonius and Tacitus the general language of Augustus.

5 *Imperator* (from which we have derived emperor) signified under the republic no more than *general*, and was emphatically bestowed by the soldiers, when on the field of battle they proclaimed their victorious leader worthy of that title. When the Roman *emperors* assumed it in that sense, they placed it after their name, and marked how often they had taken it.

6 Dion, liii, 703, etc.

7 Livy, *Epitom.*, Bk xiv; Valer. Maxim., vi, 3.

8 See in the eighth book of Livy, the conduct of Manlius Torquatus and Papirius Cursor. They violated the laws of nature and humanity, but they asserted those of military discipline; and the people, who abhorred the action, were obliged to respect the principle.

9 By the lavish but unconstrained suffrages of the people, Pompey had obtained a military command scarcely inferior to that of Augustus. Among the extraordinary acts of power executed by the former, we may remark the foundation of twenty-nine cities, and the distribution of three or four millions sterling to his troops. The ratification of his acts met with some opposition and delays in the senate. See Plutarch, Appian, Dion Cassius, and the first book of the epistles to Atticus.

10 Under the commonwealth, a triumph could only be claimed by the general, who was authorised to take the Auspices in the name of the people. By an exact consequence, drawn from this principle of policy and religion, the triumph was reserved to the emperor, and his most successful lieutenants were satisfied with some marks of distinction, which, under the name of triumphal honours, were invented in their favour.

11 Cicero (*de Legibus*, iii, 3) gives the consular office the name of *regia potestas* [royal power]; and Polybius (vi, 3) observes three powers in the Roman constitution. The monarchical was represented and exercised by the consuls.

12 As the tribunitian power (distinct from the annual office) was first invented for the dictator Caesar (Dion, xliv, 384), we may easily conceive, that it was given as a reward for having so nobly asserted, by arms, the sacred rights of the tribunes and people. See his own commentaries, *de Bell. Civil.*, Bk i.

13 Augustus exercised nine annual consulships without interruption. He then most artfully refused that magistracy as well as the dictatorship, absented himself from Rome, and waited till the fatal effects of tumult and faction forced the senate to invest him with a perpetual consulship. Augustus, as well as his successors, affected, however, to conceal so invidious a title.

14 See a fragment of a Decree of the Senate, conferring on the Emperor Vespasian all the powers granted to his predecessors, Augustus, Tiberius, and Claudius. This curious and important monument is published in Gruter's *Inscriptions*, ccxlii.

15 Two consuls were created on the Calends of January; but in the course of the year others were substituted in their places, till the annual number seems to have amounted to no less than twelve. The praetors were usually sixteen or eighteen (Lipsius in *Excurs. D. ad* Tacit., *Annals*, i). I have not mentioned the Aediles or Quaestors. Officers of the police or revenue easily adapt themselves to any form of government. In the time of Nero the tribunes legally possessed the right of intercession, though it might be dangerous to exercise it (Tacitus, *Annals*, xvi, 26). In the time of Trajan, it was doubtful whether the tribuneship was an office or a name (Pliny, *Epist.*, 123).

16 The tyrants themselves were ambitious of the consulship. The virtuous princes were moderate in the pursuit, and exact in the discharge, of it. Trajan revived the ancient oath, and swore before the consul's tribunal that he would observe the laws (Pliny, *Panegyric.*, ch. 64).

17 *Quoties magistratuum comitiis interesset, tribus cum candidatis suis circuibat; supplicabatque more solemni. Ferebat et ipse suffragium in tribubus, ut unus e populo.* Suetonius in *Augustus*, ch. 56. ['Whenever he took part in the election of the magistrates, he went around the wards together with the candidates, and canvassed for them in the traditional manner. He would also cast a vote himself, in his own ward, as if he were an ordinary person.']

18 *Tum primum Comitia e campo ad patres translata sunt.* Tacitus, *Annals*, i, 15. ['It was then that the elections were first transferred from the popular assembly to the Senate.'] The word *primum* seems to allude to some faint and unsuccessful efforts, which were made towards restoring them to the people.

19 Dion Cassius (liii, 703–14) has given a very loose and partial sketch of the Imperial system. To illustrate and often to correct him, I have meditated Tacitus, examined Suetonius, and consulted the following moderns: the Abbé de la Bléterie in the *Mémoires de l'Académie des Inscriptions*, tom. xix, xxi, xxiv, xxv, xxvii. Beaufort, *République Romaine*, i, 255–75. The dissertations of Noodt and Gronovius, *de lege Regia*, printed at Leyden in the year 1731. Gravina, *de Imperio Romano*, pp. 479–544 of his *Opuscula*. Maffei, *Verona Illustrata*, i, 245, etc.

20 A weak prince will always be governed by his domestics. The power of slaves aggravated the shame of the Romans; and the senate paid court to a Pallas or a Narcissus. There is a chance that a modern favourite may be a gentleman.

21 See a treatise of Van Dale, *de Consecratione Principum*. It would be easier for me to copy, than it has been to verify, the quotations of that learned Dutchman.

22 See a dissertation of the Abbé Mongault in the first volume of the *Academy of Inscriptions*.

 * *page 59*   [Augustus]

23 *Iurandasque tuum per nomen ponimus aras* ['We set up altars in your name for the swearing of oaths'], says Horace to the emperor himself, and Horace was well acquainted with the court of Augustus.

24 See Cicero in *Philippic*, i, 6. Julian, *in Caesaribus. Inque Deum templis iurabit Roma per umbras* ['And in the temples of the Gods, Rome will swear oaths by the shades of departed mortals'] is the indignant expression of Lucan; but it is a patriotic rather than a devout indignation.

25 Dion Cassius, liii, 710, with the curious Annotations of Reimar.

26 As Octavianus advanced to the banquet of the Caesars, his colour changed like that of the chameleon; pale at first, then red, afterwards black, he at last assumed the mild livery of Venus and the Graces (*Caesars*, p. 309). This image, employed by Julian in his ingenious fiction, is just and elegant; but, when he considers this change of character as real, and ascribes it to the power of philosophy, he does too much honour to philosophy and to Octavianus.

27 Two centuries after the establishment of monarchy, the emperor Marcus Antoninus recommends the character of Brutus as a perfect model of Roman virtue.

28 It is much to be regretted that we have lost the part of Tacitus which treated of that transaction. We are forced to content ourselves with the popular rumours of Josephus, and the imperfect hints of Dion and Suetonius.

29 Augustus restored the ancient severity of discipline. After the civil wars, he dropped the endearing name of fellow-soldiers, and called them only soldiers (Suetonius in *Augustus*, ch. 25). See the use Tiberius made of the senate in the mutiny of the Pannonian legions (Tacitus, *Annals*, i).

30 These words seem to have been the constitutional language. See Tacitus, *Annals*, xiii, 4.

31 The first was Camillus Scribonianus, who took up arms in Dalmatia against Claudius, and was deserted by his own troops in five days; the second, L. Antonius, in Germany, who rebelled against Domitian; and the third, Avidius Cassius, in the reign of M. Antoninus. The two last reigned but a few months and were cut off by their own adherents. We may observe, that both Camillus and Cassius coloured their ambition with the design of restoring the republic, a task, said Cassius, peculiarly reserved for his name and family.

32 Velleius Paterculus, ii, 121. Suetonius in *Tiberius*, ch. 20.

33 Suetonius in *Titus*, ch. 6. Pliny, in *Praefat. Hist. Natur.*

34 This idea is frequently and strongly inculcated by Tacitus. See *Hist.*, i, 5, 16, ii, 76.

35 The emperor Vespasian, with his usual good sense, laughed at the genealogists, who deduced his family from Flavius, the founder of Reate (his native country), and one of the companions of Hercules. Suetonius in *Vespasian*, ch. 12.

36 Dion, lxviii, 1121. Pliny Secund. in *Panegyric*.

37 *Felicior Augusto, melior Trajano*, Eutrop., viii, 5.

38 Dion (lxix, 1249) affirms the whole to have been a fiction, on the authority of his father, who being governor of the province where Trajan died, had very good opportunities of sifting this mysterious transaction. Yet Dodwell (*Praelect. Camden*, xvii) has maintained that Hadrian was called to the certain hope of the empire during the lifetime of Trajan.

39 Dion, lxx, 1171, Aurelius Victor.

40 The deification of Antinous, his medals, statues, temples, city, oracles, and constellation are well known, and still dishonour the memory of Hadrian. Yet we may remark, that of the first fifteen emperors, Claudius was the only one whose taste in love was entirely correct. For the honours of Antinous, see Spanheim, *Commentaires sur les Caesars de Julien*, p. 80.

41 *Hist. August.*, p. 13, Aurelius Victor in *Epitom*.

42 Without the help of medals and inscriptions, we should be ignorant of this fact, so honourable to the memory of Pius.

43 During the twenty-three years of Pius's reign, Marcus was only two nights absent from the palace, and even those were at different times. *Hist. August.*, p. 25.

* *page 65* [the second of Rome's legendary kings, 716–672 BC]

44 He was fond of the theatre and not insensible to the charms of the fair sex. Marcus Antoninus, i, 16; *Hist. August.*, p. 20, 21; Julian, in *Caesar*.

45 The enemies of Marcus charged him with hypocrisy and with a want of that simplicity which distinguished Pius and even Verus (*Hist. Aug.*, p. 34.) This suspicion, unjust as it was, may serve to account for the superior applause bestowed upon personal qualifications, in preference to the social virtues. Even Marcus Antoninus has been called a hypocrite; but the wildest scepticism never insinuated that Caesar might possibly be a coward, or Tully a fool. Wit and valour are qualifications more easily ascertained than humanity or the love of justice.

46 Tacitus has characterised, in a few words, the principles of the Portico: *Doctores sapientiae secutus est, qui sola bona quae honesta, mala tantum quae turpia; potentiam, nobilitatem, ceteraque extra animum, neque bonis neque malis adnumerant.* Tacitus, *Hist.* iv, 5.

47 Before he went on the second expedition against the Germans, he read lectures of philosophy to the Roman people, during three days. He had already done the same in the cities of Greece and Asia. *Hist. August.*, p. 41, *in Cassio*, ch. 3.

† *page 65* [the founder philosopher of Stoicism]

48 Dion, lxxi, 1190, *Hist. August.*, in *Avid. Cassio*.

49 *Hist. August.*, in *Marc. Antonin.*, ch. 18.

50 Vitellius consumed in mere eating at least six millions of our money, in about seven months. It is not easy to express his vices with dignity, or even decency. Tacitus fairly calls him a hog, but it is by substituting for a coarse word a very fine image. '*At Vitellius, umbraculis hortorum abditus, ut ignava animalia, quibus si cibum suggeras iacent torpentque, praeterita, instantia, futura, pari oblivione dimiserat. Atque illum nemore Aricino desidem et marcentem,*' etc. ['But Vitellius, withdrawn to his secluded country-seat, like the brute beasts, who if food is thrown to them, lie idly by, had consigned past, present and future to the same oblivion. And so on his estate at Aricia, indolent and sated, he . . . '] Tacitus, *Hist.*, iii, 36; ii, 95. Suetonius in *Vitellius*, ch. 13. Dion Cassius, lxv, 1062.

51 The execution of Helvidius Priscus and of the virtuous Eponina disgraced the reign of Vespasian.

52 *Voyage de Chardin en Perse*, iii, 293.

53 The practice of raising slaves to the great offices of state is still more common among the Turks than among the Persians. The miserable countries of Georgia and Circassia supply rulers to the greatest part of the East.

54 Chardin says that European travellers have diffused among the Persians some ideas of the freedom and mildness of our governments. They have done them a very ill office.

55 They alleged the example of Scipio and Cato (Tacitus, *Annals*, iii, 66.) Marcellus Epirus and Crispus Vibius had acquired two millions and a half under Nero. Their wealth, which aggravated their crimes, protected them under Vespasian. See Tacitus, *Hist.*, iv, 43, *Dialog. de Orator.*, ch. 8. For one accusation, Regulus, the just object of Pliny's satire, received from the senate the consular ornaments, and a present of sixty thousand pounds.

56 The crime of *majesty* was formerly a treasonable offence against the Roman people. As tribunes of the people, Augustus and Tiberius applied it to their own persons, and extended it to an infinite latitude.

57 After the virtuous and unfortunate widow of Germanicus had been put to death, Tiberius received the thanks of the senate for his clemency. She had not been publicly strangled nor was the body drawn with a hook to the Gemoniae, where those of common malefactors were exposed. See Tacitus, *Annals*, vi, 25; Suetonius in *Tiberius*, ch. 53.

58 Seriphus was a small rocky island in the Aegean Sea, the inhabitants of which were despised for their ignorance and obscurity. The place of Ovid's exile is well known by his just but unmanly lamentations. It should seem that he only received an order to leave Rome in so many days, and to transport himself to Tomi. Guards and gaolers were unnecessary.

59 Under Tiberius, a Roman knight attempted to fly to the Parthians. He was stopped in the straits of Sicily; but so little danger did there appear in the example that the most jealous of tyrants disdained to punish it. Tacitus, *Annals*, vi, 14.

60 Cicero, *ad Familiares*, iv, 7.

CHAPTER 4

The cruelty, follies and murder of Commodus –
election of Pertinax – his attempts to reform the state –
his assassination by the Praetorian Guards

The mildness of Marcus, which the rigid discipline of the Stoics was unable to eradicate, formed, at the same time, the most amiable, and the only defective, part of his character. His excellent understanding was often deceived by the unsuspecting goodness of his heart. Artful men, who study the passions of princes and conceal their own, approached his person in the disguise of philosophic sanctity, and acquired riches and honours by affecting to despise them.[1] His excessive indulgence to his brother, his wife, and his son, exceeded the bounds of private virtue, and became a public injury, by the example and consequences of their vices.

Faustina, the daughter of Pius and the wife of Marcus, has been as much celebrated for her gallantries as for her beauty. The grave simplicity of the philosopher was ill calculated to engage her wanton levity, or to fix that unbounded passion for variety which often discovered personal merit in the meanest of mankind.[2] The Cupid of the ancients was, in general, a very sensual deity; and the amours of an empress, as they exact on her side the plainest advances, are seldom susceptible of much sentimental delicacy. Marcus was the only man in the empire who seemed ignorant or insensible of the irregularities of Faustina; which, according to the prejudices of every age, reflected some disgrace on the injured husband. He promoted several of her lovers to posts of honour and profit,[3] and, during a connection of thirty years, invariably gave her proofs of the most tender confidence, and of a respect which ended not with her life. In his Meditations he thanks the gods, who had bestowed on him a wife so faithful, so gentle, and of such a wonderful simplicity of manners.[4] The obsequious senate, at his earnest request, declared her a goddess. She was represented in her temples with the attributes of Juno, Venus, and Ceres; and it was decreed that, on the day of their nuptials, the youth of either sex should pay their vows before the altar of their chaste patroness.[5]

The monstrous vices of the son have cast a shade on the purity of the father's virtues. It has been objected to Marcus that he sacrificed the happiness of millions to a fond partiality for a worthless boy; and that he chose a successor in his own family rather than in the republic. Nothing, however, was neglected by the anxious father, and by the men of virtue and learning whom he summoned to his assistance, to expand the narrow mind of young Commodus, to correct his growing vices, and to render him worthy of the throne for which he was designed. But the power of instruction is seldom of much efficacy, except in those happy dispositions where it is almost superfluous. The distasteful lesson of a grave philosopher was, in a moment, obliterated by the whisper of a profligate favourite; and Marcus himself blasted the fruits of this laboured education, by admitting his son, at the age of fourteen or fifteen, to a full participation of the Imperial power. He lived but four years afterwards; but he lived long enough to repent a rash measure, which raised the impetuous youth above the restraint of reason and authority.

Most of the crimes which disturb the internal peace of society are produced by the restraints which the necessary, but, unequal, laws of property have imposed on the appetites of mankind, by confining to a few the possession of those objects that are coveted by many. Of all our passions and appetites, the love of power is of the most imperious and unsociable nature, since the pride of one man requires the submission of the multitude. In the tumult of civil discord the laws of society lose their force, and their place is seldom supplied by those of humanity. The ardour of contention, the pride of victory, the despair of success, the memory of past injuries, and the fear of future dangers, all contribute to inflame the mind, and to silence the voice of pity. From such motives almost every page of history has been stained with civil blood; but these motives will not account for the unprovoked cruelties of Commodus, who had nothing to wish, and everything to enjoy. The beloved son of Marcus succeeded to his father, amidst the acclamations of the senate and armies;[6] and when he ascended the throne, the happy youth saw round him neither competitor to remove, nor enemies to punish. In this calm elevated station it was surely natural that he should prefer the love of mankind to their detestation, the mild glories of his five predecessors to the ignominious fate of Nero and Domitian.

Yet Commodus was not, as he has been represented, a tiger born with an insatiate thirst of human blood, and capable, from his infancy, of the most inhuman actions.[7] Nature had formed him of a weak, rather than a wicked, disposition. His simplicity and timidity rendered him the slave of his attendants, who gradually corrupted his mind. His cruelty, which at first obeyed the dictates of others, degenerated into habit, and at length became the ruling passion of his soul.[8]

Upon the death of his father Commodus found himself embarrassed with the command of a great army, and the conduct of a difficult war against the Quadi and Marcomanni.[9] The servile and profligate youths whom Marcus had banished soon regained their station and influence about the new emperor. They exaggerated the hardships and dangers of a campaign in the wild countries beyond the Danube; and they assured the indolent prince that the terror of his name and the arms of his lieutenants would be sufficient to complete the conquest of the dismayed barbarians, or to impose such conditions as were more advantageous than any conquest. By a dexterous application to his sensual appetites, they compared the tranquillity, the splendour, the refined pleasures of Rome with the tumult of a Pannonian camp, which afforded neither leisure nor materials for luxury.[10] Commodus listened to the pleasing advice; but, whilst he hesitated between his own inclination and the awe which he still retained for his father's counsellors, the summer insensibly elapsed, and his triumphal entry into the capital was deferred till the autumn. His graceful person,[11] popular address, and imagined virtues attracted the public favour; the honourable peace which he had recently granted to the barbarians diffused an universal joy;[12] his impatience to revisit Rome was fondly ascribed to the love of his country; and his dissolute course of amusements was faintly condemned in a prince of nineteen years of age.

During the three first years of his reign, the forms, and even the spirit, of the old administration were maintained by those faithful counsellors, to whom Marcus had recommended his son, and for whose wisdom and integrity Commodus still entertained a reluctant esteem. The young prince and his profligate favourites revelled in all the licence of sovereign power; but his hands were yet unstained with blood; and he had even displayed a generosity of sentiment, which might perhaps have ripened into solid virtue.[13] A fatal incident decided his fluctuating character.

One evening, as the emperor was returning to the palace through a dark and narrow portico in the amphitheatre,[14] an assassin, who waited his passage, rushed upon him with a drawn sword, loudly exclaiming, *The senate sends you this.* The menace prevented the deed; the assassin was seized by the guards, and immediately revealed the authors of the conspiracy. It had been formed, not in the state, but within the walls of the palace. Lucilla, the emperor's sister, and widow of Lucius Verus, impatient of the second rank, and jealous of the reigning empress, had armed the murderer against her brother's life. She had not ventured to communicate the black design to her second husband, Claudius Pompeianus, a senator of distinguished merit and unshaken loyalty; but among the crowd of her lovers (for she imitated the manners of Faustina) she found men of desperate fortunes and wild ambition, who were prepared to serve her more violent as well as her tender passions. The conspirators experienced the rigour of justice, and the abandoned princess was punished, first with exile, and afterwards with death.[15]

But the words of the assassin sunk deep into the mind of Commodus, and left an indelible impression of fear and hatred against the whole body of the senate. Those whom he had dreaded as importunate ministers, he now suspected as secret enemies. The Delators,* a race of men discouraged, and almost extinguished, under the former reigns, again became formidable as soon as they discovered that the emperor was desirous of finding disaffection and treason in the senate. That assembly, whom Marcus had ever considered as the great council of the nation, was composed of the most distinguished of the Romans; and distinction of every kind soon became criminal. The possession of wealth stimulated the diligence of the informers; rigid virtue implied a tacit censure of the irregularities of Commodus; important services implied a dangerous superiority of merit, and the friendship of the father always insured the aversion of the son. Suspicion was equivalent to proof; trial to condemnation. The execution of a considerable senator was attended with the death of all who might lament or revenge his fate; and when Commodus had once tasted human blood, he became incapable of pity or remorse.

Of these innocent victims of tyranny, none died more lamented than the two brothers of the Quintilian family, Maximus and Condianus, whose fraternal love has saved their names from oblivion, and endeared their memory to posterity. Their studies and their occupations, their pursuits and their pleasures, were still the same. In the enjoyment of a great estate, they never admitted the idea of a separate interest: some fragments are now extant of a treatise which they composed in common; and in every action of life it was observed that their two bodies were animated by one soul. The Antonines, who valued their virtues and delighted in their union, raised them, in the same year, to the consulship; and Marcus afterwards intrusted to their joint care the civil administration of Greece, and a great military command, in which they obtained a signal victory over the Germans. The kind cruelty of Commodus united them in death.[16]

The tyrant's rage, after having shed the noblest blood of the senate, at length recoiled on the principal instrument of his cruelty. Whilst Commodus was immersed in blood and luxury, he devolved the detail of the public business on Perennis; a servile and ambitious minister, who had obtained his post by the murder of his predecessor, but who possessed a considerable share of vigour and ability. By acts of extortion, and the forfeited estates of the nobles sacrificed to his avarice, he had accumulated an immense treasure. The Praetorian guards were under his immediate command; and his son, who already discovered a military genius, was at the head of the Illyrian legions. Perennis aspired to the empire; or what, in the eyes of Commodus, amounted to the same crime, he was capable of aspiring to it, had he not been prevented, surprised, and put to death. The fall of a minister is a very trifling incident in the general history of the empire; but it was hastened by an extraordinary circumstance, which proved how much the nerves of discipline were already relaxed. The legions of Britain, discontented with the administration of Perennis, formed a deputation of fifteen hundred select men, with instructions to march to Rome, and lay their complaints before the emperor. These military petitioners, by their own determined behaviour, by inflaming the divisions of the guards, by exaggerating the strength of the British army, and by alarming the fears of Commodus, exacted and obtained the minister's death, as the only redress of their grievances.[17] This presumption of a distant army, and their discovery of the weakness of government, was a sure presage of the most dreadful convulsions.

The negligence of the public administration was betrayed soon afterwards by a new disorder, which arose from the smallest beginnings. A spirit of desertion began to prevail among the troops, and the deserters, instead of seeking their safety in flight or concealment, infested the highways. Maternus, a private soldier, of a daring boldness above his station, collected these bands of robbers into a little army, set open the prisons, invited the slaves to assert their freedom, and plundered with impunity the rich and defenceless cities of Gaul and Spain. The governors of the provinces, who had long been the spectators, and perhaps the partners, of his depredations, were, at length, roused from their supine indolence by the threatening commands of the emperor. Maternus found that he was encompassed, and foresaw that he must be overpowered. A great effort of despair was his last resource. He ordered his followers to disperse, to pass the Alps in small parties and various disguises, and to assemble at Rome during the licentious tumult of the festival of Cybele.[18] To murder Commodus, and to ascend the vacant throne, was the ambition of no vulgar robber. His measures were so ably concerted that his concealed troops already filled the streets of Rome. The envy of an accomplice discovered and ruined this singular enterprise in the moment when it was ripe for execution.[19]

Suspicious princes often promote the last of mankind, from a vain persuasion that those who have no dependence except on their favour will have no attachment except to the person of their benefactor. Cleander, the successor of Perennis, was a Phrygian by birth; of a nation, over whose stubborn but servile temper blows only could prevail.[20] He had been sent from his native country to Rome, in the capacity of a slave. As a slave he entered the imperial palace, rendered himself useful to his master's passions, and rapidly ascended to the most exalted station which a subject could enjoy. His influence over the mind of Commodus was much greater than that of his predecessor; for Cleander was devoid of any ability or virtue which could inspire the emperor with envy or distrust. Avarice was the reigning passion of his soul, and the great principle of his administration. The rank of consul, of patrician, of senator, was exposed to public sale; and it would have been considered as disaffection if any one had refused to purchase these empty and disgraceful honours with the greatest part of his fortune.[21] In the lucrative provincial employments the minister shared with the governor the spoils of the people. The execution of the laws was venal and arbitrary. A wealthy criminal might obtain not only the reversal of the sentence by which he was justly condemned; but might likewise inflict whatever punishment he pleased on the accuser, the witnesses, and the judge.

By these means Cleander, in the space of three years, had accumulated more wealth than had ever yet been possessed by any freedman.[22] Commodus was perfectly satisfied with the magnificent presents which the artful courtier laid at his feet in the most seasonable moments. To divert the public envy, Cleander, under the emperor's name, erected baths, porticos, and places of exercise, for the use of the people.[23] He flattered himself that the Romans, dazzled and amused by this apparent liberality, would be less affected by the bloody scenes which were daily exhibited; that they would forget the death of Byrrhus, a senator to whose superior merit the late emperor had granted one of his daughters; and that they would forgive the execution of Arrius Antoninus, the last representative of the name and virtues of the Antonines. The former, with more integrity than prudence, had attempted to disclose to his brother-in-law the true character of Cleander. An equitable sentence pronounced by the latter, when proconsul of Asia, against a worthless creature of the favourite, proved fatal to him.[24] After the fall of Perennis the terrors of Commodus had, for a short time, assumed the appearance of a return to virtue. He repealed the most odious of his acts, loaded his memory with the public execration, and ascribed to the pernicious counsels of that wicked minister all the errors of his inexperienced youth. But his repentance lasted only thirty days; and, under Cleander's tyranny, the administration of Perennis was often regretted.

Pestilence and famine contributed to fill up the measure of the calamities of Rome.[25] The first could only be imputed to the just indignation of the gods; but a monopoly of corn, supported by the riches and power of the minister, was considered as the immediate cause of the second. The popular discontent, after it had long circulated in whispers, broke out in the assembled circus. The people quitted their favourite amusements for the more delicious pleasure of revenge, rushed in crowds towards a palace in the suburbs, one of the emperor's retirements, and demanded, with angry clamours, the head of the pubic enemy. Cleander, who commanded the Praetorian guards,[26] ordered a body of cavalry to sally forth and disperse the seditious multitude. The multitude fled with precipitation towards the city; several were slain, and many more were trampled to death; but, when the cavalry entered the streets, their pursuit was checked by a shower of stones and darts from the roofs and windows of the houses. The foot guards,[27] who had been long jealous of the prerogatives and insolence of the Praetorian cavalry, embraced the party of the people. The tumult became a regular engagement, and threatened a general massacre. The Praetorians at length gave way, oppressed with numbers; and the tide of popular fury returned with redoubled violence against the gates of the palace, where Commodus lay dissolved in luxury, and alone unconscious of the civil war. It was death to approach his person with the unwelcome news. He would have perished in this supine security had not two women, his eldest sister Fadilla, and Marcia, the most favoured of his concubines, ventured to break into his presence. Bathed in tears, and with dishevelled hair, they threw themselves at his feet, and, with all the pressing eloquence of fear, discovered to the affrighted emperor the crimes of the minister, the rage of the people, and the impending ruin which in a few minutes would burst over his palace and person. Commodus started from his dream of pleasure, and commanded that the head of Cleander should be thrown out to the people. The desired spectacle instantly appeased the tumult; and the son of Marcus might even yet have regained the affection and confidence of his subjects.[28]

But every sentiment of virtue and humanity was extinct in the mind of Commodus. Whilst he thus abandoned the reins of empire to these unworthy favourites, he valued nothing in sovereign power except the unbounded licence of indulging his sensual appetites. His hours were spent in a seraglio of three hundred beautiful women and as many boys, of every rank and of every province; and, wherever the arts of seduction proved ineffectual, the brutal lover had recourse to violence. The ancient historians[29] have expatiated on these abandoned scenes of prostitution, which scorned every restraint of nature or modesty; but it would not be easy to translate their too faithful descriptions into the decency of modern language. The intervals of lust were filled up with the basest amusements. The influence of a polite age and the labour of an attentive education had never been able to infuse into his rude and brutish mind the least tincture of learning; and he was the first of the Roman emperors totally devoid of taste for the pleasures of the understanding. Nero himself excelled, or affected to excel, in the elegant arts of music and poetry; nor should we despise his pursuits, had he not converted the pleasing relaxation of a leisure hour into the serious business and ambition of his life. But Commodus, from his earliest infancy, discovered an aversion to whatever was rational or liberal, and a fond attachment to the amusements of the populace – the sports of the circus and amphitheatre, the combats of gladiators, and the hunting of wild beasts. The masters in every branch of learning, whom Marcus provided for his son, were heard with inattention and disgust; whilst the Moors and Parthians, who taught him to dart the javelin and to shoot with the bow, found a disciple who delighted in his application, and soon equalled the most skilful of his instructors in the steadiness of the eye and the dexterity of the hand.

The servile crowd, whose fortune depended on their master's vices, applauded these ignoble pursuits. The perfidious voice of flattery reminded him that, by exploits of the same nature, by the defeat of the Nemean lion, and the slaughter of the wild boar of Erymanthus, the Grecian Hercules had acquired a place among the gods, and an immortal memory among men. They only forgot to observe that, in the first ages of society, when the fiercer animals often dispute with man the possession of an unsettled country, a successful war against those savages* is one of the most innocent and beneficial labours of heroism. In the civilised state of the Roman empire the wild beasts had long since retired from the face of man and the neighbourhood of populous cities. To surprise them in their solitary haunts, and to transport them to Rome, that they might be slain in pomp by the hand of an emperor, was an enterprise equally ridiculous for the prince and oppressive for the people.[30] Ignorant of these distinctions, Commodus eagerly embraced the glorious resemblance, and styled himself (as we still read on his medals)[31] the *Roman Hercules*. The club and the lion's hide were placed by the side of the throne amongst the ensigns of sovereignty; and statues were erected, in which Commodus was represented in the character and with the attributes of the god whose valour and dexterity he endeavoured to emulate in the daily course of his ferocious amusements.[32]

Elated with these praises, which gradually extinguished the innate sense of shame, Commodus resolved to exhibit, before the eyes of the Roman people, those exercises which till then he had decently confined within the walls of his palace and to the presence of a few favourites. On the appointed day the various motives of flattery, fear, and curiosity attracted to the amphitheatre an innumerable multitude of spectators; and some degree of applause was deservedly bestowed on the uncommon skill of the Imperial performer. Whether he aimed at the head or heart of the animal, the wound was alike certain and mortal. With arrows, whose point was shaped into the form of a crescent, Commodus often intercepted the rapid career, and cut asunder the long bony neck, of the ostrich.[33] A panther was let loose; and the archer waited till he had leaped upon a trembling malefactor. In the same instant the shaft flew, the beast dropped dead, and the man remained unhurt. The dens of the amphitheatre disgorged at once a hundred lions; a hundred darts from the unerring hand of Commodus laid them dead as they ran raging round the arena. Neither the huge bulk of the elephant nor the scaly hide of the rhinoceros could defend them from his stroke. Ethiopia and India yielded their most extraordinary productions; and several animals were slain in the amphitheatre which had been seen only in the representations of art, or perhaps of fancy.[34] In all these exhibitions, the surest precautions were used to protect the person of the Roman Hercules from the desperate spring of any savage* who might possibly disregard the dignity of the emperor and the sanctity of the god.[35]

But the meanest of the populace were affected with shame and indignation, when they beheld their sovereign enter the gladiator lists as a gladiator, and glory in a profession which the laws and manners of the Romans had branded with the justest note of infamy.[36] He chose the habit and arms of the *secutor*, whose combat with the *retiarius* formed one of the most lively scenes in the bloody sports of the amphitheatre. The *secutor* was armed with an helmet, sword, and buckler; his naked antagonist had only a large net and a trident; with the one he endeavoured to entangle, with the other to dispatch, his enemy. If he missed the first throw he was obliged to fly from the pursuit of the *secutor* till he had prepared his net for a second cast.[37] The emperor fought in this character seven hundred and thirty-five several times. These glorious achievements were carefully recorded in the public acts of the empire; and, that he might omit no circumstance of infamy, he received from the common fund of gladiators a stipend so exorbitant that it became a new and most ignominious tax upon the Roman people.[38] It may be easily supposed that in these engagements the master of the world was always successful: in the amphitheatre his victories were not often sanguinary; but when he exercised his skill in the school of gladiators, or his own palace, his wretched antagonists were frequently honoured with a mortal wound from the hand of Commodus, and obliged to seal their flattery with their blood.[39] He now disdained the appellation of Hercules. The name of Paulus, a celebrated *secutor*, was the only one which delighted his ear. It was inscribed on his colossal statues, and repeated in the redoubled acclamations[40] of the mournful and applauding senate.[41] Claudius Pompeianus, the virtuous husband of Lucilla, was the only senator who asserted the honour of his rank. As a father he permitted his sons to consult their safety by attending the amphitheatre. As a Roman he declared that his own life was in the emperor's hands, but that he would never behold the son of Marcus prostituting his person and dignity. Notwithstanding his manly resolution, Pompeianus escaped the resentment of the tyrant, and, with his honour, had the good fortune to preserve his life.[42]

Commodus had now attained the summit of vice and infamy. Amidst the acclamations of a flattering court, he was unable to disguise from himself that he had deserved the contempt and hatred of every man of sense and virtue in his empire. His ferocious spirit was irritated by the consciousness of that hatred, by the envy of every kind of merit, by the just apprehension of danger, and by the habit of slaughter which he contracted in his daily amusements. History has preserved a long list of consular senators sacrificed to his wanton suspicion, which sought out, with peculiar anxiety, those unfortunate persons connected, however remotely, with the family of the Antonines, without sparing even the ministers of his crimes or pleasures.[43] His cruelty proved at last fatal to himself. He had shed with impunity the noblest blood of Rome: he perished as soon as he was dreaded by his own domestics. Marcia, his favourite concubine, Eclectus, his chamberlain, and Laetus, his Praetorian prefect, alarmed by the fate of their companions and predecessors, resolved to prevent the destruction which every hour hung over their heads, either from the mad caprice of the tyrant, or the sudden indignation of the people. Marcia seized the occasion of presenting a draught of wine to her lover, after he had fatigued himself with hunting some wild beasts. Commodus retired to sleep; but, whilst he was labouring with the effects of poison and drunkenness, a robust youth, by profession a wrestler, entered his chamber, and strangled him without resistance. The body was secretly conveyed out of the palace, before the least suspicion was entertained in the city, or even in the court, of the emperor's death.

Such was the fate of the son of Marcus, and so easy was it to destroy a
hated tyrant, who, by the artificial powers of government, had oppressed,
during thirteen years, so many millions of subjects, every one of whom
was equal to their master in personal strength and personal abilities.[44]

The measures of the conspirators were conducted with the deliberate
coolness and celerity which the greatness of the occasion required. They
resolved instantly to fill the vacant throne with an emperor whose
character would justify and maintain the action that had been committed.
They fixed on Pertinax, prefect of the city, an ancient senator of consular
rank, whose conspicuous merit had broke through the obscurity of his
birth, and raised him to the first honours of the state. He had successively
governed most of the provinces of the empire; and in all his great
employments, military as well as civil, he had uniformly distinguished
himself, by the firmness, the prudence, and the integrity of his conduct.[45]
He now remained almost alone of the friends and ministers of Marcus;
and, when, at a late hour of the night, he was awakened with the news
that the chamberlain and the prefect were at his door, he received them
with intrepid resignation, and desired they would execute their master's
orders. Instead of death, they offered him the throne of the Roman world.
During some moments he distrusted their intentions and assurances.
Convinced at length of the death of Commodus, he accepted the purple
with a sincere reluctance, the natural effect of his knowledge both of the
duties and of the dangers of the supreme rank.[46]

Laetus conducted without delay his new emperor to the camp of the
Praetorians, diffusing at the same time through the city a seasonable
report that Commodus died suddenly of an apoplexy; and that the
virtuous Pertinax had *already* succeeded to the throne. The guards were
rather surprised than pleased with the suspicious death of a prince whose
indulgence and liberality they alone had experienced; but the emergency
of the occasion, the authority of their prefect, the reputation of Pertinax,
and the clamours of the people, obliged them to stifle their secret
discontents, to accept the donative promised by the new emperor, to
swear allegiance to him, and, with joyful acclamations and laurels in their
hands, to conduct him to the senate-house, that the military consent
might be ratified by the civil authority.

This important night was now far spent; with the dawn of day, and
the commencement of the new year, the senators expected a summons
to attend an ignominious ceremony. In spite of all remonstrances, even
of those of his creatures who yet preserved any regard for prudence or
decency, Commodus had resolved to pass the night in the gladiators'
school, and from thence to take possession of the consulship, in the habit
and with the attendance of that infamous crew. On a sudden, before the
break of day, the senate was called together in the temple of Concord, to
meet the guards, and to ratify the election of a new emperor. For a few
minutes they sat in silent suspense, doubtful of their unexpected

deliverance, and suspicious of the cruel artifices of Commodus: but, when at length they were assured that the tyrant was no more, they resigned themselves to all the transports of joy and indignation. Pertinax, who modestly represented the meanness of his extraction, and pointed out several noble senators more deserving than himself of the empire, was constrained by their dutiful violence to ascend the throne, and received all the titles of Imperial power, confirmed by the most sincere vows of fidelity. The memory of Commodus was branded with eternal infamy. The names of tyrant, of gladiator, of public enemy, resounded in every corner of the house They decreed in tumultuous votes, that his honours should be reversed, his titles erased from the public monuments, his statues thrown down, his body dragged with a hook into the stripping-room of the gladiators, to satiate the public fury; and they expressed some indignation against those officious servants who had already presumed to screen his remains from the justice of the senate. But Pertinax could not refuse those last rites to the memory of Marcus and the tears of his first protector Claudius Pompeianus, who lamented the cruel fate of his brother-in-law, and lamented still more that he had deserved it.[47]

These effusions of impotent rage against a dead emperor, whom the senate had flattered when alive with the most abject servility, betrayed a just but ungenerous spirit of revenge. The legality of these decrees was, however, supported by the principles of the Imperial constitution. To censure, to depose, or to punish with death, the first magistrate of the republic who had abused his delegated trust, was the ancient and undoubted prerogative of the Roman senate;[48] but that feeble assembly was obliged to content itself with inflicting on a fallen tyrant that public justice from which, during his life and reign, he had been shielded by the strong arm of military despotism.

Pertinax found a nobler way of condemning his predecessor's memory – by the contrast of his own virtues with the vices of Commodus. On the day of his accession he resigned over to his wife and son his whole private fortune, that they might have no pretence to solicit favours at the expense of the state. He refused to flatter the vanity of the former with the title of Augusta, or to corrupt the inexperienced youth of the latter by the rank of Caesar. Accurately distinguishing between the duties of a parent and those of a sovereign, he educated his son with a severe simplicity, which, while it gave him no assured prospect of the throne, might in time have rendered him worthy of it. In public the behaviour of Pertinax was grave and affable. He lived with the virtuous part of the senate (and, in a private station, he had been acquainted with the true character of each individual), without either pride or jealousy; considered them as friends and companions, with whom he had shared the dangers of the tyranny, and with whom he wished to enjoy the security of the present time. He very frequently invited them to familiar entertainments, the frugality of which was ridiculed by those who remembered and regretted the luxurious prodigality of Commodus.[49]

To heal, as far as it was possible, the wounds inflicted by the hand of tyranny, was the pleasing, but melancholy, task of Pertinax. The innocent victims who yet survived were recalled from exile, released from prison, and restored to the full possession of their honours and fortunes. The unburied bodies of murdered senators (for the cruelty of Commodus endeavoured to extend itself beyond death) were deposited in the sepulchres of their ancestors; their memory was justified; and every consolation was bestowed on their ruined and afflicted families. Among these consolations, one of the most grateful was the punishment of the Delators, the common enemies of their master, of virtue, and of their country. Yet, even in the inquisition of these legal assassins, Pertinax proceeded with a steady temper, which gave everything to justice, and nothing to popular prejudice and resentment.

The finances of the state demanded the most vigilant care of the emperor. Though every measure of injustice and extortion had been adopted which could collect the property of the subject into the coffers of the prince, the rapaciousness of Commodus had been so very inadequate to his extravagance that, upon his death, no more than eight thousand pounds were found in the exhausted treasury,[50] to defray the current expenses of government, and to discharge the pressing demand of a liberal donative, which the new emperor had been obliged to promise to the Praetorian guards. Yet, under these distressed circumstances, Pertinax had the generous firmness to remit all the oppressive taxes invented by Commodus, and to cancel all the unjust claims of the treasury; declaring, in a decree of the senate, 'that he was better satisfied to administer a poor republic with innocence, than to acquire riches by the ways of tyranny and dishonour.' Economy and industry he considered as the pure and genuine sources of wealth; and from them he soon derived a copious supply for the public necessities. The expense of the household was immediately reduced to one half. All the instruments of luxury Pertinax exposed to public auction,[51] gold and silver plate, chariots of a singular construction, a superfluous wardrobe of silk and embroidery, and a great number of beautiful slaves of both sexes; excepting only, with attentive humanity, those who were born in a state of freedom, and had been ravished from the arms of their weeping parents. At the same time that he obliged the worthless favourites of the tyrant to resign a part of their ill-gotten wealth, he satisfied the just creditors of the state, and unexpectedly discharged the long arrears of honest services. He removed the oppressive restrictions which had been laid upon commerce, and granted all the uncultivated lands in Italy and the provinces to those who would improve them; with an exemption from tribute during the term of ten years.[52]

Such an uniform conduct had already secured to Pertinax the noblest reward of a sovereign, the love and esteem of his people. Those who remembered the virtues of Marcus were happy to contemplate in their new emperor the features of that bright original, and flattered themselves that they should long enjoy the benign influence of his administration. A hasty zeal to reform the corrupted state, accompanied with less prudence than might have been expected from the years and experience of Pertinax, proved fatal to himself and to his country. His honest indiscretion united against him the servile crowd, who found their private benefit in the public disorders, and who preferred the favour of a tyrant to the inexorable equality of the laws.[53]

Amidst the general joy the sullen and angry countenance of the Praetorian guards betrayed their inward dissatisfaction. They had reluctantly submitted to Pertinax; they dreaded the strictness of the ancient discipline, which he was preparing to restore; and they regretted the licence of the former reign. Their discontents were secretly fomented by Laetus, their prefect, who found, when it was too late, that his new emperor would reward a servant, but would not be ruled by a favourite. On the third day of his reign, the soldiers seized on a noble senator, with a design to carry him to the camp, and to invest him with the Imperial purple. Instead of being dazzled by the dangerous honour, the affrighted victim escaped from their violence, and took refuge at the feet of Pertinax. A short time afterwards Sosius Falco, one of the consuls of the year, a rash youth,[54] but of an ancient and opulent family, listened to the voice of ambition; and a conspiracy was formed during a short absence of Pertinax, which was crushed by his sudden return to Rome and his resolute behaviour. Falco was on the point of being justly condemned to death as a public enemy, had he not been saved by the earnest and sincere entreaties of the injured emperor; who conjured the senate that the purity of his reign might not be stained by the blood even of a guilty senator.

These disappointments served only to irritate the rage of the Praetorian guards. On the twenty-eighth of March, eighty-six days only after the death of Commodus, a general sedition broke out in the camp, which the officers wanted either power or inclination to suppress. Two or three hundred of the most desperate soldiers marched at noonday, with arms in their hands and fury in their looks, towards the Imperial palace. The gates were thrown open by their companions upon guard; and by the domestics of the old court, who had already formed a secret conspiracy against the life of the too virtuous emperor. On the news of their approach, Pertinax, disdaining either flight or concealment, advanced to meet his assassins; and recalled to their minds his own innocence, and the sanctity of their recent oath. For a few moments they stood in silent suspense, ashamed of their atrocious design, and awed by the venerable aspect and majestic firmness of their sovereign, till at length, the despair of pardon reviving their fury, a barbarian of the country of Tongres[55] levelled the first blow against Pertinax, who was instantly dispatched with a multitude of wounds. His head, separated from his body, and placed on a lance, was carried in triumph to the Praetorian camp, in the sight of a mournful and indignant people, who lamented the unworthy fate of that excellent prince, and the transient blessings of a reign, the memory of which could serve only to aggravate their approaching misfortunes.[56]

NOTES TO CHAPTER 4

1 See the complaints of Avidius Cassius, *Hist. August.*, p. 45. These are, it is true, the complaints of faction; but even faction exaggerates, rather than invents.

2 *Faustinam satis constat apud Cayetam, conditiones sibi et nauticas et gladiatorias elegisse.* ['It is fairly well-known that at Caieta, Faustina picked sailors and gladiators for her lovers.' The Latin word *conditio* also meant a lover.] *Hist. August.*, p. 30. Lampridius explains the sort of merit which Faustina chose, and the *conditions* which she exacted, *Hist. August.*, p. 102.

3 *Hist. August.*, p. 34.

4 *Meditat.*, Bk i. The world has laughed at the credulity of Marcus; but Madame Dacier assures us (and we may credit a lady) that the husband will always be deceived, if the wife condescends to dissemble.

5 Dion Cassius, lxxi, 1195. *Hist. August.*, p. 33. Commentaire de Spanheim sur les *Caesars* de Julien, p. 289. The deification of Faustina is the only defect which Julian's criticism is able to discover in the accomplished character of Marcus.

6 Commodus was the first *Porphyrogenitus* (born since his father's accession to the throne). By a new strain of flattery, the Egyptian medals date by the years of his life as if they were synonymous to those of his reign. Tillemont, *Hist. des Empereurs*, ii, 752.

7 *Hist. August.*, p. 46.

8 Dion Cassius, lxxii, 1203.

9 According to Tertullian (*Apolog.*, ch. 25.) he died at Sirmium. But the situation of Vindobona, or Vienna, where both the Victors place his death, is better adapted to the operations of the war against the Marcomanni and Quadi.

10 Herodian, i, 12.

11 Herodian, i, 16.

12 This universal joy is well described (from the medals as well as historians) by Mr Wotton, *Hist. of Rome*, pp. 192, 193.

13 Manilius, the confidential secretary of Avidius Cassius, was discovered after he had lain concealed for several years. The emperor nobly relieved the public anxiety by refusing to see him, and burning his papers without opening them; Dion Cassius, lxxii, 1209.

14 See Maffei, *degli Amphitheatri*, p. 126.

15 Dion, lxxii, 1205; Herodian, i, 16; *Hist. August.*, p. 46.

* *page 76* [informers]

16 In a note upon the *Augustan History*, Casaubon has collected a number of particulars concerning these celebrated brothers. See p. 94 of his learned commentary.

17 Dion, lxxii, 1210; Herodian, i, 22; *Hist. August.*, p 48. Dion gives a much less odious character of Perennis than the other historians. His moderation is almost a pledge of his veracity.

18 During the second Punic war, the Romans imported from Asia the worship of the mother of the gods. Her festival, the *Megalesia*, began on the fourth of April, and lasted six days. The streets were crowded with mad processions, the theatres with spectators, and the public tables with unbidden guests. Order and police were suspended, and pleasure was the only serious business of the city. See Ovid *de Fastis*, iv, 189, etc.

19 Herodian, i, 23, 28.

20 Cicero, *pro Flacco*, ch. 27.

21 One of these dear-bought promotions occasioned a current bon mot, that Julius Solon was *banished* into the senate.

22 Dion (lxxii, 1213) observes that no freedman had possessed riches equal to those of Cleander. The fortune of Pallas amounted, however, to upwards of five and twenty hundred thousand pounds – *ter millies*.

23 Dion, lxxii, 1213; Herodian, i, 29; *Hist. August.*, p. 52. These baths were situated near the *Porta Capena*. See Nardini, *Roma Antica*, p. 79.

24 *Hist. August.*, p. 48.

25 Herodian, i, 28; Dion, lxxii, 1215. The latter says that two thousand persons died every day at Rome, during a considerable length of time.

26 *Tuncque primum tres praefecti praetorio fuere: inter quos libertinus.* ['There were then, for the first time, three praetorian prefects; including a freedman']. From some remains of modesty, Cleander declined the title, whilst he assumed the powers, of Praetorian Prefect. As the other freedmen were styled, from their several departments, *a rationibus, ab epistolis* [minister in charge of public accounts, minister in charge of correspondence]; Cleander called himself *a pugione* [imperial bodyguard], as entrusted with the defence of his master's person. Salmasius and Casaubon seem to have talked very idly upon this passage.

27 οἱ τῆς πόλεως πεζοὶ στρατιῶται [the city infantry], Herodian, i, 31. It is doubtful whether he means the Praetorian infantry, or the *cohortes urbanae*, a body of six thousand men, but whose rank and discipline were not equal to their numbers. Neither Tillemont nor Wotton choose to decide this question.

28 Dion Cassius, lxxii, 1215; Herodian, i, 32; *Hist. August.*, p. 48.

29 *Sororibus suis constupratis, ipsas concubinas suas sub oculis suis stuprari iubebat. Nec irruentium in se iuvenum carebat infamia, omni parte corporis atque ore in sexum utrumque pollutus. Hist. August.*, p. 47. ['He debauched his own sisters. He had his concubines debauched in his presence. He went to the depths of submitting to the embraces of young men, defiling himself with both sexes in every part of his body, including his mouth.]

* *page 80* [i.e. wild beasts]

30 The African lions, when pressed by hunger, infested the open villages and cultivated country; and they infested them with impunity. The royal beast was reserved for the pleasures of the emperor and the capital; and the unfortunate peasant who killed one of them, though in his own defence, incurred a very heavy penalty. This extraordinary *game law* was mitigated by Honorius, and finally repealed by Justinian. *Codex Theodos.*, v, 92, et *Comment*. Gothofred.

31 Spanheim, *de Numismat. Dissertat.* xii, ii, 493.

32 Dion, lxxii, 1216; *Hist. August.*, p. 49.

33 The ostrich's neck is three feet long, and composed of seventeen vertebrae. See Buffon, *Hist. Naturelle*.

34 Commodus killed a camelopardalis or giraffe (Dion, lxxii, 1211), the tallest, the

most gentle, and the most useless of the large quadrupeds. This singular animal, a native only of the interior parts of Africa, has not been seen in Europe since the revival of letters, and though M. de Buffon (*Hist. Naturelle*. tom. xiii) has endeavoured to describe, he has not ventured to delineate, the giraffe.

* *page 81*   [wild beast]

35 Herodian, i, 37; *Hist. August.*, p. 50.

36 The virtuous, and even the wise, princes forbade the senators and knights to embrace this scandalous profession, under pain of infamy, or what was more dreaded by those profligate wretches, of exile. The tyrants allured them to dishonour by threats and rewards. Nero once produced, in the arena, forty senators and sixty knights. See Lipsius, *Saturnalia*, ii, 2. He has happily corrected a passage of Suetonius, *in Nerone*, ch. 12.

37 Lipsius, ii, 7, 8. Juvenal in the eighth satire gives a picturesque description of this combat.

38 *Hist. August.*, p. 50; Dion, lxxii, 1220. He received, for each time, *decies*, about £8000 pounds sterling.

39 Victor tells us that Commodus only allowed his antagonists a leaden weapon, dreading most probably the consequences of their despair.

40 They were obliged to repeat six hundred and twenty-six times, *Paulus, first of the Secutors*, etc.

41 Dion, lxxii, 1221. He speaks of his own baseness and danger.

42 He mixed however some prudence with his courage, and passed the greatest part of his time in a country retirement; alleging his advanced age, and the weakness of his eyes. 'I never saw him in the senate,' says Dion, 'except during the short reign of Pertinax.' All his infirmities had suddenly left him, and they returned as suddenly upon the murder of that excellent prince. Dion, lxxiii, 1227.

43 The prefects were changed almost hourly or daily; and the caprice of Commodus was often fatal to his most favoured chamberlains. *Hist. August.*, 46, 51.

44 Dion, lxxii, 1222; Herodian, i, 43; *Hist. August.*, p. 52.

45 Pertinax was a native of Alba Pompeia, in Piedmont, and son of a timber merchant. The order of his employments (it is marked by Capitolinus) well deserves to be set down as expressive of the form of government and manners of the age. 1. He was a centurion. 2. Prefect of a cohort in Syria, in the Parthian war, and in Britain. 3. He obtained an *Ala*, or squadron of horse, in Maesia. 4. He was commissary of provisions on the Aemilian way. 5. He commanded the fleet upon the Rhine. 6. He was procurator of Dacia, with a salary of about £1600 a year. 7. He commanded the Veterans of a legion. 8. He obtained the rank of senator. 9. Of praetor. 10. With the command of the first legion in Rhaetia and Noricum. 11. He was consul about the year 175. 12. He attended Marcus into the East. 13. He commanded an army on the Danube. 14. He was consular legate of Maesia. 15. Of Dacia. 16. Of Syria. 17. Of Britain. 18. He had the care of the public provisions at Rome. 19. He was proconsul of Africa. 20. Prefect of the city. Herodian (i, 48) does justice to his disinterested spirit; but Capitolinus, who collected every popular rumour, charges him with a great fortune acquired by bribery and corruption.

46 Julian, in the *Caesars*, taxes him with being accessory to the death of Commodus.

47 Capitolinus gives us the particulars of these tumultuary votes, which were moved by one senator, and repeated, or rather chanted, by the whole body. *Hist. August.*, p. 52.

48 The senate condemned Nero to be put to death *more maiorum* [in accordance with ancestral custom]. Suetonius, ch. 49.

49 Dion (lxxiii, 122) speaks of these entertainments as a senator who had supped with the emperor; Capitolinus (*Hist. August.*, p. 58) like a slave who had received his intelligence from one of the scullions.

50 *Decies*. The blameless economy of Pius left his successors a treasure of *vicies septies millies*, above two and twenty millions sterling. Dion, lxxiii, 1231.

51 Besides the design of converting these useless ornaments into money, Dion (lxxiii, 1229) assigns two secret motives of Pertinax. He wished to expose the vices of Commodus, and to discover by the purchasers those who most resembled him.

52 Though Capitolinus has picked up many idle tales of the private life of Pertinax, he joins with Dion and Herodian in admiring his public conduct.

53 *leges, rem surdam, inexorabilem esse* ['the law is deaf and inexorable'], Livy, ii, 3.

54 If we credit Capitolinus (which is rather difficult), Falco behaved with the most petulant indecency to Pertinax on the day of his accession. The wise emperor only admonished him of his youth and inexperience. *Hist. August.*, p. 55.

55 The modern bishopric of Liège. This soldier probably belonged to the Batavian horse-guards, who were mostly raised in the Duchy of Gueldres and the neighbourhood, and were distinguished by their valour and by the boldness with which they swam their horses across the broadest and most rapid rivers. Tacitus, *Hist.*, iv, 12; Dion, lv, 797; Lipsius, *de magnitudine Romana*, i, 4.

56 Dion, lxxiii, 1232; Herodian, ii, 60; *Hist. August.*, p. 58; Victor in *Epitom.* and in *Caesaribus*; Eutropius, viii, 16.

CHAPTER 5

Public sale of the Empire to Didius Julianus by the Praetorian Guards – Clodius Albinus in Britain, Pescennius Niger in Syria, and Septimius Severus in Pannonia, declare against the murderers of Pertinax – civil wars, and victory of Severus over his three rivals – relaxation of discipline – new maxims of government

The power of the sword is more sensibly felt in an extensive monarchy than in a small community. It has been calculated by the ablest politicians that no state, without being soon exhausted, can maintain above the hundredth part of its members in arms and idleness. But, although this relative proportion may be uniform, its influence over the rest of the society will vary according to the degree of its positive strength. The advantages of military science and discipline cannot be exerted, unless a proper number of soldiers are united into one body, and actuated by one soul. With a handful of men, such an union would be ineffectual; with an unwieldy host, it would be impracticable; and the powers of the machine would be alike destroyed by the extreme minuteness, or the excessive weight, of its springs. To illustrate this observation we need only reflect that there is no superiority of natural strength, artificial weapons, or acquired skill, which could enable one man to keep in constant subjection one hundred of his fellow-creatures: the tyrant of a single town, or a small district, would soon discover that an hundred armed followers were a weak defence against ten thousand peasants or citizens; but an hundred thousand well-disciplined soldiers will command, with despotic sway, ten millions of subjects; and a body of ten or fifteen thousand guards will strike terror into the most numerous populace that ever crowded the streets of an immense capital.

The Praetorian bands, whose licentious fury was the first symptom and cause of the decline of the Roman empire, scarcely amounted to the last mentioned number.[1] They derived their institution from Augustus. That crafty tyrant, sensible that laws might colour, but that arms alone could maintain, his usurped dominion, had gradually formed this powerful body of guards, in constant readiness to protect his person, to awe the senate, and either to prevent or to crush the first motions of rebellion. He distinguished these favoured troops by a double pay and superior privileges; but, as their formidable aspect would at once have alarmed and irritated the Roman people, three cohorts only were stationed in the capital; whilst the remainder was dispersed in the adjacent towns of Italy.[2] But after fifty years of peace and servitude, Tiberius ventured on a decisive measure, which for ever riveted the fetters of his country. Under the fair pretences of relieving Italy from the heavy burden of military quarters, and of introducing a stricter discipline among the guards, he assembled them at Rome, in a permanent camp,[3] which was fortified with skilful care,[4] and placed on a commanding situation.[5]

Such formidable servants are always necessary, but often fatal, to the throne of despotism. By thus introducing the Praetorian guards, as it were, into the palace and the senate, the emperors taught them to perceive their own strength, and the weakness of the civil government; to view the vices of their masters with familiar contempt, and to lay aside that reverential awe which distance only, and mystery, can preserve towards an imaginary power. In the luxurious idleness of an opulent city, their pride was nourished by the sense of their irresistible weight; nor was it possible to conceal from them that the person of the sovereign, the authority of the senate, the public treasure, and the seat of empire were all in their hands. To divert the Praetorian bands from these dangerous reflections the firmest and best established princes were obliged to mix blandishments with commands, rewards with punishments, to flatter their pride, indulge their pleasures, connive at their irregularities, and to purchase their precarious faith by a liberal donative; which, since the elevation of Claudius, was exacted as a legal claim on the accession of every new emperor.[6]

The advocates of the guards endeavoured to justify by arguments the power which they asserted by arms; and to maintain that, according to the purest principles of the constitution, *their* consent was essentially necessary in the appointment of an emperor. The election of consuls, of generals, and of magistrates, however it had been recently usurped by the senate, was the ancient and undoubted right of the Roman people.[7] But where was the Roman people to be found? Not surely amongst the mixed multitude of slaves and strangers that filled the streets of Rome; a servile populace, as devoid of spirit as destitute of property. The defenders of the state, selected from the flower of Italian youth,[8] and trained in the exercise of arms and virtue, were the genuine representatives of the people, and the best entitled to elect the military chief of the republic. These assertions, however defective in reason, became unanswerable, when the fierce Praetorians increased their weight, by throwing, like the barbarian conqueror of Rome, their swords into the scale.[9]

The Praetorians had violated the sanctity of the throne, by the atrocious murder of Pertinax; they dishonoured the majesty of it, by their subsequent conduct. The camp was without a leader, for even the prefect Laetus, who had excited the tempest, prudently declined the public indignation. Amidst the wild disorder, Sulpicianus, the emperor's father-in-law, and governor of the city, who had been sent to the camp on the first alarm of mutiny, was endeavouring to calm the fury of the multitude, when he was silenced by the clamorous return of the murderers, bearing on a lance the head of Pertinax. Though history has accustomed us to observe every principle and every passion yielding to the imperious dictates of ambition, it is scarcely credible that, in these moments of horror, Sulpicianus should have aspired to ascend a throne polluted with the recent blood of so near a relation and so excellent a prince. He had already begun to use the only effectual argument, and to treat for the Imperial dignity; but the more prudent of the Praetorians, apprehensive that, in this private contract, they should not obtain a just price for so valuable a commodity, ran out upon the ramparts; and, with a loud voice, proclaimed that the Roman world was to be disposed of to the best bidder by public auction.[10]

This infamous offer, the most insolent excess of military licence, diffused an universal grief, shame, and indignation throughout the city. It reached at length the ears of Didius Julianus, a wealthy senator, who, regardless of the public calamities, was indulging himself in the luxury of the table.[11] His wife and his daughter, his freedmen and his parasites, easily convinced him that he deserved the throne, and earnestly conjured him to embrace so fortunate an opportunity. The vain old man hastened to the Praetorian camp, where Sulpicianus was still in treaty with the guards; and began to bid against him from the foot of the rampart. The unworthy negotiation was transacted by faithful emissaries, who passed alternately from one candidate to the other, and acquainted each of them with the offers of his rival. Sulpicianus had already promised a donative of five thousand drachms (above one hundred and sixty pounds) to each soldier; when Julian, eager for the prize, rose at once to the sum of six thousand two hundred and fifty drachms, or upwards of two hundred pounds sterling. The gates of the camp were instantly thrown open to the purchaser; he was declared emperor, and received an oath of allegiance from the soldiers, who retained humanity enough to stipulate that he should pardon and forget the competition of Sulpicianus.

It was now incumbent on the Praetorians to fulfil the conditions of the sale. They placed their new sovereign, whom they served and despised, in the centre of their ranks, surrounded him on every side with their shields, and conducted him in close order of battle through the deserted streets of the city. The senate was commanded to assemble, and those who had been the distinguished friends of Pertinax, or the personal enemies of Julian, found it necessary to affect a more than common share of satisfaction at this happy revolution.[12] After Julian had filled the senate house with armed soldiers, he expatiated on the freedom of his election, his own eminent virtues, and his full assurance of the affections of the senate. The obsequious assembly congratulated their own and the public felicity; engaged their allegiance, and conferred on him all the several branches of the Imperial power.[13] From the senate Julian was conducted by the same military procession, to take possession of the palace. The first objects which struck his eyes were the abandoned trunk of Pertinax, and the frugal entertainment prepared for his supper. The one he viewed with indifference; the other with contempt. A magnificent feast was prepared by his order, and he amused himself till a very late hour, with dice, and the performances of Pylades, a celebrated dancer. Yet it was observed that, after the crowd of flatterers dispersed, and left him to darkness, solitude, and terrible reflection, he passed a sleepless night; revolving most probably in his mind his own rash folly, the fate of his virtuous predecessor, and the doubtful and dangerous tenure of an empire, which had not been acquired by merit, but purchased by money.[14]

He had reason to tremble. On the throne of the world he found himself without a friend, and even without an adherent. The guards themselves were ashamed of the prince whom their avarice had persuaded them to accept; nor was there a citizen who did not consider his elevation with horror, as the last insult on the Roman name. The nobility, whose conspicuous station and ample possessions exacted the strictest caution, dissembled their sentiments, and met the affected civility of the emperor with smiles of complacency and professions of duty. But the people, secure in their numbers and obscurity, gave a free vent to their passions. The streets and public places of Rome resounded with clamours and imprecations. The enraged multitude affronted the person of Julian, rejected his liberality, and, conscious of the impotence of their own resentment, they called aloud on the legions of the frontiers to assert the violated majesty of the Roman empire.

The public discontent was soon diffused from the centre to the frontiers of the empire. The armies of Britain, of Syria, and of Illyricum, lamented the death of Pertinax, in whose company, or under whose command, they had so often fought and conquered. They received with surprise, with indignation, and perhaps with envy, the extraordinary intelligence that the Praetorians had disposed of the empire by public auction; and they sternly refused to ratify the ignominious bargain. Their immediate and unanimous revolt was fatal to Julian, but it was fatal at the same time to the public peace; as the generals of the respective armies, Clodius Albinus, Pescennius Niger, and Septimius Severus, were still more anxious to succeed than to revenge the murdered Pertinax. Their forces were exactly balanced. Each of them was at the head of three legions,[15] with a numerous train of auxiliaries; and, however different in their characters, they were all soldiers of experience and capacity.

Clodius Albinus, governor of Britain, surpassed both his competitors in the nobility of his extraction, which he derived from some of the most illustrious names of the old republic.[16] But the branch, from whence he claimed his descent, was sunk into mean circumstances, and transplanted into a remote province. It is difficult to form a just idea of his true character. Under the philosophic cloak of austerity, he stands accused of concealing most of the vices which degrade human nature.[17] But his accusers are those venal writers who adored the fortune of Severus, and trampled on the ashes of an unsuccessful rival. Virtue, or the appearances of virtue, recommended Albinus to the confidence and good opinion of Marcus; and his preserving with the son* the same interest which he had acquired with the father is a proof at least that he was possessed of a very flexible disposition. The favour of a tyrant does not always suppose a want of merit in the object of it; he may, without intending it, reward a man of worth and ability, or he may find such a man useful to his own service. It does not appear that Albinus served the son of Marcus, either as the minister of his cruelties, or even as the associate of his pleasures. He was employed in a distant honourable command, when he received a confidential letter from the emperor, acquainting him of the treasonable designs of some discontented generals, and authorising him to declare himself the guardian and successor of the throne, by assuming the title and ensigns of Caesar.[18] The governor of Britain wisely declined the dangerous honour, which would have marked him for the jealousy, or involved him in the approaching ruin, of Commodus. He courted power by nobler, or, at least, by more specious, arts. On a premature report of the death of the emperor, he assembled his troops; and, in an eloquent discourse, deplored the inevitable mischiefs of despotism, described the happiness and glory which their ancestors had enjoyed under the consular government, and declared his firm resolution to reinstate the senate and people in their legal authority. This popular harangue was answered by the loud acclamations of the British legions, and received at Rome with a secret murmur of applause. Safe in the possession of his little world, and in the command of an army less distinguished indeed for discipline than for numbers and valour,[19] Albinus braved the menaces of Commodus, maintained towards Pertinax a stately ambiguous reserve, and instantly declared against the usurpation of Julian. The convulsions of the capital added new weight to his sentiments, or rather to his professions, of patriotism. A regard to decency induced him to decline the lofty titles of Augustus and Emperor, and he imitated perhaps the example of Galba, who, on a similar occasion, had styled himself the Lieutenant of the senate and people.[20]

Personal merit alone had raised Pescennius Niger from an obscure birth and station to the government of Syria; a lucrative and important command, which in times of civil confusion gave him a near prospect of the throne. Yet his parts seem to have been better suited to the second than to the first rank; he was an unequal rival, though he might have approved himself an excellent lieutenant, to Severus, who afterwards displayed the greatness of his mind by adopting several useful institutions from a vanquished enemy.[21] In his government, Niger acquired the esteem of the soldiers and the love of the provincials. His rigid discipline fortified the valour and confirmed the obedience of the former, whilst the voluptuous Syrians were less delighted with the mild firmness of his administration than with the affability of his manners and the apparent pleasure with which he attended their frequent and pompous festivals.[22]

As soon as the intelligence of the atrocious murder of Pertinax had reached Antioch, the wishes of Asia invited Niger to assume the Imperial purple and revenge his death. The legions of the eastern frontier embraced his cause; the opulent but unarmed provinces, from the frontiers of Ethiopia[23] to the Hadriatic, cheerfully submitted to his power; and the kings beyond the Tigris and the Euphrates congratulated his election, and offered him their homage and services. The mind of Niger was not capable of receiving this sudden tide of fortune; he flattered himself that his accession would be undisturbed by competition, and unstained by civil blood; and, whilst he enjoyed the vain pomp of triumph, he neglected to secure the means of victory. Instead of entering into an effectual negotiation with the powerful armies of the West, whose resolution might decide, or at least must balance, the mighty contest; instead of advancing without delay towards Rome and Italy, where his presence was impatiently expected,[24] Niger trifled away in the luxury of Antioch those irretrievable moments which were diligently improved by the decisive activity of Severus.[25]

The country of Pannonia and Dalmatia, which occupied the space between the Danube and the Hadriatic, was one of the last and most difficult conquests of the Romans. In the defence of national freedom, two hundred thousand of these barbarians had once appeared in the field, alarmed the declining age of Augustus, and exercised the vigilant prudence of Tiberius at the head of the collected force of the empire.[26] The Pannonians yielded at length to the arms and institutions of Rome. Their recent subjection, however, the neighbourhood, and even the mixture of the unconquered tribes, and perhaps the climate, adapted, as it has been observed, to the production of great bodies and slow minds,[27] all contributed to preserve some remains of their original ferocity, and, under the tame resemblance of Roman provincials, the hardy features of the natives were still to be discerned. Their warlike youth afforded an inexhaustible supply of recruits to the legions stationed on the banks of the Danube, and which, from a perpetual warfare against the Germans and Sarmatians, were deservedly esteemed the best troops in the service.

The Pannonian army was at this time commanded by Septimius Severus, a native of Africa, who, in the gradual ascent of private honours, had concealed his daring ambition, which was never diverted from its steady course by the allurements of pleasure, the apprehension of danger, or the feelings of humanity.[28] On the first news of the murder of Pertinax, he assembled his troops, painted in the most lively colours the crime, the insolence, and the weakness of the Praetorian guards, and animated the legions to arms and to revenge. He concluded (and the peroration was thought extremely eloquent) with promising every soldier about four hundred pounds; an honourable donative, double in value to the infamous bribe with which Julian had purchased the empire.[29] The acclamations of the army immediately saluted Severus with the names of Augustus,

Pertinax, and Emperor; and he thus attained the lofty station to which he was invited by conscious merit and a long train of dreams and omens, the fruitful offspring either of his superstition or policy.[30]

The new candidate for empire saw and improved the peculiar advantage of his situation. His province extended to the Julian Alps, which gave an easy access into Italy; and he remembered the saying of Augustus, That a Pannonian army might in ten days appear in sight of Rome.[31] By a celerity proportioned to the greatness of the occasion, he might reasonably hope to revenge Pertinax, punish Julian, and receive the homage of the senate and people, as their lawful emperor, before his competitors, separated from Italy by an immense tract of sea and land, were apprised of his success, or even of his election. During the whole expedition, he scarcely allowed himself any moments for sleep or food; marching on foot, and in complete armour, at the head of his columns, he insinuated himself into the confidence and affection of his troops, pressed their diligence, revived their spirits, animated their hopes, and was well satisfied to share the hardships of the meanest soldier, whilst he kept in view the infinite superiority of his reward.

The wretched Julian had expected, and thought himself prepared, to dispute the empire with the governor of Syria; but in the invincible and rapid approach of the Pannonian legions he saw his inevitable ruin. The hasty arrival of every messenger increased his just apprehensions. He was successively informed that Severus had passed the Alps; that the Italian cities, unwilling or unable to oppose his progress, had received him with the warmest professions of joy and duty; that the important place of Ravenna had surrendered without resistance, and that the Hadriatic fleet was in the hands of the conqueror. The enemy was now within two hundred and fifty miles of Rome; and every moment diminished the narrow span of life and empire allotted to Julian.

He attempted, however, to prevent, or at least to protract, his ruin. He implored the venal faith of the Praetorians, filled the city with unavailing preparations for war, drew lines round the suburbs, and even strengthened the fortifications of the palace; as if those last intrenchments could be defended, without hope of relief, against a victorious invader. Fear and shame prevented the guards from deserting his standard; but they trembled at the name of the Pannonian legions, commanded by an experienced general, and accustomed to vanquish the barbarians on the frozen Danube.[32] They quitted, with a sigh, the pleasures of the baths and theatres, to put on arms, whose use they had almost forgotten, and beneath the weight of which they were oppressed. The unpractised elephants, whose uncouth appearance, it was hoped, would strike terror into the army of the north, threw their unskilful riders; and the awkward evolutions of the marines, drawn from the fleet of Misenum, were an object of ridicule to the populace; whilst the senate enjoyed, with secret pleasure, the distress and weakness of the usurper.[33]

Every motion of Julian betrayed his trembling perplexity. He insisted that Severus should be declared a public enemy by the senate. He entreated that the Pannonian general might be associated to the empire. He sent public ambassadors of consular rank to negotiate with his rival; he dispatched private assassins to take away his life. He designed that the Vestal virgins, and all the colleges of priests, in their sacerdotal habits, and bearing before them the sacred pledges of the Roman religion, should advance, in solemn procession, to meet the Pannonian legions; and, at the same time, he vainly tried to interrogate, or to appease, the fates, by magic ceremonies and unlawful sacrifices.[34]

Severus, who dreaded neither his arms nor his enchantments, guarded himself from the only danger of secret conspiracy by the faithful attendance of six hundred chosen men, who never quitted his person or their cuirasses, either by night or by day, during the whole march. Advancing with a steady and rapid course, he passed, without difficulty, the defiles of the Apennine, received into his party the troops and ambassadors sent to retard his progress, and made a short halt at Interamna, about seventy miles from Rome. His victory was already secure; but the despair of the Praetorians might have rendered it bloody; and Severus had the laudable ambition of ascending the throne without drawing the sword.[35] His emissaries, dispersed in the capital, assured the guards that, provided they would abandon their worthless prince, and the perpetrators of the murder of Pertinax, to the justice of the conqueror, he would no longer consider that melancholy event as the act of the whole body. The faithless Praetorians, whose resistance was supported only by sullen obstinacy, gladly complied with the easy conditions, seized the greatest part of the assassins, and signified to the senate that they no longer defended the cause of Julian. That assembly, convoked by the consul, unanimously acknowledged Severus as lawful emperor, decreed divine honours to Pertinax, and pronounced a sentence of deposition and death against his unfortunate successor. Julian was conducted into a private apartment of the baths of the palace, and beheaded as a common criminal, after having purchased, with an immense treasure, an anxious and precarious reign of only sixty-six days.[36] The almost incredible expedition of Severus, who, in so short a space of time, conducted a numerous army from the banks of the Danube to those of the Tiber, proves at once the plenty of provisions produced by agriculture and commerce, the goodness of the roads, the discipline of the legions, and the indolent subdued temper of the provinces.[37]

The first cares of Severus were bestowed on two measures, the one dictated by policy, the other by decency; the revenge and the honours due to the memory of Pertinax. Before the new emperor entered Rome, he issued his commands to the Praetorian guards, directing them to wait his arrival on a large plain near the city, without arms, but in the habits of ceremony in which they were accustomed to attend their sovereign. He was obeyed by those haughty troops, whose contrition was the effect of their just terrors. A chosen part of the Illyrian army encompassed them with levelled spears. Incapable of flight or resistance, they expected their fate in silent consternation. Severus mounted the tribunal, sternly reproached them with perfidy and cowardice, dismissed them with ignominy from the trust which they had betrayed, despoiled them of their splendid ornaments, and banished them, on pain of death, to the distance of an hundred miles from the capital. During the transaction, another detachment had been sent to seize their arms, occupy their camp, and prevent the hasty consequences of their despair.[38]

The funeral and consecration of Pertinax was next solemnised with every circumstance of sad magnificence.[39] The senate, with a melancholy pleasure, performed the last rites to that excellent prince, whom they had loved and still regretted. The concern of his successor was probably less sincere. He esteemed the virtues of Pertinax, but those virtues would for ever have confined his ambition to a private station. Severus pronounced his funeral oration with studied eloquence, inward satisfaction, and well-acted sorrow; and, by this pious regard to his memory, convinced the credulous multitude that *he alone* was worthy to supply his place. Sensible, however, that arms, not ceremonies, must assert his claim to the empire, he left Rome at the end of thirty days; and, without suffering himself to be elated by this easy victory, prepared to encounter his more formidable rivals.

The uncommon abilities and fortune of Severus have induced an elegant historian to compare him with the first and greatest of the Caesars.[40] The parallel is, at least, imperfect. Where shall we find, in the character of Severus, the commanding superiority of soul, the generous clemency, and the various genius, which could reconcile and unite the love of pleasure, the thirst of knowledge, and the fire of ambition?[41] In one instance only, they may be compared, with some degree of propriety, in the celerity of their motion, and their civil victories. In less than four years,[42] Severus subdued the riches of the east, and the valour of the west. He vanquished two competitors of reputation and ability, and defeated numerous armies, provided with weapons and discipline equal to his own. In that age, the art of fortification and the principles of tactics were well understood by all the Roman generals; and the constant superiority of Severus was that of an artist, who uses the same instruments with more skill and industry than his rivals. I shall not, however, enter into a minute narrative of these military operations; but as the two civil wars against Niger and against Albinus were almost the same in their conduct, event, and consequences, I shall collect into one point of view the most striking circumstances, tending to develop the character of the conqueror, and the state of the empire.

Falsehood and insincerity, unsuitable as they seem to the dignity of public transactions, offend us with a less degrading idea of meanness than when they are found in the intercourse of private life. In the latter, they discover a want of courage; in the other, only a defect of power; and, as it is impossible for the most able statesman to subdue millions of followers and enemies by their own personal strength, the world, under the name of policy, seems to have granted them a very liberal indulgence of craft and dissimulation. Yet the arts of Severus cannot be justified by the most ample privileges of state-reason. He promised only to betray, he flattered only to ruin; and however he might occasionally bind himself by oaths and treaties, his conscience, obsequious to his interest, always released him from the inconvenient obligation.[43]

If his two competitors, reconciled by their common danger, had advanced upon him without delay, perhaps Severus would have sunk under their united effort. Had they even attacked him at the same time, with separate views and separate armies, the contest might have been long and doubtful. But they fell, singly and successively, an easy prey to the arts as well as arms of their subtle enemy, lulled into security by the moderation of his professions, and overwhelmed by the rapidity of his action. He first marched against Niger, whose reputation and power he the most dreaded: but he declined any hostile declarations, suppressed the name of his antagonist, and only signified to the senate and people his intention of regulating the eastern provinces. In private he spoke of Niger, his old friend and intended successor,[44] with the most affectionate regard, and highly applauded his generous design of revenging the murder of Pertinax. To punish the vile usurper of the throne was the duty of every Roman general. To persevere in arms, and to resist a lawful emperor, acknowledged by the senate, would alone render him criminal.[45] The sons of Niger had fallen into his hands among the children of the provincial governors, detained at Rome as pledges for the loyalty of their parents.[46] As long as the power of Niger inspired terror, or even respect, they were educated with the most tender care, with the children of Severus himself; but they were soon involved in their father's ruin, and removed, first by exile, and afterwards by death, from the eye of public compassion.[47]

Whilst Severus was engaged in his eastern war, he had reason to apprehend that the governor of Britain might pass the sea and the Alps, occupy the vacant seat of empire, and oppose his return with the authority of the senate and the forces of the West. The ambiguous conduct of Albinus, in not assuming the Imperial title, left room for negotiation. Forgetting at once his professions of patriotism and the jealousy of sovereign power, he accepted the precarious rank of Caesar, as a reward for his fatal neutrality. Till the first contest was decided, Severus treated the man whom he had doomed to destruction with every mark of esteem and regard. Even in the letter in which he announced his victory over Niger he styles Albinus the brother of his soul and empire, sends him the affectionate salutations of his wife Julia, and his young family, and entreats him to preserve the armies and the republic faithful to their common interest. The messengers charged with this letter were instructed to accost the Caesar with respect, to desire a private audience, and to plunge their daggers into his heart.[48] The conspiracy was discovered, and the too credulous Albinus at length passed over to the continent, and prepared for an unequal contest with his rival, who rushed upon him at the head of a veteran and victorious army.

The military labours of Severus seem inadequate to the importance of his conquests. Two engagements, the one near the Hellespont, the other in the narrow defiles of Cilicia, decided the fate of his Syrian competitor; and the troops of Europe asserted their usual ascendant over the effeminate natives of Asia.[49] The battle of Lyons, where one hundred and fifty thousand Romans[50] were engaged, was equally fatal to Albinus. The valour of the British army maintained, indeed, a sharp and doubtful contest with the hardy discipline of the Illyrian legions. The fame and person of Severus appeared, during a few moments, irrecoverably lost, till that warlike prince rallied his fainting troops, and led them on to a decisive victory.[51] The war was finished by that memorable day.

The civil wars of modern Europe have been distinguished, not only by the fierce animosity, but likewise by the obstinate perseverance, of the contending factions. They have generally been justified by some principle, or, at least, coloured by some pretext, of religion, freedom, or loyalty. The leaders were nobles of independent property and hereditary influence. The troops fought like men interested in the decision of the quarrel; and, as military spirit and party zeal were strongly diffused throughout the whole community, a vanquished chief was immediately supplied with new adherents, eager to shed their blood in the same cause. But the Romans, after the fall of the republic, combated only for the choice of masters. Under the standard of a popular candidate for empire, a few enlisted from affection, some from fear, many from interest, none from principle. The legions, uninflamed by party zeal, were allured into civil war by liberal donatives, and still more liberal promises. A defeat, by disabling the chief from the performance of his engagements, dissolved the mercenary allegiance of his followers, and left them to consult their own safety by a timely desertion of an unsuccessful cause. It was of little moment to the provinces under whose name they were oppressed or governed; they were driven by the impulsion of the present power, and as soon as that power yielded to a superior force they hastened to implore the clemency of the conqueror, who, as he had an immense debt to discharge, was obliged to sacrifice the most guilty countries to the avarice of his soldiers. In the vast extent of the Roman empire there were few fortified cities capable of protecting a routed army; nor was there any person, or family, or order of men, whose natural interest, unsupported by the powers of government, was capable of restoring the cause of a sinking party.[52]

Yet, in the contest between Niger and Severus, a single city deserves an honourable exception. As Byzantium was one of the greatest passages from Europe into Asia, it had been provided with a strong garrison, and a fleet of five hundred vessels was anchored in the harbour.[53] The impetuosity of Severus disappointed this prudent scheme of defence; he left to his generals the siege of Byzantium, forced the less guarded passage of the Hellespont, and, impatient of a meaner enemy, pressed forward to encounter his rival. Byzantium, attacked by a numerous and increasing army, and afterwards by the whole naval power of the empire, sustained a siege of three years, and remained faithful to the name and memory of Niger. The citizens and soldiers (we know not from what cause) were animated with equal fury; several of the principal officers of Niger, who despaired of, or who disdained, a pardon, had thrown themselves into this last refuge; the fortifications were esteemed impregnable, and, in the defence of the place, a celebrated engineer displayed all the mechanic powers known to the ancients.[54] Byzantium, at length, surrendered to famine. The magistrates and soldiers were put to the sword, the walls demolished, the privileges suppressed, and the destined capital of the East subsisted only as an open village, subject to the insulting jurisdiction of Perinthus.* The historian Dion, who had admired the flourishing, and lamented the desolate, state of Byzantium, accused the revenge of Severus for depriving the Roman people of the strongest bulwark against the barbarians of Pontus and Asia.[55] The truth of this observation was but too well justified in the succeeding age, when the Gothic fleets covered the Euxine, and passed through the undefended Bosphorus into the centre of the Mediterranean.

Both Niger and Albinus were discovered and put to death in their flight from the field of battle. Their fate excited neither surprise nor compassion. They had staked their lives against the chance of empire, and suffered what they would have inflicted; nor did Severus claim the arrogant superiority of suffering his rivals to live in a private station. But his unforgiving temper, stimulated by avarice, indulged a spirit of revenge, where there was no room for apprehension. The most considerable of the provincials, who, without any dislike to the fortunate candidate, had obeyed the governor under whose authority they were accidentally placed, were punished by death, exile, and especially by the confiscation of their estates. Many cities of the East were stripped of their ancient honours, and obliged to pay, into the treasury of Severus, four times the amount of the sums contributed by them for the service of Niger.[56]

Till the final decision of the war, the cruelty of Severus was, in some measure, restrained by the uncertainty of the event and his pretended reverence for the senate. The head of Albinus, accompanied with a menacing letter, announced to the Romans that he was resolved to spare none of the adherents of his unfortunate competitors. He was irritated by the just suspicion that he had never possessed the affections of the senate, and he concealed his old malevolence under the recent discovery of some treasonable correspondences. Thirty-five senators, however, accused of having favoured the party of Albinus, he freely pardoned; and, by his subsequent behaviour, endeavoured to convince them that he had forgotten, as well as forgiven, their supposed offences. But, at the same time, he condemned forty-one[57] other senators, whose names history has recorded; their wives, children, and clients attended them in death, and the noblest provincials of Spain and Gaul were involved in the same ruin. Such rigid justice, for so he termed it, was, in the opinion of Severus, the only conduct capable of ensuring peace to the people, or stability to the prince; and he condescended slightly to lament that, to be mild, it was necessary that he should first be cruel.[58]

The true interest of an absolute monarch generally coincides with that of his people. Their numbers, their wealth, their order, and their security, are the best and only foundations of his real greatness; and, were he totally devoid of virtue, prudence might supply its place, and would dictate the same rule of conduct. Severus considered the Roman empire as his property, and had no sooner secured the possession, than he bestowed his care on the cultivation and improvement of so valuable an acquisition. Salutary laws, executed with inflexible firmness, soon corrected most of the abuses with which, since the death of Marcus, every part of the government had been infected. In the administration of justice, the judgments of the emperor were characterised by attention, discernment, and impartiality; and, whenever he deviated from the strict line of equity, it was generally in favour of the poor and oppressed; not so much indeed from any sense of humanity, as from the natural propensity of a despot to humble the pride of greatness, and to sink all his subjects to the same common level of absolute dependence. His expensive taste for building, magnificent shows, and, above all, a constant and liberal distribution of corn and provisions, were the surest means of captivating the affection of the Roman people.[59] The misfortunes of civil discord were obliterated. The calm of peace and prosperity was once more experienced in the provinces, and many cities, restored by the munificence of Severus, assumed the title of his colonies, and attested by public monuments their gratitude and felicity.[60] The fame of the Roman arms was revived by that warlike and successful emperor,[61] and he boasted, with a just pride, that, having received the empire oppressed with foreign and domestic wars, he left it established in profound, universal, and honourable peace.[62]

Although the wounds of civil war appeared completely healed, its mortal poison still lurked in the vitals of the constitution. Severus possessed a considerable share of vigour and ability; but the daring soul of the first Caesar, or the deep policy of Augustus, were scarcely equal to the task of curbing the insolence of the victorious legions. By gratitude, by misguided policy, by seeming necessity, Severus was induced to relax the nerves of discipline.[63] The vanity of his soldiers was flattered with the honour of wearing gold rings; their ease was indulged in the permission of living with their wives in the idleness of quarters. He increased their pay beyond the example of former times, and taught them to expect, and soon to claim, extraordinary donatives on every public occasion of danger or festivity. Elated by success, enervated by luxury, and raised above the level of subjects by their dangerous privileges,[64] they soon became incapable of military fatigue, oppressive to the country, and impatient of a just sub ordination. Their officers asserted the superiority of rank by a more profuse and elegant luxury. There is still extant a letter of Severus, lamenting the licentious state of the army, and exhorting one of his generals to begin the necessary reformation from the tribunes themselves; since, as he justly observes, the officer who has forfeited the esteem, will never command the obedience, of his soldiers.[65] Had the emperor pursued the train of reflection, he would have discovered that the primary cause of this general corruption might be ascribed, not indeed to the example, but to the pernicious indulgence, however, of the commander-in-chief.

The Praetorians, who murdered their emperor and sold the empire, had received the just punishment of their treason, but the necessary, though dangerous, institution of guards was soon restored on a new model by Severus, and increased to four times the ancient number.[66] Formerly these troops had been recruited in Italy; and, as the adjacent provinces gradually imbibed the softer manners of Rome, the levies were extended to Macedonia, Noricum and Spain. In the room of these elegant troops, better adapted to the pomp of courts than to the uses of war, it was established by Severus, that, from all the legions of the frontiers, the soldiers most distinguished for strength, valour, and fidelity should be occasionally draughted, and promoted, as an honour and reward, into the more eligible service of the guard.[67] By this new institution, the Italian youth were diverted from the exercise of arms, and the capital was terrified by the strange aspect and manners of a multitude of barbarians. But Severus flattered himself that the legions would consider these chosen Praetorians as the representatives of the whole military order; and that the present aid of fifty thousand men, superior in arms and appointments to any force that could be brought into the field against them, would for ever crush the hopes of rebellion, and secure the empire to himself and his posterity.

The command of these favoured and formidable troops soon became the first office of the empire. As the government degenerated into military despotism, the Praetorian prefect, who in his origin had been a simple captain of the guards, was placed, not only at the head of the army, but of the finances, and even of the law. In every department of administration, he represented the person, and exercised the authority, of the emperor. The first prefect who enjoyed and abused this immense power was Plautianus, the favourite minister of Severus. His reign lasted above ten years, till the marriage of his daughter with the eldest son of the emperor, which seemed to assure his fortune, proved the occasion of his ruin.[68] The animosities of the palace, by irritating the ambition and alarming the fears of Plautianus, threatened to produce a revolution and obliged the emperor, who still loved him, to consent with reluctance to his death.[69] After the fall of Plautianus, an eminent lawyer, the celebrated Papinian, was appointed to execute the motley office of Praetorian prefect.

Till the reign of Severus, the virtue, and even the good sense, of the emperors had been distinguished by their zeal or affected reverence for the senate, and by a tender regard to the nice frame of civil policy instituted by Augustus. But the youth of Severus had been trained in the implicit obedience of camps, and his riper years spent in the despotism of military command. His haughty and inflexible spirit could not discover, or would not acknowledge, the advantage of preserving an intermediate power, however imaginary, between the emperor and the army. He disdained to profess himself the servant of an assembly that detested his person and trembled at his frown; he issued his commands, where his request would have proved as effectual; assumed the conduct and style of a sovereign and a conqueror, and exercised, without disguise, the whole legislative as well as the executive power.

The victory over the senate was easy and inglorious. Every eye and every passion were directed to the supreme magistrate, who possessed the arms and treasure of the state; whilst the senate, neither elected by the people, nor guarded by the military force, nor animated by public spirit, rested its declining authority on the frail and crumbling basis of ancient opinion. The fine theory of a republic insensibly vanished, and made way for the more natural and substantial feelings of monarchy. As the freedom and honours of Rome were successfully communicated to the provinces, in which the old government had been either unknown, or was remembered with abhorrence, the tradition of republican maxims was gradually obliterated. The Greek historians of the age of the Antonines[70] observe, with a malicious pleasure, that, although the sovereign of Rome, in compliance with an obsolete prejudice, abstained from the name of king, he possessed the full measure of regal power. In the reign of Severus, the senate was filled with polished and eloquent slaves from the eastern provinces, who justified personal flattery by speculative principles of servitude. These new advocates of prerogative were heard with pleasure by the court, and with patience by the people, when they inculcated the duty of passive obedience, and descanted on the inevitable mischiefs of freedom. The lawyers and the historians concurred in teaching that the Imperial authority was held, not by the delegated commission, but by the irrevocable resignation, of the senate; that the emperor was freed from the restraint of civil laws, could command by his arbitrary will the lives and fortunes of his subjects, and might dispose of the empire as of his private patrimony.[71] The most eminent of the civil lawyers, and particularly Papinian, Paulus, and Ulpian, flourished under the house of Severus; and the Roman jurisprudence, having closely united itself with the system of monarchy, was supposed to have attained its full maturity and perfection.

The contemporaries of Severus, in the enjoyment of the peace and glory of his reign, forgave the cruelties by which it had been introduced. Posterity, who experienced the fatal effect of his maxims and example, justly considered him as the principal author of the decline of the Roman empire.

NOTES TO CHAPTER 5

1 They were originally nine or ten thousand men (for Tacitus and Dion are not agreed upon the subject), divided into as many cohorts. Vitellius increased them to sixteen thousand, and, as far as we can learn from inscriptions, they never afterwards sunk much below that number. See Lipsius, *de magnitudine Romana*, i, 4.

2 Suetonius in *Augustus*, ch. 49.

3 Tacitus, *Annals*, iv, 2; Suetonius in *Tiberius*, ch. 37; Dion Cassius, lvii, 867.

4 In the civil war between Vitellius and Vespasian, the Praetorian camp was attacked and defended with all the machines used in the siege of the best fortified cities. Tacitus, *Hist.*, iii, 84.

5 Close to the walls of the city, on the broad summit of the Quirinal and Viminal hills. See Nardini, *Roma Antica*, p. 174; Donatus, *de Roma Antiqua*, p. 46.

6 Claudius, raised by the soldiers to the empire, was the first who gave a donative. He gave *quina dena*, £120 (Suetonius in *Claudius*, ch. 10): when Marcus, with his colleague Lucius Verus, took quiet possession of the throne, he gave *vicena*, £160, to each of the guards. *Hist. August.*, p. 25 (Dion, lxxiii, 1231). We may form some idea of the amount of these sums, by Hadrian's complaint, that the promotion of a Caesar had cost him *ter millies*, two millions and a half sterling.

7 Cicero, *de Legibus*, iii. 3. The first book of Livy, and the second of Dionysius of Halicarnassus, show the authority of the people, even in the election of the kings.

8 They were originally recruited in Latium, Etruria, and the old colonies (Tacitus, *Annals*, iv, 5). The emperor Otho compliments their vanity, with the flattering titles of *Italiae Alumni, Romana vere iuventus* ['Sons of Italy, Rome's true youth']. Tacitus, *Hist.*, i, 84.

9 In the siege of Rome by the Gauls. See Livy, v, 48. Plutarch in *Camill.*, p. 143.

10 Dion, lxxiii, 1234; Herodian, ii, 63; *Hist. August.*, p. 60. Though the three historians agree that it was in fact an auction, Herodian alone affirms that it was proclaimed as such by the soldiers.

11 Spartianus softens the most odious parts of the character and elevation of Julian.

12 Dion Cassius, at that time praetor, had been a personal enemy to Julian, lxxiii, 1235.

13 *Hist. August.*, p. 61. We learn from thence one curious circumstance, that the new emperor, whatever had been his birth, was immediately aggregated to the number of Patrician families.

14 Dion, lxxiii, 1235; *Hist. August.*, p. 61. I have endeavoured to blend into one consistent story the seeming contradictions of the two writers.

15 Dion, lxxiii, 1235.

16 The Postumian and the Cejonian: the former of whom was raised to the consulship in the fifth year after its institution.

17 Spartianus, in his undigested collections, mixes up all the virtues and all the vices that enter into the human composition, and bestows them on the same object. Such, indeed, are many of the characters in the *Augustan History*.

 * *page 95*   [Commodus]

18 *Hist. August.*, pp. 80, 84.

19 Pertinax, who governed Britain a few years before, had been left for dead in a mutiny of the soldiers. *Hist. August.*, p. 54. Yet they loved and regretted him; *admirantibus eam virtutem cui irascebantur* ['they admired the virtue which annoyed them'].

20 Suetonius in *Galba*, ch. 10.

21 *Hist. August.*, p. 76.

22 Herod., ii, 68. The Chronicle of John Malala, of Antioch, shows the zealous attachment of his countrymen to these festivals, which at once gratified their superstition, and their love of pleasure.

23 A king of Thebes, in Egypt, is mentioned in the *Augustan History*, as an ally and, indeed, as a personal friend of Niger. If Spartianus is not, as I strongly suspect, mistaken, he has brought to light a dynasty of tributary princes totally unknown to history.

24 Dion, lxxiii, 1238. Herod., ii, 67. A verse in every one's mouth at that time, seems to express the general opinion of the three rivals; *Optimus est Niger, bonus Afer, pessimus Albus. Hist. August.*, p. 75. ['The Black candidate (i.e. Niger) is the best, the African (i.e. Septimius Severus) is a good candidate, the white candidate (i.e. Albinus) is the worst.']

25 Herodian, ii, 71.

26 See an account of that memorable war in Velleius Paterculus, ii, 119, etc., who served in the army of Tiberius.

27 Such is the reflection of Herodian, ii, 74. Will the modern Austrians allow the influence?

28 In the letter to Albinus, already mentioned, Commodus accuses Severus as one of the ambitious generals who censured his conduct, and wished to occupy his place. *Hist. August.*, p. 80.

29 Pannonia was too poor to supply such a sum. It was probably promised in the camp, and paid at Rome, after the victory. In fixing the sum, I have adopted the conjecture of Casaubon. See *Hist. August.*, p. 65, *Comment.* p. 115.

30 Herodian, ii, 78. Severus was declared emperor on the banks of the Danube, either at Carnuntum, according to Spartianus (*Hist. August.*, p. 65), or else at Sabaria, according to Victor. Mr Hume, in supposing that the birth and dignity of Severus were too much inferior to the Imperial crown, and that he marched into Italy as general only, has not considered this transaction with his usual accuracy. (*Essay on the original contract.*)

31 Velleius Paterculus, ii, 111. We must reckon the march from the nearest verge of Pannonia, and extend the sight of the city, as far as two hundred miles.

32 This is not a puerile figure of rhetoric, but an allusion to a real fact recorded by Dion, lxxi, 1181. It probably happened more than once.

33 Dion, lxxiii, 1238; Herodian, ii, 81. There is no surer proof of the military skill of the Romans, than their first surmounting the idle terror, and afterwards disdaining the dangerous use, of elephants in war.

34 *Hist. August.*, pp. 62, 63.

35 Victor and Eutropius, viii, 17, mention a combat near the Milvian Bridge, the Ponte Molle, unknown to the better and more ancient writers.

36 Dion, lxxiii, 1240; Herodian, ii, 83; *Hist. August.*, p. 63.

37 From these sixty-six days we must first deduct sixteen, as Pertinax was murdered on the 28th of March, and Severus most probably elected on the 13th of April. (See *Hist. August.*, p. 65, and Tillemont, *Hist. des Empereurs*, iii, 393, note 7.) We cannot allow less than ten days after his election, to put a numerous army in motion. Forty days remain for this rapid march, and, as we may compute about eight hundred miles from Rome to the neighbourhood of Vienna, the army of Severus marched twenty miles every day, without halt or intermission.

38 Dion, lxxiv, 1241; Herodian, ii, 84.

39 Dion, lxxiv. 1244, who assisted at the ceremony as a senator, gives a most pompous description of it.

40 Herodian, iii, 112.

41 Though it is not, most assuredly, the intention of Lucan to exalt the character of Caesar, yet the idea he gives of that hero, in the tenth book of the *Pharsalia*, where he describes him, at the same time, making love to Cleopatra, sustaining a siege against the power of Egypt, and conversing with the sages of the country, is, in reality, the noblest panegyric.

42 Reckoning from his election, April 13, 193, to the death of Albinus, February 19, 197. See Tillemont's Chronology.

43 Herodian, ii, 85.

44 Whilst Severus was very dangerously ill, it was industriously given out that he intended to appoint Niger and Albinus his successors. As he could not be sincere with respect to both, he might not be so with regard to either. Yet Severus carried his hypocrisy so far as to profess that intention in the memoirs of his own life.

45 *Hist. August.*, p. 65.

46 This practice, invented by Commodus, proved very useful to Severus. He found, at Rome, the children of many of the principal adherents of his rivals; and he employed them more than once to intimidate, or seduce, the parents.

47 Herodian, iii, 96; *Hist. August.*, pp. 67, 68.

48 *Hist. August.*, p. 81. Spartianus has inserted this curious letter at full length.

49 Consult the third book of Herodian, and the seventy-fourth book of Dion Cassius.

50 Dion, lxxv, 1260.

51 Dion, lxxv, 1261; Herodian, iii, 110; *Hist. August.*, p. 68. The battle was fought in the plain of Trevoux, three or four leagues from Lyons. See Tillemont, iii, 406, note 18.

52 Montesquieu, *Considérations sur la Grandeur et la Décadence des Romains*, ch. xii.

53 Most of these, as may be supposed, were small open vessels; some, however, were galleys of two, and a few of three, ranks of oars.

54 The engineer's name was Priscus. His skill saved his life, and he was taken into the service of the conqueror. For the particular facts of the siege consult Dion Cassius (lxxiv, 1251) and Herodian (iii, 95): for the theory of it, the fanciful Chevalier de Folard may be looked into. See *Polybe*, i, 76.

* *page 102*   [a city in Thrace]

55 Notwithstanding the authority of Spartianus and some modern Greeks, we may be assured, from Dion and Herodian, that Byzantium, many years after the death of Severus, lay in ruins.

56 Dion, lxxiv, 1250.

57 Dion, lxxv, 1262; only twenty-nine senators are mentioned by him but forty-one are named in the *Augustan History*, p. 69, among whom were six of the name of Pescennius. Herodian (iii, 115) speaks in general of the cruelties of Severus.

58 Aurelius Victor.

59 Dion, lxxvi, 1272; *Hist. August.*, p. 67. Severus celebrated the secular games with extraordinary magnificence, and he left in the public granaries a provision of corn for seven years, at the rate of 75,000 modii, or about 2500 quarters per day. I am persuaded that the granaries of Severus were supplied for a long term, but I am not less persuaded that policy on one hand, and admiration on the other, magnified the hoard far beyond its true contents.

60 See Spanheim's treatise of ancient medals, the inscriptions, and our learned travellers Spon and Wheeler, Shaw, Pocock, etc., who, in Africa, Greece, and Asia, have found more monuments of Severus, than of any other Roman emperor whatsoever.

61 He carried his victorious arms to Seleucia and Ctesiphon, the capitals of the Parthian monarchy. I shall have occasion to mention this war in its proper place.

62 *etiam in Britannis* ['even among the Britons'] was his own just and emphatic expression. *Hist. August.*, p. 73.

63 Herodian, iii, 115; *Hist. August.*, p. 68.

64 Upon the insolence and privileges of the soldiers, the 16th satire, falsely ascribed to Juvenal, may be consulted; the style and circumstances of it would induce me to believe that it was composed under the reign of Severus or that of his son. [Regarded now as genuinely by Juvenal.]

65 *Hist. August.*, p. 75.

66 Herodian, iii, 131.

67 Dion, lxxiv, 1243.

68 One of his most daring and wanton acts of power was the castration of a hundred free Romans, some of them married men, and even fathers of families; merely that his daughter, on her marriage with the young emperor, might be attended by a train of eunuchs worthy of an Eastern queen. Dion, lxxvi, 1271.

69 Dion, lxxvi, 1274; Herodian, iii, 122, 129. The grammarian of Alexandria [i.e. Herodian] seems, as it is not unusual, much better acquainted with this mysterious transaction; and more assured of the guilt of Plautianus, than the Roman senator ventures to be.

70 Appian in *Proem*.

71 Dion Cassius seems to have written with no other view, than to form these opinions into an historical system. The Pandects [a collection of imperial laws collated under Justinian] will show how assiduously the lawyers, on their side, laboured in the cause of prerogative.

CHAPTER 6

The death of Severus – tyranny of Caracalla – usurpation of Macrinus – follies of Elagabalus – virtues of Alexander Severus – licentiousness of the army – general state of the Roman finances

The ascent to greatness, however steep and dangerous, may entertain an active spirit with the consciousness and exercise of its own powers: but the possession of a throne could never yet afford a lasting satisfaction to an ambitious mind. This melancholy truth was felt and acknowledged by Severus. Fortune and merit had, from an humble station, elevated him to the first place among mankind. He had been 'all things,' as he said himself, 'and all was of little value.'[1] Distracted with the care, not of acquiring, but of preserving, an empire, oppressed with age and infirmities, careless of fame,[2] and satiated with power, all his prospects of life were closed. The desire of perpetuating the greatness of his family was the only remaining wish of his ambition and paternal tenderness.

Like most of the Africans, Severus was passionately addicted to the vain studies of magic and divination, deeply versed in the interpretation of dreams and omens, and perfectly acquainted with the science of judicial astrology; which, in almost every age except the present, has maintained its dominion over the mind of man. He had lost his first wife whilst he was governor of the Lyonnese Gaul.[3] In the choice of a second, he sought only to connect himself with some favourite of fortune; and, as soon as he had discovered that a young lady of Emesa in Syria had *a royal nativity*, he solicited and obtained her hand.[4] Julia Domna (for that was her name) deserved all that the stars could promise her. She possessed, even in an advanced age, the attractions of beauty,[5] and united to a lively imagination a firmness of mind, and strength of judgment, seldom bestowed on her sex. Her amiable qualities never made any deep impression on the dark and jealous temper of her husband; but, in her son's reign, she administered the principal affairs of the empire with a prudence that supported his authority; and with a moderation that sometimes corrected his wild extravagancies.[6] Julia applied herself to letters and philosophy with some success, and with the most splendid reputation. She was the patroness of every art, and the friend of every man of genius.[7] The grateful flattery of the learned has celebrated her virtues; but, if we may credit the scandal of ancient history, chastity was very far from being the most conspicuous virtue of the Empress Julia.[8]

Two sons, Caracalla[9] and Geta, were the fruit of this marriage, and the destined heirs of the empire. The fond hopes of the father, and of the Roman world, were soon disappointed by these vain youths, who displayed the indolent security of hereditary princes, and a presumption that fortune would supply the place of merit and application. Without any emulation of virtue or talents, they discovered, almost from their infancy, a fixed and implacable antipathy for each other.

Their aversion, confirmed by years, and fomented by the arts of their interested favourites, broke out in childish, and gradually in more serious, competitions; and at length divided the theatre, the circus, and the court into two factions, actuated by the hopes and fears of their respective leaders. The prudent emperor endeavoured, by every expedient of advice and authority, to allay this growing animosity. The unhappy discord of his sons clouded all his prospects, and threatened to overturn a throne raised with so much labour, cemented with so much blood, and guarded with every defence of arms and treasure. With an impartial hand he maintained between them an exact balance of favour, conferred on both the rank of Augustus, with the revered name of Antoninus; and for the first time the Roman world beheld three emperors.[10] Yet even this equal conduct served only to inflame the contest, whilst the fierce Caracalla asserted the right of primogeniture, and the milder Geta courted the affections of the people and the soldiers. In the anguish of a disappointed father, Severus foretold that the weaker of his sons would fall a sacrifice to the stronger; who, in his turn, would be ruined by his own vices.[11]

In these circumstances the intelligence of a war in Britain, and of an invasion of the province by the barbarians of the North, was received with pleasure by Severus. Though the vigilance of his lieutenants might have been sufficient to repel the distant enemy, he resolved to embrace the honourable pretext of withdrawing his sons from the luxury of Rome, which enervated their minds and irritated their passions, and of inuring their youth to the toils of war and government. Notwithstanding his advanced age (for he was above threescore), and his gout, which obliged him to be carried in a litter, he transported himself in person into that remote island, attended by his two sons, his whole court, and a formidable army. He immediately passed the walls of Hadrian and Antoninus, and entered the enemy's country, with the design of completing the long-attempted conquest of Britain. He penetrated to the northern extremity of the island without meeting an enemy. But the concealed ambuscades of the Caledonians, who hung unseen on the rear and flanks of his army, the coldness of the climate, and the severity of a winter march across the hills and morasses of Scotland, are reported to have cost the Romans above fifty thousand men. The Caledonians at length yielded to the powerful and obstinate attack, sued for peace, and surrendered a part of their arms, and a large tract of territory. But their apparent submission lasted no longer than the present terror. As soon as the Roman legions had retired, they resumed their hostile independence. Their restless spirit provoked Severus to send a new army into Caledonia, with the most bloody orders, not to subdue, but to extirpate the natives. They were saved by the death of their haughty enemy.[12]

This Caledonian war, neither marked by decisive events nor attended with any important consequences, would ill deserve our attention; but it is supposed, not without a considerable degree of probability, that the invasion of Severus is connected with the most shining period of the British history or fable. Fingal, whose fame, with that of his heroes and bards, has been revived in our language by a recent publication, is said to have commanded the Caledonians in that memorable juncture, to have eluded the power of Severus, and to have obtained a signal victory on the banks of the Carun, in which the son of *the King of the World*, Caracul, fled from his arms along the fields of his pride.[13] Something of a doubtful mist still hangs over these Highland traditions; nor can it be entirely dispelled by the most ingenious researches of modern criticism:[14] but if we could, with safety, indulge the pleasing supposition that Fingal lived, and that Ossian sung, the striking contrast of the situation and manners of the contending nations might amuse a philosophic mind. The parallel would be little to the advantage of the more civilised people, if we compared the unrelenting revenge of Severus with the generous clemency of Fingal; the timid and brutal cruelty of Caracalla, with the bravery, the tenderness, the elegant genius of Ossian; the mercenary chiefs who, from motives of fear or interest, served under the Imperial standard, with the freeborn warriors who started to arms at the voice of the King of Morven; if, in a word, we contemplated the untutored Caledonians, glowing with the warm virtues of nature, and the degenerate Romans, polluted with the mean vices of wealth and slavery.

The declining health and last illness of Severus inflamed the wild ambition and black passions of Caracalla's soul. Impatient of any delay or division of empire, he attempted, more than once, to shorten the small remainder of his father's days, and endeavoured, but without success, to excite a mutiny among the troops.[15] The old emperor had often censured the misguided lenity of Marcus, who, by a single act of justice, might have saved the Romans from the tyranny of his worthless son. Placed in the same situation, he experienced how easily the rigour of a judge dissolves away in the tenderness of a parent. He deliberated, he threatened, but he could not punish; and this last and only instance of mercy was more fatal to the empire than a long series of cruelty.[16] The disorder of his mind irritated the pains of his body; he wished impatiently for death, and hastened the instant of it by his impatience. He expired at York in the sixty-fifth year of his life and in the eighteenth of a glorious and successful reign. In his last moments he recommended concord to his sons, and his sons to the army. The salutary advice never reached the heart, or even the understanding, of the impetuous youths; but the more obedient troops, mindful of their oath of allegiance, and of the authority of their deceased master, resisted the solicitations of Caracalla, and proclaimed both brothers emperors of Rome. The new princes soon left the Caledonians in peace, returned to the capital, celebrated their father's funeral with divine honours, and were cheerfully acknowledged as lawful sovereigns by the senate, the people, and the provinces. Some pre-eminence of rank seems to have been allowed to the elder brother; but they both administered the empire with equal and independent power.[17]

Such a divided form of government would have proved a source of discord between the most affectionate brothers. It was impossible that it could long subsist between two implacable enemies, who neither desired nor could trust a reconciliation. It was visible that one only could reign, and that the other must fall; and each of them, judging of his rival's designs by his own, guarded his life with the most jealous vigilance from the repeated attacks of poison or the sword. Their rapid journey through Gaul and Italy, during which they never ate at the same table, or slept in the same house, displayed to the provinces the odious spectacle of fraternal discord. On their arrival at Rome, they immediately divided the vast extent of the Imperial palace.[18] No communication was allowed between their apartments; the doors and passages were diligently fortified, and guards posted and relieved with the same strictness as in a besieged place. The emperors met only in public, in the presence of their afflicted mother; and each surrounded by a numerous train of armed followers. Even on these occasions of ceremony, the dissimulation of courts could ill disguise the rancour of their hearts.[19]

This latent civil war already distracted the whole government, when a scheme was suggested that seemed of mutual benefit to the hostile brothers. It was proposed, that, since it was impossible to reconcile their minds, they should separate their interest, and divide the empire between them. The conditions of the treaty were already drawn with some accuracy. It was agreed that Caracalla, as the elder brother, should remain in possession of Europe and the western Africa; and that he should relinquish the sovereignty of Asia and Egypt to Geta, who might fix his residence at Alexandria or Antioch, cities little inferior to Rome itself in wealth and greatness; that numerous armies should be constantly encamped on either side of the Thracian Bosphorus, to guard the frontiers of the rival monarchies; and that the senators of European extraction should acknowledge the sovereign of Rome, whilst the natives of Asia followed the emperor of the East. The tears of the empress Julia interrupted the negotiation, the first idea of which had filled every Roman breast with surprise and indignation. The mighty mass of conquest was so intimately connected by the hand of time and policy, that it required the most forcible violence to rend it asunder. The Romans had reason to dread that the disjointed members would soon be reduced by a civil war under the dominion of one master; but, if the separation was permanent, the division of the provinces must terminate in the dissolution of an empire whose unity had hitherto remained inviolate.[20]

Had the treaty been carried into execution, the sovereign of Europe might soon have been the conqueror of Asia; but Caracalla obtained an easier though a more guilty victory. He artfully listened to his mother's entreaties, and consented to meet his brother in her apartment, on terms of peace and reconciliation. In the midst of their conversation, some centurions, who had contrived to conceal themselves, rushed with drawn swords upon the unfortunate Geta. His distracted mother strove to protect him in her arms; but in the unavailing struggle, she was wounded in the hand, and covered with the blood of her younger son, while she saw the elder animating and assisting[21] the fury of the assassins. As soon as the deed was perpetrated, Caracalla, with hasty steps and horror in his countenance, ran towards the Praetorian camp, as his only refuge, and threw himself on the ground before the statues of the tutelar deities.[22] The soldiers attempted to raise and comfort him. In broken and disordered words he informed them of his imminent danger and fortunate escape, insinuating that he had prevented the designs of his enemy, and declared his resolution to live and die with his faithful troops. Geta had been the favourite of the soldiers; but complaint was useless, revenge was danger- ous, and they still reverenced the son of Severus. Their discontent died away in idle murmurs, and Caracalla soon convinced them of the justice of his cause, by distributing in one lavish donative the accumulated treasures of his father's reign.[23] The real *sentiments* of the soldiers alone were of importance to his power or safety. Their declaration in his favour commanded the dutiful *professions* of the senate. The obsequious assembly was always prepared to ratify the decision of fortune; but, as Caracalla wished to assuage the first emotions of public indignation, the name of Geta was mentioned with decency, and he received the funeral honours of a Roman emperor.[24] Posterity, in pity to his misfortune, has cast a veil over his vices. We consider that young prince as the innocent victim of his brother's ambition, without recollecting that he himself wanted power, rather than inclination, to consummate the same attempts of revenge and murder.

The crime went not unpunished. Neither business, nor pleasure, nor flattery, could defend Caracalla from the stings of a guilty conscience; and he confessed, in the anguish of a tortured mind, that his disordered fancy often beheld the angry forms of his father and his brother rising into life, to threaten and upbraid him.[25] The consciousness of his crime should have induced him to convince mankind, by the virtues of his reign, that the bloody deed had been the involuntary effect of fatal necessity. But the repentance of Caracalla only prompted him to remove from the world whatever could remind him of his guilt, or recall the memory of his murdered brother. On his return from the senate to the palace, he found his mother in the company of several noble matrons, weeping over the untimely fate of her younger son. The jealous emperor threatened them with instant death: the sentence was executed against Fadilla, the last remaining daughter of the Emperor Marcus; and even the afflicted Julia was obliged to silence her lamentations, to suppress her sighs, and to receive the assassin with smiles of joy and approbation. It was computed that, under the vague appellation of the friends of Geta, above twenty thousand persons of both sexes suffered death. His guards and freedmen, the ministers of his serious business, and the companions of his looser hours, those who by his interest had been promoted to any commands in the army or provinces, with the long connected chain of their depend-ants, were included in the proscription; which endeavoured to reach every one who had maintained the smallest correspondence with Geta, who lamented his death, or who even mentioned his name.[26] Helvius Pertinax, son to the prince of that name, lost his life by an unseasonable witticism.[27] It was a sufficient crime of Thrasea Priscus to be descended from a family in which the love of liberty seemed an hereditary quality.[28] The particular causes of calumny and suspicion were at length exhausted; and when a senator was accused of being a secret enemy to the government, the emperor was satisfied with the general proof that he was a man of property and virtue. From this well-grounded principle he frequently drew the most bloody inferences.

The execution of so many innocent citizens was bewailed by the secret tears of their friends and families. The death of Papinian, the Praetorian prefect, was lamented as a public calamity. During the last seven years of Severus, he had exercised the most important offices of the state, and, by his salutary influence, guided the emperor's steps in the paths of justice and moderation. In full assurance of his virtue and abilities, Severus, on his deathbed, had conjured him to watch over the prosperity and union of the Imperial family.[29] The honest labours of Papinian served only to inflame the hatred which Caracalla had already conceived against his father's minister. After the murder of Geta, the prefect was commanded to exert the powers of his skill and eloquence in a studied apology for that atrocious deed. The philosophic Seneca had condescended to compose a similar epistle to the senate, in the name of the son* and assassin of Agrippina.[30] 'That it was easier to commit than to justify a parricide,' was the glorious reply of Papinian,[31] who did not hesitate between the loss of life and that of honour. Such intrepid virtue, which had escaped pure and unsullied from the intrigues of courts, the habits of business, and the arts of his profession, reflects more lustre on the memory of Papinian than all his great employments, his numerous writings, and the superior reputa-tion as a lawyer, which he has preserved through every age of the Roman jurisprudence.[32]

It had hitherto been the peculiar felicity of the Romans, and in the worst of times their consolation, that the virtue of the emperors was active, and their vice indolent. Augustus, Trajan, Hadrian, and Marcus visited their extensive dominions in person, and their progress was marked by acts of wisdom and beneficence. The tyranny of Tiberius, Nero, and Domitian, who resided almost constantly at Rome, or in the adjacent villas, was confined to the senatorial and equestrian orders.[33] But Caracalla was the common enemy of mankind. He left the capital (and he never returned to it) about a year after the murder of Geta. The rest of his reign was spent in the several provinces of the empire, particularly those of the East, and every province was, by turns, the scene of his rapine and cruelty. The senators, compelled by fear to attend his capricious motions, were obliged to provide daily entertainments at an immense expense, which he abandoned with contempt to his guards; and to erect, in every city, magnificent palaces and theatres, which he either disdained to visit, or ordered to be immediately thrown down. The most wealthy families were ruined by partial fines and confiscations, and the great body of his subjects oppressed by ingenious and aggravated taxes.[34] In the midst of peace, and upon the slightest provocation, he issued his commands, at Alexandria in Egypt, for a general massacre. From a secure post in the temple of Serapis, he viewed and directed the slaughter of many thousand citizens, as well as strangers, without distinguishing either the number or the crime of the sufferers; since, as he coolly informed the senate, *all* the Alexandrians, those who had perished and those who had escaped, were alike guilty.[35]

The wise instructions of Severus never made any lasting impression on the mind of his son, who, although not destitute of imagination and eloquence, was equally devoid of judgment and humanity.[36] One dangerous maxim, worthy of a tyrant, was remembered and abused by Caracalla, 'To secure the affections of the army, and to esteem the rest of his subjects as of little moment'.[37] But the liberality of the father had been restrained by prudence, and his indulgence to the troops was tempered by firmness and authority. The careless profusion of the son was the policy of one reign, and the inevitable ruin both of the army and of the empire. The vigour of the soldiers, instead of being confirmed by the severe discipline of camps, melted away in the luxury of cities. The excessive increase of their pay and donatives[38] exhausted the state to enrich the military order, whose modesty in peace, and service in war, is best secured by an honourable poverty. The demeanour of Caracalla was haughty and full of pride; but with the troops he forgot even the proper dignity of his rank, encouraged their insolent familiarity, and, neglecting the essential duties of a general, affected to imitate the dress and manners of a common soldier.

It was impossible that such a character and such a conduct as that of Caracalla could inspire either love or esteem; but, as long as his vices were beneficial to the armies, he was secure from the danger of rebellion. A secret conspiracy, provoked by his own jealousy, was fatal to the tyrant. The Praetorian prefecture was divided between two ministers. The military department was intrusted to Adventus, an experienced rather than an able soldier; and the civil affairs were transacted by Opilius Macrinus, who, by his dexterity in business, had raised himself, with a fair character, to that high office. But his favour varied with the caprice of the emperor, and his life might depend on the slightest suspicion, or the most casual circumstance. Malice or fanaticism had suggested to an African, deeply skilled in the knowledge of futurity, a very dangerous prediction, that Macrinus and his son were destined to reign over the empire. The report was soon diffused through the province; and, when the man was sent in chains to Rome, he still asserted, in the presence of the prefect of the city, the faith of his prophecy. That magistrate, who had received the most pressing instructions to inform himself of the *successors* of Caracalla, immediately communicated the examination of the African to the Imperial court, which at that time resided in Syria. But, notwithstanding the diligence of the public messengers, a friend of Macrinus found means to apprise him of the approaching danger. The emperor received the letters from Rome; and, as he was then engaged in the conduct of a chariot race, he delivered them unopened to the Praetorian prefect, directing him to dispatch the ordinary affairs, and to report the more important business that might be contained in them. Macrinus read his fate and resolved to prevent it. He inflamed the discontents of some inferior officers, and employed the hand of Martialis, a desperate soldier, who had been refused the rank of centurion. The devotion of Caracalla had prompted him to make a pilgrimage from Edessa to the celebrated temple of the Moon at Carrhae. He was attended by a body of cavalry; but having stopped on the road for some necessary occasion, his guards preserved a respectful distance, and Martialis, approaching his person under a pretence of duty, stabbed him with a dagger. The bold assassin was instantly killed by a Scythian archer of the Imperial guard. Such was the end of a monster whose life disgraced human nature, and whose reign accused the patience of the Romans.[39] The grateful soldiers forgot his vices, remembered only his partial liberality, and obliged the senate to prostitute their own dignity and that of religion by granting him a place among the gods. Whilst he was upon earth, Alexander the Great was the only hero whom this god* deemed worthy his admiration. He assumed the name and ensigns of Alexander, formed a Macedonian phalanx of guards, persecuted the disciples of Aristotle, and displayed with a puerile enthusiasm the only sentiment by which he discovered any regard for virtue or glory. We can easily conceive that, after the battle of Narva[†] and the conquest of Poland, Charles the Twelfth[‡] (though he still wanted the more elegant accomplishments of the son of Philip) might boast of having rivalled his valour and magnanimity; but in no one action of his life did Caracalla express the faintest resemblance of the Macedonian hero, except in the murder of a great number of his own and of his father's friends.[40]

After the extinction of the house of Severus, the Roman world remained three days without a master. The choice of the army (for the authority of a distant and feeble senate was little regarded) hung in anxious suspense; as no candidate presented himself whose distinguished birth and merit could engage their attachment and unite their suffrages.

The decisive weight of the Praetorian guards elevated the hopes of their prefects, and these powerful ministers began to assert their *legal* claim to fill the vacancy of the Imperial throne. Adventus, however, the senior prefect, conscious of his age and infirmities, of his small reputation and his smaller abilities, resigned the dangerous honour to the crafty ambition of his colleague Macrinus, whose well-dissembled grief removed all suspicion of his being accessory to his master's death.[41] The troops neither loved nor esteemed his character. They cast their eyes around in search of a competitor, and at last yielded with reluctance to his promises of unbounded liberality and indulgence. A short time after his accession he conferred on his son Diadumenianus, at the age of only ten years, the Imperial title and the popular name of Antoninus. The beautiful figure of the youth, assisted by an additional donative, for which the ceremony furnished a pretext, might attract, it was hoped, the favour of the army, and secure the doubtful throne of Macrinus.

The authority of the new sovereign had been ratified by the cheerful submission of the senate and provinces. They exulted in their unexpected deliverance from a hated tyrant, and it seemed of little consequence to examine into the virtues of the successor of Caracalla. But, as soon as the first transports of joy and surprise had subsided, they began to scrutinise the merits of Macrinus with a critical severity, and to arraign the hasty choice of the army. It had hitherto been considered as a fundamental maxim of the constitution that the emperor must always be chosen in the senate, and the sovereign power, no longer exercised by the whole body, was always delegated to one of its members. But Macrinus was not a senator.[42] The sudden elevation of the Praetorian prefects betrayed the meanness of their origin; and the equestrian order was still in possession of that great office, which commanded with arbitrary sway the lives and fortunes of the senate. A murmur of indignation was heard, that a man, whose obscure[43] extraction had never been illustrated by any signal service, should dare to invest himself with the purple, instead of bestowing it on some distinguished senator, equal in birth and dignity to the splendour of the Imperial station. As soon as the character of Macrinus was surveyed by the sharp eye of discontent, some vices, and many defects, were easily discovered. The choice of his ministers was in several instances justly censured, and the dissatisfied people, with their usual candour, accused at once his indolent tameness and his excessive severity.[44]

His rash ambition had climbed a height where it was difficult to stand with firmness, and impossible to fall without instant destruction. Trained in the arts of courts and the forms of civil business, he trembled in the presence of the fierce and undisciplined multitude, over whom he had assumed the command: his military talents were despised, and his personal courage suspected: a whisper that circulated in the camp disclosed the fatal secret of the conspiracy against the late emperor, aggravated the guilt of murder by the baseness of hypocrisy, and heightened contempt by detestation. To alienate the soldiers, and to provoke inevitable ruin, the character of a reformer was only wanting; and such was the peculiar hardship of his fate that Macrinus was compelled to exercise that invidious office. The prodigality of Caracalla had left behind it a long train of ruin and disorder: and, if that worthless tyrant had been capable of reflecting on the sure consequences of his own conduct, he would perhaps have enjoyed the dark prospect of the distress and calamities which he bequeathed to his successors.

In the management of this necessary reformation, Macrinus proceeded with a cautious prudence which would have restored health and vigour to the Roman army in an easy and almost imperceptible manner. To the soldiers already engaged in the service he was constrained to leave the dangerous privileges and extravagant pay given by Caracalla; but the new recruits were received on the more moderate, though liberal, establish-ment of Severus, and gradually formed to modesty and obedience.[45] One fatal error destroyed the salutary effects of this judicious plan. The numerous army, assembled in the East by the late emperor, instead of being immediately dispersed by Macrinus through the several provinces, was suffered to remain united in Syria during the winter that followed his elevation. In the luxurious idleness of their quarters, the troops viewed their strength and numbers, communicated their complaints, and re-volved in their minds the advantages of another revolution. The veterans, instead of being flattered by the advantageous distinction, were alarmed by the first steps of the emperor, which they considered as the presage of his future intentions. The recruits, with sullen reluctance, entered on a service, whose labours were increased while its rewards were diminished by a covetous and unwarlike sovereign. The murmurs of the army swelled with impunity into seditious clamours; and the partial mutinies betrayed a spirit of discontent and disaffection, that waited only for the slightest occasion to break out on every side into a general rebellion. To minds thus disposed the occasion soon presented itself.

The Empress Julia had experienced all the vicissitudes of fortune. From an humble station, she had been raised to greatness, only to taste the superior bitterness of an exalted rank. She was doomed to weep over the death of one of her sons, and over the life of the other. The cruel fate of Caracalla, though her good sense must have long taught her to expect it, awakened the feelings of a mother and of an empress. Notwithstanding the respectful civility expressed by the usurper towards the widow of Severus, she descended with a painful struggle into the condition of a subject, and soon withdrew herself by a voluntary death from the anxious and humiliating dependence.[46] Julia Maesa, her sister, was ordered to leave the court and Antioch. She retired to Emesa with an immense fortune, the fruit of twenty years' favour, accompanied by her two daughters, Soaemias and Mamaea, each of whom was a widow, and each had an only son. Bassianus, for that was the name of the son of Soaemias, was consecrated to the honourable ministry of high priest of the Sun; and this holy vocation, embraced either from prudence or superstition, contributed to raise the Syrian youth to the empire of Rome. A numerous body of troops were stationed at Emesa; and, as the severe discipline of Macrinus had constrained them to pass the winter encamped, they were eager to revenge the cruelty of such unaccustomed hardships. The soldiers, who resorted in crowds to the temple of the Sun, beheld with veneration and delight the elegant dress and figure of the young pontiff: they recognised, or thought that they recognised, the features of Caracalla, whose memory they now adored. The artful Maesa saw and cherished their rising partiality, and, readily sacrificing her daughter's reputation to the fortune of her grandson, she insinuated that Bassianus was the natural son of their murdered sovereign. The sums distributed by her emissaries with a lavish hand silenced every objection, and the profusion sufficiently proved the affinity, or at least the resemblance, of Bassianus with the great original. The young Antoninus (for he had assumed and polluted that respectable name) was declared emperor by the troops of Emesa, asserted his hereditary right, and called aloud on the armies to follow the standard of a young and liberal prince, who had taken up arms to revenge his father's death and the oppression of the military order.[47]

Whilst a conspiracy of women and eunuchs was concerted with prudence, and conducted with rapid vigour, Macrinus, who by a decisive motion might have crushed his infant enemy, floated between the opposite extremes of terror and security, which alike fixed him inactive at Antioch. A spirit of rebellion diffused itself through all the camps and garrisons of Syria; successive detachments murdered their officers[48] and joined the party of the rebels; and the tardy restitution of military pay and privileges was imputed to the acknowledged weakness of Macrinus. At length he marched out of Antioch, to meet the increasing and zealous army of the young pretender. His own troops seemed to take the field with faintness and reluctance; but, in the heat of battle[49] the Praetorian guards, almost by an involuntary impulse, asserted the superiority of their valour and discipline. The rebel ranks were broken; when the mother and the grandmother of the Syrian prince, who, according to their eastern custom, had attended the army, threw themselves from their covered chariots, and, by exciting the compassion of the soldiers, endeavoured to animate their drooping courage. Antoninus himself, who in the rest of his life never acted like a man, in this important crisis of his fate approved himself a hero, mounted his horse, and, at the head of his rallied troops, charged sword in hand among the thickest of the enemy; whilst the eunuch Gannys, whose occupation had been confined to female cares and the soft luxury of Asia, displayed the talents of an able and experienced general. The battle still raged with doubtful violence, and Macrinus might have obtained the victory, had he not betrayed his own cause by a shameful and precipitate flight. His cowardice served only to protract his life a few days, and to stamp deserved ignominy on his misfortunes. It is scarcely necessary to add that his son Diadumenianus was involved in the same fate. As soon as the stubborn Praetorians could be convinced that they fought for a prince who had basely deserted them, they surrendered to the conqueror; the contending parties of the Roman army, mingling tears of joy and tenderness, united under the banners of the imagined son of Caracalla, and the East acknowledged with pleasure the first emperor of Asiatic extraction.

The letters of Macrinus had condescended to inform the senate of the slight disturbance occasioned by an impostor in Syria, and a decree immediately passed, declaring the rebel and his family public enemies; with a promise of pardon, however, to such of his deluded adherents as should merit it by an immediate return to their duty. During the twenty days that elapsed from the declaration to the victory of Antoninus (for in so short an interval was the fate of the Roman world decided), the capital and the provinces, more especially those of the East, were distracted with hopes and fears, agitated with tumult, and stained with a useless effusion of civil blood, since whosoever of the rivals prevailed in Syria must reign over the empire. The specious letters in which the young conqueror announced his victory to the obedient senate were filled with profession of virtue and moderation; the shining examples of Marcus* and Augustus he should ever consider as the great rule of his administration; and he affected to dwell with pride on the striking resemblance of his own age and fortunes with those of Augustus, who in the earliest youth had revenged by a successful war the murder of his father. By adopting the style of Marcus Aurelius Antoninus, son of Antoninus, and grandson of Severus, he tacitly asserted his hereditary claim to empire; but, by assuming the tribunitian and proconsular powers before they had been conferred on him by a decree of the senate, he offended the delicacy of Roman prejudice. This new and injudicious violation of the constitution was probably dictated either by the ignorance of his Syrian courtiers or the fierce disdain of his military followers.[50]

As the attention of the new emperor was diverted by the most trifling amusements, he wasted many months in his luxurious progress from Syria to Italy, passed at Nicomedia the first winter after his victory, and deferred till the ensuing summer his triumphal entry into the capital. A faithful picture, however, which preceded his arrival, and was placed by his immediate order over the altar of Victory in the senate-house, conveyed to the Romans the just but unworthy resemblance of his person and manners. He was drawn in his sacerdotal robes of silk and gold, after the loose flowing fashion of the Medes and Phoenicians; his head was covered with a lofty tiara, his numerous collars and bracelets were adorned with gems of an inestimable value. His eyebrows were tinged with black, and his cheeks painted with an artificial red and white.[51] The grave senators confessed with a sigh, that, after having long experienced the stern tyranny of their own countrymen, Rome was at length humbled beneath the effeminate luxury of Oriental despotism.

The sun was worshipped at Emesa under the name of Elagabalus,[52] and under the form of a black conical stone, which, as it was universally believed, had fallen from heaven on that sacred place. To this protecting deity, Antoninus, not without some reason, ascribed his elevation to the throne. The display of superstitious gratitude was the only serious business of his reign. The triumph of the god of Emesa over all the religions of the earth was the great object of his zeal and vanity; and the appellation of Elagabalus (for he presumed as pontiff and favourite to adopt that sacred name) was dearer to him than all the titles of Imperial greatness. In a solemn procession through the streets of Rome, the way was strewed with gold dust; the black stone, set in precious gems, was placed on a chariot drawn by six milk-white horses richly caparisoned. The pious emperor held the reins, and, supported by his ministers, moved slowly backwards, that he might perpetually enjoy the felicity of the divine presence. In a magnificent temple raised on the Palatine Mount, the sacrifices of the god Elagabalus were celebrated with every circumstance of cost and solemnity. The richest wines, the most extraordinary victims, and the rarest aromatics were profusely consumed on his altar. Around the altar a chorus of Syrian damsels performed their lascivious dances to the sound of barbarian music, whilst the gravest personages of the state and army, clothed in long Phoenician tunics, officiated in the meanest functions, with affected zeal and secret indignation.[53]

To this temple, as to the common centre of religious worship, the Imperial fanatic attempted to remove the *Ancilia*,* the Palladium†[54] and all the sacred pledges of the faith of Numa. A crowd of inferior deities attended in various stations the majesty of the god of Emesa; but his court was still imperfect, till a female of distinguished rank was admitted to his bed. Pallas had been first chosen for his consort; but, as it was dreaded that her warlike terrors might affright the soft delicacy of a Syrian deity, the Moon, adored by the Africans under the name of Astarte, was deemed a more suitable companion for the Sun. Her image, with the rich offerings of her temple as a marriage portion, was transported with solemn pomp from Carthage to Rome, and the day of these mystic nuptials was a general festival in the capital and throughout the empire.[55]

A rational voluptuary adheres with invariable respect to the temperate dictates of nature, and improves the gratifications of sense by social intercourse, endearing connections, and the soft colouring of taste and imagination. But Elagabalus (I speak of the emperor of that name), corrupted by his youth, his country, and his fortune, abandoned himself to the grossest pleasures with ungoverned fury, and soon found disgust and satiety in the midst of his enjoyments. The inflammatory powers of art were summoned to his aid: the confused multitudes of women, of wines, and of dishes, and the studied variety of attitudes and sauces, served to revive his languid appetites. New terms and new inventions in these sciences, the only ones cultivated and patronised by the monarch,[56] signalised his reign, and transmitted his infamy to succeeding times. A capricious prodigality supplied the want of taste and elegance; and, whilst Elagabalus lavished away the treasures of his people in the wildest extravagance, his own voice and that of his flatterers applauded a spirit and magnificence unknown to the tameness of his predecessors. To confound the order of seasons and climates,[57] to sport with the passions and prejudices of his subjects, and to subvert every law of nature and decency, were in the number of his most delicious amusements. A long train of concubines, and a rapid succession of wives, among whom was a vestal virgin, ravished by force from her sacred asylum,[58] were insufficient to satisfy the impotence* of his passions. The master of the Roman world affected to copy the dress and manners of the female sex, preferred the distaff to the sceptre, and dishonoured the principal dignities of the empire by distributing them among his numerous lovers; one of whom was publicly invested with the title and authority of the emperor's, or, as he more properly styled himself, of the empress's husband.[59]

It may seem probable the vices and follies of Elagabalus have been adorned by fancy and blackened by prejudice.[60] Yet, confining ourselves to the public scenes displayed before the Roman people, and attested by grave and contemporary historians, their inexpressible infamy surpasses that of any other age or country. The licence of an eastern monarch is secluded from the eye of curiosity by the inaccessible walls of the seraglio. The sentiments of honour and gallantry have introduced a refinement of pleasure, a regard for decency, and a respect for the public opinion, into the modern courts of Europe; but the corrupt and opulent nobles of Rome gratified every vice that could be collected from the mighty conflux of nations and manners. Secure of impunity, careless of censure, they lived without restraint in the patient and humble society of their slaves and parasites. The emperor, in his turn, viewing every rank of his subjects with the same contemptuous indifference, asserted without control his sovereign privilege of lust and luxury.

The most worthless of mankind are not afraid to condemn in others the same disorders which they allow in themselves; and can readily discover some nice difference of age, character, or station, to justify the partial distinction. The licentious soldiers, who had raised to the throne the dissolute son of Caracalla, blushed at their ignominious choice, and turned with disgust from that monster, to contemplate with pleasure the opening virtues of his cousin Alexander, the son of Mamaea. The crafty Maesa, sensible that her grandson Elagabalus must inevitably destroy himself by his own vices, had provided another and surer support of her family. Embracing a favourable moment of fondness and devotion, she had persuaded the young emperor to adopt Alexander, and to invest him with the title of Caesar, that his own divine occupations might be no longer interrupted by the care of the earth. In the second rank, that amiable prince soon acquired the affections of the public, and excited the tyrant's jealousy, who resolved to terminate the dangerous competition either by corrupting the manners, or by taking away the life, of his rival. His arts proved unsuccessful; his vain designs were constantly discovered by his own loquacious folly, and disappointed by those virtuous and faithful servants whom the prudence of Mamaea had placed about the person of her son. In a hasty sally of passion, Elagabalus resolved to execute by force what he had been unable to compass by fraud, and by a despotic sentence degraded his cousin from the rank and honours of Caesar. The message was received in the senate with silence, and in the camp with fury. The Praetorian guards swore to protect Alexander, and to revenge the dishonoured majesty of the throne. The tears and promises of the trembling Elagabalus, who only begged them to spare his life, and to leave him in the possession of his beloved Hierocles, diverted their just indignation; and they contented themselves with empowering their prefects to watch over the safety of Alexander and the conduct of the emperor.[61]

It was impossible that such a reconciliation should last, or that even the mean soul of Elagabalus could hold an empire on such humiliating terms of dependence. He soon attempted, by a dangerous experiment, to try the temper of the soldiers. The report of the death of Alexander, and the natural suspicion that he had been murdered, inflamed their passions into fury, and the tempest of the camp could only be appeased by the presence and authority of the popular youth. Provoked at this new instance of their affection for his cousin, and their contempt for his person, the emperor ventured to punish some of the leaders of the mutiny. His unseasonable severity proved instantly fatal to his minions, his mother, and himself. Elagabalus was massacred by the indignant Praetorians, his mutilated corpse dragged through the streets of the city and thrown into the Tiber. His memory was branded with eternal infamy by the senate; the justice of whose decree has been ratified by posterity.[62]

In the room of Elagabalus, his cousin Alexander was raised to the throne by the Praetorian guards. His relation to the family of Severus, whose name he assumed, was the same as that of his predecessor; his virtue and his danger had already endeared him to the Romans, and the eager liberality of the senate conferred upon him, in one day, the various titles and powers of the Imperial dignity.[63] But, as Alexander was a modest and dutiful youth of only seventeen years of age, the reins of government were in the hands of two women, of his mother Mamaea, and of Maesa, his grandmother. After the death of the latter, who survived but a short time the elevation of Alexander, Mamaea remained the sole regent of her son and of the empire.

In every age and country, the wiser, or at least the stronger, of the two sexes has usurped the powers of the state, and confined the other to the cares and pleasures of domestic life. In hereditary monarchies, however, and especially in those of modern Europe, the gallant spirit of chivalry, and the law of succession, have accustomed us to allow a singular exception; and a woman is often acknowledged the absolute sovereign of a great kingdom, in which she would be deemed incapable of exercising the smallest employment, civil or military. But, as the Roman emperors were still considered as the generals and magistrates of the republic, their wives and mothers, although distinguished by the name of Augusta, were never associated to their personal honours; and a female reign would have appeared an inexpiable prodigy in the eyes of those primitive Romans, who married without love, or loved without delicacy and respect.[64] The haughty Agrippina* aspired, indeed, to share the honours of the empire, which she had conferred on her son; but her mad ambition, detested by every citizen who felt for the dignity of Rome, was disappointed by the artful firmness of Seneca and Burrhus.[65] The good sense, or the indifference, of succeeding princes restrained them from offending the prejudices of their subjects; and it was reserved for the profligate Elagabalus to disgrace the acts of the senate with the name of his mother Soaemias, who was placed by the side of the consuls, and subscribed, as a regular member, the decrees of the legislative assembly. Her more prudent sister, Mamaea, declined the useless and odious prerogative, and a solemn law was enacted, excluding women for ever from the senate, and devoting to the infernal gods the head of the wretch by whom this sanction should be violated.[66] The substance, not the pageantry, of power was the object of Mamaea's manly ambition. She maintained an absolute and lasting empire over the mind of her son, and in his affection the mother could not brook a rival. Alexander, with her consent, married the daughter of a Patrician; but his respect for his father-in-law, and love for the empress, were inconsistent with the tenderness or interest of Mamaea. The Patrician was executed on the ready accusation of treason, and the wife of Alexander driven with ignominy from the palace, and banished into Africa.[67]

Notwithstanding this act of jealous cruelty, as well as some instances of avarice, with which Mamaea is charged, the general tenor of her administration was equally for the benefit of her son and of the empire. With the approbation of the senate, she chose sixteen of the wisest and most virtuous senators, as a perpetual council of state, before whom every public business of moment was debated and determined. The celebrated Ulpian, equally distinguished by his knowledge of, and his respect for, the laws of Rome, was at their head; and the prudent firmness of this aristocracy restored order and authority to the government. As soon as they had purged the city from foreign superstition and luxury, the remains of the capricious tyranny of Elagabalus, they applied themselves to remove his worthless creatures from every department of public administration, and to supply their places with men of virtue and ability. Learning, and the love of justice, became the only recommendations for civil offices; valour, and the love of discipline, the only qualifications for military employments.[68]

But the most important care of Mamaea and her wise counsellors was to form the character of the young emperor, on whose personal qualities the happiness or misery of the Roman world must ultimately depend. The fortunate soil assisted, and even prevented,* the hand of cultivation. An excellent understanding soon convinced Alexander of the advantages of virtue, the pleasure of knowledge, and the necessity of labour. A natural mildness and moderation of temper preserved him from the assaults of passion and the allurements of vice. His unalterable regard for his mother, and his esteem for the wise Ulpian, guarded his unexperienced youth from the poison of flattery.

The simple journal of his ordinary occupations exhibits a pleasing picture of an accomplished emperor,[69] and, with some allowance for the difference of manners, might well deserve the imitation of modern princes. Alexander rose early; the first moments of the day were consecrated to private devotion, and his domestic chapel was filled with the images of those heroes who, by improving or reforming human life, had deserved the grateful reverence of posterity. But, as he deemed the service of mankind the most acceptable worship of the gods, the greatest part of his morning hours was employed in his council, where he discussed public affairs, and determined private causes, with a patience and discretion above his years. The dryness of business was relieved by the charms of literature; and a portion of time was always set apart for his favourite studies of poetry, history, and philosophy. The works of Virgil and Horace, the republics of Plato and Cicero, formed his taste, enlarged his understanding, and gave him the noblest ideas of man and government. The exercises of the body succeeded to those of the mind; and Alexander, who was tall, active, and robust, surpassed most of his equals in the gymnastic arts. Refreshed by the use of the bath and a slight dinner, he resumed, with new vigour, the business of the day, and, till the hour of supper, the principal meal of the Romans, he was attended by his secretaries, with whom he read and answered the multitude of letters, memorials, and petitions, that must have been addressed to the master of the greatest part of the world. His table was served with the most frugal simplicity; and, whenever he was at liberty to consult his own inclination, the company consisted of a few select friends, men of learning and virtue, amongst whom Ulpian was constantly invited. Their conversation was familiar and instructive; and the pauses were occasionally enlivened by the recital of some pleasing composition, which supplied the place of the dancers, comedians, and even gladiators, so frequently summoned to the tables of the rich and luxurious Romans.[70] The dress of Alexander was plain and modest, his demeanour courteous and affable: at the proper hours his palace was open to all his subjects, but the voice of a crier was heard, as in the Eleusinian mysteries, pronouncing the same salutary admonition: 'Let none enter these holy walls, unless he is conscious of a pure and innocent mind.'[71]

Such an uniform tenor of life, which left not a moment for vice or folly, is a better proof of the wisdom and justice of Alexander's government than all the trifling details preserved in the compilation of Lampridius. Since the accession of Commodus the Roman world had experienced, during a term of forty years, the successive and various vices of four tyrants. From the death of Elagabalus it enjoyed an auspicious calm of thirteen years. The provinces, relieved from the oppressive taxes invented by Caracalla and his pretended son, flourished in peace and prosperity under the administration of magistrates, who were convinced by experience that to deserve the love of the subjects was their best and only method of obtaining the favour of their sovereign. While some gentle restraints were imposed on the innocent luxury of the Roman people, the price of provisions and the interest of money were reduced by the paternal care of Alexander, whose prudent liberality, without distressing the industrious, supplied the wants and amusements of the populace. The dignity, the freedom, the authority of the senate was restored; and every virtuous senator might approach the person of the emperor without a fear and without a blush.

The name of Antoninus, ennobled by the virtues of Pius and Marcus, had been communicated by adoption to the dissolute Verus, and by descent to the cruel Commodus. It became the honourable appellation of the sons of Severus, was bestowed on young Diadumenianus, and at length prostituted to the infamy of the high priest of Emesa. Alexander, though pressed by the studied, and perhaps sincere, importunity of the senate, nobly refused the borrowed lustre of a name; whilst in his whole conduct he laboured to restore the glories and felicity of the age of the genuine Antonines.[72]

In the civil administration of Alexander, wisdom was enforced by power, and the people, sensible of the public felicity, repaid their benefactor with their love and gratitude. There still remained a greater, a more necessary, but a more difficult enterprise: the reformation of the military order, whose interest and temper, confirmed by long impunity, rendered them impatient of the restraints of discipline, and careless of the blessings of public tranquillity. In the execution of his design the emperor affected to display his love, and to conceal his fear, of the army. The most rigid economy in every other branch of the administration supplied a fund of gold and silver for the ordinary pay and the extraordinary rewards of the troops. In their marches he relaxed the severe obligation of carrying seventeen days' provision on their shoulders. Ample magazines were formed along the public roads, and as soon as they entered the enemy's country, a numerous train of mules and camels waited on their haughty laziness. As Alexander despaired of correcting the luxury of his soldiers, he attempted, at least, to direct it to objects of martial pomp and ornament, fine horses, splendid armour, and shields enriched with silver and gold. He shared whatever fatigues he was obliged to impose, visited, in person, the sick and wounded, preserved an exact register of their services and his own gratitude, and expressed, on every occasion, the warmest regard for a body of men, whose welfare, as he affected to declare, was so closely connected with that of the state.[73] By the most gentle arts he laboured to inspire the fierce multitude with a sense of duty, and to restore at least a faint image of that discipline to which the Romans owed their empire over so many other nations, as warlike and more powerful than themselves. But his prudence was vain, his courage fatal, and the attempt towards a reformation served only to inflame the ills it was meant to cure.

The Praetorian guards were attached to the youth of Alexander. They loved him as a tender pupil, whom they had saved from a tyrant's fury, and placed on the Imperial throne. That amiable prince was sensible of the obligation; but, as his gratitude was restrained within the limits of reason and justice, they soon were more dissatisfied with the virtues of Alexander than they had ever been with the vices of Elagabalus. Their prefect, the wise Ulpian, was the friend of the laws and of the people; he was considered as the enemy of the soldiers, and to his pernicious counsels every scheme of reformation was imputed. Some trifling accident blew up their discontent into a furious mutiny; and a civil war raged, during three days, in Rome, whilst the life of that excellent minister was defended by the grateful people. Terrified, at length, by the sight of some houses in flames, and by the threats of a general conflagration, the people yielded with a sigh, and left the virtuous but unfortunate Ulpian to his fate. He was pursued into the Imperial palace, and massacred at the feet of his master, who vainly strove to cover him with the purple, and to obtain his pardon from the inexorable soldiers. Such was the deplorable weakness of government that the emperor was unable to revenge his murdered friend and his insulted dignity, without stooping to the arts of patience and dissimulation. Epagathus, the principal leader of the mutiny, was removed from Rome, by the honourable employment of prefect of Egypt; from that high rank he was gently degraded to the government of Crete; and when, at length, his popularity among the guards was effaced by time and absence, Alexander ventured to inflict the tardy, but deserved, punishment of his crimes.[74] Under the reign of a just and virtuous prince, the tyranny of the army threatened with instant death his most faithful ministers, who were suspected of an intention to correct their intolerable disorders. The historian Dion Cassius had commanded the Pannonian legions with the spirit of ancient discipline. Their brethren of Rome, embracing the common cause of military licence, demanded the head of the reformer. Alexander, however, instead of yielding to their seditious clamours, showed a just sense of his merit and services, by appointing him his colleague in the consulship, and defraying from his own treasury the expense of that vain dignity; but, as it was justly apprehended that if the soldiers beheld him with the ensigns of his office they would revenge the insult in his blood, the nominal first magistrate of the staff retired, by the emperor's advice, from the city, and spent the greatest part of his consulship at his villas in Campania.[75]

The lenity of the emperor confirmed the insolence of the troops; the legions imitated the example of the guards, and defended their prerogative of licentiousness with the same furious obstinacy. The administration of Alexander was an unavailing struggle against the corruption of his age. In Illyricum, in Mauritania, in Armenia, in Mesopotamia, in Germany, fresh mutinies perpetually broke out; his officers were murdered, his authority was insulted, and his life at last sacrificed to the fierce discontents of the army.[76] One particular fact well deserves to be recorded, as it illustrates the manners of the troops, and exhibits a singular instance of their return to a sense of duty and obedience. Whilst the emperor lay at Antioch, in his Persian expedition, the particulars of which we shall hereafter relate, the punishment of some soldiers, who had been discovered in the baths with women, excited a sedition in the legion to which they belonged. Alexander ascended his tribunal, and with a modest firmness represented to the armed multitude the absolute necessity, as well as his inflexible resolution, of correcting the vices introduced by his impure predecessor, and of maintaining the discipline, which could not be relaxed without the ruin of the Roman name and empire. Their clamours interrupted his mild expostulation. 'Reserve your shouts,' said the undaunted emperor, 'till you take the field against the Persians, the Germans, and the Sarmatians. Be silent in the presence of your sovereign and benefactor, who bestows upon you the corn, the clothing, and the money of the provinces. Be silent, or I shall no longer style you soldiers, but *citizens*,[77] if those indeed who disclaim the laws of Rome deserve to be ranked among the meanest of the people.' His menaces inflamed the fury of the legion, and their brandished arms already threatened his person. 'Your courage,' resumed the intrepid Alexander, 'would be more nobly displayed in the field of battle; *me* you may destroy, you cannot intimidate; and the severe justice of the republic would punish your crime and revenge my death.' The legion still persisted in clamorous sedition, when the emperor pronounced, with a loud voice, the decisive sentence, 'Citizens! lay down your arms, and depart in peace to your respective habitations.' The tempest was instantly appeased; the soldiers, filled with grief and shame, silently confessed the justice of their punishment and the power of discipline, yielded up their arms and military ensigns, and retired in confusion, not to their camp, but to the several inns of the city. Alexander enjoyed, during thirty days, the edifying spectacle of their repentance; nor did he restore them to their former rank in the army, till he had punished with death those tribunes whose connivance had occasioned the mutiny. The grateful legion served the emperor whilst living, and revenged him when dead.[78]

The resolutions of the multitude generally depend on a moment; and the caprice of passion might equally determine the seditious legion to lay down their arms at the emperor's feet, or to plunge them into his breast. Perhaps, if the singular transaction had been investigated by the penetration of a philosopher, we should discover the secret causes which on that occasion authorised the boldness of the prince, and commanded the obedience of the troops; and perhaps, if it had been related by a judicious historian, we should find this action, worthy of Caesar himself, reduced nearer to the level of probability and the common standard of the character of Alexander Severus. The abilities of that amiable prince seem to have been inadequate to the difficulties of his situation, the firmness of his conduct inferior to the purity of his intentions. His virtues, as well as the vices of Elagabalus, contracted a tincture of weakness and effeminacy from the soft climate of Syria, of which he was a native; though he blushed at his foreign origin, and listened with a vain complacency to the flattering genealogists, who derived his race from the ancient stock of Roman nobility.[79] The pride and avarice of his mother cast a shade on the glories of his reign; and by exacting from his riper years the same dutiful obedience which she had justly claimed from his unexperienced youth, Mamaea exposed to public ridicule both her son's character and her own.[80] The fatigues of the Persian war irritated the military discontent; the unsuccessful event degraded the reputation of the emperor as a general, and even as a soldier. Every cause prepared, and every circumstance hastened, a revolution, which distracted the Roman empire with a long series of intestine calamities.

The dissolute tyranny of Commodus, the civil wars occasioned by his death, and the new maxims of policy introduced by the house of Severus, had all contributed to increase the dangerous power of the army, and to obliterate the faint image of laws and liberty that was still impressed on the minds of the Romans. This internal change, which undermined the foundations of the empire, we have endeavoured to explain with some degree of order and perspicuity. The personal characters of the emperors, their victories, laws, follies and fortunes, can interest us no further than as they are connected with the general history of the Decline and Fall of the monarchy. Our constant attention to that great object will not suffer us to overlook a most important edict of Antoninus Caracalla, which communicated to all the free inhabitants of the empire the name and privileges of Roman citizens. His unbounded liberality flowed not, however, from the sentiments of a generous mind; it was the sordid result of avarice, and will naturally be illustrated by some observations on the finances of that state, from the victorious ages of the commonwealth to the reign of Alexander Severus.

The siege of Veii in Tuscany, the first considerable enterprise of the Romans, was protracted to the tenth year, much less by the strength of the place than by the unskilfulness of the besiegers. The unaccustomed hardships of so many winter campaigns, at the distance of near twenty miles from home,[81] required more than common encouragements; and the senate wisely prevented the clamours of the people, by the institution of a regular pay for the soldiers, which was levied by a general tribute, assessed according to an equitable proportion on the property of the citizens.[82] During more than two hundred years after the conquest of Veii, the victories of the republic added less to the wealth than to the power of Rome. The states of Italy paid their tribute in military service only, and the vast force, both by sea and land, which was exerted in the Punic wars, was maintained at the expense of the Romans themselves. That high-spirited people (such is often the generous enthusiasm of freedom) cheerfully submitted to the most excessive but voluntary burdens, in the just confidence that they should speedily enjoy the rich harvest of their labours. Their expectations were not disappointed. In the course of a few years, the riches of Syracuse, of Carthage, of Macedonia, and of Asia, were brought in triumph to Rome. The treasures of Perseus alone amounted to near two millions sterling, and the Roman people, the sovereign of so many nations, was for ever delivered from the weight of taxes.[83] The increasing revenue of the provinces was found sufficient to defray the ordinary establishment of war and government, and the superfluous mass of gold and silver was deposited in the temple of Saturn, and reserved for any unforeseen emergency of the state.[84]

History has never perhaps suffered a greater or more irreparable injury than in the loss of that curious register bequeathed by Augustus to the senate, in which that experienced prince so accurately balanced the revenues and expenses of the Roman empire.[85] Deprived of this clear and comprehensive estimate, we are reduced to collect a few imperfect hints from such of the ancients as have accidentally turned aside from the splendid to the more useful parts of history. We are informed that, by the conquests of Pompey, the tributes of Asia were raised from fifty to one hundred and thirty-five millions of drachms, or about four millions and a half sterling.[86] Under the last and most indolent of the Ptolemies, the revenue of Egypt is said to have amounted to twelve thousand five hundred talents; a sum equivalent to more than two millions and a half of our money, but which was afterwards considerably improved by the more exact economy of the Romans, and the increase of the trade of Ethiopia and India.[87] Gaul was enriched by rapine, as Egypt was by commerce, and the tributes of those two great provinces have been compared as nearly equal to each other in value.[88] The ten thousand Euboic or Phoenician talents, about four millions sterling,[89] which vanquished Carthage was condemned to pay within the term of fifty years, were a slight acknowledgment of the superiority of Rome,[90] and cannot bear the least proportion with the taxes afterwards raised both on the lands and on the persons of the inhabitants, when the fertile coast of Africa was reduced into a province.[91]

Spain, by a very singular fatality, was the Peru and Mexico of the old world. The discovery of the rich western continent by the Phoenicians, and the oppression of the simple natives, who were compelled to labour in their own mines for the benefit of strangers, form an exact type of the more recent history of Spanish America.[92] The Phoenicians were acquainted only with the sea-coast of Spain; avarice as well as ambition carried the arms of Rome and Carthage into the heart of the country, and almost every part of the soil was found pregnant with copper, silver, and gold. Mention is made of a mine near Carthagena which yielded every day twenty-five thousand drachms of silver, or about three hundred thousand pounds a year.[93] Twenty thousand pounds weight of gold was annually received from the provinces of Asturia, Gallicia, and Lusitania.[94]

We want both leisure and materials to pursue this curious inquiry through the many potent states that were annihilated in the Roman empire. Some notion, however, may be formed of the revenue of the provinces where considerable wealth had been deposited by nature, or collected by man, if we observe the severe attention that was directed to the abodes of solitude and sterility. Augustus once received a petition from the inhabitants of Gyarus, humbly praying that they might be relieved from one third of their excessive impositions. Their whole tax amounted indeed to no more than one hundred and fifty drachms, or about five pounds; but Gyarus was a little island, or rather a rock, of the Aegean Sea, destitute of fresh water and every necessary of life, and inhabited only by a few wretched fishermen.[95]

From the faint glimmerings of such doubtful and scattered lights, we should be inclined to believe, first, that (with every fair allowance for the difference of times and circumstances) the general income of the Roman provinces could seldom amount to less than fifteen or twenty millions of our money;[96] and, secondly, that so ample a revenue must have been fully adequate to all the expenses of the moderate government instituted by Augustus, whose court was the modest family of a private senator, and whose military establishment was calculated for the defence of the frontiers, without any aspiring views of conquest, or any serious apprehension of a foreign invasion.

Notwithstanding the seeming probability of both these conclusions, the latter of them at least is positively disowned by the language and conduct of Augustus. It is not easy to determine whether, on this occasion, he acted as the common father of the Roman world, or as the oppressor of liberty; whether he wished to relieve the provinces, or to impoverish the senate and the equestrian order. But no sooner had he assumed the reins of government than he frequently intimated the insufficiency of the tributes, and the necessity of throwing an equitable proportion of the public burden upon Rome and Italy. In the prosecution of this unpopular design, he advanced, however, by cautious and well-weighed steps. The introduction of customs was followed by the establishment of an excise, and the scheme of taxation was completed by an artful assessment on the real and personal property of the Roman citizens, who had been exempted from any kind of contribution above a century and a half.

I.   In a great empire like that of Rome, a natural balance of money must have gradually established itself. It has been already observed that, as the wealth of the provinces was attracted to the capital by the strong hand of conquest and power, so a considerable part of it was restored to the industrious provinces by the gentle influence of commerce and arts. In the reign of Augustus and his successors, duties were imposed on every kind of merchandise, which through a thousand channels flowed to the great centre of opulence and luxury; and in whatsoever manner the law was expressed, it was the Roman purchaser, and not the provincial merchant, who paid the tax.[97] The rate of the customs varied from the eighth to the fortieth part of the value of the commodity; and we have a right to suppose that the variation was directed by the unalterable maxims of policy: that a higher duty was fixed on the articles of luxury than on those of necessity, and that the productions raised or manufactured by the labour of the subjects of the empire were treated with more indulgence than was shown to the pernicious, or at least the unpopular, commerce of Arabia and India.[98] There is still extant a long but imperfect catalogue of eastern commodities, which about the time of Alexander Severus were subject to the payment of duties: cinnamon, myrrh, pepper, ginger, and the whole tribe of aromatics; a great variety of precious stones, among which the diamond was the most remarkable for its price, and the emerald for its beauty;[99] Parthian and Babylonian leather, cottons, silks, both raw and manufactured, ebony, ivory, and eunuchs.[100] We may observe that the use and value of those effeminate slaves gradually rose with the decline of the empire.

II.   The excise, introduced by Augustus after the civil wars, was extremely moderate, but it was general. It seldom exceeded one per cent; but it comprehended whatever was sold in the markets or by public auction, from the most considerable purchases of land and houses to those minute objects which can only derive a value from their infinite multitude and daily consumption. Such a tax, as it affects the body of the people, has ever been the occasion of clamour and discontent. An emperor well acquainted with the wants and resources of the state was obliged to declare, by a public edict, that the support of the army depended in a great measure on the produce of the excise.[101]

III.   When Augustus resolved to establish a permanent military force for the defence of his government against foreign and domestic enemies, he instituted a peculiar treasury for the pay of the soldiers, the rewards of the veterans, and the extraordinary expenses of war. The ample revenue of the excise, though peculiarly appropriated to those uses, was found inadequate. To supply the deficiency, the emperor suggested a new tax of five per cent on all legacies and inheritances. But the nobles of Rome were more tenacious of property than of freedom. Their indignant murmurs were received by Augustus with his usual temper. He candidly referred the whole business to the senate, and exhorted them to provide for the public service by some other expedient of a less odious nature. They were divided and perplexed. He insinuated to them that their obstinacy would oblige him to *propose* a general land-tax and capitation. They acquiesced in silence.[102] The new imposition on legacies and inheritances was however mitigated by some restrictions. It did not take place unless the object was of a certain value, most probably of fifty or an hundred pieces of gold:[103] nor could it be exacted from the nearest of kin on the father's side.[104] When the rights of nature and property were thus secured, it seemed reasonable that a stranger, or a distant relation, who acquired an unexpected accession of fortune, should cheerfully resign a twentieth part of it for the benefit of the state.[105]

Such a tax, plentiful as it must prove in every wealthy community, was most happily suited to the situation of the Romans, who could frame their arbitrary wills, according to the dictates of reason or caprice, without any restraint from the modern fetters of entails and settlements. From various causes, the partiality of paternal affection often lost its influence over the stern patriots of the commonwealth and the dissolute nobles of the empire; and if the father bequeathed to his son the fourth part of his estate, he removed all ground of legal complaint.[106] But a rich childless old man was a domestic tyrant, and his power increased with his years and infirmities. A servile crowd, in which he frequently reckoned praetors and consuls, courted his smiles, pampered his avarice, applauded his follies, served his passions, and waited with impatience for his death. The arts of attendance and flattery were formed into a most lucrative science; those who professed it acquired a peculiar appellation; and the whole city, according to the lively descriptions of satire, was divided between two parties, the hunters and their game.[107] Yet, while so many unjust and extravagant wills were every day dictated by cunning, and subscribed by folly, a few were the result of rational esteem and virtuous gratitude. Cicero, who had so often defended the lives and fortunes of his fellow-citizens, was rewarded with legacies to an amount of an hundred and seventy thousand pounds;[108] nor do the friends of the younger Pliny seem to have been less generous to that amiable orator.[109] Whatever was the motive of the testator, the treasury claimed, without distinction, the twentieth part of his estate; and in the course of two or three generations the whole property of the subject must have gradually passed through the coffers of the state.

In the first and golden years of the reign of Nero, that prince, from a desire of popularity, and perhaps from a blind impulse of benevolence, conceived a wish of abolishing the oppression of the customs and excise.

The wisest senators applauded his magnanimity: but they diverted him from the execution of a design which would have dissolved the strength and resources of the republic.[110] Had it indeed been possible to realise this dream of fancy, such princes as Trajan and the Antonines would surely have embraced with ardour the glorious opportunity of conferring so signal an obligation on mankind. Satisfied, however, with alleviating the public burden, they attempted not to remove it. The mildness and precision of their laws ascertained the rule and measure of taxation, and protected the subject of every rank against arbitrary interpretations, antiquated claims, and the insolent vexation of the farmers of the revenue.[111] For it is somewhat singular that, in every age, the best and wisest of the Roman governors persevered in this pernicious method of collecting the principal branches at least of the excise and customs.[112]

The sentiments, and indeed the situation, of Caracalla were very different from those of the Antonines. Inattentive, or rather averse, to the welfare of his people, he found himself under the necessity of gratifying the insatiate avarice which he had excited in the army. Of the several impositions introduced by Augustus, the twentieth on inheritances and legacies was the most fruitful as well as the most comprehensive. As its influence was not confined to Rome or Italy, the produce continually increased with the gradual extension of the Roman City. The new citizens, though charged on equal terms[113] with the payment of new taxes which had not affected them as subjects, derived an ample compensation from the rank they obtained, the privileges they acquired, and the fair prospect of honours and fortune that was thrown open to their ambition. But the favour which implied a distinction was lost in the prodigality of Caracalla, and the reluctant provincials were compelled to assume the vain title and the real obligations of Roman citizens. Nor was the rapacious son of Severus contented with such a measure of taxation as had appeared sufficient to his moderate predecessors. Instead of a twentieth, he exacted a tenth of all legacies and inheritances; and during his reign (for the ancient proportion was restored after his death) he crushed alike every part of the empire under the weight of his iron sceptre.[114]

When all the provincials became liable to the peculiar impositions of Roman citizens, they seemed to acquire a legal exemption from the tributes which they had paid in their former condition of subjects. Such were not the maxims of government adopted by Caracalla and his pretended son. The old as well as the new taxes were, at the same time, levied in the provinces. It was reserved for the virtue of Alexander to relieve them in a great measure from this intolerable grievance, by reducing the tributes to a thirtieth part of the sum exacted at the time of his accession.[115] It is impossible to conjecture the motive that engaged him to spare so trifling a remnant of the public evil; but the noxious weed, which had not been totally eradicated, again sprang up with the most luxuriant growth, and in the succeeding age darkened the Roman world with its deadly shade. In the course of this history, we shall be too often summoned to explain the land-tax, the capitation, and the heavy contributions of corn, wine, oil, and meat, which were exacted from the provinces for the use of the court, the army, and the capital.

As long as Rome and Italy were respected as the centre of government, a national spirit was preserved by the ancient, and insensibly imbibed by the adopted, citizens. The principal commands of the army were filled by men who had received a liberal education, were well instructed in the advantages of laws and letters, and who had risen by equal steps through the regular succession of civil and military honours.[116] To their influence and example we may partly ascribe the modest obedience of the legions during the two first centuries of the Imperial history.

But when the last enclosure of the Roman constitution was trampled down by Caracalla, the separation of possessions gradually succeeded to the distinction of ranks. The more polished citizens of the internal provinces were alone qualified to act as lawyers and magistrates. The rougher trade of arms was abandoned to the peasants and barbarians of the frontiers, who knew no country but their camp, no science but that of war, no civil laws, and scarcely those of military discipline. With bloody hands, savage manners, and desperate revolutions, they sometimes guarded, but much oftener subverted, the throne of the emperors.

NOTES TO CHAPTER 6

1 *Hist. August.*, p. 71. *Omnia fui, et nihil expedit.*

2 Dion Cassius, lxxvi, 1284.

3 About the year 186. M. de Tillemont is miserably embarrassed with a passage of Dion, in which the Empress Faustina, who died in the year 175, is introduced as having contributed to the marriage of Severus and Julia (lxxiv, 1243). The learned compiler forgot that Dion is relating, not a real fact, but a dream of Severus; and dreams are circumscribed to no limits of time or space. Did M. de Tillemont imagine that marriages were *consummated* in the Temple of Venus at Rome? *Hist. des Empereurs*, tom. iii, 389, note 6.

4 *Hist. August.*, p. 65.

5 *Hist. August.*, p. 85.

6 Dion Cassius, lxxvii, 1304, 1312.

7 See a Dissertation of Menage, at the end of his edition of Diogenes Laertius, *de Feminis Philosophis*.

8 Dion, lxxvi, 1285; Aurelius Victor.

9 Bassianus was his first name, as it had been that of his maternal grandfather. During his reign he assumed the appellation of Antoninus, which is employed by lawyers and ancient historians. After his death, the public indignation loaded him with the nick-names of Tarantus and Caracalla. The first was borrowed from a celebrated Gladiator, the second from a long Gallic gown which he distributed to the people of Rome.

10 The elevation of Caracalla is fixed by the accurate M. de Tillemont to the year 198; the association of Geta, to the year 208.

11 Herodian, iii, 130. The lives of Caracalla and Geta, in the *Augustan History*.

12 Dion, lxxvi, 1280, etc; Herodian, iii, 132, etc.

13 Ossian's Poems, i, 175. [For Ossian, see Chapter 1, footnote 12.]

14 That the Caracul of Ossian is the Caracalla of the Roman history, is, perhaps, the only point of British antiquity in which Mr Macpherson and Mr Whitaker are of the same opinion, and yet the opinion is not without difficulty. In the Caledonian war, the son of Severus was known only by the appellation of Antoninus; and it may seem strange that the Highland bard should describe him by a nickname, invented four years afterwards, scarcely used by the Romans till after the death of that emperor, and seldom employed by the most ancient historians. See Dion, lxxviii, 1317; *Hist. August.*, p. 89; Aurel. Victor; Euseb. in *Chron. ad ann.* 214.

15 Dion, lxxvi, 1282; *Hist. August.*, p. 72; Aurel. Victor.

16 Dion, lxxvi, 1283; *Hist. August.*, p. 89.

17 Dion, lxxvi, 1284; Herodian, iii, 135.

18 Mr Hume is justly surprised at a passage of Herodian (iv, 139), who, on this occasion, represents the Imperial palace as equal in extent to the rest of Rome. The whole region of the Palatine Mount on which it was built occupied, at most, a circumference of eleven or twelve thousand feet. (See the Notitia and Victor, in Nardini's *Roma Antica*.) But we should recollect that the opulent senators had almost surrounded the city with their extensive gardens and suburb palaces, the greatest part of which had been gradually confiscated by the emperors. If Geta resided in the gardens that bore his name on the Janiculum and if Caracalla inhabited the gardens of Maecenas on the Esquiline, the rival brothers were separated from each other by the distance of several miles; and yet the intermediate space was filled by the Imperial gardens of Sallust, of Lucullus, of Agrippa, of Domitian, of Caius, etc., all skirting round the city, and all connected with each other, and with the palace by bridges thrown over the Tiber and the streets. But this explanation of Herodian would require, though it ill deserves, a particular dissertation, illustrated by a map of ancient Rome.

19 Herodian, iv, 139.

20 Herodian, iv, 144.

21 Caracalla consecrated, in the temple of Serapis, the sword with which, as he boasted, he had slain his brother Geta; Dion, lxxvii, 1307.

22 Herodian, iv, 147. In every Roman camp there was a small chapel near the headquarters, in which the statues of the tutelar deities were preserved and adored; and we may remark that the eagles, and other military ensigns, were in the first rank of these deities; an excellent institution, which confirmed discipline by the sanction of religion. See Lipsius, *de Militia Romana*, iv, 5; v, 2.

23 Herodian, iv, 148; Dion, lxxvii, 1289.

24 Geta was placed among the gods. *Sit divus, dum non sit vivus*, said his brother ['Let him be deified, as long as he is not alive']. *Hist. August.*, p. 91. Some marks of Geta's consecration are still found upon medals.

25 Dion, lxxvii, 1301.

26 Dion, lxxvii, 1290; Herodian, iv, 150. Dion (p. 1298) says that the comic poets no longer durst employ the name of Geta in their plays, and that the estates of those who mentioned it in their testaments were confiscated.

27 Caracalla had assumed the names of several conquered nations; Pertinax observed, that the name of *Geticus* (he had obtained some advantage over the Goths or Getae) would be a proper addition to Parthicus, Alemannicus, etc. *Hist. August.*, p. 89.

28 Dion, lxxvii, 1291. He was probably descended from Helvidius Priscus, and Thrasea Paetus, those patriots whose firm, but useless and unseasonable, virtue has been immortalised by Tacitus.

29 It is said that Papinian was himself a relation of the empress Julia.

* *page 115* [i.e. Nero]

30 Tacitus, *Annals*, xiv, 2.

31 *Hist. August.*, p. 88.

32 With regard to Papinian, see Heineccius's *Historia Juris Romani*, 330, etc.

33 Tiberius and Domitian never moved from the neighbourhood of Rome. Nero made a short journey into Greece. '*Et laudatorum Principum usus ex aequo quamvis procul agentibus. Saevi proximis ingruunt.*' Tacitus, *Hist.* iv, 75. ['Those who praise the emperors are usually far distant. Those at hand become their victims.']

34 Dion, lxxvii, 1294.

35 Dion, lxxvii, 1307; Herodian, iv, p. 158. The former represents it as a cruel massacre, the latter as a perfidious one too. It seems probable that the Alexandrians had irritated the tyrant by their railleries, and perhaps by their tumults.

36 Dion, lxxvii, 1296.

37 Dion, lxxvi, 1284. Mr Wotton (*Hist. of Rome*, p. 330) suspects that this maxim was invented by Caracalla himself and attributed to his father.

38 Dion (lxxviii, 1343) informs us that the extraordinary gifts of Caracalla to the army amounted annually to seventy millions of drachmae (about two millions three hundred and fifty thousand pounds). There is another passage in Dion, concerning the military pay, infinitely curious; were it not obscure, imperfect, and probably corrupt. The best sense seems to be, that the Praetorian guards received twelve hundred and fifty drachma (forty pounds) a year (Dion, lxxvii, 1307). Under the reign of Augustus, they were paid at the rate of two drachmae, or denarii, per day, 720 a year (Tacitus, *Annals*, i, 17). Domitian, who increased the soldiers' pay one-fourth, must have raised the Praetorians' to 960 drachmae (Gronovius, *de Pecunia Veteri*, iii, 2). These successive augmentations ruined the empire, for, with the soldiers' pay, their numbers too were increased. We have seen the Praetorians alone increased from 10,000 to 50,000 men.

39 Dion, lxxviii, 1312; Herodian, iv, 168.

* *page 117* [Caracalla]

† *page 117* [in 1700]

‡ *page 117* [Charles XII of Sweden (1682–1718)]

40 The fondness of Caracalla for the name and ensigns of Alexander, is still preserved on the medals of that emperor. See Spanheim, *de Usu Numismatum, Dissertat.* xii. Herodian (iv, 154) had seen very ridiculous pictures, in which a figure was drawn with one side of the face like Alexander, and the other like Caracalla.

41 Herodian, iv, 169; *Hist. August.*, p. 94.

42 Dion, lxxxix, 1350. Elagabalus reproached his predecessor with daring to seat himself on the throne; though, as Praetorian prefect, he could not have been admitted into the senate after the voice of the crier had cleared the house. The personal favour of Plautianus and Sejanus had broke through the established

rule. They rose indeed from the equestrian order; but they preserved the prefecture with the rank of senator, and even with the consulship.

43 He was a native of Caesarea, in Numidia, and began his fortune by serving in the household of Plautian, from whose ruin he narrowly escaped. His enemies asserted that he was born a slave, and had exercised, among other infamous professions, that of Gladiator. The fashion of aspersing the birth and condition of the adversary seems to have lasted from the time of the Greek orators to the learned grammarians of the last age.

44 Both Dion and Herodian speak of the virtues and vices of Macrinus with candour and impartiality; but the author of his Life, in the *Augustan History*, seems to have implicitly copied some of the venal writers employed by Elagabalus to blacken the memory of his predecessor.

45 Dion, lxxviii, 1336. The sense of the author is as clear as the intention of the emperor; but Mr Wotton has mistaken both, by understanding the distinction, not of veterans and recruits, but of old and new legions. *History of Rome*, p. 347.

46 Dion, lxxviii, 1330. The abridgment of Xiphilin, though less particular, is in this place clearer than the original.

47 According to Lampridius (*Hist. August.*, p. 135) Alexander Severus lived twenty-nine years, three months, and seven days. As he was killed March 19, 235, he was born December 12, 205, and was consequently about this time thirteen years old, as his elder cousin might be about seventeen. This computation suits much better the history of the young princes than that of Herodian (v, 181), who represents them as three years younger: whilst, by an opposite error of chronology, he lengthens the reign of Elagabalus two years beyond its real duration. For the particulars of the conspiracy, see Dion, lxxviii, 1339; Herodian, v, 184.

48 By a most dangerous proclamation of the pretended Antoninus, every soldier who brought in his officer's head became entitled to his private estate, as well as to his military commission.

49 Dion, lxxviii, 1344; Herodian, v, 186. The battle was fought near the village of Immae, about two and twenty miles from Antioch.

 * *page 121* [Marcus Aurelius]

50 Dion, lxxix, 1353.

51 Dion, lxxix, 1363; Herodian, v, 189.

52 This name is derived by the learned, from two Syriac words, *Ela*, a god, and *Gabal*, to form, the forming, or plastic God; a proper, and even happy epithet for the Sun. Wotton's *History of Rome*, p. 378.

53 Herodian, v, 190.

 * *page 122* [sacred shields associated with the protection of Rome from the time of Numa]

 † *page 122* [statue of Pallas Athene]

54 He broke into the sanctuary of Vesta, and carried away a statue, which he supposed to be the Palladium; but the vestals boasted that, by a pious fraud, they had imposed a counterfeit image on the profane intruder. *Hist. August.*, p. 103.

55 Dion, lxxix, 1360; Herodian, v, 193. The subjects of the empire were obliged to make liberal presents to the new-married couple, and whatever they had promised during the life of Elagabalus was carefully exacted under the administration of Mamaea.

56 The invention of a new sauce was liberally rewarded: but if it was not relished,

the inventor was confined to eat of nothing else, till he had discovered another more agreeable to the Imperial palate. *Hist. August.*, p. 111.

57 He never would eat sea-fish except at a great distance from the sea; he then would distribute vast quantities of the rarest sorts, brought at an immense expense, to the peasants of the inland country. *Hist. August.*, p. 109.

58 Dion, lxxix, 1358. Herodian, v, 192.

* *page 123* [ungovernable nature]

59 Hierocles enjoyed that honour, but he would have been supplanted by one Zoticus, had he not contrived by a potion, to enervate the powers of his rival, who, being found on trial unequal to his reputation, was driven with ignominy from the palace. Dion, lxxix, 1363, 1364. A dancer was made prefect of the city, a charioteer prefect of the watch, a barber prefect of the provisions. These three ministers, with many inferior officers, were all recommended *enormitate membrorum* ['for the enormous size of their genitals']. *Hist. August.*, p. 105.

60 Even the credulous compiler of his Life, in the *Augustan History* (p. 111), is inclined to suspect that his vices may have been exaggerated.

61 Dion, lxxix; 1366. Herodian, v, 195–210; *Hist. August.*, p 105. The last of the three historians [Lampridius] seems to have followed the best authors in his account of the revolution.

62 The era of the death of Elagabalus, and of the accession of Alexander, has employed the learning and ingenuity of Pagi, Tillemont, Valsecchi, Vignoli, and Torre, bishop of Adria. The question is most assuredly intricate; but I still adhere to the authority of Dion, the truth of whose calculations is undeniable, and the purity of whose text is justified by the agreement of Xiphilin, Zonaras, and Cedrenus. Elagabalus reigned three years, nine months, and four days, from his victory over Macrinus, and was killed March 10, 222. But what shall we reply to the medals, undoubtedly genuine, which reckon the fifth year of his tribunitian power? We shall reply, with the learned Valsecchi, that the usurpation of Macrinus was annihilated, and that the son of Caracalla dated his reign from his father's death. After resolving this great difficulty, the smaller knots of this question may be easily untied, or cut asunder.

63 *Hist. August.*, p. 114. By this unusual precipitation, the senate meant to confound the hopes of pretenders, and prevent the factions of the armies.

64 Metellus Numidicus, the censor, acknowledged to the Roman people, in a public oration, that, had kind Nature allowed us to exist without the help of women, we should be delivered from a very troublesome companion; and he could recommend matrimony only as the sacrifice of private pleasure to public duty. Aulus Gellius, i, 6.

* *page 125* [mother of Nero]

65 Tacitus, *Annals*, xiii, 5.

66 *Hist. August.*, pp. 102, 107.

67 Dion, lxxx, 1369; Herodian, vi, 206; *Hist. August.*, p. 131. Herodian represents the patrician as innocent. The *Augustan History*, on the authority of Dexippus, condemns him as guilty of a conspiracy against the life of Alexander. It is impossible to pronounce between them: but Dion is an irreproachable witness of the jealousy and cruelty of Mamaea towards the young empress, whose hard fate Alexander lamented, but durst not oppose.

68 Herodian, vi, 203. *Hist. August.*, p. 119. The latter insinuates that, when any law was to be passed, the council was assisted by a number of able lawyers and

experienced senators, whose opinions were separately given and taken down in writing.

* *page 126* [anticipated]

69 See his life in the *Augustan History*. The undistinguishing compiler has buried these interesting anecdotes under a load of trivial and unmeaning circumstances.

70 See the 13th Satire of Juvenal.

71 *Hist. August.*, p. 119.

72 See in the *Hist. August.*, pp. 116, 117, the whole contest between Alexander and the senate, extracted from the journals of that assembly. It happened on the sixth of March, probably of the year 223, when the Romans had enjoyed, almost a twelvemonth, the blessings of his reign. Before the appellation of Antoninus was offered him as a title of honour, the senate waited to see whether Alexander would not assume it as a family name.

73 It was a favourite saying of the emperor's, '*se milites magis servare, quam seipsum; quod salus publica in his esset.*' *Hist. August.*, p. 130. ['that he pursued the soldiers' interests rather than his own, since the public safety depended on them.']

74 Though the author of the life of Alexander (*Hist. August.*, p. 132) mentions the sedition raised against Ulpian by the soldiers, he conceals the catastrophe, as it might discover a weakness in the administration of his hero. From this designed omission, we may judge of the weight and candour of that author.

75 For an account of Ulpian's fate and his own danger, see the mutilated conclusion of Dion's *History*, lxxx, 1371.

76 Annotat. Reimar. ad Dion Cassius, lxxx, 1369.

77 Julius Caesar had appeased a sedition with the same word, *Quirites*: which, thus opposed to *Soldiers*, was used in a sense of contempt, and reduced the offenders to the less honourable condition of mere citizens. Tacitus, *Annals*, i. 43.

78 *Hist. August.*, p. 132.

79 From the Metelli. *Hist. August.*, p. 129. The choice was judicious. In one short period of twelve years, the Metelli could reckon seven consulships, and five triumphs. See Velleius Paterculus, ii. 11, and the *Fasti*.

80 The life of Alexander, in the *Augustan History*, is the mere idea of a perfect prince, an awkward imitation of the *Cyropaedia* [an idealised life of Cyrus, founder of the Persian empire, by Xenophon]. The account of his reign, as given by Herodian, is rational and moderate, consistent with the general history of the age; and, in some of the most invidious particulars, confirmed by the decisive fragments of Dion. Yet from a very paltry prejudice, the greater number of our modern writers abuse Herodian, and copy the *Augustan History*. See Mess. de Tillemont and Wotton. From the opposite prejudice, the Emperor Julian (*in Caesarib.*, p. 315) dwells with a visible satisfaction on the effeminate weakness of the Syrian, and the ridiculous avarice of his mother.

81 According to the more accurate Dionysius, the city itself was only an hundred stadia, or twelve miles and a half from Rome; though some out-posts might be advanced farther on the side of Etruria. Nardini, in a professed treatise, has combated the popular opinion and the authority of two popes, and has removed Veii from Civita Castellana, to a little spot called Isola, in the midway between Rome and the lake Bracciano.

82 See the 4th and 5th books of Livy. In the Roman census, property, power and taxation, were commensurate with each other.

83 Pliny, *Hist. Natur.*, xxxiii. 3; Cicero *de Officiis*, ii, 22; Plutarch in *P. Aemil.*, p. 275.

84 See a fine description of this accumulated wealth of ages, in Lucan's *Phars.* iii, 155, etc.

85 Tacitus in *Annals*, i, 11. It seems to have existed in the time of Appian [Alexandrian historian, 2nd century ad].

86 Plutarch *in Pompeio*, p. 642.

87 Strabo, xvii, 798.

88 Velleius Paterculus, ii, 39. He seems to give the preference to the revenue of Gaul.

89 The Euboic, the Phoenician, and Alexandrian talents, were double in weight to the Attic. See Hooper on ancient weights and measures, p. iv. c. 5. It is very probable that the same talent was carried from Tyre to Carthage.

90 Polyb. xv, 2.

91 Appian *in Punicis*, p. 84.

92 Diodorus Siculus, Bk v. Cadiz was built by the Phoenicians a little more than a thousand years before Christ. See Vell. Patercul., i. 2.

93 Strabo, iii, 148.

94 Pliny, *Hist. Natur.*, xxxiii, 3. He mentions likewise a silver mine in Dalmatia, that yielded every day fifty pounds to the state.

95 Strabo, x, 485. Tacitus, *Annals*, iii, 69, and iv, 30. See in Tournefort (*Voyages au Levant*, Lettre viii) a very lively picture of the actual misery of Gyarus.

96 Lipsius, *de magnitudine Romana* (ii, 3) computes the revenue at one hundred and fifty millions of gold crowns; but his whole book, though learned and ingenious, betrays a very heated imagination.

97 Tacitus, *Annals*, xiii, 31.

98 See Pliny (*Hist. Natur.*, vi, 28, and xii, 18). His observation, that the Indian commodities were sold at Rome at a hundred times their original price, may give us some notion of the produce of the customs, since that original price amounted to more than eight hundred thousand pounds.

99 The ancients were unacquainted with the art of cutting diamonds.

100 M. Bouchaud, in his treatise *de l'Impôt chez les Romains*, has transcribed this catalogue from the *Digest*, and attempts to illustrate it by a very prolix commentary.

101 Tacitus, *Annals*, i, 78. Two years afterwards, the reduction of the poor kingdom of Cappadocia gave Tiberius a pretence for diminishing the excise to one half; but the relief was of a very short duration.

102 Dion Cassius, lv, 799, and lvi, 825.

103 The sum is only fixed by conjecture.

104 As the Roman law subsisted for many ages, the *cognati*, or relations on the mother's side, were not called to the succession. This harsh institution was gradually undermined by humanity, and finally abolished by Justinian.

105 Pliny, *Panegyricus*, c. 37.

106 See Heineccius in the *Antiquit. Juris Romani*, Bk ii.

107 Horace, II *Sat.* v; Petron. c. 116, etc. Pliny, *Epist.* ii, 20.

108 Cicero in *Philipp.* ii, 16.

109 See his epistles. Every such will gave him an occasion of displaying his

reverence to the dead, and his justice to the living. He reconciled both, in his behaviour to a son who had been disinherited by his mother (v, 1).

110 Tacitus, *Annals*, xiii, 50; *Esprit des Loix*, xii, 19. [Montesquieu]

111 See Pliny's *Panegyric*, the *Augustan History*, and Burman. *de Vectigal.* passim.

112 The tributes (properly so called) were not farmed; since the good princes often remitted many millions of arrears.

113 The situation of the new citizens is minutely described by Pliny (*Panegyric.* 37, 38, 39). Trajan published a law very much in their favour.

114 Dion, lxxvii, 1295.

115 He who paid ten *aurei*, the usual tribute, was charged with no more than the third part of an *aureus*, and proportional pieces of gold were coined by Alexander's order. *Hist. August.*, p. 127 with the commentary of Salmasius.

116 See the lives of Agricola, Vespasian, Trajan, Severus, and his three competitors; and indeed of all the eminent men of those times.

CHAPTER 7

*The elevation and tyranny of Maximin – rebellion in Africa
and Italy, under the authority of the Senate – civil wars
and seditions – violent deaths of Maximin and his son,
of Maximus and Balbinus, and of the three Gordians –
usurpation and secular games of Philip*

Of the various forms of government which have prevailed in the world, an hereditary monarchy seems to present the fairest scope for ridicule. Is it possible to relate without an indignant smile, that, on the father's decease, the property of a nation, like that of a drove of oxen, descends to his infant son, as yet unknown to mankind and to himself, and that the bravest warriors and the wisest statesmen, relinquishing their natural right to empire, approach the royal cradle with bended knees and protestations of inviolable fidelity? Satire and declamation may paint these obvious topics in the most dazzling colours, but our more serious thoughts will respect a useful prejudice, that establishes a rule of succession, independent of the passions of mankind; and we shall cheerfully acquiesce in any expedient which deprives the multitude of the dangerous, and indeed the ideal, power of giving themselves a master.

In the cool shade of retirement, we may easily devise imaginary forms of government, in which the sceptre shall be constantly bestowed on the most worthy by the free and incorrupt suffrage of the whole community. Experience overturns these airy fabrics, and teaches us that in a large society the election of a monarch can never devolve to the wisest or to the most numerous part of the people. The army is the only order of men sufficiently united to concur in the same sentiments, and powerful enough to impose them on the rest of their fellow-citizens; but the temper of soldiers, habituated at once to violence and to slavery, renders them very unfit guardians of a legal or even a civil constitution. Justice, humanity, or political wisdom, are qualities they are too little acquainted with in themselves to appreciate them in others. Valour will acquire their esteem, and liberality will purchase their suffrage; but the first of these merits is often lodged in the most savage breasts; the latter can only exert itself at the expense of the public; and both may be turned against the possessor of the throne by the ambition of a daring rival.

The superior prerogative of birth, when it has obtained the sanction of time and popular opinion, is the plainest and least invidious of all distinctions among mankind. The acknowledged right extinguishes the hopes of faction, and the conscious security disarms the cruelty of the monarch. To the firm establishment of this idea we owe the peaceful succession and mild administration of European monarchies. To the defect of it we must attribute the frequent civil wars, through which an Asiatic despot is obliged to cut his way to the throne of his fathers. Yet, even in the East, the sphere of contention is usually limited to the princes of the reigning house, and, as soon as the more fortunate competitor has removed his brethren, by the sword and the bow-string, he no longer entertains any jealousy of his meaner subjects. But the Roman empire, after the authority of the senate had sunk into contempt, was a vast scene of confusion. The royal, and even noble, families of the provinces had long since been led in triumph before the car of the haughty republicans. The ancient families of Rome had successively fallen beneath the tyranny of the Caesars; and, whilst those princes were shackled by the forms of a commonwealth, and disappointed by the repeated failure of their posterity,[1] it was impossible that any idea of hereditary succession should have taken root in the minds of their subjects. The right to the throne, which none could claim from birth, every one assumed from merit. The daring hopes of ambition were set loose from the salutary restraints of law and prejudice, and the meanest of mankind might, without folly, entertain a hope of being raised by valour and fortune to a rank in the army, in which a single crime would enable him to wrest the sceptre of the world from his feeble and unpopular master. After the murder of Alexander Severus and the elevation of Maximin, no emperor could think himself safe upon the throne, and every barbarian peasant of the frontier might aspire to that august but dangerous station.

About thirty-two years before that event, the emperor Severus, returning from an Eastern expedition, halted in Thrace, to celebrate, with military games, the birthday of his younger son, Geta. The country flocked in crowds to behold their sovereign, and a young barbarian of gigantic stature earnestly solicited, in his rude dialect, that he might be allowed to contend for the prize of wrestling. As the pride of discipline would have been disgraced in the overthrow of a Roman soldier by a Thracian peasant, he was matched with the stoutest followers of the camp, sixteen of whom he successively laid on the ground. His victory was rewarded by some trifling gifts, and a permission to enlist in the troops. The next day the happy barbarian was distinguished above a crowd of recruits, dancing and exulting after the fashion of his country. As soon as he perceived that he had attracted the emperor's notice, he instantly ran up to his horse, and followed him on foot, without the least appearance of fatigue, in a long and rapid career. 'Thracian,' said Severus, with astonishment, 'art thou disposed to wrestle after thy race?' 'Most willingly, Sir,' replied the unwearied youth, and, almost in a breath, overthrew seven of the strongest soldiers in the army. A gold collar was the prize of his matchless vigour and activity, and he was immediately appointed to serve in the horse-guards who always attended on the person of the sovereign.[2]

Maximin, for that was his name, though born on the territories of the empire, descended from a mixed race of barbarians. His father was a Goth, and his mother of the nation of the Alani. He displayed on every occasion a valour equal to his strength; and his native fierceness was soon tempered or disguised by the knowledge of the world. Under the reign of Severus and his son, he obtained the rank of centurion, with the favour and esteem of both those princes, the former of whom was an excellent judge of merit. Gratitude forbade Maximin to serve under the assassin of Caracalla. Honour taught him to decline the effeminate insults of Elagabalus. On the accession of Alexander he returned to court, and was placed by that prince in a station useful to the service and honourable to himself. The fourth legion, to which he was appointed tribune, soon became, under his care, the best disciplined of the whole army. With the general applause of the soldiers, who bestowed on their favourite hero the names of Ajax and Hercules, he was successively promoted to the first military command,[3] and had not he still retained too much of his savage origin, the emperor might perhaps have given his own sister in marriage to the son of Maximin.[4]

Instead of securing his fidelity, these favours served only to inflame the ambition of the Thracian peasant, who deemed his fortune inadequate to his merit as long as he was constrained to acknowledge a superior. Though a stranger to real wisdom, he was not devoid of a selfish cunning, which showed him that the emperor had lost the affection of the army, and taught him to improve their discontent to his own advantage. It is easy for faction and calumny to shed their poison on the administration of the best of princes, and to accuse even their virtues by artfully confounding them with those vices to which they bear the nearest affinity. The troops listened with pleasure to the emissaries of Maximin. They blushed at their own ignominious patience, which, during thirteen years, had supported the vexatious discipline imposed by an effeminate Syrian, the timid slave of his mother and of the senate. It was time, they cried, to cast away that useless phantom of the civil power, and to elect for their prince and general a real soldier, educated in camps, exercised in war, who would assert the glory, and distribute among his companions the treasures, of the empire. A great army was at that time assembled on the banks of the Rhine, under the command of the emperor himself, who, almost immediately after his return from the Persian war, had been obliged to march against the barbarians of Germany. The important care of training and reviewing the new levies was intrusted to Maximin. One day, as he entered the field of exercise, the troops either from a sudden impulse or a formed conspiracy, saluted him emperor, silenced by their loud acclamations his obstinate refusal, and hastened to consummate their rebellion by the murder of Alexander Severus.

The circumstances of his death are variously related. The writers who suppose that he died in ignorance of the ingratitude and ambition of

Maximin affirm that, after taking a frugal repast in the sight of the army, he retired to sleep, and that about the seventh hour of the day a party of his own guards broke into the Imperial tent, and, with many wounds, assassinated their virtuous and unsuspecting prince.[5] If we credit another, and indeed a more probable, account, Maximin was invested with the purple by a numerous detachment, at the distance of several miles from the head quarters, and he trusted for success rather to the secret wishes than to the public declarations of the great army. Alexander had sufficient time to awaken a faint sense of loyalty among his troops; but their reluctant professions of fidelity quickly vanished on the appearance of Maximin, who declared himself the friend and advocate of the military order, and was unanimously acknowledged emperor of the Romans by the applauding legions. The son of Mamaea, betrayed and deserted, withdrew into his tent, desirous at least to conceal his approaching fate from the insults of the multitude. He was soon followed by a tribune and some centurions, the ministers of death; but instead of receiving with manly resolution the inevitable stroke, his unavailing cries and entreaties disgraced the last moments of his life, and converted into contempt some portion of the just pity which his innocence and misfortunes must inspire. His mother, Mamaea, whose pride and avarice he loudly accused as the cause of his ruin, perished with her son. The most faithful of his friends were sacrificed to the first fury of the soldiers. Others were reserved for the more deliberate cruelty of the usurper, and those who experienced the mildest treatment were stripped of their employments and ignomini-ously driven from the court and army.[6]

The former tyrants Caligula and Nero, Commodus and Caracalla, were all dissolute and unexperienced youths,[7] educated in the purple, and corrupted by the pride of empire, the luxury of Rome, and the perfidious voice of flattery. The cruelty of Maximin was derived from a different source, the fear of contempt. Though he depended on the attachment of the soldiers, who loved him for virtues like their own, he was conscious that his mean and barbarian origin, his savage appearance, and his total ignorance of the arts and institutions of civil life,[8] formed a very unfavourable contrast with the amiable manners of the unhappy Alexander. He remembered that, in his humbler fortune, he had often waited before the doors of the haughty nobles of Rome, and had been denied admittance by the insolence of their slaves. He recollected too the friendship of a few who had relieved his poverty, and assisted his rising hopes. But those who had spurned, and those who had protected, the Thracian, were guilty of the same crime, the knowledge of his original obscurity. For this crime many were put to death; and by the execution of several of his benefactors Maximin published, in characters of blood, the indelible history of his baseness and ingratitude.[9]

The dark and sanguinary soul of the tyrant was open to every suspicion against those among his subjects who were the most distinguished by their birth or merit. Whenever he was alarmed with the sound of treason, his cruelty was unbounded and unrelenting. A conspiracy against his life was either discovered or imagined, and Magnus, a consular senator, was named as the principal author of it. Without a witness, without a trial, and without an opportunity of defence, Magnus, with four thousand of his supposed accomplices, were put to death. Italy and the whole empire were infested with innumerable spies and informers. On the slightest accusation, the first of the Roman nobles, who had governed provinces, commanded armies, and been adorned with the consular and triumphal ornaments, were chained on the public carriages, and hurried away to the emperor's presence. Confiscation, exile, or simple death, were esteemed uncommon instances of his lenity. Some of the unfortunate sufferers he ordered to be sewed up in the hides of slaughtered animals, others to be exposed to wild beasts, others again to be beaten to death with clubs. During the three years of his reign he disdained to visit either Rome or Italy. His camp, occasionally removed from the banks of the Rhine to those of the Danube, was the seat of his stern despotism, which trampled on every principle of law and justice, and was supported by the avowed power of the sword.[10] No man of noble birth, elegant accomplishments, or knowledge of civil business, was suffered near his person; and the court of a Roman emperor revived the idea of those ancient chiefs of slaves and gladiators, whose savage power had left a deep impression of terror and detestation.[11]

As long as the cruelty of Maximin was confined to the illustrious senators, or even to the bold adventurers who in the court or army expose themselves to the caprice of fortune, the body of the people viewed their sufferings with indifference, or perhaps with pleasure. But the tyrant's avarice, stimulated by the insatiate desires of the soldiers, at length attacked the public property. Every city of the empire was possessed of an independent revenue, destined to purchase corn for the multitude, and to supply the expenses of the games and entertainments. By a single act of authority, the whole mass of wealth was at once confiscated for the use of the Imperial treasury. The temples were stripped of their most valuable offerings of gold and silver, and the statues of gods, heroes, and emperors, were melted down and coined into money. These impious orders could not be executed without tumults and massacres, as in many places the people chose rather to die in the defence of their altars than to behold in the midst of peace their cities exposed to the rapine and cruelty of war. The soldiers themselves, among whom this sacrilegious plunder was distributed, received it with a blush; and, hardened as they were in acts of violence, they dreaded the just reproaches of their friends and relations. Throughout the Roman world a general cry of indignation was heard, imploring vengeance on the common enemy of human kind; and at length, by an act of private oppression, a peaceful and unarmed province was driven into rebellion against him.[12]

The procurator of Africa was a servant worthy of such a master, who considered the fines and confiscations of the rich as one of the most fruitful branches of the Imperial revenue. An iniquitous sentence had been pronounced against some opulent youths of that country, the execution of which would have stripped them of far the greater part of their patrimony. In this extremity, a resolution that must either complete or prevent their ruin was dictated by despair. A respite of three days, obtained with difficulty from the rapacious treasurer, was employed in collecting from their estates a great number of slaves and peasants blindly devoted to the commands of their lords, and armed with the rustic weapons of clubs and axes. The leaders of the conspiracy, as they were admitted to the audience of the procurator, stabbed him with the daggers concealed under their garments, and, by the assistance of their tumultuary train, seized on the little town of Thysdrus,[13] and erected the standard of rebellion against the sovereign of the Roman empire. They rested their hopes on the hatred of mankind against Maximin, and they judiciously resolved to oppose to that detested tyrant an emperor whose mild virtues had already acquired the love and esteem of the Romans, and whose authority over the province would give weight and stability to the enterprise. Gordianus, their proconsul, and the object of their choice, refused, with unfeigned reluctance, the dangerous honour, and begged with tears that they should suffer him to terminate in peace a long and innocent life, without staining his feeble age with civil blood. Their menaces compelled him to accept the Imperial purple, his only refuge indeed against the jealous cruelty of Maximin; since, according to the reasoning of tyrants, those who have been esteemed worthy of the throne deserve death, and those who deliberate have already rebelled.[14]

The family of Gordianus was one of the most illustrious of the Roman senate. On the father's side he was descended from the Gracchi; on his mother's, from the emperor Trajan. A great estate enabled him to support the dignity of his birth, and in the enjoyment of it he displayed an elegant taste and beneficent disposition. The palace in Rome formerly inhabited by the great Pompey had been, during several generations, in the possession of Gordian's family.[15] It was distinguished by ancient trophies of naval victories, and decorated with the works of modern painting. His villa on the road to Praeneste was celebrated for baths of singular beauty and extent, for three stately rooms of an hundred feet in length, and for a magnificent portico, supported by two hundred columns of the four most curious and costly sorts of marble.[16] The public shows exhibited at his expense, and in which the people were entertained with many hundreds of wild beasts and gladiators,[17] seem to surpass the fortune of a subject; and, whilst the liberality of other magistrates was confined to a few solemn festivals in Rome, the magnificence of Gordian was repeated, when he was aedile, every month in the year, and extended, during his consulship, to the principal cities of Italy. He was twice elevated to the last-mentioned dignity, by Caracalla and by Alexander; for he possessed the uncommon talent of acquiring the esteem of virtuous princes, without alarming the jealousy of tyrants. His long life was innocently spent in the study of letters and the peaceful honours of Rome; and, till he was named proconsul of Africa by the voice of the senate and the approbation of Alexander,[18] he appears prudently to have declined the command of armies and the government of provinces. As long as that emperor lived, Africa was happy under the administration of his worthy representative; after the barbarous Maximin had usurped the throne, Gordianus alleviated the miseries which he was unable to prevent. When he reluctantly accepted the purple, he was above fourscore years old; a last and valuable remains of the happy age of the Antonines, whose virtues he revived in his own conduct, and celebrated in an elegant poem of thirty books. With the venerable proconsul, his son, who had accompanied him into Africa as his lieutenant, was likewise declared emperor. His manners were less pure, but his character was equally amiable with that of his father. Twenty-two acknowledged concubines, and a library of sixty-two thousand volumes, attested the variety of his inclinations; and from the productions which he left behind him, it appears that both the one and the other were designed for use rather than for ostentation.[19] The Roman people acknowledged in the features of the younger Gordian the resemblance of Scipio Africanus, recollected with pleasure that his mother was the granddaughter of Antoninus Pius, and rested the public hope on those latent virtues which had hitherto, as they fondly imagined, lain concealed in the luxurious indolence of a private life.

As soon as the Gordians had appeased the first tumult of a popular election they removed their court to Carthage. They were received with the acclamations of the Africans, who honoured their virtues, and who, since the visit of Hadrian, had never beheld the majesty of a Roman emperor. But these vain acclamations neither strengthened nor confirmed the title of the Gordians. They were induced by principle, as well as interest, to solicit the approbation of the senate; and a deputation of the noblest provincials was sent, without delay, to Rome, to relate and justify the conduct of their countrymen, who, having long suffered with patience, were at length resolved to act with vigour. The letters of the new princes were modest and respectful, excusing the necessity which had obliged them to accept the Imperial title, but submitting their election and their fate to the supreme judgment of the senate.[20]

The inclinations of the senate were neither doubtful nor divided. The birth and noble alliances of the Gordians had intimately connected them with the most illustrious houses of Rome. Their fortune had created many dependants in that assembly, their merit had acquired many friends. Their mild administration opened the flattering prospect of the restoration, not only of the civil but even of the republican government. The terror of military violence, which had first obliged the senate to forget the murder of

Alexander, and to ratify the election of a barbarian peasant,[21] now produced a contrary effect, and provoked them to assert the injured rights of freedom and humanity. The hatred of Maximin towards the senate was declared and implacable; the tamest submission had not appeased his fury, the most cautious innocence would not remove his suspicions; and even the care of their own safety urged them to share the fortune of an enterprise, of which (if unsuccessful) they were sure to be the first victims. These considerations, and perhaps others of a more private nature, were debated in a previous conference of the consuls and the magistrates. As soon as their resolution was decided, they convoked in the temple of Castor the whole body of the senate, according to an ancient form of secrecy,[22] calculated to awaken their attention and to conceal their decrees. 'Conscript fathers,' said the consul Syllanus, 'the two Gordians, both of consular dignity, the one your proconsul, and the other your lieutenant, have been declared emperors by the general consent of Africa. Let us return thanks,' he boldly continued, 'to the youth of Thysdrus; let us return thanks to the faithful people of Carthage, our generous deliverers from a horrid monster. – Why do you hear me thus coolly, thus timidly? Why do you cast these anxious looks on each other? why hesitate? Maximin is a public enemy! may his enmity soon expire with him, and may we long enjoy the prudence and felicity of Gordian the father, the valour and constancy of Gordian the son!'[23] The noble ardour of the consul revived the languid spirit of the senate. By an unanimous decree the election of the Gordians was ratified; Maximin, his son, and his adherents were pronounced enemies of their country, and liberal rewards were offered to whomsoever had the courage and good fortune to destroy them.

During the emperor's absence a detachment of the Praetorian guards remained at Rome, to protect, or rather to command, the capital. The prefect Vitalianus had signalised his fidelity to Maximin by the alacrity with which he had obeyed, and even prevented,* the cruel mandates of the tyrant. His death alone could rescue the authority of the senate, and the lives of the senators, from a state of danger and suspense. Before their resolves had transpired, a quaestor and some tribunes were commissioned to take his devoted† life. They executed the order with equal boldness and success; and, with their bloody daggers in their hands, ran through the streets, proclaiming to the people and the soldiers the news of the happy revolution. The enthusiasm of liberty was seconded by the promise of a large donative in lands and money; the statues of Maximin were thrown down; the capital of the empire acknowledged, with transport, the authority of the two Gordians and the senate;[24] and the example of Rome was followed by the rest of Italy.

A new spirit had arisen in that assembly, whose long patience had been insulted by wanton despotism and military licence. The senate assumed the reins of government, and, with a calm intrepidity, prepared to vindicate by arms the cause of freedom. Among the consular senators recommended by their merit and services to the favour of the emperor Alexander, it was easy to select twenty, not unequal to the command of an army and the conduct of a war. To these was the defence of Italy intrusted. Each was appointed to act in his respective department, authorised to enrol and discipline the Italian youth, and instructed to fortify the ports and highways against the impending invasion of Maximin. A number of deputies, chosen from the most illustrious of the senatorian and equestrian orders, were despatched at the same time to the governors of the several provinces, earnestly conjuring them to fly to the assistance of their country, and to remind the nations of their ancient ties of friendship with the Roman senate and people. The general respect with which these deputies were received, and the zeal of Italy and the provinces in favour of the senate, sufficiently prove that the subjects of Maximin were reduced to that uncommon distress, in which the body of the people has more to fear from oppression than from resistance. The consciousness of that melancholy truth inspires a degree of persevering fury seldom to be found in those civil wars which are artificially supported for the benefit of a few factious and designing leaders.[25]

For, while the cause of the Gordians was embraced with such diffusive ardour, the Gordians themselves were no more. The feeble court of Carthage was alarmed with the rapid approach of Capelianus, governor of Mauritania, who, with a small band of veterans and a fierce host of barbarians, attacked a faithful but unwarlike province. The younger Gordian sallied out to meet the enemy at the head of a few guards, and a numerous undisciplined multitude, educated in the peaceful luxury of Carthage. His useless valour served only to procure him an honourable death in the field of battle. His aged father, whose reign had not exceeded thirty-six days, put an end to his life on the first news of the defeat. Carthage, destitute of defence, opened her gates to the conqueror, and Africa was exposed to the rapacious cruelty of a slave, obliged to satisfy his unrelenting master with a large account of blood and treasure.[26]

The fate of the Gordians filled Rome with just, but unexpected, terror. The senate, convoked in the temple of Concord, affected to transact the common business of the day; and seemed to decline, with trembling anxiety, the consideration of their own, and the public, danger. A silent consternation prevailed on the assembly, till a senator, of the name and family of Trajan, awakened his brethren from their fatal lethargy. He represented to them that the choice of cautious dilatory measures had been long since out of their power; that Maximin, implacable by nature and exasperated by injuries, was advancing towards Italy, at the head of the military force of the empire; and that their only remaining alternative was either to meet him bravely in the field, or tamely to expect the tortures and ignominious death reserved for unsuccessful rebellion. 'We have lost,' continued he, 'two excellent princes; but, unless we desert ourselves, the hopes of the republic have not perished with the Gordians.

Many are the senators whose virtues have deserved, and whose abilities would sustain, the Imperial dignity. Let us elect two emperors, one of whom may conduct the war against the public enemy, whilst his colleague remains at Rome to direct the civil administration. I cheerfully expose myself to the danger and envy of the nomination, and give my vote in favour of Maximus and Balbinus. Ratify my choice, conscript fathers, or appoint, in their place, others more worthy of the empire.' The general apprehension silenced the whispers of jealousy; the merit of the candidates was universally acknowledged; and the house resounded with the sincere acclamations of 'Long life and victory to the Emperors Maximus and Balbinus. You are happy in the judgment of the senate; may the republic be happy under your administration!'[27]

The virtues and the reputation of the new emperors justified the most sanguine hopes of the Romans. The various nature of their talents seemed to appropriate to each his peculiar department of peace and war, without leaving room for jealous emulation. Balbinus was an admired orator, a poet of distinguished fame, and a wise magistrate, who had exercised with innocence and applause the civil jurisdiction in almost all the interior provinces of the empire. His birth was noble,[28] his fortune affluent, his manners liberal and affable. In him, the love of pleasure was corrected by a sense of dignity, nor had the habits of ease deprived him of a capacity for business. The mind of Maximus was formed in a rougher mould. By his valour and abilities he had raised himself from the meanest origin to the first employments of the state and army. His victories over the Sarmatians and the Germans, the austerity of his life, and the rigid impartiality of his justice whilst he was prefect of the city, commanded the esteem of a people whose affections were engaged in favour of the more amiable Balbinus. The two colleagues had both been consul (Balbinus had twice enjoyed that honourable office), both had been named among the twenty lieutenants of the senate; and, since the one was sixty and the other seventy-four years old,[29] they had both attained the full maturity of age and experience.

After the senate had conferred on Maximus and Balbinus an equal portion of the consular and tribunitian powers, the title of Fathers of their country, and the joint office of Supreme Pontiff, they ascended to the Capitol to return thanks to the gods, protectors of Rome.[30] The solemn rites of sacrifice were disturbed by a sedition of the people. The licentious multitude neither loved the rigid Maximus, nor did they sufficiently fear the mild and humane Balbinus. Their increasing numbers surrounded the temple of Jupiter; with obstinate clamours they asserted their inherent right of consenting to the election of their sovereign: and demanded, with an apparent moderation, that, besides the two emperors chosen by the senate, a third should be added of the family of the Gordians, as a just return of gratitude to those princes who had sacrificed their lives for the republic. At the head of the city guards and the youth of the equestrian order, Maximus and Balbinus attempted to cut their way through the seditious multitude. The multitude, armed with sticks and stones, drove them back into the Capitol. It is prudent to yield, when the contest, whatever may be the issue of it, must be fatal to both parties. A boy, only thirteen years of age, the grandson of the elder and nephew of the younger Gordian, was produced to the people, invested with the ornaments and title of Caesar. The tumult was appeased by this easy condescension; and the two emperors, as soon as they had been peaceably acknowledged in Rome, prepared to defend Italy against the common enemy.

Whilst in Rome and Africa revolutions succeeded each other with such amazing rapidity, the mind of Maximin was agitated by the most furious passions. He is said to have received the news of the rebellion of the Gordians, and of the decree of the senate against him, not with the temper of a man, but the rage of a wild beast; which, as it could not discharge itself on the distant senate, threatened the life of his son, of his friends, and of all who ventured to approach his person. The grateful intelligence of the death of the Gordians was quickly followed by the assurance that the senate, laying aside all hopes of pardon or accommodation, had substituted in their room two emperors, with whose merit he could not be unacquainted. Revenge was the only consolation left to Maximin, and revenge could only be obtained by arms. The strength of the legions had been assembled by Alexander from all parts of the empire. Three successful campaigns against the Germans and the Sarmatians had raised their fame, confirmed their discipline, and even increased their numbers, by filling the ranks with the flower of the barbarian youth. The life of Maximin had been spent in war, and the candid severity of history cannot refuse him the valour of a soldier, or even the abilities of an experienced general.[31] It might naturally be expected that a prince of such a character, instead of suffering the rebellion to gain stability by delay, should immediately have marched from the banks of the Danube to those of the Tiber, and that his victorious army, instigated by contempt for the senate, and eager to gather the spoils of Italy, should have burned with impatience to finish the easy and lucrative conquest. Yet, as far as we can trust to the obscure chronology of that period,[32] it appears that the operations of some foreign war deferred the Italian expedition till the ensuing spring. From the prudent conduct of Maximin, we may learn that the savage features of his character have been exaggerated by the pencil of party; that his passions, however impetuous, submitted to the force of reason; and that the barbarian possessed something of the generous spirit of Sylla, who subdued the enemies of Rome before he suffered himself to revenge his private injuries.[33]

When the troops of Maximin, advancing in excellent order, arrived at the foot of the Julian Alps, they were terrified by the silence and desolation that reigned on the frontiers of Italy. The villages and open towns had been abandoned, on their approach, by the inhabitants, the cattle was driven away, the provisions removed or destroyed, the bridges broken down, nor was anything left which could afford either shelter or subsistence to an invader. Such had been the wise orders of the generals of the senate, whose design was to protract the war, to ruin the army of Maximin by the slow operation of famine, and to consume his strength in the sieges of the principal cities of Italy, which they had plentifully stored with men and provisions from the deserted country. Aquileia received and withstood the first shock of the invasion. The streams that issue from the head of the Hadriatic gulf, swelled by the melting of the winter snows,[34] opposed an unexpected obstacle to the arms of Maximin. At length, on a singular bridge, constructed, with art and difficulty, of large hogsheads, he transported his army to the opposite bank, rooted up the beautiful vineyards in the neighbourhood of Aquileia, demolished the suburbs, and employed the timber of the buildings in the engines and towers with which on every side he attacked the city. The walls, fallen to decay during the security of a long peace, had been hastily repaired on this sudden emergency; but the firmest defence of Aquileia consisted in the constancy of the citizens; all ranks of whom, instead of being dismayed, were animated by the extreme danger, and their knowledge of the tyrant's unrelenting temper. Their courage was supported and directed by Crispinus and Menophilus, two of the twenty lieutenants of the senate, who, with a small body of regular troops, had thrown themselves into the besieged place. The army of Maximin was repulsed in repeated attacks, his machines destroyed by showers of artificial fire; and the generous enthusiasm of the Aquileians was exalted into a confidence of success, by the opinion that Belenus, their tutelar deity, combated in person in the defence of his distressed worshippers.[35]

The Emperor Maximus, who had advanced as far as Ravenna to secure that important place, and to hasten the military preparations, beheld the event of the war in the more faithful mirror of reason and policy. He was too sensible that a single town could not resist the persevering efforts of a great army; and he dreaded lest the enemy, tired with the obstinate resistance of Aquileia, should on a sudden relinquish the fruitless siege and march directly towards Rome. The fate of the empire and the cause of freedom must then be committed to the chance of a battle; and what arms could he oppose to the veteran legions of the Rhine and Danube? Some troops newly levied among the generous but enervated youth of Italy, and a body of German auxiliaries, on whose firmness, in the hour of trial, it was dangerous to depend. In the midst of these just alarms, the stroke of domestic conspiracy punished the crimes of Maximin and delivered Rome and the senate from the calamities that would surely have attended the victory of an enraged barbarian.

The people of Aquileia had scarcely experienced any of the common miseries of a siege; their magazines were plentifully supplied, and several fountains within the walls assured them of an inexhaustible resource of fresh water. The soldiers of Maximin were, on the contrary, exposed to the inclemency of the season, the contagion of disease, and the horrors of famine. The naked country was ruined, the rivers filled with the slain and polluted with blood. A spirit of despair and disaffection began to diffuse itself among the troops; and, as they were cut off from all intelligence, they easily believed that the whole empire had embraced the cause of the senate, and that they were left as devoted victims to perish under the impregnable walls of Aquileia. The fierce temper of the tyrant was exasperated by disappointments, which he imputed to the cowardice of his army; and his wanton and ill-timed cruelty, instead of striking terror, inspired hatred and a just desire of revenge. A party of Praetorian guards, who trembled for their wives and children in the camp of Alba, near Rome, executed the sentence of the senate. Maximin, abandoned by his guards, was slain in his tent, with his son (whom he had associated to the honours of the purple), Anulinus the prefect, and the principal ministers of his tyranny.[36] The sight of their heads, borne on the point of spears, convinced the citizens of Aquileia that the siege was at an end; the gates of the city were thrown open, a liberal market was provided for the hungry troops of Maximin, and the whole army joined in solemn protestations of fidelity to the senate and people of Rome, and to their lawful emperors Maximus and Balbinus. Such was the deserved fate of a brutal savage, destitute, as he has generally been represented, of every sentiment that distinguishes a civilised, or even a human being. The body was suited to the soul. The stature of Maximin exceeded the measure of eight feet, and circumstances almost incredible are related of his matchless strength and appetite.[37] Had he lived in a less enlightened age, tradition and poetry might well have described him as one of those monstrous giants, whose supernatural power was constantly exerted for the destruction of mankind.

It is easier to conceive than to describe the universal joy of the Roman world on the fall of the tyrant, the news of which is said to have been carried in four days from Aquileia to Rome. The return of Maximus was a triumphal procession; his colleague and young Gordian went out to meet him, and the three princes made their entry into the capital, attended by the ambassadors of almost all the cities of Italy, saluted with the splendid offerings of gratitude and superstition, and received with the unfeigned acclamations of the senate and people, who persuaded themselves that a golden age would succeed to an age of iron.[38] The conduct of the two emperors corresponded with these expectations. They administered justice in person; and the rigour of the one was tempered by the other's clemency. The oppressive taxes with which Maximin had loaded the rights of inheritance and succession were repealed, or at least moderated. Discipline was revived, and with the advice of the senate many wise laws were enacted by their Imperial ministers, who endeavoured to restore a civil constitution on the ruins of military tyranny. 'What reward may we expect for delivering Rome from a monster?' was the question asked by Maximus, in a moment of freedom and confidence. Balbinus answered it without hesitation, 'The love of the senate, of the people, and of all mankind.' 'Alas!' replied his more penetrating colleague, 'Alas! I dread the hatred of the soldiers, and the fatal effects of their resentment.'[39] His apprehensions were but too well justified by the event.

Whilst Maximus was preparing to defend Italy against the common foe, Balbinus, who remained at Rome, had been engaged in scenes of blood and intestine* discord. Distrust and jealousy reigned in the senate; and even in the temples where they assembled every senator carried either open or concealed arms. In the midst of their deliberations, two veterans of the guards, actuated either by curiosity or a sinister motive, audaciously thrust themselves into the house, and advanced by degrees beyond the altar of Victory. Gallicanus, a consular, and Maecenas, a praetorian, senator viewed with indignation their insolent intrusion: drawing their daggers, they laid the spies, for such they deemed them, dead at the foot of the altar, and then, advancing to the door of the senate, imprudently exhorted the multitude to massacre the Praetorians as the secret adherents of the tyrant. Those who escaped the first fury of the tumult took refuge in the camp, which they defended with superior advantage against the reiterated attacks of the people, assisted by the numerous bands of gladiators, the property of opulent nobles. The civil war lasted many days, with infinite loss and confusion on both sides. When the pipes were broken that supplied the camp with water, the Praetorians were reduced to intolerable distress; but, in their turn, they made desperate sallies into the city, set fire to a great number of houses, and filled the streets with the blood of the inhabitants. The emperor Balbinus attempted, by ineffectual edicts and precarious truces, to reconcile the factions of Rome. But their animosity, though smothered for a while, burnt with redoubled violence. The soldiers, detesting the senate and the people, despised the weakness of a prince who wanted either the spirit or the power to command the obedience of his subjects.[40]

After the tyrant's death his formidable army had acknowledged, from necessity rather than from choice, the authority of Maximus, who transported himself without delay to the camp before Aquileia. As soon as he had received their oath of fidelity, he addressed them in terms full of mildness and moderation; lamented rather than arraigned the wild disorders of the times, and assured the soldiers that, of all their past conduct, the senate would remember only their generous desertion of the tyrant and their voluntary return to their duty. Maximus enforced his exhortations by a liberal donative, purified the camp by a solemn sacrifice of expiation, and then dismissed the legions to their several provinces, impressed, as he hoped, with a lively sense of gratitude and obedience.[41] But nothing could reconcile the haughty spirit of the Praetorians. They attended the emperors on the memorable day of their public entry into Rome; but, amidst the general acclamations, the sullen dejected countenance of the guards sufficiently declared that they considered themselves as the object, rather than the partners, of the triumph. When the whole body was united in their camp, those who had served under Maximin, and those who had remained at home, insensibly communicated to each other their complaints and apprehensions. The emperors chosen by the army had perished with ignominy; those elected by the senate were seated on the throne.[42] The long discord between the civil and military powers was decided by a war in which the former had obtained a complete victory. The soldiers must now learn a new doctrine of submission to the senate; and, whatever clemency was affected by that politic assembly, they dreaded a slow revenge, coloured by the name of discipline, and justified by fair pretences of the public good. But their fate was still in their own hands; and, if they had courage to despise the vain terrors of an impotent republic, it was easy to convince the world that those who were masters of the arms were masters of the authority of the state.

When the senate elected two princes, it is probable that, besides the declared reason of providing for the various emergencies of peace and war, they were actuated by the secret desire of weakening by division the despotism of the supreme magistrate. Their policy was effectual, but it proved fatal both to their emperors and to themselves. The jealousy of power was soon exasperated by the difference of character. Maximus despised Balbinus as a luxurious noble, and was in his turn disdained by his colleague as an obscure soldier. Their silent discord was understood rather than seen;[43] but the mutual consciousness prevented them from uniting in any vigorous measures of defence against their common enemies of the Praetorian camp. The whole city was employed in the Capitoline games, and the emperors were left almost alone in the palace. On a sudden they were alarmed by the approach of a troop of desperate assassins. Ignorant of each other's situation or designs, for they already occupied very distant apartments, afraid to give or to receive assistance, they wasted the important moments in idle debates and fruitless recriminations. The arrival of the guards put an end to the vain strife. They seized on these emperors of the senate, for such they called them with malicious contempt, stripped them of their garments, and dragged them in insolent triumph through the streets of Rome, with a design of inflicting a slow and cruel death on these unfortunate princes. The fear of a rescue from the faithful Germans of the Imperial guards shortened their tortures; and their bodies, mangled with a thousand wounds, were left exposed to the insults or to the pity of the populace.[44]

In the space of a few months six princes had been cut off by the sword. Gordian, who had already received the title of Caesar, was the only person that occurred to the soldiers as proper to fill the vacant throne.[45] They carried him to the camp and unanimously saluted him Augustus and Emperor. His name was dear to the senate and people; his tender age promised a long impunity of military licence; and the submission of Rome and the provinces to the choice of the Praetorian guards saved the republic, at the expense indeed of its freedom and dignity, from the horrors of a new civil war in the heart of the capital.[46]

As the third Gordian was only nineteen years of age at the time of his death, the history of his life, were it known to us with greater accuracy than it really is, would contain little more than the account of his education and the conduct of the ministers who by turns abused or guided the simplicity of his inexperienced youth. Immediately after his accession he fell into the hands of his mother's eunuchs, that pernicious vermin of the East, who, since the days of Elagabalus, had infested the Roman palace. By the artful conspiracy of these wretches an impenetrable veil was drawn between an innocent prince and his oppressed subjects, the virtuous disposition of Gordian was deceived, and the honours of the empire sold without his knowledge, though in a very public manner, to the most worthless of mankind. We are ignorant by what fortunate accident the emperor escaped from this ignominious slavery, and devolved his confidence on a minister whose wise counsels had no object except the glory of the sovereign and the happiness of the people. It should seem that love and learning introduced Misitheus to the favour of Gordian. The young prince married the daughter of his master of rhetoric, and promoted his father-in-law to the first offices of the empire. Two admirable letters that passed between them are still extant. The minister, with the conscious dignity of virtue, congratulates Gordian that he is delivered from the tyranny of the eunuchs,[47] and still more, that he is sensible of his deliverance. The emperor acknowledges, with an amiable confusion, the errors of his past conduct; and laments, with singular propriety, the misfortune of a monarch from whom a venal tribe of courtiers perpetually labour to conceal the truth.[48]

The life of Misitheus had been spent in the profession of letters, not of arms; yet such was the versatile genius of that great man that, when he was appointed Praetorian prefect, he discharged the military duties of his place with vigour and ability. The Persians had invaded Mesopotamia, and threatened Antioch. By the persuasion of his father-in-law, the young emperor quitted the luxury of Rome, opened, for the last time recorded in history, the temple of Janus,* and marched in person into the East. On his approach with a great army, the Persians withdrew their garrisons from the cities which they had already taken, and retired from the Euphrates to the Tigris. Gordian enjoyed the pleasure of announcing to the senate the first success of his arms, which he ascribed with a becoming modesty and gratitude to the wisdom of his father and prefect. During the whole expedition, Misitheus watched over the safety and discipline of the army; whilst he prevented their dangerous murmurs by maintaining a regular plenty in the camp, and by establishing ample magazines of vinegar, bacon, straw, barley, and wheat, in all the cities of the frontier.[49] But the prosperity of Gordian expired with Misitheus, who died of a flux, not without very strong suspicions of poison. Philip, his successor in the prefecture, was an Arab by birth, and consequently, in the earlier part of his life, a robber by profession. His rise from so obscure a station to the first dignities of the empire seems to prove that he was a bold and able leader. But his boldness prompted him to aspire to the throne, and his abilities were employed to supplant, not to serve, his indulgent master. The minds of the soldiers were irritated by an artificial scarcity, created by his contrivance in the camp; and the distress of the army was attributed to the youth and incapacity of the prince. It is not in our power to trace the successive steps of the secret conspiracy and open sedition which were at length fatal to Gordian. A sepulchral monument was erected to his memory on the spot[50] where he was killed, near the conflux of the Euphrates with the little river Aboras.[51] The fortunate Philip, raised to the empire by the votes of the soldiers, found a ready obedience from the senate and the provinces.[52]

We cannot forbear transcribing the ingenious, though somewhat fanciful, description, which a celebrated writer of our own times has traced of the military government of the Roman empire. 'What in that age was called the Roman empire was only an irregular republic, not unlike the aristocracy[53] of Algiers,[54] where the militia, possessed of the sovereignty, creates and deposes a magistrate, who is styled a Dey. Perhaps, indeed, it may be laid down as a general rule, that a military government is, in some respects, more republican than monarchical. Nor can it be said that the soldiers only partook of the government by their disobedience and rebellions. The speeches made to them by the emperors, were they not at length of the same nature as those formerly pronounced to the people by the consuls and the tribunes? And, although the armies had no regular place or forms of assembly, though their debates were short, their action sudden, and their resolves seldom the result of cool reflection, did they not dispose, with absolute sway, of the public fortune? What was the emperor, except the minister of a violent government, elected for the private benefit of the soldiers?

'When the army had elected Philip, who was Praetorian prefect to the third Gordian, the latter demanded that he might remain sole emperor; he was unable to obtain it. He requested that the power might be equally divided between them; the army would not listen to his speech. He consented to be degraded to the rank of Caesar; the favour was refused him. He desired, at least, he might be appointed Praetorian prefect; his prayer was rejected. Finally, he pleaded for his life. The army, in these several judgments, exercised the supreme magistracy.' According to the historian, whose doubtful narrative the president de Montesquieu* has adopted, Philip, who, during the whole transaction, had preserved a sullen silence, was inclined to spare the innocent life of his benefactor; till, recollecting that his innocence might excite a dangerous compassion in the Roman world, he commanded, without regard to his suppliant cries, that he should be seized, stripped, and led away to instant death. After a moment's pause the inhuman sentence was executed.[55]

On his return from the East to Rome, Philip, desirous of obliterating the memory of his crimes, and of captivating the affections of the people, solemnised the secular games with infinite pomp and magnificence. Since their institution or revival by Augustus,[56] they had been celebrated by Claudius, by Domitian, and by Severus, and were now renewed, the fifth time, on the accomplishment of the full period of a thousand years from the foundation of Rome. Every circumstance of the secular games was skilfully adapted to inspire the superstitious mind with deep and solemn reverence. The long interval between them[57] exceeded the term of human life; and, as none of the spectators had already seen them, none could flatter themselves with the expectation of beholding them a second time. The mystic sacrifices were performed, during three nights, on the banks of the Tiber; and the Campus Martius resounded with music and dances, and was illuminated with innumerable lamps and torches. Slaves and strangers were excluded from any participation in these national ceremonies. A chorus of twenty-seven youths, and as many virgins, of noble families, and whose parents were both alive, implored the propitious gods in favour of the present, and for the hope of the rising, generation; requesting, in religious hymns, that, according to the faith of their ancient oracles, they would still maintain the virtue, the felicity, and the empire of the Roman people.[58] The magnificence of Philip's shows and entertainments dazzled the eyes of the multitude. The devout were employed in the rites of superstition, whilst the reflecting few revolved in their anxious minds the past history and the future fate of the empire.

Since Romulus, with a small band of shepherds and outlaws, fortified himself on the hills near the Tiber, ten centuries had already elapsed.[59] During the four first ages, the Romans, in the laborious school of poverty, had acquired the virtues of war and government: by the vigorous exertion of those virtues, and by the assistance of fortune, they had obtained, in the course of the three succeeding centuries, an absolute empire over many countries of Europe, Asia, and Africa. The last three hundred years had been consumed in apparent prosperity and internal decline. The nation of soldiers, magistrates, and legislators, who composed the thirty-five tribes of the Roman people, was dissolved into the common mass of mankind, and confounded with the millions of servile provincials, who had received the name, without adopting the spirit, of Romans. A mercenary army, levied among the subjects and barbarians of the frontier, was the only order of men who preserved and abused their independence. By their tumultuary election, a Syrian, a Goth, or an Arab, was exalted to the throne of Rome, and invested with despotic power over the conquests and over the country of the Scipios.

The limits of the Roman empire still extended from the Western Ocean to the Tigris, and from Mount Atlas to the Rhine and the Danube. To the undiscerning eye of the vulgar, Philip appeared a monarch no less powerful than Hadrian or Augustus had formerly been. The form was still the same, but the animating health and vigour were fled. The industry of the people was discouraged and exhausted by a long series of oppression. The discipline of the legions, which alone, after the extinction of every other virtue, had propped the greatness of the state, was corrupted by the ambition, or relaxed by the weakness, of the emperors. The strength of the frontiers, which had always consisted in arms rather than in fortifications, was insensibly undermined; and the fairest provinces were left exposed to the rapaciousness or ambition of the barbarians, who soon discovered the decline of the Roman empire.

NOTES TO CHAPTER 7

1 There had been no example of three successive generations on the throne; only three instances of sons who succeeded their fathers. The marriages of the Caesars (notwithstanding the permission, and the frequent practice, of divorces) were generally unfruitful.

2 *Hist. August.*, p. 138.

3 *Hist. August.*, p. 140; Herodian, vi, 223; Aurelius Victor. By comparing these authors, it should seem that Maximin had the particular command of the Triballian horse, with the general commission of disciplining the recruits of the whole army. His biographer ought to have marked, with more care, his exploits, and the successive steps of his military promotions.

4 See the original letter of Alexander Severus, *Hist. August.*, p. 149.

5 *Hist. August.*, p. 135. I have softened some of the most improbable circumstances of this wretched biographer. From this ill-worded narration, it should seem that, the prince's buffoon having accidentally entered the tent, and awakened the slumbering monarch, the fear of punishment urged him to persuade the disaffected soldiers to commit the murder.

6 Herodian, vi, 223–227.

7 Caligula, the eldest of the four, was only twenty-five years of age when he ascended the throne; Caracalla was twenty-three, Commodus nineteen, and Nero no more than seventeen.

8 It appears that he was totally ignorant of the Greek language; which, from its universal use in conversation and letters, was an essential part of every liberal education.

9 *Hist. August.*, p. 141; Herodian, vii, 237. The latter of these historians has been most unjustly censured for sparing the vices of Maximin.

10 The wife of Maximin, by insinuating wise counsels with female gentleness, sometimes brought back the tyrant to the way of truth and humanity. See Ammianus Marcellinus, xiv, I, where he alludes to the fact which he had more fully related under the reign of the Gordians. We may collect from the medals that Paulina was the name of this benevolent empress; and from the title of *Diva*, that she died before Maximin. (Valesius *ad loc. cit.* Ammian.) Spanheim, *de U. et P. N.* ii, 300.

11 He was compared to Spartacus and Athenio. *Hist. August.*, p. 141.

12 Herodian, vii, 238; Zosimus, i, 15.

13 In the fertile territory of Byzacium, one hundred and fifty miles to the south of Carthage. This city was decorated, probably by the Gordians, with the title of colony, and with a fine amphitheatre, which is still in a very perfect state. See *Itinerar.* Wesseling, p. 59, and Shaw's *Travels*, p. 117.

14 Herodian, vii, 239; *Hist. August.*, p. 153.

15 *Hist. August.*, p. 152. The celebrated house of Pompey *in carinis* [in Carinae – a district of Rome] was usurped by Marc Antony, and consequently became, after the Triumvir's death, a part of the Imperial domain. The emperor Trajan allowed and even encouraged the rich senators to purchase those magnificent and useless palaces (Pliny, *Panegyric.*, 50), and it may seem probable that on this occasion Pompey's house came into the possession of Gordian's great-grandfather.

16 The Claudian, the Numidian, the Carystian, and the Synnadian. The colours of Roman marble have been faintly described and imperfectly distinguished. It appears, however, that the Carystian was a sea green, and that the marble of Synnada was white mixed with oval spots of purple. See Salmasius *ad Hist. August.*, p. 164.

17 *Hist. August.*, pp. 151, 152. He sometimes gave five hundred pair of Gladiators, never less than one hundred and fifty. He once gave for the use of the Circus one hundred Sicilian, and as many Cappadocian horses. The animals designed for hunting were chiefly bears, boars, bulls, stags, elks, wild asses, etc. Elephants and lions seem to have been appropriated to Imperial magnificence.

18 See the original letter, in the *Augustan History*, p. 152, which at once shows Alexander's respect for the authority of the senate, and his esteem for the proconsul appointed by that assembly.

19 By each of his concubines, the younger Gordian left three or four children. His literary productions, though less numerous, were by no means contemptible.

20 Herodian, vii, 243; *Hist. August.*, p. 144.

21 *Quod tamen patres, dum periculosum existimant inermes armato resistere, approbaverunt*: Aurelius Victor. ['The senators gave their sanction for as long as they deemed it dangerous, being unarmed, to oppose an armed man.']

22 Even the servants of the house, the scribes, etc., were excluded, and their office was filled by the senators themselves. We are obliged to the *Augustan History*, p. 157, for preserving this curious example of the old discipline of the commonwealth.

23 This spirited speech, translated from the Augustan historian, p. 156, seems transcribed by him from the original registers of the senate.

 * *page 151*   [anticipated]
 † *page 151*   [condemned, doomed]

24 Herodian, vii, 244.

25 Herodian, vii, 247, viii, 277; *Hist. August.*, pp. 156–8.

26 Herodian, vii, 254; *Hist. August.*, pp. 158–160. We may observe that one month and six days for the reign of Gordian is a just correction of Casaubon and Panvinius, instead of the absurd reading of one year and six months. See Commentar. p. 193. Zosimus relates, i. p. 17, that the two Gordians perished by a tempest in the midst of their navigation. A strange ignorance of history, or a strange abuse of metaphors!

27 See the *Augustan History*, p. 166, from the registers of the senate; the date is confessedly faulty, but the coincidence of the Apollinarian games enables us to correct it.

28 He was descended from Cornelius Balbus, a noble Spaniard, and the adopted son of Theophanes the Greek historian. Balbus obtained the freedom of Rome by the favour of Pompey, and preserved it by the eloquence of Cicero (see *Orat. pro Cornel. Balbo*). The friendship of Caesar (to whom he rendered the most important secret services in the civil war) raised him to the consulship and the pontificate, honours never yet possessed by a stranger. The nephew of this Balbus triumphed over the Garamantes. See *Dictionnaire* de Bayle, au mot *Balbus*, where he distinguishes the several persons of that name, and rectifies, with his usual accuracy, the mistakes of former writers concerning them.

29 Zonaras, xii, 622. But little dependence is to be had on the authority of a modern Greek, so grossly ignorant of the history of the third century that he creates several imaginary emperors, and confounds those who really existed.

30 Herodian, vii, 256, supposes that the senate was at first convoked in the Capitol, and is very eloquent on the occasion. The *Augustan History*, p. 166, seems much more authentic.

31 In Herodian, vii, 249, and in the *Augustan History* we have three several orations of Maximin to his army, on the rebellion of Africa and Rome: M. de Tillemont has very justly observed, that they neither agree with each other, nor with truth. *Histoire des Empereurs*, iii, 799.

32 The carelessness of the writers of that age leaves us in a singular perplexity.   1. We know that Maximus and Balbinus were killed during the Capitoline games: Herodian, viii, 285. The authority of Censorinus (*de Die Natali*, ch. 18) enables us to fix those games: with certainty to the year 238, but leaves us in ignorance of the month or day.   2. The election of Gordian by the senate is fixed, with equal certainty, to the 27th of May; but we are at a loss to discover, whether it was in the same or the preceding year. Tillemont and Muratori, who maintain the two opposite opinions, bring into the field a desultory troop of authorities, conjectures, and probabilities. The one seems to draw out, the other to contract, the series of events, between those periods, more than can be well reconciled to reason and history. Yet it is necessary to choose between them.

33 Velleius Paterculus, ii, 24. The president de Montesquieu (in his dialogue between Sylla and Eucrates) expresses the sentiments of the dictator in a spirited and even sublime manner.

34 Muratori (*Annali d'Italia*, ii, 294) thinks the melting of the snows suits better with the months of June or July, than with that of February. The opinion of a man who passed his life between the Alps and the Apennines is undoubtedly of great weight; yet I observe,   1. That the long winter, of which Muratori takes advantage, is to be found only in the Latin version, and not in the Greek text, of Herodian.   2. That the vicissitude of suns and rains, to which the soldiers of Maximin were exposed (Herodian, viii, 277), denotes the spring rather than the summer. We may observe likewise, that these several streams, as they melted into one, composed the Timavus, so poetically (in every sense of the word) described by Virgil. They are about twelve miles to the east of Aquileia. See Cluver, *Italia Antiqua*, i, 189, etc.

35 Herodian, viii, 272. The Celtic deity was supposed to be Apollo, and received under that name the thanks of the senate. A temple was likewise built to Venus

the Bald, in honour of the women of Aquileia, who had given up their hair to make ropes for the military engines.

36 Herodian, viii, 279; *Hist. August.*, p. 146. The duration of Maximin's reign has not been defined with much accuracy, except by Eutropius, who allows him three years and a few days (ix, 1); we may depend on the integrity of the text, as the Latin original is checked by the Greek version of Paeanius.

37 Eight Roman feet and one third, which are equal to above eight English feet, as the two measures are to each other in the proportion of 967 to 1000. See Graves's discourse on the Roman foot. We are told that Maximin could drink in a day an amphora (or about seven gallons) of wine and eat thirty or forty pounds of meat. He could move a loaded waggon, break a horse's leg with his fist, crumble stones in his hand, and tear up small trees by the roots. See his Life in the *Augustan History*.

38 See the congratulatory letter of Claudius Julianus the consul, to the two emperors, in the *Augustan History*.

39 *Hist. August.*, p. 171.

 * *page 157* [internal]

40 Herodian, viii, 258.

41 Herodian, viii, 213.

42 The observation had been made imprudently enough in the acclamations of the senate, and with regard to the soldiers it carried the appearance of a wanton insult. *Hist. August.*, p. 170.

43 *Discordiae tacitae et quae intelligerentur potius quam viderentur. Hist. August.*, p. 170. This well chosen expression is probably stolen from some better writer.

44 Herodian, viii, 287, 288.

45 *quia non alius erat in praesenti* ['because there was no one else available'], is the expression of the *Augustan History*.

46 Quintus Curtius (x, 9), pays an elegant compliment to the emperor of the day, for having, by his happy accession, extinguished so many fire-brands, sheathed so many swords, and put an end to the evils of a divided government. After weighing with attention every word of the passage, I am of opinion that it suits better with the elevation of Gordian than with any other period of the *Roman History*. In that case, it may serve to decide the age of Quintus Curtius. Those who place him under the first Caesars argue from the purity of his style, but are embarrassed by the silence of Quintilian in his accurate list of Roman historians.

47 *Hist. August.*, p. 161. From some hints in the two letters, I should expect that the eunuchs were not expelled the palace without some degree of gentle violence, and that young Gordian rather approved of, than consented to, their disgrace.

48 *Duxit uxorem filiam Misithei, quem causa eloquentiae dignum parentela sua putavit; et praefectum statim fecit; post quod non puerile iam et contemptibile videbatur imperium.* ['He married the daughter of Misitheus, whom he deemed worthy to be a relative by reason of his eloquence; and he at once made him prefect; after which his rule no longer seemed childish and contemptible.']

 * *page 159* [The temple of Janus was opened in time of war.]

49 *Hist. August.*, p. 162; Aurelius Victor; Porphyrius in *Vit. Plotin. ap. Fabricium Biblioth. Graec.*, iv, 36. The philosopher Plotinus accompanied the army, prompted by the love of knowledge, and by the hope of penetrating as far as India.

50 About twenty miles from the little town of Circesium, on the frontier of the two empires.

51 The inscription (which contained a very singular pun) [on the name of Philip] was erased by the order of Licinius, who claimed some degree of relationship to Philip (*Hist. August.*, p. 165); but the *tumulus*, or mound of earth which formed the sepulchre, still subsisted in the time of Julian. See Ammianus Marcellinus, xxiii, 5.

52 Aurelius Victor; Eutrop., ix, 2; Orosius, vii, 20; Ammianus Marcellinus, xxiii, 5; Zosimus, i, 19. Philip, who was a native of Bostra, was about forty years of age.

53 Can the epithet of *aristocracy* be applied, with any propriety, to the government of Algiers? Every military government floats between the extremes of absolute monarchy and wild democracy.

54 The military republic of the Mamalukes in Egypt would have afforded M. de Montesquieu (see *Considérations sur la Grandeur et la Décadence des Romains*, ch. 16) a juster and more noble parallel.

 * *page 160*   [French philosopher and author (1689–1755)]

55 The *Augustan History* (pp. 163, 164) cannot, in this instance, be reconciled with itself or with probability. How could Philip condemn his predecessor, and yet consecrate his memory? How could he order his public execution, and yet, in his letters to the senate, exculpate himself from the guilt of his death? Philip, though an ambitious usurper, was by no means a mad tyrant. Some chronological difficulties have likewise been discovered by the nice eyes of Tillemont and Muratori, in this supposed association of Philip to the empire.

56 The account of the last supposed celebration, though in an enlightened period of history, was so very doubtful and obscure, that the alternative seems not doubtful. When the popish jubilees, the copy of the secular games, were invented by Boniface VIII, the crafty pope pretended that he only revived an ancient institution. See M. le Chais, *Lettres sur les Jubilés*.

57 Either of a hundred, or a hundred and ten years. Varro and Livy adopted the former opinion, but the infallible authority of the Sybil consecrated the latter (Censorinus, *de Die Natal.*, ch. 17). The emperors Claudius and Philip, however, did not treat the oracle with implicit respect.

58 The idea of the secular games is best understood from the poem of Horace, and the description of Zosimus, ii, 167, etc.

59 The received calculation of Varro assigns to the foundation of Rome an era that corresponds with the 754th year before Christ. But so little is the chronology of Rome to be depended on in the more early ages that Sir Isaac Newton has brought the same event as low as the year 627.

CHAPTER 8

Of the state of Persia after the restoration of the monarchy by Artaxerxes

Whenever Tacitus indulges himself in those beautiful episodes, in which he relates some domestic transaction of the Germans or of the Parthians, his principal object is to relieve the attention of the reader from a uniform scene of vice and misery. From the reign of Augustus to the time of Alexander Severus, the enemies of Rome were in her bosom – the tyrants, and the soldiers; and her prosperity had a very distant and feeble interest in the revolutions that might happen beyond the Rhine and the Euphrates. But, when the military order had levelled in wild anarchy the power of the prince, the laws of the senate, and even the discipline of the camp, the barbarians of the North and of the East, who had long hovered on the frontier, boldly attacked the provinces of a declining monarchy. Their vexatious inroads were changed into formidable irruptions, and, after a long vicissitude of mutual calamities, many tribes of the victorious invaders established themselves in the provinces of the Roman empire. To obtain a clearer knowledge of these great events we shall endeavour to form a previous idea of the character, forces, and designs of those nations who avenged the cause of Hannibal and Mithridates.*

In the more early ages of the world, whilst the forest that covered Europe afforded a retreat to a few wandering savages, the inhabitants of Asia were already collected into populous cities, and reduced under extensive empires, the seat of the arts, of luxury, and of despotism. The Assyrians reigned over the East,[1] till the sceptre of Ninus and Semiramis dropped from the hands of their enervated successors. The Medes and the Babylonians divided their power, and were themselves swallowed up in the monarchy of the Persians, whose arms could not be confined within the narrow limits of Asia. Followed, as it is said, by two millions of *men*, Xerxes, the descendant of Cyrus, invaded Greece. Thirty thousand *soldiers*, under the command of Alexander, the son of Philip, who was entrusted by the Greeks with their glory and revenge, were sufficient to subdue Persia. The princes of the house of Seleucus usurped and lost the Macedonian command over the East. About the same time that, by an ignominious treaty, they resigned to the Romans the country on this side Mount Taurus, they were driven by the Parthians, an obscure horde of Scythian origin, from all the provinces of Upper Asia. The formidable power of the Parthians, which spread from India to the frontiers of Syria, was in its turn subverted by Ardshir, or Artaxerxes; the founder of a new dynasty, which, under the name of Sassanides, governed Persia till the invasion of the Arabs. This great revolution, whose fatal influence was soon experienced by the Romans, happened in the fourth year of Alexander Severus, two hundred and twenty-six years after the Christian era.[2]

Artaxerxes had served with great reputation in the armies of Artaban, the last king of the Parthians, and it appears that he was driven into exile and rebellion by royal ingratitude, the customary reward for superior merit. His birth was obscure, and the obscurity equally gave room to the aspersions of his enemies, and the flattery of his adherents. If we credit the scandal of the former, Artaxerxes sprang from the illegitimate commerce of a tanner's wife with a common soldier.[3] The latter represents him as descended from a branch of the ancient kings of Persia, though time and misfortune had gradually reduced his ancestors to the humble station of private citizens.[4] As the lineal heir of the monarchy, he asserted his right to the throne, and challenged the noble task of delivering the Persians from the oppression under which they groaned above five centuries since the death of Darius. The Parthians were defeated in three great battles. In the last of these their king Artaban was slain, and the spirit of the nation was for ever broken.[5] The authority of Artaxerxes was solemnly acknowledged in a great assembly held at Balch in Khorasan. Two younger branches of the royal house of Arsaces were confounded among the prostrate satraps. A third, more mindful of ancient grandeur than of present necessity, attempted to retire with a numerous train of vassals, towards their kinsman, the king of Armenia; but this little army of deserters was intercepted and cut off by the vigilance of the conqueror,[6] who boldly assumed the double diadem, and the title of King of Kings, which had been enjoyed by his predecessor. But these pompous titles, instead of gratifying the vanity of the Persian, served only to admonish him of his duty, and to inflame in his soul the ambition of restoring, in their full splendour, the religion and empire of Cyrus.

I.   During the long servitude of Persia under the Macedonian and the Parthian yoke, the nations of Europe and Asia had mutually adopted and corrupted each other's superstitions. The Arsacides, indeed, practised the worship of the Magi; but they disgraced and polluted it with a various mixture of foreign idolatry. The memory of Zoroaster, the ancient prophet and philosopher of the Persians,[7] was still revered in the East; but the obsolete and mysterious language in which the Zendavesta was composed[8] opened a field of dispute to seventy sects, who variously explained the fundamental doctrines of their religion, and were all equally derided by a crowd of infidels, who rejected the divine mission and miracles of the prophet. To suppress the idolaters, reunite the schismatics, and confute the unbelievers by the infallible decision of a general council, the pious Artaxerxes summoned the Magi from all parts of his dominions. These priests, who had so long sighed in contempt and obscurity, obeyed the welcome summons; and on the appointed day appeared to the number of about eighty thousand. But, as the debates of so tumultuous an assembly could not have been directed by the authority of reason, or influenced by the art of policy, the Persian synod was reduced, by successive operations, to forty thousand, to four thousand, to four hundred, to forty, and at last to seven Magi, the most respected for their learning and piety. One of these, Erdaviraph, a young but holy prelate, received from the hands of his brethren three cups of soporiferous wine. He drank them off, and instantly fell into a long and profound sleep. As soon as he waked, he related to the king and to the believing multitude his journey to Heaven, and his intimate conferences with the Deity. Every doubt was silenced by this supernatural evidence; and the articles of the faith of Zoroaster were fixed with equal authority and precision.[9] A short delineation of that celebrated system will be found useful, not only to display the character of the Persian nation, but to illustrate many of their most important transactions, both in peace and war, with the Roman empire.[10]

The great and fundamental article of the system was the celebrated doctrine of the two principles: a bold and injudicious attempt of Eastern philosophy to reconcile the existence of moral and physical evil with the attributes of a beneficent Creator and Governor of the world. The first and original Being, in whom, or by whom, the universe exists, is denominated in the writings of Zoroaster, *Time without bounds*; but it must be confessed that this infinite substance seems rather a metaphysical abstraction of the mind than a real object endowed with self-consciousness, or possessed of moral perfections. From either the blind or the intelligent operation of this infinite Time, which bears but too near an affinity with the Chaos of the Greeks, the two secondary but active principles of the universe were from all eternity produced, Ormusd and Ahriman, each of them possessed of the powers of creation, but each disposed, by his invariable nature, to exercise them with different designs. The principle of good is eternally absorbed in light: the principle of evil eternally buried in darkness. The wise benevolence of Ormusd formed man capable of virtue, and abundantly provided his fair habitation with the materials of happiness. By his vigilant providence, the motion of the planets, the order of the seasons, and the temperate mixture of the elements are preserved. But the malice of Ahriman has long since pierced *Ormusd's egg*; or, in other words, has violated the harmony of his works. Since that fatal eruption, the most minute particles of good and evil are intimately intermingled and agitated together, the rankest poisons spring up amidst the most salutary plants; deluges, earthquakes, and conflagrations attest the conflict of Nature; and the little world of man is perpetually shaken by vice and misfortune. Whilst the rest of humankind are led away captives in the chains of their infernal enemy, the faithful Persian alone reserves his religious adoration for his friend and protector Ormusd, and fights under his banner of light, in the full confidence that he shall, in the last day, share the glory of his triumph. At that decisive period the enlightened wisdom of goodness will render the power of Ormusd superior to the furious malice of his rival. Ahriman and his followers, disarmed and subdued, will sink into their native darkness; and virtue will maintain the eternal peace and harmony of the universe.[11]

The theology of Zoroaster was darkly comprehended by foreigners, and even by the far greater number of his disciples; but the most careless observers were struck with the philosophic simplicity of the Persian worship. 'That people,' says Herodotus,[12] 'rejects the use of temples, of altars, and of statues, and smiles at the folly of those nations, who imagine that the gods are sprung from, or bear any affinity with, the human nature. The tops of the highest mountains are the places chosen for sacrifices. Hymns and prayers are the principal worship; the Supreme God who fills the wide circle of heaven, is the object to whom they are addressed.' Yet, at the same time, in the true spirit of a polytheist, he accuses them of adoring Earth, Water, Fire, the Winds, and the Sun and Moon. But the Persians of every age have denied the charge, and explained the equivocal conduct which might appear to give a colour to it. The elements, and more particularly Fire, Light, and the Sun, whom they called Mithra, were the objects of their religious reverence, because they considered them as the purest symbols, the noblest productions, and the most powerful agents of the Divine Power and Nature.[13]

Every mode of religion, to make a deep and lasting impression on the human mind, must exercise our obedience by enjoining practices of devotion, for which we can assign no reason; and must acquire our esteem, by inculcating moral duties analogous to the dictates of our own hearts. The religion of Zoroaster was abundantly provided with the former, and possessed a sufficient portion of the latter. At the age of puberty the faithful Persian was invested with a mysterious girdle, the badge of the divine protection; and from that moment all the actions of his life, even the most indifferent or the most necessary, were sanctified by their peculiar prayers, ejaculations, or genuflexions; the omission of which, under any circumstances, was a grievous sin, not inferior in guilt to the violation of the moral duties. The moral duties, however, of justice, mercy, liberality, etc., were in their turn required of the disciple of Zoroaster, who wished to escape the persecution of Ahriman, and to live with Ormusd in a blissful eternity, where the degree of felicity will be exactly proportioned to the degree of virtue and piety.[14]

But there are some remarkable instances in which Zoroaster lays aside the prophet, assumes the legislator, and discovers a liberal concern for private and public happiness, seldom to be found among the grovelling or visionary schemes of superstition. Fasting and celibacy, the common means of purchasing the divine favour, he condemns with abhorrence, as a criminal rejection of the best gifts of providence. The saint, in the

Magian religion, is obliged to beget children, to plant useful trees, to destroy noxious animals, to convey water to the dry lands of Persia, and to work out his salvation by pursuing all the labours of agriculture. We may quote from the Zend Avesta a wise and benevolent maxim, which compensates for many an absurdity. 'He who sows the ground with care and diligence acquires a greater stock of religious merit than he could gain by the repetition of ten thousand prayers.'[15] In the spring of every year a festival was celebrated, destined to represent the primitive equality, and the present connection, of mankind. The stately kings of Persia, exchanging their vain pomp for more genuine greatness, freely mingled with the humblest but most useful of their subjects. On that day the husbandmen were admitted, without distinction, to the table of the king and his satraps. The monarch accepted their petitions, inquired into their grievances, and conversed with them on the most equal terms. 'From your labours,' was he accustomed to say (and to say with truth, if not with sincerity), 'from your labours we receive our subsistence; you derive your tranquillity from our vigilance: since, therefore, we are mutually necessary to each other, let us live together like brothers in concord and love.'[16] Such a festival must indeed have degenerated, in a wealthy and despotic empire, into a theatrical representation; but it was at least a comedy well worthy of a royal audience, and which might sometimes imprint a salutary lesson on the mind of a young prince.

Had Zoroaster, in all his institutions, invariably supported this exalted character, his name would deserve a place with those of Numa and Confucius, and his system would be justly entitled to all the applause which it has pleased some of our divines, and even some of our philosophers, to bestow on it. But in that motley composition, dictated by reason and passion, by enthusiasm and by selfish motives, some useful and sublime truths were disgraced by a mixture of the most abject and dangerous superstition. The Magi, or sacerdotal order, were extremely numerous, since, as we have already seen, fourscore thousand of them were convened in a general council. Their forces were multiplied by discipline. A regular hierarchy was diffused through all the provinces of Persia; and the Archimagus, who resided at Balch, was respected as the visible head of the church, and the lawful successor of Zoroaster.[17] The property of the Magi was very considerable. Besides the less invidious possession of a large tract of the most fertile lands of Media,[18] they levied a general tax on the fortunes and the industry of the Persians.[19] 'Though your good works,' says the interested* prophet, 'exceed in number the leaves of the trees, the drops of rain, the stars in the heaven, or the sands on the seashore, they will all be unprofitable to you, unless they are accepted by the *destour*, or priest. To obtain the acceptation of this guide to salvation, you must faithfully pay him *tithes* of all you possess, of your goods, of your lands, and of your money. If the destour be satisfied, your soul will escape hell tortures; you will secure praise in this world and happiness in the next. For the destours are the teachers of religion; they know all things, and they deliver all men.'[20]

These convenient maxims of reverence and implicit faith were doubtless imprinted with care on the tender minds of youth; since the Magi were the masters of education in Persia, and to their hands the children even of the royal family were intrusted.[21] The Persian priests, who were of a speculative genius, preserved and investigated the secrets of Oriental philosophy; and acquired, either by superior knowledge or superior art, the reputation of being well versed in some occult sciences, which have derived their appellation from the Magi.[22] Those of more active dispositions mixed with the world in courts and cities; and it is observed that the administration of Artaxerxes was in a great measure directed by the counsels of the sacerdotal order, whose dignity, either from policy or devotion, that prince restored to its ancient splendour.[23]

The first counsel of the Magi was agreeable to the unsociable genius of their faith,[24] to the practice of ancient kings,[25] and even to the example of their legislator, who had fallen a victim to a religious war excited by his own intolerant zeal.[26] By an edict of Artaxerxes, the exercise of every worship, except that of Zoroaster, was severely prohibited. The temples of the Parthians, and the statues of their deified monarchs, were thrown down with ignominy.[27] The sword of Aristotle (such was the name given by the Orientals to the polytheism and philosophy of the Greeks) was easily broken:[28] the flames of persecution soon reached the more stubborn Jews and Christians;[29] nor did they spare the heretics of their own nation and religion. The majesty of Ormusd, who was jealous of a rival, was seconded by the despotism of Artaxerxes, who could not suffer a rebel; and the schismatics within his vast empire were soon reduced to the inconsiderable number of eighty thousand.[30] This spirit of persecution reflects dishonour on the religion of Zoroaster; but, as it was not productive of any civil commotion, it served to strengthen the new monarchy by uniting all the various inhabitants of Persia in the bands of religious zeal.

II.   Artaxerxes, by his valour and conduct, had wrested the sceptre of the East from the ancient royal family of Parthia. There still remained the more difficult task of establishing, throughout the vast extent of Persia, a uniform and vigorous administration. The weak indulgence of the Arsacides had resigned to their sons and brothers the principal provinces and the greatest offices of the kingdom, in the nature of hereditary possessions. The *vitaxae*, or eighteen most powerful satraps, were permitted to assume the regal title, and the vain pride of the monarch was delighted with a nominal dominion over so many vassal kings. Even tribes of barbarians in their mountains, and the Greek cities of Upper Asia,[31] within their walls, scarcely acknowledged, or seldom obeyed, any superior; and the Parthian empire exhibited, under other names, a lively image of the feudal system[32] which has since prevailed in Europe. But the active victor, at the head of a numerous and disciplined army, visited in person every province of Persia. The defeat of the boldest rebels and the reduction of the strongest fortifications[33] diffused the terror of his arms and prepared the way for the peaceful reception of his authority. An obstinate resistance was fatal to the chiefs; but their followers were treated with lenity.[34] A cheerful submission was rewarded with honours and riches; but the prudent Artaxerxes, suffering no person except himself to assume the title of king, abolished every intermediate power between the throne and the people. His kingdom, nearly equal in extent to modern Persia, was, on every side, bounded by the sea or by great rivers – by the Euphrates, the Tigris, the Araxes, the Oxus, and the Indus; by the Caspian Sea and the Gulf of Persia.[35] That country was computed to contain, in the last century, five hundred and fifty-four cities, sixty thousand villages, and about forty millions of souls.[36] If we compare the administration of the house of Sassan with that of the house of Sesi, the political influence of the Magian with that of the Mahometan religion, we shall probably infer that the kingdom of Artaxerxes contained at least as great a number of cities, villages, and inhabitants. But it must likewise be confessed that in every age the want of harbours on the sea-coast, and the scarcity of fresh water in the inland provinces, have been very unfavourable to the commerce and agriculture of the Persians; who, in the calculation of their numbers, seem to have indulged one of the meanest, though most common, artifices of national vanity.

As soon as the ambitious mind of Artaxerxes had triumphed over the resistance of his vassals, he began to threaten the neighbouring states, who, during the long slumber of his predecessors, had insulted Persia with impunity. He obtained some easy victories over the wild Scythians and the effeminate Indians; but the Romans were an enemy who, by their past injuries and present power, deserved the utmost efforts of his arms. A forty years' tranquillity, the fruit of valour and moderation, had succeeded the victories of Trajan. During the period that elapsed from the accession of Marcus to the reign of Alexander, the Roman and the Parthian empires were twice engaged in war; and, although the whole strength of the Arsacides contended with a part only of the forces of Rome, the event was most commonly in favour of the latter. Macrinus, indeed, prompted by his precarious situation and pusillanimous temper, purchased a peace at the expense of near two millions of our money;[37] but the generals of Marcus, the emperor Severus, and his son, erected many trophies in Armenia, Mesopotamia, and Assyria. Among their exploits, the imperfect relation of which would have unseasonably interrupted the more important series of domestic revolutions, we shall only mention the repeated calamities of the two great cities of Seleucia and Ctesiphon.

Seleucia, on the western bank of the Tigris, about forty-five miles to the north of ancient Babylon, was the capital of the Macedonian conquests in Upper Asia.[38] Many ages after the fall of their empire, Seleucia retained the genuine characters of a Grecian colony – arts, military virtue, and the love of freedom. The independent republic was governed by a senate of three hundred nobles; the people consisted of six hundred thousand citizens; the walls were strong, and, as long as concord prevailed among the several orders of the state, they viewed with contempt the power of the Parthian: but the madness of faction was sometimes provoked to implore the dangerous aid of the common enemy, who was posted almost at the gates of the colony.[39] The Parthian monarchs, like the Mogul sovereigns of Hindostan, delighted in the pastoral life of their Scythian ancestors; and the Imperial camp was frequently pitched in the plain of Ctesiphon, on the eastern bank of the Tigris, at the distance of only three miles from Seleucia.[40] The innumerable attendants on luxury and despotism resorted to the court, and the little village of Ctesiphon insensibly swelled into a great city.[41] Under the reign of Marcus, the Roman generals penetrated as far as Ctesiphon and Seleucia. They were received as friends by the Greek colony; they attacked as enemies the seat of the Parthian kings; yet both cities experienced the same treatment. The sack and conflagration of Seleucia, with the massacre of three hundred thousand of the inhabitants, tarnished the glory of the Roman triumph.[42] Seleucia, already exhausted by the neighbourhood of a too powerful rival, sunk under the fatal blow; but Ctesiphon, in about thirty-three years, had sufficiently recovered its strength to maintain an obstinate siege against the emperor Severus. The city was, however, taken by assault; the king, who defended it in person, escaped with precipitation; an hundred thousand captives and a rich booty rewarded the fatigues of the Roman soldiers.[43] Notwithstanding these misfortunes, Ctesiphon succeeded to Babylon and to Seleucia as one of the great capitals of the East. In summer, the monarch of Persia enjoyed at Ecbatana the cool breezes of the mountains of Media; but the mildness of the climate engaged him to prefer Ctesiphon for his winter residence.

From these successful inroads the Romans derived no real or lasting benefit; nor did they attempt to preserve such distant conquests, separated from the provinces of the empire by a large tract of intermediate desert. The reduction of the kingdom of Osrhoene was an acquisition of less splendour indeed, but of a far more solid advantage. That little state occupied the northern and most fertile part of Mesopotamia, between the Euphrates and the Tigris. Edessa, its capital, was situated about twenty miles beyond the former of those rivers, and the inhabitants, since the time of Alexander, were a mixed race of Greeks, Arabs, Syrians, and Armenians.[44] The feeble sovereigns of Osrhoene, placed on the dangerous verge of two contending empires, were attached from inclination to the Parthian cause; but the superior power of Rome exacted from them a reluctant homage, which is still attested by their medals. After the conclusion of the Parthian war under Marcus, it was judged prudent to secure some substantial pledges of their doubtful fidelity. Forts were constructed in several parts of the country, and a Roman garrison was fixed in the strong town of Nisibis. During the troubles that followed the death of Commodus, the princes of Osrhoene attempted to shake off the yoke; but the stern policy of Severus confirmed their dependence,[45] and the perfidy of Caracalla completed the easy conquest. Abgarus, the last king of Edessa, was sent in chains to Rome, his dominions reduced into a province, and his capital dignified with the rank of colony; and thus the Romans, about ten years before the fall of the Parthian monarchy, obtained a firm and permanent establishment beyond the Euphrates.[46]

Prudence as well as glory might have justified a war on the side of Artaxerxes, had his views been confined to the defence or the acquisition of a useful frontier. But the ambitious Persian openly avowed a far more extensive design of conquest; and he thought himself able to support his lofty pretensions by the arms of reason as well as by those of power. Cyrus, he alleged, had first subdued, and his successors had for a long time possessed, the whole extent of Asia, as far as the Propontis and the Aegean Sea; the provinces of Caria and Ionia, under their empire, had been governed by Persian satraps; and all Egypt, to the confines of Ethiopia, had acknowledged their sovereignty.[47] Their rights had been suspended, but not destroyed, by a long usurpation; and, as soon as he received the Persian diadem, which birth and successful valour had placed upon his head, the first great duty of his station called upon him to restore the ancient limits and splendour of the monarchy. The Great King, therefore (such was the haughty style of his embassies to the Emperor Alexander), commanded the Romans instantly to depart from all the provinces of his ancestors, and, yielding to the Persians the empire of Asia, to content themselves with the undisturbed possession of Europe. This haughty mandate was delivered by four hundred of the tallest and most beautiful of the Persians; who, by their fine horses, splendid arms, and rich apparel, displayed the pride and greatness of their master.[48] Such an embassy was much less an offer of negotiation than a declaration of war. Both Alexander Severus and Artaxerxes, collecting the military force of the Roman and Persian monarchies, resolved in this important contest to lead their armies in person.

If we credit what should seem the most authentic of all records, an oration, still extant, and delivered by the emperor himself to the senate, we must allow that the victory of Alexander Severus was not inferior to any of those formerly obtained over the Persians by the son of Philip. The army of the Great King consisted of one hundred and twenty thousand horse, clothed in complete armour of steel; of seven hundred elephants, with towers filled with archers on their backs; and of eighteen hundred chariots armed with scythes. This formidable host, the like of which is not to be found in eastern history, and has scarcely been imagined in eastern romance,[49] was discomfited in a great battle, in which the Roman Alexander approved himself an intrepid soldier and a skilful general. The Great King fled before his valour: an immense booty and the conquest of Mesopotamia were the immediate fruits of this signal victory. Such are the circumstances of this ostentatious and improbable relation, dictated, as it too plainly appears, by the vanity of the monarch, adorned by the unblushing servility of his flatterers, and received without contradiction by a distant and obsequious senate.[50] Far from being inclined to believe that the arms of Alexander obtained any memorable advantage over the Persians, we are induced to suspect that all this blaze of imaginary glory was designed to conceal some real disgrace.

Our suspicions are confirmed by the authority of a contemporary historian, who mentions the virtues of Alexander with respect, and his faults with candour. He describes the judicious plan which had been formed for the conduct of the war. Three Roman armies were destined to invade Persia at the same time, and by different roads. But the operations of the campaign, though wisely concerted, were not executed either with ability or success. The first of these armies, as soon as it had entered the marshy plains of Babylon, towards the artificial conflux of the Euphrates and the Tigris,[51] was encompassed by the superior numbers, and destroyed by the arrows, of the enemy. The alliance of Chosroes, king of Armenia,[52] and the long tract of mountainous country, in which the Persian cavalry was of little service, opened a secure entrance into the heart of Media to the second of the Roman armies. These brave troops laid waste the adjacent provinces, and by several successful actions against Artaxerxes gave a faint colour to the emperor's vanity. But the retreat of this victorious army was imprudent, or at least unfortunate. In repassing the mountains, great numbers of soldiers perished by the badness of the roads and the severity of the winter season. It had been resolved that, whilst these two great detachments penetrated into the opposite extremes of the Persian dominions, the main body, under the command of Alexander himself, should support their attack by invading the centre of the kingdom. But the unexperienced youth, influenced by his mother's counsels, and perhaps by his own fears, deserted the bravest troops and the fairest prospect of victory; and, after consuming in Mesopotamia an inactive and inglorious summer, he led back to Antioch an army diminished by sickness, and provoked by disappointment. The behaviour of Artaxerxes had been very different. Flying with rapidity from the hills of Media to the marshes of the Euphrates, he had everywhere opposed the invaders in person; and in either fortune had united with the ablest conduct the most undaunted resolution. But in several obstinate engagements against the veteran legions of Rome the Persian monarch had lost the flower of his troops. Even his victories had weakened his power. The favourable opportunities of the absence of Alexander, and of the confusions that followed that emperor's death, presented themselves in vain to his ambition. Instead of expelling the Romans, as he pretended, from the continent of Asia, he found himself unable to wrest from their hands the little province of Mesopotamia.[53]

The reign of Artaxerxes, which from the last defeat of the Parthians lasted only fourteen years, forms a memorable era in the history of the East, and even in that of Rome. His character seems to have been marked by those bold and commanding features that generally distinguish the princes who conquer, from those who inherit, an empire. Till the last period of the Persian monarchy, his code of laws was respected as the groundwork of their civil and religious policy.[54] Several of his sayings are preserved. One of them in particular discovers a deep insight into the constitution of government. 'The authority of the prince,' said Artaxerxes, 'must be defended by a military force; that force can only be maintained by taxes; all taxes must, at last, fall upon agriculture; and agriculture can never flourish except under the protection of justice and moderation.'[55] Artaxerxes bequeathed his new empire, and his ambitious designs against the Romans, to Sapor, a son not unworthy of his great father; but those designs were too extensive for the power of Persia, and served only to involve both nations in a long series of destructive wars and reciprocal calamities.

The Persians, long since civilised and corrupted, were very far from possessing the martial independence, and the intrepid hardiness, both of mind and body, which have rendered the northern barbarians masters of the world. The science of war, that constituted the more rational force of Greece and Rome, as it now does of Europe, never made any considerable progress in the East. Those disciplined evolutions which harmonise and animate a confused multitude were unknown to the Persians. They were equally unskilled in the arts of constructing, besieging, or defending, regular fortifications. They trusted more to their numbers than to their courage; more to their courage than to their discipline. The infantry was a half-armed, spiritless crowd of peasants, levied in haste by the allurements of plunder, and as easily dispersed by a victory as by a defeat. The monarch and his nobles transported into the camp the pride and luxury of the seraglio. Their military operations were impeded by a useless train of women, eunuchs, horses, and camels; and in the midst of a successful campaign the Persian host was often separated or destroyed by an unexpected famine.[56]

But the nobles of Persia, in the bosom of luxury and despotism, preserved a strong sense of personal gallantry and national honour. From the age of seven years they were taught to speak truth, to shoot with the bow, and to ride; and it was universally confessed that in the two last of these arts they had made a more than common proficiency.[57] The most distinguished youth were educated under the monarch's eye, practised their exercises in the gate of his palace, and were severely trained up to the habits of temperance and obedience in their long and laborious parties of hunting. In every province the satrap maintained a like school of military virtue. The Persian nobles (so natural is the idea of feudal tenures) received from the king's bounty lands and houses on the condition of their service in war. They were ready on the first summons to mount on horseback, with a martial and splendid train of followers, and to join the numerous bodies of guards, who were carefully selected from among the most robust slaves and the bravest adventurers of Asia. These armies, both of light and of heavy cavalry, equally formidable by the impetuosity of their charge and the rapidity of their motions, threatened, as an impending cloud, the eastern provinces of the declining empire of Rome.[58]

NOTES TO CHAPTER 8

* *page 167* [King of Pontus, who declared war on the Roman republic and was defeated by Sulla in 84 bc.]

1 An ancient chronologist quoted by Velleius Paterculus (i, 6) observes that the Assyrians, the Medes, the Persians, and the Macedonians, reigned over Asia one thousand nine hundred and ninety-five years, from the accession of Ninus to the defeat of Antiochus by the Romans. As the latter of these great events happened 189 years before Christ, the former may be placed 2184 years before the same era. The Astronomical Observations, found at Babylon by Alexander, went fifty years higher.

2 In the five hundred and thirty-eighth year of the era of Seleucus. See Agathias, ii, 63. This great event (such is the carelessness of the Orientals) is placed by Eutychius as high as the tenth year of Commodus, and by Moses of Chorene as low as the reign of Philip. Ammianus Marcellinus has so servilely copied (xxiii, 6) his ancient materials, which are indeed very good, that he describes the family of the Arsacides as still seated on the Persian throne in the middle of the fourth century.

3 The tanner's name was Babec; the soldier's, Sassan; from the former Artaxerxes obtained the surname of Babegan; from the latter all his descendants have been styled Sassanides.

4 d'Herbelot, *Bibliothèque Orientale*, Ardshir.

5 Dion Cassius, Bk lxxx; Herodian, vi, 207; Abulpharagius, *Dynast.*, p. 80.

6 See Moses Chorenensis, ii, 65–71.

7 Hyde and Prideaux, working up the Persian legends and their own conjectures into a very agreeable story, represent Zoroaster as a contemporary of Darius Hystaspis. But it is sufficient to observe that the Greek writers, who lived almost in the same age, agree in placing the era of Zoroaster many hundred, or even thousand, years before their own time. The judicious criticism of Mr Moyle perceived, and maintained against his uncle Dr Prideaux, the antiquity of the Persian prophet. See his work, vol. ii.

8 That ancient idiom was called the *Zend*. The language of the commentary, the Pehlvi, though much more modern, has ceased many ages ago to be a living tongue. This fact alone (if it is allowed as authentic) sufficiently warrants the antiquity of those writings, which M. d'Anquetil has brought into Europe, and translated into French.

9 Hyde, *de Religione veterum Pers.*, ch. 21.

10 I have principally drawn this account from the *Zendavesta* of M. d'Anquetil and the *Sadder*, subjoined to Dr Hyde's treatise. It must, however, be confessed, that the studied obscurity of a prophet, the figurative style of the East, and the deceitful medium of a French or Latin version, may have betrayed us into error and heresy, in this abridgment of Persian theology.

11 The modern Parsees (and in some degree the *Sadder*) exalt Ormusd into the first and omnipotent cause, whilst they degrade Ahriman into an inferior but rebellious spirit. Their desire of pleasing the Mahometans may have contributed to refine their theological system.

12 Herodotus, i, 131. But Dr Prideaux thinks, with reason, that the use of temples was afterwards permitted in the Magian religion.

13 Hyde, *de Relig. Pers.*, ch. 8. Notwithstanding all their distinctions and protestations, which seem sincere enough, their tyrants, the Mahometans, have constantly stigmatised them as idolatrous worshippers of the fire.

14 See the *Sadder*, the smallest part of which consists of moral precepts. The ceremonies enjoined are infinite and trifling. Fifteen genuflexions, prayers, etc., were required whenever the devout Persian cut his nails or made water; or as often as he put on the sacred girdle. *Sadder*, Art. 14, 50, 60.

15 Zend Avesta, i, 224, and *Précis du Système de Zoroastre*, tom. iii.

16 Hyde, *de Religione Persarum*, ch. 19.

17 *idem*, ch. 28. Both Hyde and Prideaux affect to apply to the Magian, the terms consecrated to the Christian, hierarchy.

18 Ammian. Marcellin., xxiii, 6. He informs us (as far as we may credit him) of two curious particulars; (1) that the Magi derived some of the most secret doctrines from the Indian Brachmans; and, (2) that they were a tribe or family, as well as order.

19 The divine institution of tithes exhibits a singular instance of conformity between the law of Zoroaster and that of Moses. Those who cannot otherwise account for it may suppose, if they please, that the Magi of the latter times inserted so useful an interpolation into the writings of their prophet.

  * *page 171*   [personally concerned]

20 *Sadder*, Art. 8.

21 Plato in *Alcibiad.*

22 Pliny (*Hist. Natur.*, xxx, 1) observes that magic held mankind by the triple chain of religion, of physic, and of astronomy.

23 Agathias, iv, 134.

24 Mr Hume, in the *Natural History of Religion*, sagaciously remarks that the most refined and philosophic sects are constantly the most intolerant.

25 Cicero, *de Legibus*, ii, 10. Xerxes, by the advice of the Magi, destroyed the temples of Greece.

26 Hyde, *de Rel. Persar.*, ch. 23, 24; d'Herbelot, *Bibliothèque Orientale, Zerdusht; Life of Zoroaster* in tom. ii of the Zendavesta.

27 Compare Moses of Chorene, ii, 74, with Ammian. Marcellin., xxiii., 6. Hereafter I shall make use of these passages.

28 Rabbi Abraham, in the *Tarikh Schickard*, pp. 108, 109.

29 Basnage, *Histoire des Juifs*, viii, 3; Sozomen, i, 1. Manes, who suffered an ignominious death, may be deemed a Magian, as well as a Christian, heretic.

30 Hyde, *de Religione Persar.* ch. 21.

31 These colonies were extremely numerous. Seleucus Nicator founded thirty-nine cities, all named from himself, or some of his relations (see Appian in *Syriac.*, p. 124). The era of Seleucus (still in use among the eastern Christians) appears as late as the year 508, of Christ 196, on the medals of the Greek cities within the Parthian empire. See Moyle's works, i, 273, etc., and M. Freret, *Mém. de l'Académie*, tom. xix.

32 The modern Persians distinguish that period as the dynasty of the kings of the nations. See Pliny, *Hist. Nat.*, vi. 25.

33 Eutychius (i, 367, 371, 375) relates the siege of the island of Mesene in the Tigris, with some circumstances not unlike the story of Nisus and Scylla.

34 Agathias, ii, 64. The princes of Segestan defended their independence during many years. As romances generally transport to an ancient period the events of their own time, it is not impossible that the fabulous exploits of Rustan Prince of Segestan may have been grafted on this real history.

35 We can scarcely attribute to the Persian monarchy the sea coast of Gedrosia or Macran, which extends along the Indian Ocean from Cape Jask (the promontory Capella) to Cape Goadel. In the time of Alexander, and probably many ages afterwards, it was thinly inhabited by a savage people of Ichthyophagi, or Fishermen, who knew no arts, who acknowledged no master, and who were divided by inhospitable deserts from the rest of the world. (See Arrian *de Reb. Indicis*.) In the twelfth century, the little town of Taiz (supposed by M. d'Anville to be the Tesa of Ptolemy) was peopled and enriched by the resort of the Arabian merchants. (See *Geographia Nubiens.*, p. 58, and d'Anville, *Géographie Ancienne*, ii, 283.) In the last age the whole country was divided between three princes, one Mahometan and two Idolaters, who maintained their independence against the successors of Shaw Abbas. (*Voyages* de Tavernier, i, v, 635.)

36 Chardin, iii, 1, 2, 3.

37 Dion, xxviii, 1335.

38 For the precise situation of Babylon, Seleucia, Ctesiphon, Modain, and Bagdad, cities often confounded with each other, see an excellent Geographical Tract of M. d'Anville, in *Mém. de l'Académie*, tom. xxx.

39 Tacitus, *Annals*, vi, 42; Pliny, *Hist. Nat.*, vi, 26.

40 This may be inferred from Strabo, xvi, 743.

41 That most curious traveller, Bernier (see *Hist. de Voyages*, tom. x), who followed the camp of Aurengzebe from Delhi to Cashmir, describes with great accuracy the immense moving city. The guard of cavalry consisted of 35,000 men, that of infantry of 10,000. It was computed that the camp contained 150,000 horses, mules, and elephants, 50,000 camels, 50,000 oxen, and between 300,000 and 400,000 persons. Almost all Delhi followed the court, whose magnificence supported its industry.

42 Dion, lxxi, 1178; *Hist. August.*, p. 38; Eutrop., viii, 10; Euseb. in *Chronic.* Quadratus (quoted in the *Augustan History*) attempted to vindicate the Romans by alleging that the citizens of Seleucia had first violated their faith.

43 Dion, lxxv, 1263; Herodian, iii, 120; *Hist. August.*, p. 70.

44 The polished citizens of Antioch called those of Edessa mixed barbarians. It was, however, some praise, that, of the three dialects of the Syriac, the purest and most elegant (the Aramaean) was spoke at Edessa. This remark M. Bayer (*Hist. Edess.*, p. 5) has borrowed from George of Malatia, a Syrian writer.

45 Dion, lxxv, 1248, 1249, 1250. M. Bayer has neglected to use this most important passage.

46 This kingdom, from Osrhoes, who gave a new name to the country, to the last Abgarus, had lasted 353 years. See the learned work of M. Bayer, *Historia Osrhoena et Edessena.*

47 Xenophon, in the preface to the *Cyropaedia*, gives a clear and magnificent idea of the extent of the empire of Cyrus. Herodotus (iii, 79, etc.) enters into a curious and particular description of the twenty great satrapies into which the Persian empire was divided by Darius Hystaspis.

48 Herodian, vi, 209, 212.

49 There were two hundred scythed chariots at the battle of Arbela, in the host of Darius. In the vast army of Tigranes, which was vanquished by Lucullus, seventeen thousand horse only were completely armed. Antiochus brought fifty-four elephants into the field against the Romans: by his frequent wars and negotiations with the princes of India, he had once collected an hundred and fifty of those great animals; but it may be questioned, whether the most powerful monarch of Hindostan ever formed a line of battle of seven hundred elephants. Instead of three or four thousand elephants, which the Great Mogul was supposed to possess, Tavernier (*Voyages*, part ii, i, 198) discovered, by a more accurate inquiry, that he had only five hundred for his baggage, and eighty or ninety for the service of war. The Greeks have varied with regard to the number which Porus brought into the field; but Quintus Curtius (viii, 13), in this instance judicious and moderate, is contented with eighty-five elephants, distinguished by their size and strength. In Siam, where these animals are the most numerous and the most esteemed, eighteen elephants are allowed as a sufficient proportion for each of the nine brigades into which a just army is divided. The whole number, of one hundred and sixty-two elephants of war, may sometimes be doubled. *Hist. des Voyages*, ix, 260.

50 *Hist. August.*, p. 133.

51 M. de Tillemont has already observed that Herodian's geography is somewhat confused.

52 Moses of Chorene (*Hist. Armen.*, ii, 71) illustrates this invasion of Media, by asserting that Chosroes, King of Armenia, defeated Artaxerxes, and pursued him to the confines of India. The exploits of Chosroes have been magnified, and he acted as a dependent ally to the Romans.

53 For the account of this war, see Herodian, vi, 209, 212. The old abbreviators and modern compilers have blindly followed the *Augustan History*.

54 Eutychius, ii, 180, vers. Pocock. The great Chosroes Noushirwan sent the code of Artaxerxes to all his satraps, as the invariable rule of their conduct.

55 d'Herbelot, *Bibliothèque Orientale*, au mot *Ardshir*. We may observe that after an ancient period of fables, and a long interval of darkness, the modern histories of Persia begin to assume an air of truth with the dynasty of the Sassanides.

56 Herodian, vi, 214; Ammianus Marcellinus, xxiii, 6. Some differences may be observed between the two historians, the natural effects of the changes produced by a century and a half.

57 The Persians are still the most skilful horsemen, and their horses the finest, in the East.

58 From Herodotus, Xenophon, Herodian, Ammianus, Chardin, etc., I have extracted such probable accounts of the Persian nobility, as seem either common to every age, or particular to that of the Sassanides.

CHAPTER 9

The state of Germany till the invasion of the Barbarians, in the time of the Emperor Decius

The government and religion of Persia have deserved some notice from their connection with the decline and fall of the Roman empire. We shall occasionally mention the Scythian or Sarmatian tribes, which, with their arms and horses, their flocks and herds, their wives and families, wandered over the immense plains which spread themselves from the Caspian Sea to the Vistula, from the confines of Persia to those of Germany. But the warlike Germans, who first resisted, then invaded, and at length over-turned, the Western monarchy of Rome, will occupy a much more important place in this history, and possess a stronger, and, if we may use the expression, a more domestic, claim to our attention and regard. The most civilised nations of modern Europe issued from the woods of Germany, and in the rude institutions of those barbarians we may still distinguish the original principles of our present laws and manners. In their primitive state of simplicity and independence, the Germans were surveyed by the discerning eye, and delineated by the masterly pencil, of Tacitus, the first of historians who applied the science of philosophy to the study of facts. The expressive conciseness of his descriptions has deserved to exercise the diligence of innumerable antiquarians, and to excite the genius and penetration of the philosophic historians of our own times. The subject, however various and important, has already been so frequently, so ably, and so successfully discussed, that it is now grown familiar to the reader, and difficult to the writer. We shall therefore content ourselves with observing, and indeed with repeating, some of the most important circumstances of climate, of manners, and of institutions, which rendered the wild barbarians of Germany such formidable enemies to the Roman power.

Ancient Germany, excluding from its independent limits the province westward of the Rhine, which had submitted to the Roman yoke, extended itself over a third part of Europe. Almost the whole of modern Germany, Denmark, Norway, Sweden, Finland, Livonia, Prussia, and the greater part of Poland, were peopled by the various tribes of one great nation, whose complexion, manners, and language denoted a common origin, and preserved a striking resemblance. On the west, ancient Germany was divided by the Rhine from the Gallic, and on the south by the Danube from the Illyrian, provinces of the empire. A ridge of hills, rising from the Danube, and called the Carpathian Mountains, covered Germany on the side of Dacia or Hungary. The eastern frontier was faintly marked by the mutual fears of the Germans and the Sarmatians, and was often confounded by the mixture of warring and confederating tribes of the two nations. In the remote darkness of the north the ancients imperfectly descried a frozen ocean that lay beyond the Baltic Sea and beyond the peninsula, or islands,[1] of Scandinavia.

Some ingenious writers[2] have suspected that Europe was much colder formerly than it is at present; and the most ancient descriptions of the climate of Germany tend exceedingly to confirm their theory. The general complaints of intense frost and eternal winter are perhaps little to be regarded, since we have no method of reducing to the accurate standard of the thermometer the feelings or the expressions of an orator born in the happier regions of Greece or Asia. But I shall select two remarkable circumstances of a less equivocal nature. 1. The great rivers which covered the Roman provinces, the Rhine and the Danube, were frequently frozen over, and capable of supporting the most enormous weights. The barbarians, who often chose that severe season for their inroads, transported, without apprehension or danger, their numerous armies, their cavalry, and their heavy waggons, over a vast and solid bridge of ice.[3] Modern ages have not presented an instance of a like phenomenon. 2. The reindeer, that useful animal, from whom the savage of the North derives the best comforts of his dreary life, is of a constitution that supports, and even requires, the most intense cold. He is found on the rock of Spitzberg, within ten degrees of the pole; he seems to delight in the snows of Lapland and Siberia; but at present he cannot subsist, much less multiply, in any country to the south of the Baltic.[4] In the time of Caesar, the reindeer, as well as the elk and the wild bull, was a native of the Hercynian forest, which then overshadowed a great part of Germany and Poland.[5] The modern improvements sufficiently explain the causes of the diminution of the cold. These immense woods have been gradually cleared, which intercepted from the earth the rays of the sun.[6] The morasses have been drained, and, in proportion as the soil has been cultivated, the air has become more temperate. Canada, at this day, is an exact picture of ancient Germany. Although situate in the same parallel with the finest provinces of France and England, that country experiences the most rigorous cold. The reindeer are very numerous, the ground is covered with deep and lasting snow, and the great river of St Lawrence is regularly frozen, in a season when the waters of the Seine and the Thames are usually free from ice.[7]

It is difficult to ascertain, and easy to exaggerate, the influence of the climate of ancient Germany over the minds and bodies of the natives. Many writers have supposed, and most have allowed, though, as it should seem, without any adequate proof, that the rigorous cold of the North was favourable to long life and generative vigour, that the women were more fruitful, and the human species more prolific, than in warmer or more temperate climates.[8] We may assert, with greater confidence, that the keen air of Germany formed the large and masculine limbs of the natives, who were, in general, of a more lofty stature than the people of the South,[9] gave them a kind of strength better adapted to violent exertions than to patient labour, and inspired them with constitutional bravery, which is the result of nerves and spirits. The severity of a winter campaign, that chilled the courage of the Roman troops, was scarcely felt by these hardy children of the North,[10] who, in their turn, were unable to resist the summer heats, and dissolved away in languor and sickness under the beams of an Italian sun.[11]

There is not anywhere upon the globe a large tract of country which we have discovered destitute of inhabitants or whose first population can be fixed with any degree of historical certainty. And yet, as the most philosophic minds can seldom refrain from investigating the infancy of great nations, our curiosity consumes itself in toilsome and disappointed efforts. When Tacitus considered the purity of the German blood, and the forbidding aspect of the country, he was disposed to pronounce those barbarians *indigenae*, or natives of the soil. We may allow with safety, and perhaps with truth, that ancient Germany was not originally peopled by any foreign colonies already formed into a political society;[12] but that the name and nation received their existence from the gradual union of some wandering savages of the Hercynian woods. To assert those savages to have been the spontaneous production of the earth which they inhabited would be a rash inference, condemned by religion, and unwarranted by reason.

Such rational doubt is but ill suited with the genius of popular vanity. Among the nations who have adopted the Mosaic history of the world, the ark of Noah has been of the same use, as was formerly to the Greeks and Romans the siege of Troy. On a narrow basis of acknowledged truth, an immense but rude superstructure of fable has been erected; and the wild Irishman,[13] as well as the wild Tartar,[14] could point out the individual son of Japhet from whose loins his ancestors were lineally descended. The last century abounded with antiquarians of profound learning and easy faith, who, by the dim light of legends and traditions, of conjectures and etymologies, conducted the great-grandchildren of Noah from the Tower of Babel to the extremities of the globe. Of these judicious critics, one of the most entertaining was Olaus Rudbeck, professor in the university of Upsal.[15] Whatever is celebrated either in history or fable, this zealous patriot ascribes to his country. From Sweden (which formed so considerable a part of ancient Germany) the Greeks themselves derived their alphabetical characters, their astronomy, and their religion. Of that delightful region (for such it appeared to the eyes of a native) the Atlantis of Plato, the country of the Hyperboreans, the gardens of the Hesperides, the Fortunate Islands, and even the Elysian Fields, were all but faint and imperfect transcripts. A clime so profusely favoured by Nature could not long remain desert after the flood. The learned Rudbeck allows the family of Noah a few years to multiply from eight to about twenty thousand persons. He then disperses them into small colonies to replenish the earth, and to propagate the human species. The German or Swedish detachment (which marched, if I am not mistaken, under the command of Askenaz, the son of Gomer, the son of Japhet) distinguished itself by a more than common diligence in the prosecution of this great work. The northern hive cast its swarms over the greatest part of Europe, Africa, and Asia; and (to use the author's metaphor) the blood circulated back from the extremities to the heart.

But all this well-laboured system of German antiquities is annihilated by a single fact, too well attested to admit of any doubt, and of too decisive a nature to leave room for any reply. The Germans, in the age of Tacitus, were unacquainted with the use of letters;[16] and the use of letters is the principal circumstance that distinguishes a civilised people from a herd of savages, incapable of knowledge or reflection. Without that artificial help the human memory soon dissipates or corrupts the ideas entrusted to her charge; and the nobler faculties of the mind, no longer supplied with models or with materials, gradually forget their powers: the judgment becomes feeble and lethargic, the imagination languid or irregular. Fully to apprehend this important truth, let us attempt, in an improved society, to calculate the immense distance between the man of learning and the *illiterate* peasant. The former, by reading and reflection, multiplies his own experience, and lives in distant ages and remote countries; whilst the latter, rooted to a single spot, and confined to a few years of existence, surpasses but very little his fellow-labourer the ox in the exercise of his mental faculties. The same and even a greater difference will be found between nations than between individuals; and we may safely pronounce that without some species of writing no people has ever preserved the faithful annals of their history, ever made any considerable progress in the abstract sciences, or ever possessed, in any tolerable degree of perfection, the useful and agreeable arts of life.

Of these arts the ancient Germans were wretchedly destitute. They passed their lives in a state of ignorance and poverty, which it has pleased some declaimers to dignify with the appellation of virtuous simplicity. Modern Germany is said to contain about two thousand three hundred walled towns.[17] In a much wider extent of country the geographer Ptolemy could discover no more than ninety places which he decorates with the name of cities;[18] though, according to our ideas, they would but ill deserve that splendid title. We can only suppose them to have been rude fortifications, constructed in the centre of the woods, and designed to secure the women, children, and cattle, whilst the warriors of the tribe marched out to repel a sudden invasion.[19] But Tacitus asserts, as a well-known fact, that the Germans, in his time, had *no* cities;[20] and that they affected to despise the works of Roman industry as places of confinement rather than of security.[21] Their edifices were not even contiguous, or formed into regular villages;[22] each barbarian fixed his independent dwelling on the spot to which a plain, a wood, or a stream of fresh water had induced him to give the preference. Neither stone, nor brick, nor tiles were employed in these slight habitations.[23] They were indeed no more than low huts of a circular figure, built of rough timber, thatched with straw, and pierced at the top to leave free passage for the smoke. In the most inclement winter, the hardy German was satisfied with a scanty garment made of the skin of some animal. The nations who dwelt towards the North clothed themselves in furs; and the women manufactured for their own use a coarse kind of linen.[24] The game of various sorts with which the forests of Germany were plentifully stocked supplied its inhabitants with food and exercise.[25] Their monstrous herds of cattle, less remarkable indeed for their beauty than for their utility,[26] formed the principal object of their wealth. A small quantity of corn was the only produce exacted from the earth: the use of orchards or artificial meadows was unknown to the Germans; nor can we expect any improvements in agriculture from a people whose property every year experienced a general change by a new division of the arable lands, and who, in that strange operation, avoided disputes by suffering a great part of their territory to lie waste and without tillage.[27]

Gold, silver, and iron were extremely scarce in Germany. Its barbarous inhabitants wanted both skill and patience to investigate those rich veins of silver, which have so liberally rewarded the attention of the princes of Brunswick and Saxony. Sweden, which now supplies Europe with iron, was equally ignorant of its own riches; and the appearance of the arms of the Germans furnished a sufficient proof how little iron they were able to bestow on what they must have deemed the noblest use of that metal. The various transactions of peace and war had introduced some Roman coins (chiefly silver) among the borderers of the Rhine and Danube; but the more distant tribes were absolutely unacquainted with the use of money, carried on their confined traffic by the exchange of commodities, and prized their rude earthen vessels as of equal value with the silver vases, the presents of Rome to their princes and ambassadors.[28] To a mind capable of reflection such leading facts convey more instruction than a tedious detail of subordinate circumstances. The value of money has been settled by general consent to express our wants and our property, as letters were invented to express our ideas, and both these institutions, by giving more active energy to the powers and passions of human nature, have contributed to multiply the objects they were designed to represent. The use of gold and silver is in a great measure factitious; but it would be impossible to enumerate the important and various services which agriculture, and all the arts, have received from iron, when tempered and fashioned by the operation of fire and the dexterous hand of man. Money, in a word, is the most universal incitement, iron the most powerful instrument, of human industry; and it is very difficult to conceive by what means a people, neither actuated by the one nor seconded by the other, could emerge from the grossest barbarism.[29]

If we contemplate a savage nation in any part of the globe, a supine indolence and a carelessness of futurity will be found to constitute their general character. In a civilised state every faculty of man is expanded and exercised; and the great chain of mutual dependence connects and embraces the several members of society. The most numerous portion of it is employed in constant and useful labour. The select few, placed by fortune above that necessity, can, however, fill up their time by the pursuits of interest or glory, by the improvement of their estate or of their understanding, by the duties, the pleasures, and even the follies, of social life. The Germans were not possessed of these varied resources. The care of the house and family, the management of the land and cattle, were delegated to the old and the infirm, to women and slaves. The lazy warrior, destitute of every art that might employ his leisure hours, consumed his days and nights in the animal gratifications of sleep and food. And yet, by a wonderful diversity of nature (according to the remark of a writer who had pierced into its darkest recesses), the same barbarians are by turns the most indolent and the most restless of mankind. They delight in sloth, they detest tranquillity.[30] The languid soul, oppressed with its own weight, anxiously required some new and powerful sensation; and war and danger were the only amusements adequate to its fierce temper. The sound that summoned the German to arms was grateful to his ear. It roused him from his uncomfortable lethargy, gave him an active pursuit, and, by strong exercise of the body, and violent emotions of the mind, restored him to a more lively sense of his existence. In the dull intervals of peace these barbarians were immoderately addicted to deep gaming and excessive drinking; both of which, by different means, the one by inflaming their passions, the other by extinguishing their reason, alike relieved them from the pain of thinking. They gloried in passing whole days and nights at table; and the blood of friends and relations often stained their numerous and drunken assemblies.[31] Their debts of honour (for in that light they have transmitted to us those of play) they discharged with the most romantic fidelity. The desperate gamester, who had staked his person and liberty on a last throw of the dice, patiently submitted to the decision of fortune, and suffered himself to be bound, chastised, and sold into remote slavery, by his weaker but more lucky antagonist.[32]

Strong beer, a liquor extracted with very little art from wheat or barley, and *corrupted* (as it is strongly expressed by Tacitus) into a certain semblance of wine, was sufficient for the gross purposes of German debauchery. But those who had tasted the rich wines of Italy, and afterwards of Gaul, sighed for that more delicious species of intoxication. They attempted not, however (as has since been executed with so much success), to naturalise the vine on the banks of the Rhine and Danube; nor

did they endeavour to procure by industry the materials of an advantageous commerce. To solicit by labour what might be ravished by arms was
esteemed unworthy of the German spirit.[33] The intemperate thirst of
strong liquors often urged the barbarians to invade the provinces on which
art or nature had bestowed those much envied presents. The Tuscan who
betrayed his country to the Celtic nations attracted them into Italy by the
prospect of the rich fruits and delicious wines, the productions of a happier
climate.[34] And in the same manner the German auxiliaries, invited into
France during the civil wars of the sixteenth century, were allured by the
promise of plenteous quarters in the provinces of Champagne and
Burgundy.[35] Drunkenness, the most illiberal but not the most dangerous
of *our* vices, was sometimes capable, in a less civilised state of mankind, of
occasioning a battle, a war, or a revolution.

The climate of ancient Germany has been mollified, and the soil
fertilised, by the labour of ten centuries from the time of Charlemagne.
The same extent of ground, which at present maintains, in ease and
plenty, a million of husbandmen and artificers, was unable to supply an
hundred thousand lazy warriors with the simple necessaries of life.[36] The
Germans abandoned their immense forests to the exercise of hunting,
employed in pasturage the most considerable part of their lands, bestowed
on the small remainder a rude and careless cultivation, and then accused
the scantiness and sterility of a country that refused to maintain the
multitude of its inhabitants. When the return of famine severely admonished them of the importance of the arts, the national distress was
sometimes alleviated by the emigration of a third, perhaps, or a fourth
part of their youth.[37] The possession and the enjoyment of property are
the pledges which bind a civilised people to an improved country. But
the Germans, who carried with them what they most valued, their arms,
their cattle, and their women, cheerfully abandoned the vast silence of
their woods for the unbounded hopes of plunder and conquest. The
innumerable swarms, that issued, or seemed to issue, from the great
storehouse of nations, were multiplied by the fears of the vanquished and
by the credulity of succeeding ages. And from facts thus exaggerated, an
opinion was gradually established, and has been supported by writers of
distinguished reputation, that, in the age of Caesar and Tacitus, the
inhabitants of the North were far more numerous than they are in our
days.[38] A more serious inquiry into the causes of population seems to
have convinced modern philosophers of the falsehood, and indeed the
impossibility, of the supposition. To the names of Mariana and of
Machiavel[39] we can oppose the equal names of Robertson and Hume.[40]

A warlike nation like the Germans, without either cities, letters, arts, or
money, found some compensation for this savage state in the enjoyment
of liberty. Their poverty secured their freedom, since our desires and our
possessions are the strongest fetters of despotism. 'Among the Suiones
(says Tacitus) riches are held in honour. They are *therefore* subject to an

absolute monarch, who instead of entrusting his people with the free use of arms, as is practised in the rest of Germany, commits them to the safe custody, not of a citizen, or even of a freedman, but of a slave. The neighbours of the Suiones, the Sitones, are sunk even below servitude; they obey a woman.'[41] In the mention of these exceptions, the great historian sufficiently acknowledges the general theory of government. We are only at a loss to conceive by what means riches and despotism could penetrate into a remote corner of the North, and extinguish the generous flame that blazed with such fierceness on the frontier of the Roman provinces, or how the ancestors of those Danes and Norwegians, so distinguished in later ages by their unconquered spirit, could thus tamely resign the great character of German liberty.[42] Some tribes, however, on the coast of the Baltic, acknowledged the authority of kings, though without relinquishing the rights of men;[43] but in the far greater part of Germany the form of government was a democracy, tempered, indeed, and controlled, not so much by general and positive laws as by the occasional ascendant of birth or valour, of eloquence or superstition.[44]

Civil governments, in their first institutions, are voluntary associations for mutual defence. To obtain the desired end it is absolutely necessary that each individual should conceive himself obliged to submit his private opinion and actions to the judgment of the greater number of his associates. The German tribes were contented with this rude but liberal outline of political society. As soon as a youth, born of free parents, had attained the age of manhood, he was introduced into the general council of his countrymen, solemnly invested with a shield and spear, and adopted as an equal and worthy member of the military commonwealth. The assembly of the warriors of the tribe was convened at stated seasons, or on sudden emergencies. The trial of public offences, the election of magistrates, and the great business of peace and war, were determined by its independent voice. Sometimes, indeed, these important questions were previously considered and prepared in a more select council of the principal chieftains.[45] The magistrates might deliberate and persuade, the people only could resolve and execute; and the resolutions of the Germans were for the most part hasty and violent. Barbarians accustomed to place their freedom in gratifying the present passion, and their courage in overlooking all future consequences, turned away with indignant contempt from the remonstrances of justice and policy, and it was the practice to signify by a hollow murmur their dislike of such timid councils. But, whenever a more popular orator proposed to vindicate the meanest citizen from either foreign or domestic injury, whenever he called upon his fellow-countrymen to assert the national honour, or to pursue some enterprise full of danger and glory, a loud clashing of shields and spears expressed the eager applause of the assembly. For the Germans always met in arms, and it was constantly to be dreaded lest an irregular multitude, inflamed with faction and strong liquors, should use those arms to enforce, as well as to declare, their furious resolves. We may recollect how often the diets of Poland have been polluted with blood, and the more numerous party has been compelled to yield to the more violent and seditious.[46]

A general of the tribe was elected on occasions of danger; and, if the danger was pressing and extensive, several tribes concurred in the choice of the same general. The bravest warrior was named to lead his country-men into the field, by his example rather than by his commands. But this power, however limited, was still invidious. It expired with the war, and in time of peace, the German tribes acknowledged not any supreme chief.[47] *Princes* were, however, appointed, in the general assembly, to administer justice, or rather to compose differences,[48] in their respective districts. In the choice of these magistrates as much regard was shown to birth as to merit.[49] To each was assigned, by the public, a guard, and a council of an hundred persons, and the first of the princes appears to have enjoyed a pre-eminence of rank and honour which sometimes tempted the Romans to compliment him with the regal title.[50]

The comparative view of the powers of the magistrates, in two remarkable instances, is alone sufficient to represent the whole system of German manners. The disposal of the landed property within their district was absolutely vested in their hands, and they distributed it every year according to a new division.[51] At the same time they were not authorised to punish with death, to imprison, or even to strike a private citizen.[52] A people thus jealous of their persons, and careless of their possessions, must have been totally destitute of industry and the arts, but animated with a high sense of honour and independence.

The Germans respected only those duties which they imposed on themselves. The most obscure soldier resisted with disdain the authority of the magistrates. 'The noblest youths blushed not to be numbered among the faithful companions of some renowned chief, to whom they devoted their arms and service. A noble emulation prevailed, among the companions to obtain the first place in the esteem of their chief; amongst the chiefs, to acquire the greatest number of valiant companions. To be ever surrounded by a band of select youths was the pride and strength of the chiefs, their ornament in peace, their defence in war. The glory of such distinguished heroes diffused itself beyond the narrow limits of their own tribe. Presents and embassies solicited their friendship, and the fame of their arms often ensured victory to the party which they espoused. In the hour of danger it was shameful for the chief to be surpassed in valour by his companions; shameful for the companions not to equal the valour of their chief. To survive his fall in battle was indelible infamy. To protect his person, and to adorn his glory with the trophies of their own exploits, were the most sacred of their duties. The chiefs combated for victory, the companions for the chief. The noblest warriors, whenever their native country was sunk in the laziness of peace, maintained their numerous bands in some distant scene of action, to exercise their restless spirit, and to acquire renown by voluntary dangers. Gifts worthy of soldiers, the warlike steed, the bloody and ever victorious lance, were the rewards which the companions claimed from the liberality of their chief. The rude plenty of his hospitable board was the only pay that *he* could bestow, or *they* would accept. War, rapine, and the free-will offerings of his friends, supplied the materials of this munificence.'[53] This institution, however it might accidentally weaken the several republics, invigorated the general character of the Germans, and even ripened amongst them all the virtues of which barbarians are susceptible – the faith and valour, the hospitality and the courtesy, so conspicuous long afterwards in the ages of chivalry. The honourable gifts, bestowed by the chief on his brave companions, have been supposed, by an ingenious writer, to contain the first rudiments of the fiefs, distributed after the conquest of the Roman provinces, by the barbarian lords among their vassals, with a similar duty of homage and military service.[54] These conditions are, however, very repugnant to the maxims of the ancient Germans, who delighted in mutual presents, but without either imposing or accepting the weight of obligation.[55]

'In the days of chivalry, or more properly of romance, all the men were brave, and all the women were chaste;' and, notwithstanding the latter of these virtues is acquired and preserved with much more difficulty than the former, it is ascribed, almost without exception, to the wives of the ancient Germans. Polygamy was not in use, except among the princes, and among them only for the sake of multiplying their alliances. Divorces were prohibited by manners rather than by laws. Adulteries were punished as rare and inexpiable crimes; nor was seduction justified by example and fashion.[56] We may easily discover that Tacitus indulges an honest pleasure in the contrast of barbarian virtue with the dissolute conduct of the Roman ladies: yet there are some striking circumstances that give an air of truth, or at least of probability, to the conjugal faith and chastity of the Germans.

Although the progress of civilisation has undoubtedly contributed to assuage the fiercer passions of human nature, it seems to have been less favourable to the virtue of chastity, whose most dangerous enemy is the softness of the mind. The refinements of life corrupt while they polish the intercourse of the sexes. The gross appetite of love becomes most dangerous, when it is elevated, or rather, indeed, disguised, by sentimental passion. The elegance of dress, of motion, and of manners, gives a lustre to beauty, and inflames the senses through the imagination. Luxurious entertainments, midnight dances, and licentious spectacles present at once temptation and opportunity to female frailty.[57] From such dangers the unpolished wives of the barbarians were secured by poverty, solitude, and the painful cares of a domestic life. The German huts, open on every side to the eye of indiscretion or jealousy, were a better safeguard of conjugal fidelity than the walls, the bolts, and the eunuchs of a Persian harem. To this reason another may be added of a more honourable nature. The Germans treated their women with esteem and confidence, consulted them on every occasion of importance, and fondly believed that in their breasts resided a sanctity and wisdom more than human. Some of these interpreters of fate, such as Velleda, in the Batavian war, governed, in the name of the deity, the fiercest nations of Germany.[58] The rest of the sex, without being adored as goddesses, were respected as the free and equal companions of soldiers; associated even by the marriage ceremony to a life of toil, of danger, and of glory.[59] In their great invasions, the camps of the barbarians were filled with a multitude of women, who remained firm and undaunted amidst the sound of arms, the various forms of destruction, and the honourable wounds of their sons and husbands.[60] Fainting armies of Germans have more than once been driven back upon the enemy by the generous despair of the women, who dreaded death much less than servitude. If the day was irrecoverably lost, they well knew how to deliver themselves and their children, with their own hands, from an insulting victor.[61] Heroines of such a cast may claim our admiration; but they were most assuredly neither lovely nor very susceptible of love. Whilst they affected to emulate the stern virtues of *man*, they must have resigned that attractive softness in which principally consist the charm and weakness of *woman*. Conscious pride taught the German females to suppress every tender emotion that stood in competition with honour, and the first honour of the sex has ever been that of chastity. The sentiments and conduct of these high-spirited matrons may, at once, be considered as a cause, as an effect, and as a proof, of the general character of the nation. Female courage, however it may be raised by fanaticism, or confirmed by habit, can be only a faint and imperfect imitation of the manly valour that distinguishes the age or country in which it may be found.

The religious system of the Germans (if the wild opinions of savages can deserve that name) was dictated by their wants, their fears, and their ignorance.[62] They adored the great visible objects and agents of Nature, the Sun and the Moon, the Fire and the Earth; together with those imaginary deities who were supposed to preside over the most important occupations of human life. They were persuaded that, by some ridiculous arts of divination, they could discover the will of the superior beings, and that human sacrifices were the most precious and acceptable offering to their altars. Some applause has been hastily bestowed on the sublime notion entertained by that people of the Deity whom they neither confined within the walls of a temple nor represented by any human figure; but when we recollect that the Germans were unskilled in architecture, and totally unacquainted with the art of sculpture, we shall readily assign the true reason of a scruple, which arose not so much from a superiority of reason as from a want of ingenuity. The only temples in Germany were dark and ancient groves, consecrated by the reverence of succeeding generations. Their secret gloom, the imagined residence of an invisible power, by presenting no distinct object of fear or worship, impressed the mind with a still deeper sense of religious horror;[63] and the priests, rude and illiterate as they were, had been taught by experience the use of every artifice that could preserve and fortify impressions so well suited to their own interest.

The same ignorance which renders barbarians incapable of conceiving or embracing the useful restraints of laws exposes them naked and unarmed to the blind terrors of superstition. The German priests, improving this favourable temper of their countrymen, had assumed a jurisdiction even in temporal concerns which the magistrate could not venture to exercise; and the haughty warrior patiently submitted to the lash of correction, when it was inflicted, not by any human power, but by the immediate order of the god of war.[64] The defects of civil policy were sometimes supplied by the interposition of ecclesiastical authority. The latter was constantly exerted to maintain silence and decency in the popular assemblies; and was sometimes extended to a more enlarged concern for the national welfare. A solemn procession was occasionally celebrated in the present countries of Mecklenburgh and Pomerania. The unknown symbol of the *Earth*, covered with a thick veil, was placed on a carriage drawn by cows; and in this manner the goddess, whose common residence was in the isle of Rugen, visited several adjacent tribes of her worshippers. During her progress, the sound of war was hushed, quarrels were suspended, arms laid aside, and the restless Germans had an opportunity of tasting the blessings of peace and harmony.[65] The *truce of God*, so often and so ineffectually proclaimed by the clergy of the eleventh century, was an obvious imitation of this ancient custom.[66]

But the influence of religion was far more powerful to inflame than to moderate the fierce passions of the Germans. Interest and fanaticism often prompted its ministers to sanctify the most daring and the most unjust enterprises, by the approbation of Heaven, and full assurances of success. The consecrated standards, long revered in the groves of superstition, were placed in the front of the battle;[67] and the hostile army was devoted with dire execrations to the gods of war and of thunder.[68] In the faith of soldiers (and such were the Germans) cowardice is the most unpardonable of sins. A brave man was the worthy favourite of their martial deities; the wretch who had lost his shield was alike banished from the religious and the civil assemblies of his countrymen. Some tribes of the north seem to have embraced the doctrine of transmigration,[69] others imagined a gross paradise of immortal drunkenness.[70] All agreed that a life spent in arms, and a glorious death in battle, were the best preparations for a happy futurity, either in this or in another world.

The immortality so vainly promised by the priests was, in some degree, conferred by the bards. That singular order of men has most deservedly attracted the notice of all who have attempted to investigate the antiquities of the Celts, the Scandinavians, and the Germans. Their genius and character, as well as the reverence paid to that important office, have been sufficiently illustrated. But we cannot so easily express, or even conceive, the enthusiasm of arms and glory which they kindled in the breast of their audience. Among a polished people, a taste for poetry is rather an amusement of the fancy than a passion of the soul. And yet, when in calm retirement we peruse the combats described by Homer or Tasso, we are insensible seduced by the fiction, and feel a momentary glow of martial ardour. But how faint, how cold is the sensation which a peaceful mind can receive from solitary study! It was in the hour of battle, or in the feast of victory, that the bards celebrated the glory of heroes of ancient days, the ancestors of those warlike chieftains who listened with transport to their artless but animated strains. The view of arms and of danger heightened the effect of the military song; and the passions which it tended to excite, the desire of fame and the contempt of death, were the habitual sentiments of a German mind.[71]

Such was the situation and such were the manners of the ancient Germans. Their climate, their want of learning, of arts, and of laws, their notions of honour, of gallantry, and of religion, their sense of freedom, impatience of peace, and thirst of enterprise, all contributed to form a people of military heroes. And yet we find that, during more than two hundred and fifty years that elapsed from the defeat of Varus to the reign of Decius, these formidable barbarians made few considerable attempts, and not any material impression, on the luxurious and enslaved provinces of the empire. Their progress was checked by their want of arms and discipline, and their fury was diverted by the intestine divisions of ancient Germany.

I.   It has been observed, with ingenuity, and not without truth, that the command of iron soon gives a nation the command of gold. But the rude tribes of Germany, alike destitute of both those valuable metals, were reduced slowly to acquire, by their unassisted strength, the possession of the one as well as the other. The face of a German army displayed their poverty of iron. Swords and the longer kind of lances they could seldom use. Their *frameae* (as they called them in their own language) were long spears headed with a sharp but narrow iron point, and which, as occasion required, they either darted from a distance, or pushed in close onset. With this spear and with a shield their cavalry was contented. A multitude of darts, scattered[72] with incredible force, were an additional resource of the infantry. Their military dress, when they wore any, was nothing more than a loose mantle. A variety of colours was the only ornament of their wooden or their osier shields. Few of the chiefs were distinguished by cuirasses, scarce any by helmets. Though the horses of Germany were neither beautiful, swift, nor practised in the skilful evolutions of the Roman manage, several of the nations obtained renown by their cavalry; but, in general, the principal strength of the Germans consisted in their infantry,[73] which was drawn up in several deep columns, according to the distinction of tribes and families. Impatient of fatigue or delay, these half-armed warriors rushed to battle with dissonant shouts and disordered ranks; and sometimes, by the effort of native valour, prevailed over the constrained and more artificial bravery of the Roman mercenaries. But as the barbarians poured forth their whole souls on the first onset, they knew not how to rally or to retire. A repulse was a sure defeat; and a defeat was most commonly total destruction. When we recollect the complete armour of the Roman soldiers, their discipline, exercises, evolutions, fortified camps, and military engines, it appears a just matter of surprise how the naked and unassisted valour of the barbarians could dare to encounter in the field the strength of the legions and the various troops of the auxiliaries, which seconded their operations. The contest was too unequal, till the introduction of luxury had enervated the vigour, and a spirit of disobedience and sedition had relaxed the discipline, of the Roman armies. The introduction of barbarian auxiliaries into those armies was a measure attended with very obvious dangers, as it might gradually instruct the Germans in the arts of war and of policy. Although they were admitted in small numbers and with the strictest precaution, the example of Civilis was proper to convince the Romans that the danger was not imaginary, and that their precautions were not always sufficient.[74] During the civil wars that followed the death of Nero, that artful and intrepid Batavian, whom his enemies condescended to compare with Hannibal and Sertorius,[75] formed a great design of freedom and ambition. Eight Batavian cohorts, renowned in the wars of Britain and Italy, repaired to his standard. He introduced an army of Germans into Gaul, prevailed on the powerful cities of Treves and Langres to embrace his cause, defeated the legions, destroyed their fortified camps, and employed against the Romans the military knowledge which he had acquired in their service. When at length, after an obstinate struggle, he yielded to the power of the empire, Civilis secured himself and his country by an honourable treaty. The Batavians still continued to occupy the islands of the Rhine,[76] the allies, not the servants, of the Roman monarchy.

II.   The strength of ancient Germany appears formidable when we consider the effects that might have been produced by its united effort. The wide extent of country might very possibly contain a million of warriors, as all who were of an age to bear arms were of a temper to use them. But this fierce multitude, incapable of concerting or executing any plan of national greatness, was agitated by various and often hostile intentions. Germany was divided into more than forty independent states; and even in each state the union of the several tribes was extremely loose and precarious. The barbarians were easily provoked; they knew not how to forgive an injury, much less an insult; their resentments were bloody and implacable. The casual disputes that so frequently happened in their tumultuous parties of hunting or drinking were sufficient to inflame the minds of whole nations; the private feud of any considerable chieftains diffused itself among their followers and allies. To chastise the insolent, or to plunder the defenceless, were alike causes of war. The most formidable states of Germany affected to encompass their territories with a wide frontier of solitude and devastation. The awful distance preserved by their neighbours attested the terror of their arms, and in some measure defended them from the danger of unexpected incursions.[77]

'The Bructeri (it is Tacitus who now speaks) were totally exterminated by the neighbouring tribes,[78] provoked by their insolence, allured by the hopes of spoil, and perhaps inspired by the tutelar deities of the empire. Above sixty thousand barbarians were destroyed, not by the Roman arms, but in our sight, and for our entertainment. May the nations, enemies of Rome, ever preserve this enmity to each other! We have now attained the utmost verge of prosperity,[79] and have nothing left to demand of fortune except the discord of the barbarians.'[80] These sentiments, less worthy of the humanity than of the patriotism of Tacitus, express the invariable maxims of the policy of his countrymen. They deemed it a much safer expedient to divide than to combat the barbarians, from whose defeat they could derive neither honour nor advantage. The money and negotiations of Rome insinuated themselves into the heart of Germany, and every art of seduction was used with dignity to conciliate those nations whom their proximity to the Rhine or Danube might render the most useful friends as well as the most troublesome enemies. Chiefs of renown and power were flattered by the most trifling presents, which they received either as marks of distinction or as the instruments of luxury. In civil dissensions, the weaker faction endeavoured to strengthen its interest by entering into secret connections with the governors of the frontier provinces. Every quarrel among the Germans was fomented by the intrigues of Rome; and every plan of union and public good was defeated by the stronger bias of private jealousy and interest.[81]

The general conspiracy which terrified the Romans under the reign of Marcus Antoninus comprehended almost all the nations of Germany, and even Sarmatia, from the mouth of the Rhine to that of the Danube.[82] It is impossible for us to determine whether this hasty confederation was formed by necessity, by reason, or by passion; but we may rest assured that the barbarians were neither allured by the indolence nor provoked by the ambition of the Roman monarch. This dangerous invasion required all the firmness and vigilance of Marcus. He fixed generals of ability in the several stations of attack, and assumed in person the conduct of the most important province on the Upper Danube. After a long and doubtful conflict, the spirit of the barbarians was subdued. The Quadi and the Marcomanni,[83] who had taken the lead in the war, were the most severely punished in its catastrophe. They were commanded to retire five miles[84] from their own banks of the Danube, and to deliver up the flower of the youth, who were immediately sent into Britain, a remote island, where they might be secure as hostages and useful as soldiers.[85] On the frequent rebellions of the Quadi and Marcomanni, the irritated emperor resolved to reduce their country into the form of a province. His designs were disappointed by death. This formidable league, however, the only one that appears in the two first centuries of the Imperial history, was entirely dissipated without leaving any traces behind in Germany.

In the course of this introductory chapter, we have confined ourselves to the general outlines of the manners of Germany, without attempting to describe or to distinguish the various tribes which filled that great country in the time of Caesar, of Tacitus, or of Ptolemy.* As the ancient or as new tribes successively present themselves in the series of this history, we shall concisely mention their origin, their situation, and their particular character. Modern nations are fixed and permanent societies, connected among themselves by laws and government, bound to their native soil by arts and agriculture. The German tribes were voluntary and fluctuating associations of soldiers, almost of savages. The same territory often changed its inhabitants in the tide of conquest and emigration. The same communities, uniting in a plan of defence or invasion, bestowed a new title on their new confederacy. The dissolution of an ancient confederacy restored to the independent tribes their peculiar but long forgotten appellation. A victorious state often communicated its own name to a vanquished people. Sometimes crowds of volunteers flocked from all parts to the standard of a favourite leader; his camp became their country, and some circumstance of the enterprise soon gave a common denomination to the mixed multitude. The distinctions of the ferocious invaders were perpetually varied by themselves, and confounded by the astonished subjects of the Roman empire.[86]

Wars and the administration of public affairs are the principal subjects of history; but the number of persons interested in these busy scenes is very different, according to the different conditions of mankind. In great monarchies millions of obedient subjects pursue their useful occupations in peace and obscurity. The attention of the writer, as well as of the reader, is solely confined to a court, a capital, a regular army, and the districts which happen to be the occasional scene of military operations. But a state of freedom and barbarism, the season of civil commotions, or the situation of petty republics,[87] raises almost every member of the community into action and consequently into notice. The irregular divisions and the restless motions of the people of Germany dazzle our imagination, and seem to multiply their numbers. The profuse enumeration of kings and warriors, of armies and nations, inclines us to forget that the same objects are continually repeated under a variety of appellations, and that the most splendid appellations have been frequently lavished on the most inconsiderable objects.

NOTES TO CHAPTER 9

1 The modern philosophers of Sweden seem agreed that the waters of the Baltic gradually sink in a regular proportion, which they have ventured to estimate at half an inch every year. Twenty centuries ago, the flat country of Scandinavia must have been covered by the sea; while the high lands rose above the waters, as so many islands of various forms and dimensions. Such indeed is the notion given us by Mela, Pliny, and Tacitus, of the vast countries round the Baltic. See in the *Bibliothèque Raisonnée*, tom. xl and xlv, a large abstract of Dalin's *History of Sweden*, composed in the Swedish language.

2 In particular, Mr Hume, and the Abbé du Bos, and M. Pelloutier, *Hist. des Celtes*, tom. i.

3 Diodorus Siculus, v, 340, edit. Wessel; Herodian, vi, 221; Jornandes, ch. 55. On the banks of the Danube, the wine, when brought to table, was frequently frozen into great lumps, *frusta vini* [lumps of wine]. Ovid *Epist. ex Ponto*, iv, 7, 7–10. Virgil, *Georgics*, iii, 355. The fact is confirmed by a soldier and a philosopher, who had experienced the intense cold of Thrace. See Xenophon, *Anabasis*, vii, 560, edit. Hutchinson.

4 Buffon, *Histoire Naturelle*, xii, 79, 116.

5 Caesar, *de Bell. Gallic.*, vi, 23, etc. The most inquisitive of the Germans were ignorant of its utmost limits, although some of them had travelled in it more than sixty days' journey.

6 Cluverius (*Germania Antiqua*, iii, 47) investigates the small and scattered remains of the Hercynian Wood.

7 Charlevoix, *Histoire du Canada*.

8 Olaus Rudbeck asserts that the Swedish women often bear ten or twelve children, and not uncommonly twenty or thirty; but the authority of Rudbeck is much to be suspected.

9 *In hos artus, in haec corpora, quae miramur, excrescunt.* ['They fill out into these limbs and bodies at which we marvel.'] Tacitus, *Germania*, 20, Cluverius, i, 14.

10 Plutarch, *in Mario*. The Cimbri, by way of amusement, often slid down mountains of snow on their broad shields.

11 The Romans made war in all climates, and by their excellent discipline were in a great measure preserved in health and vigour. It may be remarked that man is the only animal which can live and multiply in every country from the equator to the poles. The hog seems to approach the nearest to our species in that privilege.

12 Tacitus, *Germania*, 3. The emigration of the Gauls followed the course of the Danube, and discharged itself on Greece and Asia. Tacitus could discover only one inconsiderable tribe that retained any traces of a Gallic origin.

13 According to Dr Keating (*History of Ireland*, pp. 13, 14), the giant Partholanus, who was the son of Seara, the son of Esra, the son of Sru, the son of Framant, the son of Fathaclan, the son of Magog, the son of Japhet, the son of Noah, landed on the coast of Munster, the 14th day of May, in the year of the world one tbousand nine hundred and seventy-eight. Though he succeeded in his great enterprise, the loose behaviour of his wife rendered his domestic life very unhappy, and provoked him to such a degree, that he killed – her favourite greyhound. This, as the learned historian very properly observes, was the first instance of female falsehood and infidelity ever known in Ireland.

14 *Genealogical History of the Tartars* by Abulghazi Bahadur Khan.

15 His work, entitled *Atlantica*, is uncommonly scarce. Bayle has given two most curious extracts from it. *République des Lettres*, Janvier et Février, 1685.

16 Tacitus, *Germania*, ii, 19. *Litterarum secreta viri pariter ac feminae ignorant.* ['Men and woman alike are ignorant of the art of reading and writing.'] We may rest contented with this decisive authority, without entering into the obscure disputes concerning the antiquity of the Runic characters. The learned Celsius, a Swede, a scholar and a philosopher, was of opinion, that they were nothing more than the Roman letters, with the curves changed into straight lines for the ease of engraving. See Pelloutier, *Histoire des Celtes*, ii, 11. *Dictionnaire Diplomatique*, i, 223. We may add, that the oldest Runic inscriptions are supposed to be of the third century, and the most ancient writer who mentions the Runic characters is Venantius Fortunatus (*Carm*, vii, 18). who lived towards the end of the sixth century. *Barbara fraxineis pingatur Runa tabellis.* ['The barbarous runes are painted on tablets made of ash wood.']

17 *Recherches Philosophiques sur les Américains*, iii, 228. The author of that very curious work is, if I am not misinformed, a German by birth.

18 The Alexandrian Geographer is often criticised by the accurate Cluverius.

19 See Caesar, and the learned Mr Whitaker in his *History of Manchester*, vol. i.

20 Tacitus, *Germania*, 16.

21 When the Germans commanded the Ubii of Cologne to cast off the Roman yoke, and with their new freedom to resume their ancient manners, they insisted on the immediate demolition of the walls of the colony. *'Postulamus a vobis muros coloniae, munimenta servitii, detrahatis; etiam fera animalia, si clausa teneas, virtutis obliviscuntur.'* Tacitus, *Hist.*, iv, 64. ['We call on you to tear down the walls of the colony, the symbols of slavery; even wild animals, if you lock them up, lose their courage.']

22 The straggling villages of Silesia are several miles in length. See Cluverius, i, 13.

23 One hundred and forty years after Tacitus a few more regular structures were erected near the Rhine and Danube. Herodian, vii, 234.

24 Tacitus, *Germania*, 17.

25 Tacitus, *Germania*, 5.

26 Caesar, *de Bell. Gall.*, vi, 21.

27 Tacitus, *Germania*, 26; Caesar, vi, 22.

28 Tacitus, *Germania*, 5.

29 It is said that the Mexicans and Peruvians, without the use of either money or iron, had made a very great progress in the arts. Those arts, and the monuments they produced, have been strangely magnified. See *Recherches sur les Américains*, ii, 153, etc.

30 Tacitus, *Germania*, 15.

31 Tacitus, *Germania*, 22, 23.

32 Tacitus, *Germania*, 24. The Germans might borrow the *arts* of play from the Romans, but the *passion* is wonderfully inherent in the human species.

33 Tacitus, *Germania*, 14.

34 Plutarch *in Camillo*; Livy, v, 33.

35 Dubos, *Hist. de la Monarchie Françoise*, i, 193.

36 The Helvetian nation, which issued from the country called Switzerland, contained, of every age and sex, 368,000 persons (Caesar, *de Bell. Gall.*, i. 29). At present, the number of people in the Pays de Vaud (a small district on the

banks of the Leman Lake, much more distinguished for politeness than for industry) amounts to 112,591. See an excellent Tract of M. Muret, in the *Mémoires de la Société de Berne*.

37 Paul Diaconus, chs 1, 2, 3. Machiavel, Davila, and the rest of Paul's followers represent these emigrations too much as regular and concerted measures.

38 Sir William Temple and Montesquieu have indulged, on this subject, the usual liveliness of their fancy.

39 Machiavel, *Hist. di Firenze*, Bk i; Mariana, *Hist. Hispan.*, v, 1.

40 Robertson's *Charles V*; Hume's *Politic. Ess*.

41 Tacitus, *Germania*, 44, 45. Freinshemius (who dedicated his supplement to Livy to Christina of Sweden) thinks proper to be very angry with the Roman who expressed so very little reverence for Northern queens.

42 May we not suspect that superstition was the parent of despotism? The descendants of Odin (whose race was not extinct till the year 1060) are said to have reigned in Sweden above a thousand years. The temple of Upsal was the ancient seat of religion and empire. In the year 1153 I find a singular law prohibiting the use and possession of arms to any, except the king's guards. Is it not probable that it was coloured by the pretence of reviving an old institution? See Dalin's *History of Sweden* in the *Bibliothèque Raisonnée*, xl and xlv.

43 Tacitus, *Germania*, 43.

44 *Id.*, 11, 12, 13, etc.

45 Grotius changes an expression of Tacitus, *pertractantur* into *praetractantur*. The correction is equally just and ingenious. [*pertractantur*, i.e. are thoroughly considered; *praetractantur*, i.e. are previously considered.]

46 Even in *our* ancient parliament, the barons often carried a question not so much by the number of votes as by that of their armed followers.

47 Caesar, *de Bell. Gall.*, vi, 23.

48 *Minuunt controversias*, is a very happy expression of Caesar's.

49 *Reges ex nobilitate, duces ex virtute sumunt*. Tacitus, *Germania*, 7.

50 Cluverius, *Germania Antiqua,* i, 38.

51 Caesar, vi, 22; Tacitus, *Germania*, 26.

52 Tacitus, *Germania*, 7.

53 Tacitus, *Germania*, 13, 14.

54 *Esprit des Loix*, xxx, 3. The brilliant imagination of Montesquieu is corrected, however, by the dry cold reason of the Abbé de Mably. *Observations sur l'Histoire de France*, i, 356.

55 *Gaudent muneribus, sed nec data imputant, nec acceptis obligantur*. Tacitus, *Germania*, 21.

56 The adulteress was whipped through the village. Neither wealth nor beauty could inspire compassion, or procure her a second husband. [Tacitus, *Germania*] 18, 19.

57 Ovid employs two hundred lines in the research of places the most favourable to love. Above all he considers the theatre as the best adapted to collect the beauties of Rome, and to melt them into tenderness and sensuality.

58 Tacitus, *Hist.*, iv, 61, 65.

59 The marriage present was a yoke of oxen, horses, and arms. See *Germania*, 18. Tacitus is somewhat too florid on the subject.

60 The change of *exigere* into *exugere* is a most excellent correction [ch. 7] [*exigere*, to examine; *exugere*, to suck out (the wounds)].

61 Tacitus, *Germania*, 7; Plutarch *in Mario*. Before the wives of the Teutones destroyed themselves and their children, they had offered to surrender, on condition that they should be received as the slaves of the vestal virgins.

62 Tacitus has employed a few lines, and Cluverius one hundred and twenty-four pages, on this obscure subject. The former discovers in Germany the gods of Greece and Rome. The latter is positive that, under the emblems of the sun, the moon, and the fire, his pious ancestors worshipped the Trinity in unity.

63 The sacred wood, described with such sublime horror by Lucan, was in the neighbourhood of Marseilles; but there were many of the same kind in Germany.

64 Tacitus, *Germania*, 7.

65 Tacitus, *Germania*, 40.

66 See Dr Robertson's *History of Charles V*, vol. i, note 10.

67 Tacitus, *Germania*, 7. These standards were only the heads of wild beasts.

68 See an instance of this custom, Tacitus, *Annals*, xiii, 57.

69 Caesar, Diodorus, and Lucan, seem to ascribe this doctrine to the Gauls, but M. Pelloutier (*Histoire des Celtes*, iii, 18) labours to reduce their expressions to a more orthodox sense.

70 Concerning this gross but alluring doctrine of the Edda, see Fable xx in the curious version of that book, published by M. Mallet, in his Introduction to the *History of Denmark*.

71 See Tacitus, *Germania*, 3; Diodorus Siculus, v; Strabo, iv, 197. The classical reader may remember the rank of Demodocus in the Phaeacian court, and the ardour infused by Tyrtaeus into the fainting Spartans. Yet there is little probability that the Greeks and the Germans were the same people. Much learned trifling might be spared, if our antiquarians would condescend to reflect that similar manners will naturally be produced by similar situations.

72 *Missilia spargunt*, Tacitus, *Germania*, 6. ['They scatter the missiles.'] Either that historian used a vague expression, or he meant that they were thrown at random.

73 It was the principal distinction from the Sarmatians, who generally fought on horseback.

74 The relation of this enterprise occupies a great part of the fourth and fifth books of the *History* of Tacitus, and is more remarkable for its eloquence than perspicuity. Sir Henry Saville has observed several inaccuracies.

75 Tacitus, *Hist.*, iv, 13. Like them he had lost an eye.

76 It was contained between the two branches of the old Rhine, as they subsisted before the face of the country was changed by art and nature. See Cluverius, *Germania Antiqua,* iii, ch. 30, 37.

77 Caesar, *de Bell. Gall.*, vi, 23.

78 They are mentioned however in the fourth and fifth centuries by Nazarius, Ammianus, Claudian, etc., as a tribe of Franks. See Cluverius, *Germania Antiqua,* iii, 13.

79 *Urgentibus* is the common reading, but good sense, Lipsius, and some manuscripts declare for *Vergentibus*. [*Urgentibus*, i.e. driving on; *Vergentibus*, i.e. on the verge of.]

80 Tacitus, *Germania*, 33. The pious Abbé de la Bléterie is very angry with Tacitus, talks of the devil who was a murderer from the beginning, etc., etc.

81 Many traces of this policy may be discovered in Tacitus and Dion; and many more may be inferred from the principles of human nature.

82 *Hist. August.*, p. 31; Ammian. Marcellin., xxxi, 5; Aurelius Victor. The Emperor Marcus was reduced to sell the rich furniture of the palace, and to enlist slaves and robbers.

83 The Marcomanni, a colony, who, from the banks of the Rhine, occupied Bohemia and Moravia, had once erected a great and formidable monarchy under their king Maroboduus. See Strabo, vii; Velleius Paterculus, ii, 105; Tacitus, *Annals*, ii, 63.

84 Mr Wotton (*History of Rome*, p. 166) increases the prohibition to ten times the distance. His reasoning is specious [i.e. attractive] but not conclusive. Five miles were sufficient for a fortified barrier.

85 Dion, lxxi and lxxii.

* *page 197*   [the geographer, fl. AD 127–145]

86 See an excellent dissertation on the origin and migrations of nations, in the *Mémoires de l'Académie des Inscriptions*, xviii, 48–71. It is seldom that the antiquarian and the philosopher are so happily blended.

87 Should we suspect that Athens contained only 21,000 citizens, and Sparta no more than 39,000? See Hume and Wallace on the number of mankind in ancient and modern times.

CHAPTER 10 (Summary)

The Emperors Decius, Gallus, Aemilianus, Valerian,
and Gallienus – the general irruption of the Barbarians –
the thirty Tyrants

Gibbon describes the first serious inroads into the Roman empire by the Goths, the Franks, the Alemanni and the Persians in the years AD 250–268. He gives an account of the obscure origins of the Goths and indicates the ultimate disgrace for the Romans when Sapor, King of Persia, took prisoner the emperor Valerian in AD 260. By the end of the period, the population of the empire had been significantly reduced by invasions, rebellions, famine and plague.

CHAPTER 11 (Summary)

Reign of Claudius – defeat of the Goths – victories,
triumph, and death of Aurelian

Under the emperors Claudius and Aurelian, however, military discipline was restored, and the fortunes of the Roman Empire revived (AD 268–75). The Goths and the Alemanni were repelled, although the province of Dacia was surrendered. Rivals to the emperors who had established themselves in Gaul and Palmyra, namely, Tetricus and Zenobia, Queen of the East, were defeated by Aurelian. Gibbon describes the triumph given to Aurelian on his return to Rome in AD 274 with Tetricus and Zenobia as his prisoners. His rule was severe, however, and he was murdered when campaigning against Persia in the following year.

CHAPTER 12 (Summary)

Conduct of the army and senate after the death of Aurelian –
reigns of Tacitus, Probus, Carus and his sons

Gibbon describes how the authority of the Roman senate was partly restored in AD 275 by the election as emperor of Tacitus, an elderly senator and descendant of the historian of that name. He died in a campaign in Asia Minor in the following year, but the military commander Probus was a worthy successor. He restored order to the Roman world in a reign of six years. After his death, there was more internal conflict when the senator and Praetorian Prefect, Carus, and his two sons, Carinus and Numerian, became emperors. Carinus entertained the Roman populace with games in the Coliseum, and Gibbon uses the occasion to describe in detail the splendour of the amphitheatre at that time. Meanwhile, Diocletian was elected emperor by the army in AD 284 and subsequently defeated Carinus on the Danube.

CHAPTER 13

The reign of Diocletian and his three associates, Maximian,
Galerius, and Constantius – general re-establishment of
order and tranquillity – the Persian war, victory, and triumph –
the new form of administration – abdication and
retirement of Diocletian and Maximian

As the reign of Diocletian was more illustrious than that of any of his predecessors, so was his birth more abject and obscure. The strong claims of merit and of violence had frequently superseded the ideal prerogatives of nobility; but a distinct line of separation was hitherto preserved between the free and the servile part of mankind. The parents of Diocletian had been slaves in the house of Anulinus, a Roman senator; nor was he himself distinguished by any other name than that which he derived from a small town in Dalmatia, from whence his mother deduced her origin.[1] It is, however, probable, that his father obtained the freedom of the family, and that he soon acquired an office of scribe, which was commonly exercised by persons of his condition.[2] Favourable oracles, or rather the consciousness of superior merit, prompted his aspiring son to pursue the profession of arms and the hopes of fortune; and it would be extremely curious to observe the gradation of arts* and accidents which enabled him in the end to fulfil those oracles, and to display that merit to the world. Diocletian was successively promoted to the government of Maesia, the honours of the consulship, and the important command of the guards of the palace. He distinguished his abilities in the Persian war; and, after the death of Numerian, the slave, by the confession and judgment of his rivals, was declared the most worthy of the Imperial throne. The malice of religious zeal, whilst it arraigns the savage fierceness of his colleague Maximian, has affected to cast suspicions on the personal courage of the Emperor Diocletian.³ It would not be easy to persuade us of the cowardice of a soldier of fortune, who acquired and preserved the esteem of the legions, as well as the favour of many warlike princes. Yet even calumny is sagacious enough to discover and to attack the most vulnerable part. The valour of Diocletian was never found inadequate to his duty, or to the occasion; but he appears not to have possessed the daring and generous spirit of a hero, who courts danger and fame, disdains artifice, and boldly challenges the allegiance of his equals. His abilities were useful rather than splendid; a vigorous mind, improved by the experience and study of mankind, dexterity and application in business; a judicious mixture of liberality and economy, of mildness and rigour; profound dissimulation under the disguise of military frankness; steadiness to pursue his ends; flexibility to vary his means; and above all the great art of submitting his own passions, as well as those of others, to the interest of his ambition, and of colouring his ambition with the most specious pretences of justice and public utility. Like Augustus, Diocletian may be considered as the founder of a new empire. Like the adopted son of Caesar, he was distinguished as a statesman rather than a warrior; nor did either of those princes employ force, whenever their purpose could be effected by policy.

The victory of Diocletian was remarkable for its singular mildness. A people accustomed to applaud the clemency of the conqueror, if the usual punishments of death, exile and confiscation were inflicted with any degree of temper and equity, beheld with the most pleasing astonishment a civil war, the flames of which were extinguished in the field of battle. Diocletian received into his confidence Aristobulus, the principal minister of the house of Carus, respected the lives, the fortunes, and the dignity of his adversaries, and even continued in their respective stations the greater number of the servants of Carinus.⁴ It is not improbable that motives of prudence might assist the humanity of the artful Dalmatian; of these servants many had purchased his favour by secret treachery; in others, he esteemed their grateful fidelity to an unfortunate master. The discerning judgment of Aurelian, of Probus, and of Carus, had filled the several departments of the state and army with officers of approved merit, whose removal would have injured the public service, without promoting the interest of the successor. Such a conduct, however, displayed to the Roman world the fairest prospect of the new reign, and the emperor affected to confirm this favourable prepossession by declaring that, among all the virtues of his predecessors, he was the most ambitious of imitating the humane philosophy of Marcus Antoninus.*[5]

The first considerable action of his reign seemed to evince his sincerity as well as his moderation. After the example of Marcus, he gave himself a colleague in the person of Maximian, on whom he bestowed at first the title of Caesar, and afterwards that of Augustus.[6] But the motives of his conduct, as well as; the object of his choice, were of a very different nature from those of his admired predecessor. By investing a luxurious youth with the honours of the purple, Marcus had discharged a debt of private gratitude, at the expense, indeed, of the happiness of the state. By associating a friend and a fellow-soldier to the labours of government, Diocletian, in a time of public danger, provided for the defence both of the East and of the West. Maximian was born a peasant, and, like Aurelian, in the territory of Sirmium. Ignorant of letters,[7] careless of laws, the rusticity of his appearance and manners still betrayed in the most elevated fortune the meanness of his extraction. War was the only art which he professed. In a long course of service, he had distinguished himself on every frontier of the empire; and, though his military talents were formed to obey rather than to command, though, perhaps, he never attained the skill of a consummate general, he was capable, by his valour, constancy, and experience, of executing the most arduous undertakings. Nor were the vices of Maximian less useful to his benefactor. Insensible to pity, and fearless of consequences, he was the ready instrument of every act of cruelty which the policy of that artful prince might at once suggest and disclaim. As soon as a bloody sacrifice had been offered to prudence or to revenge, Diocletian, by his seasonable intercession, saved the remaining few whom he had never designed to punish, gently censured the severity of his stern colleague, and enjoyed the comparison of a golden and an iron age, which was universally applied to their opposite maxims of government. Notwithstanding the difference of their characters, the two emperors maintained, on the throne, that friendship which they had contracted in a private station. The haughty turbulent spirit of Maximian, so fatal afterwards to himself and to the public peace, was accustomed to respect the genius of Diocletian, and confessed the ascendant of reason over brutal violence.[8] From a motive either of pride or superstition, the two emperors assumed the titles, the one of Jovius, the other of Herculius. Whilst the motion of the world (such was the language of their venal orators) was maintained by the all-seeing wisdom of Jupiter, the invincible arm of Hercules purged the earth of monsters and tyrants.[9]

But even the omnipotence of Jovius and Herculius was insufficient to sustain the weight of the public administration. The prudence of

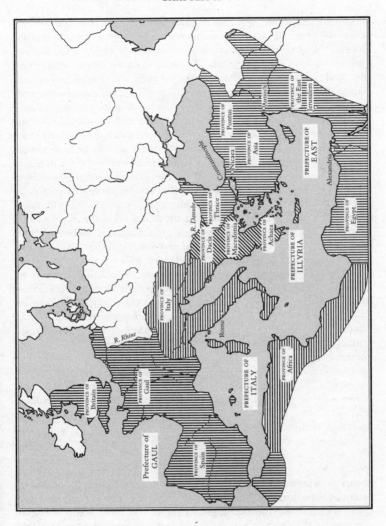

The Roman empire under Diocletian, AD *c.*300

Diocletian discovered that the empire, assailed on every side by the barbarians, required on every side the presence of a great army, and of an emperor. With this view he resolved once more to divide his unwieldy power, and, with the inferior title of *Caesars*, to confer on two generals of approved merit an equal share of the sovereign authority.[10] Galerius, surnamed Armentarius, from his original profession of a herdsman, and Constantius, who from his pale complexion had acquired the denomination of Chlorus,[11] were the two persons invested with the second honours of the Imperial purple. In describing the country, extraction, and manners of Herculius, we have already delineated those of Galerius, who was often, and not improperly, styled the younger Maximian, though in many instances both of virtue and ability he appears to have possessed a manifest superiority over the elder. The birth of Constantius was less obscure than that of his colleagues. Eutropius, his father, was one of the most considerable nobles of Dardania, and his mother was the niece of the Emperor Claudius.[12] Although the youth of Constantius had been spent in arms, he was endowed with a mild and amiable disposition, and the popular voice had long since acknowledged him worthy of the rank which he at last attained. To strengthen the bonds of political, by those of domestic, union, each of the emperors assumed the character of a father to one of the Caesars, Diocletian to Galerius, and Maximian to Constantius; and each, obliging him to repudiate their former wives, bestowed his daughter in marriage on his adopted son.[13] These four princes distributed among themselves the wide extent of the Roman empire. The defence of Gaul, Spain,[14] and Britain, was intrusted to Constantius: Galerius was stationed on the banks of the Danube, as the safeguard of the Illyrian provinces. Italy and Africa were considered as the department of Maximian, and, for his peculiar portion, Diocletian reserved Thrace, Egypt, and the rich countries of Asia. Every one was sovereign within his own jurisdiction; but their united authority extended over the whole monarchy; and each of them was prepared to assist his colleagues with his counsels or presence. The Caesars, in their exalted rank, revered the majesty of the emperors, and the three younger princes invariably acknowledged, by their gratitude and obedience, the common parent of their fortunes. The suspicious jealousy of power found not any place among them; and the singular happiness of their union has been compared to a chorus of music, whose harmony was regulated and maintained by the skilful hand of the first artist.[15]

This important measure was not carried into execution till about six years after the association of Maximian, and that interval of time had not been destitute of memorable incidents. But we have preferred, for the sake of perspicuity, first to describe the more perfect form of Diocletian's government, and afterwards to relate the actions of his reign, following rather the natural order of the events than the dates of a very doubtful chronology.

The first exploit of Maximian, though it is mentioned in a few words by our imperfect writers, deserves, from its singularity, to be recorded in a history of human manners. He suppressed the peasants of Gaul, who, under the appellation of Bagaudae,[16] had risen in a general insurrection; very similar to those which in the fourteenth century successively afflicted both France and England.[17] It should seem that very many of those institutions, referred by an easy solution to the feudal system, are derived from the Celtic barbarians. When Caesar subdued the Gauls, that great nation was already divided into three orders of men; the clergy, the nobility, and the common people. The first governed by superstition, the second by arms, but the third and last was not of any weight or account in their public councils. It was very natural for the Plebeians, oppressed by debt or apprehensive of injuries, to implore the protection of some powerful chief, who acquired over their persons and property the same absolute rights as, among, the Greeks and Romans, a master exercised over his slaves.[18] The greatest part of the nation was gradually reduced into a state of servitude; compelled to perpetual labour on the estates of the Gallic nobles, and confined to the soil, either by the real weight of fetters, or by the no less cruel and forcible restraints of the laws. During the long series of troubles which agitated Gaul, from the reign of Gallienus to that of Diocletian, the condition of these servile peasants was peculiarly miserable; and they experienced at once the complicated tyranny of their masters, of the barbarians, of the soldiers, and of the officers of the revenue.[19]

Their patience was at last provoked into despair. On every side they rose in multitudes, armed with rustic weapons, and with irresistible fury. The ploughman became a foot-soldier, the shepherd mounted on horseback, the deserted villages and open towns were abandoned to the flames, and the ravages of the peasants equalled those of the fiercest barbarians.[20] They asserted the natural rights of men, but they asserted those rights with the most savage cruelty. The Gallic nobles, justly dreading their revenge, either took refuge in the fortified cities, or fled from the wild scene of anarchy. The peasants reigned without control; and two of their most daring leaders had the folly and rashness to assume the Imperial ornaments.[21] Their power soon expired at the approach of the legions. The strength of union and discipline obtained an easy victory over a licentious and divided multitude.[22] A severe retaliation was inflicted on the peasants who were found in arms; the affrighted remnant returned to their respective habitations, and their unsuccessful effort for freedom served only to confirm their slavery. So strong and uniform is the current of popular passions that we might almost venture, from very scanty materials, to relate the particulars of this war; but we are not disposed to believe that the principal leaders Aelianus and Amandus were Christians,[23] or to insinuate that the rebellion, as it happened in the time of Luther, was occasioned by the abuse of those benevolent principles of Christianity which inculcate the natural freedom of mankind.

Maximian had no sooner recovered Gaul from the hands of the peasants, than he lost Britain by the usurpation of Carausius. Ever since the rash but successful enterprise of the Franks under the reign of Probus, their daring countrymen had constructed squadrons of light brigantines, in which they incessantly ravaged the provinces adjacent to the ocean.[24] To repel their desultory incursions, it was found necessary to create a naval power; and the judicious measure was pursued with prudence and vigour. Gessoriacum or Boulogne, in the straits of the British channel, was chosen by the emperor for the station of the Roman fleet; and the command of it was entrusted to Carausius, a Menapian of the meanest origin,[25] but who had long signalised his skill as a pilot, and his valour as a soldier. The integrity of the new admiral corresponded not with his abilities. When the German pirates sailed from their own harbours, he connived at their passage, but he diligently intercepted their return, and appropriated to his own use an ample share of the spoil which they had acquired. The wealth of Carausius was, on this occasion, very justly considered as an evidence of his guilt; and Maximian had already given orders for his death. But the crafty Menapian foresaw and prevented the severity of the emperor. By his liberality he had attached to his fortunes the fleet which he commanded, and secured the barbarians in his interest. From the port of Boulogne he sailed over to Britain, persuaded the legion and the auxiliaries which guarded that island to embrace his party, and boldly assuming, with the Imperial purple, the title of Augustus, defied the justice and the arms of his injured sovereign.[26]

When Britain was thus dismembered from the empire, its importance was sensibly felt, and its loss sincerely lamented. The Romans celebrated, and perhaps magnified, the extent of that noble island, provided on every side with convenient harbours; the temperature of the climate, and the fertility of the soil, alike adapted for the production of corn or of vines; the valuable minerals with which it abounded; its rich pastures covered with innumerable flocks, and its woods free from wild beasts or venomous serpents. Above all, they regretted the large amount of the revenue of Britain, whilst they confessed that such a province well deserved to become the seat of an independent monarchy.[27] During the space of seven years, it was possessed by Carausius; and fortune continued propitious to a rebellion supported with courage and ability. The British emperor defended the frontiers of his dominions against the Caledonians of the North, invited from the continent a great number of skilful artists, and displayed, on a variety of coins that are still extant, his taste and opulence. Born on the confines of the Franks, he courted the friendship of that formidable people, by the flattering imitation of their dress and manners. The bravest of their youth he enlisted among his land or sea forces; and, in return for their useful alliance, he communicated to the barbarians the dangerous knowledge of military and naval arts. Carausius still preserved the possession of Boulogne and the adjacent country. His fleets rode triumphant in the channel, commanded the mouths of the Seine and of the Rhine, ravaged the coasts of the ocean, and diffused, beyond the Columns of Hercules, the terror of his name. Under his command, Britain, destined in a future age to obtain the empire of the sea, already assumed its natural and respectable station of a maritime power.[28]

By seizing the fleet of Boulogne, Carausius had deprived his master of the means of pursuit and revenge. And, when, after vast expense of time and labour, a new armament was launched into the water,[29] the Imperial troops, unaccustomed to that element, were easily baffled and defeated by the veteran sailors of the usurper. This disappointed effort was soon productive of a treaty of peace. Diocletian and his colleague, who justly dreaded the enterprising spirit of Carausius, resigned to him the sovereignty of Britain, and reluctantly admitted their perfidious servant to a participation of the Imperial honours.[30] But the adoption of the two Caesars restored new vigour to the Roman arms; and, while the Rhine was guarded by the presence of Maximian, his brave associate, Constantius, assumed the conduct of the British war. His first enterprise was against the important place of Boulogne. A stupendous mole, raised across the entrance of the harbour, intercepted all hopes of relief. The town surrendered after an obstinate defence; and a considerable part of the naval strength of Carausius fell into the hands of the besiegers. During the three years which Constantius employed in preparing a fleet adequate to the conquest of Britain, he secured the coast of Gaul, invaded the country of the Franks, and deprived the usurper of the assistance of those powerful allies.

Before the preparations were finished, Constantius received the intelligence of the tyrant's death, and it was considered as a sure presage of the approaching victory. The servants of Carausius imitated the example of treason which he had given. He was murdered by his first minister Allectus, and the assassin succeeded to his power and to his danger. But he possessed not equal abilities either to exercise the one, or to repel the other. He beheld, with anxious terror, the opposite shores of the continent, already filled with arms, with troops, and with vessels; for Constantius had very prudently divided his forces, that he might likewise divide the attention and resistance of the enemy. The attack was at length made by the principal squadron, which, under the command of the prefect Asclepiodotus, an officer of distinguished merit, had been assembled in the mouth of the Seine. So imperfect in those times was the art of navigation that orators have celebrated the daring courage of the Romans, who ventured to set sail with a side-wind, and on a stormy day. The weather proved favourable to their enterprise. Under the cover of a thick fog, they escaped the fleet of Allectus, which had been stationed off the Isle of Wight to receive them, landed in safety on some part of the western coast, and convinced the Britons that a superiority of naval strength will not always protect their country from a foreign invasion.

Asclepiodotus had no sooner disembarked the Imperial troops than he set fire to his ships; and, as the expedition proved fortunate, his heroic conduct was universally admired. The usurper had posted himself near London, to expect the formidable attack of Constantius, who commanded in person the fleet of Boulogne; but the descent of a new enemy required his immediate presence in the West. He performed this long march in so precipitate a manner that he encountered the whole force of the prefect with a small body of harassed and disheartened troops. The engagement was soon terminated by the total defeat and death of Allectus; a single battle, as it has often happened, decided the fate of this great island; and, when Constantius landed on the shores of Kent, he found them covered with obedient subjects. Their acclamations were loud and unanimous; and the virtues of the conqueror may induce us to believe that they sincerely rejoiced in a revolution which, after a separation of ten years, restored Britain to the body of the Roman empire.[31]

Britain had none but domestic enemies to dread; and, as long as the governors preserved their fidelity, and the troops their discipline, the incursions of the naked savages of Scotland or Ireland could never materially affect the safety of the province. The peace of the continent, and the defence of the principal rivers which bounded the empire, were objects of far greater difficulty and importance. The policy of Diocletian, which inspired the councils of his associates, provided for the public tranquillity, by encouraging a spirit of dissension among the barbarians and by strengthening the fortifications of the Roman limit.* In the East he fixed a line of camps from Egypt to the Persian dominions, and, for every camp, he instituted an adequate number of stationary troops, commanded by their respective officers, and supplied with every kind of arms, from the new arsenals which he had formed at Antioch, Emesa, and Damascus.[32] Nor was the precaution of the emperor less watchful against the well-known valour of the barbarians of Europe. From the mouth of the Rhine to that of the Danube, the ancient camps, towns, and citadels were diligently re-established, and, in the most exposed places, new ones were skilfully constructed; the strictest vigilance was introduced among the garrisons of the frontier, and every expedient was practised that could render the long chain of fortifications firm and impenetrable.[33] A barrier so respectable was seldom violated, and the barbarians often turned against each other their disappointed rage. The Goths, the Vandals, the Gepidae, the Burgundians, the Alemanni, wasted each other's strength by destructive hostilities: and whosoever vanquished, they vanquished the enemies of Rome. The subjects of Diocletian enjoyed the bloody spectacle, and congratulated each other that the mischiefs of civil war were now experienced only by the barbarians.[34]

Notwithstanding the policy of Diocletian, it was impossible to maintain an equal and undisturbed tranquillity during a reign of twenty years, and along a frontier of many hundred miles. Sometimes the barbarians suspended their domestic animosities, and the vigilance of the garrisons sometimes gave a passage to their strength or dexterity. Whenever the provinces were invaded, Diocletian conducted himself with that calm dignity which he always affected or possessed; reserved his presence for such occasions as were worthy of his interposition, never exposed his person or reputation to any unnecessary danger, ensured his success by every means that prudence could suggest, and displayed, with ostentation, the consequences of his victory. In wars of a more difficult nature and more doubtful event, he employed the rough valour of Maximian, and that faithful soldier was content to ascribe his own victories to the wise counsels and auspicious influence of his benefactor. But, after the adoption of the two Caesars, the emperors, themselves retiring to a less laborious scene of action, devolved on their adopted sons the defence of the Danube and of the Rhine. The vigilant Galerius was never reduced to the necessity of vanquishing an army of barbarians on the Roman territory.[35] The brave and active Constantius delivered Gaul from a very furious inroad of the Alemanni; and his victories of Langres and Vindonissa appear to have been actions of considerable danger and merit. As he traversed the open country with a feeble guard he was encompassed on a sudden by the superior multitude of the enemy. He retreated with difficulty towards Langres; but, in the general consternation, the citizens refused to open their gates, and the wounded prince was drawn up the wall by the means of a rope. But on the news of his distress the Roman troops hastened from all sides to his relief, and before the evening he had satisfied his honour and revenge by the slaughter of six thousand Alemanni.[36] From the monuments of those times, the obscure traces of several other victories over the barbarians of Sarmatia and Germany might possibly be collected; but the tedious search would not be rewarded either with amusement* or with instruction.

The conduct which the emperor Probus had adopted in the disposal of the vanquished was imitated by Diocletian and his associates. The captive barbarians, exchanging death for slavery, were distributed among the provincials, and assigned to those districts (in Gaul, the territories of Amiens, Beauvais, Cambray, Treves, Langres, and Troyes, are particularly specified[37]) which had been depopulated by the calamities of war. They were usefully employed as shepherds and husbandmen, but were denied the exercise of arms, except when it was found expedient to enrol them in the military service. Nor did the emperors refuse the property of lands, with a less servile tenure, to such of the barbarians as solicited the protection of Rome. They granted a settlement to several colonies of the Carpi, the Bastarnae, and the Sarmatians; and, by a dangerous indulgence, permitted them in some measure to retain their national manners and independence.[38] Among the provincials, it was a subject of flattering exultation that the barbarian, lately an object of terror, now cultivated their lands, drove their cattle to the neighbouring fair, and contributed by his labour to the public plenty. They congratulated their masters on the powerful accession of subjects and soldiers; but they forgot to observe that multitudes of secret enemies, insolent from favour, or desperate from oppression, were introduced into the heart of the empire.[39]

While the Caesars exercised their valour on the banks of the Rhine and Danube, the presence of the emperors was required on the southern confines of the Roman world. From the Nile to Mount Atlas, Africa was in arms. A confederacy of five Moorish nations issued from their deserts to invade the peaceful provinces.[40] Julian had assumed the purple at Carthage,[41] Achilleus at Alexandria; and even the Blemmyes renewed, or rather continued, their incursions into the Upper Egypt. Scarcely any circumstances have been preserved of the exploits of Maximian in the western parts of Africa; but it appears, by the event, that the progress of his arms was rapid and decisive; that he vanquished the fiercest barbarians of Mauritania, and that he removed them from the mountains, whose inaccessible strength had inspired their inhabitants with a lawless confidence and habituated them to a life of rapine and violence.[42] Diocletian, on his side, opened the campaign in Egypt by the siege of Alexandria, cut off the aqueducts which conveyed the waters of the Nile into every quarter of that immense city,[43] and, rendering his camp impregnable to the sallies of the besieged multitude, he pushed his reiterated attacks with caution and vigour. After a siege of eight months, Alexandria, wasted by the sword and by fire, implored the clemency of the conqueror; but it experienced the full extent of his severity. Many thousands of the citizens perished in a promiscuous slaughter, and there were few obnoxious persons in Egypt who escaped a sentence either of death or at least of exile.[44] The fate of Busiris and of Coptos was still more melancholy than that of Alexandria; those proud cities, the former distinguished by its antiquity, the latter enriched by the passage of the Indian trade, were utterly destroyed by the arms and by the severe order of Diocletian.[45] The character of the Egyptian nation, insensible to kindness, but extremely susceptible of fear, could alone justify this excessive rigour. The seditions of Alexandria had often affected the tranquillity and subsistence of Rome itself. Since the usurpation of Firmus,* the province of Upper Egypt, incessantly relapsing into rebellion, had embraced the alliance of the savages of Ethiopia. The number of the Blemmyes, scattered between the Island of Meroe and the Red Sea, was very inconsiderable, their disposition was unwarlike, their weapons rude and inoffensive.[46] Yet in the public disorders these barbarians, whom antiquity, shocked with the deformity of their figure, had almost excluded from the human species, presumed to rank themselves among the enemies of Rome.[47] Such had been the unworthy allies of the Egyptians; and, while the attention of the state was engaged in more serious wars, their vexatious inroads might again harass the repose of the province. With a view of opposing to the

Blemmyes a suitable adversary, Diocletian persuaded the Nobatae, or people of Nubia, to remove from their ancient habitations in the deserts of Libya, and resigned to them an extensive but unprofitable territory, above Syene and the cataracts of the Nile, with the stipulation that they should ever respect and guard the frontier of the empire. The treaty long subsisted; and till the establishment of Christianity introduced stricter notions of religious worship, it was annually ratified by a solemn sacrifice in the isle of Elephantine, in which the Romans, as well as the barbarians, adored the same visible or invisible powers of the universe.[48]

At the same time that Diocletian chastised the past crimes of the Egyptians, he provided for their future safety and happiness by many wise regulations, which were confirmed and enforced under the succeeding reigns.[49] One very remarkable edict, which he published, instead of being condemned as the effect of jealous tyranny, deserves to be applauded as an act of prudence and humanity. He caused a diligent inquiry to be made 'for all the ancient books which treated of the admirable art of making gold and silver, and without pity committed them to the flames; apprehensive, as we are assured, lest the opulence of the Egyptians should inspire them with confidence to rebel against the empire.'[50] But, if Diocletian had been convinced of the reality of that valuable art, far from extinguishing the memory, he would have converted the operation of it to the benefit of the public revenue. It is much more likely that his good sense discovered to him the folly of such magnificent pretensions, and that he was desirous of preserving the reason and fortunes of his subjects from the mischievous pursuit. It may be remarked that these ancient books, so liberally ascribed to Pythagoras, to Solomon, or to Hermes,* were the pious frauds of more recent adepts. The Greeks were inattentive either to the use or to the abuse of chemistry. In that immense register where Pliny has deposited the discoveries, the arts, and the errors of mankind, there is not the least mention of the transmutation of metals; and the persecution of Diocletian is the first authentic event in the history of alchemy. The conquest of Egypt by the Arabs diffused that vain science over the globe. Congenial to the avarice of the human heart, it was studied in China as in Europe, with equal eagerness, and with equal success. The darkness of the middle ages ensured a favourable reception to every tale of wonder, and the revival of learning gave new vigour to hope, and suggested more specious arts of deception. Philosophy, with the aid of experience, has at length banished the study of alchemy; and the present age, however desirous of riches, is content to seek them by the humbler means of commerce and industry.[51]

The reduction of Egypt was immediately followed by the Persian war. It was reserved for the reign of Diocletian to vanquish that powerful nation, and to extort a confession from the successors of Artaxerxes, of the superior majesty of the Roman empire.

We have observed, under the reign of Valerian,* that Armenia was subdued by the perfidy and the arms of the Persians, and that, after the assassination of Chosroes, his son Tiridates, the infant heir of the monarchy, was saved by the fidelity of his friends, and educated under the protection of the emperors. Tiridates derived from his exile such advantages as he could never have attained on the throne of Armenia; the early knowledge of adversity, of mankind, and of the Roman discipline. He signalised his youth by deeds of valour, and displayed a matchless dexterity, as well as strength, in every martial exercise, and even in the less honourable contests of the Olympian games.[52] Those qualities were more nobly exerted in the defence of his benefactor Licinius.[53] That officer, in the sedition which occasioned the death of Probus, was exposed to the most imminent danger, and the enraged soldiers were forcing their way into his tent, when they were checked by the single arm of the Armenian prince. The gratitude of Tiridates contributed soon afterwards to his restoration. Licinius was in every station the friend and companion of Galerius, and the merit of Galerius, long before he was raised to the dignity of Caesar, had been known and esteemed by Diocletian. In the third year of that emperor's reign, Tiridates was invested with the kingdom of Armenia. The justice of the measure was not less evident than its expediency. It was time to rescue from the usurpation of the Persian monarch an important territory, which, since the reign of Nero, had been always granted under the protection of the empire to a younger branch of the house of Arsaces.[54]

When Tiridates appeared on the frontiers of Armenia, he was received with an unfeigned transport of joy and loyalty. During twenty-six years, the country had experienced the real and imaginary hardships of a foreign yoke. The Persian monarchs had adorned their new conquest with magnificent buildings; but those monuments had been erected at the expense of the people, and were abhorred as badges of slavery. The apprehension of a revolt had inspired the most rigorous precautions: oppression had been aggravated by insult, and the consciousness of the public hatred had been productive of every measure that could render it still more implacable. We have already remarked the intolerant spirit of the Magian religion.* The statues of the deified kings of Armenia, and the sacred images of the sun and moon, were broke in pieces by the zeal of the conqueror; and the perpetual fire of Ormuzd was kindled and preserved upon an altar erected on the summit of Mount Bagavant.[55] It was natural that a people exasperated by so many injuries should arm with zeal in the cause of their independence, their religion, and their hereditary sovereign. The torrent bore down every obstacle, and the Persian garrison retreated before its fury. The nobles of Armenia flew to the standard of Tiridates, all alleging their past merit, offering their future service, and soliciting from the new king those honours and rewards from which they had been excluded with disdain under the foreign government.[56] The command of the army was bestowed on Artavasdes, whose father had saved the infancy of Tiridates, and whose family had been massacred for that generous action. The brother of Artavasdes obtained the government of a province. One of the first military dignities was conferred on the satrap Otas, a man of singular temperance and fortitude, who presented to the king his sister[57] and a considerable treasure, both of which, in a sequestered fortress, Otas had preserved from violation. Among the Armenian nobles appeared an ally, whose fortunes are too remarkable to pass unnoticed. His name was Mamgo, his origin was Scythian, and the horde which acknowledged his authority had encamped a very few years before on the skirts of the Chinese empire,[58] which at that time extended as far as the neighbourhood of Sogdiana.[59] Having incurred the displeasure of his master, Mamgo, with his followers, retired to the banks of the Oxus, and implored the protection of Sapor. The emperor of China claimed the fugitive, and alleged the rights of sovereignty. The Persian monarch pleaded the laws of hospitality, and with some difficulty avoided a war, by the promise that he would banish Mamgo to the uttermost parts of the West: a punishment, as he described it, not less dreadful than death itself. Armenia was chosen for the place of exile, and a large district was assigned to the Scythian horde, on which they might feed their flocks and herds, and remove their encampment from one place to another according to the different seasons of the year. They were employed to repel the invasion of Tiridates; but their leader, after weighing the obligations and injuries which he had received from the Persian monarch, resolved to abandon his party. The Armenian prince, who was well acquainted with the merit as well as power of Mamgo, treated him with distinguished respect; and, by admitting him into his confidence, acquired a brave and faithful servant, who contributed very effectually to his restoration.[60]

For a while, fortune appeared to favour the enterprising valour of Tiridates. He not only expelled the enemies of his family and country from the whole extent of Armenia, but in the prosecution of his revenge he carried his arms, or at least his incursions, into the heart of Assyria. The historian who has preserved the name of Tiridates from oblivion celebrates, with a degree of national enthusiasm, his personal prowess; and, in the true spirit of eastern romance, describes the giants and the elephants that fell beneath his invincible arm. It is from other information that we discover the distracted state of the Persian monarchy, to which the king of Armenia was indebted for some part of his advantages. The throne was disputed by the ambition of contending brothers; and Hormuz, after exerting without success the strength of his own party, had recourse to the dangerous assistance of the barbarians who inhabited the banks of the Caspian Sea.[61] The civil war was, however, soon terminated, either by a victory or by a reconciliation; and Narses, who was universally acknowledged as King of Persia, directed his whole force against the foreign enemy. The contest then became too unequal; nor was the valour of the hero able to withstand the power of the monarch. Tiridates, a second time expelled from the throne of Armenia, once more took refuge in the court of the emperors. Narses soon re-established his authority over the revolted province; and, loudly complaining of the protection afforded by the Romans to rebels and fugitives, aspired to the conquest of the East.[62]

Neither prudence nor honour could permit the emperors to forsake the cause of the Armenian king, and it was resolved to exert the force of the empire in the Persian war. Diocletian, with the calm dignity which he constantly assumed, fixed his own station in the city of Antioch, from whence he prepared and directed the military operations.[63] The conduct of the legions was entrusted to the intrepid valour of Galerius, who, for that important purpose, was removed from the banks of the Danube to those of the Euphrates. The armies soon encountered each other in the plains of Mesopotamia, and two battles were fought with various and doubtful success: but the third engagement was of a more decisive nature; and the Roman army received a total overthrow, which is attributed to the rashness of Galerius, who, with an inconsiderable body of troops, attacked the innumerable host of the Persians.[64] But the consideration of the country that was the scene of action may suggest another reason for his defeat. The same ground, on which Galerius was vanquished, had been rendered memorable by the death of Crassus and the slaughter of ten legions.* It was a plain of more than sixty miles, which extended from the hills of Carrhae to the Euphrates; a smooth and barren surface of sandy desert, without a hillock, without a tree, and without a spring of fresh water.[65] The steady infantry of the Romans, fainting with heat and thirst, could neither hope for victory, if they preserved their ranks, nor break their ranks without exposing themselves to the most imminent danger. In this situation, they were gradually encompassed by the superior numbers, harassed by the rapid evolutions, and destroyed by the arrows of the barbarian cavalry. The king of Armenia had signalised his valour in the battle, and acquired personal glory by the public misfortune. He was pursued as far as the Euphrates; his horse was wounded, and it appeared impossible for him to escape the victorious enemy. In this extremity, Tiridates embraced the only refuge which he saw before him: he dismounted and plunged into the stream. His armour was heavy, the river very deep, and in those parts at least half a mile in breadth;[66] yet such was his strength and dexterity that he reached in safety the opposite bank.[67] With regard to the Roman general, we are ignorant of the circumstances of his escape; but, when he returned to Antioch, Diocletian received him, not with the tenderness of a friend and colleague, but with the indignation of an offended sovereign. The haughtiest of men, clothed in his purple, but humbled by the sense of his fault and misfortune, was obliged to follow the emperor's chariot above a mile on foot, and to exhibit before the whole court the spectacle of his disgrace.[68]

As soon as Diocletian had indulged his private resentment, and asserted the majesty of supreme power, he yielded to the submissive entreaties of the Caesar, and permitted him to retrieve his own honour as well as that of the Roman arms. In the room of the unwarlike troops of Asia, which had most probably served in the first expedition, a second army was drawn from the veterans and new levies of the Illyrian frontier, and a considerable body of Gothic auxiliaries were taken into the Imperial pay.[69] At the head of a chosen army of twenty-five thousand men, Galerius again passed the Euphrates; but, instead of exposing his legions in the open plains of Mesopotamia, he advanced through the mountains of Armenia, where he found the inhabitants devoted to his cause, and the country as favourable to the operations of infantry as it was inconvenient for the motions of cavalry.[70] Adversity had confirmed the Roman discipline, whilst the barbarians, elated by success, were become so negligent and remiss that, in the moment when they least expected it, they were surprised by the active conduct of Galerius, who, attended only by two horsemen, had, with his own eyes, secretly examined the state and position of their camp. A surprise, especially in the night-time, was for the most part fatal to a Persian army. 'Their horses were tied, and generally shackled, to prevent their running away; and, if an alarm happened, a Persian had his housing to fix, his horse to bridle, and his corslet to put on, before he could mount.'[71] On this occasion, the impetuous attack of Galerius spread disorder and dismay over the camp of the barbarians. A slight resistance was followed by a dreadful carnage, and, in the general confusion, the wounded monarch (for Narses commanded his armies in person) fled towards the deserts of Media. His sumptuous tents, and those of his satraps, afforded an immense booty to the conqueror; and an incident is mentioned, which proves the rustic but martial ignorance of the legions in the elegant superfluities of life. A bag of shining leather, filled with pearls, fell into the hands of a private soldier; he carefully preserved the bag, but he threw away its contents, judging that whatever was of no use could not possibly be of any value.[72] The principal loss of Narses was of a much more affecting nature. Several of his wives, his sisters, and children, who had attended the army, were made captives in the defeat. But, though the character of Galerius had in general very little affinity with that of Alexander, he imitated, after his victory, the amiable behaviour of the Macedonian towards the family of Darius. The wives and children of Narses were protected from violence and rapine, conveyed to a place of safety, and treated with every mark of respect and tenderness that was due, from a generous enemy, to their age, their sex, and their royal dignity.[73]

Whilst the East anxiously expected the decision of this great contest, the emperor Diocletian, having assembled in Syria a strong army of observation, displayed from a distance the resources of the Roman power, and reserved himself for any future emergency of the war. On the intelligence of the victory, he condescended to advance towards the frontier, with a view of moderating, by his presence and counsels, the pride of Galerius. The interview of the Roman princes at Nisibis was accompanied with every expression of respect on one side, and of esteem on the other. It was in that city that they soon afterwards gave audience to the ambassador of the Great King.[74] The power, or at least the spirit, of Narses had been broken by his last defeat; and he considered an immediate peace as the only means that could stop the progress of the Roman arms. He dispatched Apharban, a servant who possessed his favour and confidence, with a commission to negotiate a treaty, or rather to receive whatever conditions the conqueror should impose. Apharban opened the conference by expressing his master's gratitude for the generous treatment of his family, and by soliciting the liberty of those illustrious captives. He celebrated the valour of Galerius, without degrading the reputation of Narses, and thought it no dishonour to confess the superiority of the victorious Caesar over a monarch who had surpassed in glory all the princes of his race. Notwithstanding the justice of the Persian cause, he was empowered to submit the present differences to the decision of the emperors themselves; convinced as he was that, in the midst of prosperity, they would not be unmindful of the vicissitudes of fortune. Apharban concluded his discourse in the style of Eastern allegory, by observing that the Roman and Persian monarchies were the two eyes of the world, which would remain imperfect and mutilated, if either of them should be put out.

'It well becomes the Persians,' replied Galerius, with a transport of fury, which seemed to convulse his whole frame, 'it well becomes the Persians to expatiate on the vicissitudes of fortune and calmly to read us lectures on the virtues of moderation. Let them remember their own *moderation* towards the unhappy Valerian. They vanquished him by fraud, they treated him with indignity. They detained him till the last moment of his life in shameful captivity, and, after his death, they exposed his body to perpetual ignominy.'* Softening, however, his tone, Galerius insinuated to the ambassador that it had never been the practice of the Romans to trample on a prostrate enemy; and that on this occasion they should consult their own dignity rather than the Persian merit. He dismissed Apharban with a hope that Narses would soon be informed on what conditions he might obtain, from the clemency of the emperors, a lasting peace, and the restoration of his wives and children. In this conference we may discover the fierce passions of Galerius, as well as his deference to the superior wisdom and authority of Diocletian. The ambition of the former grasped at the conquest of the East and had proposed to reduce Persia into the state of a province. The prudence of the latter, who adhered to the moderate policy of Augustus and the Antonines, embraced the favourable opportunity of terminating a successful war by an honourable and advantageous peace.[75]

In pursuance of their promise, the emperors soon afterwards appointed

Sicorius Probus, one of their secretaries, to acquaint the Persian court with their final resolution. As the minister of peace, he was received with every mark of politeness and friendship; but, under the pretence of allowing him the necessary repose after so long a journey, the audience of Probus was deferred from day to day; and he attended the slow motions of the king, till at length he was admitted to his presence, near the river Asprudus in Media. The secret motive of Narses, in this delay, had been to collect such a military force as might enable him, though sincerely desirous of peace, to negotiate with the greater weight and dignity. Three persons only assisted at this important conference; the minister Apharban, the prefect of the guards, and an officer who had commanded on the Armenian frontier.[76] The first condition, proposed by the ambassador, is not at present of a very intelligible nature; that the city of Nisibis might be established for the place of mutual exchange, or, as we should formerly have termed it, for the staple of trade between the two empires. There is no difficulty in conceiving the intention of the Roman princes to improve their revenue by some restraints upon commerce; but, as Nisibis was situated within their own dominions, and as they were masters both of the imports and exports, it should seem that such restraints were the objects of an internal law rather than of a foreign treaty. To render them more effectual, some stipulations were probably required on the side of the king of Persia, which appeared so very repugnant either to his interest or to his dignity that Narses could not be persuaded to subscribe them. As this was the only article to which he refused his consent, it was no longer insisted on; and the emperors either suffered the trade to flow in its natural channels, or contented themselves with such restrictions as it depended on their own authority to establish.

As soon as this difficulty was removed, a solemn peace was concluded and ratified between the two nations. The conditions of a treaty so glorious to the empire, and so necessary to Persia, may deserve a more peculiar attention, as the history of Rome presents very few transactions of a similar nature; most of her wars having either been terminated by absolute conquest, or waged against barbarians ignorant of the use of letters.

I.   The Aboras, or, as it is called by Xenophon, the Araxes, was fixed as the boundary between the two monarchies.[77] That river, which rose near the Tigris, was increased, a few miles below Nisibis, by the little stream of the Mygdonius, passed under the walls of Singara, and fell into the Euphrates at Circesium, a frontier town which, by the care of Diocletian, was very strongly fortified.[78] Mesopotamia, the object of so many wars, was ceded to the empire; and the Persians, by this treaty, renounced all pretensions to that great province.

II. They relinquished to the Romans five provinces beyond the Tigris.[79] Their situation formed a very useful barrier, and their natural strength was soon improved by art and military skill. Four of these, to the north of the river, were districts of obscure fame and inconsiderable extent: Intiline, Zabdicene, Arzanene, and Moxoene; but, on the east of the Tigris, the empire acquired the large and mountainous territory of Carduene, the ancient seat of the Carduchians, who preserved for many ages their manly freedom in the heart of the despotic monarchies of Asia. The ten thousand Greeks traversed their country, after a painful march, or rather engagement, of seven days; and it is confessed by their leader, in his incomparable relation of the retreat, that they suffered more from the arrows of the Carduchians than from the power of the Great King.[80] Their posterity, the Curds, with very little alteration either of name or manners, acknowledged the nominal sovereignty of the Turkish sultan.

III. It is almost needless to observe that Tiridates, the faithful ally of Rome, was restored to the throne of his fathers, and that the rights of the Imperial supremacy were fully asserted and secured. The limits of Armenia were extended as far as the fortress of Sintha in Media, and this increase of dominion was not so much an act of liberality as of justice. Of the provinces already mentioned beyond the Tigris, the four first had been dismembered by the Parthians from the crown of Armenia;[81] and, when the Romans acquired the possession of them, they stipulated, at the expense of the usurpers, an ample compensation, which invested their ally with the extensive and fertile country of Atropatene. Its principal city, in the same situation perhaps as the modern Tauris, was frequently honoured with the residence of Tiridates; and, as it sometimes bore the name of Ecbatana, he imitated, in the buildings and fortifications, the splendid capital of the Medes.[82]

IV. The country of Iberia was barren, its inhabitants rude and savage. But they were accustomed to the use of arms, and they separated from the empire barbarians much fiercer and more formidable than themselves. The narrow defiles of Mount Caucasus were in their hands, and it was in their choice either to admit or to exclude the wandering tribes of Sarmatia, whenever a rapacious spirit urged them to penetrate into the richer climates of the South.[83] The nomination of the kings of Iberia, which was resigned by the Persian monarch to the emperors, contributed to the strength and security of the Roman power in Asia.[84] The East enjoyed a profound tranquillity during forty years; and the treaty between the rival monarchies was strictly observed till the death of Tiridates; when a new generation, animated with different views and different passions, succeeded to the government of the world; and the grandson of Narses undertook a long and memorable war against the princes of the house of Constantine.

The arduous work of rescuing the distressed empire from tyrants and barbarians had now been completely achieved by a succession of Illyrian peasants. As soon as Diocletian entered into the twentieth year of his reign, he celebrated that memorable era, as well as the success of his arms, by the pomp of a Roman triumph.[85] Maximian, the equal partner of his power, was his only companion in the glory of that day. The two Caesars had fought and conquered, but the merit of their exploits was ascribed, according to the rigour of ancient maxims, to the auspicious influence of their fathers and emperors.[86] The triumph of Diocletian and Maximian was less magnificent, perhaps, than those of Aurelian and Probus,* but it was dignified by several circumstances of superior fame and good fortune. Africa and Britain, the Rhine, the Danube, and the Nile, furnished their respective trophies; but the most distinguished ornament was of a more singular nature, a Persian victory followed by an important conquest. The representations of rivers, mountains, and provinces were carried before the Imperial car. The images of the captive wives, the sisters, and the children of the Great King afforded a new and grateful spectacle to the vanity of the people.[87] In the eyes of posterity this triumph is remarkable by a distinction of a less honourable kind. It was the last that Rome ever beheld. Soon after this period, the emperors ceased to vanquish, and Rome ceased to be the capital of the empire.

The spot on which Rome was founded had been consecrated by ancient ceremonies and imaginary miracles. The presence of some god, or the memory of some hero, seemed to animate every part of the city, and the empire of the world had been promised to the Capitol.[88] The native Romans felt and confessed the power of this agreeable illusion. It was derived from their ancestors, had grown up with their earliest habits of life, and was protected, in some measure, by the opinion of political utility. The form and the seat of government were intimately blended together, nor was it esteemed possible to transport the one without destroying the other.[89] But the sovereignty of the capital was gradually annihilated in the extent of conquest; the provinces rose to the same level, and the vanquished nations acquired the name and privileges, without imbibing the partial† affections, of Romans. During a long period, however, the remains of the ancient constitution, and the influence of custom, preserved the dignity of Rome. The emperors, though perhaps of African or Illyrian extraction, respected their adopted country, as the seat of their power, and the centre of their extensive dominions. The emergencies of war very frequently required their presence on the frontiers; but Diocletian and Maximian were the first Roman princes who fixed, in time of peace, their ordinary residence in the provinces; and their conduct, however it might be suggested by private motives, was justified by very specious‡ considerations of policy. The court of the Emperor of the West was, for the most part, established at Milan, whose situation, at the foot of the Alps, appeared far more convenient than that of Rome, for the important purpose of watching the motions of the barbarians of Germany. Milan soon assumed the splendour of an Imperial city. The houses are described as numerous and well built; the manners of the people as polished and liberal. A circus, a theatre, a mint, a palace, baths, which bore the name of their founder Maximian; porticoes adorned with statues, and a double circumference of walls, contributed to the beauty of the new capital; nor did it seem oppressed even by the proximity of Rome.[90] To rival the majesty of Rome was the ambition likewise of Diocletian, who employed his leisure, and the wealth of the East, in the embellishment of Nicomedia, a city placed on the verge of Europe and Asia, almost at an equal distance between the Danube and the Euphrates. By the taste of the monarch, and at the expense of the people, Nicomedia acquired, in the space of a few years, a degree of magnificence which might appear to have required the labour of ages, and became inferior only to Rome, Alexandria, and Antioch, in extent or populousness.[91] The life of Diocletian and Maximian was a life of action, and a considerable portion of it was spent in camps, or in their long and frequent marches; but, whenever the public business allowed them any relaxation, they seem to have retired with pleasure to their favourite residences of Nicomedia and Milan. Till Diocletian, in the twentieth year of his reign, celebrated his Roman triumph, it is extremely doubtful whether he ever visited the ancient capital of the empire. Even on that memorable occasion his stay did not exceed two months. Disgusted with the licentious familiarity of the people, he quitted Rome with precipitation thirteen days before it was expected that he should have appeared in the senate, invested with the ensigns of the consular dignity.[92]

The dislike expressed by Diocletian towards Rome and Roman freedom was not the effect of momentary caprice, but the result of the most artful policy. That crafty prince had framed a new system of Imperial government, which was afterwards completed by the family of Constantine, and, as the image of the old constitution was religiously preserved in the senate, he resolved to deprive that order of its small remains of power and consideration. We may recollect, about eight years before the elevation of Diocletian, the transient greatness, and the ambitious hopes, of the Roman senate. As long as that enthusiasm prevailed, many of the nobles imprudently displayed their zeal in the cause of freedom; and, after the successors of Probus had withdrawn their countenance from the republican party, the senators were unable to disguise their impotent resentment. As the sovereign of Italy, Maximian was entrusted with the care of extinguishing this troublesome, rather than dangerous, spirit, and the task was perfectly suited to his cruel temper. The most illustrious members of the senate, whom Diocletian always affected to esteem, were involved, by his colleague, in the accusation of imaginary plots; and the possession of an elegant villa, or a well-cultivated estate, was interpreted as a convincing evidence of guilt.[93] The camp of the Praetorians, which had so long oppressed, began to protect, the majesty of Rome; and as those haughty troops were conscious of the decline of their power, they were naturally disposed to unite their strength with the authority of the senate. By the prudent measures of Diocletian, the numbers of the Praetorians were insensibly reduced, their privileges abolished,[94] and their place supplied by two faithful legions of Illyricum, who, under the new titles of Jovians and Herculians, were appointed to perform the service of the Imperial guards.[95] But the most fatal though secret wound, which the senate received from the hands of Diocletian and Maximian, was inflicted by the inevitable operation of their absence. As long as the emperors resided at Rome, that assembly might be oppressed, but it could scarcely be neglected. The successors of Augustus exercised the power of dictating whatever laws their wisdom or caprice might suggest; but those laws were ratified by the sanction of the senate. The model of ancient freedom was preserved in its deliberations and decrees; and wise princes, who respected the prejudices of the Roman people, were in some measure obliged to assume the language and behaviour suitable to the general and first magistrate of the republic. In the armies and in the provinces, they displayed the dignity of monarchs; and, when they fixed their residence at a distance from the capital, they for ever laid aside the dissimulation which Augustus had recommended to his successors. In the exercise of the legislative as well as of the executive power, the sovereign advised with his ministers, instead of consulting the great council of the nation. The name of the senate was mentioned with honour till the last period of the empire; the vanity of its members was still flattered with honorary distinctions;[96] but the assembly, which had so long been the source, and so long the instrument, of power, was respectfully suffered to sink into oblivion. The senate of Rome, losing all connection with the Imperial court and the actual constitution, was left a venerable but useless monument of antiquity on the Capitoline hill.

When the Roman princes had lost sight of the senate and of their ancient capital, they easily forgot the origin and nature of their legal power. The civil offices of consul, of proconsul, of censor, and of tribune, by the union of which it had been formed, betrayed to the people its republican extraction. Those modest titles were laid aside;[97] and, if they still distinguished their high station by the appellation of Emperor, or Imperator, that word was understood in a new and more dignified sense, and no longer denoted the general of the Roman armies, but the sovereign of the Roman world. The name of Emperor, which was at first of a military nature, was associated with another of a more servile kind. The epithet of Dominus, or Lord, in its primitive signification, was expressive, not of the authority of a prince over his subjects, or of a commander over his soldiers, but of the despotic power of a master over his domestic slaves.[98] Viewing it in that odious light, it had been rejected with abhorrence by the first Caesars. Their resistance insensibly became more feeble, and the name less odious; till at length the style of *our Lord and Emperor* was not only bestowed by flattery, but was regularly admitted into the laws and public monuments. Such lofty epithets were sufficient to elate and satisfy the most excessive vanity; and, if the successors of Diocletian still declined the title of King, it seems to have been the effect not so much of their moderation as of their delicacy. Wherever the Latin tongue was in use (and it was the language of government throughout the empire), the Imperial title, as it was peculiar to themselves, conveyed a more respectable idea than the name of king, which they must have shared with an hundred barbarian chieftains; or which, at the best, they could derive only from Romulus or from Tarquin. But the sentiments of the East were very different from those of the West. From the earliest period of history, the sovereigns of Asia had been celebrated in the Greek language by the title of *Basileus*, or King; and, since it was considered as the first distinction among men, it was soon employed by the servile provincials of the East in their humble addresses to the Roman throne.[99] Even the attributes, or at least the titles, of the Divinity, were usurped by Diocletian and Maximian, who transmitted them to a succession of Christian emperors.[100] Such extravagant compliments, however, soon lose their impiety by losing their meaning; and, when the ear is once accustomed to the sound, they are heard with indifference as vague though excessive professions of respect.

From the time of Augustus to that of Diocletian, the Roman princes, conversing in a familiar manner among their fellow citizens, were saluted only with the same respect that was usually paid to senators and magistrates. Their principal distinction was the Imperial or military robe of purple; whilst the senatorial garment was marked by a broad, and the equestrian by a narrow, band or stripe of the same honourable colour. The pride, or rather the policy, of Diocletian engaged that artful prince to introduce the stately magnificence of the court of Persia.[101] He ventured to assume the diadem, an ornament detested by the Romans as the odious ensign of royalty, and the use of which had been considered as the most desperate act of the madness of Caligula. It was no more than a broad white fillet set with pearls, which encircled the emperor's head. The sumptuous robes of Diocletian and his successors were of silk and gold; and it is remarked, with indignation, that even their shoes were studded with the most precious gems. The access to their sacred person was every day rendered more difficult, by the institution of new forms and ceremonies. The avenues of the palace were strictly guarded by the various *schools*, as they began to be called, of domestic officers. The interior apartments were entrusted to the jealous vigilance of the eunuchs; the increase of whose numbers and influence was the most infallible symptom of the progress of despotism. When a subject was at length admitted to the Imperial presence, he was obliged, whatever might be his rank, to fall prostrate on the ground, and to adore, according to the eastern fashion, the divinity of his lord and master.[102] Diocletian was a man of sense, who, in the course of private as well as public life, had formed a just estimate both of himself and of mankind: nor is it easy to conceive that, in substituting the manners of Persia to those of Rome, he was seriously actuated by so mean a principle as that of vanity. He flattered himself that an ostentation of splendour and luxury would subdue the imagination of the multitude; that the monarch would be less exposed to the rude licence of the people and the soldiers, as his person was secluded from the public view; and that habits of submission would insensibly be productive of sentiments of veneration. Like the modesty affected by Augustus, the state maintained by Diocletian was a theatrical representation; but it must be confessed that, of the two comedies, the former was of a much more liberal and manly character than the latter. It was the aim of the one to disguise, and the object of the other to display, the unbounded power which the emperors possessed over the Roman world.

Ostentation was the first principle of the new system instituted by Diocletian. The second was division. He divided the empire, the provinces, and every branch of the civil as well as military administration. He multiplied the wheels of the machine of government, and rendered its operations less rapid but more secure. Whatever advantages, and whatever defects, might attend these innovations, they must be ascribed in a very great degree to the first inventor; but, as the new frame of policy was gradually improved and completed by succeeding princes, it will be more satisfactory to delay the consideration of it till the season of its full maturity and perfection.[103] Reserving, therefore, for the reign of Constantine a more exact picture of the new empire, we shall content ourselves with describing the principal and decisive outline, as it was traced by the hand of Diocletian. He had associated three colleagues in the exercise of the supreme power; and, as he was convinced that the abilities of a single man were inadequate to the public defence, he considered the joint administration of four princes not as a temporary expedient, but as a fundamental law of the constitution. It was his intention that the two elder princes should be distinguished by the use of the diadem, and the title of *Augusti*: that, as affection or esteem might direct their choice, they should regularly call to their assistance two subordinate colleagues; and that the *Caesars*, rising in their turn to the first rank, should supply an uninterrupted succession of emperors. The empire was divided into four parts. The East and Italy were the most honourable, the Danube and the Rhine the most laborious stations. The former claimed the presence of the *Augusti*, the latter were entrusted to the administration of the *Caesars*. The strength of the legions was in the hands of the four partners of sovereignty, and the despair of successively vanquishing four formidable rivals might intimidate the ambition of an aspiring general. In their civil government, the emperors were supposed to exercise the undivided power of the monarch, and their edicts, inscribed with their joint names, were received in all the provinces, as promulgated by their mutual councils and authority. Notwithstanding these precautions, the political union of the Roman world was gradually dissolved, and a principle of division was introduced, which, in the course of a few years, occasioned the perpetual separation of the eastern and western empires.

The system of Diocletian was accompanied with another very material disadvantage, which cannot even at present be totally overlooked; a more expensive establishment, and consequently an increase of taxes, and the oppression of the people. Instead of a modest family of slaves and freedmen, such as had contented the simple greatness of Augustus and Trajan, three or four magnificent courts were established in the various parts of the empire, and as many Roman *kings* contended with each other and with the Persian monarch for the vain superiority of pomp and luxury. The number of ministers, of magistrates, of officers, and of servants, who filled the different departments of the state, was multiplied beyond the example of former times; and (if we may borrow the warm expression of a contemporary) 'when the proportion of those who received exceeded the proportion of those who contributed, the provinces were oppressed by the weight of tributes.'[104] From this period to the extinction of the empire, it would be easy to deduce an uninterrupted series of clamours and complaints. According to his religion and situation, each writer chooses either Diocletian, or Constantine, or Valens,* or Theodosius,† for the object of his invectives; but they unanimously agree in representing the burden of the public impositions, and particularly the land-tax and capitation, as the intolerable and increasing grievance of their own times. From such a concurrence, an impartial historian, who is obliged to extract truth from satire as well as from panegyric, will be inclined to divide the blame among the princes whom they accuse, and to ascribe their exactions much less to their personal vices than to the uniform system of their administration. The emperor Diocletian was, indeed, the author of that system; but during his reign the growing evil was confined within the bounds of modesty and discretion, and he deserves the reproach of establishing pernicious precedents, rather than of exercising actual oppression.[105] It may be added that his revenues were managed with prudent economy; and that, after all the current expenses were discharged, there still remained in the Imperial treasury an ample position either for judicious liberality or for any emergency of the state.

It was in the twenty-first year of his reign that Diocletian executed his memorable resolution of abdicating the empire: an action more naturally to have been expected from the elder or the younger Antoninus, than from a prince who had never practised the lessons of philosophy either in the attainment or in the use of supreme power. Diocletian acquired the glory of giving to the world the first example of a resignation,[106] which has not been very frequently imitated by succeeding monarchs. The parallel of Charles the Fifth, however, will naturally offer itself to our mind, not only since the eloquence of a modern historian* has rendered that name so familiar to an English reader, but from the very striking resemblance between the characters of the two emperors, whose political abilities were superior to their military genius, and whose specious virtues were much less the effect of nature than of art. The abdication of Charles appears to have been hastened by the vicissitude of fortune; and the disappointment of his favourite schemes urged him to relinquish a power which he found inadequate to his ambition. But the reign of Diocletian had flowed with a tide of uninterrupted success; nor was it till after he had vanquished all his enemies, and accomplished all his designs, that he seems to have entertained any serious thoughts of resigning the empire. Neither Charles nor Diocletian were arrived at a very advanced period of life; since the one was only fifty-five, and the other was no more than fifty-nine, years of age; but the active life of those princes, their wars and journeys, the cares of royalty, and their application to business, had already impaired their constitution, and brought on the infirmities of a premature old age.[107]

Notwithstanding the severity of a very cold and rainy winter, Diocletian left Italy soon after the ceremony of his triumph, and began his progress towards the East round the circuit of the Illyrian provinces. Prom the inclemency of the weather, and the fatigue of the journey, he soon contracted a slow illness; and, though he made easy marches, and was generally carried in a close litter, his disorder, before he arrived at Nicomedia, about the end of the summer, was become very serious and alarming. During the whole winter he was confined to his palace; his danger inspired a general and unaffected concern; but the people could only judge of the various alterations of his health from the joy or consternation which they discovered in the countenances and behaviour of his attendants. The rumour of his death was for some time universally believed, and it was supposed to be concealed with a view to prevent the troubles that might have happened during the absence of the Caesar Galerius. At length, however, on the first of March, Diocletian once more appeared in public, but so pale and emaciated that he could scarcely have been recognised by those to whom his person was the most familiar. It was time to put an end to the painful struggle, which he had sustained during more than a year, between the care of his health and that of his dignity. The former required indulgence and relaxation, the latter compelled him to direct, from the bed of sickness, the administration of a great empire. He resolved to pass the remainder of his days in honourable repose, to place his glory beyond the reach of fortune, and to relinquish the theatre of the world to his younger and more active associates.[108]

The ceremony of his abdication was performed in a spacious plain, about three miles from Nicomedia. The emperor ascended a lofty throne, and in a speech, full of reason and dignity, declared his intention, both to the people and to the soldiers who were assembled on this extraordinary occasion. As soon as he had divested himself of the purple, he withdrew from the gazing multitude, and, traversing the city in a covered chariot, proceeded, without delay, to the favourite retirement which he had chosen in his native country of Dalmatia. On the same day, which was the first of May,[109] Maximian, as it had been previously concerted, made his resignation of the Imperial dignity at Milan. Even in the splendour of the Roman triumph, Diocletian had meditated his design of abdicating the government. As he wished to secure the obedience of Maximian, he exacted from him either a general assurance that he would submit his actions to the authority of his benefactor, or a particular promise that he would descend from the throne, whenever he should receive the advice and the example. This engagement, though it was confirmed by the solemnity of an oath before the altar of the Capitoline Jupiter,[110] would have proved a feeble restraint on the fierce temper of Maximian, whose passion was the love of power, and who neither desired present tranquillity nor future reputation. But he yielded, however reluctantly, to the ascendant which his wiser colleague had acquired over him, and retired, immediately after his abdication, to a villa in Lucania, where it was almost impossible that such an impatient spirit could find any lasting tranquillity.

Diocletian, who, from a servile origin, had raised himself to the throne, passed the nine last years of his life in a private condition. Reason had dictated, and content seems to have accompanied, his retreat, in which he enjoyed for a long time the respect of those princes to whom he had resigned the possession of the world.[111] It is seldom that minds long exercised in business have formed any habits of conversing with themselves, and in the loss of power they principally regret the want of occupation. The amusements of letters and of devotion, which afford so many resources in solitude, were incapable of fixing the attention of Diocletian; but he had preserved, or at least he soon recovered, a taste for the most innocent as well as natural pleasures; and his leisure hours were sufficiently employed in building, planting, and gardening. His answer to Maximian is deservedly celebrated. He was solicited by that restless old man to reassume the reins of government and the Imperial purple. He rejected the temptation with a smile of pity, calmly observing that, if he could show Maximian the cabbages which he had planted with his own hands at Salona, he should no longer be urged to relinquish the enjoyment of happiness for the pursuit of power.[112] In his conversations with his friends, he frequently acknowledged that, of all arts, the most difficult was the art of reigning; and he expressed himself on that favourite topic with a degree of warmth which could be the result only of experience. 'How often,' was he accustomed to say, 'is it the interest of four or five ministers to combine together to deceive their sovereign! Secluded from mankind by his exalted dignity, the truth is concealed from his knowledge; he can see only with their eyes, he hears nothing but their misrepresentations. He confers the most important offices upon vice and weakness, and disgraces the most virtuous and deserving among his subjects. By such infamous arts,' added Diocletian, 'the best and wisest princes are sold to the venal corruption of their courtiers.'[113] A just estimate of greatness, and the assurance of immortal fame, improve our relish for the pleasures of retirement; but the Roman emperor had filled too important a character in the world to enjoy without allay the comforts and security of a private condition. It was impossible that he could remain ignorant of the troubles which afflicted the empire after his abdication. It was impossible that he could be indifferent to their consequences. Fear, sorrow and discontent sometimes pursued him into the solitude of Salona. His tenderness, or at least his pride, was deeply wounded by the misfortunes of his wife and daughter; and the last moments of Diocletian were embittered by some affronts, which Licinius and Constantine might have spared the father of so many emperors, and the first author of their own fortune. A report, though of a very doubtful nature, has reached our times, that he prudently withdrew himself from their power by a voluntary death.[114]

Before we dismiss the consideration of the life and character of Diocletian, we may, for a moment, direct our view to the place of his retirement. Salona, a principal city of his native province of Dalmatia, was near two hundred Roman miles (according to the measurement of the public highways) from Aquileia and the confines of Italy, and about two hundred and seventy from Sirmium, the usual residence of the emperors whenever they visited the Illyrian frontier.[115] A miserable village still preserves the name of Salona, but so late as the sixteenth century, the remains of a theatre, and a confused prospect of broken arches and marble columns, continued to attest its ancient splendour.[116] About six or seven miles from the city, Diocletian constructed a magnificent palace, and we may infer from the greatness of the work, how long he had meditated his design of abdicating the empire. The choice of a spot which united all that could contribute either to health or to luxury did not require the partiality of a native. 'The soil was dry and fertile, the air is pure and wholesome, and, though extremely hot during the summer months, this country seldom feels those sultry and noxious winds to which the coast of Istria and some parts of Italy are exposed. The views from the palace are no less beautiful than the soil and climate were inviting. Towards the west lies the fertile shore that stretches along the Hadriatic, in which a number of small islands are scattered in such a manner as to give this part of the sea the appearance of a great lake. On the north side lies the bay, which led to the ancient city of Salona, and the country beyond it, appearing in sight, forms a proper contrast to that more extensive prospect of water, which the Hadriatic presents both to the south and to the east. Towards the north, the view is terminated by high and irregular mountains, situated at a proper distance, and, in many places, covered with villages, woods and vineyards.'[117]

Though Constantine, from a very obvious prejudice, affects to mention the palace of Diocletian with contempt,[118] yet one of their successors, who could only see it in a neglected and mutilated state, celebrates its magnificence in terms of the highest admiration.[119] It covered an extent of ground consisting of between nine and ten English acres. The form was quadrangular, flanked with sixteen towers. Two of the sides were near six hundred, and the other two near seven hundred, feet in length. The whole was constructed of a beautiful freestone, extracted from the neighbouring quarries of Trau or Tragutium, and very little inferior to marble itself. Four streets, intersecting each other at right angles, divided the several parts of this great edifice, and the approach to the principal apartment was from a very stately entrance, which is still denominated the Golden Gate. The approach was terminated by a *peristylium** of granite columns, on one side of which we discover the square temple of Aesculapius, on the other the octagon temple of Jupiter. The latter of those deities Diocletian revered as the patron of his fortunes, the former as the protector of his health. By comparing the present remains with the precepts of Vitruvius,[†] the several parts of the building, the baths, bedchamber, the *atrium*,[‡] the *basilica*,[§] and the Cyzicene, Corinthian, and Egyptian halls have been described with some degree of precision, or at least of probability. Their forms were various, their proportions just, but they were all attended with two imperfections, very repugnant to our modern notions of taste and conveniency. These stately rooms had neither windows nor chimneys. They were lighted from the top (for the building seems to have consisted of no more than one storey), and they received their heat by the help of pipes that were conveyed along the walls. The range of principal apartments was protected towards the southwest by a portico five hundred and seventeen feet long, which must have formed a very noble and delightful walk, when the beauties of painting and sculpture were added to those of the prospect.

Had this magnificent edifice remained in a solitary country, it would have been exposed to the ravages of time; but it might, perhaps, have escaped the rapacious industry of man. The village of Aspalathus,[120] and, long afterwards, the provincial town of Spalatro, have grown out of its ruins. The Golden Gate now opens into the market place. St John the Baptist has usurped the honours of Aesculapius; and the temple of Jupiter, under the protection of the Virgin, is converted into the cathedral church. For this account of Diocletian's palace we are principally indebted to an ingenious artist of our own time and country, whom a very liberal curiosity carried into the heart of Dalmatia.[121] But there is room to suspect that the elegance of his designs and engraving has somewhat flattered the objects which it was their purpose to represent. We are informed by a more recent and very judicious traveller that the awful ruins of Spalatro are not less expressive of the decline of the arts than of the greatness of the Roman empire in the time of Diocletian.[122] If such was indeed the state of architecture, we must naturally believe that painting and sculpture had experienced a still more sensible decay. The practice of architecture is directed by a few general and even mechanical rules. But sculpture, and, above all, painting, propose to themselves the imitation not only of the forms of nature, but of the characters and passions of the human soul. In those sublime arts, the dexterity of the hand is of little avail, unless it is animated by fancy and guided by the most correct taste and observation.

It is almost unnecessary to remark that the civil distractions of the empire, the licence of the soldiers, the inroads of the barbarians, and the progress of despotism had proved very unfavourable to genius, and even to learning. The succession of Illyrian princes restored the empire, without restoring the sciences. Their military education was not calculated to inspire them with the love of letters; and even the mind of Diocletian, however active and capacious in business, was totally uninformed by study or speculation. The professions of law and physic are of such common use and certain profit that they will always secure a sufficient number of practitioners endowed with a reasonable degree of abilities and knowledge; but it does not appear that the students in those two faculties appeal to any celebrated masters who have flourished within that period. The voice of poetry was silent. History was reduced to dry and confused abridgments, alike destitute of amusement and instruction. A languid and affected eloquence was still retained in the pay and service of the emperors, who encouraged not any arts except those which contributed to the gratification of their pride or the defence of their power.[123]

The declining age of learning and of mankind is marked, however, by the rise and rapid progress of the new Platonists. The school of Alexandria silenced those of Athens; and the ancient sects enrolled themselves under the banners of the more fashionable teachers, who recommended their system by the novelty of their method and the austerity of their manners. Several of these masters, Ammonius, Plotinus, Amelius, and Porphyry,[124] were men of profound thought and intense application; but, by mistaking the true object of philosophy, their labours contributed much less to improve than to corrupt the human understanding. The knowledge that is suited to our situation and powers, the whole compass of moral, natural, and mathematical science, was neglected by the new Platonists, whilst they exhausted their strength in the verbal disputes of metaphysics, attempted to explore the secrets of the invisible world, and studied to reconcile Aristotle with Plato, on subjects of which both these philosophers were as ignorant as the rest of mankind. Consuming their reason in these deep but unsubstantial meditations, their minds were exposed to illusions of fancy. They flattered themselves that they possessed the secret of disengaging the soul from its corporeal prison; claimed a familiar intercourse with daemons and spirits; and, by a very singular revolution, converted the study of philosophy into that of magic. The ancient sages had derided the popular superstition; after disguising its extravagance by the thin pretence of allegory, the disciples of Plotinus and Porphyry became its most zealous defenders. As they agreed with the Christians in a few mysterious points of faith, they attacked the remainder of their theological system with all the fury of civil war. The new Platonists would scarcely deserve a place in the history of science, but in that of the church the mention of them will very frequently occur.

NOTES TO CHAPTER 13

1 Eutrop., ix, 19; Victor in *Epitom*. The town seems to have been properly Doclia, from the small tribe of Illyrians (see Cellarius, *Geograph. Antiqua*, i, 393); and the original name of the fortunate slave was probably Docles; he first lengthened it to the Grecian harmony of Diocles, and at length to the Roman majesty of Diocletianus. He likewise assumed the Patrician name of Valerius, and it is usually given him by Aurelius Victor.

2 See Dacier on the sixth satire of the second book of Horace; Cornel. Nepos, in *Vit. Eumen.*, ch. 1.

* *page 205* [skills, stratagems]

3 Lactantius (or whoever was the author of the little treatise *De Mortibus Persecutorum*) accuses Diocletian of timidity in two places, ch. 7, 8. In ch. 9, he says of him, *erat in omni tumultu meticulosus et animi disiectus* ['in every emergency he was frightened and indecisive'].

4 In this encomium, Aurelius Victor seems to convey a just, though indirect, censure of the cruelty of Constantius. It appears from the *Fasti*, that Aristobulus remained prefect of the city, and that he ended with Diocletian the consulship which he had commenced with Carinus.

* *page 206* [Marcus Aurelius]

5 Aurelius Victor styles Diocletian, *parentem potius quam dominum* ['a father rather than a master']. See *Hist. August.*, p. 30.

6 The question of the time when Maximian received the honours of Caesar and Augustus has divided modern critics, and given occasion to a great deal of learned wrangling. I have followed M. de Tillemont (*Histoire des Empereurs*, iv, 500–5), who has weighed the several reasons and difficulties with his scrupulous accuracy.

7 In an oration delivered before him (*Panegyr. Vet.*, ii, 8), Mamertinus expresses a doubt whether his hero, in imitating the conduct of Hannibal and Scipio, had ever heard of their names. From thence we may fairly infer that Maximian was more desirous of being considered as a soldier, than as a man of letters, and it is in this manner that we can often translate the language of flattery into that of truth.

8 Lactantius, *de M. P.*, ch. 8; Aurelius Victor. As among the *Panegyrics* we find orations pronounced in praise of Maximian, and others which flatter his enemies at his expense, we derive some knowledge from the contrast.

9 See the second and third Panegyrics, particularly iii, 3, 10, 14, but it would be tedious to copy the diffuse and affected expressions of their false eloquence. With regard to the titles, consult Aurelius Victor, Lactantius, *de M. P.*, ch. 52. Spanheim, *de Usu Numismatum, etc., Dissertat.*, xii, 8.

10 Aurelius Victor; Victor in *Epitome;* Eutrop., ix, 22; Lactant., *de M. P.*, ch. 8, Hieronym. in *Chron.*

11 It is only among the modern Greeks that Tillemont can discover his appellation of Chlorus. Any remarkable degree of paleness seems inconsistent with the *rubor* mentioned in *Panegyric.* v, 19.

12 Julian, the grandson of Constantius, boasts that his family was derived from the warlike Maesians. *Misopogon*, p. 348. The Dardanians dwelt on the [southern] edge of Maesia.

13 Galerius married Valeria the daughter of Diocletian; if we speak with strictness, Theodora, the wife of Constantius, was daughter only to the wife of Maximian. Spanheim, *Dissertat.*, xi, 2

14 This division agrees with that of the four prefectures; yet there is some reason to doubt whether Spain was not a province of Maximian. See Tillemont, iv, 517.

15 Julian *in Caesaribus*, p. 315. Spanheim's notes to the French translation, p. 122.

16 The general name of *Bagaudae* (in the signification of *rebels*) continued till the fifth century in Gaul. Some critics derive it from a Celtic word, *Bagad*, a tumultuous assembly. Scaliger *ad* Euseb. Du Cange, *Glossar.*

17 *Chronique* de Froissart, i, 182, ii, 73–79. The naiveté of his story is lost in our best modern writers.

18 Caesar, *de Bell. Gallic.*, vi, 13. Orgetorix, the Helvetian, could arm for his defence a body of ten thousand slaves.

19 Their oppression and misery are acknowledged by Eumenius (*Panegyr.*, vi, 8): *Gallias efferatas injuriis.* ['Gaul was driven wild by the wrongs it suffered.']

20 *Panegyr. Vet.*, ii, 4; Aurelius Victor.

21 Aelianus and Amandus. We have medals coined by them. Goltzius in *Thes. R. A.*, pp. 117, 121.

22 *Levibus proeliis domuit.* ['Victory was easily won.'] Eutrop., ix, 20.

23 The fact rests indeed on very slight authority, a life of St Babolinus, which is probably of the seventh century. See Duchesne, *Scriptores Rer. Francicar.*, i, 662.

24 Aurelius Victor calls them Germans. *Eutropius* (ix, 21) gives them the name of Saxons. But Eutropius lived in the ensuing century, and seems to use the language of his time.

25 The three expressions of Eutropius, Aurelius Victor, and Eumenius, '*vilissime natus*', '*Bataviae alumnus*', and '*Menapiae civis*', [of very humble birth, a native of Batavia, and a citizen of Menapia] give us a very doubtful account of the birth of Carausius. Stukely, however (*Hist. of Carausius*, p. 62), chooses to make him a native of St David's and a prince of the blood royal of Britain. The former idea he had found in Richard of Cirencester, p. 44.

26 *Panegyr.*, v, 12. Britain at this time was secure, and slightly guarded.

27 *Panegyr. Vet.*, v, 11; vii, 9. The orator Eumenius wished to exalt the glory of the hero (Constantius) with the importance of the conquest, Notwithstanding our laudable partiality for our native country, it is difficult to conceive that in the beginning of the fourth century England deserved *all* these commendations. A century and a half before, it hardly paid its own establishment. See Appian in *Proem.*

28 As a great number of medals of Carausius are still preserved, he is become a very favourite object of antiquarian curiosity, and every circumstance of his life and actions has been investigated with sagacious accuracy. Dr Stukely in particular

has devoted a large volume to the British emperor. I have used his materials, and rejected most of his fanciful conjectures.

29 When Mamertinus pronounced his first Panegyric, the naval preparations of Maximian were completed: and the orator presaged an assured victory. His silence in the second Panegyric might alone inform us that the expedition had not succeeded.

30 Aurelius Victor, Eutropius, and the medals (Pax Aug.) inform us of the temporary reconciliation: though I will not presume (as Dr Stukely has done, *Medallic History of Carausius*, p. 86, etc.) to insert the identical articles of the treaty.

31 With regard to the recovery of Britain, we obtain a few hints from Aurelius Victor and Eutropius.

* *page 212* [frontier]

32 John Malala, in *Chron. Antiochen.*, i, 408, 409.

33 Zosimus, i, 3. That partial historian seems to celebrate the vigilance of Diocletian, with the design of exposing the negligence of Constantine; we may, however, listen to an orator: '*Nam quid ego alarum et cohortium castra percenseam, toto Rheni et Istri et Euphratis limite restituta?*' Panegyr. *Vet.*, iv, 18. ['Why should I enumerate the encampments of the cavalry and infantry, refurbished along the entire length of the Rhine, Danube and Euphrates border?']

34 *Ruunt omnes in sanguinem suum populi, quibus non contigit esse Romanis, obstinataeque feritatis poenas nunc sponte persolvunt.* Panegyr. *Vet.*, iii, 16. ['All the non-Roman peoples indulge in mutual slaughter and pay the penalty of their inveterate ferocity.'] Mamertinus illustrates the fact by the example of almost all the nations of the world.

35 He complained, though not with the strictest truth: *iam fluxisse annos quindecim in quibus, in Illyrico, ad ripam Danubii relegatus cum gentibus barbaris luctaret* ['that he had spent fifteen years in Illyricum defending the Danube frontier against the barbarians'] Lactant., *de M. P.*, ch. 18.

36 In the Greek text of Eusebius, we read six thousand, a number which I have preferred to the sixty thousand of Jerome, Orosius, Eutropius, and his Greek translator Paeanius.

* *page 213* [pleasure]

37 Panegyr. *Vet.*, vii, 21.

38 There was a settlement of the Sarmatians in the neighbourhood of Treves, which seems to have been deserted by those lazy barbarians: Ausonius speaks of them in his Moselle.

> *Unde iter ingrediens nemorosa per avia solum*
> *Et nulla humani spectans vestigia cultus*
> . . .
> *Arvaque Sauromatum nuper metata colonis.*

['Beginning the journey through deserted woodlands without seeing any trace of civilisation . . . in the territories recently allocated as settlements for the Sarmatians.'] There was a town of the Carpi in the Lower Maesia.

39 See the rhetorical exultation of Eumenius. *Panegyr.*, vii, 9.

40 Scaliger (*Animadvers.* ad Euseb., p. 243) decides, in his usual manner, that the Quinque gentiani, or five African nations, were the five great cities, the Pentapolis of the inoffensive province of Cyrene.

41 After this defeat, Julian stabbed himself with a dagger, and immediately leaped into the flames. Victor in *Epitome*.

42 *Tu ferocissimos Mauritaniae populos inaccessis montium iugis et naturali munitione fidentes, expugnasti, recepisti, transtulisti. Panegyr. Vet.*, vi, 8 ['The fiercest tribes of Mauritania, who relied on the natural defence of their inaccessible mountain ridges – you have routed, captured and driven out.']

43 See the description of Alexandria in Hirtius, *de Bel. Alexandrin.*, ch. 5.

44 Eutrop., ix, 24. Orosius, vii, 25. John Malala in *Chron. Antioch.*, pp. 409, 410. Yet Eumenius assures us that Egypt was pacified by the clemency of Diocletian.

45 Eusebius (*Chron.*) places their destruction several years sooner, and at a time when Egypt itself was in a state of rebellion against the Romans.

 * *page 214*   [an ally of Zenobia in the reign of Aurelian]

46 Strabo, xvii, 1, 172. Pomponius Mela, i, 4. His words are curious, *Intra, si credere libet, vix homines magisque semiferi; Aegipanes, et Blemmyes, et Satyri.* ['In the interior, if the sources are to be believed, are peoples scarcely human, more like half-beasts; Aegipanes, Blemmyes, and Satyrs.']

47 *Ausus sese inserere fortunae et provocare arma Romana.* ['They dared to hazard fortune and to challenge the military might of Rome.']

48 See Procopius, *De Bell. Persic.*, i, 19.

49 He fixed the public allowance of corn for the people of Alexandria, at two millions of *medimni*; about four hundred thousand quarters. *Chron. Paschal.*, p. 276. Procopius, *Hist. Arcan.*, ch. 26.

50 John Antioch. in *Excerp. Valesian.*, p. 834. Suidas in *Diocletian.*

 * *page 215*   [Hermes Trismegistus was the Greek equivalent of the Egyptian god Thoth, with his title 'very great'.]

51 See a short history and confutation of alchemy, in the works of that philosophical compiler, La Mothe le Vayer, i, 327–53.

 * *page 215*   [in Chapter 10]

52 See the education and strength of Tiridates in the *Armenian History* of Moses of Chorene, ii, 76. He could seize two wild bulls by the horns, and break them off with his hands.

53 If we give credit to the younger Victor, who supposes that, in the year 323, Licinius was only sixty years of age, he could scarcely be the same person as the patron of Tiridates; but we know from much better authority (Euseb. *Hist. Ecclesiast.*, x, 8) that Licinius was at that time in the last period of old age: sixteen years before, he is represented with grey hairs, and as the contemporary of Galerius. See Lactant., ch. 32. Licinius was probably born about the year 250.

54 See the sixty-second and sixty-third books of Dion Cassius.

 * *page 216*   [in Chapter 8]

55 Moses of Chorene, *Hist. Armen.*, ii, 74. The statues had been erected by Valarsaces, who reigned in Armenia about 130 years before Christ, and was the first king of the family of Arsaces (see Moses, *Hist. Armen.*, ii, 2, 3). The deification of the Arsacides is mentioned by Justin (xli, 5) and by Ammianus Marcellinus (xxiii, 6).

56 The Armenian nobility was numerous and powerful. Moses mentions many families which were distinguished under the reign of Valarsaces (ii, 7) and which still subsisted in his own time, about the middle of the fifth century. See the preface of his Editors.

57 She was named Chosroiduchta, and had not the *os patulum* [literally 'open mouth'] like other women. (*Hist. Armen.*, ii, 79.) I do not understand the expression.

58 In the *Armenian History* (ii, 78) as well as in the *Geography* (p. 367) China is called
    Zenia, or Zenastan. It is characterised by the production of silk, the opulence
    of the natives, and by their love of peace, above all the other nations of the earth.

59 Vou-ti, the first emperor of the seventh dynasty, who then reigned in China,
    had political transactions with Fergana, a province of Sogdiana, and is said to
    have received a Roman embassy. (*Histoire des Huns*, i, 38.) In those ages the
    Chinese kept a garrison at Kashgar, and one of their generals, about the time
    of Trajan, marched as far as the Caspian Sea. With regard to the intercourse
    between China and the Western countries, a curious memoir of M. de Guignes
    may be consulted in the *Académie des Inscriptions*, xxxii, 355.

60 See *Hist. Armen.*, ii, 81.

61 *Ipsos Persas ipsumque Regem ascitis Sacis, et Rufiis, et Gellis petit frater Ormies.*
    Panegyric. Vet., iii, 1. ['His brother Hormuz, joined by the Sacae, the Rufii and
    the Gelli, attacked the Persians and the King himself.'] The Sacae were a nation
    of wandering Scythians, who encamped towards the sources of the Oxus and
    the Jaxartes. The Gelli were the inhabitants of Ghilan along the Caspian Sea,
    and who so long, under the name of Dilemites, infested the Persian Monarchy.
    See d'Herbelot, *Bibliothèque Orientale*.

62 Moses of Chorene takes no notice of this second revolution, which I have been
    obliged to collect from a passage of Ammianus Marcellinus (xxiii, 5). Lactantius
    speaks of the ambition of Narses: *Concitatus domesticis exemplis avi sui Saporis ad*
    occupandum orientem magnis copiis inhiabat. De Mort. Persecut. ch. 9. ['Inspired by
    the example of his grandfather, Sapor, he aspired to the military conquest of the
    East.']

63 We may readily believe that Lactantius ascribes to cowardice the conduct of
    Diocletian. Julian, in his oration, says that he remained with all the forces of the
    empire: a very hyperbolical expression.

64 Our five abbreviators, Eutropius, Festus, the two Victors, and Orosius, all relate
    the last and great battle; but Orosius is the only one who speaks of the two former.
    * *page 218* [in 53 BC at Carrhae]

65 The nature of the country is finely described by Plutarch, in the life of Crassus,
    and by Xenophon, in the first book of the *Anabasis*.

66 See Foster's Dissertation, in the second volume of the translation of the *Anabasis*
    by Spelman; which I will venture to recommend as one of the best versions extant.

67 *Hist. Armen.*, ii, 76. I have transferred this exploit of Tiridates from an imaginary
    defeat to the real one of Galerius.

68 Ammianus Marcellinus, xiv. The mile, in the hands of Eutropius (ix, 24), of
    Festus (ch. 25), and of Orosius (vii, 25), easily increased to *several* miles.

69 Aurelius Victor; Jornandes, *de rebus Geticis*, ch. 21.

70 Aurelius Victor says, *Per Armeniam in hostes contendit, quae ferme sola, seu facilior*
    vincendi via est. ['He sought out the enemy by way of Armenia – practically the
    only route, and the route most likely to lead to victory.'] He followed the
    conduct of Trajan, and the idea of Julius Caesar.

71 Xenophon's *Anabasis*, iii. For that reason, the Persian cavalry encamped sixty
    stadia from the enemy.

72 The story is told by Ammianus, xxii. Instead of *saccum* some read *scutum*.

73 The Persians confessed the Roman superiority in morals as well as in arms.
    Eutrop., ix, 24. But this respect and gratitude of enemies is very seldom to be
    found in their own accounts.

74 The account of the negotiation is taken from the fragments of Peter the Patrician, in the *Excerpta Legationum*, published in the Byzantine Collection. Peter lived under Justinian; but it is very evident, by the nature of his materials, that they are drawn from the most authentic and respectable writers.

* *page 220* The emperor Valerian was defeated by the Persian king, Sapor, in AD 260 and languished in captivity. In Chapter 10, Gibbon writes: 'when Valerian sunk under the weight of shame and grief, his skin, stuffed with straw, and formed into the likeness of a human figure, was preserved for ages in the most celebrated temple of Persia.'

75 *Adeo victor* (says Aurelius) *ut ni Valerius, cuius nutu omnia gerebantur, abnuisset, Romani fasces in provinciam novam ferrentur. Verum pars terrarum tamen nobis utilior quaesita* ['Such was the extent of his victory that had not Diocletian, who enjoyed responsibility for everything, refused, the Roman *fasces* would have been carried into a new province. But a far more useful territory (i.e. Mesopotamia) was the objective of the Romans.']

76 He had been governor of Sumium. (Pet. Patricius in *Excerpt. Legat.*, p. 30.) This province seems to be mentioned by Moses of Chorene (*Geograph.*, p. 360), and lay to the east of Mount Ararat.

77 By an error of the geographer Ptolemy, the position of Singara is removed from the Aboras to the Tigris, which may have produced the mistake of Peter in assigning the latter river for the boundary, instead of the former. The line of the Roman frontier traversed, but never followed, the course of the Tigris.

78 Procopius, *de Aedificiis*, ii, 6.

79 Three of the provinces, Zabdicene, Arzanene, and Carduene, are allowed on all sides. But instead of the other two, Peter (in *Excerpt. Leg.*, p. 30) inserts Rehimene and Sophene. I have preferred Ammianus (xxv, 7), because it might be proved that Sophene was never in the hand of the Persians, either before the reign of Diocletian, or after that of Jovian. For want of correct maps, like those of M. d'Anville, almost all the moderns, with Tillemont and Valesius at their head, have imagined that it was in respect to Persia, and not to Rome, that the five provinces were situate beyond the Tigris.

80 Xenophon's *Anabasis*, iv. Their bows were three cubits in length, their arrows two; they rolled down stones that were each a waggon load. The Greeks found a great many villages in that rude country.

81 According to Eutropius (vi, 9, as the text is represented by the best manuscripts) the city of Tigranocerta was in Arzanene. The names and situation of the other three may be faintly traced.

82 Compare Herodotus, i, 97, with Moses Chorenens., *Hist. Armen.*, ii, 84, and the map of Armenia given by his editors.

83 *Hiberi, locorum potentes, Caspia via Sarmatam in Armenios raptim effundunt.* Tacitus, *Annals*, vi, 33. See Strabon. *Geograph.*, xi, 764. ['The Iberians, who hold the fastnesses, suddenly release the Sarmatians en masse against the Armenians through the pass across the Caucasus.']

84 Peter Patricius (in *Excerpt. Leg.*, p. 30) is the only writer who mentions the Iberian article of the treaty.

85 Eusebius in *Chron.* Pagi *ad annum*. Till the discovery of the treatise *de Mortibus Persecutorum*, it was not certain that the triumph and the Vicennalia [i.e. 20th anniversary] were celebrated at the same time.

86 At the time of the Vicennalia, Galerius seems to have kept his station on the Danube. See Lactant. *de M. P.,* ch. 38.

* *page 223*   [in AD 274 and AD 281]

87 Eutropius (ix, 27) mentions them as a part of the triumph. As the *persons* had been restored to Narses, nothing more than their *images* could be exhibited.

88 Livy gives us a speech of Camillus on that subject (v, 51–55 [54]), full of eloquence and sensibility, in opposition to a design of removing the seat of government from Rome to the neighbouring city of Veii.

89 Julius Caesar was reproached with the intention of removing the empire to Ilium [Troy] or Alexandria. See Suetonius in *Caesar,* ch. 79. According to the ingenious conjecture of Le Fèvre and Dacier, the third ode of the third book of Horace was intended to divert Augustus from the execution of a similar design.

† *page 223*   [prejudiced in favour of Rome]

‡ *page 223*   [plausible]

90 See Aurelius Victor, who likewise mentions the buildings erected by Maximian at Carthage, probably during the Moorish war. We shall insert some verses of Ausonius, *de Clar. Urb.,* v.

> *Et Mediolani mira omnia: copia rerum:*
> *Innumerae cultaeque domus; fecunda virorum*
> *Ingenia, et mores laeti; tum duplice muro*
> *Amplificata loci species; populique voluptas*
> *Circus; et inclusi moles cuneata Theatri;*
> *Templa, Palatinaeque arces, opulensque Moneta,*
> *Et regio Herculei celebris sub honore lavacri.*
> *Cunctaque marmoreis ornata Peristyla signis;*
> *Moeniaque in valli formam circumdata labro,*
> *Omnia quae magnis operum velut aemula formis*
> *Excellunt: nec iuncta premit vicinia Romae.*

[Everything at Milan is remarkable, its affluence, its many fine houses, its versatile people and civilised manners; its prospect enhanced by a double wall, its circus for the people's entertainment; the wedge-shaped mass of the enclosed theatre; its temples, citadel, well-stocked mint, and the well-known baths of Hercules. Its arcades, all in marble, its walls forming a rampart: everything is of the best and seems to rival the finest public works, and is not put in the shade by the proximity of Rome.]

91 Lactant., *de M. P.,* ch. 7. Libanius, *Orat.,* viii, 203.

92 Lactant., *de M. P.,* ch. 17. On a similar occasion Ammianus mentions the *dicacitas plebis* [the raillery of the common people] as not very agreeable to an Imperial ear. (See xvi, 10.)

93 Lactantius accuses Maximian of destroying *fictis criminationibus lumina senatus* ['the most brilliant men of the senate by false charges'] (*de M. P.,* ch. 8). Aurelius Victor speaks very doubtfully of the faith of Diocletian towards his friends.

94 *Truncatae vires urbis, imminuto praetoriarum cohortium atque in armis vulgi numero*: Aurelius Victor. ['The urban forces were cut back, with a reduction in the number of the praetorian units and in the arms of the common people.'] Lactantius attributes to Galerius the prosecution of the same plan (ch. 26).

95 They were old corps stationed in Illyricum and, according to the ancient establishment, they each consisted of six thousand men. They had acquired

much reputation by the use of the *plumbatae*, or darts loaded with lead. Each soldier carried five of these, which he darted from a considerable distance, with great strength and dexterity. See Vegetius, i, 17.

96 See the Theodosian Code, vi, ii with Godefroy's commentary.

97 See the twelth dissertation in Spanheim's excellent work *de Usu Numismatum*. From medals, inscriptions, and historians, he examines every title separately, and traces it from Augustus to the moment of its disappearing.

98 Pliny (in *Panegyr.*, 3, 55, etc.) speaks of *Dominus* with execration, as synonymous to Tyrant, and opposite to Prince. And the same Pliny regularly gives that title (in the tenth book of his epistles) to his friend rather than master, the virtuous Trajan. This strange expression puzzles the commentators who think, and the translators who can write.

99 Synesius, *de Regno*, Edit. Petav., p. 15. I am indebted for this quotation to the Abbé de la Bléterie.

100 See Van Dale, *de Consecratione*, p. 534, etc. It was customary for the emperors to mention (in the preamble of laws) their *numen* [i.e. godhead], *sacred majesty*, *divine oracles*, etc. According to Tillemont, Gregory of Nazianzen complains most bitterly of the profanation, especially when it was practised by an Arian emperor.

101 See Spanheim *de Usu Numismat. Dissert.* xii.

102 Aurelius Victor; Eutropius, ix, 20. It appears by the Panegyrists that the Romans were soon reconciled to the name and ceremony of adoration.

103 The innovations introduced by Diocletian are chiefly deduced, first, from some very strong passages in Lactantius; and secondly, from the new and various offices, which, in the Theodosian code, appear already established in the beginning of the reign of Constantine.

104 Lactant., *de. M. P.*, ch. 7.

  * *page 228* [emperor AD 364–378]

  † *page 228* [emperor AD 379–395]

105 *Indicta lex nova quae sane illorum temporum modestia tolerabilis, in perniciem processit.* ['A new law was introduced, which, though certainly made tolerable by the moderation with which it was applied at the time, subsequently went from bad to worse.'] Aurelius Victor, who has treated the character of Diocletian with good sense, though in bad Latin.

106 *Solus omnium post conditum Romanum Imperium, qui ex tanto fastigio sponte ad privatae vitae statum civilitatemque remearet.* Eutrop. ix, 28. ['He was the only man since the establishment of the Roman empire, who resigned that lofty office of his own accord and retired into private life as a citizen.']

  * *page ooo* [William Robertson, in his *The History of the Reign of the Emperor Charles V* (1769)]

107 The particulars of the journey and illness are taken from Lactantius (ch. 17), who may *sometimes* be admitted as an evidence of public facts, though very seldom of private anecdotes.

108 Aurelius Victor ascribes the abdication, which had been so variously accounted for, to two causes: first, Diocletian's contempt of ambition; and secondly, his apprehension of impending troubles. One of the panegyrists (vi, 9) mentions the age and infirmities of Diocletian as a very natural reason for his retirement.

109 The difficulties as well as mistakes attending the dates both of the year and of

the day of Diocletian's abdication are perfectly cleared up by Tillemont, *Hist. des Empereurs*, iv, 525, Note 19, and by Pagi *ad annum*.

110 See *Panegyr. Veter.*, vi, 9. The oration was pronounced after Maximian had reassumed the purple.

111 Eumenius pays him a very fine compliment, *At enim divinum illum virum, qui primus imperium et participavit et posuit, consilii et facti sui non paenitet; nec amisisse se putat quod sponte transcripsit. Felix beatusque vere quem vestra, tantorum principum, colunt obsequia privatum. Panegyr. Vet.*, vii, 15. ['That godlike man, the first who both shared and resigned the supreme power, does not regret his decision nor his act, nor regard as a loss what he voluntarily made over. A fortunate and happy man is he, being as a private man the object of the praises of so many emperors.']

112 We are obliged to the younger Victor for this celebrated *bon mot*. Eutropius mentions the thing in a more general manner.

113 *Hist. August.*, pp. 223, 224. Vopiscus had learned this conversation from his father.

114 The younger Victor slightly mentions the report. But, as Diocletian had disobliged a powerful and successful party, his memory has been loaded with every crime and misfortune. It has been affirmed that he died raving mad, that he was condemned as a criminal by the Roman senate, etc.

115 See the *Itiner.*, pp. 269, 272, edit. Wessel.

116 The Abate Fortis, in his *Viaggio in Dalmazia*, p. 43 (printed at Venice in the year 1774, in two small volumes in quarto), quotes a manuscript account of the antiquities of Salona, composed by Giambattista Giustiniani about the middle of the sixteenth century.

117 Adam's Antiquities of Diocletian's Palace at Spalatro, p. 6. We may add a circumstance or two from the Abate Fortis; the little stream of the Hyader, mentioned by Lucan, produces most exquisite trout, which a sagacious writer, perhaps a monk, supposes to have been one of the principal reasons that determined Diocletian in the choice of his retirement. Fortis, p. 45. The same author (p. 38) observes that a taste for agriculture is reviving at Spalatro; and that an experimental farm has lately been established near the city, by a society of gentlemen.

118 Constantin., *Orat. ad Coetum Sanct.*, ch. 25. In this sermon, the emperor, or the bishop who composed it for him, affects to relate the miserable end of all the persecutors of the church.

119 Constantin. Porphyr., *de Statu. Imper.*, p. 86.

  * *page 232* [a court or cloister]

  † *page 232* [writer and authority on architecture under Augustus]

  ‡ *page 232* [entrance hall]

  § *page 232* [portico]

120 D'Anville, *Géographie Ancienne*, i, 162.

121 Messieurs Adam and Clerisseau, attended by two draughtsmen, visited Spalatro in the month of July, 1757. The magnificent work which their journey produced was published in London seven years afterwards.

122 I shall quote the words of the Abate Fortis. *E'bastevolmente nota agli amatori dell' Architettura, e dell' Antichità, l'opera del Signor Adams, che a donato molto a que' superbi vestigi coll'abituale eleganza del suo toccalapis e del bulino. In generale la rozzezza del scalpello, e'l cattivo gusto del secolo vi gareggiano colla magnificenza del*

fabricato. See *Viaggio in Dalmazia*, p. 40. ['The works of Mr Adams (sic) are well-known to lovers of architecture and antiquity; he has given much to those superb remains with the usual elegance of his pencil and engraver's burin. In general, the roughness of the sculptor's chisel and the poor taste of the age accord ill with the magnificence of the design.']

123 The orator Eumenius was secretary to the emperors Maximian and Constantius, and Professor of Rhetoric in the College of Autun. His salary was six hundred thousand sesterces, which, according to the lowest computation of that age, must have exceeded three thousand pounds a year. He generously requested the permission of employing it in rebuilding the college. See his Oration *De restaurandis scholis*; which, though not exempt from vanity, may atone for his panegyrics.

124 Porphyry died about the time of Diocletian's abdication. The life of his master Plotinus, which he composed, will give us the most complete idea of the genius of the sect, and the manners of its professors. This very curious piece is inserted in Fabricius, *Bibliotheca Graeca*, iv, 88–148.

CHAPTER 14 (Summary)

Troubles after the abdication of Diocletian – death of Constantius – elevation of Constantine and Maxentius – six emperors at the same time – death of Maximian and Galerius – victories of Constantine over Maxentius and Licinius – reunion of the empire under the authority of Constantine

The political stability created by Diocletian within the empire did not last, and in this chapter Gibbon relates the rivalry between his successors. In AD 308 there were no less than six emperors who administered the empire between them. Constantine's rule in Gaul was the most peaceful, though Gibbon regards his policy as more expedient than humane. In contrast, Maxentius, the son of Maximian, abused his power in Rome and challenged the rule of Constantine. At the battle of the Milvian Bridge outside Rome in AD 312, Constantine's Gallic army defeated Maxentius; the Arch of Constantine was built to commemorate the event. Constantine then shared control of the empire with Licinius in the east, but there were outbreaks of civil war between them before peace was established in AD 324 with the death of Licinius.

CHAPTER 15

The progress of the Christian religion, and the sentiments, manners, numbers and condition of the primitive Christians

A candid but rational inquiry into the progress and establishment of Christianity may be considered as a very essential part of the history of the Roman empire. While that great body was invaded by open violence, or undermined by slow decay, a pure and humble religion gently insinuated itself into the minds of men, grew up in silence and obscurity, derived new vigour from opposition, and finally erected the triumphant banner of the cross on the ruins of the Capitol. Nor was the influence of Christianity confined to the period or to the limits of the Roman empire. After a revolution of thirteen or fourteen centuries, that religion is still professed by the nations of Europe, the most distinguished portion of human kind in arts and learning as well as in arms. By the industry and zeal of the Europeans it has been widely diffused to the most distant shores of Asia and Africa; and by the means of their colonies has been firmly established from Canada to Chile, in a world unknown to the ancients.

But this inquiry, however useful or entertaining, is attended with two peculiar difficulties. The scanty and suspicious materials of ecclesiastical history seldom enable us to dispel the dark cloud that hangs over the first age of the church. The great law of impartiality too often obliges us to reveal the imperfections of the uninspired teachers and believers of the gospel; and, to a careless observer, *their* faults may seem to cast a shade on the faith which they professed. But the scandal of the pious Christian, and the fallacious triumph of the Infidel, should cease as soon as they recollect not only *by whom*, but likewise *to whom*, the Divine Revelation was given. The theologian may indulge the pleasing task of describing Religion as she descended from Heaven, arrayed in her native purity. A more melancholy duty is imposed on the historian. He must discover the inevitable mixture of error and corruption which she contracted in a long residence upon earth, among a weak and degenerate race of beings.

Our curiosity is naturally prompted to inquire by what means the Christian faith obtained so remarkable a victory over the established religions of the earth. To this inquiry, an obvious but satisfactory answer may be returned; that it was owing to the convincing evidence of the doctrine itself, and to the ruling providence of its great Author. But, as truth and reason seldom find so favourable a reception in the world, and as the wisdom of Providence frequently condescends to use the passions of the human heart, and the general circumstances of mankind, as instruments to execute its purpose; we may still be permitted, though with becoming submission, to ask not indeed what were the first, but what were the secondary causes of the rapid growth of the Christian church. It will, perhaps, appear that it was most effectually favoured and assisted by the five following causes: I. The inflexible, and, if we may use the expression, the intolerant zeal of the Christians, derived, it is true, from the Jewish religion, but purified from the narrow and unsocial spirit which, instead of inviting, had deterred the Gentiles from embracing the law of Moses. II. The doctrine of a future life, improved by every additional circumstance which could give weight and efficacy to that important truth. III. The miraculous powers ascribed to the primitive church. IV. The pure and austere morals of the Christians. V. The union and discipline of the Christian republic, which gradually formed an independent and increasing state in the heart of the Roman empire.

I.   We have already described the religious harmony of the ancient world, and the facility with which the most different and even hostile nations embraced, or at least respected, each other's superstitions. A single people refused to join in the common intercourse of mankind. The Jews, who, under the Assyrian and Persian monarchies, had languished for many ages the most despised portion of their slaves,[1] emerged from obscurity under the successors of Alexander; and, as, they multiplied to a surprising degree in the East, and afterwards in the West, they soon excited the curiosity and wonder of other nations.[2] The sullen obstinacy with which they maintained their peculiar rites and unsocial manners seemed to mark them out a distinct species of men, who boldly professed, or who faintly disguised, their implacable hatred to the rest of human kind.[3] Neither the violence of Antiochus,* nor the arts of Herod,† nor the example of the circumjacent nations, could ever persuade the Jews to associate with the institutions of Moses the elegant mythology of the Greeks.[4] According to the maxims of universal toleration, the Romans protected a superstition which they despised.[5] The polite Augustus condescended to give orders that sacrifices should be offered for his prosperity in the temple of Jerusalem;[6] while the meanest of the posterity of Abraham, who should have paid the same homage to the Jupiter of the Capitol, would have been an object of abhorrence to himself and to his brethren. But the moderation of the conquerors was insufficient to appease the jealous prejudices of their subjects, who were alarmed and scandalised at the ensigns of paganism, which necessarily introduced themselves into a Roman province.[7] The mad attempt of Caligula to place his own statue in the temple of Jerusalem was defeated by the unanimous resolution of a people who dreaded death much less than such an idolatrous profanation.[8] Their attachment to the law of Moses was equal to their detestation of foreign religions. The current of zeal and devotion, as it was contracted into a narrow channel, ran with the strength, and sometimes with the fury, of a torrent.

This inflexible perseverance, which appeared so odious, or so ridiculous, to the ancient world, assumes a more awful character, since Providence has deigned to reveal to us the mysterious history of the chosen people. But the devout, and even scrupulous, attachment to the Mosaic religion, so conspicuous among the Jews who lived under the second temple, becomes still more surprising, if it is compared with the stubborn incredulity of their forefathers. When the law was given in thunder from Mount Sinai; when the tides of the ocean and the course of the planets were suspended for the convenience of the Israelites; and when temporal rewards and punishments were the immediate consequences of their piety or disobedience; they perpetually relapsed into rebellion against the visible majesty of their Divine King, placed the idols of the nations in the sanctuary of Jehovah, and imitated every fantastic ceremony that was practised in the tents of the Arabs or in the cities of Phoenicia.[9] As the protection of Heaven was deservedly withdrawn from the ungrateful race, their faith acquired a proportionable degree of vigour and purity. The contemporaries of Moses and Joshua had beheld, with careless indifference, the most amazing miracles. Under the pressure of every calamity, the belief of those miracles has preserved the Jews of a later period from the universal contagion of idolatry; and, in contradiction to every known principle of the human mind, that singular people seems to have yielded a stronger and more ready assent to the traditions of their remote ancestors than to the evidence of their own senses.[10]

The Jewish religion was admirably fitted for defence, but it was never designed for conquest; and it seems probable that the number of proselytes was never much superior to that of apostates. The divine promises were originally made, and the distinguishing rite of circumcision was enjoined, to a single family. When the posterity of Abraham had multiplied like the sands of the sea, the Deity, from whose mouth they received a system of laws and ceremonies, declared himself the proper and, as it were, the national God of Israel; and, with the most jealous care, separated his favourite people from the rest of mankind. The conquest of the land of Canaan was accompanied with so many wonderful and with so many bloody circumstances that the victorious Jews were left in a state of irreconcilable hostility with all their neighbours. They had been commanded to extirpate some of the most idolatrous tribes; and the execution of the Divine will had seldom been retarded by the weakness of humanity. With the other nations they were forbidden to contract any marriages or alliances; and the prohibition of receiving them into the congregation, which, in some cases, was perpetual, almost always extended to the third, to the seventh, or even to the tenth generation. The obligation of preaching to the Gentiles the faith of Moses had never been inculcated as a precept of the law, nor were the Jews inclined to impose it on themselves as a voluntary duty. In the admission of new citizens, that unsocial people was actuated by the selfish vanity of the Greeks, rather

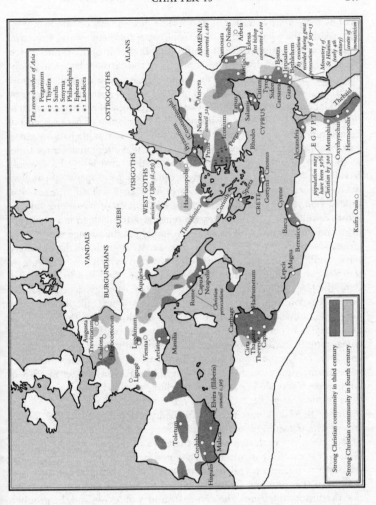

The seven churches of Asia
*1 Pergamum
*2 Thyatira
*3 Sardis
*4 Smyrna
*5 Philadelphia
*6 Ephesus
*7 Laodicea

ALANS

ARMENIA
converted c.280

Samosata
Nisibis
Edessa
first bishop
consecrated c.200
Arbela

Cappadocia

Ancyra
Nicaea
council 325
Iconium
Perga
Tarsus
Antioch
Cnidum
Sidon
Tyre
Caesarea
Jerusalem
Bethlehem
Gaza
Bostra

85 executions
recorded during great
persecutions of 303–13

Monastery of
St Hilarion
(early 4th
century)

OSTROGOTHS

Constantinople

Prusa
Pergamum
Smyrna
Rhodes
Salamis
CYPRUS
Gortyna
Cnossus
CRETE
Barca
Cyrene
Berenice

Alexandria
EGYPT
Memphis
Oxyrhynchus
Hermopolis

Thebaid

centre of
monasticism

VISIGOTHS

WEST GOTHS
mission of Ulfila (d.383)

Hadrianopolis

Thessalonica
Corinth
Sparta

SUEBI

population may
have been 50%
Christian by 300

Kufra Oasis

VANDALS

BURGUNDIANS

Aquileia

Lepcis
Magna

Augusta
Treverorum
Chalons
Dingocortorum
Lugdunum
Vienna
Arelate
Massilia

Rome
Capua
Neapolis

Christian
persecutions

Hadrumetum

Liguge

Cirta
Thagaste
Theveste
Caput

Carthage

Toletum

Elvira (Illiberis)
council c.305

Corduba
Malaca
Hispalis

Strong Christian community in third century

Strong Christian community in fourth century

The early growth of Christianity

than by the generous policy of Rome. The descendants of Abraham were flattered by the opinion that they alone were the heirs of the covenant; and they were apprehensive of diminishing the value of their inheritance, by sharing it too easily with the strangers of the earth. A larger acquaintance with mankind extended their knowledge without correcting their prejudices; and whenever the God of Israel acquired any new votaries, he was much more indebted to the inconstant humour of polytheism than to the active zeal of his own missionaries.[11] The religion of Moses seems to be instituted for a particular country, as well as for a single nation; and, if a strict obedience had been paid to the order that every male, three times in the year, should present himself before the Lord Jehovah, it would have been impossible that the Jews could ever have spread themselves beyond the narrow limits of the promised land.[12] That obstacle was indeed removed by the destruction of the temple of Jerusalem; but the most considerable part of the Jewish religion was involved in its destruction; and the Pagans, who had long wondered at the strange report of an empty sanctuary,[13] were at a loss to discover what could be the object, or what could be the instruments, of a worship which was destitute of temples and of altars, of priests and of sacrifices. Yet even in their fallen state, the Jews, still asserting their lofty and exclusive privileges, shunned, instead of courting, the society of strangers. They still insisted with inflexible rigour on those parts of the law which it was in their power to practise. Their peculiar distinctions of days, of meats, and a variety of trivial though burdensome observances, were so many objects of disgust and aversion for the other nations, to whose habits and prejudices they were diametrically opposite. The painful and even dangerous rite of circumcision was alone capable of repelling a willing proselyte from the door of the synagogue.[14]

Under these circumstances, Christianity offered itself to the world, armed with the strength of the Mosaic law, and delivered from the weight of its fetters. An exclusive zeal for the truth of religion and the unity of God was as carefully inculcated in the new as in the ancient system; and whatever was now revealed to mankind, concerning the nature and designs of the Supreme Being, was fitted to increase their reverence for that mysterious doctrine. The divine authority of Moses and the prophets was admitted, and even established, as the firmest basis of Christianity. From the beginning of the world an uninterrupted series of predictions had announced and prepared the long expected coming of the Messiah, who, in compliance with the gross apprehensions of the Jews, had been more frequently represented under the character of a King and Conqueror, than under that of a Prophet, a Martyr, and the Son of God. By his expiatory sacrifice, the imperfect sacrifices of the temple were at once consummated and abolished. The ceremonial law, which consisted only of types and figures, was succeeded by a pure and spiritual worship, equally adapted to all climates, as well as to every condition of mankind, and to the initiation of blood was substituted a more harmless initiation of water. The promise of divine favour, instead of being partially confined to the posterity of Abraham, was universally proposed to the freeman and the slave, to the Greek and to the barbarian, to the Jew and to the Gentile. Every privilege that could raise the proselyte from earth to Heaven, that could exalt his devotion, secure his happiness, or even gratify that secret pride which, under the semblance of devotion, insinuates itself into the human heart, was still reserved for the members of the Christian church; but at the same time all mankind was permitted, and even solicited, to accept the glorious distinction, which was not only proffered as a favour, but imposed as an obligation. It became the most sacred duty of a new convert to diffuse among his friends and relations the inestimable blessing which he had received, and to warn them against a refusal that would be severely punished as a criminal disobedience to the will of a benevolent but all-powerful deity.

The enfranchisement of the church from the bonds of the synagogue was a work however of some time and of some difficulty. The Jewish converts, who acknowledged Jesus in the character of the Messiah foretold by their ancient oracles, respected him as a prophetic teacher of virtue and religion; but they obstinately adhered to the ceremonies of their ancestors, and were desirous of imposing them on the Gentiles, who continually augmented the number of believers. These Judaising Christians seem to have argued with some degree of plausibility from the divine origin of the Mosaic law, and from the immutable perfections of its great Author. They affirmed *that*, if the Being, who is the same through all eternity, had designed to abolish those sacred rites which had served to distinguish his chosen people, the repeal of them would have been no less clear and solemn than their first promulgation: *that*, instead of those frequent declarations, which either suppose or assert the perpetuity of the Mosaic religion, it would have been represented as a provisionary scheme intended to last only till the coming of the Messiah, who should instruct mankind in a more perfect mode of faith and of worship:[15] *that* the Messiah himself, and his disciples who conversed with him on earth, instead of authorising by their example the most minute observances of the Mosaic law,[16] would have published to the world the abolition of those useless and obsolete ceremonies, without suffering Christianity to remain during so many years obscurely confounded among the sects of the Jewish church. Arguments like these appear to have been used in the defence of the expiring cause of the Mosaic law; but the industry of our learned divines has abundantly explained the ambiguous language of the Old Testament, and the ambiguous conduct of the apostolic teachers. It was proper gradually to unfold the system of the Gospel, and to pronounce, with the utmost caution and tenderness, a sentence of condemnation so repugnant to the inclination and prejudices of the believing Jews.

The history of the church of Jerusalem affords a lively proof of the necessity of those precautions, and of the deep impression which the Jewish religion had made on the minds of its sectaries. The first fifteen bishops of Jerusalem were all circumcised Jews; and the congregation over which they presided, united the law of Moses with the doctrine of Christ.[17] It was natural that the primitive tradition of a church which was founded only forty days after the death of Christ, and was governed almost as many years under the immediate inspection of his apostles, should be received as the standard of orthodoxy.[18] The distant churches very frequently appealed to the authority of their venerable Parent, and relieved her distresses by a liberal contribution of alms. But, when numerous and opulent societies were established in the great cities of the empire, in Antioch, Alexandria, Ephesus, Corinth, and Rome, the reverence which Jerusalem had inspired to all the Christian colonies insensibly diminished. The Jewish converts, or, as they were afterwards called, the Nazarenes, who had laid the foundations of the church, soon found themselves overwhelmed by the increasing multitudes that from all the various religions of polytheism enlisted under the banner of Christ; and the Gentiles, who with the approbation of their peculiar apostle had rejected the intolerable weight of Mosaic ceremonies, at length refused to their more scrupulous brethren the same toleration which at first they had humbly solicited for their own practice. The ruin of the temple, of the city, and of the public religion of the Jews, was severely felt by the Nazarenes; as in their manners, though not in their faith, they maintained so intimate a connection with their impious countrymen, whose misfortunes were attributed by the Pagans to the contempt, and more justly ascribed by the Christians to the wrath, of the Supreme Deity. The Nazarenes retired from the ruins of Jerusalem to the little town of Pella beyond the Jordan, where that ancient church languished above sixty years in solitude and obscurity.[19] They still enjoyed the comfort of making frequent and devout visits to the *Holy City*, and the hope of being one day restored to those seats which both nature and religion taught them to love as well as to revere. But at length, under the reign of Hadrian, the desperate fanaticism of the Jews filled up the measure of their calamities; and the Romans, exasperated by their repeated rebellions, exercised the rights of victory with unusual rigour. The emperor founded, under the name of Aelia Capitolina, a new city on Mount Sion,[20] to which he gave the privileges of a colony; and, denouncing the severest penalties against any of the Jewish people who should dare to approach its precincts, he fixed a vigilant garrison of a Roman cohort to enforce the execution of his orders. The Nazarenes had only one way left to escape the common proscription, and the force of truth was, on this occasion, assisted by the influence of temporal advantages. They elected Marcus for their bishop, a prelate of the race of the Gentiles, and most probably a native either of Italy or of some of the Latin provinces. At his persuasion, the most considerable part of the congregation renounced the Mosaic law, in the practice of which they had persevered above a century. By this sacrifice of their habits and prejudices they purchased a free admission into the colony of Hadrian, and more firmly cemented their union with the Catholic church.[21]

When the name and honours of the church of Jerusalem had been restored to Mount Sion, the crimes of heresy and schism were imputed to the obscure remnant of the Nazarenes which refused to accompany their Latin bishop. They still preserved their former habitation of Pella, spread themselves into the villages adjacent to Damascus, and formed an inconsiderable church in the city of Beroea, or, as it is now called, of Aleppo, in Syria.[22] The name of Nazarenes was deemed too honourable for those Christian Jews, and they soon received from the supposed poverty of their understanding, as well as of their condition, the contemptuous epithet of Ebionites.[23] In a few years after the return of the church of Jerusalem, it became a matter of doubt and controversy whether a man who sincerely acknowledged Jesus as the Messiah, but who still continued to observe the law of Moses, could possibly hope for salvation. The humane temper of Justin Martyr inclined him to answer this question in the affirmative; and, though he expressed himself with the most guarded diffidence, he ventured to determine in favour of such an imperfect Christian, if he were content to practise the Mosaic ceremonies without pretending to assert their general use or necessity. But, when Justin was pressed to declare the sentiment of the church, he confessed that there were very many among the orthodox Christians, who not only excluded their Judaising brethren from the hope of salvation, but who declined any intercourse with them in the common offices of friendship, hospitality, and social life.[24] The more rigorous opinion prevailed, as it was natural to expect, over the milder; and an eternal bar of separation was fixed between the disciples of Moses and those of Christ. The unfortunate Ebionites, rejected from one religion as apostates, and from the other as heretics, found themselves compelled to assume a more decided character; and, although some traces of that obsolete sect may be discovered as late as the fourth century, they insensibly melted away either into the church or the synagogue.[25]

While the orthodox church preserved a just medium between excessive veneration and improper contempt for the law of Moses, the various heretics deviated into equal but opposite extremes of error and extravagance. From the acknowledged truth of the Jewish religion, the Ebionites had concluded that it could never be abolished. From its supposed imperfections the Gnostics as hastily inferred that it never was instituted by the wisdom of the Deity. There are some objections against the authority of Moses and the prophets, which too readily present themselves to the sceptical mind; though they can only be derived from our ignorance of remote antiquity, and from our incapacity to form an adequate judgment of the divine economy.* These objections were eagerly embraced, and as petulantly urged, by the vain science of the Gnostics.[26] As those heretics were, for the most part, averse to the pleasures of sense, they morosely arraigned the polygamy of the patri- archs, the gallantries of David, and the seraglio of Solomon. The conquest of the land of Canaan, and the extirpation of the unsuspecting natives, they were at a loss how to reconcile with the common notions of humanity and justice. But, when they recollected the sanguinary list of murders, of executions, and of massacres, which stain almost every page of the Jewish annals, they acknowledged that the barbarians of Palestine had exercised as much compassion towards their idolatrous enemies as they had ever shown to their friends or countrymen.[27] Passing from the sectaries of the law to the law itself, they asserted that it was impossible that a religion which consisted only of bloody sacrifices and trifling ceremonies, and whose rewards as well as punishments were all of a carnal and temporal nature, could inspire the love of virtue, or restrain the impetuosity of passion. The Mosaic account of the creation and fall of man was treated with profane derision by the Gnostics, who would not listen with patience to the repose of the Deity after six days' labour, to the rib of Adam, the garden of Eden, the trees of life and of knowledge, the speaking serpent, the forbidden fruit, and the condemnation pronounced against human kind for the venial offence of their first progenitors.[28] The God of Israel was impiously represented by the Gnostics as a being liable to passion and to error, capricious in his favour, implacable in his resentment, meanly jealous of his superstitious worship, and confining his partial providence to a single people and to this transitory life. In such a character they could discover none of the features of the wise and omnipotent father of the universe.[29] They allowed that the religion of the Jews was somewhat less criminal than the idolatry of the Gentiles; but it was their fundamental doctrine that the Christ whom they adored as the first and brightest emanation of the Deity appeared upon earth to rescue mankind from their various errors, and to reveal a *new* system of truth and perfection. The most learned of the fathers, by a very singular condescen- sion, have imprudently admitted the sophistry of the Gnostics. Acknowledging that the literal sense is repugnant to every principle of faith as well as reason, they deem themselves secure and invulnerable behind the ample veil of allegory, which they carefully spread over every tender part of the Mosaic dispensation.[30]

It has been remarked, with more ingenuity than truth, that the virgin purity of the church was never violated by schism or heresy before the reign of Trajan or Hadrian, about one hundred years after the death of Christ.[31] We may observe, with much more propriety, that, during that period, the disciples of the Messiah were indulged in a freer latitude both of faith and practice than has ever been allowed in succeeding ages. As the terms of communion were insensibly narrowed, and the spiritual author- ity of the prevailing party was exercised with increasing severity, many of its most respectable adherents, who were called upon to renounce, were provoked to assert, their private opinions, to pursue the consequences of their mistaken principles, and openly to erect the standard of rebellion against the unity of the church. The Gnostics were distinguished as the most polite, the most learned, and the most wealthy of the Christian name, and that general appellation which expressed a superiority of knowledge was either assumed by their own pride or ironically bestowed by the envy of their adversaries. They were almost without exception of the race of the Gentiles, and their principal founders seem to have been natives of Syria or Egypt, where the warmth of the climate disposes both the mind and the body to indolent devotion. The Gnostics blended with the faith of Christ many sublime but obscure tenets which they derived from oriental philosophy, and even from the religion of Zoroaster, concerning the eternity of matter, the existence of two principles, and the mysterious hierarchy of the invisible world.[32] As soon as they launched out into that vast abyss, they delivered themselves to the guidance of a disordered imagination; and, as the paths of error are various and infinite, the Gnostic were imperceptibly divided into more than fifty particular sects,[33] of whom the most celebrated appear to have been the Basilidians, the Valentinians, the Marcionites, and, in a still later period, the Manichaeans. Each of these sects could boast of its bishops and congregations, of its doctors and martyrs,[34] and, instead of the four gospels adopted by the church, the heretics produced a multitude of histories, in which the actions and discourses of Christ and of his apostles were adapted to their respective tenets.[35] The success of the Gnostics was rapid and extensive.[36] They covered Asia and Egypt, established themselves in Rome, and sometimes penetrated into the provinces of the West. For the most part they arose in the second century, flourished during the third, and were suppressed in the fourth or fifth, by the prevalence of more fashionable controversies, and by the superior ascendant of the reigning power. Though they constantly disturbed the peace, and frequently disgraced the name, of religion, they contributed to assist rather than to retard the progress of Christianity. The Gentile converts, whose strongest objections and prejudices were directed against the law of Moses, could find admission into many Christian societies, which required not from their untutored mind any belief of an antecedent revelation. Their faith was insensibly fortified and enlarged, and the church was ultimately benefited by the conquests of its most inveterate enemies.[37]

But, whatever difference of opinion might subsist between the Orthodox, the Ebionites, and the Gnostics, concerning the divinity or the obligation of the Mosaic law, they were all equally animated by the same exclusive zeal and by the same abhorrence for idolatry which had distinguished the Jews from the other nations of the ancient world. The philosopher, who considered the system of polytheism as a composition of human fraud and error, could disguise a smile of contempt under the mask of devotion, without apprehending that either the mockery or the compliance would expose him to the resentment of any invisible, or, as he conceived them, imaginary powers. But the established religions of Paganism were seen by the primitive Christians in a much more odious and formidable light. It was the universal sentiment both of the church and of heretics that the daemons were the authors, the patrons, and the objects of idolatry.[38] Those rebellious spirits who had been degraded from the rank of angels, and cast down into the infernal pit, were still permitted to roam upon earth, to torment the bodies, and to seduce the minds of sinful men. The daemons soon discovered and abused the natural propensity of the human heart towards devotion, and, artfully withdrawing the adoration of mankind from their Creator, they usurped the place and honours of the Supreme Deity. By the success of their malicious contrivances, they at once gratified their own vanity and revenge, and obtained the only comfort of which they were yet susceptible, the hope of involving the human species in the participation of their guilt and misery. It was confessed, or at least it was imagined, that they had distributed among themselves the most important characters of polytheism, one daemon assuming the name and attributes of Jupiter, another of Aesculapius,* a third of Venus, and a fourth perhaps of Apollo;[39] and that, by the advantage of their long experience and aerial nature, they were enabled to execute, with sufficient skill and dignity, the parts which they had undertaken. They lurked in the temples, instituted festivals and sacrifices, invented fables, pronounced oracles, and were frequently allowed to perform miracles. The Christians, who, by the interposition of evil spirits, could so readily explain every praeternatural appearance, were disposed and even desirous to admit the most extravagant fictions of the Pagan mythology. But the belief of the Christian was accompanied with horror. The most trifling mark of respect to the national worship he considered as a direct homage yielded to the daemon, and as an act of rebellion against the majesty of God.

In consequence of this opinion, it was the first but arduous duty of a Christian to preserve himself pure and undefiled by the practice of idolatry. The religion of the nations was not merely a speculative doctrine professed in the schools† or preached in the temples. The innumerable deities and rites of polytheism were closely interwoven with every circumstance of business or pleasure, of public or of private life, and it seemed impossible to escape the observance of them, without, at the same time, renouncing the commerce of mankind and all the offices and amusements of society.[40] The important transactions of peace and war were prepared or concluded by solemn sacrifices, in which the magistrate, the senator, and the soldier were obliged to preside or to participate.[41] The public spectacles were an essential part of the cheerful devotion of the Pagans, and the gods were supposed to accept, as the most grateful offering, the games that the prince and people celebrated in honour of their peculiar festivals.[42] The Christian, who with pious horror avoided the abomination of the circus or the theatre, found himself encompassed with infernal snares in every convivial entertainment, as often as his friends, invoking the hospitable deities, poured out libations to each other's happiness.[43] When the bride, struggling with well-affected reluctance, was forced in hymenaeal pomp over the threshold of her new habitation,[44] or when the sad procession of the dead slowly moved towards the funeral pile,[45] the Christian, on these interesting occasions, was compelled to desert the persons who were the dearest to him, rather than contract the guilt inherent to those impious ceremonies. Every art and every trade that was in the least concerned in the framing or adorning of idols was polluted by the stain of idolatry;[46] a severe sentence, since it devoted to eternal misery the far greater part of the community, which is employed in the exercise of liberal or mechanic professions. If we cast our eyes over the numerous remains of antiquity, we shall perceive that, besides the immediate representations of the Gods and the holy instruments of their worship, the elegant forms and agreeable fictions, consecrated by the imagination of the Greeks, were introduced as the richest ornaments of the houses, the dress, and the furniture, of the Pagans.[47] Even the arts of music and painting, of eloquence and poetry, flowed from the same impure origin. In the style of the fathers, Apollo and the Muses were the organs of the infernal spirit, Homer and Virgil were the most eminent of his servants, and the beautiful mythology which pervades and animates the compositions of their genius is destined to celebrate the glory of the daemons. Even the common language of Greece and Rome abounded with familiar but impious expressions, which the imprudent Christian might too carelessly utter, or too patiently hear.[48]

The dangerous temptations which on every side lurked in ambush to surprise the unguarded believer assailed him with redoubled violence on the days of solemn festivals. So artfully were they framed and disposed throughout the year that superstition always wore the appearance of pleasure, and often of virtue.[49] Some of the most sacred festivals in the Roman ritual were destined to salute the new calends of January with vows of public and private felicity, to indulge the pious remembrance of the dead and living, to ascertain the inviolable bounds of property, to hail, on the return of spring, the genial powers of fecundity, to perpetuate the two memorable eras of Rome, the foundation of the city and that of the republic, and to restore, during the humane licence of the Saturnalia, the primitive equality of mankind. Some idea may be conceived of the abhorrence of the Christians for such impious ceremonies, by the scrupulous delicacy which they displayed on a much less alarming occasion. On days of general festivity, it was the custom of the ancients to adorn their doors with lamps and with branches of laurel, and to crown their heads with a garland of flowers. This innocent and elegant practice might, perhaps, have been tolerated as a mere civil institution. But it most unluckily happened that the doors were under the protection of the household gods, that the laurel was sacred to the lover of Daphne,* and that garlands of flowers, though frequently worn as a symbol either of joy or mourning, had been dedicated in their first origin to the service of superstition. The trembling Christians, who were persuaded in this instance to comply with the fashion of their country and the commands of the magistrate, laboured under the most gloomy apprehensions, from the reproaches of their own conscience, the censures of the church, and the denunciations of divine vengeance.[50]

Such was the anxious diligence which was required to guard the chastity of the gospel from the infectious breath of idolatry. The superstitious observances of public or private rites were carelessly practised, from education and habit, by the followers of the established religion. But, as often as they occurred, they afforded the Christians an opportunity of declaring and confirming their zealous opposition. By these frequent protestations, their attachment to the faith was continually fortified, and, in proportion to the increase of zeal, they combated with the more ardour and success in the holy war which they had undertaken against the empire of the daemons.

II.   The writings of Cicero[51] present, in the most lively colours, the ignorance, the errors, and the uncertainty of the ancient philosophers, with regard to the immortality of the soul. When they are desirous of arming their disciples against the fear of death, they inculcate, as an obvious though melancholy position, that the fatal stroke of our dissolution releases us from the calamities of life, and that those can no longer suffer who no longer exist. Yet there were a few sages of Greece and Rome who had conceived a more exalted, and, in some respects, a juster idea of human nature; though it must be confessed that, in the sublime inquiry, their reason had been often guided by their imagination, and that their imagination had been prompted by their vanity. When they viewed with complacency the extent of their own mental powers, when they exercised the various faculties of memory, of fancy, and of judgment, in the most profound speculations, or the most important labours, and when they reflected on the desire of fame, which transported them into future ages far beyond the bounds of death and of the grave; they were unwilling to confound themselves with the beasts of the field, or to suppose that a being, for whose dignity they entertained the most sincere admiration, could be limited to a spot of earth and to a few years of duration. With this favourable prepossession, they summoned to their aid the science, or rather the language, of Metaphysics. They soon discovered that, as none of the properties of matter will apply to the operations of the mind, the human soul must consequently be a substance distinct from the body, pure, simple, and spiritual, incapable of dissolution, and susceptible of a much higher degree of virtue and happiness after the release from its corporeal prison.

From these specious and noble principles, the philosophers who trod in the footsteps of Plato deduced a very unjustifiable conclusion, since they asserted, not only the future immortality, but the past eternity of the human soul, which they were too apt to consider as a portion of the infinite and self-existing spirit which pervades and sustains the universe.[52] A doctrine thus removed beyond the senses and the experience of mankind might serve to amuse the leisure of a philosophic mind; or, in the silence of solitude, it might sometimes impart a ray of comfort to desponding virtue; but the faint impression which had been received in the schools was soon obliterated by the commerce and business of active life. We are sufficiently acquainted with the eminent persons who flourished in the age of Cicero, and of the first Caesars, with their actions, their characters, and their motives, to be assured that their conduct in this life was never regulated by any serious conviction of the rewards or punishments of a future state. At the bar and in the senate of Rome the ablest orators were not apprehensive of giving offence to their hearers by exposing that doctrine as an idle and extravagant opinion, which was rejected with contempt by every man of a liberal education and understanding.[53]

Since, therefore, the most sublime efforts of philosophy can extend no farther than feebly to point out the desire, the hope, or at most the probability, of a future state, there is nothing, except a divine revelation, that can ascertain the existence, and describe the condition, of the invisible country which is destined to receive the souls of men after their separation from the body. But we may perceive several defects inherent to the popular religions of Greece and Rome, which rendered them very unequal to so arduous a task. 1. The general system of their mythology was unsupported by any solid proofs; and the wisest among the Pagans had already disclaimed its usurped authority. 2. The description of the infernal regions had been abandoned to the fancy of painters and of poets, who peopled them with so many phantoms and monsters, who dispensed their rewards and punishments with so little equity, that a solemn truth, the most congenial to the human heart, was oppressed and disgraced by the absurd mixture of the wildest fictions.[54] 3. The doctrine of a future state was scarcely considered among the devout polytheists of Greece and Rome as a fundamental article of faith. The providence of the gods, as it related to public communities rather than to private individuals, was principally displayed on the visible theatre of the present world. The petitions which were offered on the altars of Jupiter or Apollo expressed the anxiety of their worshippers for temporal happiness, and their ignorance or indifference concerning a future life.[55] The important truth of the immortality of the soul was inculcated with more diligence as well as success in India, in Assyria, in Egypt, and in Gaul; and, since we cannot attribute such a difference to the superior knowledge of the barbarians, we must ascribe it to the influence of an established priesthood, which employed the motives of virtue as the instrument of ambition.[56]

We might naturally expect that a principle, so essential to religion, would have been revealed in the clearest terms to the chosen people of Palestine, and that it might safely have been entrusted to the hereditary priesthood of Aaron. It is incumbent on us to adore the mysterious dispensations of Providence[57], when we discover that the doctrine of the immortality of the soul is omitted in the law of Moses; it is darkly insinuated by prophets, and during the long period which elapsed between the Egyptian and the Babylonian servitudes, the hopes as well as the fears of the Jews appear to have been confined within the narrow compass of the present life.[58] After Cyrus had permitted the exiled nation to return into the promised land, and after Ezra had restored the ancient records of their religion, two celebrated sects, the Sadducees and the Pharisees, insensibly arose at Jerusalem.[59] The former, selected from the more opulent and distinguished ranks of society, were strictly attached to the literal sense of the Mosaic law, and they piously rejected the immortality of the soul, as an opinion that received no countenance from the Divine book, which they revered as the only rule of their faith. To the authority of scripture the Pharisees added that of tradition, and they accepted, under the name of traditions, several speculative tenets from the philosophy or religion of the eastern nations. The doctrines of fate or predestination, of angels and spirits, and of a future state of rewards and punishments, were in the number of these new articles of belief; and, as the Pharisees, by the austerity of their manners, had drawn into their party the body of the Jewish people, the immortality of the soul became the prevailing sentiment of the synagogue, under the reign of the Asmonaean princes and pontiffs. The temper of the Jews was incapable of contenting itself with such a cold and languid assent as might satisfy the mind of a Polytheist; and, as soon as they admitted the idea of a future state, they embraced it with the zeal which has always formed the characteristic of the nation. Their zeal, however, added nothing to its evidence, or even probability: and it was still necessary that the doctrine of life and immortality, which had been dictated by nature, approved by reason, and received by superstition, should obtain the sanction of Divine truth from the authority and example of Christ.

When the promise of eternal happiness was proposed to mankind, on condition of adopting the faith and of observing the precepts of the gospel, it is no wonder that so advantageous an offer should have been accepted by great numbers of every religion, of every rank, and of every province in the Roman empire. The ancient Christians were animated by a contempt for their present existence, and by a just confidence of immortality, of which the doubtful and imperfect faith of modern ages cannot give us any adequate notion. In the primitive church, the influence of truth was very powerfully strengthened by an opinion which, however it may deserve respect for its usefulness and antiquity, has not been found agreeable to experience. It was universally believed that the end of the world and the kingdom of Heaven were at hand. The near approach of this wonderful event had been predicted by the apostles; the tradition of it was preserved by their earliest disciples, and those who understood in their literal sense the discourses of Christ himself were obliged to expect the second and glorious coming of the Son of Man in the clouds, before that generation was totally extinguished, which had beheld his humble condition upon earth and which might still be witness of the calamities of the Jews under Vespasian or Hadrian. The revolution of seventeen centuries has instructed us not to press too closely the mysterious language of prophecy and revelation; but, as long as, for wise purposes, this error was permitted to subsist in the church, it was productive of the most salutary effects on the faith and practice of Christians, who lived in the awful expectation of that moment when the globe itself, and all the various race of mankind, should tremble at the appearance of their divine judge.[60]

The ancient and popular doctrine of the Millennium was intimately connected with the second coming of Christ. As the works of the creation had been finished in six days, their duration in their present state, according to a tradition which was attributed to the prophet Elijah, was fixed to six thousand years.[61] By the same analogy it was inferred that this long period of labour and contention, which was now almost elapsed,[62] would be succeeded by a joyful Sabbath of a thousand years; and that Christ, with the triumphant band of the saints and the elect who had escaped death, or who had been miraculously revived, would reign upon earth till the time appointed for the last and general resurrection. So pleasing was this hope to the mind of believers that the *New Jerusalem*, the seat of this blissful kingdom, was quickly adorned with all the gayest colours of the imagination. A felicity consisting only of pure and spiritual pleasure would have appeared too refined for its inhabitants, who were still supposed to possess their human nature and senses. A garden of Eden, with the amusements of the pastoral life, was no longer suited to the advanced state of society which prevailed under the Roman empire. A city was therefore erected of gold and precious stones, and a supernatural plenty of corn and wine was bestowed on the adjacent territory; in the free enjoyment of whose spontaneous productions the happy and be-nevolent people was never to be restrained by any jealous laws of exclusive property.[63] The assurance of such a Millennium was carefully inculcated by a succession of fathers from Justin Martyr[64] and Irenaeus, who conversed with the immediate disciples of the apostles, down to Lactantius, who was preceptor to the son of Constantine.[65] Though it might not be universally received, it appears to have been the reigning sentiment of the orthodox believers; and it seems so well adapted to the desires and apprehensions of mankind, that it must have contributed, in a very considerable degree, to the progress of the Christian faith. But, when the edifice of the church was almost completed, the temporary support was laid aside. The doctrine of Christ's reign upon earth was at first treated as a profound allegory, was considered by degrees as a doubtful and useless opinion, and was at length rejected as the absurd invention of heresy and fanaticism.[66] A mysterious prophecy, which still forms a part of the sacred canon, but which was thought to favour the exploded sentiment, has very narrowly escaped the proscription of the church.[67]

Whilst the happiness and glory of a temporal reign were promised to the disciples of Christ, the most dreadful calamities were denounced against an unbelieving world. The edification* of the new Jerusalem was to advance by equal steps with the destruction of the mystic Babylon; and, as long as the emperors who reigned before Constantine persisted in the profession of idolatry, the epithet of Babylon was applied to the city and to the empire of Rome. A regular series was prepared of all the moral and physical evils which can afflict a flourishing nation; intestine discord, and the invasion of the fiercest barbarians from the unknown regions of the North; pestilence and famine, comets and eclipses, earthquakes and inundations.[68] All these were only so many preparatory and alarming signs of the great catastrophe of Rome, when the country of the Scipios and Caesars should be consumed by a flame from Heaven, and the city of the seven hills, with her palaces, her temples, and her triumphal arches, should be buried in a vast lake of fire and brimstone. It might, however, afford some consolation to Roman vanity, that the period of their empire would be that of the world itself; which, as it had once perished by the element of water, was destined to experience a second and a speedy destruction from the element of fire. In the opinion of a general conflagration, the faith of the Christian very happily coincided with the tradition of the East, the philosophy of the Stoics, and the analogy of Nature; and even the country which, from religious motives, had been chosen for the origin and principal scene of the conflagration, was the best adapted for that purpose by natural and physical causes; by its deep caverns, beds of sulphur, and numerous volcanoes, of which those of Etna, of Vesuvius, and of Lipari, exhibit a very imperfect representation. The calmest and most intrepid sceptic could not refuse to acknowledge that the destruction of the present system of the world by fire was in itself extremely probable. The Christian, who founded his belief much less on the fallacious arguments of reason than on the authority of tradition and the interpretation of scripture, expected it with terror and confidence, as a certain and approaching event; and, as his mind was perpetually filled with the solemn idea, he considered every disaster that happened to the empire as an infallible symptom of an expiring world.[69]

The condemnation of the wisest and most virtuous of the Pagans, on account of their ignorance or disbelief of the divine truth, seems to offend the reason and the humanity of the present age.[70] But the primitive church, whose faith was of a much firmer consistence, delivered over, without hesitation, to eternal torture the far greater part of the human species. A charitable hope might perhaps be indulged in favour of Socrates, or some other sages of antiquity, who had consulted the light of reason before that of the gospel had arisen.[71] But it was unanimously affirmed that those who, since the birth or the death of Christ, had obstinately persisted in the worship of the daemons, neither deserved, nor could expect, a pardon from the irritated justice of the Deity. These rigid sentiments, which had been unknown to the ancient world, appear to have infused a spirit of bitterness into a system of love and harmony. The ties of blood and friendship were frequently torn asunder by the difference of religious faith; and the Christians, who, in this world, found themselves oppressed by the power of the Pagans, were sometimes seduced by resentment and spiritual pride to delight in the prospect of their future triumph. 'You are fond of spectacles,' exclaims the stern Tertullian; 'expect the greatest of all spectacles, the last and eternal judgment of the universe. How shall I admire, how laugh, how rejoice, how exult, when I behold so many proud monarchs, and fancied gods, groaning in the lowest abyss of darkness; so many magistrates, who persecuted the name of the Lord, liquefying in fiercer fires than they ever kindled against the Christians; so many sage philosophers blushing in red-hot flames with their deluded scholars; so many celebrated poets trembling before the tribunal, not of Minos, but of Christ; so many tragedians, more tuneful in the expression of their own sufferings; so many dancers – !' But the humanity of the reader will permit me to draw a veil over the rest of this infernal description, which the zealous African pursues in a long variety of affected and unfeeling witticisms.[72]

   Doubtless there were many among the primitive Christians of a temper more suitable to the meekness and charity of their profession. There were many who felt a sincere compassion for the danger of their friends and countrymen, and who exerted the most benevolent zeal to save them from the impending destruction. The careless Polytheist, assailed by new and unexpected terrors, against which neither his priests nor his philosophers could afford him any certain protection, was very frequently terrified and subdued by the menace of eternal tortures. His fears might assist the progress of his faith and reason; and, if he could once persuade himself to suspect that the Christian religion might possibly be true, it became an easy task to convince him that it was the safest and most prudent party that he could possibly embrace.

III.   The supernatural gifts, which even in this life were ascribed to the Christians above the rest of mankind, must have conduced to their own comfort, and very frequently to the conviction of infidels. Besides the occasional prodigies, which might sometimes be affected by the immediate interposition of the Deity when he suspended the laws of Nature for the service of religion, the Christian church, from the time of the apostles and their first disciples,[73] has claimed an uninterrupted succession of miraculous powers, the gift of tongues, of vision and of prophecy, the power of expelling daemons, of healing the sick, and of raising the dead. The knowledge of foreign languages was frequently communicated to the contemporaries of Irenaeus, though Irenaeus himself was left to struggle with the difficulties of a barbarous dialect whilst he preached the gospel to the natives of Gaul.[74] The divine inspiration, whether it was conveyed in the form of a waking or of a sleeping vision, is described as a favour very liberally bestowed on all ranks of the faithful, on women as on elders, on boys as well as upon bishops. When their devout minds were sufficiently prepared by a course of prayer, of fasting, and of vigils, to receive the extraordinary impulse, they were transported out of their senses, and delivered in ecstasy what was inspired, being mere organs of the Holy Spirit, just as a pipe or flute is of him who blows into it.[75] We may add that the design of these visions was, for the most part, either to disclose the future history, or to guide the present administration, of the church. The expulsion of the daemons from the bodies of those unhappy persons whom they had been permitted to torment was considered as a signal, though ordinary, triumph of religion, and is repeatedly alleged by the ancient apologists as the most convincing evidence of the truth of Christianity. The awful ceremony was usually performed in a public manner, and in the presence of a great number of spectators; the patient was relieved by the power or skill of the exorcist, and the vanquished daemon was heard to confess that he was one of the fabled gods of antiquity, who had impiously usurped the adoration of mankind.[76] But the miraculous cure of diseases, of the most inveterate or even preternatural kind, can no longer occasion any surprise, when we recollect that in the days of Irenaeus, about the end of the second century, the resurrection of the dead was very far from being esteemed an uncommon event, that the miracle was frequently performed on necessary occasions, by great fasting and the joint supplication of the church of the place, and that the persons thus restored to their prayers had lived afterwards among them many years.[77] At such a period, when faith could boast of so many wonderful victories over death, it seems difficult to account for the scepticism of those philosophers who still rejected and derided the doctrine of the resurrection. A noble Grecian had rested on this important ground the whole controversy, and promised Theophilus, bishop of Antioch, that, if he could be gratified with the sight of a single person who had been actually raised from the dead, he would immediately embrace the Christian religion. It is somewhat remarkable that the prelate of the first eastern church, however anxious for the conversion of his friend, thought proper to decline this fair and reasonable challenge.[78]

The miracles of the primitive church, after obtaining the sanction of ages, have been lately attacked in a very free and ingenious inquiry;[79] which, though it has met with the most favourable reception from the public, appears to have excited a general scandal among the divines of our

own as well as of the other Protestant churches of Europe.[80] Our different
sentiments on this subject will be much less influenced by any particular
arguments than by our habits of study and reflection; and, above all, by
the degree of the evidence which we have accustomed ourselves to
require for the proof of a miraculous event. The duty of an historian does
not call upon him to interpose his private judgment in this nice and
important controversy; but he ought not to dissemble the difficulty of
adopting such a theory as may reconcile the interest of religion with that
of reason, of making a proper application of that theory, and of defining
with precision the limits of that happy period, exempt from error and
from deceit, to which we might be disposed to extend the gift of
supernatural powers. From the first of the fathers to the last of the popes,
a succession of bishops, of saints, of martyrs, and of miracles is continued
without interruption, and the progress of superstition was so gradual and
almost imperceptible that we know not in what particular link we should
break the chain of tradition. Every age bears testimony to the wonderful
events by which it was distinguished, and its testimony appears no less
weighty and respectable than that of the preceding generation, till we are
insensibly led on to accuse our own inconsistency, if in the eighth or in
the twelfth century we deny to the venerable Bede, or to the holy
Bernard, the same degree of confidence which, in the second century, we
had so liberally granted to Justin or to Irenaeus.[81] If the truth of any of
those miracles is appreciated by their apparent use and propriety, every
age had unbelievers to convince, heretics to confute, and idolatrous
nations to convert; and sufficient motives might always be produced to
justify the interposition of Heaven. And yet, since every friend to
revelation is persuaded of the reality, and every reasonable man is
convinced of the cessation, of miraculous powers, it is evident that there
must have been *some period* in which they were either suddenly or
gradually withdrawn from the Christian church. Whatever era is chosen
for that purpose, the death of the apostles, the conversion of the Roman
empire, or the extinction of the Arian heresy,[82] the insensibility of the
Christians who lived at that time will equally afford a just matter of
surprise. They still supported their pretensions after they had lost their
power. Credulity performed the office of faith; fanaticism was permitted
to assume the language of inspiration, and the effects of accident or
contrivance were ascribed to supernatural causes. The recent experience
of genuine miracles should have instructed the Christian world in the
ways of Providence, and habituated their eye (if we may use a very
inadequate expression) to the style of the divine artist. Should the most
skilful painter of modern Italy presume to decorate his feeble imitations
with the name of Raphael or of Correggio, the insolent fraud would be
soon discovered and indignantly rejected.

Whatever opinion may be entertained of the miracles of the primitive
church since the time of the apostles, this unresisting softness of temper,

so conspicuous among the believers of the second and third centuries, proved of some accidental benefit to the cause of truth and religion. In modern times, a latent, and even involuntary, scepticism adheres to the most pious dispositions. Their admission of supernatural truths is much less an active consent than a cold and passive acquiescence. Accustomed long since to observe and to respect the invariable order of Nature, our reason, or at least our imagination, is not sufficiently prepared to sustain the visible action of the Deity. But, in the first ages of Christianity, the situation of mankind was extremely different. The most curious, or the most credulous, among the Pagans were often persuaded to enter into a society which asserted an actual claim of miraculous powers. The primitive Christians perpetually trod on mystic ground, and their minds were exercised by the habits of believing the most extraordinary events. They felt, or they fancied, that on every side they were incessantly assaulted by daemons, comforted by visions, instructed by prophecy, and surprisingly delivered from danger, sickness, and from death itself, by the supplications of the church. The real or imaginary prodigies, of which they so frequently conceived themselves to be the objects, the instruments, or the spectators, very happily disposed them to adopt, with the same ease, but with far greater justice, the authentic wonders of the evangelic history; and thus miracles that exceeded not the measure of their own experience inspired them with the most lively assurance of mysteries which were acknowledged to surpass the limits of their understanding. It is this deep impression of supernatural truths which has been so much celebrated under the name of faith; a state of mind described as the surest pledge of the divine favour and of future felicity, and recommended as the first or perhaps the only merit of a Christian. According to the more rigid doctors, the moral virtues, which may be equally practised by infidels, are destitute of any value or efficacy in the work of our justification.

IV.   But the primitive Christian demonstrated his faith by his virtues; and it was very justly supposed that the divine persuasion, which enlightened or subdued the understanding, must, at the same time, purify the heart, and direct the actions, of the believer. The first apologists of Christianity who justify the innocence of their brethren, and the writers of a later period who celebrate the sanctity of their ancestors, display, in the most lively colours, the reformation of manners which was introduced into the world by the preaching of the gospel. As it is my intention to remark only such human causes as were permitted to second the influence of revelation, I shall slightly mention two motives which might naturally render the lives of the primitive Christians much purer and more austere than those of their Pagan contemporaries, or their degenerate successors; repentance for their past sins, and the laudable desire of supporting the reputation of the society in which they were engaged.

It is a very ancient reproach, suggested by the ignorance or the malice of infidelity, that the Christians allured into their party the most atrocious criminals, who, as soon as they were touched by a sense of remorse, were easily persuaded to wash away, in the water of baptism, the guilt of their past conduct, for which the temples of the gods refused to grant them any expiation. But this reproach, when it is cleared from misrepresentation, contributes as much to the honour as it did to the increase of the church.[83] The friends of Christianity may acknowledge without a blush that many of the most eminent saints had been before their baptism the most abandoned sinners. Those persons who in the world had followed, though in an imperfect manner, the dictates of benevolence and propriety, derived such a calm satisfaction from the opinion of their own rectitude, as rendered them much less susceptible of the sudden emotions of shame, of grief, and of terror, which had given birth to so many wonderful conversions. After the example of their Divine Master, the missionaries of the gospel disdained not the society of men, and especially of women, oppressed by the consciousness, and very often by the effects, of their vices. As they emerged from sin and superstition to the glorious hope of immortality, they resolved to devote themselves to a life, not only of virtue, but of penitence. The desire of perfection became the ruling passion of their soul; and it is well known that, while reason embraces a cold mediocrity, our passions hurry us, with rapid violence, over the space which lies between the most opposite extremes.

When the new converts had been enrolled in the number of the faithful and were admitted to the sacraments of the church, they found themselves restrained from relapsing into their past disorders by another consideration of a less spiritual, but of a very innocent and respectable nature. Any particular society that has departed from the great body of the nation or the religion to which it belonged immediately becomes the object of universal as well as invidious observation. In proportion to the smallness of its numbers, the character of the society may be affected by the virtue and vices of the persons who compose it; and every member is engaged to watch with the most vigilant attention over his own behaviour and over that of his brethren, since, as he must expect to incur a part of the common disgrace, he may hope to enjoy a share of the common reputation. When the Christians of Bithynia were brought before the tribunal of the younger Pliny, they assured the proconsul that, far from being engaged in any unlawful conspiracy, they were bound by a solemn obligation to abstain from the commission of those crimes which disturb the private or public peace of society, from theft, robbery, adultery, perjury, and fraud.[84] Near a century afterwards, Tertullian, with an honest pride, could boast that very few Christians had suffered by the hand of the executioner, except on account of their religion.[85] Their serious and sequestered life, averse to the gay luxury of the age, inured them to chastity, temperance, economy, and all the sober and domestic virtues. As the greater number were of some trade or profession, it was incumbent on them, by the strictest integrity and the fairest dealing, to remove the suspicions which the profane are too apt to conceive against the appearances of sanctity. The contempt of the world exercised them in the habits of humility, meekness, and patience. The more they were persecuted, the more closely they adhered to each other. Their mutual charity and unsuspecting confidence has been remarked by infidels, and was too often abused by perfidious friends.[86]

It is a very honourable circumstance for the morals of the primitive Christians, that even their faults, or rather errors, were derived from an excess of virtue. The bishops and doctors of the church, whose evidence attests, and whose authority might influence, the professions, the principles, and even the practice of their contemporaries, had studied the Scriptures with less skill than devotion; and they often received in the most literal sense those rigid precepts of Christ and the apostles to which the prudence of succeeding commentators has applied a looser and more figurative mode of interpretation. Ambitious to exalt the perfection of the Gospel above the wisdom of philosophy, the zealous fathers have carried the duties of self-mortification, of purity, and of patience, to a height which it is scarcely possible to attain, and much less to preserve, in our present state of weakness and corruption. A doctrine so extraordinary and so sublime must inevitably command the veneration of the people; but it was ill calculated to obtain the suffrage of those worldly philosophers who, in the conduct of this transitory life, consult only the feelings of nature and the interest of society.[87]

There are two very natural propensities which we may distinguish in the most virtuous and liberal dispositions, the love of pleasure and the love of action. If the former is refined by art and learning, improved by the charms of social intercourse, and corrected by a just regard to economy, to health, and to reputation, it is productive of the greatest part of the happiness of private life. The love of action is a principle of a much stronger and more doubtful nature. It often leads to anger, to ambition, and to revenge; but, when it is guided by the sense of propriety and benevolence, it becomes the parent of every virtue, and, if those virtues are accompanied with equal abilities, a family, a state, or an empire may be indebted for their safety and prosperity to the undaunted courage of a single man. To the love of pleasure we may therefore ascribe most of the agreeable, to the love of action we may attribute most of the useful and respectable, qualifications. The character in which both the one and the other should be united and harmonised would seem to constitute the most perfect idea of human nature. The insensible and inactive disposition, which should be supposed alike destitute of both, would be rejected, by the common consent of mankind, as utterly incapable of procuring any happiness to the individual, or any public benefit to the world. But it was not in *this* world that the primitive Christians were desirous of making themselves either agreeable or useful.

The acquisition of knowledge, the exercise of our reason or fancy, and the cheerful flow of unguarded conversation, may employ the leisure of a liberal mind. Such amusements, however, were rejected with abhorrence, or admitted with the utmost caution, by the severity of the fathers, who despised all knowledge that was not useful to salvation, and who considered all levity of discourse as a criminal abuse of the gift of speech. In our present state of existence the body is so inseparably connected with the soul, that it seems to be our interest to taste, with innocence and moderation, the enjoyments of which that faithful companion is susceptible. Very different was the reasoning of our devout predecessors; vainly aspiring to imitate the perfection of angels, they disdained, or they affected to disdain, every earthly and corporeal delight.[88] Some of our senses indeed are necessary for our preservation, others for our subsistence, and others again for our information, and thus far it was impossible to reject the use of them. The first sensation of pleasure was marked as the first moment of their abuse. The unfeeling candidate for Heaven was instructed, not only to resist the grosser allurements of the taste or smell, but even to shut his ears against the profane harmony of sounds, and to view with indifference the most finished productions of human art. Gay apparel, magnificent houses, and elegant furniture were supposed to unite the double guilt of pride and of sensuality: a simple and mortified appearance was more suitable to the Christian who was certain of his sins and doubtful of his salvation. In their censures of luxury, the fathers are extremely minute and circumstantial;[89] and among the various articles which excite their pious indignation, we may enumerate false hair, garments of any colour except white, instruments of music, vases of gold or silver, downy pillows (as Jacob reposed his head on a stone), white bread, foreign wines, public salutations, the use of warm baths, and the practice of shaving the beard, which, according to the expression of Tertullian, is a lie against our own faces, and an impious attempt to improve the works of the Creator.[90] When Christianity was introduced among the rich and the polite, the observation of these singular laws was left, as it would be at present, to the few who were ambitious of superior sanctity. But it is always easy, as well as agreeable, for the inferior ranks of mankind to claim a merit from the contempt of that pomp and pleasure which fortune has placed beyond their reach. The virtue of the primitive Christians, like that of the first Romans, was very frequently guarded by poverty and ignorance.

The chaste severity of the fathers, in whatever related to the commerce of the two sexes, flowed from the same principle; their abhorrence of every enjoyment which might gratify the sensual, and degrade the spiritual, nature of man. It was their favourite opinion that, if Adam had preserved his obedience to the Creator, he would have lived for ever in a state of virgin purity, and that some harmless mode of vegetation might have peopled paradise with a race of innocent and immortal beings.[91] The use of marriage was permitted only to his fallen posterity, as a necessary expedient to continue the human species, and as a restraint, however imperfect, on the natural licentiousness of desire. The hesitation of the orthodox casuists on this interesting subject betrays the perplexity of men, unwilling to approve an institution which they were compelled to tolerate.[92] The enumeration of the very whimsical laws, which they most circumstantially imposed on the marriage-bed, would force a smile from the young, and a blush from the fair. It was their unanimous sentiment that a first marriage was adequate to all the purposes of nature and of society. The sensual connection was refined into a resemblance of the mystic union of Christ with his church, and was pronounced to be indissoluble either by divorce or by death. The practice of second nuptials was branded with the name of a legal adultery; and the persons who were guilty of so scandalous an offence against Christian purity were soon excluded from the honours, and even from the alms, of the church.[93] Since desire was imputed as a crime, and marriage was tolerated as a defect, it was consistent with the same principles to consider a state of celibacy as the nearest approach to the divine perfection. It was with the utmost difficulty that ancient Rome could support the institution of six vestals;[94] but the primitive church was filled with a great number of persons of either sex who had devoted themselves to the profession of perpetual chastity.[95] A few of these, among whom we may reckon the learned Origen, judged it the most prudent to disarm the tempter.[96] Some were insensible and some were invincible against the assaults of the flesh. Disdaining an ignominious flight, the virgins of the warm climate of Africa encountered the enemy in the closest engagement; they permitted priests and deacons to share their bed, and gloried amidst the flames in their unsullied purity. But insulted Nature sometimes vindicated her rights, and this new species of martyrdom served only to introduce a new scandal into the church.[97] Among the Christian ascetics, however (a name which they soon acquired from their painful exercise),* many, as they were less presumptuous, were probably more successful. The loss of sensual pleasure was supplied and compensated by spiritual pride. Even the multitude of Pagans were inclined to estimate the merit of the sacrifice by its apparent difficulty; and it was in the praise of these chaste spouses of Christ that the fathers have poured forth the troubled stream of their eloquence.[98] Such are the early traces of monastic principles and institutions which, in a subsequent age, have counterbalanced all the temporal advantages of Christianity.[99]

The Christians were not less averse to the business than to the pleasures of this world. The defence of our persons and property they knew not how to reconcile with the patient doctrine which enjoined an unlimited forgiveness of past injuries and commanded them to invite the repetition of fresh insults. Their simplicity was offended by the use of oaths, by the pomp of magistracy, and by the active contention of public life, nor could their humane ignorance be convinced that it was lawful on any occasion to shed the blood of our fellow-creatures, either by the sword of justice or by that of war; even though their criminal or hostile attempts should threaten the peace and safety of the whole community.[100] It was acknowledged that, under a less perfect law, the powers of the Jewish constitution had been exercised, with the approbation of Heaven, by inspired prophets and by anointed kings. The Christians felt and confessed that such institutions might be necessary for the present system of the world, and they cheerfully submitted to the authority of their Pagan governors. But while they inculcated the maxims of passive obedience, they refused to take any active part in the civil administration or the military defence of the empire. Some indulgence might perhaps be allowed to those persons who, before their conversion, were already engaged in such violent and sanguinary occupations;[101] but it was impossible that the Christians, without renouncing a more sacred duty, could assume the character of soldiers, of magistrates, or of princes.[102] This indolent, or even criminal disregard to the public welfare, exposed them to the contempt and reproaches of the Pagans, who very frequently asked, what must be the fate of the empire, attacked on every side by the barbarians, if all mankind should adopt the pusillanimous sentiments of the new sect?[103] To this insulting question the Christian apologists returned obscure and ambiguous answers, as they were unwilling to reveal the secret cause of their security; the expectation that, before the conversion of mankind was accomplished, war, government, the Roman empire, and the world itself, would be no more. It may be observed that, in this instance likewise, the situation of the first Christians coincided very happily with their religious scruples, and that their aversion to an active life contributed rather to excuse them from the service, than to exclude them from the honours, of the state and army.

V. But the human character, however it may be exalted or depressed by a temporary enthusiasm, will return by degrees to its proper and natural level, and will resume those passions that seem the most adapted to its present condition. The primitive Christians were dead to the business and pleasures of the world; but their love of action, which could never be entirely extinguished, soon revived, and found a new occupation in the government of the church. A separate society, which attacked the established religion of the empire, was obliged to adopt some form of internal policy, and to appoint a sufficient number of ministers, entrusted not only with the spiritual functions, but even with the temporal direction, of the Christian commonwealth. The safety of that society, its honour, its aggrandisement, were productive, even in the most pious minds, of a spirit of patriotism, such as the first of the Romans had felt for the republic, and sometimes, of a similar indifference in the use of whatever means might probably conduce to so desirable an end. The ambition of raising themselves or their friends to the honours and offices of the church was disguised by the laudable intention of devoting to the public benefit the power and consideration which, for that purpose only, it became their duty to solicit. In the exercise of their functions, they were frequently called upon to detect the errors of heresy, or the arts of faction, to oppose the designs of perfidious brethren, to stigmatise their characters with deserved infamy, and to expel them from the bosom of a society whose peace and happiness they had attempted to disturb. The ecclesiastical governors of the Christians were taught to unite the wisdom of the serpent with the innocence of the dove; but, as the former was refined, so the latter was insensibly corrupted, by the habits of government. In the church as well as in the world the persons who were placed in any public station rendered themselves considerable by their eloquence and firmness, by their knowledge of mankind, and by their dexterity in business; and, while they concealed from others, and, perhaps, from themselves, the secret motives of their conduct, they too frequently relapsed into all the turbulent passions of active life, which were tinctured with an additional degree of bitterness and obstinacy from the infusion of spiritual zeal.

The government of the church has often been the subject, as well as the prize, of religious contention. The hostile disputants of Rome, of Paris, of Oxford and of Geneva have alike struggled to reduce the primitive and apostolic model[104] to the respective standards of their own policy. The few who have pursued this inquiry with more candour and impartiality are of opinion[105] that the apostles declined the office of legislation, and rather chose to endure some partial scandals and divisions, than to exclude the Christians of a future age from the liberty of varying their forms of ecclesiastical government according to the changes of times and circumstances. The scheme of policy which, under their approbation, was adopted for the use of the first century, may be discovered from the practice of Jerusalem, of Ephesus, or of Corinth. The societies which were instituted in the cities of the Roman empire were united only by the ties of faith and charity. Independence and equality formed the basis of their internal constitution. The want of discipline and human learning was supplied by the occasional assistance of the *prophets*,[106] who were called to that function without distinction of age, of sex, or of natural abilities, and who, as often as they felt the divine impulse, poured forth the effusions of the Spirit in the assembly of the faithful. But these extraordinary gifts were frequently abused or misapplied by the prophetic teachers. They displayed them at an improper season, presumptuously disturbed the service of the assembly, and by their pride or mistaken zeal they introduced, particularly into the apostolic church of Corinth, a long and melancholy train of disorders.[107] As the institution of prophets became useless, and even pernicious, their powers were withdrawn, and their office abolished. The public functions of religion were solely entrusted to the established ministers of the church, the *bishops* and the *presbyters*; two appellations which, in their first origin, appear to have distinguished the same office and the same order of persons. The name of Presbyter was expressive of their age,* or rather of their gravity and wisdom. The title of Bishop denoted their inspection over the faith and manners of the Christians who were committed to their pastoral care. In proportion to the respective numbers of the faithful, a larger or smaller number of these *episcopal presbyters* guided each infant congregation with equal authority and with united councils.[108]

But the most perfect equality of freedom requires the directing hand of a superior magistrate; and the order of public deliberations soon introduces the office of a president, invested at least with the authority of collecting the sentiments, and of executing the resolutions, of the assembly. A regard for the public tranquillity, which would so frequently have been interrupted by annual or by occasional elections, induced the primitive Christians to constitute an honourable and perpetual magistracy, and to choose one of the wisest and most holy among their presbyters to execute, during his life, the duties of their ecclesiastical governor. It was under these circumstances that the lofty title of Bishop began to raise itself above the humble appellation of presbyter; and, while the latter remained the most natural distinction for the members of every Christian senate, the former was appropriated to the dignity of its new president.[109] The advantages of this episcopal form of government, which appears to have been introduced before the end of the first century,[110] were so obvious, and so important for the future greatness, as well as the present peace, of Christianity, that it was adopted without delay by all the societies which were already scattered over the empire, had acquired in a very early period the sanction of antiquity,[111] and is still revered by the most powerful churches, both of the East and of the West, as a primitive and even as a divine establishment.[112] It is needless to observe that the pious and humble presbyters who were first dignified with the episcopal title could not possess, and would probably have rejected, the power and pomp which now encircles the tiara of the Roman pontiff, or the mitre of a German prelate. But we may define in a few words the narrow limits of their original jurisdiction, which was chiefly of a spiritual, though in some instances of a temporal, nature.[113] It consisted in the administration of the sacraments and discipline of the church, the superintendency of religious ceremonies, which imperceptibly increased in number and variety, the consecration of ecclesiastical ministers, to whom the bishop assigned their respective functions, the management of the public fund, and the determination of all such differences as the faithful were unwilling to expose before the tribunal of an idolatrous judge. These powers, during a short period, were exercised according to the advice of the presbyteral college, and with the consent and approbation of the assembly of Christians. The primitive bishops were considered only as the first of their equals, and the honourable servants of a free people. Whenever the episcopal chair became vacant by death, a new president was chosen among the presbyters by the suffrage of the whole congregation, every member of which supposed himself invested with a sacred and sacerdotal character.[114]

Such was the mild and equal constitution by which the Christians were governed more than an hundred years after the death of the apostles. Every society formed within itself a separate and independent republic; and, although the most distant of these little states maintained a mutual as well as friendly intercourse of letters and deputations, the Christian world was not yet connected by any supreme authority or legislative assembly. As the numbers of the faithful were gradually multiplied, they discovered the advantages that might result from a closer union of their interest and designs. Towards the end of the second century, the churches of Greece and Asia adopted the useful institutions of provincial synods, and they may justly be supposed to have borrowed the model of a representative council from the celebrated examples of their own country, the Amphictyons, the Achaean league, or the assemblies of the Ionian cities. It was soon established as a custom and as a law that the bishops of the independent churches should meet in the capital of the province at the stated periods of spring and autumn. Their deliberations were assisted by the advice of a few distinguished presbyters, and moderated by the presence of a listening multitude.[115] Their decrees, which were styled Canons, regulated every important controversy of faith and discipline; and it was natural to believe that a liberal effusion of the Holy Spirit would be poured on the united assembly of the delegates of the Christian people. The institution of synods was so well suited to private ambition and to public interest that in the space of a few years it was received throughout the whole empire. A regular correspondence was established between the provincial councils, which mutually communicated and approved their respective proceedings; and the Catholic church soon assumed the form, and acquired the strength, of a great federative republic.[116]

As the legislative authority of the particular churches was insensibly superseded by the use of councils, the bishops obtained by their alliance a much larger share of executive and arbitrary power; and, as soon as they were connected by a sense of their common interest, they were enabled to attack, with united vigour, the original rights of their clergy and people. The prelates of the third century imperceptibly changed the language of exhortation into that of command, scattered the seeds of future usurpations, and supplied, by scripture, allegories and declamatory rhetoric, their deficiency of force and of reason. They exalted the unity and power of the church, as it was represented in the *episcopal office*, of which every bishop enjoyed an equal and undivided portion.[117] Princes and magistrates, it was often repeated, might boast an earthly claim to a transitory dominion; it was the episcopal authority alone which was derived from the Deity, and extended itself over this and over another world. The bishops were the vice-regents of Christ, the successors of the apostles, and the mystic substitutes of the high priest of the Mosaic law. Their exclusive privilege of conferring the sacerdotal character invaded the freedom both of clerical and of popular elections; and if, in the administration of the church, they still consulted the judgment of the presbyters or the inclination of the people, they most carefully inculcated the merit of such a voluntary condescension. The bishops acknowledged the supreme authority which resided in the assembly of their brethren; but, in the government of his peculiar diocese, each of them exacted from his *flock* the same implicit obedience as if that favourite metaphor had been literally just, and as if the shepherd had been of a more exalted nature than that of his sheep.[118] This obedience, however, was not imposed without some efforts on one side, and some resistance on the other. The democratical part of the constitution was, in many places, very warmly supported by the zealous or interested opposition of the inferior clergy. But their patriotism received the ignominious epithets of faction and schism; and the episcopal cause was indebted for its rapid progress to the labours of many active prelates, who, like Cyprian of Carthage, could reconcile the arts of the most ambitious statesman with the Christian virtues which seem adapted to the character of a saint and martyr.[119]

The same causes which at first had destroyed the equality of the presbyters introduced among the bishops a pre-eminence of rank, and from thence a superiority of jurisdiction. As often as in the spring and autumn they met in provincial synod, the difference of personal merit and reputation was very sensibly felt among the members of the assembly, and the multitude was governed by the wisdom and eloquence of the few. But the order of public proceedings required a more regular and less invidious distinction; the office of perpetual presidents in the councils of each province was conferred on the bishops of the principal city, and these aspiring prelates, who soon acquired the lofty titles of Metropolitans and Primates, secretly prepared themselves to usurp over their episcopal brethren the same authority which the bishops had so lately assumed above the college of presbyters.[120] Nor was it long before an emulation of pre-eminence and power prevailed among the metropolitans themselves, each of them affecting to display, in the most pompous terms, the temporal honours and advantages of the city over which he presided; the numbers and opulence of the Christians who were subject to their pastoral care; the saints and martyrs who had arisen among them; and the purity with which they preserved the tradition of the faith, as it had been transmitted through a series of orthodox bishops from the apostle or the apostolic disciple, to whom the foundation of their church was ascribed.[121] From every cause, either of a civil or of an ecclesiastical nature, it was easy to foresee that Rome must enjoy the respect, and would soon claim the obedience, of the provinces. The society of the faithful bore a just proportion to the capital of the empire; and the Roman church was the greatest, the most numerous, and, in regard to the West, the most ancient of all the Christian establishments, many of which had received their religion from the pious labours of her missionaries. Instead of *one* apostolic founder, the utmost boast of Antioch, of Ephesus, or of Corinth, the banks of the Tiber were supposed to have been honoured with the preaching and martyrdom of the *two* most eminent among the apostles;[122] and the bishops of Rome very prudently claimed the inheritance of whatsoever prerogatives were attributed either to the person or to the office of St Peter.[123] The bishops of Italy and of the provinces were disposed to allow them a primacy of order and association (such was their very accurate expression) in the Christian aristocracy.[124] But the power of a monarch was rejected with abhorrence, and the aspiring genius of Rome experienced from the nations of Asia and Africa a more vigorous resistance to her spiritual than she had formerly done to her temporal dominion. The patriotic Cyprian, who ruled with the most absolute sway the church of Carthage and the provincial synods, opposed with resolution and success the ambition of the Roman pontiff, artfully connected his own cause with that of the eastern bishops, and, like Hannibal, sought out new allies in the heart of Asia.[125] If this Punic war was carried on without any effusion of blood, it was owing much less to the moderation than to the weakness of the contending prelates. Invectives and excommunications were *their* only weapons, and these, during the progress of the whole controversy, they hurled against each other with equal fury and devotion. The hard necessity of censuring either a pope, or a saint and martyr, distresses the modern Catholics whenever they are obliged to relate the particulars of a dispute in which the champions of religion indulged such passions as seem much more adapted to the senate or to the camp.[126]

The progress of the ecclesiastical authority gave birth to the memorable distinction of the laity and of the clergy, which had been unknown to the Greeks and Romans.[127] The former of these appellations comprehended the body of the Christian people; the latter, according to the signification of the word, was appropriated to the chosen portion that had been set apart for the service of religion: a celebrated order of men which has furnished the most important, though not always the most edifying, subjects for modern history. Their mutual hostilities sometimes disturbed the peace of the infant church, but their zeal and activity were united in the common cause, and the love of power, which (under the most artful disguises) could insinuate itself into the breasts of bishops and martyrs, animated them to increase the number of their subjects, and to enlarge the limits of the Christian empire. They were destitute of any temporal force, and they were for a long time discouraged and oppressed, rather than assisted, by the civil magistrate; but they had acquired, and they employed within their own society, the two most efficacious instruments of government, rewards and punishments: the former derived from the pious liberality, the latter from the devout apprehensions, of the faithful.

I. The community of goods, which had so agreeably amused the imagination of Plato,[128] and which subsisted in some degree among the austere sect of the Essenians,[129] was adopted for a short time in the primitive church. The fervour of the first proselytes prompted them to sell those worldly possessions which they despised, to lay the price of them at the feet of the apostles, and to content themselves with receiving an equal share out of the general distribution.[130] The progress of the Christian religion relaxed, and gradually abolished, this generous institution, which, in hands less pure than those of the apostles, would too soon have been corrupted and abused by the returning selfishness of human nature; and the converts who embraced the new religion were permitted to retain the possession of their patrimony, to receive legacies and inheritances, and to increase their separate property by all the lawful means of trade and industry. Instead of an absolute sacrifice, a moderate proportion was accepted by the ministers of the Gospel; and in their weekly or monthly assemblies, every believer, according to the exigency of the occasion, and the measure of his wealth and piety, presented his voluntary offering for the use of the common fund.[131] Nothing, however inconsiderable, was refused; but it was diligently inculcated that, in the article of Tythes, the Mosaic law was still of divine obligation; and that, since the Jews, under a less perfect discipline, had been commanded to pay a tenth part of all that they possessed, it would become the disciples of Christ to distinguish themselves by a superior degree of liberality,[132] and to acquire some merit by resigning a superfluous treasure, which must so soon be annihilated with the world itself.[133] It is almost unnecessary to observe that the revenue of each particular church, which was of so uncertain and fluctuating a nature, must have varied with the poverty or the opulence of the faithful, as they were dispersed in obscure villages, or collected in the great cities of the empire. In the time of the emperor Decius, it was the opinion of the magistrates that the Christians of Rome were possessed of very considerable wealth; that vessels of gold and silver were used in their religious worship; and that many among their proselytes had sold their lands and houses to increase the public riches of the sect, at the expense, indeed, of their unfortunate children, who found themselves beggars, because their parents had been saints.[134] We should listen with distrust to the suspicions of strangers and enemies: on this occasion, however, they receive a very specious and probable colour from the two following circumstances, the only ones that have reached our knowledge, which define any precise sums, or convey any distinct idea. Almost at the same period, the bishop of Carthage, from a society less opulent than that of Rome, collected a hundred thousand sesterces (above eight hundred and fifty pounds sterling), on a sudden call of charity, to redeem the brethren of Numidia, who had been carried away captives by the barbarians of the desert.[135] About an hundred years before the reign of Decius, the Roman church had received, in a single donation, the sum of two hundred thousand sesterces from a stranger of Pontus, who proposed to fix his residence in the capital.[136] These oblations, for the most part, were made in money; nor was the society of Christians either desirous or capable of acquiring, to any considerable degree, the incumbrance of landed property. It had been provided by several laws, which were enacted with the same design as our statutes of mortmain, that no real estates should be given or bequeathed to any corporate body, without either a special privilege or a particular dispensation from the emperor or from the senate;[137] who were seldom disposed to grant them in favour of a sect, at first the object of their contempt, and at last of their fears and jealousy. A transaction, however, is related under the reign of Alexander Severus, which discovers that the restraint was sometimes eluded or suspended, and that the Christians were permitted to claim and to possess lands within the limits of Rome itself.[138] The progress of Christianity and the civil confusion of the empire contributed to relax the severity of the laws; and, before the close of the third century, many considerable estates were bestowed on the opulent churches of Rome, Milan, Carthage, Antioch, Alexandria, and the other great cities of Italy and the provinces.

The bishop was the natural steward of the church; the public stock was entrusted to his care, without account or control; the presbyters were confined to their spiritual functions, and the more dependent order of deacons was solely employed in the management and distribution of the ecclesiastical revenue.[139] If we may give credit to the vehement declamations of Cyprian, there were too many among his African brethren who, in the execution of their charge, violated every precept, not only of evangelic perfection, but even of moral virtue. By some of these unfaithful stewards, the riches of the church were lavished in sensual pleasures, by others they were perverted to the purposes of private gain, of fraudulent purchases, and of rapacious usury.[140] But, as long as the contributions of the Christian people were free and unconstrained, the abuse of their confidence could not be very frequent, and the general uses to which their liberality was applied reflected honour on the religious society. A decent portion was reserved for the maintenance of the bishop and his clergy; a sufficient sum was allotted for the expenses of the public worship, of which the feasts of love, the *agapae*, as they were called, constituted a very pleasing part. The whole remainder was the sacred patrimony of the poor. According to the discretion of the bishop, it was distributed to support widows and orphans, the lame, the sick, and the aged of the community; to comfort strangers and pilgrims, and to alleviate the misfortunes of prisoners and captives, more especially when their sufferings had been occasioned by their firm attachment to the cause of religion.[141] A generous intercourse of charity united the most distant provinces, and the smaller congregations were cheerfully assisted by the alms of their more opulent brethren.[142] Such an institution, which paid less regard to the merit than to the distress of the object, very materially conduced to the progress of Christianity. The Pagans, who were actuated by a sense of humanity, while they derided the doctrines, acknowledged the benevolence, of the new sect.[143] The prospect of immediate relief and of future protection allured into its hospitable bosom many of those unhappy persons whom the neglect of the world would have abandoned to the miseries of want, of sickness, and of old age. There is some reason likewise to believe that great numbers of infants who, according to the inhuman practice of the times, had been exposed by their parents were frequently rescued from death, baptised, educated, and maintained by the piety of the Christians, and at the expense of the public treasure.[144]

II.   It is the undoubted right of every society to exclude from its communion and benefits such among its members as reject or violate those regulations which have been established by general consent. In the exercise of this power, the censures of the Christian church were chiefly directed against scandalous sinners, and particularly those who were guilty of murder, of fraud, or of incontinence; against the authors, or the followers, of any heretical opinions which had been condemned by the judgment of the episcopal order; and against those unhappy persons who, whether from choice or from compulsion, had polluted themselves after their baptism by any act of idolatrous worship. The consequences of excommunication were of a temporal as well as a spiritual nature. The Christian against whom it was pronounced was deprived of any part in the oblations of the faithful. The ties both of religious and of private friendship were dissolved; he found himself a profane object of abhorrence to the persons whom he the most esteemed, or by whom he had been the most tenderly beloved; and, as far as an expulsion from a respectable society could imprint on his character a mark of disgrace, he was shunned or suspected by the generality of mankind. The situation of these unfortunate exiles was in itself very painful and melancholy; but, as it usually happens, their apprehensions far exceeded their sufferings. The benefits of the Christian communion were those of eternal life, nor could they erase from their minds the awful opinion, that to those ecclesiastical governors by whom they were condemned the Deity had committed the keys of Hell and of Paradise. The heretics, indeed, who might be supported by the consciousness of their intentions, and by the flattering hope that they alone had discovered the true path of salvation, endeavoured to regain, in their separate assemblies, those comforts, temporal as well as spiritual, which they no longer derived from the great society of Christians. But almost all those who had reluctantly yielded to the power of vice or idolatry were sensible of their fallen condition, and anxiously desirous of being restored to the benefits of the Christian communion.

With regard to the treatment of these penitents, two opposite opin-ions, the one of justice, the other of mercy, divided the primitive church. The more rigid and inflexible casuists refused them for ever, and without exception, the meanest place in the holy community, which they had disgraced or deserted, and, leaving them to the remorse of a guilty conscience, indulged them only with a faint ray of hope that the contrition of their life and death might possibly be accepted by the Supreme Being.[145] A milder sentiment was embraced, in practice as well as in theory, by the purest and most respectable of the Christian churches.[146] The gates of reconciliation and of Heaven were seldom shut against the returning penitent; but a severe and solemn form of discipline was instituted, which, while it served to expiate his crime, might powerfully deter the spectators from the imitation of his example. Humbled by a public confession, emaciated by fasting, and clothed in sackcloth, the penitent lay prostrate at the door of the assembly, imploring, with tears, the pardon of his offences, and soliciting the prayers of the faithful.[147] If the fault was of a very heinous nature, whole years of penance were esteemed an inadequate satisfaction to the Divine Justice; and it was always by slow and painful gradations that the sinner, the heretic, or the apostate was readmitted into the bosom of the church. A sentence of perpetual excommunication was, however, reserved for some crimes of an extraordinary magnitude, and particularly for the inexcusable relapses of those penitents who had already experienced and abused the clemency of their ecclesiastical superiors. According to the circumstances or the number of the guilty, the exercise of the Christian discipline was varied by the discretion of the bishops. The councils of Ancyra and Illiberis were held about the same time, the one in Galatia, the other in Spain; but their respective canons, which are still extant, seem to breathe a very different spirit. The Galatian, who after his baptism had repeatedly sacrificed to idols, might obtain his pardon by a penance of seven years, and, if he had seduced others to imitate his example, only three years more were added to the term of his exile. But the unhappy Spaniard, who had committed the same offence, was deprived of the hope of reconciliation, even in the article of death; and his idolatry was placed at the head of a list of seventeen other crimes, against which a sentence, no less terrible, was pronounced. Among these we may distinguish the inexpiable guilt of calumniating a bishop, a presbyter, or even a deacon.[148]

The well-tempered mixture of liberality and rigour, the judicious dispensation of rewards and punishments, according to the maxims of policy as well as justice, constituted the *human* strength of the church. The bishops, whose paternal care extended itself to the government of both worlds, were sensible of the importance of these prerogatives, and, covering their ambition with the fair pretence of the love of order, they were jealous of any rival in the exercise of a discipline so necessary to prevent the desertion of those troops which had enlisted themselves under the banner of the cross, and whose numbers every day became more considerable. From the imperious declamations of Cyprian we should naturally conclude that the doctrines of excommunication and penance formed the most essential part of religion; and that it was much less dangerous for the disciples of Christ to neglect the observance of the moral duties than to despise the censures and authority of their bishops. Sometimes we might imagine that we were listening to the voice of Moses, when he commanded the earth to open, and to swallow up, in consuming flames, the rebellious race which refused obedience to the priesthood of Aaron; and we should sometimes suppose that we heard a Roman consul asserting the majesty of the republic, and declaring his inflexible resolution to enforce the rigour of the laws. 'If such irregularities are suffered with impunity' (it is thus that the bishop of Carthage chides the lenity of his colleague), 'if such irregularities are suffered, there is an end of Episcopal vigour;[149] an end of the sublime and divine power of governing the church; an end of Christianity itself.' Cyprian had renounced those temporal honours which it is probable he would never have obtained; but the acquisition of such absolute command over the consciences and understanding of a congregation, however obscure or despised by the world, is more truly grateful to the pride of the human heart than the possession of the most despotic power imposed by arms and conquest on a reluctant people.

In the course of this important, though perhaps tedious, inquiry, I have attempted to display the secondary causes which so efficaciously assisted the truth of the Christian religion. If among these causes we have discovered any artificial ornaments, any accidental circumstances, or any mixture of error and passion, it cannot appear surprising that mankind should be the most sensibly affected by such motives as were suited to their imperfect nature. It was by the aid of these causes, exclusive zeal, the immediate expectation of another world, the claim of miracles, the practice of rigid virtue, and the constitution of the primitive church, that Christianity spread itself with so much success in the Roman empire. To the first of these the Christians were indebted for their invincible valour, which disdained to capitulate with the enemy whom they were resolved to vanquish. The three succeeding causes supplied their valour with the most formidable arms. The last of these causes united their courage, directed their arms, and gave their efforts that irresistible weight which even a small band of well-trained and intrepid volunteers has so often possessed over an undisciplined multitude, ignorant of the subject, and careless of the event of the war. In the various religions of Polytheism, some wandering fanatics of Egypt and Syria, who addressed themselves to the credulous superstition of the populace, were perhaps the only order of priests[150] that derived their whole support and credit from their sacerdotal profession, and were very deeply affected by a personal concern for the safety or prosperity of their tutelar deities. The ministers of Polytheism, both in Rome and in the provinces, were, for the most part, men of a noble birth, and of an affluent fortune, who received, as an honourable distinction, the care of a celebrated temple, or of a public sacrifice, exhibited, very frequently at their own expense, the sacred games,[151] and with cold indifference performed the ancient rites, according to the laws and fashion of their country. As they were engaged in the ordinary occupations of life, their zeal and devotion were seldom animated by a sense of interest, or by the habits of an ecclesiastical character. Confined to their respective temples and cities, they remained without any connection of discipline or government; and, whilst they acknowledged the supreme jurisdiction of the senate, of the college of pontiffs, and of the emperor, those civil magistrates contented themselves with the easy task of maintaining, in peace and dignity, the general worship of mankind. We have already seen how various, how loose, and how uncertain were the religious sentiments of Polytheists. They were abandoned, almost without control, to the natural workings of a superstitious fancy. The accidental circumstances of their life and situation determined the object, as well as the degree, of their devotion; and, as long as their adoration was successively prostituted to a thousand deities, it was scarcely possible that their hearts could be susceptible of a very sincere or lively passion for any of them.

When Christianity appeared in the world, even these faint and imperfect impressions had lost much of their original power. Human reason, which by its unassisted strength is incapable of perceiving the mysteries of faith, had already obtained an easy triumph over the folly of Paganism; and, when Tertullian or Lactantius employ their labours in exposing its falsehood and extravagance, they are obliged to transcribe the eloquence of Cicero or the wit of Lucian. The contagion of these sceptical writings had been diffused far beyond the number of their readers. The fashion of incredulity was communicated from the philosopher to the man of pleasure or business, from the noble to the plebeian, and from the master to the menial slave who waited at his table, and who eagerly listened to the freedom of his conversation. On public occasions the philosophic part of mankind affected to treat with respect and decency the religious institutions of their country; but their secret contempt penetrated through the thin and awkward disguise; and even the people, when they discovered that their deities were rejected and derided by those whose rank or understanding they were accustomed to reverence, were filled with doubts and apprehensions concerning the truth of those doctrines to which they had yielded the most implicit belief. The decline of ancient prejudice exposed a very numerous portion of human kind to the danger of a painful and comfortless situation. A state of scepticism and suspense may amuse a few inquisitive minds. But the practice of superstition is so congenial to the multitude that, if they are forcibly awakened, they still regret the loss of their pleasing vision. Their love of the marvellous and supernatural, their curiosity with regard to future events, and their strong propensity to extend their hopes and fears beyond the limits of the visible world, were the principal causes which favoured the establishment of Polytheism. So urgent on the vulgar is the necessity of believing, that the fall of any system of mythology will most probably be succeeded by the introduction of some other mode of superstition. Some deities of a more recent and fashionable cast might soon have occupied the deserted temples of Jupiter and Apollo, if, in the decisive moment, the wisdom of Providence had not interposed a genuine revelation, fitted to inspire the most rational esteem and conviction, whilst, at the same time, it was adorned with all that could attract the curiosity, the wonder, and the veneration of the people. In their actual disposition, as many were almost disengaged from their artificial prejudices, but equally susceptible and desirous of a devout attachment; an object much less deserving would have been sufficient to fill the vacant place in their hearts, and to gratify the uncertain eagerness of their passions. Those who are inclined to pursue this reflection, instead of viewing with astonishment the rapid progress of Christianity, will perhaps be surprised that its success was not still more rapid and still more universal.

It has been observed, with truth as well as propriety, that the conquests of Rome prepared and facilitated those of Christianity. In the second chapter of this work we have attempted to explain in what manner the most civilised provinces of Europe, Asia, and Africa were united under the dominion of one sovereign, and gradually connected by the most intimate ties of laws, of manners, and of language. The Jews of Palestine, who had fondly expected a temporal deliverer, gave so cold a reception to the miracles of the divine prophet, that it was found unnecessary to publish, or at least to preserve, any Hebrew gospel.[152] The authentic histories of the actions of Christ were composed in the Greek language, at a considerable distance from Jerusalem, and after the Gentile converts were grown extremely numerous.[153] As soon as those histories were translated into the Latin tongue they were perfectly intelligible to all the subjects of Rome, excepting only to the peasants of Syria and Egypt, for whose benefit particular versions were afterwards made. The public highways, which had been constructed for the use of the legions, opened an easy passage for the Christian missionaries from Damascus to Corinth, and from Italy to the extremity of Spain or Britain; nor did those spiritual conquerors encounter any of the obstacles which usually retard or prevent the introduction of a foreign religion into a distant country. There is the strongest reason to believe that before the reigns of Diocletian and Constantine the faith of Christ had been preached in every province, and in all the great cities of the empire; but the foundation of the several congregations, the members of the faithful who composed them, and their proportion to the unbelieving multitude, are now buried in obscurity, or disguised by fiction and declamation. Such imperfect circumstances, however, as have reached our knowledge concerning the increase of the Christian name in Asia and Greece, in Egypt, in Italy, and in the West, we shall now proceed to relate, without neglecting the real or imaginary acquisitions which lay beyond the frontiers of the Roman empire.

The rich provinces that extend from the Euphrates to the Ionian sea were the principal theatre on which the apostle of the Gentiles* displayed his zeal and piety. The seeds of the Gospel, which he had scattered in a fertile soil, were diligently cultivated by his disciples; and it should seem that, during the two first centuries, the most considerable body of Christians was contained within those limits. Among the societies which were instituted in Syria, none were more ancient or more illustrious than those of Damascus, of Beroea or Aleppo, and of Antioch. The prophetic introduction of the Apocalypse has described and immortalised the seven churches of Asia – Ephesus, Smyrna, Pergamus, Thyatira,[154] Sardes, Laodicea, and Philadelphia; and their colonies were soon diffused over that populous country. In a very early period, the islands of Cyprus and Crete, the provinces of Thrace and Macedonia, gave a favourable reception to the new religion; and Christian republics were soon founded in the cities of Corinth, of Sparta, and of Athens.[155] The antiquity of the Greek and Asiatic churches allowed a sufficient space of time for their increase and multiplication, and even the swarms of Gnostics and other heretics serve to display the flourishing condition of the orthodox church, since the appellation of heretics has always been applied to the less numerous party. To these domestic testimonies we may add the confession, the complaints, and the apprehensions of the Gentiles themselves. From the writings of Lucian, a philosopher who had studied mankind, and who describes their manners in the most lively colours, we may learn that, under the reign of Commodus, his native country of Pontus was filled with Epicureans and *Christians*.[156] Within fourscore years after the death of Christ,[157] the humane Pliny laments the magnitude of the evil which he vainly attempted to eradicate. In his very curious epistle to the emperor Trajan, he affirms that the temples were almost deserted, that the sacred victims scarcely found any purchasers, and that the superstition had not only infected the cities, but had even spread itself into the villages and the open country of Pontus and Bithynia.[158]

Without descending into a minute scrutiny of the expressions, or of the motives of those writers who either celebrate or lament the progress of Christianity in the East, it may in general be observed that none of them have left us any grounds from whence a just estimate might be formed of the real numbers of the faithful in those provinces. One circumstance, however, has been fortunately preserved, which seems to cast a more distinct light on this obscure but interesting subject. Under the reign of Theodosius, after Christianity had enjoyed, during more than sixty years, the sunshine of Imperial favour, the ancient and illustrious church of Antioch consisted of one hundred thousand persons, three thousand of whom were supported out of the public oblations.[159] The splendour and dignity of the queen of the East, the acknowledged populousness of Caesarea, Seleucia, and Alexandria, and the destruction of two hundred and fifty thousand souls in the earthquake which afflicted Antioch under the elder Justin,[160] are so many convincing proofs that the whole number of its inhabitants was not less than half a million, and that the Christians, however multiplied by zeal and power, did not exceed a fifth part of that great city. How different a proportion must we adopt when we compare the persecuted with the triumphant church, the West with the East, remote villages with populous towns, and countries recently converted to the faith with the place where the believers first received the appellation of Christians! It must not, however, be dissembled that, in another passage, Chrysostom,* to whom we are indebted for this useful information, computes the multitude of the faithful as even superior to that of the Jews and Pagans.[161] But the solution of this apparent difficulty is easy and obvious. The eloquent preacher draws a parallel between the civil and the ecclesiastical constitution of Antioch; between the list of Christians who had acquired heaven by baptism, and the list of citizens who had a right to share the public liberality. Slaves, strangers, and infants were comprised in the former; they were excluded from the latter.

The extensive commerce of Alexandria, and its proximity to Palestine, gave an easy entrance to the new religion. It was at first embraced by great numbers of the Therapeutae, or Essenians, of the lake Mareotis, a Jewish sect which had abated much of its reverence for the Mosaic ceremonies. The austere life of the Essenians, their fasts and excommunications, the community of goods, the love of celibacy, their zeal for martyrdom, and the warmth though not the purity of their faith, already offered a very lively image of the primitive discipline.[162] It was in the school of Alexandria that the Christian theology appears to have assumed a regular and scientifical form; and, when Hadrian visited Egypt, he found a church, composed of Jews and of Greeks, sufficiently important to attract the notice of that inquisitive prince.[163] But the progress of Christianity was for a long time confined within the limits of a single city, which was itself a foreign colony, and, till the close of the second century, the predecessors of Demetrius were the only prelates of the Egyptian church. Three bishops were consecrated by the hands of Demetrius, and the number was increased to twenty by his successor Heraclas.[164] The body of the natives, a people distinguished by a sullen inflexibility of temper,[165] entertained the new doctrine with coldness and reluctance; and even in the time of Origen it was rare to meet with an Egyptian who had surmounted his early prejudices in favour of the sacred animals of his country.[166] As soon, indeed, as Christianity ascended the throne, the zeal of those barbarians obeyed the prevailing impulsion; the cities of Egypt were filled with bishops, and the deserts of Thebais swarmed with hermits.

A perpetual stream of strangers and provincials flowed into the capacious bosom of Rome. Whatever was strange or odious, whoever was guilty or suspected, might hope, in the obscurity of that immense capital, to elude the vigilance of the law. In such a various conflux of nations, every teacher, either of truth or of falsehood, every founder, whether of a virtuous or a criminal association, might easily multiply his disciples or accomplices. The Christians of Rome, at the time of the accidental* persecution of Nero, are represented by Tacitus as already amounting to a very great multitude,[167] and the language of that great historian is almost similar to the style employed by Livy, when he relates the introduction and the suppression of the rites of Bacchus. After the Bacchanals had awakened the severity of the senate, it was likewise apprehended that a very great multitude, as it were *another people*, had been initiated into those abhorred mysteries. A more careful inquiry soon demonstrated that the offenders did not exceed seven thousand: a number, indeed, sufficiently alarming when considered as the object of public justice.[168] It is with the same candid allowance that we should interpret the vague expressions of Tacitus, and in a former instance of Pliny, when they exaggerate the crowds of deluded fanatics who had forsaken the established worship of the gods. The church of Rome was undoubtedly the first and most populous of the empire; and we are possessed of an authentic record which attests the state of religion in that city, about the middle of the third century, and after a peace of thirty-eight years. The clergy, at that time, consisted of a bishop, forty-six presbyters, seven deacons, as many sub-deacons, forty-two acolytes, and fifty readers, exorcists, and porters. The number of widows, of the infirm, and of the poor, who were maintained by the oblations of the faithful, amounted to fifteen hundred.[169] From reason, as well as from the analogy of Antioch, we may venture to estimate the Christians of Rome at about fifty thousand. The populousness of that great capital cannot, perhaps, be exactly ascertained; but the most modest calculation will not surely reduce it lower than a million of inhabitants, of whom the Christians might constitute at the most a twentieth part.[170]

The western provincials appeared to have derived the knowledge of Christianity from the same source which had diffused among them the language, the sentiments, and the manners of Rome. In this more important circumstance, Africa, as well as Gaul, was gradually fashioned to the imitation of the capital. Yet, notwithstanding the many favourable occasions which might invite the Roman missionaries to visit their Latin provinces, it was late before they passed either the sea or the Alps;[171] nor can we discover in those great countries any assured traces either of faith or of persecution that ascend higher than the reign of the Antonines.[172] The slow progress of the gospel in the cold climate of Gaul was extremely different from the eagerness with which it seems to have been received on the burning sands of Africa. The African Christians soon formed one of the principal members of the primitive church. The practice introduced into that province of appointing bishops to the most inconsiderable towns, and very frequently to the most obscure villages, contributed to multiply the splendour and importance of their religious societies, which during the course of the third century were animated by the zeal of Tertullian, directed by the abilities of Cyprian, and adorned by the eloquence of Lactantius. But if, on the contrary, we turn our eyes towards Gaul, we must content ourselves with discovering, in the time of Marcus Antoninus, the feeble and united congregations of Lyons and Vienna; and, even as late as the reign of Decius, we are assured that in a few cities only, Arles, Narbonne, Toulouse, Limoges, Clermont, Tours, and Paris, some scattered churches were supported by the devotion of a small number of Christians.[173] Silence is indeed very consistent with devotion; but as it is seldom compatible with zeal, we may perceive and lament the languid state of Christianity in those provinces which had exchanged the Celtic for the Latin tongue; since they did not, during the three first centuries, give birth to a single ecclesiastical writer. From Gaul, which claimed a just pre-eminence of learning and authority over all the countries on this side of the Alps, the light of the Gospel was more faintly reflected on the remote provinces of Spain and Britain; and, if we may credit the vehement assertions of Tertullian, they had already received the first rays of the faith when he addressed his Apology to the magistrates of the emperor Severus.[174] But the obscure and imperfect origin of the western churches of Europe has been so negligently recorded, that, if we would relate the time and manner of their foundation, we must supply the silence of antiquity by those legends which avarice or superstition long afterwards dictated to the monks in the lazy gloom of their convents.[175] Of these holy romances, that of the apostle St James can alone, by its singular extravagance, deserve to be mentioned. From a peaceful fisherman of the lake of Gennesareth, he was transformed into a valorous knight, who charged at the head of the Spanish chivalry in their battles against the Moors. The gravest historians have celebrated his exploits; the miraculous shrine of Compostella displayed his power; and the sword of a military order, assisted by the terrors of the Inquisition, was sufficient to remove every objection of profane criticism.[176]

The progress of Christianity was not confined to the Roman empire; and, according to the primitive fathers, who interpret facts by prophecy, the new religion, within a century after the death of its divine author, had already visited every part of the globe. 'There exists not,' says Justin Martyr, 'a people, whether Greek or barbarian, or any other race of men, by whatsoever appellation or manners they may be distinguished, however ignorant of arts or agriculture, whether they dwell under tents, or wander about in covered waggons, among whom prayers are not offered up in the name of a crucified Jesus to the Father and Creator of all things.'[177] But this splendid exaggeration, which even at present it would be extremely difficult to reconcile with the real state of mankind, can be considered only as the rash sally of a devout but careless writer, the measure of whose belief was regulated by that of his wishes. But neither the belief nor the wishes of the fathers can alter the truth of history. It will still remain an undoubted fact that the barbarians of Scythia and Germany who afterwards subverted the Roman monarchy were involved in the darkness of paganism; and that even the conversion of Iberia, of Armenia, or of Ethiopia, was not attempted with any degree of success till the sceptre was in the hands of an orthodox emperor.[178] Before that time the various accidents of war and commerce might indeed diffuse an imperfect knowledge of the gospel among the tribes of Caledonia,[179] and among the borderers of the Rhine, the Danube, and the Euphrates.[180] Beyond the last mentioned river, Edessa was distinguished by a firm and early adherence to the faith.[181] From Edessa the principles of Christianity were easily introduced into the Greek and Syrian cities which obeyed the successors of Artaxerxes; but they do not appear to have made any deep impression on the minds of the Persians, whose religious system, by the labours of a well-disciplined order of priests, had been constructed with much more art and solidity than the uncertain mythology of Greece and Rome.[182]

From this impartial, though imperfect, survey of the progress of Christianity, it may, perhaps, seem probable that the number of its proselytes has been excessively magnified by fear on the one side and by devotion on the other. According to the irreproachable testimony of Origen,[183] the proportion of the faithful was very inconsiderable when compared with the multitude of an unbelieving world; but, as we are left without any distinct information, it is impossible to determine, and it is difficult even to conjecture, the real numbers of the primitive Christians. The most favourable calculation, however, that can be deduced from the examples of Antioch and of Rome will not permit us to imagine that more than a twentieth part of the subjects of the empire had enlisted themselves under the banner of the cross before the important conversion of Constantine.* But their habits of faith, of zeal, and of union seemed to multiply their numbers; and the same causes which contributed to their future increase served to render their actual strength more apparent and more formidable.

Such is the constitution of civil society that, whilst a few persons are distinguished by riches, by honours, and by knowledge, the body of the people is condemned to obscurity, ignorance, and poverty. The Christian religion, which addressed itself to the whole human race, must consequently collect a far greater number of proselytes from the lower than from the superior ranks of life. This innocent and natural circumstance has been improved into a very odious imputation, which seems to be less strenuously denied by the apologists than it is urged by the adversaries of the faith; that the new sect of Christians was almost entirely composed of the dregs of the populace, of peasants and mechanics, of boys and women, of beggars and slaves; the last of whom might sometimes introduce the missionaries into the rich and noble families to which they belonged. These obscure teachers (such was the charge of malice and infidelity) are as mute in public as they are loquacious and dogmatical in private. Whilst they cautiously avoid the dangerous encounter of philosophers, they mingle with the rude and illiterate crowd, and insinuate themselves into those minds, whom their age, their sex, or their education has the best disposed to receive the impression of superstitious terrors.[184]

This unfavourable picture, though not devoid of a faint resemblance, betrays, by its dark colouring and distorted features, the pencil of an enemy. As the humble faith of Christ diffused itself through the world, it was embraced by several persons who derived some consequence from the advantages of nature or fortune. Aristides, who presented an eloquent apology to the emperor Hadrian, was an Athenian philosopher.[185] Justin Martyr had sought divine knowledge in the schools of Zeno, of Aristotle, of Pythagoras, and of Plato, before he fortunately was accosted by the old man, or rather the angel, who turned his attention to the study of the Jewish prophets.[186] Clemens of Alexandria had acquired much various reading in the Greek, and Tertullian in the Latin, language. Julius Africanus and Origen possessed a very considerable share of the learning of their times; and, although the style of Cyprian is very different from that of Lactantius, we might almost discover that both those writers had been public teachers of rhetoric. Even the study of philosophy was at length introduced among the Christians, but it was not always productive of the most salutary effects; knowledge was as often the parent of heresy as of devotion, and the description which was designed for the followers of Artemon may, with equal propriety, be applied to the various sects that resisted the successors of the apostles. 'They presume to alter the holy scriptures, to abandon the ancient rule of faith, and to form their opinions according to the subtle precepts of logic. The science of the church is neglected for the study of geometry, and they lose sight of Heaven while they are employed in measuring the earth. Euclid is perpetually in their hands. Aristotle and Theophrastus are the objects of their admiration; and they express an uncommon reverence for the works of Galen. Their errors are derived from the abuse of the arts and sciences of the infidels, and they corrupt the simplicity of the Gospel by the refinements of human reason.'[187]

Nor can it be affirmed with truth that the advantages of birth and fortune were always separated from the profession of Christianity. Several Roman citizens were brought before the tribunal of Pliny, and he soon discovered that a great number of persons of *every order* of men in Bithynia had deserted the religion of their ancestors.[188] His unsuspected testimony may, in this instance, obtain more credit than the bold challenge of Tertullian, when he addresses himself to the fears as well as to the humanity of the proconsul of Africa, by assuring him that, if he persists in his cruel intentions, he must decimate Carthage, and that he will find among the guilty many persons of his own rank, senators and matrons of noblest extraction, and the friends or relations of his most intimate friends.[189] It appears, however, that about forty years afterwards the emperor Valerian was persuaded of the truth of this assertion, since in one of his rescripts he evidently supposes that senators, Roman knights, and ladies of quality were engaged in the Christian sect.[190] The church still continued to increase its outward splendour as it lost its internal purity; and in the reign of Diocletian the palace, the courts of justice, and even the army concealed a multitude of Christians who endeavoured to reconcile the interests of the present with those of a future life.

And yet these exceptions are either too few in number, or too recent in time, entirely to remove the imputation of ignorance and obscurity which has been so arrogantly cast on the first proselytes of Christianity. Instead of employing in our defence the fictions of later ages, it will be more prudent to convert the occasion of scandal into a subject of edification. Our serious thoughts will suggest to us that the apostles themselves were chosen by providence among the fishermen of Galilee, and that, the lower we depress the temporal condition of the first Christians, the more reason we shall find to admire their merit and success. It is incumbent on us diligently to remember that the kingdom of heaven was promised to the poor in spirit, and that minds afflicted by calamity and the contempt of mankind cheerfully listen to the divine promise of future happiness; while, on the contrary, the fortunate are satisfied with the possession of this world; and the wise abuse in doubt and dispute their vain superiority of reason and knowledge.

We stand in need of such reflections to comfort us for the loss of some illustrious characters, which in our eyes might have seemed the most worthy of the heavenly present. The names of Seneca, of the elder and the younger Pliny, of Tacitus, of Plutarch, of Galen, of the slave Epictetus, and of the emperor Marcus Antoninus, adorn the age in which they flourished, and exalt the dignity of human nature. They filled with glory their respective stations, either in active or contemplative life; their excellent understandings were improved by study; Philosophy had purified their minds from the prejudices of the popular superstition; and their days were spent in the pursuit of truth and the practice of virtue. Yet all these sages (it is no less an object of surprise than of concern) overlooked or rejected the perfection of the Christian system. Their language or their silence equally discover their contempt for the growing sect, which in their time had diffused itself over the Roman empire. Those among them who condescend to mention the Christians consider them only as obstinate and perverse enthusiasts, who exacted an implicit submission to their mysterious doctrines, without being able to produce a single argument that could engage the attention of men of sense and learning.[191]

It is at least doubtful whether any of these philosophers perused the apologies which the primitive Christians repeatedly published in behalf of themselves and of their religion; but it is much to be lamented that such a cause was not defended by abler advocates. They expose with superfluous wit and eloquence the extravagance of Polytheism. They interest our compassion by displaying the innocence and sufferings of their injured brethren. But, when they would demonstrate the divine origin of Christianity, they insist much more strongly on the predictions which announced, than on the miracles which accompanied, the appearance of the Messiah. Their favourite argument might serve to edify a Christian or to convert a Jew, since both the one and the other acknowledge the authority of those prophecies, and both are obliged, with devout reverence, to search for their sense and their accomplishment. But this mode of persuasion loses much of its weight and influence, when it is addressed to those who neither understand nor respect the Mosaic dispensation and the prophetic style.[192] In the unskilful hands of Justin and of the succeeding apologists, the sublime meaning of the Hebrew oracles evaporates in distant types, affected conceits, and cold allegories; and even their authenticity was rendered suspicious to an unenlightened Gentile by the mixture of pious forgeries, which, under the names of Orpheus, Hermes, and the Sibyls,[193] were obtruded on him as of equal value with the genuine inspirations of Heaven. The adoption of fraud and sophistry in the defence of revelation too often reminds us of the injudicious conduct of those poets who load their *invulnerable* heroes with a useless weight of cumbersome and brittle armour.

But how shall we excuse the supine inattention of the Pagan and philosophic world to those evidences which were presented by the hand of Omnipotence, not to their reason, but to their senses? During the age of Christ, of his apostles, and of their first disciples, the doctrine which they preached was confirmed by innumerable prodigies. The lame walked, the blind saw, the sick were healed, the dead were raised, daemons were expelled, and the laws of Nature were frequently suspended for the benefit of the church. But the sages of Greece and Rome turned aside from the awful spectacle, and, pursuing the ordinary occupations of life and study, appeared unconscious of any alterations in the moral or physical government of the world. Under the reign of Tiberius, the whole earth,[194] or at least a celebrated province of the Roman empire,[195] was involved in a preternatural darkness of three hours. Even this miraculous event, which ought to have excited the wonder, the curiosity, and the devotion of mankind, passed without notice in an age of science and history.[196] It happened during the lifetime of Seneca and the elder Pliny, who must have experienced the immediate effects, or received the earliest intelligence, of the prodigy. Each of these philosophers, in a laborious work, has recorded all the great phenomena of Nature, earthquakes, meteors, comets, and eclipses, which his indefatigable curiosity could collect.[197] Both the one and the other have omitted to mention the greatest phenomenon to which the mortal eye has been witness since the creation of the globe. A distinct chapter of Pliny[198] is designed for eclipses of an extraordinary nature and unusual duration; but he contents himself with describing the singular defect of light which followed the murder of Caesar, when, during the greatest part of the year, the orb of the sun appeared pale and without splendour. This season of obscurity, which cannot surely be compared with the preternatural darkness of the Passion, had been already celebrated by most of the poets[199] and historians of that memorable age.[200]

NOTES TO CHAPTER 15

1 *Dum Assyrios penes, Medosque, et Persas Oriens fuit, despectissima pars servientium.* Tacitus, *Hist.*, v, 8. Herodotus, who visited Asia whilst it obeyed the last of those empires, slightly mentions the Syrians of Palestine, who, according to their own confession, had received from Egypt the rite of circumcision. See ii, 104.

2 Diodorus Siculus, xl; Dion Cassius, xxxvii, 121; Tacitus, *Hist.*, v, 1–9; Justin., xxxvi, 2, 3.

3   *Tradidit arcano quaecunque volumine Moses:*
      Non monstrare vias eadem nisi sacra colenti,
      Quaesitum ad fontem solos deducere verpos.   [Juvenal, xiv, 102]
['Moses handed down these commandments in a secret volume: to teach the way only to their co-religionists, to lead only the circumcised to the desired well-spring.'] The letter of this law is not to be found in the present volume of Moses. But the wise, the humane Maimonides [Jewish philosopher, ad 1135–1204] openly teaches that, if an idolater fall into the water, a Jew ought not to save him from instant death. See Basnage, *Histoire des Juifs*, vi, 28.

* *page 245*   [King of Syria, 175–164 bc]

† *page 245*   [Herod the Great, King of Judaea, 40–4 bc]

4 A Jewish sect, which indulged themselves in a sort of occasional conformity, derived from Herod, by whose example and authority they had been seduced, the name of Herodians. But their numbers were so inconsiderable, and their duration so short, that Josephus has not thought them worthy of his notice. See Prideaux's *Connection*, ii, 285.

5 Cicero, *pro Flacco*, ch. 28.

6 Philo, *de Legatione*. Augustus left a foundation for a perpetual sacrifice. Yet he approved of the neglect which his grandson Caius expressed towards the temple of Jerusalem. See Suetonius in *Augustus*, ch. 93, and Casaubon's notes on that passage.

7 See, in particular, Joseph., *Antiquitat.*, xvii, 6, xviii, 3, and *de Bel. Judaic.*, i, 33, and ii, 9, edit. Havercamp.

8 *Iussi a Caio Caesare effigiem eius in templo locare arma potius sumpsere.* Tacitus, *Hist.*, v, 9. ['When ordered by the Emperor Caligula to place his statue in the temple, they refused and took up arms.'] Philo and Josephus gave a very circumstantial, but a very rhetorical, account of this transaction, which exceedingly perplexed

the governor of Syria. At the first mention of this idolatrous proposal, King Agrippa fainted away; and did not recover his senses till the third day.

9 For the enumeration of the Syrian and Arabian deities, it may be observed that Milton has comprised, in one hundred and thirty very beautiful lines, the two large and learned syntagmas [collections of doctrines] which Selden had composed on that abstruse subject. [John Selden, 1584–1654, jurist]

10 'How long will this people provoke me? and how long will it be ere they believe me, for all the signs which I have shewn among them?' (Numbers, xiv, 11). It would be easy, but it would be unbecoming, to justify the complaint of the Deity, from the whole tenor of the Mosaic history.

11 All that relates to the Jewish proselytes has been very ably treated by Basnage, *Hist. des Juifs*, vi, 6, 7.

12 See Exod., xxiv, 23, Deut., xvi, 16, the commentators, and a very sensible note in the *Universal History*, i, 603, edit. fol.

13 When Pompey, using or abusing the right of conquest, entered into the Holy of Holies, it was observed with amazement, *Nulla intus Deum effigie, vacuam sedem et inania arcana.* Tacitus, *Hist.*, v, 9. ['There was no statue of the Gods inside the temple; only a bare shrine and empty sanctuary.'] It was a popular saying, with regard to the Jews,

Nil praeter nubes et caeli numen adorant.

[They worship only the clouds and the heavens.]

14 A second kind of circumcision was inflicted on a Samaritan or Egyptian proselyte. The sullen indifference of the Talmudists, with respect to the conversion of strangers, may be seen in Basnage, *Histoire des Juifs*, vi, 6.

15 These arguments were urged with great ingenuity by the Jew Orobio, and refuted with equal ingenuity and candour by the Christian Limborch. See the *Amica Collatio* [Friendly Comparison] (it well deserves that name) or account of the dispute between them.

16 *Jesus . . . circumcisus erat; cibis utebatur Judaicis; vestitu simili; purgatos scabie mittebat ad sacerdotes; Paschata et alios dies festos religiose observabat: si quos sanavit sabbato, ostendit non tantum ex lege, sed ex receptis sententiis talia opera sabbato non interdicta.* ['Jesus . . . was circumcised; he observed the Jewish dietary laws and dress. Those whom he cured of leprosy he directed to the priests. He strictly observed the Passover and other holy days. If he cured people on the Sabbath, he demonstrated, not so much to Mosaic law as to received opinion, that such work was not forbidden on the Sabbath.'] Grotius, *de veritate Religionis Christianae*, v, 7. A little afterwards (ch. 12) he expatiates on the condescension of the apostles.

17 *Paene omnes Christum Deum sub legis observatione credebant.* ['They nearly all derived their belief in the divinity of Christ from their observation of the Judaic law.'] Sulpicius Severus, ii, 31. See Eusebius, *Hist. Ecclesiast.*, iv, 5.

18 Mosheim, *de Rebus Christianis ante Constantinum Magnum*, p. 153. In this masterly performance, which I shall often have occasion to quote, he enters much more fully into the state of the primitive church than he has an opportunity of doing in his General History.

19 Eusebius, iii, 5; Le Clerc, *Hist. Ecclesiast.*, p. 605. During this occasional absence, the bishop and church of Pella still retained the title of Jerusalem. In the same manner, the Roman pontiffs resided seventy years at Avignon; and the patriarchs of Alexandria have long since transferred their episcopal seat to Cairo.

20 Dion Cassius, lxix. The exile of the Jewish nation from Jerusalem is attested by Aristo of Pella (*apud* Euseb., iv, 6), and is mentioned by several ecclesiastical writers; though some of them too hastily extend this interdiction to the whole country of Palestine.

21 Eusebius, iv, 6; Sulpicius Severus, ii, 31. By comparing their unsatisfactory accounts, Mosheim (p. 327, etc) has drawn out a very distinct representation of the circumstances and motives of this revolution.

22 Le Clerc (*Hist. Ecclesiast.*, p. 477, 535) seems to have collected from Eusebius, Jerome, Epiphanius, and other writers, all the principal circumstances that relate to the Nazarenes, or Ebionites. The nature of their opinions soon divided them into a stricter and a milder sect; and there is some reason to conjecture that the family of Jesus Christ remained members, at least, of the latter and more moderate party.

23 Some writers have been pleased to create an Ebion, the imaginary author of their sect and name. But we can more safely rely on the learned Eusebius than on the vehement Tertullian or the credulous Epiphanius. According to Le Clerc, the Hebrew word *Ebjonim* may be translated into Latin by that of *Pauperes* [the poor]. See *Hist. Ecclesiast.*, p. 477.

24 See the very curious Dialogue of Justin Martyr with the Jew Tryphon. The conference between them was held at Ephesus, in the reign of Antoninus Pius, and about twenty years after the return of the church of Pella to Jerusalem. For this date consult the accurate note of Tillemont, *Mémoires Ecclésiastiques*, ii, 511.

25 Of all the systems of Christianity, that of Abyssinia is the only one which still adheres to the Mosaic rites (Geddes, *Church History of Aethiopia*, and *Dissertations de La Grand sur la Relation du P. Lobo*). The eunuch of the queen Candace might suggest some suspicions; but, as we are assured (Socrates, i, 19; Sozomen, ii, 24; Ludolphus, p. 281) that the Ethiopians were not converted till the fourth century, it is more reasonable to believe that they respected the Sabbath, and distinguished the forbidden meats, in imitation of the Jews, who, in a very early period, were seated on both sides of the Red Sea. Circumcision had been practised by the most ancient Ethiopians, from motives of health and cleanliness, which seem to be explained in the *Recherches Philosophiques sur les Américains*, ii, 117.

* *page 252* [system]

26 Beausobre, *Histoire du Manichéisme*, i, 3, has stated their objections, particularly those of Faustus, the adversary of Augustine, with the most learned impartiality.

27 *Apud ipsos fides obstinata, misericordia in promptu: adversus omnes alios hostile odium.* Tacitus. *Hist.*, v, 4. ['They are fiercely loyal to their own people, and quick to help one another; towards everyone else they show inveterate hostility.'] Surely Tacitus had seen the Jews with too favourable an eye. The perusal of Josephus must have destroyed the antithesis.

28 Dr Burnet (*Archaeologia*, ii, 7) has discussed the first chapters of Genesis with too much wit and freedom.

29 The milder Gnostics considered Jehovah, the Creator, as a Being of a mixed nature between God and the Daemon. Others confounded him with the evil principle. Consult the second century of the general history of Mosheim, which gives a very distinct, though concise, account of their strange opinions on this subject.

30 See Beausobre, *Hist. du Manichéisme*, i, 4. Origen and St Augustine were among the Allegorists.

31 Hegesippus, *ap.* Euseb., iii, 32, iv, 22. Clemens Alexandrin., *Stromat.*, vii.

32 In the account of the Gnostics of the second and third centuries, Mosheim is ingenious and candid; Le Clerc dull, but exact; Beausobre almost always an apologist; and it is much to be feared that the primitive fathers are very frequently calumniators.

33 See the catalogues of Irenaeus and Epiphanius. It must indeed be allowed that those writers were inclined to multiply the number of sects which opposed the unity of the church.

34 Eusebius, iv, 15; Sozomen, ii, 32. See in Bayle, in the article of Marcion, a curious detail of a dispute on that subject. It should seem that some of the Gnostics (the Basilidians) declined, and even refused, the honour of martyrdom. Their reasons were singular and abstruse. See Mosheim, p. 359.

35 See a very remarkable passage of Origen (*Proem. ad Lucam*). That indefatigable writer, who had consumed his life in the study of the scriptures, relies for their authenticity on the inspired authority of the church. It was impossible that the Gnostics could receive our present gospels, many parts of which (particularly in the resurrection of Christ) are directly, and as it might seem designedly, pointed against their favourite tenets. It is therefore somewhat singular that Ignatius (*Epist. ad Smyrn. Patr. Apostol.*, ii, 34) should choose to employ a vague and doubtful tradition, instead of quoting the certain testimony of the evangelists.

36 *Faciunt favos et vespae; faciunt ecclesias et Marcionitae* ['The Marcionites build churches as wasps build honeycombs'], is the strong expression of Tertullian, which I am obliged to quote from memory. In the time of Epiphanius (*advers. Haereses*, p. 302), the Marcionites were very numerous in Italy, Syria, Egypt, Arabia, and Persia.

37 Augustine is a memorable instance of this gradual progress from reason to faith. He was, during several years, engaged in the Manichaean sect.

38 The unanimous sentiment of the primitive church is very clearly explained by Justin Martyr, *Apolog. Major*, by Athenagoras, *Legat.* ch. 22 etc., and by Lactantius, *Institut. Divin.*, ii, 14–19.

 * *page 254* [god of the healing arts]

39 Tertullian (*Apolog.* ch. 23) alleges the confession of the Daemons themselves as often as they were tormented by the Christian exorcists.

 † *page 254* [schools of philosophy]

40 Tertullian has written a most severe treatise against idolatry, to caution his brethren against the hourly danger of incurring that guilt. *Recogita silvam, et quantae latitant spinae.* ['Consider how many thorns lie hidden in a forest.'] *de Corona Militis*, ch. 10.

41 The Roman senate was always held in a temple or consecrated place (Aulus Gellius, xiv, 7). Before they entered on business, every senator dropped some wine and frankincense on the altar. Suetonius in *Augustus*, ch. 35.

42 See Tertullian, *de Spectaculis*. This severe reformer shows no more indulgence to a tragedy of Euripides than to a combat of gladiators. The dress of the actors particularly offends him. By the use of the lofty buskin, they impiously strive to add a cubit to their stature, ch. 23.

43 The ancient practice of concluding the entertainment with libations may be found in every classic. Socrates and Seneca, in their last moments, made a noble application of this custom. *Postquam stagnum calidae aquae introiit, respergens proximos servorum, addita voce, libare se liquorem illum Jovi Liberatori.* ['Having

entered a warm bath, he sprinkled water on his most faithful servants, saying that he was pouring a libation to Jupiter the Deliverer.'] Tacitus, *Annals*, xv. 64.

44 See the elegant but idolatrous hymn of Catullus, on the nuptials of Manlius and Julia. *O Hymen, Hymenaee io! Quis huic Deo compararier ausit?* ['O Hymen, rejoice! Who has dared to be compared to this God?']

45 The ancient funerals (in those of Misenus and Pallas) are no less accurately described by Virgil than they are illustrated by his commentator Servius. The pile itself was an altar, the flames were fed with the blood of victims, and all the assistants were sprinkled with lustral water.

46 Tertullian, *de Idololatria*, ch. 11.

47 See every part of Montfaucon's Antiquities. Even the reverses of the Greek and Roman coins were frequently of an idolatrous nature. Here indeed the scruples of the Christian were suspended by a stronger passion.

48 Tertullian, *de Idololatria*, chs 20, 21, 22. If a Pagan friend (on the occasion perhaps of sneezing) used the familiar expression of 'Jupiter bless you', the Christian was obliged to protest against the divinity of Jupiter.

49 Consult the most laboured work of Ovid, his imperfect *Fasti*. He finished no more than the first six months of the year. The compilation of Macrobius is called the *Saturnalia*, but it is only a small part of the first book that bears any relation to the title.

* *page 256* [Apollo]

50 Tertullian has composed a defence, or rather panegyric, of the rash action of a Christian soldier, who, by throwing away his crown of laurel, had exposed himself and his brethren to the most imminent danger. By the mention of the emperors (Severus and Caracalla) it is evident, notwithstanding the wishes of M. de Tillemont, that Tertullian composed his treatise *de Corona* long before he was engaged in the errors of the Montanists. See *Mémoires Ecclésiastiques*, iii, 384.

51 In particular, the first book of the *Tusculan Questions*, and the treatise *de Senectute*, and the *Somnium Scipionis* contain, in the most beautiful language, everything that Grecian philosophy, or Roman good sense, could possibly suggest on this dark but important object.

52 The pre-existence of human souls, so far at least as that doctrine is compatible with religion, was adopted by many of the Greek and Latin fathers. See Beausobre, *Hist. du Manichéisme*, vi, 4.

53 See Cicero, *pro Cluent.*, ch. 61; Caesar *ap.* Sallust., *de Bell. Catilin.*, ch. 50; Juvenal, *Satir.*, ii, 149.

> *Esse aliquos manes, et subterranea regna,*
> . . .
> *Nec pueri credunt, nisi qui nondum aere lavantur.*

['Only little boys believe in the spirits of the dead or the kingdom of the underworld.']

54 The eleventh book of the *Odyssey* gives a very dreary and incoherent account of the infernal shades. Pindar and Virgil have embellished the picture; but even those poets, though more correct than their great model, are guilty of very strange inconsistencies. See Bayle, *Responses aux Questions d'un Provincial*, iii, 22.

55 See the sixteenth epistle of the first book of Horace, the thirteenth Satire of Juvenal, and the second Satire of Persius: these popular discourses express the sentiment and language of the multitude.

56 If we confine ourselves to the Gauls, we may observe that they entrusted not only their lives, but even their money, to the security of another world. *Vetus ille mos Gallorum occurrit* (says Valerius Maximus, ii, 6, 10), *quos memoria proditum est, pecunias mutuas, quae his apud inferos redderentur, dare solitos.* ['It is the immemorial custom of the Gauls to lend money for repayment in the underworld.'] The same custom is more darkly insinuated by Mela, iii, 2. It is almost needless to add that the profits of trade hold a just proportion to the credit of the merchant, and that the Druids derived from their holy profession a character of responsibility which could scarcely be claimed by any other order of men.

57 The right reverend author of the *Divine Legation of Moses* [Warburton, 1698–1779, bishop of Gloucester] assigns a very curious reason for the omission, and most ingeniously retorts it on the unbelievers.

58 See Le Clerc (*Prolegomena ad Hist. Ecclesiast.*, 1, 8). His authority seems to carry the greater weight, as he has written a learned and judicious commentary on the books of the Old Testament.

59 Josephus, *Antiquitat.*, xiii, 10, *de Bell. Jud.*, ii, 8. According to the most natural interpretation of his words, the Sadducees admitted only the Pentateuch; but it has pleased some modern critics to add the prophets to their creed, and to suppose that they contented themselves with rejecting the traditions of the Pharisees. Dr Jortin has argued that point in his *Remarks on Ecclesiastical History*, ii, 103.

60 This expectation was countenanced by the twenty-fourth chapter of St Matthew, and by the first epistle of St Paul to the Thessalonians. Erasmus removes the difficulty by the help of allegory and metaphor; and the learned Grotius ventures to insinuate that, for wise purposes, the pious deception was permitted to take place.

61 See Burnet's *Sacred Theory*, iii, 5. This tradition may be traced as high as the author of the Epistle of Barnabas, who wrote in the first century, and who seems to have been half a Jew.

62 The primitive church of Antioch computed almost 6000 years from the creation of the world to the birth of Christ. Africanus, Lactantius, and the Greek church have reduced that number to 5500, and Eusebius has contented himself with 5200 years. These calculations were formed on the Septuagint, which was universally received during the six first centuries. The authority of the Vulgate and of the Hebrew text has determined the moderns, Protestants as well as Catholics, to prefer a period of about 4000 years; though, in the study of profane antiquity, they often find themselves straitened by those narrow limits.

63 Most of these pictures were borrowed from a misrepresentation of Isaiah, Daniel, and the Apocalypse. One of the grossest images may be found in Irenaeus (v, 455), the disciple of Papias, who had seen the apostle St John.

64 See the second dialogue of Justin with Tryphon, and the seventh book of Lactantius. It is unnecessary to allege all the intermediate fathers, as the fact is not disputed. Yet the curious reader may consult Daillé, *de Usu Patrum*, iii, 4.

65 The testimony of Justin, of his own faith and that of his orthodox brethren, in the doctrine of a Millennium, is delivered in the clearest and most solemn manner (*Dialog. cum Tryphonte Jud.*, pp. 177, 178, edit. Benedictin). If in the beginning of this important passage there is anything like an inconsistency, we may impute it, as we think proper, either to the author or to his transcribers.

66 Dupin, *Bibliothèque Ecclésiastique*, i, 223, ii, 366; and Mosheim, p. 720; though the latter of these learned divines is not altogether candid on this occasion.

67 In the council of Laodicea (about the year 360) the Apocalypse was tacitly excluded from the sacred canon by the same churches of Asia to which it is addressed; and we may learn from the complaint of Sulpicius Severus that their sentence had been ratified by the greater number of Christians of his time. From what causes, then, is the Apocalypse at present so generally received by the Greek, the Roman, and the Protestant churches? The following ones may be assigned: 1. The Greeks were subdued by the authority of an impostor who, in the sixth century, assumed the character of Dionysius the Areopagite. 2. A just apprehension that the grammarians might become more important than the theologians engaged the council of Trent to fix the seal of their infallibility on all the books of Scripture contained in the Latin Vulgate, in the number of which the Apocalypse was fortunately included (Fra Paolo, *Istoria del Concilio Tridentino*, Bk ii). 3. The advantage of turning those mysterious prophecies against the See of Rome inspired the Protestants with uncommon veneration for so useful an ally. See the ingenious and elegant discourses of the present bishop of Lichfield on that unpromising subject.

 * *page 260*   [building]

68 Lactantius (*Institut. Divin.*, vii, 15, etc.) relates the dismal tale of futurity with great spirit and eloquence.

69 On this subject every reader of taste will be entertained with the third part of Burnet's *Sacred Theory*. He blends philosophy, scripture, and tradition, into one magnificent system; in the description of which he displays a strength of fancy not inferior to that of Milton himself.

70 And yet, whatever may be the language of individuals, it is still the public doctrine of all the Christian churches; nor can even our own refuse to admit her conclusions which must be drawn from the eighth and the eighteenth of her Articles. [Gibbon refers to the Articles of the Church of England.] The Jansenists, who have so diligently studied the works of the fathers, maintain this sentiment with distinguished zeal; and the learned M. de Tillemont never dismisses a virtuous emperor without pronouncing his damnation. Zuinglius is perhaps the only leader of a party who has ever adopted the milder sentiment, and he gave no less offence to the Lutherans than to the Catholics. See Bossuet, *Histoire des Variations des Eglises Protestantes*, ii, 19–22.

71 Justin and Clemens of Alexandria allow that some of the philosophers were instructed by the Logos; confounding its double signification of the human reason and of the Divine Word.

72 Tertullian, *de Spectaculis*, ch. 30. In order to ascertain the degree of authority which the zealous African had acquired, it may be sufficient to allege the testimony of Cyprian, the doctor and guide of all the western churches (see Prudent., *Hymn.*, xiii, 100). As often as he applied himself to his daily study of the writings of Tertullian, he was accustomed to say, '*Da mihi magistrum,* Give me my master.' (Hieronym., *de Viris Illustribus*, i, 284.)

73 Notwithstanding the evasions of Dr Middleton, it is impossible to overlook the clear traces of visions and inspiration which may be found in the apostolic fathers.

74 Irenaeus, *Adv. Haeres. Proem.*, p. 3. Dr Middleton (*Free Inquiry*, p. 96, etc.) observes that, as this pretension of all others was the most difficult to support by art, it was the soonest given up. The observation suits his hypothesis.

75 Athenagoras, *in Legatione*; Justin Martyr, *Cohort. ad Gentes*; Tertullian, *advers. Marcionit.*, Bk iv. These descriptions are not very unlike the prophetic fury for which Cicero (*de Divinat.*, ii, 54) expresses so little reverence.

76 Tertullian (*Apolog.*, ch. 23) throws out a bold defiance to the Pagan magistrates. Of the primitive miracles, the power of exorcising is the only one which has been assumed by Protestants.

77 Irenaeus, *adv. Haereses*, ii, 56, 57; v, 6. Mr Dodwell (*Dissertat. ad Irenaeum*, ii, 42) concludes that the second century was still more fertile in miracles than the first.

78 Theophilus, *ad Autolycum*, i, 345, edit. Benedictin. Paris, 1742.

79 Dr Middleton sent out his Introduction in the year 1747, published his *Free Inquiry* in 1749, and before his death, which happened in 1750, he had prepared a vindication of it against his numerous adversaries.

80 The university of Oxford conferred degrees on his opponents. From the indignation of Mosheim (p. 221), we may discover the sentiments of the Lutheran divines.

81 It may seem somewhat remarkable that Bernard of Clairvaux, who records so many miracles of his friend St Malachi, never takes any notice of his own, which, in their turn, however, are carefully related by his companions and disciples. In the long series of ecclesiastical history, does there exist a single instance of a saint asserting that he himself possessed the gift of miracles?

82 The conversion of Constantine is the era which is most usually fixed by Protestants. The more rational divines are unwilling to admit the miracles of the fourth, whilst the more credulous are unwilling to reject those of the fifth, century.

83 The imputations of Celsus and Julian, with the defence of the fathers, are very fairly stated by Spanheim, *Commentaire sur les Césars de Julian*, p. 468.

84 Pliny, *Epist.*, x, 97.

85 Tertullian, *Apolog.*, ch. 44. He adds, however, with some degree of hesitation, *Aut si aliud, iam non Christianus.* ['Or if it was for some other charge, then they were no longer Christians.']

86 The philosopher Peregrinus (of whose life and death Lucian has left us so entertaining an account) imposed, for a long time, on the credulous simplicity of the Christians of Asia.

87 See a very judicious treatise of Barbeyrac *sur la Morale des Pères*.

88 Lactant., *Institut. Divin.*, vi, 20, 21, 22.

89 Consult a work of Clemens of Alexandria, entitled the *Paedagogue*, which contains the rudiments of ethics, as they were taught in the most celebrated of the Christian schools.

90 Tertullian, *de Spectaculis*, ch. 23. Clemens Alexandrin., *Paedagog.*, iii, 8.

91 Beausobre, *Hist. Critique du Manichéisme*, vii, 3. Justin, Gregory of Nyssa, Augustine, etc., strongly inclined to this opinion.

92 Some of the Gnostic heretics were more consistent; they rejected the use of marriage.

93 See a chain of tradition, from Justin Martyr to Jerome, in the *Morale des Pères*, iv, 6–26.

94 See a very curious Dissertation on the Vestals, in the *Mémoires de l'Académie des Inscriptions*, iv, 161–227. Notwithstanding the honours and rewards which were bestowed on those virgins, it was difficult to procure a sufficient number; nor could the dread of the most horrible death always restrain their incontinence.

95 *Cupiditatem procreandi aut unam scimus aut nullam.* ['The desire to procreate we know to be either single or non-existent.'] Minucius Felix, ch. 31; Justin., *Apolog. Major* [29]; Athenagoras in *Legat.*, ch. 28; Tertullian, *de Cultu Femin.*, Bk ii.

96 Eusebius, vi, 8. Before the fame of Origen had excited envy and persecution, this extraordinary action was rather admired than censured. As it was his general practice to allegorise Scripture, it seems unfortunate that, in this instance only, he should have adopted the literal sense. [Origen castrated himself.]

97 Cyprian, *Epist.*, 4, and Dodwell, *Dissertat. Cyprianic.*, iii. Something like this rash attempt was long afterwards imputed to the founder of the order of Fontevrault. Bayle has amused himself and his readers on that very delicate subject.

* *page 268*   [from the Greek IÛÎ¤ˆ, 'I exercise']

98 Dupin (*Bibliothèque. Ecclésiastique*, i, 195) gives a particular account of the dialogue of the ten virgins, as it was composed by Methodius, bishop of Tyre. The praises of virginity are excessive.

99 The Ascetics (as early as the second century) made a public profession of mortifying their bodies, and of abstaining from the use of flesh and wine. Mosheim, p. 310.

100 See the *Morale des Pères*. The same patient principles have been revived since the Reformation by the Socinians, the modern Anabaptists, and the Quakers. Barclay, the apologist of the Quakers, has protected his brethren by the authority of the primitive Christians; pp. 542–549.

101 Tertullian, *Apolog.*, ch. 21; *de Idololatria*, chs 17, 18. Origen *contra Celsum*, v, 253; vii, 348; viii, 423–28.

102 Tertullian (*de Corona Militis*, ch. 11) suggests to them the expedient of deserting; a counsel which, if it had been generally known, was not very proper to conciliate the favour of the emperors towards the Christian sect.

103 As well as we can judge from the mutilated representation of Origen (viii, 423), his adversary, Celsus, had urged his objection with great force and candour.

104 The aristocratical party in France, as well as in England, has strenuously maintained the divine origin of bishops. But the Calvinistical presbyters were impatient of a superior; and the Roman Pontiff refused to acknowledge an equal. See Fra Paolo.

105 In the history of the Christian hierarchy, I have, for the most part, followed the learned and candid Mosheim.

106 For the prophets of the primitive church, see Mosheim, *Dissertationes ad Hist. Eccles. pertinentes*, ii, 132–208.

107 See the epistles of St Paul, and of Clemens, to the Corinthians.

* *page 271*   [i.e., an elder]

108 Hooker's *Ecclesiastical Polity*, Bk vii.

109 See Jerome, *ad Titum*, ch. i. and *Epistol.*, 85 (in the Benedictine edition, 101), and the elaborate apology of Blondel, *pro sententia Hieronymi*. The ancient state, as it is described by Jerome, of the bishop and presbyters of Alexandria, receives a remarkable confirmation from the patriarch Eutychius (*Annal.*, i, 330, Vers. Pocock); whose testimony I know not how to reject, in spite of all the objections of the learned Pearson in his *Vindiciae Ignatianae*, i, 11.

110 See the introduction to the Apocalypse. Bishops, under the name of angels, were already instituted in the seven cities of Asia. And yet the epistle of Clemens (which is probably of as ancient a date) does not lead us to discover any traces of episcopacy either at Corinth or Rome.

111 *Nulla ecclesia sine episcopo* [No church without bishops] has been a fact as well as a maxim since the time of Tertullian and Irenaeus.

112 After we have passed the difficulties of the first century, we find the episcopal government universally established, till it was interrupted by the republican genius of the Swiss and German reformers.

113 See Mosheim in the first and second centuries. Ignatius (*ad Smyrnaeos*, ch. 3, etc.) is fond of exalting the episcopal dignity. Le Clerc (*Hist. Eccles.*, p. 569) very bluntly censures his conduct. Mosheim, with a more critical judgment (p. 161), suspects the purity even of the smaller epistles.

114 *Nonne et Laici sacerdotes sumus?* ['Are not we laymen also priests?'] Tertullian, *Exhort. ad Castitat.*, ch. 7. As the human heart is still the same, several of the observations which Mr Hunt has made on Enthusiasm (*Essays*, i, 76, quarto edit.) may be applied even to real inspiration.

115 *Acta Concil. Carthag. apud* Cyprian., edit. Fell, p. 158. This council was composed of eighty-seven bishops from the provinces of Mauritania, Numidia, and Africa; some presbyters and deacons assisted at the assembly; *praesente plebis maxima parte* ['most of those present were of the common people'].

116 *Aguntur praeterea per Graecias illas, certis in locis concilia*, etc. Tertullian, *de Ieiuniis*, ch. 13. ['Henceforth throughout Greece, councils were held in certain places, etc.'] The African mentions it as a recent and foreign institution. The coalition of the Christian churches is very ably explained by Mosheim, pp. 164–70.

117 Cyprian, in his admired treatise, *de Unitate Ecclesiae*, pp. 75–86.

118 We may appeal to the whole tenor of Cyprian's conduct, of his doctrine, and of his epistles. Le Clerc, in a short life of Cyprian (*Bibliothèque Universelle*, xii, 207–378), has laid him open with great freedom and accuracy.

119 If Novatus, Felicissimus, etc., whom the bishop of Carthage expelled from his church, and from Africa, were not the most detestable monsters of wickedness, the zeal of Cyprian must occasionally have prevailed over his veracity. For a very just account of these obscure quarrels, see Mosheim, pp. 497–512.

120 Mosheim, pp. 269, 574. Dupin, *Antiquae Eccles. Disciplin.*, pp. 19, 20.

121 Tertullian, in a distinct treatise, has pleaded against the heretics the right of prescription, as it was held by the apostolic churches.

122 The journey of St Peter to Rome is mentioned by most of the ancients (see Eusebius, ii, 25), maintained by all the Catholics, allowed by some Protestants (see Pearson and Dodwell, *de Success. Episcop. Roman.*), but has been vigorously attacked by Spanheim (*Miscellanea Sacra*, iii, 3). According to father Hardouin, the monks of the thirteenth century, who composed the *Aeneid*, represented St Peter under the allegorical character of the Trojan hero.

123 It is in French only that the famous allusion to St Peter's name is exact. *Tu es Pierre, et sur cette pierre*. The same is imperfect in Greek, Latin, Italian, etc., and totally unintelligible in our Teutonic languages.

124 Irenaeus, *Adv. Haereses*, iii. 3; Tertullian, *de Praescription.*, ch. 36; and Cyprian, *Epistol.*, 27, 55, 71, 75. Le Clerc (*Hist. Eccles.*, p. 764) and Mosheim (pp. 258, 578) labour in the interpretation of these passages. But the loose and rhetorical style of the fathers often appears favourable to the pretensions of Rome.

125 See the sharp epistle from Firmilianus, bishop of Caesarea, to Stephen, bishop of Rome, Cyprian., *Epistol.*, 75.

126 Concerning this dispute of the re-baptism of heretics, see the epistles of Cyprian, and the seventh Book of Eusebius.

127 For the origin of these words, see Mosheim, p. 141. Spanheim, *Hist. Ecclesiast.*, p. 633. The distinction of *Clerus* and *Laicus* was established before the time of Tertullian.

128 The community instituted by Plato is more perfect than that which Sir Thomas More had imagined for his Utopia. The community of women, and that of temporal goods, may be considered as inseparable parts of the same system.

129 Josephus, *Antiquitat.*, xxiii, 2; Philo, *de Vit. Comtemplativ.*

130 See the Acts of the Apostles, ii, 4, 5, with Grotius's Commentary. Mosheim, in a particular dissertation, attacks the common opinion with very inconclusive arguments.

131 Justin. Martyr, *Apolog. Major*, ch. 89; Tertullian, *Apolog.*, ch. 39.

132 Irenaeus, *ad Haeres.*, iv, 27, 34; Origen in *Num. Hom.*, ii; Cyprian, *de Unitat. Eccles. Constitut. Apostol.*, ii, 34, 35, with the notes of Cotelerius. The *Constitutions* introduce this divine precept by declaring that priests are as much above kings as the soul is above the body. Among the tythable articles, they enumerate corn, wine, oil, and wood. On this interesting subject, consult Prideaux's History of Tythes, and Fra Paolo, *della Materie Beneficiarie*; two writers of a very different character.

133 The same opinion, which prevailed about the year one thousand, was productive of the same effects. Most of the donations express their motive, *appropinquante mundi fine* ['the end of the world being nigh']. See Mosheim's *General History of the Church*, i, 457.

134
> *Tum summa cura est fratribus*
> *(Ut sermo testatur loquax)*
> *Offerre fundis venditis*
> *Sestertiorum milia.*
> *Addicta avorum praedia*
> *Foedis sub auctionibus,*
> *Successor exheres gemit,*
> *Sanctis egens parentibus.*
> *Haec occuluntur abditis*
> *Ecclesiarum in angulis.*
> *Et summa pietas creditur*
> *Nudare dulces liberos.*
>
> Prudent., περὶ στεφάνων, Hymn 2.

['The Christians' chief concern (as common gossip testifies) is to sell their properties and make offerings of thousands of sesterces. The disgraceful auctioning off of the grandparents' goods is bemoaned by the heir, cut off without a penny, the needy son of saintly parents. The goods are hidden away in the corners of the churches, and it is thought the height of religious piety to leave one's beloved children penniless.']

The subsequent conduct of the deacon Laurence only proves how proper a use was made of the wealth of the Roman church; it was undoubtedly very considerable; but Fra Paolo (ch. 3) appears to exaggerate when he supposes that the successors of Commodus were urged to persecute the Christians by their own avarice, or that of their Praetorian prefects.

135 Cyprian, *Epistol.*, 62.

136 Tertullian, *de Praescriptionibus*, ch. 30.

137 Diocletian gave a rescript, which is only a declaration of the old law: *Collegium, si nullo speciali privilegio subnixum sit, haereditatem capere non posse, dubium non est.* ['There is no doubt that a corporate body, unless it relies on some special privilege, cannot inherit.'] Fra Paolo (ch. 4) thinks that these regulations had been much neglected since the reign of Valerian.

138 *Hist. August.*, p. 131. The ground had been public; and was now disputed between the society of Christians and that of butchers.

139 *Constitut. Apostol.*, ii, 35.

140 Cyprian, *de Lapsis*, p. 89, *Epistol.*, 65. The charge is confirmed by the 19th and 20th canon of the council of Illiberis.

141 See the apologies of Justin, Tertullian, etc.

142 The wealth and liberality of the Romans to their most distant brethren is gratefully celebrated by Dionysius of Corinth: Eusebius, iv, 23.

143 See Lucian in *Peregrin.* Julian (*Epist.* 49) seems mortified that the Christian charity maintains not only their own, but likewise the heathen poor.

144 Such, at least, has been the laudable conduct of more modern missionaries, under the same circumstances Above three thousand new-born infants are annually exposed in the streets of Pekin. See Le Comte, *Mémoires sur la Chine*, and the *Recherches sur les Chinois et les Egyptiens*, i, 61.

145 The Montanists and the Novatians, who adhered to this opinion with the greatest rigour and obstinacy, found *themselves* at last in the number of excommunicated heretics. See the learned and copious Mosheim, *Secul.*, ii and iii.

146 Dionysius, *ap.* Euseb., iv. 23. Cyprian, *de Lapsis.*

147 Cave's *Primitive Christianity*, iii, 5. The admirers of antiquity regret the loss of this public penance.

148 See in Dupin, *Bibliothèque Ecclésiastique*, ii, 304–13, a short but rational exposition of the canons of those councils, which were assembled in the first moments of tranquillity after the persecution of Diocletian. This persecution had been much less severely felt in Spain than in Galatia; a difference which may, in some measure, account for the contrast of their regulations.

149 Cyprian, *Epist.*, 69.

150 The arts, the manners, and the vices of the priests of the Syrian goddess are very humorously described by Apuleius, in the eighth book of his *Metamorphoses.*

151 The office of Asiarch was of this nature, and it is frequently mentioned in Aristides, the Inscriptions, etc. It was annual and elective. None but the vainest citizens could desire the honour; none but the most wealthy could support the expense. See in the *Patres Apostol.*, ii, 200, with how much indifference Philip the Asiarch conducted himself in the martyrdom of Polycarp. There were likewise Bithyniarchs, Lyciarchs, etc.

152 The modern critics are not disposed to believe what the fathers almost unanimously assert, that St Matthew composed a Hebrew gospel, of which only the Greek translation is extant. It seems, however, dangerous to reject their testimony.

153 Under the reigns of Nero and Domitian, and in the cities of Alexandria, Antioch, Rome, and Ephesus. See Mill, *Prolegomena* ad Nov. Testament., and Dr Lardner's fair and extensive collection, vol. xv.

  * *page 282*   [St Paul]

154 The Alogians (Epiphanius, *de Haeres.*, 51) disputed the genuineness of the Apocalypse, because the church of Thyatira was not yet founded. Epiphanius, who allows the fact, extricates himself from the difficulty by ingeniously supposing that St John wrote in the spirit of prophecy. See Abauzit, *Discours sur l'Apocalypse.*

155 The epistles of Ignatius and Dionysius (*ap.* Eusebius, iv. 23) point out many churches in Asia and Greece. That of Athens seems to have been one of the least flourishing.

156 Lucian *in Alexandro*, ch. 25. Christianity, however, must have been very unequally diffused over Pontus; since in the middle of the third century there were no more than seventeen believers in the extensive diocese of Neo-Caesarea. See M. de Tillemont, *Mémoires Ecclésiast.*, iv, 675, from Basil and Gregory of Nyssa, who were themselves natives of Cappadocia.

157 According to the ancients, Jesus Christ suffered under the consulship of the two Gemini, in the year 29 of our present era. Pliny was sent into Bithynia (according to Pagi) in the year 110.

158 Pliny, *Epistles*, x, 97.

159 Chrysostom., *Opera*, vii, 658, 810.

160 John Malala, ii, 144. He draws the same conclusion with regard to the populousness of Antioch.

 * *page 283* [St John Chrysostom, AD 347–407, Archbishop of Constantinople]

161 Chrysostom., i, 592. I am indebted for these passages, though not for my inference, to the learned Dr Lardner. *Credibility of the Gospel History*, xii, 370.

162 Basnage, *Histoire des Juifs*, 2, chs 20, 21, 22 and 23, has examined, with the most critical accuracy, the curious treatise of Philo which describes the Therapeutae. By proving that it was composed as early as the time of Augustus, Basnage has demonstrated, in spite of Eusebius (ii, 17), and a crowd of modern Catholics, that the Therapeutae were neither Christians nor monks. It still remains probable that they changed their name, preserved their manners, adopted some new articles of faith, and gradually became the fathers of the Egyptian Ascetics.

163 See a letter of Hadrian, in the *Augustan History*, p. 245.

164 For the succession of Alexandrian bishops, consult Renaudot's *History*, p. 24, etc. This curious fact is preserved by the patriarch Eutychius (*Annals*, i, 334, Vers. Pocock [date 10th century]), and its internal evidence would alone be a sufficient answer to all the objections which Bishop Pearson has urged in the *Vindiciae Ignatianae.*

165 Ammianus Marcellinus, xxii, 16.

166 Origen, *contra Celsum*, i, 40.

 * *page 284* [fortuitous, happening by chance]

167 *Ingens multitudo* [a huge multitude] is the expression of Tacitus, xv, 44.

168 Livy, xxxix, 13, 15,16,17. Nothing could exceed the horror and consternation of the senate on the discovery of the Bacchanalians, whose depravity is described, and perhaps exaggerated, by Livy.

169 Eusebius, vi, 43. The Latin translator (M. de Valois) has thought proper to reduce the number of presbyters to forty-four.

170 This proportion of the presbyters and of the poor to the rest of the people was originally fixed by Burnet (*Travels into Italy*, p. 168), and is approved by Moyle (ii, 151). They were both unacquainted with the passage of Chrysostom which converts their conjecture almost into a fact.

171 *Serius trans Alpes, religione Dei suscepta.* ['Christianity spread later across the Alps.'] Sulpicius Severus, Bk ii. With regard to Africa, see Tertullian, *ad Scapulam*, ch. 3. According to the Donatists, whose assertion is confirmed by the tacit acknowledgment of Augustine, Africa was the last of the provinces which received the gospel. Tillemont, *Mém. Ecclésiast.*, i, 754.

172 *Tum primum intra Gallias martyria visa.* ['This was the first time that martyrdom made its appearance in Gaul.'] Sulpicius Severus, Bk ii. These were the celebrated martyrs of Lyons. See Eusebius, v, 1; Tillemont, *Mém. Ecclésiast.*, ii, 316. It is imagined that the Scyllitan martyrs were the first (*Acta Sincera Ruinart.*, p. 34). One of the adversaries of Apuleius seems to have been a Christian. *Apolog.*, pp. 496, 497, edit. Delphin.

173 *Rarae in aliquibus civitatibus ecclesiae, paucorum Christianorum devotione, resurgerent. Acta Sincera*, p. 130; Gregory of Tours, i, 28; Mosheim, pp. 207, 449. There is some reason to believe that, in the beginning of the fourth century, the extensive dioceses of Liège, of Treves, and of Cologne composed a single bishopric, which had been very recently founded. See *Mémoires* de Tillemont, vi, i, 43 and 411.

174 The date of Tertullian's Apology is fixed, in a dissertation of Mosheim, to the year 198.

175 In the fifteenth century, there were few who had either inclination or courage to question, whether Joseph of Arimathea founded the monastery of Glastonbury, and whether Dionysius the Areopagite preferred the residence of Paris to that of Athens.

176 The stupendous metamorphosis was performed in the ninth century. See Mariana (*Hist. Hispan.*, vii, 13; i, 285, edit. Hag. Com. 1733), who, in every sense, imitates Livy, and the honest detection of the legend of St James by Dr Geddes, *Miscellanies*, ii, 221.

177 Justin Martyr, *Dialog. cum Tryphon.*, p. 341; Irenaeus, *adv. Haeres.*, i, 10; Tertullian, *adv. Jud.*, ch. 7. See Mosheim, p. 203.

178 See the fourth century of Mosheim's *History of the Church*. Many, though very confused circumstances, that relate to the conversion of Iberia and Armenia, may be found in Moses of Chorene, ii, 78–89.

179 According to Tertullian, the Christian faith had penetrated into parts of Britain inaccessible to the Roman arms. About a century afterwards, Ossian, the son of Fingal, is said to have disputed, in his extreme old age, with one of the foreign missionaries, and the dispute is still extant, in verse, and in the Erse language. See Mr Macpherson's Dissertation on the Antiquity of Ossian's Poems, p. 10.

180 The Goths, who ravaged Asia in the reign of Gallienus, carried away great numbers of captives; some of whom were Christians, and became missionaries. See Tillemont, *Mémoires Ecclésiast.*, iv, 44.

181 The legend of Abgarus, fabulous as it is, affords a decisive proof that, many years before Eusebius wrote his history, the greatest part of the inhabitants of Edessa had embraced Christianity. Their rivals, the citizens of Carrhae, adhered, on the contrary, to the cause of Paganism, as late as the sixth century.

182 According to Bardesanes (*ap.* Eusebius, *Praepar. Evangel.*), there were some Christians in Persia before the end of the second century. In the time of Constantine (see his *Epistle to Sapor, Vit.*, iv, 13), they composed a flourishing church. Consult Beausobre, *Hist. Critique du Manichéisme*, i, 180, and the *Bibliotheca Orientalis* of Assemani.

183 Origen, *contra Celsum*, viii, 424.

   * *page 286* [Between AD 306 and AD 337; see Chapter 20.]

184 Minucius Felix, ch. 8, with Wowerus's notes. Celsus *ap.* Origen, iii, 138 and142; Julian *ap.* Cyril., vi, 206, edit. Spanheim.

185 Eusebius, *Hist. Eccles.*, iv, 3; Hieronym., *Epist.*, 83.

186 The story is prettily told in Justin's Dialogues. Tillemont (*Mém. Ecclésiast.*, ii, 384), who relates it after him, is sure that the old man was a disguised angel.

187 Eusebius, v, 28. It may be hoped that none, except the heretics gave occasion to the complaint of Celsus (*ap.* Origen, ii, 77) that the Christians were perpetually correcting and altering their Gospels.

188 Pliny, *Epist.*, x, 97. *Fuerunt alii similis amentiae, cives Romani . . . Multi enim omnis aetatis, omnis ordinis, utriusque sexus, etiam vocantur in periculum et vocabuntur.* ['Others have been subject to a similar madness, including Roman citizens . . . For many of every age, of every class, and either sex, continue and will continue to be brought to trial.']

189 Tertullian, *ad Scapulam*. Yet even his rhetoric rises no higher than to claim a *tenth* part of Carthage.

190 Cyprian, *Epist.*, 79.

191 Dr Lardner, in his first and second volume of Jewish and Christian testimonies, collects and illustrates those of Pliny the younger, of Tacitus, of Galen, of Marcus Antoninus, and perhaps of Epictetus (for it is doubtful whether that philosopher means to speak of the Christians). The new sect is totally unnoticed by Seneca, the elder Pliny, and Plutarch.

192 If the famous prophecy of the Seventy Weeks had been alleged to a Roman philosopher, would he not have replied in the words of Cicero, *'Quae tandem ista auguratio est, annorum potius quam aut mensium aut dierum?' de Divinatione*, ii, 80.['Will this prophecy come about in years, rather than in months or days?'] Observe with what irreverence Lucian (*in Alexandro*, ch. 13), and his friend Celsus *ap.* Origen (vii, 327), express themselves concerning the Hebrew prophets.

193 The philosophers, who derided the more ancient predictions of the Sibyls, would easily have detected the Jewish and Christian forgeries, which have been so triumphantly quoted by the fathers, from Justin Martyr to Lactantius. When the Sibylline verses had performed their appointed task, they, like the system of the millennium, were quietly laid aside. The Christian Sibyl had unluckily fixed the ruin of Rome for the year 195, AUC 948. [In AD 195, or the year 948 since the foundation of Rome, *ab urbe condita*. Sibyls were female soothsayers who expressed their prophecies in verse.]

194 The fathers, as they are drawn out in battle array by Dom Calmet (*Dissertations sur la Bible*, iii, 295–308), seem to cover the whole earth with darkness, in which they are followed by most of the moderns.

195 Origen, *ad* Matth. ch. 27, and a few modern critics, Beza, Le Clerc, Lardner, etc., are desirous of confining it to the land of Judaea.

196 The celebrated passage of Phlegon is now wisely abandoned. When Tertullian assures the Pagans that the mention of the prodigy is found in *Arcanis* (not *Archivis*) *vestris* (see his *Apology*, ch. 21), he probably appeals to the Sibylline verses, which relate it exactly in the words of the gospel.

197 Seneca, *Quaest. Natur.*, i, 1 and 15; vi, 1; vii, 17; Pliny, *Hist. Natur.*, Bk ii.

198 Pliny, *Hist. Natur.*, ii, 30.

199 Virgil, *Georgics*, i, 466; *Tibullus*, Bk ii *Eleg.*, v, 75; Ovid, *Metamorph.*, xv, 782; Lucan, *Pharsal.*, i, 540. The last of these poets places this prodigy before the civil war.

200 See a public epistle of M. Antony in Josephus, *Antiquit.*, xiv, 12; Plutarch in *Caesar*, p. 471; Appian, *Bell. Civil.*, Bk iv; Dion Cassius, xlv, 431; Julius Obsequens, ch. 128. His little treatise is an abstract of Livy's prodigies.

CHAPTER 16

The conduct of the Roman government towards the Christians,
from the reign of Nero to that of Constantine

If we seriously consider the purity of the Christian religion, the sanctity of
its moral precepts, and the innocent as well as austere lives of the greater
number of those who, during the first ages, embraced the faith of the
gospel, we should naturally suppose that so benevolent a doctrine would
have been received with due reverence, even by the unbelieving world;
that the learned and the polite, however they might deride the miracles,
would have esteemed the virtues of the new sect; and that the magistrates,
instead of persecuting, would have protected an order of men who
yielded the most passive obedience to the laws, though they declined the
active cares of war and government. If, on the other hand, we recollect
the universal toleration of Polytheism, as it was invariably maintained by
the faith of the people, the incredulity of philosophers, and the policy of
the Roman senate and emperors, we are at a loss to discover what new
offence the Christians had committed, what new provocation could
exasperate the mild indifference of antiquity, and what new motives
could urge the Roman princes, who beheld, without concern, a thousand
forms of religion subsisting in peace under their gentle sway, to inflict a
severe punishment on any part of their subjects, who had chosen for
themselves a singular, but an inoffensive, mode of faith and worship.

The religious policy of the ancient world seems to have assumed a more
stern and intolerant character, to oppose the progress of Christianity.
About fourscore years after the death of Christ, his innocent disciples
were punished with death, by the sentence of a proconsul of the most
amiable and philosophic character, and according to the laws of an
emperor distinguished by the wisdom and justice of his general administration. The apologies which were repeatedly addressed to the successors
of Trajan are filled with the most pathetic complaints that the Christians,
who obeyed the dictates and solicited the liberty of conscience, were
alone, among all the subjects of the Roman empire, excluded from the
common benefits of their auspicious government. The deaths of a few
eminent martyrs have been recorded with care; and from the time that
Christianity was invested with the supreme power, the governors of the
church have been no less diligently employed in displaying the cruelty,
than in imitating the conduct, of their Pagan adversaries. To separate (if it
be possible) a few authentic as well as interesting facts from an undigested
mass of fiction and error, and to relate, in a clear and rational manner, the
causes, the extent, the duration, and the most important circumstances of

the persecutions to which the first Christians were exposed, is the design of the present chapter.

The sectaries of a persecuted religion, depressed by fear, animated with resentment, and perhaps heated by enthusiasm, are seldom in a proper temper of mind calmly to investigate, or candidly to appreciate, the motives of their enemies, which often escape the impartial and discerning view even of those who are placed at a secure distance from the flames of persecution. A reason has been assigned for the conduct of the emperors towards the primitive Christians, which may appear the more specious and probable as it is drawn from the acknowledged genius of Polytheism. It has already been observed that the religious concord of the world was principally supported by the implicit assent and reverence which the nations of antiquity expressed for their respective traditions and ceremonies. It might therefore be expected that they would unite with indignation against any sect or people which should separate itself from the communion of mankind, and, claiming the exclusive possession of divine knowledge, should disdain every form of worship except its own as impious and idolatrous. The rights of toleration were held by mutual indulgence: they were justly forfeited by a refusal of the accustomed tribute. As the payment of this tribute was inflexibly refused by the Jews, and by them alone, the consideration of the treatment which they experienced from the Roman magistrates will serve to explain how far these speculations are justified by facts, and will lead us to discover the true causes of the persecution of Christianity.

Without repeating what has been already mentioned of the reverence of the Roman princes and governors for the temple of Jerusalem, we shall only observe that the destruction of the temple and city was accompanied and followed by every circumstance that could exasperate the minds of the conquerors, and authorise religious persecution by the most specious arguments of political justice and the public safety. From the reign of Nero to that of Antoninus Pius, the Jews discovered a fierce impatience of the dominion of Rome, which repeatedly broke out in the most furious massacres and insurrections. Humanity is shocked at the recital of the horrid cruelties which they committed in the cities of Egypt, of Cyprus, and of Cyrene, where they dwelt in treacherous friendship with the unsuspecting natives;[1] and we are tempted to applaud the severe retaliation which was exercised by the arms of the legions against a race of fanatics, whose dire and credulous superstition seemed to render them the implacable enemies not only of the Roman government, but of human kind.[2] The enthusiasm of the Jews was supported by the opinion that it was unlawful for them to pay taxes to an idolatrous master; and by the flattering promise which they derived from their ancient oracles, that a conquering Messiah would soon arise, destined to break their fetters and to invest the favourites of heaven with the empire of the earth. It was by announcing himself as their long-expected deliverer, and by calling on all the descendants of Abraham to assert the hope of Israel, that the famous Barchochebas* collected a formidable army, with which he resisted, during two years, the power of the emperor Hadrian.[3]

Notwithstanding these repeated provocations, the resentment of the Roman princes expired after the victory; nor were their apprehensions continued beyond the period of war and danger. By the general indulgence of polytheism, and by the mild temper of Antoninus Pius, the Jews were restored to their ancient privileges, and once more obtained the permission of circumcising their children, with the easy restraint that they should never confer on any foreign proselyte that distinguishing mark of the Hebrew race.[4] The numerous remains of that people, though they were still excluded from the precincts of Jerusalem, were permitted to form and to maintain considerable establishments both in Italy and in the provinces, to acquire the freedom of Rome, to enjoy municipal honours, and to obtain, at the same time, an exemption from the burdensome and expensive offices of society. The moderation or the contempt of the Romans gave a legal sanction to the form of ecclesiastical police which was instituted by the vanquished sect. The patriarch, who had fixed his residence at Tiberias, was empowered to appoint his subordinate ministers and apostles, to exercise a domestic jurisdiction, and to receive from his dispersed brethren an annual contribution.[5] New synagogues were frequently erected in the principal cities of the empire; and the sabbaths, the fasts, and the festivals, which were either commanded by the Mosaic law or enjoined by the traditions of the Rabbis, were celebrated in the most solemn and public manner.[6] Such gentle treatment insensibly assuaged the stern temper of the Jews. Awakened from their dream of prophecy and conquest, they assumed the behaviour of peaceable and industrious subjects. Their irreconcilable hatred of mankind, instead of flaming out in acts of blood and violence, evaporated in less dangerous gratifications. They embraced every opportunity of over-reaching the idolaters in trade; and they pronounced secret and ambiguous imprecations against the haughty kingdom of Edom.[7]

Since the Jews, who rejected with abhorrence the deities adored by their sovereign and by their fellow-subjects, enjoyed, however, the free exercise of their unsocial religion; there must have existed some other cause, which exposed the disciples of Christ to those severities from which the posterity of Abraham was exempt. The difference between them is simple and obvious; but, according to the sentiments of antiquity, it was of the highest importance. The Jews were a *nation*; the Christians were a *sect*; and, if it was natural for every community to respect the sacred institutions of their neighbours, it was incumbent on them to persevere in those of their ancestors. The voice of oracles, the precepts of philosophers, and the authority of the laws, unanimously enforced this national obligation. By their lofty claim of superior sanctity, the Jews might provoke the Polytheists to consider them as an odious and impure race.

By disdaining the intercourse of other nations they might deserve their contempt. The laws of Moses might be for the most part frivolous or absurd; yet, since they had been received during many ages by a large society, his followers were justified by the example of mankind; and it was universally acknowledged that they had a right to practise what it would have been criminal in them to neglect. But this principle which protected the Jewish synagogue afforded not any favour or security to the primitive church. By embracing the faith of the Gospel, the Christians incurred the supposed guilt of an unnatural and unpardonable offence. They dissolved the sacred ties of custom and education, violated the religious institutions of their country, and presumptuously despised whatever their fathers had believed as true, or had reverenced as sacred. Nor was this apostasy (if we may use the expression) merely of a partial or local kind; since the pious deserter who withdrew himself from the temples of Egypt or Syria would equally disdain to seek an asylum in those of Athens or Carthage. Every Christian rejected with contempt the superstitions of his family, his city, and his province. The whole body of Christians unanimously refused to hold any communion with the gods of Rome, of the empire, and of mankind. It was in vain that the oppressed believer asserted the inalienable rights of conscience and private judgment. Though his situation might excite the pity, his arguments could never reach the understanding, either of the philosophic or of the believing part of the Pagan world. To their apprehensions, it was no less a matter of surprise that any individuals should entertain scruples against complying with the established mode of worship, than if they had conceived a sudden abhorrence to the manners, the dress, or the language of their native country.[8]

The surprise of the Pagans was soon succeeded by resentment; and the most pious of men were exposed to the unjust but dangerous imputation of impiety. Malice and prejudice concurred in representing the Christians as a society of atheists, who, by the most daring attack on the religious constitution of the empire, had merited the severest animadversion of the civil magistrate. They had separated themselves (they gloried in the confession) from every mode of superstition which was received in any part of the globe by the various temper of polytheism; but it was not altogether so evident what deity or form of worship they had substituted to the gods and temples of antiquity. The pure and sublime idea which they entertained of the Supreme Being escaped the gross conception of the Pagan multitude, who were at a loss to discover a spiritual and solitary God, that was neither represented under any corporeal figure or visible symbol, nor was adored with the accustomed pomp of libations and festivals, of altars and sacrifices.[9] The sages of Greece and Rome, who had elevated their minds to the contemplation of the existence and attributes of the First Cause, were induced, by reason or by vanity, to reserve for themselves and their chosen disciples the privilege of this philosophical devotion.[10] They were far from admitting the prejudices of mankind as the standard of truth; but they considered them as flowing from the original disposition of human nature; and they supposed that any popular mode of faith and worship which presumed to disclaim the assistance of the senses would, in proportion as it receded from superstition, find itself incapable of restraining the wanderings of the fancy and the visions of fanaticism. The careless glance which men of wit and learning condescended to cast on the Christian revelation served only to confirm their hasty opinion, and to persuade them that the principle, which they might have revered, of the divine unity was defaced by the wild enthusiasm, and annihilated by the airy speculations, of the new sectaries. The author of a celebrated dialogue which has been attributed to Lucian, whilst he affects to treat the mysterious subject of the Trinity in a style of ridicule and contempt, betrays his own ignorance of the weakness of human reason, and of the inscrutable nature of the divine perfections.[11]

It might appear less surprising that the founder of Christianity should not only be revered by his disciples as a sage and a prophet, but that he should be adored as a God. The Polytheists were disposed to adopt every article of faith which seemed to offer any resemblance, however distant or imperfect, with the popular mythology; and the legends of Bacchus, of Hercules, and of Aesculapius had, in some measure, prepared their imagination for the appearance of the Son of God under a human form.[12] But they were astonished that the Christians should abandon the temples of those ancient heroes who, in the infancy of the world, had invented arts, instituted laws, and vanquished the tyrants or monsters who infested the earth; in order to choose, for the exclusive object of their religious worship, an obscure teacher who, in a recent age, and among a barbarous people, had fallen a sacrifice either to the malice of his own countrymen or to the jealousy of the Roman government. The Pagan multitude, reserving their gratitude for temporal benefits alone, rejected the inestimable present of life and immortality which was offered to mankind by Jesus of Nazareth. His mild constancy in the midst of cruel and voluntary sufferings, his universal benevolence, and the sublime simplicity of his actions and character, were insufficient, in the opinion of those carnal men, to compensate for the want of fame, of empire, and of success; and whilst they refused to acknowledge his stupendous triumph over the powers of darkness and of the grave, they misrepresented, or they insulted, the equivocal birth, wandering life, and ignominious death, of the divine Author of Christianity.[13]

The personal guilt which every Christian had contracted, in thus preferring his private sentiment to the national religion, was aggravated in a very high degree by the number and union of the criminals. It is well known, and has been already observed, that Roman policy viewed with the utmost jealousy and distrust any association among its subjects; and that the privileges of private corporations, though formed for the most harmless or beneficial purposes, were bestowed with a very sparing hand.[14] The religious assemblies of the Christians, who had separated themselves from the public worship, appeared of a much less innocent nature: they were illegal in their principle, and in their consequences might become dangerous; nor were the emperors conscious that they violated the laws of justice, when, for the peace of society, they prohibited those secret and sometimes nocturnal meetings.[15] The pious disobedience of the Christians made their conduct, or perhaps their designs, appear in a much more serious and criminal light; and the Roman princes, who might perhaps have suffered themselves to be disarmed by a ready submission, deeming their honour concerned in the execution of their commands, sometimes attempted by rigorous punishments to subdue this independent spirit, which boldly acknowledged an authority superior to that of the magistrate. The extent and duration of this spiritual conspiracy seemed to render it every day more deserving of his animadversion. We have already seen that the active and successful zeal of the Christians had insensibly diffused them through every province and almost every city of the empire. The new converts seemed to renounce their family and country, that they might connect themselves in an indissoluble band of union with a peculiar society, which everywhere assumed a different character from the rest of mankind. Their gloomy and austere aspect, their abhorrence of the common business and pleasures of life, and their frequent predictions of impending calamities,[16] inspired the Pagans with the apprehension of some danger which would arise from the new sect, the more alarming as it was the more obscure. 'Whatever,' says Pliny, 'may be the principle of their conduct, their inflexible obstinacy appeared deserving of punishment.'[17]

The precautions with which the disciples of Christ performed the offices of religion were at first dictated by fear and necessity; but they were continued from choice. By imitating the awful secrecy which reigned in the Eleusinian mysteries, the Christians had flattered themselves that they should render their sacred institutions more respectable in the eyes of the Pagan world.[18] But the event, as it often happens to the operations of subtle policy, deceived their wishes and their expectations. It was concluded that they only concealed what they would have blushed to disclose. Their mistaken prudence afforded an opportunity for malice to invent, and for suspicious credulity to believe, the horrid tales which described the Christians as the most wicked of human kind, who practised in their dark recesses every abomination that a depraved fancy could suggest, and who solicited the favour of their unknown God by the sacrifice of every moral virtue. There were many who pretended to confess or to relate the ceremonies of this abhorred society. It was asserted, 'that a newborn infant, entirely covered over with flour, was presented, like some mystic symbol of initiation, to the knife of the proselyte, who unknowingly inflicted many a secret and mortal wound on the innocent victim of his error; that, as soon as the cruel deed was perpetrated, the sectaries drank up the blood, greedily tore asunder the quivering members, and pledged themselves to eternal secrecy, by a mutual consciousness of guilt. It was as confidently affirmed that this inhuman sacrifice was succeeded by a suitable entertainment, in which intemperance served as a provocative to brutal lust; till, at the appointed moment, the lights were suddenly extinguished, shame was banished, nature was forgotten; and, as accident might direct, the darkness of the night was polluted by the incestuous commerce of sisters and brothers, of sons and of mothers.'[19]

But the perusal of the ancient apologies was sufficient to remove even the slightest suspicion from the mind of a candid adversary. The Christians, with the intrepid security of innocence, appeal from the voice of rumour to the equity of the magistrates. They acknowledge that, if any proof can be produced of the crimes which calumny has imputed to them, they are worthy of the most severe punishment. They provoke the punishment, and they challenge the proof. At the same time they urge, with equal truth and propriety, that the charge is not less devoid of probability than it is destitute of evidence; they ask whether anyone can seriously believe that the pure and holy precepts of the Gospel, which so frequently restrain the use of the most lawful enjoyments, should inculcate the practice of the most abominable crimes; that a large society should resolve to dishonour itself in the eyes of its own members; and that a great number of persons of either sex, and every age and character, insensible to the fear of death or infamy, should consent to violate those principles which nature and education had imprinted most deeply in their minds.[20] Nothing, it should seem, could weaken the force or destroy the effect of so unanswerable a justification, unless it were the injudicious conduct of the apologists themselves, who betrayed the common cause of religion, to gratify their devout hatred to the domestic enemies of the church. It was sometimes faintly insinuated, and sometimes boldly asserted, that the same bloody sacrifices, and the same incestuous festivals, which were so falsely ascribed to the orthodox believers, were in reality celebrated by the Marcionites, by the Carpocratians, and by several other sects of the Gnostics, who, notwithstanding they might deviate into the paths of heresy, were still actuated by the sentiments of men, and still governed by the precepts of Christianity.[21] Accusations of a similar kind were retorted upon the church by the schismatics who had departed from its communion;[22] and it was confessed on all sides that the most scandalous licentiousness of manners prevailed among great numbers of those who affected the name of Christians. A Pagan magistrate, who possessed neither leisure nor abilities to discern the almost imperceptible line which divides the orthodox faith from heretical pravity, might easily have imagined that their mutual animosity had extorted the discovery of their common guilt. It was fortunate for the repose, or at least for the reputation, of the first Christians, that the magistrates sometimes proceeded with more temper and moderation than is usually consistent with religious zeal, and that they reported, as the impartial result of their judicial inquiry, that the sectaries who had deserted the established worship appeared to them sincere in their professions and blameless in their manners; however they might incur, by their absurd and excessive superstition, the censure of the laws.[23]

History, which undertakes to record the transactions of the past, for the instruction of future, ages, would ill deserve that honourable office, if she condescended to plead the cause of tyrants, or to justify the maxims of persecution. It must, however, be acknowledged that the conduct of the emperors who appeared the least favourable to the primitive church is by no means so criminal as that of modern sovereigns who have employed the arm of violence and terror against the religious opinions of any part of their subjects. From their reflections, or even from their own feelings, a Charles V or a Louis XIV might have acquired a just knowledge of the rights of conscience, of the obligation of faith, and of the innocence of error. But the princes and magistrates of ancient Rome were strangers to those principles which inspired and authorised the inflexible obstinacy of the Christians in the cause of truth, nor could they themselves discover in their own breasts any motive which would have prompted them to refuse a legal, and as it were a natural, submission to the sacred institutions of their country. The same reason which contributes to alleviate the guilt, must have tended to abate the rigour, of their persecutions. As they were actuated, not by the furious zeal of bigots, but by the temperate policy of legislators, contempt must often have relaxed, and humanity must frequently have suspended, the execution of those laws which they enacted against the humble and obscure followers of Christ. From the general view of their character and motives we might naturally conclude: I. That a considerable time elapsed before they considered the new sectaries as an object deserving of the attention of government. II. That, in the conviction of any of their subjects who were accused of so very singular a crime, they proceeded with caution and reluctance. III. That they were moderate in the use of punishments; and IV. That the afflicted church enjoyed many intervals of peace and tranquillity. Notwithstanding the careless indifference which the most copious and the most minute of the Pagan writers have shown to the affairs of the Christians,[24] it may still be in our power to confirm each of these probable suppositions by the evidence of authentic facts.

I.   By the wise dispensation of Providence, a mysterious veil was cast over the infancy of the church, which, till the faith of the Christians was matured and their numbers were multiplied, served to protect them not only from the malice, but even from the knowledge, of the Pagan world. The slow and gradual abolition of the Mosaic ceremonies afforded a safe and innocent disguise to the more early proselytes of the Gospel. As they were far the greater part of the race of Abraham, they were distinguished by the peculiar mark of circumcision, offered up their devotions in the Temple of Jerusalem till its final destruction, and received both the Law and the Prophets as the genuine inspirations of the Deity. The Gentile converts, who by a spiritual adoption had been associated to the hope of Israel, were likewise confounded under the garb and appearance of Jews,[25] and, as the Polytheists paid less regard to articles of faith than to the external worship, the new sect, which carefully concealed, or faintly announced, its future greatness and ambition, was permitted to shelter itself under the general toleration which was granted to an ancient and celebrated people in the Roman empire. It was not long, perhaps, before the Jews themselves, animated with a fiercer zeal and a more jealous faith, perceived the gradual separation of their Nazarene brethren from the doctrine of the synagogue; and they would gladly have extinguished the dangerous heresy in the blood of its adherents. But the decrees of heaven had already disarmed their malice; and, though they might sometimes exert the licentious privilege of sedition, they no longer possessed the administration of criminal justice; nor did they find it easy to infuse into the calm breast of a Roman magistrate the rancour of their own zeal and prejudice. The provincial governors declared themselves ready to listen to any accusation that might affect the public safety; but, as soon as they were informed that it was a question not of facts but of words, a dispute relating only to the interpretation of the Jewish laws and prophecies, they deemed it unworthy of the majesty of Rome seriously to discuss the obscure differences which might arise among a barbarous and superstitious people. The innocence of the first Christians was protected by ignorance and contempt; and the tribunal of the Pagan magistrate often proved their most assured refuge against the fury of the synagogue.[26] If, indeed, we were disposed to adopt the traditions of a too credulous antiquity, we might relate the distant peregrinations, the wonderful achievements, and the various deaths, of the twelve apostles; but a more accurate inquiry will induce us to doubt whether any of those persons who had been witnesses to the miracles of Christ were permitted, beyond the limits of Palestine, to seal with their blood the truth of their testimony.[27] From the ordinary term of human life, it may very naturally be presumed that most of them were deceased before the discontent of the Jews broke out into that furious war which was terminated only by the ruin of Jerusalem. During a long period, from the death of Christ to that memorable rebellion, we cannot discover any traces of Roman intolerance, unless they are to be found in the sudden, the transient, but the cruel persecution, which was exercised by Nero against the Christians of the capital, thirty-five years after the former, and only two years before the latter of those great events. The character of the philosophic historian,* to whom we are principally indebted for the knowledge of this singular transaction, would alone be sufficient to recommend it to our most attentive consideration.

In the tenth year of the reign of Nero, the capital of the empire was afflicted by a fire which raged beyond the memory or example of former ages.[28] The monuments of Grecian art and of Roman virtue, the trophies of the Punic and Gallic wars, the most holy temples, and the most splendid palaces were involved in one common destruction. Of the fourteen regions or quarters into which Rome was divided, four only subsisted entire, three were levelled with the ground, and the remaining seven, which had experienced the fury of the flames, displayed a melancholy prospect of ruin and desolation. The vigilance of government appears not to have neglected any of the precautions which might alleviate the sense of so dreadful a calamity. The Imperial gardens were thrown open to the distressed multitude, temporary buildings were erected for their accommodation, and a plentiful supply of corn and provisions was distributed at a very moderate price.[29] The most generous policy seemed to have dictated the edicts which regulated the disposition of the streets and the construction of private houses; and, as it usually happens in an age of prosperity, the conflagration of Rome, in the course of a few years, produced a new city, more regular and more beautiful than the former. But all the prudence and humanity affected by Nero on this occasion were insufficient to preserve him from the popular suspicion. Every crime might be imputed to the assassin of his wife and mother; nor could the prince who prostituted his person and dignity on the theatre be deemed incapable of the most extravagant folly. The voice of rumour accused the emperor as the incendiary of his own capital; and, as the most incredible stories are the best adapted to the genius* of an enraged people, it was gravely reported, and firmly believed, that Nero, enjoying the calamity which he had occasioned, amused himself with singing to his lyre the destruction of ancient Troy.[30] To divert a suspicion which the power of despotism was unable to suppress, the emperor resolved to substitute in his own place some fictitious criminals. 'With this view (continues Tacitus) he inflicted the most exquisite tortures on those men, who, under the vulgar appellation of Christians, were already branded with deserved infamy. They derived their name and origin from Christ, who, in the reign of Tiberius, had suffered death, by the sentence of the procurator Pontius Pilate.[31] For a while this dire superstition was checked; but it again burst forth, and not only spread itself over Judaea, the first seat of this mischievous sect, but was even introduced into Rome, the common asylum which receives and protects whatever is impure, whatever is atrocious. The confessions of those who were seized, discovered a great multitude of their accomplices, and they were all convicted, not so much for the crime of setting fire to the city, as for their hatred of human kind.[32] They died in torments, and their torments were embittered by insult and derision. Some were nailed on crosses; others sewn up in the skins of wild beasts, and exposed to the fury of dogs; others again, smeared over with combustible materials, were used as torches to illuminate the darkness of the night. The gardens of Nero were destined for the melancholy spectacle, which was accompanied with a horse race, and honoured with the presence of the emperor, who mingled with the populace in the dress and attitude of a charioteer. The guilt of the Christians deserved, indeed, the most exemplary punishment, but the public abhorrence was changed into commiseration, from the opinion that those unhappy wretches were sacrificed, not so much to the public welfare, as to the cruelty of a jealous tyrant.'[33] Those who survey, with a curious eye, the revolutions of mankind may observe that the gardens and circus of Nero on the Vatican, which were polluted with the blood of the first Christians, have been rendered still more famous by the triumph and by the abuse of the persecuted religion. On the same spot,[34] a temple, which far surpasses the ancient glories of the Capitol, has been since erected by the Christian Pontiffs, who, deriving their claim of universal dominion from an humble fisherman of Galilee, have succeeded to the throne of the Caesars, given laws to the barbarian conquerors of Rome, and extended their spiritual jurisdiction from the coast of the Baltic to the shores of the Pacific Ocean.

But it would be improper to dismiss this account of Nero's persecution, till we have made some observations, that may serve to remove the difficulties with which it is perplexed and to throw some light on the subsequent history of the church.

1. The most sceptical criticism is obliged to respect the truth of this extraordinary fact, and the integrity of this celebrated passage of Tacitus. The former is confirmed by the diligent and accurate Suetonius, who mentions the punishment which Nero inflicted on the Christians, a sect of men who had embraced a new and criminal superstition.[35] The latter may be proved by the consent of the most ancient manuscripts; by the inimitable character of the style of Tacitus; by his reputation, which guarded his text from the interpolations of pious fraud; and by the purport of his narration, which accused the first Christians of the most atrocious crimes, without insinuating that they possessed any miraculous or even magical powers above the rest of mankind.[36]

2. Notwithstanding it is probable that Tacitus was born some years before the fire of Rome,[37] he could derive only from reading and conversation the knowledge of an event which happened during his infancy. Before he gave himself to the public, he calmly waited till his genius had attained its full maturity, and he was more than forty years of age, when a grateful regard for the memory of the virtuous Agricola* extorted from him the most early of those historical compositions which will delight and instruct the most distant posterity. After making a trial of his strength in the life of Agricola and the description of Germany, he conceived, and at length executed, a more arduous work: the history of

Rome, in thirty books, from the fall of Nero to the accession of Nerva. The administration of Nerva introduced an age of justice and prosperity, which Tacitus had destined for the occupation of his old age;[38] but, when he took a nearer view of his subject, judging, perhaps, that it was a more honourable or a less invidious office to record the vices of past tyrants than to celebrate the virtues of a reigning monarch, he chose rather to relate, under the form of annals, the actions of the four immediate successors of Augustus. To collect, to dispose, and to adorn a series of fourscore years in an immortal work, every sentence of which is pregnant with the deepest observations and the most lively images, was an undertaking sufficient to exercise the genius of Tacitus himself during the greatest part of his life. In the last years of the reign of Trajan, whilst the victorious monarch extended the power of Rome beyond its ancient limits, the historian was describing, in the second and fourth books of his annals, the tyranny of Tiberius;[39] and the emperor Hadrian must have succeeded to the throne, before Tacitus, in the regular prosecution of his work, could relate the fire of the capital and the cruelty of Nero towards the unfortunate Christians. At the distance of sixty years, it was the duty of the annalist to adopt the narratives of contemporaries; but it was natural for the philosopher to indulge himself in the description of the origin, the progress, and the character of the new sect, not so much according to the knowledge or prejudices of the age of Nero, as according to those of the time of Hadrian.

3. Tacitus very frequently trusts to the curiosity or reflection of his readers to supply those intermediate circumstances and ideas which, in his extreme conciseness, he has thought proper to suppress. We may, therefore, presume to imagine some probable cause which could direct the cruelty of Nero against the Christians of Rome, whose obscurity, as well as innocence, should have shielded them from his indignation, and even from his notice. The Jews, who were numerous in the capital, and oppressed in their own country, were a much fitter object for the suspicions of the emperor and of the people; nor did it seem unlikely that a vanquished nation, who already discovered their abhorrence of the Roman yoke, might have recourse to the most atrocious means of gratifying their implacable revenge. But the Jews possessed very powerful advocates in the palace, and even in the heart of the tyrant; his wife and mistress, the beautiful Poppaea, and a favourite player of the race of Abraham, who had already employed their intercession in behalf of the obnoxious people.[40] In their room it was necessary to offer some other victims, and it might easily be suggested that, although the genuine followers of Moses were innocent of the fire of Rome, there had arisen among them a new and pernicious sect of Galilaeans, which was capable of the most horrid crimes. Under the appellation of Galilaeans, two distinctions of men were confounded, the most opposite to each other in their manners and principles: the disciples who had embraced the faith of

Jesus of Nazareth,[41] and the zealots who had followed the standard of Judas the Gaulonite.[42] The former were the friends, and the latter were the enemies, of human kind; and the only resemblance between them consisted in the same inflexible constancy which, in the defence of their cause, rendered them insensible of death and tortures. The followers of Judas, who impelled their countrymen into rebellion, were soon buried under the ruins of Jerusalem; whilst those of Jesus, known by the more celebrated name of Christians, diffused themselves over the Roman empire. How natural was it for Tacitus, in the time of Hadrian, to appropriate to the Christians the guilt and the sufferings which he might, with far greater truth and justice, have attributed to a sect whose odious memory was almost extinguished!

4. Whatever opinion may be entertained of this conjecture (for it is no more than a conjecture), it is evident that the effect, as well as the cause, of Nero's persecution were confined to the walls of Rome;[43] that the religious tenets of the Galilaeans, or Christians, were never made a subject of punishment or even of inquiry; and that, as the idea of their sufferings was, for a long time, connected with the idea of cruelty and injustice, the moderation of succeeding princes inclined them to spare a sect, oppressed by a tyrant whose rage had been usually directed against virtue and innocence.

It is somewhat remarkable that the flames of war consumed almost at the same time the temple of Jerusalem and the Capitol of Rome;[44] and it appears no less singular that the tribute which devotion had destined to the former should have been converted by the power of an assaulting victor to restore and adorn the splendour of the latter.[45] The emperors levied a general capitation tax on the Jewish people; and, although the sum assessed on the head of each individual was inconsiderable, the use for which it was designed, and the severity with which it was exacted, were considered as an intolerable grievance.[46] Since the officers of the revenue extended their unjust claim to many persons who were strangers to the blood or religion of the Jews, it was impossible that the Christians, who had so often sheltered themselves under the shade of the synagogue, should now escape this rapacious persecution. Anxious as they were to avoid the slightest infection of idolatry, their conscience forbade them to contribute to the honour of that daemon who had assumed the character of the Capitoline Jupiter. As a very numerous, though declining, party among the Christians still adhered to the law of Moses, their efforts to dissemble their Jewish origin were detected by the decisive test of circumcision,[47] nor were the Roman magistrates at leisure to inquire into the difference of their religious tenets. Among the Christians who were brought before the tribunal of the emperor, or, as it seems more probable, before that of the procurator of Judaea, two persons are said to have appeared, distinguished by their extraction, which was more truly noble than that of the greatest monarchs. These were the grandsons of St Jude the apostle, who himself was the brother of Jesus Christ.[48] Their natural pretensions to the throne of David might perhaps attract the respect of the people, and excite the jealousy of the governor; but the meanness of their garb and the simplicity of their answers soon convinced him that they were neither desirous nor capable of disturbing the peace of the Roman empire. They frankly confessed their royal origin and their near relation to the Messiah; but they disclaimed any temporal views, and professed that his kingdom, which they devoutly expected, was purely of a spiritual and angelic nature. When they were examined concerning their fortune and occupation, they showed their hands hardened with daily labour, and declared that they derived their whole subsistence from the cultivation of a farm near the village of Cocaba, of the extent of about twenty-four English acres,[49] and of the value of nine thousand drachms, or three hundred pounds sterling. The grandsons of St Jude were dismissed with compassion and contempt.[50]

But, although the obscurity of the house of David might protect them from the suspicions of a tyrant, the present greatness of his own family alarmed the pusillanimous temper of Domitian, which could only be appeased by the blood of those Romans whom he either feared, or hated, or esteemed. Of the two sons of his uncle Flavius Sabinus,[51] the elder was soon convicted of treasonable intentions, and the younger, who bore the name of Flavius Clemens, was indebted for his safety to his want of courage and ability.[52] The emperor, for a long time, distinguished so harmless a kinsman by his favour and protection, bestowed on him his own niece Domitilla, adopted the children of that marriage to the hope of the succession, and invested their father with the honours of the consulship. But he had scarcely finished the term of his annual magistracy, when, on a slight pretence, he was condemned and executed; Domitilla was banished to a desolate island on the coast of Campania;[53] and sentences either of death or of confiscation were pronounced against a great number of persons who were involved in the same accusation. The guilt imputed to their charge was that of *Atheism* and *Jewish manners*:[54] a singular association of ideas, which cannot with any propriety be applied except to the Christians, as they were obscurely and imperfectly viewed by the magistrates and by the writers of that period. On the strength of so probable an interpretation, and too eagerly admitting the suspicions of a tyrant as an evidence of their honourable crime, the church has placed both Clemens and Domitilla among its first martyrs, and has branded the cruelty of Domitian with the name of the second persecution. But this persecution (if it deserves that epithet) was of no long duration. A few months after the death of Clemens and the banishment of Domitilla, Stephen, a freedman belonging to the latter, who had enjoyed the favour, but who had not surely embraced the faith, of his mistress, assassinated the emperor in his palace.[55] The memory of Domitian was condemned by the senate; his acts were rescinded; his exiles recalled; and under the gentle administration of Nerva, while the innocent were restored to their rank and fortunes, even the most guilty either obtained pardon or escaped punishment.[56]

II.   About ten years afterwards, under the reign of Trajan, the younger Pliny was entrusted by his friend and master with the government of Bithynia and Pontus. He soon found himself at a loss to determine by what rule of justice or of law he should direct his conduct in the execution of an office the most repugnant to his humanity. Pliny had never assisted at any judicial proceedings against the Christians, with whose name alone he seems to be acquainted; and he was totally uninformed with regard to the nature of their guilt, the method of their conviction, and the degree of their punishment. In this perplexity he had recourse to his usual expedient, of submitting to the wisdom of Trajan an impartial and, in some respects, a favourable account of the new superstition, requesting the emperor that he would condescend to resolve his doubts and to instruct his ignorance.[57] The life of Pliny had been employed in the acquisition of learning, and in the business of the world. Since the age of nineteen he had pleaded with distinction in the tribunals of Rome,[58] filled a place in the senate, had been invested with the honours of the consulship, and had formed very numerous connections with every order of men, both in Italy and in the provinces. From *his* ignorance, therefore, we may derive some useful information. We may assure ourselves that when he accepted the government of Bithynia there were no general laws or decrees of the senate in force against the Christians; that neither Trajan nor any of his virtuous predecessors, whose edicts were received into the civil and criminal jurisprudence, had publicly declared their intentions concerning the new sect; and that, whatever proceedings had been carried on against the Christians, there were none of sufficient weight and authority to establish a precedent for the conduct of a Roman magistrate.

The answer of Trajan, to which the Christians of the succeeding age have frequently appealed, discovers as much regard for justice and humanity as could be reconciled with his mistaken notions of religious policy.[59] Instead of displaying the implacable zeal of an inquisitor, anxious to discover the most minute particles of heresy and exulting in the number of his victims, the emperor expresses much more solicitude to protect the security of the innocent than to prevent the escape of the guilty. He acknowledges the difficulty of fixing any general plan; but he lays down two salutary rules, which often accorded relief and support to the distressed Christians. Though he directs the magistrates to punish such persons as are legally convicted, he prohibits them, with a very humane inconsistency, from making any inquiries concerning the supposed criminals. Nor was the magistrate allowed to proceed on every kind of information. Anonymous charges the emperor rejects, as too repugnant to the equity of his government; and he strictly requires, for the conviction of those to whom the guilt of Christianity is imputed, the positive evidence of a fair and open accuser. It is likewise probable that the persons who assumed so invidious an office were obliged to declare the grounds of their suspicions, to specify (both in respect to time and place) the secret assemblies which their Christian adversary had frequented, and to disclose a great number of circumstances which were concealed with the most vigilant jealousy from the eye of the profane. If they succeeded in their prosecution, they were exposed to the resentment of a considerable and active party, to the censure of the more liberal portion of mankind, and to the ignominy which, in every age and country, has attended the character of an informer. If, on the contrary, they failed in their proofs, they incurred the severe, and perhaps capital, penalty which, according to a law published by the emperor Hadrian, was inflicted on those who falsely attributed to their fellow-citizens the crime of Christianity. The violence of personal or superstitious animosity might sometimes prevail over the most natural apprehensions of disgrace and danger; but it cannot surely be imagined that accusations of so unpromising an appearance were either lightly or frequently undertaken by the Pagan subjects of the Roman empire.[60]

The expedient which was employed to elude the prudence of the laws affords a sufficient proof how effectually they disappointed the mischievous designs of private malice or superstitious zeal. In a large and tumultuous assembly, the restraints of fear and shame, so forcible on the minds of individuals, are deprived of the greatest part of their influence. The pious Christian, as he was desirous to obtain or to escape the glory of martyrdom, expected, either with impatience or with terror, the stated returns of the public games and festivals. On those occasions, the inhabitants of the great cities of the empire were collected in the circus or the theatre, where every circumstance of the place, as well as of the ceremony, contributed to kindle their devotion and to extinguish their humanity. Whilst the numerous spectators, crowned with garlands, perfumed with incense, purified with the blood of victims, and surrounded with the altars and statues of their tutelar deities, resigned themselves to the enjoyment of pleasures which they considered as an essential part of their religious worship; they recollected that the Christians alone abhorred the gods of mankind, and by their absence and melancholy on these solemn festivals seemed to insult or to lament the public felicity. If the empire had been afflicted by any recent calamity, by a plague, a famine, or an unsuccessful war; if the Tiber had, or if the Nile had not, risen beyond its banks; if the earth had shaken, or if the temperate order of the seasons had been interrupted, the superstitious Pagans were convinced that the crimes and the impiety of the Christians, who were spared by the excessive lenity of the government, had at length provoked the Divine Justice. It was not among a licentious and exasperated populace that the forms of legal proceedings could be observed; it was not in an amphitheatre, stained with the blood of wild beasts and gladiators, that the voice of compassion could be heard. The impatient clamours of the multitude denounced the Christians as the enemies of gods and men, doomed them to the severest tortures, and, venturing to accuse by name some of the most distinguished of the new sectaries, required, with irresistible vehemence, that they should be instantly apprehended and cast to the lions.[61] The provincial governors and magistrates who presided in the public spectacles were usually inclined to gratify the inclinations, and to appease the rage, of the people by the sacrifice of a few obnoxious victims. But the wisdom of the emperors protected the church from the danger of these tumultuous clamours and irregular accusations, which they justly censured as repugnant both to the firmness and to the equity of their administration. The edicts of Hadrian and of Antoninus Pius expressly declared that the voice of the multitude should never be admitted as legal evidence to convict or to punish those unfortunate persons who had embraced the enthusiasm of the Christians.[62]

III.   Punishment was not the inevitable consequence of conviction, and the Christians, whose guilt was the most clearly proved by the testimony of witnesses, or even by their voluntary confession, still retained in their own power the alternative of life or death. It was not so much the past offence, as the actual resistance, which excited the indignation of the magistrate. He was persuaded that he offered them an easy pardon, since, if they consented to cast a few grains of incense upon the altar, they were dismissed from the tribunal in safety and with applause. It was esteemed the duty of a humane judge to endeavour to reclaim, rather than to punish, those deluded enthusiasts. Varying his tone according to the age, the sex, or the situation of the prisoners, he frequently condescended to set before their eyes every circumstance which could render life more pleasing, or death more terrible; and to solicit, nay, to entreat them, that they would show some compassion to themselves, to their families, and to their friends.[63] If threats and persuasions proved ineffectual, he had often recourse to violence; the scourge and the rack were called in to supply the deficiency of argument, and every art of cruelty was employed to subdue such inflexible and, as it appeared to the Pagans, such criminal obstinacy. The ancient apologists of Christianity have censured, with equal truth and severity, the irregular conduct of their persecutors, who, contrary to every principle of judicial proceeding, admitted the use of torture, in order to obtain not a confession but a denial of the crime which was the object of their inquiry.[64] The monks of succeeding ages, who, in their peaceful solitudes, entertained themselves with diversifying the death and sufferings of the primitive martyrs, have frequently invented torments of a much more refined and ingenious nature. In particular, it has pleased them to suppose that the zeal of the Roman magistrates, disdaining every consideration of moral virtue or public decency, endeavoured to seduce those whom they were unable to vanquish, and that, by their orders, the most brutal violence was offered to those whom they found it impossible to seduce. It is related that pious females, who were prepared to despise death, were sometimes condemned to a more severe trial, and called upon to determine whether they set a higher value on their religion or on their chastity. The youths to whose licentious embraces they were abandoned received a solemn exhortation from the judge to exert their most strenuous efforts to maintain the honour of Venus against the impious virgin who refused to burn incense on her altars. Their violence, however, was commonly disappointed; and the seasonable interposition of some miraculous power preserved the chaste spouses of Christ from the dishonour even of an involuntary defeat. We should not, indeed, neglect to remark that the more ancient, as well as authentic, memorials of the church are seldom polluted with these extravagant and indecent fictions.[65]

The total disregard of truth and probability in the representation of these primitive martyrdoms was occasioned by a very natural mistake. The ecclesiastical writers of the fourth or fifth centuries ascribed to the magistrates of Rome the same degree of implacable and unrelenting zeal which filled their own breasts against the heretics or the idolaters of their own times. It is not improbable that some of those persons who were raised to the dignities of the empire might have imbibed the prejudices of the populace, and that the cruel disposition of others might occasionally be stimulated by motives of avarice or of personal resentment.[66] But it is certain, and we may appeal to the grateful confessions of the first Christians, that the greatest part of those magistrates who exercised in the provinces the authority of the emperor, or of the senate, and to whose hands alone the jurisdiction of life and death was entrusted, behaved like men of polished manners and liberal educations, who respected the rules of justice, and who were conversant with the precepts of philosophy. They frequently declined the odious task of persecution, dismissed the charge with contempt, or suggested to the accused Christian some legal evasion by which he might elude the severity of the laws.[67] Whenever they were invested with a discretionary power,[68] they used it much less for the oppression than for the relief and benefit of the afflicted church. They were far from condemning all the Christians who were accused before their tribunal, and very far from punishing with death all those who were convicted of an obstinate adherence to the new superstition. Contenting themselves, for the most part, with the milder chastisements of imprisonment, exile, or slavery in the mines,[69] they left the unhappy victims of their justice some reason to hope that a prosperous event, the accession, the marriage, or the triumph of an emperor, might speedily restore them, by a general pardon, to their former state. The martyrs, devoted* to immediate execution by the Roman magistrates, appear to have been selected from the most opposite extremes. They were either bishops and presbyters, the persons the most distinguished among the Christians by their rank and influence, and whose example might strike terror into the whole sect;[70] or else they were the meanest and most abject among them, particularly those of the servile condition, whose lives were esteemed of little value, and whose sufferings were viewed by the ancients with too careless an indifference.[71] The learned Origen, who, from his experience as well as reading, was intimately acquainted with the history of the Christians, declares, in the most express terms, that the number of martyrs was very inconsiderable.[72] His authority would alone be sufficient to annihilate that formidable army of martyrs whose relics, drawn for the most part from the catacombs of Rome, have replenished so many churches,[73] and whose marvellous achievements have been the subject of so many volumes of holy romance.[74] But the general assertion of Origen may be explained and confirmed by the particular testimony of his friend Dionysius, who, in the immense city of Alexandria, and under the rigorous persecution of Decius, reckons only ten men and seven women who suffered for the profession of the Christian name.[75]

During the same period of persecution, the zealous, the eloquent, the ambitious Cyprian, governed the church, not only of Carthage, but even of Africa. He possessed every quality which could engage the reverence of the faithful or provoke the suspicions and resentment of the Pagan magistrates. His character as well as his station seemed to mark out that holy prelate as the most distinguished object of envy and of danger.[76] The experience, however, of the life of Cyprian is sufficient to prove that our fancy has exaggerated the perilous situation of a Christian bishop; and that the dangers to which he was exposed were less imminent than those which temporal ambition is always prepared to encounter in the pursuit of honours. Four Roman emperors, with their families, their favourites, and their adherents, perished by the sword in the space of ten years, during which the bishop of Carthage guided, by his authority and eloquence, the counsels of the African church. It was only in the third year of his administration that he had reason, during a few months, to apprehend the severe edicts of Decius, the vigilance of the magistrate, and the clamours of the multitude, who loudly demanded that Cyprian, the leader of the Christians, should be thrown to the lions. Prudence suggested the necessity of a temporary retreat, and the voice of prudence was obeyed. He withdrew himself into an obscure solitude, from whence he could maintain a constant correspondence with the clergy and people of Carthage; and, concealing himself till the tempest was past, he preserved his life, without relinquishing either his power or his reputation. His extreme caution did not, however, escape the censure of the more rigid Christians who lamented, or the reproaches of his personal enemies who insulted, a conduct which they considered as a pusillanimous and criminal desertion of the most sacred duty.[77] The propriety of reserving himself for the future exigencies of the church, the example of several holy bishops,[78] and the divine admonitions which, as he declares himself, he frequently received in visions and ecstasies, were the reasons alleged in his justification.[79] But his best apology may be found in the cheerful resolution with which, about eight years afterwards, he suffered death in the cause of religion. The authentic history of his martyrdom has been recorded with unusual candour and impartiality. A short abstract, therefore, of its most important circumstances will convey the clearest information of the spirit, and of the forms, of the Roman persecutions.[80]

When Valerian was consul for the third, and Gallienus for the fourth, time, Paternus, proconsul of Africa, summoned Cyprian to appear in his private council-chamber. He there acquainted him with the Imperial mandate which he had just received,[81] that those who had abandoned the Roman religion should immediately return to the practice of the ceremonies of their ancestors. Cyprian replied without hesitation that he was a Christian and a bishop, devoted to the worship of the true and only Deity, to whom he offered up his daily supplications for the safety and prosperity of the two emperors, his lawful sovereigns. With modest confidence he pleaded the privilege of a citizen, in refusing to give any answer to some invidious and, indeed, illegal questions which the proconsul had proposed. A sentence of banishment was pronounced as the penalty of Cyprian's disobedience; and he was conducted, without delay, to Curubis, a free and maritime city of Zeugitana, in a pleasant situation, a fertile territory, and at the distance of about forty miles from Carthage.[82] The exiled bishop enjoyed the conveniences of life and the consciousness of virtue. His reputation was diffused over Africa and Italy; an account of his behaviour was published for the edification of the Christian world;[83] and his solitude was frequently interrupted by the letters, the visits, and the congratulations of the faithful. On the arrival of a new proconsul in the province, the fortune of Cyprian appeared for some time to wear a still more favourable aspect. He was recalled from banishment; and, though not yet permitted to return to Carthage, his own gardens in the neighbourhood of the capital were assigned for the place of his residence.[84]

At length, exactly one year[85] after Cyprian was first apprehended, Galerius Maximus, proconsul of Africa, received the Imperial warrant for the execution of the Christian teachers. The bishop of Carthage was sensible that he should be singled out for one of the first victims; and the frailty of nature tempted him to withdraw himself, by a secret flight, from the danger and the honour of martyrdom; but, soon recovering that fortitude which his character required, he returned to his gardens, and patiently expected the ministers of death. Two officers of rank, who were entrusted with that commission, placed Cyprian between them in a chariot; and, as the proconsul was not then at leisure, they conducted him, not to a prison, but to a private house in Carthage, which belonged to one of them. An elegant supper was provided for the entertainment of the bishop, and his Christian friends were permitted for the last time to enjoy his society, whilst the streets were filled with a multitude of the faithful, anxious and alarmed at the approaching fate of their spiritual father.[86] In the morning he appeared before the tribunal of the proconsul, who, after informing himself of the name and situation of Cyprian, commanded him to offer sacrifice, and pressed him to reflect on the consequences of his disobedience. The refusal of Cyprian was firm and decisive; and the magistrate, when he had taken the opinion of his council, pronounced with some reluctance the sentence of death. It was conceived in the following terms: 'That Thascius Cyprianus should be immediately beheaded, as the enemy of the gods of Rome, and as the chief and ringleader of a criminal association, which he had seduced into an impious resistance against the laws of the most holy emperors, Valerian and Gallienus.'[87] The manner of his execution was the mildest and least painful that could be inflicted on a person convicted of any capital offence; nor was the use of torture admitted to obtain from the bishop of Carthage either the recantation of his principles or the discovery of his accomplices.

As soon as the sentence was proclaimed, a general cry of 'We will die with him' arose at once among the listening multitude of Christians who waited before the palace gates. The generous effusions of their zeal and affection were neither serviceable to Cyprian nor dangerous to themselves. He was led away under a guard of tribunes and centurions, without resistance and without insult, to the place of his execution, a spacious and level plain near the city, which was already filled with great numbers of spectators. His faithful presbyters and deacons were permitted to accompany their holy bishop. They assisted him in laying aside his upper garment, spread linen on the ground to catch the precious relics of his blood, and received his orders to bestow five-and-twenty pieces of gold on the executioner. The martyr then covered his face with his hands, and at one blow his head was separated from his body. His corpse remained during some hours exposed to the curiosity of the Gentiles; but in the night it was removed, and transported in a triumphal procession and with a splendid illumination to the burial place of the Christians. The funeral of Cyprian was publicly celebrated without receiving any interruption from the Roman magistrates; and those among the faithful who had performed the last offices to his person and his memory were secure from the danger of inquiry or of punishment. It is remarkable that of so great a multitude of bishops in the province of Africa, Cyprian was the first who was esteemed worthy to obtain the crown of martyrdom.[88]

It was in the choice of Cyprian either to die a martyr or to live an apostate, but on that choice depended the alternative of honour or infamy. Could we suppose that the bishop of Carthage had employed the profession of the Christian faith only as the instrument of his avarice or ambition, it was still incumbent on him to support the character which he had assumed;[89] and, if he possessed the smallest degree of manly fortitude, rather to expose himself to the most cruel tortures than by a single act to exchange the reputation of a whole life for the abhorrence of his Christian brethren and the contempt of the Gentile world. But, if the zeal of Cyprian was supported by the sincere conviction of the truth of those doctrines which he preached, the crown of martyrdom must have appeared to him as an object of desire rather than of terror. It is not easy to extract any distinct ideas from the vague though eloquent declamations of the Fathers or to ascertain the degree of immortal glory and happiness which they confidently promised to those who were so fortunate as to shed their blood in the cause of religion.[90] They inculcated with becoming diligence that the fire of martyrdom supplied every defect and expiated every sin; that, while the souls of ordinary Christians were obliged to pass through a slow and painful purification, the triumphant sufferers entered into the immediate fruition of eternal bliss, where, in the society of the patriarchs, the apostles, and the prophets, they reigned with Christ, and acted as his assessors in the universal judgment of mankind. The assurance of a lasting reputation upon earth, a motive so congenial to the vanity of human nature, often served to animate the courage of the martyrs. The honours which Rome or Athens bestowed on those citizens who had fallen in the cause of their country were cold and unmeaning demonstrations of respect, when compared with the ardent gratitude and devotion which the primitive church expressed towards the victorious champions of the faith. The annual commemoration of their virtues and sufferings was observed as a sacred ceremony, and at length terminated in religious worship. Among the Christians who had publicly confessed their religious principles, those who (as it very frequently happened) had been dismissed from the tribunal or the prisons of the Pagan magistrates obtained such honours as were justly due to their imperfect martyrdom and their generous resolution. The most pious females courted the permission of imprinting kisses on the fetters which they had worn and on the wounds which they had received. Their persons were esteemed holy, their decisions were admitted with deference, and they too often abused, by their spiritual pride and licentious manners, the pre-eminence which their zeal and intrepidity had acquired.[91] Distinctions like these, whilst they display the exalted merit, betray the inconsiderable number, of those who suffered and of those who died for the profession of Christianity.

The sober discretion of the present age will more readily censure than admire, but can more easily admire than imitate, the fervour of the first Christians; who, according to the lively expression of Sulpicius Severus, desired martyrdom with more eagerness than his own contemporaries solicited a bishopric.[92] The epistles which Ignatius composed as he was carried in chains through the cities of Asia breathe sentiments the most repugnant to the ordinary feelings of human nature. He earnestly beseeches the Romans that, when he should be exposed in the amphitheatre, they would not, by their kind but unseasonable intercession, deprive him of the crown of glory; and he declares his resolution to provoke and irritate the wild beasts which might be employed as the instruments of his death.[93] Some stories are related of the courage of martyrs who actually performed what Ignatius had intended; who exasperated the fury of the lions, pressed the executioner to hasten his office, cheerfully leaped into the fires which were kindled to consume them, and discovered a sensation of joy and pleasure in the midst of the most exquisite tortures. Several examples have been preserved of a zeal impatient of those restraints which the emperors had provided for the security of the church. The Christians sometimes supplied by their voluntary declaration the want of an accuser, rudely disturbed the public service of Paganism,[94] and, rushing in crowds round the tribunal of the magistrates, called upon them to pronounce and to inflict the sentence of the law. The behaviour of the Christians was too remarkable to escape the notice of the ancient philosophers; but they seem to have considered it with much less admiration than astonishment. Incapable of conceiving the motives which sometimes transported the fortitude of believers beyond the bounds of prudence or reason, they treated such an eagerness to die as the strange result of obstinate despair, of stupid insensibility, or of superstitious frenzy.[95] 'Unhappy men!' exclaimed the proconsul Antoninus to the Christians of Asia; 'unhappy men! if you are thus weary of your lives, is it so difficult for you to find ropes and precipices?'[96] He was extremely cautious (as it is observed by a learned and pious historian) of punishing men who had found no accusers but themselves, the Imperial laws not having made any provision for so unexpected a case; condemning, therefore, a few as a warning to their brethren, he dismissed the multitude with indignation and contempt.[97] Notwithstanding this real or affected disdain, the intrepid constancy of the faithful was productive of more salutary effects on those minds which nature or grace had disposed for the easy reception of religious truth. On these melancholy occasions, there were many among the Gentiles who pitied, who admired, and who were converted. The generous enthusiasm was communicated from the sufferer to the spectators; and the blood of martyrs, according to a well known observation, became the seed of the church.

But, although devotion had raised, and eloquence continued to inflame, this fever of the mind, it insensibly gave way to the more natural hopes and fears of the human heart, to the love of life, the apprehension of pain, and the horror of dissolution. The more prudent rulers of the church found themselves obliged to restrain the indiscreet ardour of their followers, and to distrust a constancy which too often abandoned them in the hour of trial.[98] As the lives of the faithful became less mortified and austere, they were every day less ambitious of the honours of martyrdom; and the soldiers of Christ, instead of distinguishing themselves by voluntary deeds of heroism, frequently deserted their post, and fled in confusion before the enemy whom it was their duty to resist. There were three methods, however, of escaping the flames of persecution, which were not attended with an equal degree of guilt: the first, indeed, was generally allowed to be innocent; the second was of a doubtful, or at least of a venial, nature; but the third implied a direct and criminal apostasy from the Christian faith.

1. A modern inquisitor would hear with surprise that, whenever an information was given to a Roman magistrate of any person within his jurisdiction who had embraced the sect of the Christians, the charge was communicated to the party accused, and that a convenient time was allowed him to settle his domestic concerns and to prepare an answer to the crime which was imputed to him.[99] If he entertained any doubt of his own constancy, such a delay afforded him the opportunity of preserving his life and honour by flight, of withdrawing himself into some obscure retirement or some distant province, and of patiently expecting the return of peace and security. A measure so consonant to reason was soon authorised by the advice and example of the most holy prelates, and seems to have been censured by few, except by the Montanists, who deviated into heresy by their strict and obstinate adherence to the rigour of ancient discipline.[100] 2. The provincial governors, whose zeal was less prevalent than their avarice, had countenanced the practice of selling certificates (or libels as they were called), which attested that the persons therein mentioned had complied with the laws and sacrificed to the Roman deities. By producing these false declarations, the opulent and timid Christians were enabled to silence the malice of an informer and to reconcile, in some measure, their safety with their religion. A slight penance atoned for this profane dissimulation.[101] 3. In every persecution there were great numbers of unworthy Christians who publicly disowned or renounced the faith which they had professed; and who confirmed the sincerity of their abjuration by the legal acts of burning incense or of offering sacrifices. Some of these apostates had yielded on the first menace or exhortation of the magistrate; whilst the patience of others had been subdued by the length and repetition of tortures. The affrighted countenances of some betrayed their inward remorse, while others advanced, with confidence and alacrity, to the altars of the gods.[102] But the disguise which fear had imposed subsisted no longer than the present danger. As soon as the severity of the persecution was abated, the doors of the churches were assailed by the returning multitude of penitents, who detested their idolatrous submission, and who solicited, with equal ardour, but with curious success, their readmission into the society of Christians.[103]

IV. Notwithstanding the general rules established for the conviction and punishment of the Christians, the fate of those sectaries, in an extensive and arbitrary government, must still, in a great measure, have depended on their own behaviour, the circumstances of the times, and the temper of their supreme as well as subordinate rulers. Zeal might sometimes provoke, and prudence might sometimes avert or assuage, the superstitious fury of the Pagans. A variety of motives might dispose the provincial governors either to enforce or to relax the execution of the laws; and of these motives the most forcible was their regard not only for the public edicts, but for the secret intentions of the emperor, a glance from whose eye was sufficient to kindle or to extinguish the flames of persecution. As often as any occasional severities were exercised in the different parts of the empire, the primitive Christians lamented and perhaps magnified their own sufferings; but the celebrated number of *ten* persecutions has been determined by the ecclesiastical writers of the fifth century, who possessed a more distinct view of the prosperous or adverse fortunes of the church, from the age of Nero to that of Diocletian. The ingenious parallels of the *ten* plagues of Egypt and of the *ten* horns of the Apocalypse first suggested this calculation to their minds; and in their application of the faith of prophecy to the truth of history they were careful to select these reigns which were indeed the most hostile to the Christian cause.[104] But these transient persecutions served only to revive the zeal, and to restore the discipline, of the faithful: and the moments of extraordinary rigour were compensated by much longer intervals of peace and security. The indifference of some princes and the indulgence of others permitted the Christians to enjoy, though not perhaps a legal, yet an actual and public, toleration of their religion.

The apology of Tertullian contains two very ancient, very singular, but at the same time very suspicious, instances of Imperial clemency; the edicts published by Tiberius and by Marcus Antoninus, and designed not only to protect the innocence of the Christians, but even to proclaim those stupendous miracles which had attested the truth of their doctrine. The first of these examples is attended with some difficulties which might perplex the sceptical mind.[105] We are required to believe *that* Pontius Pilate informed the emperor of the unjust sentence of death which he had pronounced against an innocent, and, as it appeared, a divine, person; and that, without acquiring the merit, he exposed himself to the danger, of martyrdom; *that* Tiberius, who avowed his contempt for all religion, immediately conceived the design of placing the Jewish Messiah among the gods of Rome; *that* his servile senate ventured to disobey the commands of their master; *that* Tiberius, instead of resenting their refusal, contented himself with protecting the Christians from the severity of the laws, many years before such laws were enacted, or before the church had assumed any distinct name or existence; and lastly, *that* the memory of this extraordinary transaction was preserved in the most public and authentic records, which escaped the knowledge of the historians of Greece and Rome, and were only visible to the eyes of an African Christian, who composed his apology one hundred and sixty years after the death of Tiberius. The edict of Marcus Antoninus is supposed to have been the effect of his devotion and gratitude for the miraculous deliverance which he had obtained in the Marcomannic war. The distress of the legions, the seasonable tempest of rain and hail, of thunder and lightning, and the dismay and defeat of the barbarians, have been celebrated by the eloquence of several Pagan writers. If there were any Christians in that army, it was natural that they should ascribe some merit to the fervent prayers which, in the moment of danger, they had offered up for their own and the public safety. But we are still assured by monuments of brass and marble, by the Imperial medals, and by the Antonine column, that neither the prince nor the people entertained any sense of this signal obligation, since they unanimously attribute their deliverance to the providence of Jupiter and to the interposition of Mercury. During the whole course of his reign, Marcus despised the Christians as a philosopher, and punished them as a sovereign.[106]

By a singular fatality, the hardships which they had endured under the government of a virtuous prince immediately ceased on the accession of a tyrant, and, as none except themselves had experienced the injustices of Marcus, so they alone were protected by the lenity of Commodus. The celebrated Marcia, the most favoured of his concubines, and who at length contrived the murder of her Imperial lover, entertained a singular affection for the oppressed church; and, though it was impossible that she could reconcile the practice of vice with the precepts of the Gospel, she might hope to atone for the frailties of her sex and profession, by declaring herself the patroness of the Christians.[107] Under the gracious protection of Marcia, they passed in safety the thirteen years of a cruel tyranny; and, when the empire was established in the house of Severus, they formed a domestic but more honourable connection with the new court. The emperor was persuaded that, in a dangerous sickness, he had derived some benefit, either spiritual or physical, from the holy oil with which one of his slaves had anointed him. He always treated with peculiar distinction several persons of both sexes who had embraced the new religion. The nurse as well as the preceptor of Caracalla were Christians; and, if that young prince ever betrayed a sentiment of humanity, it was occasioned by an incident which, however trifling, bore some relation to the cause of Christianity.[108] Under the reign of Severus, the fury of the populace was checked; the rigour of ancient laws was for some time suspended; and the provincial governors were satisfied with receiving an annual present from the churches within their jurisdiction, as the price, or as the reward, of their moderation.[109] The controversy concerning the precise time of the celebration of Easter armed the bishops of Asia and Italy against each other, and was considered as the most important business of this period of leisure and tranquillity.[110] Nor was the peace of the church interrupted till the increasing numbers of proselytes seem at length to have attracted the attention, and to have alienated the mind, of Severus. With the design of restraining the progress of Christianity, he published an edict which, though it was designed to affect only the new converts, could not be carried into strict execution without exposing to danger and punishment the most zealous of their teachers and missionaries. In this mitigated persecution, we may still discover the indulgent spirit of Rome and of Polytheism, which so readily admitted every excuse in favour of those who practised the religious ceremonies of their fathers.[111]

But the laws which Severus had enacted soon expired with the authority of that emperor; and the Christians, after this accidental tempest, enjoyed a calm of thirty-eight years.[112] Till this period they had usually held their assemblies in private houses and sequestered places. They were now permitted to erect and consecrate convenient edifices for the purpose of religious worship;[113] to purchase lands, even at Rome itself, for the use of the community; and to conduct the elections of their ecclesiastical ministers in so public, but at the same time in so exemplary, a manner as to deserve the respectful attention of the Gentiles.[114] This long repose of the church was accompanied with dignity. The reigns of those princes who derived their extraction from the Asiatic provinces proved the most favourable to the Christians; the eminent persons of the sect, instead of being reduced to implore the protection of a slave or concubine, were admitted into the palace in the honourable characters of priests and philosophers; and their mysterious doctrines, which were already diffused among the people, insensibly attracted the curiosity of their sovereign. When the empress Mammaea passed through Antioch, she expressed a desire of conversing with the celebrated Origen, the fame of whose piety and learning was spread over the East. Origen obeyed so flattering an invitation, and, though he could not expect to succeed in the conversion of an artful and ambitious woman, she listened with pleasure to his eloquent exhortations, and honourably dismissed him to his retirement in Palestine.[115] The sentiments of Mammaea were adopted by her son Alexander, and the philosophic devotion of that emperor was marked by a singular but injudicious regard for the Christian religion. In his domestic chapel he placed the statues of Abraham, of Orpheus, of Apollonius, and of Christ, as an honour justly due to those respectable sages who had instructed mankind in the various modes of addressing their homage to the supreme and universal deity.[116] A purer faith, as well as worship, was openly professed and practised among his household. Bishops, perhaps for the first time, were seen at court; and after the death of Alexander, when the inhuman Maximin discharged his fury on the favourites and servants of his unfortunate benefactor, a great number of Christians, of every rank, and of both sexes, were involved in the promiscuous massacre, which, on their account, has improperly received the name of Persecution.[117]

Notwithstanding the cruel disposition of Maximin, the effects of his resentment against the Christians were of a very local and temporary nature, and the pious Origen, who had been proscribed as a devoted victim, was still reserved to convey the truths of the Gospel to the ear of monarchs.[118] He addressed several edifying letters to the emperor Philip, to his wife, and to his mother; and, as soon as that prince, who was born in the neighbourhood of Palestine, had usurped the Imperial sceptre, the Christians acquired a friend and a protector. The public and even partial favour of Philip towards the sectaries of the new religion, and his constant reverence for the ministers of the church, gave some colour to the suspicion, which prevailed in his own times, that the emperor himself was become a convert to the faith;[119] and afforded some grounds for a fable which was afterwards invented, that he had been purified by confession and penance from the guilt contracted by the murder of his innocent predecessor.[120] The fall of Philip introduced, with the change of masters, a new system of government, so oppressive to the Christians that their former condition, ever since the time of Domitian, was represented as a state of perfect freedom and security, if compared with the rigorous treatment which they experienced under the short reign of Decius.[121] The virtues of that prince will scarcely allow us to suspect that he was actuated by a mean resentment against the favourites of his predecessor, and it is more reasonable to believe that, in the prosecution of his general design to restore the purity of Roman manners, he was desirous of delivering the empire from what he condemned as a recent and criminal superstition. The bishops of the most considerable cities were removed by exile or death; the vigilance of the magistrates prevented the clergy of Rome during sixteen months from proceeding to a new election; and it was the opinion of the Christians that the emperor would more patiently endure a competitor for the purple than a bishop in the capital.[122] Were it possible to suppose that the penetration of Decius had discovered pride under the disguise of humility, or that he could foresee the temporal dominion which might insensibly arise from the claims of spiritual authority, we might be less surprised that he should consider the successors of St Peter as the most formidable rivals to those of Augustus.

The administration of Valerian was distinguished by a levity and inconstancy, ill suited to the gravity of the *Roman Censor*. In the first part of his reign, he surpassed in clemency those princes who had been suspected of an attachment to the Christian faith. In the last three years and a half, listening to the insinuations of a minister addicted to the superstitions of Egypt, he adopted the maxims, and imitated the severity, of his predecessor Decius.[123] The accession of Gallienus, which increased the calamities of the empire, restored peace to the church; and the Christians obtained the free exercise of their religion, by an edict addressed to the bishops and conceived in such terms as seemed to acknowledge their office and public character.[124] The ancient laws, without being formally repealed, were suffered to sink into oblivion; and (excepting only some hostile intentions which are attributed to the emperor Aurelian[125]) the disciples of Christ passed above forty years in a state of prosperity, far more dangerous to their virtue than the severest trials of persecution.

The story of Paul of Samosata, who filled the metropolitan see of Antioch, while the East was in the hands of Odenathus and Zenobia, may serve to illustrate the condition and character of the times. The wealth of that prelate was a sufficient evidence of his guilt, since it was neither derived from the inheritance of his fathers nor acquired by the arts of honest industry. But Paul considered the service of the church as a very lucrative profession.[126] His ecclesiastical jurisdiction was venal and rapacious; he exhorted frequent contributions from the most opulent of the faithful, and converted to his own use a considerable part of the public revenue. By his pride and luxury the Christian religion was rendered odious in the eyes of the Gentiles. His council-chamber and his throne, the splendour with which he appeared in public, the suppliant crowd who solicited his attention, the multitude of letters and petitions to which he dictated his answers, and the perpetual hurry of business in which he was involved, were circumstances much better suited to the state of a civil magistrate[127] than to the humility of a primitive bishop. When he harangued his people from the pulpit, Paul affected the figurative style and the theatrical gestures of an Asiatic sophist, while the cathedral resounded with the loudest and most extravagant acclamations in the praise of his divine eloquence. Against those who resisted his power, or refused to flatter his vanity, the prelate of Antioch was arrogant, rigid, and inexorable; but he relaxed the discipline, and lavished the treasures, of the church on his dependent clergy, who were permitted to imitate their master in the gratification of every sensual appetite. For Paul indulged himself very freely in the pleasures of the table, and he had received into the episcopal palace two young and beautiful women, as the constant companions of his leisure moments.[128]

Notwithstanding these scandalous vices, if Paul of Samosata had preserved the purity of the orthodox faith, his reign over the capital of Syria would have ended only with his life; and, had a seasonable persecution intervened, an effort of courage might perhaps have placed him in the rank of saints and martyrs. Some nice and subtle errors, which he imprudently adopted and obstinately maintained, concerning the doctrine of the Trinity, excited the zeal and indignation of the eastern churches.[129] From Egypt to the Euxine sea, the bishops were in arms and in motion. Several councils were held, confutations were published, excommunications were pronounced, ambiguous explanations were by turns accepted and refused, treaties were concluded and violated, and, at length, Paul of Samosata was degraded from his episcopal character, by the sentence of seventy or eighty bishops, who assembled for that purpose at Antioch, and who, without consulting the rights of the clergy or people, appointed a successor by their own authority. The manifest irregularity of this proceeding increased the numbers of the discontented faction; and as Paul, who was no stranger to the arts of courts, had insinuated himself into the favour of Zenobia, he maintained above four years the possession of the episcopal house and office. The victory of Aurelian changed the face of the East, and the two contending parties, who applied to each other the epithets of schism and heresy, were either commanded or permitted to plead their cause before the tribunal of the conqueror. This public and very singular trial affords a convincing proof that the existence, the property, the privileges, and the internal policy of the Christians were acknowledged, if not by the laws, at least by the magistrates, of the empire. As a Pagan and as a soldier, it could scarcely be expected that Aurelian should enter into the discussion, whether the sentiments of Paul or those of his adversaries were most agreeable to the true standard of the orthodox faith. His determination, however, was founded on the general principles of equity and reason. He considered the bishops of Italy as the most impartial and respectable judges among the Christians, and, as soon as he was informed that they had unanimously approved the sentence of the council, he acquiesced in their opinion, and immediately gave orders that Paul should be compelled to relinquish the temporal possessions belonging to an office of which, in the judgment of his brethren, he had been regularly deprived. But, while we applaud the justice, we should not overlook the policy, of Aurelian; who was desirous of restoring and cementing the dependence of the provinces on the capital by every means which could bind the interests or prejudices of any part of his subjects.[130]

Amidst the frequent revolutions of the empire, the Christians still flourished in peace and prosperity; and, notwithstanding a celebrated era of martyrs has been deduced from the accession of Diocletian,[131] the new system of policy, introduced and maintained by the wisdom of that prince, continued, during more than eighteen years, to breathe the mildest and most liberal spirit of religious toleration. The mind of Diocletian himself was less adapted indeed to speculative inquiries than to the active labours of war and government. His prudence rendered him averse to any great innovation, and, though his temper was not very susceptible of zeal or enthusiasm, he always maintained an habitual regard for the ancient deities of the empire. But the leisure of the two empresses, of his wife Prisca and of Valeria his daughter, permitted them to listen with more attention and respect to the truths of Christianity, which in every age has acknowledged its important obligations to female devotion.[132] The principal eunuchs, Lucian[133] and Dorotheus, Gorgonius and Andrew, who attended the person, possessed the favour, and governed the household of Diocletian, protected by their powerful influence the faith which they had embraced. Their example was imitated by many of the most considerable officers of the palace, who, in their respective stations, had the care of the Imperial ornaments, of the robes, of the furniture, of the jewels, and even of the private treasury; and, though it might sometimes be incumbent on them to accompany the emperor when he sacrificed in the temple,[134] they enjoyed, with their wives, their children, and their slaves, the free exercise of the Christian religion. Diocletian and his colleagues frequently conferred the most important offices on those persons who avowed their abhorrence for the worship of the gods, but who had displayed abilities proper for the service of the state. The bishops held an honourable rank in their respective provinces, and were treated with distinction and respect, not only by the people, but by the magistrates themselves. Almost in every city, the ancient churches were found insufficient to contain the increasing multitude of proselytes; and in their place more stately and capacious edifices were erected for the public worship of the faithful. The corruption of manners and principles, so forcibly lamented by Eusebius,[135] may be considered, not only as a consequence, but as a proof, of the liberty which the Christians enjoyed and abused under the reign of Diocletian. Prosperity had relaxed the nerves of discipline. Fraud, envy, and malice prevailed in every congregation. The presbyters aspired to the episcopal office, which every day became an object more worthy of their ambition. The bishops, who contended with each other for ecclesiastical pre-eminence, appeared by their conduct to claim a secular and tyrannical power in the church; and the lively faith which still distinguished the Christians from the Gentiles was shown much less in their lives than in their controversial writings.

Notwithstanding this seeming security, an attentive observer might discern some symptoms that threatened the church with a more violent persecution than any which she had yet endured. The zeal and rapid progress of the Christians awakened the Polytheists from their supine indifference in the cause of those deities whom custom and education had taught them to revere. The mutual provocations of a religious war, which had already continued above two hundred years, exasperated the animosity of the contending parties. The Pagans were incensed at the rashness of a recent and obscure sect which presumed to accuse their countrymen of error and to devote their ancestors to eternal misery. The habits of justifying the popular mythology against the invectives of an implacable enemy produced in their minds some sentiments of faith and reverence for a system which they had been accustomed to consider with the most careless levity. The supernatural powers assumed by the church inspired at the same time terror and emulation. The followers of the established religion entrenched themselves behind a similar fortification of prodigies; invented new modes of sacrifice, of expiation, and of initiation;[136] attempted to revive the credit of their expiring oracles;[137] and listened with eager credulity to every impostor who flattered their prejudices by a tale of wonders.[138] Both parties seemed to acknowledge the truth of those miracles which were claimed by their adversaries; and, while they were contented with ascribing them to the arts of magic and to the power of daemons, they mutually concurred in restoring and establishing the reign of superstition.[139] Philosophy, her most dangerous enemy, was now converted into her most useful ally. The groves of the academy, the gardens of Epicurus, and even the portico of the Stoics, were almost deserted, as so many different schools of scepticism or impiety;[140] and many among the Romans were desirous that the writings of Cicero should be condemned and suppressed by the authority of the senate.[141] The prevailing sect of the new Platonicians judged it prudent to connect themselves with the priests, whom perhaps they despised, against the Christians, whom they had reason to fear. These fashionable philosophers prosecuted the design of extracting allegorical wisdom from the fictions of the Greek poets; instituted mysterious rites of devotion for the use of their chosen disciples; recommended the worship of the ancient gods as the emblems or ministers of the Supreme Deity; and composed against the faith of the Gospel many elaborate treatises,[142] which have since been committed to the flames by the prudence of orthodox emperors.[143]

Although the policy of Diocletian and the humanity of Constantius inclined them to preserve inviolate the maxims of toleration, it was soon discovered that their two associates Maximian and Galerius entertained the most implacable aversion for the name and religion of the Christians. The minds of those princes had never been enlightened by science; education had never softened their temper. They owed their greatness to their swords, and in their most elevated fortune they still retained their superstitious prejudices of soldiers and peasants. In the general administration of the provinces they obeyed the laws which their benefactor had established; but they frequently found occasions of exercising within their camp and palaces a secret persecution,[144] for which the imprudent zeal of the Christians sometimes offered the most specious pretences. A sentence of death was executed upon Maximilianus, an African youth, who had been produced by his own father before the magistrate as a sufficient and legal recruit, but who obstinately persisted in declaring that his conscience would not permit him to embrace the profession of a soldier.[145] It could scarcely be expected that any government should suffer the action of Marcellus the centurion to pass with impunity. On the day of a public festival, that officer threw away his belt, his arms, and the ensigns of his office, and exclaimed with a loud voice that he would obey none but Jesus Christ the eternal King, and that he renounced for ever the use of carnal weapons and the service of an idolatrous master. The soldiers, as soon as they recovered from their astonishment, secured the person of Marcellus. He was examined in the city of Tingi by the president of that part of Mauritania; and, as he was convicted by his own confession, he was condemned and beheaded for the crime of desertion.[146] Examples of such a nature savour much less of religious persecution than of martial or even civil law: but they served to alienate the mind of the emperors, to justify the severity of Galerius, who dismissed a great number of Christian officers from their employments, and to authorise the opinion that a sect of enthusiasts which avowed principles so repugnant to the public safety must either remain useless, or would soon become dangerous, subjects of the empire.

After the success of the Persian war had raised the hopes and the reputation of Galerius, he passed a winter with Diocletian in the palace of Nicomedia; and the fate of Christianity became the object of their secret consultations.[147] The experienced emperor was still inclined to pursue measures of lenity; and, though he readily consented to exclude Christians from holding any employments in the household or the army, he urged in the strongest terms the danger as well as cruelty of shedding the blood of those deluded fanatics. Galerius at length extorted from him the permission of summoning a council, composed of a few persons the most distinguished in the civil and military departments of the state. The important question was agitated in their presence, and those ambitious courtiers easily discerned that it was incumbent on them to second, by their eloquence, the importunate violence of the Caesar. It may be presumed that they insisted on every topic which might interest the pride, the piety, or the fears, of their sovereign in the destruction of Christianity. Perhaps they represented that the glorious work of the deliverance of the empire was left imperfect, as long as an independent people was permitted to subsist and multiply in the heart of the provinces. The Christians (it might speciously be alleged), renouncing the gods and the institutions of Rome, had constituted a distinct republic, which might yet be suppressed before it had acquired any military force; but which was already governed by its own laws and magistrates, was possessed of a public treasure, and was intimately connected in all its parts by the frequent assemblies of the bishops, to whose decrees their numerous and opulent congregations yielded an implicit obedience. Arguments like these may seem to have determined the reluctant mind of Diocletian to embrace a new system of persecution: but, though we may suspect, it is not in our power to relate, the secret intrigues of the palace, the private views and resentments, the jealousy of women or eunuchs, and all those trifling but decisive causes which so often influence the fate of empires and the councils of the wisest monarchs.[148]

The pleasure of the emperors was at length signified to the Christians, who, during the course of this melancholy winter, had expected, with anxiety, the result of so many secret consultations. The twenty-third of February, which coincided with the Roman festival of the Terminalia,[149] was appointed (whether from accident or design) to set bounds to the progress of Christianity. At the earliest dawn of day, the Praetorian prefect,[150] accompanied by several generals, tribunes, and officers of the revenue, repaired to the principal church of Nicomedia, which was situated on an eminence in the most populous and beautiful part of the city. The doors were instantly broken open; they rushed into the sanctuary; and, as they searched in vain for some visible object of worship, they were obliged to content themselves with committing to the flames the volumes of holy scripture. The ministers of Diocletian were followed by a numerous body of guards and pioneers, who marched in order of battle, and were provided with all the instruments used in the destruction of fortified cities. By their incessant labour, a sacred edifice, which towered above the Imperial palace, and had long excited the indignation and envy of the Gentiles, was in a few hours levelled with the ground.[151]

The next day the general edict of persecution was published;[152] and, though Diocletian, still averse to the effusion of blood, had moderated the fury of Galerius, who proposed that everyone refusing to offer sacrifice should immediately be burnt alive, the penalties inflicted on the obstinacy of the Christians might be deemed sufficiently rigorous and effectual. It was enacted that their churches, in all the provinces of the empire, should be demolished to their foundations; and the punishment of death was denounced against all who should presume to hold any secret assemblies for the purpose of religious worship. The philosophers who now assumed the unworthy office of directing the blind zeal of persecution, had diligently studied the nature and genius of the Christian religion; and, as they were not ignorant that the speculative doctrines of the faith were supposed to be contained in the writings of the prophets, of the evangelists, and of the apostles, they most probably suggested the order that the bishops and presbyters should deliver all their sacred books into the hands of the magistrates; who were commanded, under the severest penalties, to burn them in a public and solemn manner. By the same edict, the property of the church was at once confiscated; and the several parts of which it might consist were either sold to the highest bidder, united to the Imperial domain, bestowed on the cities and corporations, or granted to the solicitations of rapacious courtiers. After taking such effectual measures to abolish the worship, and to dissolve the government, of the Christians, it was thought necessary to subject to the most intolerable hardships the condition of those perverse individuals who should still reject the religion of Nature, of Rome, and of their ancestors. Persons of a liberal birth were declared incapable of holding any honours or employments; slaves were for ever deprived of the hopes of freedom, and the whole body of the people were put out of the protection of the law. The judges were authorised to hear and to determine every action that was brought against a Christian. But the Christians were not permitted to complain of any injury which they themselves had suffered; and thus those unfortunate sectaries were exposed to the severity, while they were excluded from the benefits, of public justice. This new species of martyrdom, so painful and lingering, so obscure and ignominious, was, perhaps, the most proper to weary the constancy of the faithful; nor can it be doubted that the passions and interest of mankind were disposed on this occasion to second the designs of the emperors. But the policy of a well-ordered government must sometimes have interposed in behalf of the oppressed Christians; nor was it possible for the Roman princes entirely to remove the apprehension of punishment, or to connive at every act of fraud and violence, without exposing their own authority and the rest of their subjects to the most alarming dangers.[153]

This edict was scarcely exhibited to the public view, in the most conspicuous place of Nicomedia, before it was torn down by the hands of a Christian, who expressed, at the same time, by the bitterest invectives, his contempt as well as abhorrence for such impious and tyrannical governors. His offence, according to the mildest laws, amounted to treason, and deserved death. And, if it be true that he was a person of rank and education, those circumstances could serve only to aggravate his guilt. He was burnt, or rather roasted, by a slow fire; and his executioners, jealous to revenge the personal insult which had been offered to the emperors, exhausted every refinement of cruelty, without being able to subdue his patience, or to alter the steady and insulting smile which in his dying agonies he still preserved in his countenance. The Christians, though they confessed that his conduct had not been strictly conformable to the laws of prudence, admired the divine fervour of his zeal; and the excessive commendations which they lavished on the memory of their hero and martyr contributed to fix a deep impression of terror and hatred in the mind of Diocletian.[154]

His fears were soon alarmed by the view of a danger from which he very narrowly escaped. Within fifteen days the palace of Nicomedia, and even the bedchamber of Diocletian, were twice in flames; and, though both times they were extinguished without any material damage, the singular repetition of the fire was justly considered as an evident proof that it had not been the effect of chance or negligence. The suspicion naturally fell on the Christians; and it was suggested, with some degree of probability, that those desperate fanatics, provoked by their present sufferings and apprehensive of impending calamities, had entered into a conspiracy with their faithful brethren, the eunuchs of the palace, against the lives of two emperors, whom they detested as the irreconcilable enemies of the Church of God. Jealousy and resentment prevailed in every breast, but especially in that of Diocletian. A great number of persons, distinguished either by the offices which they had filled or by the favour which they had enjoyed, were thrown into prison. Every mode of torture was put in practice, and the court, as well as city, was polluted with many bloody executions.[155] But, as it was found impossible to extort any discovery of this mysterious transaction, it seems incumbent on us either to presume the innocence, or to admire the resolution, of the sufferers. A few days afterwards Galerius hastily withdrew himself from Nicomedia, declaring that, if he delayed his departure from that devoted palace, he should fall a sacrifice to the rage of the Christians. The ecclesiastical historians, from whom alone we derive a partial and imperfect knowledge of this persecution, are at a loss how to account for the fears and dangers of the emperors. Two of these writers, a prince and a rhetorician, were eye-witnesses of the fire of Nicomedia. The one ascribes it to lightning and the divine wrath; the other affirms that it was kindled by the malice of Galerius himself.[156]

As the edict against the Christians was designed for a general law of the whole empire, and as Diocletian and Galerius, though they might not wait for the consent, were assured of the concurrence, of the western princes, it would appear more consonant to our ideas of policy that the governors of all the provinces should have received secret instructions to publish, on one and the same day, this declaration of war within their respective departments. It was at least to be expected that the convenience of the public highways and established posts would have enabled the emperors to transmit their orders with the utmost dispatch from the palace of Nicomedia to the extremities of the Roman world; and that they would not have suffered fifty days to elapse before the edict was published in Syria, and near four months before it was signified to the cities of Africa.[157] This delay may perhaps be imputed to the cautious temper of Diocletian, who had yielded a reluctant consent to the measures of persecution, and who was desirous of trying the experiment under his more immediate eye, before he gave way to the disorders and discontent which it must inevitably occasion in the distant provinces. At first, indeed, the magistrates were restrained from the effusion of blood; but the use of every other severity was permitted and even recommended to their zeal; nor could the Christians, though they cheerfully resigned the ornaments of their churches, resolve to interrupt their religious assemblies or to deliver their sacred books to the flames. The pious obstinacy of Felix, an African bishop, appears to have embarrassed the subordinate ministers of the government. The curator of his city sent him in chains to the proconsul. The proconsul transmitted him to the Praetorian prefect of Italy; and Felix, who disdained even to give an evasive answer, was at length beheaded at Venusia, in Lucania, a place on which the birth of Horace* has conferred fame.[158] This precedent, and perhaps some Imperial rescript, which was issued in consequence of it, appeared to authorise the governors of provinces in punishing with death the refusal of the Christians to deliver up their sacred books. There were undoubtedly many persons who embraced this opportunity of obtaining the crown of martyrdom; but there were likewise too many who purchased an ignominious life by discovering and betraying the holy scripture into the hands of infidels. A great number even of bishops and presbyters acquired, by this criminal compliance, the opprobrious epithet of *traditors*;† and their offence was productive of much present scandal, and of much future discord, in the African church.[159]

The copies, as well as the versions, of scripture were already so multiplied in the empire that the most severe inquisition could no longer be attended with any fatal consequences; and even the sacrifice of those volumes which, in every congregation, were preserved for public use required the consent of some treacherous and unworthy Christians. But the ruin of the churches was easily effected by the authority of the government and by the labour of the Pagans. In some provinces, however, the magistrates contented themselves with shutting up the places of religious worship. In others, they more literally complied with the terms of the edict; and, after taking away the doors, the benches, and the pulpit, which they burnt, as it were in a funeral pile, they completely demolished the remainder of the edifice.[160] It is perhaps to this melancholy occasion that we should apply a very remarkable story, which is related with so many circumstances of variety and improbability that it serves rather to excite than to satisfy our curiosity. In a small town in Phrygia, of whose name as well as situation we are left ignorant, it should seem that the magistrates and the body of the people had embraced the Christian faith; and, as some resistance might be apprehended to the execution of the edict, the governor of the province was supported by a numerous detachment of legionaries. On their approach the citizens threw themselves into the church, with the resolution either of defending by arms that sacred edifice or of perishing in its ruins. They indignantly rejected the notice and permission which was given them to retire, till the soldiers, provoked by their obstinate refusal, set fire to the building on all sides, and consumed, by this extraordinary kind of martyrdom, a great number of Phrygians, with their wives and children.[161]

Some slight disturbances, though they were suppressed almost as soon as excited, in Syria and the frontiers of Armenia, afforded the enemies of the church a very plausible occasion to insinuate that those troubles had been secretly fomented by the intrigues of the bishops, who had already forgotten their ostentatious professions of passive and unlimited obedience.[162] The resentment, or the fears, of Diocletian at length transported him beyond the bounds of moderation which he had hitherto preserved, and he declared, in a series of cruel edicts, his intention of abolishing the Christian name. By the first of these edicts, the governors of the provinces were directed to apprehend all persons of the ecclesiastical order; and the prisons, destined for the vilest criminals, were soon filled with a multitude of bishops, presbyters, deacons, readers, and exorcists. By a second edict, the magistrates were commanded to employ every method of severity which might reclaim them from their odious superstition and oblige them to return to the established worship of the gods. This rigorous order was extended by a subsequent edict to the whole body of Christians, who were exposed to a violent and general persecution.[163] Instead of those salutary restraints, which had required the direct and solemn testimony of an accuser, it became the duty as well as the interest of the imperial officers to discover, to pursue, and to torment the most obnoxious among the faithful. Heavy penalties were denounced against all who should presume to save a proscribed sectary from the just indignation of the gods, and of the emperors. Yet, notwithstanding the severity of this law, the virtuous courage of many of the Pagans, in concealing their friends or relations, affords an honourable proof that the rage of superstition had not extinguished in their minds the sentiments of nature and humanity.[164]

Diocletian had no sooner published his edicts against the Christians than, as if he had been desirous of committing to other hands the work of persecution, he divested himself of the Imperial purple. The character and situation of his colleagues and successors sometimes urged them to enforce, and sometimes inclined them to suspend, the execution of these rigorous laws; nor can we acquire a just and distinct idea of this important period of ecclesiastical history, unless we separately consider the state of Christianity, in the different parts of the empire, during the space of ten years, which elapsed between the first edicts of Diocletian and the final peace of the church.

The mild and humane temper of Constantius was averse to the oppression of any part of his subjects. The principal offices of his palace were exercised by Christians. He loved their persons, esteemed their fidelity, and entertained not any dislike to their religious principles. But, as long as Constantius remained in the subordinate station of Caesar, it was not in his power openly to reject the edicts of Diocletian or to disobey the commands of Maximian. His authority contributed, however, to alleviate the sufferings which he pitied and abhorred. He consented, with reluctance, to the ruin of the churches; but he ventured to protect the Christians themselves from the fury of the populace and from the rigour of the laws. The provinces of Gaul (under which we may probably include those of Britain) were indebted for the singular tranquillity which they enjoyed to the gentle interposition of their sovereign.[165] But Datianus, the president or governor of Spain, actuated either by zeal or policy, chose rather to execute the public edicts of the emperors than to understand the secret intentions of Constantius; and it can scarcely be doubted that his provincial administration was stained with the blood of a few martyrs.[166] The elevation of Constantius to the supreme and independent dignity of Augustus gave a free scope to the exercise of his virtues, and the shortness of his reign did not prevent him from establishing a system of toleration, of which he left the precept and the example to his son Constantine. His fortunate son, from the first moment of his accession declaring himself the protector of the church, at length deserved the appellation of the first emperor who publicly professed and established the Christian religion. The motives of his conversion, as they may variously be deduced from benevolence, from policy, from conviction, or from remorse; and the progress of the revolution which, under his powerful influence, and that of his sons, rendered Christianity the reigning religion of the Roman empire, will form a very interesting and important chapter in the second volume of this history. At present it may be sufficient to observe that every victory of Constantine was productive of some relief or benefit to the church.

The provinces of Italy and Africa experienced a short but violent persecution. The rigorous edicts of Diocletian were strictly and cheerfully executed by his associate Maximian, who had long hated the Christians, and who delighted in acts of blood and violence. In the autumn of the first year of the persecution, the two emperors met at Rome to celebrate their triumph; several oppressive laws appear to have issued from their secret consultations, and the diligence of the magistrates was animated by the presence of their sovereigns. After Diocletian had divested himself of the purple, Italy and Africa were administered under the name of Severus, and were exposed, without defence, to the implacable resentment of his master Galerius. Among the martyrs of Rome, Adauctus deserves the notice of posterity. He was of a noble family in Italy, and had raised himself, through the successive honours of the palace, to the important office of treasurer of the private demesnes. Adauctus is the more remarkable for being the only person of rank and distinction who appears to have suffered death during the whole course of this general persecution.[167]

The revolt of Maxentius immediately restored peace to the churches of Italy and Africa; and the same tyrant who oppressed every other class of his subjects showed himself just, humane, and even partial, towards the afflicted Christians. He depended on their gratitude and affection, and very naturally presumed that the injuries which they had suffered, and the dangers which they still apprehended from his most inveterate enemy, would secure the fidelity of a party already considerable by their numbers and opulence.[168] Even the conduct of Maxentius towards the bishops of Rome and Carthage may be considered as the proof of his toleration, since it is probable that the most orthodox princes would adopt the same measures with regard to their established clergy. Marcellus, the former of those prelates, had thrown the capital into confusion by the severe penance which he imposed on a great number of Christians, who, during the late persecution, had renounced or dissembled their religion. The rage of faction broke out in frequent and violent seditions; the blood of the faithful was shed by each other's hands; and the exile of Marcellus, whose prudence seems to have been less eminent than his zeal, was found to be the only measure capable of restoring peace to the distracted church of Rome.[169] The behaviour of Mensurius, bishop of Carthage, appears to have been still more reprehensible. A deacon of that city had published a libel against the emperor. The offender took refuge in the episcopal palace; and, though it was somewhat early to advance any claims of ecclesiastical immunities, the bishop refused to deliver him up to the officers of justice. For this treasonable resistance, Mensurius was summoned to court, and, instead of receiving a legal sentence of death or banishment, he was permitted, after a short examination, to return to his diocese.[170] Such was the happy condition of the Christian subjects of Maxentius that, whenever they were desirous of procuring for their own use any bodies of martyrs, they were obliged to purchase them from the most distant provinces of the East. A story is related of Aglae; a Roman lady, descended from a consular family, and possessed of so ample an estate that it required the management of seventy-three stewards. Among these, Boniface was the favourite of his mistress; and, as Aglae mixed love with devotion, it is reported that he was admitted to share her bed. Her fortune enabled her to gratify the pious desire of obtaining some sacred relics from the East. She entrusted Boniface with a considerable sum of gold and a large quantity of aromatics; and her lover, attended by twelve horsemen and three covered chariots, undertook a remote pilgrimage, as far as Tarsus in Cilicia.[171]

The sanguinary temper of Galerius, the first and principal author of the persecution, was formidable to those Christians whom their misfortunes had placed within the limits of his dominions; and it may fairly be presumed that many persons of a middle rank, who were not confined by the chains either of wealth or of poverty, very frequently deserted their native country, and sought a refuge in the milder climate of the West. As long as he commanded only the armies and provinces of Illyricum, he could with difficulty either find or make a considerable number of martyrs in a  country which had entertained the missionaries of coldness and reluctance than any other part of the Galerius had obtained the supreme power and the st, he indulged in their fullest extent his zeal and e provinces of Thrace and Asia, which acknowl- urisdiction, but in those of Syria, Palestine, and gratified his own inclination by yielding a rigorous commands of his benefactor.[173] The frequent ambitious views, the experience of six years of lutary reflections which a lingering and painful he mind of Galerius, at length convinced him that most violent efforts of despotism are insufficient to extirpate a whole people or to subdue their religious prejudices. Desirous of repairing the mischief that he had occasioned, he published in his own name, and in those of Licinius and Constantine, a general edict, which, after a pompous recital of the Imperial titles, proceeded in the following manner.

'Among the important cares which have occupied our mind for the utility and preservation of the empire, it was our intention to correct and reestablish all things according to the ancient laws and public discipline of the Romans. We were particularly desirous of reclaiming, into the way of reason and nature, the deluded Christians, who had renounced the religion and ceremonies instituted by their fathers, and, presumptuously despising the practice of antiquity, had invented extravagant laws and opinions, according to the dictates of their fancy, and had collected a various society from the different provinces of our empire. The edicts which we have published to enforce the worship of the gods, having exposed many of the Christians to danger and distress, many having suffered death, and many more, who still persist in their impious folly, being left destitute of any public exercise of religion, we are disposed to extend to those unhappy men the effects of our wonted clemency. We permit them, therefore, freely to profess their private opinions, and to assemble in their conventicles without fear of molestation, provided always that they preserve a due respect to the established laws and government. By another rescript we shall signify our intentions to the judges and magistrates; and we hope that our indulgence will engage the Christians to offer up their prayers to the Deity whom they adore, for our safety and prosperity, for their own, and for that of the republic.'[174] It is not usually in the language of edicts and manifestoes that we should search for the real character or the secret motives of princes; but, as these were the words of a dying emperor, his situation, perhaps, may be admitted as a pledge of his sincerity.

When Galerius subscribed this edict of toleration, he was well assured that Licinius would readily comply with the inclinations of his friend and benefactor, and that any measures in favour of the Christians would obtain the approbation of Constantine. But the emperor would not venture to insert in the preamble the name of Maximin, whose consent was of the greatest importance, and who succeeded a few days afterwards to the provinces of Asia. In the first six months, however, of his new reign, Maximin affected to adopt the prudent counsels of his predecessor; and, though he never condescended to secure the tranquillity of the church by a public edict, Sabinus, his Praetorian prefect, addressed a circular letter to all the governors and magistrates of the provinces, expatiating on the Imperial clemency, acknowledging the invincible obstinacy of the Christians, and directing the officers of justice to cease their ineffectual prosecutions and to connive at the secret assemblies of those enthusiasts. In consequence of these orders, great numbers of Christians were released from prison or delivered from the mines. The confessors, singing hymns of triumph, returned into their own countries; and those who had yielded to the violence of the tempest solicited with tears of repentance their readmission into the bosom of the church.[175]

But this treacherous calm was of short duration; nor could the Christians of the East place any confidence in the character of their sovereign. Cruelty and superstition were the ruling passions of the soul of Maximin. The former suggested the means, the latter pointed out the objects, of persecution. The emperor was devoted to the worship of the gods, to the study of magic, and to the belief of oracles. The prophets or philosophers, whom he revered as the favourites of heaven, were frequently raised to the government of provinces and admitted into his most secret counsels. They easily convinced him that the Christians had been indebted for their victories to their regular discipline, and that the weakness of Polytheism had principally flowed from a want of union and subordination among the ministers of religion. A system of government was therefore instituted, which was evidently copied from the policy of the church. In all the great cities of the empire, the temples were repaired and beautified by the order of Maximin; and the officiating priests of the various deities were subjected to the authority of a superior pontiff, destined to oppose the bishop and to promote the cause of Paganism. These pontiffs acknowledged, in their turn, the supreme jurisdiction of the metropolitans or high priests of the province, who acted as the immediate vicegerents of the emperor himself. A white robe was the ensign of their dignity; and these new prelates were carefully selected from the most noble and opulent families. By the influence of the magistrates and of the sacerdotal order, a great number of dutiful addresses were obtained, particularly from the cities of Nicomedia, Antioch, and Tyre, which artfully represented the well-known intentions of the court as the general sense of the people; solicited the emperor to consult the laws of justice rather than the dictates of his clemency; expressed their abhorrence of the Christians; and humbly prayed that those impious sectaries might at least be excluded from the limits of their respective territories. The answer of Maximin to the address which he obtained from the citizens of Tyre is still extant. He praises their zeal and devotion in terms of the highest satisfaction, descants on the obstinate impiety of the Christians, and betrays, by the readiness with which he consents to their banishment, that he considered himself as receiving, rather than as conferring, an obligation. The priests, as well as the magistrates, were empowered to enforce the execution of his edicts, which were engraved on tables of brass; and, though it was recommended to them to avoid the effusion of blood, the most cruel and ignominious punishments were inflicted on the refractory Christians.[176]

The Asiatic Christians had everything to dread from the severity of a bigoted monarch, who prepared his measures of violence with such deliberate policy. But a few months had scarcely elapsed before the edicts published by the two western emperors obliged Maximin to suspend the prosecution of his designs: the civil war, which he so rashly undertook against Licinius, employed all his attention; and the defeat and death of Maximin soon delivered the church from the last and most implacable of her enemies.[177]

In this general view of the persecution, which was first authorised by the edicts of Diocletian, I have purposely refrained from describing the particular sufferings and deaths of the Christian martyrs. It would have been an easy task, from the history of Eusebius, from the declamations of Lactantius, and from the most ancient acts, to collect a long series of horrid and disgustful pictures, and to fill many pages with racks and scourges, with iron hooks, and red-hot beds, and with all the variety of tortures which fire and steel, savage beasts and more savage executioners, could inflict on the human body. These melancholy scenes might be enlivened by a crowd of visions and miracles destined either to delay the death, to celebrate the triumph, or to discover the relics, of those canonised saints who suffered for the name of Christ. But I cannot determine what I ought to transcribe, till I am satisfied how much I ought to believe. The gravest of the ecclesiastical historians, Eusebius himself, indirectly confesses that he has related whatever might redound to the glory, and that he has suppressed all that could tend to the disgrace, of religion.[178] Such an acknowledgment will naturally excite a suspicion that a writer who has so openly violated one of the fundamental laws of history has not paid a very strict regard to the observance of the other; and the suspicion will derive additional credit from the character of Eusebius, which was less tinctured with credulity, and more practised in the arts of courts, than that of almost any of his contemporaries. On some particular occasions, when the magistrates were exasperated by some personal motives of interest or resentment, when the zeal of the martyrs urged them to forget the rules of prudence, and perhaps of decency, to overturn the altars, to pour out imprecations against the emperors, or to strike the judge as he sat on his tribunal, it may be presumed that every mode of torture, which cruelty could invent or constancy could endure, was exhausted on those devoted victims.[179] Two circumstances, however, have been unwarily mentioned, which insinuate that the general treatment of the Christians who had been apprehended by the officers of justice was less intolerable than it is usually imagined to have been. 1. The confessors who were condemned to work in the mines were permitted, by the humanity or the negligence of their keepers, to build chapels and freely to profess their religion in the midst of those dreary habitations.[180] 2. The bishops were obliged to check and to censure the forward zeal of the Christians, who voluntarily threw themselves into the hands of the magistrates. Some of these were persons oppressed by poverty and debts, who blindly sought to terminate a miserable existence by a glorious death. Others were allured by the hope that a short confinement would expiate the sins of a whole life; and others, again, were actuated by the less honourable motive of deriving a plentiful subsistence, and perhaps a considerable profit, from the alms which the charity of the faithful bestowed on the prisoners.[181] After the church had triumphed over all her enemies, the interest as well as vanity of the captives prompted them to magnify the merit of their respective suffering. A convenient distance of time or place gave an ample scope to the progress of fiction; and the frequent instances which might be alleged of holy martyrs, whose wounds had been instantly healed, whose strength had been renewed, and whose lost members had miraculously been restored, were extremely convenient for the purpose of removing every difficulty and of silencing every objection. The most extravagant legends, as they conduced to the honour of the church, were applauded by the credulous multitude, countenanced by the power of the clergy, and attested by the suspicious evidence of ecclesiastical history.

The vague descriptions of exile and imprisonment, of pain and torture, are so easily exaggerated or softened by the pencil of an artful orator that we are naturally induced to inquire into a fact of a more distinct and stubborn kind: the number of persons who suffered death, in consequence of the edicts published by Diocletian, his associates, and his successors. The recent legendaries* record whole armies and cities, which were at once swept away by the undistinguishing rage of persecution. The more ancient writers content themselves with pouring out a liberal effusion of loose and tragical invectives, without condescending to ascertain the precise number of those persons who were permitted to seal with their blood their belief of the gospel. From the history of Eusebius, it may however be collected that only nine bishops were punished with death; and we are assured, by his particular enumeration of the martyrs of Palestine, that no more than ninety-two Christians were entitled to that honourable appellation.[182] As we are unacquainted with the degree of episcopal zeal and courage which prevailed at that time, it is not in our power to draw any useful inferences from the former of these facts; but the latter may serve to justify a very important and probable conclusion. According to the distribution of Roman provinces, Palestine may be considered as the sixteenth part of the Eastern empire;[183] and since there were some governors who, from a real or affected clemency, had preserved their hands unstained with the blood of the faithful,[184] it is reasonable to believe that the country which had given birth to Christianity produced at least the sixteenth part of the martyrs who suffered death within the dominions of Galerius and Maximin; the whole might consequently amount to about fifteen hundred: a number which, if it is equally divided between the ten years of the persecution, will allow an annual consumption of one hundred and fifty martyrs. Allotting the same proportion to the provinces of Italy, Africa, and perhaps Spain, where, at the end of two or three years, the rigour of the penal laws was either suspended or abolished, the multitude of Christians in the Roman empire on whom a capital punishment was inflicted by a judicial sentence will be reduced to somewhat less than two thousand persons. Since it cannot be doubted that the Christians were more numerous, and their enemies more exasperated, in the time of Diocletian, than they had ever been in any former persecution, this probable and moderate computation may teach us to estimate the number of primitive saints and martyrs who sacrificed their lives for the important purpose of introducing Christianity into the world.

We shall conclude this chapter by a melancholy truth which obtrudes itself on the reluctant mind; that even admitting, without hesitation, or inquiry, all that history has recorded, or devotion has feigned, on the subject of martyrdoms, it must still be acknowledged that the Christians, in the course of their intestine dissensions, have inflicted far greater severities on each other than they had experienced from the zeal of infidels. During the ages of ignorance which followed the subversion of the Roman empire in the West, the bishops of the Imperial city extended their dominion over the laity as well as clergy of the Latin church. The fabric of superstition which they had erected, and which might long have defied the feeble efforts of reason, was at length assaulted by a crowd of daring fanatics, who, from the twelfth to the sixteenth century, assumed the popular character of reformers. The church of Rome defended by violence the empire which she had acquired by fraud; a system of peace and benevolence was soon disgraced by proscriptions, wars, massacres, and the institution of the holy office.* And, as the reformers were animated by the love of civil, as well as of religious, freedom, the Catholic princes connected their own interest with that of the clergy, and enforced by fire and the sword the terrors of spiritual censures. In the Netherlands alone, more than one hundred thousand of the subjects of Charles the Fifth† are said to have suffered by the hand of the executioner; and this extraordinary number is attested by Grotius,[185] a man of genius and learning,‡ who preserved his moderation amidst the fury of contending sects, and who composed the annals of his own age and country, at a time when the invention of printing had facilitated the means of intelligence and increased the danger of detection. If we are obliged to submit our belief to the authority of Grotius, it must be allowed that the number of Protestants who were executed in a single province and a single reign far exceeded that of the primitive martyrs in the space of three centuries and of the Roman empire. But, if the improbability of the fact itself should prevail over the weight of evidence; if Grotius should be convicted of exaggerating the merit and sufferings of the Reformers;[186] we shall be naturally led to inquire what confidence can be placed in the doubtful and imperfect monuments of ancient credulity; what degree of credit can be assigned to a courtly bishop, and a passionate declaimer, who, under the protection of Constantine, enjoyed the exclusive privilege of recording the persecutions inflicted on the Christians by the vanquished rivals or disregarded predecessors of their gracious sovereign.

NOTES TO CHAPTER 16

1 In Cyrene they massacred 220,000 Greeks; in Cyprus, 240,000; in Egypt, a very great multitude. Many of these unhappy victims were sawed asunder, according to a precedent to which David had given the sanction of his example. The victorious Jews devoured the flesh, licked up the blood and twisted the entrails like a girdle round their bodies. See Dion Cassius, lxviii, 1145.

2 Without repeating the well-known narratives of Josephus, we may learn from Dion (lxix, 1162) that in Hadrian's war 580,000 Jews were cut off by the sword, besides an infinite number which perished by famine, by disease, and by fire.

* *page 308*   [Bar-Cochba, the leader of a rebellion in ad 132–135]

3 For the sect of the Zealots, see Basnage, *Histoire des Juifs*, i, 17, for the characters of the Messiah, according to the Rabbis, v, 11, 12 and 13, for the actions of Barchochebas, vii, 12.

4 It is to Modestinus, a Roman lawyer (Bk vi, *regular.*), that we are indebted for a distinct knowledge of the Edict of Antoninus. See Casaubon, *ad Hist. August.*, p. 27.

5 See Basnage, *Histoire des Juifs*, iii, 2 and 3. The office of Patriarch was suppressed by Theodosius the younger.

6 We need only mention the *purim*, or deliverance of the Jews from the rage of Haman, which, till the reign of Theodosius, was celebrated with insolent triumph and riotous intemperance. Basnage, *Hist. des Juifs*, vi, 17; viii, 6.

7 According to the false Josephus, Tsepho, the grandson of Esau, conducted into Italy the army of Aeneas, king of Carthage. Another colony of Idumaeans, flying from the sword of David, took refuge in the dominions of Romulus. For these, or for other reasons of equal weight, the name of Edom was applied by the Jews to the Roman empire.

8 From the arguments of Celsus, as they are represented and refuted by Origen (v, pp. 247–259), we may clearly discover the distinction that was made between the Jewish *people* and the Christian *sect*. See in the Dialogue of Minucius Felix (chs 5 and 6) a fair and not inelegant description of the popular sentiments with regard to the desertion of the established worship.

9 *Cur nullas aras habent? templa nulla? nulla nota simulacra? . . . Unde autem, vel quis ille, aut ubi, Deus unicus, solitarius, destitutus?* Minucius Felix, ch. 10. ['Why do they have no altars, no temples, no known statues . . . What is the origin, identity or location of the one and only and yet destitute God?'] The Pagan interlocutor goes on to make a distinction in favour of the Jews, who had once a temple, altars, victims, etc.

10 It is difficult (says Plato) to attain, and dangerous to publish, the knowledge of the true God. See the *Théologie des Philosophes*, in the Abbé d'Olivet's French translation of Tully, *de Natura Deorum*, i, 275.

11 The author of the *Philopatris* perpetually treats the Christians as a company of dreaming enthusiasts, δαιμόνιοι αἰθέριοι αἰθεροβατοῦντες ἀεροβατοῦντες, etc. ['ethereal creatures, ethereal, aerial travellers, etc.'], and in one place manifestly alludes to the vision in which St Paul was transported to the third heaven. In another place, Triephon, who personates a Christian, after deriding the Gods of Paganism, proposes a mysterious oath,

Ὑψιμέδοντα θεὸν, μέγαν, ἄμβροτον, οὐρανίωνα,

Υἱὸν πατρὸς, πνεῦμα ἐκ πατρὸς ἐκπορευόμενον

Ἐν ἐκ τριῶν, καὶ ἐξ ἑνὸς τρία.

[By the great god on high, immortal, heavenly, son of the father, one in three, and three in one.]

Ἀριθμέειν με διδάσκεις (is the profane answer of Critias) καὶ ὅρκος ἡ ἀριθμητική· οὐκ οἶδα γὰρ τί λέγεις· ἐν τρία, τρία ἕν! ['You are teaching me to count, an arithmetical oath, forsooth! I know not what you are saying. One equals three, three equals one!']

12 According to Justin Martyr (*Apolog. Major*, chs 70–85), the daemon, who had gained some imperfect knowledge of the prophecies, purposely contrived this resemblance, which might deter, though by different means, both the people and the philosophers from embracing the faith of Christ.

13 In the first and second books of Origen, Celsus treats the birth and character of our Saviour with the most impious contempt. The orator Libanius praises Porphyry and Julian [emperor, AD 361–363] for confuting the folly of a sect which styled a dead man of Palestine God, and the Son of God. Socrates, *Hist. Ecclesiast.*, iii, 23.

14 The emperor Trajan refused to incorporate a company of 150 firemen, for the use of the city of Nicomedia. He disliked all associations. See Pliny, *Epist.*, x, 42 and 43.

15 The proconsul Pliny had published a general edict against unlawful meetings. The prudence of the Christians suspended their Agapae; but it was impossible for them to omit the exercise of public worship.

16 As the prophecies of the Antichrist, approaching conflagration, etc., provoked those Pagans whom they did not convert, they were mentioned with caution and reserve; and the Montanists were censured for disclosing too freely the dangerous secret. See Mosheim, p. 413.

17 *Neque enim dubitabam, quodcunque esset quod faterentur* (such are the words of Pliny), *pervicaciam certe et inflexibilem obstinationem debere puniri.*

18 See Mosheim's *Ecclesiastical History*, i, 101, and Spanheim, *Remarques sur les Césars de Julien*, p. 468, etc.

19 See Justin Martyr, *Apolog.*, i. 35, ii, 14; Athenagoras in *Legation.*, ch. 27; Tertullian, *Apolog.*, chs. 7, 8 and 9; Minucius Felix, chs. 9, 10, 30, 31. The last of these writers relates the accusation in the most elegant and circumstantial manner. The answer of Tertullian is the boldest and most vigorous.

20 In the persecution of Lyons, some Gentile slaves were compelled, by the fear of tortures, to accuse their Christian master. The church of Lyons, writing to their brethren of Asia, treat the horrid charge with proper indignation and contempt. Eusebius, *Hist. Eccles.*, v, 1.

21 See Justin Martyr, *Apolog.*, i, 35; Irenaeus, *Adv. Haeres.*, i, 24; Clemens Alexandrin., *Stromat.*, iii, 438; Eusebius, iv. 8. It would be tedious and disgusting to relate all that the succeeding writers have imagined, all that Epiphanius has received, and all that Tillemont has copied. M de Beausobre (*Hist. du Manichéisme*, ix, 8 and 9) has exposed, with great spirit, the disingenuous arts of Augustine and Pope Leo I.

22 When Tertullian became a Montanist, he aspersed the morals of the church which he had so resolutely defended. *Sed maioris est Agape, quia per hanc adolescentes tui cum sororibus dormiunt, appendices scilicet gulae lascivia et luxuria.* ['But more popular is the Love Feast, because it is there that your young men sleep with their sisters; it combines gluttony, sexual indulgence and excess.'] *de Ieiuniis*, ch. 17. The thirty-fifth canon of the council of Illiberis provides against the scandals which too often polluted the vigils of the church and disgraced the Christian name in the eyes of unbelievers.

23 Tertullian (*Apolog.*, ch. 2) expatiates on the fair and honourable testimony of Pliny, with much reason, and some declamation.

24 In the various compilation of the *Augustan History* (a part of which was composed under the reign of Constantine), there are not six lines which relate to the Christians; nor has the diligence of Xiphilin discovered their name in the large history of Dion Cassius.

25 An obscure passage of Suetonius (in *Claudius*, ch. 25) may seem to offer a proof how strangely the Jews and Christians of Rome were confounded with each other.

26 See in the eighteenth and twenty-fifth chapters of the Acts of the Apostles, the behaviour of Gallio, proconsul of Achaia, and of Festus, procurator of Judaea.

27 In the time of Tertullian and Clemens of Alexandria, the glory of martyrdom was confined to St Peter, St Paul, and St James. It was gradually bestowed on the rest of the apostles, by the more recent Greeks, who prudently selected for the theatre of their preaching and sufferings, some remote country beyond the limits of the Roman empire. See Mosheim, p. 81, and Tillemont, *Mémoires Ecclésiastiques*, i, iii.

* *page 314*   [Tacitus]

28 Tacitus, *Annals*, xv, 38–44; Suetonius, in *Nero*, ch. 38; Dion Cassius, lxii, 1014; Orosius, vii, 7.

29 The price of wheat (probably of the *modius* [the standard Roman measure of corn, a peck]) was reduced as low as *terni nummi* [three sesterces]; which would be equivalent to about fifteen shillings the English quarter.

* *page 315*   [character]

30 We may observe, that the rumour is mentioned by Tacitus with a very becoming distrust and hesitation, whilst it is greedily transcribed by Suetonius, and solemnly confirmed by Dion.

31 This testimony is alone sufficient to expose the anachronism of the Jews who place the birth of Christ near a century sooner (Basnage, *Histoire des Juifs*, v, 14 and 15). We may learn from Josephus (*Antiquitat.*, xviii, 3), that the procuratorship of Pilate corresponded with the last ten years of Tiberius, AD 27–37. As to the particular time of the death of Christ, a very early tradition fixed it to the 25th of March, AD 29, under the consulship of the two Gemini (Tertullian, *Adv. Judaeos*, ch. 8). This date, which is adopted by Pagi, cardinal Noris, and Le Clerc, seems at least as probable as the vulgar era, which is placed (I know not from what conjectures) four years later.

32 *Odio humani generis convicti.* These words may either signify the hatred of mankind towards the Christians, or the hatred of the Christians towards mankind. I have preferred the latter sense, as the most agreeable to the style of Tacitus, and to the popular error, of which a precept of the Gospel (see Luke, xiv, 26) had been, perhaps, the innocent occasion. My interpretation is justified by the authority of Lipsius; of the Italian, the French, and the English translators of Tacitus; of Mosheim (p. 102), of Le Clerc (*Historia Ecclesiast.*, p. 427), of Dr Lardner (*Testimonies*, i, 345), and of the bishop of Gloucester (*Divine Legation*, vol. iii, p. 38). But as the word *convicti* does not unite very happily with the rest of the sentence, James Gronovius has preferred the reading of *coniuncti*, which is authorised by the valuable manuscript of Florence.

33 Tacitus, *Annals*, xv, 44.

34 Nardini, *Roma Antica*, p. 487; Donatus, *de Roma Antiqua*, iii, 449.

35 Suetonius, in *Nero*, ch. 16. The epithet of *malefica* [harmful], which some sagacious commentators have translated 'magical', is considered by the more rational Mosheim as only synonymous to the *exitiabilis* [dangerous] of Tacitus.

36 The passage concerning Jesus Christ, which was inserted into the text of Josephus between the time of Origen and that of Eusebius, may furnish an example of no vulgar forgery. The accomplishment of the prophecies, the virtues, miracles and resurrection of Jesus are distinctly related. Josephus acknowledges that he was the Messiah, and hesitates whether he should call him a man. If any doubt can still remain concerning this celebrated passage, the

reader may examine the pointed objections of Le Fevre (Havercamp. *Joseph.*, ii, 267–73), the laboured answers of Daubuz (pp. 187–232) and the masterly reply (*Bibliothèque Ancienne et Moderne*, vii, 287–88) of an anonymous critic, whom I believe to have been the learned Abbé de Longuerue.

37 See the lives of Tacitus, by Lipsius and the Abbé de la Bléterie, *Dictionnaire* de Bayle à *l'article Tacite*; and Fabricius, *Biblioth. Latin.*, ii, 386, edit. Ernest.

 * *page 316*   [father-in-law of Tacitus and governor of the province of Britain]

38 *Principatum Divi Nervae et imperium Traiani, uberiorem securioremque materiam senectuti seposui.* Tacitus, *Hist.*, i. ['The reigns of Nerva and Trajan, which furnish richer and more reliable material, I have put aside in order to cover them in my old age.']

39 See Tacitus, *Annals*, ii. 61; iv, 4.

40 The player's name was Aliturus. Through the same channel, Josephus (*de Vita Sua*, 3) about two years before, had obtained the pardon and release of some Jewish priests, who were prisoners at Rome.

41 The learned Dr Lardner (*Jewish and Heathen Testimonies*, ii, 102 and 103) has proved that the name of Galilaeans was a very ancient and, perhaps, the primitive appellation of the Christians.

42 Josephus, *Antiquitat.*, xviii, 1 and 2. Tillemont, *Ruine des Juifs*, p. 742, The sons of Judas were crucified in the time of Claudius. His grandson Eleazar, after Jerusalem was taken, defended a strong fortress [Masada] with 960 of his most desperate followers. When the battering ram had made a breach, they turned their swords against their wives, their children, and at length against their own breasts. They died to the last man.

43 See Dodwell, *Paucitat. Mart.*, Bk xiii. The Spanish Inscription in Gruter, p. 238, No. 9, is a manifest and acknowledged forgery, contrived by that noted impostor Cyriacus of Ancona, to flatter the pride and prejudices of the Spaniards. See Ferreras, *Histoire d'Espagne*, i, 192.

44 The Capitol was burnt during the civil war between Vitellius and Vespasian, the 19th of December, AD 69. On the 10th of August, AD 70, the Temple of Jerusalem was destroyed by the hands of the Jews themselves, rather than by those of the Romans.

45 The new Capitol was dedicated by Domitian. Suetonius, in *Domitian*, ch. 5; Plutarch, in *Poplicola*, i, 230, edit. Bryan. The gilding alone cost 12,000 talents (above two millions and a half). It was the opinion of Martial (ix, 3) that, if the emperor had called in his debts, Jupiter himself, even though he had made a general auction of Olympus, would have been unable to pay two shillings in the pound.

46 With regard to the tribute, see Dion Cassius, lxvi, 1082, with Reimarus's notes. Spanheim, *de Usu Numismatum*, ii, 571, and Basnage, *Histoire des Juifs*, vii, 2.

47 Suetonius (in *Domitian*, p. 12) had seen an old man of ninety publicly examined before the procurator's tribunal. This is what Martial calls, *mentula tributis damnata* [a taxable penis].

48 This appellation was at first understood in the most obvious sense, and it was supposed that the brothers of Jesus were the lawful issue of Joseph and of Mary. A devout respect for the virginity of the Mother of God suggested to the Gnostics, and afterwards to the orthodox Greeks, the expedient of bestowing a second wife on Joseph. The Latins (from the time of Jerome) improved on that hint, asserted the perpetual celibacy of Joseph, and justified, by many similar

examples, the new interpretation that Jude, as well as Simon and James, who are styled the brothers of Jesus Christ, were only his first cousins. See Tillemont, *Mém. Ecclésiast.*, i, iii, and Beausobre, *Hist. Critique du Manichéisme*, ii, 2.

49 Thirty-nine πλέθρα, squares of an hundred feet each, which, if strictly computed, would scarcely amount to nine acres. But the probability of circumstances, the practice of other Greek writers, and the authority of M. de Valois inclined me to believe that the πλέθρον is used to express the Roman *iugerum* [acre].

50 Eusebius, iii, 20. The story is taken from Hegesippus.

51 See the death and character of Sabinus in Tacitus (*Hist.*, iii, 74, 75). Sabinus was the elder brother, and, till the accession of Vespasian, had been considered as the principal support of the Flavian family.

52 *Flavium Clementem patruelem suum contemptissimae inertiae . . . ex tenuissima suspicione interemit.* Suetonius, in *Domitian*, ch. 15. ['Flavius Clemens, his own cousin, a man of quite despicable idleness, he (Domitian) put to death on the slenderest of suspicions.']

53 The isle of Pandataria, according to Dion. Bruttius Praesens (*apud* Euseb., iii, 18) banishes her to that of Pontia, which was not far distant from the other. That difference, and a mistake, either of Eusebius or of his transcribers, have given occasion to suppose two Domitillas, the wife and the niece of Clemens. See Tillemont, *Mémoires Ecclésiastiques*, ii, 224.

54 Dion, lxvii, 1112. If the Bruttius Praesens, from whom it is probable that he collected this account, was the correspondent of Pliny (*Epist.*, vii, 3), we may consider him as a contemporary writer.

55 Suetonius, in *Domitian*, ch. 17; Philostratus, in *Vit. Apollon.*, Bk viii.

56 Dion, lxviii, p. 1118; Pliny, *Epist.*, iv, 22.

57 Pliny, *Epist.*, x, 97. The learned Mosheim expresses himself (pp. 147, 232) with the highest approbation of Pliny's moderate and candid temper. Notwithstanding Dr Lardner's suspicions (see *Jewish and Heathen Testimonies*, ii, 46), I am unable to discover any bigotry in his language or proceedings.

58 Pliny, *Epist.*, v, 8. He pleaded his first cause AD 81; the year after the famous eruptions of Mount Vesuvius, in which his uncle lost his life.

59 Pliny, *Epist.*, x, 98. Tertullian (*Apolog.*, ch. 5) considers this rescript as a relaxation of the ancient penal laws *quas Traianus ex parte frustratus est* ['which Trajan repealed in part']; and yet Tertullian, in another part of his *Apology*, exposes the inconsistency of prohibiting inquiries and enjoining punishments.

60 Eusebius (*Hist. Ecclesiast.*, iv, 9) has preserved the edict of Hadrian. He has likewise (ch. 13) given us one still more favourable under the name of Antoninus; the authenticity of which is not so universally allowed. The second *Apology* of Justin contains some curious particulars relative to the accusations of Christians.

61 See Tertullian (*Apolog.*, ch. 40). The acts of the martyrdom of Polycarp exhibit a lively picture of these tumults, which were usually fomented by the malice of the Jews.

62 These regulations are inserted in the above-mentioned edicts of Hadrian and Pius. See the apology of Melito (*apud* Euseb., iv, 26).

63 See the rescript of Trajan, and the conduct of Pliny. The most authentic acts of the martyrs abound in these exhortations.

64 In particular, see Tertullian (*Apolog.*, chs 2 and 3), and Lactantius (*Institut.*

Divin., v, 9). Their reasonings are almost the same; but we may discover that one of these apologists had been a lawyer and the other a rhetorician.

65 See two instances of this kind of torture in the *Acta Sincera Martyrum* published by Ruinart, pp. 160 and 399. Jerome, in his Legend of Paul the Hermit, tells a strange story of a young man who was chained naked on a bed of flowers, and assaulted by a beautiful and wanton courtesan. He quelled the rising temptation by biting off his tongue.

66 The conversion of his wife provoked Claudius Herminianus, governor of Cappadocia, to treat the Christians with uncommon severity. Tertullian, *ad Scapulam*, ch. 8.

67 Tertullian, in his epistle to the governor of Africa, mentions several remarkable instances of lenity and forbearance which had happened within his knowledge.

68 *Neque enim in universum aliquid quod quasi certam formam habeat constitui potest* ['Particular fixed offences are not to be construed beyond the letter of the law']: an expression of Trajan which gave a very great latitude to the governors of provinces.

69 *In metalla damnamur, in insulas relegamur.* Tertullian, *Apolog.*, ch. 12. ['We are sentenced to the mines, we are banished to the islands.'] The mines of Numidia contained nine bishops, with a proportionable number of their clergy and people, to whom Cyprian addressed a pious epistle of praise and comfort. See Cyprian, *Epistol.*, 76 and 77.

 * *page 323* [condemned]

70 Though we cannot receive with entire confidence either the epistles or the acts of Ignatius (they may be found in the second volume of the Apostolic Fathers) yet we may quote that bishop of Antioch as one of those *exemplary* martyrs. He was sent in chains to Rome as a public spectacle; and, when he arrived at Troas, he received the pleasing intelligence that the persecution of Antioch was already at an end.

71 Among the martyrs of Lyons (Eusebius, v, 1), the slave Blandina was distinguished by more exquisite tortures. Of the five martyrs so much celebrated in the acts of Felicitas and Perpetua, two were of a servile, and two others of a very mean, condition.

72 Origen, *Advers. Celsum.*, iii, 116. His words deserve to be transcribed: Ὀλίγοι κατὰ καιροὺς, καὶ σφόδρα εὐαρίθμητοι περὶ τῶν Χριστιανῶν θεοσεβείας τεθνήκασι. ['On appropriate occasions, a few, very insignificant in number, died on account of their Christian religion.']

73 If we recollect that *all* the Plebeians of Rome were not Christians, and that all the Christians were not saints and martyrs, we may judge with how much safety religious honours can be ascribed to bones or urns indiscriminately taken from the public burial-place. After ten centuries of a very free and open trade, some suspicions have arisen among the more learned Catholics. They now require, as a proof of sanctity and martyrdom, the letters B. M., a vial full of red liquor, supposed to be blood, or the figure of a palm tree. But the two former signs are of little weight, and with regard to the last it is observed by the critics, 1. That the figure, as it is called, of a palm is perhaps a cypress, and perhaps only a stop, the flourish of a comma, used in the monumental inscriptions. 2. That the palm was the symbol of victory among the Pagans. 3. That among the Christians it served as the emblem, not only of martyrdom, but in general of a joyful resurrection. See the epistle of P. Mabillon, on the worship of unknown saints, and Muratori, *Sopra le Antichità Italiane, Dissertat.*, lviii.

74 As a specimen of these legends, we may be satisfied with 10,000 Christian soldiers crucified in one day, either by Trajan or Hadrian, on Mount Ararat. See Baronius *ad Martyrologium Romanum*; Tillemont, *Mém. Ecclésiast.*, ii, ii, 438; and Geddes's *Miscellanies*, ii, 203. The abbreviation of MIL, which may signify either soldiers or thousands, is said to have occasioned some extraordinary mistakes.

75 Dionysius, *apud* Euseb., vi, 41. One of the seventeen was likewise accused of robbery.

76 The letters of Cyprian exhibit a very curious and original picture both of the man and of the times. See likewise the two lives of Cyprian, composed with equal accuracy, though with very different views; the one by Le Clerc (*Bibliothèque Universelle*, xii, 208–378), the other by Tillemont, *Mémoires Ecclésiastiques*, iv, i, 76–459.

77 See the polite but severe epistle of the clergy of Rome to the bishop of Carthage (Cyprian, *Epist.*, 8, 9). Pontius labours with the greatest care and diligence to justify his master against the general censure.

78 In particular those of Dionysius of Alexandria and Gregory Thaumaturgus of Neo-Caesarea. See Eusebius, *Hist. Ecclesiast.*, vi, 40, and *Mémoires* de Tillemont, iv, ii, 685.

79 See Cyprian, *Epist.*, 16, and his life by Pontius.

80 We have an original life of Cyprian by the deacon Pontius, the companion of his exile, and the spectator of his death; and we likewise possess the ancient proconsular acts of his martyrdom. These two relations are consistent with each other and with probability, and, what is somewhat remarkable, they are both unsullied by any miraculous circumstances.

81 It should seem that these were circular orders, sent at the same time to all the governors. Dionysius (*apud* Euseb., vii, 11) relates the history of his own banishment from Alexandria almost in the same manner. But, as he escaped and survived the persecution, we must account him either more or less fortunate than Cyprian.

82 See Pliny, *Hist. Natur.*, v, 3; Cellarius, *Geograph. Antiq.*, iii, 96; Shaw's *Travels*, p. 90; and for the adjacent country (which is terminated by Cape Bona, or the promontory of Mercury), *L'Afrique* de Marmol., ii, 494. There are the remains of an aqueduct near Curubis, or Curbis, at present altered into Gurbes; and Dr Shaw read an inscription which styles that city *Colonia Fulvia*. The deacon Pontius (in *Vit. Cyprian.*, ch. 12) calls it *apricum et competentem locum, hospitium pro voluntate secretum, et quicquid apponi eis ante promissum est, qui regnum et iustitiam Dei quaerunt.* ['A sunny and convenient spot, a desirable secret refuge, and a foretaste of the kingdom of heaven and God's justice.']

83 See Cyprian, *Epistol.*, 77. Edit. Fell.

84 Upon his conversion, he had sold those gardens for the benefit of the poor. The indulgence of God (most probably the liberality of some Christian friend) restored them to Cyprian. See Pontius, ch. 15.

85 When Cyprian, a twelvemonth before, was sent into exile, he dreamt that he would be put to death the next day. The event made it necessary to explain that word as signifying a year. Pontius, ch. 12.

86 Pontius (ch. 15) acknowledges that Cyprian, with whom he supped, passed the night *custodia delicata* [in pleasant custody]. The bishop exercised a last and very proper act of jurisdiction, by directing that the younger females who watched

in the street should be removed from the dangers and temptations of a nocturnal crowd. *Act. Proconsularia*, ch. 2.

87 See the original sentence in the *Acts*, ch. 4, and in Pontius, ch. 17. The latter expresses it in a more rhetorical manner.

88 Pontius, ch. 19. M. de Tillemont (*Mémoires*, iv, i, 450, note 50) is not pleased with so positive an exclusion of any former martyrs of the episcopal rank.

89 Whatever opinion we may entertain of the character or principles of Thomas Becket, we must acknowledge that he suffered death with a constancy not unworthy of the primitive martyrs. See Lord Lyttelton's *History of Henry II*, ii, 592, etc.

90 See, in particular, the treatise of Cyprian *de Lapsis*, pp. 87–98, edit. Fell. The learning of Dodwell (*Dissertat. Cyprianic.*, xii, xiii) and the ingenuity of Middleton (*Free Inquiry*, p. 162, etc.) have left scarcely anything to add concerning the merit, the honours, and the motives of the martyrs.

91 Cyprianus, *Epistol.*, 5, 6, 7, 22 and 24, and *de Unitat. Ecclesiae*. The number of pretended martyrs has been much multiplied by the custom which was introduced of bestowing that honourable name on confessors.

92 *Certatim gloriosa in certamina ruebatur; multoque avidius tum martyria gloriosis mortibus quaerebantur, quam nunc Episcopatus pravis ambitionibus appetuntur.* Sulpicius Severus, Bk ii. ['They rushed to compete in this glorious contest; and they sought a glorious death by martyrdom more avidly than the base and ambitious seek a bishopric now.'] He might have omitted the word *nunc* [now].

93 See *Epist. ad Roman.*, chs 4 and 5; *apud Patres Apostol.*, ii, 27. It suited the purpose of Bishop Pearson (see *Vindiciae Ignatianae*, ii, 9) to justify, by a profusion of examples and authorities, the sentiments of Ignatius.

94 The story of Polyeuctes, on which Corneille has founded a very beautiful tragedy, is one of the most celebrated, though not perhaps the most authentic, instances of this excessive zeal. We should observe that the sixtieth canon of the council of Illiberis refuses the title of martyrs to those who exposed themselves to death by publicly destroying the idols.

95 See Epictetus, iv, 7 (though there is some doubt whether he alludes to the Christians); Marcus Antoninus, *de Rebus Suis*, xi, 3; Lucian, in *Peregrin*.

96 Tertullian, *ad Scapul.*, ch. 5. The learned are divided between three persons of the same name, who were all proconsuls of Asia. I am inclined to ascribe this story to Antoninus Pius, who was afterwards emperor, and who may have governed Asia under the reign of Trajan.

97 Mosheim, *de Rebus Christ. ante Constantin.*, p. 235.

98 See the Epistle of the Church at Smyrna, *ap*. Euseb., *Hist. Eccles.*, iv, 15.

99 In the second apology of Justin, there is a particular and very curious instance of this legal delay. The same indulgence was granted to accused Christians in the persecution of Decius; and Cyprian (*de Lapsis*) expressly mentions the *dies negantibus praestitutus* [day set aside for people to recant].

100 Tertullian considers flight from persecution as an imperfect, but very criminal apostasy, as an impious attempt to elude the will of God, etc. etc. He has written a treatise on this subject (see pp. 536–44, edit. Rigalt), which is filled with the wildest fanaticism and the most incoherent declamation. It is, however, somewhat remarkable that Tertullian did not suffer martyrdom himself.

101 The *Libellatici* [i.e., those Christians who procured the certificates], who are chiefly known by the writings of Cyprian, are described, with the utmost precision, in the copious commentary of Mosheim, pp. 483–89.

102 Pliny, *Epistol.*, x, 97, Dionysius Alexandrin. *apud* Euseb., vi, 41. *Ad prima statim verba minantis inimici maximus fratrum numerus fidem suam prodidit; nec prostratus est persecutionis impetu, sed voluntario lapsu seipsum prostravit.* ['At the first threatening words of a denouncer, a very large number of Christians immediately betrayed their faith; and humbly submitted, not as a result of persecution, but of their own accord.'] Cyprianus, *Opera*, p. 89. Among these deserters were many priests, and even bishops.

103 It was on this occasion that Cyprian wrote his treatise *de Lapsis* and many of his epistles. The controversy concerning the treatment of penitent apostates does not occur among the Christians of the preceding century. Shall we ascribe this to the superiority of their faith and courage or to our less intimate knowledge of their history?

104 See Mosheim, p. 97. Sulpicius Severus was the first author of this computation; though he seemed desirous of reserving the tenth and greatest persecution for the coming of the Antichrist.

105 The testimony given by Pontius Pilate is first mentioned by Justin. The successive improvements which the story has acquired (as it passed through the hands of Tertullian, Eusebius, Epiphanius, Chrysostom, Orosius, Gregory of Tours, and the authors of the several editions of the acts of Pilate) are very fairly stated by Dom. Calmet, *Dissertat. sur l'Ecriture*, iii, 651, etc.

106 On this miracle, as it is commonly called, of the Thundering Legion, see the admirable criticism of Mr Moyle, in his Works, ii, 81–390.

107 Dion Cassius, or rather his abbreviator Xiphilin, lxxii, 1206. Mr Moyle (p. 266) has explained the condition of the church under the reign of Commodus.

108 Compare the life of Caracalla in the *Augustan History* with the epistle of Tertullian to Scapula. Dr Jortin (*Remarks on Ecclesiastical History*, ii, 5, etc.) considers the cure of Severus by the means of holy oil, with a strong desire to convert it into a miracle.

109 Tertullian, *de Fuga*, ch. 13. The present was made during the feast of the Saturnalia; and it is a matter of serious concern to Tertullian that the faithful should be confounded with the most infamous professions which purchased the connivance of the government.

110 Eusebius, v, 23 and 24; Mosheim, pp. 435–47.

111 *Iudaeos fieri sub gravi poena vetuit. Idem etiam de Christianis sanxit.* ['He ordered that the Jews should not be subjected to severe punishment, and he even issued the same instructions in the case of the Christians.'] *Hist. August.*, p. 70.

112 Sulpicius Severus, ii, 384. This computation (allowing for a single exception) is confirmed by the history of Eusebius, and by the writings of Cyprian.

113 The antiquity of Christian churches is discussed by Tillemont (*Mémoires Ecclésiastiques*, iii, ii, pp. 68–72), and by Mr Moyle (i, 378–98). The former refers the first construction of them to the peace of Alexander Severus, the latter to the peace of Gallienus.

114 See the *Augustan History*, p. 130. The emperor Alexander adopted their method of publicly proposing the names of those persons who were candidates for ordination. It is true that the honour of this practice is likewise attributed to the Jews.

115 Eusebius, *Hist. Ecclesiast.*, vi, 21: Hieronym., *de Script. Eccles.* ch. 54. Mammaea was styled a holy and pious woman, both by the Christians and the Pagans. From the former, therefore, it was impossible that she should deserve that honourable epithet.

116 See the *Augustan History*, p. 123. Mosheim (p. 465) seems to refine too much on the domestic religion of Alexander. His design of building a public temple to Christ (*Hist. August.*, p. 129), and the objection which was suggested either to him, or in similar circumstances to Hadrian, appear to have no other foundation than an improbable report, invented by the Christians and credulously adopted by an historian of the age of Constantine.

117 Eusebius, vi, 28. It may be presumed that the success of the Christians had exasperated the increasing bigotry of the Pagans. Dion Cassius, who composed his history under the former reign, had most probably intended for the use of his master those counsels of persecution which he ascribes to a better age and to the favourite of Augustus. Concerning this oration of Maecenas, or rather of Dion, I may refer to my own unbiased opinion (i, 37, note 28) [Chapter 2, note 25] and to the Abbé de la Bléterie (*Mémoires de l'Académie*, xxiv, 303; xxv, 432).

118 Orosius, vii, 19, mentions Origen as the object of Maximin's resentment, and Firmilianus, a Cappadocian bishop of that age, gives a just and confined idea of this persecution (*apud* Cyprian., *Epist.* 75).

119 The mention of those princes who were publicly supposed to be Christians, as we find it in an epistle of Dionysius of Alexandria (*ap* Euseb., vii, 10), evidently alludes to Philip and his family, and forms a contemporary evidence that such a report had prevailed; but the Egyptian bishop, who lived at an humble distance from the court of Rome, expresses himself with a becoming diffidence concerning the truth of the fact. The epistles of Origen (which were extant in the time of Eusebius, see vi, 36) would most probably decide this curious, rather than important, question.

120 Eusebius, vi, 34. The story, as is usual, has been embellished by succeeding writers, and is confuted, with much superfluous learning, by Frederick Spanheim (*Opera Varia*, ii, 400, etc.).

121 Lactantius, *de Mortibus Persecutorum*, chs 3 and 4. After celebrating the felicity and increase of the church, under a long succession of good princes he adds, *Extitit post annos plurimos, execrabile animal, Decius, qui vexerat Ecclesiam.* ['After a long period of years there appeared that detestable creature, Decius, who persecuted the church.']

122 Eusebius, vi, 39; Cyprian, *Epist.*, 55. The see of Rome remained vacant from the martyrdom of Fabianus, the 20th of January, AD 250, till the election of Cornelius, the 4th of June, AD 251. Decius had probably left Rome, since he was killed before the end of that year.

123 Eusebius, vii, 10; Mosheim (p. 548) has very clearly shown that the Prefect Macrianus and the Egyptian *Magus* are one and the same person.

124 Eusebius (vii, 13) gives us a Greek version of this Latin edict, which seems to have been very concise. By another edict he directed that the *Coemeteria* [cemeteries] should be restored to the Christians.

125 Eusebius, vii, 30; Lactantius, *de M. P.*, ch. 6; Hieronym., in *Chron.* p. 177; Orosius, vii, ch 23. Their language is in general so ambiguous and incorrect that we are at a loss to determine how far Aurelian had carried his intentions before

he was assassinated. Most of the moderns (except Dodwell, *Dissertat. Cyprian.*, xi, 64) have seized the occasion of gaining a few extraordinary martyrs.

126 Paul was better pleased with the title of *Ducenarius*, than with that of bishop. The *Ducenarius* was an Imperial procurator, so called from his salary of two hundred *sestertia*, or £1600 a year. (See Salmasius *ad Hist. August.* p. 124.) Some critics suppose that the bishop of Antioch had actually obtained such an office from Zenobia, while others considered it only as a figurative expression of his pomp and insolence.

127 Simony [the sale of ecclesiastical offices] was not unknown in those times; and the clergy sometimes bought what they intended to sell. It appears that the bishopric of Carthage was purchased by a wealthy matron, named Lucilla, for her servant Majorinus. The price was 400 *folles*. (*Monument. Antiq. ad calcem Optati*, p. 263.) Every *follis* contained 125 pieces of silver, and the whole sum may be computed at about £2400.

128 If we are desirous of extenuating the vices of Paul, we must suspect the assembled bishops of the East of publishing the most malicious calumnies in circular epistles addressed to all the churches of the empire (*ap.* Euseb., vii, 30).

129 His heresy (like those of Noetus and Sabellius, in the same century) tended to confound the mysterious distinction of the divine persons. See Mosheim, p. 702, etc.

130 Eusebius, *Hist. Ecclesiast.*, vii, 30. We are entirely indebted to him for the curious story of Paul of Samosata.

131 The era of Martyrs, which is still in use among the Copts and the Abyssinians, must be reckoned from the 29th of August, AD 284; as the beginning of the Egyptian year was nineteen days earlier than the real accession of Diocletian. See *Dissertation Préliminaire à l'Art de vérifier les Dates*.

132 The expression of Lactantius (*de M. P.*, ch. 15), *sacrificio pollui coegit* ['he forced them to become polluted through sacrifice to the gods'], implies their antecedent conversion to the faith; but does not seem to justify the assertion of Mosheim (p. 912) that they had been privately baptised.

133 M. de Tillemont (*Mémoires Ecclésiastiques*, v, i, 11 and 12) has quoted, from the *Spicilegium* of Dom. Luc d'Acheri, a very curious introduction which bishop Theonas composed for the use of Lucian.

134 Lactantius, *de M. P.*, ch. 10.

135 Eusebius, *Hist. Ecclesiast.*, viii, i. The reader who consults the original will not accuse me of heightening the picture. Eusebius was about sixteen years of age at the accession of the emperor Diocletian.

136 We might quote, among a great number of instances, the mysterious worship of Mithras, and the Taurobolia; the latter of which became fashionable in the time of the Antonines (see a Dissertation of M. de Boze, in the *Mémoires de l'Académie des Inscriptions*, ii, 443). The romance of Apuleius is as full of devotion as of satire.

137 The impostor Alexander very strongly recommended the oracle of Trophonius at Mallos, and those of Apollo at Claros and Miletus (Lucian, ii, 236, edit. Reitz). The last of these, whose singular history would furnish a very curious episode, was consulted by Diocletian before he published his edicts of persecution (Lactantius, *de M. P.*, ch. 11).

138 Besides the ancient stories of Pythagoras and Aristeas, the cures performed at the shrine of Aesculapius and the fables related of Apollonius of Tyana were

frequently opposed to the miracles of Christ; though I agree with Dr Lardner (see *Testimonies*, iii, 253, 352) that, when Philostratus composed the life of Apollonius, he had no such intention.

139 It is seriously to be lamented that the Christian fathers, by acknowledging the supernatural or, as they deem it, the infernal part of Paganism, destroy with their own hands the great advantage which we might otherwise derive from the liberal concessions of our adversaries.

140 Julian (p. 301, edit. Spanheim) expresses a pious joy that the providence of the gods had extinguished the impious sects, and for the most part destroyed the books of the Pyrrhonians and Epicureans, which had been very numerous, since Epicurus himself composed no less than 300 volumes. See Diogenes Laertius, x, 26.

141 *Cumque alios audiam mussitare indignanter, et dicere oportere statui per Senatum, aboleantur ut haec scripta, quibus Christiana religio comprobetur et vetustatis opprimatur auctoritas.* Arnobius, *adversus Gentes*, iii, 103, 104. ['I hear some people mutter indignantly and say that the Senate should decree the suppression of these writings against which the Christian religion is tested and the authority of tradition is brought into question.'] He adds very properly, *Erroris convincite Ciceronem . . . nam intercipere scripta, et publicatam velle submergere lectionem, non est Deum [Deos] defendere sed veritatis testificationem timere.* ['You should demonstrate Cicero's errors . . . for to seize his writings and to wish to stop the public from reading them is not to defend God but to fear the evidence of truth.']

142 Lactantius (*Divin. Institut.*, v, 2, 3) gives a very clear and spirited account of two of these philosophic adversaries of the faith. The large treatise of Porphyry against the Christians consisted of thirty books, and was composed in Sicily about the year 270.

143 See Socrates, *Hist. Ecclesiast.*, i, 9; and *Codex Justinian.*, i, tit. i, 3.

144 Eusebius, viii, 4, 17. He limits the number of military martyrs, by a remarkable expression (σπανίως τούτων εἰς που καὶ δεύτερος) [perhaps the odd one or two], of which neither his Latin nor French translations have rendered the energy. Notwithstanding the authority of Eusebius and the silence of Lactantius, Ambrose, Sulpicius, Orosius, etc. it has been long believed that the Thebaean legion, consisting of 6000 Christians, suffered martyrdom, by the order of Maximian, in the valley of the Pennine Alps. The story was first published about the middle of the fifth century by Eucherius, bishop of Lyons, who received it from certain persons, who received it from Isaac, bishop of Geneva, who is said to have received it from Theodore, bishop of Octodurum. The abbey of St Maurice still subsists, a rich monument of the credulity of Sigismund, king of Burgundy. See an excellent Dissertation in the thirty-sixth volume of the *Bibliothèque Raisonnée*, pp. 427–454.

145 See the *Acta Sincera*, p. 299. The accounts of his martyrdom and of that of Marcellus bear every mark of truth and authenticity.

146 *Acta Sincera*, p. 302.

147 *De M. P.*, ch. 11. Lactantius (or whoever was the author of this little treatise) was, at the time, an inhabitant of Nicomedia; but it seems difficult to conceive how he could acquire so accurate a knowledge of what passed in the Imperial cabinet.

148 The only circumstance which we can discover is the devotion and jealousy of

the mother of Galerius. She is described by Lactantius as *deorum montium cultrix; mulier admodum superstitiosa* [worshipper of the mountain gods; a quite superstitious woman]. She had a great influence over her son, and was offended by the disregard of some of her Christian servants.

149   The worship and festival of the god Terminus are elegantly illustrated by M. de Boze, *Mém. de l'Académie des Inscriptions*, i, 50.

150   In our only manuscript of Lactantius, we read *profectus* [having set forth]; but reason and the authority of all the critics allow us, instead of that word, which destroys the sense of the passage, to substitute *praefectus* [prefect].

151   Lactantius, *de M. P.*, ch. 12, gives a very lively picture of the destruction of the church.

152   Mosheim (pp. 922–26), from many scattered passages of Lactantius and Eusebius, has collected a very just and accurate notion of this edict; though he sometimes deviates into conjecture and refinement.

153   Many ages afterwards, Edward I practised with great success the same mode of persecution against the clergy of England. See Hume's *History of England*, ii, 300, last 4to edition.

154   Lactantius only calls him *quidam, etsi non recte, magno tamen animo, etc.* ['one who, even if not rightly, yet with great courage, etc.'], ch. 12. Eusebius (viii, 5) adorns him with secular honours. Neither have condescended to mention his name; but the Greeks celebrate his memory under that of John. See Tillemont, *Mémoires Ecclésiastiques*, v, ii, 320.

155   Lactantius, *de M. P.*, chs 13 and 14. *Potentissimi quondam eunuchi necati, per quos palatium et ipse constabat.* ['The once all-powerful eunuchs, on whom the palace and the emperor himself relied, were put to death.'] Eusebius (viii, 6) mentions the cruel executions of the eunuchs Gorgonius and Dorotheus, and of Anthimius, bishop of Nicomedia: and both those writers describe, in a vague but tragical manner, the horrid scenes which were acted even in the Imperial presence.

156   See Lactantius, Eusebius, and Constantine, *ad Coetum Sanctorum*, ch. 25. Eusebius confesses his ignorance of the cause of the fire.

157   Tillemont, *Mémoires Ecclésiast.*, v, i, 43.

  *   *page 341*   [the poet, 65–8 BC]

158   See the *Acta Sincera* of Ruinart, p. 353; those of Felix of Thibara, or Tibiur, appear much less corrupted than in the other editions, which afford a lively specimen of legendary licence.

  †   *page 341*   [betrayers]

159   See the first book of Optatus of Milevis, *Against the Donatists*, Paris, 1700 [*leg.* 1702], edit. Dupin. He lived under the reign of Valens.

160   The ancient monuments, published at the end of Optatus, p. 261, etc. describe, in a very circumstantial manner, the proceedings of the governors in the destruction of churches. They made a minute inventory of the plate, etc. which they found in them. That of the Church of Cirta, in Numidia, is still extant. It consisted of two chalices of gold, and six of silver; six urns, one kettle, seven lamps, all likewise of silver; besides a large quantity of brass utensils, and wearing apparel.

161   Lactantius (*Institut. Divin.*, v, 11) confines the calamity to the *conventiculum* [the church], with its congregation. Eusebius (viii, 11) extends it to a whole city, and introduces something very like a regular siege. His ancient Latin translator,

Rufinus, adds the important circumstance of the permission given to the inhabitants of retiring from thence. As Phrygia reached to the confines of Isauria, it is possible that the restless temper of those independent Barbarians may have contributed to this misfortune.

162 Eusebius, viii, 6. M. de Valois (with some probability) thinks that he has discovered the Syrian rebellion in an oration of Libanius, and that it was a rash attempt of the tribune Eugenius, who with only five hundred men seized Antioch, and might perhaps allure the Christians by the promise of religious toleration. From Eusebius (ix, 8), as well as from Moses of Chorene (*Hist. Armen.*, ii, 77, etc.), it may be inferred that Christianity was already introduced into Armenia.

163 See Mosheim, p. 938; the text of Eusebius very plainly shows that the governors, whose powers were enlarged, not restrained, by the new laws, could punish with death the most obstinate Christians, as an example to their brethren.

164 Athanasius, p. 833, *ap.* Tillemont, *Mém. Ecclésiast.*, v, i, 90.

165 Eusebius, viii, 13; Lactantius, *de M. P.*, ch. 15; Dodwell (*Dissertat. Cyprian.*, xi, 75) represents them as inconsistent with each other. But the former evidently speaks of Constantius in the station of Caesar, and the latter of the same prince in the rank of Augustus.

166 Datianus is mentioned in Gruter's Inscriptions as having determined the limits between the territories of Pax Julia, and those of Ebora, both cities in the southern part of Lusitania. If we recollect the neighbourhood of those places to Cape St Vincent, we may suspect that the celebrated deacon and martyr of that name has been inaccurately assigned by Prudentius, etc. to Saragossa, or Valentia. See the pompous history of his sufferings, in the *Mémoires* de Tillemont, v, ii, 58–85. Some critics are of opinion that the department of Constantius, as Caesar, did not include Spain, which still continued under the immediate jurisdiction of Maximian.

167 Eusebius, viii, 11; Gruter, *Inscript.*, 1171, No. 18. Rufinus has mistaken the office of Adauctus, as well as the place of his martyrdom.

168 Eusebius, viii, 14. But, as Maxentius was vanquished by Constantine, it suited the purpose of Lactantius to place his death among those of the persecutors.

169 The epitaph of Marcellus is to be found in Gruter, *Inscrip.*, 1172, No. 3, and it contains all that we know of his history. Marcellinus and Marcellus, whose names follow in the list of popes, are supposed by many critics to be different persons; but the learned Abbé de Longuerue was convinced that they were one and the same.

> *Veredicus rector, lapsis quia crimina flere*
> *Praedixit, miseris fuit omnibus hostis amarus.*
> *Hinc furor, hinc odium; sequitur discordia, lites,*
> *Seditio, caedes; solvuntur foedera pacis.*
> *Crimen ob alterius, Christum qui in pace negavit,*
> *Finibus expulsus patriae est feritate Tyranni.*
> *Haec breviter Damasus voluit comperta referre:*
> *Marcelli populus meritum cognescere posset.*

['A truthful ruler – for he foretold that the lapsed Christians would be punished – he proved a bitter enemy to all these wretches. This was the cause of madness and hatred; followed by discord, lawsuits, insurrection and slaughter.

Agreements to live in peace were broken. One man who denied Christ in a time of peace, was for this offence expelled from his country through the tyrant's cruelty. Damasus decided to make a brief report of these facts, so that the people should know of Marcellus's worthy deeds.']

We may observe, that Damasus was made bishop of Rome, AD 366.

170 Optatus, *contr. Donatist.*, i, 17 and 18.

171 The Acts of the Passion of St Boniface, which abound in miracles and declamation, are published by Ruinart (pp. 283–91) both in Greek and Latin, from the authority of very ancient manuscripts.

172 During the four first centuries there exist few traces of either bishops or bishoprics in the western Illyricum. It has been thought probable that the primate of Milan extended his jurisdiction over Sirmium, the capital of that great province. See the *Geographia Sacra* of Charles de St Paul, pp. 68–76, with the observations of Lucas Holstenius.

173 The eighth book of Eusebius, as well as the supplement concerning the martyrs of Palestine, principally relate to the persecution of Galerius and Maximin. The general lamentations with which Lactantius opens the fifth book of his *Divine Institutions* allude to their cruelty.

174 Eusebius (viii, 17) has given us a Greek version, and Lactantius (*de M. P.*, ch. 34) the Latin original, of this memorable edict. Neither of these writers seems to recollect how directly it contradicts whatever they have just affirmed of the remorse and repentance of Galerius.

175 Eusebius, ix, 1. He inserts the epistle of the prefect.

176 See Eusebius, viii, 14; ix, 2–8; Lactantius, *de M. P.*, ch. 36. These writers agree in representing the arts of Maximin; but the former relates the execution of several martyrs, while the latter expressly affirms, *occidi servos Dei vetuit* ['he forbade the killing of the servants of God'].

177 A few days before his death, he published a very ample edict of toleration, in which he imputes all the severities which the Christians suffered to the judges and governors, who had misunderstood his intentions. See the edict in Eusebius, ix, 10.

178 Such is the *fair* deduction from two remarkable passages in Eusebius, viii, 2, and *de Martyr. Palestin.*, ch. 12. The prudence of the historian has exposed his own character to censure and suspicion. It is well known that he himself had been thrown into prison; and it was suggested that he had purchased his deliverance by some dishonourable compliance. The reproach was urged in his lifetime, and even in his presence, at the council of Tyre. See Tillemont, *Mémoires Ecclésiastiques*, viii, i, 67.

179 The ancient, and perhaps authentic, account of the sufferings of Tarachus and his companions (*Acta Sincera*, Ruinart, pp. 419–48) is filled with strong expressions of resentment and contempt, which could not fail of irritating the magistrate. The behaviour of Aedesius to Hierocles, prefect of Egypt, was still more extraordinary, λόγοις τε καὶ ἔργοις τὸν δικαστὴν . . . περιβαλών ['verbally and physically assaulting the prefect'].

180 Eusebius, *de Martyr. Palestin.*, ch. 13.

181 Augustin., *Collat. Carthagin. Dei*, iii, 13, *ap.* Tillemont, *Mémoires Ecclésiastiques*, v, i, 46. The controversy with the Donatists has reflected some, though perhaps a partial, light on the history of the African church.

  * *page 349* [compilers or collectors of legends concerning Christian martyrs]

182 Eusebius, *de Martyr. Palestin.*, ch. 13. He closes his narration by assuring us that these were the martyrdoms inflicted in Palestine during the whole course of the persecution. The fifth chapter of his eighth book, which relates to the province of Thebais in Egypt, may seem to contradict our moderate computation; but it will only lead us to admire the artful management of the historian. Choosing for the scene of the most exquisite cruelty the most remote and sequestered country of the Roman empire, he relates that in Thebais from ten to one hundred persons had frequently suffered martyrdom in the same day. But when he proceeds to mention his own journey into Egypt, his language insensibly becomes more cautious and moderate. Instead of a large, but definite number, he speaks of many Christians (πλείους), and most artfully selected two ambiguous words (ἱστορήσαμεν, and ὑπομείναντας), which may signify either what he had seen or what he had heard; either the expectation or the execution of the punishment. Having thus provided a secure evasion, he commits the equivocal passage to his readers and translators; justly conceiving that their piety would induce them to prefer the most favourable sense. There was perhaps some malice in the remark of Theodorus Metochita, that all who, like Eusebius, had been conversant with the Egyptians delighted in an obscure and intricate style. (See Valesius, *ad loc.*)

183 When Palestine was divided into three, the prefecture of the East contained forty-eight provinces. As the ancient distinctions of nations were long since abolished, the Romans distributed the provinces according to a general proportion of their extent and opulence.

184 *Ut gloriari possint nullum se innocentium peremisse, nam et ipse audivi aliquos gloriantes, quia administratio sua in hac parte fuerit incruenta.* ['In order to boast that they put no innocents to death, for I myself have heard some boast, because their administration of this region was without bloodshed.'] Lactantius, *Instit. Divin.*, v, 11.

 * *page 350* [the Inquisition]

 † *page 350* [Emperor of Germany and King of Spain, 1500–1558]

185 Grot., *Annal. de Rebus Belgicis*, i, 12, edit. fol.

 ‡ *page 350* [Dutch jurist and historian, 1583–1645]

186 Fra Paolo (*Istoria del Concilio Tridentino*, Bk iii) reduces the number of Belgic martyrs to 50,000. In learning and moderation, Fra Paolo was not inferior to Grotius. The priority of time gives some advantage to the evidence of the former, which he loses on the other hand by the distance of Venice from the Netherlands.

CHAPTER 17 (Summary)

Foundation of Constantinople – political system of Constantine and his successors – military discipline – the palace – the finances

The second and third volumes of *The Decline and Fall* were published in 1781, five years after the first sixteen chapters appeared. Gibbon resumes the history of the Roman empire with an account of the building of Constantinople as the new capital. He then reviews the laws and manners of the empire in the period from the dedication of Constantinople in AD 330 to the year of the Theodosian Code, AD 438. The hierarchy of officials is described according to their administrative, financial and military functions. He concludes the review with a detailed examination of the heavy taxation of the empire under Constantine.

CHAPTER 18 (Summary)

Character of Constantine – Gothic war – death of Constantine – division of the empire among his three sons – Persian war – tragic death of Constantine the Younger, and Constans – usurpation of Magnentius – civil war – victory of Constantius

Gibbon's assessment of Constantine's character contains praise for his military valour and criticism of his lack of justice: the crimes of his later years included the murder of his son, Crispus, in AD 326. Yet, despite involvement in wars between the Goths and the Sarmatians beyond the Danube, his reign ended in glory, and he died from natural causes in AD 337. Gibbon describes the bloodshed within Constantine's family over the succession of three of his sons, Constantine II, Constantius II and Constans. Constantius in the east was soon engaged in a conflict with the Persians lasting twenty-three years. Meanwhile, civil war within the empire caused the death of Constantine II in AD 340 and the murder of Constans in AD 350. A rival emperor in the west, Magnentius, was defeated by Constantius at the battle of Mursa in Lower Hungary in AD 353.

CHAPTER 19 (Summary)

*Constantius sole emperor – elevation and death of Gallus –
danger and elevation of Julian – Sarmatian and
Persian wars – victories of Julian in Gaul*

Chapter 19 deals with the later years of the reign of Constantius, when he allowed himself to be governed by eunuchs. In AD 354 they procured the death of his cousin, Gallus, who had ruled in Antioch as Caesar. Julian, another cousin of the emperor, was exiled to Athens, but was allowed to marry Helena, sister of Constantius, and was appointed Caesar to administer the western provinces. Constantius meanwhile visited Rome in AD 357 and had an obelisk transported from Egypt to commemorate his visit. Later, he quelled disturbances across the Danube in campaigns known as the Sarmatian War. Meanwhile, the Persians under Sapor II laid claim to Armenia and Mesopotamia, and Gaul was invaded by the Franks and the Alemanni. Julian repelled the German tribes and restored the cities of Gaul.

CHAPTER 20

*The motives, progress, and effects of the conversion
of Constantine – legal establishment and
constitution of the Christian or Catholic church*

The public establishment of Christianity may be considered as one of those important and domestic revolutions which excite the most lively curiosity and afford the most valuable instruction. The victories and the civil policy of Constantine no longer influence the state of Europe; but a considerable portion of the globe still retains the impression which it received from the conversion of that monarch; and the ecclesiastical institutions of his reign are still connected, by an indissoluble chain, with the opinions, the passions, and the interests of the present generation.

In the consideration of a subject which may be examined with impartiality, but cannot be viewed with indifference, a difficulty immediately arises of a very unexpected nature: that of ascertaining the real and precise date of the conversion of Constantine. The eloquent Lactantius, in the midst of his court, seems impatient[1] to proclaim to the world the glorious example of the sovereign of Gaul; who, in the first moments of his reign, acknowledged and adored the majesty of the true and only God.[2] The learned Eusebius has ascribed the faith of Constantine to the miraculous sign which was displayed in the heavens whilst he meditated and prepared the Italian expedition.[3] The historian Zosimus maliciously asserts that the emperor had imbrued his hands in the blood of his eldest son, before he publicly renounced the gods of Rome and of his ancestors.[4] The perplexity produced by these discordant authorities is derived from the behaviour of Constantine himself. According to the strictness of ecclesiastical language, the first of the *Christian* emperors was unworthy of that name, till the moment of his death; since it was only during his last illness that he received, as a catechumen,* the imposition of hands,[5] and was afterwards admitted, by the initiatory rites of baptism, into the number of the faithful.[6] The Christianity of Constantine must be allowed in a much more vague and qualified sense; and the nicest accuracy is required in tracing the slow and almost imperceptible gradations by which the monarch declared himself the protector, and at length the proselyte, of the church. It was an arduous task to eradicate the habits and prejudices of his education, to acknowledge the divine power of Christ, and to understand that the truth of *his* revelation was incompatible with the worship of the gods. The obstacles which he had probably experienced in his own mind instructed him to proceed with caution in the momentous change of a national religion; and he insensibly discovered his new opinions, as far as he could enforce them with safety and with effect. During the whole course of his reign, the stream of Christianity flowed with a gentle, though accelerated, motion; but its general direction was sometimes checked, and sometimes diverted, by the accidental circumstances of the times, and by the prudence, or possibly by the caprice, of the monarch. His ministers were permitted to signify the intentions of their master in the various language which was best adapted to their respective principles;[7] and he artfully balanced the hopes and fears of his subjects by publishing in the same year two edicts: the first of which enjoined the solemn observance of Sunday,[8] and the second directed the regular consultation of the Aruspices.[9] While this important revolution yet remained in suspense, the Christians and the Pagans watched the conduct of their sovereign with the same anxiety, but with very opposite sentiments. The former were prompted by every motive of zeal, as well as vanity, to exaggerate the marks of his favour, and the evidences of his faith. The latter, till their just apprehensions were changed into despair and resentment, attempted to conceal from the world, and from themselves, that the gods of Rome could no longer reckon the emperor in the number of their votaries. The same passions and prejudices have engaged the partial writers of the times to connect the public profession of Christianity with the most glorious or the most ignominious era of the reign of Constantine.

Whatever symptoms of Christian piety might transpire in the discourses

or actions of Constantine, he persevered till he was near forty years of age
in the practice of the established religion;[10] and the same conduct, which
in the court of Nicomedia might be imputed to his fear, could be ascribed
only to the inclination or policy of the sovereign of Gaul. His liberality
restored and enriched the temples of the gods: the medals which issued
from his Imperial mint are impressed with the figures and attributes of
Jupiter and Apollo, of Mars and Hercules; and his filial piety increased the
council of Olympus by the solemn apotheosis of his father Constantius.[11]
But the devotion of Constantine was more peculiarly directed to the
genius of the Sun, the Apollo of Greek and Roman mythology; and he
was pleased to be represented with the symbols of the God of Light and
Poetry. The unerring shafts of that deity, the brightness of his eyes, his
laurel wreath, immortal beauty, and elegant accomplishments, seem to
point him out as the patron of a young hero. The altars of Apollo were
crowned with the votive offerings of Constantine; and the credulous
multitude were taught to believe that the emperor was permitted to
behold with mortal eyes the visible majesty of their tutelar deity, and that,
either waking or in a vision, he was blessed with the auspicious omens of
a long and victorious reign. The Sun was universally celebrated as the
invincible guide and protector of Constantine; and the Pagans might
reasonably expect that the insulted god would pursue with unrelenting
vengeance the impiety of his ungrateful favourite.[12]

As long as Constantine exercised a limited sovereignty over the
provinces of Gaul, his Christian subjects were protected by the authority,
and perhaps by the laws, of a prince who wisely left to the gods the care
of vindicating their own honour. If we may credit the assertion of
Constantine himself, he had been an indignant spectator of the savage
cruelties which were inflicted, by the hands of Roman soldiers, on those
citizens whose religion was their only crime.[13] In the East and in the
West, he had seen the different effects of severity and indulgence; and, as
the former was rendered still more odious by the example of Galerius, his
implacable enemy, the latter was recommended to imitation by the
authority and advice of a dying father. The son of Constantius immediately suspended or repealed the edicts of persecution, and granted the free
exercise of their religious ceremonies to all those who had already
professed themselves members of the church. They were soon encouraged to depend on the favour as well as on the justice of their sovereign,
who had imbibed a secret and sincere reverence for the name of Christ
and for the God of the Christians.[14]

About five months after the conquest of Italy, the emperor made a
solemn and authentic declaration of his sentiments, by the celebrated
edict of Milan, which restored peace to the Catholic Church. In the
personal interview of the two western princes, Constantine, by the
ascendant of genius and power, obtained the ready concurrence of his
colleague Licinius; the union of their names and authority disarmed the

fury of Maximin; and, after the death of the tyrant of the East,* the edict
of Milan was received as a general and fundamental law of the Roman
world.[15] The wisdom of the emperors provided for the constitution of all
the civil and religious rights of which the Christians had been so unjustly
deprived. It was enacted that the places of worship, and public lands,
which had been confiscated, should be restored to the church, without
dispute, without delay, and without expense; and this severe injunction
was accompanied with a gracious promise that, if any of the purchasers
had paid a fair and adequate price, they should be indemnified from the
Imperial treasury. The salutary regulations which guard the future
tranquillity of the faithful are framed on the principles of enlarged and
equal toleration; and such an equality must have been interpreted by a
recent sect as an advantageous and honourable distinction. The two
emperors proclaim to the world that they have granted a free and
absolute power to the Christians, and to all others, of following the
religion which each individual thinks proper to prefer, to which he has
addicted his mind, and which he may deem the best adapted to his own
use. They carefully explain every ambiguous word, remove every
exception, and exact from the governors of the provinces a strict
obedience to the true and simple meaning of an edict which was
designed to establish and secure, without any limitation, the claims of
religious liberty. They condescend to assign two weighty reasons which
have induced them to allow this universal toleration: the humane
intention of consulting the peace and happiness of their people; and the
pious hope that, by such a conduct, they shall appease and propitiate *the
Deity*, whose seat is in heaven. They gratefully acknowledge the many
signal proofs which they have received of the divine favour; and they
trust that the same Providence will for ever continue to protect the
prosperity of the prince and people. From these vague and indefinite
expressions of piety, three suppositions may be deduced, of a different,
but not of an incompatible, nature. The mind of Constantine might
fluctuate between the Pagan and the Christian religions. According to
the loose and complying notions of Polytheism, he might acknowledge
the God of the Christians as *one* of the *many* deities who composed the
hierarchy of heaven. Or perhaps he might embrace the philosophic and
pleasing idea that, notwithstanding the variety of names, of rites, and of
opinions, all the sects and all the nations of mankind are united in the
worship of the common Father and Creator of the universe.[16]

But the counsels of princes are more frequently influenced by views of
temporal advantage than by considerations of abstract and speculative
truth. The partial and increasing favour of Constantine may naturally be
referred to the esteem which he entertained for the moral character of the
Christians; and to a persuasion that the propagation of the gospel would
inculcate the practice of private and public virtue. Whatever latitude an
absolute monarch may assume in his own conduct, whatever indulgence

he may claim for his own passions, it is undoubtedly his interest that all his subjects should respect the natural and civil obligations of society. But the operation of the wisest laws is imperfect and precarious. They seldom inspire virtue, they cannot always restrain vice. Their power is insufficient to prohibit all that they condemn, nor can they always punish the actions which they prohibit. The legislators of antiquity had summoned to their aid the powers of education and of opinion. But every principle which had once maintained the vigour and purity of Rome and Sparta was long since extinguished in a declining and despotic empire. Philosophy still exercised her temperate sway over the human mind, but the cause of virtue derived very feeble support from the influence of the Pagan superstition. Under these discouraging circumstances, a prudent magistrate might observe with pleasure the progress of a religion, which diffused among the people a pure, benevolent, and universal system of ethics, adapted to every duty and every condition of life; recommended as the will and reason of the Supreme Deity, and enforced by the sanction of eternal rewards or punishments. The experience of Greek and Roman history could not inform the world how far the system of national manners might be reformed and improved by the precepts of a divine revelation; and Constantine might listen with some confidence to the flattering, and indeed reasonable, assurances of Lactantius. The eloquent apologist seemed firmly to expect, and almost ventured to promise, *that* the establishment of Christianity would restore the innocence and felicity of the primitive age; *that* the worship of the true God would extinguish war and dissension among those who mutually considered themselves as the children of a common parent; *that* every impure desire, every angry or selfish passion, would be restrained by the knowledge of the gospel; and *that* the magistrates might sheathe the sword of justice among a people who would be universally actuated by the sentiments of truth and piety, of equity and moderation, of harmony and universal love.[17]

The passive and unresisting obedience which bows under the yoke of authority, or even of oppression, must have appeared, in the eyes of an absolute monarch, the most conspicuous and useful of the evangelic virtues.[18] The primitive Christians derived the institution of civil government, not from the consent of the people, but from the decrees of heaven. The reigning emperor, though he had usurped the sceptre by treason and murder, immediately assumed the sacred character of vice gerent of the Deity. To the Deity alone he was accountable for the abuse of his power; and his subjects were indissolubly bound, by their oath of fidelity, to a tyrant who had violated every law of nature and society. The humble Christians were sent into the world as sheep among wolves; and, since they were not permitted to employ force, even in the defence of their religion, they should be still more criminal if they were tempted to shed the blood of their fellow-creatures in disputing the vain privileges, or the sordid possessions, of this transitory life. Faithful to the doctrine of the apostle* who in the reign of Nero had preached the duty of unconditional submission, the Christians of the three first centuries preserved their conscience pure and innocent of the guilt of secret conspiracy or open rebellion. While they experienced the rigour of persecution, they were never provoked either to meet their tyrants in the field or indignantly to withdraw themselves into some remote and sequestered corner of the globe.[19] The Protestants of France, of Germany, and of Britain[†] who asserted with such intrepid courage their civil and religious freedom, have been insulted by the invidious comparison between the conduct of the primitive and of the reformed Christians.[20] Perhaps, instead of censure, some applause may be due to the superior sense and spirit of our ancestors, who had convinced themselves that religion cannot abolish the unalienable rights of human nature.[21] Perhaps the patience of the primitive church may be ascribed to its weakness, as well as to its virtue. A sect of unwarlike plebeians, without leaders, without arms, without fortifications, must have encountered inevitable destruction in a rash and fruitless resistance to the master of the Roman legions. But the Christians, when they deprecated the wrath of Diocletian, or solicited the favour of Constantine, could allege, with truth and confidence, that they held the principle of passive obedience, and that, in the space of three centuries, their conduct had always been conformable to their principles. They might add that the throne of the emperors would be established on a fixed and permanent basis, if all their subjects, embracing the Christian doctrine, should learn to suffer and to obey.

In the general order of Providence, princes and tyrants are considered as the ministers of Heaven, appointed to rule or to chastise the nations of the earth. But sacred history affords many illustrious examples of the more immediate interposition of the Deity in the government of his chosen people. The sceptre and the sword were committed to the hands of Moses, of Joshua, of Gideon, of David, of the Maccabees; the virtues of those heroes were the motive or the effect of the divine favour, the success of their arms was destined to achieve the deliverance or the triumph of the church. If the judges of Israel were occasional and temporary magistrates, the kings of Judah derived from the royal unction of their great ancestor an hereditary and indefeasible right, which could not be forfeited by their own vices, nor recalled by the caprice of their subjects. The same extraordinary providence, which was no longer confined to the Jewish people, might elect Constantine and his family as the protectors of the Christian world; and the devout Lactantius announces, in a prophetic tone, the future glories of his long and universal reign.[22] Galerius and Maximin, Maxentius and Licinius, were the rivals who shared with the favourite of Heaven the provinces of the empire. The tragic deaths of Galerius and Maximin soon gratified the resentment, and fulfilled the sanguine expectations, of the Christians. The success of

Constantine against Maxentius and Licinius removed the two formidable competitors who still opposed the triumph of the second David, and his cause might seem to claim the peculiar interposition of Providence. The character of the Roman tyrant* disgraced the purple and human nature; and, though the Christians might enjoy his precarious favour, they were exposed, with the rest of his subjects, to the effects of his wanton and capricious cruelty. The conduct of Licinius soon betrayed the reluctance with which he had consented to the wise and humane regulations of the edict of Milan. The convocation of provincial synods was prohibited in his dominions; his Christian officers were ignominiously dismissed; and, if he avoided the guilt, or rather danger, of a general persecution, his partial oppressions were rendered still more odious by the violation of a solemn and voluntary engagement.[23] While the East, according to the lively expression of Eusebius, was involved in the shades of infernal darkness, the auspicious rays of celestial light warmed and illuminated the provinces of the West. The piety of Constantine was admitted as an unexceptionable proof of the justice of his arms; and his use of victory confirmed the opinion of the Christians, that their hero was inspired and conducted by the Lord of Hosts. The conquest of Italy produced a general edict of toleration; and, as soon as the defeat of Licinius had invested Constantine with the sole dominion of the Roman world, he immediately, by circular letters, exhorted all his subjects to imitate, without delay, the example of their sovereign, and to embrace the divine truth of Christianity.[24]

The assurance that the elevation of Constantine was intimately connected with the designs of Providence instilled into the minds of the Christians two opinions, which, by very different means, assisted the accomplishment of the prophecy. Their warm and active loyalty exhausted in his favour every resource of human industry; and they confidently expected that their strenuous efforts would be seconded by some divine and miraculous aid. The enemies of Constantine have imputed to interested motives the alliance which he insensibly contracted with the Catholic church, and which apparently contributed to the success of his ambition. In the beginning of the fourth century, the Christians still bore a very inadequate proportion to the inhabitants of the empire; but among a degenerate people, who viewed the change of masters with the indifference of slaves, the spirit and union of a religious party might assist the popular leader to whose service, from a principle of conscience, they had devoted their lives and fortunes.[25] The example of his father had instructed Constantine to esteem and to reward the merit of the Christians; and in the distribution of public offices, he had the advantage of strengthening his government, by the choice of ministers or generals in whose fidelity he could repose a just and unreserved confidence. By the influence of these dignified missionaries, the proselytes of the new faith must have multiplied in the court and army; the Barbarians of Germany, who filled the ranks of the legions, were of a careless temper, which acquiesced without resistance in the religion of their commander; and, when they passed the Alps, it may fairly be presumed that a great number of the soldiers had already consecrated their swords to the service of Christ and of Constantine.[26] The habits of mankind, and the interest of religion, gradually abated the horror of war and bloodshed, which had so long prevailed among the Christians; and, in the councils which were assembled under the gracious protection of Constantine, the authority of the bishops was seasonably employed to ratify the obligation of the military oath, and to inflict the penalty of excommunication on those soldiers who threw away their arms during the peace of the church.[27] While Constantine, in his own dominions, increased the number and zeal of his faithful adherents, he could depend on the support of a powerful faction in those provinces which were still possessed or usurped by his rivals. A secret disaffection was diffused among the Christian subjects of Maxentius and Licinius; and the resentment which the latter did not attempt to conceal served only to engage them still more deeply in the interest of his competitor. The regular correspondence which connected the bishops of the most distant provinces enabled them freely to communicate their wishes and their designs, and to transmit without danger any useful intelligence, or any pious contributions, which might promote the service of Constantine, who publicly declared that he had taken up arms for the deliverance of the church.[28]

The enthusiasm which inspired the troops, and perhaps the emperor himself, had sharpened their swords, while it satisfied their conscience. They marched to battle with the full assurance that the same God, who had formerly opened a passage to the Israelites through the waters of Jordan, and had thrown down the walls of Jericho at the sound of the trumpets of Joshua, would display his visible majesty and power in the victory of Constantine. The evidence of ecclesiastical history is prepared to affirm that their expectations were justified by the conspicuous miracle to which the conversion of the first Christian emperor has been almost unanimously ascribed. The real or imaginary cause of so important an event deserves and demands the attention of posterity; and I shall endeavour to form a just estimate of the famous vision of Constantine, by a distinct consideration of the *standard*, the *dream*, and the *celestial sign*; by separating the historical, the natural, and the marvellous parts of this extraordinary story, which, in the composition of a specious argument, have been artfully confounded in one splendid and brittle mass.

I. An instrument of the tortures which were inflicted only on slaves and strangers became an object of horror in the eyes of a Roman citizen; and the ideas of guilt, of pain, and of ignominy were closely united with the idea of the cross.[29] The piety rather than the humanity of Constantine soon abolished in his dominions the punishment which the Saviour of

mankind had condescended to suffer;[30] but the emperor had already
learned to despise the prejudices of his education, and of his people,
before he could erect in the midst of Rome his own statue, bearing a cross
in its right hand, with an inscription which referred the victory of his
arms, and the deliverance of Rome, to the virtue of that salutary sign, the
true symbol of force and courage.[31] The same symbol sanctified the arms
of the soldiers of Constantine; the cross glittered on their helmets, was
engraved on their shields, was interwoven into their banners; and the
consecrated emblems which adorned the person of the emperor himself
were distinguished only by richer materials and more exquisite workmanship.[32] But the principal standard which displayed the triumph of the cross
was styled the *Labarum*,[33] an obscure though celebrated name, which has
been vainly derived from almost all the languages of the world. It is
described[34] as a long pike intersected by a transversal beam. The silken veil
which hung down from the beam was curiously enwrought with the
images of the reigning monarch and his children. The summit of the pike
supported a crown of gold which enclosed the mysterious monogram, at
once expressive of the figure of the cross and the initial letters of the name
of Christ.[35] The safety of the labarum was entrusted to fifty guards, of
approved valour and fidelity; their station was marked by honours and
emoluments; and some fortunate accidents soon introduced an opinion
that, as long as the guards of the labarum were engaged in the execution
of their office, they were secure and invulnerable amidst the darts of the
enemy. In the second civil war Licinius felt and dreaded the power of this
consecrated banner, the sight of which, in the distress of battle, animated
the soldiers of Constantine with an invincible enthusiasm, and scattered
terror and dismay through the ranks of the adverse legions.[36] The
Christian emperors, who respected the example of Constantine, displayed in all their military expeditions the standard of the cross; but, when
the degenerate successors of Theodosius had ceased to appear in person at
the head of their armies, the labarum was deposited as a venerable but
useless relic in the palace of Constantinople.[37] Its honours are still
preserved on the medals of the Flavian family. Their grateful devotion has
placed the monogram of Christ in the midst of the ensigns of Rome. The
solemn epithets of safety of the republic, glory of the army, restoration of
public happiness, are equally applied to the religious and military trophies;
and there is still extant a medal of the emperor Constantius, where the
standard of the labarum is accompanied with these memorable words, 'BY
THIS SIGN THOU SHALT CONQUER'.[38]

II. In all occasions of danger or distress, it was the practice of the primitive
Christians to fortify their minds and bodies by the sign of the cross, which
they used, in all their ecclesiastical rites, in all the daily occurrences of life,
as an infallible preservative against every species of spiritual or temporal
evil.[39] The authority of the church might alone have had sufficient weight

to justify the devotion of Constantine, who, in the same prudent and gradual progress, acknowledged the truth, and assumed the symbol, of Christianity. But the testimony of a contemporary writer, who in a formal treatise has avenged the cause of religion, bestows on the piety of the emperor a more awful and sublime character. He affirms, with the most perfect confidence, that, in the night which preceded the last battle against Maxentius, Constantine was admonished in a dream to inscribe the shields of his soldiers with the *celestial sign of God*, the sacred monogram of the name of Christ; that he executed the commands of heaven; and that his valour and obedience were rewarded by the decisive victory of the Milvian Bridge. Some considerations might perhaps incline a sceptical mind to suspect the judgment or the veracity of the rhetorician, whose pen, either from zeal or interest, was devoted to the cause of the prevailing faction.[40] He appears to have published his deaths of the persecutors at Nicomedia about three years after the Roman victory; but the interval of a thousand miles, and a thousand days, will allow an ample latitude for the invention of declaimers, the credulity of party, and the tacit approbation of the emperor himself; who might listen without indignation to a marvellous tale, which exalted his fame and promoted his designs. In favour of Licinius, who still dissembled his animosity to the Christians, the same author has provided a similar vision, of a form of prayer, which was communicated by an angel, and repeated by the whole army before they engaged the legions of the tyrant Maximin. The frequent repetition of miracles serves to provoke, where it does not subdue, the reason of mankind;[41] but, if the dream of Constantine is separately considered, it may be naturally explained either by the policy or the enthusiasm of the emperor. Whilst his anxiety for the approaching day, which must decide the fate of the empire, was suspended by a short and interrupted slumber, the venerable form of Christ, and the well-known symbol of his religion, might forcibly offer themselves to the active fancy of a prince who reverenced the name, and had perhaps secretly implored the power, of the God of the Christians. As readily might a consummate statesman indulge himself in the use of one of those military stratagems, one of those pious frauds, which Philip* and Sertorius† had employed with such art and effect.[42] The preternatural origin of dreams was universally admitted by the nations of antiquity, and a considerable part of the Gallic army was already prepared to place their confidence in the salutary sign of the Christian religion. The secret vision of Constantine could be disproved only by the event; and the intrepid hero who had passed the Alps and the Apennine might view with careless despair the consequences of a defeat under the walls of Rome. The senate and people, exulting in their own deliverance from an odious tyrant, acknowledged that the victory of Constantine surpassed the powers of man, without daring to insinuate that it had been obtained by the protection of the *Gods*. The triumphal arch which was erected about three years after the event proclaims, in ambiguous language, that, by the greatness of his own mind and by an *instinct* or impulse of the Divinity, he had saved and avenged the Roman republic.[43] The pagan orator, who had seized an earlier opportunity of celebrating the virtues of the conqueror, supposes that he alone enjoyed a secret and intimate commerce with the Supreme Being, who delegated the care of mortals to his subordinate deities; and thus assigns a very plausible reason why the subjects of Constantine should not presume to embrace the new religion of their sovereign.[44]

III. The philosopher, who with calm suspicion examines the dreams and omens, the miracles and prodigies, of profane or even of ecclesiastical history, will probably conclude that, if the eyes of the spectators have sometimes been deceived by fraud, the understanding of the readers has much more frequently been insulted by fiction. Every event, or appearance, or accident, which seems to deviate from the ordinary course of nature, has been rashly ascribed to the immediate action of the Deity; and the astonished fancy of the multitude has sometimes given shape and colour, language and motion, to the fleeting but uncommon meteors of the air.[45] Nazarius and Eusebius are the two most celebrated orators who, in studied panegyrics, have laboured to exalt the glory of Constantine. Nine years after the Roman victory, Nazarius[46] describes an army of divine warriors, who seemed to fall from the sky: he marks their beauty, their spirit, their gigantic forms, the stream of light which beamed from their celestial armour, their patience in suffering themselves to be heard, as well as seen, by mortals; and their declaration that they were sent, that they flew, to the assistance of the great Constantine. For the truth of this prodigy, the Pagan orator appeals to the whole Gallic nation, in whose presence he was then speaking; and seems to hope that the ancient apparitions[47] would now obtain credit from this recent and public event. The Christian fable of Eusebius, which in the space of twenty-six years might arise from the original dream, is cast in a much more correct and elegant mould. In one of the marches of Constantine, he is reported to have seen with his own eyes the luminous trophy of the cross, placed above the meridian sun, and inscribed with the following words: BY THIS CONQUER. This amazing object in the sky astonished the whole army, as well as the emperor himself, who was yet undetermined in the choice of a religion: but his astonishment was converted into faith by the vision of the ensuing night. Christ appeared before his eyes; and, displaying the same celestial sign of the cross, he directed Constantine to frame a similar standard, and to march, with an assurance of victory, against Maxentius and all his enemies.[48] The learned bishop of Caesarea appears to be sensible that the recent discovery of this marvellous anecdote would excite some surprise and distrust among the most pious of his readers. Yet instead of ascertaining the precise circumstances of time and place, which always serve to detect falsehood or establish truth;[49] instead of collecting and recording the evidence of so many living witnesses, who must have been spectators of this stupendous miracle;[50] Eusebius contents himself with alleging a very singular testimony: that of the deceased Constantine, who, many years after the event, in the freedom of conversation, had related to him this extraordinary incident of his own life, and had attested the truth of it by a solemn oath. The prudence and gratitude of the learned prelate forbade him to suspect the veracity of his victorious master, but he plainly intimates that, in a fact of such a nature, he should have refused his assent to any meaner authority. This motive of credibility could not survive the power of the Flavian family; and the celestial sign, which the Infidels might afterwards deride,[51] was disregarded by the Christians of the age which immediately followed the conversion of Constantine.[52] But the Catholic Church, both of the East and of the West, has adopted a prodigy, which favours, or seems to favour, the popular worship of the cross. The vision of Constantine maintained an honourable place in the legend of superstition, till the bold and sagacious spirit of criticism presumed to depreciate the triumph, and to arraign the truth, of the first Christian emperor.[53]

The protestant and philosophic readers of the present age will incline to believe that, in the account of his own conversion, Constantine attested a wilful falsehood by a solemn and deliberate perjury. They may not hesitate to pronounce that, in the choice of a religion, his mind was determined only by a sense of interest; and that (according to the expression of a profane poet[54]) he used the altars of the church as a convenient footstool to the throne of the empire. A conclusion so harsh and so absolute is not, however, warranted by our knowledge of human nature, of Constantine, or of Christianity. In an age of religious fervour, the most artful statesmen are observed to feel some part of the enthusiasm which they inspire; and the most orthodox saints assume the dangerous privilege of defending the cause of truth by the arms of deceit and falsehood. Personal interest is often the standard of our belief, as well as of our practice; and the same motives of temporal advantage which might influence the public conduct and professions of Constantine would insensibly dispose his mind to embrace a religion so propitious to his fame and fortunes. His vanity was gratified by the flattering assurance that *he* had been chosen by Heaven to reign over the earth; success had justified his divine title to the throne, and that title was founded on the truth of the Christian revelation. As real virtue is sometimes excited by undeserved applause, the specious piety of Constantine, if at first it was only specious, might gradually, by the influence of praise, of habit, and of example, be matured into serious faith and fervent devotion. The bishops and teachers of the new sect, whose dress and manners had not qualified them for the residence of a court, were admitted to the Imperial table; they accompanied the monarch in his expeditions; and the ascendant which one of them, an Egyptian or a Spaniard,[55] acquired over his mind was imputed by the Pagans to the effect of magic.[56] Lactantius, who has adorned the precepts of the gospel with the eloquence of Cicero,[57] and Eusebius, who has consecrated the learning and philosophy of the Greeks to the service of religion,[58] were both received into the friendship and familiarity of their sovereign: and those able masters of controversy could patiently watch the soft and yielding moments of persuasion, and dexterously apply the arguments which were the best adapted to his character and understanding. Whatever advantages might be derived from the acquisition of an Imperial proselyte, he was distinguished by the splendour of his purple, rather than by the superiority of wisdom or virtue, from the many thousands of his subjects who had embraced the doctrines of Christianity. Nor can it be deemed incredible that the mind of an unlettered soldier should have yielded to the weight of evidence, which, in a more enlightened age, has satisfied or subdued the reason of a Grotius,* a Pascal,† or a Locke.‡ In the midst of the incessant labours of his great office, this soldier employed, or affected to employ, the hours of the night in the diligent study of the Scriptures and the composition of theological discourses; which he afterwards pronounced in the presence of a numerous and applauding audience. In a very long discourse, which is still extant, the royal preacher expatiates on the various proofs of religion; but he dwells with peculiar complacency on the Sibylline verses,[59] and the fourth eclogue of Virgil.[60] Forty years before the birth of Christ, the Mantuan bard, as if inspired by the celestial muse of Isaiah, had celebrated, with all the pomp of oriental metaphor, the return of the Virgin, the fall of the serpent, the approaching birth of a God-like child, the offspring of the great Jupiter, who should expiate the guilt of human kind, and govern the peaceful universe with the virtues of his father; the rise and appearance of an heavenly race, a primitive nation throughout the world; and the gradual restoration of the innocence and felicity of the golden age. The poet was perhaps unconscious of the secret sense and object of these sublime predictions, which have been so unworthily applied to the infant son of a consul or a triumvir;[61] but, if a more splendid, and indeed specious, interpretation of the fourth eclogue contributed to the conversion of the first Christian emperor, Virgil may deserve to be ranked among the most successful missionaries of the gospel.[62]

The awful mysteries of the Christian faith and worship were concealed from the eyes of strangers, and even of catechumens, with an affected secrecy, which served to excite their wonder and curiosity.[63] But the severe rules of discipline which the prudence of the bishops had instituted were relaxed by the same prudence in favour of an Imperial proselyte, whom it was so important to allure, by every gentle condescension, into the pale of the church; and Constantine was permitted, at least by a tacit dispensation, to enjoy most of the privileges, before he had contracted any of the obligations, of a Christian. Instead of retiring from the congregation when the voice of the deacon dismissed the profane multitude, he prayed with the faithful, disputed with the bishops, preached on the most sublime and intricate subjects of theology, celebrated with sacred rites the vigil of Easter, and publicly declared himself, not only a partaker, but in some measure a priest and hierophant of the Christian mysteries.[64] The pride of Constantine might assume, and his services had deserved, some extraordinary distinction: an ill-timed rigour might have blasted the unripened fruits of his conversion; and, if the doors of the church had been strictly closed against a prince who had deserted the altars of the gods, the master of the empire would have been left destitute of any form of religious worship. In his last visit to Rome, he piously disclaimed and insulted the superstition of his ancestors by refusing to lead the military procession of the equestrian order and to offer the public vows to the Jupiter of the Capitoline Hill.[65] Many years before his baptism and death, Constantine had proclaimed to the world that neither his person nor his image should ever more be seen within the walls of an idolatrous temple; while he distributed through the provinces a variety of medals and pictures, which represented the emperor in an humble and suppliant posture of Christian devotion.[66]

The pride of Constantine, who refused the privileges of a catechumen, cannot easily be explained or excused; but the delay of his baptism may be justified by the maxims and the practice of ecclesiastical antiquity. The sacrament of baptism[67] was regularly administered by the bishop himself, with his assistant clergy, in the cathedral church of the diocese, during the fifty days between the solemn festivals of Easter and Pentecost; and this holy term admitted a numerous band of infants and adult persons into the bosom of the church. The discretion of parents often suspended the baptism of their children till they could understand the obligations which they contracted; the severity of ancient bishops exacted from the new converts a noviciate of two or three years; and the catechumens themselves, from different motives of a temporal or a spiritual nature, were seldom impatient to assume the character of perfect and initiated Christians. The sacrament of baptism was supposed to contain a full and absolute expiation of sin; and the soul was instantly restored to its original purity, and entitled to the promise of eternal salvation. Among the proselytes of Christianity, there were many who judged it imprudent to precipitate a salutary rite, which could not be repeated; to throw away an inestimable privilege, which could never be recovered. By the delay of their baptism, they could venture freely to indulge their passions in the enjoyments of this world, while they still retained in their own hands the means of a sure and easy absolution.[68] The sublime theory of the gospel had made a much fainter impression on the heart than on the understanding of Constantine himself. He pursued the great object of his ambition through the dark and bloody paths of war and policy; and, after the victory, he abandoned himself, without moderation, to the abuse of his fortune. Instead of asserting his just superiority above the imperfect heroism and profane philosophy of Trajan and the Antonines, the mature age of Constantine forfeited the reputation which he had acquired in his youth. As he gradually advanced in the knowledge of truth, he proportionably declined in the practice of virtue; and the same year of his reign in which he convened the council of Nicaea was polluted by the execution, or rather murder, of his eldest son.* This date is alone sufficient to refute the ignorant and malicious suggestions of Zosimus,[69] who affirms that, after the death of Crispus, the remorse of his father accepted from the ministers of Christianity the expiation which he had vainly solicited from the Pagan Pontiffs. At the time of the death of Crispus, the emperor could no longer hesitate in the choice of a religion; he could no longer be ignorant that the church was possessed of an infallible remedy, though he chose to defer the application of it, till the approach of death had removed the temptation and danger of a relapse. The bishops, whom he summoned in his last illness to the palace of Nicomedia, were edified by the fervour with which he requested and received the sacrament of baptism, by the solemn protestation that the remainder of his life should be worthy of a disciple of Christ, and by his humble refusal to wear the imperial purple after he had been clothed in the white garment of a neophyte.† The example and reputation of Constantine seemed to countenance the delay of baptism.[70] Future tyrants were encouraged to believe that the innocent blood which they might shed in a long reign would instantly be washed away in the waters of regeneration; and the abuse of religion dangerously undermined the foundations of moral virtue.

The gratitude of the church has exalted the virtues and excused the failings of a generous patron, who seated Christianity on the throne of the Roman world; and the Greeks, who celebrate the festival of the Imperial saint, seldom mention the name of Constantine without adding the title of *equal to the Apostles*.[71] Such a comparison, if it allude to the character of those divine missionaries, must be imputed to the extravagance of impious flattery. But, if the parallel is confined to the extent and number of their evangelic victories, the success of Constantine might perhaps equal that of the Apostles themselves. By the edicts of toleration he removed the temporal disadvantages which had hitherto retarded the progress of Christianity; and its active and numerous ministers received a free permission, a liberal encouragement, to recommend the salutary truths of revelation by every argument which could affect the reason or piety of mankind. The exact balance of the two religions continued but a moment; and the piercing eye of ambition and avarice soon discovered that the profession of Christianity might contribute to the interest of the present, as well as of a future, life.[72] The hopes of wealth and honours, the example of an emperor, his exhortations, his irresistible smiles, diffused conviction among the venal and obsequious crowds which usually fill the apartments of a palace. The cities which signalised a forward zeal by the voluntary destruction of their temples were distinguished by municipal privileges, and rewarded with popular donatives; and the new capital of the East gloried in the singular advantage that Constantinople was never profaned by the worship of idols.[73] As the lower ranks of society are governed by imitation, the conversion of those who possessed any eminence of birth, of power, or of riches, was soon followed by dependent multitudes.[74] The salvation of the common people was purchased at an easy rate, if it be true that, in one year, twelve thousand men were baptised at Rome, besides a proportionable number of women and children; and that a white garment, with twenty pieces of gold, had been promised by the emperor to every convert.[75] The powerful influence of Constantine was not circumscribed by the narrow limits of his life, or of his dominions. The education which he bestowed on his sons and nephews secured to the empire a race of princes whose faith was still more lively and sincere, as they imbibed, in their earliest infancy, the spirit, or at least the doctrine, of Christianity. War and commerce had spread the knowledge of the gospel beyond the confines of the Roman provinces; and the Barbarians, who had disdained an humble and proscribed sect, soon learned to esteem a religion which had been so lately embraced by the greatest monarch and the most civilised nation of the globe.[76] The Goths and Germans who enlisted under the standard of Rome revered the cross which glittered at the head of the legions, and their fierce countrymen received at the same time the lessons of faith and of humanity. The kings of Iberia* and Armenia worshipped the God of their protector; and their subjects, who have invariably preserved the name of Christians, soon formed a sacred and perpetual connection with their Roman brethren. The Christians of Persia were suspected, in time of war, of preferring their religion to their country; but, as long as peace subsisted between the two empires, the persecuting spirit of the Magi was effectually restrained by the interposition of Constantine.[77] The rays of the gospel illuminated the coast of India. The colonies of Jews, who had penetrated into Arabia and Ethiopia,[78] opposed the progress of Christianity; but the labour of the missionaries was in some measure facilitated by a previous knowledge of the Mosaic revelation; and Abyssinia still reveres the memory of Frumentius, who, in the time of Constantine, devoted his life to the conversion of those sequestered regions. Under the reign of his son Constantius, Theophilus,[79] who was himself of Indian extraction, was invested with the double character of ambassador and bishop. He embarked on the Red Sea with two hundred horses of the purest breed of Cappadocia, which were sent by the emperor to the prince of the Sabaeans, or Homerites. Theophilus was entrusted with many other useful or curious presents, which might raise the admiration and conciliate the friendship of the Barbarians; and he successfully employed several years in a pastoral visit to the churches of the torrid zone.[80]

The irresistible power of the Roman emperors was displayed in the important and dangerous change of the national religion. The terrors of a military force silenced the faint and unsupported murmurs of the Pagans, and there was reason to expect that the cheerful submission of the Christian clergy, as well as people, would be the result of conscience and gratitude. It was long since established, as a fundamental maxim of the Roman constitution, that every rank of citizens were alike subject to the laws, and that the care of religion was the right as well as duty of the civil magistrate. Constantine and his successors could not easily persuade themselves that they had forfeited, by their conversion, any branch of the Imperial prerogatives, or that they were incapable of giving laws to a religion which they had protected and embraced. The emperors still continued to exercise a supreme jurisdiction over the ecclesiastical order; and the sixteenth book of the Theodosian code represents, under a variety of titles, the authority which they assumed in the government of the Catholic church.

But the distinction of the spiritual and temporal powers,[81] which had never been imposed on the free spirit of Greece and Rome, was introduced and confirmed by the legal establishment of Christianity. The office of supreme pontiff, which, from the time of Numa to that of Augustus, had always been exercised by one of the most eminent of the senators, was at length united to the Imperial dignity. The first magistrate of the state, as often as he was prompted by superstition or policy, performed with his own hands the sacerdotal functions;[82] nor was there any order of priests, either at Rome or in the provinces, who claimed a more sacred character among men, or a more intimate communication with the Gods. But in the Christian church, which entrusts the service of the altar to a perpetual succession of consecrated ministers, the monarch, whose spiritual rank is less honourable than that of the meanest deacon, was seated below the rails of the sanctuary, and confounded with the rest of the faithful multitude.[83] The emperor might be saluted as the father of his people, but he owed a filial duty and reverence to the fathers of the church; and the same marks of respect which Constantine had paid to the persons of saints and confessors were soon exacted by the pride of the episcopal order.[84] A secret conflict between the civil and ecclesiastical jurisdictions embarrassed the operations of the Roman government; and a pious emperor was alarmed by the guilt and danger of touching with a profane hand the ark of the covenant. The separation of men into the two orders of the clergy and of the laity was, indeed, familiar to many nations of antiquity; and the priests of India, of Persia, of Assyria, of Judea, of Ethiopia, of Egypt, and of Gaul, derived from a celestial origin the temporal power and possessions which they had acquired. These venerable institutions had gradually assimilated themselves to the manners and government of their respective countries;[85] but the opposition or contempt of the civil power served to cement the discipline of the primitive church. The Christians had been obliged to elect their own magistrates, to raise and distribute a peculiar revenue, and to regulate the internal policy of their republic by a code of laws, which were ratified by the consent of the people and the practice of three hundred years. When Constantine embraced the faith of the Christians, he seemed to contract a perpetual alliance with a distinct and independent society; and the privileges granted or confirmed by that emperor, or by his successors, were accepted, not as the precarious favours of the court, but as the just and unalienable rights of the ecclesiastical order.

The Catholic church was administered by the spiritual and legal jurisdiction of eighteen hundred bishops;[86] Of whom one thousand were seated in the Greek, and eight hundred in the Latin, provinces of the empire. The extent and boundaries of their respective dioceses had been variously and accidentally decided by the zeal and success of the first missionaries, by the wishes of the people, and by the propagation of the gospel. Episcopal churches were closely planted along the banks of the Nile, on the seacoast of Africa, in the proconsular Asia, and through the southern provinces of Italy. The bishops of Gaul and Spain, of Thrace and Pontus, reigned over an ample territory, and delegated their rural suffragans to execute the subordinate duties of the pastoral office.[87] A Christian diocese might be spread over a province or reduced to a village; but all the bishops possessed an equal and indelible character: they all derived the same powers and privileges from the apostles, from the people, and from the laws. While the *civil* and *military* professions were separated by the policy of Constantine, a new and perpetual order of *ecclesiastical* ministers, always respectable, sometimes dangerous, was established in the church and state. The important review of their station and attributes may be distributed under the following heads: I. Popular election. II. Ordination of the clergy. III. Property. IV. Civil jurisdiction. V. Spiritual censures. VI. Exercise of public oratory. VII. Privilege of legislative assemblies.

I. The freedom of elections subsisted long after the legal establishment of Christianity;[88] and the subjects of Rome enjoyed in the church the privilege which they had lost in the republic, of choosing the magistrates whom they were bound to obey. As soon as a bishop had closed his eyes, the metropolitan issued a commission to one of his suffragans to administer the vacant see, and prepare, within a limited time, the future election. The right of voting was vested in the inferior clergy, who were best qualified to judge of the merit of the candidates; in the senators or nobles of the city, all those who were distinguished by their rank or property; and finally in the whole body of the people, who, on the appointed day, flocked in multitudes from the most remote parts of the diocese,[89] and sometimes silenced, by their tumultuous acclamations, the voice of reason and the laws of discipline. These acclamations might accidentally fix on the head of the most deserving competitor; of some ancient presbyter, some holy monk, or some layman, conspicuous for his zeal and piety. But the episcopal chair was solicited, especially in the great and opulent cities of the empire, as a temporal rather than as a spiritual dignity. The interested views, the selfish and angry passions, the arts of perfidy and dissimulation, the secret corruption, the open and even bloody violence, which had formerly disgraced the freedom of election in the commonwealths of Greece and Rome, too often influenced the choice of the successors of the apostles. While one of the candidates boasted the honours of his family, a second allured his judges by the delicacies of a plentiful table, and a third, more guilty than his rivals, offered to share the plunder of the church among the accomplices of his sacrilegious hopes.[90] The civil as well as ecclesiastical laws attempted to exclude the populace from this solemn and important transaction. The canons of ancient discipline, by requiring several episcopal qualifications of age, station, etc., restrained in some measure the indiscriminate caprice of the electors. The authority of the provincial bishops, who were assembled in the vacant church to consecrate the choice of the people, was interposed to moderate their passions and to correct their mistakes. The bishops could refuse to ordain an unworthy candidate, and the rage of contending factions sometimes accepted their impartial mediation. The submission, or the resistance, of the clergy and people, on various occasions, afforded different precedents, which were insensibly converted into positive laws and provincial customs;[91] but it was everywhere admitted, as a fundamental maxim of religious policy, that no bishop could be imposed on an orthodox church without the consent of its members. The emperors, as the guardians of the public peace, and as the first citizens of Rome and Constantinople, might effectually declare their wishes in the choice of a primate; but those absolute monarchs respected the freedom of ecclesiastical elections; and, while they distributed and resumed the honours of the state and army, they allowed eighteen hundred perpetual magistrates to receive their important offices from the free suffrages of the people.[92] It was agreeable to the dictates of justice, that these magistrates should not desert an honourable station from which they could not be removed; but the wisdom of councils endeavoured, without much success, to enforce the residence, and to prevent the translation,* of bishops. The discipline of the West was indeed less relaxed than that of the East; but the same passions which made those regulations necessary rendered them ineffectual. The reproaches which angry prelates have so vehemently urged against each other serve only to expose their common guilt and their mutual indiscretion.

II. The bishops alone possessed the faculty of *spiritual* generation; and this extraordinary privilege might compensate, in some degree, for the painful celibacy[93] which was imposed as a virtue, as a duty, and at length as a positive obligation. The religions of antiquity, which established a separate order of priests, dedicated a holy race, a tribe or family, to the perpetual service of the Gods.[94] Such institutions were founded for possession rather than conquest. The children of the priests enjoyed, with proud and indolent security, their sacred inheritance; and the fiery spirit of enthusiasm was abated by the cares, the pleasures, and the endearments of domestic life. But the Christian sanctuary was open to every ambitious candidate who aspired to its heavenly promises or temporal possessions. The office of priests, like that of soldiers or magistrates, was strenuously exercised by those men whose temper and abilities had prompted them to embrace the ecclesiastical profession, or who had been selected by a discerning bishop as the best qualified to promote the glory and interest of the church. The bishops[95] (till the abuse was restrained by the prudence of the laws) might constrain the reluctant, and protect the distressed; and the imposition of hands for ever bestowed some of the most valuable privileges of civil society. The whole body of the Catholic clergy, more numerous perhaps than the legions, was exempted by the emperors from all service, private or public, all municipal offices, and all personal taxes and contributions which pressed on their fellow-citizens with intolerable weight; and the duties of their holy profession were accepted as a full discharge of their obligations to the republic.[96] Each bishop acquired an absolute and indefeasible right to the perpetual obedience of the clerk whom he ordained: the clergy of each episcopal church, with its dependent parishes, formed a regular and permanent society; and the cathedrals of Constantinople[97] and Carthage[98] maintained their peculiar establishment of five hundred ecclesiastical ministers. The ranks[99] and numbers were insensibly multiplied by the superstition of the times, which introduced into the church the splendid ceremonies of a Jewish or Pagan temple; and a long train of priests, deacons, sub-deacons, acolytes, exorcists, readers, singers, and door-keepers, contributed, in their respective stations, to swell the pomp and harmony of religious worship. The clerical name and privilege were extended to many pious fraternities, who devoutly supported the ecclesiastical throne.[100] Six hundred *parabolani*, or adventurers, visited the sick at Alexandria; eleven hundred *copiatae*, or gravediggers, buried the dead at Constantinople; and the swarms of monks, who arose from the Nile, overspread and darkened the face of the Christian world.

III. The edict of Milan secured the revenue as well as the peace of the church.[101] The Christians not only recovered the lands and houses of which they had been stripped by the persecuting laws of Diocletian, but they acquired a perfect title to all the possessions which they had hitherto enjoyed by the connivance of the magistrate. As soon as Christianity became the religion of the emperor and the empire, the national clergy might claim a decent and honourable maintenance: and the payment of an annual tax might have delivered the people from the more oppressive tribute which superstition imposes on her votaries. But, as the wants and expenses of the church increased with her prosperity, the ecclesiastical order was still supported and enriched by the voluntary oblations of the faithful. Eight years after the edict of Milan, Constantine granted to all his subjects the free and universal permission of bequeathing their fortunes to the holy Catholic church;[102] and their devout liberality, which during their lives was checked by luxury or avarice, flowed with a profuse stream at the hour of their death. The wealthy Christians were encouraged by the example of their sovereign. An absolute monarch, who is rich without patrimony, may be charitable without merit; and Constantine too easily believed that he should purchase the favour of Heaven, if he maintained the idle at the expense of the industrious, and distributed among the saints the wealth of the republic. The same messenger who carried over to Africa the head of Maxentius* might be entrusted with an epistle to Caecilian, bishop of Carthage. The emperor acquaints him that the treasurers of the province are directed to pay into his hands the sum of three thousand *folles*, or eighteen thousand pounds sterling, and to obey his farther requisitions for the relief of the churches of Africa, Numidia, and Mauritania.[103] The liberality of Constantine increased in a just proportion to his faith, and to his vices. He assigned in each city a regular allowance of corn, to supply the fund of ecclesiastical charity; and the persons of both sexes who embraced the monastic life became the peculiar favourites of their sovereign. The Christian temples of Antioch, Alexandria, Jerusalem, Constantinople, etc. displayed the ostentatious piety of a prince ambitious, in a declining age, to equal the perfect labours of antiquity.[104] The form of these religious edifices was simple and oblong; though they might sometimes swell into the shape of a dome, and sometimes branch into the figure of a cross. The timbers were framed for the most part of cedars of Libanus;† the roof was covered with tiles, perhaps of gilt brass; and the walls, the columns, the pavement, were encrusted with variegated marbles. The most precious ornaments of gold and silver, of silk and gems, were profusely dedicated to the service of the altar; and this specious magnificence was supported on the solid and perpetual basis of landed property. In the space of two centuries, from the reign of Constantine to that of Justinian, the eighteen hundred churches of the empire were enriched by the frequent and unalienable gifts of the prince and people. An annual income of six hundred pounds sterling may be reasonably assigned to the bishops, who were placed at an equal distance between riches and poverty,[105] but the standard of their wealth insensibly rose with the dignity and opulence of the cities which they governed. An authentic but imperfect[106] rent-roll specifies some houses, shops, gardens, and farms, which belonged to the three *Basilicae* of Rome, St Peter, St Paul, and St John Lateran, in the provinces of Italy, Africa, and the East. They produce, besides a reserved rent of oil, linen, paper, aromatics, etc. a clear annual revenue of twenty-two thousand pieces of gold, or twelve thousand pounds sterling. In the age of Constantine and Justinian, the bishops no longer possessed, perhaps they no longer deserved, the unsuspecting confidence of their clergy and people. The ecclesiastical revenues of each diocese were divided into four parts; for the respective uses, of the bishop himself, of his inferior clergy, of the poor, and of the public worship; and the abuse of this sacred trust was strictly and repeatedly checked.[107] The patrimony of the church was still subject to all the public impositions of the state.[108] The clergy of Rome, Alexandria, Thessalonica, etc. might solicit and obtain some partial exemptions; but the premature attempt of the great council of Rimini, which aspired to universal freedom, was successfully resisted by the son of Constantine.[109]

IV. The Latin clergy, who erected their tribunal on the ruins of the civil and common law, have modestly accepted as the gift of Constantine[110] the independent jurisdiction which was the fruit of time, of accident, and of their own industry. But the liberality of the Christian emperors had actually endowed them with some legal prerogatives, which secured and dignified the sacerdotal character.[111] 1. Under a despotic government, the bishops alone enjoyed and asserted the inestimable privilege of being tried only by their *peers*; and even in a capital accusation, a synod of their brethren were the sole judges of their guilt or innocence. Such a tribunal, unless it was inflamed by personal resentment or religious discord, might be favourable, or even partial, to the sacerdotal order; but Constantine was satisfied[112] that secret impunity would be less pernicious than public scandal; and the Nicene council was edified by his public declaration that, if he surprised a bishop in the act of adultery, he should cast his Imperial mantle over the episcopal sinner. 2. The domestic jurisdiction of the bishops was at once a privilege and a restraint of the ecclesiastical order, whose civil causes were decently withdrawn from the cognisance of a secular judge. Their venial offences were not exposed to the shame of a public trial or punishment; and the gentle correction, which the tenderness of youth may endure from its parents or instructors, was inflicted by the temperate severity of the bishops. But, if the clergy were guilty of any crime which could not be sufficiently expiated by their degradation from an honourable and beneficial profession, the Roman magistrate drew the sword of justice without any regard to ecclesiastical immunities. 3. The arbitration of the bishops was ratified by a positive law; and the judges were instructed to execute, without appeal or delay, the episcopal decrees, whose validity had hitherto depended on the consent of the parties. The conversion of the magistrates themselves, and of the whole empire, might gradually remove the fears and scruples of the Christians. But they still resorted to the tribunal of the bishops, whose abilities and integrity they esteemed; and the venerable Austin* enjoyed the satisfaction of complaining that his spiritual functions were perpetually interrupted by the invidious labour of deciding the claim or the possession of silver and gold, of lands and cattle. 4. The ancient privilege of sanctuary was transferred to the Christian temples, and extended, by the liberal piety of the younger Theodosius, to the precincts of consecrated ground.[113] The fugitive, and even guilty, suppliants were permitted to implore either the justice or the mercy of the Deity and his ministers. The rash violence of despotism was suspended by the mild interposition of the church; and the lives or fortunes of the most eminent subjects might be protected by the mediation of the bishop.

V. The bishop was the perpetual censor of the morals of his people. The discipline of penance was digested into a system of canonical jurisprudence,[114] which accurately defined the duty of private or public confession, the rules of evidence, the degrees of guilt, and the measure of punishment. It was impossible to execute this spiritual censure, if the Christian pontiff, who punished the obscure sins of the multitude, respected the conspicuous vices and destructive crimes of the magistrate; but it was impossible to arraign the conduct of the magistrate without controlling the administration of civil government. Some considerations of religion, or loyalty, or fear, protected the sacred persons of the emperors from the zeal or resentment of the bishops; but they boldly censured and excommunicated the sub-ordinate tyrants who were not invested with the majesty of the purple. St Athanasius excommunicated one of the ministers of Egypt; and the interdict which he pronounced, of fire and water, was solemnly transmitted to the churches of Cappadocia.[115] Under the reign of the younger Theodosius, the polite and eloquent Synesius, one of the descendants of Hercules,[116] filled the episcopal seat of Ptolemais, near the ruins of ancient Cyrene,[117] and the philosophic bishop supported, with dignity, the character which he had assumed with reluctance.[118] He vanquished the monster of Libya, the president Andronicus, who abused the authority of a venal office, invented new modes of rapine and torture, and aggravated the guilt of oppression by that of sacrilege.[119] After a fruitless attempt to reclaim the haughty magistrate by mild and religious admonition, Synesius proceeds to inflict the last sentence of ecclesiastical justice,[120] which devotes Andronicus, with his associates and their *families*, to the abhorrence of earth and heaven. The impenitent sinners, more cruel than Phalaris* or Sennacherib,† more destructive than war, pestilence, or a cloud of locusts, are deprived of the name and privileges of Christians, of the participation of the sacraments, and of the hope of Paradise. The bishop exhorts the clergy, the magistrates, and the people, to renounce all society with the enemies of Christ; to exclude them from their houses and tables; and to refuse them the common offices of life and the decent rites of burial. The church of Ptolemais, obscure and contemptible as she may appear, addresses this declaration to all her sister churches of the world; and the profane who reject her decrees will be involved in the guilt and punishment of Andronicus and his impious followers. These spiritual terrors were enforced by a dexterous application to the Byzantine court; the trembling president implored the mercy of the church; and the descendant of Hercules enjoyed the satisfaction of raising a prostrate tyrant from the ground.[121] Such principles and such examples insensibly prepared the triumph of the Roman pontiffs, who have trampled on the necks of kings.

VI. Every popular government has experienced the effects of rude or artificial eloquence. The coldest nature is animated, the firmest reason is moved, by the rapid communication of the prevailing impulse; and each hearer is affected by his own passions, and by those of the surrounding multitude. The ruin of civil liberty had silenced the demagogues of Athens and the tribunes of Rome; the custom of preaching, which seems to constitute a considerable part of Christian devotion, had not been introduced into the temples of antiquity; and the ears of monarchs were never invaded by the harsh sound of popular eloquence, till the pulpits of the empire were filled with sacred orators who possessed some advantages unknown to their profane predecessors.[122] The arguments and rhetoric of the tribune were instantly opposed, with equal arms, by skilful and resolute antagonists; and the cause of truth and reason might derive an accidental support from the conflict of hostile passions. The bishop, or some distinguished presbyter, to whom he cautiously delegated the powers of preaching, harangued, without the danger of interruption or reply, a submissive multitude, whose minds had been prepared and subdued by the awful ceremonies of religion. Such was the strict subordination of the Catholic church that the same concerted sounds might issue at once from an hundred pulpits of Italy or Egypt, if they were tuned[123] by the master hand of the Roman or Alexandrian primate. The design of this institution was laudable, but the fruits were not always salutary. The preachers recommended the practice of the social duties; but they exalted the perfection of monastic virtue, which is painful to the individual and useless to mankind. Their charitable exhortations betrayed a secret wish that the clergy might be permitted to manage the wealth of the faithful for the benefit of the poor. The most sublime representations of the attributes and laws of the Deity were sullied by an idle mixture of metaphysical subtleties, puerile rites, and fictitious miracles: and they expatiated, with the most fervent zeal, on the religious merit of hating the adversaries, and obeying the ministers, of the church. When the public peace was distracted by heresy and schism, the sacred orators sounded the trumpet of discord, and perhaps of sedition. The understandings of their congregations were perplexed by mystery, their passions were inflamed by invectives: and they rushed from the Christian temples of Antioch or

Alexandria, prepared either to suffer or to inflict martyrdom. The corruption of taste and language is strongly marked in the vehement declarations of the Latin bishops; but the compositions of Gregory* and Chrysostom† have been compared with the most splendid models of Attic, or at least of Asiatic, eloquence.[124]

VII. The representatives of the Christian republic were regularly assembled in the spring and autumn of each year; and these synods diffused the spirit of ecclesiastical discipline and legislation through the hundred and twenty provinces of the Roman world.[125] The archbishop or metropolitan was empowered, by the laws, to summon the suffragan bishops of his province, to revise their conduct, to vindicate their rights, to declare their faith, and to examine the merit of the candidates who were elected by the clergy and people to supply the vacancies of the episcopal college. The primates of Rome, Alexandria, Antioch, Carthage, and afterwards Constantinople, who exercised a more ample jurisdiction, convened the numerous assembly of their dependent bishops. But the convocation of great and extraordinary synods was the prerogative of the emperor alone. Whenever the emergencies of the church required this decisive measure, he dispatched a peremptory summons to the bishops, or the deputies of each province, with an order for the use of post-horses, and a competent allowance for the expenses of their journey. At an early period, when Constantine was the protector, rather than the proselyte, of Christianity, he referred the African controversy to the council of Arles; in which the bishops of York, of Treves, of Milan, and of Carthage, met as friends and brethren, to debate in their native tongue on the common interest of the Latin or Western church.[126] Eleven years afterwards, a more numerous and celebrated assembly was convened at Nicaea in Bithynia, to extinguish, by their final sentence, the subtle disputes which had arisen in Egypt on the subject of the Trinity. Three hundred and eighteen bishops obeyed the summons of their indulgent master; the ecclesiastics, of every rank and sect and denomination, have been computed at two thousand and forty-eight persons;[127] the Greeks appeared in person; and the consent of the Latins was expressed by the legates of the Roman pontiff. The session, which lasted about two months, was frequently honoured by the presence of the emperor. Leaving his guards at the door, he seated himself (with the permission of the council) on a low stool in the midst of the hall. Constantine listened with patience and spoke with modesty: and, while he influenced the debates, he humbly professed that he was the minister, not the judge, of the successors of the apostles, who had been established as priests and as gods upon earth.[128] Such profound reverence of an absolute monarch towards a feeble and unarmed assembly of his own subjects can only be compared to the respect with which the senate had been treated by the Roman princes, who adopted the policy of Augustus. Within the space of fifty years, a philosophic spectator of the vicissitude of human affairs might have contemplated Tacitus* in the senate of Rome, and Constantine in the council of Nicaea. The fathers of the capitol and those of the church had alike degenerated from the virtues of their founders; but, as the bishops were more deeply rooted in the public opinion, they sustained their dignity with more decent pride, and sometimes opposed, with a manly spirit, the wishes of their sovereign. The progress of time and superstition erased the memory of the weakness, the passion, the ignorance, which disgraced these ecclesiastical synods; and the Catholic world has unanimously submitted[129] to the *infallible* decrees of the general councils.[130]

NOTES ON CHAPTER 20

1 The date of the *Divine Institutions* of Lactantius has been accurately discussed, difficulties have been started, solutions proposed, and an expedient imagined of two *original* editions: the former published during the persecution of Diocletian, the latter under that of Licinius. See Dufresnoy, *Prefat.*, p. v; Tillemont, *Mém. Ecclésiast.*, vi, 465–470; Lardner's *Credibility*, ii, vii, 78–86. For my own part, I am *almost* convinced that Lactantius dedicated his *Institutions* to the sovereign of Gaul, at a time when Galerius, Maximin, and even Licinius, persecuted the Christians; that is, between the years 306 and 311.

2 Lactant., *Divin. Institut.*, i, 1; vii, 27. The first and most important of these passages is indeed wanting in twenty-eight manuscripts; but it is found in nineteen. If we weigh the comparative value of those manuscripts, one of 900 years old, in the king of France's library, may be alleged in its favour; but the passage is omitted in the correct manuscript of Bologna, which the P. de Montfaucon ascribes to the sixth or seventh century (*Diarium Italic.*, p. 409). The taste of most of the editors (except Isaeus, see Lactant. edit. Dufresnoy, i, 596) has felt the genuine style of Lactantius.

3 Euseb., *in Vit. Constant.*, i, 27–32.

4 Zosimus, ii, p. 104.

* *page 369* [convert undergoing instruction before baptism]

5 That rite was *always* used in making a catechumen (see Bingham's *Antiquities*, x, 1, p. 419; Dom. Chardon, *Hist. des Sacremens*, i, 62), and Constantine received it for the *first* time (Euseb., *in Vit. Constant.*, iv, 61) immediately before his baptism and death. From the connection of these two facts, Valesius (*ad loc.* Euseb.) has drawn the conclusion, which is reluctantly admitted by Tillemont (*Hist. des Empereurs*, iv, 628), and opposed with feeble arguments by Mosheim (p. 968).

6 Euseb., *in Vit. Constant.*, iv, 61, 62, 63. The legend of Constantine's baptism at Rome, thirteen years before his death, was invented in the eighth century, as a proper motive for his *donation*. Such has been the gradual progress of knowledge that a story of which Cardinal Baronius (*Annal. Ecclesiast.* ad 324, No. 43–49) declared himself the unblushing advocate is now feebly supported, even within the verge of the Vatican. See the *Antiquitates Christianae*, ii, 232;

a work published with six approbations at Rome, in the year 1751, by Father Mamachi, a learned Dominican.

7 The quaestor, or secretary, who composed the law of the *Theodosian Code*, makes his master say with indifference, *hominibus supradictae religionis* (xvi, ii, 1) ['persons of the aforesaid religion']. The minister of ecclesiastical affairs was allowed a more devout and respectful style, τῆς ἐνθέσμου καὶ ἁγιωτάτης καθολικῆς θρησκεία̃, the legal, most holy, and catholic worship. See Euseb., *Hist. Eccl.*, x, 6.

8 *Cod. Theodos.*, ii, viii, 1. *Cod. Justinian.*, iii, xii, iii. Constantine styles the Lord's day *dies solis* [i.e. 'sun-day'], a name which could not offend the ears of his Pagan subjects.

† *page 369* [(H)aruspices – an order of priests who foretold the future by examining the entrails of sacrificial beasts.]

9 *Cod. Theod.*, xvi, x, 1, Godefroy, in the character of a commentator endeavours (vi, 257) to excuse Constantine; but the more zealous Baronius (*Annal. Eccl.*, ad 321, No. 18) censures his profane conduct with truth and asperity.

10 Theodoret (i, 18) seems to insinuate that Helena gave her son a Christian education, but we may be assured, from the superior authority of Eusebius (*in Vit. Constant.*, iii, 47), that she herself was indebted to Constantine for the knowledge of Christianity.

11 See the medals of Constantine in Ducange and Banduri. As few cities had retained the privilege of coining, almost all the medals of that age issued from the mint under the sanction of the Imperial authority.

12 The panegyric of Eumenius (vii, *inter Panegyr. Vet.*), which was pronounced a few months before the Italian war, abounds with the most unexceptionable evidence of the Pagan superstition of Constantine, and of his particular veneration for Apollo, or the Sun, to which Julian alludes (*Orat.* vii, 228, ἀπολείπων σε [abandoning you]). See *Commentaire* de Spanheim *sur les Césars*, p. 317.

13 Constantin., *Orat. ad Sanctos*, ch. 25. But it might easily be shown that the Greek translator has improved the sense of the Latin original; and the aged emperor might recollect the persecution of Diocletian with a more lively abhorrence than he had actually felt in the days of his youth and Paganism.

14 See Euseb., *Hist. Eccles.*, viii, 13; ix, 9, and *in Vit. Const.*, i, 16, 17; Lactant., *Divin. Institut.*, i, 1; Caecilius, *de Mort. Persecut.*, ch. 25.

* *page 371* [Maximin, in AD 313]

15 Caecilius (*de Mort. Persecut.*, ch. 48) has preserved the Latin original; and Eusebius (*Hist. Eccles.*, x, 5) has given a Greek translation of this perpetual edict, which refers to some provisional regulations.

16 A panegyric of Constantine, pronounced seven or eight months after the edict of Milan (see Gothofred., *Chronolog. Legum*, p. 7, and Tillemont, *Hist. des Empereurs*, iv, 246), uses the following remarkable expression: *Summe rerum sator, cuius tot nomina sunt, quot linguas gentium esse voluisti, quem enim te ipse dici velis, scire non possumus.* ['Supreme creator of the universe, whose names are as many as the languages which it has pleased thee to bestow upon the human race – we cannot know by what name thou desirest to be known.'] *Panegyr. Vet.*, ix, 26. In explaining Constantine's progress in the faith, Mosheim (p. 971, etc.) is ingenious, subtle, prolix.

17 See the elegant description of Lactantius (*Divin. Institut.*, v, 8), who is much more perspicuous and positive than it becomes a discreet prophet.

18 The political system of the Christians is explained by Grotius, *de Iure Belli et Pacis*, i, 3, 4. Grotius was a republican and an exile, but the mildness of his temper inclined him to support the established powers.

* *page 373* [St Paul]

19 Tertullian, *Apolog.*, chs 32, 34, 35, 36. *Tamen nunquam Albiniani, nec Nigriani vel Cassiani inveniri potuerunt Christiani.* ['Nor was it possible to find that the followers of Albinus, of Niger, or of Cassius had at any time been Christians.'] *ad Scapulam*, ch. 2. If this assertion be strictly true, it excludes the Christians of that age from all civil and military employments, which would have compelled them to take an active part in the service of their respective governors. See Moyle's *Works*, ii, 349.

† *page 373* [during the Reformation in the sixteenth century]

20 See the artful Bossuet (*Hist. des Variations des Eglises Protestantes*, iii. pp. 210–258), and the malicious Bayle (ii, 620). I *name* Bayle, for he was certainly the author of the *Avis aux Réfugiés*; consult the *Dictionnaire Critique* de Chauffepié, i, ii, 145.

21 Buchanan is the earliest, or at least the most celebrated, of the reformers, who has justified the theory of resistance [George Buchanan, Scottish humanist, 1506–82]. See his *Dialogue de Jure Regni apud Scotos*, ii, 28, 30, edit. fol. Ruddiman.

22 Lactant., *Divin. Institut.*, i, 1. Eusebius, in the course of his history, his life, and his oration, repeatedly inculcates the divine right of Constantine to the empire.

* *page 374* [Maxentius]

23 Our imperfect knowledge of the persecution of Licinius is derived from Eusebius (*Hist. Eccles.*, x, 8. *Vit. Constantin.*, i, 49–56; ii, 1, 2). Aurelius Victor mentions his cruelty in general terms.

24 Euseb., *in Vit. Constant.*, ii, 24–42, 48–60.

25 In the beginning of the last century, the Papists of England were only a *thirtieth*, and the Protestants of France only a *fifteenth*, part of the respective nations, to whom their spirit and power were a constant object of apprehension. See the relations which Bentivoglio (who was then nuncio at Brussels, and afterwards cardinal) transmitted to the court of Rome (*Relazione*, ii, 211, 241). Bentivoglio was curious, well-informed, but somewhat partial.

26 This careless temper of the Germans appears almost uniformly in the history of the conversion of each of the tribes. The legions of Constantine were recruited with Germans (Zosimus, ii, 86); and the court even of his father had been filled with Christians. See the first book of the *Life of Constantine*, by Eusebius.

27 *De his qui arma proiiciunt in pace, placuit eos abstinere a communione. Concil. Arelat.*, Canon iii. The best critics apply these words to the *peace of the church*.

28 Eusebius always considers the second civil war against Licinius as a sort of religious crusade. At the invitation of the tyrant, some Christian officers had resumed their *zones*; or, in other words, had returned to the military service. Their conduct was afterwards censured by the 12th canon of the Council of Nicaea; if this particular application may be received, instead of the loose and general sense of the Greek interpreters, Balsamon, Zonaras, and Alexis Aristenus. See Beveridge, *Pandect. Eccles. Graec.*, i, 72; ii, 78, Annotation.

29 *Nomen ipsum crucis absit non modo a corpore civium Romanorum, sed etiam a cogitatione, oculis, auribus.* ['Let the very name of the cross be absent not just from the body of the citizens of Rome, but even from their thoughts, sight and

hearing.'] Cicero, *pro Rabirio*, ch. 5. The Christian writers, Justin, Minucius Felix, Tertullian, Jerom, and Maximus of Turin, have investigated with tolerable success the figure or likeness of a cross in almost every object of nature or art; in the intersection of the meridian and equator, the human face, a bird flying, a man swimming, a mast and yard, a plough, a *standard*, etc. See Lipsius, *de Cruce*, i, 9.

30 See Aurelius Victor, who considers this law as one of the examples of Constantine's piety. An edict so honourable to Christianity deserved a place in the Theodosian Code, instead of the indirect mention of it, which seems to result from the comparison of the fifth and eighteenth titles of the ninth book.

31 Eusebius, *in Vit. Constantin.*, i, 40. The statue, or at least the cross and inscription, may be ascribed with more probability to the second, or even the third, visit of Constantine to Rome. Immediately after the defeat of Maxentius, the minds of the senate and people were scarcely ripe for this public monument.

32
> *Agnoscas regina libens mea signa necesse est;*
> *In quibus effigies crucis aut gemmata refulget*
> *Aut longis solido ex auro praefertur in hastis.*
> *Hoc signo invictus, transmissis Alpibus Ultor*
> *Servitium solvit miserabile Constantinus.*
>
> * * *
>
> *Christus purpureum gemmanti textus in auro*
> *Signabat Labarum, clypeorum insignia Christus*
> *Scripserat; ardebat summis crux addita cristis.*

Prudentius, *in Symmachum*, ii, 464, 486.

['You must readily recognise my standards, O queen, from the emblem of the cross, either studded with glittering gems, or made of solid gold, borne aloft on long spears. Rendered invincible by this symbol, Constantine the avenger, having crossed the Alps, has delivered the city from its wretched servitude . . . The purple *Labarum* featured the name of Christ woven in sparkling gold; Christ appeared on the insignia of the shields, a gleaming cross adorned the helmets' crests.']

33 The derivation and meaning of the word *Labarum* or *Laborum*, which is employed by Gregory Nazianzen, Ambrose, Prudentius, etc. still remain totally unknown, in spite of the efforts of the critics, who have ineffectually tortured the Latin, Greek, Spanish, Celtic, Teutonic, Illyric, Armenian, etc. in search of an etymology. See Ducange, in *Gloss. Med. et infim. Latinitat. sub voce Labarum*, and Godefroy, *ad Cod. Theodos.*, ii, 143.

34 Euseb., *in Vit. Constant.*, i, 30, 31. Baronius (*Annal. Eccles.*, AD 312, No. 26) has engraved a representation of the Labarum.

35 *Transversa X litera, summo capite circumflexo, Christum in scutis notat.* ['Christ is signified on the shields by the letter X turned on its side (i.e. +) with the top bent round.'] Caecilius, *de M. P.*, ch. 44. Cuper (*ad. M.P.*, in edit. Lactant., ii, 500) and Baronius (AD 312, No. 25) have engraved from ancient monuments several specimens (as thus ☧ or ☧) of these monograms, which became extremely fashionable in the Christian world.

36 Euseb., *in Vit. Constantin.*, ii, 7, 8, 9. He introduces the Labarum before the Italian expedition; but his narrative seems to indicate that it was never shown at the head of an army, till Constantine, above ten years afterwards, declared himself the enemy of Licinius and the deliverer of the church.

37 See *Cod. Theod.*, vi, xxv; Sozomen, i, 2; Theophan., *Chronogr.*, p. 11. Theophanes lived towards the end of the eighth century, almost five hundred years after Constantine. The modern Greeks were not inclined to display in the field the standard of the empire and of Christianity; and, though they depended on every superstitious hope of *defence*, the promise of *victory* would have appeared too bold a fiction.

38 The Abbé du Voisin, p. 103, etc. alleges several of these medals, and quotes a particular dissertation of a Jesuit, the Père de Grainville, on this subject.

39 Tertullian, *de Corona*, ch. 3; Athanasius, i, 101. The learned Jesuit Petavius (*Dogmata Theolog.*, xv, 9, 10) has collected many similar passages on the virtues of the cross, which in the last age embarrassed our Protestant disputants.

40 Caecilius, *de M. P.*, ch. 44. It is certain that this historical declamation was composed and published while Licinius, sovereign of the East, still preserved the friendship of Constantine and of the Christians. Every reader of taste must perceive that the style is of a very different and inferior character to that of Lactantius; and such indeed is the judgment of Le Clerc and Lardner (*Bibliothèque Ancienne et Moderne*, iii, p. 438; *Credibility of the Gospel*, etc., ii, vii, 94). Three arguments from the title of the book, and from the names of Donatus and Caecilius, are produced by the advocates for Lactantius (see the P. Lestocq., ii, 46–60). Each of these proofs is singly weak and defective; but their concurrence has great weight. I have often fluctuated, and shall *tamely* follow the Colbert MS. in calling the author (whoever he was) Caecilius.

41 Caecilius, *de M. P.*, ch. 46. There seems to be some reason in the observation of M. de Voltaire (*Oeuvres*, xiv, 307), who ascribes to the success of Constantine the superior fame of his Labarum above the angel of Licinius. Yet even this angel is favourably entertained by Pagi, Tillemont, Fleury, etc. who are fond of increasing their stock of miracles.

* *page 377*   [Philip of Macedon, 382–336 BC, father of Alexander the Great]

† *page 377*   [Quintus Sertorius, Roman general, murdered in 72 BC]

42 Besides these well-known examples, Tollius (Preface to Boileau's translation of Longinus) has discovered a vision of Antigonus, who assured his troops that he had seen a pentagon (the symbol of safety) with these words, 'In this conquer'. But Tollius has most inexcusably omitted to produce his authority; and his own character, literary as well as moral, is not free from reproach (see Chauffepié, *Dictionnaire Critique*, iv, 460). Without insisting on the silence of Diodorus, Plutarch, Justin, etc., it may be observed that Polyaenus, who in a separate chapter (iv, 6) has collected nineteen military stratagems of Antigonus, is totally ignorant of this remarkable vision.

43 *Instinctu Divinitatis, mentis magnitudine.* The inscription on the triumphal arch of Constantine, which has been copied by Baronius, Gruter, etc., may still be perused by every curious traveller.

44 *Habes profecto aliquid cum illa mente Divina secretum; quae delegata nostra Diis Minoribus cura uni se tibi dignatur ostendere.* ['You certainly have a secret communion with the divine spirit, which deigns to reveal itself to you alone, leaving us to the care of the lesser gods.'] *Panegyr. Vet.* ix, 2.

45 M. Freret (*Mémoires de l'Académie des Inscriptions*, iv, 411–437) explains, by physical causes, many of the prodigies of antiquity; and Fabricius, who is abused by both parties, vainly tries to introduce the celestial cross of Constantine among the solar halos. *Bibliothec. Graec.*, vi, 8–29.

46 Nazarius, *inter Panegyr. Vet.*, x, 14, 15. It is unnecessary to name the moderns whose undistinguishing and ravenous appetite has swallowed even the Pagan bait of Nazarius.

47 The apparitions of Castor and Pollux, particularly to announce the Macedonian victory, are attested by historians and public monuments. See Cicero, *de Natura Deorum*, ii, 2; iii, 5, 6; Florus, ii, 12; Valerius Maximus, i, 8, No. 1. Yet the most recent of these miracles is omitted, and indirectly denied, by Livy (xlv, 1).

48 Eusebius, i, 28, 29, 30. The silence of the same Eusebius, in his *Ecclesiastical History*, is deeply felt by those advocates for the miracle who are not absolutely callous.

49 The narrative of Constantine seems to indicate that he saw the cross in the sky before he passed the Alps against Maxentius. The scene has been fixed by provincial vanity at Treves, Besançon, etc. See Tillemont, *Hist. des Empereurs*, iv, 573.

50 The pious Tillemont (*Mém. Ecclés.*, vii, 1317) rejects with a sigh the useful Acts of Artemius, a veteran and a martyr, who attests as an eye-witness the vision of Constantine.

51 Gelasius Cyzic., in *Act. Concil. Nicen.*, i, 4.

52 The advocates for the vision are unable to produce a single testimony from the Fathers of the fourth and fifth centuries, who, in their voluminous writings, repeatedly celebrate the triumph of the church and of Constantine. As these venerable men had not any dislike to a miracle, we may suspect (and the suspicion is confirmed by the ignorance of Jerom) that they were all unacquainted with the life of Constantine by Eusebius. This tract was recovered by the diligence of those who translated or continued his *Ecclesiastical History*, and who have represented in various colours the vision of the cross.

53 Godefroy was the first who, in the year 1643 (not. *ad* Philostorgius, i, 6, 16), expressed any doubt of a miracle which had been supported with equal zeal by Cardinal Baronius and the Centuriators of Magdeburg. Since that time, many of the Protestant critics have inclined towards doubt and disbelief. The objections are urged, with great force, by M. Chauffepié (*Dictionnaire Critique*, iv, 6–11), and, in the year 1774, a doctor of Sorbonne, the Abbé du Voisin, published an Apology, which deserves the praise of learning and moderation.

54
> *Lors Constantin dit ces propres paroles:*
>
> *J'ai renversé le culte des idoles;*
> *Sur les débris de leurs temples fumans*
> *Au Dieu du Ciel j'ai prodigué l'encens.*
> *Mais tous mes soins pour sa grandeur suprême*
> *N'eurent jamais d'autre objet que moi-même ;*
> *Les saints autels n'étoient à mes regards*
> *Qu'un marchepié du trône des Césars.*
> *L'ambition, la fureur, les délices*
> *Etoient mes Dieux, avoient mes sacrifices.*
> *L'or des Chrétiens, leurs intrigues, leur sang*
> *Ont cimenté ma fortune et mon rang.*

x['Then Constantine spoke as follows: I have done away with idol-worship, and on the ruins of their smoking temples, I offered up clouds of incense to the God of Heaven. But all my solicitude for his supreme greatness had one object only: myself. As far as I was concerned, the holy altars were merely a footstool to the imperial throne. Ambition, madness, pleasure – these were my gods and the objects of my sacrifices. Christian gold, Christian intrigues and Christian blood have secured my good fortune and my lofty rank.']

The poem which contains these lines may be read with pleasure, but cannot be named with decency. [Voltaire's 'La Pucelle', a poem on the virginity of Joan of Arc.]

55 This favourite was probably the great Osius, bishop of Cordova, who preferred the pastoral care of the whole church to the government of a particular diocese. His character is magnificently, though concisely, expressed by Athanasius (i, 703). See Tillemont, *Mém. Ecclés.*, vii, 521–561. Osius was accused, perhaps unjustly, of retiring from court with a very ample fortune.

56 See Eusebius (*in Vit. Constant.*, *passim*), and Zosimus, ii, 104.

57 The Christianity of Lactantius was of a moral rather than of a mysterious cast. *Erat paene rudis* (says the orthodox Bull) *disciplinae Christianae, et in rhetorica melius quam in theologia versatus.* ['He was almost ignorant of Christian doctrine, and better versed in rhetoric than in theology.'] *Defensio Fidei Nicenae*, ii, 14.

58 Fabricius, with his usual diligence, has collected a list of between three and four hundred authors quoted in the *Evangelical Preparation* of Eusebius. See *Bibl. Graec.*, v, 4, vi, pp. 37–56.

 * *page 380* [Dutch jurist and historian, 1583–1645]

 † *page 380* [French philosopher, 1623–62]

 ‡ *page 380* [English philosopher, 1632–1704]

59 See Constantin., *Orat. ad Sanctos*, chs 19, 20. He chiefly depends on a mysterious acrostic, composed in the sixth age after the Deluge by the Erythraean Sibyl, and translated by Cicero into Latin. The initial letters of the thirty-four Greek verses form this prophetic sentence: Jesus Christ, Son of God, Saviour of the World

60 In his paraphrase of Virgil, the emperor has frequently assisted and improved the literal sense of the Latin text. See Blondel, *des Sybilles*, i, 14, 15, 16.

61 The different claims of an elder and younger son of Pollio, of Julia, of Drusus, of Marcellus, are found to be incompatible with chronology, history, and the good sense of Virgil.

62 See Lowth, *de Sacra Poesi Hebraeorum Praelect.*, xxi, 289–293. In the examination of the fourth eclogue, the respectable bishop of London has displayed learning, taste, ingenuity, and a temperate enthusiasm, which exalts his fancy without degrading his judgment.

63 The distinction between the public and the secret parts of divine service, the *missa catechumenorum*, and the *missa fidelium* [the mass for converts under instruction, and the mass for the faithful], and the mysterious veil which piety or policy had cast over the latter, are very judiciously explained by Thiers, *Exposition du Saint Sacrement*, i, chs 8–12, pp. 59–91; but as, on this subject, the Papists may reasonably be suspected, a Protestant reader will depend with more confidence on the learned Bingham, *Antiquities*, x, 5.

64 See Eusebius, *in Vit. Const.*, iv, 15–32, and the whole tenor of Constantine's sermon. The faith and devotion of the emperor has furnished Baronius with a specious argument in favour of his early baptism.

65 Zosimus, ii, 105.

66 Eusebius, *in Vit. Constant.*, iv, 15, 16.

67 The theory and practice of antiquity with regard to the sacrament of baptism, have been copiously explained by Dom. Chardon, *Hist. des Sacremens*, i, 3–405;

Dom. Martenne, *de Ritibus Ecclesiae Antiquis*, tom. i; and by Bingham, in the tenth and eleventh books of his *Christian Antiquities*. One circumstance may be observed, in which the modern churches have materially departed from the ancient custom. The sacrament of baptism (even when it was administered to infants) was immediately followed by confirmation and the holy communion.

68 The Fathers, who censured this criminal delay, could not deny the certain and victorious efficacy even of a deathbed baptism. The ingenious rhetoric of Chrysostom could find only three arguments against these prudent Christians. 1. That we should love and pursue virtue for her own sake, and not merely for the reward. 2. That we may be surprised by death without an opportunity of baptism. 3. That, although we shall be placed in heaven, we shall only twinkle like little stars, when compared to the suns of righteousness who have run their appointed course with labour, with success, and with glory. Chrysostom, in *Epist. ad Hebraeos*, Homil. xiii. apud Chardon, *Hist. des Sacremens*, i, 49. I believe that this delay of baptism, though attended with the most pernicious consequences, was never condemned by any general or provincial council, or by any public act or declaration of the church. The zeal of the bishops was easily kindled on much slighter occasions.

* *page 382* [Crispus, in AD 326. (Gibbon relates his death in Chapter 18.)]

69 Zosimus, ii, 104. For this disingenuous falsehood he has deserved and experienced the harshest treatment from all the ecclesiastical writers, except Cardinal Baronius (AD 324, No. 15–28), who had occasion to employ the Infidel on a particular service against the Arian Eusebius.

† *page 382* [a new convert]

70 Eusebius, iv, 61, 62, 63. The bishop of Caesarea supposes the salvation of Constantine with the most perfect confidence.

71 See Tillemont, *Hist. des Empereurs*, iv, 429. The Greeks, the Russians, and, in the darker ages, the Latins themselves have been desirous of placing Constantine in the catalogue of saints.

72 See the third and fourth books of his Life. He was accustomed to say that, whether Christ was preached in pretence or in truth, he should still rejoice (iii, 58).

73 M. de Tillemont (*Hist. des Empereurs*, iv, 374, 616) has defended, with strength and spirit, the virgin purity of Constantinople against some malevolent insinuations of the Pagan Zosimus.

74 The author of the *Histoire Politique et Philosophique des deux Indes* (i, 9) [the Abbé Raynal (1713–96)] condemns a law of Constantine which gave freedom to all the slaves who should embrace Christianity. The emperor did indeed publish a law which restrained the Jews from circumcising, perhaps from keeping, any Christian slaves (see Euseb., *in Vit. Constant.*, iv, 27, and *Cod. Theod.*, xvi, ix, with Godefroy's *Commentary*, vi, 247). But this imperfect exception related only to the Jews; and the great body of slaves, who were the property of Christian or Pagan masters, could not improve their temporal condition by changing their religion. I am ignorant by what guides the Abbé Raynal was deceived, as the total absence of quotations is the unpardonable blemish of his entertaining history. [It is now thought that the work was masterminded by Diderot.]

75 See *Acta Sti. Silvestri*, and *Hist. Eccles. Nicephor. Callist.*, vii, 34. *ap.* Baronium *Annal. Eccles.* AD 324, No. 67, 74. Such evidence is contemptible enough; but these circumstances are in themselves so probable, that the learned Dr Howell (*History of the World*, iii, 14) has not scrupled to adopt them .

76 The conversion of the barbarians under the reign of Constantine is celebrated by the ecclesiastical historians (see Sozomen, ii, 6, and Theodoret, i, 23, 24). But Rufinus, the Latin translator of Eusebius, deserves to be considered as an original authority. His information was curiously collected from one of the companions of the Apostle of Ethiopia, and from Bacurius, an Iberian prince, who was count of the domestics. Father Mamachi has given an ample compilation on the progress of Christianity, in the first and second volumes of his great but imperfect work.

* *page 383* [Georgia]

77 See in Eusebius (*in Vit. Constant.*, iv, 9) the pressing and pathetic epistle of Constantine in favour of his Christian brethren of Persia.

78 See Basnage, *Hist. des Juifs*, vii, 182; viii, 333; ix, 810. The curious diligence of this writer pursues the Jewish exiles to the extremities of the globe.

79 Theophilus had been given in his infancy as a hostage by his countrymen of the isle of Diva, and was educated by the Romans in learning and piety. The Maldives, of which Male, or *Diva*, may be the capital, are a cluster of 1900 or 2000 minute islands in the Indian Ocean. The ancients were imperfectly acquainted with the Maldives, but they are described in the two Mahometan travellers of the ninth century, published by Renaudot, *Geograph. Nubiensis.* pp. 30, 31. D'Herbelot, *Bibliothèque Orientale*, p. 704. *Hist. Générale des Voyages*, tom. viii.

80 Philostorgius, iii, 4, 5, 6, with Godefroy's learned observations. The historical narrative is soon lost in an inquiry concerning the seat of Paradise, strange monsters, etc.

81 See the epistle of Osius, *ap.* Athanasium, i. 840. The public remonstrance which Osius was forced to address to the son contained the same principles of ecclesiastical and civil government which he had secretly instilled into the mind of the father [i.e. Constantine – see note 55 of this chapter].

82 M. de la Bastie (*Mémoires de l'Académie des Inscriptions*, xv, 38–61) has evidently proved that Augustus and his successors exercised in person all the sacred functions of *pontifex maximus*, or high priest, of the Roman empire.

83 Something of a contrary practice had insensibly prevailed in the church of Constantinople; but the rigid Ambrose commanded Theodosius to retire below the rails, and taught him to know the difference between a king and a priest. See Theodoret, v, 18.

84 At the table of the emperor Maximus [the usurper who raised a rebellion in Britain and was defeated in Italy by the emperor Theodosius in AD 388], Martin, bishop of Tours, received the cup from an attendant, and gave it to the presbyter his companion, before he allowed the emperor to drink; the empress waited on Martin at table. Sulpicius Severus, in *Vit. Sti. Martin.*, ch. 23, and *Dialogue*, ii. 7. Yet it may be doubted whether these extraordinary compliments were paid to the bishop or the saint. The honours usually granted to the former character may be seen in Bingham's *Antiquities*, ii, 9, and Vales., *ad Theodoret.*, iv, 6. See the haughty ceremonial which Leontius, bishop of Tripoli, imposed on the empress. Tillemont, *Hist. des Empereurs*, iv, 754. *Patres Apostol.*, ii, 179.

85 Plutarch, in his treatise of Isis and Osiris, informs us that the kings of Egypt, who were not already priests, were initiated, after their election, into the sacerdotal order.

86 The numbers are not ascertained by any ancient writer or original catalogue; for the partial lists of the eastern churches are comparatively modern. The patient diligence of Charles a Sto Paolo, of Luke Holstenius, and of Bingham, has

laboriously investigated all the episcopal sees of the Catholic church, which was almost commensurate with the Roman empire. The ninth book of the *Christian Antiquities* is a very accurate map of ecclesiastical geography.

87 On the subject of the rural bishops, or *Chorepiscopi,* who voted in synods, and conferred the minor orders, see Thomassin, *Discipline de l'Eglise,* i, 447, etc., and Chardon, *Hist. des Sacramens,* v, 395, &c. They do not appear till the fourth century; and this equivocal character, which had excited the jealousy of the prelates, was abolished before the end of the tenth, both in the East and the West.

88 Thomassin (*Discipline de l'Eglise,* ii, ii, 1–8, 673–721) has copiously treated of the election of bishops during the five first centuries, both in the East and in the West; but he shows a very partial bias in favour of the episcopal aristocracy. Bingham (iv, 2) is moderate; and Chardon (*Hist. des Sacremens,* v, 108–128) is very clear and concise.

89 *Incredibilis multitudo, non solum ex eo oppido* (Tours), *sed etiam ex vicinis urbibus ad suffragia ferenda convenerat,* etc. ['An incredible multitude, not only from that town (Tours), but even from the neighbouring cities, had come to vote.'] Sulpicius Severus, *in Vit. Martin.,* ch. 7. The council of Laodicea (canon xiii) prohibits mobs and tumults; and Justinian confines the right of election to the nobility: *Novell.,* cxxiii, 1.

90 The epistles of Sidonius Apollinaris (iv, 25; vii, 5, 9) exhibit some of the scandals of the Gallican church; and Gaul was less polished and less corrupt than the East.

91 A compromise was sometimes introduced by law or by consent; either the bishops or the people chose one of the three candidates who had been named by the other party.

92 All the examples quoted by Thomassin (*Discipline de l'Eglise,* ii, 6, 704–14) appear to be extraordinary acts of power, and even of oppression. The confirmation of the bishop of Alexandria is mentioned by Philostorgius as a more regular proceeding (*Hist. Eccles.,* ii, 11).

* *page 386*   [transfer to another diocese]

93 The celibacy of the clergy during the first five or six centuries is a subject of discipline, and indeed of controversy, which has been very diligently examined. See in particular Thomassin, *Discipline de l'Eglise,* i, ii, lx and lxi, 886–902; and Bingham's *Antiquities,* iv, 5. By each of these learned but partial critics, one half of the truth is produced, and the other is concealed.

94 Diodorus Siculus attests and approves the hereditary succession of the priesthood among the Egyptians, the Chaldeans, and the Indians (i, 84; ii, 142, 153, edit. Wesseling). The Magi are described by Ammianus as a very numerous family: *Per saecula multa ad praesens una eademque prosapia multitudo creata, Deorum cultibus dedicatur* ['For many centuries up to the present day a large number, all from the same stock, has been created, dedicated to the worship of the Gods.'] (xxiii, 6). Ausonius celebrates the *Stirps Druidarum* [the race of Druids] (*de Professorib. Burdigal,* iv); but we may infer from the remark of Caesar (*Bell. Gall.,* vi, 13), that in the Celtic hierarchy some room was left for choice and emulation.

95 The subject of the vocation, ordination, obedience, etc., of the clergy, is laboriously discussed by Thomassin (*Discipline de l'Eglise,* ii, 1–83) and Bingham (in the 4th book of his *Antiquities,* more especially the 4th, 6th, and 7th chapters). When the brother of St Jerome was ordained in Cyprus, the deacons forcibly stopped his mouth, lest he should make a solemn protestation which might invalidate the holy rites.

96 The charter of immunities, which the clergy obtained from the Christian emperors, is contained in the 16th book of the Theodosian code; and is illustrated with tolerable candour by the learned Godefroy, whose mind was balanced by the opposite prejudices of a civilian [i.e. an expert in Roman law] and a Protestant.

97 Justinian., *Novell.*, ciii. Sixty presbyters or priests, one hundred deacons, forty deaconesses, ninety sub-deacons, one hundred and ten readers, twenty-five chanters, and one hundred doorkeepers; in all, five hundred and twenty-five. This moderate number was fixed by the emperor, to relieve the distress of the church, which had been involved in debt and usury by the expense of a much higher establishment.

98 *Universus clerus ecclesiæ Carthaginiensis . . . fere quinginti vel amplius; inter quos quamplurimi erant lectores infantuli.* Victor Vitensis, *de Persecut. Vandal.*, 9, 78, edit. Ruinart. ['The clergy of the church at Carthage totalled some five hundred or more, among whom were very many child officials.']. This remnant of a more prosperous state still subsisted under the oppression of the Vandals.

99 The number of *seven* orders has been fixed in the Latin church, exclusive of the episcopal character. But the four inferior ranks, the minor orders, are now reduced to empty and useless titles.

100 See *Cod. Theodos.*, xvi, 2, 42, 43. Godefroy's *Commentary*, and the *Ecclesiastical History of Alexandria*, show the danger of these pious institutions, which often disturbed the peace of that turbulent capital.

101 The edict of Milan (*de M. P.*, ch. 48) acknowledges, by reciting, that there existed a species of landed property, *ad ius corporis eorum, id est, ecclesiarum non hominum singulorum pertinentia* ['corporate property, that is, belonging to the churches, not to individuals']. Such a solemn declaration of the supreme magistrate must have been received in all the tribunals as a maxim of civil law.

102 *Habeat unusquisque licentiam sanctissimo Catholicae (ecclesiae) venerabilique concilio, decedens bonorum quod optavit relinquere.* ['Let each and every man have the right to bequeath such of his goods as he wishes to the holy Catholic (church) and to its venerable council.'] *Cod. Theodos.*, xvi, ii, 4. This law was published at Rome, AD 321, at a time when Constantine might foresee the probability of a rupture with the emperor of the East.

 * *page 388* [One of six emperors in AD 308, who was defeated by Constantine near Rome in AD 312.]

103 Eusebius, *Hist. Eccles.*, x, 6; *in Vit. Constant.*, iv, 28. He repeatedly expatiates on the liberality of the Christian hero, which the bishop himself had an opportunity of knowing, and even of tasting.

104 Eusebius, *Hist. Eccles.*, x, 2, 3, 4. The bishop of Caesarea, who studied and gratified the taste of his master, pronounced in public an elaborate description of the church of Jerusalem (*in Vit. Const.*, iv, 46). It no longer exists, but he has inserted in the *Life of Constantine* (iii, 36) a short account of the architecture and ornaments. He likewise mentions the church of the holy Apostles at Constantinople (iv, 59).

 † *page 388* [Lebanon]

105 See Justinian, *Novell.*, cxxiii, 3. The revenue of the patriarchs, and the most wealthy bishops, is not expressed: the highest annual valuation of a bishopric is stated at *thirty*, and the lowest at *two*, pounds of gold; the medium might be taken at *sixteen*, but these valuations are much below the real value.

106 See Baronius (*Annal. Eccles.*, AD 324, No. 58, 65, 70, 71). Every record which comes from the Vatican is justly suspected; yet these rent-rolls have an ancient and authentic colour; and it is at least evident that, if forged, they were forged in a period when *farms*, not *kingdoms*, were the objects of papal avarice.

107 See Thomassin, *Discipline de l'Eglise*, iii, ii, 13, 14, 15, 689–706. The legal division of the ecclesiastical revenue does not appear to have been established in the time of Ambrose and Chrysostom [i.e. second half of the fourth century]. Simplicius and Gelasius, who were bishops of Rome in the latter part of the fifth century, mention it in their pastoral letters as a general law, which was already confirmed by the custom of Italy.

108 Ambrose, the most strenuous asserter of ecclesiastical privileges, submits without a murmur to the payment of the land-tax. *Si tributum petit Imperator non negamus; agri ecclesiae solvunt tributum; solvimus quae sunt Caesaris, Caesari, et quae sunt Dei, Deo; tributum Caesaris est; non negatur.* ['If the Emperor demands the tax, we do not refuse. The church lands yield the tax. We render under Caesar what is Caesar's, and to God what is God's. The tax is Caesar's; it is not refused.'] Baronius labours to interpret this tribute as an act of charity rather than of duty (*Annal. Eccles.*, AD 387); but the words, if not the intentions, of Ambrose, are more candidly explained by Thomassin, *Discipline de l'Eglise*, iii, i, 34, 268.

109 *In Ariminense synodo super ecclesiarum et clericorum privilegiis tractatu habito, usque eo dispositio progressa est, ut iuga quae viderentur ad ecclesiam pertinere a publica functione cessarent inquietudine desistente; quod nostra videtur dudum sanctio repulisse.* ['At the council of Rimini, in a debate concerning the privileges of the churches and clergy, it was proposed that land which appeared to belong to the church should cease to be in public ownership once disquiet should have subsided; but we decided to reject this proposal.'] *Cod. Theod.* xvi, ii, 15. Had the synod of Rimini carried this point, such practical merit might have atoned for some speculative heresies.

110 From Eusebius (*in Vit. Constant.*, iv, 27) and Sozomen (i, 9) we are assured that the episcopal jurisdiction was extended and confirmed by Constantine; but the forgery of a famous edict, which was never fairly inserted in the *Theodosian Code* (see at the end, vi, 303), is demonstrated by Godefroy in the most satisfactory manner. It is strange that M. de Montesquieu, who was a lawyer as well as a philosopher, should allege this edict of Constantine (*Esprit des Loix*, xxix, 16) without intimating any suspicion.

111 The subject of ecclesiastical jurisdiction has been involved in a mist of passion, of prejudice, and of interest. Two of the fairest books which have fallen into my hands are the *Institutes of Canon Law*, by the Abbé de Fleury, and the *Civil History of Naples*, by Giannone. Their moderation was the effect of situation as well as of temper. Fleury was a French ecclesiastic, who respected the authority of the parliaments; Giannone was an Italian lawyer, who dreaded the power of the church. And here let me observe that, as the general propositions which I advance are the result of *many* particular and imperfect facts, I must either refer the reader to those modern authors who have expressly treated the subject, or swell these notes to a disagreeable and disproportioned size.

112 Tillemont has collected from Rufinus, Theodoret, etc., the sentiments and language of Constantine. *Mém. Ecclés.*, iii, 749, 750.

* *page 389*   [St Augustine]

113 See *Cod. Theod.*, ix, xlv, 4. In the works of Fra Paolo (iv, 192, etc.) there is an excellent discourse on the origin, claims, abuses, and limits of sanctuaries. He justly observes that ancient Greece might perhaps contain fifteen or twenty *asyla* or sanctuaries; a number which at present may be found in Italy within the walls of a single city.

114 The penitential jurisprudence was continually improved by the canons of the councils. But, as many cases were still left to the discretion of the bishops, they occasionally published, after the example of the Roman praetor, the rules of discipline which they proposed to observe. Among the canonical epistles of the fourth century, those of Basil the Great were the most celebrated. They are inserted in the *Pandects* of Beveridge (ii, 47–151) [a collection of the canon law and decisions of the councils of the Greek church, edited by William Beveridge, Bishop of St Asaph (Oxford, 1672)], and are translated by Chardon, *Hist. des Sacremens*, iv, 219–277.

115 Basil, *Epistol.*, xlviii. in Baronius (*Annal. Eccles.*, AD 370, No. 91), who declares that he purposely relates it, to convince governors that they were not exempt from a sentence of excommunication. In his opinion, even a royal head is not safe from the thunders of the Vatican; and the cardinal shows himself much more consistent than the lawyers and theologians of the Gallican church.

116 The long series of his ancestors, as high as Eurysthenes, the first Doric king of Sparta, and the fifth in lineal descent from Hercules, was inscribed in the public registers of Cyrene, a Lacedaemonian colony. (Synes., *Epist.*, lvii, 197, edit. Petav.) Such a pure and illustrious pedigree of seventeen hundred years, without adding the royal ancestors of Hercules, cannot be equalled in the history of mankind.

117 Synesius (*de Regno*, p. 2) pathetically deplores the fallen and ruined state of Cyrene, πόλις Ἑλληνὶς, παλαιὸν ὄνομα καὶ σεμνὸν καὶ ἐν ᾠδῇ μυρία τῶν πάλαι σοφῶν, νῦν πένης καὶ κατηφὴς, καὶ μέγα ἐρείπιον. ['A Greek city, of ancient and august renown and celebrated time and again by the wise men of old, now poor and obscure, a great heap of ruins.'] Ptolemais, a new city, 82 miles to the westward of Cyrene, assumed the metropolitan honours of the Pentapolis, or Upper Libya, which were afterwards transferred to Sozusa. See Wesseling, *Itinerar.*, pp. 67, 68, 732. Cellarius, *Geograph.*, ii, ii, 72, 74. Carolus a Sto Paulo, *Geograph. Sacra*, p. 273. D'Anville, *Géographie Ancienne*, iii, 43, 44. *Mémoires de l'Acad. des Inscriptions*, xxxvii, 363–391.

118 Synesius had previously represented his own disqualifications (*Epist.*, cv, 246–50). He loved profane studies and profane sports; he was incapable of supporting a life of celibacy; he disbelieved the resurrection, and he refused to preach *fables* to the people, unless he might be permitted to *philosophise* at home. Theophilus, primate of Egypt, who knew his merit, accepted this extraordinary compromise. See the Life of Synesius in Tillemont, *Mém. Ecclés.*, xii, 499–554.

119 See the invective of Synesius, *Epist.*, lvii, 191–201. The promotion of Andronicus was illegal, since he was a native of Berenice, in the same province. The instruments of tortures are curiously specified, the πιεστήριον or press, the δακτυλήθρα, the ποδοστράβη, the ῥινολαβίς, the ὠτάγρα, and the χειλοστρόφιον, that variously pressed or distended the fingers, the feet, the nose, the ears, and the lips of the victims.

120 The sentence of excommunication is expressed in a rhetorical style (Synesius,

Epist., lviii, 201–203.) The method of involving whole families, though somewhat unjust, was improved into national interdicts.

* *page 390*   [tyrant of Agrigentum in Sicily]

† *page 390*   [King of Assyria, 704–681 BC]

121 See Synesius, *Epist.*, xlvii, 186, 187; *Epist.*, lxxii, 218, 219; *Epist.*, lxxxix, 230, 231.

122 See Thomassin (*Discipline de l'Eglise*, ii, iii, 83, 1761–1770) and Bingham (*Antiquities*, i, xiv, 4, 688–717). Preaching was considered as the most important office of the bishop; but this function was sometimes entrusted to such presbyters as Chrysostom and Augustine.

123 Queen Elizabeth used this expression, and practised this art, whenever she wished to prepossess the minds of her people in favour of any extraordinary measure of government. The hostile effects of this *music* were apprehended by her successor, and severely felt by his son. 'When pulpit, drum ecclesiastic', etc., see Heylin's *Life of Archbishop Laud*, p. 153.

* *page 392*   [St Gregory of Nazianzen, ad *c*.330–389]

† *page 392*   [St John Chrysostom ('Golden-mouth'), ad *c*.347–407]

124 Those modest orators acknowledged that, as they were destitute of the gift of miracles, they endeavoured to acquire the arts of eloquence.

125 The council of Nicaea, in the fourth, fifth, sixth, and seventh canons, has made some fundamental regulations concerning synods, metropolitans, and primates. The Nicene canons have been variously tortured, abused, interpolated, or forged, according to the interest of the clergy. The *Suburbicarian* churches, assigned (by Rufinus) to the bishop of Rome, have been made the subject of vehement controversy. See Sirmond, *Opera*, iv, 1–238.

126 We have only thirty-three or forty-seven episcopal subscriptions; but Ado, a writer indeed of small account, reckons six hundred bishops in the council of Arles. Tillemont, *Mém. Ecclés.*, vi, 422.

127 See Tillemont, vi, 915, and Beausobre, *Hist. du Manichéisme*, i, 529. The name of *bishop*, which is given by Eutychius to the 2048 ecclesiastics (*Annal.*, i, 440, vers. Pocock), must be extended far beyond the limits of an orthodox or even episcopal ordination.

128 See Euseb., *in Vit. Constantin.*, iii, 6–21; Tillemont, *Mém. Ecclésiastiques*, vi, 669–759.

* *page 393*   [the emperor Tacitus, ad 275–76]

129 *Sancimus igitur vicem legum obtinere, quae a quatuor Sanctis Conciliis . . expositae sunt aut firmatae. Praedictarum enim quatuor synodorum dogmata sicut sanctas Scripturas et regulas sicut leges observamus.* ['We therefore give legal force to those decrees which have been formulated or confirmed by the four holy Councils. For we regard the dogmas of the four aforesaid synods as equal to the Holy Scriptures and their rulings as equal to the laws.'] Justinian, *Novell.*, cxxxi. Beveridge (*ad Pandect.*, proleg., p. 2) remarks that the emperors never made new laws in ecclesiastical matters; and Giannone observes, in a very different spirit, that they gave a legal sanction to the canons of councils. *Istoria Civile di Napoli*, i, 136.

130 See the article 'Concile' in the *Encyclopédie*, iii, 668–679, édition de Lucques. The author, M. le docteur Bouchaud, has discussed, according to the principles of the Gallican church, the principal questions which relate to the form and constitution of general, national, and provincial councils. The editors (see Preface, p. xvi) have reason to be proud of *this* article. Those who consult their immense compilation seldom depart so well satisfied.

CHAPTER 21

*Persecution of heresy – the schism of the Donatists – the Arian
controversy – Athanasius – distracted state of the Church and
empire under Constantine and his sons – toleration of Paganism*

The grateful applause of the clergy has consecrated the memory of a
prince who indulged their passions and promoted their interest.
Constantine gave them security, wealth, honours, and revenge; and the
support of the orthodox faith was considered as the most sacred and
important duty of the civil magistrate. The edict of Milan, the great
charter of toleration, had confirmed to each individual of the Roman
world the privilege of choosing and professing his own religion. But this
inestimable privilege was soon violated: with the knowledge of truth, the
emperor imbibed the maxims of persecution; and the sects which
dissented from the Catholic church were afflicted and oppressed by the
triumph of Christianity. Constantine easily believed that the Heretics,
who presumed to dispute *his* opinions or to oppose *his* commands, were
guilty of the most absurd and criminal obstinacy; and that a seasonable
application of moderate severities might save those unhappy men from
the danger of an everlasting condemnation. Not a moment was lost in
excluding the ministers and teachers of the separated congregations from
any share of the rewards and immunities which the emperor had so
liberally bestowed on the orthodox clergy. But, as the sectaries might still
exist under the cloud of royal disgrace, the conquest of the East was
immediately followed by an edict which announced their total destruction.[1] After a preamble filled with passion and reproach, Constantine
absolutely prohibits the assemblies of the Heretics, and confiscates their
public property to the use either of the revenue or of the Catholic church.
The sects against whom the Imperial severity was directed appear to have
been the adherents of Paul of Samosata; the Montanists of Phrygia, who
maintained an enthusiastic succession of prophecy; the Novatians, who
sternly rejected the temporal efficacy of repentance; the Marcionites and
Valentinians,* under whose leading banners the various Gnostics of Asia
and Egypt had insensibly† rallied; and perhaps the Manichaeans, who had
recently imported from Persia a more artful composition of Oriental and
Christian theology.[2] The design of extirpating the name, or at least of
restraining the progress, of these odious Heretics was prosecuted with
vigour and effect. Some of the penal regulations were copied from the
edicts of Diocletian; and this method of conversion was applauded by the
same bishops who had felt the hand of oppression and had pleaded for the
rights of humanity. Two immaterial‡ circumstances may serve, however,

to prove that the mind of Constantine was not entirely corrupted by the spirit of zeal and bigotry. Before he condemned the Manichaeans and their kindred sects, he resolved to make an accurate enquiry into the nature of their religious principles. As if he distrusted the impartiality of his ecclesiastical counsellors, this delicate commission was entrusted to a civil magistrate, whose learning and moderation he justly esteemed, and of whose venal character he was probably ignorant.[3] The emperor was soon convinced that he had too hastily proscribed the orthodox faith and the exemplary morals of the Novatians, who had dissented from the church in some articles of discipline which were not perhaps essential to salvation. By a particular edict, he exempted them from the general penalties of the law;[4] allowed them to build a church at Constantinople, respected the miracles of their saints, invited their bishop Acesius to the council of Nicaea, and gently ridiculed the narrow tenets of his sect by a familiar jest, which, from the mouth of a sovereign, must have been received with applause and gratitude.[5]

The complaints and mutual accusations which assailed the throne of Constantine, as soon as the death of Maxentius had submitted Africa to his victorious arms, were ill adapted to edify an imperfect proselyte. He learned with surprise that the provinces of that great country, from the confines of Cyrene to the columns of Hercules, were distracted with religious discord.[6] The source of the division was derived from a double election in the church of Carthage; the second, in rank and opulence, of the ecclesiastical thrones of the West. Caecilian and Majorinus were the two rival primates of Africa; and the death of the latter soon made room for Donatus, who, by his superior abilities and apparent virtues, was the firmest support of his party. The advantage which Caecilian might claim from the priority of his ordination was destroyed by the illegal, or at least indecent, haste with which it had been performed, without expecting the arrival of the bishops of Numidia. The authority of these bishops, who, to the number of seventy, condemned Caecilian and consecrated Majorinus, is again weakened by the infamy of some of their personal characters; and by the female intrigues, sacrilegious bargains, and tumultuous proceedings which are imputed to this Numidian council.[7] The bishops of the contending factions maintained, with equal ardour and obstinacy, that their adversaries were degraded, or at least dishonoured, by the odious crime of delivering the Holy Scriptures to the officers of Diocletian. From their mutual reproaches, as well as from the story of this dark transaction, it may justly be inferred that the late persecution had embittered the zeal, without reforming the manners, of the African Christians. That divided church was incapable of affording an impartial judicature; the controversy was solemnly tried in five successive tribunals which were appointed by the emperor; and the whole proceeding, from the first appeal to the final sentence, lasted above three years. A severe inquisition, which was taken by the Praetorian vicar and the proconsul of Africa, the report of two episcopal visitors who had been sent to Carthage, the decrees of the councils of Rome and of Arles, and the supreme judgment of Constantine himself in his sacred consistory, were all favourable to the cause of Caecilian; and he was unanimously acknowledged by the civil and ecclesiastical powers as the true and lawful primate of Africa. The honours and estates of the church were attributed to *his* suffragan bishops, and it was not without difficulty that Constantine was satisfied with inflicting the punishment of exile on the principal leaders of the Donatist faction. As their cause was examined with attention, perhaps it was determined with justice. Perhaps their complaint was not without foundation, that the credulity of the emperor had been abused by the insidious arts of his favourite Osius. The influence of falsehood and corruption might procure the condemnation of the innocent, or aggravate the sentence of the guilty. Such an act, however, of injustice, if it concluded an importunate dispute, might be numbered among the transient evils of a despotic administration, which are neither felt nor remembered by posterity.

But this incident, so inconsiderable that it scarcely deserves a place in history, was productive of a memorable schism, which afflicted the provinces of Africa above three hundred years, and was extinguished only with Christianity itself. The inflexible zeal of freedom and fanaticism animated the Donatists to refuse obedience to the usurpers whose election they disputed and whose spiritual powers they denied. Excluded from the civil and religious communion of mankind, they boldly excommunicated the rest of mankind, who had embraced the impious party of Caecilian, and of the Traditors,* from whom he derived his pretended ordination. They asserted with confidence, and almost with exultation, that the Apostolical succession was interrupted; that *all* the bishops of Europe and Asia were infected by the contagion of guilt and schism; and that the prerogatives of the Catholic church were confined to the chosen portion of the African believers, who alone had preserved inviolate the integrity of their faith and discipline. This rigid theory was supported by the most uncharitable conduct. Whenever they acquired a proselyte, even from the distant provinces of the East, they carefully repeated the sacred rites of baptism[8] and ordination; as they rejected the validity of those which he had already received from the hands of heretics or schismatics. Bishops, virgins, and even spotless infants were subjected to the disgrace of a public penance, before they could be admitted to the communion of the Donatists. If they obtained possession of a church which had been used by their Catholic adversaries, they purified the unhallowed building with the same jealous care which a temple of idols might have required. They washed the pavement, scraped the walls, burnt the altar, which was commonly of wood, melted the consecrated plate, and cast the Holy Eucharist to the dogs, with every circumstance of ignominy which could provoke and perpetuate the animosity of religious factions.[9] Notwithstanding this irreconcilable aversion, the two parties, who were mixed and separated in all the cities of Africa, had the same language and manners, the same zeal and learning, the same faith and worship. Proscribed by the civil and ecclesiastical powers of the empire, the Donatists still maintained in some provinces, particularly in Numidia, their superior numbers; and four hundred bishops acknowledged the jurisdiction of their primate. But the invincible spirit of the sect sometimes preyed on its own vitals; and the bosom of their schismatical church was torn by intestine divisions. A fourth part of the Donatist bishops followed the independent standard of the Maximianists. The narrow and solitary path which their first leaders had marked out continued to deviate from the great society of mankind. Even the imperceptible sect of the Rogatians could affirm, without a blush, that, when Christ should descend to judge the earth, he would find his true religion preserved only in a few nameless villages of the Caesarean Mauritania.[10]

The schism of the Donatists was confined to Africa: the more diffusive mischief of the Trinitarian controversy successively penetrated into every part of the Christian world. The former was an accidental quarrel, occasioned by the abuse of freedom; the latter was a high and mysterious argument, derived from the abuse of philosophy. From the age of Constantine to that of Clovis and Theodoric,* the temporal interests both of the Romans and Barbarians were deeply involved in the theological disputes of Arianism. The historian may therefore be permitted respectfully to withdraw the veil of the sanctuary, and to deduce the progress of reason and faith, of error and passion, from the school of Plato to the decline and fall of the empire.

The genius of Plato, informed by his own meditation, or by the traditional knowledge of the priests of Egypt,[11] had ventured to explore the mysterious nature of the Deity. When he had elevated his mind to the sublime contemplation of the first self-existent, necessary cause of the universe, the Athenian sage was incapable of conceiving *how* the simple unity of his essence could admit the infinite variety of distinct and successive ideas which compose the model of the intellectual world; *how* a Being purely incorporeal could execute that perfect model, and mould with a plastic hand the rude and independent chaos. The vain hope of extricating himself from these difficulties, which must ever oppress the feeble powers of the human mind, might induce Plato to consider the divine nature under the threefold modification: of the first cause, the reason or *Logos*, and the soul or spirit of the universe. His poetical imagination sometimes fixed and animated these metaphysical abstractions: the three *archical* or original principles were represented in the Platonic system as three Gods, united with each other by a mysterious and ineffable generation; and the Logos was particularly considered under the more accessible character of the Son of an Eternal Father, and the Creator and Governor of the world. Such appear to have been the secret doctrines which were cautiously whispered in the gardens of the academy; and which, according to the more recent disciples of Plato, could not be perfectly understood, till after an assiduous study of thirty years.[12]

The arms of the Macedonians diffused over Asia and Egypt the language and learning of Greece; and the theological system of Plato was taught with less reserve, and perhaps with some improvements, in the celebrated school of Alexandria.[13] A numerous colony of Jews had been invited, by the favour of the Ptolemies, to settle in their new capital.[14] While the bulk of the nation practised the legal ceremonies, and pursued the lucrative occupations of commerce, a few Hebrews, of a more liberal spirit, devoted their lives to religious and philosophical contemplation.[15] They cultivated with diligence, and embraced with ardour, the theological system of the Athenian sage. But their national pride would have been mortified by a fair confession of their former poverty: and they boldly marked, as the sacred inheritance of their ancestors, the gold and jewels which they had so lately stolen from their Egyptian masters. One hundred years before the birth of Christ, a philosophical treatise, which manifestly betrays the style and sentiments of the school of Plato, was produced by the Alexandrian Jews and unanimously received as a genuine and valuable relic of the inspired Wisdom of Solomon.[16] A similar union of the Mosaic faith and the Grecian philosophy distinguishes the works of Philo, which were composed, for the most part, under the reign of Augustus.[17] The material soul of the universe[18] might offend the piety of the Hebrews; but they applied the character of the *Logos* to the Jehovah of Moses and the patriarchs; and the Son of God was introduced upon earth under a visible, and even human, appearance, to perform those familiar offices which seem incompatible with the nature and attributes of the Universal Cause.[19]

The eloquence of Plato, the name of Solomon, the authority of the school of Alexandria, and the consent of the Jews and Greeks, were insufficient to establish the truth of a mysterious doctrine which might please, but could not satisfy, a rational mind. A prophet or apostle, inspired by the Deity, can alone exercise a lawful dominion over the faith of mankind; and the theology of Plato might have been for ever confounded with the philosophical visions of the Academy, the Porch, and the Lyceum,* if the name and divine attributes of the *Logos* had not been confirmed by the celestial pen of the last and most sublime of the Evangelists.[20] The Christian Revelation, which was consummated under the reign of Nerva, disclosed to the world the amazing secret that the *Logos*, who was with God from the beginning and was God, who had made all things and for whom all things had been made, was incarnate in the person of Jesus of Nazareth; who had been born of a virgin, and suffered death on the cross. Besides the general design of fixing on a perpetual basis the divine honours of Christ, the most ancient and respectable of the ecclesiastical writers have ascribed to the evangelic theologian a particular intention to confute two opposite heresies, which disturbed the peace of the primitive church.[21] I. The faith of the Ebionites,[22] perhaps of the Nazarenes,[23] was gross and imperfect. They revered Jesus as the greatest of the prophets, endowed with supernatural virtue and power. They ascribed to his person and to his future reign all the predictions of the Hebrew oracles which relate to the spiritual and everlasting kingdom of the promised Messiah.[24] Some of them might confess that he was born of a virgin; but they obstinately rejected the preceding existence and divine perfections of the *Logos*, or Son of God, which are so clearly defined in the Gospel of St John. About fifty years afterwards the Ebionites, whose errors are mentioned by Justin Martyr with less severity than they seem to deserve,[25] formed a very inconsiderable portion of the Christian name. II. The Gnostics, who were distinguished by the epithet of *Docetes*, deviated into the contrary extreme, and betrayed the human, while they asserted the divine, nature of Christ. Educated in the school of Plato, accustomed to the sublime idea of the *Logos*, they readily conceived that the brightest *Aeon*, or *Emanation* of the Deity, might assume the outward shape and visible appearances of a mortal;[26] but they vainly pretended that the imperfections of matter are incompatible with the purity of a celestial substance. While the blood of Christ yet smoked on Mount Calvary, the Docetes invented the impious and extravagant hypothesis that, instead of issuing from the womb of the Virgin,[27] he had descended on the banks of the Jordan in the form of perfect manhood; that he had imposed on the senses of his enemies, and of his disciples; and that the ministers of Pilate had wasted their impotent rage on an airy phantom, who *seemed* to expire on the cross and, after three days, to rise from the dead.[28]

The divine sanction which the Apostle had bestowed on the fundamental principle of the theology of Plato encouraged the learned proselytes of the second and third centuries to admire and study the writings of the Athenian sage, who had thus marvellously anticipated one of the most surprising discoveries of the Christian revelation. The respectable name of Plato was used by the orthodox,[29] and abused by the heretics,[30] as the common support of truth and error: the authority of his skilful commentators, and the science of dialectics, were employed to justify the remote consequences of his opinions, and to supply the discreet silence of the inspired writers. The same subtle and profound questions concerning the nature, the generation, the distinction, and the equality of the three divine persons of the mysterious *Triad*, or Trinity,[31] were agitated in the philosophical, and in the Christian, schools of Alexandria. An eager spirit of curiosity urged them to explore the secrets of the abyss; and the pride of the professors and of their disciples was satisfied with the science of words. But the most sagacious of the Christian theologians, the great Athanasius* himself, has candidly confessed[32] that, whenever he forced his understanding to meditate on the divinity of the *Logos*, his toilsome and unavailing efforts recoiled on themselves; that the more he thought, the less he comprehended; and the more he wrote, the less capable was he of expressing his thoughts. In every step of the enquiry, we are compelled to feel and acknowledge the immeasurable disproportion between the size of the object and the capacity of the human mind. We may strive to abstract the notions of time, of space, and of matter, which so closely adhere to all the perceptions of our experimental knowledge. But, as soon as we presume to reason of infinite substance, of spiritual generation; as often as we deduce any positive conclusions from a negative idea, we are involved in darkness, perplexity, and inevitable contradiction. As these difficulties arise from the nature of the subject, they oppress, with the same insuperable weight, the philosophic and the theological disputant; but we may observe two essential and peculiar circumstances which discriminated the doctrines of the Catholic church from the opinions of the Platonic school.

I. A chosen society of philosophers, men of a liberal education and curious disposition, might silently meditate, and temperately discuss, in the gardens of Athens or the library of Alexandria, the abstruse questions of metaphysical science. The lofty speculations which neither convinced the understanding, nor agitated the passions, of the Platonists themselves were carelessly overlooked by the idle, the busy, and even the studious part of mankind.[33] But, after the *Logos* had been revealed as the sacred object of the faith, the hope, and the religious worship of the Christians, the mysterious system was embraced by a numerous and increasing multitude in every province of the Roman world. Those persons who, from their age, or sex, or occupations, were the least qualified to judge, who were the least exercised in the habits of abstract reasoning, aspired to contemplate the economy of the Divine Nature; and it is the boast of Tertullian[34] that a Christian mechanic could readily answer such questions as had perplexed the wisest of the Grecian sages. Where the subject lies so far beyond our reach, the difference between the highest and the lowest of human understandings may indeed be calculated as infinitely small; yet the degree of weakness may perhaps be measured by the degree of obstinacy and dogmatic confidence. These speculations, instead of being treated as the amusement of a vacant hour, became the most serious business of the present, and the most useful preparation for a future, life. A theology, which it was incumbent to believe, which it was impious to doubt, and which it might be dangerous, and even fatal, to mistake, became the familiar topic of private meditation and popular discourse. The cold indifference of philosophy was inflamed by the fervent spirit of devotion; and even the metaphors of common language suggested the fallacious prejudices of sense and experience. The Christians, who abhorred the gross and impure generation of the Greek mythology,[35] were tempted to argue from the familiar analogy of the filial and paternal relations. The character of *Son* seemed to imply a perpetual subordination to the voluntary author of his existence;[36] but, as the act of generation, in the most spiritual and abstracted sense, must be supposed to transmit the properties of a common nature,[37] they durst not presume to circumscribe the powers or the duration of the Son of an eternal and omnipotent Father. Fourscore years after the death of Christ, the Christians of Bithynia declared before the tribunal of Pliny that they invoked him as a god; and his divine honours have been perpetuated in every age and country by the various sects who assume the name of his disciples.[38] Their tender reverence for the memory of Christ and their horror for the profane worship of any created being would have engaged them to assert the equal and absolute divinity of the *Logos*, if their rapid ascent towards the throne of heaven had not been imperceptibly checked by the apprehension of violating the unity and sole supremacy of the great Father of Christ, and of the Universe. The suspense and fluctuation produced in the minds of the Christians by these opposite tendencies may be observed in the writings of the theologians who flourished after the end if the apostolic age and before the origin of the Arian controversy. Their suffrage is claimed, with equal confidence, by the orthodox and by the heretical parties; and the most inquisitive critics have fairly allowed that, if they had the good fortune of possessing the Catholic verity, they have delivered their conceptions in loose, inaccurate, and sometimes contradictory language.[39]

II. The devotion of individuals was the first circumstance which distinguished the Christians from the Platonists; the second was the authority of the church. The disciples of philosophy asserted the rights of intellectual freedom, and their respect for the sentiments of their teachers was a liberal and voluntary tribute, which they offered to superior reason. But the Christians formed a numerous and disciplined society; and the jurisdiction of their laws and magistrates was strictly exercised over the minds of the faithful. The loose wanderings of the imagination were gradually confined by creeds and confessions;[40] the freedom of private judgment submitted to the public wisdom of synods; the authority of a theologian was determined by his ecclesiastical rank, and the episcopal successors of the apostles inflicted the censures of the church on those who deviated from the orthodox belief. But in an age of religious controversy every act of oppression adds new force to the elastic vigour of the mind; and the zeal or obstinacy of a spiritual rebel was sometimes stimulated by secret motives of ambition or avarice. A metaphysical argument became the cause or pretence of political contests; the subtleties of the Platonic school were used as the badges of popular factions, and the distance which separated their respective tenets was enlarged or magnified by the acrimony of dispute. As long as the dark heresies of Praxeas and Sabellius laboured to confound the *Father* with the *Son*,[41] the orthodox party might be excused if they adhered more strictly and more earnestly to the *distinction*, than to the *equality*, of the divine persons. But, as soon as the heat of controversy had subsided, and the progress of the Sabellians was no longer an object of terror to the churches of Rome, of Africa, or of Egypt; the tide of theological opinion began to flow with a gentle but steady motion toward the contrary extreme; and the most orthodox doctors allowed themselves the use of the terms and definitions which had been censured in the mouth of the sectaries.[42] After the edict of toleration had restored peace and leisure to the Christians, the Trinitarian controversy was revived in the ancient seat of Platonism, the learned, the opulent, the tumultuous city of Alexandria; and the flame of religious discord was rapidly communicated from the schools to the clergy, the people, the province, and the East. The abstruse question of the eternity of the *Logos* was agitated in ecclesiastical conferences and popular sermons; and the heterodox opinions of Arius[43] were soon made public by his own zeal and by that of his adversaries. His most implacable adversaries have acknowledged the learning and blameless life of that eminent presbyter, who, in a former election, had declared, and perhaps generously declined, his pretensions to the episcopal throne.[44] His competitor Alexander assumed the office of his judge. The important cause was argued before him; and, if at first he seemed to hesitate, he at length pronounced his final sentence, as an absolute rule of faith.[45] The undaunted presbyter, who presumed to resist the authority of his angry bishop, was separated from the communion of the church. But the pride of Arius was supported by the applause of a numerous party. He reckoned among his immediate followers two bishops of Egypt, seven presbyters, twelve deacons, and (what may appear almost incredible) seven hundred virgins. A large majority of the bishops of Asia appeared to support or favour his cause; and their measures were conducted by Eusebius of Caesarea, the most learned of the Christian prelates, and by Eusebius of Nicomedia, who had acquired the reputation of a statesman without forfeiting that of a saint. Synods in Palestine and Bithynia were opposed to the synods of Egypt. The attention of the prince and people was attracted by this theological dispute; and the decision, at the end of six years,[46] was referred to the supreme authority of the general council of Nicaea.

When the mysteries of the Christian faith were dangerously exposed to public debate, it might be observed that the human understanding was capable of forming three distinct, though imperfect, systems concerning the nature of the Divine Trinity; and it was pronounced that none of these systems, in a pure and absolute sense, were exempt from heresy and error.[47] I. According to the first hypothesis, which was maintained by Arius and his disciples, the *Logos* was a dependent and spontaneous production, created from nothing by the will of the Father. The Son, by whom all things were made,[48] had been begotten before all worlds, and the longest of the astronomical periods could be compared only as a fleeting moment to the extent of his duration; yet this duration was not infinite,[49] and there *had* been a time which preceded the ineffable generation of the *Logos*. On this only-begotten Son the Almighty Father had transfused his ample spirit, and impressed the effulgence of his glory. Visible image of invisible perfection, he saw, at an immeasurable distance beneath his feet, the thrones of the brightest archangels; yet he shone only with a reflected light, and, like the sons of the Roman emperors who were invested with the titles of Caesar or Augustus,[50] he governed the universe in obedience to the will of his Father and Monarch. II. In the second hypothesis, the *Logos* possessed all the inherent, incommunicable perfections which religion and philosophy appropriate to the Supreme God. Three distinct and infinite minds or substances, three co-equal and co-eternal beings, composed the Divine Essence;[51] and it would have implied contradiction that any of them should not have existed or that they should ever cease to exist.[52] The advocates of a system which seemed to establish three independent Deities attempted to preserve the unity of the First Cause, so conspicuous in the design and order of the world, by the perpetual concord of their administration and the essential agreement of their will. A faint resemblance of this unity of action may be discovered in the societies of men, and even of animals. The causes which disturb their harmony proceed only from the imperfection and inequality of their faculties; but the omnipotence which is guided by infinite wisdom and goodness cannot fail of choosing the same means for the accomplishment of the same ends. III. Three Beings, who, by the self-derived necessity of their existence, possess all the divine attributes in the most perfect degree; who are eternal in duration, infinite in space and intimately present to each other and to the whole universe; irresistibly force themselves on the astonished mind as one and the same Being,[53] who, in the economy of grace, as well as in that of nature, may manifest himself under different forms, and be considered under different aspects. By this hypothesis, a real substantial Trinity is refined into a trinity of names and abstract modifications, that subsist only in the mind which conceives them. The *Logos* is no longer a person, but an attribute; and it is only in a figurative sense that the epithet of Son can be applied to the eternal reason which was with God from the beginning, and by *which*, not by *whom*, all things were made. The incarnation of the *Logos* is reduced to a mere inspiration of the Divine Wisdom, which filled the soul, and directed all the actions, of the man Jesus. Thus, after revolving round the theological circle, we are surprised to find that the Sabellian ends where the Ebionite had begun; and that the incomprehensible mystery which excites our adoration eludes our enquiry.[54]

If the bishops of the council of Nice[55] had been permitted to follow the unbiased dictates of their conscience, Arius and his associates could scarcely have flattered themselves with the hopes of obtaining a majority of votes, in favour of an hypothesis so directly adverse to the two most popular opinions of the Catholic world. The Arians soon perceived the danger of their situation, and prudently assumed those modest virtues which, in the fury of civil and religious dissensions, are seldom practised, or even praised, except by the weaker party. They recommended the exercise of Christian charity and moderation; urged the incomprehensible nature of the controversy; disclaimed the use of any terms or definitions which could not be found in the scriptures; and offered, by very liberal concessions, to satisfy their adversaries without renouncing the integrity of their own principles. The victorious faction received all their proposals with haughty suspicion; and anxiously sought for some irreconcilable mark of distinction, the rejection of which might involve the Arians in the guilt and consequences of heresy. A letter was publicly read, and ignominiously torn, in which their patron, Eusebius of Nicomedia, ingenuously confessed that the admission of the Homoousion, or Consubstantial, a word already familiar to the Platonists, was incompatible with the principles of their theological system. The fortunate opportunity was eagerly embraced by the bishops who governed the resolutions of the synod; and, according to the lively expression of Ambrose,*[56] they used the sword, which heresy itself had drawn from the scabbard, to cut off the head of the hated monster. The consubstantiality of the Father and the Son was established by the council of Nicaea, and has been unanimously received as a fundamental article of the Christian faith, by the consent of the Greek, the Latin, the Oriental, and the Protestant churches. But, if the same word had not served to stigmatise the heretics and to unite the Catholics, it would have been inadequate to the purpose of the majority by whom it was introduced into the orthodox creed. This majority was divided into two parties, distinguished by a contrary tendency to the sentiments of the Tritheists and of the Sabellians. But, as those opposite extremes seemed to overthrow the foundations either of natural or revealed religion, they mutually agreed to qualify the rigour of their principles and to disavow the just, but invidious, consequences which might be urged by their antagonists. The interest of the common cause inclined them to join their numbers and to conceal their differences; their animosity was softened by the healing counsels of toleration, and their disputes were suspended by the use of the mysterious *Homoousion*, which either party was free to interpret according to their peculiar tenets. The Sabellian sense, which, about fifty years before, had obliged the council of Antioch[57] to prohibit this celebrated term, had endeared it to those theologians who entertained a secret but partial affection for a nominal Trinity. But the more fashionable saints of the Arian times, the intrepid Athanasius, the learned Gregory Nazianzen,† and the other pillars of the church, who supported with ability and success the Nicene doctrine, appeared to consider the expression of *substance* as if it had been synonymous with that of *nature*; and they ventured to illustrate their meaning by affirming that three men, as they belong to the same common species, are consubstantial or homoousian to each other.[58] This pure and distinct equality was tempered, on the one hand, by the internal connection, and spiritual penetration, which indissolubly unites the divine persons;[59] and on the other, by the pre-eminence of the Father, which was acknowledged as far as it is compatible with the independence of the Son.[60] Within these limits the almost invisible and tremulous ball of orthodoxy was allowed securely to vibrate. On either side, beyond this consecrated ground, the heretics and the demons lurked in ambush to surprise and devour the unhappy wanderer. But, as the degrees of theological hatred depend on the spirit of the war rather than on the importance of the controversy, the heretics who degraded, were treated with more severity than those who annihilated, the person of the Son. The life of Athanasius was consumed in irreconcilable opposition to the impious *madness* of the Arians;[61] but he defended above twenty years the Sabellianism of Marcellus of Ancyra; and, when at last he was compelled to withdraw himself from his communion, he continued to mention, with an ambiguous smile, the venial errors of his respectable friend.[62]

The authority of a general council, to which the Arians themselves had been compelled to submit, inscribed on the banners of the orthodox party the mysterious characters of the word *Homoousion*, which essentially contributed, notwithstanding some obscure disputes, some nocturnal combats, to maintain and perpetuate the uniformity of faith, or at least of language. The Consubstantialists, who by their success have deserved and obtained the title of Catholics, gloried in the simplicity and steadiness of their own creed, and insulted the repeated variations of their adversaries, who were destitute of any certain rule of faith. The sincerity or the cunning of the Arian chiefs, the fear of the laws or of the people, their reverence for Christ, their hatred of Athanasius, all the causes, human and divine, that influence and disturb the counsels of a theological faction, introduced among the sectaries a spirit of discord and inconstancy, which, in the course of a few years, erected eighteen different models of religion,[63] and avenged the violated dignity of the church. The zealous Hilary,*[64] who, from the peculiar hardships of his situation, was inclined to extenuate rather than to aggravate the errors of the Oriental clergy, declares that in the wide extent of the ten provinces of Asia to which he had been banished, there could be found very few prelates who had preserved the knowledge of the true God.[65] The oppression which he had felt, the disorders of which he was the spectator and the victim, appeased, during a short interval, the angry passions of his soul; and in the following passage, of which I shall transcribe a few lines, the bishop of Poitiers unwarily deviates into the style of a Christian philosopher. 'It is a thing,' says Hilary, 'equally deplorable and dangerous, that there are as many creeds as opinions among men, as many doctrines as inclinations, and as many sources of blasphemy as there are faults among us; because we make creeds arbitrarily, and explain them as arbitrarily. The Homoousion is rejected, and received, and explained away by successive synods. The partial or total resemblance of the Father and of the Son is a subject of dispute for these unhappy times. Every year, nay every moon, we make new creeds to describe invisible mysteries. We repent of what we have done, we defend those who repent, we anathematise those whom we defended. We condemn either the doctrine of others in ourselves or our own in that of others; and, reciprocally tearing one another to pieces, we have been the cause of each other's ruin.'[66]

It will not be expected, it would not perhaps be endured, that I should swell this theological digression by a minute examination of the eighteen creeds, the authors of which, for the most part, disclaimed the odious name of their parent Arius. It is amusing enough to delineate the form, and to trace the vegetation, of a singular plant; but the tedious detail of leaves without flowers, and of branches without fruit, would soon exhaust the patience, and disappoint the curiosity, of the laborious student. One question which gradually arose from the Arian controversy may however be noticed, as it served to produce and discriminate the three sects who were united only by their common aversion to the Homoousion of the Nicene synod. 1. If they were asked, whether the Son was *like* unto the Father, the question was resolutely answered in the negative by the heretics who adhered to the principles of Arius, or indeed to those of philosophy; which seem to establish an infinite difference between the Creator and the most excellent of his creatures. This obvious consequence was maintained by Aetius,[67] on whom the zeal of his adversaries bestowed the surname of the Atheist. His restless and aspiring spirit urged him to try almost every profession of human life. He was successively a slave, or at least a husbandman, a travelling tinker, a goldsmith, a physician, a school-master, a theologian, and at last the apostle of a new church, which was propagated by the abilities of his disciple Eunomius.[68] Armed with texts of scripture, and with captious* syllogisms from the logic of Aristotle, the subtle Aetius had acquired the fame of an invincible disputant, whom it was impossible either to silence or to convince. Such talents engaged the friendship of the Arian bishops, till they were forced to renounce and even to persecute a dangerous ally, who by the accuracy of his reasoning had prejudiced their cause in the popular opinion and offended the piety of their most devoted followers. 2. The omnipotence of the Creator suggested a specious and respectful solution of the *likeness* of the Father and the Son; and faith might humbly receive what reason could not presume to deny, that the Supreme God might communicate his infinite perfections, and create a being similar only to himself.[69] These Arians were powerfully supported by the weight and abilities of their leaders, who had succeeded to the management of the Eusebian interest and who occupied the principal thrones of the East. They detested, perhaps with some affectation, the impiety of Aetius: they professed to believe, either without reserve, or according to the scriptures, that the Son was different from all *other* creatures and similar only to the Father. But they denied that he was either of the same or of a similar substance: sometimes boldly justifying their dissent, and sometimes objecting to the use of the word substance, which seems to imply an adequate, or at least a distinct, notion of the nature of the Deity. 3. The sect which asserted the doctrine of a similar substance was the most numerous, at least in the provinces of Asia; and, when the leaders of both parties were assembled in the council of Seleucia,[70] *their* opinion would have prevailed by a majority of one hundred and five to forty-three bishops. The Greek word which was chosen to express this mysterious resemblance bears so close an affinity to the orthodox symbol, that the profane of every age have derided the furious contests which the difference of a single diphthong excited between the Homoousians and the Homoiousians. As it frequently happens that the sounds and characters which approach the nearest to each other accidentally represent the most opposite ideas, the observation would be itself ridiculous, if it were possible to mark any real and sensible distinction between the doctrine of the Semi-Arians, as they were improperly styled, and that of the Catholics themselves. The bishop of Poitiers, who in his Phrygian exile very wisely aimed at a coalition of parties, endeavours to prove that, by a pious and faithful interpretation,[71] the *Homoiousion* may be reduced to a consubstantial sense. Yet he confesses that the word has a dark and suspicious aspect; and, as if darkness were congenial to theological disputes, the Semi-Arians, who advanced to the doors of the church, assailed them with the most unrelenting fury.

The provinces of Egypt and Asia, which cultivated the language and manners of the Greeks, had deeply imbibed the venom of the Arian controversy. The familiar study of the Platonic system, a vain and argumentative disposition, a copious and flexible idiom, supplied the clergy and people of the East with an inexhaustible flow of words and distinctions; and, in the midst of their fierce contentions, they easily forgot the doubt which is recommended by philosophy, and the submission which is enjoined by religion. The inhabitants of the West were of a less inquisitive spirit; their passions were not so forcibly moved by invisible objects; their minds were less frequently exercised by the habits of dispute, and such was the happy ignorance of the Gallican church that Hilary himself, above thirty years after the first general council, was still a stranger to the Nicene creed.[72] The Latins had received the rays of divine knowledge through the dark and doubtful medium of a translation. The poverty and stubbornness of their native tongue was not always capable of affording just equivalents for the Greek terms, for the technical words of the Platonic philosophy,[73] which had been consecrated by the gospel or by the church to express the mysteries of the Christian faith; and a verbal defect might introduce into the Latin theology a long train of error or perplexity.[74] But, as the western provincials had the good fortune of deriving their religion from an orthodox source, they preserved with steadiness the doctrine which they had accepted with docility; and, when the Arian pestilence approached their frontiers, they were supplied with the seasonable preservative of the Homoousion, by the paternal care of the Roman pontiff. Their sentiments and their temper were displayed in the memorable synod of Rimini, which surpassed in numbers the council of Nicaea, since it was composed of above four hundred bishops of Italy, Africa, Spain, Gaul, Britain and Illyricum. From the first debates it appeared that only four score prelates adhered to the party, though *they* affected to anathematise the name and memory of Arius. But this inferiority was compensated by the advantages of skill, of experience, and of discipline; and the minority was conducted by Valens and Ursacius, two bishops of Illyricum, who had spent their lives in the intrigues of courts and councils, and who had been trained under the Eusebian banner in the religious wars of the East. By their arguments and negotiations, they embarrassed, they confounded, they at last deceived, the honest simplicity of the Latin bishops; who suffered the palladium* of the faith to be extorted from their hands by fraud and importunity rather than by open violence. The council of Rimini was not allowed to separate, till the members had imprudently subscribed a captious creed, in which some expressions, susceptible of an heretical sense, were inserted in the room of the Homoousion. It was on this occasion that, according to Jerome, the world was surprised to find itself Arian.[75] But the bishops of the Latin provinces had no sooner reached their respective dioceses than they discovered their mistake and repented of their weakness. The ignominious capitulation was rejected with disdain and abhorrence; and the Homoousian standard, which had been shaken but not overthrown, was more firmly replanted in all the churches of the West.[76]

Such was the rise and progress and such were the natural revolutions of these theological disputes which disturbed the peace of Christianity under the reigns of Constantine and of his sons. But, as those princes presumed to extend their despotism over the faith, as well as over the lives and fortunes, of their subjects; the weight of their suffrage sometimes inclined the ecclesiastical balance; and the prerogatives of the King of Heaven were settled, or changed, or modified, in the cabinet of an earthly monarch.

The unhappy spirit of discord which pervaded the provinces of the East interrupted the triumph of Constantine; but the emperor continued for some time to view, with cool and careless indifference, the object of the dispute. As he was yet ignorant of the difficulty of appeasing the quarrels of theologians, he addressed to the contending parties, to Alexander and to Arius, a moderating epistle;[77] which may be ascribed, with far greater reason, to the untutored sense of a soldier and statesman than to the dictates of any of his episcopal counsellors. He attributes the origin of the whole controversy to a trifling and subtle question, concerning an incomprehensible point of the law, which was foolishly asked by the bishop, and imprudently resolved by the presbyter. He laments that the

Christian people, who had the same God, the same religion, and the same worship, should be divided by such inconsiderable distinctions; and he seriously recommends to the clergy of Alexandria the example of the Greek philosophers; who could maintain their arguments without losing their temper, and assert their freedom without violating their friendship. The indifference and contempt of the sovereign would have been, perhaps, the most effectual method of silencing the dispute, if the popular current had been less rapid and impetuous, and if Constantine himself, in the midst of faction and fanaticism, could have preserved the calm possession of his own mind. But his ecclesiastical ministers soon contrived to seduce the impartiality of the magistrate, and to awaken the zeal of the proselyte. He was provoked by the insults which had been offered to his statues; he was alarmed by the real, as well as the imaginary, magnitude of the spreading mischief; and he extinguished the hope of peace and toleration, from the moment that he assembled three hundred bishops within the walls of the same palace. The presence of the monarch swelled the importance of the debate; his attention multiplied the arguments; and he exposed his person with a patient intrepidity, which animated the valour of the combatants. Notwithstanding the applause which has been bestowed on the eloquence and sagacity of Constantine,[78] a Roman general, whose religion might be still a subject of doubt, and whose mind had not been enlightened either by study or by inspiration, was indifferently qualified to discuss, in the Greek language, a metaphysical question, or an article of faith. But the credit of his favourite Osius, who appears to have presided in the council of Nicaea, might dispose the emperor in favour of the orthodox party; and a well-timed insinuation that the same Eusebius of Nicomedia, who now protected the heretic, had lately assisted the tyrant,*[79] might exasperate him against their adversaries. The Nicene creed was ratified by Constantine; and his firm declaration, that those who resisted the divine judgment of the synod must prepare themselves for an immediate exile, annihilated the murmurs of a feeble opposition; which from seventeen, was almost instantly reduced to two protesting bishops. Eusebius of Caesarea yielded a reluctant and ambiguous consent to the Homoousion;[80] and the wavering conduct of the Nicomedian Eusebius served only to delay, about three months, his disgrace and exile.[81] The impious Arius was banished into one of the remote provinces of Illyricum; his person and disciples were branded by law with the odious name of Porphyrians, his writings were condemned to the flames, and a capital punishment was denounced against those in whose possession they should be found. The emperor had now imbibed the spirit of controversy, and the angry sarcastic style of his edicts was designed to inspire his subjects with the hatred which he had conceived against the enemies of Christ.[82]

But, as if the conduct of the emperor had been guided by passion instead of principle, three years from the council of Nicaea were scarcely elapsed before he discovered some symptoms of mercy, and even of indulgence, towards the proscribed sect, which was secretly protected by his favourite sister. The exiles were recalled; and Eusebius, who gradually resumed his influence over the mind of Constantine, was restored to the episcopal throne from which he had been ignominiously degraded. Arius himself was treated by the whole court with the respect which would have been due to an innocent and oppressed man. His faith was approved by the synod of Jerusalem; and the emperor seemed impatient to repair his injustice, by issuing an absolute command that he should be solemnly admitted to the communion in the cathedral of Constantinople. On the same day which had been fixed for the triumph of Arius, he expired; and the strange and horrid circumstances of his death might excite a suspicion that the orthodox saints had contributed more efficaciously than by their prayers to deliver the church from the most formidable of her enemies.[83] The three principal leaders of the Catholics, Athanasius of Alexandria, Eustathius of Antioch, and Paul of Constantinople, were deposed on various accusations, by the sentence of numerous councils; and were afterwards banished into distant provinces by the first of the Christian emperors, who, in the last moments of his life, received the rites of baptism from the Arian bishop of Nicomedia. The ecclesiastical government of Constantine cannot be justified from the reproach of levity and weakness. But the credulous monarch, unskilled in the stratagems of theological warfare, might be deceived by the modest and specious professions of the heretics, whose sentiments he never perfectly understood; and, while he protected Arius, and persecuted Athanasius, he still considered the council of Nicaea as the bulwark of the Christian faith and the peculiar glory of his own reign.[84]

The sons of Constantine must have been admitted from their childhood into the rank of catechumens, but they imitated, in the delay of their baptism, the example of their father. Like him, they presumed to pronounce their judgment on mysteries into which they had never been regularly initiated,[85] and the fate of the Trinitarian controversy depended, in a great measure, on the sentiments of Constantius; who inherited the provinces of the East, and acquired the possession of the whole empire. The Arian presbyter or bishop,* who had secreted for his use the testament of the deceased emperor, improved the fortunate occasion which had introduced him to the familiarity of a prince whose public counsels were always swayed by his domestic favourites. The eunuchs and slaves diffused the spiritual poison through the palace, and the dangerous infection was communicated, by the female attendants to the guards, and by the empress to her unsuspicious husband.[86] The partiality which Constantius always expressed towards the Eusebian faction was insensibly fortified by the dexterous management of their leaders; and his victory over the tyrant Magnentius† increased his inclination, as well as ability, to employ the arms of power in the cause of Arianism. While the two armies were engaged in the plains of Mursa, and the fate of the two rivals depended on the chance of war, the son of Constantine passed the anxious moments in a church of the martyrs, under the walls of the city. His spiritual comforter, Valens, the Arian bishop of the diocese, employed the most artful precautions to obtain such early intelligence as might secure either his favour or his escape. A secret chain of swift and trusty messengers informed him of the vicissitudes of the battle; and, while the courtiers stood trembling round their affrighted master, Valens assured him that the Gallic legions gave way; and insinuated with some presence of mind that the glorious event had been revealed to him by an angel. The grateful emperor ascribed his success to the merits and intercession of the bishop of Mursa, whose faith had deserved the public and miraculous approbation of Heaven.[87] The Arians, who considered as their own the victory of Constantius, preferred his glory to that of his father.[88] Cyril, bishop of Jerusalem, immediately composed the description of a celestial cross encircled with a splendid rainbow; which during the festival of Pentecost, about the third hour of the day, had appeared over the Mount of Olives, to the edification of the devout pilgrims and the people of the holy city.[89] The size of the meteor was gradually magnified; and the Arian historian has ventured to affirm that it was conspicuous to the two armies in the plains of Pannonia; and that the tyrant, who is purposely represented as an idolater, fled before the auspicious sign of orthodox Christianity.[90]

The sentiments of a judicious stranger, who has impartially considered the progress of civil or ecclesiastical discord, are always entitled to our notice: and a short passage of Ammianus, who served in the armies, and studied the character, of Constantius, is perhaps of more value than many pages of theological invectives. 'The Christian religion, which, in itself,' says that moderate historian, 'is plain and simple, *he* confounded by the dotage of superstition. Instead of reconciling the parties by the weight of his authority, he cherished and propagated, by verbal disputes, the differences which his vain curiosity had excited. The highways were covered with troops of bishops, galloping from every side to the assemblies, which they call synods; and, while they laboured to reduce the whole sect to their own particular opinions, the public establishment of the posts was almost ruined by their hasty and repeated journeys.'[91] Our more intimate knowledge of the ecclesiastical transactions of the reign of Constantius would furnish an ample commentary on this remarkable passage; which justifies the rational apprehensions of Athanasius that the restless activity of the clergy, who wandered round the empire in search of the true faith, would excite the contempt and laughter of the unbelieving world.[92] As soon as the emperor was relieved from the terrors of the civil war, he devoted the leisure of his winter quarters at Arles, Milan, Sirmium, and Constantinople, to the amusement or toils of controversy: the sword of the magistrate, and even of the tyrant, was unsheathed, to enforce the reasons of the theologian; and, as he opposed the orthodox faith of Nicaea, it is readily confessed that his incapacity and ignorance were equal to his presumption.[93] The eunuchs, the women, and the bishops, who governed the vain and feeble mind of the emperor, had inspired him with an insuperable dislike to the Homoousion; but his timid conscience was alarmed by the impiety of Aetius. The guilt of that atheist was aggravated by the suspicious favour of the unfortunate Gallus; and even the deaths of the Imperial ministers who had been massacred at Antioch were imputed to the suggestions of that dangerous sophist. The mind of Constantius, which could neither be moderated by reason nor fixed by faith, was blindly impelled to either side of the dark and empty abyss by his horror of the opposite extreme: he alternately embraced and condemned the sentiments, he successively banished and recalled the leaders, of the Arian and Semi-Arian factions.[94] During the season of public business or festivity, he employed whole days, and even nights, in selecting the words, and weighing the syllables, which composed his fluctuating creeds. The subject of his meditation still pursued and occupied his slumbers; the incoherent dreams of the emperor were received as celestial visions; and he accepted with complacency the lofty title of bishop of bishops, from those ecclesiastics who forgot the interest of their order for the gratification of their passions. The design of establishing an uniformity of doctrine, which had engaged him to convene so many synods in Gaul, Italy, Illyricum, and Asia, was repeatedly baffled by his own levity, by the divisions of the Arians, and by the resistance of the Catholics; and he resolved, as the last and decisive effort, imperiously to dictate the decrees of a general council. The destructive earthquake of Nicomedia, the difficulty of finding a convenient place, and perhaps some secret motives of policy, produced an alteration in the summons. The bishops of the East were directed to meet at Seleucia, in Isauria; while those of the West held their deliberations at Rimini, on the coast of the Adriatic; and, instead of two or three deputies from each province, the whole episcopal body was ordered to march. The eastern council, after consuming four days in fierce and unavailing debate, separated without any definitive conclusion. The council of the West was protracted till the seventh month. Taurus, the praetorian prefect, was instructed not to dismiss the prelates till they should all be united in the same opinion; and his efforts were supported by a power of banishing fifteen of the most refractory, and a promise of the consulship if he achieved so difficult an adventure. His prayers and threats, the authority of the sovereign, the sophistry of Valens and Ursacius, the distress of cold and hunger, and the tedious melancholy of hopeless exile, at length extorted the reluctant consent of the bishops of Rimini. The deputies of the East and of the West attended the emperor in the palace of Constantinople, and he enjoyed the satisfaction of imposing on the world a profession of faith which established the *likeness*, without expressing the *consubstantiality*, of the Son of

God.[95] But the triumph of Arianism had been preceded by the removal of the orthodox clergy, whom it was impossible either to intimidate or to corrupt; and the reign of Constantius was disgraced by the unjust and ineffectual persecution of the great Athanasius.

We have seldom an opportunity of observing, either in active or speculative life, what effect may be produced, or what obstacles may be surmounted, by the force of a single mind when it is inflexibly applied to the pursuit of a single object. The immortal name of Athanasius*[96] will never be separated from the Catholic doctrine of the Trinity, to whose defence he consecrated every moment and every faculty of his being. Educated in the family of Alexander, he had vigorously opposed the early progress of the Arian heresy: he exercised the important functions of secretary under the aged prelate; and the fathers of the Nicene council beheld, with surprise and respect, the rising virtues of the young deacon. In a time of public danger, the dull claims of age and of rank are sometimes superseded; and within five months after his return from Nicaea, the deacon Athanasius was seated on the archiepiscopal throne of Egypt. He filled that eminent station above forty-six years, and his long administration was spent in a perpetual combat against the powers of Arianism. Five times was Athanasius expelled from his throne; twenty years he passed as an exile or a fugitive; and almost every province of the Roman empire was successively witness to his merit, and his sufferings in the cause of the Homoousion, which he considered as the sole pleasure and business, as the duty, and as the glory, of his life. Amidst the storms of persecution, the archbishop of Alexandria was patient of labour, jealous of fame, careless of safety; and, although his mind was tainted by the contagion of fanaticism, Athanasius displayed a superiority of character and abilities, which would have qualified him, far better than the degenerate sons of Constantine, for the government of a great monarchy. His learning was much less profound and extensive than that of Eusebius of Caesarea, and his rude eloquence could not be compared with the polished oratory of Gregory or Basil; but, whenever the primate of Egypt was called upon to justify his sentiments or his conduct, his unpremeditated style, either of speaking or writing, was clear, forcible, and persuasive. He has always been revered in the orthodox school, as one of the most accurate masters of the Christian theology; and he was supposed to possess two profane sciences, less adapted to the episcopal character, the knowledge of jurisprudence[97] and that of divination.[98] Some fortunate conjectures of future events, which impartial reasoners might ascribe to the experience and judgment of Athanasius, were attributed by his friends to heavenly inspiration, and imputed by his enemies to infernal magic.

But, as Athanasius was continually engaged with the prejudices and passions of every order of men, from the monk to the emperor, the knowledge of human nature was his first and most important science. He preserved a distinct and unbroken view of a scene which was incessantly shifting; and never failed to improve those decisive moments which are irrecoverably past before they are perceived by a common eye. The archbishop of Alexandria was capable of distinguishing how far he might boldly command, and where he must dexterously insinuate; how long he might contend with power, and when he must withdraw from persecution; and, while he directed the thunders of the church against heresy and rebellion, he could assume, in the bosom of his own party, the flexible and indulgent temper of a prudent leader. The election of Athanasius has not escaped the reproach of irregularity and precipitation;[99] but the propriety of his behaviour conciliated the affections both of the clergy and of the people. The Alexandrians were impatient to rise in arms for the defence of an eloquent and liberal pastor. In his distress he always derived support, or at least consolation, from the faithful attachment of his parochial clergy; and the hundred bishops of Egypt adhered, with unshaken zeal, to the cause of Athanasius. In the modest equipage* which pride and policy would affect, he frequently performed the episcopal visitation of his provinces, from the mouth of the Nile to the confines of Ethiopia; familiarly conversing with the meanest of the populace, and humbly saluting the saints and hermits of the desert.[100] Nor was it only in ecclesiastical assemblies, among men whose education and manners were similar to his own, that Athanasius displayed the ascendancy of his genius. He appeared with easy and respectful firmness in the courts of princes; and in the various turns of his prosperous and adverse fortune, he never lost the confidence of his friends or the esteem of his enemies.

In his youth, the primate of Egypt resisted the great Constantine, who had repeatedly signified his will that Arius should be restored to the Catholic communion.[101] The emperor respected, and might forgive, this inflexible resolution; and the faction who considered Athanasius as their most formidable enemy were constrained to dissemble their hatred, and silently to prepare an indirect and distant assault. They scattered rumours and suspicions, represented the archbishop as a proud and oppressive tyrant, and boldly accused him of violating the treaty which had been ratified in the Nicene council with the schismatic followers of Meletius.[102] Athanasius had openly disapproved that ignominious peace, and the emperor was disposed to believe that he had abused his ecclesiastical and civil power, to persecute those odious sectaries; that he had sacrilegiously broken a chalice in one of their churches of Mareotis; that he had whipped or imprisoned six of their bishops; and that Arsenius, a seventh bishop of the same party, had been murdered, or at least mutilated, by the cruel hand of the primate.[103] These charges, which affected his honour and his life, were referred by Constantine to his brother Dalmatius the censor, who resided at Antioch; the synods of Caesarea and Tyre were successively convened; and the bishops of the East were instructed to judge the cause of Athanasius before they proceeded to consecrate the new church of the Resurrection at Jerusalem. The primate might be conscious of his innocence; but he was sensible that the same implacable spirit which had dictated the accusation would direct the proceeding, and pronounce the sentence. He prudently declined the tribunal of his enemies; despised the summons of the synod of Caesarea; and, after a long and artful delay, submitted to the peremptory commands of the emperor, who threatened to punish his criminal disobedience if he refused to appear in the council of Tyre.[104] Before Athanasius, at the head of fifty Egyptian prelates, sailed from Alexandria, he had wisely secured the alliance of the Meletians; and Arsenius himself, his imaginary victim and his secret friend, was privately concealed in his train. The synod of Tyre was conducted by Eusebius of Caesarea with more passion, and with less art, than his learning and experience might promise; his numerous faction repeated the names of homicide and tyrant; and their clamours were encouraged by the seeming patience of Athanasius; who expected the decisive moment to produce Arsenius alive and unhurt in the midst of the assembly. The nature of the other charges did not admit of such clear and satisfactory replies; yet the archbishop was able to prove that, in the village where he was accused of breaking a consecrated chalice, neither church nor altar nor chalice could really exist. The Arians, who had secretly determined the guilt and condemnation of their enemy, attempted, however, to disguise their injustice by the imitation of judicial forms: the synod appointed an episcopal commission of six delegates to collect evidence on the spot; and this measure, which was vigorously opposed by the Egyptian bishops, opened new scenes of violence and perjury.[105] After the return of the deputies from Alexandria, the majority of the council pronounced the final sentence of degradation and exile against the primate of Egypt. The decree, expressed in the fiercest language of malice and revenge, was communicated to the emperor and the Catholic church; and the bishops immediately resumed a mild and devout aspect, such as became their holy pilgrimage to the sepulchre of Christ.[106]

But the injustice of these ecclesiastical judges had not been countenanced by the submission, or even by the presence, of Athanasius. He resolved to make a bold and dangerous experiment, whether the throne was inaccessible to the voice of truth; and, before the final sentence could be pronounced at Tyre, the intrepid primate threw himself into a bark which was ready to hoist sail for the Imperial city. The request of a formal audience might have been opposed or eluded; but Athanasius concealed his arrival, watched the moment of Constantine's return from an adjacent villa, and boldly encountered his angry sovereign as he passed on horseback through the principal street of Constantinople. So strange an apparition excited his surprise and indignation; and the guards were ordered to remove the importunate suitor; but his resentment was subdued by involuntary respect; and the haughty spirit of the emperor was awed by the courage and eloquence of a bishop, who implored his justice and awakened his conscience.[107] Constantine listened to the complaints of Athanasius with impartial and even gracious attention; the members of the synod of Tyre were summoned to justify their proceedings; and the arts of the Eusebian faction would have been confounded, if they had not aggravated the guilt of the primate by the dexterous supposition of an unpardonable offence: a criminal design to intercept and detain the corn-fleet of Alexandria, which supplied the subsistence of the new capital.[108] The emperor was satisfied that the peace of Egypt would be secured by the absence of a popular leader; but he refused to fill the vacancy of the archiepiscopal throne; and the sentence which, after a long hesitation, he pronounced was that of a jealous ostracism, rather than of an ignominious exile. In the remote province of Gaul, but in the hospitable court of Treves, Athanasius passed about twenty-eight months. The death of the emperor changed the face of public affairs; and, amidst the general indulgence of a young reign, the primate was restored to his country by an honourable edict of the younger Constantine, who expressed a deep sense of the innocence and merit of his venerable guest.[109]

The death of that prince exposed Athanasius to a second persecution; and the feeble Constantius, the sovereign of the East, soon became the secret accomplice of the Eusebians. Ninety bishops of that sect or faction assembled at Antioch, under the specious pretence of dedicating the cathedral. They composed an ambiguous creed, which is faintly tinged with the colours of Semi-Arianism, and twenty-five canons, which still regulate the discipline of the orthodox Greeks.[110] It was decided, with some appearance of equity, that a bishop, deprived by a synod, should not resume his episcopal functions, till he had been absolved by the judgment of an equal synod; the law was immediately applied to the case of Athanasius, the council of Antioch pronounced, or rather confirmed, his degradation: a stranger, named Gregory, was seated on his throne; and Philagrius,[111] the prefect of Egypt, was instructed to support the new primate with the civil and military powers of the province. Oppressed by the conspiracy of the Asiatic prelates, Athanasius withdrew from Alexandria, and passed three[112] years as an exile and a suppliant on the holy threshold of the Vatican.[113] By the assiduous study of the Latin language, he soon qualified himself to negotiate with the western clergy; his decent flattery swayed and directed the haughty Julius: the Roman Pontiff was persuaded to consider his appeal as the peculiar interest of the Apostolic see; and his innocence was unanimously declared in a council of fifty bishops of Italy. At the end of three years, the primate was summoned to the court of Milan by the emperor Constans, who, in the indulgence of unlawful pleasures, still professed a lively regard for the orthodox faith. The cause of truth and justice was promoted by the influence of gold,[114] and the ministers of Constans advised their sovereign to require the convocation of an ecclesiastical assembly, which might act as the representatives of the Catholic church. Ninety-four bishops of the West, seventy-six bishops of the East, encountered each other at Sardica on the verge of the two empires, but in the dominions of the protector of Athanasius. Their debates soon degenerated into hostile altercations; the Asiatics, apprehensive for their personal safety, retired to Philippopolis in Thrace; and the rival synods reciprocally hurled their spiritual thunders against their enemies, whom they piously condemned as the enemies of the true God. Their decrees were published and ratified in their respective provinces; and Athanasius, who in the West was revered as a saint, was exposed as a criminal to the abhorrence of the East.[115] The council of Sardica reveals the first symptoms of discord and schism between the Greek and Latin churches, which were separated by the accidental difference of faith and the permanent distinction of language.

During the second exile in the West, Athanasius was frequently admitted to the imperial presence; at Capua, Lodi, Milan, Verona, Padua, Aquileia, and Treves. The bishop of the diocese usually assisted at these interviews; the master of the offices stood before the veil or curtain of the sacred apartment; and the uniform moderation of the primate might be attested by these respectable witnesses, to whose evidence he solemnly appeals.[116] Prudence would undoubtedly suggest the mild and respectful tone that became a subject and a bishop. In these familiar conferences with the sovereign of the West, Athanasius might lament the error of Constantius; but he boldly arraigned the guilt of his eunuchs and his Arian prelates; deplored the distress and danger of the Catholic church; and excited Constans to emulate the zeal and glory of his father. The emperor declared his resolution of employing the troops and treasures of Europe in the orthodox cause; and signified, by a concise and peremptory epistle to his brother Constantius, that, unless he consented to the immediate restoration of Athanasius, he himself, with a fleet and army, would seat the archbishop on the throne of Alexandria.[117] But this religious war, so horrible to nature, was prevented by the timely compliance of Constantius; and the emperor of the East condescended to solicit a reconciliation with a subject whom he had injured. Athanasius waited with decent pride, till he had received three successive epistles full of the strongest assurances of the protection, the favour, and the esteem of his sovereign; who invited him to resume his episcopal seat, and who added the humiliating precaution of engaging his principal ministers to attest the sincerity of his intentions. They were manifested in a still more public manner by the strict orders which were dispatched into Egypt to recall the adherents of Athanasius, to restore their privileges, to proclaim their innocence, and to erase from the public registers the illegal proceedings which had been obtained during the prevalence of the Eusebian faction. After every satisfaction and security had been given, which justice or even delicacy could require, the primate proceeded, by slow journeys, through the provinces of Thrace, Asia, and Syria; and his progress was marked by the abject homage of the oriental bishops, who excited his contempt without deceiving his penetration.[118] At Antioch he saw the emperor Constantius; sustained, with modest firmness, the embraces and protestations of his master, and eluded the proposal of allowing the Arians a single church at Alexandria, by claiming, in the other cities of the empire, a similar toleration for his own party: a reply which might have appeared just and moderate in the mouth of an independent prince. The entrance of the archbishop into his capital was a triumphal procession; absence and persecution had endeared him to the Alexandrians; his authority, which he exercised with rigour, was more firmly established; and his fame was diffused from Ethiopia to Britain, over the whole extent of the Christian world.[119]

But the subject who has reduced his prince to the necessity of dissembling can never expect a sincere and lasting forgiveness; and the tragic fate of Constans soon deprived Athanasius of a powerful and generous protector. The civil war between the assassin and the only surviving brother* of Constans, which afflicted the empire above three years, secured an interval of repose to the Catholic church; and the two contending parties were desirous to conciliate the friendship of a bishop who, by the weight of his personal authority, might determine the fluctuating resolutions of an important province. He gave audience to the ambassadors of the tyrant, with whom he was afterwards accused of holding a secret correspondence;[120] and the emperor Constantius repeatedly assured his dearest father, the most reverend Athanasius, that, notwithstanding the malicious rumours which were circulated by their common enemies, he had inherited the sentiments, as well as the throne, of his deceased brother.[121] Gratitude and humanity would have disposed the primate of Egypt to deplore the untimely fate of Constans, and to abhor the guilt of Magnentius; but, as he clearly understood that the apprehensions of Constantius were his only safeguard, the fervour of his prayers for the success of the righteous cause might perhaps be somewhat abated. The ruin of Athanasius was no longer contrived by the obscure malice of a few bigoted or angry bishops, who abused the authority of a credulous monarch. The monarch himself avowed the resolution, which he had so long suppressed, of avenging his private injuries;[122] and the first winter after his victory, which he passed at Arles, was employed against an enemy more odious to him than the vanquished tyrant of Gaul.

If the emperor had capriciously decreed the death of the most eminent and virtuous citizen of the republic, the cruel order would have been executed without hesitation, by the ministers of open violence or of specious injustice. The caution, the delay, the difficulty with which he proceeded in the condemnation and punishment of a popular bishop, discovered to the world that the privileges of the church had already revived a sense of order and freedom in the Roman government. The sentence which was pronounced in the synod of Tyre, and subscribed by a large majority of the eastern bishops, had never been expressly repealed; and, as Athanasius had been once degraded from his episcopal dignity by the judgment of his brethren, every subsequent act might be considered as irregular, and even criminal. But the memory of the firm and effectual support which the primate of Egypt had derived from the attachment of the western church engaged Constantius to suspend the execution of the sentence, till he had obtained the concurrence of the Latin bishops. Two years were consumed in ecclesiastical negotiations; and the important cause between the emperor and one of his subjects was solemnly debated, first in the synod of Arles, and afterwards in the great council of Milan,[123] which consisted of above three hundred bishops. Their integrity was gradually undermined by the arguments of the Arians, the dexterity of the eunuchs, and the pressing solicitations of a prince, who gratified his revenge at the expense of his dignity, and exposed his own passions, whilst he influenced those of the clergy. Corruption, the most infallible symptom of constitutional liberty, was successfully practised: honours, gifts, and immunities were offered and accepted as the price of an episcopal vote;[124] and the condemnation of the Alexandrian primate was artfully represented as the only measure which could restore the peace and union of the Catholic church. The friends of Athanasius were not, however, wanting to their leader, or to their cause. With a manly spirit, which the sanctity of their character rendered less dangerous, they maintained in public debate, and in private conference with the emperor, the eternal obligation of religion and justice. They declared that neither the hope of his favour nor the fear of his displeasure should prevail on them to join in the condemnation of an absent, an innocent, a respectable brother.[125] They affirmed with apparent reason, that the illegal and obsolete decrees of the council of Tyre had long since been tacitly abolished by the Imperial edicts, the honourable re-establishment of the archbishop of Alexandria, and the silence or recantation of his most clamorous adversaries. They alleged that his innocence had been attested by the unanimous bishops of Egypt, and had been acknowledged, in the councils of Rome and Sardica,[126] by the impartial judgment of the Latin church. They deplored the hard condition of Athanasius, who, after enjoying so many years his seat, his reputation, and the seeming confidence of his sovereign, was again called upon to confute the most groundless and extravagant accusations. Their language was specious; their conduct was honourable; but in this long and obstinate contest, which fixed the eyes of the whole empire on a single bishop, the ecclesiastical factions were prepared to sacrifice truth and justice to the more interesting object of defending, or removing, the intrepid champion of the Nicene faith. The Arians still thought it prudent to disguise, in ambiguous language, their real sentiments and designs; but the orthodox bishops, armed with the favour of the people and the decrees of a general council, insisted on every occasion, and particularly at Milan, that their adversaries should purge themselves from the suspicion of heresy, before they presumed to arraign the conduct of the great Athanasius.[127]

But the voice of reason (if reason was indeed on the side of Athanasius) was silenced by the clamours of a factious or venal majority; and the councils of Arles and Milan were not dissolved, till the archbishop of Alexandria had been solemnly condemned and deposed by the judgment of the Western, as well as of the Eastern, church. The bishops who had opposed, were required to subscribe, the sentence; and to unite in religious communion with the suspected leaders of the adverse party. A formulary of consent was transmitted by the messengers of state to the absent bishops; and all those who refused to submit their private opinion to the public and inspired wisdom of the councils of Arles and Milan were immediately banished by the emperor, who affected to execute the decrees of the Catholic church. Among those prelates who led the honourable band of confessors and exiles, Liberius of Rome, Osius of Cordova, Paulinus of Treves, Dionysius of Milan, Eusebius of Vercellae, Lucifer of Cagliari, and Hilary of Poitiers, may deserve to be particularly distinguished. The eminent station of Liberius, who governed the capital of the empire; the personal merit and long experience of the venerable Osius, who was revered as the favourite of the great Constantine, and the father of the Nicene faith; placed those prelates at the head of the Latin church; and their example, either of submission or resistance, would probably be imitated by the episcopal crowd. But the repeated attempts of the emperor to seduce or to intimidate the bishops of Rome and Cordova were for some time ineffectual. The Spaniard declared himself ready to suffer under Constantius, as he had suffered threescore years before under his grandfather Maximian. The Roman, in the presence of his sovereign, asserted the innocence of Athanasius, and his own freedom. When he was banished to Beroea in Thrace, he sent back a large sum which had been offered for the accommodation of his journey; and insulted the court of Milan by the haughty remark that the emperor and his eunuchs might want that gold to pay their soldiers and their bishops.[128] The resolution of Liberius and Osius was at length subdued by the hardships of exile and confinement. The Roman pontiff purchased his return by some criminal compliances; and afterwards expiated his guilt by a seasonable repentance. Persuasion and violence were employed to extort the reluctant signature of the decrepit bishop of Cordova, whose strength was broken, and whose faculties were perhaps impaired, by the weight of an hundred years; and the insolent triumph of the Arians provoked some of the orthodox party to treat with inhuman severity the character, or rather the memory, of an unfortunate old man, to whose former services Christianity itself was so deeply indebted.[129]

The fall of Liberius and Osius reflected a brighter lustre on the firmness of those bishops who still adhered, with unshaken fidelity, to the cause of Athanasius and religious truth. The ingenious malice of their enemies had deprived them of the benefit of mutual comfort and advice, separated those illustrious exiles into distant provinces, and carefully selected the most inhospitable spots of a great empire.[130] Yet they soon experienced that the deserts of Libya and the most barbarous tracts of Cappadocia were less inhospitable than the residence of those cities in which an Arian bishop could satiate, without restraint, the exquisite rancour of theological hatred.[131] Their consolation was derived from the consciousness of rectitude and independence, from the applause, the visits, the letters, and the liberal alms of their adherents,[132] and from the satisfaction which they soon enjoyed of observing the intestine divisions of the adversaries of the Nicene faith. Such was the nice and capricious taste of the emperor Constantius, and so easily was he offended by the slightest deviation from his imaginary standard of Christian truth, that he persecuted, with equal zeal, those who defended the *consubstantiality*, those who asserted the *similar substance*, and those who denied the *likeness*, of the Son of God. Three bishops, degraded and banished for those adverse opinions, might possibly meet in the same place of exile; and, according to the difference of their temper, might either pity or insult the blind enthusiasm of their antagonists, whose present sufferings would never be compensated by future happiness.

The disgrace and exile of the orthodox bishops of the West were designed as so many preparatory steps to the ruin of Athanasius himself.[133] Six and twenty months had elapsed, during which the Imperial court secretly laboured, by the most insidious arts, to remove him from Alexandria, and to withdraw the allowance which supplied his popular liberality. But, when the primate of Egypt, deserted and proscribed by the Latin church, was left destitute of any foreign support, Constantius dispatched two of his secretaries with a verbal commission to announce and execute the order of his banishment. As the justice of the sentence was publicly avowed by the whole party, the only motive which could restrain Constantius from giving his messengers the sanction of a written mandate must be imputed to his doubt of the event; and to a sense of the danger to which he might expose the second city, and the most fertile province of the empire, if the people should persist in the resolution of defending, by force of arms, the innocence of their spiritual father. Such extreme caution afforded Athanasius a specious pretence respectfully to dispute the truth of an order, which he could not reconcile either with the equity, or with the former declarations, of his gracious master. The civil powers of Egypt found themselves inadequate to the task of persuading or compelling the primate to abdicate his episcopal throne; and they were obliged to conclude a treaty with the popular leaders of Alexandria, by which it was stipulated that all proceedings and hostilities should be suspended till the emperor's pleasure had been more distinctly ascertained. By this seeming moderation, the Catholics were deceived into a false and fatal security; while the legions of the Upper Egypt and of Libya advanced, by secret orders and hasty marches, to besiege, or rather to surprise, a capital habituated to sedition and inflamed by religious zeal.[134] The position of Alexandria, between the sea and the lake Mareotis, facilitated the approach and landing of the troops; who were introduced into the heart of the city, before any effectual measures could be taken either to shut the gates or to occupy the important posts of defence. At the hour of midnight, twenty-three days after the signature of the treaty, Syrianus, duke of Egypt, at the head of five thousand soldiers, armed and prepared for an assault, unexpectedly invested the Church of St Theonas, where the archbishop, with a party of his clergy and people, performed their nocturnal devotions. The doors of the sacred edifice yielded to the impetuosity of the attack, which was accompanied with every horrid circumstance of tumult and bloodshed; but, as the bodies of the slain and the fragments of military weapons remained the next day an unexceptionable evidence in the possession of the Catholics, the enterprise of Syrianus may be considered as a successful irruption, rather than as an absolute conquest. The other churches of the city were profaned by similar outrages; and, during at least four months, Alexandria was exposed to the insults of a licentious army, stimulated by the ecclesiastics of an hostile faction. Many of the faithful were killed; who may deserve the name of martyrs, if their deaths were neither provoked nor revenged; bishops and presbyters were treated with cruel ignominy; consecrated virgins were stripped naked, scourged, and violated; the houses of wealthy citizens were plundered; and, under the mask of religious zeal, lust, avarice, and private resentment were gratified with impunity, and even with applause. The Pagans of Alexandria, who still formed a numerous and discontented party, were easily persuaded to desert a bishop whom they feared and esteemed. The hopes of some peculiar favours, and the apprehension of being involved in the general penalties of rebellion, engaged them to promise their support to the destined successor of Athanasius, the famous George of Cappadocia. The usurper, after receiving the consecration of an Arian synod, was placed on the episcopal throne by the arms of Sebastian, who had been appointed Count of Egypt for the execution of that important design. In the use, as well as in the acquisition, of power, the tyrant George disregarded the laws of religion, of justice, and of humanity; and the same scenes of violence and scandal which had been exhibited in the capital were repeated in more than ninety episcopal cities of Egypt. Encouraged by success, Constantius ventured to approve the conduct of his ministers. By a public and passionate epistle, the emperor congratulates the deliverance of Alexandria from a popular tyrant, who deluded his blind votaries by the magic of his eloquence; expatiates on the virtues and piety of the most reverend George, the elected bishop; and aspires, as the patron and benefactor of the city, to surpass the fame of Alexander himself. But he solemnly declares his unalterable resolution to pursue with fire and sword the seditious adherents of the wicked Athanasius, who, by flying from justice, has confessed his guilt, and escaped the ignominious death which he had so often deserved.[135]

Athanasius had indeed escaped from the most imminent dangers; and the adventures of that extraordinary man deserve and fix our attention. On the memorable night when the church of St Theonas was invested by the troops of Syrianus, the archbishop, seated on his throne, expected, with calm and intrepid dignity, the approach of death. While the public devotion was interrupted by shouts of rage and cries of terror, he animated his trembling congregation to express their religious confidence, by chanting one of the psalms of David, which celebrates the triumph of the God of Israel over the haughty and impious tyrant of Egypt. The doors were at length burst open; a cloud of arrows was discharged among the people; the soldiers, with drawn swords, rushed forwards into the sanctuary; and the dreadful gleam of their armour was reflected by the holy luminaries which burnt round the altar.[136] Athanasius still rejected the pious importunity of the Monks and Presbyters, who were attached to his person; and nobly refused to desert his episcopal station, till he had dismissed in safety the last of the congregation. The darkness and tumult of the night favoured the retreat of the archbishop; and, though he was oppressed by the waves of an agitated multitude, though he was thrown to the ground, and left without sense or motion, he still recovered his undaunted courage, and eluded the eager search of the soldiers, who were instructed by their Arian guides that the head of Athanasius would be the most acceptable present to the emperor. From that moment the primate of Egypt disappeared from the eyes of his enemies, and remained above six years concealed in impenetrable obscurity.[137]

The despotic power of his implacable enemy filled the whole extent of the Roman world; and the exasperated monarch had endeavoured, by a very pressing epistle to the Christian princes of Ethiopia, to exclude Athanasius from the most remote and sequestered regions of the earth. Counts, prefects, tribunes, whole armies, were successively employed to pursue a bishop and a fugitive; the vigilance of the civil and military powers was excited by the Imperial edicts; liberal rewards were promised to the man who should produce Athanasius, either alive or dead; and the most severe penalties were denounced against those who should dare to protect the public enemy.[138] But the deserts of Thebais were now peopled by a race of wild yet submissive fanatics, who preferred the commands of their abbot to the laws of their sovereign. The numerous disciples of Anthony and Pachomius received the fugitive primate as their father, admired the patience and humility with which he conformed to their strictest institutions, collected every word which dropt from his lips as the genuine effusions of inspired wisdom; and persuaded themselves that their prayers, their fasts, and their vigils, were less meritorious than the zeal which they expressed, and the dangers which they braved, in the defence of truth and innocence.[139] The monasteries of Egypt were seated in lonely and desolate places, on the summit of mountains, or in the islands of the Nile; and the sacred horn or trumpet of Tabenne was the well-known signal which assembled several thousand robust and determined Monks, who, for the most part, had been the peasants of the adjacent country. When their dark retreats were invaded by a military force, which it was impossible to resist, they silently stretched out their necks to the executioner, and supported their national character that tortures could never wrest from an Egyptian the confession of a secret which he was resolved not to disclose.[140] The archbishop of Alexandria, for whose safety they eagerly devoted their lives, was lost among a uniform and well-disciplined multitude; and on the nearer approach of danger, he was swiftly removed, by their officious hands, from one place of concealment to another, till he reached the formidable deserts, which the gloomy and credulous temper of superstition had peopled with demons and savage monsters. The retirement of Athanasius, which ended only with the life of Constantius, was spent, for the most part, in the society of the Monks, who faithfully served him as guards, as secretaries, and as messengers; but the importance of maintaining a more intimate connection with the Catholic party tempted him, whenever the diligence of the pursuit was abated, to emerge from the desert, to introduce himself into Alexandria, and to trust his person to the discretion of his friends and adherents. His various adventures might have furnished the subject of a very entertaining romance. He was once secreted in a dry cistern, which he had scarcely left before he was betrayed by the treachery of a female slave;[141] and he was once concealed in a still more extraordinary asylum, the house of a virgin, only twenty years of age, and who was celebrated in the whole city for her exquisite beauty. At the hour of midnight, as she related the story many years afterwards, she was surprised by the appearance of the archbishop in a loose undress, who, advancing with hasty steps, conjured her to afford him the protection which he had been directed by a celestial vision to seek under her hospitable roof. The pious maid accepted and preserved the sacred pledge which was entrusted to her prudence and courage. Without imparting the secret to anyone, she instantly conducted Athanasius into her most secret chamber, and watched over his safety with the tenderness of a friend and the assiduity of a servant. As long as the danger continued, she regularly supplied him with books and provisions, washed his feet, managed his correspondence, and dexterously concealed from the eye of suspicion this familiar and solitary intercourse between a saint whose character required the most unblemished chastity and a female whose charms might excite the most dangerous emotions.[142] During the six years of persecution and exile,

Athanasius repeated his visits to his fair and faithful companion; and the formal declaration that he *saw* the councils of Rimini and Seleucia[143] forces us to believe that he was secretly present at the time and place of their convocation. The advantage of personally negotiating with his friends, and of observing and improving the divisions of his enemies, might justify, in a prudent statesman, so bold and dangerous an enterprise; and Alexandria was connected by trade and navigation with every seaport of the Mediterranean. From the depth of his inaccessible retreat, the intrepid primate waged an incessant and offensive war against the protector of the Arians; and his seasonable writings, which were diligently circulated and eagerly perused, contributed to unite and animate the orthodox party. In his public apologies, which he addressed to the emperor himself, he sometimes affected the praise of moderation; whilst at the same time, in secret and vehement invectives, he exposed Constantius as a weak and wicked prince, the executioner of his family, the tyrant of the republic, and the antichrist of the church. In the height of his prosperity, the victorious monarch, who had chastised the rashness of Gallus, and suppressed the revolt of Sylvanus, who had taken the diadem from the head of Vetranio, and vanquished in the field the legions of Magnentius, received from an invisible hand a wound which he could neither heal nor revenge; and the son of Constantine was the first of the Christian princes who experienced the strength of those principles which, in the cause of religion, could resist the most violent exertions of the civil power.[144]

The persecution of Athanasius and of so many respectable bishops, who suffered for the truth of their opinions, or at least for the integrity of their conscience, was a just subject of indignation and discontent to all Christians, except those who were blindly devoted to the Arian faction. The people regretted the loss of their faithful pastors, whose banishment was usually followed by the intrusion of a stranger[145] into the episcopal chair; and loudly complained that the right of election was violated, and that they were condemned to obey a mercenary usurper, whose person was unknown, and whose principles were suspected. The Catholics might prove to the world that they were not involved in the guilt and heresy of their ecclesiastical governor, by publicly testifying their dissent, or by totally separating themselves from his communion. The first of these methods was invented at Antioch, and practised with such success that it was soon diffused over the Christian world. The doxology or sacred hymn, which celebrates the *glory* of the Trinity, is susceptible of very nice, but material, inflexions; and the substance of an orthodox, or an heretical, creed may be expressed by the difference of a disjunctive, or a copulative, particle. Alternate responses, and a more regular psalmody,[146] were introduced into the public service by Flavianus and Diodorus, two devout and active laymen, who were attached to the Nicene faith. Under their conduct, a swarm of monks issued from the adjacent desert, bands of well-disciplined singers were stationed in the cathedral of Antioch, the Glory to the Father, AND the Son, AND the Holy Ghost,[147] was triumphantly chanted by a full chorus of voices; and the Catholics insulted, by the purity of their doctrine, the Arian prelate who had usurped the throne of the venerable Eustathius. The same zeal which inspired their songs prompted the more scrupulous members of the orthodox party to form separate assemblies, which were governed by the presbyters, till the death of their exiled bishop allowed the election and consecration of a new episcopal pastor.[148] The revolutions of the court multiplied the number of pretenders; and the same city was often disputed, under the reign of Constantius, by two, or three, or even four bishops, who exercised their spiritual jurisdiction over their respective followers, and alternately lost and regained the temporal possessions of the church. The abuse of Christianity introduced into the Roman government new causes of tyranny and sedition; the bands of civil society were torn asunder by the fury of religious factions; and the obscure citizen, who might calmly have surveyed the elevation and fall of successive emperors, imagined and experienced that his own life and fortune were connected with the interests of a popular ecclesiastic. The example of the two capitals, Rome and Constantinople, may serve to represent the state of the empire, and the temper of mankind, under the reign of the sons of Constantine.

I. The Roman pontiff, as long as he maintained his station – and his principles, was guarded by the warm attachment of a great people; and could reject with scorn the prayers, the menaces, and the oblations of an heretical prince. When the eunuchs had secretly pronounced the exile of Liberius, the well-grounded apprehension of a tumult engaged them to use the utmost precautions in the execution of the sentence. The capital was invested on every side, and the prefect was commanded to seize the person of the bishop, either by stratagem or by open force. The order was obeyed; and Liberius, with the greatest difficulty, at the hour of midnight, was swiftly conveyed beyond the reach of the Roman people, before their consternation was turned into rage. As soon as they were informed of his banishment into Thrace, a general assembly was convened, and the clergy of Rome bound themselves, by a public and solemn oath, never to desert their bishop, never to acknowledge the usurper Felix; who, by the influence of the eunuchs, had been irregularly chosen and consecrated within the walls of a profane palace. At the end of two years, their pious obstinacy subsisted entire and unshaken; and, when Constantius visited Rome, he was assailed by the importunate solicitations of a people, who had preserved, as the last remnant of their ancient freedom, the right of treating their sovereign with familiar insolence. The wives of many of the senators and most honourable citizens, after pressing their husbands to intercede in favour of Liberius, were advised to undertake a commission, which, in their hands, would be less dangerous and might prove more successful. The emperor received with politeness these female deputies, whose wealth and dignity were displayed in the magnificence of their dress and ornaments: he admired their inflexible resolution of following their beloved pastor to the most distant regions of the earth, and consented that the two bishops, Liberius and Felix, should govern in peace their respective congregations. But the ideas of toleration were so repugnant to the practice, and even to the sentiments, of those times that, when the answer of Constantius was publicly read in the Circus of Rome, so reasonable a project of accommodation was rejected with contempt and ridicule. The eager vehemence which animated the spectators in the decisive moment of a horse-race was now directed towards a different object; and the Circus resounded with the shout of thousands, who repeatedly exclaimed, 'One God, One Christ, One Bishop'. The zeal of the Roman people in the cause of Liberius was not confined to words alone; and the dangerous and bloody sedition which they excited soon after the departure of Constantius determined that prince to accept the submission of the exiled prelate, and to restore him to the undivided dominion of the capital. After some ineffectual resistance, his rival was expelled from the city by the permission of the emperor, and the power of the opposite faction; the adherents of Felix were inhumanly murdered in the streets, in the public places, in the baths, and even in the churches; and the face of Rome, upon the return of a Christian bishop, renewed the horrid image of the massacres of Marius* and the proscriptions of Sulla.[†149]

II. Notwithstanding the rapid increase of Christians under the reign of the Flavian family, Rome, Alexandria, and the other great cities of the empire, still contained a strong and powerful faction of Infidels, who envied the prosperity, and who ridiculed, even on their theatres, the theological disputes of the church. Constantinople alone enjoyed the advantage of being born and educated in the bosom of the faith. The capital of the East had never been polluted by the worship of idols; and the whole body of the people had deeply imbibed the opinions, the virtues, and the passions, which distinguished the Christians of that age from the rest of mankind. After the death of Alexander, the episcopal throne was disputed by Paul and Macedonius. By their zeal and abilities they both deserved the eminent station to which they aspired; and, if the moral character of Macedonius was less exceptionable, his competitor had the advantage of a prior election and a more orthodox doctrine. His firm attachment to the Nicene creed, which has given Paul a place in the calendar among saints and martyrs, exposed him to the resentment of the Arians. In the space of fourteen years he was five times driven from the throne; to which he was more frequently restored by the violence of the people than by the permission of the prince; and the power of Macedonius could be secured only by the death of his rival. The unfortunate Paul was dragged in chains from the sandy deserts of Mesopotamia to the most desolate places of Mount Taurus,[150] confined in a dark and narrow dungeon, left six days without food, and at length strangled, by the order of Philip, one of the principal ministers of the emperor Constantius.[151] The first blood which stained the new capital was spilt in this ecclesiastical contest; and many persons were slain on both sides, in the furious and obstinate seditions of the people. The commission of enforcing a sentence of banishment against Paul had been entrusted to Hermogenes, the master-general of the cavalry; but the execution of it was fatal to himself. The Catholics rose in the defence of their bishop; the palace of Hermogenes was consumed; the first military officer of the empire was dragged by the heels through the streets of Constantinople, and, after he expired, his lifeless corpse was exposed to their wanton insults.[152] The fate of Hermogenes instructed Philip, the Praetorian prefect, to act with more precaution on a similar occasion. In the most gentle and honourable terms, he required the attendance of Paul in the baths of Zeuxippus, which had a private communication with the palace and the sea. A vessel, which lay ready at the garden-stairs, immediately hoisted sail; and, while the people were still ignorant of the meditated sacrilege, their bishop was already embarked on his voyage to Thessalonica. They soon beheld, with surprise and indignation, the gates of the palace thrown open, and the usurper Macedonius seated by the side of the prefect on a lofty chariot, which was surrounded by troops of guards with drawn swords. The military procession advanced towards the cathedral; the Arians and the Catholics eagerly rushed to occupy that important post; and three thousand one hundred and fifty persons lost their lives in the confusion of the tumult. Macedonius, who was supported by a regular force, obtained a decisive victory; but his reign was disturbed by clamour and sedition; and the causes which appeared the least connected with the subject of dispute were sufficient to nourish and to kindle the flame of civil discord. As the chapel in which the body of the great Constantine had been deposited was in a ruinous condition, the bishops transported those venerable remains into the church of St Acacius. This prudent and even pious measure was represented as a wicked profanation by the whole party which adhered to the Homoousian doctrine. The factions immediately flew to arms, the consecrated ground was used as their field of battle; and one of the ecclesiastical historians has observed, as a real fact, not as a figure of rhetoric, that the well before the church overflowed with a stream of blood, which filled the porticoes and the adjacent courts. The writer who should impute these tumults solely to a religious principle would betray a very imperfect knowledge of human nature; yet it must be confessed that the motive which misled the sincerity of zeal, and the pretence which disguised the licentiousness of passion, suppressed the remorse which, in another cause, would have succeeded to the rage of the Christians of Constantinople.[153]

The cruel and arbitrary disposition of Constantius, which did not

always require the provocations of guilt and resistance, was justly exasperated by the tumults of his capital and the criminal behaviour of a faction,
which opposed the authority and religion of their sovereign. The
ordinary punishments of death, exile, and confiscation were inflicted with
partial rigour;* and the Greeks still revere the holy memory of two clerks,
a reader and a sub-deacon, who were accused of the murder of
Hermogenes, and beheaded at the gates of Constantinople. By an edict of
Constantius against the Catholics, which has not been judged worthy of
a place in the Theodosian code, those who refused to communicate† with
the Arian bishops, and particularly with Macedonius, were deprived of
the immunities of ecclesiastics and of the rights of Christians; they were
compelled to relinquish the possession of the churches; and were strictly
prohibited from holding their assemblies within the walls of the city. The
execution of this unjust law, in the provinces of Thrace and Asia Minor,
was committed to the zeal of Macedonius; the civil and military powers
were directed to obey his commands; and the cruelties exercised by this
Semi-Arian tyrant in the support of the *Homoiousion*, exceeded the
commission, and disgraced the reign, of Constantius. The sacraments of
the church were administered to the reluctant victims, who denied the
vocation, and abhorred the principles, of Macedonius. The rites of
baptism were conferred on women and children, who, for that purpose,
had been torn from the arms of their friends and parents; the mouths of
the communicants were held open, by a wooden engine, while the
consecrated bread was forced down their throat; the breasts of tender
virgins were either burnt with red-hot eggshells or inhumanly com-
pressed between sharp and heavy boards.[154] The Novatians of
Constantinople and the adjacent country, by their firm attachment to the
Homoousian standard, deserved to be confounded with the Catholics
themselves. Macedonius was informed that a large district of Paphlagonia
was almost entirely inhabited by those sectaries. He resolved either to
convert or to extirpate them; and, as he distrusted, on this occasion, the
efficacy of an ecclesiastical mission, he commanded a body of four
thousand legionaries to march against the rebels, and to reduce the
territory of Mantinium[155] under his spiritual dominion. The Novatian
peasants, animated by despair and religious fury, boldly encountered the
invaders of their country; and, though many of the Paphlagonians were
slain, the Roman legions were vanquished by an irregular multitude,
armed only with scythes and axes; and, except a few who escaped by an
ignominious flight, four thousand soldiers were left dead on the field of
battle. The successor of Constantius has expressed, in a concise but lively
manner, some of the theological calamities which afflicted the empire,
and more especially the East, in the reign of a prince who was the slave of
his own passions and of those of his eunuchs. 'Many were imprisoned,
and persecuted, and driven into exile. Whole troops of those who were
styled heretics were massacred, particularly at Cyzicus, and at Samosata.

In Paphlagonia, Bithynia, Galatia, and in many other provinces, towns and villages were laid waste and utterly destroyed.'[156]

While the flames of the Arian controversy consumed the vitals of the empire, the African provinces were infested by their peculiar enemies the savage fanatics, who, under the name of *Circumcellions*, formed the strength and scandal of the Donatist party.[157] The severe execution of the laws of Constantine had excited a spirit of discontent and resistance; the strenuous efforts of his son Constans to restore the unity of the church exasperated the sentiments of mutual hatred which had first occasioned the separation; and the methods of force and corruption employed by the two imperial commissioners, Paul and Macarius, furnished the schismatics with a specious contrast between the maxims of the apostles and the conduct of their pretended successors.[158] The peasants who inhabited the villages of Numidia and Mauritania were a ferocious race, who had been imperfectly reduced under the authority of the Roman laws; who were imperfectly converted to the Christian faith; but who were actuated by a blind and furious enthusiasm in the cause of their Donatist teachers. They indignantly supported the exile of their bishops, the demolition of their churches, and the interruption of their secret assemblies. The violence of the officers of justice, who were usually sustained by a military guard, was sometimes repelled with equal violence; and the blood of some popular ecclesiastics, which had been shed in the quarrel, inflamed their rude followers with an eager desire of revenging the death of these holy martyrs. By their own cruelty and rashness, the ministers of persecution sometimes provoked their fate; and the guilt of an accidental tumult precipitated the criminals into despair and rebellion. Driven from their native villages, the Donatist peasants assembled in formidable gangs on the edge of the Gaetulian desert; and readily exchanged the habits of labour for a life of idleness and rapine, which was consecrated by the name of religion and faintly condemned by the doctors of the sect. The leaders of the Circumcellions assumed the title of captains of the saints; their principal weapon, as they were indifferently provided with swords and spears, was a huge and weighty club, which they termed an *Israelite*; and the well-known sound of 'Praise be to God,' which they used as their cry of war, diffused consternation over the unarmed provinces of Africa. At first their depredations were coloured by the plea of necessity; but they soon exceeded the measure of subsistence, indulged without control their intemperance and avarice, burnt the villages which they had pillaged, and reigned the licentious tyrants of the open country. The occupations of husbandry, and the administration of justice, were interrupted; and, as the Circumcellions pretended to restore the primitive equality of mankind and to reform the abuses of civil society, they opened a secure asylum for the slaves and debtors, who flocked in crowds to their holy standard. When they were not resisted, they usually contented themselves with plunder, but the slightest opposition provoked them to acts of violence and murder; and some Catholic priests, who had imprudently signalised their zeal, were tortured by the fanatics with the most refined and wanton barbarity. The spirit of the Circumcellions was not always exerted against their defenceless enemies; they engaged, and sometimes defeated, the troops of the province; and in the bloody action of Bagai, they attacked in the open field, but with unsuccessful valour, an advanced guard of the Imperial cavalry. The Donatists who were taken in arms received, and they soon deserved, the same treatment which might have been shown to the wild beasts of the desert. The captives died, without a murmur, either by the sword, the axe, or the fire; and the measures of retaliation were multiplied in a rapid proportion, which aggravated the horrors of rebellion, and excluded the hope of mutual forgiveness. In the beginning of the present century, the example of the Circumcellions has been renewed in the persecution, the boldness, the crimes, and the enthusiasm of the Camisards;* and, if the fanatics of Languedoc surpassed those of Numidia by their military achievements, the Africans maintained their fierce independence with more resolution and perseverance.[159]

Such disorders are the natural effects of religious tyranny; but the rage of the Donatists was inflamed by a frenzy of a very extraordinary kind; and which, if it really prevailed among them in so extravagant a degree, cannot surely be paralleled in any country or in any age. Many of these fanatics were possessed with the horror of life, and the desire of martyrdom; and they deemed it of little moment by what means, or by what hands, they perished, if their conduct was sanctified by the intention of devoting themselves to the glory of the true faith and the hope of eternal happiness.[160] Sometimes they rudely disturbed the festivals and profaned the temples of paganism, with the design of exciting the most zealous of the idolaters to revenge the insulted honour of their gods. They sometimes forced their way into the courts of justice, and compelled the affrighted judge to give orders for their immediate execution. They frequently stopped travellers on the public highways, and obliged them to inflict the stroke of martyrdom, by the promise of a reward, if they consented, and by the threat of instant death, if they refused to grant so very singular a favour. When they were disappointed of every other resource, they announced the day on which, in the presence of their friends and brethren, they should cast themselves headlong from some lofty rock; and many precipices were shown, which had acquired fame by the number of religious suicides. In the actions of these desperate enthusiasts, who were admired by one party as the martyrs of God, and abhorred by the other as the victims of Satan, an impartial philosopher may discover the influence and the last abuse of that inflexible spirit, which was originally derived from the character and principles of the Jewish nation.

The simple narrative of the intestine divisions, which distracted the peace, and dishonoured the triumph, of the church, will confirm the remark of a pagan historian, and justify the complaint of a venerable bishop. The experience of Ammianus had convinced him that the enmity of the Christians towards each other surpassed the fury of savage beasts against man;[161] and Gregory Nazianzen most pathetically laments that the kingdom of heaven was converted, by discord, into the image of chaos, of a nocturnal tempest, and of hell itself.[162] The fierce and partial writers of the times, ascribing *all* virtue to themselves, and imputing *all* guilt to their adversaries, have painted the battle of the angels and daemons. Our calmer reason will reject such pure and perfect monsters of vice or sanctity, and will impute an equal, or at least an indiscriminate, measure of good and evil to the hostile sectaries, who assumed and bestowed the appellations of orthodox and heretics. They had been educated in the same religion, and the same civil society. Their hopes and fears in the present, or in a future, life were balanced in the same proportion. On either side, the error might be innocent, the faith sincere, the practice meritorious or corrupt. Their passions were excited by similar objects; and they might alternately abuse the favour of the court, or of the people. The metaphysical opinions of the Athanasians and the Arians could not influence their moral character; and they were alike actuated by the intolerant spirit which has been extracted from the pure and simple maxims of the gospel.

A modern writer,* who, with a just confidence, has prefixed to his own history the honourable epithets of political and philosophical,[163] accuses the timid prudence of Montesquieu for neglecting to enumerate, among the causes of the decline of the empire, a law of Constantine, by which the exercise of the pagan worship was absolutely suppressed, and a considerable part of his subjects was left destitute of priests, of temples, and of any public religion. The zeal of the philosophic historian for the rights of mankind has induced him to acquiesce in the ambiguous testimony of those ecclesiastics, who have too lightly ascribed to their favourite hero the *merit* of a general persecution.[164] Instead of alleging this imaginary law, which would have blazed in the front of the Imperial codes, we may safely appeal to the original epistle which Constantine addressed to the followers of the ancient religion; at a time when he no longer disguised his conversion nor dreaded the rivals of his throne. He invites and exhorts, in the most pressing terms, the subjects of the Roman empire to imitate the example of their master; but he declares that those who still refuse to open their eyes to the celestial light may freely enjoy their temples and their fancied gods. A report that the ceremonies of paganism were suppressed is formally contradicted by the emperor himself, who wisely assigns, as the principle of his moderation, the invincible force of habit, of prejudice, and of superstition.[165] Without violating the sanctity of his promise, without alarming the fears of the pagans, the artful monarch advanced, by slow and cautious steps, to undermine the irregular and decayed fabric of polytheism. The partial acts of severity which he occasionally exercised, though they were secretly prompted by a Christian zeal, were coloured by the fairest pretences of justice and the public good; and, while Constantine designed to ruin the foundations, he seemed to reform the abuses, of the ancient religion. After the example of the wisest of his predecessors, he condemned, under the most rigorous penalties, the occult and impious arts of divination; which excited the vain hopes, and sometimes the criminal attempts, of those who were discontented with their present condition. An ignominious silence was imposed on the oracles, which had been publicly convicted of fraud and falsehood; the effeminate priests of the Nile were abolished; and Constantine discharged the duties of a Roman censor, when he gave orders for the demolition of several temples of Phoenicia, in which every mode of prostitution was devoutly practised in the face of day, and to the honour of Venus.[166] The Imperial city of Constantinople was, in some measure, raised at the expense, and was adorned with the spoils, of the opulent temples of Greece and Asia; the sacred property was confiscated; the statues of gods and heroes were transported, with rude familiarity, among a people who considered them as objects, not of adoration, but of curiosity: the gold and silver were restored to circulation; and the magistrates, the bishops, and the eunuchs, improved the fortunate occasion of gratifying at once their zeal, their avarice, and their resentment. But these depredations were confined to a small part of the Roman world; and the provinces had been long since accustomed to endure the same sacrilegious rapine, from the tyranny of princes and proconsuls, who could not be suspected of any design to subvert the established religion.[167]

The sons of Constantine trod in the footsteps of their father, with more zeal and with less discretion. The pretences of rapine and oppression were insensibly multiplied;[168] every indulgence was shown to the illegal behaviour of the Christians; every doubt was explained to the disadvantage of paganism; and the demolition of the temples was celebrated as one of the auspicious events of the reign of Constans and Constantius.[169] The name of Constantius is prefixed to a concise law, which might have superseded the necessity of any future prohibitions. 'It is our pleasure that in all places, and in all cities, the temples be immediately shut, and carefully guarded, that none may have the power of offending. It is likewise our pleasure that all our subjects should abstain from sacrifices. If anyone should be guilty of such an act, let him feel the sword of vengeance, and, after his execution, let his property be confiscated to the public use. We denounce the same penalties against the governors of the provinces, if they neglect to punish the criminals.'[170] But there is the strongest reason to believe that this formidable edict was either composed without being published, or was published without being executed. The evidence of facts, and the monuments which are still extant of brass and marble, continue to prove the public exercise of the pagan worship during the whole reign of the sons of Constantine. In the east, as well as in the west, in cities, as well as in the country, a great number of temples were respected, or at least were spared; and the devout multitude still enjoyed the luxury of sacrifices, of festivals, and of processions, by the permission, or by the connivance, of the civil government. About four years after the supposed date of his bloody edict, Constantius visited the temples of Rome; and the decency of his behaviour is recommended by a pagan orator as an example worthy of the imitation of succeeding princes. 'That emperor,' says Symmachus, 'suffered the privileges of the vestal virgins to remain inviolate; he bestowed the sacerdotal dignities on the nobles of Rome, granted the customary allowance to defray the expenses of the public rites and sacrifices; and, though he had embraced a different religion, he never attempted to deprive the empire of the sacred worship of antiquity.'[171] The senate still presumed to consecrate, by solemn decrees, the *divine* memory of their sovereigns; and Constantine himself was associated, after his death, to those gods whom he had renounced and insulted during his life. The title, the ensigns, the prerogatives of SOVEREIGN PONTIFF, which had been instituted by Numa, and assumed by Augustus, were accepted, without hesitation, by seven Christian emperors; who were invested with a more absolute authority over the religion which they had deserted than over that which they professed.[172]

The divisions of Christianity suspended the ruin of *paganism*;[173] and the holy war against the infidels was less vigorously prosecuted by princes and bishops who were more immediately alarmed by the guilt and danger of domestic rebellion. The extirpation of *idolatry*[174] might have been justified by the established principles of intolerance; but the hostile sects, which alternately reigned in the imperial court, were mutually apprehensive of alienating, and perhaps exasperating, the minds of a powerful, though declining, faction. Every motive of authority and fashion, of interest and reason, now militated on the side of Christianity; but two or three generations elapsed before their victorious influence was universally felt. The religion which had so long and so lately been established in the Roman empire was still revered by a numerous people, less attached indeed to speculative opinion than to ancient custom. The honours of the state and army were indifferently bestowed on all the subjects of Constantine and Constantius; and a considerable portion of knowledge and wealth and valour was still engaged in the service of polytheism. The superstition of the senator and of the peasant, of the poet and the philosopher, was derived from very different causes, but they met with equal devotion in the temples of the gods. Their zeal was insensibly provoked by the insulting triumph of a proscribed sect; and their hopes were revived by the well-grounded confidence that the presumptive heir of the empire, a young and valiant hero, who had delivered Gaul from the arms of the Barbarians, had secretly embraced the religion of his ancestors.

1 Eusebius, *in Vit. Constantin.*, iii, 63, 64, 65, 66.

* *page 407* [These various sects are referred to in Chapters 15 and 16.]

† *page 407* [imperceptibly, gradually]

2 After some examination of the various opinions of Tillemont, Beausobre, Lardner, etc., I am convinced that Manes did not propagate this sect, even in Persia, before the year 270. It is strange that a philosophic and foreign heresy should have penetrated so rapidly into the African provinces; yet I cannot easily reject the edict of Diocletian against the Manichaeans, which may be found in Baronius (*Annal. Eccl.*, ad 287.)

‡ *page 407* [unimportant]

3 *Constantinus enim, cum limatius superstitionum quaereret sectas, Manichaeorum et similium*, etc., ['Constantine sought to investigate more closely the heretical Manichaeans and other sects.'] Ammian., xv, 15. Strategius, who from this commission obtained the surname of *Musonianus* [a follower of the Stoics], was a Christian of the Arian sect. He acted as one of the counts at the council of Sardica. Libanius praises his mildness and prudence. Vales., *ad locum* Ammian.

4 *Cod. Theod.*, xvi, v, 2. As the general law is not inserted in the Theodosian Code, it is probable that in the year 438 the sects which it had condemned were already extinct.

5 Sozomen, i, 22; Socrates, i, 10. These historians have been suspected, but I think without reason, of an attachment to the Novatian doctrine. The emperor said to the bishop, 'Acesius, take a ladder, and get up to Heaven by yourself.' Most of the Christian sects have, by turns, borrowed the ladder of Acesius.

6 The best materials for this part of ecclesiastical history may be found in the edition of Optatus Milevitanus, published (Paris, 1700) by M. Dupin, who has enriched it with critical notes, geographical discussions, original records, and an accurate abridgment of the whole controversy. M. de Tillemont has bestowed on the Donatists the greatest part of a volume (vi, i): and I am indebted to him for an ample collection of all the passages of his favourite St Augustine which relate to those heretics.

7 *Schisma igitur illo tempore confusae mulieris iracundia peperit; ambitus nutrivit, avaritia roboravit.* ['And so the anger of a distracted woman caused a schism, which was fuelled by intrigue and consolidated by greed.'] Optatus, i, 19. The language of Purpurius is that of a furious madman. *Dicitur te necasse filios sororis tuae duos. Purpurius respondit, Putas me terreri a te . . . occidi; et occido eos qui contra me faciunt.* ['It is alleged that you murdered your sister's two sons. Purpurius replied: "You think that you can frighten me . . . I killed them; and I kill those who oppose me."'] Acta Concil. Cirtensis, *ad calc. Optat.* p. 274. When Caecilian was invited to an assembly of bishops, Purpurius said to his brethren, or rather to his accomplices, 'Let him come hither to receive our imposition of hands, and we will break his head by way of penance.' Optat., i, 19.

* *page 409* [those who had handed over holy vessels and sacred writings to the officers of Diocletian]

8 The councils of Arles, of Nicaea, and of Trent, confirmed the wise and moderate practice of the church of Rome. The Donatists, however, had the

advantage of maintaining the sentiment of Cyprian, and of a considerable part of the primitive church. Vincentius Lirinensis (p. 332, *ap*. Tillemont, *Mém. Ecclés*., vi, 138) has explained why the Donatists are eternally burning with the Devil, while St Cyprian reigns in heaven with Jesus Christ.

9 See the sixth book of Optatus Milevitanus, pp. 91–100.

10 Tillemont, *Mém. Ecclésiastiques*, vi, i, 253. He laughs at their partial credulity. He revered Augustine, the great doctor of the system of predestination.

* *page 410* [at the end of the fifth century]

11 *Plato Aegyptum peragravit ut a sacerdotibus Barbaris numeros et* caelestia *acciperet.* ['Plato travelled across Egypt in order to learn mathematics and astronomy from the Barbarian priests.'] Cicero, *de Finibus*, v, 25. The Egyptians might still preserve the traditional creed of the patriarchs. Josephus has persuaded many of the Christian fathers that Plato derived a part of his knowledge from the Jews; but this vain opinion cannot be reconciled with the obscure state and unsocial manners of the Jewish people, whose scriptures were not accessible to Greek curiosity till more than one hundred years after the death of Plato. See Marsham, *Canon. Chron.*, p. 144; Le Clerc, *Epistol. Critic.*, vii, 177–94.

12 The modern guides who lead me to the knowledge of the Platonic system are Cudworth (*Intellectual System*, pp. 568–620), Basnage (*Hist. des Juifs*, iv, 4, 53–86), Le Clerc (*Epist. Crit.*, ii, 194–209), and Brucker (*Hist. Philosoph.*, i, 675–706). As the learning of these writers was equal, and their intention different, an inquisitive observer may derive instruction from their disputes, and certainty from their agreement.

13 Brucker, *Hist. Philosoph.*, i, 1349–1357. The Alexandrian school is celebrated by Strabo (xvii) and Ammianus (xxii, 6).

14 Joseph., *Antiquitat.*, xii, 1, 3; Basnage, *Hist. des Juifs*, vii, 7.

15 For the origin of the Jewish philosophy, see Eusebius, *Praeparat. Evangel.*, viii, 9,10. According to Philo, the Therapeutae studied philosophy; and Brucker has proved (*Hist. Philosoph.*, ii, 787) that they gave the preference to that of Plato.

16 See Calmet, *Dissertations sur la Bible*, ii, 277. The book of the Wisdom of Solomon was received by many of the fathers as the work of that monarch; and although rejected by the Protestants for want of a Hebrew original, it has obtained, with the rest of the Vulgate, the sanction of the council of Trent.

17 The Platonism of Philo, which was famous to a proverb, is proved beyond a doubt by Le Clerc (*Epist. Crit.*, viii, 211–28). Basnage (*Hist. des Juifs*, iv, 5) has clearly ascertained that the theological works of Philo were composed before the death, and most probably before the birth, of Christ. In such a time of darkness, the knowledge of Philo is more astonishing than his errors. Bull, *Defens. Fid. Nicen.*, i, i, 12.

18 *Mens agitat molem, et magno se corpore miscet.* ['An intelligence moves the universe and intermingles with the physical world.' Virgil, *Aeneid*, vi, 727.] Besides this material soul, Cudworth has discovered (p. 562) in Amelius, Porphyry, Plotinus, and, as he thinks, in Plato himself, a superior, spiritual, *hupercosmian* soul of the universe. But this double soul is exploded by Brucker, Basnage, and Le Clerc, as an idle fancy of the latter Platonists.

19 Petav., *Dogmata Theologica.*, ii, viii, 2, 791. Bull, *Defens. Fid. Nicen.*, i, i, 8,13. This notion, till it was abused by the Arians, was freely adopted in the Christian theology. Tertullian (*adv. Praxeam.*, ch. 16) has a remarkable and dangerous passage. After contrasting, with indiscreet wit, the nature of God and the actions

of Jehovah, he concludes: *Scilicet ut haec de filio Dei non credenda fuisse, si non scripta essent; fortasse non credenda de Patre licet scripta.* ['Just as what is here said about the son of God would not have been believable had it not been written down, so perhaps things that should not be believed have been written about the Father.']

* *page 411* [Schools of philosophy at Athens]

20 The Platonists admired the beginning of the Gospel of St John, as containing an exact transcript of their own principles. Augustine, *de Civitat. Dei*, x, 29. Amelius, *apud* Cyril. *advers Julian.*, viii, 283. But in the third and fourth centuries the Platonists of Alexandria might improve their Trinity by the secret study of the Christian theology.

21 See Beausobre, *Hist Critique du Manichéisme*, i, 377. The Gospel according to St John is supposed to have been published about seventy years after the death of Christ.

22 The sentiments of the Ebionites are fairly stated by Mosheim (p. 331) and Le Clerc (*Hist. Ecclés.*, p. 535). The Clementines, published among the apostolical Fathers, are attributed by the critics to one of these sectaries.

23 Staunch polemics, like Bull (*Judicium Eccles. Cathol.*, ch. 2), insist on the orthodoxy of the Nazarenes; which appears less pure and certain in the eyes of Mosheim (p. 330).

24 The humble condition and sufferings of Jesus have always been a stumbling block to the Jews. *Deus . . contrariis coloribus Messiam depinxerat; futurus erat Rex, Iudex, Pastor,* etc. ['God . . . had depicted the Messiah in very different colours; he was to be king, judge, shepherd,' etc.] See Limborch et Orobio, *Amica Collat.*, pp. 8, 19, 53–76, 192–234. But this objection has obliged the believing Christians to lift up their eyes to a spiritual and everlasting kingdom.

25 Justin Martyr., *Dialog. cum Tryphonte*, pp. 143, 144. See Le Clerc, *Hist. Ecclés.*, p. 615. Bull and his editor Grabe (*Judicium Eccles. Cathol.*, ch. 7, and Appendix), attempt to distort either the sentiments or the words of Justin; but their violent correction of the text is rejected even by the Benedictine editors.

26 The Arians reproached the orthodox party with borrowing their Trinity from the Valentinians and Marcionites. See Beausobre, *Hist. du Manichéisme*, iii, 5,7.

27 *Non dignum est ex utero credere Deum, et Deum Christum . . . non dignum est ut tanta maiestas per sordes et squalores mulieris transire credatur.* ['It is not fitting to believe that God, and God as Christ, came from the womb . . . it is not fitting that such majesty should be thought of as emerging through a woman's filth and squalor.'] The Gnostics asserted the impurity of matter, and of marriage; and they were scandalised by the gross interpretations of the fathers, and even of Augustine himself. See Beausobre, ii, 523.

28 *Apostolis adhuc in saeculo superstitibus apud Iudaeam Christi sanguine recente et phantasma corpus Domini asserebatur.* ['It was claimed by the Apostles still living in Judaea at that time that Christ was alive and that the Lord's dead body was a mere vision.'] Cotelerius thinks (*Patres Apostol.*, ii, 24) that those who will not allow the *Docetes* to have arisen in the time of the Apostles may with equal reason deny that the sun shines at noonday. These *Docetes*, who formed the most considerable party among the Gnostics, were so called, because they granted only a *seeming* body to Christ.

29 Some proofs of the respect which the Christians entertained for the person and doctrine of Plato may be found in De la Mothe le Vayer, v, 135, etc., edit. 1757; and Basnage, *Hist. des Juifs*, iv, 29, 79, etc.

30 *Doleo bona fide, Platonem omnium haereticorum condimentarium factum.* ['I sincerely grieve that Plato has become the inspiration of all the heretics.'] Tertullian, *de Anima*, ch. 23. Petavius (*Dogm. Theolog.*, iii, 2) shows that this was a general complaint. Beausobre (i, iii, 9, 10) has deduced the Gnostic errors from Platonic principles; and as, in the school of Alexandria, those principles were blended with the oriental philosophy (Brucker, i, 1356), the sentiment of Beausobre may be reconciled with the opinion of Mosheim (*General History of the Church*, i, 37).

31 If Theophilus, bishop of Antioch (see Dupin, *Bibilothèque Ecclésiastique*, i, 66), was the first who employed the word *Triad, Trinity*, that abstract term, which was already familiar to the schools of philosophy, must have been introduced into the theology of the Christians after the middle of the second century.

* *page 412* [St Athanasius, *c.*AD 296–373, bishop of Alexandria]

32 Athanasius, i. 808. His expressions have an uncommon energy; and, as he was writing to monks, there could not be any occasion for him to *affect* a rational language.

33 In a treatise which professed to explain the opinions of the ancient philosophers concerning the nature of the gods, we might expect to discover the theological Trinity of Plato. But Cicero very honestly confessed that, though he had translated the *Timaeus*, he could not understand that mysterious dialogue. See Hieronym., *praef. ad* xii *in Isaiam*, v, 154.

34 Tertullian, in *Apolog.*, ch. 46. See Bayle, *Dictionnaire, au mot Simonide*. His remarks on the presumption of Tertullian are profound and interesting.

35 Lactantius, iv, 8. Yet the *Probole*, or *Prolatio*, which the most orthodox divines borrowed without scruple from the Valentinians, and illustrated by the comparisons of a fountain and stream, the sun and its rays, etc., either meant nothing, or favoured a material idea of the divine generation. See Beausobre, i, iii, 7, 548.

36 Many of the primitive writers have frankly confessed that the Son owed his being to the *will* of the Father. See Clarke's *Scripture Trinity*, pp. 280–87. On the other hand, Athanasius and his followers seem unwilling to grant what they are afraid to deny. The schoolmen extricate themselves from this difficulty by the distinction of a *preceding* and a *concomitant* will. Petav., *Dogm. Theolog.*, ii, vi, 8, 587–603.

37 See Petav., *Dogm. Theolog.*, ii, ii, 10, 159.

38 *Carmenque Christo quasi Deo dicere secum invicem.* Plin., *Epist.*, x. 97. The sense of *Deus*, Θεός, *Elohim* ['God' in Latin, Greek and Hebrew], in the ancient languages, is critically examined by Le Clerc (*Ars Critica*, pp. 150–56), and the propriety of worshipping a very excellent creature is ably defended by the Socinian Emlyn (*Tracts*, pp. 29–36, 51–145).

39 See Daillé, *de Usu Patrum*, and Le Clerc, *Bibliothèque Universelle*, x, 409. To arraign the faith of the Ante-Nicene fathers was the object, or at least has been the effect, of the stupendous work of Petavius on the Trinity (*Dogm. Theolog.*, tom. i); nor has the deep impression been erased by the learned defence of Bishop Bull.

40 The most ancient creeds were drawn up with the greatest latitude. See Bull (*Judicium Eccles. Cathol.*), who tries to prevent Episcopius from deriving any advantage from this observation.

41 The heresies of Praxeas, Sabellius, etc., are accurately explained by Mosheim (p. 425, 680–714). Praxeas, who came to Rome about the end of the second

century, deceived, for some time, the simplicity of the bishop, and was confuted by the pen of the angry Tertullian.

42 Socrates [a historian and theologian of the fifth century AD] acknowledges that the heresy of Arius proceeded from his strong desire to embrace an opinion the most diametrically opposite to that of Sabellius.

43 The figure and manners of Arius, the character and numbers of his first proselytes, are painted in very lively colours by Epiphanius (i *Haeres.*, lxix, 3, 729); and we cannot but regret that he should soon forget the historian, to assume the task of controversy.

44 See Philostorgius (i, 3), and Godefroy's ample Commentary. Yet the credibility of Philostorgius is lessened, in the eyes of the orthodox, by his Arianism; and in those of rational critics, by his passion, his prejudice, and his ignorance.

45 Sozomen (i, 15) represents Alexander as indifferent, and even ignorant, in the beginning of the controversy; while Socrates (i, 5) ascribes the origin of the dispute to the vain curiosity of his theological speculations. Dr Jortin (*Remarks on Ecclesiastical History*, ii, 178) has censured, with his usual freedom, the conduct of Alexander: πρὸς ὀργὴν ἐξάπτεται . . . ὁμοίως φρονεῖν ἐκέλευσε ['he angrily harassed him . . . he ordered him to follow the same mode of thought'].

46 The flames of Arianism might burn for some time in secret; but there is reason to believe that they burst out with violence as early as the year 319. Tillemont, *Mém. Ecclés.*, vi, 774–80.

47 *Quid credidit? Certe, aut tria nomina audiens tres Deos esse credidit, et idololatra effectus est; aut in tribus vocabulis trinominem credens Deu, in Sabelli haeresim incurrit; aut edoctus ab Arianis unum esse verum Deum, Patrem, filium et spiritum sanctum credidit creaturas. Aut extra haec quid credere potuerit nescio.* ['What did he believe? One or other of the following. *Either,* when he heard the three names, he believed that there are three Gods, and was therefore an idolater; *or,* believing God to have three different names, he was guilty of the heresy of Sabellius; *or,* having learned from the Arians that there is only one true God the Father, he believed that the Son and Holy Spirit were created. What else he could have believed other than these three alternatives, I do not know.'] Hieronym., *adv. Luciferianos.* Jerome reserves for the last the orthodox system, which is more complicated and difficult.

48 As the doctrine of absolute creation from nothing was gradually introduced among the Christians (Beausobre, ii, 165–215), the dignity of the *workman* very naturally rose with that of the *work*.

49 The metaphysics of Dr Clarke (*Scripture Trinity*, pp. 276–80) could digest an eternal generation from an infinite cause.

50 This profane and absurd simile is employed by several of the primitive fathers, particularly by Athenagoras, in his Apology to the emperor Marcus and his son; and it is alleged, without censure, by Bull himself. See *Defens. Fid. Nicen.*, iii, 5, 4.

51 See Cudworth's *Intellectual System*, pp. 559, 579. This dangerous hypothesis was countenanced by the two Gregories, of Nyssa and Nazianzen, by Cyril of Alexandria, John of Damascus, etc. See Cudworth, p. 603. Le Clerc, *Bibliothèque Universelle*, xviii, 97–105.

52 Augustine seems to envy the freedom of the philosophers. *Liberis verbis loquuntur philosophi . . . Nos autem non dicimus duo vel tria principia, duos vel tres Deos.* ['The philosophers speak freely . . . But we for our part do not speak of two or three principles, or two or three Gods.'] *de Civitat. Dei*, x, 23.

53 Boethius, who was deeply versed in the philosophy of Plato and Aristotle, explains the unity of the Trinity by the *indifference* of the three persons. See the judicious remarks of Le Clerc, *Bibliothèque Choisie*, xvi, 225, etc.

54 If the Sabellians were startled at this conclusion, they were driven down another precipice into the confession that the Father was born of a virgin, that he had suffered on the cross; and thus deserved the odious epithet of *Patripassians* [believers that God the Father also suffered crucifixion], with which they were branded by their adversaries. See the invectives of Tertullian against Praxeas, and the temperate reflections of Mosheim (pp. 423, 681); and Beausobre, i, iii, 6, 533.

55 The transactions of the council of Nicaea are related by the ancients, not only in a partial, but in a very imperfect manner. Such a picture as Fra Paolo would have drawn can never be recovered; but such rude sketches as have been traced by the pencil of bigotry, and that of reason, may be seen in Tillemont (*Mém. Ecclés.*, vi, 669–759), and in Le Clerc (*Bibliothèque Universelle*, x, 435–54).

* *page 417* [St Ambrose, *c.*AD 339–397, bishop of Milan]

56 We are indebted to Ambrose (*de Fide*, iii. cap. ult.) for the knowledge of this curious anecdote. *Hoc verbum posuerunt Patres, quod viderunt adversariis esse formidini; ut tanquam evaginato ab ipsis gladio, ipsum nefandae caput haereseos amputarent.*

57 See Bull, *Defens. Fid. Nicen.*, ii, i, pp. 25–36. He thinks it his duty to reconcile two orthodox synods.

† *page 417* [St Gregory Nazianzen, *c.*AD 330–389, archbishop of Constantinople]

58 According to Aristotle, the stars were homoousian to each other. 'That *Homoousius* means of one substance in *kind*, hath been shown by Petavius, Curcellaeus, Cudworth, Le Clerc, etc., and to prove it would be *actum agere*' ['to do what already has been done']. This is the just remark of Dr Jortin (ii, 212), who examines the Arian controversy with learning, candour, and ingenuity.

59 See Petavius (*Dogm. Theolog.*, ii, iv, 16, p. 453, etc.), Cudworth (p. 559), Bull (iv, 285–290, edit. Grab.). The περιχώρησις, or *circumincessio* [the mysterious connection between the different persons of the Trinity] is perhaps the deepest and darkest corner of the whole theological abyss.

60 The third section of Bull's *Defence of the Nicene Faith*, which some of his antagonists have called nonsense, and others heresy, is consecrated to the supremacy of the Father.

61 The ordinary appellation with which Athanasius and his followers chose to compliment the Arians was that of *Ariomanites* [mad followers of Arius].

62 Epiphanius, i, lxxii, 4, 837. See the adventures of Marcellus, in Tillemont (*Mém. Ecclés.*, vii, 880–99). His work, in *one* book, of the unity of God, was answered in the *three* books, which are still extant, of Eusebius. After a long and careful examination, Petavius (ii, i, 14, 78) has reluctantly pronounced the condemnation of Marcellus.

63 Athanasius, in his epistle concerning the synods of Seleucia and Rimini (i, 886–905), has given an ample list of Arian creeds, which has been enlarged and improved by the labours of the indefatigable Tillemont (*Mém. Ecclés.*, vi, 477).

* *page 418* [St Hilary, *c.*AD 315–367, bishop of Poitiers]

64 Erasmus, with admirable sense and freedom, has delineated the just character of Hilary. To revise his text, to compose the annals of his life, and to justify his sentiments and conduct, is the province of the Benedictine editors.

65 *Absque episcopo Eleusio et paucis cum eo, ex maiore parte Asianae decem provinciae, inter quas consisto, vere Deum nesciunt. Atque utinam penitus nescirent! cum procliviore enim venia ignorarent quam obtrectarent.* ['Apart from the bishop of Eleusis and a few of his followers, in the greater part, of the ten provinces of Asia, where I find myself, they have no proper understanding of God. And would that they knew Him not at all! It would be more pardonable if they knew nothing about Him rather than defame Him.'] Hilar., *de Synodis, sive de Fide Orientalium,* 63, 1186, edit. Benedict. In the celebrated parallel between atheism and superstition, the bishop of Poitiers would have been surprised in the philosophic society of Bayle and Plutarch.

66 Hilarius, *ad Constantium,* ii, 4, 5, 1227, 1228. This remarkable passage deserved the attention of Mr Locke, who has transcribed it (iii, 470) into the model of his new commonplace book.

67 In Philostorgius (iii, 15) the character and adventures of Aetius appear singular enough, though they are carefully softened by the hand of a friend. The editor Godefroy (p. 153), who was more attached to his principles than to his author, has collected the odious circumstances which his various adversaries have preserved or invented.

68 According to the judgment of a man who respected both those sectaries, Aetius had been endowed with a stronger understanding, and Eunomius had acquired more art and learning (Philostorgius, viii, 18). The confession and apology of Eunomius (Fabricius, *Biblioth. Græc.,* viii, 258–305) is one of the few heretical pieces which have escaped.

* *page 419* [fallacious]

69 Yet, according to the opinion of Estius and Bull (p. 297), there is one power, that of creation, which God *cannot* communicate to a creature. Estius, who so accurately defined the limits of omnipotence, was a Dutchman by birth, and by trade a scholastic divine. Dupin, *Biblioth. Eccles.,* xvii, 45.

70 Sabinus (*ap.* Socrat., ii, 39) had copied the acts; Athanasius and Hilary have explained the divisions of this Arian synod; the other circumstances which are relative to it are carefully collected by Baronius and Tillemont.

71 *Fideli et pia intelligentia . . . de Synod.,* 77, p. 1193. In his short apologetical notes (first published by the Benedictines from a manuscript of Chartres) he observes that he used this cautious expression, *qui intelligerem et impiam* ['in order that I should also understand an impious interpretation'], p. 1206. See p. 1146. Philostorgius, who saw those objects through a different medium, is inclined to forget the difference of the important diphthong. See in particular viii, 17, and Godefroy, p. 352.

72 *Testor Deum caeli atque terrae me cum neutrum audissem, semper tamen utrumque sensisse . . . Regeneratus pridem et in episcopatu aliquantisper manens fidem Nicenam nunquam nisi exsulaturus audivi.* ['I swear by the God of heaven and earth that, though I had heard of neither, I sensed both intuitively . . . Though long since spiritually reborn and having been some little time in my diocese, I never heard the Nicene creed until just before I went into exile.'] Hilar., *de Synodis,* xci, 1205. The Benedictines are persuaded that he governed the diocese of Poitiers several years before his exile.

73 Seneca (*Epist.,* lviii.) complains that even the τό ὄν [that which is] of the Platonists (the *ens* of the bolder schoolmen) could not be expressed by a Latin noun.

74 The preference which the fourth council of the Lateran at length gave to a *numerical* rather than a *generical* unity (see Petav., ii, iv, 13, p. 424) was favoured by the Latin language: τριάς seems to excite the idea of substance, *trinitas* of qualities.

 * *page 421* [symbol and guarantee]

75 *Ingemuit totus orbis, et Arianum se esse miratus est.* Hieronym., *adv. Lucifer.*, i, 145.

76 The story of the council of Rimini is very elegantly told by Sulpicius Severus (*Hist. Sacra*, ii, pp. 419–30, edit. Lugd. Bat. 1647), and by Jerome in his dialogue against the Luciferians. The design of the latter is to apologise for the conduct of the Latin bishops, who were deceived, and who repented.

77 Eusebius, *in Vit. Constantin.*, ii, 64–72. The principles of toleration and religious indifference, contained in this epistle, have given great offence to Baronius, Tillemont, etc. who suppose that the emperor had some evil counsellor, either Satan or Eusebius, at his elbow. See Jortin's *Remarks*, ii, 183.

78 Eusebius, *in Vit. Constantin.*, iii, 13.

 * *page 422* [Licinius]

79 Theodoret has preserved (i, 20) an epistle from Constantine to the people of Nicomedia, in which the monarch declares himself the public accuser of one of his subjects; he styles Eusebius, ὁ τῆς τυραννικῆς ὠμότητος συμμύστης ['the fellow participant in tyrannical cruelty'], and complains of his hostile behaviour during the civil war.

80 See in Socrates (i, 8), or rather in Theodoret (i, 12), an original letter of Eusebius of Cæsarea, in which he attempts to justify his subscribing the Homoousion. The character of Eusebius has always been a problem, but those who have read the second critical epistle of Le Clerc (A*rs Crit.*, iii, 30–69) must entertain a very unfavourable opinion of the orthodoxy and sincerity of the bishop of Caesarea.

81 Athanasius, i, 727; Philostorgius, i, 10, and Godefroy, *Commentary*, p. 41.

82 Socrates, i, 9. In his circular letters, which were addressed to the several cities, Constantine employed against the heretics the arms of ridicule and *comic* raillery.

83 We derive the original story from Athanasius (i, 670), who expresses some reluctance to stigmatise the memory of the dead. He might exaggerate; but the perpetual commerce of Alexandria and Constantinople would have rendered it dangerous to invent. Those who press the literal narrative of the death of Arius (his bowels suddenly burst out in a privy) must make their option between *poison* and *miracle*.

84 The change in the sentiments, or at least in the conduct, of Constantine, may be traced in Eusebius (*in Vit. Constant.*, iii, 23; iv, 41), Socrates (i, 23–39), Sozomen (ii, 16–34), Theodoret (i, 14–34), and Philostorgius, (ii, 1–17). But the first of these writers was too near the scene of action and the others were too remote from it. It is singular enough that the important task of continuing the history of the church should have been left for two laymen and a heretic.

85 *Quia etiam tum catechumenus sacramentum fidei merito videretur potuisse nescire* ['because even as a new convert under instruction, it seemed quite proper for him to be ignorant of a sacrament of faith']. Sulp. Sever., *Hist. Sacra.*, ii, 410.

 * *page 423* [Eusebius of Nicomedia]

86 Socrates, ii, 2; Sozomen, iii, 18; Athanas., i, 813, 834. He observes that the eunuchs are the natural enemies of the *Son*. Compare Dr Jortin's *Remarks on Ecclesiastical History*, iv, 3, with a certain genealogy in *Candide* (ch. ix), which

ends with one of the first companions of Christopher Columbus [and records the spread of venereal disease].

† *page 423* [the usurper who was defeated in AD 351]

87 Sulpicius Severus, *in Hist. Sacra.*, ii, 405, 406.

88 Cyril (*apud* Baron., AD 353, No. 26) expressly observes that in the reign of Constantine the cross had been found in the bowels of the earth; but that it had appeared, in the reign of Constantius, in the midst of the heavens. This opposition evidently proves that Cyril was ignorant of the stupendous miracle to which the conversion of Constantine is attributed; and this ignorance is the more surprising, since it was no more than twelve years after his death that Cyril was consecrated bishop of Jerusalem by the immediate successor of Eusebius of Cæsarea. See Tillemont, *Mém. Ecclés.*, viii, 715.

89 It is not easy to determine how far the ingenuity of Cyril might be assisted by some natural appearances of a solar halo.

90 Philostorgius, iii, 26. He is followed by the author of the Alexandrian Chronicle, by Cedrenus, and by Nicephorus (see Gothofred., *Dissert.*, p. 188). They could not refuse a miracle, even from the hand of an enemy.

91 So curious a passage well deserves to be transcribed. *Christianam religionem absolutam et simplicem, anili superstitione confundens; in qua scrutanda perplexius quam componenda gravius excitaret discidia plurima; quae progressa fusius aluit concertatione verborum, ut catervis antistitum iumentis publicis ultro citroque discurrentibus, per synodos (quas appellant) dum ritum omnem ad suum trahere conantur* (Valesius reads *conatur*) *rei vehiculariae concideret nervos.* Ammianus, xxi, 16.

92 Athanas., i, 870.

93 Socrates, ii, 35–47; Sozomen, iv, 12–30; Theodoret, ii, 18–32; Philostorg., iv, 4–12; v, 1–4; vi, 1–5.

94 Sozomen, iv, 23; Athanas., i, 831. Tillemont (*Mém. Ecclés.*, vii, 947) has collected several instances of the haughty fanaticism of Constantius from the detached treatises of Lucifer of Cagliari. The very titles of these treatises inspire zeal and terror; *Moriendum pro Dei Filio* ['The necessity of dying for the Son of God'], *De Regibus Apostaticis* ['On the Apostate Rulers'], *De non conveniendo cum Hæretico* ['On the necessity of not coming to agreement with a Heretic'], *De non parcendo in Deum delinquentibus* ['On the necessity of not sparing those who sin against God'].

95 Sulp. Sever., *Hist. Sacra.*, ii, 418–30. The Greek historians were very ignorant of the affairs of the West.

* *page 426* ['Athanasius' literally means immortal.]

96 We may regret that Gregory Nazianzen composed a panegyric instead of a life of Athanasius, but we should enjoy and improve the advantage of drawing our most authentic materiaìs from the rich fund of his own epistles and apologies (i, 670–951). I shall not imitate the example of Socrates (ii, 1), who published the first edition of his history without giving himself the trouble to consult the writings of Athanasius. Yet even Socrates, the more curious Sozomen, and the learned Theodoret, connect the life of Athanasius with the series of ecclesiastical history. The diligence of Tillemont (tom. viii) and of the Benedictine editors has collected every fact, and examined every difficulty.

97 Sulpicius Severus (*Hist. Sacra*, ii, 396) calls him a lawyer, a jurisconsult. This character cannot now be discovered either in the life or writings of Athanasius.

98 *Dicebatur enim fatidicarum sortium fidem, quaeve augurales portenderent alites*

scientissime callens aliquoties praedixisse futura. ['He was said to possess the art of soothsaying, to have been a considerable expert in interpreting omens and sometimes to have predicted the future.'] Ammianus, xv, 7. A prophecy, or rather a joke, is related by Sozomen (iv, 10), which evidently proves (if the crows speak Latin) that Athanasius understood the language of the crows.

99 The irregular ordination of Athanasius was slightly mentioned in the councils which were held against him. See Philostorg., ii, 11, and Godefroy, p. 71; but it can scarcely be supposed that the assembly of the bishops of Egypt would solemnly attest a *public* falsehood. Athanas., i, 726.

* *page 427* [vehicle]

100 See the *History of the Fathers of the Desert*, published by Rosweide, and Tillemont, *Mém. Ecclés.*, tom. vii, in the lives of Anthony, Pachomius, etc. Athanasius himself, who did not disdain to compose the life of his friend Anthony, has carefully observed how often the holy monk deplored and prophesied the mischiefs of the Arian heresy. Athanas., ii, 492, 498, etc.

101 At first Constantine threatened in *speaking*, but requested in *writing*: καὶ ἀγράφως μὲν ἠπείλει, γράφων δὲ, ἠξίου. His letters gradually assumed a menacing tone; but, while he required that the entrance of the church should be open to *all*, he avoided the odious name of Arius. Athanasius, like a skilful politician, has accurately marked these distinctions (i, 788), which allowed him some scope for excuse and delay.

102 The Meletians in Egypt, like the Donatists in Africa, were produced by an episcopal quarrel which arose from the persecution. I have not leisure to pursue the obscure controversy, which seems to have been misrepresented by the partiality of Athanasius, and the ignorance of Epiphanius. See Mosheim's *General History of the Church*, i, 201.

103 The treatment of the six bishops is specified by Sozomen (ii, 25); but Athanasius himself, so copious on the subject of Arsenius and the chalice, leaves this grave accusation without a reply.

104 Athanas., i, 788; Socrates, i, 28; Sozomen, ii, 25. The emperor, in his epistle of Convocation (Euseb., *in Vit. Constant.*, iv, 42), seems to prejudge some members of the clergy, and it was more than probable that the synod would apply those reproaches to Athanasius.

105 See, in particular, the second Apology of Athanasius (i, 763–808) and his *Epistles to the Monks* (p. 808–66). They are justified by original and authentic documents; but they would inspire more confidence if he appeared less innocent, and his enemies less absurd.

106 Eusebius, *in Vit. Constantin.*, iv, 41–47.

107 Athanas., i, 804. In a church dedicated to St Athanasius this situation would afford a better subject for a picture than most of the stories of miracles and martyrdoms.

108 Athanas., i, 729. Eunapius has related (in *Vit. Sophist.*, pp. 36, 37, edit. Commelin) a strange example of the cruelty and credulity of Constantine on a similar occasion. The eloquent Sopater, a Syrian philosopher, enjoyed his friendship, and provoked the resentment of Ablavius, his Prætorian præfect. The corn-fleet was detained for want of a south wind; the people of Constantinople were discontented; and Sopater was beheaded, on a charge that he had *bound* the winds by the power of magic. Suidas adds that

Constantine wished to prove, by this execution, that he had absolutely renounced the superstition of the Gentiles.

109 In his return he saw Constantius twice, at Viminiacum and at Caesarea in Cappadocia (Athanas., i, 676). Tillemont supposes that Constantine introduced him to the meeting of the three royal brothers in Pannonia (*Mémoires Ecclés.*, viii, 69).

110 See Beveridge, *Pandect.*, i, 429–52, and ii, annotation p. 182. Tillemont, *Mém. Ecclés.*, vi, 310–24. St Hilary of Poitiers has mentioned this synod of Antioch with too much favour and respect. He reckons ninety-seven bishops.

111 This magistrae, so odious to Athanasius, is praised by Gregory Nazianzen, i, orat. xxi, 390, 391.

> Saepe premente Deo fert Deus alter opem.
>
> ['Often when one god oppresses, another brings help.']

For the credit of human nature, I am always pleased to discover some good qualities in those men whom party has represented as tyrants and monsters.

112 The chronological difficulties which perplex the residence of Athanasius at Rome are strenuously agitated by Valesius (*Observat. ad Calcem*, tom. ii, *Hist. Eccles.*, i, 1–5) and Tillemont (*Mém. Ecclés.*, viii, 674, etc). I have followed the simple hypothesis of Valesius, who allows only one journey after the intrusion of Gregory.

113 I cannot forbear transcribing a judicious observation of Wetstein (Prolegomen. N. T. p. 19): *Si tamen Historiam Ecclesiasticam velimus consulere patebit iam inde a seculo quarto, cum, ortis controversiis, ecclesiae Graeciae doctores in duas partes scinderentur, ingenio, eloquentia, numero, tantum non aequales, eam partem quae vincere cupiebat Romam confugisse, maiestatemque pontificis comiter coluisse, eoque pacto oppressis per pontificem et episcopos Latinos adversariis praevaluisse, atque orthodoxiam in consiliis stabilivisse. Eam ob causam Athanasius, non sine comitatu, Romam petiit, pluresque annos ibi haesit.* ['If, however, we wish to consider the history of the Church, it will emerge, beginning from the fourth century, when the controversies arose, that the teachers of the Greek church split into two parties. In talent, eloquence and number, these were far from equal; for the party which longed to overcome fled to Rome, and won over the pope in friendly concord; and by virtue of this agreement it succeeded, though the oppression of the opposite party by the pope and the Latin bishops; and established orthodoxy on a firm basis at the Councils. It was for this reason that Athanasius – and he was not the only one – went to Rome and remained there for several years.']

114 Philostor., iii, 12. If any corruption was used to promote the interest of religion, an advocate of Athanasius might justify or excuse this questionable conduct by the example of Cato and Sidney [Cato, Roman statesman, 234–149 BC; Sidney, Elizabethan soldier and poet, AD 1554–86], the former of whom is *said* to have given, and the latter to have received, a bribe, in the cause of liberty.

115 The Canon which allows appeals to the Roman pontiffs has almost raised the council of Sardica to the dignity of a general council; and its acts have been ignorantly or artfully confounded with those of the Nicene synod. See Tillemont, viii, 689, and Geddes's *Tracts*, ii, 419–60.

116 As Athanasius dispersed secret invectives against Constantius (see the *Epistle to the Monks*), at the same time that he assured him of his profound respect, we might distrust the professions of the archbishop, i, 677.

117 Notwithstanding the discreet silence of Athanasius, and the manifest forgery of a letter inserted by Socrates, these menaces are proved by the unquestionable evidence of Lucifer of Cagliari, and even of Constantius himself. See Tillemont, viii, 693.

118 I have always entertained some doubts concerning the retractation of Ursacius and Valens (Athanas., i, 776). Their epistles to Julius, bishop of Rome, and to Athanasius himself, are of so different a cast from each other that they cannot both be genuine. The one speaks the language of criminals who confess their guilt and infamy; the other of enemies who solicit on equal terms an honourable reconciliation.

119 The circumstances of his second return may be collected from Athanasius himself, i, 769 and 822, 843; Socrates, ii, 18; Sozomen, iii, 19; Theodoret, ii, 11, 12; Philostorgius, iii, 12.

  * *page 431*   [Constantius II. Constans had been overthrown by Magnentius, who had assumed the Empire in Gaul.]

120 Athanasius (i, 677, 678) defends his innocence by pathetic complaints, solemn assertions, and specious arguments. He admits that letters had been forged in his name, but he requests that his own secretaries, and those of the tyrant, may be examined, whether those letters had been written by the former or received by the latter.

121 Athanas., i, pp. 825–844.

122 Athanas., i, p. 861; Theodoret, ii, 16. The emperor declared that he was more desirous to subdue Athanasius than he had been to vanquish Magnentius or Sylvanus.

123 The affairs of the council of Milan are so imperfectly and erroneously related by the Greek writers that we must rejoice in the supply of some letters of Eusebius, extracted by Baronius from the archives of the church of Vercellae, and of an old life of Dionysius of Milan, published by Bollandus. See Baronius, AD 355, and Tillemont, vii, 1415.

124 The honours, presents, feasts, which seduced so many bishops, are mentioned with indignation by those who were too pure or too proud to accept them. 'We combat (says Hilary of Poitiers) against Constantius the antichrist; who strokes the belly instead of scourging the back;' *qui non dorsa caedit, sed ventrem palpat.* Hilarius, *contra Constant.*, 5, 1240.

125 Something of this opposition is mentioned by Ammianus (xv, 7), who had a very dark and superficial knowledge of ecclesiastical history. *Liberius . . . perserveranter renitebatur, nec visum hominem, nec auditum damnare nefas ultimum saepe exclamans; aperte scilicet recalcitrans Imperatoris arbitrio. Id enim ille Athanasio semper infestus,* etc.

126 More properly by the orthodox part of the council of Sardica. If the bishops of both parties had fairly voted, the division would have been 94 to 76. M. de Tillemont (see viii, 1147–58) is justly surprised that so small a majority should have proceeded so vigorously against their adversaries, the principal of whom they immediately deposed.

127 Sulp. Severus, in *Hist. Sacra*, ii, 412.

128 The exile of Liberius is mentioned by Ammianus, xv, 7. See Theodoret, ii, 16; Athanas., i, 834–837; Hilar., *Fragment.*, i.

129 The life of Osius is collected by Tillemont (vii, 524–61), who in the most extravagant terms first admires, and then reprobates, the bishop of Cordova.

In the midst of their lamentations on his fall, the prudence of Athanasius may be distinguished from the blind and intemperate zeal of Hilary.

130 The confessors of the West were successively banished to the deserts of Arabia or Thebais, the lonely places of Mount Taurus, the wildest parts of Phrygia, which were in the possession of the impious Montanists, etc. When the heretic Aetius was too favourably entertained at Mopsuestia in Cilicia, the place of his exile was changed, by the advice of Acacius, to Amblada, a district inhabited by savages and infested by war and pestilence. Philostorg., v, 2.

131 See the cruel treatment and strange obstinacy of Eusebius, in his own letters, published by Baronius, AD 356, No. 92–102.

132 *Ceterum exules satis constat, totius orbis studiis celebratos pecuniasque eis in sumptum affatim congestas legationibus quoque eos plebis Catholicae ex omnibus fere provinciis frequentatos.* Sulp. Sever., *Hist. Sacra,* p. 414; Athanas., i, 836, 840.

133 Ample materials for the history of this third persecution of Athanasius may be found in his own works. See particularly his very able Apology to Constantius (i, 673), his first Apology for his flight (p. 701), his prolix Epistle to the Solitaries (p. 808), and the original Protest of the People of Alexandria against the violences committed by Syrianus (p. 866). Sozomen (iv, 9) has thrown into the narrative two or three luminous and important circumstances.

134 Athanasius had lately sent for Anthony and some of his chosen Monks. They descended from their mountain, announced to the Alexandrians the sanctity of Athanasius, and were honourably conducted by the archbishop as far as the gates of the city. Athanas., ii, 491, 492. See likewise Rufinus, iii, 164, in *Vit. Patr.,* p. 524.

135 Athanas., i, 694. The emperor, or his Arian secretaries, while they express their resentment, betray their fears and esteem of Athanasius.

136 These minute circumstances are curious, as they are literally transcribed from the protest which was publicly presented three days afterwards by the Catholics of Alexandria. See Athanas., i, 867.

137 The Jansenists have often compared Athanasius and Arnauld [a leading Jansenist thinker whose order was persecuted by Louis XIV in the seventeenth century], and have expatiated with pleasure on the faith and zeal, the merit and exile, of those celebrated doctors. This concealed parallel is very dexterously managed by the Abbé de la Blêterie, *Vie de Jovien,* i, 130.

138 *Hince iam toto orbe profugus Athanasius, nec ullus ei tutus ad latendum supererat locus. Tribuni, Praefecti, Comites, exercitus quoque, ad pervestigandum eum moventur edictis imperialibus: praemia delatoribus proponuntur, si quis eum vivum, si id minus, caput certe Athanasii detulisset.* Rufin., i, 16.

139 Gregor. Nazianzen, i, xxi, 384, 385. See Tillemont, *Mém. Ecclés.,* vii, 176–410, 820–80.

140 *Et nulla tormentorum vis inveniri adhuc potuit, quae obdurato illius tractus latroni invito elicere potuit, ut nomen proprium dicat.* Ammian., xxii, 16 and Valesius, *ad locum.*

141 Rufin., i, 18; Sozomen, iv, 10. This and the following story will be rendered impossible, if we suppose that Athanasius always inhabited the asylum which he accidentally or occasionally had used.

142 Palladius (*Hist. Lausiac.,* ch. 136, in *Vit. Patr.,* 776), the original author of this anecdote, had conversed with the damsel, who in her old age still remembered with pleasure so pious and honourable a connection. I cannot indulge the

delicacy of Baronius, Valesius, Tillemont, etc. who almost reject a story so unworthy, as they deem it, of the gravity of ecclesiastical history.

143 Athanas., i, 869. I agree with Tillemont (viii, 1197), that his expressions imply a personal, though perhaps secret, visit to the synods.

144 The Epistle of Athanasius to the Monks is filled with reproaches, which the public must feel to be true (i, 834, 856); and, in compliment to his readers, he has introduced the comparisons of Pharaoh, Ahab, Belshazzar, etc. The boldness of Hilary was attended with less danger, if he published his invective in Gaul after the revolt of Julian; but Lucifer sent his libels to Constantius, and almost challenged the reward of martyrdom. See Tillemont, vii, 905.

145 Athanasius (i, 811) complains in general of this practice, which he afterwards exemplifies (p. 861) in the pretended election of Felix. Three eunuchs represented the Roman people, and three prelates, who followed the court, assumed the functions of the bishops of the Suburbicarian provinces.

146 Thomassin (*Discipline de l'Eglise*, i, ii, 72, 73, 966–984) has collected many curious facts concerning the origin and progress of church-singing, both in the East and West.

147 Philostorgius, iii, 13. Godefroy has examined this subject with singular accuracy (p. 147, etc.). There were three heterodox forms: 'To the Father *by* the Son, *and* in the Holy Ghost', 'To the Father *and* the Son *in* the Holy Ghost', and 'To the Father *in* the Son *and* the Holy Ghost'.

148 After the exile of Eustathius, under the reign of Constantine, the rigid party of the orthodox formed a separation, which afterwards degenerated into a schism, and lasted above fourscore years. See Tillemont, *Mém. Ecclés.*, vii, 35–54, 1137–1158; viii, 573–632, 1314–1332. In many churches, the Arians and Homoousians, who had renounced each other's *communion*, continued for some time to join in prayer. Philostorgius, iii, 14.

* *page 440* [Roman general, 155–86 BC]

† *page 440* [rival of Marius, 138–78 BC]

149 See, on this ecclesiastical revolution of Rome, Ammianus, xv, 7; Athanas., i, 834, 861; Sozomen, iv, 15; Theodoret, ii, 17; Sulp. Sever., *Hist. Sacra*, ii, 413; Hieronym., *Chron. Marcellin. et Faustin. Libell.*, pp. 3, 4; Tillemont, *Mém. Ecclés.*, vi, 336.

150 Cucusus was the last stage of his life and sufferings. The situation of that lonely town on the confines of Cappadocia, Cilicia, and the Lesser Armenia, has occasioned some geographical perplexity; but we are directed to the true spot by the course of the Roman road from Caesarea to Anazarbus. See Cellarii, *Geograph.*, ii, 213; Wesseling, *ad Itinerar.*, pp. 179, 703.

151 Athanasius (i, 703, 813, 814) affirms, in the most positive terms, that Paul was murdered; and appeals, not only to common fame, but even to the unsuspicious testimony of Philagrius, one of the Arian persecutors. Yet he acknowledges that the heretics attributed to disease the death of the bishop of Constantinople. Athanasius is servilely copied by Socrates (ii, 26); but Sozomen, who discovers a more liberal temper, presumes (iv, 2) to insinuate a prudent doubt.

152 Ammianus (xiv, 10) refers to his own account of this tragic event. But we no longer possess that part of his history.

153 See Socrates, ii, 6, 7, 12, 13, 15, 16, 26, 27, 38, and Sozomen, iii, 3, 4, 7, 9; iv, 2, 21. The acts of St Paul of Constantinople, of which Photius has made an

abstract (Phot., *Bibliot.*, pp. 1419–30), are an indifferent copy of these historians; but a modern Greek, who could write the life of a saint without adding fables and miracles, is entitled to some commendation.

* *page 442* [in a biased manner, with extra rigour]

† *page 442* [to take communion]

154 Socrates, ii, 27, 38; Sozomen, iv, 21. The principal assistants of Macedonius, in the work of persecution, were the two bishops of Nicomedia and Cyzicus, who were esteemed for their virtues, and especially for their charity. I cannot forbear reminding the reader that the difference between the *Homoousion* and *Homoiousion* is almost invisible to the nicest theological eye.

155 We are ignorant of the precise situation of Mantinium. In speaking of these *four* bands of legionaries, Socrates, Sozomen, and the author of the Acts of St Paul, use the indefinite terms of ἀριθμοί, φάλαγγες, τάγματα [companies, phalanxes, divisions], which Nicephorus very properly translates *thousands*. Vales., *ad* Socrat., ii, 38.

156 Julian., *Epistol.*, lii, 436, edit. Spanheim.

157 See Optatus Milevitanus (particularly iii, 4), with the Donatist history, by M. Dupin, and the original pieces at the end of his edition. The numerous circumstances which Augustine has mentioned of the fury of the Circumcellions against others, and against themselves, have been laboriously collected by Tillemont, *Mém Ecclés.*, vi, 147–65; and he has often, though without design, exposed the injuries which had provoked those fanatics.

158 It is amusing enough to observe the language of opposite parties, when they speak of the same men and things. Gratus, bishop of Carthage, begins the acclamations of an orthodox synod, *Gratias Deo omnipotenti et Christo Jesu . . . qui imperavit religiosissimo Constanti Imperatori, ut votum gereret unitatis, et mitteret ministros sancti operis* famulos Dei *Paulum et Macarium.* ['Thanks be to Almighty God and to Jesus Christ, who commanded the most devout emperor Constans to bring about the desired unity and to send out as ministers of this holy work Paul and Macarius, the *servants of God*.'] *Mon. Vet., ad Calcem Optati*, p. 313. *Ecce subito* (says the Donatist author of the Passion of Marculus), *de Constantis regis tyrannica domo . . . pollutum Macarianae persecutionis murmur increpuit, et* duabus bestiis *ad Africam missis, eodem scilicet Macario et Paulo, execrandum prorsus ac dirum ecclesiae certamen indictum est; ut populus Christianus ad unionem cum traditoribus faciendam, nudatis militum gladiis et draconum praesentibus signis et tubarum vocibus cogeretur.* ['Suddenly from the house of the tyrant Constans, the roaring of the Macarian persecution was heard, and the *two beasts* sent out to Africa, namely that same Macarius and Paul, launched a thoroughly hateful and dreadful campaign against the church; in order to force the Christian community to join in union with the apostates, they employed soldiers with drawn swords, standards with the images of dragons, and clarion calls.'] *Monument.*, p. 304.

* *page 444* [the rebellious protestant communities of the Cevennes, in Languedoc, persecuted by Louis XIV in the early eighteenth century]

159 The *Histoire des Camisards*, in 3 vols. 12mo. Villefranche, 1760, may be recommended as accurate and impartial. It requires some attention to discover the religion of the author.

160 The Donatist suicides alleged in their justification the example of Razias, which is related in the 14th chapter of the second book of the Maccabees.

161 *Nullas infestas hominibus bestias, ut sunt sibi ferales plerique Christianorum expertus.* Ammian., xxii, 5.

162 Gregor. Nazianzen, *Orat.* i, 33. See Tillemont, vi, 501, quarto edit.

* *page 445* [the Abbé Raynal, 1713–96]

163 The *Histoire Politique et Philosophique des Etablissemens des Européens dans les deux Indes*, i, 9.

164 According to Eusebius (*in Vit. Constantin.*, ii, 45) the emperor prohibited, both in cities and in the country, τὰ μυσαρὰ . . . τῆς εἰδωλολατρείας; the abominable acts or parts of idolatry. Socrates (i, 17) and Sozomen (ii, 4, 5) have represented the conduct of Constantine with a just regard to truth and history; which has been neglected by Theodoret (v, 21) and Orosius (vii, 28). *Tum deinde* (says the latter) *primus Constantinus iusto ordine et pio vicem vertit edicto; siquidem statuit citra ullam hominum caedem paganorum templa claudi.* ['Then at last Constantine I brought about a revolution by his just order and pious edict, whereby he commanded the pagan temples to be closed on pain of death.']

165 See Eusebius, *in Vit. Constantin.*, ii, 56, 60. In the sermon to the assembly of saints, which the emperor pronounced when he was mature in years and piety, he declares to the idolaters (c. xi) that they are permitted to offer sacrifices and to exercise every part of their religious worship.

166 See Eusebius, *in Vit. Constantin.*, iii, 54–58, and iv, 23, 25. These acts of authority may be compared with the suppression of the Bacchanals, and the demolition of the temple of Isis, by the magistrates of pagan Rome.

167 Eusebius (*in Vit. Constant.*, iii, 54) and Libanius (*Orat. pro Templis*, pp. 9, 10, edit. Gothofred.) both mention the pious sacrilege of Constantine, which they viewed In very different lights. The latter expressly declares that 'he made use of the sacred money, but made no alteration in the legal worship; the temples indeed were impoverished, but the sacred rites were performed there.' Lardner's *Jewish and Heathen Testimonies*, iv, 140.

168 Ammianus (xxii, 4) speaks of some court eunuchs who were *spoliis templorum pasti* ['fed on the spoils from the temples']. Libanius says (*Orat. pro Templ.*, p. 23), that the emperor often gave away a temple, like a dog, or a horse, or a slave, or a gold cup; but the devout philosopher takes care to observe that these sacrilegious favourites very seldom prospered.

169 See Gothofred., *Cod. Theodos.*, vi, 262; Liban., *Orat. Parental.*, ch. x, in Fabric., *Bibl. Graec.*, vii, 235.

170 *Placuit omnibus locis atque urbibus universis claudi protinus templa, et accessu vetitis omnibus licentiam delinquendi perditis abnegari. Volumus etiam cunctos a sacrificiis abstinere. Quod siquis aliquid forte huiusmodi perpetraverit, gladio sternatur: facultates etiam perempti fisco decernimus vindicari: et similiter adfligi rectores provinciarum si facinora vindicare neglexerint. Cod. Theodos.*, xvi, x, 4. Chronology has discovered some contradiction in the date of this extravagant law: the only one, perhaps, by which the negligence of magistrates is punished by death and confiscation. M. de la Bastie (*Mém. de l'Académie*, xv, 98) conjectures, with a show of reason, that this was no more than the minutes of a law, the heads of an intended bill, which were found *in Scriniis Memoriae* [in the imperial archives], among the papers of Constantius, and afterwards inserted, as a worthy model, in the Theodosian Code.

171 Symmach., *Epistol.* x, 54.

172 The fourth Dissertation of M. de la Bastie, 'sur le Souverain Pontificat des

Empereurs Romains' (*in Mém. de l'Acad.*, xv, 75–144), is a very learned and judicious performance, which explains the state, and proves the toleration, of paganism from Constantine to Gratian. The assertion of Zosimus that Gratian was the first who refused the pontifical robe is confirmed beyond a doubt; and the murmurs of bigotry, on that subject, are almost silenced.

173 As I have freely anticipated the use of *pagans* and paganism, I shall now trace the singular revolutions of those celebrated words. 1. παγή [*pagê*], in the Doric dialect, so familiar to the Italians, signifies a fountain; and the rural neighbourhood which frequented the same fountain derived the common appellation of *pagus* and *pagans* (Festus, *sub voce,* and Servius, *ad* Virgil. *Georgic.*, ii, 382). [Gibbon's derivation of 'pagan' from Greek *pagê* or *pêgê* (a well) is incorrect. The Latin *pagus* means district or village.] 2. By an easy extension of the word, *pagan* and rural became almost synonymous (Plin., *Hist. Natur.*, xxviii, 5); and the meaner rustics acquired that name, which has been corrupted into *peasants* in the modern languages of Europe. 3. The amazing increase of the military order introduced the necessity of a correlative term (Hume's *Essays*, i, 555); and all the *people* who were not enlisted in the service of the prince were branded with the contemptuous epithet of *pagans* (Tacit., *Hist.*, iii, 24, 43, 77; Juvenal, *Satir.*, xvi, Tertullian, *de Pallio*, ch. 4). 4. The Christians were the soldiers of Christ; their adversaries, who refused his *sacrament*, or military oath of baptism, might deserve the metaphorical name of pagans; and this popular reproach was introduced as early as the reign of Valentinian (AD 365) into Imperial laws (*Cod. Theodos.*, xvi, ii, 18) and theological writings. 5. Christianity gradually filled the cities of the empire; the old religion, in the time of Prudentius (*advers. Symmachum*, i, *ad fin.*) and Orosius (in *Praefat. Hist.*), retired and languished in obscure villages; and the word *pagans*, with its new signification, reverted to its primitive origin. 6. Since the worship of Jupiter and his family has expired, the vacant title of pagans has been successively applied to all the idolaters and polytheists of the old and new world. 7. The Latin Christians bestowed it, without scruple, on their mortal enemies the Mahometans; and the purest *unitarians* were branded with the unjust reproach of idolatry and paganism. See Gerard Vossius, *Etymologicon Linguae Latinae*, in his works, i, 420; Godefroy's *Commentary on the Theodosian Code*, vi, 250; and Ducange, *mediae Latinitat. Glossar.*

174 In the pure language of Ionia and Athens, εἴδωλον [eidolon] and λατρεία [latreia] were ancient and familiar words. The former expressed a likeness, an apparition (Homer, *Odyss.*, xi, 601), a representation, an *image*, created either by fancy or art. The latter denoted any sort of *service* or slavery. The Jews of Egypt, who translated the Hebrew scriptures, restrained the use of these words (Exodus xx: 4, 5) to the religious worship of an image. The peculiar idiom of the Hellenists, or Grecian Jews, has been adopted by the sacred and ecclesiastical writers; and the reproach of *idolatry* (εἰδωλολατρεία) has stigmatised that visible and abject mode of superstition which some sects of Christianity should not hastily impute to the polytheists of Greece and Rome.

CHAPTER 22 (Summary)

Julian is declared emperor by the legions of Gaul – his march and success – the death of Constantius – civil administration of Julian

Gibbon returns to political narrative, describing how Constantius, driven by envy, might have undermined the victories of Julian in Gaul by summoning the Gallic army to a campaign in Persia. The army revolted and declared Julian to be emperor. After vain efforts to negotiate a treaty, Julian renounced Constantius and his religion in favour of the pagan divinities. He swiftly travelled down the Danube, and only the death of Constantius in AD 361 prevented civil war. Julian was received in triumph at Constantinople. Gibbon praises Julian for his devotion to duty and to study, calling him 'the philosophic warrior'. He despised the pomp of the imperial palaces and brought the most venal ministers to justice. In Gibbon's view, no emperor since Alexander Severus was so concerned with the welfare of his subjects.

CHAPTER 23

The religion of Julian – universal toleration – he attempts to restore and reform the Pagan worship; to rebuild the temple of Jerusalem – his artful persecution of the Christians – mutual zeal and injustice

The character of Apostate has injured the reputation of Julian; and the enthusiasm which clouded his virtues has exaggerated the real and apparent magnitude of his faults. Our partial ignorance may represent him as a philosophic monarch, who studied to protect, with an equal hand, the religious factions of the empire; and to allay the theological fever which had inflamed the minds of the people from the edicts of Diocletian to the exile of Athanasius. A more accurate view of the character and conduct of Julian will remove this favourable prepossession for a prince who did not escape the general contagion of the times. We enjoy the singular advantage of comparing the pictures which have been delineated by his fondest admirers and his implacable enemies. The actions of Julian are faithfully related by a judicious and candid historian,* the impartial spectator of his life and death. The unanimous evidence of his contemporaries is confirmed by the public and private declarations of the emperor himself; and his various writings express the uniform tenor of his religious sentiments, which policy would have prompted him to dissemble rather than to affect. A devout and sincere attachment for the gods of Athens and Rome constituted the ruling passion of Julian;[1] the powers of an enlightened understanding were betrayed and corrupted by the influence of superstitious prejudice; and the phantoms which existed only in the mind of the emperor had a real and pernicious effect on the government of the empire. The vehement zeal of the Christians, who despised the worship, and overturned the altars, of those fabulous deities, engaged their votary in a state of irreconcilable hostility with a very numerous party of his subjects; and he was sometimes tempted, by the desire of victory or the shame of a repulse, to violate the laws of prudence, and even of justice. The triumph of the party which he deserted and opposed has fixed a stain of infamy on the name of Julian; and the unsuccessful apostate has been overwhelmed with a torrent of pious invectives, of which the signal was given by the sonorous trumpet[2] of Gregory Nazianzen.[3] The interesting nature of the events which were crowded into the short reign of this active emperor deserves a just and circumstantial narrative. His motives, his counsels, and his actions, as far as they are connected with the history of religion, will be the subject of the present chapter.

The cause of his strange and fatal apostasy may be derived from the early period of his life, when he was left an orphan in the hands of the murderers of his family. The names of Christ and of Constantius, the ideas of slavery and of religion, were soon associated in a youthful imagination, which was susceptible of the most lively impressions. The care of his infancy was entrusted to Eusebius, bishop of Nicomedia,[4] who was related to him on the side of his mother; and, till Julian reached the twentieth year of his age, he received from his Christian preceptors the education, not of a hero, but of a saint. The emperor, less jealous of a heavenly than of an earthly crown, contented himself with the imperfect character of a catechumen, while he bestowed the advantages of baptism[5] on the nephews of Constantine.[6] They were even admitted to the inferior offices of the ecclesiastical order; and Julian publicly read the Holy Scriptures in the church of Nicomedia. The study of religion, which they assiduously cultivated, appeared to produce the fairest fruits of faith and devotion.[7] They prayed, they fasted, they distributed alms to the poor, gifts to the clergy, and oblations to the tombs of the martyrs; and the splendid monument of St Mamas, at Caesarea, was erected, or at least was undertaken, by the joint labour of Gallus and Julian.[8] They respectfully conversed with the bishops who were eminent for superior sanctity, and solicited the benediction of the monks and hermits who had introduced into Cappadocia the voluntary hardships of the ascetic life.[9] As the two princes advanced towards the years of manhood, they discovered, in their religious sentiments, the difference of their characters. The dull and obstinate understanding of Gallus embraced, with implicit zeal, the doctrines of Christianity; which never influenced his conduct or moderated his passions. The mild disposition of the younger brother was less repugnant to the precepts of the gospel; and his active curiosity might have been gratified by a theological system which explains the mysterious essence of the Deity and opens the boundless prospect of invisible and future worlds. But the independent spirit of Julian refused to yield the passive and unresisting obedience which was required, in the name of religion, by the haughty ministers of the church. Their speculative opinions were imposed as positive laws, and guarded by the terrors of eternal punishments; but, while they prescribed the rigid formulary of the thoughts, the words, and the actions of the young prince; whilst they silenced his objections and severely checked the freedom of his enquiries, they secretly provoked his impatient genius to disclaim the authority of his ecclesiastical guides. He was educated in the Lesser Asia, amidst the scandals of the Arian controversy.[10] The fierce contests of the eastern bishops, the incessant alterations of their creeds, and the profane motives which appeared to actuate their conduct, insensibly strengthened the prejudice of Julian, that they neither understood nor believed the religion for which they so fiercely contended. Instead of listening to the proofs of Christianity with that favourable attention which adds weight to the most respectable evidence, he heard with suspicion, and disputed with obstinacy and acuteness, the doctrines for which he already entertained an invincible aversion. Whenever the young princes were directed to compose declamations on the subject of the prevailing controversies, Julian always declared himself the advocate of Paganism; under the specious excuse that, in the defence of the weaker cause, his learning and ingenuity might be more advantageously exercised and displayed.

As soon as Gallus was invested with the honours of the purple, Julian was permitted to breathe the air of freedom, of literature, and of Paganism.[11] The crowd of sophists, who were attracted by the taste and liberality of their royal pupil, had formed a strict alliance between the learning and the religion of Greece; and the poems of Homer, instead of being admired as the original productions of human genius, were seriously ascribed to the heavenly inspiration of Apollo and the muses. The deities of Olympus, as they are painted by the immortal bard, imprint themselves on the minds which are the least addicted to superstitious credulity. Our familiar knowledge of their names and characters, their forms and attributes, *seems* to bestow on these airy beings a real and substantial existence; and the pleasing enchantment produces an imperfect and momentary assent of the imagination to those fables which are the most repugnant to our reason and experience. In the age of Julian every circumstance contributed to prolong and fortify the illusion: the magnificent temples of Greece and Asia; the works of those artists who had expressed, in painting or in sculpture, the divine conceptions of the poet; the pomp of festivals and sacrifices; the successful arts of divination;

the popular traditions of oracles and prodigies; and the ancient practice of two thousand years. The weakness of polytheism was, in some measure, excused by the moderation of its claims; and the devotion of the Pagans was not incompatible with the most licentious scepticism.[12] Instead of an indivisible and regular system, which occupies the whole extent of the believing mind, the mythology of the Greeks was composed of a thousand loose and flexible parts, and the servant of the gods was at liberty to define the degree and measure of his religious faith. The creed which Julian adopted for his own use was of the largest dimensions; and, by a strange contradiction, he disdained the salutary yoke of the gospel, whilst he made a voluntary offering of his reason on the altars of Jupiter and Apollo. One of the orations of Julian is consecrated to the honour of Cybele, the mother of the gods, who required from her effeminate priests the bloody sacrifice,* so rashly performed by the madness of the Phrygian boy. The pious emperor condescends to relate, without a blush, and without a smile, the voyage of the goddess from the shores of Pergamus to the mouth of the Tiber, and the stupendous miracle, which convinced the senate and people of Rome that the lump of clay which their ambassadors had transported over the seas was endowed with life, and sentiment, and divine power.[13] For the truth of this prodigy, he appeals to the public monuments of the city; and censures, with some acrimony, the sickly and affected taste of those men who impertinently derided the sacred traditions of their ancestors.[14]

But the devout philosopher, who sincerely embraced and warmly encouraged the superstition of the people, reserved for himself the privilege of a liberal interpretation; and silently withdrew from the foot of the altars into the sanctuary of the temple. The extravagance of the Grecian mythology proclaimed with a clear and audible voice that the pious inquirer, instead of being scandalised or satisfied with the literal sense, should diligently explore the occult wisdom which had been disguised, by the prudence of antiquity, under the mask of folly and of fable.[15] The philosophers of the Platonic school,[16] Plotinus, Porphyry, and the divine Iamblichus, were admired as the most skilful masters of this allegorical science which laboured to soften and harmonise the deformed features of Paganism. Julian himself, who was directed in the mysterious pursuit by Aedesius, the venerable successor of Iamblichus, aspired to the possession of a treasure which he esteemed, if we may credit his solemn asseverations, far above the empire of the world.[17] It was indeed a treasure which derived its value only from opinion; and every artist who flattered himself that he had extracted the precious ore from the surrounding dross claimed an equal right of stamping the name and figure the most agreeable to his peculiar fancy. The fable of Atys and Cybele had been already explained by Porphyry; but his labours served only to animate the pious industry of Julian, who invented and published his own allegory of that ancient and mystic tale. This freedom of interpretation, which might gratify the pride of the Platonists, exposed the vanity of their art. Without a tedious detail, the modern reader could not form a just idea of the strange allusions, the forced etymologies, the solemn trifling, and the impenetrable obscurity of these sages, who professed to reveal the system of the universe. As the traditions of Pagan mythology were variously related, the sacred interpreters were at liberty to select the most convenient circumstances; and, as they translated an arbitrary cypher, they could extract from *any* fable *any* sense which was adapted to their favourite system of religion and philosophy. The lascivious form of a naked Venus was tortured into the discovery of some moral precept or some physical truth: and the castration of Atys explained the revolution of the sun between the tropics or the separation of the human soul from vice and error.[18]

The theological system of Julian appears to have contained the sublime and important principles of natural religion. But, as the faith which is not founded on revelation must remain destitute of any firm assurance, the disciple of Plato imprudently relapsed into the habits of vulgar superstition; and the popular and philosophic notion of the Deity seems to have been confounded in the practice, writings, and even in the mind of Julian.[19] The pious emperor acknowledged and adored the Eternal Cause of the universe, to whom he ascribed all the perfections of an infinite nature, invisible to the eyes, and inaccessible to the understanding, of feeble mortals. The Supreme God had created, or rather, in the Platonic language, had generated, the gradual succession of dependent spirits, of gods, of daemons, of heroes, and of men; and every being which derived its existence immediately from the First Cause received the inherent gift of immortality. That so precious an advantage might not be lavished upon unworthy objects, the Creator had entrusted to the skill and power of the inferior gods, the office of forming the human body, and of arranging the beautiful harmony of the animal, the vegetable, and the mineral kingdoms. To the conduct of these divine ministers he delegated the temporal government of this lower world; but their imperfect administration is not exempt from discord or error. The earth, and its inhabitants, are divided among them, and the characters of Mars or Minerva, of Mercury or Venus, may be distinctly traced in the laws and manners of their peculiar votaries. As long as our immortal souls are confined in a mortal prison, it is our interest, as well as our duty, to solicit the favour, and to deprecate the wrath, of the powers of heaven; whose pride is gratified by the devotion of mankind; and whose grosser parts may be supposed to derive some nourishment from the fumes of sacrifice.[20] The inferior gods might sometimes condescend to animate the statues, and to inhabit the temples, which were dedicated to their honour. They might occasionally visit the earth, but the heavens were the proper throne and symbol of their glory. The invariable order of the sun, moon, and stars, was hastily admitted by Julian as a proof of their *eternal* duration; and their eternity was a sufficient evidence that they were the workmanship, not of an inferior deity, but of the Omnipotent King. In the system of the Platonists, the visible, was a type of the invisible, world. The celestial bodies, as they were informed by a divine spirit, might be considered as the objects the most worthy of religious worship. The *Sun*, whose genial influence pervades and sustains the universe, justly claimed the adoration of mankind, as the bright representative of the *Logos*, the lively, the rational, the beneficent image of the intellectual Father.[21]

In every age, the absence of genuine inspiration is supplied by the strong illusions of enthusiasm and the mimic arts of imposture. If, in the time of Julian, these arts had been practised only by the Pagan priests, for the support of an expiring cause, some indulgence might perhaps be allowed to the interest and habits of the sacerdotal character. But it may appear a subject of surprise and scandal that the philosophers themselves should have contributed to abuse the superstitious credulity of mankind,[22] and that the Grecian mysteries should have been supported by the magic or theurgy* of the modern Platonists. They arrogantly pretended to control the order of nature, to explore the secrets of futurity, to command the service of the inferior daemons, to enjoy the view and conversation of the superior gods, and, by disengaging the soul from her material bands, to reunite that immortal particle with the Infinite and Divine Spirit.

The devout and fearless curiosity of Julian tempted the philosophers with the hopes of an easy conquest; which, from the situation of their young proselyte, might be productive of the most important consequences.[23] Julian imbibed the first rudiments of the Platonic doctrines from the mouth of Aedesius, who had fixed at Pergamus his wandering and persecuted school. But, as the declining strength of that venerable sage was unequal to the ardour, the diligence, the rapid conception of his pupil, two of his most learned disciples, Chrysanthius and Eusebius, supplied, at his own desire, the place of their aged master. These philosophers seem to have prepared and distributed their respective parts; and they artfully contrived, by dark hints and affected disputes, to excite the impatient hopes of the *aspirant*, till they delivered him into the hands of their associate Maximus, the boldest and most skilful master of the theurgic science. By his hands Julian was secretly initiated at Ephesus, in the twentieth year of his age. His residence at Athens confirmed this unnatural alliance of philosophy and superstition. He obtained the privilege of a solemn initiation into the mysteries of Eleusis,[†] which, amidst the general decay of the Grecian worship, still retained some vestiges of their primaeval sanctity; and such was the zeal of Julian that he afterwards invited the Eleusinian pontiff to the court of Gaul, for the sole purpose of consummating, by mystic rites and sacrifices, the great work of his sanctification. As these ceremonies were performed in the depth of caverns, and in the silence of the night, and as the inviolable secret of the mysteries was preserved by the discretion of the initiated, I shall not presume to describe the horrid sounds and fiery apparitions, which were presented to the senses, or the imagination, of the credulous aspirant,[24] till the visions of comfort and knowledge broke upon him in a blaze of celestial light.[25] In the caverns of Ephesus and Eleusis, the mind of Julian was penetrated with sincere, deep, and unalterable enthusiasm; though he might sometimes exhibit the vicissitudes of pious fraud and hypocrisy, which may be observed, or at least suspected, in the characters of the most conscientious fanatics. From that moment he consecrated his life to the service of the gods; and, while the occupations of war, of government, and of study, seemed to claim the whole measure of his time, a stated portion of the hours of the night was invariably reserved for the exercise of private devotion. The temperance which adorned the severe manners of the soldier and the philosopher was connected with some strict and frivolous rules of religious abstinence; and it was in honour of Pan or Mercury, of Hecate or Isis, that Julian, on particular days, denied himself the use of some particular food, which might have been offensive to his tutelar deities. By these voluntary fasts, he prepared his senses and his understanding for the frequent and familiar visits with which he was honoured by the celestial powers. Notwithstanding the modest silence of Julian himself, we may learn from his faithful friend, the orator Libanius, that he lived in a perpetual intercourse with the gods and goddesses; that they descended upon earth, to enjoy the conversation of their favourite hero; that they gently interrupted his slumbers, by touching his hand or his hair; that they warned him of every impending danger, and conducted him, by their infallible wisdom, in every action of his life; and that he had acquired such an intimate knowledge of his heavenly guests, as readily to distinguish the voice of Jupiter from that of Minerva, and the form of Apollo from the figure of Hercules.[26] These sleeping or waking visions, the ordinary effects of abstinence and fanaticism, would almost degrade the emperor to the level of an Egyptian monk. But the useless lives of Antony or Pachomius were consumed in these vain occupations. Julian could break from the dream of superstition to arm himself for battle; and, after vanquishing in the field the enemies of Rome, he calmly retired into his tent, to dictate the wise and salutary laws of an empire, or to indulge his genius in the elegant pursuits of literature and philosophy.

The important secret of the apostasy of Julian was entrusted to the fidelity of the *initiated*, with whom he was united by the sacred ties of friendship and religion.[27] The pleasing rumour was cautiously circulated among the adherents of the ancient worship; and his future greatness became the object of the hopes, the prayers, and the predictions of the pagans, in every province of the empire. From the zeal and virtues of their royal proselyte, they fondly expected the cure of every evil and the restoration of every blessing; and, instead of disapproving of the ardour of their pious wishes, Julian ingenuously confessed that he was ambitious to attain a situation in which he might be useful to his country and to his religion. But this religion was viewed with an hostile eye by the successor of Constantine,* whose capricious passions alternately saved and threatened the life of Julian. The arts of magic and divination were strictly prohibited under a despotic government which condescended to fear them; and, if the pagans were reluctantly indulged in the exercise of their superstition, the rank of Julian would have excepted him from the general toleration. The apostate soon became the presumptive heir of the monarchy, and his death could alone have appeased the just apprehensions of the Christians.[28] But the young prince, who aspired to the glory of a hero rather than of a martyr, consulted his safety by dissembling his religion; and the easy temper of polytheism permitted him to join in the public worship of a sect which he inwardly despised. Libanius has considered the hypocrisy of his friend as a subject, not of censure, but of praise. 'As the statues of the gods,' says that orator, 'which have been defiled with filth, are again placed in a magnificent temple; so the beauty of truth was seated in the mind of Julian, after it had been purified from the errors and follies of his education. His sentiments were changed; but, as it would have been dangerous to have avowed his sentiments, his conduct still continued the same. Very different from the ass in Aesop, who disguised himself with a lion's hide, our lion was obliged to conceal himself under the skin of an ass; and, while he embraced the dictates of reason, to obey the laws of prudence and necessity.'[29] The dissimulation of Julian lasted above ten years, from his secret initiation at Ephesus to the beginning of the civil war; when he declared himself at once the implacable enemy of Christ and of Constantius. This state of constraint might contribute to strengthen his devotion; and, as soon as he had satisfied the obligation of assisting, on solemn festivals, at the assemblies of the Christians, Julian returned, with the impatience of a lover, to burn his free and voluntary incense on the domestic chapels of Jupiter and Mercury. But, as every act of dissimulation must be painful to an ingenuous spirit, the profession of Christianity increased the aversion of Julian for a religion which oppressed the freedom of his mind and compelled him to hold a conduct repugnant to the noblest attributes of human nature, sincerity and courage.

The inclination of Julian might prefer the gods of Homer, and of the Scipios, to the new faith which his uncle had established in the Roman empire; and in which he himself had been sanctified by the sacrament of baptism. But, as a philosopher, it was incumbent on him to justify his dissent from Christianity, which was supported by the number of its converts, by the chain of prophecy, the splendour of miracles, and the weight of evidence. The elaborate work,[30] which he composed amidst the preparations of the Persian war, contained the substance of those arguments which he had long revolved in his mind. Some fragments have been transcribed and preserved by his adversary, the vehement Cyril of

Alexandria;[31] and they exhibit a very singular mixture of wit and learning, of sophistry and fanaticism. The elegance of the style, and the rank of the author, recommended his writings to the public attention;[32] and in the impious list of the enemies of Christianity, the celebrated name of Porphyry was effaced by the superior merit or reputation of Julian. The minds of the faithful were either seduced, or scandalised, or alarmed; and the pagans, who sometimes presumed to engage in the unequal dispute, derived from the popular work of their Imperial missionary an inexhaustible supply of fallacious objections. But in the assiduous prosecution of these theological studies, the emperor of the Romans imbibed the illiberal prejudices and passions of a polemic divine. He contracted an irrevocable obligation to maintain and propagate his religious opinions; and, whilst he secretly applauded the strength and dexterity with which he wielded the weapons of controversy, he was tempted to distrust the sincerity, or to despise the understandings, of his antagonists, who could obstinately resist the force of reason and eloquence.

The Christians, who beheld with horror and indignation the apostasy of Julian, had much more to fear from his power than from his arguments. The pagans, who were conscious of his fervent zeal, expected, perhaps with impatience, that the flames of persecution should be immediately kindled against the enemies of the gods; and that the ingenious malice of Julian would invent some cruel refinements of death and torture, which had been unknown to the rude and inexperienced fury of his predecessors. But the hopes, as well as the fears, of the religious factions were apparently disappointed by the prudent humanity of a prince[33] who was careful of his own fame, of the public peace, and of the rights of mankind. Instructed by history and reflection, Julian was persuaded that, if the diseases of the body may sometimes be cured by salutary violence, neither steel nor fire can eradicate the erroneous opinions of the mind. The reluctant victim may be dragged to the foot of the altar; but the heart still abhors and disclaims the sacrilegious act of the hand. Religious obstinacy is hardened and exasperated by oppression; and, as soon as the persecution subsides, those who have yielded are restored as penitents, and those who have resisted are honoured as saints and martyrs. If Julian adopted the unsuccessful cruelty of Diocletian and his colleagues, he was sensible that he should stain his memory with the name of tyrant, and add new glories to the Catholic church, which had derived strength and increase from the severity of the pagan magistrates. Actuated by these motives, and apprehensive of disturbing the repose of an unsettled reign, Julian surprised the world by an edict which was not unworthy of a statesman or a philosopher. He extended to all the inhabitants of the Roman world the benefits of a free and equal toleration; and the only hardship which he inflicted on the Christians was to deprive them of the power of tormenting their fellow-subjects, whom they stigmatised with the odious titles of idolaters and heretics. The pagans received a gracious permission, or rather an express order, to open all their temples;[34] and they were at once delivered from the oppressive laws and arbitrary vexations which they had sustained under the reign of Constantine and of his sons. At the same time, the bishops and clergy who had been banished by the Arian monarch were recalled from exile and restored to their respective churches; the Donatists, the Novatians, the Macedonians, the Eunomians, and those who, with a more prosperous fortune, adhered to the doctrine of the council of Nicaea. Julian, who understood and derided their theological disputes, invited to the palace the leaders of the hostile sects, that he might enjoy the agreeable spectacle of their furious encounters. The clamour of controversy sometimes provoked the emperor to exclaim, 'Hear me! the Franks have heard me, and the Alemanni'; but he soon discovered that he was now engaged with more obstinate and implacable enemies; and, though he exerted the powers of oratory to persuade them to live in concord, or at least in peace, he was perfectly satisfied, before he dismissed them from his presence, that he had nothing to dread from the union of the Christians. The impartial Ammianus has ascribed this affected clemency to the desire of fomenting the intestine divisions of the church; and the insidious design of undermining the foundations of Christianity was inseparably connected with the zeal which Julian professed to restore the ancient religion of the empire.[35]

As soon as he ascended the throne, he assumed, according to the custom of his predecessors, the character of supreme pontiff; not only as the most honourable title of Imperial greatness, but as a sacred and important office, the duties of which he was resolved to execute with pious diligence. As the business of the state prevented the emperor from joining every day in the public devotion of his subjects, he dedicated a domestic chapel to his tutelar deity the Sun; his gardens were filled with statues and altars of the gods; and each apartment of the palace displayed the appearance of a magnificent temple. Every morning he saluted the parent of light with a sacrifice; the blood of another victim was shed at the moment when the Sun sunk below the horizon; and the Moon, the Stars, and the Genii of the night, received their respective and seasonable honours from the indefatigable devotion of Julian. On solemn festivals, he regularly visited the temple of the god or goddess to whom the day was peculiarly consecrated, and endeavoured to excite the religion of the magistrates and people by the example of his own zeal. Instead of maintaining the lofty state of a monarch, distinguished by the splendour of his purple, and encompassed by the golden shields of his guards, Julian solicited, with respectful eagerness, the meanest offices which contributed to the worship of the gods. Amidst the sacred but licentious crowd of priests, of inferior ministers, and of female dancers, who were dedicated to the service of the temple, it was the business of the emperor to bring the wood, to blow the fire, to handle the knife, to slaughter the victim, and, thrusting his bloody hand into the bowels of the expiring animal, to draw forth the heart or liver, and to read, with the consummate skill of an haruspex,* the imaginary signs of future events. The wisest of the pagans censured this extravagant superstition, which affected to despise the restraints of prudence and decency. Under the reign of a prince who practised the rigid maxims of economy, the expense of religious worship consumed a very large portion of the revenue; a constant supply of the scarcest and most beautiful birds was transported from distant climates, to bleed on the altars of the gods; an hundred oxen were frequently sacrificed by Julian on one and the same day; and it soon became a popular jest that, if he should return with conquest from the Persian war, the breed of horned cattle must infallibly be extinguished. Yet this expense may appear inconsiderable, when it is compared with the splendid presents which were offered, either by the hand or by order of the emperor, to all the celebrated places of devotion in the Roman world; and with the sums allotted to repair and decorate the ancient temples, which had suffered the silent decay of time or the recent injuries of Christian rapine. Encouraged by the example, the exhortations, the liberality, of their pious sovereign, the cities and families resumed the practice of their neglected ceremonies. 'Every part of the world,' exclaims Libanius with devout transport, 'displayed the triumph of religion; and the grateful prospect of flaming altars, bleeding victims, the smoke of incense, and a solemn train of priests and prophets, without fear and without danger. The sound of prayer and of music was heard on the tops of the highest mountains; and the same ox afforded a sacrifice for the gods and a supper for their joyous votaries.'[36]

But the genius and power of Julian were unequal to the enterprise of restoring a religion which was destitute of theological principles, of moral precepts, and of ecclesiastical discipline; which rapidly hastened to decay and dissolution, and was not susceptible of any solid or consistent reformation. The jurisdiction of the supreme pontiff, more especially after that office had been united with the Imperial dignity, comprehended the whole extent of the Roman empire. Julian named for his vicars, in the several provinces, the priests and philosophers whom he esteemed the best qualified to co-operate in the execution of his great design; and his pastoral letters,[37] if we may use that name, still represent a very curious sketch of his wishes and intentions. He directs that in every city the sacerdotal order should be composed, without any distinction of birth or fortune, of those persons who were the most conspicuous for their love of the gods and of men. 'If they are guilty,' continues he, 'of any scandalous offence, they should be censured or degraded by the superior pontiff; but, as long as they retain their rank, they are entitled to the respect of the magistrates and people. Their humility may be shown in the plainness of their domestic garb; their dignity, in the pomp of holy vestments. When they are summoned in their turn to officiate before the altar, they ought not, during the appointed number of days, to depart from the precincts of the temple; nor should a single day be suffered to elapse without the prayers and the sacrifice, which they are obliged to offer for the prosperity of the state and of individuals. The exercise of their sacred functions requires an immaculate purity, both of mind and body; and, even when they are dismissed from the temple to the occupations of common life, it is incumbent on them to excel in decency and virtue the rest of their fellow-citizens. The priest of the gods should never be seen in theatres or taverns. His conversation should be chaste, his diet temperate, his friends of honourable reputation; and, if he sometimes visits the Forum or the Palace, he should appear only as the advocate of those who have vainly solicited either justice or mercy. His studies should be suited to the sanctity of his profession. Licentious tales, or comedies, or satires, must be banished from his library; which ought solely to consist of historical and philosophical writings; of history which is founded in truth, and of philosophy which is connected with religion. The impious opinions of the Epicureans and Sceptics deserve his abhorrence and contempt;[38] but he should diligently study the systems of Pythagoras, of Plato, and of the Stoics, which unanimously teach that there *are* gods; that the world is governed by their providence; that their goodness is the source of every temporal blessing; and that they have prepared for the human soul a future state of reward or punishment.' The Imperial pontiff inculcates, in the most persuasive language, the duties of benevolence and hospitality; exhorts his inferior clergy to recommend the universal practice of those virtues; promises to assist their indigence from the public treasury; and declares his resolution of establishing hospitals in every city, where the poor should be received without any invidious distinction of country or of religion. Julian beheld with envy the wise and humane regulations of the church; and he very frankly confesses his intention to deprive the Christians of the applause, as well as advantage, which they had acquired by the exclusive practice of charity and beneficence.[39] The same spirit of imitation might dispose the emperor to adopt several ecclesiastical institutions, the use and importance of which were approved by the success of his enemies. But, if these imaginary plans of reformation had been realised, the forced and imperfect copy would have been less beneficial to Paganism than honourable to Christianity.[40] The Gentiles, who peaceably followed the customs of their ancestors, were rather surprised than pleased with the introduction of foreign manners; and, in the short period of his reign, Julian had frequent occasions to complain of the want of fervour of his own party.[41]

The enthusiasm of Julian prompted him to embrace the friends of Jupiter as his personal friends and brethren; and, though he partially overlooked the merit of Christian constancy, he admired and rewarded the noble perseverance of those Gentiles who had preferred the favour of the gods to that of the emperor.[42] If they cultivated the literature, as well as the religion, of the Greeks, they acquired an additional claim to the friendship of Julian, who ranked the Muses in the number of his tutelar deities. In the religion which he had adopted, piety and learning were almost synonymous;[43] and a crowd of poets, of rhetoricians, and of philosophers, hastened to the Imperial court, to occupy the vacant places of the bishops who had seduced the credulity of Constantius. His successor esteemed the ties of common initiation as far more sacred than those of consanguinity: he chose his favourites among the sages who were deeply skilled in the occult sciences of magic and divination; and every impostor who pretended to reveal the secrets of futurity was assured of enjoying the present hour in honour and affluence.[44] Among the philosophers, Maximus obtained the most eminent rank in the friendship of his royal disciple, who communicated, with unreserved confidence, his actions, his sentiments, and his religious designs, during the anxious suspense of the civil war.[45] As soon as Julian had taken possession of the palace of Constantinople, he dispatched an honourable and pressing invitation to Maximus; who then resided at Sardes in Lydia, with Chrysanthius, the associate of his art and studies. The prudent and superstitious Chrysanthius refused to undertake a journey which showed itself, according to the rules of divination, with the most threatening and malignant aspect; but his companion, whose fanaticism was of a bolder cast, persisted in his interrogations, till he had extorted from the gods a seeming consent to his own wishes and those of the emperor. The journey of Maximus through the cities of Asia displayed the triumph of philosophic vanity; and the magistrates vied with each other in the honourable reception which they prepared for the friend of their sovereign. Julian was pronouncing an oration before the senate, when he was informed of the arrival of Maximus. The emperor immediately interrupted his discourse, advanced to meet him, and, after a tender embrace, conducted him by the hand into the midst of the assembly; where he publicly acknowledged the benefits which he had derived from the instructions of the philosopher. Maximus,[46] who soon acquired the confidence, and influenced the councils, of Julian, was insensibly corrupted by the temptations of a court. His dress became more splendid, his demeanour more lofty, and he was exposed, under a succeeding reign, to a disgraceful inquiry into the means by which the disciple of Plato had accumulated, in the short duration of his favour, a very scandalous proportion of wealth. Of the other philosophers and sophists, who were invited to the Imperial residence by the choice of Julian or by the success of Maximus, few were able to preserve their innocence or their reputation.[47] The liberal gifts of money, lands, and houses, were insufficient to satiate their rapacious avarice; and the indignation of the people was justly excited by the remembrance of their abject poverty and disinterested professions. The penetration of Julian could not always be deceived; but he was unwilling to despise the characters of those men whose talents deserved his esteem; he desired to escape the double reproach of imprudence and inconstancy; and he was apprehensive of degrading, in the eyes of the profane, the honour of letters and of religion.[48]

The favour of Julian was almost equally divided between the Pagans, who had firmly adhered to the worship of their ancestors, and the Christians, who prudently embraced the religion of their sovereign. The acquisition of new proselytes[49] gratified the ruling passions of his soul, superstition and vanity; and he was heard to declare with the enthusiasm of a missionary that, if he could render each individual richer than Midas, and every city greater than Babylon, he should not esteem himself the benefactor of mankind, unless, at the same time, he could reclaim his subjects from their impious revolt against the immortal gods.[50] A prince, who had studied human nature, and who possessed the treasures of the Roman empire, could adapt his arguments, his promises, and his rewards, to every order of Christians;[51] and the merit of a seasonable conversion was allowed to supply the defects of a candidate, or even to expiate the guilt of a criminal. As the army is the most forcible engine of absolute power, Julian applied himself, with peculiar diligence, to corrupt the religion of his troops, without whose hearty concurrence every measure must be dangerous and unsuccessful; and the natural temper of soldiers made this conquest as easy as it was important. The legions of Gaul devoted themselves to the faith, as well as to the fortunes, of their victorious leader; and even before the death of Constantius, he had the satisfaction of announcing to his friends that they assisted with fervent devotion, and voracious appetite, at the sacrifices, which were repeatedly offered in his camp, of whole hecatombs of fat oxen.[52] The armies of the East, which had been trained under the standard of the cross, and of Constantius, required a more artful and expensive mode of persuasion. On the days of solemn and public festivals, the emperor received the homage, and rewarded the merits, of the troops. His throne of state was encircled with the military ensigns of Rome and the republic; the holy name of Christ was erased from the *Labarum*; and the symbols of war, of majesty, and of pagan superstition, were so dexterously blended, that the faithful subject incurred the guilt of idolatry, when he respectfully saluted the person or image of his sovereign. The soldiers passed successively in review; and each of them, before he received from the hand of Julian a liberal donative, proportioned to his rank and services, was required to cast a few grains of incense into the flame which burnt upon the altar. Some Christian confessors might resist, and others might repent; but the far greater number, allured by the prospect of gold and awed by the presence of the emperor, contracted the criminal engagement; and their future perseverance in the worship of the gods was enforced by every consideration of duty and of interest. By the frequent repetition of these arts, and at the expense of sums which would have purchased the service of half the nations of Scythia, Julian gradually acquired for his troops the imaginary protection of the gods, and for himself the firm and effectual support of the Roman legions.[53] It is indeed more than probable that the restoration and encouragement of Paganism revealed a multitude of pretended Christians, who, from motives of temporal advantage, had acquiesced in the religion of the former reign; and who afterwards returned, with the same flexibility of conscience, to the faith which was professed by the successors of Julian.

While the devout monarch incessantly laboured to restore and propagate the religion of his ancestors, he embraced the extraordinary design of rebuilding the temple of Jerusalem. In a public epistle[54] to the nation or community of the Jews, dispersed through the provinces, he pities their misfortunes, condemns their oppressors, praises their constancy, declares himself their gracious protector, and expresses a pious hope that, after his return from the Persian war, he may be permitted to pay his grateful vows to the Almighty in his holy city of Jerusalem. The blind superstition and abject slavery of those unfortunate exiles must excite the contempt of a philosophic emperor; but they deserved the friendship of Julian by their implacable hatred of the Christian name. The barren synagogue abhorred and envied the fecundity of the rebellious church: the power of the Jews was not equal to their malice; but their gravest rabbis approved the private murder of an apostate;[55] and their seditious clamours had often awakened the indolence of the pagan magistrates. Under the reign of Constantine, the Jews became the subjects of their revolted children, nor was it long before they experienced the bitterness of domestic tyranny. The civil immunities which had been granted, or confirmed, by Severus were gradually repealed by the Christian princes; and a rash tumult excited by the Jews of Palestine[56] seemed to justify the lucrative modes of oppression, which were invented by the bishops and eunuchs of the court of Constantius. The Jewish patriarch, who was still permitted to exercise a precarious jurisdiction, held his residence at Tiberias;[57] and the neighbouring cities of Palestine were filled with the remains of a people who fondly adhered to the promised land. But the edict of Hadrian was renewed and enforced; and they viewed from afar the walls of the holy city, which were profaned in their eyes by the triumph of the cross and the devotion of the Christians.[58]

In the midst of a rocky and barren country, the walls of Jerusalem[59] enclosed the two mountains of Sion and Acra, within an oval figure of about three English miles.[60] Towards the south, the upper town and the fortress of David were erected on the lofty ascent of Mount Sion: on the north side, the buildings of the lower town covered the spacious summit of Mount Acra; and a part of the hill, distinguished by the name of Moriah and levelled by human industry, was crowned with the stately temple of the Jewish nation. After the final destruction of the temple, by the arms of Titus and Hadrian, a ploughshare was drawn over the consecrated ground, as a sign of perpetual interdiction. Sion was deserted; and the vacant space of the lower city was filled with the public and private edifices of the Aelian colony, which spread themselves over the adjacent hill of Calvary. The holy places were polluted with monuments of idolatry; and, either from design or accident, a chapel was dedicated to Venus on the spot which had been sanctified by the death and resurrection of Christ.[61] Almost three hundred years after those stupendous events, the profane chapel of Venus was demolished by the order of Constantine; and the removal of the earth and stones revealed the holy sepulchre to the eyes of mankind. A magnificent church was erected on that mystic ground, by the first Christian emperor; and the effects of his pious munificence were extended to every spot which had been consecrated by the footsteps of patriarchs, of prophets, and of the Son of God.[62]

The passionate desire of contemplating the original monuments of their redemption attracted to Jerusalem a successive crowd of pilgrims, from the shores of the Atlantic ocean and the most distant countries of the East;[63] and their piety was authorised by the example of the empress Helena,* who appears to have united the credulity of age with the warm feelings of a recent conversion. Sages and heroes, who have visited the memorable scenes of ancient wisdom or glory, have confessed the inspiration of the genius of the place;[64] and the Christian who knelt before the holy sepulchre ascribed his lively faith and his fervent devotion to the more immediate influence of the Divine spirit. The zeal, perhaps the avarice, of the clergy of Jerusalem cherished and multiplied these beneficial visits. They fixed, by unquestionable tradition, the scene of each memorable event. They exhibited the instruments which had been used in the passion of Christ: the nails and the lance that had pierced his hands, his feet, and his sides; the crown of thorns that was planted on his head, the pillar at which he was scourged; and, above all, they showed the cross on which he suffered, and which was dug out of the earth in the reign of those princes who inserted the symbol of Christianity in the banners of the Roman legions.[65] Such miracles as seemed necessary to account for its extraordinary preservation and seasonable discovery were gradually propagated without opposition. The custody of the *true cross*, which on Easter Sunday was solemnly exposed to the people, was entrusted to the bishop of Jerusalem; and he alone might gratify the curious devotion of the pilgrims, by the gift of small pieces, which they enchased in gold or gems, and carried away in triumph to their respective countries. But, as this gainful branch of commerce must soon have been annihilated, it was found convenient to suppose that the marvellous wood possessed a secret power of vegetation; and that its substance, though continually diminished, still remained entire and unimpaired.[66] It might perhaps have been expected that the influence of the place, and the belief of a perpetual miracle, should have produced some salutary effects on the morals as well as on the faith of the people. Yet the most respectable of the ecclesiastical writers have been obliged to confess, not only that the streets of Jerusalem were filled with the incessant tumult of business and pleasure,[67] but that every species of vice, adultery, theft, idolatry, poisoning, murder, was familiar to the inhabitants of the holy city.[68] The wealth and pre-eminence of the church of Jerusalem excited the ambition of Arian, as well as orthodox, candidates; and the virtues of Cyril, who, since his death, has been honoured with the title of Saint, were displayed in the exercise, rather than in the acquisition, of his episcopal dignity.[69]

The vain and ambitious mind of Julian might aspire to restore the ancient glory of the temple of Jerusalem.[70] As the Christians were firmly persuaded that a sentence of everlasting destruction had been pronounced against the whole fabric of the Mosaic law, the imperial sophist would have converted the success of his undertaking into a specious argument against the faith of the prophecy and the truth of revelation.[71] He was displeased with the spiritual worship of the synagogue; but he approved the institutions of Moses, who had not disdained to adopt many of the rites and ceremonies of Egypt.[72] The local and national deity of the Jews was sincerely adored by a polytheist who desired only to multiply the number of the gods;[73] and such was the appetite of Julian for bloody sacrifice that his emulation might be excited by the piety of Solomon, who had offered, at the feast of the dedication, twenty-two thousand oxen and one hundred and twenty thousand sheep.[74] These considerations might influence his designs; but the prospect of an immediate and important advantage would not suffer the impatient monarch to expect the remote and uncertain event of the Persian war. He resolved to erect, without delay, on the commanding eminence of Moriah, a stately temple which might eclipse the splendour of the church of the Resurrection on the adjacent hill of Calvary; to establish an order of priests, whose interested zeal would detect the arts, and resist the ambition, of their Christian rivals; and to invite a numerous colony of Jews, whose stern fanaticism would be always prepared to second, and even to anticipate, the hostile measures of the pagan government. Among the friends of the emperor (if the names of emperor and of friend are not incompatible) the first place was assigned, by Julian himself, to the virtuous and learned Alypius.[75] The humanity of Alypius was tempered by severe justice and manly fortitude; and, while he exercised his abilities in the civil administration of Britain, he imitated, in his poetical compositions, the harmony and softness of the odes of Sappho. This minister, to whom Julian communicated, without reserve, his most careless levities and his most serious counsels, received an extraordinary commission to restore, in its pristine beauty, the temple of Jerusalem; and the diligence of Alypius required and obtained the strenuous support of the governor of Palestine. At the call of their great deliverer, the Jews, from all the provinces of their empire, assembled on the holy mountain of their fathers; and their insolent triumph alarmed and exasperated the

Christian inhabitants of Jerusalem. The desire of rebuilding the temple has, in every age, been the ruling passion of the children of Israel. In this propitious moment the men forgot their avarice, and the women their delicacy; spades and pick-axes of silver were provided by the vanity of the rich, and the rubbish was transported in mantles of silk and purple. Every purse was opened in liberal contributions, every hand claimed a share in the pious labour; and the commands of a great monarch were executed by the enthusiasm of a whole people.[76]

Yet, on this occasion, the joint efforts of power and enthusiasm were unsuccessful; and the ground of the Jewish temple, which is now covered by a Mahometan mosque,[77] still continued to exhibit the same edifying spectacle of ruin and desolation. Perhaps the absence and death of the emperor, and the new maxims of a Christian reign, might explain the interruption of an arduous work, which was attempted only in the last six months of the life of Julian.[78] But the Christians entertained a natural and pious expectation that, in this memorable contest, the honour of religion would be vindicated by some signal miracle. An earthquake, a whirlwind, and a fiery eruption, which overturned and scattered the new foundations of the temple, are attested, with some variations, by contemporary and respectable evidence.[79] This public event is described by Ambrose,[80] bishop of Milan, in an epistle to the emperor Theodosius, which must provoke the severe animadversion of the Jews; by the eloquent Chrysostom,[81] who might appeal to the memory of the elder part of his congregation at Antioch; and by Gregory Nazianzen,[82] who published his account of the miracle before the expiration of the same year. The last of these writers has boldly declared that this preternatural event was not disputed by the infidels; and his assertion, strange as it may seem, is confirmed by the unexceptionable testimony of Ammianus Marcellinus.[83] The philosophic soldier, who loved the virtues, without adopting the prejudices, of his master, has recorded, in his judicious and candid history of his own times, the extraordinary obstacles which interrupted the restoration of the temple of Jerusalem. 'Whilst Alypius, assisted by the governor of the province, urged with vigour and diligence the execution of the work, horrible balls of fire breaking out near the foundations with frequent and reiterated attacks, rendered the place, from time to time, inaccessible to the scorched and blasted workmen; and, the victorious element continuing in this manner obstinately and resolutely bent, as it were, to drive them to a distance, the undertaking was abandoned.' Such authority should satisfy a believing, and must astonish an incredulous, mind. Yet a philosopher may still require the original evidence of impartial and intelligent spectators. At this important crisis, any singular accident of nature would assume the appearance, and produce the effects, of a real prodigy. This glorious deliverance would be speedily improved and magnified by the pious art of the clergy of Jerusalem and the active credulity of the Christian world; and, at the distance of twenty years, a

Roman historian, careless of theological disputes, might adorn his work with the specious and splendid miracle.[84]

The restoration of the Jewish temple was secretly connected with the ruin of the Christian church. Julian still continued to maintain the freedom of religious worship, without distinguishing whether this universal toleration proceeded from his justice or his clemency. He affected to pity the unhappy Christians, who were mistaken in the most important object of their lives; but his pity was degraded by contempt, his contempt was embittered by hatred; and the sentiments of Julian were expressed in a style of sarcastic wit, which inflicts a deep and deadly wound whenever it issues from the mouth of a sovereign. As he was sensible that the Christians gloried in the name of their Redeemer, he countenanced, and perhaps enjoined, the use of the less honourable appellation of *Galilaeans*.[85] He declared that, by the folly of the Galilaeans, whom he describes as a sect of fanatics, contemptible to men, and odious to the gods, the empire had been reduced to the brink of destruction, and he insinuates in a public edict that a frantic patient might sometimes be cured by salutary violence.[86] An ungenerous distinction was admitted into the mind and counsels of Julian, that, according to the difference of their religions sentiments, one part of his subjects deserved his favour and friendship, while the other was entitled only to the common benefits that his justice could not refuse to an obedient people.[87] According to a principle, pregnant with mischief and oppression, the emperor transferred to the pontiffs of his own religion the management of the liberal allowances from the public revenue which had been granted to the church by the piety of Constantine and his sons. The proud system of clerical honours and immunities, which had been constructed with so much art and labour, was levelled to the ground; the hopes of testamentary donations were intercepted by the rigour of the laws; and the priests of the Christian sect were confounded with the last and most ignominious class of the people. Such of these regulations as appeared necessary to check the ambition and avarice of the ecclesiastics were soon afterwards imitated by the wisdom of an orthodox prince. The peculiar distinctions which policy has bestowed, or superstition has lavished, on the sacerdotal order *must* be confined to those priests who profess the religion of the state. But the will of the legislator was not exempt from prejudice and passion; and it was the object of the insidious policy of Julian to deprive the Christians of all the temporal honours and advantages, which rendered them respectable in the eyes of the world.[88]

A just and severe censure has been inflicted on the law which prohibited the Christians from teaching the arts of grammar and rhetoric.[89] The motives alleged by the emperor to justify this partial and oppressive measure might command, during his lifetime, the silence of slaves and the applause of flatterers. Julian abuses the ambiguous meaning of a word which might be indifferently applied to the language and the religion of the Greeks: he contemptuously observes that the men who exalt the merit of implicit faith are unfit to claim or to enjoy the advantages of science; and he vainly contends that, if they refuse to adore the gods of Homer and Demosthenes, they ought to content themselves with expounding Luke and Matthew in the churches of the Galilaeans.[90] In all the cities of the Roman world, the education of the youth was entrusted to masters of grammar and rhetoric; who were elected by the magistrates, maintained at the public expense, and distinguished by many lucrative and honourable privileges. The edict of Julian appears to have included the physicians, and professors of all the liberal arts; and the emperor, who reserved to himself the approbation of the candidates, was authorised by the laws to corrupt, or to punish, the religious constancy of the most learned of the Christians.[91] As soon as the resignation of the more obstinate[92] teachers had established the unrivalled dominion of the Pagan sophists, Julian invited the rising generation to resort with freedom to the public schools, in a just confidence that their tender minds would receive the impressions of literature and idolatry. If the greatest part of the Christian youth should be deterred by their own scruples, or by those of their parents, from accepting this dangerous mode of instruction, they must at the same time relinquish the benefits of a liberal education. Julian had reason to expect that, in the space of a few years, the church would relapse into its primaeval simplicity, and that the theologians, who possessed an adequate share of the learning and eloquence of the age, would be succeeded by a generation of blind and ignorant fanatics, incapable of defending the truth of their own principles or of exposing the various follies of Polytheism.[93]

It was undoubtedly the wish and the design of Julian to deprive the Christians of the advantages of wealth, of knowledge, and of power; but the injustice of excluding them from all offices of trust and profit seems to have been the result of his general policy rather than the immediate consequence of any positive law.[94] Superior merit might deserve, and obtain, some extraordinary exceptions; but the greater part of the Christian officers were gradually removed from their employments in the state, the army, and the provinces. The hopes of future candidates were extinguished by the declared partiality of a prince who maliciously reminded them that it was unlawful for a Christian to use the sword either of justice or of war; and who studiously guarded the camp and the tribunals with the ensigns of idolatry. The powers of government were entrusted to the Pagans, who professed an ardent zeal for the religion of their ancestors; and, as the choice of the emperor was often directed by the rules of divination, the favourites whom he preferred as the most agreeable to the gods did not always obtain the approbation of mankind.[95] Under the administration of their enemies, the Christians had much to suffer, and more to apprehend. The temper of Julian was averse to cruelty; and the care of his reputation, which was exposed to the eyes of the universe, restrained the philosophic monarch from violating the laws of justice and toleration which he himself had so recently established. But the provincial ministers of his authority were placed in a less conspicuous station. In the exercise of arbitrary power, they consulted the wishes, rather than the commands, of their sovereign; and ventured to exercise a secret and vexatious tyranny against the sectaries, on whom they were not permitted to confer the honours of martyrdom. The emperor, who dissembled as long as possible his knowledge of the injustice that was exercised in his name, expressed his real sense of the conduct of his officers by gentle reproofs and substantial rewards.[96]

The most effectual instrument of oppression with which they were armed was the law that obliged the Christians to make full and ample satisfaction for the temples which they had destroyed under the preceding reign. The zeal of the triumphant church had not always expected the sanction of the public authority; and the bishops, who were secure of impunity, had often marched, at the head of their congregations, to attack and demolish the fortresses of the prince of darkness. The consecrated lands, which had increased the patrimony of the sovereign or of the clergy, were clearly defined, and easily restored. But on these lands, and on the ruins of Pagan superstition, the Christians had frequently erected their own religious edifices: and, as it was necessary to remove the church before the temple could be rebuilt, the justice and piety of the emperor were applauded by one party, while the other deplored and execrated his sacrilegious violence.[97] After the ground was cleared, the restitution of those stately structures which had been levelled with the dust and of the precious ornaments which had been converted to Christian uses swelled into a very large account of damages and debt. The authors of the injury had neither the ability nor the inclination to discharge this accumulated demand; and the impartial wisdom of a legislator would have been displayed in balancing the adverse claims and complaints, by an equitable and temperate arbitration. But the whole empire, and particularly the East, was thrown into confusion by the rash edicts of Julian; and the Pagan magistrates, inflamed by zeal and revenge, abused the rigorous privilege of the Roman law, which substitutes, in the place of his inadequate property, the person of the insolvent debtor. Under the preceding reign, Mark, bishop of Arethusa,[98] had laboured in the conversion of his people with arms more effectual than those of persuasion.[99] The magistrates required the full value of a temple which had been destroyed by his intolerant zeal: but, as they were satisfied of his poverty, they desired only to bend his inflexible spirit to the promise of the slightest compensation. They apprehended the aged prelate, they inhumanly scourged him, they tore his beard; and his naked body, anointed with honey, was suspended in a net between heaven and earth, and exposed to the stings of insects and the rays of a Syrian sun.[100] From this lofty station, Mark still persisted to glory in his crime and to insult the impotent rage of his persecutors. He was at length rescued from their hands, and dismissed to enjoy the honour of his divine triumph. The Arians celebrated the virtue of their pious confessor; the Catholics ambitiously claimed his alliance;[101] and the Pagans, who might be susceptible of shame or remorse, were deterred from the repetition of such unavailing cruelty[102] Julian spared his life; but, if the bishop of Arethusa had saved the infancy of Julian,*[103] posterity will condemn the ingratitude, instead of praising the clemency, of the emperor.

At the distance of five miles from Antioch, the Macedonian kings of Syria had consecrated to Apollo one of the most elegant places of devotion in the Pagan world.[104] A magnificent temple rose in honour of the god of light; and his colossal figure[105] almost filled the capacious sanctuary, which was enriched with gold and gems, and adorned by the skill of the Grecian artists. The deity was represented in a bending attitude, with a golden cup in his hand, pouring out a libation on the earth, as if he supplicated the venerable mother to give to his arms the cold and beauteous Daphne; for the spot was ennobled by fiction, and the fancy of the Syrian poets had transported the amorous tale from the banks of the Peneus† to those of the Orontes. The ancient rites of Greece were imitated by the royal colony of Antioch. A stream of prophecy, which rivalled the truth and reputation of the Delphic oracle, flowed from the *Castalian*‡ fountain of Daphne.[106] In the adjacent fields a stadium was built by a special privilege,[107] which had been purchased from Elis;§ the Olympic games were celebrated at the expense of the city; and a revenue of thirty thousand pounds sterling was annually applied to the public pleasures.[108] The perpetual resort of pilgrims and spectators insensibly formed, in the neighbourhood of the temple, the stately and populous village of Daphne, which emulated the splendour, without acquiring the title, of a provincial city. The temple and the village were deeply bosomed in a thick grove of laurels and cypresses, which reached as far as a circumference of ten miles, and formed in the most sultry summers a cool and impenetrable shade. A thousand streams of the purest water, issuing from every hill, preserved the verdure of the earth and the temperature of the air; the senses were gratified with harmonious sounds and aromatic odours; and the peaceful grove was consecrated to health and joy, to luxury and love. The vigorous youth pursued, like Apollo, the object of his desires; and the blushing maid was warned, by the fate of Daphne,** to shun the folly of unseasonable coyness. The soldier and the philosopher wisely avoided the temptation of this sensual paradise;[109] where pleasure, assuming the character of religion, imperceptibly dissolved the firmness of manly virtue. But the groves of Daphne continued for many ages to enjoy the veneration of natives and strangers; the privileges of the holy ground were enlarged by the munificence of succeeding emperors; and every generation added new ornaments to the splendour of the temple.[110]

When Julian, on the day of the annual festival, hastened to adore the Apollo of Daphne, his devotion was raised to the highest pitch of eagerness and impatience. His lively imagination anticipated the grateful pomp of victims, of libations, and of incense; a long procession of youths and virgins, clothed in white robes, the symbol of their innocence; and the tumultuous concourse of an innumerable people. But the zeal of Antioch was diverted, since the reign of Christianity, into a different channel. Instead of hecatombs of fat oxen sacrificed by the tribes of a wealthy city to their tutelar deity, the emperor complains that he found only a single goose, provided at the expense of a priest, the pale and solitary inhabitant of this decayed temple.[111] The altar was deserted, the oracle had been reduced to silence, and the holy ground was profaned by the introduction of Christian and funereal rites. After Babylas[112] (a bishop of Antioch, who died in prison in the persecution of Decius) had rested near a century in his grave, his body, by the order of the Caesar Gallus, was transported into the midst of the grove of Daphne. A magnificent church was erected over his remains; a portion of the sacred lands was usurped for the maintenance of the clergy, and for the burial of the Christians of Antioch who were ambitious of lying at the feet of their bishop; and the priests of Apollo retired, with their affrighted and indignant votaries. As soon as another revolution seemed to restore the fortune of Paganism, the church of St Babylas was demolished, and new buildings were added to the mouldering edifice which had been raised by the piety of Syrian kings. But the first and most serious care of Julian was to deliver his oppressed deity from the odious presence of the dead and living Christians who had so effectually suppressed the voice of fraud or enthusiasm.[113] The scene of infection was purified, according to the forms of ancient rituals; the bodies were decently removed; and the ministers of the church were permitted to convey the remains of St Babylas to their former habitation within the walls of Antioch. The modest behaviour which might have assuaged the jealousy of an hostile government was neglected on this occasion by the zeal of the Christians. The lofty car that transported the relics of Babylas was followed, and accompanied, and received, by an innumerable multitude; who chanted, with thundering acclamations, the Psalms of David the most expressive of their contempt for idols and idolaters. The return of the saint was a triumph; and the triumph was an insult on the religion of the emperor, who exerted his pride to dissemble his resentment. During the night which terminated this indiscreet procession, the temple of Daphne was in flames; the statue of Apollo was consumed; and the walls of the edifice were left a naked and awful monument of ruin. The Christians of Antioch asserted, with religious confidence, that the powerful intercession of St Babylas had pointed the lightnings of heaven against the devoted roof; but, as Julian was reduced to the alternative of believing either a crime or a miracle, he chose, without hesitation, without evidence, but with some colour of probability, to impute the fire of Daphne to the revenge of the Galilaeans.[114] Their offence, had it been sufficiently proved, might have justified the retaliation which was immediately executed by the order of Julian, of shutting the doors, and confiscating the wealth, of the cathedral of Antioch. To discover the criminals who were guilty of the tumult, of the fire, or of secreting the riches of the church, several ecclesiastics were tortured;[115] and a presbyter, of the name of Theodoret, was beheaded by the sentence of the Count of the East. But this hasty act was blamed by the emperor; who lamented, with real or affected concern, that the imprudent zeal of his ministers would tarnish his reign with the disgrace of persecution.[116]

The zeal of the ministers of Julian was instantly checked by the frown of their sovereign; but, when the father of his country declares himself the leader of a faction, the licence of popular fury cannot easily be restrained nor consistently punished. Julian, in a public composition, applauds the devotion and loyalty of the holy cities of Syria, whose pious inhabitants had destroyed, at the first signal, the sepulchres of the Galilaeans; and faintly complains that they had revenged the injuries of the gods with less moderation than he should have recommended.[117] This imperfect and reluctant confession may appear to confirm the ecclesiastical narratives: that in the cities of Gaza, Ascalon, Caesarea, Heliopolis, etc. the Pagans abused, without prudence or remorse, the moment of their prosperity; that the unhappy objects of their cruelty were released from torture only by death; that, as their mangled bodies were dragged through the streets, they were pierced (such was the universal rage) by the spits of cooks and the distaffs of enraged women; and that the entrails of Christian priests and virgins, after they had been tasted by those bloody fanatics, were mixed with barley, and contemptuously thrown to the unclean animals of the city.[118] Such scenes of religious madness exhibit the most contemptible and odious picture of human nature; but the massacre of Alexandria attracts still more attention, from the certainty of the fact, the rank of the victims, and the splendour of the capital of Egypt.

George,[119] from his parents or his education surnamed the Cappadocian, was born at Epiphania in Cilicia, in a fuller's shop. From this obscure and servile origin he raised himself by the talents of a parasite; and the patrons, whom he assiduously flattered, procured for their worthless dependent a lucrative commission, or contract, to supply the army with bacon. His employment was mean; he rendered it infamous. He accumulated wealth by the basest arts of fraud and corruption; but his malversations were so notorious that George was compelled to escape from the pursuits of justice. After this disgrace, in which he appears to have saved his fortune at the expense of his honour, he embraced, with real or affected zeal, the profession of Arianism. From the love, or the ostentation, of learning, he collected a valuable library of history, rhetoric, philosophy, and theology;[120] and the choice of the prevailing faction promoted George of

Cappadocia to the throne of Athanasius. The entrance of the new archbishop was that of a Barbarian conqueror; and each moment of his reign was polluted by cruelty and avarice. The Catholics of Alexandria and Egypt were abandoned to a tyrant, qualified, by nature and education, to exercise the office of persecution; but he oppressed with an impartial hand the various inhabitants of his extensive diocese. The primate of Egypt assumed the pomp and insolence of his lofty station; but he still betrayed the vices of his base and servile extraction. The merchants of Alexandria were impoverished by the unjust, and almost universal, monopoly, which he acquired, of nitre, salt, paper, funerals, etc.; and the spiritual father of a great people condescended to practise the vile and pernicious arts of an informer. The Alexandrians could never forget nor forgive the tax which he suggested on all the houses of the city; under an obsolete claim that the royal founder had conveyed to his successors, the Ptolemies and the Caesars, the perpetual property of the soil. The Pagans, who had been flattered with the hopes of freedom and toleration, excited his devout avarice; and the rich temples of Alexandria were either pillaged or insulted by the haughty prelate, who exclaimed, in a loud and threatening tone, 'How long will these sepulchres be permitted to stand?' Under the reign of Constantius, he was expelled by the fury, or rather by the justice, of the people; and it was not without a violent struggle that the civil and military powers of the state could restore his authority and gratify his revenge. The messenger who proclaimed at Alexandria the accession of Julian announced the downfall of the archbishop. George, with two of his obsequious ministers, count Diodorus, and Dracontius, master of the mint, were ignominiously dragged in chains to the public prison. At the end of twenty-four days, the prison was forced open by the rage of a superstitious multitude, impatient of the tedious forms of judicial proceedings. The enemies of gods and men expired under their cruel insults; the lifeless bodies of the archbishop and his associates were carried in triumph through the streets on the back of a camel; and the inactivity of the Athanasian party[121] was esteemed a shining example of evangelical patience. The remains of these guilty wretches were thrown into the sea; and the popular leaders of the tumult declared their resolution to disappoint the devotion of the Christians, and to intercept the future honours of these *martyrs*, who had been punished, like their predecessors, by the enemies of their religion.[122] The fears of the Pagans were just, and their precautions ineffectual. The meritorious death of the archbishop obliterated the memory of his life. The rival of Athanasius was dear and sacred to the Arians, and the seeming conversion of those sectaries introduced his worship into the bosom of the Catholic church.[123] The odious stranger, disguising every circumstance of time and place, assumed the mask of a martyr, a saint, and a Christian hero;[124] and the infamous George of Cappadocia has been transformed[125] into the renowned St George of England, the patron of arms, of chivalry, and of the garter.[126]

About the same time that Julian was informed of the tumult of Alexandria, he received intelligence from Edessa that the proud and wealthy faction of the Arians had insulted the weakness of the Valentinians, and committed such disorders as ought not to be suffered with impunity in a well-regulated state. Without expecting the slow forms of justice, the exasperated prince directed his mandate to the magistrates of Edessa,[127] by which he confiscated the whole property of the church: the money was distributed among the soldiers; the lands were added to the domain; and this act of oppression was aggravated by the most ungenerous irony. 'I show myself,' says Julian, 'the true friend of the Galilaeans. Their *admirable* law has promised the kingdom of heaven to the poor; and they will advance with more diligence in the paths of virtue and salvation, when they are relieved by my assistance from the load of temporal possessions. Take care,' pursued the monarch, in a more serious tone, 'take care how you provoke my patience and humanity. If these disorders continue, I will revenge on the magistrates the crimes of the people; and you will have reason to dread, not only confiscation and exile, but fire and the sword.' The tumults of Alexandria were doubtless of a more bloody and dangerous nature; but a Christian bishop had fallen by the hands of the Pagans; and the public epistle of Julian affords a very lively proof of the partial spirit of his administration. His reproaches to the citizens of Alexandria are mingled with expressions of esteem and tenderness; and he laments that on this occasion they should have departed from the gentle and generous manners which attested their Grecian extraction. He gravely censures the offence which they had committed against the laws of justice and humanity; but he recapitulates, with visible complacency, the intolerable provocations which they had so long endured from the impious tyranny of George of Cappadocia. Julian admits the principle that a wise and vigorous government should chastise the insolence of the people; yet, in consideration of their founder Alexander and of Serapis their tutelar deity, he grants a free and gracious pardon to the guilty city, for which he again feels the affection of a brother.[128]

After the tumult of Alexandria had subsided, Athanasius, amidst the public acclamations, seated himself on the throne from whence his unworthy competitor had been precipitated; and, as the zeal of the archbishop was tempered with discretion, the exercise of his authority tended not to inflame, but to reconcile, the minds of the people. His pastoral labours were not confined to the narrow limits of Egypt. The state of the Christian world was present to his active and capacious mind; and the age, the merit, the reputation of Athanasius enabled him to assume, in a moment of danger, the office of Ecclesiastical Dictator.[129] Three years were not yet elapsed since the majority of the bishops of the West had ignorantly, or reluctantly, subscribed the Confession of Rimini. They repented, they believed; but they dreaded the unseasonable rigour of their orthodox brethren, and, if their pride was stronger than their faith, they might throw themselves into the arms of the Arians, to escape the indignity of a public penance, which must degrade them to the condition of obscure laymen. At the same time, the domestic differences concerning the union and distinction of the divine persons were agitated with some heat among the Catholic doctors; and the progress of this metaphysical controversy seemed to threaten a public and lasting division of the Greek and Latin churches. By the wisdom of a select synod, to which the name and presence of Athanasius gave the authority of a general council, the bishops who had unwarily deviated into error were admitted to the communion of the church, on the easy condition of subscribing the Nicene Creed; without any formal acknowledgment of their past fault or any minute definition of their scholastic opinions. The advice of the primate of Egypt had already prepared the clergy of Gaul and Spain, of Italy and Greece, for the reception of this salutary measure; and, notwith-standing the opposition of some ardent spirits,[130] the fear of the common enemy promoted the peace and harmony of the Christians.[131]

The skill and diligence of the primate of Egypt had improved the season of tranquillity, before it was interrupted by the hostile edicts of the emperor.[132] Julian, who despised the Christians, honoured Athanasius with his sincere and peculiar hatred. For his sake alone, he introduced an arbitrary distinction, repugnant, at least, to the spirit of his former declarations. He maintained that the Galilaeans whom he had recalled from exile were not restored, by that general indulgence, to the posses-sion of their respective churches: and he expressed his astonishment that a criminal, who had been repeatedly condemned by the judgment of the emperors, should dare to insult the majesty of the laws, and insolently usurp the archiepiscopal throne of Alexandria, without expecting the orders of his sovereign. As a punishment for the imaginary offence, he again banished Athanasius from the city; and he was pleased to suppose that this act of justice would be highly agreeable to his pious subjects. The pressing solicitations of the people soon convinced him that the majority of the Alexandrians were Christians; and that the greatest part of the Christians were firmly attached to the cause of their oppressed primate. But the knowledge of their sentiments, instead of persuading him to recall his decree, provoked him to extend to all Egypt the term of the exile of Athanasius. The zeal of the multitude rendered Julian still more inex-orable: he was alarmed by the danger of leaving at the head of a tumultuous city a daring and popular leader; and the language of his resentment discovers the opinion which he entertained of the courage and abilities of Athanasius. The execution of the sentence was still delayed, by the caution or negligence of Ecdicius, prefect of Egypt, who was at length awakened from his lethargy by a severe reprimand. 'Though you neglect,' says Julian, 'to write to me on any other subject, at least it is your duty to inform me of your conduct towards Athanasius, the enemy of the gods. My intentions have been long since communicated to you. I swear by the great Serapis that unless, on the calends* of December, Athanasius has departed from Alexandria, nay from Egypt, the officers of your government shall pay a fine of one hundred pounds of gold. You know my temper: I am slow to condemn, but I am still slower to forgive.' This epistle was enforced by a short postscript, written with the emperor's own hand. 'The contempt that is shown for all the gods fills me with grief and indignation. There is nothing that I should see, nothing that I should hear with more pleasure than the expulsion of Athanasius from all Egypt. The abominable wretch! Under my reign, the baptism of several Grecian ladies of the highest rank has been the effect of his persecutions.'[133] The death of Athanasius was not *expressly* commanded; but the prefect of Egypt understood that it was safer for him to exceed, than to neglect, the orders of an irritated master. The archbishop prudently retired to the monasteries of the Desert; eluded, with his usual dexterity, the snares of the enemy; and lived to triumph over the ashes of a prince who, in words of formidable import, had declared his wish that the whole venom of the Galilaean school were contained in the single person of Athanasius.[134]

I have endeavoured faithfully to represent the artful system by which Julian proposed to obtain the effects, without incurring the guilt, or reproach, of persecution. But, if the deadly spirit of fanaticism perverted the heart and understanding of a virtuous prince, it must, at the same time, be confessed, that the *real* sufferings of the Christians were inflamed and magnified by human passions and religious enthusiasm. The meekness and resignation which had distinguished the primitive disciples of the gospel was the object of the applause rather than of the imitation of their successors. The Christians, who had now possessed about forty years the civil and ecclesiastical government of the empire, had contracted the insolent vices of prosperity,[135] and the habit of believing that the saints alone were entitled to reign over the earth. As soon as the enmity of Julian deprived the clergy of the privileges which had been conferred by the favour of Constantine, they complained of the most cruel oppression; and the free toleration of idolaters and heretics was a subject of grief and scandal to the orthodox party.[136] The acts of violence, which were no longer countenanced by the magistrates, were still committed by the zeal of the people. At Pessinus,† the altar of Cybele was overturned almost in the presence of the emperor; and in the city of Caesarea in Cappadocia, the temple of Fortune, the sole place of worship which had been left to the Pagans, was destroyed by the rage of a popular tumult. On these occasions, a prince who felt for the honour of the gods was not disposed to interrupt the course of justice; and his mind was still more deeply exasperated, when he found that the fanatics, who had deserved and suffered the punishment of incendiaries, were rewarded with the honours of martyrdom.[137] The Christian subjects of Julian were assured of the hostile designs of their sovereign; and, to their jealous apprehension, every circumstance of his government might afford some grounds of discontent and suspicion. In the ordinary administration of the laws, the Christians, who formed so large a part of the people, must frequently be condemned; but their indulgent brethren, without examining the merits of the cause, presumed their innocence, allowed their claims, and imputed the severity of their judge to the partial malice of religious persecution.[138] These present hardships, intolerable as they might appear, were represented as a slight prelude of the impending calamities. The Christians considered Julian as a cruel and crafty tyrant, who suspended the execution of his revenge, till he should return victorious from the Persian war. They expected that, as soon as he had triumphed over the foreign enemies of Rome, he would lay aside the irksome mask of dissimulation; that the amphitheatres would stream with the blood of hermits and bishops; and that the Christians, who still persevered in the profession of the faith, would be deprived of the common benefits of nature and society.[139] Every calumny[140] that could wound the reputation of the Apostate was credulously embraced by the fears and hatred of his adversaries; and their indiscreet clamours provoked the temper of a sovereign whom it was their duty to respect and their interest to flatter. They still protested that prayers and tears were their only weapons against the impious tyrant, whose head they devoted to the justice of offended Heaven. But they insinuated with sullen resolution, that their submission was no longer the effect of weakness; and that, in the imperfect state of human virtue, the patience which is founded on principle may be exhausted by persecution. It is impossible to determine how far the zeal of Julian would have prevailed over his good sense and humanity; but, if we seriously reflect on the strength and spirit of the church, we shall be convinced that, before the emperor could have extinguished the religion of Christ, he must have involved his country in the horrors of a civil war.[141]

NOTES TO CHAPTER 23

* *page 465*   [Ammianus Marcellinus (*c.*ad 330–395)]

1 I shall transcribe some of his own expressions from a short religious discourse which the imperial pontiff composed to censure the bold impiety of a Cynic: Ἀλλ ὅμως οὕτω δή τι τοὺς θεοὺς πέφρικα, καὶ φιλῶ, καὶ σέβω, καὶ ἄζομαι, καὶ πάνθ' ἁπλῶς τὰ τοιαῦτα πάσχω, ὅσαπερ ἄν τις καὶ οἷα πρὸς ἀγαθοὺς δεσπότας, πρὸς διδασκάλους, πρὸς πατέρας, πρὸς κηδεμόνας. ['I fear the gods, and love, honour and revere them, and feel towards them in all respects as one does towards good masters and teachers, parents and friends.'] *Orat.*, vii, 212. The variety and copiousness of the Greek tongue seems inadequate to the fervour of his devotion.

2 The orator, with some eloquence, much enthusiasm, and more vanity, addresses his discourse to heaven and earth, to men and angels, to the living and the dead; and above all, to the great Constantius (εἴ τις αἴσθησις ['if he has any consciousness'], an odd Pagan expression). He concludes with a bold assurance that he has erected a monument not less durable, and much more portable, than the columns of Hercules. See Greg. Nazianzen, *Orat.*, iii, 50; iv, 134.

3 See this long invective, which has been injudiciously divided into two orations in Gregory's works, i, 49–134, Paris, 1630. It was published by Gregory and his friend Basil (iv, 133) about six months after the death of Julian, when his remains had been carried to Tarsus (iv, 120), but while Jovian was still on the throne (iii, 54; iv, 117). I have derived much assistance from a French version and remarks, printed at Lyons 1735.

4 *Nicomediae ab Eusebio educatus Episcopo, quem genere longius contingebat* (Ammian., xxii, 9). Julian never expresses any gratitude towards that Arian prelate; but he celebrates his preceptor, the eunuch Mardonius, and describes his mode of education, which inspired his pupil with a passionate admiration for the genius, and perhaps the religion, of Homer. *Misopogon*, pp. 351, 352.

5 Greg. Naz., iii, 70. He laboured to efface that holy mark in the blood, perhaps, of a Taurobolium [a bull-sacrifice, part of the religion of Mithras]. Baron., *Annal. Eccles.*, ad 361, No. 3, 4.

6 Julian himself (*Epist.*, li, 434) assures the Alexandrians that he had been a Christian (he must mean a sincere one) till the twentieth year of his age.

7 See his Christian and even ecclesiastical education, in Gregory (iii, 58), Socrates (iii, 1), and Sozomen (v, 2). He escaped very narrowly from being a bishop, and perhaps a saint.

8 The share of the work which had been allotted to Gallus was prosecuted with vigour and success; but the earth obstinately rejected and subverted the structures which were imposed by the sacrilegious hand of Julian. Greg., iii, 59, 60, 61 [ch. 26 *sqq.*]. Such a partial earthquake, attested by many living spectators, would form one of the clearest miracles in ecclesiastical story.

9   The *philosopher* (Fragment, p. 228) ridicules the iron chains, etc. of these solitary fanatics (see Tillemont, *Mém. Ecclés.*, ix, 661, 662), who had forgot that man is by nature a gentle and social animal, ἀνθρώπου φύσει πολιτικοῦ ζώου καὶ ἡμέρου. The *Pagan* supposes that, because they had renounced the gods, they were possessed and tormented by evil daemons.

10 See Julian, *apud* Cyril., vi, 206; viii, 253, 262. 'You persecute,' says he, 'those heretics who do not mourn the dead man precisely in the way which you approve.' He shows himself a tolerable theologian; but he maintains that the Christian Trinity is not derived from the doctrine of Paul, of Jesus, or of Moses.

11 Libanius, *Orat. Parentalis*, 9, 10, 232, etc.; Greg. Nazianzen, *Orat.*, iii, 61; Eunap., *Vit. Sophist. in Maximo*, pp. 68, 69, 70, edit. Commelin.

12 A modern philosopher has ingeniously compared the different operation of theism and polytheism, with regard to the doubt or conviction which they produce in the human mind. See Hume's *Essays* ii, pp. 444–457 in 8vo edit. 1777.

* *page 468* [i.e. castration. Cybele fell in love with Attis, or Atys ('the Phrygian boy'), and to prevent him from marrying anyone else, deprived him of his reason.]

13 The Idaean mother [Cybele] landed in Italy about the end of the second Punic war. The miracle of Claudia, either virgin or matron, who cleared her fame by disgracing the graver modesty of the Roman ladies, is attested by a cloud of

witnesses. [The ship carrying the image of Cybele had stuck in the shallows. Claudia, a vestal virgin accused of unchastity, brought the ship safely ashore by removing her girdle and using it to tow the vessel. 'This stupendous miracle' was considered as proof of her innocence.] Their evidence is collected by Drakenborch (ad Silium Italicum, xvii, 33): but we may observe that Livy (xxix, 14) slides over the transaction with discreet ambiguity.

14 I cannot refrain from transcribing the emphatical words of Julian: ἐμοὶ δὲ δοκεῖ ταῖς πόλεσι πιστεύειν μᾶλλον τὰ τοιαῦτα, ἢ τουτοισὶ τοῖς κομψοῖς, ὧν τὸ ψυχάριον δριμὺ μὲν, ὑγιὲς δὲ οὐδὲ ἐν βλέπει. ['It seems to me preferable to rely on the evidence of the cities rather than on those affected persons whose petty minds perceive what is shocking, but not what is wholesome.'] Orat., v, 161. Julian likewise declares his firm belief in the ancilia, the holy shields, which dropped from heaven on the Quirinal hill; and pities the strange blindness of the Christians, who preferred the cross to those celestial trophies. Apud Cyril., vi, 194.

15 See the principles of allegory in Julian (Orat., vii, 216, 222). His reasoning is less absurd than that of some modern theologians, who assert that an extravagant or contradictory doctrine must be divine, since no man alive could have thought of inventing it.

16 Eunapius has made these sophists the subject of a partial and fanatical history; and the learned Brucker (Hist. Philosoph., ii, 217–303) has employed much labour to illustrate their obscure lives and incomprehensible doctrines.

17 Julian., Orat., vii, 222. He swears with the most fervent and enthusiastic devotion; and trembles lest he should betray too much of these holy mysteries, which the profane might deride with an impious sardonic laugh.

18 See the fifth oration of Julian. But all the allegories which ever issued from the Platonic school are not worth the short poem of Catullus [87–54 BC] on the same extraordinary subject. The transition of Atys from the wildest enthusiasm to sober pathetic complaint, for his irretrievable loss, must inspire a man with pity, an eunuch with despair.

19 The true religion of Julian may be deduced from the Caesars, p. 308, with Spanheim's notes and illustrations, from the fragments in Cyril, ii, 57, 58, and especially from the theological oration in Solem Regem, pp. 130–58, addressed, in the confidence of friendship, to the prefect Sallust.

20 Julian adopts this gross conception, by ascribing it to his favourite Marcus Antoninus (Caesares, p. 333). The Stoics and Platonists hesitated between the analogy of the bodies and the purity of spirits; yet the gravest philosophers inclined to the whimsical fancy of Aristophanes and Lucian that an unbelieving age might starve the immortal gods. See Observations de Spanheim, pp. 284, 444, etc.

21 Ἥλιον λέγω, τὸ ζῶν ἄγαλμα καὶ ἔμψυχον, καὶ ἔννουν, καὶ ἀγαθόεργον τοῦ νοητοῦ πατρός. Julian, Epist., xli. In another place (apud Cyril., ii, 69) he calls the Sun, God, and the throne of God. Julian believed the Platonician Trinity; and only blames the Christians for preferring a mortal, to an immortal, Logos.

22 The sophists of Eunapius perform as many miracles as the saints of the desert; and the only circumstance in their favour is that they are of a less gloomy complexion. Instead of devils with horns and tails, Iamblichus evoked the genii of love, Eros and Anteros, from two adjacent fountains. Two beautiful boys issued from the water, fondly embraced him as their father, and retired at his command, pp. 26, 27.

* page 470 [supernatural agency]

23 The dexterous management of these sophists, who played their credulous pupil into each other's hands, is fairly told by Eunapius (pp. 69–76), with unsuspecting simplicity. The Abbé de la Bléterie understands, and neatly describes, the whole comedy (*Vie de Julien*, pp. 61–67).

† *page 470*   [a city in Attica]

24 When Julian, in a momentary panic, made the sign of the cross, the daemons instantly disappeared (Greg. Naz., *Orat.*, iii, 71). Gregory supposes that they were frightened, but the priests declared that they were indignant. The reader, according to the measure of his faith, will determine this profound question.

25 A dark and distant view of the terrors and joys of initiation is shown by Dion Chrysostom, Themistius, Proclus, and Stobaeus. The learned author of the *Divine Legation* has exhibited their words (i, 239, 247, 248, 280, edit. 1765), which he dexterously or forcibly applies to his own hypothesis.

26 Julian's modesty confined him to obscure and occasional hints; but Libanius expatiates with pleasure on the fasts and visions of the religious hero (*Legat. ad Julian.*, p. 157 and *Orat. Parental.*, lxxxiii, 309, 310).

27 Libanius, *Orat. Parent.*, x, 233, 234. Gallus had some reasons to suspect the secret apostasy of his brother; and in a letter, which may be received as genuine, he exhorts Julian to adhere to the religion of their *ancestors*; an argument which, as it should seem, was not yet perfectly ripe. See Julian., *Op.*, p. 454, and *Hist. de Jovien*, ii, 141.

* *page 472*   [Constantius II]

28 Gregory (iii, 50), with inhuman zeal, censures Constantius for sparing the infant apostate (κακῶς σωθέντα). His French translator (p. 265) cautiously observes that such expressions must not be *prises à la lettre* [taken literally].

29 Libanius, *Orat. Parental.*, ix, 233.

30 Fabricius (*Biblioth. Graec.*, v, viii, 88–90) and Lardner (*Heathen Testimonies*, iv, 44–47) have accurately compiled all that can now be discovered of Julian's work against the Christians.

31 About seventy years after the death of Julian, he executed a task which had been feebly attempted by Philip of Side, a prolix and contemptible writer. Even the work of Cyril has not entirely satisfied the most favourable judges, and the Abbé de la Bléterie (Preface à *L'Hist. de Jovien*, p. 30, 32) wishes that some *théologien philosophe* (a strange centaur) would undertake the refutation of Julian.

32 Libanius (*Orat. Parent.*, lxxxvii, 313), who has been suspected of assisting his friend, prefers this divine vindication (*Orat.*, ix, *in necem Julian.*, p. 255, edit. Morel) to the writings of Porphyry. His judgment may be arraigned (Socrates, iii, 23), but Libanius cannot be accused of flattery to a dead prince.

33 Libanius (*Orat. Parent.*, lviii, 283, 284) has eloquently explained the tolerating principles and conduct of his Imperial friend. In a very remarkable epistle to the people of Bostra, Julian himself (*Epist.*, lii) professes his moderation, and betrays his zeal; which is acknowledged by Ammianus, and exposed by Gregory, *Orat.*, iii, 72.

34 In Greece the temples of Minerva were opened by his express command, before the death of Constantius (Liban., *Orat. Parent.*, 55, 280); and Julian declares himself a pagan in his public manifesto to the Athenians. This unquestionable evidence may correct the hasty assertion of Ammianus, who seems to suppose Constantinople to be the place where he discovered [i.e. revealed] his attachment to the gods.

35 Ammian., xxii, 5. Sozomen, v, 5. *Bestia moritur, tranquillitas redit . . . omnes episcopi, qui de propriis sedibus fuerant exterminati, per indulgentiam novi principis ad ecclesias redeunt.* ['The beast is dead, tranquillity returns . . . All the bishops, who had been expelled from their sees, return to their churches, thanks to the indulgence of the new ruler.'] Jerom., *adversus Luciferianos*, ii, 143. Optatus accuses the Donatists for owing their safety to an apostate (ii, 16, 36, 37, edit. Dupin).

* *page 475* [priest, who inspected the entrails of the sacrificial animals]

36 The restoration of the pagan worship is described by Julian (*Misopogon*, p. 346), Libanius (*Orat. Parent.*, 60, 286, 287, and *Orat. Consular. ad Julian.*, pp. 245, 246, edit. Morel), Ammianus (xxii, 12), and Gregory Nazianzen (*Orat.*, iv, 121). These writers agree in the essential, and even minute, facts; but the different lights in which they view the extreme devotion of Julian are expressive of the gradations of self-applause, passionate admiration, mild reproof, and partial invective.

37 See Julian., *Epistol.*, xlix, lxii, lxiii, and a long and curious fragment without beginning or end, pp. 288–305. The supreme pontiff derides the Mosaic history and the Christian discipline, prefers the Greek poets to the Hebrew prophets, and palliates, with the skill of a Jesuit, the *relative* worship of images.

38 The exultation of Julian (p. 301) that these impious sects, and even their writings, are extinguished may be consistent enough with the sacerdotal character: but it is unworthy of a philosopher to wish that any opinions and arguments the most repugnant to his own should be concealed from the knowledge of mankind.

39 Yet he insinuates that the Christians, under the pretence of charity, inveigled children from their religion and parents, conveyed them on shipboard, and devoted those victims to a life of poverty or servitude in a remote country (p. 305). Had the charge been proved, it was his duty, not to complain, but to punish.

40 Gregory Nazianzen is facetious, ingenious, and argumentative; *Orat.*, iii, 101, 102, etc. He ridicules the folly of such vain imitation; and amuses himself with inquiring, what lessons, moral or theological, could be extracted from the Grecian fables.

41 He accuses one of his pontiffs of a secret confederacy with the Christian bishops and presbyters: *Epist.* lxii. Ὁρῶν οὖν πολλὴν μὲν ὀλιγωρίαν οὖσαν ἡμῖν πρὸς τοὺς θεούς, and again, ἡμᾶς δὲ οὕτω ῥαθύμως, etc. ['seeing much indifference towards the gods among our co-religionists, so light-heartedly do we, etc.'] *Epist.*, lxiii.

42 He praises the fidelity of Callixene, priestess of Ceres, who had been twice as constant as Penelope, and rewards her with the priesthood of the Phrygian goddess at Pessinus. (Julian., *Epist.*, xxi.) He applauds the firmness of Sopater of Hierapolis, who had been repeatedly pressed by Constantius and Gallus to *apostatise.* (*Epist.*, xxvii, 401).

43 Ὁ δὲ νομίζων ἀδελφὰ λόγους τε καὶ θεῶν ἱερά, *Orat. Parent.*, 77, 302. The same sentiment is frequently inculcated by Julian, Libanius, and the rest of their party.

44 The curiosity and credulity of the emperor, who tried every mode of divination, are fairly exposed by Ammianus, xxii, 12.

45 Julian., *Epist.*, xxxviii. Three other epistles (xv, xvi, xxxix) in the same style of friendship and confidence are addressed to the philosopher Maximus.

46 Eunapius (*in Maximo*, pp. 77, 78, 79, and *in Chrysanthio*, pp. 147, 148) has minutely related these anecdotes, which he conceives to be the most important

events of the age. Yet he fairly confesses the frailty of Maximus. His reception at Constantinople is described by Libanius (*Orat. Parent.*, 86, p. 301) and Ammianus (xxii, 7).

47 Chrysanthius, who had refused to quit Lydia, was created high priest of the province. His cautious and temperate use of power secured him after the revolution; and he lived in peace; while Maximus, Priscus, etc. were persecuted by the Christian ministers. See the adventures of those fanatic sophists, collected by Brucker, ii, 281–93.

48 See Libanius (*Orat. Parent.*, chs 101, 102; pp. 324, 325, 326) and Eunapius (*Vit. Sophist. in Proaeresio*, p. 126). Some students, whose expectations perhaps were groundless or extravagant, retired in disgust. Greg. Naz., *Orat.*, iv, 120. It is strange that we should not be able to contradict the title of one of Tillemont's chapters (*Hist. des Empereurs*, iv, 960): *La Cour de Julien est pleine de philosophes et de gens perdus.* ['The court of Julian is full of philosophers and lost souls.'].

49 Under the reign of Lewis XIV his subjects of every rank aspired to the glorious title of *Convertisseur* [i.e. converter], expressive of their zeal and success in making proselytes. The word and idea are growing obsolete in France; may they never be introduced into England!

50 See the strong expressions of Libanius, which were probably those of Julian himself. (*Orat. Parent.*, 59, 285.)

51 When Gregory Nazianzen (*Orat.*, x, p. 167) is desirous to magnify the Christian firmness of his brother Caesarius, physician to the Imperial court, he owns that Caesarius disputed with a formidable adversary, πολὺν ἐν ὅπλοις, καὶ μέγαν ἐν λόγων δεινότητι ['mighty in war and with great cleverness in argument']. In his invectives he scarcely allows any share of wit or courage to the apostate.

52 Julian., *Epist.*, xxxviii; Ammianus, xxii, 12. *Adeo ut in dies paene singulos milites carnis distentiore sagina victitantes incultius, potusque aviditate corrupti, humeris impositi transeuntium per plateas, ex publicis aedibus . . . ad sua diversoria portarentur.* The devout prince and the indignant historian describe the same scene; and in Illyricum or Antioch similar causes must have produced similar effects.

53 Gregory (*Orat.*, iii, 74, 75, 83–86) and Libanius (*Orat. Parent.*, lxxxi, lxxxii, pp. 307, 308) περὶ ταύτην τὴν σπουδὴν, οὐκ ἀρνοῦμαι πλοῦτον ἀνηλῶσθαι μέγαν. ['I do not deny that large sums were spent in the cause of this zeal.'] The sophist owns and justifies the expense of these military conversions.

54 Julian's epistle (xxv) is addressed to the community of the Jews. Aldus (Venet. 1499) has branded it with an εἰ γνήσιος [if it is genuine]; but this stigma is justly removed by the subsequent editors, Petavius and Spanheim. The epistle is mentioned by Sozomen (v, 22), and the purport of it is confirmed by Gregory (*Orat.*, iv, 111) and by Julian himself (*Fragment*, p. 295).

55 The Misnah [usually Mishnah, Jewish book of commentary on the Bible] denounced death against those who abandoned the foundation. The judgment of zeal is explained by Marsham (*Canon. Chron.*, pp. 161, 162, edit. fol. London, 1672) and Basnage (*Hist. des Juifs.*, viii, 120). Constantine made a law to protect Christian converts from Judaism. *Cod. Theod.*, xvi, viii, 1; Godefroy, vi, 215.

56 *Et interea* (during the civil war of Magnentius) *Iudaeorum seditio, qui Patricium nefarie in regni speciem sustulerunt, oppressa.* ['Meanwhile . . . there took place the suppression of a rebellion of the Jews, who wickedly supported Patricius as a sort of independent ruler.'] Aurelius Victor, *in Constantio*, ch. xlii. See Tillemont, *Hist. des Empereurs*, iv, 379 in 4to.

57 The city and synagogue of Tiberias are curiously described by Reland, *Palestin.*, ii, 1036–42.

58 Basnage has fully illustrated the state of the Jews under Constantine and his successors (viii, iv, 111–53).

59 Reland (*Palestin.*, i, 309, 390; iii, 838) describes, with learning and perspicuity, Jerusalem, and the face of the adjacent country.

60 I have consulted a rare and curious treatise of M. d'Anville (*sur l'ancienne Jerusalem*, Paris, 1747, p. 75). The circumference of the ancient city (Euseb., *Praeparat. Evangel.*, ix, 36) was twenty-seven stadia, or 2550 *toises*. A plan taken on the spot assigns no more than 1980 for the modern town. The circuit is defined by natural landmarks which cannot be mistaken or removed.

61 See two curious passages in Jerome (i, 102; vi, 315), and the ample details of Tillemont (*Hist. des Empereurs*, i, 569; ii, 289, 294, 4to edition).

62 Eusebius, *in Vit. Constantin.*, iii, 25–47, 51–53. The emperor likewise built churches at Bethlem, the Mount of Olives, and the oak of Mambre. The holy sepulchre is described by Sandys (*Travels*, pp. 125–33), and curiously delineated by Le Bruyn (*Voyage au Levant*, pp. 288–96).

63 The Itinerary from Bourdeaux to Jerusalem was composed in the year 333, for the use of pilgrims; among whom Jerome (i, 126) mentions the Britons and the Indians. The causes of this superstitious fashion are discussed in the learned and judicious preface of Wesseling (*Itin.*, pp. 537–45).

* *page 480* [mother of Constantine I]

64 Cicero (*de Finibus*, v, 1) has beautifully expressed the common sense of mankind.

65 Baronius (*Annal. Eccles.*, AD 326, No. 42–50) and Tillemont (*Mém. Ecclés.*, vii, 8–16) are the historians and champions of the miraculous *invention* of the cross, under the reign of Constantine. Their oldest witnesses are Paulinus, Sulpicius Severus, Rufinus, Ambrose, and perhaps Cyril of Jerusalem. The silence of Eusebius and the Bourdeaux pilgrim, which satisfies those who think, perplexes those who believe. See Jortin's sensible remarks, ii, 238–48.

66 This multiplication is asserted by Paulinus (*Epist.*, xxxvii. See Dupin, *Biblioth. Ecclés.*, iii, 149), who seems to have improved a rhetorical flourish of Cyril into a real fact. The same supernatural privilege must have been communicated to the Virgin's milk (Erasmi *Opera*, i, 778, Lug. Bat. 1703, *in Colloq. de Peregrinat. Religionis ergo*), saints' heads, etc. and other relics, which were repeated in so many different churches.

67 Jerome (i, 103), who resided in the neighbouring village of Bethlehem, describes the vices of Jerusalem from his personal experience.

68 Gregor. Nyssen., *apud* Wesseling, p. 539. The whole epistle, which condemns either the use or the abuse of religious pilgrimage, is painful to the Catholic divines, while it is dear and familiar to our Protestant polemics.

69 He renounced his orthodox ordination, officiated as a deacon, and was reordained by the hands of the Arians. But Cyril afterwards changed with the times, and prudently conformed to the Nicene faith. Tillemont (*Mém. Ecclés.*, tom. viii), who treats his memory with tenderness and respect, has thrown his virtues into the text, and his faults into the notes, in decent obscurity, at the end of the volume.

70 *Imperii sui memoriam magnitudine operum gestiens propagare* ['desirous of spreading the fame of his rule by the grandeur of his works']. Ammian., xxiii, 1. The temple

of Jerusalem had been famous even among the Gentiles. *They* had many temples in each city (at Sichem five, at Gaza eight, at Rome four hundred and twenty-four); but the wealth and religion of the Jewish nation was centred in one spot.

71 The secret intentions of Julian are revealed by the late bishop of Gloucester, the learned and dogmatic Warburton; who, with the authority of a theologian, prescribes the motives and conduct of the Supreme Being. The discourse entitled *Julian* (2nd editon, London, 1751) is strongly marked with all the peculiarities which are imputed to the Warburtonian school.

72 I shelter myself behind Maimonides, Marsham, Spencer, Le Clerc, Warburton, etc. who have fairly derided the fears, the folly, and the falsehood of some superstitious divines. See *Divine Legation*, iv, 25, etc.

73 Julian (*Fragment*, p. 295) respectfully styles him μέγας θεός [a great god], and mentions him elsewhere (*Epist.* lxiii) with still higher reverence. He doubly condemns the Christians, for believing and for renouncing the religion of the Jews. Their Deity was a *true*, but not the *only*, God. Apud Cyril., ix, 305, 306.

74 1 Kings, viii, 63; 2 Chronicles, vii, 5; Joseph., *Antiquitat. Judaic.*, viii, 4, 431, edit. Havercamp. As the blood and smoke of so many hecatombs might be inconvenient, Lightfoot, the Christian Rabbi, removes them by a miracle. Le Clerc (*ad loca*) is bold enough to suspect the fidelity of the numbers.

75 Julian, *Epist.* xxix, xxx. La Blèterie has neglected to translate the second of these epistles.

76 See the zeal and impatience of the Jews in Gregory Nazianzen (*Orat.*, iv, 111) and Theodoret (iii, 20).

77 Built by Omar, the second Khalif, who died AD 644. This great mosque covers the whole consecrated ground of the Jewish temple, and constitutes almost a square of 760 *toises*, or one Roman mile in circumference. See d'Anville, *Jérusalem*, p. 45.

78 Ammianus records the consuls of the year 363, before he proceeds to mention the *thoughts* of Julian. *Templum . . . instaurare sumptibus cogitabat immodicis.* ['He contemplated restoring the temple on a lavish scale.'] Warburton has a secret wish to anticipate the design; but he must have understood, from former examples, that the execution of such a work would have demanded many years.

79 The subsequent witnesses, Socrates, Sozomen, Theodoret, Philostorgius, etc. add contradictions rather than authority. Compare the objections of Basnage (*Hist. des Juifs*, viii, 157–68) with Warburton's answer (*Julian*, 174–258). The bishop has ingeniously explained the miraculous crosses which appeared on the garments of the spectators by a similar instance, and the natural effects of lightning.

80 Ambros., ii, xl, 946, edit. Benedictin. He composed this fanatic epistle (AD 388) to justify a bishop, who had been condemned by the civil magistrate for burning a synagogue.

81 Chrysostom, i, 580, *advers. Iudaeos et Gentes*; ii, 574, *de Sancto Babyla*, edit. Montfaucon. I have followed the common and natural supposition; but the learned Benedictine, who dates the composition of these sermons in the year 383, is confident they were never pronounced from the pulpit.

82 Greg. Nazianzen, *Orat.*, iv, 110–13. Τὸ δὲ οὖν περιβόητον πᾶσι θαῦμα, καὶ οὐδὲ τοῖς ἀθέοις αὐτοῖς ἀπιστούμενον λέξων ἔρχομαι. ['The miracle which I am about to relate is well known to all and is not disbelieved even by atheists.']

83 Ammian., xxiii, 1. *Cum itaque rei fortiter instaret Alypius, iuvaretque provinciae*

rector, metuendi globi flammarum prope fundamenta crebris assultibus erumpentes fecere locum exustis aliquoties operantibus inaccessum: hocque modo elemento destinatius repellente, cessavit inceptum. Warburton labours (pp. 60–90) to extort a confession of the miracle from the mouths of Julian and Libanius, and to employ the evidence of a rabbi who lived in the fifteenth century. Such witnesses can only be received by a very favourable judge.

84 Dr Lardner, perhaps alone of the Christian critics, presumes to doubt the truth of this famous miracle (*Jewish and Heathen Testimonies*, iv, 47–71). The silence of Jerome would lead to a suspicion that the same story, which was celebrated at a distance, might be despised on the spot.

85 Greg. Naz., *Orat.*, iii., 81. And this law was confirmed by the invariable practice of Julian himself. Warburton has justly observed (p. 35) that the Platonists believed in the mysterious virtue of words; and Julian's dislike for the name of Christ might proceed from superstition, as well as from contempt.

86 *Fragment*, Julian, p. 288. He derides the μωρία Γαλιλαίων [the folly of the Galilaeans] (*Epist.* vii), and so far loses sight of the principles of toleration as to wish (*Epist.* xlii) ἄκοντας ἰᾶσθαι [to cure them against their will].

87 οὐ γάρ μοι θέμις ἐστὶ κομιζέμεν ἢ ἐλεαίρειν
ἄνδρας οἵ κε θεοῖσιν ἀπέχθωντ᾽ ἀθανάτοισιν.

['It is not right for me to show solicitude or pity for men who make themselves hateful to the immortal gods.'] These two lines, which Julian has changed and perverted in the true spirit of a bigot (*Epist.* xlix), are taken from the speech of Aeolus, when he refuses to grant Ulysses a fresh supply of winds (*Odyss.*, x, 73). Libanius (*Orat. Parental.*, lix, 286) attempts to justify this partial behaviour by an apology in which persecution peeps through the mask of candour.

88 These laws which affected the clergy may be found in the slight hints of Julian himself (*Epist.* lii), in the vague declarations of Gregory (*Orat.*, iii, 86, 87), and in the positive assertions of Sozomen (v, 5).

89 *Inclemens . . . perenni obruendum silentio.* ['Lacking in mercy . . . should be buried in eternal silence.'] Ammian., xxii, 10; xxv, 5.

90 The edict itself, which is still extant among the epistles of Julian (xlii), may be compared with the loose invectives of Gregory (*Orat.*, iii, 96). Tillemont (*Mém. Ecclés.*, vii, 1291–94) has collected the seeming differences of ancients and moderns. They may be easily reconciled. The Christians were *directly* forbid to teach, they were *indirectly* forbid to learn; since they would not frequent the schools of the Pagans.

91 *Codex Theodos.*, xiii, iii, *de medicis et professoribus*, leg. 5 (published the 17th June, received, at Spoleto in Italy, the 29th of July, AD 363), with Godefroy's Illustrations, v, 31.

92 Orosius celebrates their disinterested resolution, *Sicut a maioribus nostris compertum habemus, omnes ubique propemodum . . . officium quam fidem deserere maluerunt* ['As we know from our ancestors, they all nearly everywhere . . . preferred to abandon their positions rather than their faith'], vii, 30. Proaeresius, a Christian sophist, refused to accept the partial favour of the emperor. Hieronym., *in Chron.*, 185, edit. Scaliger. Eunapius, *in Proaeresio*, p. 126.

93 They had recourse to the expedient of composing books for their own schools. Within a few months Apollinaris produced his Christian imitations of Homer (a sacred history in xxiv books), Pindar, Euripides, and Menander; and Sozomen is satisfied that they equalled, or excelled, the originals.

94 It was the instruction of Julian to his magistrates (*Epist.* vii), προτιμᾶσθαι μέν τοι τοὺς θεοσεβεῖς καὶ πάνυ φημὶ δεῖν. ['I insist that special preference be given to those who honour the gods.'] Sozomen (v, 18) and Socrates (iii, 13) must be reduced to the standard of Gregory (*Orat.*, iii, 95), not less prone to exaggeration, but more restrained by the actual knowledge of his contemporary readers.

95 ψήφῳ θεῶν καὶ διδοὺς καὶ μὴ διδούς. ['He gave or withheld at the gods' choice.'] Libanius, *Orat. Parent.*, 88, 314.

96 Greg. Naz., *Orat.*, iii, 74, 91, 92; Socrates, iii, 14; Theodoret, iii, 6. Some drawback may however be allowed for the violence of *their* zeal, not less partial than the zeal of Julian.

97 If we compare the gentle language of Libanius (*Orat. Parent.*, 60, 286) with the passionate exclamations of Gregory (*Orat.*, iii, 86, 87), we may find it difficult to persuade ourselves that the two orators are really describing the same events.

98 Restan, or Arethusa, at the equal distance of sixteen miles between Emesa (Hems) and Epiphania (Hamath) was founded, or at least named, by Seleucus Nicator. Its peculiar era dates from the year of Rome 685 according to the medals of the city. In the decline of the Seleucides, Emesa and Arethusa were usurped by the Arab Sampsiceramus, whose posterity, the vassals of Rome, were not extinguished in the reign of Vespasian. See d'Anville's Maps and *Géographie Ancienne*, ii, 134. Wesseling, *Itineraria*, p. 188 and Noris., *Epoch. Syro-Macedon.*, pp. 80, 481, 482.

99 Sozomen, v, 10. It is surprising that Gregory and Theodoret should suppress a circumstance which, in their eyes, must have enhanced the religious merit of the confessor.

100 The sufferings and constancy of Mark, which Gregory has so tragically painted (*Orat.*, iii, 88–91), are confirmed by the unexceptionable and reluctant evidence of Libanius. Μάρκος ἐκεῖνος κρεμάμενος, καὶ μαστιγούμενος, και τοῦ πώγωνος αὐτῷ τιλλομένου πάντα ἐνεγκὼν ἀνδρείως νῦν ἰσόθεός ἐστι ταῖς τιμαῖς, κᾶν φανῇ που περιμάχητος εὐθύς. *Epist.* 730, p. 350, 351, edit. Wolf. Amstel. 1738. ['Mark, who was hung up, flogged, and had his beard pulled out, bore everything bravely, and is now equal in honour to a god, and mobbed if he makes an appearance.']

101 περιμάχητος *certatim eum sibi (Christiani) vindicant*. ['The Christians zealously claim him as a saint.'] It is thus that La Croze and Wolfius (*ad loc.*) have explained a Greek word whose true signification had been mistaken by former interpreters, and even by Le Clerc (*Bibliothèque Ancienne et Moderne*, iii, 371). Yet Tillemont is strangely puzzled to understand (*Mém. Ecclés.*, vii, 1309) *how* Gregory and Theodoret could mistake a Semi-Arian bishop for a saint.

102 See the probable advice of Sallust (Greg. Nazianzen, *Orat.*, iii, 90, 91). Libanius intercedes for a similar offender, lest they should find many *Marks;* yet he allows that, if Orion had secreted the consecrated wealth, he deserved to suffer the punishment of Marsyas: to be flayed alive (*Epist.*, 730, 349–551).

* *page 486* [In Chapter 19, Gibbon refers to the evidence of Gregory Nazianzen that Julian had been saved from the violence of the soldiers by the bishop of Arethusa when Constantius had become emperor.]

103 Gregory (*Orat.*, iii, 90) is satisfied that, by saving the apostate, Mark had deserved still more than he had suffered.

104 The grove and temple of Daphne are described by Strabo (xvi, 1089, 1090,

edit. Amstel. 1707), Libanius (*Nenia*, pp. 185, 188, *Antiochic. Orat.* xi, p 380, 381), and Sozomen (v, 19). Wesseling (*Itinerar.* p. 581) and Casaubon (*ad Hist. August.*, p. 64) illustrate this curious subject.

105 *Simulacrum in eo Olympiaci Iovis imitamenti aequiparans magnitudinem.* ['His statue was equal in size to that of the statue of Jupiter at Olympia.'] Ammian., xxii, 13. The Olympic Jupiter was sixty feet high, and his bulk was consequently equal to that of a thousand men. See a curious *Mémoire* of the Abbé Gedoyn (*Académie des Inscriptions*, ix, p. 198).

† *page 486* [in Greece]

‡ *page 486* [Castalia, a fountain on Mount Parnassus in Greece, sacred to Apollo and the muses]

106 Hadrian read the history of his future fortunes on a leaf dipped in the Castalian stream: a trick which, according to the physician Vandale (*de Oraculis*, pp. 281, 282), might be easily performed by chemical preparations. The emperor stopped the source of such dangerous knowledge; which was again opened by the devout curiosity of Julian.

107 It was purchased, AD 44, in the year 92 of the era of Antioch (Noris., *Epoch. Syro-Maced.*, pp. 139–74) for the term of ninety Olympiads. But the Olympic games of Antioch were not regularly celebrated till the reign of Commodus. See the curious details in the Chronicle of John Malala (i, 293, 372–81), a writer whose merit and authority are confined within the limits of his native city.

* *page 486* [a Greek city near Olympia]

108 Fifteen talents of gold, bequeathed by Sosibius, who died in the reign of Augustus. The theatrical merits of the Syrian cities, in the age of Constantine, are compared in the *Expositio totius Mundi*, p. 6 (Hudson, *Geograph. Minor.*, tom. iii).

** *page 486* [Daphne was turned into a laurel-tree.]

109 *Avidio Cassio Syriacas legiones dedi luxuria diffluentes et* Daphnicis *moribus.* ['I entrusted to Avidius Cassius the legions of Syria, enervated by luxurious living and the customs of the groves of Daphne.'] These are the words of the emperor Marcus Antoninus in an original letter preserved by his biographer in *Hist. August.*, p. 41. Cassius dismissed or punished every soldier who was seen at Daphne.

110 *Aliquantum agrorum Daphnensibus dedit* (Pompey), *quo lucus ibi spatiosior fieret; delectatus amoenitate loci et aquarum abundantia.* ['He (Pompey) donated some land to enlarge the groves of Daphne, charmed by the delights of the place and its many fountains.'] Eutropius, vi, 14. Sextus Rufus, *de Provinciis*, ch. 16.

111 Julian (*Misopogon*, pp. 361, 362) discovers his own character with that naïveté, that unconscious simplicity, which always constitutes genuine humour.

112 Babylas is named by Eusebius in the sucession of the bishops of Antioch (*Hist. Ecclés.*, vi, 29, 39). His triumph over two emperors (the first fabulous, the second historical) is diffusely celebrated by Chrysostom (ii, 536–79, edit. Montfaucon). Tillemont (*Mém. Ecclés.*, iii, ii, 287–302, 459–65) becomes almost a sceptic.

113 Ecclesiastical critics, particularly those who love relics, exult in the confession of Julian (*Misopogon*, p. 361) and Libanius (*Nenia*, p. 185), that Apollo was disturbed by the vicinity of *one* dead man. Yet Ammianus (xxii, 12) clears and purifies the whole ground, according to the rites which the Athenians formerly practised in the isle of Delos.

114 Julian (in *Misopogon*, p. 361) rather insinuates than affirms their guilt. Ammianus (xxii, 13) treats the imputation as *levissimus rumor* [a very faint rumour], and relates the story with extraordinary candour.

115 *Quo non atroci casu repente consumpto, ad id usque imperatoris ira provexit, ut quaestiones agitare iuberet solito acriores* (yet Julian blames the lenity of the magistrates of Antioch), *et maiorem ecclesiam Antiochiae claudi*. ['After this not very serious incident, the emperor's anger was such that he ordered more painful forms of torture than usual to be applied, and the great church of Antioch to be closed.'] This interdiction was performed with some circumstances of indignity and profanation; and the seasonable death of the principal actor, Julian's uncle, is related with much superstitious complacency by the Abbé de la Bléterie. *Vie de Julien*, pp. 362–69.

116 Besides the ecclesiastical historians, who are more or less to be suspected, we may allege the passion of St Theodore, in the *Acta Sincera* of Ruinart, p 591. The complaint of Julian gives it an original and authentic air.

117 Julian, *Misopogon*, p. 361.

118 See Gregory Nazianzen, *Orat.*, iii, 87. Sozomen (v, c. 9) may be considered as an original, though not impartial, witness. He was a native of Gaza, and had conversed with the confessor Zeno, who, as bishop of Maiuma, lived to the age of an hundred (vii, 28). Philostorgius (vii, 4, with Godefroy's *Dissertations*, p. 284) adds some tragic circumstances of Christians who were *literally* sacrificed at the altars of the gods, etc.

119 The life and death of George of Cappadocia are described by Ammianus (xxii, 11), Gregory Nazianzen (*Orat.*, xxi, 382, 385, 389, 390), and Epiphanius (*Haeres.*, lxxvi). The invectives of the two saints might not deserve much credit, unless they were confirmed by the testimony of the cool and impartial infidel.

120 After the massacre of George, the emperor Julian repeatedly sent orders to preserve the library for his own use, and to torture the slaves who might be suspected of secreting any books. He praises the merit of the collection, from whence he had borrowed and transcribed several manuscripts while he pursued his studies in Cappadocia. He could wish indeed that the works of the Galilaeans might perish; but he requires an exact account even of those theological volumes, lest other treatises more valuable should be confounded in their loss. Julian., *Epist.*, ix, xxxvi.

121 Philostorgius, with cautious malice, insinuates their guilt, καὶ τοῦ Ἀθανασίου γνώμην στρατηγῆσαι τῆς πράξεως [Athanasius was behind this]. vii, 2, Godefroy, p. 267.

122 *Cineres proiecit in mare, id metuens, ut clamabat, ne, collectis supremis, aedes illis exstruerent ut reliquis, qui deviare a religione compulsi pertulere cruciabiles poenas, ad usque gloriosam mortem intemerata fide progressi, et nunc martyres appellantur*. Ammian., xxii, 11. Epiphanius proves to the Arians that George was not a martyr.

123 Some Donatists (Optatus Milev., pp. 60, 303, edit. Dupin; and Tillemont, *Mém. Ecclés.*, vi, 713, in 4to) and Priscillianists (Tillemont, *Mém Ecclés.*, viii, 517, in 4to) have in like manner usurped the honours of Catholic saints and martyrs.

124 The saints of Cappadocia, Basil and the Gregories, were ignorant of their holy companion. Pope Gelasius (AD 494), the first Catholic who acknowledges St

George, places him among the martyrs, *qui Deo magis quam hominibus noti sunt* ['better known to God than to men']. He rejects his Acts as the composition of heretics. Some, perhaps not the oldest, of the spurious Acts are still extant; and, through a cloud of fiction, we may yet distinguish the combat which St George of Cappadocia sustained, in the presence of Queen *Alexandra*, against the *magician Athanasius*.

125 This transformation is not given as absolutely certain, but as *extremely* probable. See the *Longueruana*, i, 194.

126 A curious history of the worship of St George, from the sixth century (when he was already revered in Palestine, in Armenia, at Rome, and at Treves in Gaul), might be extracted from Dr Heylin (*History of* [that most famous saynt and souldier of Christ Jesus] *St George*, 2nd edition, London, 1633, in 4to, p. 429), and the Bollandists (Act. SS. Mens. April., iii, 120–63). His fame and popularity in Europe, and especially in England, proceeded from the Crusades.

127 Julian., *Epist.*, xliii.

128 Julian., *Epist.*, x. He allowed his friends to assuage his anger. Ammian., xxii, 11.

129 See Athanas., *ad Rufin.*, ii, 40, 41; and Greg. Nazianzen, *Orat.*, iii, [*leg.* xxi] pp. 395, 396, who justly states the temperate zeal of the primate as much more meritorious than his prayers, his fasts, his persecutions, etc.

130 I have not leisure to follow the blind obstinacy of Lucifer of Cagliari. See his adventures in Tillemont (*Mém. Ecclés.*, vii, 900–16); and observe how the colour of the narrative insensibly changes, as the confessor becomes a schismatic.

131 *Assensus est huic sententiae Occidens, et, per tam necessarium concilium, Satanae faucibus mundus ereptus.* ['The West assented to this verdict, and thanks to that very necessary council, the world was snatched from the jaws of Satan.']. The lively and artful Dialogue of Jerome against the Luciferians (ii, 135–55) exhibits an original picture of the ecclesiastical policy of the time.

132 Tillemont, who supposes that George was massacred in August, crowds the actions of Athanasius into a narrow space (*Mém. Ecclés.*, viii, 360). An original fragment, published by the Marquis Maffei, from the old Chapter-library of Verona (*Osservazioni Litterarie*, iii, 60–92) affords many important dates, which are authenticated by the computation of Egyptian months.

* *page 492* [the first day]

133 τὸν μιαρὸν, ὃς ἐτόλμησεν Ἑλληνίδας, ἐπ᾽ ἐμοῦ, γυναῖκας τῶν ἐπισήμων βαπτίσαι διώκεσθαι. I have preserved the ambiguous sense of the last word, the ambiguity of a tyrant who wished to find, or to create, guilt.

134 The three epistles of Julian which explain his intentions and conduct with regard to Athanasius should be disposed in the following chronological order, xxvi, x, vi. See likewise Greg. Nazianzen, xxi, 393; Sozomen, v, 15; Socrates, iii, 14; Theodoret, iii, 9; and Tillemont, *Mém. Ecclés.*, viii, 361–68, who has used some materials prepared by the Bollandists.

135 See the fair confession of Gregory (*Orat.*, iii, 61, 62).

136 Hear the furious and absurd complaint of Optatus (*de Schismat. Donatist.*, ii, 16, 17).

† *page 492* [in Asia Minor]

137 Greg. Nazianzen., *Orat.*, iii, 91; iv, 133. He praises the rioters of Caesarea, τούτων δὲ τῶν μεγαλοφυῶν καὶ θερμῶν εἰς εὐσέβειαν [these noble-minded people,

zealous in the cause of piety]. See Sozomen, v, 4, 11. Tillemont (*Mém. Ecclés.*, vii, 649, 650) owns that their behaviour was not *dans l'ordre commun* [i.e. conventional]: but he is perfectly satisfied, as the great St Basil always celebrated the festival of these blessed martyrs.

138 Julian determined a lawsuit against the new Christian city at Maiuma, the port of Gaza; and his sentence, though it might be imputed to bigotry, was never reversed by his successors. Sozomen, v, 3; Reland, *Palestine*, ii, 791.

139 Gregory (*Orat.*, iii, 93, 94, 95; *Orat.*, iv, 114) pretends to speak from the information of Julian's confidants, whom Orosius (vii, 30) could not have seen.

140 Gregory (*Orat.*, iii, 91) charges the Apostate with secret sacrifices of boys and girls; and positively affirms that the dead bodies were thrown into the Orontes. See Theodoret, iii, 26, 27; and the equivocal candour of the Abbé de la Bléterie, *Vie de Julien*, pp. 351, 352. Yet *contemporary* malice could not impute to Julian the troops of martyrs, more especially in the West, which Baronius so greedily swallows, and Tillemont so faintly rejects (*Mém. Ecclés.*, vii, 1295– 1315).

141 The resignation of Gregory is truly edifying (*Orat.*, iv, 123, 124). Yet, when an officer of Julian attempted to seize the Church of Nazianzus, he would have lost his life, if he had not yielded to the zeal of the bishop and people (*Orat.*, xix, 308). See the reflections of Chrysostom, as they are alleged by Tillemont (*Mém. Ecclés.*, vii, 575).

CHAPTER 24

*Residence of Julian at Antioch – his successful expedition
against the Persians – passage of the Tigris – the retreat
and death of Julian – election of Jovian – he saves
the Roman army by a disgraceful treaty*

The philosophical fable which Julian composed under the name of the *Caesars*[1] is one of the most agreeable and instructive productions of ancient wit.[2] During the freedom and equality of the days of the Saturnalia,* Romulus prepared a feast for the deities of Olympus, who had adopted him as a worthy associate, and for the Roman princes, who had reigned over his martial people and the vanquished nations of the earth. The immortals were placed in just order on their thrones of state, and the table of the Caesars was spread below the Moon, in the upper region of the air. The tyrants, who would have disgraced the society of gods and men, were thrown headlong, by the inexorable Nemesis, into the Tartarean abyss. The rest of the Caesars successively advanced to their seats; and, as they passed, the vices, the defects, the blemishes of their respective characters were maliciously noticed by old Silenus, a laughing moralist, who disguised the wisdom of a philosopher under the mask of a Bacchanal.[3] As soon as the feast was ended, the voice of Mercury proclaimed the will of Jupiter, that a celestial crown should be the reward of superior merit. Julius Caesar, Augustus, Trajan, and Marcus Antoninus were selected as the most illustrious candidates; the effeminate Constantine[4] was not excluded from this honourable competition, and the great Alexander was invited to dispute the prize of glory with the Roman heroes. Each of the candidates was allowed to display the merit of his own exploits; but, in the judgment of the gods, the modest silence of Marcus pleaded more powerfully than the elaborate orations of his haughty rivals. When the judges of this awful contest proceeded to examine the heart and to scrutinise the springs of action, the superiority of the Imperial Stoic appeared still more decisive and conspicuous.[5] Alexander and Caesar, Augustus, Trajan, and Constantine, acknowledged with a blush that fame or power or pleasure had been the important object of *their* labours; but the gods themselves beheld, with reverence and love, a virtuous mortal, who had practised on the throne the lessons of philosophy; and who, in a state of human imperfection, had aspired to imitate the moral attributes of the Deity. The value of this agreeable composition (the *Caesars* of Julian) is enhanced by the rank of the author. A prince, who delineates with freedom the vices and virtues of his predecessors, subscribes,* in every line, the censure or approbation of his own conduct.

In the cool moments of reflection, Julian preferred the useful and benevolent virtues of Antoninus; but his ambitious spirit was inflamed by the glory of Alexander; and he solicited, with equal ardour, the esteem of the wise and the applause of the multitude. In the season of life, when the powers of the mind and body enjoy the most active vigour, the emperor, who was instructed by the experience, and animated by the success, of the German war, resolved to signalise his reign by some more splendid and memorable achievement. The ambassadors of the East, from the continent of India and the isle of Ceylon,[6] had respectfully saluted the Roman purple.[7] The nations of the West esteemed and dreaded the personal virtues of Julian, both in peace and war. He despised the trophies of a Gothic victory,[8] and was satisfied that the rapacious Barbarians of the Danube would be restrained from any future violation of the faith of treaties by the terror of his name and the additional fortifications with which he strengthened the Thracian and Illyrian frontiers. The successor of Cyrus and Artaxerxes was the only rival whom he deemed worthy of his arms; and he resolved, by the final conquest of Persia, to chastise the haughty nation which had so long resisted and insulted the majesty of Rome.[9] As soon as the Persian monarch[†] was informed that the throne of Constantius was filled by a prince of a very different character, he condescended to make some artful, or perhaps sincere, overtures towards a negotiation of peace. But the pride of Sapor was astonished by the firmness of Julian; who sternly declared that he would never consent to hold a peaceful conference among the flames and ruins of the cities of Mesopotamia; and who added, with a smile of contempt, that it was needless to treat by ambassadors, as he himself had determined to visit speedily the court of Persia. The impatience of the emperor urged the diligence of the military preparations. The generals were named; a formidable army was destined for this important service; and Julian, marching from Constantinople through the provinces of Asia Minor, arrived at Antioch about eight months after the death of his predecessor. His ardent desire to march into the heart of Persia was checked by the indispensable duty of regulating the state of the empire; by his zeal to revive the worship of the gods; and by the advice of his wisest friends, who represented the necessity of allowing the salutary interval of winter quarters, to restore the exhausted strength of the legions of Gaul and the discipline and spirit of the Eastern troops. Julian was persuaded to fix, till the ensuing spring, his residence at Antioch, among a people maliciously disposed to deride the haste, and to censure the delays, of their sovereign.[10]

If Julian had flattered himself that his personal connection with the capital of the East would be productive of mutual satisfaction to the prince and people, he made a very false estimate of his own character,

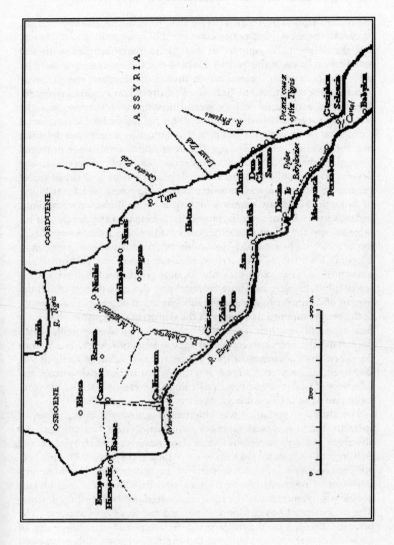

Julian's campaign against the Persians, AD 363

and of the manners of Antioch.[11] The warmth of the climate disposed the natives to the most intemperate enjoyment of tranquillity and opulence; and the lively licentiousness of the Greeks was blended with the hereditary softness of the Syrians. Fashion was the only law, pleasure the only pursuit, and the splendour of dress and furniture was the only distinction of the citizens of Antioch. The arts of luxury were honoured; the serious and manly virtues were the subject of ridicule; and the contempt for female modesty and reverent age announced the universal corruption of the capital of the East. The love of spectacles was the taste, or rather passion, of the Syrians: the most skilful artists were procured from the adjacent cities;[12] a considerable share of the revenue was devoted to the public amusements; and the magnificence of the games of the theatre and circus was considered as the happiness, and as the glory, of Antioch. The rustic manners of a prince who disdained such glory, and was insensible of such happiness, soon disgusted the delicacy of his subjects; and the effeminate Orientals could neither imitate nor admire the severe simplicity which Julian always maintained and sometimes affected. The days of festivity, consecrated by ancient custom to the honour of the gods, were the only occasions in which Julian relaxed his philosophic severity; and those festivals were the only days in which the Syrians of Antioch could reject the allurements of pleasure. The majority of the people supported the glory of the Christian name, which had been first invented by their ancestors;[13] they contented themselves with disobeying the moral precepts, but they were scrupulously attached to the speculative doctrines, of their religion. The church of Antioch was distracted by heresy and schism; but the Arians and the Athanasians, the followers of Meletius and those of Paulinus,[14] were actuated by the same pious hatred of their common adversary.

The strongest prejudice was entertained against the character of an apostate, the enemy and successor of a prince who had engaged the affections of a very numerous sect; and the removal of St Babylas excited an implacable opposition to the person of Julian. His subjects complained, with superstitious indignation, that famine had pursued the emperor's steps from Constantinople to Antioch; and the discontent of a hungry people was exasperated by the injudicious attempt to relieve their distress. The inclemency of the season had affected the harvests of Syria; and the price of bread,[15] in the markets of Antioch, had naturally risen in proportion to the scarcity of corn. But the fair and reasonable proportion was soon violated by the rapacious arts of monopoly. In this unequal contest, in which the produce of the land is claimed by one party as his exclusive property, is used by another as a lucrative object of trade, and is required by a third for the daily and necessary support of life; all the profits of the intermediate agents are accumulated on the head of the defenceless consumers. The hardships of their situation were exaggerated and increased by their own impatience and anxiety; and the apprehension of a scarcity gradually produced the appearances of a famine. When the luxurious citizens of Antioch complained of the high price of poultry and fish, Julian publicly declared that a frugal city ought to be satisfied with a regular supply of wine, oil, and bread; but he acknowledged that it was the duty of a sovereign to provide for the subsistence of his people. With this salutary view, the emperor ventured on a very dangerous and doubtful step, of fixing, by legal authority, the value of corn. He enacted that, in a time of scarcity, it should be sold at a price which had seldom been known in the most plentiful years; and, that his own example might strengthen his laws, he sent into the market four hundred and twenty-two thousand *modii*, or measures, which were drawn by his order from the granaries of Hierapolis, of Chalcis, and even of Egypt. The consequences might have been foreseen, and were soon felt. The Imperial wheat was purchased by the rich merchants; the proprietors of land, or of corn, withheld from the city the accustomed supply; and the small quantities that appeared in the market were secretly sold at an advanced and illegal price. Julian still continued to applaud his own policy, treated the complaints of the people as a vain and ungrateful murmur, and convinced Antioch that he had inherited the obstinacy, though not the cruelty, of his brother Gallus.*[16] The remonstrances of the municipal senate served only to exasperate his inflexible mind. He was persuaded, perhaps with truth, that the senators of Antioch who possessed lands, or were concerned in trade, had themselves contributed to the calamities of their country; and he imputed the disrespectful boldness which they assumed to the sense, not of public duty, but of private interest. The whole body, consisting of two hundred of the most noble and wealthy citizens, were sent under a guard from the palace to the prison; and, though they were permitted, before the close of evening, to return to their respective houses,[17] the emperor himself could not obtain the forgiveness which he had so easily granted. The same grievances were still the subject of the same complaints, which were industriously circulated by the wit and levity of the Syrian Greeks. During the licentious days of the Saturnalia, the streets of the city resounded with insolent songs, which derided the laws, the religion, the personal conduct, and even the *beard*, of the emperor; and the spirit of Antioch was manifested by the connivance of the magistrates and the applause of the multitude.[18] The disciple of Socrates was too deeply affected by these popular insults; but the monarch, endowed with quick sensibility, and possessed of absolute power, refused his passions the gratification of revenge. A tyrant might have proscribed, without distinction, the lives and fortunes of the citizens of Antioch; and the unwarlike Syrians must have patiently submitted to the lust, the rapaciousness, and the cruelty of the faithful legions of Gaul. A milder sentence might have deprived the capital of the East of its honours and privileges; and the courtiers, perhaps the subjects, of Julian would have applauded an act of justice which asserted the dignity of the supreme magistrate of the republic.[19] But, instead of abusing, or exerting, the authority of the state to revenge his personal injuries, Julian contented himself with an inoffensive mode of retaliation, which it would be in the power of few princes to employ. He had been insulted by satires and libels; in his turn he composed, under the title of the *Enemy of the Beard*, an ironical confession of his own faults, and a severe satire of the licentious and effeminate manners of Antioch. This Imperial reply was publicly exposed before the gates of the palace; and the *Misopogon*[20] still remains a singular monument of the resentment, the wit, the humanity, and the indiscretion, of Julian. Though he affected to laugh, he could not forgive.[21] His contempt was expressed, and his revenge might be gratified, by the nomination of a governor[22] worthy only of such subjects; and the emperor, for ever renouncing the ungrateful city, proclaimed his resolution to pass the ensuing winter at Tarsus in Cilicia.[23]

Yet Antioch possessed one citizen, whose genius and virtues might atone, in the opinion of Julian, for the vice and folly of his country. The sophist Libanius was born in the capital of the East; he publicly professed the arts of rhetoric and declamation at Nicaea, Nicomedia, Constantinople, Athens, and, during the remainder of his life, at Antioch. His school was assiduously frequented by the Grecian youth; his disciples, who sometimes exceeded the number of eighty, celebrated their incomparable master; and the jealousy of his rivals, who persecuted him from one city to another, confirmed the favourable opinion which Libanius ostentatiously displayed of his superior merit. The preceptors of Julian had extorted a rash but solemn assurance that he would never attend the lectures of their adversary: the curiosity of the royal youth was checked and inflamed: he secretly procured the writings of this dangerous sophist, and gradually surpassed, in the perfect imitation of his style, the most laborious of his domestic pupils.[24] When Julian ascended the throne, he declared his impatience to embrace and reward the Syrian sophist, who had preserved, in a degenerate age, the Grecian purity of taste, of manners and of religion. The emperor's prepossession was increased and justified by the discreet pride of his favourite. Instead of pressing, with the foremost of the crowd, into the palace of Constantinople, Libanius calmly expected his arrival at Antioch; withdrew from court on the first symptoms of coldness and indifference; required a formal invitation for each visit; and taught his sovereign an important lesson, that he might command the obedience of a subject, but that he must deserve the attachment of a friend. The sophists of every age, despising, or affecting to despise, the accidental distinctions of birth and fortune,[25] reserve their esteem for the superior qualities of the mind, with which they themselves are so plentifully endowed. Julian might disdain the acclamations of a venal court, who adored the Imperial purple; but he was deeply flattered by the praise, the admonition, the freedom, and the envy of an independent philosopher, who refused his favours, loved his person, celebrated his fame, and protected his memory. The voluminous writings of Libanius still exist: for the most part, they are the vain and idle compositions of an orator, who cultivated the science of words; the productions of a recluse student, whose mind, regardless of his contemporaries, was incessantly fixed on the Trojan war and the Athenian commonwealth. Yet the sophist of Antioch sometimes descended from this imaginary elevation; he entertained a various and elaborate correspondence;[26] he praised the virtues of his own times; he boldly arraigned the abuses of public and private life; and he eloquently pleaded the cause of Antioch against the just resentment of Julian and Theodosius. It is the common calamity of old age,[27] to lose whatever might have rendered it desirable; but Libanius experienced the peculiar misfortune of surviving the religion and the sciences to which he had consecrated his genius. The friend of Julian was an indignant spectator of the triumph of Christianity; and his bigotry, which darkened the prospect of the visible world, did not inspire Libanius with any lively hopes of celestial glory and happiness.[28]

The martial impatience of Julian urged him to take the field in the beginning of the spring; and he dismissed, with contempt and reproach, the senate of Antioch, who accompanied the emperor beyond the limits of their own territory, to which he was resolved never to return. After a laborious march of two days,[29] he halted on the third at Beroea, or Aleppo, where he had the mortification of finding a senate almost entirely Christian; who received with cold and formal demonstrations of respect the eloquent sermon of the apostle of paganism. The son of one of the most illustrious citizens of Beroea, who had embraced, either from interest or conscience, the religion of the emperor, was disinherited by his angry parent. The father and the son were invited to the Imperial table. Julian, placing himself between them, attempted, without success, to inculcate the lesson and example of toleration; supported, with affected calmness, the indiscreet zeal of the aged Christian, who seemed to forget the sentiments of nature and the duty of a subject; and at length turning towards the afflicted youth, 'Since you have lost a father,' said he, 'for my sake, it is incumbent on me to supply his place.'[30] The emperor was received in a manner much more agreeable to his wishes at Batnae, a small town pleasantly seated in a grove of cypresses, about twenty miles from the city of Hierapolis. The solemn rites of sacrifice were decently prepared by the inhabitants of Batnae, who seemed attached to the worship of their tutelar deities, Apollo and Jupiter; but the serious piety of Julian was offended by the tumult of their applause; and he too clearly discerned that the smoke which arose from their altars was the incense of flattery rather than of devotion. The ancient and magnificent temple, which had sanctified, for so many ages, the city of Hierapolis,[31] no longer subsisted; and the consecrated wealth, which afforded a liberal maintenance to more than three hundred priests, might hasten its downfall. Yet

Julian enjoyed the satisfaction of embracing a philosopher and a friend, whose religious firmness had withstood the pressing and repeated solicitations of Constantius and Gallus, as often as those princes lodged at his house, in their passage through Hierapolis. In the hurry of military preparation, and the careless confidence of a familiar correspondence, the zeal of Julian appears to have been lively and uniform. He had now undertaken an important and difficult war; and the anxiety of the event rendered him still more attentive to observe and register the most trifling presages from which, according to the rules of divination, any knowledge of futurity could be derived.[32] He informed Libanius of his progress as far as Hierapolis, by an elegant epistle,[33] which displays the facility of his genius and his tender friendship for the sophist of Antioch.

Hierapolis, situate almost on the banks of the Euphrates,[34] had been appointed for the general rendezvous of the Roman troops, who immediately passed the great river on a bridge of boats, which was previously constructed.[35] If the inclinations of Julian had been similar to those of his predecessor, he might have wasted the active and important season of the year in the circus of Samosata, or in the churches of Edessa. But, as the warlike emperor, instead of Constantius, had chosen Alexander for his model, he advanced without delay to Carrhae,[36] a very ancient city of Mesopotamia, at the distance of fourscore miles from Hierapolis. The temple of the Moon attracted the devotion of Julian; but the halt of a few days was principally employed in completing the immense preparations of the Persian war. The secret of the expedition had hitherto remained in his own breast; but, as Carrhae is the point of separation of the two great roads, he could no longer conceal whether it was his design to attack the dominions of Sapor on the side of the Tigris or on that of the Euphrates. The emperor detached an army of thirty thousand men, under the command of his kinsman Procopius, and of Sebastian, who had been duke of Egypt. They were ordered to direct their march towards Nisibis, and to secure the frontier from the desultory incursions of the enemy, before they attempted the passage of the Tigris. Their subsequent operations were left to the discretion of the generals; but Julian expected that, after wasting with fire and sword the fertile districts of Media and Adiabene, they might arrive under the walls of Ctesiphon* about the same time that he himself, advancing with equal steps along the banks of the Euphrates, should besiege the capital of the Persian monarchy. The success of this well-concerted plan depended, in a great measure, on the powerful and ready assistance of the king of Armenia, who, without exposing the safety of his own dominions, might detach an army of four thousand horse, and twenty thousand foot, to the assistance of the Romans.[37] But the feeble Arsaces Tiranus,[38] king of Armenia, had degenerated still more shamefully than his father Chosroes from the manly virtues of the great Tiridates;[†] and, as the pusillanimous monarch was averse to any enterprise of danger and glory, he could disguise his timid indolence by the more decent excuses of religion and gratitude. He expressed a pious attachment to the memory of Constantius, from whose hands he had received in marriage Olympias, the daughter of the prefect Ablavius; and the alliance of a female who had been educated as the destined wife of the emperor Constans exalted the dignity of a Barbarian king.[39] Tiranus professed the Christian religion; he reigned over a nation of Christians; and he was restrained, by every principle of conscience and interest, from contributing to the victory, which would consummate the ruin of the church. The alienated mind of Tiranus was exasperated by the indiscretion of Julian, who treated the king of Armenia as *his* slave, and as the enemy of the gods. The haughty and threatening style of the Imperial mandates[40] awakened the secret indignation of a prince who, in the humiliating state of dependence, was still conscious of his royal descent from the Arsacides, the lords of the East and the rivals of the Roman power.

The military dispositions of Julian were skilfully contrived to deceive the spies, and to divert the attention, of Sapor. The legions appeared to direct their march towards Nisibis and Tigris. On a sudden they wheeled to the right; traversed the level and naked plain of Carrhae; and reached, on the third day, the banks of the Euphrates, where the strong town of Nicephorium, or Callinicum, had been founded by the Macedonian kings. From thence the emperor pursued his march, above ninety miles, along the winding stream of the Euphrates, till, at length, about one month after his departure from Antioch, he discovered* the towers of Circesium, the extreme limit of the Roman dominions. The army of Julian, the most numerous that any of the Caesars had ever led against Persia, consisted of sixty-five thousand effective and well-disciplined soldiers. The veteran bands of cavalry and infantry, of Romans and Barbarians, had been selected from the different provinces; and a just pre-eminence of loyalty and valour was claimed by the hardy Gauls, who guarded the throne and person of their beloved prince. A formidable body of Scythian auxiliaries had been transported from another climate, and almost from another world, to invade a distant country, of whose name and situation they were ignorant. The love of rapine and war allured to the Imperial standard several tribes of Saracens, or roving Arabs, whose service Julian had commanded, while he sternly refused the payment of the accustomed subsidies. The broad channel of the Euphrates[41] was crowded by a fleet of eleven hundred ships, destined to attend the motions, and to satisfy the wants, of the Roman army. The military strength of the fleet was composed of fifty armed galleys; and these were accompanied by an equal number of flat-bottomed boats, which might occasionally be connected into the form of temporary bridges. The rest of the ships, partly constructed of timber and partly covered with raw hides, were laden with an almost inexhaustible supply of arms and engines, of utensils and provisions. The vigilant humanity of Julian had embarked a very large magazine of vinegar and biscuit for the use of the soldiers, but he prohibited the indulgence of wine; and rigorously stopped a long string of superfluous camels that attempted to follow the rear of the army. The river Chaboras falls into the Euphrates at Circesium;[42] and, as soon as the trumpet gave the signal of march, the Romans passed the little stream which separated two mighty and hostile empires. The custom of ancient discipline required a military oration; and Julian embraced every opportunity of displaying his eloquence. He animated the impatient and attentive legions by the example of the inflexible courage and glorious triumphs of their ancestors. He excited their resentment by a lively picture of the insolence of the Persians; and he exhorted them to imitate his firm resolution, either to extirpate that perfidious nation or to devote* his life in the cause of the republic. The eloquence of Julian was enforced by a donative of one hundred and thirty pieces of silver to every soldier; and the bridge of the Chaboras was instantly cut away, to convince the troops that they must place their hopes of safety in the success of their arms. Yet the prudence of the emperor induced him to secure a remote frontier, perpetually exposed to the inroads of the hostile Arabs. A detachment of four thousand men was left at Circesium, which completed, to the number of ten thousand, the regular garrison of that important fortress.[43]

From the moment that the Romans entered the enemy's country,[44] the country of an active and artful enemy, the order of march was disposed in three columns.[45] The strength of the infantry, and consequently of the whole army, was placed in the centre, under the peculiar command of their master-general Victor. On the right, the brave Nevitta led a column of several legions along the banks of the Euphrates, and almost always in sight of the fleet. The left flank of the army was protected by the column of cavalry. Hormisdas and Arinthaeus were appointed generals of the horse; and the singular adventures of Hormisdas[46] are not undeserving of our notice. He was a Persian prince, of the royal race of the Sassanides, who, in the troubles of the minority of Sapor, had escaped from prison to the hospitable court of the great Constantine. Hormisdas at first excited the compassion, and at length acquired the esteem, of his new masters; his valour and fidelity raised him to the military honours of the Roman service; and, though a Christian, he might indulge the secret satisfaction of convincing his ungrateful country that an oppressed subject may prove the most dangerous enemy. Such was the disposition of the three principal columns. The front and flanks of the army were covered by Lucillianus with a flying detachment of fifteen hundred light-armed soldiers, whose active vigilance observed the most distant signs, and conveyed the earliest notice, of any hostile approach. Dagalaiphus, and Secundinus duke of Osrhoene, conducted the troops of the rearguard; the baggage, securely, proceeded in the intervals of the columns; and the ranks, from a motive either of use or ostentation, were formed in such open order that the whole line of march extended almost ten miles. The ordinary post of Julian was at the head of the centre column; but, as he preferred the duties of a general to the state of a monarch, he rapidly moved, with a small escort of light cavalry, to the front, the rear, the flanks, wherever his presence could animate or protect the march of the Roman army. The country which they traversed from the Chaboras to the cultivated lands of Assyria may be considered as a part of the desert of Arabia, a dry and barren waste, which could never be improved by the most powerful arts of human industry. Julian marched over the same ground which had been trod above seven hundred years before by the footsteps of the younger Cyrus, and which is described by one of the companions of his expedition, the sage and heroic Xenophon.[47] 'The country was a plain throughout, as even as the sea, and full of wormwood; and, if any other kind of shrubs or reeds grew there, they had all an aromatic smell; but no trees could be seen. Bustards and ostriches, antelopes and wild asses,[48] appeared to be the only inhabitants of the desert; and the fatigues of the march were alleviated by the amusements of the chase.' The loose sand of the desert was frequently raised by the wind into clouds of dust; and a great number of the soldiers of Julian, with their tents, were suddenly thrown to the ground by the violence of an unexpected hurricane.

The sandy plains of Mesopotamia were abandoned to the antelopes and wild asses of the desert; but a variety of populous towns and villages were pleasantly situated on the banks of the Euphrates, and in the islands which are occasionally formed by that river. The city of Annah, or Anatho,[49] the actual* residence of an Arabian Emir, is composed of two long streets, which enclose, within a natural fortification, a small island in the midst, and two fruitful spots on either side of the Euphrates. The warlike inhabitants of Anatho showed a disposition to stop the march of a Roman emperor; till they were diverted from such fatal presumption by the mild exhortations of prince Hormisdas and the approaching terrors of the fleet and army. They implored, and experienced, the clemency of Julian, who transplanted the people to an advantageous settlement near Chalcis in Syria, and admitted Pusaeus, the governor, to an honourable rank in his service and friendship. But the impregnable fortress of Thilutha could scorn the menace of a siege; and the emperor was obliged to content himself with an insulting promise that, when he had subdued the interior provinces of Persia, Thilutha would no longer refuse to grace the triumph of the conqueror. The inhabitants of the open towns, unable to resist and unwilling to yield, fled with precipitation; and their houses, filled with spoil and provisions, were occupied by the soldiers of Julian, who massacred, without remorse, and without punishment, some defenceless women. During the march, the Surenas, or Persian general, and Malek Rodosaces, the renowned Emir of the tribe of Gassan,[50] incessantly hovered round the army: every straggler was intercepted; every detachment was attacked; and the valiant Hormisdas escaped with some difficulty from their hands. But the Barbarians were finally repulsed; the country became every day less favourable to the operations of cavalry; and, when the Romans arrived at Macepracta, they perceived the ruins of the wall which had been constructed by the ancient kings of Assyria to secure their dominions from the incursions of the Medes. These preliminaries of the expedition of Julian appear to have employed about fifteen days; and we may compute near three hundred miles from the fortress of Circesium to the wall of Macepracta.[51]

The fertile province of Assyria,[52] which stretched beyond the Tigris as far as the mountains of Media,[53] extended about four hundred miles from the ancient wall of Macepracta to the territory of Basra, where the united streams of the Euphrates and Tigris discharge themselves into the Persian Gulf.[54] The whole country might have claimed the peculiar name of Mesopotamia;* as the two rivers which are never more distant than fifty, approach, between Bagdad and Babylon, within twenty-five, miles of each other. A multitude of artificial canals, dug without much labour in a soft and yielding soil, connected the rivers, and intersected the plain of Assyria. The uses of these artificial canals were various and important. They served to discharge the superfluous waters from one river into the other at the season of their respective inundations. Subdividing themselves into smaller and smaller branches, they refreshed the dry lands, and supplied the deficiency of rain. They facilitated the intercourse of peace and commerce; and, as the dams could be speedily broke down, they armed the despair of the Assyrians with the means of opposing a sudden deluge to the progress of an invading army. To the soil and climate of Assyria nature had denied some of her choicest gifts, the vine, the olive, and the fig-tree; but the food which supports the life of man, and particularly wheat and barley, were produced with inexhaustible fertility; and the husbandman who committed his seed to the earth was frequently rewarded with an increase of two, or even of three, hundred. The face of the country was interspersed with groves of innumerable palm trees;[55] and the diligent natives celebrated, either in verse or prose, the three hundred and sixty uses to which the trunk, the branches, the leaves, the juice, and the fruit, were skilfully applied. Several manufactures, especially those of leather and linen, employed the industry of a numerous people, and afforded valuable materials for foreign trade; which appears, however, to have been conducted by the hands of strangers. Babylon had been converted into a royal park; but near the ruins of the ancient capital new cities had successively arisen, and the populousness of the country was displayed in the multitude of towns and villages, which were built of bricks, dried in the sun, and strongly cemented with bitumen, the natural and peculiar production of the Babylonian soil. While the successors of Cyrus reigned over Asia, the province of Assyria alone maintained, during a third part of the year, the luxurious plenty of the table and household of the Great King. Four considerable villages were assigned for the subsistence of his Indian dogs; eight hundred stallions and sixteen thousand mares were constantly kept at the expense of the country, for the royal stables; and, as the daily tribute, which was paid to the satrap,* amounted to one English bushel of silver, we may compute the annual revenue of Assyria at more than twelve hundred thousand pounds sterling.[56]

The fields of Assyria were devoted by Julian to the calamities of war; and the philosopher retaliated on a guiltless people the acts of rapine and cruelty which had been committed by their haughty master in the Roman provinces. The trembling Assyrians summoned the rivers to their assistance; and completed, with their own hands, the ruin of their country. The roads were rendered impracticable; a flood of waters was poured into the camp; and during several days the troops of Julian were obliged to contend with the most discouraging hardships. But every obstacle was surmounted by the perseverance of the legionaries, who were inured to toil as well as to danger, and who felt themselves animated by the spirit of their leader. The damage was gradually repaired; the waters were restored to their proper channels; whole groves of palm trees were cut down and placed along the broken parts of the road; and the army passed over the broad and deeper canals on bridges of floating rafts, which were supported by the help of bladders. Two cities of Assyria presumed to resist the arms of a Roman emperor; and they both paid the severe penalty of their rashness. At the distance of fifty miles from the royal residence of Ctesiphon, Perisabor, or Anbar, held the second rank in the province; a city, large, populous, and well fortified, surrounded with a double wall, almost encompassed by a branch of the Euphrates, and defended by the valour of a numerous garrison. The exhortations of Hormisdas were repulsed with contempt; and the ears of the Persian prince were wounded by a just reproach that, unmindful of his royal birth, he conducted an army of strangers against his king and country. The Assyrians maintained their loyalty by a skilful, as well as vigorous, defence; till, the lucky stroke of a battering ram having opened a large breach by shattering one of the angles of the wall, they hastily retired into the fortifications of the interior citadel. The soldiers of Julian rushed impetuously into the town, and, after the full gratification of every military appetite, Perisabor was reduced to ashes; and the engines which assaulted the citadel were planted on the ruins of the smoking houses. The contest was continued by an incessant and mutual discharge of missile weapons; and the superiority which the Romans might derive from the mechanical powers of their balistae[†] and catapultae was counterbalanced by the advantage of the ground on the side of the besieged. But as soon as an *Helepolis*[‡] had been constructed, which could engage on equal terms with the loftiest ramparts, the tremendous aspect of a moving turret, that would leave no hope of resistance or of mercy, terrified the defenders of the citadel into an humble submission; and the place was surrendered only two days after Julian first appeared under the walls of Perisabor. Two thousand five hundred persons of both sexes, the feeble remnant of a flourishing people, were permitted to retire; the plentiful magazines of corn, of arms, and of splendid furniture were partly distributed among the troops, and partly reserved for the public service; the useless stores were destroyed by fire or thrown into the stream of the Euphrates; and the fate of Amida* was revenged by the total ruin of Perisabor.

The city, or rather fortress, of Maogamalcha, which was defended by sixteen large towers, a deep ditch, and two strong and solid walls of brick and bitumen, appears to have been constructed at the distance of eleven miles, as the safeguard of the capital of Persia. The emperor, apprehensive of leaving such an important fortress in his rear, immediately formed the siege of Maogamalcha; and the Roman army was distributed, for that, purpose, into three divisions. Victor, at the head of the cavalry, and of a detachment of heavy-armed foot, was ordered to clear the country as far as the banks of the Tigris and the suburbs of Ctesiphon. The conduct of the attack was assumed by Julian himself, who seemed to place his whole dependence in the military engines which he erected against the walls; while he secretly contrived a more efficacious method of introducing his troops into the heart of the city. Under the direction of Nevitta and Dagalaiphus, the trenches were opened at a considerable distance, and gradually prolonged as far as the edge of the ditch. The ditch was speedily filled with earth; and, by the incessant labour of the troops, a mine was carried under the foundations of the walls, and sustained, at sufficient intervals, by props of timber. Three chosen cohorts, advancing in a single file, silently explored the dark and dangerous passage; till their intrepid leader whispered back the intelligence that he was ready to issue from his confinement into the streets of the hostile city. Julian checked their ardour that he might ensure their success; and immediately diverted the attention of the garrison, by the tumult and clamour of a general assault. The Persians, who from their walls contemptuously beheld the progress of an impotent attack, celebrated, with songs of triumph, the glory of Sapor; and ventured to assure the emperor that he might ascend the starry mansion of Ormusd,† before he could hope to take the impregnable city of Maogamalcha. The city was already taken. History has recorded the name of a private soldier, the first who ascended from the mine into a deserted town. The passage was widened by his companions, who pressed forwards with impatient valour. Fifteen hundred enemies were already in the midst of the city. The astonished garrison abandoned the walls, and their only hope of safety; the gates were instantly burst open; and the revenge of the soldier, unless it were suspended by lust or avarice, was satiated by an undistinguishing massacre. The governor, who had yielded on a promise of mercy, was burnt alive, a few days afterwards, on a charge of having uttered some disrespectful words against the honour of prince

Hormisdas. The fortifications were razed to the ground; and not a vestige was left that the city of Maogamalcha had ever existed. The neighbourhood of the capital of Persia was adorned with three stately palaces, laboriously enriched with every production that could gratify the luxury and pride of an eastern monarch. The pleasant situation of the gardens along the banks of the Tigris was improved, according to the Persian taste, by the symmetry of flowers, fountains, and shady walks; and spacious parks were enclosed for the reception of the bears, lions, and wild boars, which were maintained at a considerable expense for the pleasure of the royal chase. The park-walls were broke down, the savage game was abandoned to the darts of the soldiers, and the palaces of Sapor were reduced to ashes, by the command of the Roman emperor. Julian, on this occasion, showed himself ignorant, or careless, of the laws of civility, which the prudence and refinement of polished ages have established between hostile princes. Yet these wanton ravages need not excite in our breasts any vehement emotions of pity or resentment. A simple, naked statue, finished by the hand of a Grecian artist, is of more genuine value, than all these rude and costly monuments of Barbaric labour; and, if we are more deeply affected by the ruin of a palace than by the conflagration of a cottage, our humanity must have formed a very erroneous estimate of the miseries of human life.[57]

Julian was an object of terror and hatred to the Persians, and the painters of that nation represented the invader of their country under the emblem of a furious lion, who vomited from his mouth a consuming fire.[58] To his friends and soldiers, the philosophic hero appeared in a more amiable light; and his virtues were never more conspicuously displayed than in the last, and most active, period of his life. He practised, without effort, and almost without merit, the habitual qualities of temperance and sobriety. According to the dictates of that artificial wisdom which assumes an absolute dominion over the mind and body, he sternly refused himself the indulgence of the most natural appetites.[59] In the warm climate of Assyria, which solicited a luxurious people to the gratification of every sensual desire,[60] a youthful conqueror preserved his chastity pure and inviolate; nor was Julian ever tempted, even by a motive of curiosity, to visit his female captives of exquisite beauty,[61] who, instead of resisting his power, would have disputed with each other the honour of his embraces. With the same firmness that he resisted the allurements of love, he sustained the hardships of war. When the Romans marched through the flat and flooded country, their sovereign, on foot, at the head of his legions, shared their fatigues, and animated their diligence. In every useful labour, the hand of Julian was prompt and strenuous; and the Imperial purple was wet and dirty, as the coarse garment of the meanest soldier. The two sieges allowed him some remarkable opportunities of signalising his personal valour, which, in the improved state of the military art, can seldom be exerted by a prudent general. The emperor stood before the citadel of Perisabor, insensible of his extreme danger, and encouraged his troops to burst open the gates of iron, till he was almost overwhelmed under a cloud of missile weapons and huge stones that were directed against his person. As he examined the exterior fortifications of Maogamalcha, two Persians, devoting themselves for their country, suddenly rushed upon him with drawn scimitars: the emperor dexterously received their blows on his uplifted shield; and, with a steady and well-aimed thrust, laid one of his adversaries dead at his feet. The esteem of a prince who possesses the virtues which he approves is the noblest recompense of a deserving subject; and the authority which Julian derived from his personal merit enabled him to revive and enforce the rigour of ancient discipline. He punished with death, or ignominy, the misbehaviour of three troops of horse, who, in a skirmish with the Surenas, had lost their honour, and one of their standards; and he distinguished with *obsidional*[62] crowns the valour of the foremost soldiers who had ascended into the city of Maogamalcha. After the siege of Perisabor, the firmness of the emperor was exercised by the insolent avarice of the army, who loudly complained that their services were rewarded by a trifling donative of one hundred pieces of silver. His just indignation was expressed in the grave and manly language of a Roman. 'Riches are the object of your desires? those riches are in the hands of the Persians; and the spoils of this fruitful country are proposed as the prize of your valour and discipline. Believe me,' added Julian, 'the Roman republic, which formerly possessed such immense treasures, is now reduced to want and wretchedness; since our princes have been persuaded, by weak and interested ministers, to purchase with gold the tranquillity of the Barbarians. The revenue is exhausted; the cities are ruined; the provinces are dispeopled. For myself, the only inheritance that I have received from my royal ancestors is a soul incapable of fear; and, as long as I am convinced that every real advantage is seated in the mind, I shall not blush to acknowledge an honourable poverty, which, in the days of ancient virtue, was considered as the glory of Fabricius. That glory, and that virtue, may be your own if you will listen to the voice of Heaven, and of your leader. But, if you will rashly persist, if you are determined to renew the shameful and mischievous examples of old seditions, proceed. – As it becomes an emperor who has filled the first rank among men, I am prepared to die, standing; and to despise a precarious life, which, every hour, may depend on an accidental fever. If I have been found unworthy of the command, there are now among you (I speak it with pride and pleasure), there are many chiefs, whose merit and experience are equal to the conduct of the most important war. Such has been the temper of my reign that I can retire, without regret, and without apprehension, to the obscurity of a private station.'[63] The modest resolution of Julian was answered by the unanimous applause and cheerful obedience of the Romans; who declared their confidence of victory, while they fought under the banners of their

heroic prince. Their courage was kindled by his frequent and familiar
asseverations (for such wishes were the oaths of Julian), 'So may I reduce
the Persians under the yoke!' 'Thus may I restore the strength and
splendour of the republic!' The love of fame was the ardent passion of his
soul: but it was not before he trampled on the ruins of Maogamalcha, that
he allowed himself to say, 'We have now provided some materials for the
sophist* of Antioch.'[64]

The successful valour of Julian had triumphed over all the obstacles that
opposed his march to the gates of Ctesiphon. But the reduction, or even
the siege, of the capital of Persia was still at a distance; nor can the military
conduct of the emperor be clearly apprehended without a knowledge of
the country which was the theatre of his bold and skilful operations.[65]
Twenty miles to the south of Bagdad, and on the eastern bank of the
Tigris, the curiosity of travellers has observed some ruins of the palaces of
Ctesiphon, which, in the time of Julian, was a great and populous city.
The name and glory of the adjacent Seleucia[†] were for ever extinguished;
and the only remaining quarter of that Greek colony had resumed, with
the Assyrian language and manners, the primitive appellation of Coche.
Coche was situate on the western side of the Tigris; but it was naturally
considered as a suburb of Ctesiphon, with which we may suppose it to
have been connected by a permanent bridge of boats. The united parts
contributed to form the common epithet of Al Modain, The Cities,
which the Orientals have bestowed on the winter residence of the
Sassanides; and the whole circumference of the Persian capital was
strongly fortified by the waters of the river, by lofty walls, and by
impracticable morasses. Near the ruins of Seleucia, the camp of Julian was
fixed; and secured, by a ditch and rampart, against the sallies of the
numerous and enterprising garrison of Coche. In this fruitful and pleasant
country, the Romans were plentifully supplied with water and forage; and
several forts which might have embarrassed the motions of the army
submitted, after some resistance, to the efforts of their valour. The fleet
passed from the Euphrates into an artificial derivation of that river, which
pours a copious and navigable stream into the Tigris, at a small distance
below the great city. If they had followed this royal canal, which bore the
name of Nahar-Malcha,[66] the intermediate situation of Coche would
have separated the fleet and army of Julian; and the rash attempt of
steering against the current of the Tigris, and forcing their way through
the midst of a hostile capital, must have been attended with the total
destruction of the Roman navy. The prudence of the emperor foresaw the
danger, and provided the remedy. As he had minutely studied the
operations of Trajan in the same country, he soon recollected that his
warlike predecessor had dug a new and navigable canal, which, leaving
Coche on the right hand, conveyed the waters of the Nahar-Malcha into
the river Tigris, at some distance *above* the cities. From the information of
the peasants, Julian ascertained the vestiges of this ancient work, which

were almost obliterated by design or accident. By the indefatigable labour of the soldiers, a broad and deep channel was speedily prepared for the reception of the Euphrates. A strong dyke was constructed to interrupt the ordinary current of the Nahar-Malcha: a flood of waters rushed impetuously into their new bed; and the Roman fleet, steering their triumphant course into the Tigris, derided the vain and ineffectual barriers which the Persians of Ctesiphon had erected to oppose their passage.

As it became necessary to transport the Roman army over the Tigris, another labour presented itself, of less toil, but of more danger, than the preceding expedition. The stream was broad and rapid; the ascent steep and difficult; and the entrenchments, which had been formed on the ridge of the opposite bank, were lined with a numerous army of heavy cuirassiers, dexterous archers, and huge elephants; who (according to the extravagant hyperbole of Libanius) could trample, with the same ease, a field of corn, or a legion of Romans.[67] In the presence of such an enemy, the construction of a bridge was impracticable; and the intrepid prince, who instantly seized the only possible expedient, concealed his design, till the moment of execution, from the knowledge of the Barbarians, of his own troops, and even of his generals themselves. Under the specious pretence of examining the state of the magazines, fourscore vessels were gradually unladen; and a select detachment, apparently destined for some secret expedition, was ordered to stand to their arms on the first signal. Julian disguised the silent anxiety of his own mind with smiles of confidence and joy; and amused the hostile nations with the spectacle of military games, which he insultingly celebrated under the walls of Coche. The day was consecrated to pleasure; but, as soon as the hour of supper was past, the emperor summoned the generals to his tent; and acquainted them that he had fixed that night for the passage of the Tigris. They stood in silent and respectful astonishment; but, when the venerable Sallust assumed the privilege of his age and experience, the rest of the chiefs supported with freedom the weight of his prudent remonstrances.[68] Julian contented himself with observing that conquest and safety depended on the attempt; that, instead of diminishing, the number of their enemies would be increased, by successive reinforcements; and that a longer delay would neither contract the breadth of the stream nor level the height of the bank. The signal was instantly given, and obeyed: the most impatient of the legionaries leaped into five vessels that lay nearest to the bank; and, as they plied their oars with intrepid diligence, they were lost, after a few moments, in the darkness of the night. A flame arose on the opposite side; and Julian, who too clearly understood that his foremost vessels, in attempting to land, had been fired by the enemy, dextrously converted their extreme danger into a presage of victory. 'Our fellow-soldiers,' he eagerly exclaimed, 'are already masters of the bank; see – they make the appointed signal: let us hasten to emulate and assist their courage.' The united and rapid motion of a great fleet broke the violence of the current, and they reached the eastern shore of the Tigris with sufficient speed to extinguish the flames and rescue their adventurous companions. The difficulties of a steep and lofty ascent were increased by the weight of armour and the darkness of the night. A shower of stones, darts, and fire was incessantly discharged on the heads of the assailants; who, after an arduous struggle, climbed the bank, and stood victorious upon the ramparts. As soon as they possessed a more equal field, Julian, who, with his light infantry, had led the attack,[69] darted through the ranks a skilful and experienced eye: his bravest soldiers, according to the precepts of Homer,[70] were distributed in the front and rear; and all the trumpets of the imperial army sounded to battle. The Romans, after sending up a military shout, advanced in measured steps to the animated notes of martial music; launched their formidable javelins; and rushed forwards with drawn swords, to deprive the Barbarians, by a closer onset, of the advantage of their missile weapons. The whole engagement lasted above twelve hours; till the gradual retreat of the Persians was changed into a disorderly flight, of which the shameful example was given by the principal leaders, and the Surenas himself. They were pursued to the gates of Ctesiphon; and the conquerors might have entered the dismayed city,[71] if their general, Victor, who was dangerously wounded with an arrow, had not conjured them to desist from a rash attempt, which must be fatal, if it were not successful. On *their* side, the Romans acknowledged the loss of only seventy-five men; while they affirmed that the Barbarians had left on the field of battle two thousand five hundred, or even six thousand, of their bravest soldiers. The spoil was such as might be expected from the riches and luxury of an Oriental camp: large quantities of silver and gold, splendid arms and trappings, and beds and tables of massy silver. The victorious emperor distributed, as the rewards of valour, some honourable gifts, civic and mural and naval crowns; which he, and perhaps he alone, esteemed more precious than the wealth of Asia. A solemn sacrifice was offered to the god of war, but the appearances of the victims threatened the most inauspicious events; and Julian soon discovered, by less ambiguous signs, that he had now reached the term of his prosperity.[72]

On the second day after the battle, the domestic guards, the Jovians and Herculians,* and the remaining troops, which composed near two-thirds of the whole army, were securely wafted over the Tigris.[73] While the Persians beheld from the walls of Ctesiphon the desolation of the adjacent country, Julian cast many an anxious look towards the North, in full expectation that, as he himself had victoriously penetrated to the capital of Sapor, the march and junction of his lieutenants, Sebastian and Procopius, would be executed with the same courage and diligence. His expectations were disappointed by the treachery of the Armenian king, who permitted, and most probably directed, the desertion of his auxiliary troops from the camp of the Romans;[74] and by the dissensions of the two generals, who were incapable of forming or executing any plan for the public service. When the emperor had relinquished the hope of this important reinforcement, he condescended to hold a council of war, and approved, after a full debate, the sentiment of those generals who dissuaded the siege of Ctesiphon as a fruitless and pernicious undertaking. It is not easy for us to conceive by what arts of fortification a city thrice besieged and taken by the predecessors of Julian could be rendered impregnable against an army of sixty thousand Romans, commanded by a brave and experienced general, and abundantly supplied with ships, provisions, battering engines, and military stores. But we may rest assured, from the love of glory, and contempt of danger, which formed the character of Julian, that he was not discouraged by any trivial or imaginary obstacles.[75] At the very time when he declined the siege of Ctesiphon, he rejected, with obstinacy and disdain, the most flattering offers of a negotiation of peace. Sapor, who had been so long accustomed to the tardy ostentation of Constantius, was surprised by the intrepid diligence of his successor. As far as the confines of India and Scythia, the satraps of the distant provinces were ordered to assemble their troops, and to march, without delay, to the assistance of their monarch. But their preparations were dilatory, their motions slow; and, before Sapor could lead an army into the field, he received the melancholy intelligence of the devastation of Assyria, the ruin of his palaces, and the slaughter of his bravest troops, who defended the passage of the Tigris. The pride of royalty was humbled in the dust; he took his repasts on the ground; and the disorder of his hair expressed the grief and anxiety of his mind. Perhaps he would not have refused to purchase, with one half of his kingdom, the safety of the remainder; and he would have gladly subscribed himself, in a treaty of peace, the faithful and dependent ally of the Roman conqueror. Under the pretence of private business, a minister of rank and confidence was secretly dispatched to embrace the knees of Hormisdas, and to request, in the language of a suppliant, that he might be introduced into the presence of the emperor. The Sassanian prince, whether he listened to the voice of pride or humanity, whether he consulted the sentiments of his birth or the duties of his situation, was equally inclined to promote a salutary measure, which would terminate the calamities of Persia, and secure the triumph of Rome. He was astonished by the inflexible firmness of a hero, who remembered, most unfortunately for himself and for his country, that Alexander had uniformly rejected the propositions of Darius. But, as Julian was sensible that the hope of a safe and honourable peace might cool the ardour of his troops, he earnestly requested that Hormisdas would privately dismiss the minister of Sapor and conceal this dangerous temptation from the knowledge of the camp.[76]

The honour, as well as interest, of Julian forbade him to consume his time under the impregnable walls of Ctesiphon; and, as often as he defied the Barbarians, who defended the city, to meet him on the open plain, they prudently replied that, if he desired to exercise his valour, he might seek the army of the Great King. He felt the insult, and he accepted the advice. Instead of confining his servile march to the banks of the Euphrates and Tigris, he resolved to imitate the adventurous spirit of Alexander, and boldly to advance into the inland provinces, till he forced his rival to contend with him, perhaps in the plains of Arbela, for the empire of Asia. The magnanimity of Julian was applauded and betrayed by the arts of a noble Persian, who, in the cause of his country, had generously submitted to act a part full of danger, of falsehood, and of shame.[77] With a train of faithful followers, he deserted to the Imperial camp; exposed, in a specious tale, the injuries which he had sustained; exaggerated the cruelty of Sapor, the discontent of the people, and the weakness of the monarchy; and confidently offered himself as the hostage and guide of the Roman march. The most rational grounds of suspicion were urged, without effect, by the wisdom and experience of Hormisdas; and the credulous Julian, receiving the traitor into his bosom, was persuaded to issue an hasty order, which, in the opinion of mankind, appeared to arraign his prudence, and to endanger his safety. He destroyed, in a single hour, the whole navy, which had been transported above five hundred miles, at so great expense of toil, of treasure, and of blood. Twelve, or, at the most, twenty-two, small vessels were saved, to accompany, on carriages, the march of the army, and to form occasional bridges for the passage of the rivers. A supply of twenty days' provisions was reserved for the use of the soldiers; and the rest of the magazines, with a fleet of eleven hundred vessels, which rode at anchor in the Tigris, were abandoned to the flames, by the absolute command of the emperor. The Christian bishops, Gregory and Augustine, insult the madness of the apostate, who executed, with his own hands, the sentence of divine justice. Their authority, of less weight, perhaps, in a military question, is confirmed by the cool judgment of an experienced soldier, who was himself spectator of the conflagration, and who could not disapprove the reluctant murmurs of the troops.[78] Yet there are not wanting some specious and perhaps solid reasons, which might justify the resolution of Julian. The navigation of the Euphrates never ascended above Babylon, nor that of the Tigris above Opis.[79] The distance of the last-mentioned city from the Roman camp was not very considerable; and Julian must soon have renounced the vain and impracticable attempt of forcing upwards a great fleet against the stream of a rapid river,[80] which in several places was embarrassed by natural or artificial cataracts.[81] The power of sails or oars was insufficient; it became necessary to tow the ships against the current of the river; the strength of twenty thousand soldiers was exhausted in this tedious and servile labour; and, if the Romans continued to march along the banks of the Tigris, they could only expect to return home without achieving any enterprise worthy of the genius or fortune of their leader. If, on the contrary, it was advisable to advance into the inland country, the destruction of the fleet and magazines was the only measure which could save that valuable prize from the hands of the numerous and active troops which might suddenly be poured from the gates of Ctesiphon. Had the arms of Julian been victorious, we should now admire the conduct, as well as the courage, of a hero, who, by depriving his soldiers of the hopes of a retreat, left them only the alternative of death or conquest.[82]

The cumbersome train of artillery and waggons which retards the operations of a modern army were in a great measure unknown in the camps of the Romans.[83] Yet, in every age, the subsistence of sixty thousand men must have been one of the most important cares of a prudent general; and that subsistence could only be drawn from his own or from the enemy's country. Had it been possible for Julian to maintain a bridge of communication on the Tigris, and to preserve the conquered places of Assyria, a desolated province could not afford any large or regular supplies, in a season of the year when the lands were covered by the inundation of the Euphrates,[84] and the unwholesome air was darkened with swarms of innumerable insects.[85] The appearance of the hostile country was far more inviting. The extensive region that lies between the river Tigris and the mountains of Media was filled with villages and towns; and the fertile soil, for the most part, was in a very improved state of cultivation. Julian might expect that a conqueror who possessed the two forcible instruments of persuasion, steel and gold, would easily procure a plentiful subsistence from the fears or the avarice of the natives. But on the approach of the Romans this rich and smiling prospect was instantly blasted. Wherever they moved, the inhabitants deserted the open villages, and took shelter in the fortified towns; the cattle was driven away; the grass and ripe corn were consumed with fire; and, as soon as the flames had subsided which interrupted the march of Julian, he beheld the melancholy face of a smoking and naked desert. This desperate but effectual method of defence can only be executed by the enthusiasm of a people who prefer their independence to their property; or by the rigour of an arbitrary government, which consults the public safety without submitting to their inclinations the liberty of choice. On the present occasion, the zeal and obedience of the Persians seconded the commands of Sapor; and the emperor was soon reduced to the scanty stock of provisions, which continually wasted in his hands. Before they were entirely consumed, he might still have reached the wealthy and unwarlike cities of Ecbatana or Susa, by the effort of a well-directed march;[86] but he was deprived of this last resource by his ignorance of the roads, and by the perfidy of his guides. The Romans wandered several days in the country to the eastward of Bagdad; the Persian deserter, who had artfully led them into the snare, escaped from their resentment; and his followers, as soon as they were put to the torture, confessed the secret of the conspiracy. The visionary conquests of Hyrcania* and India, which had so long amused, now tormented, the mind of Julian. Conscious that his own imprudence was the cause of the public distress, he anxiously balanced the hopes of safety or success, without obtaining a satisfactory answer either from gods or men. At length, as the only practicable measure, he embraced the resolution of directing his steps towards the banks of the Tigris, with the design of saving the army by a hasty march to the confines of Corduene, a fertile and friendly province, which acknowledged the sovereignty of Rome. The desponding troops obeyed the signal of the retreat, only seventy days after they had passed the Chaboras[†] with the sanguine expectation of subverting the throne of Persia.[87]

As long as the Romans seemed to advance into the country, their march was observed and insulted from a distance by several bodies of Persian cavalry; who, showing themselves sometimes in loose, and sometimes in closer, order, faintly skirmished with the advanced guards. These detachments were, however, supported by a much greater force; and the heads of the columns were no sooner pointed towards the Tigris than a cloud of dust arose on the plain. The Romans, who now aspired only to the permission of a safe and speedy retreat, endeavoured to persuade themselves that this formidable appearance was occasioned by a troop of wild asses, or perhaps by the approach of some friendly Arabs. They halted, pitched their tents, fortified their camp, passed the whole night in continual alarms; and discovered, at the dawn of day, that they were surrounded by an army of Persians. This army, which might be considered only as the van of the Barbarians, was soon followed by the main body of cuirassiers,[‡] archers, and elephants, commanded by Meranes, a general of rank and reputation. He was accompanied by two of the king's sons, and many of the principal satraps; and fame and expectation exaggerated the strength of the remaining powers, which slowly advanced under the conduct of Sapor himself. As the Romans continued their march, their long array, which was forced to bend, or divide, according to the varieties of the ground, afforded frequent and favourable opportunities to their vigilant enemies. The Persians repeatedly charged with fury; they were repeatedly repulsed with firmness; and the action at Maronga, which almost deserved the name of a battle, was marked by a considerable loss of satraps and elephants, perhaps of equal value in the eyes of their monarch. These splendid advantages were not obtained without an adequate slaughter on the side of the Romans: several officers of distinction were either killed or wounded; and the emperor himself, who, on all occasions of danger, inspired and guided the valour of his troops, was obliged to expose his person and exert his abilities. The weight of offensive and defensive arms, which still constituted the strength and safety of the Romans, disabled them from making any long or effectual pursuit; and, as the horsemen of the East were trained to dart their javelins, and shoot their arrows, at full speed, and in every possible direction,[88] the cavalry of Persia was never more formidable than in the moment of a rapid and disorderly flight. But the most certain and irreparable loss of the Romans was that of time. The hardy veterans, accustomed to the cold climate of Gaul and Germany, fainted under the sultry heat of an Assyrian summer; their vigour was exhausted by the incessant repetition of march and combat; and the progress of the army was suspended by the precautions of a slow and dangerous retreat in the presence of an active enemy. Every day, every hour, as the supply diminished, the value and price of subsistence increased in the Roman camp.[89] Julian, who always contented himself with such food as a hungry soldier would have disdained, distributed for the use of his troops the provisions of the imperial household, and whatever could be spared from the sumpter-horses* of the tribunes and generals. But this feeble relief served only to aggravate the sense of the public distress; and the Romans began to entertain the most gloomy apprehensions that, before they could reach the frontiers of the empire, they should all perish, either by famine or by the sword of the Barbarians.[90]

While Julian struggled with the almost insuperable difficulties of his situation, the silent hours of the night were still devoted to study and contemplation. Whenever he closed his eyes in short and interrupted slumbers, his mind was agitated with painful anxiety; nor can it be thought surprising that the Genius of the empire should once more appear before him, covering with a funeral veil his head and his horn of abundance, and slowly retiring from the Imperial tent. The monarch started from his couch, and stepping forth, to refresh his wearied spirits with the coolness of the midnight air, he beheld a fiery meteor, which shot athwart the sky, and suddenly vanished. Julian was convinced that he had seen the menacing countenance of the god of war;[91] the council which he summoned, of Tuscan haruspices,[92] unanimously pronounced that he should abstain from action; but, on this occasion, necessity and reason were more prevalent than superstition; and the trumpets sounded at the break of day. The army marched through a hilly country; and the hills had been secretly occupied by the Persians. Julian led the van, with the skill and attention of a consummate general; he was alarmed by the intelligence that his rear was suddenly attacked. The heat of the weather had tempted him to lay aside his cuirass; but he snatched a shield from one of his attendants, and hastened, with a sufficient reinforcement, to the relief of the rearguard. A similar danger recalled the intrepid prince to the defence of the front; and, as he galloped between the columns, the centre of the left was attacked, and almost overpowered, by a furious charge of the Persian cavalry and elephants. This huge body was soon defeated, by the well-timed evolution of the light infantry, who aimed their weapons, with dexterity and effect, against the backs of the horsemen and the legs of the elephants. The Barbarians fled; and Julian, who was foremost in every danger, animated the pursuit with his voice and gestures. His trembling guards, scattered and oppressed by the disorderly throng of friends and enemies, reminded their fearless sovereign that he was without armour; and conjured him to decline the fall of the impending ruin. As they exclaimed,[93] a cloud of darts and arrows was discharged from the flying squadrons; and a javelin, after razing the skin of his arm, transpierced the ribs, and fixed in the inferior part of the liver. Julian attempted to draw the deadly weapon from his side; but his fingers were cut by the sharpness of the steel, and he fell senseless from his horse. His guards flew to his relief; and the wounded emperor was gently raised from the ground, and conveyed out of the tumult of the battle into an adjacent tent. The report of the melancholy event passed from rank to rank; but the grief of the Romans inspired them with invincible valour and the desire of revenge. The bloody and obstinate conflict was maintained by the two armies, till they were separated by the total darkness of the night. The Persians derived some honour from the advantage which they obtained against the left wing, where Anatolius, master of the offices, was slain, and the prefect Sallust very narrowly escaped. But the event of the day was adverse to the Barbarians. They abandoned the field, their two generals, Meranes and Nohordates,[94] fifty nobles or satraps, and a multitude of their bravest soldiers; and the success of the Romans, if Julian had survived, might have been improved into a decisive and useful victory.

The first words that Julian uttered, after his recovery from the fainting fit into which he had been thrown by loss of blood, were expressive of his martial spirit. He called for his horse and arms, and was impatient to rush into the battle. His remaining strength was exhausted by the painful effort; and the surgeons who examined his wound discovered the symptoms of approaching death. He employed the awful moments with the firm temper of a hero and a sage; the philosophers who had accompanied him in this fatal expedition compared the tent of Julian with the prison of Socrates; and the spectators, whom duty, or friendship, or curiosity, had assembled around his couch, listened with respectful grief to the funeral oration of their dying emperor.[95] 'Friends and fellow-soldiers, the seasonable period of my departure is now arrived, and I discharge, with the cheerfulness of a ready debtor, the demands of nature. I have learned from philosophy, how much the soul is more excellent than the body; and that the separation of the nobler substance should be the subject of joy, rather than of affliction. I have learned from religion, that an early death has often been the reward of piety;[96] and I accept, as a favour of the gods, the mortal stroke that secures me from the danger of disgracing a character, which has hitherto been supported by virtue and fortitude. I die without remorse, as I have lived without guilt. I am pleased to reflect on the innocence of my private life; and I can affirm, with confidence, that the supreme authority, that emanation of the Divine Power, has been preserved in my hands pure and immaculate. Detesting the corrupt and destructive maxims of despotism, I have considered the happiness of the people as the end of government. Submitting my actions to the laws of prudence, of justice, and of moderation, I have trusted the event to the care of Providence. Peace was the object of my counsels, as long as peace was consistent with the public welfare; but, when the imperious voice of my country summoned me to arms, I exposed my person to the dangers of war, with the clear fore-knowledge (which I had acquired from the art of divination) that I was destined to fall by the sword. I now offer my tribute of gratitude to the Eternal Being, who has not suffered me to perish by the cruelty of a tyrant, by the secret dagger of conspiracy, or by the slow tortures of lingering disease. He has given me, in the midst of an honourable career, a splendid and glorious departure from this world; and I hold it equally absurd, equally base, to solicit, or to decline, the stroke of fate. – Thus much have I attempted to say; but my strength fails me, and I feel the approach of death. – I shall cautiously refrain from any word that may tend to influence your suffrages in the election of an emperor. My choice might be imprudent, or injudicious; and, if it should not be ratified by the consent of the army, it might be fatal to the person whom I should recommend. I shall only, as a good citizen, express my hopes that the Romans may be blessed with the government of a virtuous sovereign.' After this discourse, which Julian pronounced in a firm and gentle tone of voice, he distributed, by a military testament,[97] the remains of his private fortune; and, making some inquiry why Anatolius was not present, he understood, from the answer of Sallust, that Anatolius was killed; and bewailed, with amiable inconsistency, the loss of his friend. At the same time he reproved the immoderate grief of the spectators; and conjured them not to disgrace, by unmanly tears, the fate of a prince who in a few moments would be united with heaven, and with the stars.[98] The spectators were silent; and Julian entered into a metaphysical argument with the philosophers Priscus and Maximus, on the nature of the soul. The efforts which he made, of mind as well as body, most probably hastened his death. His wound began to bleed with fresh violence; his respiration was embarrassed by the swelling of the veins: he called for a draught of cold water, and, as soon as he had drunk it, expired without pain, about the hour of midnight. Such was the end of that extraordinary man, in the thirty-second year of his age, after a reign of one year and about eight months from the death of Constantius. In his last moments he displayed, perhaps with some ostentation, the love of virtue and of fame which had been the ruling passions of his life.[99]

The triumph of Christianity, and the calamities of the empire, may, in some measure, be ascribed to Julian himself, who had neglected to secure the future execution of his designs by the timely and judicious nomination of an associate and successor. But the royal race of Constantius Chlorus was reduced to his own person; and, if he entertained any serious thoughts of investing with the purple the most worthy among the

Romans, he was diverted from his resolution by the difficulty of the choice, the jealousy of power, the fear of ingratitude, and the natural presumption of health, of youth, and of prosperity. His unexpected death left the empire without a master and without an heir, in a state of perplexity and danger, which, in the space of fourscore years, had never been experienced, since the election of Diocletian. In a government which had almost forgotten the distinction of pure and noble blood, the superiority of birth was of little moment; the claims of official rank were accidental and precarious; and the candidates who might aspire to ascend the vacant throne could be supported only by the consciousness of personal merit, or by the hopes of popular favour. But the situation of a famished army, encompassed on all sides by an host of Barbarians, shortened the moments of grief and deliberation. In this scene of terror and distress, the body of the deceased prince, according to his own directions, was decently embalmed; and, at the dawn of day, the generals convened a military senate, at which the commanders of the legions and the officers, both of cavalry and infantry, were invited to assist. Three or four hours of the night had not passed away without some secret cabals; and, when the election of an emperor was proposed, the spirit of faction began to agitate the assembly. Victor and Arinthaeus collected the remains of the court of Constantius; the friends of Julian attached themselves to the Gallic chiefs, Dagalaiphus and Nevitta; and the most fatal consequences might be apprehended from the discord of two factions, so opposite in their character and interest, in their maxims of government, and perhaps in their religious principles. The superior virtues of Sallust could alone reconcile their divisions and unite their suffrages; and the venerable prefect would immediately have been declared the successor of Julian, if he himself, with sincere and modest firmness, had not alleged his age and infirmities, so unequal to the weight of the diadem. The generals, who were surprised and perplexed by his refusal, showed some disposition to adopt the salutary advice of an inferior officer,[100] that they should act as they would have acted in the absence of the emperor; that they should exert their abilities to extricate the army from the present distress; and, if they were fortunate enough to reach the confines of Mesopotamia, they should proceed with united and deliberate counsels in the election of a lawful sovereign. While they debated, a few voices saluted Jovian, who was no more than *first*[101] of the domestics, with the names of Emperor and Augustus. The tumultuary acclamation was instantly repeated by the guards who surrounded the tent, and passed, in a few minutes, to the extremities of the line. The new prince, astonished with his own fortune, was hastily invested with the Imperial ornaments and received an oath of fidelity from the generals whose favour and protection he so lately solicited. The strongest recommendation of Jovian was the merit of his father, Count Varronian, who enjoyed, in honourable retirement, the fruit of his long services. In the obscure freedom of a private station, the son indulged his taste for wine and women; yet he supported, with credit, the character of a Christian[102] and a soldier. Without being conspicuous for any of the ambitious qualifications which excite the admiration and envy of mankind, the comely person of Jovian, his cheerful temper, and familiar wit, had gained the affection of his fellow-soldiers; and the generals of both parties acquiesced in a popular election, which had not been conducted by the arts of their enemies. The pride of this unexpected elevation was moderated by the just apprehension that the same day might terminate the life and reign of the new emperor. The pressing voice of necessity was obeyed without delay; and the first orders issued by Jovian, a few hours after his predecessor had expired, were to prosecute a march which could alone extricate the Romans from their actual distress.[103]

The esteem of an enemy is most sincerely expressed by his fears; and the degree of fear may be accurately measured by the joy with which he celebrates his deliverance. The welcome news of the death of Julian, which a deserter revealed to the camp of Sapor, inspired the desponding monarch with a sudden confidence of victory. He immediately detached the royal cavalry, perhaps the ten thousand *Immortals*,[104] to second and support the pursuit; and discharged the whole weight of his united forces on the rearguard of the Romans. The rearguard was thrown into disorder; the renowned legions, which derived their titles from Diocletian and his warlike colleague, were broke and trampled down by the elephants; and three tribunes lost their lives in attempting to stop the flight of their soldiers. The battle was at length restored by the persevering valour of the Romans; the Persians were repulsed with a great slaughter of men and elephants; and the army, after marching and fighting a long summer's day, arrived, in the evening, at Samara on the banks of the Tigris, about one hundred miles above Ctesiphon.[105] On the ensuing day, the Barbarians, instead of harassing the march, attacked the camp, of Jovian which had been seated in a deep and sequestered valley. From the hills, the archers of Persia insulted and annoyed the wearied legionaries; and a body of cavalry, which had penetrated with desperate courage through the Praetorian gate, was cut in pieces, after a doubtful conflict, near the Imperial tent. In the succeeding night, the camp of Carche was protected by the lofty dykes of the river; and the Roman army, though incessantly exposed to the vexatious pursuit of the Saracens, pitched their tents near the city of Dura,[106] four days after the death of Julian. The Tigris was still on their left; their hopes and provisions were almost consumed; and the impatient soldiers, who had fondly persuaded themselves that the frontiers of the empire were not far distant, requested their new sovereign that they might be permitted to hazard the passage of the river. With the assistance of his wisest officers, Jovian endeavoured to check their rashness; by representing that, if they possessed sufficient skill and vigour to stem the torrent of a deep and rapid stream, they would only deliver themselves naked and defenceless to the Barbarians, who had occupied the opposite banks. Yielding at length to their clamorous importunities, he consented, with reluctance, that five hundred Gauls and Germans, accustomed from their infancy to the waters of the Rhine and Danube, should attempt the bold adventure, which might serve either as an encouragement, or as a warning, for the rest of the army. In the silence of the night, they swam the Tigris, surprised an unguarded post of the enemy, and displayed at the dawn of day the signal of their resolution and fortune. The success of this trial disposed the emperor to listen to the promises of his architects, who proposed to construct a floating bridge of the inflated skins of sheep, oxen, and goats, covered with a floor of earth and fascines.*[107] Two important days were spent in the ineffectual labour; and the Romans, who already endured the miseries of famine, cast a look of despair on the Tigris, and upon the Barbarians; whose numbers and obstinacy increased with the distress of the Imperial army.[108]

In this hopeless situation, the fainting spirits of the Romans were revived by the sound of peace. The transient presumption of Sapor had vanished: he observed, with serious concern, that, in the repetition of doubtful combats, he had lost his most faithful and intrepid nobles, his bravest troops, and the greatest part of his train of elephants; and the experienced monarch feared to provoke the resistance of despair, the vicissitudes of fortune, and the unexhausted powers of the Roman empire; which might soon advance to relieve, or to revenge, the successor of Julian. The Surenas himself, accompanied by another satrap, appeared in the camp of Jovian;[109] and declared that the clemency of his sovereign was not averse to signify the conditions on which he would consent to spare and to dismiss the Caesar with the relics of his captive army. The hopes of safety subdued the firmness of the Romans; the emperor was compelled, by the advice of his council and the cries of the soldiers, to embrace the offer of peace; and the prefect Sallust was immediately sent, with the general Arinthaeus, to understand the pleasure of the Great King. The crafty Persian delayed, under various pretences, the conclusion of the agreement; started difficulties, required explanations, suggested expedients, receded from his concessions, increased his demands, and wasted four days in the arts of negotiation, till he had consumed the stock of provisions which yet remained in the camp of the Romans. Had Jovian been capable of executing a bold and prudent measure, he would have continued his march with unremitting diligence; the progress of the treaty would have suspended the attacks of the Barbarians; and, before the expiration of the fourth day, he might have safely reached the fruitful province of Corduene, at the distance only of one hundred miles.[110] The irresolute emperor, instead of breaking through the toils† of the enemy, expected his fate with patient resignation; and accepted the humiliating conditions of peace, which it was no longer in his power to refuse. The five provinces beyond the Tigris, which had been ceded by the grandfather of Sapor, were restored to the Persian monarchy. He acquired, by a single article, the impregnable city of Nisibis; which had sustained, in three successive sieges, the effort of his arms. Singara, and the castle of the Moors, one of the strongest places of Mesopotamia, were likewise dismembered from the empire. It was considered as an indulgence, that the inhabitants of those fortresses were permitted to retire with their effects; but the conqueror rigorously insisted that the Romans should for ever abandon the king and kingdom of Armenia. A peace, or rather a long truce, of thirty years was stipulated between the hostile nations; the faith of the treaty was ratified by solemn oaths and religious ceremonies; and hostages of distinguished rank were reciprocally delivered to secure the performance of the conditions.[111]

The sophist of Antioch, who saw with indignation the sceptre of his hero in the feeble hand of a Christian successor, professes to admire the moderation of Sapor, in contenting himself with so small a portion of the Roman empire. If he had stretched as far as the Euphrates the claims of his ambition, he might have been secure, says Libanius, of not meeting with a refusal. If he had fixed, as the boundary of Persia, the Orontes, the Cydnus, the Sangarius,* or even the Thracian Bosphorus, flatterers would not have been wanting in the court of Jovian to convince the timid monarch that his remaining provinces would still afford the most ample gratifications of power and luxury.[112] Without adopting in its full force this malicious insinuation, we must acknowledge that the conclusion of so ignominious a treaty was facilitated by the private ambition of Jovian. The obscure domestic, exalted to the throne by fortune rather than by merit, was impatient to escape from the hands of the Persians; that he might prevent the designs of Procopius, who commanded the army of Mesopotamia, and establish his doubtful reign over the legions and provinces, which were still ignorant of the hasty and tumultuous choice of the camp beyond the Tigris.[113] In the neighbourhood of the same river, at no very considerable distance from the fatal station of Dura,[114] the ten thousand Greeks, without generals, or guides, or provisions, were abandoned, above twelve hundred miles from their native country, to the resentment of a victorious monarch.† The difference of *their* conduct and success depended much more on their character than on their situation. Instead of tamely resigning themselves to the secret deliberations and private views of a single person, the united councils of the Greeks were inspired by the generous enthusiasm of a popular assembly; where the mind of each citizen is filled with the love of glory, the pride of freedom, and the contempt of death. Conscious of their superiority over the Barbarians in arms and discipline, they disdained to yield, they refused to capitulate; every obstacle was surmounted by their patience, courage, and military skill; and the memorable retreat of the ten thousand exposed and insulted the weakness of the Persian monarchy.[115]

As the price of his disgraceful concessions, the emperor might perhaps have stipulated that the camp of the hungry Romans should be plentifully supplied;[116] and that they should be permitted to pass the Tigris on the bridge which was constructed by the hands of the Persians. But, if Jovian presumed to solicit those equitable terms, they were sternly refused by the haughty tyrant of the East; whose clemency had pardoned the invaders of his country. The Saracens sometimes intercepted the stragglers of the march; but the generals and troops of Sapor respected the cessation of arms; and Jovian was suffered to explore the most convenient place for the passage of the river. The small vessels, which had been saved from the conflagration of the fleet, performed the most essential service. They first conveyed the emperor and his favourites; and afterwards transported, in many successive voyages, a great part of the army. But, as every man was anxious for his personal safety, and apprehensive of being left on the hostile shore, the soldiers, who were too impatient to wait the slow returns of the boats, boldly ventured themselves on light hurdles, or inflated skins; and, drawing after them their horses, attempted, with various success, to swim across the river. Many of these daring adventurers were swallowed by the waves; many others, who were carried along by the violence of the stream, fell an easy prey to the avarice, or cruelty, of the wild Arabs; and the loss which the army sustained in the passage of the Tigris was not inferior to the carnage of a day of battle. As soon as the Romans had landed on the western bank, they were delivered from the hostile pursuit of the Barbarians; but, in a laborious march of two hundred miles over the plains of Mesopotamia, they endured the last extremities of thirst and hunger. They were obliged to traverse a sandy desert, which, in the extent of seventy miles, did not afford a single blade of sweet grass, nor a single spring of fresh water; and the rest of the inhospitable waste was untrod by the footsteps either of friends or enemies. Whenever a small measure of flour could be discovered in the camp, twenty pounds weight were greedily purchased with ten pieces of gold;[117] the beasts of burden were slaughtered and devoured; and the desert was strewed with the arms and baggage of the Roman soldiers, whose tattered garments and meagre countenances displayed their past sufferings and actual misery. A small convoy of provisions advanced to meet the army as far as the castle of Ur; and the supply was the more grateful, since it declared the fidelity of Sebastian and Procopius. At Thilsaphata[118] the emperor most graciously received the generals of Mesopotamia, and the remains of a once flourishing army at length reposed themselves under the walls of Nisibis. The messengers of Jovian had already proclaimed, in the language of flattery, his election, his treaty, and his return; and the new prince had taken the most effectual measures to secure the allegiance of the armies and provinces of Europe, by placing the military command in the hands of those officers who, from motives of interest or inclination, would firmly support the cause of their benefactor.[119]

The friends of Julian had confidently announced the success of his expedition. They entertained a fond persuasion that the temples of the gods would be enriched with the spoils of the East; that Persia would be reduced to the humble state of a tributary province, governed by the laws and magistrates of Rome; that the Barbarians would adopt the dress, and manners, and language, of their conquerors; and that the youth of Ecbatana and Susa would study the art of rhetoric under Grecian masters.[120] The progress of the arms of Julian interrupted his communication with the empire; and, from the moment that he passed the Tigris, his affectionate subjects were ignorant of the fate and fortunes of their prince. Their contemplation of fancied triumphs was disturbed by the melancholy rumour of his death; and they persisted to doubt, after they could no longer deny, the truth of that fatal event.[121] The messengers of Jovian promulgated the specious tale of a prudent and necessary peace: the voice of fame, louder and more sincere, revealed the disgrace of the emperor and the conditions of the ignominious treaty. The minds of the people were filled with astonishment and grief, with indignation and terror, when they were informed that the unworthy successor of Julian relinquished the five provinces which had been acquired by the victory of Galerius; and that he shamefully surrendered to the Barbarians the important city of Nisibis, the firmest bulwark of the provinces of the East.[122] The deep and dangerous question, how far the public faith should be observed, when it becomes incompatible with the public safety, was freely agitated in popular conversation; and some hopes were entertained that the emperor would redeem his pusillanimous behaviour by a splendid act of patriotic perfidy. The inflexible spirit of the Roman senate had always disclaimed the unequal conditions which were extorted from the distress of her captive armies; and, if it were necessary to satisfy the national honour by delivering the guilty general into the hands of the Barbarians, the greatest part of the subjects of Jovian would have cheerfully acquiesced in the precedent of ancient times.[123]

But the emperor, whatever might be the limits of his constitutional authority, was the absolute master of the laws and arms of the state; and the same motives which had forced him to subscribe, now pressed him to execute, the treaty of peace. He was impatient to secure an empire at the expense of a few provinces; and the respectable names of religion and honour concealed the personal fears and the ambition of Jovian. Notwithstanding the dutiful solicitations of the inhabitants, decency, as well as prudence, forbade the emperor to lodge in the palace of Nisibis; but, the next morning after his arrival, Bineses, the ambassador of Persia, entered the place, displayed from the citadel the standard of the Great King, and proclaimed, in his name, the cruel alternative of exile or servitude. The principal citizens of Nisibis, who, till that fatal moment, had confided in the protection of their sovereign, threw themselves at his feet. They conjured him not to abandon, or, at least, not to deliver, a faithful colony to the rage of a barbarian tyrant, exasperated by the three successive defeats which he had experienced under the walls of Nisibis. They still possessed arms and courage to repel the invaders of their country; they requested only the permission of using them in their own defence; and, as soon as they had asserted their independence, they should implore the favour of being again admitted into the rank of his subjects. Their arguments, their eloquence, their tears, were ineffectual. Jovian alleged, with some confusion, the sanctity of oaths; and, as the reluctance with which he accepted the present of a crown of gold convinced the citizens of their hopeless condition, the advocate Sylvanus was provoked to exclaim, 'O Emperor! may you thus be crowned by all the cities of your dominions!' Jovian, who, in a few weeks, had assumed the habits of a prince,[124] was displeased with freedom, and offended with truth; and, as he reasonably supposed that the discontent of the people might incline them to submit to the Persian government, he published an edict, under pain of death, that they should leave the city within the term of three days. Ammianus has delineated in lively colours the scene of universal despair, which he seems to have viewed with an eye of compassion.[125] The martial youth deserted, with indignant grief, the walls which they had so gloriously defended; the disconsolate mourner dropt a last tear over the tomb of a son or husband, which must soon be profaned by the rude hand of a Barbarian master; and the aged citizen kissed the threshold, and clung to the doors, of the house where he had passed the cheerful and careless hours of infancy. The highways were crowded with a trembling multitude: the distinctions of rank, and sex, and age, were lost in the general calamity. Every one strove to bear away some fragment from the wreck of his fortunes; and, as they could not command the immediate service of an adequate number of horses or waggons, they were obliged to leave behind them the greatest part of their valuable effects. The savage insensibility of Jovian appears to have aggravated the hardships of these unhappy fugitives. They were seated, however, in a new-built quarter of Amida; and that rising city, with the reinforcement of a very considerable colony, soon recovered its former splendour, and became the capital of Mesopotamia.[126] Similar orders were dispatched by the emperor for the evacuation of Singara and the castle of the Moors; and for the restitution of the five provinces beyond the Tigris. Sapor enjoyed the glory and the fruits of his victory; and this ignominious peace has justly been considered as a memorable era in the decline and fall of the Roman empire. The predecessors of Jovian had sometimes relinquished the dominion of distant and unprofitable provinces; but, since the foundation of the city, the genius* of Rome, the god Terminus, who guarded the boundaries of the republic, had never retired before the sword of a victorious enemy.[127]

After Jovian had performed those engagements which the voice of his people might have tempted him to violate, he hastened away from the scene of his disgrace, and proceeded with his whole court to enjoy the luxury of Antioch.[128] Without consulting the dictates of religious zeal, he was prompted, by humanity and gratitude, to bestow the last honours on the remains of his deceased sovereign;[129] and Procopius, who sincerely bewailed the loss of his kinsman, was removed from the command of the army, under the decent pretence of conducting the funeral. The corpse of Julian was transported from Nisibis to Tarsus, in a slow march of fifteen days; and, as it passed through the cities of the East, was saluted by the hostile factions, with mournful lamentations and clamorous insults. The Pagans already placed their beloved hero in the rank of those gods whose worship he had restored; while the invectives of the Christians pursued the soul of the apostate to hell, and his body to the grave.[130] One party lamented the approaching ruin of their altars; the other celebrated the marvellous deliverance of the church. The Christians applauded, in lofty and ambiguous strains, the stroke of divine vengeance, which had been so long suspended over the guilty head of Julian. They acknowledged that the death of the tyrant, at the instant he expired beyond the Tigris, was *revealed* to the saints of Egypt, Syria and Cappadocia;[131] and, instead of suffering him to fall by the Persian darts, their indiscretion ascribed the heroic deed to the obscure hand of some mortal or immortal champion of the faith.[132] Such imprudent declarations were eagerly adopted by the malice, or credulity, of their adversaries;[133] who darkly insinuated, or confidently asserted, that the governors of the church had instigated and directed the fanaticism of a domestic assassin.[134] Above sixteen years after the death of Julian, the charge was solemnly and vehemently urged, in a public oration, addressed by Libanius to the emperor Theodosius. His suspicions are unsupported by fact or argument; and we can only esteem the generous zeal of the sophist of Antioch for the cold and neglected ashes of his friend.[135]

It was an ancient custom in the funerals, as well as in the triumphs, of the Romans, that the voice of praise should be corrected by that of satire and ridicule; and that, in the midst of the splendid pageants, which displayed the glory of the living or of the dead, their imperfections should not be concealed from the eyes of the world.[136] This custom was practised in the funeral of Julian. The comedians, who resented his contempt and aversion for the theatre, exhibited, with the applause of a Christian audience, the lively and exaggerated representation of the faults and follies of the deceased emperor. His various character and singular manners afforded an ample scope for pleasantry and ridicule.[137] In the exercise of his uncommon talents, he often descended below the majesty of his rank. Alexander was transformed into Diogenes;* the philosopher was degraded into a priest. The purity of his virtue was sullied by excessive vanity: his superstition disturbed the peace, and endangered the safety, of a mighty empire; and his irregular sallies were the less entitled to indulgence, as they appeared to be the laborious efforts of art, or even of affectation. The remains of Julian were interred at Tarsus in Cilicia; but his stately tomb which arose in that city, on the banks of the cold and limpid Cydnus,[138] was displeasing to the faithful friends, who loved and revered the memory of that extraordinary man. The philosopher expressed a very reasonable wish that the disciple of Plato might have reposed amidst the groves of the academy;[139] while the soldiers exclaimed in bolder accents that the ashes of Julian should have been mingled with those of Caesar, in the field of Mars, and among the ancient monuments of Roman virtue.[140] The history of princes does not very frequently renew the example of a similar competition.

NOTES ON CHAPTER 24

1 See this fable or satire, pp. 306–36 of the Leipzig edition of Julian's works. The French version of the learned Ezekiel Spanheim (Paris, 1683) is coarse, languid, and incorrect; and his notes, proofs, illustrations, etc. are piled on each other till they form a mass of 557 close-printed quarto pages. The Abbé de la Bléterie (*Vie de Jovien*, i, 241–393) has more happily expressed the spirit, as well as the sense, of the original, which he illustrates with some concise and curious notes.

2 Spanheim (in his preface) has most learnedly discussed the etymology, origin, resemblance, and disagreement of the Greek *satyrs*, a dramatic piece, which was acted after the tragedy; and the Latin *satires* (from *satura*), a *miscellaneous* composition, either in prose or verse. But the *Caesars* of Julian are of such an original cast that the critic is perplexed to which class he should ascribe them.

* *page 507* [Roman festival, held in late December, in which social roles were reversed and slaves were allowed to make fun of their masters.]

3 This mixed character of Silenus is finely painted in the sixth eclogue of Virgil.

4 Every impartial reader must perceive and condemn the partiality of Julian against his uncle Constantine and the Christian religion. On this occasion the interpreters are compelled, by a more sacred interest, to renounce their allegiance, and to desert the cause of their author.

5 Julian was secretly inclined to prefer a Greek to a Roman. But, when he seriously compared a hero with a philosopher, he was sensible that mankind had much greater obligations to Socrates than to Alexander (*Orat. ad Themistium*, p. 264).

* *page 508* [acknowledges]

6 *Inde nationibus Indicis certatum cum donis optimates mittentibus . . . ab usque Divis et Serendivis.* ['He was sought out by the peoples of India, who sent their leading men with gifts . . . from as far away as the Divi and the Ceylonese.'] Ammian., xxii, 7. This island to which the names of Taprobana, Serendib, and Ceylon, have been successively applied manifests how imperfectly the seas and lands to the east of Cape Comorin were known to the Romans. 1. Under the reign of Claudius, a freedman, who farmed the customs of the Red Sea, was accidentally driven by the winds upon this strange and undiscovered coast: he conversed six months with the natives; and the king of Ceylon, who heard, for the first time, of the power and justice of Rome, was persuaded to send an embassy to the emperor (Pliny, *Hist. Nat.*, vi, 24). 2. The geographers (and even Ptolemy) have magnified, above fifteen times, the real size of this new world, which they extended as far as the equator and the neighbourhood of China.

7 These embassies had been sent to Constantius. Ammianus, who unwarily deviates into gross flattery, must have forgotten the length of the way, and the short duration of the reign of Julian.

8 *Gothos saepe fallaces et perfidos; hostes quaerere se meliores aiebat: illis enim sufficere mercatores Galatas per quos ubique sine conditionis discrimine venundantur.* ['He said the Goths were often deceitful and treacherous; he sought superior foes: for the Goths it was enough to hire the mercenary Galatians, by whom they were everywhere sold into slavery.'] Within less than fifteen years, these Gothic slaves threatened and subdued their masters.

9 Alexander reminds his rival Caesar, who deprecated the fame and merit of an Asiatic victory, that Crassus and Antony had felt the Persian arrows; and that the Romans, in a war of three hundred years, had not yet subdued the single province of Mesopotamia or Assyria (*Caesares*, p. 324).

† *page 508* [Sapor II, King of Persia from his birth in ad 310 until his death in 380.]

10 The design of the Persian war is declared by Ammianus (xxii, 7, 12), Libanius (*Orat. Parent.*, chs 79, 80, pp. 305, 306), Zosimus (iii, 158), and Socrates (iii, 19).

11 The satire of Julian and the *Homilies* of St Chrysostom exhibit the same picture of Antioch. The miniature which the Abbé de la Blétérie has copied from thence (*Vie de Julien*, p. 332) is elegant, and correct.

12 Laodicea furnished charioteers; Tyre and Berytus, comedians; Caesarea, pantomimes; Heliopolis, singers; Gaza, gladiators; Ascalon, wrestlers; and Castabala, rope-dancers. See the *Expositio totius Mundi*, p. 6, in the third tome of Hudson's *Minor Geographers*.

13 Χριστὸν δὲ ἀγαπῶντες, ἔχετε πολιοῦχον ἀντὶ τοῦ Διός. ['In adoring Christ, you have a guardian in the place of Zeus.'] The people of Antioch ingeniously professed their attachment to the *Chi* (Christ) and the *Kappa* (Constantius). Julian., *in Misopogon.*, p. 357.

14 The schism of Antioch, which lasted eighty-five years (AD 330–415), was inflamed, while Julian resided in that city, by the indiscreet ordination of Paulinus. See Tillemont, *Mém. Ecclés.*, vii, 803, of the quarto edition (Paris, 1701, etc.), which henceforward I shall quote. [See footnote 102 of Chapter 21. Paulinus was a rival to Meletius, the bishop of Antioch. The death of Meletius in AD 381 caused a schism at the Council of Constantinople. Paulinus was supported by the Western bishops as his successor, but the majority were against him.]

15 Julian states three different proportions of five, ten, or fifteen *modii* of wheat for one piece of gold, according to the degrees of plenty and scarcity (*in Misopogon.*, p. 369). From this fact, and from some collateral examples, I conclude that under the successors of Constantine the moderate price of wheat was about thirty-two shillings the English quarter, which is equal to the average price of the sixty-four first years of the present century. See Arbuthnot's *Tables of Coins, Weights, and Measures*, pp. 88, 89; Pliny, *Hist. Natur.*, xviii, 12. *Mém. de l'Académie des Inscriptions*, xxviii, 718–21; Smith's *Inquiry into the Nature and Causes of the Wealth of Nations*, i, 246. This last I am proud to quote, as the work of a sage and a friend. [Adam Smith, 1723–90, whose *Wealth of Nations* was published in 1776, the same year as the first volume of the *Decline and Fall*.]

* *page 511* [Elder brother of Julian, who was executed in AD 354 for crimes committed when he ruled as Caesar at Antioch.]

16 *Nunquam a proposito declinabat, Galli similis fratris, licet incruentus*, Ammian., xxii,

14. The ignorance of the most enlightened princes may claim some excuse: but we cannot be satisfied with Julian's own defence (*in Misopogon.*, pp. 368, 369), or the elaborate apology of Libanius (*Orat. Parental.*, xcvii, 321).

17 Their short and easy confinement is gently touched by Libanius, *Orat. Parental.*, xcviii, 322, 323.

18 Libanius (*ad Antiochenos de Imperatoris ira*, chs 17, 18, 19, in Fabricius, *Bibliot. Graec.*, vii, 221–23), like a skilful advocate, severely censures the folly of the people, who suffered for the crime of a few obscure and drunken wretches.

19 Libanius (*ad Antiochen.*, vii, 213) reminds Antioch of the recent chastisement of Caesarea: and even Julian (*in Misopogon.*, p. 355) insinuates how severely Tarentum had expiated the insult to the Roman ambassadors.

20 On the subject of the *Misopogon*, see Ammianus (xxii, 14), Libanius (*Orat. Parentalis*, xcix, 323), Gregory Nazianzen (*Orat.*, iv, 133), and the Chronicle of Antioch, by John Malala (ii, 15, 16). I have essential obligations to the translation and notes of the Abbé de la Bléterie (*Vie de Jovien*, ii, 1–138).

21 Ammianus very justly remarks, *Coactus dissimulare pro tempore ira sufflabatur interna.* ['Compelled for the time being to conceal his anger, he seethed internally.'] The elaborate irony of Julian at length bursts forth into serious and direct invective.

22 *Ipse autem Antiochiam egressurus, Heliopoliten quendam Alexandrum Syriacae iurisdictioni praefecit, turbulentum et saevum; dicebatque non illum meruisse, sed Antiochensibus avaris et contumeliosis huiusmodi iudicem convenire.* ['He appointed as governor of Syria, one Alexander from Heliopolis, a cruel and unbalanced man; and he used to say that it was not due to Alexander's merits, but rather that the greedy and quarrelsome people of Antioch deserved a governor of this kind.'] Ammian., xxiii, 2. Libanius (*Epist.*, 722, pp. 346, 347), who confesses to Julian himself that he had shared the general discontent, pretends that Alexander was an useful, though harsh, reformer of the manners and religion of Antioch.

23 Julian., *in Misopogon.*, p. 364; Ammian., xxiii, 2, and Valesius, *ad loc.* Libanius, in a professed oration, invites him to return to his loyal and penitent city of Antioch.

24 Libanius, *Orat. Parent.*, vii, 230, 231.

25 Eunapius reports that Libanius refused the honorary rank of Praetorian prefect, as less illustrious than the title of Sophist (*in Vit. Sophist.*, p. 135). The critics have observed a similar sentiment in one of the epistles (xviii, edit. Wolf) of Libanius himself.

26 Near two thousand of his letters, a mode of composition in which Libanius was thought to excel, are still extant, and already published. The critics may praise their subtle and elegant brevity; yet Dr Bentley (*Dissertation upon Phalaris*, p. 487) might justly, though quaintly, observe that 'you feel, by the emptiness and deadness of them, that you converse with some dreaming pedant with his elbow on his desk.' [Bentley, a famous classical scholar, 1662–1742.]

27 His birth is assigned to the year 314. He mentions the seventy-sixth year of his age (AD 390), and seems to allude to some events of a still later date.

28 Libanius has composed the vain, prolix, but curious, narrative of his own life (ii, 1–84, edit. Morell.), of which Eunapius (p. 130–35) has left a concise and unfavourable account. Among the moderns, Tillemont (*Hist. des Empereurs*, iv, pp. 571–76), Fabricius (*Bibliot. Graec.*, vii, 376–414) and Lardner (*Heathen Testimonies*, iv, 127–63) have illustrated the character and writings of this famous sophist.

29 From Antioch to Litarbe, on the territory of Chalcis, the road, over hills and through morasses, was extremely bad; and the loose stones were cemented only with sand. Julian., *Epist.*, xxvii. It is singular enough that the Romans should have neglected the great communication between Antioch and the Euphrates. See Wesseling, *Itinerar.*, p. 190; Bergier, *Hist. des Grands Chemins*, ii, 100.

30 Julian alludes to this incident (*Epist.*, xxvii), which is more distinctly related by Theodoret (iii, 22). The intolerant spirit of the father is applauded by Tillemont (*Hist. des Empereurs*, iv, 534), and even by La Bléterie (*Vie de Julien*, p. 413).

31 See the curious treatise *de Dea Syria*, inserted among the works of Lucian (iii, 451–90, edit. Reitz). The singular appellation of *Ninus vetus* [old Ninus] (Ammian., xiv, 8) might induce a suspicion that Hierapolis had been the royal seat of the Assyrians. [Ninus was the reputed founder of the city of the same name, otherwise known as Nineveh.]

32 Julian (*Epistle* xxviii) kept a regular account of all the fortunate omens but he suppresses the inauspicious signs, which Ammianus (xxiii, 2) has carefully recorded.

33 Julian, *Epistle* xxvii, pp. 399–402.

34 I take the earliest opportunity of acknowledging my obligations to M. d'Anville for his recent geography of the Euphrates and Tigris (Paris, 1780, in 4to), which particularly illustrates the expedition of Julian.

35 There are three passages within a few miles of each other: 1. Zeugma, celebrated by the ancients; 2. Bir, frequented by the moderns; and 3. the bridge of Menbigz, or Hierapolis, at the distance of four parasangs from the city.

36 Haran, or Carrhae, was the ancient residence of the Sabaeans and of Abraham. See the *Index Geographicus* of Schultens (*ad calcem Vit. Saladin.*), a work from which I have obtained much Oriental knowledge concerning the ancient and modern geography of Syria and the adjacent countries.

* *page 514*   [The Persian capital]

37 See Xenophon, *Cyropaed.*, iii, 189, edit. Hutchinson. Artavasdes might have supplied Mark Antony with 16,000 horse, armed and disciplined after the Parthian manner (Plutarch, *in M. Antonio*, v, 117).

38 Moses of Chorene (*Hist. Armeniac.*, iii, 11, p. 242) fixes his accession (AD 357) to the seventeenth year of Constantius.

† *page 514*   [King of Armenia in the time of the Emperor Diocletian: see Ch. 13.]

39 Ammian., xx, 11. Athanasius (i, 856) says, in general terms, that Constantius gave his brother's widow τοῖς βαρβάροις [to the Barbarians], an expression more suitable to a Roman than a Christian.

40 Ammianus (xxiii, 2) uses a word much too soft for the occasion, *monuerat* [he (Julian) had warned]. Muratori (Fabricius, *Bibliothec. Graec.*, vii, 86) has published an epistle from Julian to the satrap Arsaces; fierce, vulgar, and (though it might deceive Sozomen, vi, 5), most probably spurious. La Bléterie (*Hist. de Jovien*, ii, 339) translates and rejects it.

* *page 515*   [perceived]

41 *Latissimum flumen Euphraten artabat.* Ammian., xxiii, 3. Somewhat higher, at the fords of Thapsacus, the river is four stadia, or 800 yards, almost half an English mile broad (Xenophon, *Anabasis*, i, 41, edit. Hutchinson, with Foster's Observations, p. 29, etc. in the second volume of Spelman's translation). If the breadth of the Euphrates at Bir and Zeugma is no more than 130 yards (*Voyages*

de Niebuhr, ii, 335), the enormous difference must chiefly arise from the depth of the channel.

42 *Munimentum tutissimum et fabre politum, cuius moenia Abora* (the Orientals aspire [i.e. pronounce with an 'h'] Chaboras or Chabour) *et Euphrates ambiunt flumina, velut spatium insulare fingentes* ['a very secure fortification, ingeniously fashioned, past whose walls flow the rivers Abora and Euphrates, forming as it were an island']. Ammian., xxiii, 5.

* *page 516* [give up, sacrifice]

43 The enterprise and armament of Julian are described by himself (*Epist.*, xxvii), Ammianus Marcellinus (xxiii, 3, 4 and 5), Libanius (*Orat. Parent.*, chs 108, 109, pp. 332, 333), Zosimus (iii, 160, 161 and 162), Sozomen (vi, 1), and John Malala (ii, 17).

44 Before he enters Persia, Ammianus copiously describes (xxiii, 6, pp. 396–419, edit. Gronov. in 4to) the eighteen great satrapies, or provinces (as far as the Seric, or Chinese, frontiers), which were subject to the Sassanides.

45 Ammianus (xxiv, 1) and Zosimus (iii, 162, 163) have accurately expressed the order of march.

46 The adventures of Hormisdas are related with some mixture of fable (Zosimus, ii, 100–02, Tillemont, *Hist. des Empereurs*, iv, 198). It is almost impossible that he should be the brother (*frater germanus*) of an *eldest* and *posthumous* child: nor do I recollect that Ammianus ever gives him that title.

47 See the first book of the *Anabasis*, pp. 45, 46. This pleasing work is original and authentic. Yet Xenophon's memory, perhaps many years after the expedition, has sometimes betrayed him; and the distances which he marks are often larger than either a soldier or a geographer will allow. [Xenophon was the Greek general and historian (431–*c*.350 BC) who served with a band of Spartan mercenaries under the Persian Cyrus.]

48 Mr Spelman, the English translator of the *Anabasis* (i, 51), confounds the antelope with the roe-buck, and the wild ass with the zebra.

49 See *Voyages* de Tavernier, i, iii, 316, and more especially *Viaggi* di Pietro della Valle, i, xvii, 671, etc. He was ignorant of the old name and condition of Annah. Our blind travellers *seldom* possess any previous knowledge of the countries which they visit. Shaw and Tournefort deserve an honourable exception.

* *page 517* [present-day]

50 *Famosi nominis latro* ['a well-known bandit'], says Ammianus; an high encomium for an Arab. The tribe of Gassan had settled on the edge of Syria, and reigned some time in Damascus, under a dynasty of thirty-one kings, or emirs, from the time of Pompey to that of the Khalif Omar. D'Herbelot, *Bibliothèque Orientale*, p. 360. Pocock, *Specimen Hist. Arabicae*, pp. 75–8. The name of Rodosaces does not appear in the list.

51 See Ammianus (xxiv, 1, 2), Libanius (*Orat. Parental.*, chs 110, 111, p. 334), Zosimus (iii, 164–68).

52 The description of Assyria is furnished by Herodotus (i, 192, etc.), who sometimes writes for children, and sometimes for philosophers; by Strabo (xvi, 1070–82), and by Ammianus (xxiii, 6). The most useful of the modern travellers are Tavernier (i, ii, 226–58), Otter (ii, 35–69, and 189–224), and Niebuhr (ii, 172–288). Yet I much regret that the *Irak Arabi* of Abulfeda has not been translated.

53 Ammianus remarks that the primitive Assyria, which comprehended Ninus (Nineveh) and Arbela, had assumed the more recent and peculiar appellation

of Adiabene: and he seems to fix Teredon, Vologesia, and Apollonia, as the *extreme* cities of the actual province of Assyria.

54 The two rivers unite at Apamea, or Corna (one hundred miles from the Persian Gulf), into the broad stream of the Pasitigris, or Shat-ul-Arab. The Euphrates formerly reached the sea by a separate channel, which was obstructed and diverted by the citizens of Orchoe, about twenty miles to the south-east of modern Basra (d'Anville, in the *Mémoires de l'Acad. des Inscriptions*, xxx, 170–91).

* *page 518* ['the land between rivers' (Greek)]

55 The learned Kaempfer, as a botanist, an antiquary, and a traveller, has exhausted (*Amoenitat. Exoticae*, iv, 630–764) the whole subject of palm trees.

* *page 519* [viceroy, or ruler of a province]

56 Assyria yielded to the Persian satrap an *artaba* of silver each day. The well known proportion of weights and measures (see Bishop Hooper's elaborate *Inquiry*), the specific gravity of water and silver, and the value of that metal, will afford, after a short process, the annual revenue which I have stated. Yet the Great King received no more than 1000 Euboic, or Tyrian, talents (£252,000) from Assyria. The comparison of two passages in Herodotus (i, 192; iii, 89–96) reveals an important difference between the *gross*, and the net, revenue of Persia; the sums paid by the province, and the gold or silver deposited in the royal treasure. The monarch might annually save three millions six hundred thousand pounds, of the seventeen or eighteen millions raised upon the people.

† *page 519* [large military engines for throwing stones]

‡ *page 519* [siege-engine]

* *page 520* [Roman town on the upper Tigris besieged and taken by Sapor in AD359]

† *page 520* [The Zoroastrian God of goodness, described by Gibbon in Chapter 8 as 'eternally absorbed in light'.]

57 The operations of the Assyrian war are circumstantially related by Ammianus (xxiv, 2, 3, 4, 5), Libanius (*Orat. Parent.*, chs 112–23, pp. 335–47), Zosimus (iii, 168–80), and Gregory Nazianzen (*Orat.*, iv, 113, 144). The *military* criticisms of the saint are devoutly copied by Tillemont, his faithful slave.

58 Libanius, *de ulciscenda Juliani nece*, 13, 162.

59 The famous examples of Cyrus, Alexander, and Scipio were acts of justice. Julian's chastity was voluntary, and, in his opinion, meritorious.

60 Sallust (*ap.* Vet. Scholiast. Juvenal, *Satir.*, i, 104) observes that *nihil corruptius moribus* [nothing was more degenerate than their morals]. The matrons and virgins of Babylon freely mingled with the men in licentious banquets: and, as they felt the intoxication of wine and love, they gradually, and almost completely, threw aside the encumbrance of dress; *ad ultimum ima corporum velamenta proiiciunt*. Q. Curtius, v, 1.

61 *Ex virginibus autem, quae speciosae sunt captae, et in Perside, ubi feminarum pulchritudo excellit, nec contrectare aliquam voluit nec videre.* Ammian., xxiv, 4. The native race of Persians is small and ugly; but it has been improved by the perpetual mixture of Circassian blood (Herodot., iii, 97. Buffon, *Hist. Naturelle*, iii, 420).

62 *Obsidionalibus coronis donati.* Ammian., xxiv, 4. Either Julian or his historian were unskilful antiquaries. He should have given *mural* crowns [for tunnelling under the *walls*]. The *obsidional* were the reward of a general who had delivered a besieged city (Aulus Gellius, *Noct. Attic.*, v, 6).

63 I give this speech as original and genuine. Ammianus might hear, could

transcribe, and was incapable of inventing, it. I have used some slight freedoms, and conclude with the most forcible sentence.

* *page 523* [Libanius, who sang his praises]

64 Ammian., xxiv, 3. Libanius, *Orat. Parent.*, 122, 346.

65 M. d'Anville (*Mém. de l'Académie des Inscriptions*, xxviii, 246–59) has ascertained the true position and distance of Babylon, Seleucia, Ctesiphon, Bagdad, etc. The Roman traveller, Pietro della Valle (i, xvii, 650–780), seems to be the most intelligent spectator of that famous province. He is a gentleman and a scholar, but intolerably vain and prolix.

† *page 523* [once the capital of the Parthians]

66 The royal canal (*Nahar Malcha*) might be successively restored, altered, divided, etc. (Cellarius, *Geograph. Antiq.*, ii, 453); and these changes may serve to explain the seeming contradictions of antiquity. In the time of Julian, it must have fallen into the Euphrates [or rather, Tigris] *below* Ctesiphon.

67 καὶ μεγέθεσιν ἐλεφάντων, οἷς ἴσον ἔργον διὰ σταχύων ἐλθεῖν, καὶ φάλαγγος. *Rien n'est beau que le vrai* [truth alone is beautiful]: a maxim which should be inscribed on the desk of every rhetorician.

68 Libanius alludes to the most powerful of the generals. I have ventured to name *Sallust*. Ammianus says, of all the leaders, *quod acri metu territi duces concordi precatu fieri prohibere tentarent* ['the terror-stricken generals were united in their attempts to have the enterprise called off'].

69 *Hinc Imperator . . .* (says Ammianus) *ipse cum levis armaturae auxiliis per prima postremaque discurrens*, etc. ['The emperor himself, rushing to front and rear with his light auxiliaries. . .']. Yet Zosimus, his friend, does not allow him to pass the river till two days after the battle.

70 *secundum Homericam dispositionem*. A similar disposition is ascribed to the wise Nestor, in the fourth book of the *Iliad*; and Homer was never absent from the mind of Julian.

71 *Persas terrore subito miscuerunt, versisque agminibus totius gentis apertas Ctesiphontis portas victor miles intrasset, ni maior praedarum occasio fuisset, quam cura victoriae.* ['The Persians were suddenly panic-stricken, and having completely overthrown the enemy lines, the victorious Romans might have entered through the open gates of Ctesiphon, had they not been more concerned with booty than with victory.'] (Sextus Rufus, *de Provinciis*, ch. 28). Their avarice might dispose them to hear the advice of Victor.

72 The labour of the canal, the passage of the Tigris, and the victory are described by Ammianus (xxiv, 5, 6), Libanius (*Orat. Parent.*, chs 124–28, pp. 347–53), Greg. Nazianzen (*Orat.*, iv, 115), Zosimus (iii, 181–83), and Sextus Rufus (*de Provinciis*, ch. 28).

* *page 525* [Diocletian had given these names to two legions of Illyricum.]

73 The fleet and army were formed in three divisions, of which the first only had passed during the night (Ammian., xxiv, 6). The πᾶσα δορυφορία [the whole contingent of bodyguards], whom Zosimus transports on the third day (iii, 183), might consist of the protectors, among whom the historian Ammianus, and the future emperor Jovian, actually served, some *schools* of the *domestics*, and perhaps the Jovians and Herculians, who often did duty as guards.

74 Moses of Chorene (*Hist. Armen.*, iii, 15, 246) supplies us with a national tradition, and a spurious letter. I have borrowed only the leading circumstance, which is consistent with truth, probability, and Libanius (*Orat. Parent.*, 131, 355).

75 *Civitas inexpugnabilis, facinus audax et importunum* ['The city could not be taken by siege, an attempt would be hazardous and untimely'], Ammianus, xxiv, 7. His fellow-soldier, Eutropius, turns aside from the difficulty, *Assyriamque populatus, castra apud Ctesiphontem stativa aliquandiu habuit: remeansque victor*, etc. ['having laid waste Assyria, he fixed his rest-camp at Ctesiphon for a time; returning home in triumph, etc.'] x, 16. Zosimus is artful or ignorant, and Socrates inaccurate.

76 Libanius, *Orat. Parent.*, 130, 354; 139, 361; Socrates, iii, 21. The ecclesiastical historian imputes the refusal of peace to the advice of Maximus [the philosopher who attended Julian's court and initiated him in the Eleusinian mysteries – see Chapter 23]. Such advice was unworthy of a philosopher; but the philosopher was likewise a magician, who flattered the hopes and passions of his master.

77 The arts of this new Zopyrus [a writer on physiognomy] (Greg. Nazianzen, *Orat.*, iv, 115, 116) may derive some credit from the testimony of two abbreviators (Sextus Rufus and Victor), and the casual hints of Libanius (*Orat. Parent.*, 134, 357), and Ammianus (xxiv, 7). The course of genuine history is interrupted by a most unseasonable chasm in the text of Ammianus.

78 See Ammianus (xxiv, 7), Libanius (*Orat. Parentalis*, chs 132, 133, pp. 356, 357), Zosimus (iii, 183), Zonaras (ii, xiii, 26), Gregory (*Orat.*, iv, 116), Augustine (*de Civitate Dei*, iv, 29; v, 21). Of these, Libanius alone attempts a faint apology for his hero, who, according to Ammianus, pronounced his own condemnation, by a tardy and ineffectual attempt to extinguish the flames.

79 Consult Herodotus (i, 194), Strabo (xvi, 1074), and Tavernier (i, ii, 152).

80 *A celeritate Tigris incipit vocari, ita appellant Medi sagittam*. ['From its speed it takes its name of Tigris, which is the word the Medes use for an arrow.'] Pliny, *Hist. Natur.*, vi, 31.

81 One of these dikes [dams], which produces an artificial cascade or cataract, is described by Tavernier (i, ii, 226), and Thévenot (ii, i, 193). The Persians, or Assyrians, laboured to interrupt the navigation of the river (Strabo, xv, 1075. D'Anville, *l'Euphrate et le Tigre*, pp. 98, 99).

82 Recollect the successful and applauded rashness of Agathocles [King of Syracuse, 361–289 BC], and Cortez [conqueror of Mexico, AD 1485–1547], who burnt their ships on the coasts of Africa and Mexico.

83 See the judicious reflections of the author of the *Essai sur la Tactique*, ii, 287–353, and the learned remarks of M. Guichardt (*Nouveaux Mémoires Militaires*, i, 351–82) on the baggage and subsistence of the Roman armies.

84 The Tigris rises to the south, the Euphrates to the north, of the Armenian mountains. The former overflows in March, the latter in July. These circumstances are well explained in the Geographical Dissertation of Foster, inserted in Spelman's *Expedition of Cyrus*, ii, 26.

85 Ammianus (xxiv, 8) describes, as he had felt, the inconveniency of the flood, the heat, and the insects. The lands of Assyria, oppressed by the Turks, and ravaged by the Curds, or Arabs, yield an increase of ten, fifteen, and twentyfold for the seed which is cast into the ground by the wretched and unskilful husbandmen. *Voyages* de Niebuhr, ii, 279, 285.

86 Isidore of Charax (*Mansion. Parthic.*, pp. 5, 6, in Hudson, *Geograph. Minor.*, tom. ii) reckons 129 schoeni from Seleucia, and Thévenot (i, i, ii, 209–45) 128 hours of march from Bagdad, to Ecbatana, or Hamadam. These measures cannot exceed an ordinary parasang, or three Roman miles.

* *page 529*   [land around the Caspian Sea]

† *page 529*   [the river which marked the boundary of the Roman and Persian empires]

87 The march of Julian from Ctesiphon is circumstantially, but not clearly, described by Ammianus (xxiv, 7, 8), Libanius (*Orat. Parent.*, 134, 357), and Zosimus (iii, 183). The two last seem ignorant that their conqueror was retreating; and Libanius absurdly confines him to the banks of the Tigris.

‡ *page 529*   [horsemen wearing armour]

88 Chardin, the most judicious of modern travellers, describes (iii, 57, 58, etc. edit. in 4to) the education and dexterity of the Persian horsemen. Brissonius (*de Regno Persico*, pp. 650, 661, etc.) has collected the testimonies of antiquity.

89 In Mark Antony's retreat, an attic choenix sold for fifty drachmae, or, in other words, a pound of flour for twelve or fourteen shillings: barley bread was sold for its weight in silver. It is impossible to peruse the interesting narrative of Plutarch (v, 102–16) without perceiving that Mark Antony and Julian were pursued by the same enemies and involved in the same distress.

* *page 530*   [baggage horses]

90 Ammian., xxiv, 8, xxv, 1; Zosimus, iii, 184, 185, 186; Libanius, *Orat. Parent.*, chs 134, 135, pp. 357, 358, 359. The sophist of Antioch appears ignorant that the troops were hungry.

91 Ammian., xxv, 2. Julian had sworn in a passion, *nunquam se Marti sacra facturum* [that he would never sacrifice to Mars] (xxiv 6). Such whimsical quarrels were not uncommon between the gods and their insolent votaries, and even the prudent Augustus, after his fleet had been twice shipwrecked, excluded Neptune from the honours of public processions. See Hume's 'Philosophical Reflections', *Essays*, ii, 418.

92 They still retained the monopoly of the vain, but lucrative, science which had been invented in Etruria; and professed to derive their knowledge of signs and omens from the ancient books of Tarquitius, a Tuscan sage.

93 *Clamabant hinc inde candidati* (see the note of Valesius) *quos disiecerat terror, ut fugientium molem tanquam ruinam male compositi culminis declinaret*. Ammian., xxv, 3.

94 Sapor himself declared to the Romans that it was his practice to comfort the families of his deceased satraps by sending them, as a present, the heads of the guards and officers who had not fallen by their master's side. Libanius, *de nece Julian. ulcis.*, xiii, 163.

95 The character and situation of Julian might countenance the suspicion that he had previously composed the elaborate oration which Ammianus heard and has transcribed. The version of the Abbé de la Bléterie is faithful and elegant. I have followed him in expressing the Platonic idea of emanations [i.e. the belief that the soul partakes of the divine essence and does not perish with death], which is darkly insinuated in the original.

96 Herodotus (i, 31) has displayed that doctrine in an agreeable tale. Yet the Jupiter [Zeus] (in the 16th book of the *Iliad*) who laments with tears of blood the death of Sarpedon his son had a very imperfect notion of happiness or glory beyond the grave.

97 The soldiers who made their verbal, or nuncupatory [oral], testaments upon actual service (*in procinctu*) were exempted from the formalities of the Roman law. See Heineccius (*Antiquit. Jur. Roman.*, i, 504), and Montesquieu (*Esprit des Loix*, Bk xxvii).

98 This union of the human soul with the divine aetherial substance of the universe is the ancient doctrine of Pythagoras and Plato, but it seems to exclude any personal or conscious immortality. See Warburton's learned and rational observations, *Divine Legation*, ii, 199–216.

99 The whole relation of the death of Julian is given by Ammianus (xxv, 3), an intelligent spectator. Libanius, who turns with horror from the scene, has supplied some circumstances (*Orat. Parental.*, chs 136–40, pp. 359–62). The calumnies of Gregory, and the legends of more recent saints, may now be *silently* despised.

100 *honoratior aliquis miles*; perhaps Ammianus himself. The modest and judicious historian describes the scene of the election, at which he was undoubtedly present (xxv, 5).

101 The *primus*, or *primicerius*, enjoyed the dignity of a senator; and, though only a tribune, he ranked with the military dukes. *Cod. Theodosian.*, vi, xxiv. These privileges are perhaps more recent than the time of Jovian.

102 The ecclesiastical historians, Socrates (iii, 22), Sozomen (vi, 3), and Theodoret (iv, 1), ascribe to Jovian the merit of a confessor under the preceding reign; and piously suppose that he refused the purple, till the whole army unanimously exclaimed that they were Christians. Ammianus, calmly pursuing his narrative, overthrows the legend by a single sentence. *Hostiis pro Joviano extisque inspectis pronuntiatum est*, etc. ['The entrails of the sacrificial victims were found to be in favour of Jovian, and it was announced that', etc.] xxv, 6.

103 Ammianus (xxv, 10) has drawn from the life an impartial portrait of Jovian: to which the younger Victor has added some remarkable strokes. The Abbé de la Bléterie (*Histoire de Jovien*, i, 1–238) has composed an elaborate history of his short reign; a work remarkably distinguished by elegance of style, critical disquisition, and religious prejudice.

104 *regius equitatus*. It appears from Procopius that the Immortals, so famous under Cyrus and his successors, were revived, if we may use that improper word, by the Sassanides. Brisson, *de Regno Persico*, p. 268, etc.

105 The obscure villages of the inland country are irrecoverably lost; nor can we name the field of battle where Julian fell: but M. d'Anville has demonstrated the precise situation of Sumere, Carche, and Dura, along the banks of the Tigris (*Géographie Ancienne*, ii, 248. *L'Euphrate et le Tigre*, pp. 95, 97). In the ninth century, Sumere, or Samara, became, with a slight change of name, the royal residence of the Khalifs of the house of Abbas.

106 Dura was a fortified place in the wars of Antiochus [King of Syria in the second century BC] against the rebels of Media and Persia (Polybius, v, chs 48, 52, pp. 548, 552, edit. Casaubon, in 8vo).

* *page 535* [faggots or sticks]

107 A similar expedient was proposed to the leaders of the ten thousand [the army of Xenophon which crossed Asia Minor in 401 BC], and wisely rejected. Xenophon, *Anabasis*, iii, pp. 255, 256, 257. It appears from our modern travellers that rafts floating on bladders performed the trade and navigation of the Tigris.

108 The first military acts of the reign of Jovian are related by Ammianus (xxv, 6), Libanius (*Orat. Parent.*, 146, 364), and Zosimus (iii, pp. 189, 190, 191). Though we may distrust the fairness of Libanius, the ocular testimony of Eutropius (*uno a Persis atque altero proelio victus* ['each defeated by the Persians in a different

battle'], x, 17) must incline us to suspect that Ammianus has been too jealous of the honour of the Roman arms.

109 Sextus Rufus (*de Provinciis*, ch. 29) embraces a poor subterfuge of national vanity. *Tanta reverentia nominis Romani fuit, ut a Persis primus de pace sermo haberetur.* ['Such was their respect for the Roman name that it was the Persians who first raised the question of peace.']

110 It is presumptuous to controvert the opinion of Ammianus, a soldier and a spectator. Yet it is difficult to understand *how* the mountains of Corduene could extend over the plain of Assyria, as low as the conflux of the Tigris and the great Zab; or *how* an army of sixty thousand men could march one hundred miles in four days.

† *page 535* [snares]

111 The treaty of Dura is recorded with grief or indignation by Ammianus (xxx, 7), Libanius (*Orat. Parent.*, 142, 364), Zosimus (iii, 190, 191), Gregory Nazianzen (*Orat.*, iv, 117, 118, who imputes the distress to Julian, the deliverance to Jovian), and Eutropius (x, 17). The last-mentioned writer, who was present in a military station, styles this peace *necessariam quidem sed ignobilem* ['necessary indeed but shameful'].

* *page 536* [rivers in the provinces of Syria, Cilicia and Bithynia in Asia Minor]

112 Libanius, *Orat. Parent.*, 143, 364, 365.

113 *Conditionibus . . . dispendiosis Romanae reipublicae impositis . . . quibus cupidior regni quam gloriae Jovianus imperio rudis adquievit.* ['On these heavy terms imposed on the Roman empire, did the vulgar Jovian agree to rule, being greedier of power than of glory.'] Sextus Rufus, *de Provinciis*, ch. 29. La Bléterie has expressed, in a long direct oration, these specious considerations of public and private interest. *Hist. de Jovien*, i, 39, etc.

114 The generals were murdered on the banks of the Zabatus (*Anabasis*, ii, 156; iii, 226), or great Zab, a river of Assyria, 400 feet broad, which falls into the Tigris fourteen hours below Mosul. The error of the Greeks bestowed on the great and lesser Zab the names of the Wolf (Lycus), and the Goat (Capros). They created these animals to attend the Tiger of the East.

† *page 531* [Gibbon refers to the defeat of Cyrus near Babylon by his elder brother Artaxerxes in 401 bc. The Greeks including Xenophon had been allies of Cyrus.]

115 The *Cyropaedia* is vague and languid: the *Anabasis* circumstantial and animated. Such is the eternal difference between fiction and truth. [In the *Cyropaedia*, Xenophon purported to relate the education of the Persian King Cyrus (563–529 BC), in the *Anabasis* he reported the long march of the ten thousand from Mesopotamia to Greece.]

116 According to Rufinus, an immediate supply of provisions was stipulated by the treaty; and Theodoret affirms that the obligation was faithfully discharged by the Persians. Such a fact is probable, but undoubtedly false. See Tillemont, *Hist. des Empereurs*, iv, 702.

117 We may recollect some lines of Lucan (*Pharsal.*, iv, 95), who describes a similar distress of Caesar's army in Spain:

> *Saeva fames aderat . . .*
> *Miles eget: toto censu non prodigus emit*
> *Exiguam Cererem. Pro lucri pallida tabes!*
> *Non deest prolato ieiunus venditor auro.*

['There was cruel famine . . . the soldiers were starving: no spendthrifts, they sold all they had – to buy a crust of bread. O pale disease of greed! Once gold was offered, there was no shortage of hungry sellers.'] See Guichardt (*Nouveaux Mémoires Militaires*, i, 379–82). His Analysis of the two campaigns in Spain and Africa is the noblest monument that has ever been raised to the fame of Caesar.

118 M. d'Anville (see his maps, and *l'Euphrate et le Tigre*, pp. 92, 93) traces their march, and assigns the true position of Hatra, Ur, and Thilsaphata, which Ammianus has mentioned. He does not complain of the Samiel, the deadly hot wind, which Thévenot (*Voyages*, ii, i, 192) so much dreaded.

119 The retreat of Jovian is described by Ammianus (xxv, 9), Libanius (*Orat. Parent.*, 143, 365), and Zosimus (iii, 194).

120 Libanius, *Orat. Parent.*, 145, 366. Such were the natural hopes and wishes of a rhetorician.

121 The people of Carrhae, a city devoted to Paganism, buried the inauspicious messenger under a pile of stones. Zosimus, iii, 196. Libanius, when he received the fatal intelligence, cast his eye on his sword; but he recollected that Plato had condemned suicide, and that he must live to compose the panegyric of Julian (Libanius, *de Vita sua*, ii, 45, 46).

122 Ammianus and Eutropius may be admitted as fair and credible witnesses of the public language and opinions. The people of Antioch reviled an ignominious peace, which exposed them to the Persians on a naked and defenceless frontier. (*Excerpt. Valesiana*, p. 845, ex Johanne Antiocheno.)

123 The Abbé de la Bléterie (*Hist. de Jovien*, i, 212–27), though a severe casuist, has pronounced that Jovian was not bound to execute his promise, since he *could not* dismember the empire, nor alienate, without their consent, the allegiance of his people. I have never found much delight or instruction in such political metaphysics.

124 At Nisibis he performed a *royal* act. [Gibbon here assumes the prejudice against kings held in republican Rome.] A brave officer, his namesake, who had been thought worthy of the purple, was dragged from supper, thrown into a well, and stoned to death, without any form of trial or evidence of guilt. Ammian, xxv, 8.

125 See xxv, 9, and Zosimus, iii, 194, 195.

126 *Chron. Paschal.*, p. 300. The ecclesiastical *Notitiae* may be consulted.
   * *page 539* [guardian spirit]

127 Zosimus, iii, 192, 193; Sextus Rufus, *de Provinciis*, ch. 29; Augustine, *de Civitat. Dei*, iv, 29. This general position must be applied and interpreted with some caution.

128 Ammianus, xxv, 9; Zosimus, iii, 196. He might be *edax, et vino Venerique indulgens* ['greedy, and one who indulged in wine and fornication']. But I agree with La Bléterie (i, 148–54) in rejecting the foolish report of a Bacchanalian riot (*ap. Suidam*) celebrated at Antioch, by the emperor, his *wife*, and a troop of concubines.

129 The Abbé de la Bléterie, (i, 156, 209) handsomely exposes the brutal bigotry of Baronius, who would have thrown Julian to the dogs, *ne cespititia quidem sepultura dignus* ['not even fit to be buried'].

130 Compare the sophist and the saint (Libanius, *Monod.*, ii, 251, and *Orat. Parent.*, 145, 307; 156, 377, with Gregory Nazianzen, *Orat.*, iv, 125–32). The Christian

orator faintly mutters some exhortations to modesty and forgiveness; but he is well satisfied that the real sufferings of Julian will far exceed the fabulous torments of Ixion or Tantalus. [For making love to Juno, Ixion was fastened to a wheel; Tantalus, for divulging the secrets of the gods, was punished with an unquenchable thirst.]

131 Tillemont (*Hist. des Empereurs*, iv, 549) has collected these visions. Some saint or angel was observed to be absent in the night on a secret expedition, etc.

132 Sozomen (vi, 2) applauds the Greek doctrine of *tyrannicide*, but the whole passage, which a Jesuit might have translated, is prudently suppressed by the president Cousin. [Louis Cousin, 1627–1707, historian and editor of Greek literature]

133 Immediately after the death of Julian, an uncertain rumour was scattered *telo cecidisse Romano* ['that he fell slain by a Roman weapon']. It was carried, by some deserters, to the Persian camp; and the Romans were reproached as the assassins of the emperor by Sapor and his subjects (Ammian., xxv, 6. Libanius, *de ulciscenda Juliani nece*, xiii, 162, 163). It was urged, as a decisive proof, that no Persian had appeared to claim the promised reward (Liban., *Orat. Parent.*, 141, 363). But the flying horseman, who darted the fatal javelin, might be ignorant of its effect; or he might be slain in the same action. Ammianus neither feels nor inspires a suspicion.

134 ὅστις ἐντολὴν πληρῶν τῷ σφῶν αὐτῶν ἄρχοντι ['someone carrying out the order of one of their leaders']. This dark and ambiguous expression may point to Athanasius, the first, without a rival, of the Christian clergy (Libanius, *de ulcis. Jul. nece*, 5, 149. La Bléterie, *Hist. de Jovien*, i, 179).

135 The Orator (Fabricius, *Bibliot. Graec.*, vii, 145–79) scatters suspicions, demands an inquiry, and insinuates that proofs might still be obtained. He ascribes the success of the Huns to the criminal neglect of revenging Julian's death.

136 At the funeral of Vespasian, the comedian who personated that frugal emperor anxiously inquired, how much it cost? – Fourscore thousand pounds (*centies*). – Give me the tenth part of the sum and throw my body into the Tiber. Sueton., in *Vespasian.*, ch. 19, with the notes of Casaubon and Gronovius.

137 Gregory (*Orat.*, iv., 119, 120) compares this supposed ignominy and ridicule to the funeral honours of Constantius, whose body was chanted over mount Taurus by a choir of angels.

* *page 540* [the Cynic philosopher]

138 Quintus Curtius, i, iii, 4. The luxuriancy of his descriptions has been often censured. Yet it was almost the duty of the historian to describe a river whose waters had nearly proved fatal to Alexander.

139 Libanius, *Orat. Parent.*, 156, 377. Yet he acknowledges with gratitude the liberality of the two royal brothers in decorating the tomb of Julian (*de ulcis Jul. nece*, 7, 152).

140 *Cuius suprema et cineres, si qui tunc iuste consuleret, non Cydnus videre deberet, quamvis gratissimus amnis et liquidus: sed ad perpetuandam gloriam recte factorum praeterlambere Tiberis, intersecans urbem aeternam divorumque veterum monumenta praestringens.* Ammian., xxv, 10.

CHAPTER 25 (Summary)

The government and death of Jovian – the election of Valentinian, who associates his brother Valens, and makes his final division of the Eastern and Western empires – revolt of Procopius – civil and ecclesiastical administration – Germany – Britain – Africa – the East – the Danube – death of Valentinian – his two sons, Gratian and Valentinian II, succeed to the Western empire

Gibbon relates the death of Jovian on his way back to Constantinople, and the succession of Valentinian, an army commander, who ruled the empire in the West, with his brother Valens as emperor in the East. Magic and witchcraft were cruelly persecuted but the brothers were on the whole tolerant in matters of religion and supported learning. Gibbon reviews the five theatres of war during the period AD 364–375 under the headings of Germany, Britain, Africa, the East and the Danube. The defences of the Rhine were restored against the German tribes; the general Theodosius restored order in Britain, which had suffered from Caledonian and Saxon marauders. Theodosius also put down a rebellion in Africa; in the East, an uncertain peace prevailed; but on the Danube, the Goths were threatening to invade the empire at the time of Valentinian's death in AD 375.

CHAPTER 26 (Summary)

Manners of the pastoral nations – progress of the Huns, from China to Europe – flight of the Goths – they pass the Danube – Gothic war – defeat and death of Valens – Gratian invests Theodosius with the Eastern empire – his character and success – peace and settlement of the Goths

Gibbon dates the decline of the Roman empire from the later years of the reign of Valens (AD 375–378), when the Goths were allowed to cross the Danube to gain protection from invading Huns, whose nomadic lifestyle, ranging from the frontiers of China to eastern Europe, is vividly portrayed in Chapter 26. The Goths were alienated by their harsh treatment within the empire and were provoked into declaring war. Meanwhile, the German tribes crossed the Rhine, but were defeated by the Gallic army under Gratian, who had succeeded his father, Valentinian, as emperor in the West. Valens, however, was disastrously defeated and killed by the Goths at the battle of Hadrianople in AD 378. His successor was Theodosius, son of the general of the same name who had restored order in Britain. He slowly built up the strength of the Roman armies in the East and won the trust of the Goths, who were settled in Thrace. It was, however, an uneasy peace and 'the public safety seemed to depend on the life and abilities of a single man.'

CHAPTER 27 (Summary)

Death of Gratian – ruin of Arianism – St Ambrose – first civil war, against Maximus – character, administration, and penance of Theodosius – death of Valentinian II – second civil war, against Eugenius – death of Theodosius

Gibbon relates how Gratian belied his early promise and was ousted from power by Maximus, a military commander, who invaded Gaul from Britain in AD 383. There were now three emperors, Theodosius in the East, Valentinian II in Italy and Africa, and Maximus in the West. Theodosius imposed unity on the Christian Church by expelling the Arians. In Milan, the archbishop Ambrose resisted the Arianism of Valentinian and his mother, Justina, and when they fled to seek the protection of Theodosius, Maximus invaded Italy. He was defeated and killed and Valentinian was restored. Rebellions at Antioch and Thessalonica were quelled with contrasting mildness and brutality, and Theodosius was forced to repent of the latter by Ambrose. When Valentinian died in mysterious circumstances in AD 392, there was further civil war. When Theodosius himself died, in AD 395, he left the empire to his two sons, Honorius in the West and Arcadius in the East. The empire was now on the eve of its invasion by the Goths and the Huns, and there no longer existed the heavily armed Roman infantry to withstand the barbarian cavalry.

CHAPTER 28

*Final destruction of Paganism – introduction of the worship
of saints, and relics, among the Christians*

The ruin of Paganism, in the age of Theodosius, is perhaps the only
example of the total extirpation of any ancient and popular superstition;
and may therefore deserve to be considered as a singular event in the
history of the human mind. The Christians, more especially the clergy,
had impatiently supported the prudent delays of Constantine and the
equal toleration of the elder Valentinian; nor could they deem their
conquest perfect or secure, as long as their adversaries were permitted to
exist. The influence which Ambrose and his brethren had acquired over
the youth of Gratian and the piety of Theodosius was employed to infuse
the maxims of persecution into the breasts of their Imperial proselytes.
Two specious principles of religious jurisprudence were established, from
whence they deduced a direct and rigorous conclusion against the
subjects of the empire who still adhered to the ceremonies of their
ancestors: *that* the magistrate is, in some measure, guilty of the crimes
which he neglects to prohibit or to punish; and, *that* the idolatrous
worship of fabulous deities and real daemons is the most abominable
crime against the supreme majesty of the Creator. The laws of Moses and
the examples of Jewish history[1] were hastily, perhaps erroneously, applied
by the clergy to the mild and universal reign of Christianity.[2] The zeal of
the emperors was excited to vindicate their own honour, and that of the
Deity; and the temples of the Roman world were subverted, about sixty
years after the conversion of Constantine.

From the age of Numa to the reign of Gratian* the Romans preserved
the regular succession of the several colleges of the sacerdotal order.[3]
Fifteen Pontiffs† exercised their supreme jurisdiction over all things and
persons that were consecrated to the service of the gods; and the various
questions which perpetually arose in a loose and traditionary system
were submitted to the judgment of their holy tribunal. Fifteen grave and
learned Augurs observed the face of the heavens, and prescribed the
actions of heroes, according to the flight of birds. Fifteen keepers of the
Sibylline books‡ (their name of Quindecemvirs was derived from their
number) occasionally consulted the history of future, and as it should
seem, of contingent, events. Six Vestals devoted their virginity to the
guard of the sacred fire and of the unknown pledges of the duration of
Rome; which no mortal had been suffered to behold with impunity.[4]
Seven Epulos prepared the table of the gods, conducted the solemn
procession, and regulated the ceremonies, of the annual festival. The

three Flamens of Jupiter, of Mars, and of Quirinus,* were considered as the peculiar ministers of the three most powerful deities who watched over the fate of Rome and of the universe. The King of the Sacrifices represented the person of Numa, and of his successors, in the religious functions which could be performed only by royal hands. The confraternities of the Salians,† the Lupercals,‡ etc., practised such rites as might extort a smile of contempt from every reasonable man, with a lively confidence of recommending themselves to the favour of the immortal gods. The authority which the Roman priests had formerly obtained in the counsels of the republic was gradually abolished by the establishment of monarchy and the removal of the seat of empire. But the dignity of their sacred character was still protected by the laws and manners of their country; and they still continued, more especially the college of pontiffs, to exercise in the capital, and sometimes in the provinces, the rights of their ecclesiastical and civil jurisdiction. Their robes of purple, chariots of state, and sumptuous entertainments attracted the admiration of the people; and they received, from the consecrated lands and the public revenue, an ample stipend, which liberally supported the splendour of the priesthood and all the expenses of the religious worship of the state. As the service of the altar was not incompatible with the command of armies, the Romans, after their consulships and triumphs, aspired to the place of pontiff or of augur; the seats of Cicero[5] and Pompey were filled, in the fourth century, by the most illustrious members of the senate; and the dignity of their birth reflected additional splendour on their sacerdotal character. The fifteen priests who composed the college of pontiffs enjoyed a more distinguished rank as the companions of their sovereign; and the Christian emperors condescended to accept the robe and ensigns which were appropriated to the office of supreme pontiff. But, when Gratian ascended the throne, more scrupulous, or more enlightened, he sternly rejected those profane symbols;[6] applied to the service of the state, or of the church, the revenues of the priests and vestals; abolished their honours and immunities; and dissolved the ancient fabric of Roman superstition, which was supported by the opinions and habits of eleven hundred years. Paganism was still the constitutional religion of the senate. The hall, or temple, in which they assembled, was adorned by the statue and altar of Victory;[7] a majestic female standing on a globe, with flowing garments, expanded wings, and a crown of laurel in her outstretched hand.[8] The senators were sworn on the altar of the goddess to observe the laws of the emperor and of the empire; and a solemn offering of wine and incense was the ordinary prelude of their public deliberations.[9] The removal of this ancient monument was the only injury which Constantius had offered to the superstition of the Romans. The altar of Victory was again restored by Julian, tolerated by Valentinian, and once more banished from the senate by the zeal of

Gratian.[10] But the emperor yet spared the statues of the gods, which were exposed to the public veneration; four hundred and twenty-four temples, or chapels, still remained to satisfy the devotion of the people; and in every quarter of Rome the delicacy of the Christians was offended by the fumes of idolatrous sacrifice.[11]

But the Christians formed the least numerous party in the senate of Rome;[12] and it was only by their absence that they could express their dissent from the legal, though profane, acts of a Pagan majority. In that assembly, the dying embers of freedom were, for a moment, revived and inflamed by the breath of fanaticism. Four respectable deputations were successively voted to the Imperial court[13] to represent the grievances of the priesthood and the senate; and to solicit the restoration of the altar of Victory. The conduct of this important business was entrusted to the eloquent Symmachus,[14] a wealthy and noble senator, who united the sacred characters of pontiff and augur with the civil dignities of proconsul of Africa and prefect of the city. The breast of Symmachus was animated by the warmest zeal for the cause of expiring Paganism; and his religious antagonists lamented the abuse of his genius, and the inefficacy of his moral virtues.[15] The orator, whose petition is extant to the emperor Valentinian, was conscious of the difficulty and danger of the office which he had assumed. He cautiously avoids every topic which might appear to reflect on the religion of his sovereign; humbly declares that prayers and entreaties are his only arms; and artfully draws his arguments from the schools of rhetoric rather than from those of philosophy. Symmachus endeavours to seduce the imagination of a young prince, by displaying the attributes of the goddess of victory; he insinuates that the confiscation of the revenues, which were consecrated to the service of the gods, was a measure unworthy of his liberal and disinterested character; and he maintains that the Roman sacrifices would be deprived of their force and energy, if they were no longer celebrated at the expense, as well as in the name, of the republic. Even scepticism is made to supply an apology for superstition. The great and incomprehensible *secret* of the universe eludes the enquiry of man. Where reason cannot instruct, custom may be permitted to guide; and every nation seems to consult the dictates of prudence by a faithful attachment to those rites and opinions which have received the sanction of ages. If those ages have been crowned with glory and prosperity, if the devout people has frequently obtained the blessings which they have solicited at the altars of the gods, it must appear still more advisable to persist in the same salutary practice; and not to risk the unknown perils that may attend any rash innovations. The test of antiquity and success was applied with singular advantage to the religion of Numa; and Rome herself, the celestial genius that presided over the fates of the city, is introduced by the orator to plead her own cause before the tribunal of the emperors. 'Most excellent princes,' says the venerable matron, 'fathers of your country! pity and respect my age, which has hitherto flowed in an uninterrupted course of piety. Since I do not repent, permit me to continue in the practice of my ancient rites. Since I am born free, allow me to enjoy my domestic institutions. This religion has reduced the world under my laws. These rites have repelled Hannibal from the city, and the Gauls from the Capitol. Were my grey hairs reserved for such intolerable disgrace? I am ignorant of the new system that I am required to adopt; but I am well assured that the correction of old age is always an ungrateful and ignominious office.'[16] The fears of the people supplied what the discretion of the orator had suppressed; and the calamities which afflicted, or threatened, the declining empire were unanimously imputed, by the Pagans, to the new religion of Christ and of Constantine.

But the hopes of Symmachus were repeatedly baffled by the firm and dexterous opposition of the archbishop of Milan; who fortified the emperors against the fallacious eloquence of the advocate of Rome. In this controversy, Ambrose condescends to speak the language of a philosopher, and to ask, with some contempt, why it should be thought necessary to introduce an imaginary and invisible power, as the cause of those victories which were sufficiently explained by the valour and discipline of the legions? He justly derides the absurd reverence for antiquity which could only tend to discourage the improvements of art and to replunge the human race into their original barbarism. From thence gradually rising to a more lofty and theological tone, he pronounces that Christianity alone is the doctrine of truth and salvation, and that every mode of Polytheism conducts its deluded votaries, through the paths of error, to the abyss of eternal perdition.[17] Arguments like these, when they were suggested by a favourite bishop, had power to prevent the restoration of the altar of Victory; but the same arguments fell, with much more energy and effect, from the mouth of a conqueror; and the gods of antiquity were dragged in triumph at the chariot-wheels of Theodosius.[18] In a full meeting of the senate, the emperor proposed, according to the forms of the republic, the important question, Whether the worship of Jupiter or that of Christ should be the religion of the Romans? The liberty of suffrages, which he affected to allow, was destroyed by the hopes and fears that his presence inspired; and the arbitrary exile of Symmachus was a recent admonition that it might be dangerous to oppose the wishes of the monarch. On a regular division of the senate, Jupiter was condemned and degraded by the sense of a very large majority; and it is rather surprising that any members should be found bold enough to declare by their speeches and votes that they were still attached to the interest of an abdicated deity.[19] The hasty conversion of the senate must be attributed either to supernatural or to sordid motives; and many of these reluctant proselytes betrayed, on every favourable occasion, their secret disposition to throw aside the mask of odious dissimulation. But they were gradually fixed in the new religion, as the cause of the ancient became more hopeless; they yielded to the authority of the emperor, to the fashion of the times, and to the entreaties of their wives and children,[20] who were instigated and governed by the clergy of Rome and the monks of the East. The edifying example of the Anician family was soon imitated by the rest of the nobility: the Bassi, the Paullini, the Gracchi, embraced the Christian religion; and 'the luminaries of the world, the venerable assembly of Catos (such are the high-flown expressions of Prudentius), were impatient to strip themselves of their pontifical garment: to cast the skin of the old serpent; to assume the snowy robes of baptismal innocence; and to humble the pride of the consular fasces before the tombs of the martyrs'.[21] The citizens, who subsisted by their own industry, and the populace, who were supported by the public liberality, filled the churches of the Lateran and Vatican with an incessant throng of devout proselytes. The decrees of the senate, which proscribed the worship of idols, were ratified by the general consent of the Romans;[22] the splendour of the Capitol was defaced, and the solitary temples were abandoned to ruin and contempt.[23] Rome submitted to the yoke of the Gospel; and the vanquished provinces had not yet lost their reverence for the name and authority of Rome.

The filial piety of the emperors themselves engaged them to proceed, with some caution and tenderness, in the reformation of the eternal city. Those absolute monarchs acted with less regard to the prejudices of the provincials. The pious labour, which had been suspended near twenty years since the death of Constantius,[24] was vigorously resumed, and finally accomplished, by the zeal of Theodosius. Whilst that warlike prince yet struggled with the Goths, not for the glory, but for the safety, of the republic, he ventured to offend a considerable party of his subjects, by some acts which might perhaps secure the protection of Heaven, but which must seem rash and unseasonable in the eye of human prudence. The success of his first experiments against the Pagans encouraged the pious emperor to reiterate and enforce his edicts of proscription; the same laws which had been originally published in the provinces of the East were applied, after the defeat of Maximus,* to the whole extent of the Western empire; and every victory of the orthodox Theodosius contributed to the triumph of the Christian and Catholic faith.[25] He attacked superstition in her most vital part by prohibiting the use of sacrifices, which he declared to be criminal as well as infamous; and, if the terms of his edicts more strictly condemned the impious curiosity which examined the entrails of the victims,[26] every subsequent explanation tended to involve, in the same guilt, the general practice of *immolation*, which essentially constituted the religion of the Pagans. As the temples had been erected for the purpose of sacrifice, it was the duty of a benevolent prince to remove from his subjects the dangerous temptation of offending against the laws which he had enacted. A special commission was granted to Cynegius, the Praetorian prefect of the East, and afterwards to the counts Jovius and Gaudentius, two officers of distinguished rank in the West; by which they were directed to shut the temples, to seize or destroy the instruments of idolatry, to abolish the privileges of the priests, and to confiscate the consecrated property for the benefit of the emperor, of the church, or of the army.[27] Here the desolation might have stopped, and the naked edifices, which were no longer employed in the service of idolatry, might have been protected from the destructive rage of fanaticism. Many of those temples were the most splendid and beautiful monuments of Grecian architecture: and the emperor himself was interested not to deface the splendour of his own cities or to diminish the value of his own possessions. Those stately edifices might be suffered to remain as so many lasting trophies of the victory of Christ. In the decline of the arts, they might be usefully converted into magazines, manufactures, or places of public assembly; and perhaps, when the walls of the temple had been sufficiently purified by holy rites, the worship of the true Deity might be allowed to expiate the ancient guilt of idolatry. But, as long as they subsisted, the Pagans fondly cherished the secret hope that an auspicious revolution, a second Julian, might again restore the altars of the gods; and the earnestness with which they addressed their unavailing prayers to the throne[28] inreased the zeal of the Christian reformers to extirpate, without mercy, the root of superstition. The laws of the emperors exhibit some symptoms of a milder disposition;[29] but their cold and languid efforts were insufficient to stem the torrent of enthusiasm and rapine, which was conducted, or rather impelled, by the spiritual rulers of the church. In Gaul, the holy Martin, bishop of Tours,[30] marched at the head of his faithful monks, to destroy the idols, the temples, and the consecrated trees of his extensive diocese; and in the execution of this arduous task, the prudent reader will judge whether Martin was supported by the aid of miraculous powers or of carnal weapons. In Syria, the divine and excellent Marcellus,[31] as he is styled by Theodoret, a bishop animated with apostolic fervour, resolved to level with the ground the stately temples within the diocese of Apamea. His attack was resisted by the skill and solidity with which the temple of Jupiter had been constructed. The building was seated on an eminence; on each of the four sides, the lofty roof was supported by fifteen massy columns, sixteen feet in circumference; and the large stones, of which they were composed, were firmly cemented with lead and iron. The force of the strongest and sharpest tools had been tried without effect. It was found necessary to undermine the foundations of the columns, which fell down as soon as the temporary wooden props had been consumed with fire; and the difficulties of the enterprise are described under the allegory of a black daemon, who retarded, though he could not defeat, the operations of the Christian engineers. Elated with victory, Marcellus took the field in person against the powers of darkness; a numerous troop of soldiers and gladiators marched under the episcopal banner, and he successively attacked the villages and country temples of the diocese of Apamea. Whenever any resistance or danger was apprehended, the champion of the faith, whose lameness would not allow him either to fight or fly, placed himself at a convenient distance, beyond the reach of darts. But this prudence was the occasion of his death; he was surprised and slain by a body of exasperated rustics; and the synod of the province pronounced, without hesitation, that the holy Marcellus had sacrificed his life in the cause of God. In the support of this cause, the monks, who rushed with tumultuous fury from the desert, distinguished themselves by their zeal and diligence. They deserved the enmity of the Pagans; and some of them might deserve the reproaches of avarice and intemperance: of avarice, which they gratified with holy plunder, and of intemperance, which they indulged at the expense of the people, who foolishly admired their tattered garments, loud psalmody, and artificial paleness.[32] A small number of temples was protected by the fears, the venality, the taste, or the prudence, of the civil and ecclesiastical governors. The temple of the celestial Venus at Carthage, whose sacred precincts formed a circumference of two miles, was judiciously converted into a Christian church;[33] and a similar consecration has preserved inviolate the majestic dome of the Pantheon at Rome.[34] But, in almost every province of the Roman world, an army of fanatics, without authority and without discipline, invaded the peaceful inhabitants; and the ruin of the fairest structures of antiquity still displays the ravages of *those* Barbarians, who alone had time and inclination to execute such laborious destruction.

In this wide and various prospect of devastation, the spectator may distinguish the ruins of the temple of Serapis, at Alexandria.[35] Serapis does not appear to have been one of the native gods, or monsters, who sprung from the fruitful soil of superstitious Egypt.[36] The first of the Ptolemies had been commanded, by a dream, to import the mysterious stranger from the coast of Pontus,* where he had been long adored by the inhabitants of Sinope; but his attributes and his reign were so imperfectly understood that it became a subject of dispute, whether he represented the bright orb of day or the gloomy monarch of the subterraneous regions.[37] The Egyptians, who were obstinately devoted to the religion of their fathers, refused to admit this foreign deity within the walls of their cities.[38] But the obsequious priests, who were seduced by the liberality of the Ptolemies, submitted, without resistance, to the power of the god of Pontus; an honourable and domestic genealogy was provided; and this fortunate usurper was introduced into the throne and bed of Osiris,[39] the husband of Isis, and the celestial monarch of Egypt. Alexandria, which claimed his peculiar protection, gloried in the name of the city of Serapis. His temple,[40] which rivalled the pride and magnificence of the Capitol, was erected on the spacious summit of an artificial mount, raised one hundred steps above the level of the adjacent parts of the city; and the interior cavity was strongly supported by arches, and distributed into vaults and subterraneous apartments. The consecrated buildings were surrounded by a quadrangular portico; the stately halls, and exquisite statues, displayed the triumph of the arts; and the treasures of ancient learning were preserved in the famous Alexandrian library, which had arisen with new splendour from its ashes.[41] After the edicts of Theodosius had severely prohibited the sacrifices of the Pagans, they were still tolerated in the city and temple of Serapis; and this singular indulgence was imprudently ascribed to the superstitious terrors of the Christians themselves: as if they had feared to abolish those ancient rites which could alone secure the inundations of the Nile, the harvests of Egypt, and the subsistence of Constantinople.[42]

At that time[43] the archiepiscopal throne of Alexandria was filled by Theophilus,[44] the perpetual enemy of peace and virtue; a bold, bad man, whose hands were alternately polluted with gold and with blood. His pious indignation was excited by the honours of Serapis; and the insults which he offered to an ancient chapel of Bacchus convinced the Pagans that he meditated a more important and dangerous enterprise. In the tumultuous capital of Egypt, the slightest provocation was sufficient to inflame a civil war. The votaries of Serapis, whose strength and numbers were much inferior to those of their antagonists, rose in arms at the instigation of the philosopher Olympius,[45] who exhorted them to die in the defence of the altars of the gods. These Pagan fanatics fortified themselves in the temple, or rather fortress, of Serapis; repelled the besiegers by daring sallies and a resolute defence; and, by the inhuman cruelties which they exercised on their Christian prisoners, obtained the last consolation of despair. The efforts of the prudent magistrate were usefully exerted for the establishment of a truce till the answer of Theodosius should determine the fate of Serapis. The two parties assembled, without arms, in the principal square; and the Imperial rescript was publicly read. But, when a sentence of destruction against the idols of Alexandria was pronounced, the Christians set up a shout of joy and exultation, whilst the unfortunate Pagans, whose fury had given way to consternation, retired with hasty and silent steps, and eluded, by their flight or obscurity, the resentment of their enemies. Theophilus proceeded to demolish the temple of Serapis, without any other difficulties than those which he found in the weight and solidity of the materials; but these obstacles proved so insuperable that he was obliged to leave the foundations and to content himself with reducing the edifice itself to a heap of rubbish; a part of which was soon afterwards cleared away, to make room for a church erected in honour of the Christian martyrs. The valuable library of Alexandria was pillaged or destroyed; and, near twenty years afterwards, the appearance of the empty shelves excited the regret and indignation of every spectator whose mind was not totally darkened by religious prejudice.[46] The compositions of ancient genius, so many of which have irretrievably perished, might surely have been excepted from the wreck of idolatry, for the amusement and instruction of succeeding ages; and either the zeal or the avarice of the archbishop[47] might have been satiated with the rich spoils which were the reward of his victory. While the images and vases of gold and silver were carefully melted, and those of a less valuable metal were contemptuously broken and cast into the streets, Theophilus laboured to expose the frauds and vices of the ministers of the idols; their dexterity in the management of the loadstone;* their secret methods of introducing an human actor into a hollow statue; and their scandalous abuse of the confidence of devout husbands and unsuspecting females.[48] Charges like these may seem to deserve some degree of credit, as they are not repugnant to the crafty and interested spirit of superstition. But the same spirit is equally prone to the base practice of insulting and calumniating a fallen enemy; and our belief is naturally checked by the reflection that it is much less difficult to invent a fictitious story than to support a practical fraud. The colossal statue of Serapis[49] was involved in the ruin of his temple and religion. A great number of plates of different metals, artificially joined together, composed the majestic figure of the Deity, who touched on either side the walls of the sanctuary. The aspect of Serapis, his sitting posture, and the sceptre which he bore in his left hand, were extremely similar to the ordinary representations of Jupiter. He was distinguished from Jupiter by the basket, or bushel, which was placed on his head; and by the emblematic monster, which he held in his right hand: the head and body of a serpent branching into three tails, which were again terminated by the triple heads of a dog, a lion, and a wolf. It was confidently affirmed that, if any impious hand should dare to violate the majesty of the god, the heavens and the earth would instantly return to their original chaos. An intrepid soldier, animated by zeal and armed with a weighty battle-axe, ascended the ladder; and even the Christian multitude expected, with some anxiety, the event of the combat.[50] He aimed a vigorous stroke against the cheek of Serapis; the cheek fell to the ground; the thunder was still silent, and both the heavens and the earth continued to preserve their accustomed order and tranquillity. The victorious soldier repeated his blows; the huge idol was overthrown, and broken in pieces; and the limbs of Serapis were ignominiously dragged through the streets of Alexandria. His mangled carcase was burnt in the amphitheatre, amidst the shouts of the populace; and many persons attributed their conversion to this discovery of the impotence of their tutelar deity. The popular modes of religion that propose any visible and material objects of worship have the advantage of adapting and familiarising themselves to the senses of mankind; but this advantage is counter-balanced by the various and inevitable accidents to which the faith of the idolater is exposed. It is scarcely possible that, in every disposition of mind, he should preserve his implicit reverence for the idols or the relics which the naked eye and the profane hand are unable to distinguish from the most common productions of art or nature; and, if, in the hour of danger, their secret and miraculous virtue does not operate for their own preservation, he scorns the vain apologies of his priest, and justly derides the object, and the folly, of his superstitious attachment.[51] After the fall of Serapis, some hopes were still entertained by the Pagans that the Nile would refuse his annual supply to the impious masters of Egypt; and the extraordinary delay of the inundation seemed to announce the displeasure of the river-god. But this delay was soon compensated by the rapid swell of the waters. They suddenly rose to such an unusual height as to comfort the discontented party with the pleasing expectation of a deluge; till the peaceful river again subsided to the well-known and fertilising level of sixteen cubits, or about thirty English feet.[52]

The temples of the Roman empire were deserted, or destroyed; but the ingenious superstition of the Pagans still attempted to elude the laws of Theodosius, by which all sacrifices had been severely prohibited. The inhabitants of the country, whose conduct was less exposed to the eye of malicious curiosity, disguised their *religious*, under the appearance of *convivial*, meetings. On the days of solemn festivals, they assembled in great numbers under the spreading shade of some consecrated trees; sheep and oxen were slaughtered and roasted; and this rural entertainment was sanctified by the use of incense, and by the hymns which were sung in honour of the gods. But it was alleged that, as no part of the animal was made a burnt-offering, as no altar was provided to receive the blood, and as the previous oblation of salt cakes and the concluding ceremony of libations were carefully omitted, these festal meetings did not involve the guests in the guilt, or penalty, of an illegal sacrifice.[53] Whatever might be the truth of the facts or the merit of the distinction,[54] these vain pretences were swept away by the last edict of Theodosius; which inflicted a deadly wound on the superstition of the Pagans.[55] This prohibitory law is expressed in the most absolute and comprehensive terms. 'It is our will and pleasure,' says the emperor, 'that none of our subjects, whether magistrates or private citizens, however exalted or however humble may be their rank and condition, shall presume, in any city or in any place, to worship an inanimate idol by the sacrifice of a guiltless victim.' The act of sacrificing and the practice of divination by the entrails of the victim are declared (without any regard to the object of the enquiry) a crime of high treason against the state; which can be expiated only by the death of the guilty. The rites of Pagan superstition, which might seem less bloody and atrocious, are abolished, as highly injurious to the truth and honour of religion; luminaries, garlands, frankincense, and libations of wine, are specially enumerated and condemned; and the harmless claims of the domestic genius, of the household gods, are included in this rigorous proscription. The use of any of these profane and illegal ceremonies subjects the offender to the forfeiture of the house or estate where they have been performed; and, if he has artfully chosen the property of another for the scene of his impiety, he is compelled to discharge, without delay, a heavy fine of twenty-five pounds of gold, or more than one thousand pounds sterling. A fine, not less considerable, is imposed on the connivance of the secret enemies of religion, who shall neglect the duty of their respective stations, either to reveal or to punish the guilt of idolatry. Such was the persecuting spirit of the laws of Theodosius, which were repeatedly enforced by his sons and grandsons, with the loud and unanimous applause of the Christian world.[56]

In the cruel reigns of Decius and Diocletian, Christianity had been proscribed, as a revolt from the ancient and hereditary religion of the empire; and the unjust suspicions which were entertained of a dark and dangerous faction were, in some measure, countenanced by the inseparable union and rapid conquests of the Catholic church. But the same excuses of fear and ignorance cannot be applied to the Christian emperors, who violated the precepts of humanity and of the gospel. The experience of ages had betrayed the weakness, as well as folly, of Paganism; the light of reason and of faith had already exposed, to the greatest part of mankind, the vanity of idols; and the declining sect, which still adhered to their worship, might have been permitted to enjoy, in peace and obscurity, the religious customs of their ancestors. Had the Pagans been animated by the undaunted zeal which possessed the minds of the primitive believers, the triumph of the church must have been stained with blood; and the martyrs of Jupiter and Apollo might have embraced the glorious opportunity of devoting their lives and fortunes at the foot of their altars. But such obstinate zeal was not congenial to the loose and careless temper of polytheism. The violent and repeated strokes of the orthodox princes were broken by the soft and yielding substance against which they were directed; and the ready obedience of the Pagans protected them from the pains and penalties of the Theodosian Code.[57] Instead of asserting that the authority of the gods was superior to that of the emperor, they desisted, with a plaintive murmur, from the use of those sacred rites which their sovereign had condemned. If they were sometimes tempted, by a sally of passion or by the hopes of concealment, to indulge their favourite superstition, their humble repentance disarmed the severity of the Christian magistrate; and they seldom refused to atone for their rashness by submitting, with some secret reluctance, to the yoke of the Gospel. The churches were filled with the increasing multitude of these unworthy proselytes, who had conformed, from temporal motives, to the reigning religion; and, whilst they devoutly imitated the postures, and recited the prayers, of the faithful, they satisfied their conscience by the silent and sincere invocation of the gods of antiquity.[58] If the Pagans wanted patience to suffer, they wanted spirit to resist; and the scattered myriads, who deplored the ruin of the temples, yielded, without a contest, to the fortune of their adversaries. The disorderly opposition[59] of the peasants of Syria, and the populace of Alexandria, to the rage of private fanaticism was silenced by the name and authority of the emperor. The Pagans of the West, without contributing to the elevation of Eugenius,* disgraced, by their partial attachment, the cause and character of the usurper. The clergy vehemently exclaimed that he aggravated the crime of rebellion by the guilt of apostasy; that, by his permission, the altar of Victory was again restored; and that the idolatrous symbols of Jupiter and Hercules were displayed in the field against the invincible standard of the cross. But the vain hopes of the Pagans were soon annihilated by the defeat of Eugenius; and they were left exposed to the resentment of the conqueror, who laboured to deserve the favour of heaven by the extirpation of idolatry.[60]

A nation of slaves is always prepared to applaud the clemency of their master, who, in the abuse of absolute power, does not proceed to the last extremes of injustice and oppression. Theodosius might undoubtedly have proposed to his Pagan subjects the alternative of baptism or of death; and the eloquent Libanius has praised the moderation of a prince, who never enacted, by any positive law, that all his subjects should immediately embrace and practise the religion of their sovereign.[61] The profession of Christianity was not made an essential qualification for the enjoyment of the civil rights of society, nor were any peculiar hardships imposed on the sectaries who credulously received the fables of Ovid and obstinately rejected the miracles of the Gospel. The palace, the schools, the army, and the senate were filled with declared and devout Pagans; they obtained, without distinction, the civil and military honours of the empire. Theodosius distinguished his liberal regard for virtue and genius, by the consular dignity which he bestowed on Symmachus,[62] and by the personal friendship which he expressed to Libanius;[63] and the two eloquent apologists of Paganism were never required either to change or to dissemble their religious opinions. The Pagans were indulged in the most licentious freedom of speech and writing; the historical and philosophical remains of Eunapius, Zosimus,[64] and the fanatic teachers of the school of Plato, betray the most furious animosity, and contain the sharpest invectives, against the sentiments and conduct of their victorious adversaries. If these audacious libels were publicly known, we must applaud the good sense of the Christian princes who viewed, with a smile of contempt, the last struggles of superstition and despair.[65] But the Imperial laws which prohibited the sacrifices and ceremonies of Paganism were rigidly executed; and every hour contributed to destroy the influence of a religion which was supported by custom rather than by argument. The devotion of the poet or the philosopher may be secretly nourished by prayer, meditation, and study; but the exercise of public worship appears to be the only solid foundation of the religious sentiments of the people, which derive their force from imitation and habit. The interruption of that public exercise may consummate, in the period of a few years, the important work of a national revolution. The memory of theological opinions cannot long be preserved without the artificial helps of priests, of temples, and of books.[66] The ignorant vulgar, whose minds are still agitated by the blind hopes and terrors of superstition, will be soon persuaded by their superiors to direct their vows to the reigning deities of the age; and will insensibly imbibe an ardent zeal for the support and propagation of the new doctrine, which spiritual hunger at first compelled them to accept. The generation that arose in the world after the promulgation of the Imperial laws was attracted within the pale of the Catholic church: and so rapid, yet so gentle, was the fall of Paganism that only twenty-eight years after the death of Theodosius the faint and minute vestiges were no longer visible to the eye of the legislator.[67]

The ruin of the Pagan religion is described by the sophists as a dreadful and amazing prodigy which covered the earth with darkness and restored the ancient dominion of chaos and of night. They relate, in solemn and pathetic strains, that the temples were converted into sepulchres, and that the holy places, which had been adorned by the statues of the gods, were basely polluted by the relics of Christian martyrs. 'The monks' (a race of filthy animals, to whom Eunapius is tempted to refuse the name of men) 'are the authors of the new worship, which, in the place of one of those deities, who are conceived by the understanding, has substituted the meanest and most contemptible slaves. The heads, salted and pickled, of those infamous malefactors, who for the multitude of their crimes have suffered a just and ignominious death; their bodies, still marked by the impression of the lash, and the scars of those tortures which were inflicted by the sentence of the magistrate; such' (continues Eunapius) 'are the gods which the earth produces in our days; such are the martyrs, the supreme arbitrators of our prayers and petitions to the Deity, whose tombs are now consecrated as the objects of the veneration of the people.'[68] Without approving the malice, it is natural enough to share the surprise, of the Sophist, the spectator of a revolution which raised those obscure victims of the laws of Rome to the rank of celestial and invisible protectors of the Roman empire. The grateful respect of the Christians for the martyrs of the faith was exalted, by time and victory, into religious adoration; and the most illustrious of the saints and prophets were deservedly associated to the honours of the martyrs. One hundred and fifty years after the glorious deaths of St Peter and St Paul, the Vatican and the Ostian road were distinguished by the tombs, or rather by the trophies, of those spiritual heroes.[69] In the age which followed the conversion of Constantine, the emperors, the consuls, and the generals of armies devoutly visited the sepulchres of a tent-maker and a fisherman;[70] and their venerable bones were deposited under the altars of Christ, on which the bishops of the royal city continually offered the unbloody sacrifice.[71] The new capital of the eastern world, unable to produce any ancient and domestic trophies, was enriched by the spoils of dependent provinces. The bodies of St Andrew, St Luke, and St Timothy, had reposed, near three hundred years, in the obscure graves from whence they were sent, in solemn pomp, to the church of the Apostles, which the magnificence of Constantine had founded on the banks of the Thracian Bosphorus.[72] About fifty years afterwards, the same banks were honoured by the presence of Samuel, the judge and prophet of the people of Israel. His ashes, deposited in a golden vase and covered with a silken veil, were delivered by the bishops into each other's hands. The relics of Samuel were received by the people with the same joy and reverence which they would have shown to the living prophet; the highways, from Palestine to the gates of Constantinople, were filled with an uninterrupted procession; and the emperor Arcadius himself, at the head of the most illustrious members of the clergy and senate, advanced to meet his extraordinary guest, who had always deserved and claimed the homage of kings.[73] The example of Rome and Constantinople confirmed the faith and discipline of the Catholic world. The honours of the saints and martyrs, after a feeble and ineffectual murmur of profane reason,[74] were universally established; and in the age of Ambrose and Jerome, something was still deemed wanting to the sanctity of a Christian church, till it had been consecrated by some portion of holy relics, which fixed and inflamed the devotion of the faithful.

In the long period of twelve hundred years which elapsed between the reign of Constantine and the reformation of Luther, the worship of saints and relics corrupted the pure and perfect simplicity of the Christian model; and some symptoms of degeneracy may be observed even in the first generations which adopted and cherished this pernicious innovation.

I. The satisfactory experience that the relics of saints were more valuable than gold or precious stones[75] stimulated the clergy to multiply the treasures of the church. Without much regard for truth or probability, they invented names for skeletons and actions for names. The fame of the apostles, and of the holy men who had imitated their virtues, was darkened by religious fiction. To the invincible band of genuine and primitive martyrs, they added myriads of imaginary heroes, who had never existed except in the fancy of crafty or credulous legendaries; and there is reason to suspect that Tours might not be the only diocese in which the bones of a malefactor were adored instead of those of a saint.[76] A superstitious practice, which tended to increase the temptations of fraud and credulity, insensibly extinguished the light of history and of reason in the Christian world.

II. But the progress of superstition would have been much less rapid and victorious, if the faith of the people had not been assisted by the seasonable aid of visions and miracles, to ascertain the authenticity and virtue of the most suspicious relics. In the reign of the younger Theodosius,* Lucian,[77] a presbyter of Jerusalem, and the ecclesiastical minister of the village of Caphargamala, about twenty miles from the city, related a very singular dream, which, to remove his doubts, had been repeated on three successive Saturdays. A venerable figure stood before him, in the silence of the night, with a long beard, a white robe, and a gold rod; announced himself by the name of Gamaliel; and revealed to the astonished presbyter that his own corpse, with the bodies of his son Abibas, his friend Nicodemus, and the illustrious Stephen, the first martyr of the Christian faith, were secretly buried in the adjacent field. He added, with some impatience, that it was time to release himself and his companions from their obscure prison; that their appearance would be salutary to a distressed world; and that they had made choice of Lucian to inform the bishop of Jerusalem of their situation and their wishes. The doubts and difficulties which still retarded this important discovery were successively removed by new visions; and the ground was opened by the bishop, in the presence of an innumerable multitude. The coffins of Gamaliel, of his son, and of his friend were found in regular order; but when the fourth coffin, which contained the remains of Stephen, was shown to the light, the earth trembled, and an odour, such as that of paradise, was smelt, which instantly cured the various diseases of seventy-three of the assistants. The companions of Stephen were left in their peaceful residence of Caphargamala; but the relics of the first martyr were transported in solemn procession to a church constructed in their honour on Mount Sion; and the minute particles of those relics, a drop of blood,[78] or the scrapings of a bone, were acknowledged in almost every province of the Roman world to possess a divine and miraculous virtue. The grave and learned Augustine,[79] whose understanding scarcely admits the excuse of credulity, has attested the innumerable prodigies which were performed in Africa by the relics of St Stephen; and this marvellous narrative is inserted in the elaborate work of the *City of God*, which the bishop of Hippo designed as a solid and immortal proof of the truth of Christianity. Augustine solemnly declares that he has selected those miracles only which were publicly certified by the persons who were either the objects, or the spectators, of the power of the martyr. Many prodigies were omitted or forgotten; and Hippo had been less favourably treated than the other cities of the province. And yet the bishop enumerates above seventy miracles, of which three were resurrections from the dead, in the space of two years and within the limits of his own diocese.[80] If we enlarge our view to all the dioceses and all the saints of the Christian world, it will not be easy to calculate the fables and the errors which issued from this inexhaustible source. But we may surely be allowed to observe that a miracle, in that age of superstition and credulity, lost its name and its merit, since it could scarcely be considered as a deviation from the ordinary and established laws of nature.

III. The innumerable miracles of which the tombs of the martyrs were the perpetual theatre revealed to the pious believer the actual state and constitution of the invisible world; and his religious speculations appeared to be founded on the firm basis of fact and experience. Whatever might be the condition of vulgar souls, in the long interval between the dissolution and the resurrection of their bodies, it was evident that the superior spirits of the saints and martyrs did not consume that portion of their existence in silent and inglorious sleep.[81] It was evident (without presuming to determine the place of their habitation or the nature of their felicity) that they enjoyed the lively and active consciousness of their happiness, their virtue, and their powers; and that they had already secured the possession of their eternal reward. The enlargement of their intellectual faculties surpassed the measure of the human imagination; since it was proved by *experience* that they were capable of hearing and understanding the various petitions of their numerous votaries; who, in the same moment of time, but in the most distant parts of the world, invoked the name and assistance of Stephen or of Martin.[82] The confidence of their petitioners was founded on the persuasion that the saints, who reigned with Christ, cast an eye of pity upon earth; that they were warmly interested in the prosperity of the Catholic church; and that the individuals, who imitated the example of their faith and piety, were the peculiar and favourite objects of their most tender regard. Sometimes, indeed, their friendship might be influenced by considerations of a less exalted kind: they viewed, with partial affection, the places which had been consecrated by their birth, their residence, their death, their burial, or the possession of their relics. The meaner passions of pride, avarice, and revenge may be deemed unworthy of a celestial breast; yet the saints themselves condescended to testify their grateful approbation of the liberality of their votaries; and the sharpest bolts of punishment were hurled against those impious wretches who violated their magnificent shrines or disbelieved their supernatural power.[83] Atrocious, indeed, must have been the guilt, and strange would have been the scepticism, of those men, if they had obstinately resisted the proofs of a divine agency which the elements, the whole range of the animal creation, and even the subtle and invisible operations of the human mind were compelled to obey.[84] The immediate, and almost instantaneous, effects, that were supposed to follow the prayer or the offence, satisfied the Christians of the ample measure of favour and authority which the saints enjoyed in the presence of the Supreme God; and it seemed almost superfluous to inquire whether they were continually obliged to intercede before the throne of grace, or whether they might not be permitted to exercise, according to the dictates of their benevolence and justice, the delegated powers of their subordinate ministry. The imagination, which had been raised by a painful effort to the contemplation and worship of the Universal Cause, eagerly embraced such inferior objects of adoration as were more proportioned to its gross conceptions and imperfect faculties. The sublime and simple theology of the primitive Christians was gradually corrupted;

and the monarchy of heaven, already clouded by metaphysical subtleties, was degraded by the introduction of a popular mythology, which tended to restore the reign of polytheism.[85]

IV. As the objects of religion were gradually reduced to the standard of the imagination, the rites and ceremonies were introduced that seemed most powerfully to affect the senses of the vulgar. If, in the beginning of the fifth century,[86] Tertullian or Lactantius[87] had been suddenly raised from the dead, to assist at the festival of some popular saint or martyr,[88] they would have gazed with astonishment and indignation on the profane spectacle, which had succeeded to the pure and spiritual worship of a Christian congregation. As soon as the doors of the church were thrown open, they must have been offended by the smoke of incense, the perfume of flowers, and the glare of lamps and tapers, which diffused, at noonday, a gaudy, superfluous, and, in their opinion, a sacrilegious light. If they approached the balustrade of the altar, they made their way through the prostrate crowd, consisting, for the most part, of strangers and pilgrims, who resorted to the city on the vigil of the feast; and who already felt the strong intoxication of fanaticism, and, perhaps, of wine. Their devout kisses were imprinted on the walls and pavement of the sacred edifice; and their fervent prayers were directed, whatever might be the language of their church, to the bones, the blood, or the ashes of the saints, which were usually concealed by a linen or silken veil from the eyes of the vulgar. The Christians frequented the tombs of the martyrs, in the hope of obtaining, from their powerful intercession, every sort of spiritual, but more especially of temporal, blessings. They implored the preservation of their health or the cure of their infirmities; the fruitfulness of their barren wives or the safety and happiness of their children. Whenever they undertook any distant or dangerous journey, they requested that the holy martyrs would be their guides and protectors on the road; and, if they returned without having experienced any misfortune, they again hastened to the tombs of the martyrs, to celebrate, with grateful thanksgivings, their obligations to the memory and relics of those heavenly patrons. The walls were hung round with symbols of the favours which they had received: eyes, and hands, and feet, of gold and silver; and edifying pictures, which could not long escape the abuse of indiscreet or idolatrous devotion, represented the image, the attributes, and the miracles of the tutelar saint. The same uniform original spirit of superstition might suggest, in the most distant ages and countries, the same methods of deceiving the credulity, and of affecting the senses, of mankind;[89] but it must ingenuously be confessed that the ministers of the Catholic church imitated the profane model which they were impatient to destroy. The most respectable bishops had persuaded themselves that the ignorant rustics would more cheerfully renounce the superstitions of Paganism, if they found some resemblance, some compensation, in the bosom of Christianity. The religion of Constantine achieved, in less than a century, the final conquest of the Roman empire; but the victors themselves were insensibly subdued by the arts of their vanquished rivals.[90]

NOTES TO CHAPTER 28

1 St Ambrose (tom. ii, de Obit. Theodos., p. 1208) expressly praises and recommends the zeal of Josiah in the destruction of idolatry. The language of Julius Firmicus Maternus on the same subject (de Errore Profan. Relig., p. 467, edit. Gronov.) is piously inhuman. Nec filio iubet (the Mosaic Law) parci, nec fratri, et per amatam coniugem gladium vindicem ducit, etc. ['(The Mosaic Law) does not command us to spare the life of a son or brother, it leads the sword of vengeance against a beloved spouse, etc.']

2 Bayle (ii, 406, in his Commentaire Philosophique) justifies and limits these intolerant laws by the temporal reign of Jehovah over the Jews. The attempt is laudable.

* page 556 [from the seventh century bc to ad 367–383]

3 See the outlines of the Roman hierarchy in Cicero (de Legibus, ii, 7–8); Livy (i, 20); Dionysius Halicarnassensis (ii, 119–29, edit Hudson); Beaufort (République Romaine, i, 1–90); and Moyle (i, 10–55). The last is the work of an English Whig, as well as of a Roman antiquary.

† page 556 [Pagan high priests]

‡ page 556 [books of prophecy]

4 These mystic and perhaps imaginary symbols have given birth to various fables and conjectures. It seems probable that the Palladium was a small statue (three cubits and a half high) of Minerva, with a lance and distaff; that it was usually enclosed in a seria, or barrel; and that a similar barrel was placed by its side to disconcert curiosity or sacrilege. See Mezeriac (Comment. sur les Epîtres d'Ovide, i, 60–66) and Lipsius (iii, 610, de Vesta, etc., ch. 10).

* page 557 [name of Romulus after deification]

† page 557 [priests of Mars]

‡ page 557 [priests associated with the cult of Romulus]

5 Cicero frankly (ad Atticum, ii, epist. 5) or indirectly (ad Familiar., xv, epist. 4) confesses that the Augurate is the supreme object of his wishes. Pliny is proud to tread in the footsteps of Cicero (iv, epist. 8), and the chain of tradition might be continued from history and marbles.

6 Zosimus, iv, 249–50. I have suppressed the foolish pun about Pontifex and Maximus.

7 This statue was transported from Tarentum to Rome, placed in the Curia Julia by Caesar, and decorated by Augustus with the spoils of Egypt.

8 Prudentius (Bk ii, in initio) has drawn a very awkward portrait of Victory; but the curious reader will obtain more satisfaction from Montfaucon's Antiquities (i, 341).

9 See Suetonius (in August., ch. 35) and the Exordium of Pliny's Panegyric.

10 These facts are mutually allowed by the two advocates, Symmachus and Ambrose.

11 The Notitia Urbis, more recent than Constantine, does not find one Christian

church worthy to be named among the edifices of the city. Ambrose (ii, epist. xvii, 825) deplores the public scandals of Rome, which continually offended the eyes, the ears, and the nostrils of the faithful.

12 Ambrose repeatedly affirms, in contradiction to common sense (Moyle's *Works*, ii, 147), that the Christians had a majority in the senate.

13 The *first* (AD 382) to Gratian, who refused them audience. The *second* (AD 384) to Valentinian, when the field was disputed by Symmachus and Ambrose. The *third* (AD 388) to Theodosius; and the *fourth* (AD 392) to Valentinian. Lardner (*Heathen Testimonies*, iv, 372–99) fairly represents the whole transaction.

14 Symmachus, who was invested with all the civil and sacerdotal honours, represented the emperor under the two characters of *Pontifex Maximus* and *Princeps Senatus* [leader of the senate]. See the proud inscription at the head of his works.

15 As if anyone, says Prudentius (in *Symmach.*, i, 639), should dig in the mud with an instrument of gold and ivory. Even saints, and polemic saints, treat this adversary with respect and civility.

16 See the fifty-fourth epistle of the tenth book of Symmachus. In the form and disposition of his ten books of epistles, he imitated the younger Pliny; whose rich and florid style he was supposed, by his friends, to equal or excel (Macrob., *Saturnal.*, v, 1). But the luxuriancy of Symmachus consists of barren leaves, without fruits, and even without flowers. Few facts, and few sentiments, can be extracted from his verbose correspondence.

17 See Ambrose (ii, epist. xvii, xviii, 825–33). The former of these epistles is a short caution; the latter is a formal reply to the petition or *libel* of Symmachus. The same ideas are more copiously expressed in the poetry, if it may deserve that name, of Prudentius; who composed his two books against Symmachus (AD 404) while that senator was still alive. It is whimsical enough that Montesquieu (*Considérations*, etc., xix, iii, 487) should overlook the two professed antagonists of Symmachus; and amuse himself with descanting on the more remote and indirect confutations of Orosius, St Augustine, and Salvian.

18 See Prudentius (in *Symmach.*, i, 545, etc.). The Christian agrees with the Pagan Zosimus (iv, 283) in placing this visit of Theodosius after the *second* civil war, *gemini bis victor caede Tyranni* (i, 410) ['twice victorious by the death of the two tyrants' – a reference to the defeat of the usurper Eugenius and his general Arbogastes in AD 394]. But the time and circumstances are better suited to his first triumph.

19 Prudentius, after proving that the sense of the senate is declared by a legal majority, proceeds to say (609, etc.):

> *Adspice quam pleno subsellia nostra Senatu*
> *Decernant infame Iovis pulvinar, et omne*
> *Idolium longe purgata ex urbe fugandum.*
> *Qua vocat egregii sententia Principis, illuc*
> *Libera, cum pedibus, tum corde, frequentia transit.*

['See how our side of a full senate house succeeds in voting down the infamous worship of Jupiter, and decrees that the city should be completely purged of idol-worship. The proposal of an excellent Prince is actively and enthusiastically seconded by the crowded assembly.']

Zosimus ascribes to the conscript fathers an heathenish courage, which few of them are found to possess.

20 Jerome specifies the pontiff Albinus, who was surrounded with such a believing family of children and grand-children as would have been sufficient to convert even Jupiter himself; an extraordinary proselyte! (tom. i, *ad Laetam*, p. 54).

21   *Exsultare Patres videas, pulcherrima mundi*
                      Lumina; conciliumque senum gestire Catonum
                      Candidiore toga niveum pietatis amictum
                      Sumere, et exuvias deponere pontificales.

The fancy of Prudentius is warmed and elevated by victory.

22 Prudentius, after he has described the conversion of the senate and people, asks, with some truth and confidence,

                      Et dubitamus adhuc Romam, tibi, Christe, dicatam
                      In leges transisse tuas?

['Can we doubt that Rome, now consecrated to thee, O Christ, is now converted to thy laws?']

23 Jerome exults in the desolation of the Capitol, and the other temples of Rome (i, 54; ii, 95).

24 Libanius (*Orat. pro Templis*, p. 10, Genev. 1634, published by James Godefroy, and now extremely scarce, see below, note 29) accuses Valentinian and Valens of prohibiting sacrifices. Some partial order may have been issued by the Eastern emperor; but the idea of any general law is contradicted by the silence of the Code and the evidence of ecclesiastical history.

* *page 560* [in AD 388]

25 See his laws in the Theodosian Code, xvi, x, 7–11.

26 Homer's sacrifices are not accompanied with any inquisition of entrails (see Feithius, *Antiquitat. Homer.*, i, 10, 16). The Tuscans, who produced the first *Haruspices* [who divined from entrails], subdued both the Greeks and the Romans (Cicero, *de Divinatione*, ii, 23).

27 Zosimus, iv, 245, 249; Theodoret, v, 21; Idatius, in *Chron.*; Prosper Aquitan., iii, 38, *apud* Baronium, *Annal. Eccles.*, AD 389, No. 52. Libanius (*pro Templis*, p. 10) labours to prove that the commands of Theodosius were not direct and positive.

28 *Cod. Theodos.*, xvi, x, 8, 18. There is room to believe that this temple of Edessa, which Theodosius wished to save for civil uses, was soon afterwards a heap of ruins (Libanius, *pro Templis*, pp. 26–27, and Godefroy's notes, p. 59).

29 See this curious oration of Libanius, *pro Templis*, pronounced, or rather composed, about the year 390. I have consulted, with advantage, Dr Lardner's version and remarks (*Heathen Testimonies*, iv, 135–63).

30 See the life of Martin, by Sulpicius Severus, ch. 9–14. The saint once mistook (as Don Quixote might have done) an harmless funeral for an idolatrous procession, and imprudently committed a miracle.

31 Compare Sozomen (vii, 15) with Theodoret (v, 21). Between them, they relate the crusade and death of Marcellus.

32 Libanius, *pro Templis*, pp. 10–13. He rails at these black-garbed men, the Christian monks, who eat more than elephants. Poor elephants! *they* are temperate animals.

33 Prosper Aquitan., iii, 38, *apud* Baronium; *Annal. Eccles.*, AD 389, No. 58, etc. The temple had been shut some time, and the access to it was overgrown with brambles.

34 Donatus, *Roma Antiqua et Nova*, iv, 4, 468. This consecration was performed by Pope Boniface IV. I am ignorant of the favourable circumstances which had preserved the Pantheon above two hundred years after the reign of Theodosius.

35 Sophronius composed a recent and separate history (Jerome, in *Script. Eccles.*, i, 303), which had furnished materials to Socrates (v, 16); Theodoret (v, 22); and Rufinus (ii, 22). Yet the last, who had been at Alexandria before and after the event, may deserve the credit of an original witness.

36 Gerard Vossius (*Opera*, v, 80; and *de Idololatria*, i, 29) strives to support the strange notion of the Fathers; that the patriarch Joseph was adored in Egypt as the bull Apis and the god Serapis.

* *page 562*   [the Black Sea]

37 *Origo dei nondum nostris celebrata. Aegyptiorum antistites sic memorant,* etc. ['The origin of the god was not yet known to the Romans. The Egyptian priests commemorate him as follows, etc.'] Tacit., *Hist.*, iv, 83. The Greeks, who had travelled into Egypt, were alike ignorant of this new deity.

38 Macrobius, *Saturnal.*, i, 7. Such a living fact decisively proves his foreign extraction.

39 At Rome Isis and Serapis were united in the same temple. The precedency which the queen assumed may seem to betray her unequal alliance with the stranger of Pontus. But the superiority of the female sex was established in Egypt as a civil and religious institution (Diodor. Sicul., i, 1, 31, edit. Wesseling), and the same order is observed in Plutarch's Treatise of Isis and Osiris; whom he identifies with Serapis.

40 Ammianus (xxii, 16). The *Expositio totius Mundi* (p. 8, in Hudson's *Geograph. Minor.*, tom. iii) and Rufinus (ii, 22) celebrate the *Serapeum* [temple of Serapis] as one of the wonders of the world.

41 See *Mémoires de l'Acad. des Inscriptions*, ix, 397–416. The old library of the Ptolemies was *totally* consumed in Caesar's Alexandrian war. Marc Antony gave the whole collection of Pergamus (200,000 volumes) to Cleopatra, as the foundation of the *new* library of Alexandria.

42 Libanius (*pro Templis*, p. 21) indiscreetly provokes his Christian masters by this insulting remark.

43 We may choose between the date of Marcellinus (AD 389) or that of Prosper (AD 391). Tillemont (*Hist. des Emp.*, v, 310, 756) prefers the former, and Pagi the latter.

44 Tillemont, *Mém. Ecclés.*, xi, 441–500. The ambiguous situation of Theophilus – a *saint*, as the friend of Jerome; a *devil*, as the enemy of Chrysostom – produces a sort of impartiality; yet, upon the whole, the balance is justly inclined against him.

45 Lardner (*Heathen Testimonies*, iv, 411) has alleged a beautiful passage from Suidas, or rather from Damascius, which shows the devout and virtuous Olympius, not in the light of a warrior, but of a prophet.

46 *Nos vidimus, armaria librorum, quibus direptis exinanita ea a nostris hominibus, nostris temporibus memorant.* Orosius, vi, 15, 421, edit. Havercamp. Though a bigot, and a controversial writer, Orosius seems to blush.

47 Eunapius, in the lives of Antoninus and Aedesius, execrates the sacrilegious rapine of Theophilus. Tillemont (*Mém. Ecclés.*, xiii, 453) quotes an epistle of Isidore of Pelusium, which reproaches the primate with the idolatrous worship of gold, the *auri sacra fames* [accursed lust for gold (Virgil, *Aeneid*, iii, 57)].

* *page 564*   [tricks effected by magnetism]

48 Rufinus names the priest of Saturn, who, in the character of the god, familiarly conversed with many pious ladies of quality; till he betrayed himself, in a

moment of transport, when he could not disguise the tone of his voice. The authentic and impartial narrative of Aeschines (see Bayle, *Dictionnaire Critique*, SCAMANDRE) and the adventure of Mundus (Joseph., *Antiquitat. Judaic.*, xviii, 3, 877, edit. Havercamp) may prove that such amorous frauds have been practised with success.

49 See the images of Serapis, in Montfaucon (ii, 297); but the description of Macrobius (*Saturnal.*, i, 20) is much more picturesque and satisfactory.

50   *Sed fortes tremuere manus, motique verenda*
                Maiestate loci, si robora sacra ferirent
                In sua credebant redituras membra secures.

['But their strong hands trembled, and overcome by the solemn atmosphere of the place, they thought that if they struck the sacred oaks, the axes would fly back to hit their own bodies.'] (Lucan, iii, 429.)

'Is it true (said Augustus to a veteran of Italy, at whose house he supped) that the man who gave the first blow to the golden statue of Anaitis was instantly deprived of his eyes, and of his life?' '*I* was that man (replied the clear-sighted veteran), and you now sup on one of the legs of the goddess.' (Plin., *Hist. Natur.*, xxxiii, 24.)

51 The history of the Reformation affords frequent examples of the sudden change from superstition to contempt.

52 Sozomen, vii, 20. I have supplied the measure. The same standard of the inundation, and consequently of the cubit, has uniformly subsisted since the time of Herodotus. See Fréret, in the *Mém. de l'Académie des Inscriptions*, xvi, 344–53. Greaves's *Miscellaneous Works*, i, 233. The Egyptian cubit is about twenty-two inches of the English measure.

53 Libanius (*pro Templis*, pp. 15–17) pleads their cause with gentle and insinuating rhetoric. From the earliest age, such feasts had enlivened the country; and those of Bacchus (*Georgics*, ii, 380) had produced the theatre of Athens. See Godefroy, *ad loc.* Liban., and *Codex Theodos.*, vi, 284.

54 Honorius tolerated these rustic festivals (AD 399). *Absque ullo sacrificio, atque ulla superstitione damnabili* ['Apart from any sacrifice or any reprehensible superstitious practice']. But nine years afterwards he found it necessary to reiterate and enforce the same proviso (*Codex Theodos.*, xvi, x, 17, 19).

55 *Cod. Theodos.*, xvi, x, 12. Jortin (*Remarks on Eccles. History*, iv, 134) censures, with becoming asperity, the style and sentiments of this intolerant law.

56 Such a charge should not be lightly made; but it may surely be justified by the authority of St Augustine, who thus addresses the Donatists: *Quis nostrum, quis vestrum non laudat leges ab Imperatoribus datas adversus sacrificia Paganorum? Et certe longe ibi poena severior constituta est; illius quippe impietatis capitale supplicium est.* ['Which of us, or of you, does not approve of the imperial laws against pagan sacrifices? Certainly the penalty laid down there is far more severe; indeed for that kind of impious conduct the punishment is death.'] *Epist.* xciii, No. 10, quoted by Le Clerc (*Bibliothèque Choisie*, viii, 277), who adds some judicious reflections on the intolerance of the victorious Christians.

57 Orosius, vii, 28, 537. Augustine (*Enarrat. in Psal.* cxl, *apud* Lardner, *Heathen Testimonies*, iv, 458) insults their cowardice. *Quis eorum comprehensus est in sacrificio (cum his legibus ista prohiberentur) et non negavit?* ['Which of them has been caught performing a sacrifice (since these are forbidden by the law) and has pleaded guilty?']

58 Libanius (*pro Templis*, pp. 17–18) mentions, without censure, the occasional conformity, and as it were theatrical play, of these hypocrites.

59 Libanius concludes his apology (p. 32) by declaring to the emperor that, unless he expressly warrants the destruction of the temples, ἴσθι τοὺς τῶν ἀγρῶν δεσπότας καὶ αὐτοῖς καὶ τῷ νόμῳ βοηθήσοντας, the proprietors will defend themselves and the laws.

 * *page 567* [acclaimed as emperor in the civil war of AD 392–94]

60 Paulinus, in *Vit. Ambros.*, ch. 26; Augustine, de *Civitat. Dei*, v, 26; Theodoret, v, 24.

61 Libanius suggests the form of a persecuting edict, which Theodosius might enact (*pro Templis*, p. 32): a rash joke, and a dangerous experiment. Some princes would have taken his advice.

62   *Denique pro meritis terrestribus aequa rependens*
      Munera, sacricolis summos impertit honores.
      . . .
      Ipse magistratum tibi consulis, ipse tribunal
      Contulit.   Prudent., *in Symmach.*, i, 617, etc.

63 Libanius (*pro Templis*, p. 32) is proud that Theodosius should thus distinguish a man, who even in his *presence* would swear by Jupiter. Yet this presence seems to be no more than a figure of rhetoric.

64 Zosimus, who styles himself Count and Ex-advocate of the Treasury, reviles, with partial and indecent bigotry, the Christian princes, and even the father of his sovereign. His work must have been privately circulated, since it escaped the invectives of the ecclesiatical historians prior to Evagrius (iii, 40–42), who lived towards the end of the sixth century.

65 Yet the Pagans of Africa complained that the times would not allow them to answer with freedom the *City of God* [in which St Augustine defended Christianity]; nor does St Augustine (v, 26) deny the charge.

66 The Moors of Spain, who secretly preserved the Mahometan religion above a century, under the tyranny of the Inquisition, possessed the Koran, with the peculiar use of the Arabic tongue. See the curious and honest story of their expulsion in Geddes (*Miscellanies*, i, 1–198).

67 *Paganos qui supersunt, quanquam iam nullos esse credamus,* etc. ['The Pagans who remain, although we believe that there are none, etc.] *Cod. Theodos.*, xvi, x, 22, AD 423. The younger Theodosius was afterwards satisfied that his judgment had been somewhat premature.

68 See Eunapius, in the life of the sophist Aedesius; in that of Eustathius he foretells the ruin of Paganism, καί τι μυθῶδες, καὶ ἀειδὲς σκότος τυραννήσει τὰ ἐπὶ γῆς κάλλιστα. ['A kind of prodigy, and a formless darkness will prevail over the most beautiful things on earth.']

69 Caius (*apud* Euseb., *Hist. Eccles.*, ii, 25), a Roman presbyter, who lived in the time of Zephyrinus (AD 202–19), is an early witness of this superstitious practice.

70 Chrysostom, *Quod Christus sit Deus.*, tom. i, nov. edit., No 9. I am indebted for this quotation to Benedict the XIVth's pastoral letter on the jubilee of the year 1750. See the curious and entertaining letters of M. Chais, tom. iii.

71 *Male facit ergo Romanus episcopus? qui, super mortuorum hominum, Petri et Pauli, secundum nos, ossa veneranda . . . offert Domino sacrificia, et tumulos eorum Christi arbitratur altaria.* Jerom., tom. ii, *advers. Vigilant.* p. 153.

72 Jerome (ii, 122) bears witness to these translations, which are neglected by the ecclesiastical historians. The passion of St Andrew at Patrae is described in an epistle from the clergy of Achaia, which Baronius (*Annal. Eccles.*, AD 60, No. 35) wishes to believe and Tillemont is forced to reject. St Andrew was adopted as the spiritual founder of Constantinople (*Mém. Ecclés.*, i, 317–23, 588–94).

73 Jerome (ii, 122) pompously describes the translation of Samuel, which is noticed in the chronicles of the times.

74 The presbyter Vigilantius, the protestant of his age, firmly, though ineffectually, withstood the superstition of monks, relics, saints, fasts, etc., for which Jerome compares him to the Hydra, Cerberus, the Centaurs, etc., and considers him only as the organ of the daemon (ii, 120–26). Whoever will peruse the controversy of St Jerome and Vigilantius, and St Augustine's account of the miracles of St Stephen, may speedily gain some idea of the spirit of the Fathers.

75 M. de Beausobre (*Hist. du Manichéisme*, ii, 648) has applied a worldly sense to the pious observation of the clergy of Smyrna who carefully preserved the relics of St Polycarp the martyr.

76 Martin of Tours (see his Life, ch. 8, by Sulpicius Severus) extorted this confession from the mouth of the dead man. The error is allowed to be natural; the discovery is supposed to be miraculous. Which of the two was likely to happen most frequently?

* *page 569* [Theodosius II, emperor ad 408–50]

77 Lucian composed in Greek his original narrative, which has been translated by Avitus, and published by Baronius (*Annal. Eccles.*, AD 415, Nos 7–16). The Benedictine editors of St Augustine have given (at the end of the work *de Civitate Dei*) two several copies, with many various readings. It is the character of falsehood to be loose and inconsistent. The most incredible parts of the legend are smoothed and softened by Tillemont (*Mém. Ecclés.*, ii, 9, etc.)

78 A phial of St Stephen's blood was annually liquefied at Naples, till he was superseded by St Januarius (Ruinart., *Hist. Persecut. Vandal.*, p. 529).

79 Augustine composed the two and twenty books *de Civitate Dei* in the space of thirteen years, AD 413–26 (Tillemont, *Mém. Ecclés.*, xiv, 608, etc.). His learning is too often borrowed, and his arguments are too often his own; but the whole work claims the merit of a magnificent design, vigorously, and not unskilfully, executed.

80 See Augustine, *de Civitate Dei*, xxii, 22, and the Appendix, which contains two books of St Stephen's miracles, by Evodius, bishop of Uzalis. Freculphus (*apud* Basnage, *Hist. des Juifs*, viii, 249) has preserved a Gallic or Spanish proverb, 'Whoever pretends to have read all the miracles of St Stephen, he lies'.

81 Burnet (*de Statu Mortuorum*, pp. 56–84) collects the opinions of the fathers, as far as they assert the sleep, or repose, of human souls till the day of judgment. He afterwards exposes (pp. 91, etc.) the inconveniencies which must arise, if they possessed a more active and sensible existence.

82 Vigilantius placed the souls of the prophets and martyrs either in the bosom of Abraham (*in loco refrigerii*) [in a resting place] or else under the altar of God. *Nec posse suis tumulis et ubi voluerunt adesse praesentes.* ['They cannot still be present in their tombs and where they wished to be.'] But Jerome (ii, 122) sternly refutes this *blasphemy. Tu Deo leges pones? Tu apostolis vincula iniicies, ut usque ad diem iudicii teneantur custodia, nec sint cum Domino suo; de quibus scriptum est, Sequuntur Agnum quocunque vadit? Si Agnus ubique, ergo, et hi, qui cum Agno sunt,*

ubique esse credendi sunt. Et cum diabolus et daemones toto vagentur in orbe, etc. ['Will you impose laws on God? Will you put chains on the apostles so that they remain imprisoned until the day of judgment and are not in the company of their Lord? Of these men, it is written, they follow the Lamb wherever he goes. If the Lamb is everywhere, then those who are with the Lamb must also be assumed to be everywhere. And since the devil and the demons wander all over the world, etc.']

83 Fleury, *Discours sur l'Hist. Ecclésiastique,* iii, 80.

84 At Minorca, the relics of St Stephen converted, in eight days, 540 Jews, with the help, indeed, of some severities, such as burning the synagogue, driving the obstinate infidels to starve among the rocks, etc. See the original letter of Severus, bishop of Minorca (*ad calcem* St Augustine, *de Civ. Dei*), and the judicious remarks of Basnage (viii, 245–51).

85 Mr Hume (*Essays,* ii, 434) observes, like a philosopher, the natural flux and reflux of polytheism and theism.

86 D'Aubigné (see his own *Mémoires,* pp. 150–60) frankly offered, with the consent of the Huguenot ministers, to allow the first 400 years as the rule of faith. The Cardinal du Perron haggled for forty years more, which were indiscreetly given. Yet neither party would have found their account in this foolish bargain.

87 The worship practised and inculcated by Tertullian, Lactantius, Arnobius, etc., is so *extremely* pure and spiritual that their declamations against the Pagan, sometimes glance against the Jewish, ceremonies.

88 Faustus the Manichaean accuses the Catholics of idolatry. *Vertitis idola in martyres . . . quos votis similibus colitis.* ['You turn idols into martyrs . . . and worship them in the same way.'] M. de Beausobre (*Hist. Critique du Manichéisme,* ii, 629–700), a protestant, but a philosopher, has represented, with candour and learning, the introduction of *Christian idolatry* in the fourth and fifth centuries.

89 The resemblance of superstition, which could not be imitated, might be traced from Japan to Mexico. Warburton has seized this idea, which he distorts, by rendering it too general and absolute (*Divine Legation,* iv, 126, etc.).

90 The imitation of Paganism is the subject of Dr Middleton's agreeable letter from Rome. Warburton's animadversions obliged him to connect (iii, 120–32) the history of the two religions, and to prove the antiquity of the Christian copy.

CHAPTER 29 (Summary)

Final division of the Roman empire between the sons of
Theodosius – reign of Arcadius and Honorius – administration
of Rufinus and Stilicho – revolt and defeat of Gildo in Africa

In Chapter 29, Gibbon reverts to the political scene, describing the different fortunes of the East and the West under the young and spiritless sons of Theodosius, the emperors Arcadius and Honorius. In the East, the rapacious minister Rufinus was captured and murdered in AD 395 by an army sent from the West by Stilicho, the general and protector of Honorius. Stilicho was also responsible for suppressing, in AD 398, a rebellion in Africa by the tyrant, Gildo. Gibbon sees the disintegration of the empire beginning with the development of feuds between East and West and with the increased involvement of barbarian forces within the frontiers. Theodosius, known as the Great, had been the last emperor to lead his troops in battle, and Gibbon writes of the genius of Rome dying with him.

CHAPTER 30

Revolt of the Goths – they plunder Greece – two great
invasions of Italy by Alaric and Radagaisus – they are repulsed
by Stilicho – the Germans overrun Gaul – usurpation of
Constantine in the West – disgrace and death of Stilicho

If the subjects of Rome could be ignorant of their obligations to the great Theodosius, they were too soon convinced how painfully the spirit and abilities of their deceased emperor had supported the frail and mouldering edifice of the republic. He died in the month of January; and before the end of the winter of the same year the Gothic nation was in arms.[1] The Barbarian auxiliaries erected their independent standard; and boldly avowed the hostile designs which they had long cherished in their ferocious minds. Their countrymen, who had been condemned by the conditions of the last treaty* to a life of tranquillity and labour, deserted their farms at the first sound of the trumpet, and eagerly resumed the weapons which they had reluctantly laid down. The barriers of the Danube were thrown open; the savage warriors of Scythia issued from their forests; and the uncommon severity of the winter allowed the poet to remark 'that they rolled their ponderous waggons over the broad and icy back of the indignant river'.[2] The unhappy natives of the provinces to the south of the Danube submitted to the calamities which, in the course of twenty years, were almost grown familiar to their imagination; and the various troops of Barbarians who gloried in the Gothic name were irregularly spread from the woody shores of Dalmatia to the walls of Constantinople.[3] The interruption, or at least the diminution, of the subsidy which the Goths had received from the prudent liberality of Theodosius was the specious pretence of their revolt; the affront was embittered by their contempt for the unwarlike sons of Theodosius; and their resentment was inflamed by the weakness or treachery of the minister of Arcadius. The frequent visits of Rufinus* to the camp of the Barbarians, whose arms and apparel he affected to imitate, were considered as a sufficient evidence of his guilty correspondence; and the public enemy, from a motive either of gratitude or of policy, was attentive, amidst the general devastation, to spare the private estates of the unpopular prefect. The Goths, instead of being impelled by the blind and headstrong passions of their chiefs, were now directed by the bold and artful genius of Alaric. That renowned leader was descended from the noble race of the Balti;[4] which yielded only to the royal dignity of the Amali: he had solicited the command of the Roman armies; and the Imperial court provoked him to demonstrate the folly of their refusal and the importance of their loss. Whatever hopes might be entertained of the conquest of Constantinople, the judicious general soon abandoned an impracticable enterprise. In the midst of a divided court and a discontented people, the Emperor Arcadius was terrified by the aspect of the Gothic arms; but the want of wisdom and valour was supplied by the strength of the city; and the fortifications, both of the sea and land, might securely brave the impotent and random darts of the Barbarians. Alaric disdained to trample any longer on the prostrate and ruined countries of Thrace and Dacia, and he resolved to seek a plentiful harvest of fame and riches in a province which had hitherto escaped the ravages of war.[5]

The character of the civil and military officers, on whom Rufinus had devolved the government of Greece, confirmed the public suspicion that he had betrayed the ancient seat of freedom and learning to the Gothic invader. The proconsul Antiochus was the unworthy son of a respectable father; and Gerontius, who commanded the provincial troops, was much better qualified to execute the oppressive orders of a tyrant than to defend, with courage and ability, a country most remarkably fortified by the hand of nature. Alaric had traversed, without resistance, the plains of Macedonia and Thessaly, as far as the foot of Mount Oeta, a steep and woody range of hills, almost impervious to his cavalry. They stretched from East to West, to the edge of the seashore; and left, between the precipice and the Malian Gulf, an interval of three hundred feet, which, in some places, was contracted to a road capable of admitting only a single carriage.[6] In this narrow pass of Thermopylae, where Leonidas and the three hundred Spartans had gloriously devoted their lives,* the Goths might have been stopped, or destroyed, by a skilful general; and perhaps the view of that sacred spot might have kindled some sparks of military ardour in the breasts of the degenerate Greeks. The troops which had been posted to defend the straits of Thermopylae retired, as they were directed, without attempting to disturb the secure and rapid passage of Alaric;[7] and the fertile fields of Phocis and Boeotia were instantly covered by a deluge of barbarians, who massacred the males of an age to bear arms, and drove away the beautiful females, with the spoil and cattle, of the flaming villages. The travellers who visited Greece several years afterwards could easily discover the deep and bloody traces of the march of the Goths; and Thebes was less indebted for her preservation to the strength of her seven gates than to the eager haste of Alaric, who advanced to occupy the city of Athens and the important harbour of the Piraeus. The same impatience urged him to prevent the delay and danger of a siege, by the offer of a capitulation: and, as soon as the Athenians heard the voice of the Gothic herald, they were easily persuaded to deliver the greatest part of their wealth, as the ransom of the city of Minerva and its inhabitants. The treaty was ratified by solemn oaths, and observed with mutual fidelity. The Gothic prince, with a small and select train, was admitted within the walls; he indulged himself in the refreshment of the bath, accepted a splendid banquet which was provided by the magistrate, and affected to show that he was not ignorant of the manners of civilised nations.[8] But the whole territory of Attica, from the promontory of Sunium to the town of Megara, was blasted by his baleful presence; and, if we may use the comparison of a contemporary philosopher, Athens itself resembled the bleeding and empty skin of a slaughtered victim. The distance between Megara and Corinth could not much exceed thirty miles; but the *bad road*, an expressive name, which it still bears among the Greeks, was, or might easily have been made, impassable for the march of an enemy. The thick and gloomy woods of Mount Cithaeron covered the inland country; the Scironian rocks approached the water's edge, and hung over the narrow and winding path, which was confined above six miles along the seashore.[9] The passage of those rocks, so infamous in every age, was terminated by the isthmus of Corinth; and a small body of firm and intrepid soldiers might have successfully defended a temporary entrenchment of five or six miles from the Ionian to the Aegean sea. The confidence of the cities of Peloponnesus in their natural rampart had tempted them to neglect the care of their antique walls; and the avarice of the Roman governors had exhausted and betrayed the unhappy province.[10] Corinth, Argos, Sparta, yielded without resistance to the arms of the Goths; and the most fortunate of the inhabitants were saved by death from beholding the slavery of their families and the conflagration of their cities.[11] The vases and statues were distributed among the Barbarians, with more regard to the value of the materials than to the elegance of the workmanship; the female captives submitted to the laws of war; the enjoyment of beauty was the reward of valour; and the Greeks could not reasonably complain of an abuse, which was justified by the example of the heroic times.[12] The descendants of that extraordinary people, who had considered valour and discipline as the walls of Sparta, no longer remembered the generous reply of their ancestors to an invader* more formidable than Alaric: 'If thou art a god, thou wilt not hurt those who have never injured thee; if thou art a man, advance – and thou wilt find men equal to thyself.'[13] From Thermopylae to Sparta, the leader of the Goths pursued his victorious march without encountering any mortal antagonists; but one of the advocates of expiring Paganism has confidently asserted that the walls of Athens were guarded by the goddess Minerva, with her formidable aegis,† and by the angry phantom of Achilles;[14] and that the conqueror was dismayed by the presence of the hostile deities of Greece. In an age of miracles, it would perhaps be unjust to dispute the claim of the historian Zosimus to the common benefit; yet it cannot be dissembled that the mind of Alaric was ill prepared to receive, either in sleeping or waking visions, the impressions of Greek superstition. The songs of Homer and the fame of Achilles had probably never reached the ear of the illiterate *Barbarian*; and the *Christian* faith, which he had devoutly embraced, taught him to despise the imaginary deities of Rome and Athens. The invasion of the Goths, instead of vindicating the honour, contributed, at least accidentally, to extirpate the last remains, of Paganism; and the mysteries of Ceres, which had subsisted eighteen hundred years, did not survive the destruction of Eleusis and the calamities of Greece.[15]

The last hope of a people who could no longer depend on their arms, their gods, or their sovereign, was placed in the powerful assistance of the general of the West; and Stilicho, who had not been permitted to repulse, advanced to chastise the invaders of Greece.[16] A numerous fleet was equipped in the ports of Italy; and the troops, after a short and prosperous navigation over the Ionian sea, were safely disembarked on the isthmus, near the ruins of Corinth. The woody and mountainous country of Arcadia, the fabulous residence of Pan and the Dryads, became the scene of a long and doubtful conflict between two generals not unworthy of each other. The skill and perseverance of the Roman at length prevailed; and the Goths, after sustaining a considerable loss from disease and desertion, gradually retreated to the lofty mountain of Pholoe, near the sources of the Peneus, and on the frontiers of Elis: a sacred country, which had formerly been exempted from the calamities of war.[17] The camp of the Barbarians was immediately besieged; the waters of the river[18] were diverted into another channel; and, while they laboured under the intolerable pressure of thirst and hunger, a strong line of circumvallation was formed* to prevent their escape. After these precautions, Stilicho, too confident of victory, retired to enjoy his triumph in the theatrical games and lascivious dances of the Greeks; his soldiers, deserting their standards, spread themselves over the country of their allies, which they stripped of all that had been saved from the rapacious hands of the enemy. Alaric appears to have seized the favourable moment to execute one of those hardy enterprises, in which the abilities of a general are displayed with more genuine lustre than in the tumult of a day of battle. To extricate himself from the prison of Peloponnesus, it was necessary that he should pierce the entrenchments† which surrounded his camp; that he should perform a difficult and dangerous march of thirty miles as far as the Gulf of Corinth; and that he should transport his troops, his captives, and his spoil, over an arm of the sea which, in the narrow interval between Rhium and the opposite shore, is at least half a mile in breadth.[19] The operations of Alaric must have been secret, prudent, and rapid; since the Roman general was confounded by the intelligence that the Goths, who had eluded his efforts, were in full possession of the important province of Epirus. This unfortunate delay allowed Alaric sufficient time to conclude the treaty, which he secretly negotiated with the ministers of Constantinople. The apprehension of a civil war compelled Stilicho to retire, at the haughty mandate of his rivals, from the dominions of Arcadius; and he respected in the enemy of Rome the honourable character of the ally and servant of the emperor of the East.

A Grecian philosopher,[20] who visited Constantinople soon after the death of Theodosius, published his liberal opinions concerning the duties of kings and the state of the Roman republic. Synesius observes and deplores the fatal abuse which the imprudent bounty of the late emperor had introduced into the military service. The citizens and subjects had purchased an exemption from the indispensable duty of defending their country; which was supported by the arms of Barbarian mercenaries. The fugitives of Scythia were permitted to disgrace the illustrious dignities of the empire; their ferocious youth, who disdained the salutary restraint of laws, were more anxious to acquire the riches than to imitate the arts of a people, the object of their contempt and hatred; and the power of the Goths was the stone of Tantalus,* perpetually suspended over the peace and safety of the devoted state. The measures which Synesius recommends are the dictates of a bold and generous patriot. He exhorts the emperor to revive the courage of his subjects by the example of manly virtue; to banish luxury from the court and from the camp; to substitute in the place of the Barbarian mercenaries, an army of men interested in the defence of their laws and of their property; to force, in such a moment of public danger, the mechanic from his shop and the philosopher from his school; to rouse the indolent citizen from his dream of pleasure, and to arm, for the protection of agriculture, the hands of the laborious husbandman. At the head of such troops, who might deserve the name, and would display the spirit, of Romans, he animates the son of

Theodosius to encounter a race of Barbarians who were destitute of any real courage; and never to lay down his arms, till he had chased them far away into the solitudes of Scythia; or had reduced them to the state of ignominious servitude which the Lacedaemonians formerly imposed on the captive Helots.[21] The court of Arcadius indulged the zeal, applauded the eloquence, and neglected the advice of Synesius. Perhaps the philosopher, who addresses the emperor of the East in the language of reason and virtue which he might have used to a Spartan king, had not condescended to form a practicable scheme, consistent with the temper and circumstances of a degenerate age. Perhaps the pride of the ministers, whose business was seldom interrupted by reflection, might reject as wild and visionary every proposal which exceeded the measure of their capacity and deviated from the forms and precedents of office. While the oration of Synesius and the downfall of the Barbarians were the topics of popular conversation, an edict was published at Constantinople, which declared the promotion of Alaric to the rank of master-general of the Eastern Illyricum. The Roman provincials and the allies, who had respected the faith of treaties, were justly indignant that the ruin of Greece and Epirus should be so liberally rewarded. The Gothic conqueror was received as a lawful magistrate, in the cities which he had so lately besieged. The fathers whose sons he had massacred, the husbands whose wives he had violated, were subject to his authority; and the success of his rebellion encouraged the ambition of every leader of the foreign mercenaries. The use to which Alaric applied his new command distinguishes the firm and judicious character of his policy. He issued his orders to the four magazines and manufactures of offensive and defensive arms, Margus, Ratiaria, Naissus, and Thessalonica, to provide his troops with an extraordinary supply of shields, helmets, swords, and spears; the unhappy provincials were compelled to forge the instruments of their own destruction; and the Barbarians removed the only defect which had sometimes disappointed the efforts of their courage.[22] The birth of Alaric, the glory of his past exploits, and the confidence in his future designs, insensibly united the body of the nation under his victorious standard; and with the unanimous consent of the Barbarian chieftains, the master-general of Illyricum was elevated, according to ancient custom, on a shield, and solemnly proclaimed king of the Visigoths.[23] Armed with this double power, seated on the verge of the two empires, he alternately sold his deceitful promises to the courts of Arcadius and Honorius;[24] till he declared and executed his resolution of invading the dominions of the West. The provinces of Europe which belonged to the Eastern emperor were already exhausted; those of Asia were inaccessible; and the strength of Constantinople had resisted his attack. But he was tempted by the fame, the beauty, the wealth of Italy, which he had twice visited; and he secretly aspired to plant the Gothic standard on the walls of Rome, and to enrich his army with the accumulated spoils of three hundred triumphs.[25]

The scarcity of facts[26] and the uncertainty of dates[27] oppose our attempts to describe the circumstances of the first invasion of Italy by the arms of Alaric. His march, perhaps from Thessalonica, through the warlike and hostile country of Pannonia, as far as the foot of the Julian Alps; his passage of those mountains, which were strongly guarded by troops and entrenchments; the siege of Aquileia, and the conquest of the provinces of Istria and Venetia, appear to have employed a considerable time. Unless his operations were extremely cautious and slow, the length of the interval would suggest a probable suspicion that the Gothic king retreated towards the banks of the Danube and reinforced his army with fresh swarms of Barbarians, before he again attempted to penetrate into the heart of Italy. Since the public and important events escape the diligence of the historian, he may amuse himself with contemplating, for a moment, the influence of the arms of Alaric on the fortunes of two obscure individuals, a presbyter of Aquileia and an husbandman of Verona. The learned Rufinus, who was summoned by his enemies to appear before a Roman synod,[28] wisely preferred the dangers of a besieged city; and the Barbarians, who furiously shook the walls of Aquileia, might save him from the cruel sentence of another heretic, who, at the request of the same bishops, was severely whipped and condemned to perpetual exile on a desert island.[29] The *old man*,[30] who had passed his simple and innocent life in the neighbourhood of Verona, was a stranger to the quarrels both of kings and of bishops; *his* pleasures, his desires, his knowledge, were confined within the little circle of his paternal farm; and a staff supported his aged steps, on the same ground where he had sported in his infancy. Yet even this humble and rustic felicity (which Claudian describes with so much truth and feeling) was still exposed to the undistinguishing rage of war. His trees, his old *contemporary* trees,[31] must blaze in the conflagration of the whole country; a detachment of Gothic cavalry might sweep away his cottage and his family; and the power of Alaric could destroy this happiness which he was not able either to taste or to bestow. 'Fame,' says the poet, 'encircling with terror her gloomy wings, proclaimed the march of the Barbarian army, and filled Italy with consternation'; the apprehensions of each individual were increased in just proportion to the measure of his fortune; and the most timid, who had already embarked their valuable effects, meditated their escape to the island of Sicily or the African coast. The public distress was aggravated by the fears and reproaches of superstition.[32] Every hour produced some horrid tale of strange and portentous accidents; the Pagans deplored the neglect of omens and the interruption of sacrifices; but the Christians still derived some comfort from the powerful intercession of the saints and martyrs.[33]

The emperor Honorius was distinguished, above his subjects, by the pre-eminence of fear, as well as of rank. The pride and luxury in which he was educated had not allowed him to suspect that there existed on the earth any power presumptuous enough to invade the repose of the successor of Augustus. The arts of flattery concealed the impending danger, till Alaric approached the palace of Milan. But, when the sound of war had awakened the young emperor, instead of flying to arms with the spirit, or even the rashness, of his age, he eagerly listened to those timid counsellors who proposed to convey his sacred person and his faithful attendants to some secure and distant station in the provinces of Gaul. Stilicho alone[34] had courage and authority to resist this disgraceful measure, which would have abandoned Rome and Italy to the Barbarians; but, as the troops of the palace had been lately detached to the Rhaetian frontier, and as the resource of new levies was slow and precarious, the general of the West could only promise that, if the court of Milan would maintain their ground during his absence, he would soon return with an army equal to the encounter of the Gothic king. Without losing a moment (while each moment was so important to the public safety) Stilicho hastily embarked on the Larian lake,* ascended the mountains of ice and snow, amidst the severity of an Alpine winter, and suddenly repressed, by his unexpected presence, the enemy who had disturbed the tranquillity of Rhaetia.[35] The Barbarians, perhaps some tribes of the Alemanni, respected the firmness of a chief who still assumed the language of command; and the choice which he condescended to make of a select number of their bravest youths was considered as a mark of his esteem and favour. The cohorts, who were delivered from the neighbouring foe, diligently repaired to the Imperial standard; and Stilicho issued his orders to the most remote troops of the West to advance, by rapid marches, to the defence of Honorius and of Italy. The fortresses of the Rhine were abandoned; and the safety of Gaul was protected only by the faith[†] of the Germans and the ancient terror of the Roman name. Even the legion which had been stationed to guard the wall of Britain against the Caledonians of the north was hastily recalled;[36] and a numerous body of the cavalry of the Alani was persuaded to engage in the service of the emperor, who anxiously expected the return of his general. The prudence and vigour of Stilicho were conspicuous on this occasion, which revealed, at the same time, the weakness of the falling empire. The legions of Rome, which had long since languished in the gradual decay of discipline and courage, were exterminated by the Gothic and civil wars; and it was found impossible, without exhausting and exposing the provinces, to assemble an army for the defence of Italy.

When Stilicho seemed to abandon his sovereign in the unguarded palace of Milan, he had probably calculated the term of his absence, the distance of the enemy, and the obstacles that might retard their march. He principally depended on the rivers of Italy, the Adige, the Mincius, the Oglio, and the Addua; which, in the winter or spring, by the fall of rains, or by the melting of the snows, are commonly swelled into broad and impetuous torrents.[37] But the season happened to be remarkably dry; and the Goths could traverse, without impediment, the wide and stony beds, whose centre was faintly marked by the course of a shallow stream. The bridge and passage of the Addua were secured by a strong detachment of the Gothic army; and, as Alaric approached the walls, or rather the suburbs, of Milan, he enjoyed the proud satisfaction of seeing the emperor of the Romans fly before him. Honorius, accompanied by a feeble train of statesmen and eunuchs, hastily retreated towards the Alps, with a design of securing his person in the city of Arles, which had often been the royal residence of his predecessors. But Honorius[38] had scarcely passed the Po, before he was overtaken by the speed of the Gothic cavalry;[39] since the urgency of the danger compelled him to seek a temporary shelter within the fortification of Asta, a town of Liguria or Piemont, situate on the banks of the Tanarus.[40] The siege of an obscure place, which contained so rich a prize and seemed incapable of a long resistance, was instantly formed and indefatigably pressed by the king of the Goths; and the bold declaration, which the emperor might afterwards make, that his breast had never been susceptible of fear, did not probably obtain much credit, even in his own court.[41] In the last and almost hopeless extremity, after the Barbarians had already proposed the indignity of a capitulation, the Imperial captive was suddenly relieved by the fame, the approach, and at length the presence of the hero whom he had so long expected. At the head of a chosen and intrepid vanguard, Stilicho swam the stream of the Addua, to gain the time which he must have lost in the attack of the bridge; the passage of the Po was an enterprise of much less hazard and difficulty; and the successful action, in which he cut his way through the Gothic camp under the walls of Asta, revived the hopes, and vindicated the honour, of Rome. Instead of grasping the fruit of his victory, the Barbarian was gradually invested, on every side, by the troops of the West, who successively issued through all the passes of the Alps; his quarters were straitened; his convoys were intercepted; and the vigilance of the Romans prepared to form a chain of fortifications, and to besiege the lines of the besiegers. A military council was assembled of the long-haired chiefs of the Gothic nation; of aged warriors, whose bodies were wrapped in furs, and whose stern countenances were marked with honourable wounds. They weighed the glory of persisting in their attempt against the advantage of securing their plunder; and they recommended the prudent measure of a seasonable retreat. In this important debate, Alaric displayed the spirit of the conqueror of Rome; and, after he had reminded his countrymen of their achievements and of their designs, he concluded his animating speech by the solemn and positive assurance that he was resolved to find in Italy either a kingdom or a grave.[42]

The loose discipline of the Barbarians always exposed them to the danger of a surprise; but, instead of choosing the dissolute hours of riot and intemperance, Stilicho resolved to attack the *Christian* Goths, whilst they were devoutly employed in celebrating the festival of Easter.[43] The execution of the stratagem, or, as it was termed by the clergy, of the sacrilege, was entrusted to Saul, a Barbarian and a Pagan, who had served, however, with distinguished reputation among the veteran generals of Theodosius. The camp of the Goths, which Alaric had pitched in the neighbourhood of Pollentia,[44] was thrown into confusion by the sudden and impetuous charge of the Imperial cavalry; but, in a few moments, the undaunted genius of their leader gave them an order, and a field, of battle; and, as soon as they had recovered from their astonishment, the pious confidence, that the God of the Christians would assert their cause, added new strength to their native valour. In this engagement, which was long maintained with equal courage and success, the chief of the Alani, whose diminutive and savage form concealed a magnanimous soul, approved* his suspected loyalty by the zeal with which he fought, and fell, in the service of the republic; and the fame of this gallant Barbarian has been imperfectly preserved in the verses of Claudian, since the poet, who celebrates his virtue, has omitted the mention of his name. His death was followed by the flight and dismay of the squadrons which he commanded; and the defeat of the wing of cavalry might have decided the victory of Alaric, if Stilicho had not immediately led the Roman and Barbarian infantry to the attack. The skill of the general and the bravery of the soldiers surmounted every obstacle. In the evening of the bloody day, the Goths retreated from the field of battle; the entrenchments of their camp were forced, and the scene of rapine and slaughter made some atonement for the calamities which they had inflicted on the subjects of the empire.[45] The magnificent spoils of Corinth and Argos enriched the veterans of the West; the captive wife of Alaric, who had impatiently claimed his promise of Roman jewels and Patrician handmaids,[46] was reduced to implore the mercy of the insulting foe; and many thousand prisoners, released from the Gothic chains, dispersed through the provinces of Italy the praises of their heroic deliverer. The triumph of Stilicho[47] was compared by the poet, and perhaps by the public, to that of Marius; who, in the same part of Italy, had encountered and destroyed another army of northern Barbarians.† The huge bones, and the empty helmets, of the Cimbri and of the Goths would easily be confounded by succeeding generations; and posterity might erect a common trophy to the memory of the two most illustrious generals who had vanquished, on the same memorable ground, the two most formidable enemies of Rome.[48]

The eloquence of Claudian[49] has celebrated with lavish applause the victory of Pollentia, one of the most glorious days in the life of his patron; but his reluctant and partial muse bestows more genuine praise on the character of the Gothic king. His name is indeed branded with the reproachful epithets of pirate and robber, to which the conquerors of every age are so justly entitled; but the poet of Stilicho is compelled to acknowledge that Alaric possessed the invincible temper of mind which rises superior to every misfortune and derives new resources from adversity. After the total defeat of his infantry he escaped, or rather withdrew, from the field of battle, with the greatest part of his cavalry entire and unbroken. Without wasting a moment to lament the irreparable loss of so many brave companions, he left his victorious enemy to bind in chains the captive images of a Gothic king;[50] and boldly resolved to break through the unguarded passes of the Apennine, to spread desolation over the fruitful face of Tuscany, and to conquer or die before the gates of Rome. The capital was saved by the active and incessant diligence of Stilicho: but he respected the despair of his enemy; and, instead of committing the fate of the republic to the chance of another battle, he proposed to purchase the absence of the Barbarians. The spirit of Alaric would have rejected such terms, the permission of a retreat and the offer of a pension, with contempt and indignation; but he exercised a limited and precarious authority over the independent chieftains, who had raised him, for *their* service, above the rank of his equals; they were still less disposed to follow an unsuccessful general, and many of them were tempted to consult their interest by a private negotiation with the minister of Honorius. The king submitted to the voice of his people, ratified the treaty with the empire of the West, and repassed the Po, with the remains of the flourishing army which he had led into Italy. A considerable part of the Roman forces still continued to attend his motions; and Stilicho, who maintained a secret correspondence with some of the Barbarian chiefs, was punctually apprised of the designs that were formed in the camp and council of Alaric. The king of the Goths, ambitious to signalise his retreat by some splendid achievement, had resolved to occupy the important city of Verona, which commands the principal passage of the Rhaetian Alps; and directing his march through the territories of those German tribes, whose alliance would restore his exhausted strength, to invade, on the side of the Rhine, the wealthy and unsuspecting provinces of Gaul. Ignorant of the treason, which had already betrayed his bold and judicious enterprise, he advanced towards the passes of the mountains, already possessed by the Imperial troops; where he was exposed, almost at the same instant, to a general attack in the front, on his flanks, and in the rear. In this bloody action, at a small distance from the walls of Verona, the loss of the Goths was not less heavy than that which they had sustained in the defeat of Pollentia; and their valiant king, who escaped by the swiftness of his horse, must either have been slain or made prisoner, if the hasty rashness of the Alani had not disappointed the measures of the Roman general. Alaric secured the remains of his army on the adjacent rocks; and prepared himself with undaunted resolution to maintain a siege against the superior numbers of the enemy, who invested him on all sides. But he could not oppose the destructive progress of hunger and disease; nor was it possible for him to check the continual desertion of his impatient and capricious Barbarians. In this extremity he still found resources in his own courage, or in the moderation of his adversary; and the retreat of the Gothic king was considered as the deliverance of Italy.[51] Yet the people and even the clergy, incapable of forming any rational judgment of the business of peace and war, presumed to arraign the policy of Stilicho, who so often vanquished, so often surrounded, and so often dismissed the implacable enemy of the republic. The first moment of the public safety is devoted to gratitude and joy; but the second is diligently occupied by envy and calumny.[52]

The citizens of Rome had been astonished by the approach of Alaric; and the diligence with which they laboured to restore the walls of the capital confessed their own fears and the decline of the empire. After the retreat of the Barbarians, Honorius was directed to accept the dutiful invitation of the senate, and to celebrate in the Imperial city the auspicious era of the Gothic victory and of his sixth consulship.[53] The suburbs and the streets from the Milvian bridge to the Palatine mount were filled by the Roman people, who, in the space of an hundred years, had only thrice been honoured with the presence of their sovereigns. While their eyes were fixed on the chariot where Stilicho was deservedly seated by the side of his royal pupil, they applauded the pomp of a triumph, which was not stained, like that of Constantine, or of Theodosius, with civil blood. The procession passed under a lofty arch, which had been purposely erected; but in less than seven years the Gothic conquerors of Rome might read, if they were able to read, the superb inscription of that monument, which attested the total defeat and destruction of their nation.[54] The emperor resided several months in the capital, and every part of his behaviour was regulated with care to conciliate the affection of the clergy, the senate, and the people of Rome. The clergy was edified by his frequent visits and liberal gifts to the shrines of the apostles. The senate, who in the triumphal procession had been excused from the humiliating ceremony of preceding on foot the Imperial chariot, was treated with the decent reverence which Stilicho always affected for that assembly. The people was repeatedly gratified by the attention and courtesy of Honorius in the public games, which were celebrated on that occasion with a magnificence not unworthy of the spectator. As soon as the appointed number of chariot races was con-cluded, the decoration of the Circus was suddenly changed; the hunting of wild beasts afforded a various and splendid entertainment; and the chase was succeeded by a military dance, which seems in the lively description of Claudian to present the image of a modern tournament.

In these games of Honorius, the inhuman combats of gladiators[55] polluted, for the last time, the amphitheatre of Rome. The first Christian emperor may claim the honour of the first edict which condemned the art and amusement of shedding human blood;[56] but this benevolent law expressed the wishes of the prince, without reforming an inveterate abuse, which degraded a civilised nation below the condition of savage

cannibals. Several hundred, perhaps several thousand, victims were annually slaughtered in the great cities of the empire; and the month of
December, more peculiarly devoted to the combats of gladiators, still
exhibited to the eyes of the Roman people a grateful* spectacle of blood
and cruelty. Amidst the general joy of the victory of Pollentia, a Christian
poet exhorted the emperor to extirpate by his authority the horrid custom
which had so long resisted the voice of humanity and religion.[57] The
pathetic representations of Prudentius were less effectual than the generous boldness of Telemachus, an Asiatic monk, whose death was more
useful to mankind than his life.[58] The Romans were provoked by the
interruption of their pleasures; and the rash monk, who had descended
into the arena to separate the gladiators, was overwhelmed under a
shower of stones. But the madness of the people soon subsided; they
respected the memory of Telemachus, who had deserved the honours of
martyrdom; and they submitted, without a murmur, to the laws of
Honorius, which abolished for ever the human sacrifices of the amphitheatre. The citizens who adhered to the manners of their ancestors,
might perhaps insinuate that the last remains of a martial spirit were
preserved in this school of fortitude, which accustomed the Romans to
the sight of blood and to the contempt of death: a vain and cruel
prejudice, so nobly confuted by the valour of ancient Greece and of
modern Europe.[59]

The recent danger to which the person of the emperor had been
exposed in the defenceless palace of Milan urged him to seek a retreat in
some inaccessible fortress of Italy, where he might securely remain while
the open country was covered by a deluge of Barbarians. On the coast of
the Hadriatic, about ten or twelve miles from the most southern of the
seven mouths of the Po, the Thessalians had founded the ancient colony
of Ravenna,[60] which they afterwards resigned to the natives of Umbria.
Augustus, who had observed the opportunity of the place, prepared, at
the distance of three miles from the old town, a capacious harbour for the
reception of two hundred and fifty ships of war. This naval establishment,
which included the arsenals and magazines, the barracks of the troops, and
the houses of the artificers, derived its origin and name from the
permanent station of the Roman fleet; the intermediate space was soon
filled with buildings and inhabitants, and the three extensive and populous quarters of Ravenna gradually contributed to form one of the most
important cities of Italy. The principal canal of Augustus poured a
copious stream of the waters of the Po through the midst of the city to the
entrance of the harbour; the same waters were introduced into the
profound ditches that encompassed the walls; they were distributed by a
thousand subordinate canals into every part of the city, which they
divided into a variety of small islands; the communication was maintained
only by the use of boats and bridges; and the houses of Ravenna, whose
appearance may be compared to that of Venice, were raised on the

foundation of wooden piles. The adjacent country, to the distance of many miles, was a deep and impassable morass; and the artificial cause-way, which connected Ravenna with the continent, might be easily guarded or destroyed on the approach of an hostile army. These morasses were interspersed, however, with vineyards; and, though the soil was exhausted by four or five crops, the town enjoyed a more plentiful supply of wine than of fresh water.[61] The air, instead of receiving the sickly and almost pestilential exhalations of low and marshy grounds, was distin-guished, like the neighbourhood of Alexandria, as uncommonly pure and salubrious; and this singular advantage was ascribed to the regular tides of the Hadriatic, which swept the canals, interrupted the unwholesome stagnation of the waters, and floated every day the vessels of the adjacent country into the heart of Ravenna. The gradual retreat of the sea has left the modern city at the distance of four miles from the Hadriatic; and as early as the fifth or sixth century of the Christian era the port of Augustus was converted into pleasant orchards, and a lonely grove of pines covered the ground where the Roman fleet once rode at anchor.[62] Even this alteration contributed to increase the natural strength of the place; and the shallowness of the water was a sufficient barrier against the large ships of the enemy. This advantageous situation was fortified by art and labour; and in the twentieth year of his age the emperor of the West, anxious only for his personal safety, retired to the perpetual confinement of the walls and morasses of Ravenna. The example of Honorius was imitated by his feeble successors, the Gothic kings, and afterwards the Exarchs,* who occupied the throne and palace of the emperors; and, till the middle of the eighth century, Ravenna was considered as the seat of government and the capital of Italy.[63]

The fears of Honorius were not without foundation, nor were his precautions without effect. While Italy rejoiced in her deliverance from the Goths, a furious tempest was excited among the nations of Germany, who yielded to the irresistible impulse that appears to have been gradually communicated from the eastern extremity of the continent of Asia. The Chinese annals, as they have been interpreted by the learned industry of the present age, may be usefully applied to reveal the secret and remote causes of the fall of the Roman empire. The extensive territory to the north of the great wall was possessed, after the flight of the Huns, by the victorious Sien-pi, who were sometimes broken into independent tribes, and reunited under a supreme chief; till at length, styling themselves *Topa*, or masters of the earth, they acquired a more solid consistence and a more formidable power. The Topa soon compelled the pastoral nations of the eastern desert to acknowledge the superiority of their arms; they invaded China in a period of weakness and intestine discord; and these fortunate Tartars, adopting the laws and manners of the vanquished people, founded an Imperial dynasty, which reigned near one hundred and sixty years over the northern provinces of the monarchy. Some generations before they ascended the throne of China, one of the Topa princes had enlisted in his cavalry a slave of the name of Moko, renowned for his valour; but who was tempted by the fear of punishment to desert his standard and to range the desert at the head of an hundred followers. This gang of robbers and outlaws swelled into a camp, a tribe, a numerous people, distinguished by the appellation of *Geougen*; and their hereditary chieftains, the posterity of Moko, the slave, assumed their rank among the Scythian monarchs. The youth of Toulun, the greatest of his descendants, was exercised by those misfortunes which are the school of heroes. He bravely struggled with adversity, broke the imperious yoke of the Topa, and became the legislator of his nation and the conqueror of Tartary. His troops were distributed into regular bands of an hundred and of a thousand men; cowards were stoned to death; the most splendid honours were proposed as the reward of valour; and Toulun, who had knowledge enough to despise the learning of China, adopted only such arts and institutions as were favourable to the military spirit of his government. His tents, which he removed in the winter season to a more southern latitude, were pitched during the summer on the fruitful banks of the Selinga. His conquests stretched from Corea far beyond the river Irtish. He vanquished in the country to the North of the Caspian Sea the nation of the Huns; and the new title of *Khan* or *Cagan*, expressed the fame and power which he derived from this memorable victory.[64]

The chain of events is interrupted, or rather is concealed, as it passes from the Volga to the Vistula, through the dark interval which separates the extreme limits of the Chinese and of the Roman geography. Yet the temper of the Barbarians and the experience of successive emigrations sufficiently declare that the Huns, who were oppressed by the arms of the Geougen, soon withdrew from the presence of an insulting victor. The countries towards the Euxine were already occupied by their kindred tribes; and their hasty flight, which they soon converted into a bold attack, would more naturally be directed towards the rich and level plains through which the Vistula gently flows into the Baltic Sea. The North must again have been alarmed and agitated by the invasion of the Huns; and the nations who retreated before them must have pressed with incumbent weight on the confines of Germany.[65] The inhabitants of those regions which the ancients have assigned to the Suevi, the Vandals, and the Burgundians, might embrace the resolution of abandoning to the fugitives of Sarmatia their woods and morasses; or at least of discharging their superfluous numbers on the provinces of the Roman empire.[66] About four years after the victorious Toulun had assumed the title of Khan of the Geougen, another Barbarian, the haughty Rhodogast or Radagaisus,[67] marched from the northern extremities of Germany almost to the gates of Rome, and left the remains of his army to achieve the destruction of the West. The Vandals, the Suevi, and the Burgundians formed the strength of this mighty host; but the Alani, who had found an hospitable reception in their new seats, added their active cavalry to the heavy infantry of the Germans; and the Gothic adventurers crowded so eagerly to the standard of Radagaisus that, by some historians, he has been styled the king of the Goths. Twelve thousand warriors, distinguished above the vulgar by their noble birth or their valiant deeds, glittered in the van;[68] and the whole multitude, which was not less than two hundred thousand fighting men, might be increased by the accession of women, of children and of slaves, to the amount of four hundred thousand persons. This formidable emigration issued from the same coast of the Baltic which had poured forth the myriads of the Cimbri and Teutones to assault Rome and Italy in the vigour of the republic.* After the departure of those Barbarians, their native country, which was marked by the vestiges of their greatness, long ramparts and gigantic moles,[69] remained during some ages a vast and dreary solitude; till the human species was renewed by the powers of generation, and the vacancy was filled by the influx of new inhabitants. The nations who now usurp an extent of land which they are unable to cultivate would soon be assisted by the industrious poverty of their neighbours, if the government of Europe did not protect the claims of dominion and property.

The correspondence of nations was in that age so imperfect and precarious that the revolutions of the North might escape the know-ledge of the court of Ravenna; till the dark cloud which was collected along the coast of the Baltic burst in thunder upon the banks of the Upper Danube. The emperor of the West, if his ministers disturbed his amuse-ments by the news of the impending danger, was satisfied with being the occasion, and the spectator, of the war.[70] The safety of Rome was entrusted to the counsels and the sword of Stilicho; but such was the feeble and exhausted state of the empire that it was impossible to restore the fortifications of the Danube, or to prevent, by a vigorous effort, the invasion of the Germans.[71] The hopes of the vigilant minister of Honorius were confined to the defence of Italy. He once more abandoned the provinces, recalled the troops, pressed the new levies, which were rigorously exacted and pusillanimously eluded, employed the most effica-cious means to arrest, or allure, the deserters, and offered the gift of freedom, and of two pieces of gold, to all the slaves who would enlist.[72] By these efforts he painfully collected, from the subjects of a great empire, an army of thirty or forty thousand men, which, in the days of Scipio or Camillus, would have been instantly furnished by the free citizens of the territory of Rome.[73] The thirty legions of Stilicho were reinforced by a large body of Barbarian auxiliaries; the faithful Alani were personally attached to his service; and the troops of Huns and of Goths, who marched under the banners of their native princes, Huldin and Sarus, were animated by interest and resentment to oppose the ambition of Radagaisus. The king of the confederate Germans passed, without resist-ance, the Alps, the Po, and the Apennine, leaving on one hand the inaccessible palace of Honorius, securely buried among the marshes of Ravenna, and, on the other, the camp of Stilicho, who had fixed his headquarters at Ticinum, or Pavia, but who seems to have avoided a decisive battle, till he had assembled his distant forces. Many cities of Italy were pillaged, or destroyed, and the siege of Florence[74] by Radagaisus is one of the earliest events in the history of that celebrated republic, whose firmness checked and delayed the unskilful fury of the Barbarians. The senate and people trembled at their approach within an hundred and eighty miles of Rome, and anxiously compared the danger which they had escaped with the new perils to which they were exposed. Alaric was a Christian and a soldier, the leader of a disciplined army; who understood the laws of war, who respected the sanctity of treaties, and who had familiarly conversed with the subjects of the empire in the same camps, and the same churches. The savage Radagaisus was a stranger to the manners, the religion, and even the language, of the civilised nations of the south. The fierceness of his temper was exasperated by cruel superstition, and it was universally believed that he had bound himself by a solemn vow to reduce the city into a heap of stones and ashes, and to sacrifice the most illustrious of the Roman senators on the altars of those gods who were appeased by human blood. The public danger, which should have reconciled all domestic animosities, displayed the incurable madness of religious faction. The oppressed votaries of Jupiter and Mercury respected, in the implacable enemy of Rome, the character of a devout Pagan; loudly declared that they were more apprehensive of the sacrifices than of the arms of Radagaisus, and secretly rejoiced in the calamities of their country which condemned the faith of their Christian adversaries.[75]

Florence was reduced to the last extremity, and the fainting courage of the citizens was supported only by the authority of St Ambrose, who had communicated, in a dream, the promise of a speedy deliverance.[76] On a sudden, they beheld, from their walls, the banners of Stilicho, who advanced, with his united force, to the relief of the faithful city, and who soon marked that fatal spot for the grave of the Barbarian host. The apparent contradictions of those writers who variously relate the defeat of Radagaisus may be reconciled, without offering much violence to their respective testimonies. Orosius and Augustine, who were intimately connected by friendship and religion, ascribe this miraculous victory to the providence of God rather than to the valour of man.[77] They strictly exclude every idea of chance, or even of bloodshed, and positively affirm that the Romans, whose camp was the scene of plenty and idleness, enjoyed the distress of the Barbarians, slowly expiring on the sharp and barren ridge of the hills of Faesulae, which rise above the city of Florence. Their extravagant assertion that not a single soldier of the Christian army was killed, or even wounded, may be dismissed with silent contempt; but the rest of the narrative of Augustine and Orosius is consistent with the

state of the war and the character of Stilicho. Conscious that he commanded the *last* army of the republic, his prudence would not expose it in
the open field to the headstrong fury of the Germans. The method of
surrounding the enemy with strong lines of circumvallation, which he
had twice employed against the Gothic king, was repeated on a larger
scale, and with more considerable effect. The examples of Caesar must
have been familiar to the most illiterate of the Roman warriors; and the
fortifications of Dyrrachium,* which connected twenty-four castles by a
perpetual ditch and rampart of fifteen miles, afforded the model of an
entrenchment which might confine and starve the most numerous host of
Barbarians.[78] The Roman troops had less degenerated from the industry
than from the valour of their ancestors, and, if the servile and laborious
work offended the pride of the soldiers, Tuscany could supply many
thousand peasants who would labour, though perhaps they would not
fight, for the salvation of their native country. The imprisoned multitude
of horses and men[79] was gradually destroyed by famine rather than by the
sword; but the Romans were exposed, during the progress of such an
extensive work, to the frequent attacks of an impatient enemy. The
despair of the hungry Barbarians would precipitate them against the
fortifications of Stilicho; the general might sometimes indulge the ardour
of his brave auxiliaries, who eagerly pressed to assault the camp of the
Germans; and these various incidents might produce the sharp and bloody
conflicts which dignify the narrative of Zosimus and the Chronicles of
Prosper and Marcellinus.[80] A seasonable supply of men and provisions had
been introduced into the walls of Florence, and the famished host of
Radagaisus was in its turn besieged. The proud monarch of so many
warlike nations, after the loss of his bravest warriors, was reduced to
confide either in the faith of a capitulation or in the clemency of
Stilicho.[81] But the death of the royal captive, who was ignominiously
beheaded, disgraced the triumph of Rome and of Christianity, and the
short delay of his execution was sufficient to brand the conqueror with
the guilt of cool and deliberate cruelty.[82] The famished Germans who
escaped the fury of the auxiliaries were sold as slaves, at the contemptible
price of as many single pieces of gold; but the difference of food and
climate swept away great numbers of those unhappy strangers; and it was
observed that the inhuman purchasers, instead of reaping the fruits of
their labour, were soon obliged to provide the expense of their interment.
Stilicho informed the emperor and the senate of his success; and deserved,
a second time, the glorious title of Deliverer of Italy.[83]

The fame of the victory, and more especially of the miracle, has
encouraged a vain persuasion that the whole army, or rather nation, of
Germans, who migrated from the shores of the Baltic, miserably perished
under the walls of Florence. Such indeed was the fate of Radagaisus
himself, of his brave and faithful companions, and of more than one-third
of the various multitude of Sueves and Vandals, of Alani and

Burgundians, who adhered to the standard of their general.[84] The union of such an army might excite our surprise, but the causes of separation are obvious and forcible; the pride of birth, the insolence of valour, the jealousy of command, the impatience of subordination, and the obstinate conflict of opinions, of interests, and of passions, among so many kings and warriors, who were untaught to yield, or to obey. After the defeat of Radagaisus, two parts of the German host, which must have exceeded the number of one hundred thousand men, still remained in arms, between the Apennine and the Alps, or between the Alps and the Danube. It is uncertain whether they attempted to revenge the death of their general; but their irregular fury was soon diverted by the prudence and firmness of Stilicho, who opposed their march, and facilitated their retreat; who considered the safety of Rome and Italy as the great object of his care, and who sacrificed, with too much indifference, the wealth and tranquillity of the distant provinces.[85] The Barbarians acquired, from the junction of some Pannonian deserters, the knowledge of the country and of the roads; and the invasion of Gaul, which Alaric had designed, was executed by the remains of the great army of Radagaisus.[86]

Yet, if they expected to derive any assistance from the tribes of Germany, who inhabited the banks of the Rhine, their hopes were disappointed. The Alemanni preserved a state of inactive neutrality; and the Franks distinguished their zeal and courage in the defence of the empire. In the rapid progress down the Rhine, which was the first act of the administration of Stilicho, he had applied himself, with peculiar attention, to secure the alliance of the warlike Franks, and to remove the irreconcilable enemies of peace and of the republic. Marcomir, one of their kings, was publicly convicted before the tribunal of the Roman magistrate, of violating the faith of treaties. He was sentenced to a mild, but distant, exile in the province of Tuscany; and this degradation of the regal dignity was so far from exciting the resentment of his subjects that they punished with death the turbulent Sunno, who attempted to revenge his brother; and maintained a dutiful allegiance to the princes who were established on the throne by the choice of Stilicho.[87] When the limits of Gaul and Germany were shaken by the northern emigration, the Franks bravely encountered the single force of the Vandals, who, regardless of the lessons of adversity, had again separated their troops from the standard of their Barbarian allies. They paid the penalty of their rashness, and twenty thousand Vandals, with their king Godigisclus, were slain in the field of battle. The whole people must have been extirpated if the squadrons of the Alani, advancing to their relief, had not trampled down the infantry of the Franks, who, after an honourable resistance, were compelled to relinquish the unequal contest. The victorious confederates pursued their march; and on the last day of the year, in a season when the waters of the Rhine were most probably frozen, they entered, without opposition, the defenceless provinces of Gaul. This memorable passage of the Suevi, the Vandals, the Alani, and the Burgundians, who never afterwards retreated, may be considered as the fall of the Roman empire in the countries beyond the Alps; and the barriers, which had so long separated the savage and the civilised nations of the earth, were from that fatal moment levelled with the ground.[88]

While the peace of Germany was secured by the attachment of the Franks, and the neutrality of the Alemanni, the subjects of Rome, unconscious of their approaching calamities, enjoyed the state of quiet and prosperity, which had seldom blessed the frontiers of Gaul. Their flocks and herds were permitted to graze in the pastures of the Barbarians; their huntsmen penetrated, without fear or danger, into the darkest recesses of the Hercynian wood.[89] The banks of the Rhine were crowned, like those of the Tiber, with elegant houses, and well-cultivated farms; and, if a poet descended the river, he might express his doubt on which side was situated the territory of the Romans.[90] This scene of peace and plenty was suddenly changed into a desert; and the prospect of the smoking ruins could alone distinguish the solitude of nature from the desolation of man. The flourishing city of Mentz* was surprised and destroyed; and many thousand Christians were inhumanly massacred in the church. Worms perished after a long and obstinate siege; Strasburg, Spires, Rheims, Tournay, Arras, Amiens, experienced the cruel oppression of the German yoke; and the consuming flames of war spread from the banks of the Rhine over the greatest part of the seventeen provinces of Gaul. That rich and extensive country, as far as the ocean, the Alps, and the Pyrenees, was delivered to the Barbarians, who drove before them, in a promiscuous crowd, the bishop, the senator, and the virgin, laden with the spoils of their houses and altars.[91] The ecclesiastics, to whom we are indebted for this vague description of the public calamities, embraced the opportunity of exhorting the Christians to repent of the sins which had provoked the Divine Justice, and to renounce the perishable goods of a wretched and deceitful world. But, as the Pelagian† controversy,[92] which attempts to sound the abyss of grace and predestination, soon became the serious employment of the Latin clergy; the Providence which had decreed, or foreseen, or permitted such a train of moral and natural evils was rashly weighed in the imperfect and fallacious balance of reason. The crimes and the misfortunes of the suffering people were presumptuously compared with those of their ancestors; and they arraigned the Divine Justice, which did not exempt from the common destruction the feeble, the guiltless, the infant portion of the human species. These idle disputants overlooked the invariable laws of nature, which have connected peace with innocence, plenty with industry, and safety with valour. The timid and selfish policy of the court of Ravenna might recall the Palatine legions for the protection of Italy; the remains of the stationary troops might be unequal to the arduous task; and the Barbarian auxiliaries might prefer the unbounded licence of spoil to the benefits of a moderate and regular stipend. But the provinces of Gaul were filled with a numerous race of hardy and robust youth, who, in the defence of their houses, their families, and their altars, if they had dared to die, would have deserved to vanquish. The knowledge of their native country would have enabled them to oppose continual and insuperable obstacles to the progress of an invader; and the deficiency of the Barbarians, in arms as well as in discipline, removed the only pretence which excuses the submission of a populous country to the inferior numbers of a veteran army. When France was invaded by Charles the Fifth,* he inquired of a prisoner how many *days* Paris might be distant from the frontier. 'Perhaps *twelve*, but they will be days of battle';[93] such was the gallant answer which checked the arrogance of that ambitious prince. The subjects of Honorius and those of Francis I were animated by a very different spirit; and in less than two years the divided troops of the savages of the Baltic, whose numbers, were they fairly stated, would appear contemptible, advanced without a combat to the foot of the Pyrenaean mountains.

In the early part of the reign of Honorius, the vigilance of Stilicho had successfully guarded the remote island of Britain from her incessant enemies of the ocean, the mountains, and the Irish coast.[94] But those restless Barbarians could not neglect the fair opportunity of the Gothic war, when the walls and stations of the province were stripped of the Roman troops. If any of the legionaries were permitted to return from the Italian expedition, their faithful report of the court and character of Honorius must have tended to dissolve the bonds of allegiance and to exasperate the seditious temper of the British army. The spirit of revolt, which had formerly disturbed the age of Gallienus,† was revived by the capricious violence of the soldiers; and the unfortunate, perhaps the ambitious, candidates, who were the objects of their choice, were the instruments, and at length the victims, of their passion.[95] Marcus was the first whom they placed on the throne, as the lawful emperor of Britain, and of the West. They violated, by the hasty murder of Marcus, the oath of fidelity which they had imposed on themselves; and *their* disapprobation of his manners may seem to inscribe an honourable epitaph on his tomb. Gratian was the next whom they adorned with the diadem and the purple; and, at the end of four months, Gratian experienced the fate of his predecessor. The memory of the great Constantine, whom the British legions had given to the church and to the empire, suggested the singular motive of their third choice. They discovered in the ranks a private soldier of the name of Constantine, and their impetuous levity had already seated him on the throne, before they perceived his incapacity to sustain the weight of that glorious appellation.[96] Yet the authority of Constantine was less precarious, and his government was more successful, than the transient reigns of Marcus and of Gratian. The danger of leaving his inactive troops in those camps which had been twice polluted with blood and sedition urged him to attempt the reduction of the Western provinces. He landed at Boulogne with an inconsiderable force; and, after he had reposed himself some days, he summoned the cities of Gaul, which had escaped the yoke of the Barbarians, to acknowledge their lawful sovereign. They obeyed the summons without reluctance. The neglect of the court of Ravenna had absolved a deserted people from the duty of allegiance; their actual distress encouraged them to accept any circumstances of change, without apprehension, and perhaps with some degree of hope; and they might flatter themselves that the troops, the authority, and even the name of a Roman emperor, who fixed his residence in Gaul, would protect the unhappy country from the rage of the Barbarians. The first successes of Constantine against the detached parties of the Germans were magnified by the voice of adulation into splendid and decisive victories; which the reunion and insolence of the enemy soon reduced to their just value. His negotiations procured a short and precarious truce; and, if some tribes of the barbarians were engaged, by the liberality of his gifts and promises, to undertake the defence of the Rhine, these expensive and uncertain treaties, instead of restoring the pristine vigour of the Gallic frontier, served only to disgrace the majesty of the prince and to exhaust what yet remained of the treasures of the republic. Elated, however, with this imaginary triumph, the vain deliverer of Gaul advanced into the provinces of the South, to encounter a more pressing and personal danger. Sarus the Goth was ordered to lay the head of the rebel at the feet of the emperor Honorius; and the forces of Britain and Italy were unworthily consumed in this domestic quarrel. After the loss of his two bravest generals Justinian and Nevigastes, the former of whom was slain in the field of battle, the latter in a peaceful and treacherous interview, Constantine fortified himself within the walls of Vienna. The place was ineffectually attacked for seven days; and the Imperial army supported, in a precipitate retreat, the ignominy of purchasing a secure passage from the freebooters and outlaws of the Alps.[97] Those mountains now separated the dominions of two rival monarchs; and the fortifications of the double frontier were guarded by the troops of the empire, whose arms would have been more usefully employed to maintain the Roman limits against the Barbarians of Germany and Scythia.

On this side of the Pyrenees, the ambition of Constantine might be justified by the proximity of danger; but his throne was soon established by the conquest, or rather submission, of Spain; which yielded to the influence of regular and habitual subordination, and received the laws and magistrates of the Gallic prefecture. The only opposition which was made to the authority of Constantine proceeded not so much from the powers of government, or the spirit of the people, as from the private zeal and interest of the family of Theodosius. Four brothers[98] had obtained by the favour of their kinsman, the deceased emperor, an honourable rank, and ample possessions, in their native country; and the grateful youths resolved to risk those advantages in the service of his son. After an unsuccessful effort to maintain their ground at the head of the stationary troops of Lusitania, they retired to their estates; where they armed and levied, at their own expense, a considerable body of slaves and dependents, and boldly marched to occupy the strong posts of the Pyrenaean mountains. This domestic insurrection alarmed and perplexed the sovereign of Gaul and Britain; and he was compelled to negotiate with some troops of Barbarian auxiliaries, for the service of the Spanish war. They were distinguished by the title *Honorians*;[99] a name which might have reminded them of their fidelity to their lawful sovereign; and, if it should candidly be allowed that the *Scots* were influenced by any partial affection for a British prince, the *Moors* and *Marcomanni** could be tempted only by the profuse liberality of the usurper, who distributed among the Barbarians the military, and even the civil, honours of Spain. The nine bands of *Honorians*, which may be easily traced on the establishment of the Western empire, could not exceed the number of five thousand men; yet this inconsiderable force was sufficient to terminate a war which had threatened the power and safety of Constantine. The rustic army of the Theodosian family was surrounded and destroyed in the Pyrenees: two of the brothers had the good fortune to escape by sea to Italy, or the East; the other two, after an interval of suspense, were executed at Arles; and, if Honorius could remain insensible of the public disgrace, he might perhaps be affected by the personal misfortunes of his generous kinsmen. Such were the feeble arms which decided the possession of the Western provinces of Europe, from the wall of Antoninus to the columns of Hercules. The events of peace and war have undoubtedly been diminished by the narrow and imperfect view of the historians of the times, who were equally ignorant of the causes and of the effects of the most important revolutions. But the total decay of the national strength had annihilated even the last resource of a despotic government; and the revenue of exhausted provinces could no longer purchase the military service of a discontented and pusillanimous people.

The poet, whose flattery has ascribed to the Roman eagle the victories of Pollentia and Verona, pursues the hasty retreat of Alaric, from the confines of Italy, with a horrid train of imaginary spectres, such as might hover over an army of Barbarians, which was almost exterminated by war, famine, and disease.[100] In the course of this unfortunate expedition, the king of the Goths must indeed have sustained a considerable loss, and his harassed forces required an interval of repose, to recruit their numbers and revive their confidence. Adversity had exercised, and displayed, the genius of Alaric; and the fame of his valour invited to the Gothic standard the bravest of the Barbarian warriors, who, from the Euxine to the Rhine, were agitated by the desire of rapine and conquest. He had deserved the esteem, and he soon accepted the friendship, of Stilicho himself. Renouncing the service of the emperor of the East, Alaric concluded, with the court of Ravenna, a treaty of peace and alliance, by which he was declared master-general of the Roman armies throughout the prefecture of Illyricum; as it was claimed, according to the true and ancient limits, by the minister of Honorius.[101] The execution of the ambitious design, which was either stipulated, or implied, in the articles of the treaty, appears to have been suspended by the formidable irruption of Radagaisus; and the neutrality of the Gothic king may perhaps be compared to the indifference of Caesar, who, in the conspiracy of Catiline,* refused either to assist or to oppose the enemy of the republic. After the defeat of the Vandals, Stilicho resumed his pretensions to the provinces of the East; appointed civil magistrates for the administration of justice, and of the finances; and declared his impatience to lead to the gates of Constantinople the united armies of the Romans and of the Goths. The prudence, however, of Stilicho, his aversion to civil war, and his perfect knowledge of the weakness of the state, may countenance the suspicion that domestic peace, rather than foreign conquest, was the object of his policy; and that his principal care was to employ the forces of Alaric at a distance from Italy. This design could not long escape the penetration of the Gothic king, who continued to hold a doubtful, and perhaps a treacherous, correspondence with the rival courts, who protracted, like a dissatisfied mercenary, his languid operations in Thessaly and Epirus, and who soon returned to claim the extravagant reward of his ineffectual services. From his camp near Aemona,[102] on the confines of Italy, he transmitted, to the emperor of the West, a long account of promises, of expenses, and of demands; called for immediate satisfaction and clearly intimated the consequences of a refusal. Yet, if his conduct was hostile, his language was decent and dutiful. He humbly professed himself the friend of Stilicho, and the soldier of Honorius; offered his person and his troops to march, without delay, against the usurper of Gaul; and solicited, as a permanent retreat for the Gothic nation, the possession of some vacant province of the Western empire.

The political and secret transactions of two statesmen, who laboured to deceive each other and the world, must for ever have been concealed in the impenetrable darkness of the cabinet, if the debates of a popular assembly had not thrown some rays of light on the correspondence of Alaric and Stilicho. The necessity of finding some artificial support for a government, which, from a principle, not of moderation, but of weakness, was reduced to negotiate with its own subjects, had insensibly revived the authority of the Roman senate; and the minister of Honorius respectfully consulted the legislative council of the republic. Stilicho assembled the senate in the palace of the Caesars; represented, in a studied oration, the actual state of affairs; proposed the demands of the Gothic king, and submitted to their consideration the choice of peace or war. The senators, as if they had been suddenly awakened from a dream of four hundred years, appeared on this important occasion to be inspired by the courage, rather than by the wisdom, of their predecessors. They loudly declared, in regular speeches, or in tumultuary acclamations, that it was unworthy of the majesty of Rome to purchase a precarious and disgraceful truce from a Barbarian king; and that, in the judgment of a magnanimous people, the chance of ruin was always preferable to the certainty of dishonour. The minister, whose pacific intentions were seconded only by the voices of a few servile and venal followers, attempted to allay the general ferment, by an apology for his own conduct, and even for the demands of the Gothic prince. 'The payment of a subsidy, which had excited the indignation of the Romans, ought not (such was the language of Stilicho) to be considered in the odious light either of a tribute or of a ransom, extorted by the menaces of a Barbarian enemy. Alaric had faithfully asserted the just pretensions of the republic to the provinces which were usurped by the Greeks of Constantinople; he modestly required the fair and stipulated recompense of his services; and, if he had desisted from the prosecution of his enterprise, he had obeyed, in his retreat, the peremptory though private letters of the emperor himself. These contradictory orders (he would not dissemble the errors of his own family) had been procured by the intercession of Serena.* The tender piety of his wife had been too deeply affected by the discord of the royal brothers, the sons of her adopted father; and the sentiments of nature had too easily prevailed over the stern dictates of the public welfare.' These ostensible reasons, which faintly disguise the obscure intrigues of the palace of Ravenna, were supported by the authority of Stilicho; and obtained, after a warm debate, the reluctant approbation of the senate. The tumult of virtue and freedom subsided; and the sum of four thousand pounds of gold was granted, under the name of a subsidy, to secure the peace of Italy, and to conciliate the friendship of the king of the Goths. Lampadius alone, one of the most illustrious members of the assembly, still persisted in his dissent; exclaimed with a loud voice, 'This is not a treaty of peace, but of servitude';[103] and escaped the danger of such bold opposition by immediately retiring to the sanctuary of a Christian church.

But the reign of Stilicho drew towards its end, and the proud minister might perceive the symptoms of his approaching disgrace. The generous boldness of Lampadius had been applauded; and the senate, so patiently resigned to a long servitude, rejected with disdain the offer of invidious and imaginary freedom. The troops, who still assumed the name and prerogatives of the Roman legions, were exasperated by the partial affection of Stilicho for the Barbarians; and the people imputed to the mischievous policy of the minister the public misfortunes, which were the natural consequence of their own degeneracy. Yet Stilicho might have continued to brave the clamours of the people, and even of the soldiers, if he could have maintained his dominion over the feeble mind of his pupil. But the respectful attachment of Honorius was converted into fear, suspicion, and hatred. The crafty Olympius,[104] who concealed his vices under the mask of Christian piety, had secretly undermined the benefactor by whose favour he was promoted to the honourable offices of the Imperial palace. Olympius revealed to the unsuspecting emperor, who had attained the twenty-fifth year of his age, that he was without weight, or authority, in his own government; and artfully alarmed his timid and indolent disposition by a lively picture of the designs of Stilicho, who already meditated the death of his sovereign, with the ambitious hope of placing the diadem on the head of his son Eucherius. The emperor was instigated, by his new favourite, to assume the tone of independent dignity; and the minister was astonished to find that secret resolutions were formed in the court and council, which were repugnant to his interest or to his intentions. Instead of residing in the palace at Rome, Honorius declared that it was his pleasure to return to the secure fortress of Ravenna. On the first intelligence of the death of his brother Arcadius, he prepared to visit Constantinople, and to regulate, with the authority of a guardian, the provinces of the infant Theodosius.[105] The representation of the difficulty and expense of such a distant expedition checked this strange and sudden sally of active diligence; but the danger-ous project of showing the emperor to the camp of Pavia, which was composed of the Roman troops, the enemies of Stilicho, and his Barbar-ian auxiliaries, remained fixed and unalterable. The minister was pressed, by the advice of his confidant Justinian, a Roman advocate of a lively and penetrating genius, to oppose a journey so prejudicial to his reputation and safety. His strenuous, but ineffectual, efforts confirmed the triumph of Olympius; and the prudent lawyer withdrew himself from the impend-ing ruin of his patron.

In the passage of the emperor through Bologna, a mutiny of the guards was excited and appeased by the secret policy of Stilicho; who announced his instructions to decimate the guilty, and ascribed to his own interces-sion the merit of their pardon. After this tumult, Honorius embraced, for the last time, the minister whom he now considered as a tyrant, and proceeded on his way to the camp of Pavia, where he was received by the loyal acclamations of the troops who were assembled for the service of the Gallic war. On the morning of the fourth day, he pronounced, as he had been taught, a military oration in the presence of the soldiers, whom the charitable visits, and artful discourses, of Olympius had prepared to execute a dark and bloody conspiracy. At the first signal, they massacred the friends of Stilicho, the most illustrious officers of the empire; two Praetorian prefects, of Gaul, and of Italy; two masters-general, of the cavalry and infantry; the master of the offices; the quaestor, the treasurer, and the count of the domestics. Many lives were lost; many houses were plundered; the furious sedition continued to rage till the close of the evening; and the trembling emperor, who was seen in the streets of Pavia without his robes or diadem, yielded to the persuasions of his favourite, condemned the memory of the slain, and solemnly approved the inno-cence and fidelity of their assassins. The intelligence of the massacre of

Pavia filled the mind of Stilicho with just and gloomy apprehensions; and he instantly summoned, in the camp of Bologna, a council of the confederate leaders who were attached to his service, and would be involved in his ruin. The impetuous voice of the assembly called aloud for arms, and for revenge; to march, without a moment's delay, under the banners of a hero whom they had so often followed to victory; to surprise, to oppress, to extirpate the guilty Olympius, and his degenerate Romans; and perhaps to fix the diadem on the head of their injured general. Instead of executing a resolution, which might have been justified by success, Stilicho hesitated till he was irrecoverably lost. He was still ignorant of the fate of the emperor; he distrusted the fidelity of his own party; and he viewed with horror the fatal consequences of arming a crowd of licentious Barbarians against the soldiers and people of Italy. The confederates, impatient of his timorous and doubtful delay, hastily retired, with fear and indignation. At the hour of midnight, Sarus, a Gothic warrior, renowned among the Barbarians themselves for his strength and valour, suddenly invaded the camp of his benefactor, plundered the baggage, cut in pieces the faithful Huns, who guarded his person, and penetrated to the tent, where the minister, pensive and sleepless, meditated on the dangers of his situation. Stilicho escaped with difficulty from the sword of the Goths; and, after issuing a last and generous admonition to the cities of Italy, to shut their gates against the Barbarians, his confidence, or his despair, urged him to throw himself into Ravenna, which was already in the absolute possession of his enemies. Olympius, who had assumed the dominion of Honorius, was speedily informed that his rival had embraced, as a suppliant, the altar of the Christian church. The base and cruel disposition of the hypocrite was incapable of pity or remorse; but he piously affected to elude, rather than to violate, the privilege of the sanctuary. Count Heraclian, with a troop of soldiers, appeared, at the dawn of day, before the gates of the church of Ravenna. The bishop was satisfied by a solemn oath that the Imperial mandate only directed them to secure the person of Stilicho; but, as soon as the unfortunate minister had been tempted beyond the holy threshold, he produced the warrant for his instant execution. Stilicho supported, with calm resignation, the injurious names of traitor and parricide; repressed the unseasonable zeal of his followers, who were ready to attempt an ineffectual rescue; and, with a firmness not unworthy of the last of the Roman generals, submitted his neck to the sword of Heraclian.[106]

The servile crowd of the palace, who had so long adored the fortune of Stilicho, affected to insult his fall, and the most distant connection with the master-general of the West, which had so lately been a title to wealth and honours, was studiously denied and rigorously punished. His family, united by a triple alliance with the family of Theodosius, might envy the condition of the meanest peasant. The flight of his son Eucherius was intercepted, and the death of that innocent youth soon followed the divorce of Thermantia, who filled the place of her sister Maria,* and who, like Maria, had remained a virgin in the Imperial bed.[107] The friends of Stilicho, who had escaped the massacre of Pavia, were persecuted by the implacable revenge of Olympius, and the most exquisite cruelty was employed to extort the confession of a treasonable and sacrilegious conspiracy. They died in silence: their firmness justified the choice,[108] and perhaps absolved the innocence, of their patron, and the despotic power which could take his life without a trial, and stigmatise his memory without a proof, has no jurisdiction over the impartial suffrage of posterity.[109] The services of Stilicho are great and manifest; his crimes, as they are vaguely stated in the language of flattery and hatred, are obscure, at least, and improbable. About four months after his death an edict was published in the name of Honorius to restore the free communication of the two empires which had been so long interrupted by the *public enemy*.[110] The minister whose fame and fortune depended on the prosperity of the state was accused of betraying Italy to the Barbarians, whom he repeatedly vanquished at Pollentia, at Verona, and before the walls of Florence. His pretended design of placing the diadem on the head of his son Eucherius could not have been conducted without preparations or accomplices, and the ambitious father would not surely have left the future emperor, till the twentieth year of his age, in the humble station of tribune of the notaries. Even the religion of Stilicho was arraigned by the malice of his rival. The seasonable and almost miraculous deliverance was devoutly celebrated by the applause of the clergy, who asserted that the restoration of idols and the persecution of the church would have been the first measure of the reign of Eucherius. The son of Stilicho, however, was educated in the bosom of Christianity, which his father had uniformly professed and zealously supported.[111] Serena had borrowed her magnificent necklace from the statue of Vesta,[112] and the Pagans execrated the memory of the sacrilegious minister, by whose order the Sibylline books, the oracles of Rome, had been committed to the flames.[113] The pride and power of Stilicho constituted his real guilt. An honourable reluctance to shed the blood of his countrymen appears to have contributed to the success of his unworthy rival; and it is the last humiliation of the character of Honorius that posterity has not condescended to reproach him with his base ingratitude to the guardian of his youth and the support of his empire.

Among the train of dependents whose wealth and dignity attracted the notice of their own times our curiosity is excited by the celebrated name of the poet Claudian, who enjoyed the favour of Stilicho, and was overwhelmed in the ruin of his patron. The titular offices of tribune and notary fixed his rank in the Imperial court, he was indebted to the powerful intercession of Serena for his marriage with a very rich heiress of the province of Africa,[114] and the statue of Claudian, erected in the forum of Trajan, was a monument of the taste and liberality of the Roman senate.[115] After the praises of Stilicho became offensive and criminal, Claudian was exposed to the enmity of a powerful and unforgiving courtier, whom he had provoked by the insolence of wit. He had compared, in a lively epigram, the opposite characters of two Praetorian prefects of Italy; he contrasts the innocent repose of a philosopher, who sometimes resigned the hours of business to slumber, perhaps to study, with the interested diligence of a rapacious minister, indefatigable in the pursuit of unjust or sacrilegious gain. 'How happy,' continues Claudian, 'how happy might it be for the people of Italy if Mallius could be constantly awake, and if Hadrian would always sleep!'[116] The repose of Mallius was not disturbed by this friendly and gentle admonition, but the cruel vigilance of Hadrian watched the opportunity of revenge, and easily obtained from the enemies of Stilicho the trifling sacrifice of an obnoxious poet. The poet concealed himself, however, during the tumult of the revolution, and, consulting the dictates of prudence rather than of honour, he addressed, in the form of an epistle, a suppliant and humble recantation to the offended prefect. He deplores, in mournful strains, the fatal indiscretion into which he had been hurried by passion and folly; submits to the imitation of his adversary the generous examples of the clemency of gods, of heroes, and of lions; and expresses his hope that the magnanimity of Hadrian will not trample on a defenceless and contemptible foe, already humbled by disgrace and poverty, and deeply wounded by the exile, the tortures, and the death of his dearest friends.[117] Whatever might be the success of his prayer, or the accidents of his future life, the period of a few years levelled in the grave the minister and the poet; but the name of Hadrian is almost sunk in oblivion, while Claudian is read with pleasure in every country which has retained, or acquired, the knowledge of the Latin language. If we fairly balance his merits and his defects, we shall acknowledge that Claudian does not either satisfy or silence our reason. It would not be easy to produce a passage that deserves the epithet of sublime or pathetic; to select a verse that melts the heart or enlarges the imagination. We should vainly seek, in the poems of Claudian, the happy invention and artificial conduct* of an interesting fable, or the just and lively representation of the characters and situations of real life. For the service of his patron he published occasional panegyrics and invectives; and the design of these slavish compositions encouraged his propensity to exceed the limits of truth and nature. These imperfections, however, are compensated in some degree by the poetical virtues of Claudian. He was endowed with the rare and precious talent of raising the meanest, of adorning the most barren, and of diversifying the most similar topics; his colouring, more especially in descriptive poetry, is soft and splendid; and he seldom fails to display, and even to abuse, the advantages of a cultivated understanding, a copious fancy, an easy, and sometimes forcible, expression, and a perpetual flow of harmonious versification. To these commendations, independent of any accidents of time and place, we must add the peculiar merit which Claudian derived from the unfavourable circumstances of his birth. In the decline of arts and of empire a native of Egypt,[118] who had received the education of a Greek, assumed, in a mature age, the familiar use and absolute command of the Latin language,[119] soared above the heads of his feeble contemporaries, and placed himself, after an interval of three hundred years, among the poets of ancient Rome.[120]

NOTES TO CHAPTER 30

1   The revolt of the Goths and the blockade of Constantinople are distinctly mentioned by Claudian (in *Rufin.*, ii, 7–100); Zosimus (v, 292); and Jornandes (*de Rebus Geticis*, ch. 29).

*   * page 581   [The settlement of the Goths in Thrace was described by Gibbon at the end of Chapter 26.]

2   *alii per terga ferocis*
                  Danubii solidata ruunt expertaque remis
                  Frangunt stagna rotis.
    Claudian and Ovid often amuse their fancy by interchanging the metaphors and properties of *liquid* water and *solid* ice. Much false wit has been expended in this easy exercise.

3   Jerome, i, 26. He endeavours to comfort his friend Heliodorus, bishop of Altinum, for the loss of his nephew Nepotian, by a curious recapitulation of all the public and private misfortunes of the times. See Tillemont, *Mém. Ecclés.*, xii, 200, etc.

*   * page 582   [The chief minister or prefect of Arcadius, murdered in ad 395.]

4   *Baltha* or *bold: origo mirifica* ['a heroic derivation'], says Jornandes (ch. 29). This illustrious race long continued to flourish in France, in the Gothic province of Septimania or Languedoc, under the corrupted appellation of *Baux*; and a branch of that family afterwards settled in the kingdom of Naples (Grotius in *Prolegom. ad Hist. Gothic.*, p. 53). The lords of Baux, near Arles, and of seventy-nine subordinate places, were independent of the counts of Provence (Longuerue, *Description de la France*, i, 357).

5   Zosimus (v, 293–95) is our best guide for the conquest of Greece; but the hints and allusion of Claudian are so many rays of historic light.

6   Compare Herodotus (vii, 176) and Livy (xxxvi, 15). The narrow entrance of Greece was probably enlarged by each successive ravisher.

*   * page 583   [resisting the Persian invasion of Greece in 480 bc]

7   He passed, says Eunapius (in *Vit. Philosoph.*, p. 93, edit. Commelin, 1596), through the straits, διὰ τῶν πυλῶν (ὑὑ ὠὑὀῒῂὒὰὑῇὰὸ) παρῆλθεν, ὥσπερ διὰ σταδίου καὶ ἱπποκρότου πεδίου τρέχων ['as if running along a level race track'].

8   In obedience to Jerome and Claudian (in *Rufin.*, ii, 191), I have mixed some darker colours in the mild representation of Zosimus, who wished to soften the calamities of Athens.

                  Nec fera Cecropias traxissent vincula matres.
    ['He would not have put the mothers of Athens in chains.']

Synesius (Epist. clvi, 272, edit. Petav.) observes that Athens, whose sufferings he imputes to the proconsul's avarice, was at that time less famous for her schools of philosophy than for her trade of honey.

9   *vallata mari Scironia rupes*
                      Et duo continuo connectens aequora muro
                      Isthmos   Claudian, *de Bell. Getico*, 188.

The Scironian rocks are described by Pausanias (i, 44, 107, edit. Kuhn), and our modern travellers, Wheeler (p. 436), and Chandler (p. 298). Hadrian made the road passable for two carriages.

10 Claudian (in *Rufin.*, ii, 186, and *de Bello Getico*, 611, etc.) vaguely, though forcibly, delineates the scene of rapine and destruction.

11 Τρὶς μάκαρες Δαναοὶ καὶ τετράκις, etc. ['Thrice blessed, even four times are the Greeks, etc.'] These generous lines of Homer (*Odyss.*, v, 306) were transcribed by one of the captive youths of Corinth; and the tears of Mummius [Roman general who destroyed Corinth in 146 bc] may prove that the rude conqueror, though he was ignorant of the value of an original picture, possessed the purest source of good taste, a benevolent heart (Plutarch, *Symposiac.*, ix, ii, 737, edit. Wechel).

12 Homer perpetually describes the exemplary patience of those female captives, who gave their charms, and even their hearts, to the murderers of their fathers, brothers, etc. Such a passion (of Eriphile for Achilles) is touched with admirable delicacy by Racine [in his tragedy *Iphigenia in Aulis* (1674)].

* *page 584* [Pyrrhus, king of Epirus, in the third century BC]

13 Plutarch (*in Pyrrho*, ii, 471, edit. Brian) gives the genuine answer in the Laconic dialect. Pyrrhus attacked Sparta, with 25,000 foot, 2000 horse, and 24 elephants: and the defence of that open town is a fine comment on the laws of Lycurgus, even in the last stage of decay.

† *page 584* [shield]

14 Such, perhaps, as Homer (*Iliad*, xx, 164) has so nobly painted him.

15 Eunapius (in *Vit. Philosoph.*, pp. 90–93) intimates that a troop of Monks betrayed Greece and followed the Gothic camp.

16 For Stilicho's Greek war, compare the honest narrative of Zosimus (v, 295–96) with the curious circumstantial flattery of Claudian (*i Cons. Stilich.*, 172–86; *iv Cons. Hon.*, 459–87). As the event was not glorious, it is artfully thrown into the shade.

17 The troops who marched through Elis delivered up their arms. This security enriched the Eleans, who were lovers of a rural life. Riches begat pride; they disdained their privilege, and they suffered. Polybius advises them to retire once more within their magic circle. See a learned and judicious discourse on the Olympic games, which Mr West has prefixed to his translation of Pindar.

18 Claudian (in *iv Cons. Hon.*, 480) alludes to the fact, without naming the river: perhaps the Alpheus (*i Cons. Stil.*, i, 185).

                      et Alpheus Geticis angustus acervis
                      Tardior ad Siculos etiamnum pergit amores.

['The Alpheus, diminished by the hordes of Goths, proceeds still more slowly to its Sicilian goal.']

   Yet I should prefer the Peneus, a shallow stream in a wide and deep bed, which runs through Elis, and falls into the sea below Cyllene. It had been joined with the Alpheus, to cleanse the Augean stable (Cellarius, i, 760; Chandler's *Travels*, p. 286).

19 Strabo, viii, 517; Pliny, *Hist. Natur.*, iv, 3; Wheeler, p. 308; Chandler, p. 275. They measured from different points the distance between the two lands.

20 Synesius passed three years (AD 397–400) at Constantinople, as deputy from Cyrene to the emperor Arcadius. He presented him with a crown of gold, and pronounced before him the instructive oration *de Regno* (pp. 1–32, edit. Petav., Paris, 1612). The philosopher was made bishop of Ptolemais, AD 410, and died about 430. See Tillemont, *Mém. Ecclés.*, xii, 499, 554, 683–85.

* *page 585* [In classical mythology, according to one account, a rock was suspended over Tantalus, ever threatening to fall.]

21 Synesius, *de Regno*, pp. 21–26.

22   *qui foedera rumpit*
         Ditatur: qui servat, eget: vastator Achivae
         Gentis, et Epirum nuper populatus inultam
         Praesidet Illyrico; iam, quos obsedit, amicos
         Ingreditur muros; illis responsa daturus
         Quorum coniugibus potitur natosque peremit.

                                         Claudian, in *Eutrop.*, ii, 212.

Alaric applauds his own policy (*de Bell. Getic.*, 533–43) in the use which he had made of this Illyrian jurisdiction.

23 Jornandes, 29, 651. The Gothic historian adds, with unusual spirit, *Cum suis deliberans suasit suo labore quaerere regna, quam alienis per otium subiacere.* ['Taking counsel with his followers, he persuaded them that it was better to seek kingdoms by their own efforts than to be passively subject to foreign rule.']

24   *discors odiisque anceps civilibus orbis*
         Non sua vis tutata diu, dum foedera fallax
         Ludit, et alternae periuria venditat aulae.

                                         Claudian, de Bell. Get. 565.

25 *Alpibus Italiae ruptis penetrabis ad Urbem.* ['You will break through the Italian Alps and reach Rome.'] This authentic prediction was announced by Alaric, or at least by Claudian (*de Bell. Getico*, 547), seven years before the event. But, as it was not accomplished within the term which had been rashly fixed, the interpreters escaped through an ambiguous meaning.

26 Our best materials are 970 verses of Claudian, in the poem on the Getic war, and the beginning of that which celebrates the sixth consulship of Honorius. Zosimus is totally silent, and we are reduced to such scraps, or rather crumbs, as we can pick from Orosius and the Chronicles.

27 Notwithstanding the gross errors of Jornandes, who confounds the Italian wars of Alaric (ch. 29), his date of the consulship of Stilicho and Aurelian (AD 400) is firm and respectable. It is certain from Claudian (Tillemont, *Hist. des Emp.*, v, 804) that the battle of Pollentia was fought AD 403; but we cannot easily fill the interval.

28 *Tantum Romanae urbis iudicium fugis, ut magis obsidionem barbaricam, quam pacatae urbis iudicium velis sustinere.* Jerome, ii, 239. ['You are in such fear of appearing before a court at Rome that you prefer to undergo a siege by the Barbarians than submit yourself to judgment in a peaceful city.'] Rufinus understood his danger: the *peaceful* city was inflamed by the beldam Marcella and the rest of Jerome's faction. [Marcella was a Roman matron whom Gibbon describes in a footnote to Chapter 31 as 'equally respectable for her rank, her age and her piety'. Rufinus, who translated Greek works into Latin, had aroused Jerome's

antagonism by, allegedly, misusing the authority of his name.]

29 Jovinian, the enemy of fasts and celibacy, who was persecuted and insulted by the furious Jerom (Jortin's *Remarks*, iv, 104, etc.). See the original edict of banishment in the *Theodosian Code* xvi, v, 43.

30 This epigram (*de Sene Veronensi qui suburbium nusquam egressus est*) ['The old man of Verona who never left the outskirts of the city'], is one of the earliest and most pleasing compositions of Claudian. Cowley's [1618–67] imitation (Hurd's edition, ii, 241) has some natural and happy strokes: but it is much inferior to the original portrait, which is evidently drawn from the life.

31   *Ingentem meminit parvo qui germine quercum*
              Aequaevumque videt consenuisse nemus.

              'A neighbouring wood born with himself he sees,
              And loves his old contemporary trees.'

In this passage, Cowley is perhaps superior to his original; and the English poet, who was a good botanist, has concealed the oaks under a more general expression.

32 Claudian, *de Bell. Get.*, 192–266. He may seem prolix; but fear and superstition occupied as large a space in the minds of the Italians.

33 From the passages of Paulinus [St Paulinus of Nola, AD 353–431, the biographer of St Ambrose], which Baronius has produced (*Annal. Eccles.*, AD 403, No. 51), it is manifest that the general alarm had pervaded all Italy, as far as Nola in Campania, where that famous penitent had fixed his abode.

34 *Solus erat Stilicho*, etc., ['Stilicho was the only one, etc.'] is the exclusive commendation which Claudian bestows (*de Bell. Get.*, 267) without condescending to except the emperor. How insignificant must Honorius have appeared in his own court!

* *page 588* [Lake Como]

35 The face of the country, and the hardiness of Stilicho, are finely described (*de Bell. Get.*, 340–63).

† *page 588* [loyalty]

36   *Venit et extremis legio praetenta Britannis*
              Quae Scoto dat frena truci.   *de Bell. Get.* 416.

Yet the most rapid march from Edinburgh, or Newcastle, to Milan must have required a longer space of time than Claudian seems willing to allow for the duration of the Gothic war.

37 Every traveller must recollect the face of Lombardy (see Fontenelle, v, 279), which is often tormented by the capricious and irregular abundance of waters. The Austrians, before Genoa, were encamped in the dry bed of the Polcevera. *Ne sarebbe* (says Muratori) *mai passato per mente a que' buoni Alemanni, che quel picciolo torrente potesse, per cosi dire, in un instante cangiarsi in un terribil gigante.* ['It would never have occurred to those good Germans that that little stream could change in a moment into a terrible giant.'] (*Annali d'Italia*, xvi, 443. Milan, 1753, 8vo edit.)

38 Claudian does not clearly answer our question, Where was Honorius himself? Yet the flight is marked by the pursuit; and my idea of the Gothic war is justified by the Italian critics, Sigonius (i, ii, 369; *de Imp. Occident*, Bk x) and Muratori (*Annali d'Italia*, iv, 45).

39 One of the roads may be traced in the Itineraries (pp. 98, 288, 294, with Wesseling's notes). Asta lay some miles on the right hand.

40 Asta, or Asti, a Roman colony, is now the capital of a pleasant country, which, in the sixteenth century, devolved to the dukes of Savoy (Leandro Alberti, *Descrizzione d'Italia*, p. 382).

41 *Nec me timor impulit ullus.* ['I have never been swayed by fear.'] He might hold this proud language the next year at Rome, five hundred miles from the scene of danger (*vi Cons. Hon.*, 449).

42   *Hanc ego vel victor regno vel morte tenebo*
                    Victus humum –
The speeches (*de Bell. Get.*, 479–549) of the Gothic Nestor and Achilles are strong, characteristic, adapted to the circumstances, and possibly not less genuine than those of Livy.

43 Orosius (vii, 37) is shocked at the impiety of the Romans who attacked, on Easter Sunday, such pious Christians. Yet, at the same time, public prayers were offered at the shrine of St Thomas of Edessa, for the destruction of the Arian robber. See Tillemont (*Hist. des Emp.*, v, 529), who quotes an homily, which has been erroneously ascribed to St Chrysostom.

44 The vestiges of Pollentia are twenty-five miles to the south-east of Turin. *Urbs*, in the same neighbourhood, was a royal chace of the Kings of Lombardy, and a small river, which excused the prediction, *'penetrabis ad urbem'* ['you will reach Rome']. Cluver., *Ital. Antiq.*, i, p. 83–85. [*Urbem* (nominative *Urbs*) refers to the city of Rome, but could also be taken to mean the river Urbs referred to here. Hence the 'ambiguous meaning' mentioned in footnote 25.]

 * *page 590*   [proved]

45 Orosius wishes, in doubtful words, to insinuate the defeat of the Romans. *Pugnantes vicimus, victores victi sumus.* ['We won the fight, but though victorious, we were beaten.'] Prosper (in *Chron.*) makes it an equal and bloody battle; but the Gothic writers, Cassiodorus (in *Chron.*) and Jornandes (*de Reb. Get.*, ch. 29), claim a decisive victory.

46   *Demens Ausonidum gemmata monilia matrum,*
                    Romanasque alta famulas cervice petebat.
                                        de Bell. Get., 627.

47 Claudian (*de Bell. Get.*, 580–647) and Prudentius (in *Symmach.*, ii, 694–719) celebrate, without ambiguity, the Roman victory of Pollentia. They are poetical and party writers; yet some credit is due to the most suspicious witnesses, who are checked by the recent notoriety of facts.

 † *page 590*   [the Cimbri, in 101 BC]

48 Claudian's peroration is strong and elegant; but the identity of the Cimbric and Gothic fields must be understood (like Virgil's Philippi, *Georgics*, i, 490) according to the loose geography of a poet. Vercellae and Pollentia are sixty miles from each other; and the latitude is still greater, if the Cimbri were defeated in the wide and barren plain of Verona (Maffei, *Verona Illustrata*, i, 54–62).

49 Claudian and Prudentius must be strictly examined, to reduce the figures, and extort the historic sense, of those poets.

50   *Et gravant en airain ses frêles avantages*
                    De mes états conquis enchaîner les images.
                                        [Racine, *Mithridates* (1673)]
The practice of exposing in triumph the images of kings and provinces was familiar to the Romans. The bust of Mithridates himself was twelve feet high, of massy gold (Freinshem., *Supplement. Livian.*, ciii, 47).

51 The Getic war and the sixth consulship of Honorius obscurely connect the events of Alaric's retreat and losses.

52 *Taceo de Alarico . . . saepe victo, saepe concluso, semperque dimisso.* Orosius, vii, 37, 567. Claudian (*vi Cons. Hon.*, 320) drops the curtain with a fine image.

53 The remainder of Claudian's poem on the sixth consulship of Honorius describes the journey, the triumph, and the games (330–660).

54 See the inscription in Mascou's *History of the Ancient Germans*, viii, 12. The words are positive and indiscreet, *Getarum nationem in omne aevum domitam*, etc. ['the Goths, vanquished for all time.']

55 On the curious, though horrid, subject of the gladiators, consult the two books of the *Saturnalia* of Lipsius, who, as an *antiquarian*, is inclined to excuse the practice of *antiquity* (iii, 483–545).

56 *Cod. Theodos.*, xv, xii, 1. The commentary of Godefroy affords large materials (v, 396) for the history of gladiators.

57 See the peroration of Prudentius (in *Symmach.*, ii, 1121–31), who had doubtless read the eloquent invective of Lactantius (*Divin. Institut.*, vi, 20). The Christian apologists have not spared these bloody games, which were introduced in the religious festivals of Paganism.

58 Theodoret, v, 26. I wish to believe the story of St Telemachus. Yet no church has been dedicated, no altar has been erected, to the only monk who died a martyr in the cause of humanity.

  * *page 593* [welcome]

59 *Crudele gladiatorum spectaculum et inhumanum nonnullis videri solet, et haud scio an ita sit, ut nunc fit.* Cic. Tusculan., ii, 17. ['Some people consider gladiatorial spectacles to be cruel and unhuman. I hardly think this is the case today.'] He faintly censures the *abuse* and warmly defends the *use* of these sports; *oculis nulla poterat esse fortior contra dolorem et mortem disciplina.* ['No sight could better teach us how to face pain and death.'] Seneca (*epist.* vii) shows the feelings of a man.

60 This account of Ravenna is drawn from Strabo (v, 327); Pliny (iii, 20); Stephen of Byzantium (*sub voce* 'Ράβεννα, p. 651, edit. Berkel); Claudian (in *vi Cons. Honor.*, 494, etc.); Sidonius Apollinaris (i, epist. v, 8); Jornandes (*de Reb. Get.*, ch. 29); Procopius (*de Bell. Gothic.*, i, 1, 309, edit. Louvre); and Cluverius (*Ital. Antiq.*, i, 301–07). Yet I still want a local antiquarian, and a good topographical map.

61 Martial (*Epigram.*, iii, 56–57) plays on the trick of the knave who had sold him wine instead of water; but he seriously declares that a cistern at Ravenna is more valuable than a vineyard. Sidonius complains that the town is destitute of fountains and aqueducts, and ranks the want of fresh water among the local evils, such as the croaking of frogs, the stinging of gnats, etc.

62 The fable of Theodore and Honoria, which Dryden has so admirably transplanted from Boccaccio (*Giornata*, iii, novell. viii), was acted in the wood of *Chiassi*, a corrupt word from *Classis*, the naval station, which, with the intermediate road or suburb, the *Via Caesaris*, constituted the *triple* city of Ravenna.

  * *page 594* [governors of a province]

63 From the year 404, the dates of the Theodosian Code become sedentary at Constantinople and Ravenna. See Godefroy's Chronology of the Laws, i, cxlviii, etc.

64 See M. de Guignes, *Hist. des Huns*, i, 179–89; ii, 295, 334–38.

65 Procopius (*de Bell. Vandal.*, i, iii, 182) has observed an emigration from the Palus Maeotis [the sea of Azov] to the north of Germany, which he ascribes to famine. But his views of ancient history are strangely darkened by ignorance and error.

66 Zosimus (v, 331) uses the general description of the nations beyond the Danube and the Rhine. Their situation, and consequently their names, are manifestly shown, even in the various epithets which each ancient writer may have casually added.

67 The name of Rhadagast was that of a local deity of the Obotrites (in Mecklenburgh). A hero might naturally assume the appellation of his tutelar god; but it is not probable that the Barbarians should worship an unsuccessful hero. See Mascou, *Hist. of the Germans*, viii, 14.

68 Olympiodorus (*apud* Photium, p. 180) uses the Greek word Ὀπτιμάτοι [from Latin *optimates*, i.e. the best men, aristocrats]; which does not convey any precise idea. I suspect that they were the princes and nobles, with their faithful companions; the knights with their squires, as they would have been styled some centuries afterwards.

 * *page 596*   [at the end of the second century BC]

69 Tacit., *de Moribus Germanorum*, ch. 37.

70   *cuius agendi*
                        Spectator vel causa fui,   Claudian, *vi Cons. Hon.*, 439,
is the modest language of Honorius, in speaking of the Gothic war, which he had seen somewhat nearer.

71 Zosimus (v, 331) transports the war and the victory of Stilicho beyond the Danube. A strange error, which is awkwardly and imperfectly cured by reading Ἄρνον for Ἴστρον (Tillemont, *Hist. des Emp.*, v, 807) [the Arno for the Danube]. In good policy, we must use the service of Zosimus, without esteeming or trusting him.

72 *Codex Theodos.*, vii, xiii, 16. The date of this law (AD 406, 18th May) satisfies me, as it had done Godefroy (ii, 387), of the true year of the invasion of Radagaisus. Tillemont, Pagi, and Muratori prefer the preceding year; but they are bound, by certain obligations of civility and respect, to St Paulinus of Nola.

73 Soon after Rome had been taken by the Gauls [in 390 BC], the senate, on a sudden emergency, armed ten legions, 3000 horse, and 42,000 foot; a force which the city could not have sent forth under Augustus (Livy, vii, 25). This declaration may puzzle an antiquary, but it is clearly explained by Montesquieu.

74 Machiavel has explained, at least as a philosopher, the origin of Florence, which insensibly descended, for the benefit of trade, from the rock of Faesulae to the banks of the Arno (*Istoria Fiorentina*, i, ii, 36, Londra, 1747). The Triumvirs sent a colony to Florence, which, under Tiberius (Tacit. *Annal.*, i, 79), deserved the reputation and name of a *flourishing* city. See Cluver., *Ital. Antiq.*, i, 507, etc.

75 Yet the Jupiter of Radagaisus who worshipped Thor and Woden was very different from the Olympic or Capitoline Jove. The accommodating temper of Polytheism might unite those various and remote deities, but the genuine Romans abhorred the human sacrifices of Gaul and Germany.

76 Paulinus (in *Vit. Ambros.*, ch. 50) relates this story, which he received from the mouth of Pansophia herself, a religious matron of Florence. Yet the archbishop soon ceased to take an active part in the business of the world, and never became a popular saint.

77 Augustine, *de Civitat. Dei*, v, 23; Orosius, vii, 37, 567–71. The two friends wrote in Africa, ten or twelve years after the victory; and their authority is implicitly followed by Isidore of Seville (in *Chron.*, p. 713, edit. Grot.). How many interesting facts might Orosius have inserted in the vacant space which is devoted to pious nonsense!

* *page 598* [now Durrës, on the coast of Albania]

78   *Franguntur montes, planumque per ardua Caesar*
                        Ducit opus: pandit fossas, turritaque summis
                        Disponit castella iugis, magnoque recessu
                        Amplexus fines; saltus nemorosaque tesqua
                        Et silvas vastaque feras indagine claudit.

['Mountains are demolished and under Caesar's direction every obstacle is levelled. He digs wide moats, sets fortified towers at intervals along the hill-tops, and completes the work of circumvallation all the way around. By this vast encirclement he completely surrounds acres of woodland, groves and wild forests.']

Yet the simplicity of truth (Caesar, *de Bell. Civ.*, iii, 44) is far greater than the amplifications of Lucan (*Pharsal.*, vi, 29–63).

79 The rhetorical expressions of Orosius, *'in arido et aspero montis ijugo'*, *'in unum ac parvum verticem'*, ['On a dry and rough hill-top', 'onto one small hill-top'] are not very suitable to the encampment of a great army. But Faesulae, only three miles from Florence, might afford space for the headquarters of Radagaisus, and would be comprehended within the circuit of the Roman lines.

80 See Zosimus, v, 331, and the Chronicles of Prosper and Marcellinus.

81 Olympiodorus (*apud* Photium, p. 180) uses an expression (προσηταιρίσατο) which would denote a strict and friendly alliance, and render Stilicho still more criminal. The *pauliper detentus, deinde interfectus* ['held for a brief time, then killed'] of Orosius is sufficiently odious.

82 Orosius, piously inhuman, sacrifices the king and people, Agag and the Amalekites, without a symptom of compassion. The bloody actor is less detestable than the cool unfeeling historian.

83 And Claudian's muse, was she asleep? had she been ill paid? Methinks the seventh consulship of Honorius (AD 407) would have furnished the subject of a noble poem. Before it was discovered that the state could no longer be saved, Stilicho (after Romulus, Camillus, and Marius) might have been worthily surnamed the fourth founder of Rome.

84 A luminous passage of Prosper's Chronicle, *In tres partes, per diversos principes, divisus exercitus* ['The army was divided into three, under different chiefs'], reduces the miracle of Florence, and connects the history of Italy, Gaul and Germany.

85 Orosius and Jerome positively charge him with instigating the invasion. *Excitatae a Stilichone gentes*, etc. ['The peoples were stirred up by Stilicho.'] They must mean *indirectly*. He saved Italy at the expense of Gaul.

86 The Count de Buat is satisfied that the Germans who invaded Gaul were the *two thirds* that yet remained of the army of Radagaisus. See the *Histoire Ancienne des Peuples de l'Europe* (vii, 87–121, Paris, 1772); an elaborate work, which I had not the advantage of perusing till the year 1777. As early as 1771, I find the same idea expressed in a rough draft of the present History. I have since observed a similar intimation in Mascou (viii, 15). Such agreement, without mutual communication, may add some weight to our common sentiment.

87   *provincia missos*
                                Expellet citius fasces quam Francia reges
                                Quos dederis.

['A Roman province will sooner expel the officials sent to it than France will expel the kings whom you have assigned.']

Claudian (*i Cons. Stil.*, i, 235, etc.) is clear and satisfactory. These kings of France are unknown to Gregory of Tours; but the author of the *Gesta Francorum* mentions both Sunno and Marcomir, and names the latter as the father of Pharamond (in ii, 543). He seems to write from good materials, which he did not understand.

88 See Zosimus (vi, 373), Orosius (vii, 40, 576), and the Chronicles. Gregory of Tours (ii, 9,165, in the second volume of the *Historians of France*) has preserved a valuable fragment of Renatus Profuturus Frigeridus, whose three names denote a Christian, a Roman subject, and a Semi-barbarian.

89 Claudian (*i Cons. Stil.*, i, 221, etc., ii, 186) describes the peace and prosperity of the Gallic frontier. The Abbé Dubos (*Hist. Critique*, etc., i, 174) would read *Alba* (a nameless rivulet of the Ardennes) instead of *Albis*, and expatiates on the danger of the Gallic cattle grazing beyond the *Elbe*. Foolish enough! In poetical geography, the Elbe, and the Hercynian, signify any river, or any wood in Germany. Claudian is not prepared for the strict examination of our antiquaries.

90   *geminasque viator*
                                Cum videat ripas, quae sit Romana requirat.

* *page 600*   [Mainz]

91 Jerome, i, 93. See in the 1st vol. of the *Historians of France*, pp. 777, 782, the proper extracts from the *Carmen de Providentia Divina*, and Salvian. The anonymous poet was himself a captive, with his bishop and fellow-citizens.

† *page 600*   [Pelagius opposed the doctrine of original sin.]

92 The Pelagian doctrine, which was first agitated AD 405, was condemned, in the space of ten years, at Rome and Carthage. St Augustine fought and conquered, but the Greek Church was favourable to his adversaries; and (what is singular enough) the people did not take any part in a dispute which they could not understand.

* *page 601*   [German Emperor, AD 1519–56]

93 See *Mémoires* de Guillaume du Bellay, Bk vi. In French the original reproof is less obvious and more pointed, from the double sense of the word *journée*, which signifies a day's travel or a battle.

94 Claudian (*i Cons. Stil.*, ii, 250). It is supposed that the Scots of Ireland invaded, by sea, the whole western coast of Britain; and some slight credit may be given even to Nennius and the Irish traditions (Carte's *Hist. of England*, i, 169; Whitaker's *Genuine History of the Britons*, p. 199). The sixty-six lives of St Patrick, which were extant in the ninth century, must have contained as many thousand lies; yet we may believe that, in one of these Irish inroads, the future apostle was led away captive (Usher, *Antiquit. Eccles. Britann.*, p. 431, and Tillemont, *Mém. Ecclés.*, xvi, 456, 782, etc.).

† *page 601*   [emperor, ad 253–68]

95 The British usurpers are taken from Zosimus (vi, 371–75); Orosius (vii, 40, 576–77); Olympiodorus (*apud* Photium, pp. 180–81), the ecclesiastical historians, and the Chronicles. The Latins are ignorant of Marcus.

96 *Cum in Constantino* inconstantiam . . . *execrarentur* ['they abhorred Constantine's inconstancy'] (Sidonius Apollinaris, v, 9, 139, edit. secund.

Sirmond.). Yet Sidonius might be tempted, by so fair a pun, to stigmatise a prince who had disgraced his grandfather.

97 *Bagaudae* is the name which Zosimus applies to them; perhaps they deserved a less odious character (see Dubos, *Hist. Critique*, i, 203, and this History, i, 383). [See footnote 16 to Chapter 13.] We shall hear of them again.

98 Verinianus, Didymus, Theodosius, and Lagodius, who, in modern courts, would be styled princes of the blood, were not distinguished by any rank or privileges above the rest of their fellow-subjects.

99 These *Honoriani*, or *Honoriaci*, consisted of two bands of Scots, or Attacotti, two of Moors, two of Marcomanni, the Victores, the Ascarii, and the Gallicani (*Notitia Imperii*, sect. xxxviii, edit. Lab). They were part of the sixty-five *Auxilia Palatina* [palace auxiliaries], and are properly styled ἐν τῇ αὐλῇ τάξεις by Zosimus (vi, 374).

* *page 603* [a German tribe]

100 *comitatur euntem*
 Pallor et atra fames, et saucia lividus ora
 Luctus, et inferni stridentes agmine morbi.
   Claudian, in *vi Cons. Hon.*, 321, etc.

101 These dark transactions are investigated by the Count de Buat (*Hist. des Peuples de l'Europe*, vii, iii–viii, 69–206), whose laborious accuracy may sometimes fatigue a superficial reader.

* *page 604* [65 BC]

102 See Zosimus, v, 334–35. He interrupts his scanty narrative, to relate the fable of Aemona, and of the ship Argo, which was drawn over from that place to the Hadriatic. Sozomen (viii, 25; ix, 4) and Socrates (vii, 10) cast a pale and doubtful light; and Orosius (vii, 38, 571) is abominably partial.

* *page 605* [niece of Theodosius I and wife of Stilicho]

103 Zosimus, v, 338–39. He repeats the words of Lampadius, as they were spoke in Latin, *Non est ista pax, sed pactio servitutis*, and then translates them into Greek for the benefit of his readers.

104 He came from the coast of the Euxine, and exercised a splendid office, λαμπρᾶς δὲ στρατείας ἐν τοῖς βασιλείοις ἀξιούμενος ['his brilliant military career gave him great standing in the palace']. His actions justify his character, which Zosimus (v, 340) exposes with visible satisfaction. Augustine revered the piety of Olympius, whom he styles a true son of the church (Baronius, *Annal. Eccles.*, AD 408, No. 19, etc. Tillemont, *Mém. Eccles.*, xiii, 467–68). But these praises, which the African saint so unworthily bestows, might proceed as well from ignorance as from adulation.

105 Zosimus, v, 338–39; Sozomen, ix, 4. Stilicho offered to undertake the journey to Constantinople, that he might divert Honorius from the vain attempt. The Eastern empire would not have obeyed, and could not have been conquered.

106 Zosimus (v, 336–45) has copiously, though not clearly, related the disgrace and death of Stilicho. Olympiodorus (*apud* Phot., p. 177), Orosius (vii, 38, 571–72), Sozomen (ix, 4), and Philostorgius (xi, 3; xii, 2) afford supplemental hints.

* *page 608* [Maria and Thermantia were daughters of Stilicho and wives, in turn, of the emperor Honorius.]

107 Zosimus, v, 333. The marriage of a Christian with two sisters scandalises Tillemont (*Hist. des Empereurs*, v, 557), who expects, in vain, that Pope Innocent I should have done something in the way either of censure or of

dispensation. [Marriage with the sister of a deceased wife was contrary to canon law.]

108 Two of his friends are honourably mentioned (Zosimus, v, 346): Peter, chief of the school of notaries, and the great chamberlain Deuterius. Stilicho had secured the bedchamber, and it is surprising that, under a feeble prince, the bedchamber was not able to secure him.

109 Orosius (vii, 38, 571–72) seems to copy the false and furious manifestos which were dispersed through the provinces by the new administration.

110 See the Theodosian Code, vii, xvi, 1; ix, xlii, 22. Stilicho is branded with the name of *praedo publicus*, who employed his wealth *ad omnem ditandam inquietandamque Barbariem* ['in order to enrich and stir up all the outside world'].

111 Augustine himself is satisfied with the effectual laws which Stilicho had enacted against heretics and idolaters, and which are still extant in the Code. He only applies to Olympius for their confirmation (Baronius, *Annal. Eccles.*, AD 408, No. 19).

112 Zosimus, v, 351. We may observe the bad taste of the age in dressing their statues with such awkward finery.

113 See Rutilius Numatianus (*Itinerar.*, ii, 41–60), to whom religious enthusiasm has dictated some elegant and forcible lines. Stilicho likewise stripped the gold plates from the doors of the Capitol, and read a prophetic sentence which was engraven under them (Zosimus, v, 352). These are foolish stories: yet the charge of *impiety* adds weight and credit to the praise, which Zosimus reluctantly bestows, of his virtues.

114 At the nuptials of Orpheus (a modest comparison!) all the parts of animated nature contributed their various gifts, and the gods themselves enriched their favourite. Claudian had neither flocks, nor herds, nor vines, nor olives. His wealthy bride was heiress to them all. But he carried to Africa a recommendatory letter from Serena, his Juno, and was made happy (*Epist.* ii, *ad Serenam*).

115 Claudian feels the honour like a man who deserved it (in *praefat. Bell. Get.*). The original inscription, on marble, was found at Rome, in the fifteenth century, in the house of Pomponius Laetus. The statue of a poet, far superior to Claudian, should have been erected during his lifetime by the men of letters, his countrymen, and contemporaries. It was a noble design! [Gibbon refers to Voltaire.]

116 See Epigram xxx.

> *Mallius indulget somno noctesque diesque:*
> *Insomnis Pharius sacra, profana, rapit.*
> *Omnibus, hoc, Italae gentes, exposcite votis*
> *Mallius ut vigilet, dormiat ut Pharius.*

Hadrian was a Pharian (of Alexandria). See his public life in Godefroy, *Cod. Theodos.*, vi, 364. Mallius did not always sleep. He composed some elegant dialogues on the Greek systems of natural philosophy (Claud., in *Mall. Theodor. Cons.*, 61–112).

117 See Claudian's first Epistle. Yet, in some places, an air of irony and indignation betrays his secret reluctance.

* *page 609* [skilful treatment]

118 National vanity has made him a Florentine, or a Spaniard. But the first epistle of Claudian proves him a native of Alexandria (Fabricius, *Bibliot. Latin.*, iii, 191–202, edit. Ernest).

119 His first Latin verses were composed during the consulship of Probinus, AD 395.

Romanos bibimus primum, te consule, fontes,
Et Latiae cessit Graia Thalia togae.

Besides some Greek epigrams, which are still extant, the Latin poet had composed, in Greek, the antiquities of Tarsus, Anazarbus, Berytus, Nice, etc. It is more easy to supply the loss of good poetry than of authentic history.

120 Strada (*Prolusion*, v, vi) allows him to contend with the five heroic poets, Lucretius, Virgil, Ovid, Lucan, and Statius. His patron is the accomplished courtier Balthazar Castiglione. His admirers are numerous and passionate. Yet the rigid critics reproach the exotic weeds or flowers, which spring too luxuriantly in his Latian soil.

CHAPTER 31 (Summary)

*Invasion of Italy by Alaric – manners of the Roman senate and
people – Rome is thrice besieged, and at length pillaged by the
Goths – death of Alaric – the Goths evacuate Italy – fall
of Constantine – Gaul and Spain are occupied by the
Barbarians – independence of Britain*

After Stilicho's death in AD 408, the ministers of Honorius lost control
over the Goths within the western empire. In Chapter 31, Gibbon
describes life in Rome before Alaric, the leader of the Goths, blockaded
the city, and estimates its population at 1,200,000. It experienced famine
and plague before Alaric raised the siege on the payment of a ransom.
Honorius in Ravenna refused Alaric a command in the Danubian provinces and, in effect, condemned Rome to its sack by Alaric's army in AD
410. Alaric withdrew his troops after six days' pillage and died near
Messina, attempting to invade Sicily. His successor, Adolphus, agreed a
treaty of peace with Honorius and married his sister, Placidia. Rome was
partly restored to its former splendour but rebellion and war continued in
Africa, Spain and Gaul. The imperial usurper from Britain, Constantine,
was defeated in Gaul in AD 411 and Adolphus was killed in Spain in AD
415. Goths, Franks and Burgundians settled in Gaul, paying allegiance to
Honorius in Ravenna, but Britain and Armorica in northwestern Gaul
were irretrievably lost to Roman rule.

CHAPTER 32 (Summary)

*Arcadius emperor of the East – administration and disgrace of
Eutropius – revolt of Gainas – persecution of St John Chrysostom
– Theodosius II emperor of the East – his sister Pulcheria – his
wife Eudocia – the Persian war, and division of Armenia*

In Chapter 32, Gibbon turns to the empire in the East under Arcadius.
The chief minister after Rufinus was defeated in AD 395 was a eunuch
called Eutropius, whose rapacious and oppressive policy led to a rebellion
and his downfall in AD 399. Before his fall, John Chrysostom of Antioch
was appointed archbishop of Constantinople. Gibbon describes him as a
man 'of choleric disposition', whose passion to reform the Church

aroused hostility. He was exiled to Armenia but was venerated after his death in AD 407. Arcadius died the following year, after an undistinguished reign of thirteen years, and was succeeded by his seven-year-old son, Theodosius. His reign began peacefully under the wise ministry of Anthemius. He married the daughter of a philosopher, who became known as the empress Eudocia. She aspired to the position of Pulcheria, the elder sister of Theodosius, as the power behind the throne, and was eventually exiled to Jerusalem.

CHAPTER 33 (Summary)

Death of Honorius – Valentinian III emperor of the West – administration of his mother Placidia – Aetius and Boniface – conquest of Africa by the Vandals

Gibbon returns to the West to describe the last years of the 'long and disgraceful reign' of Honorius. On his death in AD 423, an army from the empire of the East suppressed the usurper John and, under the influence of Placidia, the daughter of Theodosius the Great, her six-year-old son became the emperor of the West, as Valentinian III. The military command was divided between Aetius and Boniface. As a result of a conspiracy against him by Aetius, Boniface invited the Vandals who had settled in Spain to aid him in Africa. Genseric, their leader, quickly asserted his independence and overran and desolated much of the province that had been the granary of Rome. Boniface was besieged and defeated at Hippo in AD 431. Gibbon describes the bishop of Hippo, Saint Augustine, as 'a strong, capacious, argumentative mind', who 'boldly sounded the dark abyss of grace, predestination, free-will, and original sin'. The Vandals, helped by a schism in the Church, went on to capture Carthage in AD 439. By this time, the barbarians had established their reign over 'the fairest provinces of Europe and Africa'.

CHAPTER 34

The character, conquests, and court of Attila, king of the Huns – death of Theodosius the Younger – elevation of Marcian to the empire of the East

The western world was oppressed by the Goths and Vandals, who fled before the Huns; but the achievements of the Huns themselves were not adequate to their power and prosperity. Their victorious hordes had spread from the Volga to the Danube; but the public force was exhausted by the discord of independent chieftains; their valour was idly consumed in obscure and predatory excursions; and they often degraded their national dignity by condescending, for the hopes of spoil, to enlist under the banners of their fugitive enemies. In the reign of Attila,[1] the Huns again became the terror of the world; and I shall now describe the character and actions of that formidable Barbarian, who alternately insulted and invaded the East and the West, and urged* the rapid downfall of the Roman empire.

In the tide of emigration which impetuously rolled from the confines of China to those of Germany, the most powerful and populous tribes may commonly be found on the verge of the Roman provinces. The accumulated weight was sustained for a while by artificial barriers; and the easy condescension of the emperors invited, without satisfying, the insolent demands of the Barbarians, who had acquired an eager appetite for the luxuries of civilised life. The Hungarians, who ambitiously insert the name of Attila among their native kings, may affirm with truth that the hordes which were subject to his uncle Roas, or Rugilas, had formed their encampments within their limits of modern Hungary,[2] in a fertile country which liberally supplied the wants of a nation of hunters and shepherds. In this advantageous situation, Rugilas and his valiant brothers, who continually added to their power and reputation, commanded the alternative of peace or war with the two empires. His alliance with the Romans of the West was cemented by his personal friendship for the great Aetius; who was always secure of finding in the Barbarian camp a hospitable reception and a powerful support. At his solicitation, in the name of John the usurper, sixty thousand Huns advanced to the confines of Italy; their march and their retreat were alike expensive to the state; and the grateful policy of Aetius abandoned the possession of Pannonia to his faithful confederates. The Romans of the East were not less apprehensive of the arms of Rugilas, which threatened the provinces, or even the capital. Some ecclesiastical historians have destroyed the

Barbarians with lightning and pestilence;[3] but Theodosius was reduced to the more humble expedient of stipulating an annual payment of three hundred and fifty pounds of gold, and of disguising this dishonourable tribute by the title of general, which the king of the Huns condescended to accept. The public tranquillity was frequently interrupted by the fierce impatience of the Barbarians and the perfidious intrigues of the Byzantine court. Four dependent nations, among whom we may distinguish the Bavarians, disclaimed the sovereignty of the Huns; and their revolt was encouraged and protected by a Roman alliance; till the just claims and formidable power of Rugilas were effectually urged by the voice of Eslaw his ambassador. Peace was the unanimous wish of the senate; their decree was ratified by the emperor; and two ambassadors were named, Plinthas, a general of Scythian extraction, but of consular rank, and the quaestor Epigenes, a wise and experienced statesman, who was recommended to that office by his ambitious colleague.

The death of Rugilas suspended the progress of the treaty. His two nephews, Attila and Bleda, who succeeded to the throne of their uncle, consented to a personal interview with the ambassadors of Constantinople; but, as they proudly refused to dismount, the business was transacted on horseback, in a spacious plain near the city of Margus in the Upper Maesia. The kings of the Huns assumed the solid benefits, as well as the vain honours, of the negotiation. They dictated the conditions of peace, and each condition was an insult on the majesty of the empire. Besides the freedom of a safe and plentiful market on the banks of the Danube, they required that the annual contribution should be augmented from three hundred and fifty to seven hundred pounds of gold; that a fine, or ransom, of eight pieces of gold should be paid for every Roman captive who had escaped from his Barbarian master; that the emperor should renounce all treaties and engagements with the enemies of the Huns; and that all the fugitives, who had taken refuge in the court or provinces of Theodosius, should be delivered to the justice of their offended sovereign. This justice was rigorously indicted on some unfortunate youths of a royal race. They were crucified on the territories of the empire, by the command of Attila: and, as soon as the king of the Huns had impressed the Romans with the terror of his name, he indulged them in a short and arbitrary respite, whilst he subdued the rebellious or independent nations of Scythia and Germany.[4]

Attila, the son of Mundzuk, deduced his noble, perhaps his regal, descent[5] from the ancient Huns, who had formerly contended with the monarchs of China. His features, according to the observation of a Gothic historian, bore the stamp of his national origin; and the portrait of Attila exhibits the genuine deformity of a modern Calmuck:* a large head, a swarthy complexion, small, deep-seated eyes, a flat nose, a few hairs in the place of a beard, broad shoulders, and a short square body, of nervous† strength, though of a disproportioned form.[6] The haughty step and demeanour of the king of the Huns expressed the consciousness of his superiority above the rest of mankind; and he had a custom of fiercely rolling his eyes, as if he wished to enjoy the terror which he inspired. Yet this savage hero was not inaccessible to pity: his suppliant enemies might confide in the assurance of peace or pardon; and Attila was considered by his subjects as a just and indulgent master. He delighted in war; but, after he had ascended the throne in a mature age, his head, rather than his hand, achieved the conquest of the North; and the fame of an adventurous soldier was usefully exchanged for that of a prudent and successful general. The effects of personal valour are so inconsiderable, except in poetry or romance, that victory, even among Barbarians, must depend on the degree of skill with which the passions of the multitude are combined and guided for the service of a single man. The Scythian conquerors, Attila and Zingis,* surpassed their rude countrymen in art rather than in courage; and it may be observed that the monarchies, both of the Huns and of the Moguls, were erected by their founders on the basis of popular superstition. The miraculous conception, which fraud and credulity ascribed to the virgin-mother of Zingis, raised him above the level of human nature; and the naked prophet, who, in the name of the Deity, invested him with the empire of the earth, pointed the valour of the Moguls with irresistible enthusiasm.[7] The religious arts of Attila were not less skilfully adapted to the character of his age and country. It was natural enough that the Scythians should adore, with peculiar devotion, the god of war; but, as they were incapable of forming either an abstract idea or a corporeal representation, they worshipped their tutelar deity under the symbol of an iron scimitar.[8] one of the shepherds of the Huns perceived that a heifer, who was grazing, had wounded herself in the foot, and curiously followed the track of the blood, till he discovered, among the long grass, the point of an ancient sword, which he dug out of the ground and presented to Attila. That magnanimous, or rather that artful, prince accepted, with pious gratitude, this celestial favour; and, as the rightful possessor of the *sword of Mars*, asserted his divine and indefeasible claim to the dominion of the earth.[9] If the rites of Scythia were practised on this solemn occasion, a lofty altar, or rather pile of faggots, three hundred yards in length and in breadth, was raised in a spacious plain; and the sword of Mars was placed erect on the summit of this rustic altar, which was annually consecrated by the blood of sheep, horses, and of the hundredth captive.[10] Whether human sacrifices formed any part of the worship of Attila, or whether he propitiated the god of war with the victims which he continually offered in the field of battle, the favourite of Mars soon acquired a sacred character, which rendered his conquests more easy, and more permanent; and the Barbarian princes confessed, in the language of devotion and flattery, that they could not presume to gaze, with a steady eye, on the divine majesty of the king of the Huns.[11] His brother Bleda, who reigned over a considerable part of the nation,

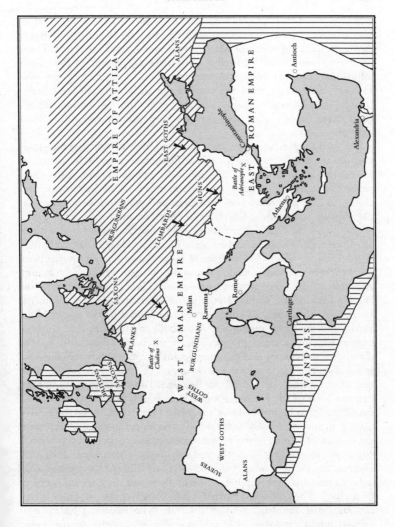

The Roman and Hun empires, AD *c.*450

was compelled to resign his sceptre and his life. Yet even this cruel act was attributed to a supernatural impulse; and the vigour with which Attila wielded the sword of Mars convinced the world that it had been reserved alone for his invincible arm.[12] But the extent of his empire affords the only remaining evidence of the number and importance of his victories; and the Scythian monarch, however ignorant of the value of science and philosophy, might, perhaps, lament that his illiterate subjects were destitute of the art which could perpetuate the memory of his exploits.

If a line of separation were drawn between the civilised and the savage climates of the globe; between the inhabitants of cities, who cultivated the earth, and the hunters and shepherds, who dwelt in tents; Attila might aspire to the title of supreme and sole monarch of the Barbarians.[13] He alone, among the conquerors of ancient and modern times, united the two mighty kingdoms of Germany and Scythia; and those vague appellations, when they are applied to his reign, may be understood with an ample latitude. Thuringia, which stretched beyond its actual limits as far as the Danube, was in the number of his provinces; he interposed, with the weight of a powerful neighbour, in the domestic affairs of the Franks; and one of his lieutenants chastised, and almost exterminated, the Burgundians of the Rhine. He subdued the islands of the ocean, the kingdoms of Scandinavia, encompassed and divided by the waters of the Baltic; and the Huns might derive a tribute of furs from that northern region which has been protected from all other conquerors by the severity of the climate and the courage of the natives. Towards the East, it is difficult to circumscribe the dominion of Attila over the Scythian deserts; yet we may be assured that he reigned on the banks of the Volga; that the king of the Huns was dreaded, not only as a warrior, but as a magician;[14] that he insulted and vanquished the Khan of the formidable Geougen; and that he sent ambassadors to negotiate an equal alliance with the empire of China. In the proud review of the nations who acknowledged the sovereignty of Attila, and who never entertained, during his lifetime, the thought of a revolt, the Gepidae* and the Ostrogoths were distinguished by their numbers, their bravery, and the personal merit of their chiefs. The renowned Ardaric, king of the Gepidae, was the faithful and sagacious counsellor of the monarch, who esteemed his intrepid genius, whilst he loved the mild and discreet virtues of the noble Walamir, king of the Ostrogoths. The crowd of vulgar kings, the leaders of so many martial tribes, who served under the standard of Attila, were ranged in the submissive order of guards and domestics, round the person of their master. They watched his nod; they trembled at his frown; and, at the first signal of his will, they executed, without murmur or hesitation, his stern and absolute commands. In time of peace, the dependent princes, with their national troops, attended the royal camp in regular succession; but, when Attila collected his military force, he was able to bring into the field an army of five, or according to another account of seven, hundred thousand Barbarians.[15]

The ambassadors of the Huns might awaken the attention of Theodosius, by reminding him that they were his neighbours both in Europe and Asia; since they touched the Danube on one hand, and reached, with the other, as far as the Tanais.* In the reign of his father Arcadius, a band of adventurous Huns had ravaged the provinces of the East; from whence they brought away rich spoils and innumerable captives.[16] They advanced, by a secret path, along the shores of the Caspian sea; traversed the snowy mountains of Armenia; passed the Tigris, the Euphrates, and the Halys;† recruited their weary cavalry with the generous‡ breed of Cappadocian horses; occupied the hilly country of Cilicia; and disturbed the festal songs and dances of the citizens of Antioch. Egypt trembled at their approach; and the monks and pilgrims of the Holy Land prepared to escape their fury by a speedy embarkation. The memory of this invasion was still recent in the minds of the Orientals. The subjects of Attila might execute, with superior forces, the design which these adventurers had so boldly attempted; and it soon became the subject of anxious conjecture, whether the tempest would fall on the dominions of Rome or of Persia. Some of the great vassals of the king of the Huns, who were themselves in the rank of powerful princes, had been sent to ratify an alliance and society of arms with the emperor, or rather with the general, of the West. They related, during their residence at Rome, the circumstances of an expedition which they had lately made into the East. After passing a desert and a morass, supposed by the Romans to be the Lake Maeotis,§ they penetrated through the mountains, and arrived, at the end of fifteen days' march, on the confines of Media; where they advanced as far as the unknown cities of Basic and Cursic. They encountered the Persian army in the plains of Media; and the air, according to their own expression, was darkened by a cloud of arrows. But the Huns were obliged to retire, before the numbers of the enemy. Their laborious retreat was effected by a different road; they lost the greatest part of their booty; and at length returned to the royal camp, with some knowledge of the country, and an impatient desire of revenge. In the free conversation of the Imperial ambassadors, who discussed, at the court of Attila, the character and designs of their formidable enemy, the ministers of Constantinople expressed their hope that his strength might be diverted and employed in a long and doubtful contest with the princes of the house of Sassan. The more sagacious Italians admonished their Eastern brethren of the folly and danger of such a hope, and convinced them that the Medes and Persians were incapable of resisting the arms of the Huns, and that the easy and important acquisition would exalt the pride, as well as power, of the conqueror. Instead of contenting himself with a moderate contribution, and a military title which equalled him only to the generals of Theodosius, Attila would proceed to impose a disgraceful and intolerable yoke on the necks of the prostrate and captive Romans, who would then be encompassed, on all sides, by the empire of the Huns.[17]

While the powers of Europe and Asia were solicitous to avert the impending danger, the alliance of Attila maintained the Vandals in the possession of Africa. An enterprise had been concerted between the courts of Ravenna and Constantinople, for the recovery of that valuable province; and the ports of Sicily were already filled with the military and naval forces of Theodosius. But the subtle Genseric, who spread his negotiations round the world, prevented their designs by exciting the king of the Huns to invade the Eastern empire; and a trifling incident soon became the motive, or pretence, of a destructive war.[18] Under the faith of the treaty of Margus, a free market was held on the northern side of the Danube, which was protected by a Roman fortress surnamed Constantia. A troop of Barbarians violated the commercial security, killed, or dispersed, the unsuspecting traders, and levelled the fortress with the ground. The Huns justified this outrage as an act of reprisal; alleged that the bishop of Margus had entered their territories, to discover and steal a secret treasure of their kings; and sternly demanded the guilty prelate, the sacrilegious spoil, and the fugitive subjects, who had escaped from the justice of Attila. The refusal of the Byzantine court was the signal of war; and the Maesians at first applauded the generous firmness of their sovereign. But they were soon intimidated by the destruction of Viminacium and the adjacent towns; and the people were persuaded to adopt the convenient maxim that a private citizen, however innocent or respectable, may be justly sacrificed to the safety of his country. The bishop of Margus, who did not possess the spirit of a martyr, resolved to prevent the designs which he suspected. He boldly treated with the princes of the Huns; secured, by solemn oaths, his pardon and reward; posted a numerous detachment of Barbarians, in silent ambush, on the banks of the Danube; and at the appointed hour opened, with his own hand, the gates of his episcopal city. This advantage, which had been obtained by treachery, served as a prelude to more honourable and decisive victories. The Illyrian frontier was covered by a line of castles and fortresses; and, though the greatest part of them consisted only of a single tower, with a small garrison, they were commonly sufficient to repel, or to intercept, the inroads of an enemy who was ignorant of the art, and impatient of the delay, of a regular siege. But these slight obstacles were instantly swept away by the inundation of the Huns.[19] They destroyed, with fire and sword, the populous cities of Sirmium and Singidunum, of Ratiaria and Marcianopolis, of Naissus and Sardica; where every circumstance, in the discipline of the people and the construction of the buildings, had been gradually adapted to the sole purpose of defence. The whole breadth of Europe, as it extends above five hundred miles from the Euxine to the Hadriatic, was at once invaded, and occupied, and desolated, by the myriads of Barbarians whom Attila led into the field. The public danger and distress could not, however, provoke Theodosius to interrupt his amusements and devotion, or to appear in person at the head of the Roman legions. But the troops which had been sent against Genseric were hastily recalled from Sicily; the garrisons on the side of Persia were exhausted; and a military force was collected in Europe, formidable by their arms and numbers, if the generals had understood the science of command, and their soldiers the duty of obedience. The armies of the Eastern empire were vanquished in three successive engagements; and the progress of Attila may be traced by the fields of battle. The two former, on the banks of the Utus, and under the walls of Marcianopolis, were fought in the extensive plains between the Danube and Mount Haemus. As the Romans were pressed by a victorious enemy, they gradually, and unskilfully, retired towards the Chersonesus of Thrace; and that narrow peninsula, the last extremity of the land, was marked by their third, and irreparable, defeat. By the destruction of this army, Attila required the indisputable possession of the field. From the Hellespont to Thermopylae and the suburbs of Constantinople, he ravaged, without resistance, and without mercy, the provinces of Thrace and Macedonia. Heraclea and Hadrianople might, perhaps, escape this dreadful irruption of the Huns; but the words the most expressive of total extirpation and erasure are applied to the calamities which they inflicted on seventy cities of the Eastern empire.[20] Theodosius, his court, and the unwarlike people, were protected by the walls of Constantinople; but those walls had been shaken by a recent earthquake, and the fall of fifty-eight towers had opened a large and tremendous breach. The damage indeed was speedily repaired; but this accident was aggravated by a superstitious fear that Heaven itself had delivered the Imperial city to the shepherds of Scythia, who were strangers to the laws, the language, and the religion, of the Romans.[21]

In all their invasions of the civilised empires of the South, the Scythian shepherds have been uniformly actuated by a savage and destructive spirit. The laws of war, that restrain the exercise of national rapine and murder, are founded on two principles of substantial interest: the knowledge of the permanent benefits which may be obtained by a moderate use of conquest; and a just apprehension lest the desolation which we inflict on the enemy's country may be retaliated on our own. But these considerations of hope and fear are almost unknown in the pastoral state of nations. The Huns of Attila may, without injustice, be compared to the Moguls and Tartars, before their primitive manners were changed by religion and luxury; and the evidence of Oriental history may reflect some light on the short and imperfect annals of Rome. After the Moguls had subdued the northern provinces of China, it was seriously proposed, not in the hour of victory and passion, but in calm deliberate council, to exterminate all the inhabitants of that populous country, that the vacant land might be converted to the pasture of cattle. The firmness of a Chinese mandarin,[22] who insinuated some principles of rational policy into the mind of Zingis, diverted him from the execution of this horrid design. But in the cities of Asia, which yielded to the Moguls, the inhuman abuse of the rights of war was exercised, with a regular form of discipline, which may, with equal reason, though not with equal authority, be imputed to the victorious Huns. The inhabitants, who had submitted to their discretion, were ordered to evacuate their houses, and to assemble in some plain adjacent to the city; where a division was made of the vanquished into three parts. The first class consisted of the soldiers of the garrison, and of the young men capable of bearing arms; and their fate was instantly decided: they were either enlisted among the Moguls, or they were massacred on the spot by the troops, who, with pointed spears and bended bows, had formed a circle round the captive multitude. The second class, composed of the young and beautiful women, of the artificers of every rank and profession, and of the more wealthy or honourable citizens, from whom a private ransom might be expected, was distributed in equal or proportionable lots. The remainder, whose life or death was alike useless to the conquerors, were permitted to return to the city; which, in the meanwhile, had been stripped of its valuable furniture; and a tax was imposed on those wretched inhabitants for the indulgence of breathing their native air. Such was the behaviour of the Moguls, when they were not conscious of any extraordinary rigour.[23] But the most casual provocation, the slightest motive of caprice or convenience, often provoked them to involve a whole people in an indiscriminate massacre; and the ruin of some flourishing cities was executed with such unrelenting perseverance that, according to their own expression, horses might run, without stumbling, over the ground where they had once stood. The three great capitals of Khorasan, Maru, Neisabour, and Herat, were destroyed by the armies of Zingis; and the exact account which was taken of the slain amounted to four millions three hundred and forty-seven thousand persons.[24] Timur, or Tamerlane, was educated in a less barbarous age, and in the profession of the Mahometan religion; yet, if Attila equalled the hostile ravages of Tamerlane,[25] either the Tartar or the Hun might deserve the epithet of the Scourge of God.[26]

It may be affirmed, with bolder assurance, that the Huns depopulated the provinces of the empire, by the number of Roman subjects whom they led away into captivity. In the hands of a wise legislator, such an industrious colony might have contributed to diffuse, through the deserts of Scythia, the rudiments of the useful and ornamental arts; but these captives, who had been taken in war, were accidentally dispersed among the hordes that obeyed the empire of Attila. The estimate of their respective value was formed by the simple judgment of unenlightened and unprejudiced Barbarians. Perhaps they might not understand the merit of a theologian, profoundly skilled in the controversies of the Trinity and the Incarnation; yet they respected the ministers of every religion; and the active zeal of the Christian missionaries, without approaching the person or the palace of the monarch, successfully laboured in the propagation of the gospel.[27] The pastoral tribes, who were ignorant of the distinction of landed property, must have disregarded the use, as well as the abuse, of civil jurisprudence; and the skill of an eloquent lawyer could excite only their contempt, or their abhorrence.[28] The perpetual intercourse of the Huns and the Goths had communicated the familiar knowledge of the two national dialects; and the Barbarians were ambitious of conversing in Latin, the military idiom even of the Eastern empire.[29] But they disdained the language, and the sciences, of the Greeks; and the vain sophist, or grave philosopher, who had enjoyed the flattering applause of the schools, was mortified to find that his robust servant was a captive of more value and importance than himself. The mechanic arts were encouraged and esteemed, as they tended to satisfy the wants of the Huns. An architect, in the service of Onegesius, one of the favourites of Attila, was employed to construct a bath; but this work was a rare example of private luxury; and the trades of the smith, the carpenter, the armourer, were much more adapted to supply a wandering people with the useful instruments of peace and war. But the merit of the physician was received with universal favour and respect; the Barbarians, who despised death, might be apprehensive of disease; and the haughty conqueror trembled in the presence of a captive, to whom he ascribed, perhaps, an imaginary power of prolonging, or preserving, his life.[30] The Huns might be provoked to insult the misery of their slaves, over whom they exercised a despotic command;[31] but their manners were not susceptible of a refined system of oppression; and the efforts of courage and diligence were often recompensed by the gift of freedom. The historian Priscus, whose embassy is a course of curious instruction, was accosted, in the camp of Attila, by a stranger, who saluted him in the Greek language, but whose dress and figure displayed the appearance of a wealthy Scythian. In the siege of Viminacium, he had lost, according to his own account, his fortune and liberty; he became the slave of Onegesius; but his faithful services, against the Romans and the Acatzires, had gradually raised him to the rank of the native Huns; to whom he was attached by the domestic pledges of a new wife and several children. The spoils of war had restored and improved his private property; he was admitted to the table of his former lord; and the apostate Greek blessed the hour of his captivity, since it had been the introduction to an happy and independent state; which he held by the honourable tenure of military service. This reflection naturally produced a dispute on the advantages, and defects, of the Roman government, which was severely arraigned by the apostate, and defended by Priscus in a prolix and feeble declamation. The freedman of Onegesius exposed, in true and lively colours, the vices of a declining empire, of which he had so long been the victim; the cruel absurdity of the Roman princes, unable to protect their subjects against the public enemy, unwilling to trust them with arms for their own defence; the intolerable weight of taxes, rendered still more oppressive by the intricate or arbitrary modes of collection; the obscurity of numerous and contradictory laws; the tedious and expensive forms of judicial proceedings; the partial administration of justice; and the universal corruption, which increased the influence of the rich, and aggravated the misfortunes of the poor. A sentiment of patriotic sympathy was at length revived in the breast of the fortunate exile; and he lamented, with a flood of tears, the guilt or weakness of those magistrates who had perverted the wisest and most salutary institutions.[32]

The timid, or selfish, policy of the Western Romans had abandoned the Eastern empire to the Huns.[33] The loss of armies, and the want of discipline or virtue, were not supplied by the personal character of the monarch. Theodosius might still affect the style, as well as the title, of *Invincible Augustus*; but he was reduced to solicit the clemency of Attila, who imperiously dictated these harsh and humiliating conditions of peace. I. The emperor of the East resigned, by an express or tacit convention, an extensive and important territory, which stretched along the southern banks of the Danube, from Singidunum, or Belgrade, as far as Novae, in the diocese of Thrace. The breadth was defined by the vague computation of fifteen days' journey; but, from the proposal of Attila to remove the situation of the national market, it soon appeared that he comprehended the ruined city of Naissus within the limits of his dominions. II. The king of the Huns required and obtained, that his tribute or subsidy should be augmented from seven hundred pounds of gold to the annual sum of two thousand one hundred; and he stipulated the immediate payment of six thousand pounds of gold to defray the expenses, or to expiate the guilt, of the war. One might imagine that such a demand, which scarcely equalled the measure of private wealth, would have been readily discharged by the opulent empire of the East; and the public distress affords a remarkable proof of the impoverished, or at least of the disorderly, state of the finances. A large proportion of the taxes, extorted from the people, was detained and intercepted in their passage, through the foulest channels, to the treasury of Constantinople. The revenue was dissipated by Theodosius and his favourites in wasteful and profuse luxury; which was disguised by the names of Imperial magnificence or Christian charity. The immediate supplies had been exhausted by the unforeseen necessity of military preparations. A personal contribution, rigorously, but capriciously, imposed on the members of the senatorian order, was the only expedient that could disarm, without loss of time, the impatient avarice of Attila; but the poverty of the nobles compelled them to adopt the scandalous resource of exposing to public auction the jewels of their wives and the hereditary ornaments of their palaces.[34] III. The king of the Huns appears to have established, as a principle of national jurisprudence, that he could never lose the property which he had once acquired in the persons who had yielded either a voluntary or reluctant submission to his authority. From this principle he concluded, and the conclusions of Attila were irrevocable laws, that the Huns who had been taken prisoners in war should be released without delay and without ransom; that every Roman captive who had presumed to escape should purchase his right to freedom at the price of twelve pieces of gold; and that all the Barbarians who had deserted the standard of Attila should be restored, without any promise, or stipulation, of pardon. In the execution of this cruel and ignominious treaty, the Imperial officers were forced to massacre several loyal and noble deserters, who refused to devote themselves to certain death; and the Romans forfeited all reasonable claims to the friendship of any Scythian people, by this public confession that they were destitute either of faith or power to protect the suppliants who had embraced the throne of Theodosius.[35]

The firmness of a single town, so obscure that, except on this occasion, it has never been mentioned by any historian or geographer, exposed the disgrace of the emperor and empire. Azimus, or Azimuntium, a small city of Thrace on the Illyrian borders,[36] had been distinguished by the martial spirit of its youth, the skill and reputation of the leaders whom they had chosen, and their daring exploits against the innumerable host of the Barbarians. Instead of tamely expecting their approach, the Azimuntines attacked, in frequent and successful sallies, the troops of the Huns, who gradually declined the dangerous neighbourhood; rescued from their hands the spoil and the captives; and recruited their domestic force by the voluntary association of fugitives and deserters. After the conclusion of the treaty, Attila still menaced the empire with implacable war, unless the Azimuntines were persuaded, or compelled, to comply with the conditions which their sovereign had accepted. The ministers of Theodosius confessed with shame, and with truth, that they no longer possessed any authority over a society of men, who so bravely asserted their natural independence; and the king of the Huns condescended to negotiate an equal exchange with the citizens of Azimus. They demanded the restitution of some shepherds, who, with their cattle, had been accidentally surprised. A strict, though fruitless, inquiry was allowed; but the Huns were obliged to swear that they did not detain any prisoners belonging to the city, before they could recover two surviving countrymen, whom the Azimuntines had reserved as pledges for the safety of their lost companions. Attila, on his side, was satisfied, and deceived, by their solemn asseveration that the rest of the captives had been put to the sword; and that it was their constant practice immediately to dismiss the Romans and the deserters, who had obtained the security of the public faith. This prudent and officious dissimulation may be condemned or excused by the casuists, as they incline to the rigid decree of St Augustine or to the milder sentiment of St Jerome and St Chrysostom; but every soldier, every statesman, must acknowledge that, if the race of the Azimuntines had been encouraged and multiplied, the Barbarians would have ceased to trample on the majesty of the empire.[37]

It would have been strange, indeed, if Theodosius had purchased, by the loss of honour, a secure and solid tranquillity; or if his tameness had not invited the repetition of injuries. The Byzantine court was insulted by five or six successive embassies;[38] and the ministers of Attila were uniformly instructed to press the tardy or imperfect execution of the last treaty; to produce the names of fugitives and deserters, who were still protected by the empire; and to declare, with seeming moderation, that, unless their sovereign obtained complete and immediate satisfaction, it would be impossible for him, were it even his wish, to check the resentment of his warlike tribes. Besides the motives of pride and interest which might prompt the king of the Huns to continue this train of negotiation, he was influenced by the less honourable view of enriching his favourites at the expense of his enemies. The Imperial treasury was exhausted, to procure the friendly offices of the ambassadors and their principal attendants, whose favourable report might conduce to the maintenance of peace. The Barbarian monarch was flattered by the liberal reception of his ministers; he computed with pleasure the value and splendour of their gifts, rigorously exacted the performance of every promise which would contribute to their private emolument, and treated as an important business of state the marriage of his secretary Constantius.[39] That Gallic adventurer, who was recommended by Aetius to the king of the Huns, had engaged his service to the ministers of Constantinople, for the stipulated reward of a wealthy and noble wife; and the daughter of count Saturninus was chosen to discharge the obligations of her country. The reluctance of the victim, some domestic troubles, and the unjust confiscation of her fortune, cooled the ardour of her interested* lover; but he still demanded, in the name of Attila, an equivalent alliance; and, after many ambiguous delays and excuses, the Byzantine court was compelled to sacrifice to this insolent stranger the widow of Armatius, whose birth, opulence, and beauty placed her in the most illustrious rank of the Roman matrons. For these importunate and oppressive embassies, Attila claimed a suitable return; he weighed, with suspicious pride, the character and station of the Imperial envoys; but he condescended to promise that he would advance as far as Sardica, to receive any ministers who had been invested with the consular dignity. The council of Theodosius eluded this proposal by representing the desolate and ruined condition of Sardica; and even ventured to insinuate that every officer of the army or household was qualified to treat with the most powerful princes of Scythia. Maximin,[40] a respectable courtier, whose abilities had been long exercised in civil and military employments, accepted with reluctance the troublesome, and, perhaps, dangerous commission of reconciling the angry spirit of the king of the Huns. His friend, the historian Priscus,[41] embraced the opportunity of observing the Barbarian hero in the peaceful and domestic scenes of life; but the secret of the embassy, a fatal and guilty secret,* was entrusted only to the interpreter Vigilius. The two last ambassadors of the Huns, Orestes, a noble subject of the Pannonian province, and Edecon, a valiant chieftain of the tribe of the Scyri, returned at the same time from Constantinople to the royal camp. Their obscure names were afterwards illustrated by the extraordinary fortune and the contrast of their sons; the two servants of Attila became the fathers of the last Roman emperor of the West[†] and of the first Barbarian king of Italy.[‡]

The ambassadors, who were followed by a numerous train of men and horses, made their first halt at Sardica, at the distance of three hundred and fifty miles, or thirteen days' journey, from Constantinople. As the remains of Sardica were still included within the limits of the empire, it was incumbent on the Romans to exercise the duties of hospitality. They provided, with the assistance of the provincials, a sufficient number of sheep and oxen; and invited the Huns to a splendid, or at least a plentiful, supper. But the harmony of the entertainment was soon disturbed by mutual prejudice and indiscretion. The greatness of the emperor and the empire was warmly maintained by their ministers; the Huns, with equal ardour, asserted the superiority of their victorious monarch: the dispute was inflamed by the rash and unseasonable flattery of Vigilius, who passionately rejected the comparison of a mere mortal with the divine Theodosius; and it was with extreme difficulty that Maximin and Priscus were able to divert the conversation, or to soothe the angry minds of the Barbarians. When they rose from table, the Imperial ambassador presented Edecon and Orestes with rich gifts of silk robes and Indian pearls, which they thankfully accepted. Yet Orestes could not forbear insinuating that *he* had not always been treated with such respect and liberality; the offensive distinction which was implied between his civil office and the hereditary rank of his colleague seems to have made Edecon a doubtful friend, and Orestes an irreconcilable enemy. After this entertainment, they travelled about one hundred miles from Sardica to Naissus. That flourishing city, which had given birth to the great Constantine, was levelled with the ground; the inhabitants were destroyed or dispersed; and the appearance of some sick persons, who were still permitted to exist among the ruins of the churches, served only to increase the horror of the prospect. The surface of the country was covered with the bones of the slain; and the ambassadors, who directed their course to the northwest, were obliged to pass the hills of modern Servia, before they descended into the flat and marshy grounds which are terminated by the Danube. The Huns were masters of the great river; their navigation was performed in large canoes, hollowed out of the trunk of a single tree; the ministers of Theodosius were safely landed on the opposite bank; and their Barbarian associates immediately hastened to the camp of Attila, which was equally prepared for the amusements of hunting or of war. No sooner had Maximin advanced about two miles from the Danube, than he began to experience the fastidious insolence of the conqueror. He was sternly forbid to pitch his tents in a pleasant valley, lest he should infringe the distant awe that was due to the royal mansion. The ministers of Attila pressed him to communicate the business and the instructions, which he reserved for the ear of their sovereign. When Maximin temperately urged the contrary practice of nations, he was still more confounded to find that the resolutions of the Sacred Consistory, those secrets (says Priscus) which should not be revealed to the gods themselves, had been treacherously disclosed to the public enemy. On his refusal to comply with such ignominious terms, the Imperial envoy was commanded instantly to depart; the order was recalled; it was again repeated; and the Huns renewed their ineffectual attempts to subdue the patient firmness of Maximin. At length, by the intercession of Scotta, the brother of Onegesius, whose friendship had been purchased by a liberal gift, he was admitted to the royal presence: but, instead of obtaining a decisive answer, he was compelled to undertake a remote journey towards the North, that Attila might enjoy the proud satisfaction of receiving, in the same camp, the ambassadors of the Eastern and Western empires. His journey was regulated by the guides, who obliged him to halt, to hasten his march, or to deviate from the common road, as it best suited the convenience of the King. The Romans who traversed the plains of Hungary suppose that they passed *several* navigable rivers, either in canoes or portable boats; but there is reason to suspect that the winding stream of the Theiss, or Tibiscus, might present itself in different places, under different names. From the contiguous villages they received a plentiful and regular supply of provisions; mead instead of wine, millet in the place of bread, and a certain liquor named *camus*, which, according to the report of Priscus, was distilled from barley.[42] Such fare might appear coarse and indelicate to men who had tasted the luxury of Constantinople; but, in their accidental distress, they were relieved by the gentleness and hospitality of the same Barbarians, so terrible and so merciless in war. The ambassadors had encamped on the edge of a large morass. A violent tempest of wind and rain, of thunder and lightning, overturned their tents, immersed their baggage and furniture in the water, and scattered their retinue, who wandered in the darkness of the night, uncertain of their road, and apprehensive of some unknown danger, till they awakened by their cries the inhabitants of a neighbouring village, the property of the widow of Bleda.* A bright illumination, and, in a few moments, a comfortable fire of reeds, was kindled by their officious benevolence; the wants, and even the desires, of the Romans were liberally satisfied; and they seem to have been embarrassed by the singular politeness of Bleda's widow, who added to her other favours the gift, or at least the loan, of a sufficient number of beautiful and obsequious damsels. The sunshine of the succeeding day was dedicated to repose; to collect and dry the baggage, and to the refreshment of the men and horses; but, in the evening, before they pursued their journey, the ambassadors expressed their gratitude to the bounteous lady of the village, by a very acceptable present of silver cups, red fleeces, dried fruits, and Indian pepper. Soon after this adventure, they rejoined the march of Attila, from whom they had been separated about six days; and slowly proceeded to the capital of an empire which did not contain, in the space of several thousand miles, a single city.

As far as we may ascertain the vague and obscure geography of Priscus, this capital appears to have been seated between the Danube, the Theiss, and the Carpathian hills, in the plains of Upper Hungary, and most probably in the neighbourhood of Jazberin, Agria, or Tokay.[43] In its origin it could be no more than an accidental camp, which, by the long and frequent residence of Attila, had insensibly swelled into a huge village, for the reception of his court, of the troops who followed his person, and of the various multitude of idle or industrious slaves and retainers.[44] The baths, constructed by Onegesius, were the only edifice of stone; the materials had been transported from Pannonia; and, since the adjacent country was destitute even of large timber, it may be presumed that the meaner habitations of the royal village consisted of straw, of mud, or of canvas. The wooden houses of the more illustrious Huns were built and adorned with rude magnificence, according to the rank, the fortune, or the taste of the proprietors. They seem to have been distributed with some degree of order and symmetry; and each spot became more honourable, as it approached the person of the sovereign. The palace of Attila, which surpassed all other houses in his dominions, was built entirely of wood, and covered an ample space of ground. The outward enclosure was a lofty wall, or palisade of smooth square timber, intersected with high towers, but intended rather for ornament than defence. This wall, which seems to have encircled the declivity of a hill, comprehended a great variety of wooden edifices, adapted to the uses of royalty. A separate house was assigned to each of the numerous wives of Attila; and, instead of the rigid and illiberal confinement imposed by Asiatic jealousy, they politely admitted the Roman ambassadors to their presence, their table, and even to the freedom of an innocent embrace. When Maximin offered his presents to Cerca, the principal queen, he admired the singular architecture of her mansion, the height of the round columns, the size and beauty of the wood, which was curiously shaped, or turned, or polished, or carved; and his attentive eye was able to discover some taste in the ornaments, and some regularity in the proportions. After passing through the guards who watched before the gate, the ambassadors were introduced into the private apartment of Cerca. The wife of Attila received their visit sitting, or rather lying, on a soft couch; the floor was covered with a carpet; the domestics formed a circle round the queen; and her damsels, seated on the ground, were employed in working the variegated embroidery which adorned the dress of the Barbaric warriors. The Huns were ambitious of displaying those riches which were the fruit and evidence of their victories: the trappings of their horses, their swords, and even their shoes, were studded with gold and precious stones; and their tables were profusely spread with plates, and goblets, and vases of gold and silver, which had been fashioned by the labour of Grecian artists. The monarch alone assumed the superior pride of still adhering to the simplicity of his Scythian ancestors.[45] The dress of Attila, his arms, and the furniture of his horse were plain, without ornament, and of a single colour. The royal table was served in wooden cups and platters; flesh was his only food; and the conqueror of the North never tasted the luxury of bread.

When Attila first gave audience to the Roman ambassadors on the banks of the Danube, his tent was encompassed with a formidable guard. The monarch himself was seated in a wooden chair. His stern countenance, angry gestures, and impatient tone astonished the firmness of Maximin; but Vigilius had more reason to tremble, since he distinctly understood the menace that, if Attila did not respect the law of nations, he would nail the deceitful interpreter to a cross and leave his body to the vultures. The Barbarian condescended, by producing an accurate list, to expose the bold falsehood of Vigilius, who had affirmed that no more than seventeen deserters could be found. But he arrogantly declared that he apprehended only the disgrace of contending with his fugitive slaves; since he despised their impotent efforts to defend the provinces which Theodosius had entrusted to their arms: 'For what fortress' (added Attila), 'what city, in the wide extent of the Roman Empire, can hope to exist, secure and impregnable, if it is our pleasure that it should be erased from the earth?' He dismissed, however, the interpreter, who returned to Constantinople with his peremptory demand of more complete restitution and a more splendid embassy. His anger gradually subsided, and his domestic satisfaction in a marriage which he celebrated on the road with the daughter of Eslam might perhaps contribute to mollify the native fierceness of his temper. The entrance of Attila into the royal village was marked by a very singular ceremony. A numerous troop of women came out to meet their hero, and their king. They marched before him, distributed into long and regular files; the intervals between the files were filled by white veils of thin linen, which the women on either side bore aloft in their hands, and which formed a canopy for a chorus of young virgins, who chanted hymns and songs in the Scythian language. The wife of his favourite Onegesius, with a train of female attendants, saluted Attila at the door of her own house, on his way to the palace; and offered, according to the custom of the country, her respectful homage, by entreating him to taste the wine and meat which she had prepared for his reception. As soon as the monarch had graciously accepted her hospitable gift, his domestics lifted a small silver table to a convenient height, as he sat on horseback; and Attila, when he had touched the goblet with his lips, again saluted the wife of Onegesius, and continued his march. During his residence at the seat of empire, his hours were not wasted in the recluse idleness of a seraglio; and the king of the Huns could maintain his superior dignity, without concealing his person from the public view. He frequently assembled his council, and gave audience to the ambassadors of the nations; and his people might appeal to the supreme tribunal, which he held at stated times, and, according to the eastern custom, before the principal gate of his wooden palace. The Romans, both of the East and of the West, were twice invited to the banquets, where Attila feasted with the princes and nobles of Scythia. Maximin and his colleagues were stopped on the threshold, till they had made a devout libation to the health and prosperity of the king of the Huns; and were conducted, after this ceremony, to their respective seats in a spacious hall. The royal table and couch, covered with carpets and fine linen, was raised by several steps in the midst of the hall; and a son, an uncle, or perhaps a favourite king, were admitted to share the simple and homely repast of Attila. Two lines of small tables, each of which contained three or four guests, were ranged in order on either hand; the right was esteemed the most honourable, but the Romans ingenuously confess that they were placed on the left; and that Beric, an unknown chieftain, most probably of the Gothic race, preceded the representatives of Theodosius and Valentinian. The Barbarian monarch received from his cup-bearer a goblet filled with wine, and courteously drank to the health of the most distinguished guest, who rose from his seat and expressed, in the same manner, his loyal and respectful vows. This ceremony was successively performed for all, or at least for the illustrious persons of the assembly; and a considerable time must have been consumed, since it was thrice repeated, as each course or service was placed on the table. But the wine still remained after the meat had been removed; and the Huns continued to indulge their intemperance long after the sober and decent ambassadors of the two empires had withdrawn themselves from the nocturnal banquet. Yet before they retired, they enjoyed a singular opportunity of observing the manners of the nation in their convivial amusements. Two Scythians stood before the couch of Attila, and recited the verses which they had composed, to celebrate his valour and his victories. A profound silence prevailed in the hall; and the attention of the guests was captivated by the vocal harmony, which revived and perpetuated the memory of their own exploits: a martial ardour flashed from the eyes of the warriors, who were impatient for battle; and the tears of the old men expressed their generous despair that they could no longer partake the danger and glory of the field.[46] This entertainment, which might be considered as a school of military virtue, was succeeded by a farce that debased the dignity of human nature. A

Moorish and a Scythian buffoon successively excited the mirth of the rude spectators, by their deformed figure, ridiculous dress, antic gestures, absurd speeches, and the strange unintelligible confusion of the Latin, the Gothic, and the Hunnic languages; and the hall resounded with loud and licentious peals of laughter In the midst of this intemperate riot, Attila alone, without a change of countenance, maintained his steadfast and inflexible gravity; which was never relaxed, except on the entrance of Irnac, the youngest of his sons: he embraced the boy with a smile of paternal tenderness, gently pinched him by the cheek, and betrayed a partial affection, which was justified by the assurance of his prophets that Irnac would be the future support of his family and empire. Two days afterwards, the ambassadors received a second invitation; and they had reason to praise the politeness as well as the hospitality of Attila. The king of the Huns held a long and familiar conversation with Maximin; but his civility was interrupted by rude expressions, and haughty reproaches; and he was provoked, by a motive of interest, to support, with unbecoming zeal, the private claims of his secretary Constantius. 'The emperor' (said Attila) 'has long promised him a rich wife; Constantius must not be disappointed; nor should a Roman emperor deserve the name of liar.' On the third day, the ambassadors were dismissed; the freedom of several captives was granted, for a moderate ransom, to their pressing entreaties; and, besides the royal presents, they were permitted to accept from each of the Scythian nobles the honourable and useful gift of a horse. Maximin returned, by the same road, to Constantinople and though he was involved in an accidental dispute with Beric, the new ambassador of Attila, he flattered himself that he had contributed, by the laborious journey, to confirm the peace and alliance of the two nations.[47]

But the Roman ambassador was ignorant of the treacherous design, which had been concealed under the mask of the public faith. The surprise and satisfaction of Edecon, when he contemplated the splendour of Constantinople, had encouraged the interpreter Vigilius to procure for him a secret interview with the eunuch Chrysaphius,[48] who governed the emperor and the empire. After some previous conversation, and a mutual oath of secrecy, the eunuch, who had not, from his own feelings or experience, imbibed any exalted notions of ministerial virtue, ventured to propose the death of Attila, as an important service, by which Edecon might deserve a liberal share of the wealth and luxury which he admired. The ambassador of the Huns listened to the tempting offer, and professed, with apparent zeal, his ability, as well as readiness, to execute the bloody deed; the design was communicated to the master of the offices, and the devout Theodosius consented to the assassination of his invincible enemy. But this perfidious conspiracy was defeated by the dissimulation, or the repentance, of Edecon; and, though he might exaggerate his inward abhorrence for the treason, which he seemed to approve, he dexterously assumed the merit of an early and voluntary confession. If we *now* review the embassy of Maximin, and the behaviour of Attila, we must applaud the Barbarian, who respected the laws of hospitality, and generously entertained and dismissed the minister of a prince who had conspired against his life. But the rashness of Vigilius will appear still more extraordinary, since he returned, conscious of his guilt and danger, to the royal camp; accompanied by his son, and carrying with him a weighty purse of gold, which the favourite eunuch had furnished, to satisfy the demands of Edecon, and to corrupt the fidelity of the guards. The interpreter was instantly seized, and dragged before the tribunal of Attila, where he asserted his innocence with specious firmness, till the threat of inflicting instant death on his son extorted from him a sincere discovery of the criminal transaction. Under the name of ransom or confiscation, the rapacious king of the Huns accepted two hundred pounds of gold for the life of the traitor, whom he disdained to punish. He pointed his just indignation against a nobler object. His ambassadors Eslaw and Orestes were immediately dispatched to Constantinople with a peremptory instruction, which it was much safer for them to execute than to disobey. They boldly entered the Imperial presence, with the fatal purse hanging down from the neck of Orestes; who interrogated the eunuch Chrysaphius, as he stood beside the throne, whether he recognised the evidence of his guilt. But the office of reproof was reserved for the superior dignity of his colleague Eslaw, who gravely addressed the Emperor of the East in the following words: 'Theodosius is the son of an illustrious and respectable parent; Attila likewise is descended from a noble race; and *he* has supported, by his actions, the dignity which he inherited from his father Mundzuk. But Theodosius has forfeited his paternal honours, and, by consenting to pay tribute, has degraded himself to the condition of a slave. It is therefore just that he should reverence the man whom fortune and merit have placed above him; instead of attempting, like a wicked slave, clandestinely to conspire against his master.' The son of Arcadius, who was accustomed only to the voice of flattery, heard with astonishment the severe language of truth; he blushed and trembled; nor did he presume directly to refuse the head of Chrysaphius, which Eslaw and Orestes were instructed to demand. A solemn embassy, armed with full powers and magnificent gifts, was hastily sent to deprecate the wrath of Attila; and his pride was gratified by the choice of Nomius and Anatolius, two ministers of consular or patrician rank, of whom the one was great treasurer, and the other was master-general of the armies of the East. He condescended to meet these ambassadors on the banks of the river Drenco; and, though he at first affected a stern and haughty demeanour, his anger was insensibly mollified by their eloquence and liberality. He condescended to pardon the emperor, the eunuch, and the interpreter; bound himself by an oath to observe the conditions of peace; to release a great number of captives; abandoned the fugitives and deserters to their fate; and resigned a large territory to the south of the

Danube, which he had already exhausted of its wealth and its inhabitants. But this treaty was purchased at an expense which might have supported a vigorous and successful war; and the subjects of Theodosius were compelled to redeem the safety of a worthless favourite by oppressive taxes, which they would more cheerfully have paid for his destruction.[49]

The emperor Theodosius did not long survive the most humiliating circumstance of an inglorious life. As he was riding, or hunting, in the neighbourhood of Constantinople, he was thrown from his horse into the river Lycus; the spine of the back was injured by the fall; and he expired some days afterwards, in the fiftieth year of his age, and the forty-third of his reign.[50] His sister Pulcheria, whose authority had been controlled both in civil and ecclesiastical affairs by the pernicious influence of the eunuchs, was unanimously proclaimed empress of the East; and the Romans, for the first time, submitted to a female reign. No sooner had Pulcheria ascended the throne than she indulged her own and the public resentment by an act of popular justice. Without any legal trial, the eunuch Chrysaphius was executed before the gates of the city; and the immense riches which had been accumulated by the rapacious favourite served only to hasten and to justify his punishment.[51] Amidst the general acclamations of the clergy and people, the empress did not forget the prejudice and disadvantage to which her sex was exposed; and she wisely resolved to prevent their murmurs by the choice of a colleague, who would always respect the superior rank and virgin chastity of his wife. She gave her hand to Marcian, a senator, about sixty years of age, and the nominal husband of Pulcheria was solemnly invested with the Imperial purple. The zeal which he displayed for the orthodox creed, as it was established by the council of Chalcedon, would alone have inspired the grateful eloquence of the Catholics. But the behaviour of Marcian in a private life, and afterwards on the throne, may support a more rational belief that he was qualified to restore and invigorate an empire which had been almost dissolved by the successive weakness of two hereditary monarchs. He was born in Thrace, and educated to the profession of arms; but Marcian's youth had been severely exercised by poverty and misfortune, since his only resource, when he first arrived at Constantinople, consisted in two hundred pieces of gold, which he had borrowed of a friend. He passed nineteen years in the domestic and military service of Aspar and his son Ardaburius; followed those powerful generals to the Persian and African wars; and obtained, by their influence, the honourable rank of tribune and senator. His mild disposition, and useful talents, without alarming the jealousy, recommended Marcian to the esteem and favour, of his patrons; he had seen, perhaps he had felt, the abuses of a venal and oppressive administration; and his own example gave weight and energy to the laws which he promulgated for the reformation of manners.[52]

1 The authentic materials for the history of Attila may be found in Jornandes (*de Rebus Geticis*, 34–50, 660–688, edit. Grot.) and Priscus (*Excerpta de Legationibus*, pp. 33–76, Paris, 1648). I have not seen the lives of Attila, composed by Juvencus Caelius Calanus Dalmatinus, in the twelfth century; or by Nicholas Olahus, archbishop of Gran, in the sixteenth. See Mascou's *History of the Germans*, ix, 23, and Maffei, *Osservazioni Litterarie*, i, 88–89. Whatever the modern Hungarians have added, must be fabulous; and they do not seem to have excelled in the art of fiction. They suppose that, when Attila invaded Gaul and Italy, married innumerable wives, etc. he was one hundred and twenty years of age. Thewrocz, *Chron.*, i, 22, in *Script. Hungar.*, i, 76.

* *page 624* [hastened]

2 Hungary has been successfully occupied by three Scythian colonies: 1. the Huns of Attila; 2. the Abares, in the sixth century; and 3. the Turks or Magyars, ad 889: the immediate and genuine ancestors of the modern Hungarians, whose connection with the two former is extremely faint and remote. The *Prodromus* and *Notitia* of Matthew Belius appear to contain a rich fund of information concerning ancient and modern Hungary. I have seen the extracts in *Bibliothèque Ancienne et Moderne*, xxii, 1–51, and *Bibliothèque Raisonnée*, xvi, 127–75.

3 Socrates, vii, 43; Theodoret, v, 36. Tillemont, who always depends on the faith of his ecclesiastical authors, strenuously contends (*Hist. des Emp.*, vi, 136, 607) that the wars and personages were not the same.

4 See Priscus, pp. 47–48, and *Hist. des Peuples de l'Europe*, vii, chs xii–xv.

5 Priscus, p. 39. The modern Hungarians have deduced his genealogy, which ascends, in the thirty-fifth degree, to Ham the son of Noah; yet they are ignorant of his father's real name (de Guignes, *Hist. des Huns*, ii, 297).

* *page 625* [of the Tartar race]

† *page 625* [muscular, sinewy]

6 Compare Jornandes (35, 661) with Buffon, *Hist. Naturelle*, iii, 380. The former had a right to observe, *originis suae signa restituens* [since he was recounting the characteristics of his own ancestors]. The character and portrait of Attila are probably transcribed from Cassiodorus.

* *page 626* [Jenghis Khan]

7 Abulpharag., *Dynast.* vers. Pocock, p. 281. *Genealogical History of the Tartars*, by Abulghazi Bahadar Khan, iii, 15; iv, 3. *Vie de Gengiscan*, par Petit de la Croix, i, 1, 6. The relations of the missionaries who visited Tartary in the thirteenth century (see the seventh volume of the *Histoire des Voyages*) express the popular language and opinions; Zingis is styled the Son of God, etc. etc.

8 *Nec templum apud eos visitur aut delubrum, ne tugurium quidem culmo tectum cerni usquam potest; sed gladius Barbarico ritu humi figitur nudus, eumque ut Martem regionum quas circumcircant praesulem verecundius colunt.* ['They have no temple or shrine, not even a hut thatched with straw; but in accordance with their barbaric rite, a naked sword is planted on the ground, and they worship it very reverently as the tutelar god of war in the areas around which they are accustomed to travel.'] Ammian. Marcellin., xxxi, 2, and the learned Notes of Lindenbrogius and Valesius.

9 Priscus relates this remarkable story, both in his own text (p. 65) and in the quotation made by Jornandes (35, 662). He might have explained the tradition, or fable, which characterised this famous sword, and the name as well as attributes of the Scythian deity, whom he has translated into the Mars of the Greeks and Romans.

10 Herodot., iv, 62. For the sake of economy, I have calculated by the smallest stadium. In the human sacrifices, they cut off the shoulder and arm of the victim, which they threw up into the air, and drew omens and presages from the manner of their falling on the pile.

11 Priscus, p. 55. A more civilised hero, Augustus himself, was pleased if the person on whom he fixed his eyes seemed unable to support their divine lustre, Sueton., in *August.*, ch. 79.

12 The count de Buat (*Hist. des Peuples de l'Europe*, vii, 428–29) attempts to clear Attila from the murder of his brother; and is almost inclined to reject the concurrent testimony of Jornandes and the contemporary Chronicles.

13 *Fortissimarum gentium dominus, qui, inaudita ante se potentia, solus Scythica et Germanica regna possedit.* Jornandes, 49, 684; Priscus; p. 64–65. M. de Guignes, by his knowledge of the Chinese, has acquired (ii, 295–301) an adequate idea of the empire of Attila.

14 See *Hist. des Huns*, ii, 296. The Geougen believed that the Huns could excite at pleasure storms of wind and rain. This phenomenon was produced by the stone *Gezi*; to whose magic power the loss of a battle was ascribed by the Mahometan Tartars of the fourteenth century. See Cherefeddin Ali, *Hist. de Timur Bec*, i, 82–83.

* *page 628* [a Gothic tribe]

15 Jornandes, 35, 661; 37, 667. See Tillemont's *Hist. des Empereurs*, vi, 129, 138. Corneille has represented the pride of Attila to his subject kings; and his tragedy opens with these two ridiculous lines:

> *Ils ne sont pas venus, nos deux rois! qu'on leur die*
> *Qu'ils se font trop attendre, et qu' Attila s'ennuie.*

The two kings of the Gepidae and the Ostrogoths are profound politicians and sentimental lovers; and the whole piece exhibits the defects, without the genius, of the poet.

* *page 629* [the Don]

16   *alii per Caspia claustra*
> *Armeniasque nives inopino tramite ducti*
> *Invadunt Orientis opes: iam pascua fumant*
> *Cappadocum, volucrumque parens Argaeus equorum.*
> *Iam rubet altus Halys, nec se defendit iniquo*
> *Monte Cilix; Syriae tractus vastantur amoeni;*
> *Assuetumque choris et laeta plebe canorum*
> *Proterit imbellem sonipes hostilis Orontem.*

Claudian, in *Rufin.*, ii, 28–35.

See likewise, in Eutrop., i, 243–51, and the strong description of Jerome, who wrote from his feelings, i, 26, *ad Heliodor.*, p. 220, *ad Ocean.* Philostorgius (ix, 8) mentions this irruption.

† *page 629* [river in Asia Minor]
‡ *page 629* [thoroughbred]
§ *page 629* [the Sea of Azov]

17 See the original conversation in Priscus, pp. 64–65.

18 Priscus, p. 331. His history contained a copious and elegant account of the war (Evagrius, i, 17), but the extracts which relate to the embassies are the only parts that have reached our times. The original work was accessible, however, to the writers from whom we borrow our imperfect knowledge: Jornandes, Theophanes, Count Marcellinus, Prosper-Tiro, and the author of the Alexandrian, or Paschal, Chronicle. M. de Buat (*Hist. des Peuples de l'Europe*, vii, xv) has examined the cause, the circumstances, and the duration, of this war; and will not allow it to extend beyond the year four hundred and forty-four.

19 Procopius, *de Aedificiis*, iv, 5. These fortresses were afterwards restored, strengthened, and enlarged, by the emperor Justinian; but they were soon destroyed by the Abares, who succeeded to the power and possessions of the Huns.

20 *Septuaginta civitates* (says Prosper-Tiro) *depraedatione vastatae*. The language of count Marcellinus is still more forcible. *Paene totam Europam, invasis excisisque civitatibus atque castellis, conrasit.*

21 Tillemont (*Hist. des Empereurs*, vi, 106–07) has paid great attention to this memorable earthquake; which was felt as far from Constantinople as Antioch and Alexandria, and is celebrated by all the ecclesiastical writers. In the hands of a popular preacher, an earthquake is an engine of admirable effect.

22 He represented to the emperor of the Moguls, that the four provinces (Petchlei, Chantong, Chansi, and Leaotong) which he already possessed might annually produce, under a mild administration, 500,000 ounces of silver, 400,000 measures of rice, and 800,000 pieces of silk. Gaubil, *Hist. de la Dynastie des Mongous*, pp. 58–59. Yelutchousay (such was the name of the mandarin) was a wise and virtuous minister, who saved his country, and civilised the conquerors. See p. 102–03.

23 Particular instances would be endless; but the curious reader may consult the life of Gengiscan, by Petit de la Croix, the *Histoire des Mongous*, and the fifteenth book of the *History of the Huns*.

24 At Maru, 1,300,000; at Herat, 1,600,000; at Neisabour, 1,747,000. D'Herbelot, *Bibliothèque Orientale*, pp. 380–1. I use the orthography of d'Anville's maps. It must, however, be allowed that the Persians were disposed to exaggerate their losses, and the Moguls to magnify their exploits.

25 Cherefeddin Ali, his servile panegyrist, would afford us many horrid examples. In his camp before Delhi, Timur massacred 100,000 Indian prisoners, who had *smiled* when the army of their countrymen appeared in sight (*Hist. de Timur Bec*, iii, 90). The people of Ispahan supplied 70,000 human skulls for the structure of several lofty towers (*id.* i, 434). A similar tax was levied on the revolt of Bagdad (iii, 370); and the exact account, which Cherefeddin was not able to procure from the proper officers, is stated by another historian (Ahmed Arabsiada, ii, 175, vers. Manger) at 90,000 heads.

26 The ancients, Jornandes, Priscus, etc. are ignorant of this epithet. The modern Hungarians have imagined that it was applied, by a hermit of Gaul, to Attila, who was pleased to insert it among the titles of his royal dignity. Mascou, ix, 23, and Tillemont, *Hist. des Empereurs*, vi, 143.

27 The missionaries of St Chrysostom had converted great numbers of the Scythians, who dwelt beyond the Danube in tents and waggons. Theodoret, v, 31; Photius, p. 1517. The Mahometans, the Nestorians, and the Latin

Christians, thought themselves secure of gaining the sons and grandsons of Zingis, who treated the rival missionaries with impartial favour.

28 The Germans, who exterminated Varus and his legions [in AD 9], had been particularly offended with the Roman laws and lawyers. One of the Barbarians, after the effectual precautions of cutting out the tongue of an advocate and sewing up his mouth, observed with much satisfaction that the viper could no longer hiss. Florus, iv, 12.

29 Priscus, p. 59. It should seem that the Huns preferred the Gothic and Latin language to their own; which was probably a harsh and barren idiom.

30 Philip de Comines, in his admirable picture of the last moments of Lewis XI (*Mémoires*, vi, 12), represents the insolence of his physician, who, in five months, extorted 54,000 crowns, and a rich bishopric, from the stern, avaricious tyrant.

31 Priscus (p. 61) extols the equity of the Roman laws, which protected the life of a slave. *Occidere solent* (says Tacitus of the Germans) *non disciplina et severitate, sed impetu et ira, ut inimicum, nisi quod impune.* ['They will kill a slave, not on principle or out of harshness, but simply on an angry impulse, just as they might an enemy, apart from the fact that the action goes unpunished.'] *de Moribus Germ.*, ch. 25. The Heruli, who were the subjects of Attila, claimed, and exercised, the power of life and death over their slaves. See a remarkable instance in the second book of Agathias.

32 See the whole conversation in Priscus, pp. 59–62 .

33 *Nova iterum Orienti assurgit ruina . . . quum nulla ab Occidentalibus ferrentur auxilia.* Prosper-Tiro composed his Chronicle in the West, and his observation implies a censure.

34 According to the description or rather invective of Chrysostom, an auction of Byzantine luxury must have been very productive. Every wealthy house possessed a semicircular table of massy silver, such as two men could scarcely lift, a vase of solid gold of the weight of forty pounds, cups, dishes of the same metal, etc.

35 The articles of the treaty, expressed without much order or precision, may be found in Priscus (pp. 34–37, 53). Count Marcellinus dispenses some comfort by observing, 1st, That Attila himself solicited the peace and presents which he had formerly refused; and, 2dly, That, about the same time, the ambassadors of India presented a fine large tame tiger to the emperor Theodosius.

36 Priscus, p. 35–36. Among the hundred and eighty-two forts, or castles, of Thrace, enumerated by Procopius (*de Aedificiis*, iv, xi; ii, 92, edit. Paris) there is one of the name of *Esimontou*, whose position is doubtfully marked in the neighbourhood of Anchialus and the Euxine Sea. The name and walls of Azimuntium might subsist till the reign of Justinian, but the race of its brave defenders had been carefully extirpated by the jealousy of the Roman princes.

37 The peevish dispute of St Jerome and St Augustine, who laboured, by different expedients, to reconcile the *seeming* quarrel of the two apostles St Peter and St Paul, depends on the solution of an important question (Middleton's *Works*, ii, 5–10) which has been frequently agitated by Catholic and Protestant divines, and even by lawyers and philosophers of every age.

38 Montesquieu (*Considérations sur la Grandeur*, etc. ch. xix) has delineated, with a bold and easy pencil, some of the most striking circumstances of the pride of Attila, and the disgrace of the Romans. He deserves the praise of having read the Fragments of Priscus, which have been too much disregarded.

39 See Priscus, pp. 69, 71–72, etc. I would fain believe that this adventurer was afterwards crucified by the order of Attila, on a suspicion of treasonable practices; but Priscus (p. 57) has too plainly distinguished *two* persons of the name of Constantius, who, from the similar events of their lives, might have been easily confounded.

* *page 636* [mercenary]

40 In the Persian treaty, concluded in the year 422, the wise and eloquent Maximin had been the assessor of Ardaburius [who had opposed the usurper John in AD 423–25, on behalf of the emperor in the East] (Socrates, vii, 20). When Marcian ascended the throne, the office of Great Chamberlain was bestowed on Maximin, who is ranked, in a public edict, among the four principal ministers of state (*Novell. ad. Calc. Cod. Theod.*, p. 31). He executed a civil and military commission in the Eastern provinces; and his death was lamented by the savages of Ethiopia, whose incursions he had repressed. See Priscus, pp. 40–41.

41 Priscus was a native of Panium in Thrace, and deserved, by his eloquence, an honourable place among the sophists of the age. His Byzantine history, which related to his own times, was comprised in seven books. See Fabricius, *Bibliot. Graec.*, vi, 235–36. Notwithstanding the charitable judgment of the critics, I suspect that Priscus was a Pagan.

* *page 637* [This is explained in the subsequent pages.]

† *page 637* [Romulus Augustulus, AD 475–76]

‡ *page 637* [Odoacer, AD 476–93]

42 The Huns themselves still continued to despise the labours of agriculture; they abused the privilege of a victorious nation, and the Goths, their industrious subjects who cultivated the earth, dreaded their neighbourhood, like that of so many ravenous wolves (Priscus, p. 45). In the same manner the Sarts and Tadgics provide for their own subsistence, and for that of the Usbec Tartars, their lazy and rapacious sovereigns. See *Genealogical History of the Tartars*, pp. 423, 455, etc.

* *page 638* [brother of Attila, who had put him to death]

43 It is evident that Priscus passed the Danube and the Theiss, and that he did not reach the foot of the Carpathian Hills. Agria, Tokay, and Jazberin, are situated in the plains circumscribed by this definition. M. de Buat (*Histoire des Peuples*, etc., vii, 461) has chosen Tokay; Otrokosci (p. 180, *apud* Mascou, ix, 23), a learned Hungarian, has preferred Jazberin, a place about thirty-six miles westward of Buda and the Danube.

44 The royal village of Attila may be compared to the city of Karacorum, the residence of the successors of Zingis; which, though it appears to have been a more stable habitation, did not equal the size or splendour of the town and abbeys of St Denys, in the thirteenth century (see Rubruquis, in the *Histoire Générale des Voyages*, vii, 286). The camp of Aurengzebe, as it is so agreeably described by Bernier (ii, 217–35), blended the manners of Scythia with the magnificence and luxury of Hindostan.

45 When the Moguls displayed the spoils of Asia, in the diet of Toncat, the throne of Zingis was still covered with the original black felt carpet on which he had been seated when he was raised to the command of his warlike countrymen. See *Vie de Gengiscan*, xv, 9.

46 If we may believe Plutarch (in *Demetrio*, v, 24), it was the custom of the Scythians, when they indulged in the pleasures of the table, to awaken their languid courage by the martial harmony of twanging their bow-strings.

47 The curious narrative of this embassy, which required few observations, and was not susceptible of any collateral evidence, may be found in Priscus, pp. 49–70. But I have not confined myself to the same order; and I had previously extracted the historical circumstances, which were less intimately connected with the journey, and business, of the Roman ambassadors.

48 M. de Tillemont has very properly given the succession of Chamberlains who reigned in the name of Theodosius. Chrysaphius was the last and, according to the unanimous evidence of history, the worst of these favourites (see *Hist. des Empereurs*, vi, 117–19; *Mém. Ecclés.*, xv, 438). His partiality for his godfather, the heresiarch Eutyches, engaged him to persecute the orthodox party.

49 This secret conspiracy and its important consequences may be traced in the fragments of Priscus, pp. 37–39, 54, 70–72. The chronology of that historian is not fixed by any precise date; but the series of negotiations between Attila and the Eastern empire must be included between the three or four years which are terminated, AD 450, by the death of Theodosius.

50 Theodorus the Reader (see Vales., *Hist. Eccles.*, iii, 563) and the Paschal Chronicle mention the fall, without specifying the injury, but the consequence was so likely to happen, and so unlikely to be invented, that we may safely give credit to Nicephorus Callistus, a Greek of the fourteenth century.

51 *Pulcheriae nutu* (says Count Marcellinus) *sua cum avaritia interemptus est.* ['At Pulcheria's nod, both he and his greed were disposed of.'] She abandoned the eunuch to the pious revenge of a son whose father had suffered at his instigation.

52 Procopius, *de Bell. Vandal.*, i, 4; Evagrius, ii, 1; Theophanes, pp. 90–91; *Novell. ad Calcem Cod. Theod.*, vi, 30. The praises which St Leo and the Catholics have bestowed on Marcian are diligently transcribed by Baronius, as an encouragement for future princes.

CHAPTER 35

Invasion of Gaul by Attila – he is repulsed by Aetius and the
Visigoths – Attila invades and evacuates Italy – the deaths
of Attila, Aetius, and Valentinian the Third

It was the opinion of Marcian that war should be avoided, as long as it is possible to preserve a secure and honourable peace; but it was likewise his opinion that peace cannot be honourable or secure, if the sovereign betrays a pusillanimous aversion to war. This temperate courage dictated his reply to the demands of Attila, who insolently pressed the payment of the annual tribute. The emperor signified to the Barbarians that they must no longer insult the majesty of Rome, by the mention of a tribute; that he was disposed to reward with becoming liberality the faithful friendship of his allies; but that if they presumed to violate the public peace, they should feel that he possessed troops, and arms, and resolution, to repel their attacks. The same language, even in the camp of the Huns, was used by his ambassador Apollonius, whose bold refusal to deliver the presents, till he had been admitted to a personal interview, displayed a sense of dignity, and a contempt of danger, which Attila was not prepared to expect from the degenerate Romans.[1] He threatened to chastise the rash successor of Theodosius; but he hesitated whether he should first direct his invincible arms against the Eastern or the Western empire. While mankind awaited his decision with awful suspense, he sent an equal defiance to the courts of Ravenna and Constantinople, and his ministers saluted the two emperors with the same haughty declaration. 'Attila, my lord, and thy lord, commands thee to provide a palace for his immediate reception.'[2] But, as the Barbarian despised, or affected to despise, the Romans of the East, whom he had so often vanquished, he soon declared his resolution of suspending the easy conquest, till he had achieved a more glorious and important enterprise. In the memorable invasions of Gaul and Italy, the Huns were naturally attracted by the wealth and fertility of those provinces; but the particular motives and provocations of Attila can only be explained by the state of the Western empire under the reign of Valentinian, or, to speak more correctly, under the administration of Aetius.[3]

After the death of his rival Boniface, Aetius had prudently retired to the tents of the Huns; and he was indebted to their alliance for his safety and his restoration. Instead of the suppliant language of a guilty exile, he solicited his pardon at the head of sixty thousand Barbarians; and the empress Placidia confessed, by a feeble resistance, that the condescension, which might have been ascribed to clemency, was the effect of weakness or fear. She delivered herself, her son Valentinian, and the Western empire, into the hands of an insolent subject; nor could Placidia protect the son-in-law of Boniface, the virtuous and faithful Sebastian,[4] from the implacable persecution, which urged him from one kingdom to another, till he miserably perished in the service of the Vandals. The fortunate Aetius, who was immediately promoted to the rank of patrician, and thrice invested with the honours of the consulship, assumed, with the title of master of the cavalry and infantry, the whole military power of the state; and he is sometimes styled, by contemporary writers, the Duke, or General, of the Romans of the West. His prudence, rather than his virtue, engaged him to leave the grandson of Theodosius in the possession of the purple; and Valentinian was permitted to enjoy the peace and luxury of Italy, while the patrician appeared in the glorious light of a hero and a patriot who supported near twenty years the ruins of the Western empire. The Gothic historian ingenuously confesses that Aetius was born for the salvation of the Roman republic;[5] and the following portrait, though it is drawn in the fairest colours, must be allowed to contain a much larger proportion of truth than of flattery. 'His mother was a wealthy and noble Italian, and his father Gaudentius, who held a distinguished rank in the province of Scythia, gradually rose from the station of a military *domestic* to the dignity of master of the cavalry. Their son, who was enrolled almost in his infancy in the guards, was given as a hostage, first to Alaric, and afterwards to the Huns; and he successively obtained the civil and military honours of the palace, for which he was equally qualified by superior merit. The graceful figure of Aetius was not above the middle stature; but his manly limbs were admirably formed for strength, beauty, and agility; and he excelled in the martial exercises of managing a horse, drawing the bow, and darting the javelin. He could patiently endure the want of food or of sleep; and his mind and body were alike capable of the most laborious efforts. He possessed the genuine courage that can despise not only dangers but injuries; and it was impossible either to corrupt, or deceive, or intimidate, the firm integrity of his soul.'[6] The Barbarians who had seated themselves in the Western provinces were insensibly taught to respect the faith and valour of the patrician Aetius. He soothed their passions, consulted their prejudices, balanced their interests, and checked their ambition. A seasonable treaty, which he concluded with Genseric, protected Italy from the depredations of the Vandals; the independent Britons implored and acknowledged his salutary aid; the Imperial authority was restored and maintained in Gaul and Spain; and he compelled the Franks and the Suevi, whom he had vanquished in the field, to become the useful confederates of the republic.

From a principle of interest, as well as gratitude, Aetius assiduously cultivated the alliance of the Huns. While he resided in their tents as a hostage or an exile, he had familiarly conversed with Attila himself, the nephew of his benefactor;* and the two famous antagonists appear to have been connected by a personal and military friendship, which they afterwards confirmed by mutual gifts, frequent embassies, and the education of Carpilio, the son of Aetius, in the camp of Attila. By the specious professions of gratitude and voluntary attachment, the patrician might disguise his apprehensions of the Scythian conqueror, who pressed the two empires with his innumerable armies. His demands were obeyed or eluded. When he claimed the spoils of a vanquished city, some vases of gold, which had been fraudulently embezzled, the civil and military governors of Noricum were immediately dispatched to satisfy his complaints;[7] and it is evident from their conversation with Maximin and Priscus in the royal village, that the valour and prudence of Aetius had not saved the Western Romans from the common ignominy of tribute. Yet his dexterous policy prolonged the advantages of a salutary peace, and a numerous army of Huns and Alani, whom he had attached to his person, was employed in the defence of Gaul. Two colonies of these Barbarians were judiciously fixed in the territories of Valence and Orleans;[8] and their active cavalry secured the important passages of the Rhone and of the Loire. These savage allies were not indeed less formidable to the subjects than to the enemies of Rome. Their original settlement was enforced with the licentious violence of conquest; and the province through which they marched was exposed to all the calamities of an hostile invasion.[9] Strangers to the emperor or the republic, the Alani of Gaul were devoted to the ambition of Aetius; and, though he might suspect that, in a contest with Attila himself, they would revolt to the standard of their national king, the patrician laboured to restrain, rather than to excite, their zeal and resentment against the Goths, the Burgundians, and the Franks.

The kingdom established by the Visigoths in the southern provinces of Gaul had gradually acquired strength and maturity; and the conduct of those ambitious Barbarians, either in peace or war, engaged the perpetual vigilance of Aetius. After the death of Wallia the Gothic sceptre devolved to Theodoric, the son of the great Alaric;[10] and his prosperous reign, of more than thirty years, over a turbulent people, may be allowed to prove that his prudence was supported by uncommon vigour, both of mind and body. Impatient of his narrow limits, Theodoric aspired to the possession of Arles, the wealthy seat of government and commerce; but the city was saved by the timely approach of Aetius; and the Gothic king, who had raised the siege with some loss and disgrace, was persuaded, for an adequate subsidy, to divert the martial valour of his subjects in a Spanish war. Yet Theodoric still watched, and eagerly seized, the favourable moment of renewing his hostile attempts. The Goths besieged Narbonne, while the Belgic provinces were invaded by the Burgundians; and the public safety was threatened on every side by the apparent union of the enemies of Rome. On every side, the activity of Aetius, and his Scythian cavalry, opposed a firm and successful resistance. Twenty thousand Burgundians were slain in battle; and the remains of the nation humbly accepted a dependent seat in the mountains of Savoy.[11] The walls of Narbonne had been shaken by the battering engines, and the inhabitants had endured the last extremities of famine, when count Litorius, approaching in silence, and directing each horseman to carry behind him two sacks of flour, cut his way through the entrenchments of the besiegers. The siege was immediately raised; and the more decisive victory, which is ascribed to the personal conduct of Aetius himself, was marked with the blood of eight thousand Goths. But in the absence of the patrician, who was hastily summoned to Italy by some public or private interest, count Litorius succeeded to the command; and his presumption soon discovered that far different talents are required to lead a wing of cavalry, or to direct the operations of an important war. At the head of an army of Huns, he rashly advanced to the gates of Toulouse, full of careless contempt for an enemy whom his misfortunes had rendered prudent and his situation made desperate. The predictions of the augurs had inspired Litorius with the profane confidence that he should enter the Gothic capital in triumph; and the trust which he reposed in his Pagan allies encouraged him to reject the fair conditions of peace, which were repeatedly proposed by the bishops in the name of Theodoric. The king of the Goths exhibited in his distress the edifying contrast of Christian piety and moderation; nor did he lay aside his sackcloth and ashes till he was prepared to arm for the combat. His soldiers, animated with martial and religious enthusiasm, assaulted the camp of Litorius. The conflict was obstinate; the slaughter was mutual. The Roman general, after a total defeat, which could be imputed only to his unskilful rashness, was actually led through the streets of Toulouse, not in his own, but in a hostile triumph; and the misery which he experienced, in a long and ignominious captivity, excited the compassion of the Barbarians themselves.[12] Such a loss, in a country whose spirit and finances were long since exhausted, could not easily be repaired; and the Goths, assuming, in their turn, the sentiments of ambition and revenge, would have planted their victorious standards on the banks of the Rhone, if the presence of Aetius had not restored strength and discipline to the Romans.[13] The two armies expected the signal of a decisive action; but the generals, who were conscious of each other's force, and doubtful of their own superiority, prudently sheathed their swords in the field of battle; and their reconciliation was permanent and sincere. Theodoric, king of the Visigoths, appears to have deserved the love of his subjects, the confidence of his allies, and the esteem of mankind. His throne was surrounded by six valiant sons, who were educated with equal care in the exercises of the Barbarian camp and in those of the Gallic schools; from the study of the Roman jurisprudence, they acquired the theory, at least, of law and justice; and the harmonious sense of Virgil contributed to soften the asperity of their native manners.[14] The two daughters of the Gothic king were given in marriage to the eldest sons of the kings of the Suevi and of the Vandals, who reigned in Spain and Africa; but these illustrious alliances were pregnant with guilt and discord. The queen of the Suevi bewailed the death of an husband, inhumanly massacred by her brother. The princess of the Vandals was the victim of a jealous tyrant, whom she called her father. The cruel Genseric suspected that his son's wife had conspired to poison him; the supposed crime was punished by the amputation of her nose and ears; and the unhappy daughter of Theodoric was ignominiously returned to the court of Toulouse in that deformed and mutilated condition. This horrid act, which must seem incredible to a civilised age, drew tears from every spectator; but Theodoric was urged, by the feelings of a parent and a king, to revenge such irreparable injuries. The Imperial ministers, who always cherished the discord of the Barbarians, would have supplied the Goths with arms and ships and treasures for the African war; and the cruelty of Genseric might have been fatal to himself, if the artful Vandal had not armed, in his cause, the formidable power of the Huns. His rich gifts and pressing solicitations inflamed the ambition of Attila; and the designs of Aetius and Theodoric were prevented by the invasion of Gaul.[15]

The Franks, whose monarchy was still confined to the neighbourhood of the Lower Rhine, had wisely established the right of hereditary succession in the noble family of the Merovingians.[16] These princes were elevated on a buckler, the symbol of military command;[17] and the royal fashion of long hair was the ensign of their birth and dignity. Their flaxen locks, which they combed and dressed with singular care, hung down in flowing ringlets on their back and shoulders; while the rest of the nation were obliged, either by law or custom, to shave the hinder part of their head, to comb their hair over the forehead, and to content themselves with the ornament of two small whiskers.[18] The lofty stature of the Franks, and their blue eyes, denoted a Germanic origin; their close apparel accurately expressed the figure of their limbs; a weighty sword was suspended from a broad belt; their bodies were protected by a large shield; and these warlike Barbarians were trained, from their earliest youth, to run, to leap, to swim; to dart the javelin or battle-axe with unerring aim; to advance, without hesitation, against a superior enemy; and to maintain, either in life or death, the invincible reputation of their ancestors.[19] Clodion, the first of the long-haired kings whose name and actions are mentioned in authentic history, held his residence at Dispargum,[20] a village or fortress whose place may be assigned between Louvain and Brussels. From the report of his spies the king of the Franks was informed that the defenceless state of the second Belgic* must yield, on the slightest attack, to the valour of his subjects. He boldly penetrated through the thickets and morasses of the Carbonarian forest;[21] occupied Tournay and Cambray, the only cities which existed in the fifth century; and extended his conquests as far as the river Somme, over a desolate country, whose cultivation and populousness are the effects of more recent industry.[22] While Clodion lay encamped in the plains of Artois,[23] and celebrated with vain and ostentatious security the marriage, perhaps, of his son, the nuptial feast was interrupted by the unexpected and unwelcome presence of Aetius, who had passed the Somme at the head of his light cavalry. The tables, which had been spread under the shelter of a hill, along the banks of a pleasant stream, were rudely overturned; the Franks were oppressed before they could recover their arms, or their ranks; and their unavailing valour was fatal only to themselves. The loaded waggons which had followed their march afforded a rich booty; and the virgin bride, with her female attendants, submitted to the new lovers who were imposed on them by the chance of war. This advantage, which had been obtained by the skill and activity of Aetius, might reflect some disgrace on the military prudence of Clodion; but the king of the Franks soon regained his strength and reputation, and still maintained the possession of his Gallic kingdom from the Rhine to the Somme.[24] Under his reign, and most probably from the enterprising spirit of his subjects, the three capitals, Mentz, Treves, and Cologne, experienced the effects of hostile cruelty and avarice. The distress of Cologne was prolonged by the perpetual dominion of the same Barbarians, who evacuated the ruins of Treves; and Treves, which, in the space of forty years, had been four times besieged and pillaged, was disposed to lose the memory of her afflictions in the vain amusements of the circus.[25] The death of Clodion, after a reign of twenty years, exposed his kingdom to the discord and ambition of his two sons. Meroveus, the younger,[26] was persuaded to implore the protection of Rome; he was received at the Imperial court as the ally of Valentinian and the adopted son of the patrician Aetius; and dismissed to his native country with splendid gifts and the strongest assurances of friendship and support. During his absence, his elder brother had solicited, with equal ardour, the formidable aid of Attila; and the king of the Huns embraced an alliance which facilitated the passage of the Rhine and justified, by a specious and honourable pretence, the invasion of Gaul.[27]

When Attila declared his resolution of supporting the cause of his allies, the Vandals and the Franks, at the same time, and almost in the spirit of romantic chivalry, the savage monarch professed himself the lover and the champion of the princess Honoria. The sister of Valentinian was educated in the palace of Ravenna; and, as her marriage might be productive of some danger to the state, she was raised, by the title of *Augusta*,[28] above the hopes of the most presumptuous subject. But the fair Honoria had no sooner attained the sixteenth year of her age than she detested the importunate greatness which must for ever exclude her from the comforts of honourable love; in the midst of vain and unsatisfactory pomp, Honoria sighed, yielded to the impulse of nature, and threw herself into the arms of her chamberlain Eugenius. Her guilt and shame (such is the absurd language of imperious man) were soon betrayed by the appearances of pregnancy; but the disgrace of the royal family was published to the world by the imprudence of the empress Placidia; who dismissed her daughter, after a strict and shameful confinement, to a remote exile at Constantinople. The unhappy princess passed twelve or fourteen years in the irksome society of the sisters of Theodosius, and their chosen virgins; to whose *crown* Honoria could no longer aspire, and whose monastic assiduity of prayer, fasting, and vigils, she reluctantly imitated. Her impatience of long and hopeless celibacy urged her to embrace a strange and desperate resolution. The name of Attila was familiar and formidable at Constantinople; and his frequent embassies entertained a perpetual intercourse between his camp and the Imperial palace. In the pursuit of love, or rather of revenge, the daughter of Placidia sacrificed every duty and every prejudice; and offered to deliver her person into the arms of a Barbarian, of whose language she was ignorant, whose figure was scarcely human, and whose religion and manners she abhorred. By the ministry of a faithful eunuch, she transmitted to Attila a ring, the pledge of her affection; and earnestly conjured him to claim her as a lawful spouse, to whom he had been secretly betrothed. These indecent advances were received, however, with coldness and disdain; and the king of the Huns continued to multiply the number of his wives, till his love was awakened by the more forcible passions of ambition and avarice. The invasion of Gaul was preceded, and justified, by a formal demand of the princess Honoria, with a just and equal share of the Imperial patrimony. His predecessors, the ancient Tanjous, had often addressed, in the same hostile and peremptory manner, the daughters of China; and the pretensions of Attila were not less offensive to the majesty of Rome. A firm, but temperate, refusal was communicated to his ambassadors. The right of a female succession, though it might derive a specious argument from the recent examples of Placidia and Pulcheria, was strenuously denied; and the indissoluble engagements of Honoria were opposed to the claims of her Scythian lover.[29] On the discovery of her connection with the king of the Huns, the guilty princess had been sent away, as an object of horror, from Constantinople to Italy; her life was spared; but the ceremony of her marriage was performed with some obscure and nominal husband, before she was immured in a perpetual prison, to bewail those crimes and misfortunes which Honoria might have escaped, had she not been born the daughter of an emperor.[30]

A native of Gaul and a contemporary, the learned and eloquent Sidonius, who was afterwards bishop of Clermont, had made a promise to one of his friends that he would compose a regular history of the war of Attila. If the modesty of Sidonius had not discouraged him from the prosecution of this interesting work,[31] the historian would have related, with the simplicity of truth, those memorable events to which the poet, in vague and doubtful metaphors, has concisely alluded.[32] The kings and nations of Germany and Scythia, from the Volga perhaps to the Danube, obeyed the warlike summons of Attila. From the royal village, in the plains of Hungary, his standard moved towards the West; and, after a march of seven or eight hundred miles, he reached the conflux of the Rhine and the Necker; where he was joined by the Franks, who adhered to his ally, the elder of the sons of Clodion. A troop of light Barbarians, who roamed in quest of plunder, might choose the winter for the convenience of passing the river on the ice; but the innumerable cavalry of the Huns required such plenty of forage and provisions, as could be procured only in a milder season; the Hercynian forest supplied materials for a bridge of boats; and the hostile myriads were poured, with resistless violence, into the Belgic provinces.[33] The consternation of Gaul was universal; and the various fortunes of its cities have been adorned by tradition with martyrdom and miracles.[34] Troyes was saved by the merits of St Lupus; St Servatius was removed from the world, that he might not behold the ruin of Tongres; and the prayers of St Genevieve diverted the march of Attila from the neighbourhood of Paris. But, as the greatest part of the Gallic cities were alike destitute of saints and soldiers, they were besieged and stormed by the Huns; who practised, in the example of Metz,[35] their customary maxims of war. They involved, in a promiscuous massacre, the priests who served at the altar, and the infants, who, in the hour of danger, had been providently baptised by the bishop; the flourishing city was delivered to the flames, and a solitary chapel of St Stephen marked the place where it formerly stood. From the Rhine and the Moselle, Attila advanced into the heart of Gaul; crossed the Seine at Auxerre; and, after a long and laborious march, fixed his camp under the walls of Orleans. He was desirous of securing his conquests by the possession of an advantageous post, which commanded the passage of the Loire; and he depended on the secret invitation of Sangiban, king of the Alani, who had promised to betray the city, and to revolt from the service of the empire. But this treacherous conspiracy was detected and disappointed: Orleans had been strengthened with recent fortifications; and the assaults of the Huns were vigorously repelled by the faithful valour of the soldiers, or citizens, who defended the place. The pastoral diligence of Anianus, a bishop of primitive sanctity and consummate prudence, exhausted every art of religious policy to support their courage, till the arrival of the expected succours. After an obstinate siege, the walls were shaken by the battering rams; the Huns had already occupied the suburbs; and the people, who were incapable of bearing arms, lay prostrate in prayer. Anianus, who anxiously counted the days and hours, dispatched a trusty messenger to observe, from the rampart, the face of the distant country. He returned twice without any intelligence that could inspire hope or comfort; but, in his third report, he mentioned a small cloud, which he had faintly descried at the extremity of the horizon. 'It is the aid of God!' exclaimed the bishop, in a tone of pious confidence; and the whole multitude repeated after him, 'It is the aid of God.' The remote object, on which every eye was fixed, became each moment larger and more distinct; the Roman and Gothic banners were gradually perceived; and a favourable wind, blowing aside the dust, discovered, in deep array, the impatient squadrons of Aetius and Theodoric, who pressed forwards to the relief of Orleans.

The facility with which Attila had penetrated into the heart of Gaul may be ascribed to his insidious policy as well as to the terror of his arms. His public declarations were skilfully mitigated by his private assurances; he alternately soothed and threatened the Romans and the Goths; and the courts of Ravenna and Toulouse, mutually suspicious of each other's intentions, beheld with supine indifference the approach of their common enemy. Aetius was the sole guardian of the public safety; but his wisest measures were embarrassed by a faction which, since the death of Placidia, infested the Imperial palace; the youth of Italy trembled at the sound of the trumpet; and the Barbarians who, from fear or affection, were inclined to the cause of Attila awaited, with doubtful and venal faith, the event of the war. The patrician passed the Alps at the head of some troops, whose strength and numbers scarcely deserved the name of an army.[36] But on his arrival at Arles, or Lyons, he was confounded by the intelligence that the Visigoths, refusing to embrace the defence of Gaul, had determined to expect, within their own territories, the formidable invader, whom they professed to despise. The senator Avitus, who, after the honourable exercise of the Praetorian prefecture, had retired to his estate in Auvergne, was persuaded to accept the important embassy, which he executed with ability and success. He represented to Theodoric that an ambitious conqueror, who aspired to the dominion of the earth, could be resisted only by the firm and unanimous alliance of the powers whom he laboured to oppress. The lively eloquence of Avitus inflamed the Gothic warriors, by the description of the injuries which their ancestors had suffered from the Huns; whose implacable fury still pursued them from the Danube to the foot of the Pyrenees. He strenuously urged that it was the duty of every Christian to save from sacrilegious violation the churches of God and the relics of the saints; that it was the interest of every Barbarian who had acquired a settlement in Gaul to defend the fields and vineyards, which were cultivated for his use, against the desolation of the Scythian shepherds. Theodoric yielded to the evidence of truth; adopted the measure at once the most prudent and the most honourable; and declared that, as the faithful ally of Aetius and the Romans, he was ready to expose his life and kingdom for the common safety of Gaul.[37] The Visigoths, who at that time were in the mature vigour of their fame and power, obeyed with alacrity the signal of war, prepared their arms and horses, and assembled under the standard of their aged king, who was resolved, with his two eldest sons, Torismond and Theodoric, to command in person his numerous and valiant people. The example of the Goths determined several tribes or nations that seemed to fluctuate between the Huns and the Romans. The indefatigable diligence of the patrician gradually collected the troops of Gaul and Germany, who had formerly acknowledged themselves the subjects or soldiers of the republic, but who now claimed the rewards of voluntary service and the rank of independent allies: the Laeti, the Armoricans, the Breones, the Saxons, the Burgundians, the Sarmatians or Alani, the Ripuarians, and the Franks who followed Meroveus as their lawful prince. Such was the various* army, which, under the conduct of Aetius and Theodoric, advanced, by rapid marches, to relieve Orleans, and to give battle to the innumerable host of Attila.[38]

On their approach the king of the Huns immediately raised the siege, and sounded a retreat to recall the foremost of his troops from the pillage of a city which they had already entered.[39] The valour of Attila was always guided by his prudence; and, as he foresaw the fatal consequences of a defeat in the heart of Gaul, he repassed the Seine and expected the enemy in the plains of Châlons, whose smooth and level surface was adapted to the operations of his Scythian cavalry. But in this tumultuary† retreat the vanguard of the Romans and their allies continually pressed, and sometimes engaged the troops whom Attila had posted in the rear; the hostile columns, in the darkness of the night, and the perplexity of the roads, might encounter each other without design; and the bloody conduct of the Franks and Gepidae, in which fifteen thousand[40] Barbarians were slain, was a prelude to a more general and decisive action. The Catalaunian fields[41] spread themselves round Châlons, and extend, according to the vague measurement of Jornandes, to the length of one hundred and fifty, and the breadth of one hundred, miles, over the whole province, which is entitled to the appellation of a *champaign*‡ country.[42] This spacious plain was distinguished, however, by some inequalities of ground; and the importance of an height, which commanded the camp of Attila, was understood, and disputed, by the two generals. The young and valiant Torismond first occupied the summit; the Goths rushed with irresistible weight on the Huns, who laboured to ascend from the opposite side; and the possession of this advantageous post inspired both the troops and their leaders with a fair assurance of victory. The anxiety of Attila prompted him to consult his priests and haruspices. It was reported that, after scrutinising the entrails of victims and scraping their bones, they revealed, in mysterious language, his own defeat, with the death of his principal adversary; and that the Barbarian, by accepting the equivalent, expressed his involuntary esteem for the superior merit of Aetius. But the unusual despondency, which seemed to prevail among the Huns, engaged Attila to use the expedient, so familiar to the generals of antiquity, of animating his troops by a military oration; and his language was that of a king who had often fought and conquered at their head.[43] He pressed them to consider their past glory, their actual danger, and their future hopes. The same fortune which opened the deserts and morasses of Scythia to their unarmed valour, which had laid so many warlike nations prostrate at their feet, had reserved the *joys* of this memorable field for the consummation of their victories. The cautious steps of their enemies, their strict alliance, and their advantageous posts, he artfully represented as the effects, not of prudence, but of fear. The Visigoths alone were the strength and nerves of the opposite army; and the Huns might securely trample on the degenerate Romans, whose close and compact order betrayed their apprehensions, and who were equally incapable of supporting the dangers or the fatigues of a day of battle. The doctrine of predestination, so favourable to martial virtue, was carefully inculcated by the king of the Huns, who assured his subjects that the warriors, protected by Heaven, were safe and invulnerable amidst the darts of the enemy; but that the unerring Fates would strike their victims in the bosom of inglorious peace. 'I myself,' continued Attila, 'will throw the first javelin, and the wretch who refuses to imitate the example of his sovereign is devoted* to inevitable death.' The spirit of the Barbarians was rekindled by the presence, the voice, and the example, of their intrepid leader; and Attila, yielding to their impatience, immediately formed his order of battle. At the head of his brave and faithful Huns he occupied in person the centre of the line. The nations subject to his empire, the Rugians, the Heruli, the Thuringians, the Franks, the Burgundians, were extended, on either hand, over the ample space of the Catalaunian fields; the right wing was commanded by Ardaric, king of the Gepidae; and the three valiant brothers who reigned over the Ostrogoths were posted on the left to oppose the kindred tribes of the Visigoths. The disposition of the allies was regulated by a different principle. Sangiban, the faithless king of the Alani, was placed in the centre; where his motions might be strictly watched, and his treachery might be instantly punished. Aetius assumed the command of the left, and Theodoric of the right wing; while Torismond still continued to occupy the heights which appear to have stretched on the flank, and perhaps the rear, of the Scythian army. The nations from the Volga to the Atlantic were assembled on the plain of Châlons; but many of these nations had been divided by faction, or conquest, or emigration; and the appearance of similar arms and ensigns, which threatened each other, presented the image of a civil war.

The discipline and tactics of the Greeks and Romans form an interesting part of their national manners. The attentive study of the military operations of Xenophon, or Caesar, or Frederic,† when they are described by the same genius which conceived and executed them, may tend to improve (if such improvement can be wished) the art of destroying the human species. But the battle of Châlons can only excite our curiosity by the magnitude of the object; since it was decided by the blind impetuosity of Barbarians, and has been related by partial writers, whose civil or ecclesiastical profession secluded them from the knowledge of military affairs. Cassiodorus, however, had familiarly conversed with many Gothic warriors, who served in that memorable engagement; 'a conflict', as they informed him, 'fierce, various, obstinate and bloody; such as could not be paralleled either in the present or in past ages.' The number of the slain amounted to one hundred and sixty-two thousand, or, according to another account, three hundred thousand persons;[44] and these incredible exaggerations suppose a real and effective loss, sufficient to justify the historian's remark that whole generations may be swept away, by the madness of kings, in the space of a single hour. After the mutual and repeated discharge of missile weapons, in which the archers of Scythia might signalise their superior dexterity, the cavalry and infantry of the two armies were furiously mingled in closer combat. The Huns, who fought under the eyes of their king, pierced through the feeble and doubtful centre of the allies, separated their wings from each other, and wheeling, with a rapid effort, to the left, directed their whole force against the Visigoths. As Theodoric rode along the ranks to animate his troops, he received a mortal stroke from the javelin of Andages, a noble Ostrogoth, and immediatiy fell from his horse. The wounded king was oppressed* in the general disorder, and trampled under the feet of his own cavalry; and this important death served to explain the ambiguous prophecy of the haruspices. Attila already exulted in the confidence of victory, when the valiant Torismond descended from the hills, and verified† the remainder of the prediction. The Visigoths, who had been thrown into confusion by the sight, or defection, of the Alani, gradually restored their order of battle; and the Huns were undoubtedly vanquished, since Attila was compelled to retreat. He had exposed his person with the rashness of a private soldier; but the intrepid troops of the centre had pushed forwards beyond the rest of the line; their attack was faintly supported; their flanks were unguarded; and the conquerors of Scythia and Germany were saved by the approach of the night from a total defeat. They retired within the circle of waggons that fortified their camp; and the dismounted squadrons prepared themselves for a defence, to which neither their arms nor their temper were adapted. The event was doubtful; but Attila had secured a last and honourable resource. The saddles and rich furniture of the cavalry were collected by his order into a funeral pile; and the magnanimous Barbarian had resolved, if his entrenchments should be forced, to rush headlong into the flames, and to deprive his enemies of the glory which they might have acquired by the death or captivity of Attila.[45]

But his enemies had passed the night in equal disorder and anxiety. The inconsiderate‡ courage of Torismond was tempted to urge the pursuit, till he unexpectedly found himself, with a few followers, in the midst of the Scythian waggons. In the confusion of a nocturnal combat, he was thrown from his horse; and the Gothic prince must have perished like his father, if his youthful strength, and the intrepid zeal of his companions, had not rescued him from this dangerous situation. In the same manner, but on the left of the line, Aetius himself, separated from his allies, ignorant of their victory, and anxious for their fate, encountered and escaped the hostile troops that were scattered over the plains of Châlons; and at length reached the camp of the Goths, which he could only fortify with a slight rampart of shields, till the dawn of day. The Imperial general was soon satisfied of the defeat of Attila, who still remained inactive within his entrenchments; and, when he contemplated the bloody scene, he observed, with secret satisfaction, that the loss had principally fallen on the Barbarians. The body of Theodoric, pierced with honourable wounds, was discovered under a heap of the slain: his subjects bewailed the death of their king and father; but their tears were mingled with songs and acclamations, and his funeral rites were performed in the face of a vanquished enemy. The Goths, clashing their arms, elevated on a buckler his eldest son Torismond, to whom they justly ascribed the glory of their success; and the new king accepted the obligation of revenge as a sacred portion of his paternal inheritance. Yet the Goths themselves were astonished by the fierce and undaunted aspect of their formidable antagonist; and their historian has compared Attila to a lion encompassed in his den, and threatening his hunters with redoubled fury. The kings and nations, who might have deserted his standard in the hour of distress, were made sensible that the displeasure of their monarch was the most imminent and inevitable danger. All his instruments of martial music incessantly sounded a loud and animating strain of defiance; and the foremost troops who advanced to the assault were checked, or destroyed, by showers of arrows from every side of the entrenchments. It was determined in a general council of war, to besiege the king of the Huns in his camp, to intercept his provisions, and to reduce him to the alternative of a disgraceful treaty or an unequal combat. But the impatience of the Barbarians soon disdained these cautious and dilatory measures; and the mature policy of Aetius was apprehensive that, after the extirpation of the Huns, the republic would be oppressed by the pride and power of the Gothic nation. The patrician exerted the superior ascendant of authority and reason, to calm the passions which the son of Theodoric considered as a duty; represented, with seeming affection, and real truth, the dangers of absence and delay; and persuaded Torismond to disappoint, by his speedy return, the ambitious designs of his brothers, who might occupy the throne and treasures of Toulouse.[46] After the departure of the Goths and the separation of the allied army, Attila was surprised at the vast silence that reigned over the plains of Châlons; the suspicion of some hostile stratagem detained him several days within the circle of his waggons; and his retreat beyond the Rhine confessed the last victory which was achieved in the name of the Western empire. Meroveus and his Franks, observing a prudent distance, and magnifying the opinion of their strength by the numerous fires which they kindled every night, continued to follow the rear of the Huns, till they reached the confines of

Thuringia. The Thuringians served in the army of Attila; they traversed, both in their march and in their return, the territories of the Franks; and it was perhaps in this war that they exercised the cruelties which, about fourscore years afterwards, were revenged by the son of Clovis. They massacred their hostages, as well as their captives: two hundred young maidens were tortured with exquisite and unrelenting rage; their bodies were torn asunder by wild horses, or their bones were crushed under the weight of rolling waggons; and their unburied limbs were abandoned on the public roads, as a prey to dogs and vultures. Such were those savage ancestors, whose imaginary virtues have sometimes excited the praise and envy of civilised ages.[47]

Neither the spirit nor the forces nor the reputation of Attila were impaired by the failure of the Gallic expedition. In the ensuing spring, he repeated his demand of the princess Honoria and her patrimonial treasures. The demand was again rejected, or eluded; and the indignant lover immediately took the field, passed the Alps, invaded Italy, and besieged Aquileia with an innumerable host of Barbarians. Those Barbarians were unskilled in the methods of conducting a regular siege, which, even among the ancients, required some knowledge, or at least some practice, of the mechanic arts. But the labour of many thousand provincials and captives, whose lives were sacrificed without pity, might execute the most painful and dangerous work. The skill of the Roman artists* might be corrupted to the destruction of their country. The walls of Aquileia were assaulted by a formidable train of battering rams, moveable turrets, and engines, that threw stones, darts, and fire;[48] and the monarch of the Huns employed the forcible impulse of hope, fear, emulation, and interest, to subvert the only barrier which delayed the conquest of Italy. Aquileia was at that period one of the richest, the most populous, and the strongest of the maritime cities of the Hadriatic coast. The Gothic auxiliaries, who appear to have served under their native princes Alaric and Antala, communicated their intrepid spirit; and the citizens still remembered the glorious and successful resistance, which their ancestors had opposed to a fierce, inexorable Barbarian,† who disgraced the majesty of the Roman purple. Three months were consumed without effect in the siege of Aquileia; till the want of provisions, and the clamours of his army, compelled Attila to relinquish the enterprise, and reluctantly to issue his orders that the troops should strike their tents the next morning and begin their retreat. But, as he rode round the walls, pensive, angry, and disappointed, he observed a stork preparing to leave her nest, in one of the towers, and to fly with her infant family towards the country. He seized, with the ready penetration of a statesman, this trifling incident, which chance had offered to superstition; and exclaimed, in a loud and cheerful tone, that such a domestic bird, so constantly attached to human society, would never have abandoned her ancient seats, unless those towers had been devoted to impending ruin and solitude.[49] The favourable omen inspired an assurance of victory; the siege was renewed, and prosecuted with fresh vigour; a large breach was made in the part of the wall from whence the stork had taken her flight; the Huns mounted to the assault with irresistible fury; and the succeeding generation could scarcely discover the ruins of Aquileia.[50] After this dreadful chastisement, Attila pursued his march; and, as he passed, the cities of Altinum, Concordia, and Padua, were reduced into heaps of stones and ashes. The inland towns, Vicenza, Verona, and Bergamo, were exposed to the rapacious cruelty of the Huns. Milan and Pavia submitted, without resistance, to the loss of their wealth; and applauded the unusual clemency, which preserved from the flames the public, as well as private, buildings; and spared the lives of the captive multitude. The popular traditions of Comum, Turin, or Modena, may justly be suspected; yet they concur with more authentic evidence to prove that Attila spread his ravages over the rich plains of modern Lombardy: which are divided by the Po, and bounded by the Alps and Apennine.[51] When he took possession of the royal palace of Milan, he was surprised, and offended, at the sight of a picture, which represented the Caesars seated on their throne and the princes of Scythia prostrate at their feet. The revenge which Attila inflicted on this monument of Roman vanity was harmless and ingenious. He commanded a painter to reverse the figures and the attitudes; and the emperors were delineated on the same canvas, approaching in a suppliant posture to empty their bags of tributary gold before the throne of the Scythian monarch.[52] The spectators must have confessed the truth and propriety of the alteration; and were perhaps tempted to apply, on this singular occasion, the well-known fable of the dispute between the lion and the man.[53]

It is a saying worthy of the ferocious pride of Attila, that the grass never grew on the spot where his horse had trod. Yet the savage destroyer undesignedly laid the foundations of a republic which revived, in the feudal state of Europe, the art and spirit of commercial industry. The celebrated name of Venice, or Venetia,[54] was formerly diffused over a large and fertile province of Italy, from the confines of Pannonia to the river Addua, and from the Po to the Rhaetian and Julian Alps. Before the irruption of the Barbarians, fifty Venetian cities flourished in peace and prosperity; Aquileia was placed in the most conspicuous station; but the ancient dignity of Padua was supported by agriculture and manufactures; and the property of five hundred citizens, who were entitled to the equestrian rank, must have amounted, at the strictest computation, to one million seven hundred thousand pounds. Many families of Aquileia, Padua, and the adjacent towns, who fled from the sword of the Huns, found a safe, though obscure, refuge in the neighbouring islands.[55] At the extremity of the Gulf, where the Hadriatic feebly imitates the tides of the ocean, near an hundred small islands are separated by shallow water from the continent, and protected from the waves by several long slips of land, which admit the entrance of vessels through some secret and narrow channels.[56] Till the middle of the fifth century, these remote and sequestered spots remained without cultivation, with few inhabitants, and almost without a name. But the manners of the Venetian fugitives, their arts and their government, were gradually formed by their new situation; and one of the epistles of Cassiodorus,[57] which describes their condition about seventy years afterwards, may be considered as the primitive monument of the republic. The minister of Theodoric compares them, in his quaint declamatory style, to waterfowl, who had fixed their nests on the bosom of the waves; and, though he allows that the Venetian provinces had formerly contained many noble families, he insinuates that they were now reduced by misfortune to the same level of humble poverty. Fish was the common, and almost the universal, food of every rank; their only treasure consisted in the plenty of salt, which they extracted from the sea; and the exchange of that commodity, so essential to human life, was substituted in the neighbouring markets to the currency of gold and silver. A people, whose habitations might be doubtfully assigned to the earth or water, soon became alike familiar with the two elements; and the demands of avarice succeeded to those of necessity. The islanders, who, from Grado to Chiozza, were intimately connected with each other, penetrated into the heart of Italy by the secure, though laborious, navigation of the rivers and inland canals. Their vessels, which were continually increasing in size and number, visited all the harbours of the Gulf; and the marriage, which Venice annually celebrates with the Hadriatic, was contracted in her early infancy. The epistle of Cassiodorus, the Praetorian prefect, is addressed to the maritime tribunes; and he exhorts them, in a mild tone of authority, to animate the zeal of their countrymen for the public service, which required their assistance to transport the magazines of wine and oil from the province of Istria to the royal city of Ravenna. The ambiguous office of these magistrates is explained by the tradition that, in the twelve principal islands, twelve tribunes, or judges, were created by an annual and popular election. The existence of the Venetian republic under the Gothic kingdom of Italy is attested by the same authentic record, which annihilates their lofty claim of original and perpetual independence.[58]

The Italians, who had long since renounced the exercise of arms, were surprised, after forty years' peace, by the approach of a formidable Barbarian, whom they abhorred, as the enemy of their religion as well as of their republic. Amidst the general consternation, Aetius alone was incapable of fear; but it was impossible that he should achieve, alone and unassisted, any military exploits worthy of his former renown. The Barbarians who had defended Gaul refused to march to the relief of Italy; and the succours promised by the Eastern emperor were distant and doubtful. Since Aetius, at the head of his domestic troops, still maintained the field, and harassed or retarded the march of Attila, he never showed himself more truly great than at the time when his conduct was blamed by an ignorant and ungrateful people.[59] If the mind of Valentinian had been susceptible of any generous sentiments, he would have chosen such a general for his example and his guide. But the timid grandson of Theodosius, instead of sharing the dangers, escaped from the sound, of war; and his hasty retreat from Ravenna to Rome, from an impregnable fortress to an open capital, betrayed his secret intention of abandoning Italy as soon as the danger should approach his Imperial person. This shameful abdication was suspended, however, by the spirit of doubt and delay, which commonly adheres to pusillanimous counsels, and sometimes corrects their pernicious tendency. The Western emperor, with the senate and people of Rome, embraced the more salutary resolution of deprecating,* by a solemn and suppliant embassy, the wrath of Attila. This important commission was accepted by Avienus, who, from his birth and riches, his consular dignity, the numerous train of his clients, and his personal abilities, held the first rank in the Roman senate. The specious and artful character of Avienus[60] was admirably qualified to conduct a negotiation either of public or private interest; his colleague Trigetius had exercised the Praetorian prefecture of Italy; and Leo, bishop of Rome, consented to expose his life for the safety of his flock. The genius of Leo[61] was exercised and displayed in the public misfortunes; and he has deserved the appellation of Great by the successful zeal with which he laboured to establish his opinions and his authority, under the venerable names of orthodox faith and ecclesiastical discipline. The Roman ambassadors were introduced to the tent of Attila, as he lay encamped at the place where the slow-winding Mincius is lost in the foaming waves of the lake Benacus,[†62] and trampled, with his Scythian cavalry, the farms of Catullus and Virgil.[63] The Barbarian monarch listened with favourable, and even respectful, attention; and the deliverance of Italy was purchased by the immense ransom, or dowry, of the princess Honoria. The state of his army might facilitate the treaty, and hasten his retreat. Their martial spirit was relaxed by the wealth and indolence of a warm climate. The shepherds of the North, whose ordinary food consisted of milk and raw flesh, indulged themselves too freely in the use of bread, of wine, and of meat prepared and seasoned by the arts of cookery; and the progress of disease revenged in some measure the injuries of the Italians.[64] When Attila declared his resolution of carrying his victorious arms to the gates of Rome, he was admonished by his friends, as well as by his enemies, that Alaric had not long survived the conquest of the eternal city. His mind, superior to real danger, was assaulted by imaginary terrors; nor could he escape the influence of superstition, which had so often been subservient to his designs.[65] The pressing eloquence of Leo, his majestic aspect and sacerdotal robes, excited the veneration of Attila for the spiritual father of the Christians. The apparition of the two apostles, St Peter and St Paul, who menaced the Barbarian with instant death, if he rejected the prayer of their successor, is one of the noblest legends of ecclesiastical tradition. The safety of Rome might deserve the interposition of celestial beings; and some indulgence is due to a fable which has been represented by the pencil of Raphael and the chisel of Algardi.[66]

Before the king of the Huns evacuated Italy, he threatened to return more dreadful and more implacable, if his bride, the princess Honoria, were not delivered to his ambassadors within the term stipulated by the treaty. Yet, in the meanwhile, Attila relieved his tender anxiety by adding a beautiful maid, whose name was Ildico, to the list of his innumerable wives.[67] Their marriage was celebrated with barbaric pomp and festivity at his wooden palace beyond the Danube; and the monarch, oppressed with wine and sleep, retired, at a late hour, from the banquet to the nuptial bed. His attendants continued to respect his pleasures, or his repose, the greatest part of the ensuing day, till the unusual silence alarmed their fears and suspicions; and, after attempting to awaken Attila by loud and repeated cries, they at length broke into the royal apartment. They found the trembling bride sitting by the bedside, hiding her face with her veil, and lamenting her own danger as well as the death of the king, who had expired during the night.[68] An artery had suddenly burst; and, as Attila lay in a supine posture, he was suffocated by a torrent of blood, which, instead of finding a passage through the nostrils, regurgitated into the lungs and stomach. His body was solemnly exposed in the midst of the plain, under a silken pavilion; and the chosen squadrons of the Huns, wheeling round in measured evolutions, chanted a funeral song to the memory of a hero, glorious in his life, invincible in his death, the father of his people, the scourge of his enemies, and the terror of the world. According to their national custom, the Barbarians cut off a part of their hair, gashed their faces with unseemly wounds, and bewailed their valiant leader as he deserved, not with the tears of women, but with the blood of warriors. The remains of Attila were enclosed within three coffins, of gold, of silver, and of iron, and privately buried in the night: the spoils of nations were thrown into his grave; the captives who had opened the ground were inhumanly massacred; and the same Huns, who had indulged such excessive grief, feasted, with dissolute and intemperate mirth, about the recent sepulchre of their king. It was reported at Constantinople that on the fortunate night in which he expired Marcian beheld in a dream the bow of Attila broken asunder; and the report may be allowed to prove how seldom the image of that formidable Barbarian was absent from the mind of a Roman emperor.[69]

The revolution which subverted the empire of the Huns established the fame of Attila, whose genius alone had sustained the huge and disjointed fabric. After his death, the boldest chieftains aspired to the rank of kings; the most powerful kings refused to acknowledge a superior; and the numerous sons, whom so many various mothers bore to the deceased monarch, divided and disputed, like a private inheritance, the sovereign command of the nations of Germany and Scythia. The bold Ardaric felt and represented the disgrace of this servile partition; and his subjects, the warlike Gepidae, with the Ostrogoths, under the conduct of three valiant brothers, encouraged their allies to vindicate the rights of freedom and royalty. In a bloody and decisive conflict on the banks of the river Netad, in Pannonia, the lance of the Gepidae, the sword of the Goths, the arrows of the Huns, the Suevic infantry, the light arms of the Heruli, and the heavy weapons of the Alani, encountered or supported each other, and the victory of Ardaric was accompanied with the slaughter of thirty thousand of his enemies. Ellac, the eldest son of Attila, lost his life and crown in the memorable battle of Netad: his early valour had raised him to the throne of the Acatzires, a Scythian people, whom he subdued; and his father, who loved the superior merit, would have envied the death, of Ellac.[70] His brother Dengisich with an army of Huns, still formidable in their fight and ruin, maintained his ground above fifteen years on the banks of the Danube. The palace of Attila, with the old country of Dacia, from the Carpathian hills to the Euxine, became the seat of a new power, which was erected by Ardaric, king of the Gepidae. The Pannonian conquests, from Vienna to Sirmium, were occupied by the Ostrogoths; and the settlements of the tribes, who had so bravely asserted their native freedom, were irregularly distributed, according to the measure of their respective strength. Surrounded and oppressed by the multitude of his father's slaves, the kingdom of Dengisich was confined to the circle of his waggons; his desperate courage urged him to invade the Eastern empire; he fell in battle; and his head, ignominiously exposed in the Hippodrome,* exhibited a grateful spectacle to the people of Constantinople. Attila had fondly or superstitiously believed that Irnac, the youngest of his sons, was destined to perpetuate the glories of his race. The character of that prince, who attempted to moderate the rashness of his brother Dengisich, was more suitable to the declining condition of the Huns; and Irnac, with his subject hordes, retired into the heart of the Lesser Scythia. They were soon overwhelmed by a torrent of new Barbarians, who followed the same road which their own ancestors had formerly discovered. The *Geougen*, or Avares, whose residence is assigned by the Greek writers to the shores of the ocean, impelled† the adjacent tribes; till at length the Igours of the North, issuing from the cold Siberian regions, which produce the most valuable furs, spread themselves over the desert, as far as the Borysthenes‡ and Caspian gates; and finally extinguished the empire of the Huns.[71]

Such an event might contribute to the safety of the Eastern empire, under the reign of a prince who conciliated the friendship, without forfeiting the esteem, of the Barbarians. But the emperor of the West, the feeble and dissolute Valentinian, who had reached his thirty-fifth year without attaining the age of reason or courage, abused this apparent security, to undermine the foundations of his own throne by the murder of the patrician Aetius. From the instinct of a base and jealous mind, he hated the man who was universally celebrated as the terror of the Barbarians and the support of the republic; and his new favourite, the eunuch Heraclius, awakened the emperor from the supine lethargy, which might be disguised, during the life of Placidia,[72] by the excuse of filial piety. The fame of Aetius, his wealth and dignity, the numerous and martial train of Barbarian followers, his powerful dependents, who filled the civil offices of the state, and the hopes of his son Gaudentius, who was already contracted to Eudoxia, the emperor's daughter, had raised him above the rank of a subject. The ambitious designs, of which he was secretly accused, excited the fears, as well as the resentment, of Valentinian. Aetius himself, supported by the consciousness of his merit, his services, and perhaps his innocence, seems to have maintained a haughty and indiscreet behaviour. The patrician offended his sovereign by an hostile declaration; he aggravated the offence by compelling him to ratify, with a solemn oath, a treaty of reconciliation and alliance; he proclaimed his suspicions, he neglected his safety; and, from a vain confidence that the enemy, whom he despised, was incapable even of a manly crime, he rashly ventured his person in the palace of Rome. Whilst he urged, perhaps with intemperate vehemence, the marriage of his son, Valentinian, drawing his sword, the first sword he had ever drawn, plunged it in the breast of a general who had saved his empire; his courtiers and eunuchs ambitiously struggled to imitate their master; and Aetius, pierced with an hundred wounds, fell dead in the royal presence. Boethius, the Praetorian prefect, was killed at the same moment; and, before the event could be divulged, the principal friends of the patrician were summoned to the palace, and separately murdered. The horrid deed, palliated by the specious names of justice and necessity, was immediately communicated by the emperor to his soldiers, his subjects, and his allies. The nations, who were strangers or enemies to Aetius, generously deplored the unworthy fate of a hero; the Barbarians, who had been attached to his service, dissembled their grief and resentment; and the public contempt which had been so long entertained for Valentinian was at once converted into deep and universal abhorrence. Such sentiments seldom pervade the walls of a palace; yet the emperor was confounded by the honest reply of a Roman, whose approbation he had not disdained to solicit: 'I am ignorant, sir, of your motives or provocations; I only know that you have acted like a man who cuts off his right hand with his left.'[73]

The luxury of Rome seems to have attracted the long and frequent visits of Valentinian; who was consequently more despised at Rome than in any other part of his dominions. A republican spirit was insensibly revived in the senate, as their authority, and even their supplies, became necessary for the support of his feeble government. The stately demeanour of an hereditary monarch offended their pride; and the pleasures of Valentinian were injurious to the peace and honour of noble families. The birth of the empress Eudoxia was equal to his own, and her charms and tender affection deserved those testimonies of love which her inconstant husband dissipated in vague and unlawful amours. Petronius Maximus, a wealthy senator of the Anician family, who had been twice consul, was possessed of a chaste and beautiful wife: her obstinate resistance served only to irritate the desires of Valentinian; and he resolved to accomplish them either by stratagem or force. Deep gaming was one of the vices of the court; the emperor, who, by chance or contrivance, had gained from Maximus a considerable sum, uncourteously exacted his ring as a security for the debt; and sent it by a trusty messenger to his wife, with an order, in her husband's name, that she should immediately attend the empress Eudoxia. The unsuspecting wife of Maximus was conveyed in her litter to the Imperial palace; the emissaries of her impatient lover conducted her to a remote and silent bedchamber; and Valentinian violated, without remorse, the laws of hospitality. Her tears, when she returned home, her deep affliction, and her bitter reproaches against her husband, whom she considered as the accomplice of his own shame, excited Maximus to a just revenge; the desire of revenge was stimulated by ambition; and he might reasonably aspire, by the free suffrage of the Roman senate, to the throne of a detested and despicable rival. Valentinian, who supposed that every human breast was devoid, like his own, of friendship and gratitude, had imprudently admitted among his guards several domestics and followers of Aetius. Two of these, of Barbarian race, were persuaded to execute a sacred and honourable duty, by punishing with death the assassin of their patron; and their intrepid courage did not long expect a favourable moment. Whilst Valentinian amused himself in the field of Mars with the spectacle of some military sports, they suddenly rushed upon him with drawn weapons, dispatched the guilty Heraclius, and stabbed the emperor to the heart, without the least opposition from his numerous train, who seemed to rejoice in the tyrant's death. Such was the fate of Valentinian the Third,[74] the last Roman emperor of the family of Theodosius. He faithfully imitated the hereditary weakness of his cousin* and his two uncles,† without inheriting the gentleness, the purity, the innocence, which alleviate, in their characters, the want of spirit and ability. Valentinian was less excusable, since he had passions, without virtues; even his religion was questionable; and, though he never deviated into the paths of heresy, he scandalised the pious Christians by his attachment to the profane arts of magic and divination.

As early as the time of Cicero and Varro, it was the opinion of the Roman augurs that the *twelve vultures*, which Romulus had seen, represented the *twelve centuries*, assigned for the fatal period of his city.[75] This prophecy, disregarded perhaps in the season of health and prosperity, inspired the people with gloomy apprehensions, when the twelfth century, clouded with disgrace and misfortune, was almost elapsed;[76] and even posterity must acknowledge with some surprise that the arbitrary interpretation of an accidental or fabulous circumstance has been seriously verified in the downfall of the Western empire. But its fall was announced by a clearer omen than the flight of vultures: the Roman government appeared every day less formidable to its enemies, more odious and oppressive to its subjects.[77] The taxes were multiplied with the public distress; economy was neglected in proportion as it became necessary; and the injustice of the rich shifted the unequal burden from themselves to the people, whom they defrauded of the *indulgencies* that might sometimes have alleviated their misery. The severe inquisition, which confiscated their goods and tortured their persons, compelled the subjects of Valentinian to prefer the more simple tyranny of the Barbarians, to fly to the woods and mountains, or to embrace the vile and abject condition of mercenary servants. They abjured and abhorred the name of Roman citizens, which had formerly excited the ambition of mankind. The Armorican provinces of Gaul, and the greatest part of Spain, were thrown into a state of disorderly independence, by the confederations of the Bagaudae; and the Imperial ministers pursued with proscriptive laws, and ineffectual arms, the rebels whom they had made.[78] If all the Barbarian conquerors had been annihilated in the same hour, their total destruction would not have restored the empire of the West; and, if Rome still survived, she survived the loss of freedom, of virtue, and of honour.

NOTES TO CHAPTER 35

1 See Priscus, pp. 39, 72.

2 The Alexandrian or Paschal Chronicle, which introduces this haughty message during the lifetime of Theodosius, may have anticipated the date; but the dull annalist was incapable of inventing the original and genuine style of Attila.

3 The second book of the *Histoire Critique de l'Etablissement de la Monarchie Françoise*, i, 189–424, throws great light on the state of Gaul, when it was invaded by Attila; but the ingenious author, the Abbé Dubos, too often bewilders himself in system and conjecture.

4 Victor Vitensis (*de Persecut. Vandal.*, i, 6, 8, edit. Ruinart) calls him, *acer consilio et strenuus in bello* ['shrewd in counsel and energetic in war']; but his courage, when he became unfortunate, was censured as desperate rashness, and Sebastian deserved, or obtained, the epithet of *praeceps* ['reckless'] (Sidon. Apollinar. *Carmen*. ix, 181). His adventures at Constantinople, in Sicily, Gaul, Spain and Africa, are faintly marked in the Chronicles of Marcellinus and Idatius. In his distress he was always followed by a numerous train; since he could ravage the Hellespont and Propontis and seize the city of Barcelona.

5 *Reipublicae Romanae singulariter natus, qui superbiam Suevorum, Francorumque barbariem immensis caedibus servire Imperio Romano coegisset.* ['A man born uniquely for the good of the Roman republic, who compelled the proud Suevi and the

barbarous Franks to serve the Roman empire with bloodshed on a huge scale.']
Jornandes, de Rebus Geticis, 34, 660.

6 This portrait is drawn by Renatus Profuturus Frigeridus, a contemporary historian, known only by some extracts, which are preserved by Gregory of Tours (ii, 8, in ii, 163). It was probably the duty, or at least the interest, of Renatus to magnify the virtues of Aetius; but he would have shown more dexterity, if he had not insisted on his patient, *forgiving* disposition.

* page 652 [Rugilas – see Chapter 34, p. 642.]

7 The embassy consisted of Count Romulus; of Promotus, president of Noricum; and of Romanus, the military duke. They were accompanied by Tatullus, an illustrious citizen of Petovio in the same province, and father of Orestes, who had married the daughter of Count Romulus. See Priscus, pp. 57, 65. Cassiodorus (*Variar.*, i, 4) mentions another embassy, which was executed by his father and Carpilio, the son of Aetius; and, as Attila was no more, he could safely boast of their manly intrepid behaviour in his presence.

8 *Deserta Valentinae urbis rura Alanis partienda traduntur.* ['The deserted countryside of Valence was given over for the Alani to share']. Prosper. Tironis, *Chron.*, in *Historiens de France*, i, 639. A few lines afterwards, Prosper observes that lands in the *ulterior* Gaul [north-western Gaul] were assigned to the Alani. Without admitting the correction of Dubos (i, 300), the reasonable supposition of *two* colonies or garrisons of Alani will confirm his arguments and remove his objections.

9 See Prosper Tiro, p. 639; Sidonius (*Panegyr. Avit.*, 246) complains, in the name of Auvergne, his native country,

> Litorius Scythicos equites tunc forte subacto
> Celsus Aremorico, Geticum rapiebat in agmen
> Per terras, Arverne, tuas, qui proxima quaeque
> Discursu, flammis, ferro, feritate, rapinis,
> Delebant, pacis fallentes nomen inane.

['Sweeping through Britanny, the proud Litorius directed the Scythian horsemen against the ranks of the Goths. Throughout the territory of the Auvergne, they laid waste everything in sight, running savagely amok, raiding, setting fire, slaughtering, looting – supposedly in the name of peace.']
Another poet, Paulinus of Perigord, confirms the complaint:

> Nam socium vix ferre queas, qui durior hoste.

['It is hard to bear an ally who is harsher than an enemy.']   See Dubos, i, 330.

10 Theodoric II, the son of Theodoric I, declares to Avitus his resolution of repairing or expiating the fault which his *grandfather* had committed.

> Quae noster peccavit avus, quem fuscat id unum,
> Quod te, Roma, capit.   Sidon., Panegyric. Avit., 505.

['Our grandfather's single sin and stain – his capture of Rome.']

This character, applicable only to the great Alaric, establishes the genealogy of the Gothic kings, which has hitherto been unnoticed.

11 The name of *Sapaudiae*, the origin of *Savoy*, is first mentioned by Ammianus Marcellinus; and two military posts are ascertained, by the *Notitia*, within the limits of that province: a cohort was stationed at Grenoble in Dauphiné; and Ebredunum, or Iverdun, sheltered a fleet of small vessels, which commanded the lake of Neufchâtel. See Valesius, *Notit. Galliarum*, p. 503; D'Anville, *Notice de l'Ancienne Gaule*, pp. 284, 579.

12 Salvian has attempted to explain the moral government of the Deity: a task which may be readily performed by supposing that the calamities of the wicked are *judgments,* and those of the righteous, *trials.*

13
> *Capto terrarum damna patebant*
> *Litorio; in Rhodanum proprios producere fines,*
> *Theudoridae fixum; nec erat pugnare necesse,*
> *Sed migrare Getis. Rabidam trux asperat iram*
> *Victor; quod sensit Scythicum sub moenibus hostem,*
> *Imputat; et nihil est gravius, si forsitan unquam*
> *Vincere contingat, trepido . . .*   Panegyr. Avit., 300, etc.

Sidonius then proceeds, according to the duty of a panegyrist, to transfer the whole merit from Aetius to his minister Avitus.

14 Theodoric II revered, in the person of Avitus, the character of his preceptor.
> *Mihi Romula dudum*
> *Per te iura placent, parvumque ediscere iussit*
> *Ad tua verba pater, docili quo prisca Maronis*
> *Carmine molliret Scythicos mihi pagina mores.*
>
> Sidon., *Panegyr. Avit.,* 495, etc.

15 Our authorities for the reign of Theodoric I are: Jornandes, *de Rebus Geticis,* ch. 34, 36, and the Chronicles of Idatius, and the two Prospers, inserted in the *Historians of France,* i, 612–40. To these we may add Salvian, *de Gubernatione Dei,* vii, 243–5, and the *Panegyric of Avitus,* by Sidonius.

16 *Reges Crinitos se creavisse de prima, et ut ita dicam nobiliori suorum familia* ['They made the Long-haired kings over them – they came from the first and as it were more noble of their families.'] (Greg. Turon., ii, 9, 166 of the second volume of the *Historians of France*). Gregory himself does not mention the *Merovingian* name, which may be traced, however, to the beginning of the seventh century as the distinctive appellation of the royal family, and even of the French monarchy. An ingenious critic has deduced the Merovingians from the great Maroboduus [chief of the Marcomanni, a tribe of the Suevi in the reign of Augustus]; and he has clearly proved that the prince who gave his name to the first race was more ancient than the father of Childeric [the father of Clovis, king of the Franks AD 481–511]. See the *Mémoires de l'Académie des Inscriptions,* xx, 52–90; xxx, 557–87.

17 This German custom, which may be traced from Tacitus to Gregory of Tours, was at length adopted by the emperors of Constantinople. From a Ms. of the tenth century Montfaucon has delineated the representation of a similar ceremony, which the ignorance of the age had applied to king David. See *Monuments de la Monarchie Françoise,* tom. i, Discourse Préliminaire.

18 *Caesaries prolixa . . . crinium flagellis per terga dimissis,* etc. See the Preface to the third volume of the *Historians of France,* and the Abbé Le Boeuf (*Dissertat.,* iii, 47–79). This peculiar fashion of the Merovingians has been remarked by natives and strangers; by Priscus (i, 608); by Agathias (ii, 49) and by Gregory of Tours, iii, 18; vi, 24; viii, 10; ii, 196, 278, 316.

19 See an original picture of the figure, dress, arms, and temper of the ancient Franks in Sidonius Apollinaris (*Panegyr. Majorian.,* 238–54); and such pictures, though coarsely drawn, have a real and intrinsic value. Father Daniel (*Hist. de la Milice Françoise,* i, 2–7) has illustrated the description.

20 Dubos, *Hist. Critique,* etc., i, 271–72. Some geographers have placed Dispargum

on the German side of the Rhine. See a note of the Benedictine Editors to the *Historians of France*, ii, 166.

* *page 655*   [i.e. province]

21 The Carbonarian wood was that part of the great forest of the Ardennes, which lay between the Escaut, or Scheld, and the Meuse. Vales., *Notit. Gall.*, p. 126.

22 Gregor. Turon., ii, 9, in ii, 166–67. Fredegar., *Epitom.*, 9, 395. *Gesta Reg. Francor.*, 5, in ii, 544. *Vit. St Remig. ab* Hincmar, in iii, 373.

23   *Francus qua Cloio patentes*
                 Atrebatum terras pervaserat.   *Panegyr. Majorian.*, 212.
The precise spot was a town or village called Vicus Helena; and both the name and the place are discovered by modern geographers at Lens. See Vales., *Notit. Gall.*, p. 246. Longuerue, *Description de la France*, ii, 88.

24 See a vague account of the action in Sidonius, *Panegyr. Majorian.*, 212–30. The French critics, impatient to establish their monarchy in Gaul, have drawn a strong argument from the silence of Sidonius, who dares not insinuate that the vanquished Franks were compelled to repass the Rhine. Dubos, i, 322.

25 Salvian (*de Gubernat. Dei*, Bk vi) has expressed, in vague and declamatory language, the misfortunes of these three cities, which are distinctly ascertained by the learned Mascou, *Hist. of the Ancient Germans*, ix, 21.

26 Priscus, in relating the contest, does not name the two brothers; the second of whom he had seen at Rome, a beardless youth, with long flowing hair (*Historians of France*, i, 607–8). The Benedictine Editors are inclined to believe that they were the sons of some unknown king of the Franks who reigned on the banks of the Necker; but the arguments of M. de Foncemagne (*Mém. de l'Académie*, viii, 464) seem to prove that the succession of Clodion was disputed by his two sons, and that the younger was Meroveus, the father of Childeric.

27 Under the Merovingian race the throne was hereditary; but all the sons of the deceased monarch were equally entitled to their share of his treasures and territories. See the Dissertations of M. de Foncemagne in the sixth and eighth volumes of the *Mémoires de l'Académie*.

28 A medal is still extant, which exhibits the pleasing countenance of Honoria, with the title of Augusta; and on the reverse the improper legend of *Salus Reipublicae* [saviour of the State] round the monogram of Christ. See Ducange, *Famil. Byzantin.*, pp. 67, 73.

29 See Priscus, pp. 39–40. It might be fairly alleged that, if females could succeed to the throne, Valentinian himself, who had married the daughter and heiress of the younger Theodosius, would have asserted her right to the eastern empire.

30 The adventures of Honoria are imperfectly related by Jornandes, *de Successione Regn.*, ch. 97, and *de Reb. Get.*, 42, 674, and in the Chronicles of Prosper and Marcellinus; but they cannot be made consistent, or probable, unless we separate, by an interval of time and place, her intrigue with Eugenius and her invitation of Attila.

31 *Exegeras mihi, ut promitterem tibi Attilae bellum stylo me posteris intimaturum . . . coeperam scribere, sed operis arrepti fasce perspecto taeduit inchoasse.*
                                             Sidon. Apoll., viii, epist. 15, 246.

32   *Subito cum rupta tumultu*
            Barbaries totas in te transfuderat arctos,
            Gallia. Pugnacem Rugum comitante Gelono
            Gepida trux sequitur; Scyrum Burgundio cogit:

> *Chunus, Bellonotus, Neurus, Bastarna, Toringus,*
> *Bructerus, ulvosa vel quem Nicer alluit unda*
> *Prorumpit Francus. Cecidit cito secta bipenni*
> *Hercynia in lintres, et Rhenum texuit alno.*
> *Et iam terrificis diffuderat Attila turmis*
> *In campos se, Belga, tuos.*

> *Panegyr. Avit.*, 319, etc.

33 The most authentic and circumstantial account of this war is contained in Jornandes (*de Reb. Geticis*, 36–41, 662–72), who has sometimes abridged, and sometimes transcribed, the larger history of Cassiodorus. Jornandes, a quotation which it would be superfluous to repeat, may be corrected and illustrated by Gregory of Tours, 2, 5–7, and the Chronicles of Idatius, Isidore, and the two Prospers. All the ancient testimonies are collected and inserted in the *Historians of France*; but the reader should be cautioned against a supposed extract from the Chronicle of Idatius (among the fragments of Fredegarius, ii, 462), which often contradicts the genuine text of the Gallician bishop.

34 The *ancient* legendaries deserve some regard, as they are obliged to connect their fables with the real history of their own times. See the lives of St Lupus, St Anianus, the bishops of Metz, St Genevieve, etc., in the *Historians of France*, i, 644–45, 649, iii, 369.

35 The scepticism of the Count de Buat (*Hist. des Peuples*, vii, 539–40) cannot be reconciled with any principles of reason or criticism. Is not Gregory of Tours precise and positive in his account of the destruction of Metz? At the distance of no more than 100 years, could he be ignorant, could the people be ignorant, of the fate of a city, the actual residence of his sovereigns, the kings of Austrasia? The learned Count, who seems to have undertaken the apology of Attila and the Barbarians, appeals to the false Idatius, *parcens civitatibus Germaniae et Gallia* ['sparing the cities of Germany and Gaul'], and forgets that the true Idatius had explicitly affirmed, *plurimae civitates effractae* ['most of the cities were taken by storm'], among which he enumerates Metz.

36
> *Vix liquerat Alpes*
> *Aetius, tenue et rarum sine milite ducens*
> *Robur in auxiliis, Geticum male credulus agmen*
> *Incassum propriis praesumens adfore castris.*

> *Panegyr. Avit.*, 328, etc.

37 The policy of Attila, of Aetius, and of the Visigoths, is imperfectly described in the *Panegyric of Avitus* and the thirty-sixth chapter of Jornandes. The poet and the historian were both biased by personal or national prejudices. The former exalts the merit and importance of Avitus; *orbis, Avite, salus,* etc.! ['Avitus, saviour of the world, etc.!'] The latter is anxious to show the Goths in the most favourable light. Yet their agreement, when they are fairly interpreted, is a proof of their veracity.

* *page 660* [varied, miscellaneous]

38 The review of the army of Aetius is made by Jornandes, 36, 664, edit. Grot.; ii, 23, of the *Historians of France*, with the notes of the Benedictine Editor. The *Laeti* were a promiscuous race of Barbarians, born or naturalised in Gaul; and the Riparii, or *Ripuarii*, derived their name from their posts on the three rivers, the Rhine, the Meuse, and the Moselle; the *Armoricans* possessed the independent cities between the Seine and the Loire. A colony of *Saxons* had been planted

in the diocese of Bayeux; the *Burgundians* were settled in Savoy; and the *Breones* were a warlike tribe of Rhaetians, to the east of the lake of Constance.

39 *Aurelianensis urbis obsidio, oppugnatio, irruptio, nec direptio.* ['The city of Orleans was invested, besieged and broken into, but not yet plundered.'] Bk v, Sidon. Apollin., viii, *epist.* 15, 246. The preservation of Orleans might be easily turned into a miracle, obtained and foretold by the holy bishop.

† *page 660* [hasty, disorderly]

40 The common editions read XCM [90,000]; but there is some authority of manuscripts (and almost any authority is sufficient) for the more reasonable number of XVM [15,000].

41 Châlons or Duro-Catalaunum, afterwards *Catalauni*, had formerly made a part of the territory of Rheims, from whence it is distant only twenty-seven miles. See Vales., *Notit. Gall.*, p. 136. D'Anville, *Notice de l'Ancienne Gaule*, pp. 212, 279.

‡ *page 660* [flat, open country; hence, the scene of military operations, or campaigns]

42 The name of Campania, or Champagne, is frequently mentioned by Gregory of Tours; and that great province, of which Rheims was the capital, obeyed the command of a duke. Vales., *Notit.*, pp. 120–23.

43 I am sensible that these military orations are usually composed by the historian; yet the old Ostrogoths, who had served under Attila, might repeat his discourse to Cassiodorus: the ideas, and even the expressions, have an original Scythian cast; and I doubt whether an Italian of the sixth century would have thought of the *huius certaminis gaudia* ['the joys of this battle'].

* *page 661* [doomed]

† *page 661* [Frederick the Great of Prussia]

44 The expressions of Jornandes, or rather of Cassiodorus, are extremely strong. *Bellum atrox, multiplex, immane, pertinax, cui simili nulla usquam narrat antiquitas: ubi talia gesta referuntur, ut nihil esset quod in vita sua conspicere potuisset egregius, qui huius miraculi privaretur aspectu.* Dubos (*Hist. Critique*, i, 392–93) attempts to reconcile the 162,000 of Jornandes with the 300,000 of Idatius and Isidore, by supposing that the larger number included the total destruction of the war, the effects of disease, the slaughter of the unarmed people, etc.

* *page 662* [hemmed in]

† *page 662* [brought to pass]

45 The Count de Buat (*Hist. des Peuples*, etc., vii, 554–73), still depending on the *false*, and again rejecting the *true*, Idatius, has divided the defeat of Attila into two great battles: the former near Orleans, the latter in Champagne: in the one, Theodoric was slain; in the other, he was revenged.

‡ *page 662* [reckless]

46 Jornandes, *de Rebus Geticis*, 41, 671. The policy of Aetius and the behaviour of Torismond are extremely natural; and the patrician, according to Gregory of Tours (ii, 7, 163), dismissed the prince of the Franks, by suggesting to him a similar apprehension. The false Idatius ridiculously pretends that Aetius paid a clandestine nocturnal visit to the kings of the Huns and of the Visigoths; from each of whom he obtained a bribe of ten thousand pieces of gold as the price of an undisturbed retreat.

47 These cruelties, which are passionately deplored by Theodoric, the son of Clovis (Gregory of Tours, iii, 10, 190), suit the time and circumstances of the invasion of Attila. His residence in Thuringia was long attested by popular tradition; and

he is supposed to have assembled a *couroultai*, or diet, in the territory of Eisenach. See Mascou, ix, 30, who settles with nice accuracy the extent of ancient Thuringia, and derives its name from the Gothic tribe of the Thervingi.

* *page 664* [engineers]

48 *Machinis constructis, omnibusque tormentorum generibus adhibitis.* Jornandes, 42, 673. In the thirteenth century, the Moguls battered the cities of China with large engines constructed by the Mahometans or Christians in their service, which threw stones from 150 to 300 pounds weight. In the defence of their country, the Chinese used gunpowder, and even bombs, above an hundred years before they were known in Europe; yet even those celestial, or infernal, arms were insufficient to protect a pusillanimous nation. See Gaubil, *Hist. des Mongous*, pp. 70–71, 155, 157, etc.

† *page 664* [Maximin, in AD 238 (Chapter 7)]

49 The same story is told by Jornandes, and by Procopius (*de Bell. Vandal.*, i, 4, 187–88); nor is it easy to decide which is the original. But the Greek historian is guilty of an inexcusable mistake in placing the siege of Aquileia *after* the death of Aetius.

50 Jornandes, about an hundred years afterwards, affirms that Aquileia was so completely ruined, *ita ut vix eius vestigia, ut appareant, reliquerint.* See Jornandes, *de Reb. Geticis*, 42, 673; Paul. Diacon., ii, 14, 785; Liutprand, *Hist.*, iii, 2. The name of Aquileia was sometimes applied to Forum Julii (Cividad del Friuli), the more recent capital of the Venetian province.

51 In describing this war of Attila, a war so famous, but so imperfectly known, I have taken for my guides two learned Italians, who considered the subject with some peculiar advantages: Sigonius, *de Imperio Occidentali*, Bk xiii, in his works, i, 495–502; and Muratori, *Annali d'Italia*, iv, 229–36, 8vo edition.

52 This anecdote may be found under two different articles (μεδιόλανον and κόρυκος) of the miscellaneous compilation of Suidas [a lexicon dating from the tenth century].

53   *Leo respondit, humana hoc pictum manu:*
                 Videres hominem deiectum, si pingere
                 Leones scirent.

['On this picture, executed by a human artist, the lion replied: "If lions could paint, you would see the man in the inferior position." ']

                            Appendix ad Phaedrum, *Fab.* xxv.

   The lion in Phaedrus very foolishly appeals from pictures to the amphitheatre; and I am glad to observe that the native taste of La Fontaine (Bk iii, fable x) has omitted this most lame and impotent conclusion.

54 Paul the Deacon (*de Gestis Langobard*, ii, 14, 784) describes the provinces of Italy about the end of the eighth century. Venetia *non solum in paucis insulis quas nunc Venetias dicimus constat; sed eius terminus a Pannoniae finibus usque Adduam fluvium protelatur.* The history of that province till the age of Charlemagne forms the first and most interesting part of the *Verona Illustrata* (pp. 1–388), in which the marquis Scipio Maffei has shown himself equally capable of enlarged views and minute disquisitions.

55 This emigration is not attested by any contemporary evidence; but the fact is proved by the event, and the circumstances might be preserved by tradition. The citizens of Aquileia retired to the isle of Gradus, those of Padua to Rivus Altus, or Rialto, where the city of Venice was afterwards built, etc.

56 The topography and antiquities of the Venetian islands, from Gradus to Clodia, or Chioggia, are accurately stated in the *Dissertatio Chronographica de Italia Medii Aevi*, pp. 151–55.

57 Cassiodor., *Variar.*, xii, *epist.* 24. Maffei (*Verona Illustrata*, i, 240–54) has translated and explained this curious letter, in the spirit of a learned antiquarian and a faithful subject, who considered Venice as the only legitimate offspring of the Roman republic. He fixes the date of the epistle, and consequently the prefecture, of Cassiodorus, AD 523; and the marquis's authority has the more weight, as he had prepared an edition of his works, and actually published a Dissertation on the true orthography of his name, See *Osservazioni Letterarie*, ii, 290–339.

58 See, in the second volume of Amelot de la Houssaie, *Histoire du Gouvernement de Vénise*, a translation of the famous *Squittinio*. This book, which has been exalted far above its merits, is stained in every line with the disingenuous malevolence of party; but the principal evidence, genuine and apocryphal, is brought together, and the reader will easily choose the fair medium.

59 Sirmond (*Not. ad* Sidon. Apollin., p. 19) has published a curious passage from the Chronicle of Prosper. *Attila redintegratis viribus, quas in Gallia amiserat, Italiam ingredi per Pannonias intendit; nihil duce nostro Aetio secundum prioris belli opera prospiciente,* etc. ['Attila, having reformed the forces which he had lost in Gaul, made to enter Italy by way of Pannonia; but our leader Aetius had learned nothing from the operations of the previous war, and made no provision, etc.'] He reproaches Aetius with neglecting to guard the Alps, and with a design to abandon Italy; but this rash censure may at least be counterbalanced by the favourable testimonies of Idatius and Isidore.

* *page 667* [averting]

60 See the original portraits of Avienus and his rival Basilius, delineated and contrasted in the epistles (i, 9, 22) of Sidonius. He had studied the characters of the two chiefs of the senate; but he attached himself to Basilius, as the more solid and disinterested friend.

61 The character and principles of Leo may be traced in one hundred and forty-one original epistles, which illustrate the ecclesiastical history of his long and busy pontificate, from AD 440–61. See Dupin, *Bibliothèque Ecclésiastique*, iii, ii, 120–65.

† *page 667* [Lake Garda]

62   *tardis ingens ubi flexibus errat*
                  Mincius, et tenera praetexit arundine ripas

                              . . .

                  Anne lacus tantos, te Lari maxime, teque
                  Fluctibus, et fremitu assurgens Benace marino.

[These lines, paraphrased by Gibbon in the text, are from Virgil's *Georgics*, III, 14–15 and II, 58–59].

63 The Marquis Maffei (*Verona Illustrata*, i, 95, 129, 221; ii, ii, 6) has illustrated with taste and learning this interesting topography. He places the interview of Attila and St Leo near Ariolica, or Ardelica, now Peschiera, at the conflux of the lake and river; ascertains the villa of Catullus, in the delightful peninsula of Sirmio; and discovers the Andes of Virgil, in the village of Bandes, precisely situate *qua se subducere colles incipiunt,* where the Veronese hills imperceptibly slope down into the plain of Mantua.

64 *Si statim infesto agmine urbem petiissent, grande discrimen esset: sed in Venetia quo fere*

tractu Italia mollissima est, ipsa soli caelique clementia robur elanguit. Ad hoc panis usu carnisque coctae, et dulcedine vini mitigatos, etc. ['If they had suddenly attacked Rome in force, the danger would have been great; but in Venice, almost the mildest part of Italy, their strength was undermined by the very softness of the locality and climate. Furthermore, weakened by the use of bread and cooked meat and the delights of sweet wine, etc.'] This passage of Florus (iii, 3) is still more applicable to the Huns than to the Cimbri, and it may serve as a commentary on the *celestial* plague, with which Idatius and Isidore have afflicted the troops of Attila.

65 The historian Priscus had positively mentioned the effect which this example produced on the mind of Attila. Jornandes, 42, 673.

66 The picture of Raphael is in the Vatican; the *basso* (or perhaps the *alto*) *relievo* of Algardi, on one of the altars of St Peter (see Dubos, *Réflexions sur la Poésie et sur la Peinture*, i, 519–20). Baronius (*Annal. Eccles.*, AD 452, No. 57–58) bravely sustains the truth of the apparition; which is rejected, however, by the most learned and pious Catholics.

67 *Attila, ut Priscus historicus refert, extinctionis suae tempore puellam Ildico nomine, decoram valde, sibi matrimonium post innumerabiles uxores . . . socians.* Jornandes, 49, 683–84. He afterwards adds (50, 686): *Filii Attilae, quorum per licentiam libidinis paene populus fuit* ['Attila's sons, of whom there was virtually a whole tribe as a result of his unbridled sexual activity.'] – Polygamy has been established among the Tartars of every age. The rank of plebeian wives is regulated only by their personal charms; and the faded matron prepares, without a murmur, the bed which is destined for her blooming rival. But in royal families the daughters of Khans communicate to their sons a prior right of inheritance. See *Genealogical History*, pp. 406–8.

68 The report of her *guilt* reached Constantinople, where it obtained a very different name; and Marcellinus observes that the tyrant of Europe was slain in the night by the hand and the knife of a woman. Corneille, who has adapted the genuine account to his tragedy, describes the irruption of blood in forty bombast lines, and Attila exclaims with ridiculous fury:

> *S'il ne veut s'arrêter* (his blood),
> *(Dt il) on me payera ce qui m'en va coûter.*

['Unless it (his blood) stops flowing, someone (says he) will pay the cost.']

69 The curious circumstances of the death and funeral of Attila are related by Jornandes (49, 683–85), and were probably transcribed from Priscus.

70 See Jornandes, *de Rebus Geticis*, 50, 685–8. His distinction of the national arms is curious and important. *Nam ibi admirandum reor fuisse spectaculum, ubi cernere erat cunctis pugnantem Gothum ense furentem, Gepidam in vulnere suorum cuncta tela frangentem, Suevum pede Hunnum sagittâ praesumere, Alanum gravi, Herulum levi, armaturâ aciem instruere.* I am not precisely informed of the situation of the river Netad.

* *page 669*   [race course]

† *page 669*   [pushed forward]

‡ *page 669*   [the Dnieper]

71 Two modern historians have thrown much new light on the ruin and division of the empire of Attila: M. de Buat, by his laborious and minute diligence (viii, 3–31, 68–94), and M. de Guignes, by his extraordinary knowledge of the Chinese language and writers. See *Hist. des Huns*, ii, 315–19.

72 Placidia died at Rome, November 27, AD 450. She was buried at Ravenna, where her sepulchre, and even her corpse, seated in a chair of cypress wood, were preserved for ages. The empress received many compliments from the orthodox clergy; and St Peter Chrysologus assured her that her zeal for the Trinity had been recompensed by an august trinity of children. See Tillemont, *Hist. des Emp.*, vi, 240.

73 *Aetium Placidus mactavit semivir amens* ['Valentinian, effeminate and deranged, slew Aetius'], is the expression of Sidonius (*Panegyr. Avit.*, 359). The poet knew the world, and was not inclined to flatter a minister who had injured or disgraced Avitus and Majorian, the successive heroes of his song.

74 With regard to the cause and circumstances of the deaths of Aetius and Valentinian, our information is dark and imperfect. Procopius (*de Bell. Vandal.*, i, 4,186–88) is a fabulous writer [i.e. a retailer of myths] for the events which precede his own memory. His narrative must therefore be supplied and corrected by five or six Chronicles, none of which were composed in Rome or Italy; and which can only express, in broken sentences, the popular rumours as they were conveyed to Gaul, Spain, Africa, Constantinople, or Alexandria.

* *page 671* [Theodosius II]

† *page 671* [the emperors Honorius and Arcadius]

75 This interpretation of Vettius, a celebrated augur, was quoted by Varro, in the xviiith book of his *Antiquities*. Censorinus, *De Die Natali*, 17, 90–91, edit. Havercamp.

76 According to Varro, the twelfth century would expire AD 447, but the uncertainty of the true era of Rome might allow some latitude of anticipation or delay. The poets of the age, Claudian (*de Bell. Getico*, 265) and Sidonius (in *Panegyr. Avit.*, 357), may be admitted as fair witnesses of the popular opinion.

> *Iam reputant annos, interceptoque volatu*
> *Vulturis incidunt properatis saecula metis.*
>
>   * * *
>
> *Tam prope fata tui bissenas vulturis alas*
> *Implebant; scis namque tuos, scis, Roma, labores.*

['Now they are counting up the years, and catching the flight of the vulture they inscribe the centuries on the turning post as it flashes by . . . Now the fates have almost brought to pass the twelve flights of your vulture: you know, O Rome, what trouble awaits you.'] See Dubos, *Hist. Critique*, i, 340–46.

77 The fifth book of Salvian is filled with pathetic lamentations and vehement invectives. His immoderate freedom serves to prove the weakness, as well as the corruption, of the Roman government. His book was published after the loss of Africa (AD 439) and before Attila's war (AD 451).

78 The Bagaudae of Spain, who fought pitched battles with the Roman troops, are repeatedly mentioned in the Chronicle of Idatius. Salvian has described their distress and rebellion in very forcible language. *Itaque nomen civium Romanorum . . . nunc ultro repudiatur ac fugitur, nec vile tamen sed etiam abominabile paene habetur . . . Et hinc est ut etiam hi qui ad Barbaros non confugiunt Barbari tamen esse coguntur, scilicet ut est pars magna Hispanorum, et non minima Gallorum . . . De Bagaudis nunc mihi sermo est, qui per malos iudices et cruentos spoliati, afflicti, necati, postquam ius Romanae libertatis amiserant, etiam honorem Romani nominis perdiderunt . . . Vocamus rebelles, vocamus perditos quos esse compulimus criminosos. De Gubernat. Dei*, v, 158–59.

CHAPTER 36

*Sack of Rome by Genseric, king of the Vandals – his naval
depredations – succession of the last emperors of the West,
Maximus, Avitus, Majorian, Severus, Anthemius, Olybrius,
Glycerius, Nepos, Augustulus – total extinction of the Western
empire – reign of Odoacer, the first Barbarian king of Italy*

The loss or desolation of the provinces, from the ocean* to the Alps,
impaired the glory and greatness of Rome; her internal prosperity was
irretrievably destroyed by the separation of Africa. The rapacious Vandals
confiscated the patrimonial estates of the senators, and intercepted the
regular subsidies which relieved the poverty, and encouraged the idleness,
of the plebeians. The distress of the Romans was soon aggravated by an
unexpected attack; and the province, so long cultivated for their use by
industrious and obedient subjects, was armed against them by an ambitious Barbarian. The Vandals and Alani, who followed the successful
standard of Genseric, had acquired a rich and fertile territory, which
stretched along the coast above ninety days' journey from Tangier to
Tripoli; but their narrow limits were pressed and confined, on either side,
by the sandy desert and the Mediterranean. The discovery and conquest
of the Black nations, that might dwell beneath the torrid zone,† could not
tempt the rational ambition of Genseric; but he cast his eyes towards the
sea; he resolved to create a naval power; and his bold resolution was
executed with steady and active perseverance. The woods of Mount Atlas
afforded an inexhaustible nursery of timber; his new subjects were skilled
in the arts of navigation and shipbuilding; he animated his daring Vandals
to embrace a mode of warfare which would render every maritime
country accessible to their arms; the Moors and Africans were allured by
the hopes of plunder; and, after an interval of six centuries, the fleets that
issued from the port of Carthage again claimed the empire of the
Mediterranean. The success of the Vandals, the conquest of Sicily, the
sack of Palermo, and the frequent descents on the coast of Lucania,
awakened and alarmed the mother of Valentinian and the sister of
Theodosius. Alliances were formed, and armaments, expensive and
ineffectual, were prepared, for the destruction of the common enemy,
who reserved his courage to encounter those dangers which his policy
could not prevent or elude. The designs of the Roman government were
repeatedly baffled by his artful delays, ambiguous promises, and apparent
concessions; and the interposition of his formidable confederate, the king
of the Huns, recalled the emperors from the conquest of Africa to the care

of their domestic safety. The revolutions of the palace, which left the Western empire without a defender and without a lawful prince, dispelled the apprehensions, and stimulated the avarice, of Genseric. He immediately equipped a numerous fleet of Vandals and Moors, and cast anchor at the mouth of the Tiber, about three months after the death of Valentinian and the elevation of Maximus to the Imperial throne.

The private life of the senator Petronius Maximus[1] was often alleged as a rare example of human felicity. His birth was noble and illustrious, since he descended from the Anician family; his dignity was supported by an adequate patrimony in land and money; and these advantages of fortune were accompanied with liberal arts and decent* manners, which adorn or imitate the inestimable gifts of genius and virtue. The luxury of his palace and table was hospitable and elegant. Whenever Maximus appeared in public, he was surrounded by a train of grateful and obsequious clients;[2] and it is possible that among these clients he might deserve and possess some real friends. His merit was rewarded by the favour of the prince† and senate; he thrice exercised the office of Praetorian prefect of Italy; he was twice invested with the consulship, and he obtained the rank of patrician. These civil honours were not incompatible with the enjoyment of leisure and tranquillity; his hours, according to the demands of pleasure or reason, were accurately distributed by a water-clock; and this avarice of time may be allowed to prove the sense which Maximus entertained of his own happiness. The injury which he received from the emperor Valentinian appears to excuse the most bloody revenge. Yet a philosopher might have reflected that, if the resistance of his wife‡ had been sincere, her chastity was still inviolate, and that it could never be restored if she had consented to the will of the adulterer. A patriot would have hesitated before he plunged himself and his country into those inevitable calamities which must follow the extinction of the royal house of Theodosius. The imprudent Maximus disregarded these salutary considerations: he gratified his resentment and ambition; he saw the bleeding corpse of Valentinian at his feet; and he heard himself saluted emperor by the unanimous voice of the senate and people. But the day of his inauguration was the last day of his happiness. He was imprisoned (such is the lively expression of Sidonius) in the palace; and, after passing a sleepless night, he sighed that he had attained the summit of his wishes, and aspired only to descend from the dangerous elevation. Oppressed by the weight of the diadem, he communicated his anxious thoughts to his friend and quaestor Fulgentius; and, when he looked back with unavailing regret on the secure pleasures of his former life, the emperor exclaimed, 'O fortunate Damocles,[3] thy reign began and ended with the same dinner': a well-known allusion, which Fulgentius afterwards repeated as an instructive lesson for princes and subjects.

The reign of Maximus continued about three months. His hours, of which he had lost the command, were disturbed by remorse, or guilt, or terror; and his throne was shaken by the seditions of the soldiers, the people, and the confederate Barbarians. The marriage of his son Palladius with the eldest daughter of the late emperor might tend to establish the hereditary succession of his family; but the violence which he offered to the empress Eudoxia could proceed only from the blind impulse of lust or revenge. His own wife, the cause of these tragic events, had been seasonably removed by death; and the widow of Valentinian was compelled to violate her decent mourning, perhaps her real grief, and to submit to the embraces of a presumptuous usurper, whom she suspected as the assassin of her deceased husband. These suspicions were soon justified by the indiscreet confession of Maximus himself; and he wantonly provoked the hatred of his reluctant bride, who was still conscious that she descended from a line of emperors. From the East, however, Eudoxia could not hope to obtain any effectual assistance; her father and her aunt Pulcheria were dead; her mother languished at Jerusalem in disgrace and exile; and the sceptre of Constantinople was in the hands of a stranger. She directed her eyes towards Carthage; secretly implored the aid of the king of the Vandals; and persuaded Genseric to improve the fair opportunity of disguising his rapacious designs by the specious names of honour, justice, and compassion.[4] Whatever abilities Maximus might have shown in a subordinate station, he was found incapable of administering an empire; and, though he might easily have been informed of the naval preparations which were made on the opposite shores of Africa, he expected with supine indifference the approach of the enemy, without adopting any measures of defence, of negotiation, or of a timely retreat. When the Vandals disembarked at the mouth of the Tiber, the emperor was suddenly roused from his lethargy by the clamours of a trembling and exasperated multitude. The only hope which presented itself to his astonished mind was that of a precipitate flight, and he exhorted the senators to imitate the example of their prince. But no sooner did Maximus appear in the streets than he was assaulted by a shower of stones; a Roman, or a Burgundian, soldier claimed the honour of the first wound; his mangled body was ignominiously cast into the Tiber; the Roman people rejoiced in the punishment which they had inflicted on the author of the public calamities; and the domestics of Eudoxia signalised their zeal in the service of their mistress.[5]

On the third day after the tumult, Genseric boldly advanced from the port of Ostia to the gates of the defenceless city. Instead of a sally of the Roman youth, there issued from the gates an unarmed and venerable procession of the bishop at the head of his clergy.[6] The fearless spirit of Leo, his authority and eloquence, *again* mitigated the fierceness of a Barbarian conqueror: the king of the Vandals promised to spare the unresisting multitude, to protect the buildings from fire, and to exempt the captives from torture; and, although such orders were neither seriously given nor strictly obeyed, the mediation of Leo was glorious to

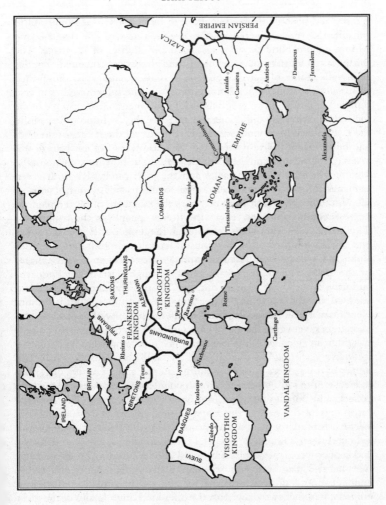

The Roman empire and the Barbarian kingdoms AD c.500

himself and in some degree beneficial to his country. But Rome and its inhabitants were delivered to the licentiousness of the Vandals and Moors, whose blind passions revenged the injuries of Carthage. The pillage lasted fourteen days and nights; and all that yet remained of public or private wealth, of sacred or profane treasure, was diligently transported to the vessels of Genseric. Among the spoils, the splendid relics of two temples, or rather of two religions, exhibited a memorable example of the vicissitude of human and divine things. Since the abolition of Paganism, the Capitol had been violated and abandoned; yet the statues of the gods and heroes were still respected, and the curious roof of gilt bronze was reserved for the rapacious hands of Genseric.[7] The holy instruments of the Jewish worship,[8] the gold table, and the gold candlestick with seven branches, originally framed according to the particular instructions of God himself, and which were placed in the sanctuary of his temple, had been ostentatiously displayed to the Roman people in the triumph of Titus. They were afterwards deposited in the temple of Peace; and at the end of four hundred years the spoils of Jerusalem were transferred from Rome to Carthage, by a Barbarian who derived his origin from the shores of the Baltic. These ancient monuments might attract the notice of curiosity, as well as of avarice. But the Christian churches, enriched and adorned by the prevailing superstition of the times, afforded more plentiful materials for sacrilege; and the pious liberality of pope Leo, who melted six silver vases, the gift of Constantine, each of an hundred pounds weight, is an evidence of the damage which he attempted to repair. In the forty-five years that had elapsed since the Gothic invasion the pomp and luxury of Rome were in some measure restored; and it was difficult either to escape or to satisfy the avarice of a conqueror who possessed leisure to collect, and ships to transport, the wealth of the capital. The Imperial ornaments of the palace, the magnificent furniture and wardrobe, the sideboards of massy plate, were accumulated with disorderly rapine; the gold and silver amounted to several thousand talents; yet even the brass and copper were laboriously removed. Eudoxia herself, who advanced to meet her friend and deliverer, soon bewailed the imprudence of her own conduct. She was rudely stripped of her jewels: and the unfortunate empress, with her two daughters, the only surviving remains of the great Theodosius, was compelled, as a captive, to follow the haughty Vandal; who immediately hoisted sail, and returned with a prosperous navigation to the port of Carthage.[9] Many thousand Romans of both sexes, chosen for some useful or agreeable qualifications, reluctantly embarked on board the fleet of Genseric; and their distress was aggravated by the unfeeling Barbarians, who, in the division of the booty, separated the wives from their husbands, and the children from their parents. The charity of Deogratias, bishop of Carthage,[10] was their only consolation and support. He generously sold the gold and silver plate of the church to purchase the freedom of some, to alleviate the slavery of others, and to assist the wants and infirmities of a captive multitude, whose health was impaired by the hardships which they had suffered in their passage from Italy to Africa. By his order, two spacious churches were converted into hospitals; the sick were distributed in convenient beds, and liberally supplied with food and medicines; and the aged prelate repeated his visits both in the day and night, with an assiduity that surpassed his strength, and a tender sympathy which enhanced the value of his services. Compare this scene with the field of Cannae;* and judge between Hannibal and the successor of St Cyprian.[11]

The deaths of Aetius and Valentinian had relaxed the ties which held the Barbarians of Gaul in peace and subordination. The sea-coast was infested by the Saxons; the Alemanni and the Franks advanced from the Rhine to the Seine; and the ambition of the Goths seemed to meditate more extensive and permanent conquests. The emperor Maximus relieved himself, by a judicious choice, from the weight of these distant cares; he silenced the solicitations of his friends, listened to the voice of fame, and promoted a stranger to the general command of the forces in Gaul. Avitus,[12] the stranger whose merit was so nobly rewarded, descended from a wealthy and honourable family in the diocese of Auvergne. The convulsions of the times urged him to embrace, with the same ardour, the civil and military professions; and the indefatigable youth blended the studies of literature and jurisprudence with the exercise of arms and hunting. Thirty years of his life were laudably spent in the public service; he alternately displayed his talents in war and negotiation; and the soldier of Aetius, after executing the most important embassies, was raised to the station of Praetorian prefect of Gaul. Either the merit of Avitus excited envy, or his moderation was desirous of repose, since he calmly retired to an estate which he possessed in the neighbourhood of Clermont. A copious stream, issuing from the mountain, and falling headlong in many a loud and foaming cascade, discharged its waters into a lake about two miles in length, and the villa was pleasantly seated on the margin of the lake. The baths, the porticoes, the summer and winter apartments, were adapted to the purposes of luxury and use; and the adjacent country afforded the various prospects of woods, pastures, and meadows.[13] In this retreat, where Avitus amused his leisure with books, rural sports, the practice of husbandry, and the society of his friends,[14] he received the Imperial diploma, which constituted him master-general of the cavalry and infantry of Gaul. He assumed the military command; the Barbarians suspended their fury; and, whatever means he might employ, whatever concessions he might be forced to make, the people enjoyed the benefits of actual tranquillity. But the fate of Gaul depended on the Visigoths; and the Roman general, less attentive to his dignity than to the public interest, did not disdain to visit Toulouse in the character of an ambassador. He was received with courteous hospitality by Theodoric, the king of the Goths; but, while Avitus laid the foundation of a solid alliance with that powerful nation, he was astonished by the intelligence that the emperor Maximus was slain and that Rome had been pillaged by the Vandals. A vacant throne, which he might ascend without guilt or danger, tempted his ambition;[15] and the Visigoths were easily persuaded to support his claim by their irresistible suffrage. They loved the person of Avitus; they respected his virtues; and they were not insensible of the advantage, as well as honour, of giving an emperor to the West. The season was now approaching in which the annual assembly of the seven provinces was held at Arles; their deliberations might perhaps be influenced by the presence of Theodoric and his martial brothers; but their choice would naturally incline to the most illustrious of their countrymen. Avitus, after a decent resistance, accepted the Imperial diadem from the representatives of Gaul; and his election was ratified by the acclamations of the Barbarians and provincials. The formal consent of Marcian, emperor of the East, was solicited and obtained; but the senate, Rome, and Italy, though humbled by their recent calamities, submitted with a secret murmur to the presumption of the Gallic usurper.

Theodoric, to whom Avitus was indebted for the purple, had acquired the Gothic sceptre by the murder of his elder brother Torismond; and he justified this atrocious deed by the design which his predecessor had formed of violating his alliance with the empire.[16] Such a crime might not be incompatible with the virtues of a Barbarian; but the manners of Theodoric were gentle and humane; and posterity may contemplate without terror the original picture of a Gothic king, whom Sidonius had intimately observed in the hours of peace and of social intercourse. In an epistle, dated from the court of Toulouse, the orator satisfies the curiosity of one of his friends, in the following description:[17] 'By the majesty of his appearance, Theodoric would command the respect of those who are ignorant of his merit; and, although he is born a prince, his merit would dignify a private station. He is of a middle stature, his body appears rather plump than fat, and in his well-proportioned limbs agility is united with muscular strength.[18] If you examine his countenance, you will distinguish a high forehead, large shaggy eyebrows, an aquiline nose, thin lips, a regular set of white teeth, and a fair complexion that blushes more frequently from modesty than from anger. The ordinary distribution of his time, as far as it is exposed to the public view, may be concisely represented. Before daybreak, he repairs, with a small train, to his domestic chapel, where the service is performed by the Arian clergy; but those who presume to interpret his secret sentiments consider this assiduous devotion as the effect of habit and policy. The rest of the morning is employed in the administration of his kingdom. His chair is surrounded by some military officers of decent aspect and behaviour; the noisy crowd of his Barbarian guards occupies the hall of audience; but they are not permitted to stand within the veils or curtains that conceal the council-chamber from vulgar eyes. The ambassadors of the nations are successively introduced: Theodoric listens with attention, answers them with discreet brevity, and either announces or delays, according to the nature of their business, his final resolution. About eight (the second hour) he rises from his throne, and visits either his treasury or his stables. If he chooses to hunt, or at least to exercise himself on horseback, his bow is carried by a favourite youth; but, when the game is marked, he bends it with his own hand, and seldom misses the object of his aim: as a king, he disdains to bear arms in such ignoble warfare; but, as a soldier, he would blush to accept any military service which he could perform himself. On common days his dinner is not different from the repast of a private citizen; but every Saturday many honourable guests are invited to the royal table, which, on these occasions, is served with the elegance of Greece, the plenty of Gaul, and the order and diligence of Italy.[19] The gold or silver plate is less remarkable for its weight than for the brightness and curious workmanship; the taste is gratified without the help of foreign and costly luxury; the size and number of the cups of wine are regulated with a strict regard to the laws of temperance; and the respectful silence that prevails is interrupted only by grave and instructive conversation. After dinner, Theodoric sometimes indulges himself in a short slumber; and, as soon as he wakes, he calls for the dice and tables, encourages his friends to forget the royal majesty, and is delighted when they freely express the passions which are excited by the incidents of play. At this game, which he loves as the image of war, he alternately displays his eagerness, his skill, his patience, and his cheerful temper. If he loses, he laughs; he is modest and silent if he wins. Yet, notwithstanding this seeming indifference, his courtiers choose to solicit any favour in the moments of victory; and I myself, in my applications to the king, have derived some benefit from my losses.[20] About the ninth hour (three o'clock) the tide of business again returns, and flows incessantly till after sunset, when the signal of the royal supper dismisses the weary crowd of suppliants and pleaders. At the supper, a more familiar repast, buffoons and pantomimes are sometimes introduced, to divert, not to offend, the company by their ridiculous wit; but female singers and the soft effeminate modes of music are severely banished, and such martial tunes as animate the soul to deeds of valour are alone grateful to the ear of Theodoric. He retires from table; and the nocturnal guards are immediately posted at the entrance of the treasury, the palace, and the private apartments.'

When the king of the Visigoths encouraged Avitus to assume the purple, he offered his person and his forces, as a faithful soldier of the republic.[21] The exploits of Theodoric soon convinced the world that he had not degenerated from the warlike virtues of his ancestors. After the establishment of the Goths in Aquitain and the passage of the Vandals into Africa, the Suevi, who had fixed their kingdom in Gallicia, aspired to the conquest of Spain, and threatened to extinguish the feeble remains of the

Roman dominion. The provincials of Carthagena and Tarragona, afflicted by an hostile invasion, represented their injuries and their apprehensions. Count Fronto was dispatched, in the name of the emperor Avitus, with advantageous offers of peace and alliance; and Theodoric interposed his weighty mediation, to declare that, unless his brother-in-law, the king of the Suevi, immediately retired, he should be obliged to arm in the cause of justice and of Rome. 'Tell him,' replied the haughty Rechiarius, 'that I despise his friendship and his arms; but that I shall soon try whether he will dare to expect my arrival under the walls of Toulouse.' Such a challenge urged Theodoric to prevent the bold designs of his enemy: he passed the Pyrenees at the head of the Visigoths; the Franks and Burgundians served under his standard; and, though he professed himself the dutiful servant of Avitus, he privately stipulated, for himself and his successors, the absolute possession of his Spanish conquests. The two armies, or rather the two nations, encountered each other on the banks of the river Urbicus, about twelve miles from Astorga; and the decisive victory of the Goths appeared for a while to have extirpated the name and kingdom of the Suevi. From the field of battle Theodoric advanced to Braga, their metropolis, which still retained the splendid vestiges of its ancient commerce and dignity.[22] His entrance was not polluted with blood, and the Goths respected the chastity of their female captives, more especially of the consecrated virgins; but the greatest part of the clergy and people were made slaves, and even the churches and altars were confounded* in the universal pillage. The unfortunate king of the Suevi had escaped to one of the ports of the ocean; but the obstinacy of the winds opposed his flight; he was delivered to his implacable rival; and Rechiarius, who neither desired nor expected mercy, received, with manly constancy, the death which he would probably have inflicted. After this bloody sacrifice to policy or resentment, Theodoric carried his victorious arms as far as Merida, the principal town of Lusitania, without meeting any resistance, except from the miraculous powers of St Eulalia; but he was stopped in the full career of success, and recalled from Spain, before he could provide for the security of his conquests. In his retreat towards the Pyrenees, he revenged his disappointment on the country through which he passed; and, in the sack of Pollentia and Astorga, he showed himself a faithless ally, as well as a cruel enemy. Whilst the king of the Visigoths fought and vanquished in the name of Avitus, the reign of Avitus had expired; and both the honour and the interest of Theodoric were deeply wounded by the disgrace of a friend, whom he had seated on the throne of the Western empire.[23]

The pressing solicitations of the senate and people persuaded the emperor Avitus to fix his residence at Rome and to accept the consulship for the ensuing year. On the first day of January, his son-in-law, Sidonius Apollinaris, celebrated his praises in a panegyric of six hundred verses; but this composition, though it was rewarded with a brass statue,[24] seems to contain a very moderate proportion either of genius or of truth. The poet, if we may degrade that sacred name, exaggerates the merit of a sovereign and a father;* and his prophecy of a long and glorious reign was soon contradicted by the event. Avitus, at a time when the Imperial dignity was reduced to a pre-eminence of toil and danger, indulged himself in the pleasures of Italian luxury; age had not extinguished his amorous inclinations; and he is accused of insulting, with indiscreet and ungenerous raillery, the husbands whose wives he had seduced or violated.[25] But the Romans were not inclined either to excuse his faults or to acknowledge his virtues. The several parts of the empire became every day more alienated from each other; and the stranger of Gaul was the object of popular hatred and contempt. The senate asserted their legitimate claim in the election of an emperor; and their authority, which had been originally derived from the old constitution, was again fortified by the actual weakness of a declining monarchy. Yet even such a monarchy might have resisted the votes of an unarmed senate, if their discontent had not been supported, or perhaps inflamed, by Count Ricimer, one of the principal commanders of the Barbarian troops, who formed the military defence of Italy. The daughter of Wallia, king of the Visigoths, was the mother of Ricimer; but he was descended on the father's side, from the nation of the Suevi;[26] his pride, or patriotism, might be exasperated by the misfortunes of his countrymen; and he obeyed, with reluctance, an emperor in whose elevation he had not been consulted. His faithful and important services against the common enemy rendered him still more formidable;[27] and, after destroying, on the coast of Corsica, a fleet of Vandals, which consisted of sixty galleys, Ricimer returned in triumph with the appellation of the Deliverer of Italy. He chose that moment to signify to Avitus that his reign was at an end; and the feeble emperor, at a distance from his Gothic allies, was compelled, after a short and unavailing struggle, to abdicate the purple. By the clemency, however, or the contempt, of Ricimer,[28] he was permitted to descend from the throne to the more desirable station of bishop of Placentia; but the resentment of the senate was still unsatisfied, and their inflexible severity pronounced the sentence of his death. He fled towards the Alps, with the humble hope, not of arming the Visigoths in his cause, but of securing his person and treasures in the sanctuary of Julian, one of the tutelar saints of Auvergne.[29] Disease, or the hand of the executioner, arrested him on the road; yet his remains were decently transported to Brivas, or Brioude, in his native province, and he reposed at the feet of his holy patron.[30] Avitus left only one daughter, the wife of Sidonius Apollinaris, who inherited the patrimony of his father-in-law; lamenting, at the same time, the disappointment of his public and private expectations. His resentment prompted him to join, or at least to countenance, the measures of a rebellious faction in Gaul; and the poet had contracted some guilt, which it was incumbent on him to expiate by a new tribute of flattery to the succeeding emperor.[31]

The successor of Avitus presents the welcome discovery of a great and heroic character, such as sometimes arise in a degenerate age, to vindicate the honour of the human species. The emperor Majorian has deserved the praises of his contemporaries, and of posterity; and these praises may be strongly expressed in the words of a judicious and disinterested historian: 'That he was gentle to his subjects; that he was terrible to his enemies; and that he excelled in *every* virtue *all* his predecessors who had reigned over the Romans.'[32] Such a testimony may justify at least the panegyric of Sidonius; and we may acquiesce in the assurance that, although the obsequious orator would have flattered, with equal zeal, the most worthless of princes, the extraordinary merit of his object confined him, on this occasion, within the bounds of truth.[33] Majorian derived his name from his maternal grandfather, who in the reign of the great Theodosius had commanded the troops of the Illyrian frontier. He gave his daughter in marriage to the father of Majorian, a respectable officer, who administered the revenues of Gaul with skill and integrity, and generously preferred the friendship of Aetius to the tempting offers of an insidious court. His son, the future emperor, who was educated in the profession of arms, displayed, from his early youth, intrepid courage, premature wisdom, and unbounded liberality in a scanty fortune. He followed the standard of Aetius, contributed to his success, shared and sometimes eclipsed his glory, and at last excited the jealousy of the patrician, or rather of his wife, who forced him to retire from the service.[34] Majorian, after the death of Aetius, was recalled, and promoted; and his intimate connection with count Ricimer was the immediate step by which he ascended the throne of the Western empire. During the vacancy that succeeded the abdication of Avitus, the ambitious Barbarian, whose birth excluded him from the Imperial dignity, governed Italy, with the title of Patrician; resigned, to his friend, the conspicuous station of master-general of the cavalry and infantry; and after an interval of some months, consented to the unanimous wish of the Romans, whose favour Majorian had solicited by a recent victory over the Alemanni.[35] He was invested with the purple at Ravenna, and the epistle which he addressed to the senate will best describe his situation and his sentiments. 'Your election, Conscript Fathers!* and the ordinance of the most valiant army, have made me your emperor.[36] May the propitious Deity direct and prosper the counsels and events of my administration, to your advantage, and to the public welfare! For my own part, I did not aspire, I have submitted, to reign; nor should I have discharged the obligations of a citizen, if I had refused, with base and selfish ingratitude, to support the weight of those labours which were imposed by the republic. Assist, therefore, the prince whom you have made; partake the duties which you have enjoined; and may our common endeavours promote the happiness of an empire which I have accepted from your hands. Be assured that, in our times, justice shall resume her ancient vigour, and that virtue shall become not only innocent but meritorious. Let none, except the authors themselves, be apprehensive of *delations*,*[37] which, as a subject, I have always condemned, and, as a prince, will severely punish. Our own vigilance, and that of our father, the patrician Ricimer, shall regulate all military affairs, and provide for the safety of the Roman world, which we have saved from foreign and domestic enemies.[38] You now understand the maxims of my government: you may confide in the faithful love and sincere assurances of a prince who has formerly been the companion of your life and dangers, who still glories in the name of senator, and who is anxious that you should never repent of the judgment which you have pronounced in his favour.' The emperor, who, amidst the ruins of the Roman world, revived the ancient language of law and liberty which Trajan would not have disclaimed, must have derived those generous sentiments from his own heart; since they were not suggested to his imitation by the customs of his age, or the example of his predecessors.[39]

The private and public actions of Majorian are very imperfectly known; but his laws, remarkable for an original cast of thought and expression, faithfully represent the character of a sovereign who loved his people, who sympathised in their distress, who had studied the causes of the decline of the empire, and who was capable of applying (as far as such reformation was practicable) judicious and effectual remedies to the public disorders.[40] His regulations concerning the finances manifestly tended to remove, or at least to mitigate, the most intolerable grievances. I. From the first hour of his own reign, he was solicitous (I translate his own words) to relieve the *weary* fortunes of the provincials, oppressed by the accumulated weight of indictions and superindictions.†[41] With this view he granted an universal amnesty, a final and absolute discharge of all arrears of tribute, of all debts, which, under any pretence, the fiscal officers might demand from the people. This wise dereliction of obsolete, vexatious, and unprofitable claims improved and purified the sources of the public revenue; and the subject who could now look back without despair might labour with hope and gratitude for himself and for his country. II. In the assessment and collection of taxes Majorian restored the ordinary jurisdiction of the provincial magistrates, and suppressed the extraordinary commissions which had been introduced in the name of the emperor himself or of the Praetorian prefects. The favourite servants, who obtained such irregular powers, were insolent in their behaviour and arbitrary in their demands; they affected to despise the subordinate tribunals, and they were discontented if their fees and profits did not twice exceed the sum which they condescended to pay into the treasury. One instance of their extortion would appear incredible, were it not authenticated by the legislator himself. They exacted the whole payment in gold; but they refused the current coin of the empire, and would accept only such ancient pieces as were stamped with the names of Faustina or the Antonines. The subject who was unprovided with these curious medals had recourse to the expedient of compounding with their rapacious demands; or, if he succeeded in the research, his imposition was doubled, according to the weight and value of the money of former times.[42] III. 'The municipal corporations (says the emperor), the lesser senates (so antiquity has justly styled them), deserve to be considered as the heart of the cities and the sinews of the republic. And yet so low are they now reduced, by the injustice of magistrates and the venality of collectors, that many of their members, renouncing their dignity and their country, have taken refuge in distant and obscure exile.' He urges, and even compels, their return to their respective cities; but he removes the grievance which had forced them to desert the exercise of their municipal functions. They are directed, under the authority of the provincial magistrates, to resume their office of levying the tribute; but, instead of being made responsible for the whole sum assessed on their district, they are only required to produce a regular account of the payments which they have actually received, and of the defaulters who are still indebted to the public. IV. But Majorian was not ignorant that these corporate bodies were too much inclined to retaliate the injustice and oppression which they had suffered; and he therefore revives the useful office of the *defenders of cities*. He exhorts the people to elect, in a full and free assembly, some man of discretion and integrity, who would dare to assert their privileges, to represent their grievances, to protect the poor from the tyranny of the rich, and to inform the emperor of the abuses that were committed under the sanction of his name and authority.

The spectator, who casts a mournful view over the ruins of ancient Rome, is tempted to accuse the memory of the Goths and Vandals, for the mischief which they had neither leisure, nor power, nor perhaps inclination, to perpetrate. The tempest of war might strike some lofty turrets to the ground; but the destruction which undermined the foundations of those massy fabrics was prosecuted, slowly and silently, during a period of ten centuries; and the motives of interest that afterwards operated without shame or control were severely checked by the taste and spirit of the emperor Majorian. The decay of the city had gradually impaired the value of the public works. The circus and theatres might still excite, but they seldom gratified, the desires of the people; the temples, which had escaped the zeal of the Christians, were no longer inhabited either by gods or men; the diminished crowds of the Romans were lost in the immense space of their baths and porticoes; and the stately libraries and halls of justice became useless to an indolent generation, whose repose was seldom disturbed either by study or business. The monuments of consular, or Imperial, greatness were no longer revered as the immortal glory of the capital; they were only esteemed as an inexhaustible mine of materials, cheaper and more convenient than the distant quarry. Specious petitions were continually addressed to the easy magistrates of Rome, which stated the want of stones or bricks for some necessary service; the fairest forms of architecture were rudely defaced for the sake of some paltry, or pretended, repairs; and the degenerate Romans, who converted the spoil to their own emolument, demolished with sacrilegious hands the labours of their ancestors. Majorian, who had often sighed over the desolation of the city, applied a severe remedy to the growing evil.[43] He reserved to the prince and senate the sole cognisance of the extreme cases which might justify the destruction of an ancient edifice; imposed a fine of fifty pounds of gold (two thousand pounds sterling) on every magistrate who should presume to grant such illegal and scandalous licence; and threatened to chastise the criminal obedience of their subordinate officers by a severe whipping and the amputation of both their hands. In the last instance, the legislature might seem to forget the proportion of guilt and punishment; but his zeal arose from a generous principle, and Majorian was anxious to protect the monuments of those ages in which he would have desired and deserved to live. The emperor conceived that it was his interest to increase the number of his subjects; that it was his duty to guard the purity of the marriage-bed; but the means which he employed to accomplish these salutary purposes are of an ambiguous, and perhaps exceptionable, kind. The pious maids, who consecrated their virginity to Christ, were restrained from taking the veil till they had reached their fortieth year. Widows under that age were compelled to form a second alliance within the term of five years, by the forfeiture of half their wealth to their nearest relations or to the state. Unequal marriages* were condemned or annulled. The punishment of confiscation and exile was deemed so inadequate to the guilt of adultery, that, if the criminal returned to Italy, he might, by the express declaration of Majorian, be slain with impunity.[44]

While the emperor Majorian assiduously laboured to restore the happiness and virtue of the Romans, he encountered the arms of Genseric, from his character and situation, their most formidable enemy. A fleet of Vandals and Moors landed at the mouth of the Liris, or Garigliano; but the Imperial troops surprised and attacked the disorderly Barbarians, who were encumbered with the spoils of Campania; they were chased with slaughter to their ships, and their leader, the king's brother-in-law, was found in the number of the slain.[45] Such vigilance might announce the character of the new reign; but the strictest vigilance and the most numerous forces were insufficient to protect the long-extended coast of Italy from the depredations of a naval war. The public opinion had imposed a nobler and more arduous task on the genius of Majorian. Rome expected from him alone the restitution of Africa; and the design which he formed, of attacking the Vandals in their new settlements, was the result of bold and judicious policy. If the intrepid emperor could have infused his own spirit into the youth of Italy; if he could have revived, in the field of Mars, the manly exercises in which he had always surpassed his equals; he might have marched against Genseric at the head of a *Roman* army. Such a reformation of national manners might be embraced by the rising generation; but it is the misfortune of those princes who laboriously sustain a declining monarchy that, to obtain some immediate advantage, or to avert some impending danger, they are forced to countenance, and even to multiply, the most pernicious abuses. Majorian, like the weakest of his predecessors, was reduced to the disgraceful expedient of substituting Barbarian auxiliaries in the place of his unwarlike subjects; and his superior abilities could only be displayed in the vigour and dexterity with which he wielded a dangerous instrument, so apt to recoil on the hand that used it. Besides the confederates, who were already engaged in the service of the empire, the fame of his liberality and valour attracted the nations of the Danube, the Borysthenes,* and perhaps of the Tanais.[†] Many thousands of the bravest subjects of Attila, the Gepidae, the Ostrogoths, the Rugians, the Burgundians, the Suevi, the Alani, assembled in the plains of Liguria; and their formidable strength was balanced by their mutual animosities.[46] They passed the Alps in a severe winter. The emperor led the way on foot, and in complete armour; sounding, with his long staff, the depth of the ice, or snow, and encouraging the Scythians, who complained of the extreme cold, by the cheerful assurance that they should be satisfied with the heat of Africa. The citizens of Lyons had presumed to shut their gates: they soon implored, and experienced, the clemency of Majorian. He vanquished Theodoric in the field; and admitted to his friendship and alliance a king whom he had found not unworthy of his arms. The beneficial, though precarious, reunion of the greatest part of Gaul and Spain was the effect of persuasion, as well as of force;[47] and the independent Bagaudae, who had escaped, or resisted, the oppression of former reigns, were disposed to confide in the virtues of Majorian. His camp was filled with Barbarian allies; his throne was supported by the zeal of an affectionate people; but the emperor had foreseen that it was impossible, without a maritime power, to achieve the conquest of Africa. In the first Punic war, the republic had exerted such incredible diligence that, within sixty days after the first stroke of the axe had been given in the forest, a fleet of one hundred and sixty galleys proudly rode at anchor in the sea.[48] Under circumstances much less favourable, Majorian equalled the spirit and perseverance of the ancient Romans. The woods of the Apennine were felled; the arsenals and manufactures of Ravenna and Misenum were restored; Italy and Gaul vied with each other in liberal contributions to the public service; and the Imperial navy, of three hundred large galleys, with an adequate proportion of transports and smaller vessels, was collected in the secure and capacious harbour of Carthagena in Spain.[49] The intrepid countenance of Majorian animated his troops with a confidence of victory; and, if we might credit the historian Procopius, his courage sometimes hurried him beyond the bounds of prudence. Anxious to explore, with his own eyes, the state of the Vandals he ventured, after disguising the colour of his hair, to visit Carthage in the character of his own ambassador; and Genseric was afterwards mortified by the discovery that he had entertained and dismissed the emperor of the Romans. Such an anecdote may be rejected as an improbable fiction; but it is a fiction which would not have been imagined, unless in the life of a hero.[50]

Without the help of a personal interview, Genseric was sufficiently acquainted with the genius and designs of his adversary. He practised his customary arts of fraud and delay, but he practised them without success. His applications for peace became each hour more submissive, and perhaps more sincere; but the inflexible Majorian had adopted the ancient maxim that Rome could not be safe as long as Carthage existed in a hostile state. The king of the Vandals distrusted the valour of his native subjects, who were enervated by the luxury of the South;[51] he suspected the fidelity of the vanquished people, who abhorred him as an Arian tyrant; and the desperate measure, which he executed, of reducing Mauritania into a desert,[52] could not defeat the operations of the Roman emperor, who was at liberty to land his troops on any part of the African coast. But Genseric was saved from impending and inevitable ruin by the treachery of some powerful subjects, envious, or apprehensive, of their master's success. Guided by their secret intelligence, he surprised the unguarded fleet in the bay of Carthagena; many of the ships were sunk, or taken, or burnt; and the preparations of three years were destroyed in a single day.[53] After this event, the behaviour of the two antagonists showed them superior to their fortune. The Vandal, instead of being elated by this accidental victory, immediately renewed his solicitations for peace. The emperor of the West, who was capable of forming great designs, and of supporting heavy disappointments, consented to a treaty, or rather to a suspension of arms; in the full assurance that, before he could restore his navy, he should be supplied with provocations to justify a second war. Majorian returned to Italy, to prosecute his labours for the public happiness; and, as he was conscious of his own integrity, he might long remain ignorant of the dark conspiracy which threatened his throne and his life. The recent misfortune of Carthagena sullied the glory which had dazzled the eyes of the multitude; almost every description of civil and military officers were exasperated against the Reformer, since they all derived some advantage from the abuses which he endeavoured to suppress; and the patrician Ricimer impelled the inconstant passions of the Barbarians against a prince whom he esteemed and hated. The virtues of Majorian could not protect him from the impetuous sedition which broke out in the camp near Tortona, at the foot of the Alps. He was compelled to abdicate the Imperial purple: five days after his abdication, it was reported that he died of a dysentery;[54] and the humble tomb, which covered his remains, was consecrated by the respect and gratitude of succeeding generations.[55] The private character of Majorian inspired love and respect. Malicious calumny and satire excited his indignation, or, if he himself were the object, his contempt; but he protected the freedom of wit, and, in the hours which the emperor gave to the familiar society of his friends, he could indulge his taste for pleasantry, without degrading the majesty of his rank.[56]

It was not perhaps without some regret that Ricimer sacrificed his friend to the interest of his ambition; but he resolved, in a second choice, to avoid the imprudent preference of superior virtue and merit. At his command the obsequious senate of Rome bestowed the Imperial title on Libius Severus, who ascended the throne of the West without emerging from the obscurity of a private condition. History has scarcely deigned to notice his birth, his elevation, his character, or his death. Severus expired, as soon as his life became inconvenient to his patron;[57] and it would be useless to discriminate* his nominal reign in the vacant interval of six years, between the death of Majorian and the elevation of Anthemius. During that period, the government was in the hands of Ricimer alone; and, although the modest Barbarian disclaimed the name of king, he accumulated treasures, formed a separate army, negotiated private alliances, and ruled Italy with the same independent and despotic authority which was afterwards exercised by Odoacer and Theodoric. But his dominions were bounded by the Alps; and two Roman generals, Marcellinus and Aegidius, maintained their allegiance to the republic, by rejecting, with disdain, the phantom which he styled an emperor. Marcellinus still adhered to the old religion; and the devout Pagans, who secretly disobeyed the laws of the church and state, applauded his profound skill in the science of divination. But he possessed the more valuable qualifications of learning, virtue, and courage;[58] the study of the Latin literature had improved his taste; and his military talents had recommended him to the esteem and confidence of the great Aetius, in whose ruin he was involved. By a timely flight, Marcellinus escaped the rage of Valentinian, and boldly asserted his liberty amidst the convulsions of the Western empire. His voluntary, or reluctant, submission to the authority of Majorian was rewarded by the government of Sicily and the command of an army, stationed in that island to oppose, or to attack, the Vandals; but his Barbarian mercenaries, after the emperor's death, were tempted to revolt by the artful liberality of Ricimer. At the head of a band of faithful followers, the intrepid Marcellinus occupied the province of Dalmatia, assumed the title of Patrician of the West, secured the love of his subjects by a mild and equitable reign, built a fleet which claimed the dominion of the Hadriatic, and alternately alarmed the coasts of Italy and of Africa.[59] Aegidius, the master-general of Gaul, who equalled, or at least who imitated, the heroes of ancient Rome,[60] proclaimed his immortal resentment against the assassins of his beloved master. A brave and numerous army was attached to his standard; and, though he was prevented by the arts of Ricimer, and the arms of the Visigoths, from marching to the gates of Rome, he maintained his independent sovereignty beyond the Alps, and rendered the name of Aegidius respectable both in peace and war. The Franks, who had punished with exile the youthful follies of Childeric, elected the Roman general for their king; his vanity, rather than his ambition, was gratified by that singular honour; and, when the nation, at the end of four years, repented of the injury which they had offered to the Merovingian family, he patiently acquiesced in the restoration of the lawful prince. The authority of Aegidius ended only with his life; and the suspicions of poison and secret violence, which derived some countenance from the character of Ricimer, were eagerly entertained by the passionate credulity of the Gauls.[61]

The kingdom of Italy, a name to which the Western empire was gradually reduced, was afflicted, under the reign of Ricimer, by the incessant depredations of the Vandal pirates.[62] In the spring of each year they equipped a formidable navy in the port of Carthage; and Genseric himself, though in a very advanced age, still commanded in person the most important expeditions. His designs were concealed with impenetrable secrecy, till the moment that he hoisted sail. When he was asked by his pilot, what course he should steer; 'Leave the determination to the winds (replied the Barbarian with pious arrogance); *they* will transport us to the guilty coast, whose inhabitants have provoked the divine justice'; but, if Genseric himself deigned to issue more precise orders, he judged the most wealthy to be the most criminal. The Vandals repeatedly visited the coasts of Spain, Liguria, Tuscany, Campania, Lucania, Bruttium, Apulia, Calabria, Venetia, Dalmatia, Epirus, Greece, and Sicily; they were tempted to subdue the island of Sardinia, so advantageously placed in the centre of the Mediterranean; and their arms spread desolation, or terror, from the columns of Hercules* to the mouth of the Nile. As they were more ambitious of spoil than of glory, they seldom attacked any fortified cities or engaged any regular troops in the open field. But the celerity of their motions enabled them, almost at the same time, to threaten and to attack the most distant objects which attracted their desires; and, as they always embarked a sufficient number of horses, they had no sooner landed than they swept the dismayed country with a body of light cavalry. Yet, notwithstanding the example of their king, the native Vandals and Alani insensibly declined this toilsome and perilous warfare; the hardy generation of the first conquerors was almost extinguished, and their sons, who were born in Africa, enjoyed the delicious baths and gardens which had been acquired by the valour of their fathers. Their place was readily supplied by a various multitude of Moors and Romans, of captives and outlaws; and those desperate wretches who had already violated the laws of their country were the most eager to promote the atrocious acts which disgrace the victories of Genseric. In the treatment of his unhappy prisoners, he sometimes consulted his avarice, and sometimes indulged his cruelty; and the massacre of five hundred noble citizens of Zant or

Zacynthus, whose mangled bodies he cast into the Ionian sea, was imputed, by the public indignation, to his latest posterity.

Such crimes could not be excused by any provocations; but the war which the king of the Vandals prosecuted against the Roman empire was justified by a specious and reasonable motive. The widow of Valentinian, Eudoxia, whom he had led captive from Rome to Carthage, was the sole heiress of the Theodosian house; her elder daughter, Eudocia, became the reluctant wife of Hunneric, his eldest son; and the stern father, asserting a legal claim, which could not easily be refuted or satisfied, demanded a just proportion of the Imperial patrimony. An adequate, or at least a valuable, compensation was offered by the Eastern emperor, to purchase a necessary peace. Eudoxia and her younger daughter, Placidia, were honourably restored, and the fury of the Vandals was confined to the limits of the Western empire. The Italians, destitute of a naval force, which alone was capable of protecting their coasts, implored the aid of the more fortunate nations of the East; who had formerly acknowledged, in peace and war, the supremacy of Rome. But the perpetual division of the two empires had alienated their interest and their inclinations; the faith of a recent treaty was alleged; and the Western Romans, instead of arms and ships, could only obtain the assistance of a cold and ineffectual mediation. The haughty Ricimer, who had long struggled with the difficulties of his situation, was at length reduced to address the throne of Constantinople, in the humble language of a subject; and Italy submitted, as the price and security of the alliance, to accept a master from the choice of the emperor of the East.[63] It is not the purpose of the present chapter, or even of the present volume,* to continue the distinct series of the Byzantine history; but a concise view of the reign and character of the emperor Leo may explain the last efforts that were attempted to save the falling empire of the West.[64]

Since the death of the younger Theodosius, the domestic repose of Constantinople had never been interrupted by war or faction. Pulcheria had bestowed her hand, and the sceptre of the East, on the modest virtue of Marcian; he gratefully reverenced her august rank and virgin chastity; and, after her death, he gave his people the example of the religious worship that was due to the memory of the Imperial saint.[65] Attentive to the prosperity of his own dominions, Marcian seemed to behold with indifference the misfortunes of Rome; and the obstinate refusal of a brave and active prince to draw his sword against the Vandals was ascribed to a secret promise, which had formerly been exacted from him when he was a captive in the power of Genseric.[66] The death of Marcian, after a reign of seven years, would have exposed the East to the danger of a popular election, if the superior weight of a single family had not been able to incline the balance in favour of the candidate whose interest they supported. The patrician Aspar might have placed the diadem on his own head, if he would have subscribed the Nicene creed.[67] During three generations the armies of the East were successively commanded by his father, by himself, and by his son Ardaburius; his Barbarian guards formed a military force that overawed the palace and the capital; and the liberal distribution of his immense treasures rendered Aspar as popular as he was powerful. He recommended the obscure name of Leo of Thrace, a military tribune, and the principal steward of his household. His nomination was unanimously ratified by the senate; and the servant of Aspar received the Imperial crown from the hands of the patriarch or bishop, who was permitted to express, by this unusual ceremony, the suffrage of the Deity.[68] This emperor, the first of the name of Leo, has been distinguished by the title of the Great, from a succession of princes, who gradually fixed, in the opinion of the Greeks, a very humble standard of heroic, or at least of royal, perfection. Yet the temperate firmness with which Leo resisted the oppression of his benefactor showed that he was conscious of his duty and of his prerogative. Aspar was astonished to find that his influence could no longer appoint a prefect of Constantinople: he presumed to reproach his sovereign with a breach of promise, and, insolently shaking his purple, 'It is not proper (said he) that the man who is invested with this garment should be guilty of lying.' 'Nor is it proper (replied Leo) that a prince should be compelled to resign his own judgment, and the public interest, to the will of a subject.'[69] After this extraordinary scene, it was impossible that the reconciliation of the emperor and the patrician could be sincere; or, at least, that it could be solid and permanent. An army of Isaurians[70] was secretly levied, and introduced into Constantinople; and, while Leo undermined the authority, and prepared the disgrace, of the family of Aspar, his mild and cautious behaviour restrained them from any rash and desperate attempts, which might have been fatal to themselves or their enemies. The measures of peace and war were affected by this internal revolution. As long as Aspar degraded the majesty of the throne, the secret correspondence of religion and interest engaged him to favour the cause of Genseric. When Leo had delivered himself from that ignominious servitude, he listened to the complaints of the Italians; resolved to extirpate the tyranny of the Vandals; and declared his alliance with his colleague, Anthemius, whom he solemnly invested with the diadem and purple of the West.

The virtues of Anthemius have perhaps been magnified, since the Imperial descent, which he could only deduce from the usurper Procopius, has been swelled into a line of emperors.[71] But the merit of his immediate parents, their honours, and their riches, rendered Anthemius one of the most illustrious subjects of the East. His father Procopius obtained, after his Persian embassy, the rank of general and patrician; and the name of Anthemius was derived from his maternal grandfather, the celebrated prefect, who protected, with so much ability and success, the infant reign of Theodosius. The grandson of the prefect was raised above the condition of a private subject, by his marriage with Euphemia, the daughter of the emperor Marcian. This splendid alliance, which might supersede the necessity of merit, hastened the promotion of Anthemius to the successive dignities of count, of master-general, of consul, and of patrician; and his merit or fortune claimed the honours of a victory which was obtained on the banks of the Danube over the Huns. Without indulging an extravagant ambition, the son-in-law of Marcian might hope to be his successor; but Anthemius supported the disappointment with courage and patience; and his subsequent elevation was universally approved by the public, who esteemed him worthy to reign, till he ascended the throne.[72] The emperor of the West marched from Constantinople, attended by several counts of high distinction, and a body of guards, almost equal to the strength and numbers of a regular army; he entered Rome in triumph, and the choice of Leo was confirmed by the senate, the people, and the Barbarian confederates of Italy.[73] The solemn inauguration of Anthemius was followed by the nuptials of his daughter and the patrician Ricimer: a fortunate event which was considered as the firmest security of the union and happiness of the state. The wealth of two empires was ostentatiously displayed; and many senators completed their ruin by an expensive effort to disguise their poverty. All serious business was suspended during this festival; the courts of justice were shut; the streets of Rome, the theatres, the places of public and private resort, resounded with hymenaeal songs and dances; and the royal bride, clothed in silken robes, with a crown on her head, was conducted to the palace of Ricimer, who had changed his military dress for the habit of a consul and a senator. On this memorable occasion, Sidonius, whose early ambition had been so fatally blasted, appeared as the orator of Auvergne, among the provincial deputies who addressed the throne with congratulations or complaints.[74] The calends of January were now approaching, and the venal poet, who had loved Avitus and esteemed Majorian, was persuaded by his friends to celebrate, in heroic verse, the merit, the felicity, the second consulship and the future triumphs of the emperor Anthemius. Sidonius pronounced, with assurance and success, a panegyric which is still extant; and, whatever might be the imperfections either of the subject or of the composition, the welcome flatterer was immediately rewarded with the prefecture of Rome; a dignity which placed him among the illustrious personages of the empire, till he wisely preferred the more respectable character of a bishop and a saint.[75]

The Greeks ambitiously commend the piety and catholic faith of the emperor whom they gave to the West; nor do they forget to observe that, when he left Constantinople, he converted his palace into the pious foundation of a public bath, a church, and an hospital for old men.[76] Yet some suspicious appearances are found to sully the theological fame of Anthemius. From the conversation of Philotheus, a Macedonian sectary, he had imbibed the spirit of religious toleration; and the heretics of Rome would have assembled with impunity, if the bold and vehement censure which pope Hilary pronounced in the church of St Peter had not obliged him to abjure the unpopular indulgence.[77] Even the Pagans, a feeble and obscure remnant, conceived some vain hopes from the indifference or partiality of Anthemius; and his singular friendship for the philosopher Severus, whom he promoted to the consulship, was ascribed to a secret project of reviving the ancient worship of the gods.[78] These idols were crumbled into dust, and the mythology which had once been the creed of nations was so universally disbelieved that it might be employed without scandal, or at least without suspicion, by Christian poets.[79] Yet the vestiges of superstition were not absolutely obliterated, and the festival of the Lupercalia, whose origin had preceded the foundation of Rome, was still celebrated under the reign of Anthemius. The savage and simple rites were expressive of an early state of society before the invention of arts and agriculture. The rustic deities who presided over the toils and pleasures of the pastoral life, Pan, Faunus, and their train of satyrs, were such as the fancy of shepherds might create, sportive, petulant, and lascivious; whose power was limited, and whose malice was inoffensive. A goat was the offering the best adapted to their character and attributes; the flesh of the victim was roasted on willow spits; and the riotous youths who crowded to the feast ran naked about the fields, with leather thongs in their hands, communicating, as it was supposed, the blessing of fecundity to the women whom they touched.[80] The altar of Pan was erected, perhaps by Evander the Arcadian,* in a dark recess in the side of the Palatine hill, watered by a perpetual fountain, and shaded by an hanging grove. A tradition that, in the same place, Romulus and Remus were suckled by the wolf rendered it still more sacred and venerable in the eyes of the Romans; and this sylvan spot was gradually surrounded by the stately edifices of the Forum.[81] After the conversion of the Imperial city, the Christians still continued, in the month of February, the annual celebration of the Lupercalia; to which they ascribed a secret and mysterious influence on the genial powers of the animal and vegetable world. The bishops of Rome were solicitous to abolish a profane custom, so repugnant to the spirit of Christianity; but their zeal was not supported by the authority of the civil magistrate: the inveterate abuse subsisted till the end of the fifth century, and pope Gelasius, who purified the capital from the last stain of idolatry, appeased, by a formal apology, the murmurs of the senate and people.[82]

In all his public declarations, the emperor Leo assumes the authority, and professes the affection, of a father for his son Anthemius, with whom he had divided the administration of the universe.[83] The situation, and perhaps the character, of Leo dissuaded him from exposing his person to the toils and dangers of an African war. But the powers of the Eastern empire were strenuously exerted to deliver Italy and the Mediterranean from the Vandals; and Genseric, who had so long oppressed both the land and the sea, was threatened from every side with a formidable invasion.

The campaign was opened by a bold and successful enterprise of the prefect Heraclius.[84] The troops of Egypt, Thebais, and Libya were embarked under his command; and the Arabs, with a train of horses and camels, opened the roads of the desert. Heraclius landed on the coast of Tripoli, surprised and subdued the cities of that province, and prepared, by a laborious march, which Cato* had formerly executed,[85] to join the Imperial army under the walls of Carthage. The intelligence of this loss extorted from Genseric some insidious and ineffectual propositions of peace; but he was still more seriously alarmed by the reconciliation of Marcellinus with the two empires. The independent patrician had been persuaded to acknowledge the legitimate title of Anthemius, whom he accompanied in his journey to Rome; the Dalmatian fleet was received into the harbours of Italy; the active valour of Marcellinus expelled the Vandals from the island of Sardinia; and the languid efforts of the West added some weight to the immense preparations of the Eastern Romans. The expense of the naval armament, which Leo sent against the Vandals, has been distinctly ascertained; and the curious and instructive account displays the wealth of the declining empire. The royal demesnes, or private patrimony of the prince, supplied seventeen thousand pounds of gold; forty-seven thousand pounds of gold, and seven hundred thousand of silver, were levied and paid into the treasury by the Praetorian prefects. But the cities were reduced to extreme poverty; and the diligent calculation of fines and forfeitures, as a valuable object of the revenue, does not suggest the idea of a just or merciful administration. The whole expense, by whatever means it was defrayed, of the African campaign amounted to the sum of one hundred and thirty thousand pounds of gold, about five millions two hundred thousand pounds sterling, at a time when the value of money appears, from the comparative price of corn, to have been somewhat higher than in the present age.[86] The fleet that sailed from Constantinople to Carthage, consisted of eleven hundred and thirteen ships, and the number of soldiers and mariners exceeded one hundred thousand men. Basiliscus, the brother of the empress Verina,† was entrusted with this important command. His sister, the wife of Leo, had exaggerated the merit of his former exploits against the Scythians. But the discovery of his guilt, or incapacity, was reserved for the African war; and his friends could only save his military reputation by asserting that he had conspired with Aspar to spare Genseric and to betray the last hope of the Western empire.

Experience has shown that the success of an invader most commonly depends on the vigour and celerity of his operations. The strength and sharpness of the first impression are blunted by delay; the health and spirit of the troops insensibly languish in a distant climate; the naval and military force, a mighty effort which perhaps can never be repeated, is silently consumed; and every hour that is wasted in negotiation accustoms the enemy to contemplate and examine those hostile terrors which, on their first appearance, he deemed irresistible. The formidable navy of Basiliscus pursued its prosperous navigation from the Thracian Bosphorus to the coast of Africa. He landed his troops at Cape Bona, or the promontory of Mercury, about forty miles from Carthage.[87] The army of Heraclius and the fleet of Marcellinus either joined or seconded the Imperial lieutenant; and the Vandals, who opposed his progress by sea or land, were successively vanquished.[88] If Basiliscus had seized the moment of consternation and boldly advanced to the capital, Carthage must have surrendered, and the kingdom of the Vandals was extinguished. Genseric beheld the danger with firmness, and eluded it with his veteran dexterity. He protested, in the most respectful language, that he was ready to submit his person and his dominions to the will of the emperor; but he requested a truce of five days to regulate the terms of his submission; and it was universally believed that his secret liberality contributed to the success of this public negotiation. Instead of obstinately refusing whatever indulgence his enemy so earnestly solicited, the guilty, or the credulous, Basiliscus consented to the fatal truce; and his imprudent security seemed to proclaim that he already considered himself as the conqueror of Africa. During this short interval, the wind became favourable to the designs of Genseric. He manned his largest ships of war with the bravest of the Moors and Vandals, and they towed after them many large barques filled with combustible materials. In the obscurity of the night these destructive vessels were impelled against the unguarded and unsuspecting fleet of the Romans, who were awakened by the sense of their instant danger. Their close and crowded order assisted the progress of the fire, which was communicated with rapid and irresistible violence; and the noise of the wind, the crackling of the flames, the dissonant cries of the soldiers and mariners, who could neither command nor obey, increased the horror of the nocturnal tumult. Whilst they laboured to extricate themselves from the fire-ships, and to save at least a part of the navy, the galleys of Genseric assaulted them with temperate and disciplined valour; and many of the Romans, who escaped the fury of the flames, were destroyed or taken by the victorious Vandals. Among the events of that disastrous night the heroic, or rather desperate, courage of John, one of the principal officers of Basiliscus, has rescued his name from oblivion. When the ship, which he had bravely defended, was almost consumed, he threw himself in his armour into the sea, disdainfully rejected the esteem and pity of Genso, the son of Genseric, who pressed him to accept honourable quarter, and sunk under the waves; exclaiming, with his last breath, that he would never fall alive into the hands of those impious dogs. Actuated by a far different spirit, Basiliscus, whose station was the most remote from danger, disgracefully fled in the beginning of the engagement, returned to Constantinople with the loss of more than half of his fleet and army, and sheltered his guilty head in the sanctuary of St Sophia, till his sister, by her tears and entreaties, could obtain his pardon from the indignant emperor.

Heraclius effected his retreat through the desert; Marcellinus retired to Sicily, where he was assassinated, perhaps at the instigation of Ricimer, by one of his own captains; and the king of the Vandals expressed his surprise and satisfaction that the Romans themselves should remove from the world his most formidable antagonists.[89] After the failure of this great expedition, Genseric again became the tyrant of the sea: the coasts of Italy, Greece and Asia were again exposed to his revenge and avarice; Tripoli and Sardinia returned to his obedience; he added Sicily to the number of his provinces; and, before he died, in the fulness of years and of glory, he beheld the final extinction of the empire of the West.[90]

During his long and active reign, the African monarch had studiously cultivated the friendship of the Barbarians of Europe, whose arms he might employ in a seasonable and effectual diversion against the two empires. After the death of Attila, he renewed his alliance with the Visigoths of Gaul; and the sons of the elder Theodoric, who successively reigned over that warlike nation, were easily persuaded, by the sense of interest, to forget the cruel affront which Genseric had inflicted on their sister.[91] The death of the emperor Majorian delivered Theodoric the Second from the restraint of fear, and perhaps of honour; he violated his recent treaty with the Romans; and the ample territory of Narbonne, which he firmly united to his dominions, became the immediate reward of his perfidy. The selfish policy of Ricimer encouraged him to invade the provinces which were in the possession of Aegidius, his rival; but the active count, by the defence of Arles and the victory of Orleans, saved Gaul, and checked, during his lifetime, the progress of the Visigoths. Their ambition was soon rekindled; and the design of extinguishing the Roman empire in Spain and Gaul was conceived, and almost completed, in the reign of Euric, who assassinated his brother Theodoric, and displayed, with a more savage temper, superior abilities both in peace and war. He passed the Pyrenees at the head of a numerous army, subdued the cities of Saragossa and Pampeluna, vanquished in battle the martial nobles of the Tarragonese province, carried his victorious arms into the heart of Lusitania, and permitted the Suevi to hold the kingdom of Gallicia under the Gothic monarchy of Spain.[92] The efforts of Euric were not less vigorous or less successful in Gaul; and, throughout the country that extends from the Pyrenees to the Rhone and the Loire, Berry and Auvergne were the only cities, or dioceses, which refused to acknowledge him as their master.[93] In the defence of Clermont, their principal town, the inhabitants of Auvergne sustained with inflexible resolution the miseries of war, pestilence and famine; and the Visigoths, relinquishing the fruitless siege, suspended the hopes of that important conquest. The youth of the province were animated by the heroic and almost incredible valour of Ecdicius, the son of the emperor Avitus,[94] who made a desperate sally with only eighteen horsemen, boldly attacked the Gothic army, and, after maintaining a flying skirmish, retired safe and victorious within the

walls of Clermont. His charity was equal to his courage: in a time of
extreme scarcity four thousand poor were fed at his expense, and his
private influence levied an army of Burgundians for the deliverance of
Auvergne. From *his* virtues alone the faithful citizens of Gaul derived any
hopes of safety or freedom; and even such virtues were insufficient to
avert the impending ruin of their country, since they were anxious to
learn from his authority and example, whether they should prefer the
alternative of exile or servitude.[95] The public confidence was lost; the
resources of the state were exhausted; and the Gauls had too much reason
to believe that Anthemius, who reigned in Italy, was incapable of
protecting his distressed subjects beyond the Alps. The feeble emperor
could only procure for their defence the service of twelve thousand
British auxiliaries. Riothamus, one of the independent kings, or chieftains, of the island, was persuaded to transport his troops to the continent
of Gaul; he sailed up the Loire, and established his quarters in Berry,
where the people complained of these oppressive allies, till they were
destroyed, or dispersed, by the arms of the Visigoths.[96]

One of the last acts of jurisdiction, which the Roman senate exercised
over their subjects of Gaul, was the trial and condemnation of Arvandus
the Praetorian prefect. Sidonius, who rejoices that he lived under a reign
in which he might pity and assist a state criminal, has expressed with
tenderness and freedom, the faults of his indiscreet and unfortunate
friend.[97] From the perils which he had escaped, Arvandus imbibed
confidence rather than wisdom; and such was the various, though
uniform, imprudence of his behaviour that his prosperity must appear
much more surprising than his downfall. The second prefecture, which
he obtained within the term of five years, abolished the merit and
popularity of his preceding administration. His easy temper was corrupted
by flattery and exasperated by opposition; he was forced to satisfy his
importunate creditors with the spoils of the province; his capricious
insolence offended the nobles of Gaul, and he sunk under the weight of
the public hatred. The mandate of his disgrace summoned him to justify
his conduct before the senate; and he passed the sea of Tuscany with a
favourable wind, the presage, as he vainly imagined, of his future
fortunes. A decent respect was still observed for the Prefectorian rank;
and, on his arrival at Rome, Arvandus was committed to the hospitality,
rather than to the custody, of Flavius Asellus, the count of the sacred
largesses, who resided in the Capitol.[98] He was eagerly pursued by his
accusers, the four deputies of Gaul, who were all distinguished by their
birth, their dignities, or their eloquence. In the name of a great province,
and according to the forms of Roman jurisprudence, they instituted a civil
and criminal action, requiring such a restitution as might compensate the
losses of individuals, and such punishment as might satisfy the justice of
the state. Their charges of corrupt oppression were numerous and
weighty; but they placed their secret dependence on a letter, which they

had intercepted, and which they could prove, by the evidence of his secretary, to have been dictated by Arvandus himself. The author of this letter seemed to dissuade the king of the Goths from a peace with the *Greek* emperor; he suggested the attack of the Britons on the Loire; and he recommended a division of Gaul, according to the law of nations, between the Visigoths and the Burgundians.[99] These pernicious schemes, which a friend could only palliate by the reproaches of vanity and indiscretion, were susceptible of a treasonable interpretation; and the deputies had artfully resolved not to produce their most formidable weapons till the decisive moment of the contest. But their intentions were discovered by the zeal of Sidonius. He immediately apprised the unsuspecting criminal of his danger; and sincerely lamented, without any mixture of anger, the haughty presumption of Arvandus, who rejected, and even resented, the salutary advice of his friends. Ignorant of his real situation, Arvandus showed himself in the Capitol in the white robe of a candidate, accepted indiscriminate salutations and offers of service, examined the shops of the merchants, the silks and gems, sometimes with the indifference of a spectator, and sometimes with the attention of a purchaser; and complained of the times, of the senate, of the prince, and of the delays of justice. His complaints were soon removed. An early day was fixed for his trial; and Arvandus appeared, with his accusers, before a numerous assembly of the Roman senate. The mournful garb which they affected excited the compassion of the judges, who were scandalised by the gay and splendid dress of their adversary; and, when the prefect Arvandus, with the first of the Gallic deputies, were directed to take their places on the senatorial benches, the same contrast of pride and modesty was observed in their behaviour. In this memorable judgment, which presented a lively image of the old republic, the Gauls exposed, with force and freedom, the grievances of the province; and, as soon as the minds of the audience were sufficiently inflamed, they recited the fatal epistle. The obstinacy of Arvandus was founded on the strange supposition that a subject could not be convicted of treason, unless he had actually conspired to assume the purple. As the paper was read, he repeatedly, and with a loud voice, acknowledged it for his genuine composition; and his astonishment was equal to his dismay, when the unanimous voice of the senate declared him guilty of a capital offence. By their decree, he was degraded from the rank of a prefect to the obscure condition of a plebeian, and ignominiously dragged by servile hands to the public prison. After a fortnight's adjournment, the senate was again convened to pronounce the sentence of his death; but, while he expected, in the island of Aesculapius,* the expiration of the thirty days allowed by an ancient law to the vilest malefactors,[100] his friends interposed, the emperor Anthemius relented, and the prefect of Gaul obtained the milder punishment of exile and confiscation. The faults of Arvandus might deserve compassion; but the impunity of Seronatus accused the justice of the republic, till he was condemned, and executed, on the complaint of the people of Auvergne. That flagitious* minister, the Catiline† of his age and country, held a secret correspondence with the Visigoths, to betray the province which he oppressed; his industry was continually exercised in the discovery of new taxes and obsolete offences; and his extravagant vices would have inspired contempt, if they had not excited fear and abhorrence.[101]

Such criminals were not beyond the reach of justice; but whatever might be the guilt of Ricimer, that powerful Barbarian was able to contend or to negotiate with the prince whose alliance he had condescended to accept. The peaceful and prosperous reign which Anthemius had promised to the West was soon clouded by misfortune and discord. Ricimer, apprehensive, or impatient, of a superior, retired from Rome, and fixed his residence at Milan, an advantageous situation either to invite or to repel the warlike tribes that were seated between the Alps and the Danube.[102] Italy was gradually divided into two independent and hostile kingdoms; and the nobles of Liguria, who trembled at the near approach of a civil war, fell prostrate at the feet of the patrician, and conjured him to spare their unhappy country. 'For my own part,' replied Ricimer in a tone of insolent moderation, 'I am still inclined to embrace the friendship of the Galatian;[103] but who will undertake to appease his anger, or to mitigate the pride which always rises in proportion to our submission?' They informed him that Epiphanius, bishop of Pavia,[104] united the wisdom of the serpent with the innocence of the dove; and appeared confident that the eloquence of such an ambassador must prevail against the strongest opposition either of interest or passion. Their recommendation was approved; and Epiphanius, assuming the benevolent office of mediation, proceeded without delay to Rome, where he was received with the honours due to his merit and reputation. The oration of a bishop in favour of peace may be easily supposed: he argued, that in all possible circumstances the forgiveness of injuries must be an act of mercy, or magnanimity, or prudence; and he seriously admonished the emperor to avoid a contest with a fierce Barbarian, which might be fatal to himself, and must be ruinous to his dominions. Anthemius acknowledged the truth of his maxims; but he deeply felt, with grief and indignation, the behaviour of Ricimer, and his passion gave eloquence and energy to his discourse. 'What favours,' he warmly exclaimed, 'have we refused to this ungrateful man? What provocations have we not endured? Regardless of the majesty of the purple, I gave my daughter to a Goth; I sacrificed my own blood to the safety of the republic. The liberality which ought to have secured the eternal attachment of Ricimer has exasperated him against his benefactor. What wars has he not excited against the empire? How often has he instigated and assisted the fury of hostile nations? Shall I now accept his perfidious friendship? Can I hope that *he* will respect the engagements of a treaty, who has already violated the duties of a son?' But the anger of Anthemius evaporated in these passionate exclamations; he insensibly yielded to the proposals of Epiphanius; and the bishop returned to his diocese with the satisfaction of restoring the peace of Italy, by a reconciliation,[105] of which the sincerity and continuance might be reasonably suspected. The clemency of the emperor was extorted from his weakness; and Ricimer suspended his ambitious designs, till he had secretly prepared the engines with which he resolved to subvert the throne of Anthemius. The mask of peace and moderation was then thrown aside. The army of Ricimer was fortified by a numerous reinforcement of Burgundians and Oriental Suevi; he disclaimed all allegiance to the Greek emperor, marched from Milan to the gates of Rome, and, fixing his camp on the banks of the Anio, impatiently expected the arrival of Olybrius, his Imperial candidate.

The senator Olybrius, of the Anician family, might esteem himself the lawful heir of the Western empire. He had married Placidia, the younger daughter of Valentinian, after she was restored by Genseric; who still detained her sister Eudoxia, as the wife, or rather as the captive, of his son. The king of the Vandals supported, by threats and solicitations, the fair pretensions of his Roman ally; and assigned, as one of the motives of the war, the refusal of the senate and people to acknowledge their lawful prince, and the unworthy preference which they had given to a stranger.[106] The friendship of the public enemy might render Olybrius still more unpopular to the Italians; but, when Ricimer meditated the ruin of the emperor Anthemius, he tempted with the offer of a diadem the candidate who could justify his rebellion by an illustrious name and a royal alliance. The husband of Placidia, who, like most of his ancestors, had been invested with the consular dignity, might have continued to enjoy a secure and splendid fortune in the peaceful residence of Constantinople; nor does he appear to have been tormented by such a genius as cannot be amused or occupied unless by the administration of an empire. Yet Olybrius yielded to the importunities of his friends, perhaps of his wife; rashly plunged into the dangers and calamities of a civil war; and, with the secret connivance of the emperor Leo, accepted the Italian purple, which was bestowed and resumed at the capricious will of a Barbarian. He landed without obstacle (for Genseric was master of the sea) either at Ravenna or the port of Ostia, and immediately proceeded to the camp of Ricimer, where he was received as the sovereign of the Western world.[107]

The patrician, who had extended his posts from the Anio to the Milvian bridge, already possessed two quarters of Rome, the Vatican and the Janiculum, which are separated by the Tiber from the rest of the city;[108] and it may be conjectured that an assembly of seceding senators imitated, in the choice of Olybrius, the forms of a legal election. But the body of the senate and people firmly adhered to the cause of Anthemius; and the more effectual support of a Gothic army enabled him to prolong his reign, and the public distress, by a resistance of three months, which produced the concomitant evils of famine and pestilence. At length Ricimer made a furious assault on the bridge of Hadrian, or St Angelo; and the narrow pass was defended with equal valour by the Goths, till the death of Gilimer their leader. The victorious troops, breaking down every barrier, rushed with irresistible violence into the heart of the city, and Rome (if we may use the language of a contemporary Pope) was subverted by the civil fury of Anthemius and Ricimer.[109] The unfortunate Anthemius was dragged from his concealment and inhumanly massacred by the command of his son-in-law; who thus added a third, or perhaps a fourth, emperor to the number of his victims. The soldiers, who united the rage of factious citizens with the savage manners of Barbarians, were indulged, without control, in the licence of rapine and murder; the crowd of slaves and plebeians, who were unconcerned in the event, could only gain by the indiscriminate pillage; and the face of the city exhibited the strange contrast of stern cruelty and dissolute intemperance.[110] Forty days after this calamitous event, the subject not of glory but of guilt, Italy was delivered, by a painful disease, from the tyrant Ricimer, who bequeathed the command of his army to his nephew Gundobald, one of the princes of the Burgundians. In the same year, all the principal actors in this great revolution were removed from the stage; and the whole reign of Olybrius, whose death does not betray any symptoms of violence, is included within the term of seven months. He left one daughter, the offspring of his marriage with Placidia; and the family of the great Theodosius, transplanted from Spain to Constantinople, was propagated in the female line as far as the eighth generation.[111]

Whilst the vacant throne of Italy was abandoned to lawless Barbarians,[112] the election of a new colleague was seriously agitated in the council of Leo. The empress Verina, studious to promote the greatness of her own family, had married one of her nieces to Julius Nepos, who succeeded his uncle Marcellinus in the sovereignty of Dalmatia, a more solid possession than the title which he was persuaded to accept, of Emperor of the West. But the measures of the Byzantine court were so languid and irresolute that many months elapsed after the death of Anthemius, and even of Olybrius, before their destined successor could show himself, with a respectable force, to his Italian subjects. During that interval, Glycerius, an obscure soldier, was invested with the purple by his patron Gundobald; but the Burgundian prince was unable, or unwilling, to support his nomination by a civil war: the pursuits of domestic ambition recalled him beyond the Alps,[113] and his client was permitted to exchange the Roman sceptre for the bishopric of Salona. After extinguishing such a competitor, the emperor Nepos was acknowledged by the senate, by the Italians, and by the provincials of Gaul; his moral virtues and military talents were loudly celebrated; and those who derived any private benefit from his government announced, in prophetic strains, the restoration of the public felicity.[114] Their hopes (if such hopes had been entertained) were confounded within the term of a single year, and the treaty of peace, which ceded Auvergne to the Visigoths, is the only event of his short and inglorious reign. The most faithful subjects of Gaul were sacrificed by the Italian emperor to the hope of domestic security;[115] but his repose was soon invaded by a furious sedition of the Barbarian confederates, who, under the command of Orestes, their general, were in full march from Rome to Ravenna. Nepos trembled at their approach; and, instead of placing a just confidence in the strength of Ravenna, he hastily escaped to his ships, and retired to his Dalmatian principality, on the opposite coast of the Hadriatic. By this shameful abdication, he protracted his life about five years, in a very ambiguous state, between an emperor and an exile, till he was assassinated at Salona by the ungrateful Glycerius, who was translated, perhaps as the reward of his crime, to the archbishopric of Milan.[116]

The nations who had asserted their independence after the death of Attila were established, by the right of possession or conquest, in the boundless countries to the north of the Danube, or in the Roman provinces between the river and the Alps. But the bravest of their youth enlisted in the army of *confederates*, who formed the defence and the terror of Italy;[117] and in this promiscuous multitude, the names of the Heruli, the Scyrri, the Alani, the Turcilingi, and the Rugians, appear to have predominated. The example of these warriors was imitated by Orestes,[118] the son of Tatullus, and the father of the last Roman emperor of the West. Orestes, who has been already mentioned in this history,* had never deserted his country. His birth and fortunes rendered him one of the most illustrious subjects of Pannonia. When that province was ceded to the Huns, he entered into the service of Attila, his lawful sovereign, obtained the office of his secretary, and was repeatedly sent ambassador to Constantinople, to represent the person, and signify the commands, of the imperious monarch. The death of that conqueror restored him to his freedom; and Orestes might honourably refuse either to follow the sons of Attila into the Scythian desert or to obey the Ostrogoths, who had usurped the dominion of Pannonia. He preferred the service of the Italian princes, the successors of Valentinian; and, as he possessed the qualifications of courage, industry, and experience, he advanced with rapid steps in the military profession, till he was elevated, by the favour of Nepos himself, to the dignities of patrician and master-general of the troops. These troops had been long accustomed to reverence the character and authority of Orestes, who affected their manners, conversed with them in their own language, and was intimately connected with their national chieftains, by long habits of familiarity and friendship. At his solicitation they rose in arms against the obscure Greek, who presumed to claim their obedience; and, when Orestes, from some secret motive, declined the purple, they consented, with the same facility, to acknowledge his son

Augustulus as the emperor of the West. By the abdication of Nepos, Orestes had now attained the summit of his ambitious hopes; but he soon discovered, before the end of the first year, that the lessons of perjury and ingratitude, which a rebel must inculcate, will be retorted* against himself; and that the precarious sovereign of Italy was only permitted to choose whether he would be the slave or the victim of his Barbarian mercenaries. The dangerous alliance of these strangers had oppressed and insulted the last remains of Roman freedom and dignity. At each revolution, their pay and privileges were augmented; but their insolence increased in a still more extravagant degree; they envied the fortune of their brethren in Gaul, Spain, and Africa, whose victorious arms had acquired an independent and perpetual inheritance; and they insisted on their peremptory demand that a *third* part of the lands of Italy should be immediately divided among them. Orestes, with a spirit which, in another situation, might be entitled to our esteem, chose rather to encounter the rage of an armed multitude than to subscribe the ruin of an innocent people. He rejected the audacious demand; and his refusal was favourable to the ambition of Odoacer: a bold Barbarian, who assured his fellow soldiers that, if they dared to associate under his command, they might soon extort the justice which had been denied to their dutiful petitions. From all the camps and garrisons of Italy, the confederates, actuated by the same resentment and the same hopes, impatiently flocked to the standard of this popular leader; and the unfortunate patrician, overwhelmed by the torrent, hastily retreated to the strong city of Pavia, the episcopal seat of the holy Epiphanius. Pavia was immediately besieged, the fortifications were stormed, the town was pillaged; and, although the bishop might labour, with much zeal and some success, to save the property of the church and the chastity of female captives, the tumult could only be appeased by the execution of Orestes.[119] His brother Paul was slain in an action near Ravenna; and the helpless Augustulus, who could no longer command the respect, was reduced to implore the clemency, of Odoacer.

That successful Barbarian was the son of Edecon: who, in some remarkable transactions, particularly described in a preceding chapter,† had been the colleague of Orestes himself. The honour of an ambassador should be exempt from suspicion; and Edecon had listened to a conspiracy against the life of his sovereign. But this apparent guilt was expiated by his merit or repentance; his rank was eminent and conspicuous; he enjoyed the favour of Attila; and the troops under his command, who guarded in their turn the royal village, consisted in a tribe of Scyrri, his immediate and hereditary subjects. In the revolt of the nations, they still adhered to the Huns; and, more than twelve years afterwards, the name of Edecon is honourably mentioned, in their unequal contest with the Ostrogoths; which was terminated, after two bloody battles, by the defeat and dispersion of the Scyrri.[120] Their gallant leader, who did not survive this national calamity, left two sons, Onulf and Odoacer, to struggle with adversity, and to maintain as they might, by rapine or service, the faithful followers of their exile. Onulf directed his steps towards Constantinople, where he sullied, by the assassination of a generous benefactor, the fame which he had acquired in arms. His brother Odoacer led a wandering life among the Barbarians of Noricum, with a mind and a fortune suited to the most desperate adventures; and, when he had fixed his choice, he piously visited the cell of Severinus, the popular saint of the country, to solicit his approbation and blessing. The lowness of the door would not admit the lofty stature of Odoacer: he was obliged to stoop; but in that humble attitude the saint could discern the symptoms of his future greatness; and, addressing him in a prophetic tone, 'Pursue' (said he) 'your design; proceed to Italy; you will soon cast away this coarse garment of skins; and your wealth will be adequate to the liberality of your mind'.[121] The Barbarian, whose daring spirit accepted and ratified the prediction, was admitted into the service of the Western empire, and soon obtained an honourable rank in the guards. His manners were gradually polished, his military skill was improved, and the confederates of Italy would not have elected him for their general, unless the exploits of Odoacer had established a high opinion of his courage and capacity.[122] Their military acclamations saluted him with the title of King; but he abstained, during his whole reign, from the use of the purple and diadem,[123] lest he should offend those princes whose subjects, by their accidental mixture, had formed the victorious army which time and policy might insensibly unite into a great nation.

Royalty was familiar to the Barbarians, and the submissive people of Italy was prepared to obey, without a murmur, the authority which he should condescend to exercise as the vice-gerent of the emperor of the West. But Odoacer had resolved to abolish that useless and expensive office; and such is the weight of antique prejudice that it required some boldness and penetration to discover the extreme facility of the enterprise. The unfortunate Augustulus was made the instrument of his own disgrace; he signified his resignation to the senate; and that assembly, in their last act of obedience to a Roman prince, still affected the spirit of freedom and the forms of the constitution. An epistle was addressed, by their unanimous decree, to the emperor Zeno, the son-in-law and successor of Leo; who had lately been restored, after a short rebellion, to the Byzantine throne. They solemnly 'disclaim the necessity, or even the wish, of continuing any longer the Imperial succession in Italy; since, in their opinion, the majesty of a sole monarch is sufficient to pervade and protect, at the same time, both the East and the West. In their own name, and in the name of the people, they consent that the seat of universal empire shall be transferred from Rome to Constantinople; and they basely renounce the right of choosing their master, the only vestige that yet remained of the authority which had given laws to the world. The republic (they repeat that name without a blush) might safely confide in the civil and military virtues of Odoacer; and they humbly request that the emperor would invest him with the title of Patrician and the administration of the *diocese* of Italy.' The deputies of the senate were received at Constantinople with some marks of displeasure and indignation; and, when they were admitted to the audience of Zeno, he sternly reproached them with their treatment of the two emperors, Anthemius and Nepos, whom the East had successively granted to the prayers of Italy. 'The first' (continued he) 'you have murdered; the second you have expelled; but the second is still alive, and whilst he lives he is your lawful sovereign.' But the prudent Zeno soon deserted the hopeless cause of his abdicated colleague. His vanity was gratified by the title of sole emperor and by the statues erected to his honour in the several quarters of Rome; he entertained a friendly, though ambiguous, correspondence with the *patrician* Odoacer; and he gratefully accepted the Imperial ensigns, the sacred ornaments of the throne and palace, which the Barbarian was not unwilling to remove from the sight of the people.[124]

In the space of twenty years since the death of Valentinian, nine emperors had successively disappeared, and the son of Orestes, a youth recommended only by his beauty, would be the least entitled to the notice of posterity, if his reign, which was marked by the extinction of the Roman empire in the West, did not leave a memorable era in the history of mankind.[125] The patrician Orestes had married the daughter of Count *Romulus*, of Petovio, in Noricum; the name of *Augustus*, notwithstanding the jealousy of power, was known at Aquileia as a familiar surname; and the appellations of the two great founders, of the city and of the monarchy, were thus strangely united in the last of their successors.[126] The son of Orestes assumed and disgraced the names of Romulus Augustus; but the first was corrupted into Momyllus by the Greeks, and the second has been changed by the Latins into the contemptible diminutive Augustulus. The life of this inoffensive youth was spared by the generous clemency of Odoacer; who dismissed him with his whole family, from the Imperial palace, fixed his annual allowance at six thousand pieces of gold, and assigned the castle of Lucullus, in Campania, for the place of his exile or retirement.[127] As soon as the Romans breathed from the toils of the Punic war, they were attracted by the beauties and the pleasures of Campania; and the country house of the elder Scipio at Liternum exhibited a lasting model of their rustic simplicity.[128] The delicious shores of the bay of Naples were crowded with villas; and Sulla applauded the masterly skill of his rival,* who had seated himself on the lofty promontory of Misenum, that commands, on every side, the sea and land, as far as the boundaries of the horizon.[129] The villa of Marius was purchased, within a few years, by Lucullus, and the price had increased from two thousand five hundred to more than fourscore thousand pounds sterling.[130] It was adorned by the new proprietor with Grecian arts, and

Asiatic treasures; and the houses and gardens of Lucullus obtained a distinguished rank in the list of Imperial palaces.[131] When the Vandals became formidable to the sea-coast, the Lucullan villa, on the promontory of Misenum, gradually assumed the strength and appellation of a strong castle, the obscure retreat of the last emperor of the West. About twenty years after that great revolution it was converted into a church and monastery, to receive the bones of St Severinus. They securely reposed, amidst the broken trophies of Cimbric and Armenian victories, till the beginning of the tenth century; when the fortifications, which might afford a dangerous shelter to the Saracens, were demolished by the people of Naples.[132]

Odoacer was the first Barbarian who reigned in Italy, over a people who had once asserted their just superiority above the rest of mankind. The disgrace of the Romans still excites our respectful compassion, and we fondly sympathise with the imaginary grief and indignation of their degenerate posterity. But the calamities of Italy had gradually subdued the proud consciousness of freedom and glory. In the age of Roman virtue, the provinces were subject to the arms, and the citizens to the laws, of the republic; till those laws were subverted by civil discord, and both the city and the provinces became the servile property of a tyrant. The forms of the constitution, which alleviated or disguised their abject slavery, were abolished by time and violence; the Italians alternately lamented the presence or the absence of the sovereigns, whom they detested or despised; and the succession of five centuries inflicted the various evils of military licence, capricious despotism, and elaborate oppression. During the same period, the Barbarians had emerged from obscurity and contempt, and the warriors of Germany and Scythia were introduced into the provinces, as the servants, the allies, and at length the masters, of the Romans, whom they insulted or protected. The hatred of the people was suppressed by fear; they respected the spirit and splendour of the martial chiefs who were invested with the honours of the empire; and the fate of Rome had long depended on the sword of those formidable strangers. The stern Ricimer, who trampled on the ruins of Italy, had exercised the power, without assuming the title, of a king; and the patient Romans were insensibly prepared to acknowledge the royalty of Odoacer and his Barbaric successors.

The King of Italy was not unworthy of the high station to which his valour and fortune had exalted him; his savage manners were polished by the habits of conversation; and he respected, though a conqueror and a Barbarian, the institutions, and even the prejudices, of his subjects. After an interval of seven years, Odoacer restored the consulship of the West. For himself, he modestly, or proudly, declined an honour which was still accepted by the emperors of the East; but the curule chair* was successively filled by eleven of the most illustrious senators;[133] and the list is adorned by the respectable name of Basilius, whose virtues claimed the friendship and grateful applause of Sidonius, his client.[134] The laws of the emperors were strictly enforced, and the civil administration of Italy was still exercised by the Praetorian prefect and his subordinate officers. Odoacer devolved on the Roman magistrates the odious and oppressive task of collecting the public revenue; but he reserved for himself the merit of seasonable and popular indulgence.[135] Like the rest of the Barbarians, he had been instructed in the Arian heresy; but he revered the monastic and episcopal characters; and the silence of the Catholics attests the toleration which they enjoyed. The peace of the city required the interposition of his prefect Basilius in the choice of a Roman pontiff; the decree which restrained the clergy from alienating* their lands was ultimately designed for the benefit of the people, whose devotion would have been taxed to repair the dilapidations of the church.[136] Italy was protected by the arms of its conqueror; and its frontiers were respected by the Barbarians of Gaul and Germany, who had so long insulted the feeble race of Theodosius. Odoacer passed the Hadriatic, to chastise the assassins of the emperor Nepos, and to acquire the maritime province of Dalmatia. He passed the Alps, to rescue the remains of Noricum from Fava, or Feletheus, king of the Rugians, who held his residence beyond the Danube. The king was vanquished in battle, and led away prisoner; a numerous colony of captives and subjects was transplanted into Italy; and Rome, after a long period of defeat and disgrace, might claim the triumph of her Barbarian master.[137]

Notwithstanding the prudence and success of Odoacer, his kingdom exhibited the sad prospect of misery and desolation. Since the age of Tiberius, the decay of agriculture had been felt in Italy; and it was a subject of complaint that the life of the Roman people depended on the accidents of the winds and waves.[138] In the division and the decline of the empire, the tributary harvests of Egypt and Africa were withdrawn; the numbers of the inhabitants continually diminished with the means of subsistence; and the country was exhausted by the irretrievable losses of war, famine,[139] and pestilence. St Ambrose has deplored the ruin of a populous district, which had been once adorned with the flourishing cities of Bologna, Modena, Regium, and Placentia.[140] Pope Gelasius was a subject of Odoacer, and he affirms, with strong exaggeration, that in Aemilia, Tuscany, and the adjacent provinces, the human species was almost extirpated.[141] The plebeians of Rome, who were fed by the hand of their master, perished or disappeared, as soon as his liberality was suppressed; the decline of the arts reduced the industrious mechanic to idleness and want; and the senators, who might support with patience the ruin of their country, bewailed their private loss of wealth and luxury. One-third of those ample estates, to which the ruin of Italy is originally imputed,[142] was extorted for the use of the conquerors. Injuries were aggravated by insults; the sense of actual sufferings was embittered by the fear of more dreadful evils; and, as new lands were allotted to new swarms of Barbarians, each senator was apprehensive lest the arbitrary surveyors should approach his favourite villa or his most profitable farm. The least unfortunate were those who submitted without a murmur to the power which it was impossible to resist. Since they desired to live, they owed some gratitude to the tyrant who had spared their lives; and, since he was the absolute master of their fortunes, the portion which he left must be accepted as his pure and voluntary gift.[143] The distress of Italy was mitigated by the prudence and humanity of Odoacer, who had bound himself, as the price of his elevation, to satisfy the demands of a licentious and turbulent multitude. The kings of the Barbarians were frequently resisted, deposed, or murdered, by their *native* subjects; and the various bands of Italian mercenaries, who associated under the standard of an elective general, claimed a larger privilege of freedom and rapine. A monarchy destitute of national union, and hereditary right, hastened to its dissolution. After a reign of fourteen years, Odoacer was oppressed by the superior genius of Theodoric, king of the Ostrogoths, a hero alike excellent in the arts of war and of government, who restored an age of peace and prosperity, and whose name still excites and deserves the attention of mankind.

NOTES TO CHAPTER 36

* *page 682* [the Atlantic]
† *page 682* [in the Tropics]
1 Sidonius Apollinaris composed the thirteenth epistle of the second book to refute the paradox of his friend Serranus, who entertained a singular, though generous, enthusiasm for the deceased emperor. This epistle, with some indulgence, may claim the praise of an elegant composition; and it throws much light on the character of Maximus.
* *page 683* [seemly, fitting]
2 *Clientum praevia, pedisequa, circumfusa populositas*, is the train which Sidonius himself (i, 9) assigns to another senator of consular rank.
† *page 683* [the *princeps* or emperor]
‡ *page 683* [Gibbon has related the story in Chapter 35.]
3   *Districtus ensis cui super impia*
                             Cervice pendet, non Siculae dapes
                             Dulcem elaborabunt saporem:
                             Non avium citharaeque cantus
                             Somnum reducent.
['He, over whose guilty neck hovers a drawn sword, will take no relish in Sicilian banquets; no birdsong or tuneful lyre will restore his slumbers.']
                                                        Horat., *Carm.*, iii, 1.
  Sidonius concludes his letter with the story of Damocles, which Cicero (*Tusculan.*, v, 20–21) had so inimitably told. [The Sicilian Damocles feasted with a sword suspended over him by a horsehair.]

4 Notwithstanding the evidence of Procopius, Evagrius, Idatius, Marcellinus, etc., the learned Muratori (*Annali d'Italia*, iv, 249) doubts the reality of this invitation, and observes, with great truth, *Non si può dir quanto sia facile il popolo a sognare e spacciar voci false*. ['It is impossible to exaggerate the people's proneness to imagine and retail false accounts.']. But his argument, from the interval of time and place, is extremely feeble. The figs which grew near Carthage were produced to the senate of Rome on the third day.

5   . . . *infidoque tibi Burgundio ductu*
                              Extorquet trepidas mactandi principis iras.

                                                     Sidon., in *Panegyr. Avit.*, 442.

['The Burgundian, with his treacherous leadership, aroused in you the rash impulse to assassinate the emperor.]' A remarkable line, which insinuates that Rome and Maximus were betrayed by their Burgundian mercenaries.

6 The apparent success of pope Leo may be justified by Prosper and the *Historia Miscellan.*; but the improbable notion of Baronius (AD 455, No. 13) that Genseric spared the three apostolical churches is not countenanced even by the doubtful testimony of the *Liber Pontificalis*.

7 The profusion of Catulus, the first who gilt the roof of the Capitol, was not universally approved (Pliny, *Hist. Natur.*, xxxiii, 18); but it was far exceeded by the emperor's, and the external gilding of the temple cost Domitian 12,000 talents (£2,400,000). The expressions of Claudian and Rutilius (*luce metalli aemula . . . fastigia astris*, and *confunduntque vagos delubra micantia visus*) ['with their glittering metal . . . the roofs rivalled the stars . . . the glittering temple dazzles the sight'] manifestly prove that this splendid covering was not removed either by the Christians or the Goths (see Donatus, *Roma Antiqua*, ii, 125). It should seem that the roof of the Capitol was decorated with gilt statues and chariots drawn by four horses.

8 The curious reader may consult the learned and accurate treatise of Hadrian Reland, *de Spoliis Templi Hierosolymitani in Arcu Titiano Romae conspicuis*, in 12mo. *Trajecti ad Rhenum*, 1716.

9 The vessel which transported the relics of the Capitol was the only one of the whole fleet that suffered shipwreck. If a bigoted sophist, a Pagan bigot, had mentioned the accident, he might have rejoiced that this cargo of sacrilege was lost in the sea.

10 See Victor Vitensis, *de Persecut. Vandal.*, i, 8, 11–12, edit. Ruinart. Deogratias governed the church of Carthage only three years. If he had not been privately buried, his corpse would have been torn piecemeal by the mad devotion of the people.

*   *page 687*   [in 216 BC, when the troops of Hannibal massacred the Roman army]

11 The general evidence for the death of Maximus and the sack of Rome by the Vandals is comprised in Sidonius (*Panegyr. Avit.*, 441–50); Procopius (*de Bell. Vandal.*, i, 4–5, 188–89; and ii, 9, 255); Evagrius (ii, 7); Jornandes (*de Reb. Geticis*, 45, 677); and the Chronicles of Idatius, Prosper, Marcellinus, and Theophanes under the proper year.

12 The private life and elevation of Avitus must be deduced, with becoming suspicion, from the panegyric pronounced by Sidonius Apollinaris, his subject and his son-in-law.

13 After the example of the younger Pliny, Sidonius (ii, 2) has laboured the florid, prolix, and obscure description of his villa, which bore the name (*Avitacum*), and

had been the property, of Avitus. The precise situation is not ascertained. Consult, however, the notes of Savaron and Sirmond.

14 Sidonius (ii, 9) has described the country life of the Gallic nobles, in a visit which he made to his friends, whose estates were in the neighbourhood of Nismes. The morning hours were spent in the *sphaeristerium*, or tennis-court; or in the library, which was furnished with *Latin* authors, profane and religious: the former for the men, the latter for the ladies. The table was twice served, at dinner and supper, with hot meat (boiled and roast) and wine. During the intermediate time, the company slept, took the air on horseback, and used the warm bath.

15 Seventy lines of Panegyric (505–78) which describe the importunity of Theodoric and of Gaul, struggling to overcome the modest reluctance of Avitus, are blown away by three words of an honest historian: *Romanum ambisset imperium* ['he aimed to rule the Roman empire'] (Greg. Turon., ii, 11, in ii, 168).

16 Isidore, archbishop of Seville, who was himself of the blood-royal of the Goths, acknowledges and almost justifies (*Hist. Goth.*, p. 718) the crime which their slave Jornandes had basely dissembled (43, 673).

17 This elaborate description (i, ii, 2–7) was dictated by some political motive. It was designed for the public eye, and had been shown by the friends of Sidonius, before it was inserted in the collection of his epistles. The first book was published separately. See Tillemont, *Mémoires Ecclés.*, xvi, 264.

18 I have suppressed in this portrait of Theodoric several minute circumstances and technical phrases, which could be tolerable, or indeed intelligible, to those only who, like the contemporaries of Sidonius, had frequented the markets where naked slaves were exposed to sale (Dubos, *Hist. Critique*, i, 404).

19 *Videas ibi elegantiam Graecam, abundantiam Gallicanam, celeritatem Italam; publicam pompam, privatam diligentiam, regiam disciplinam.*

20 *Tunc etiam ego aliquid obsecraturus feliciter vincor, et mihi tabula perit ut causa salvetur.* Sidonius of Auvergne was not a subject of Theodoric; but he might be compelled to solicit either justice or favour at the court of Toulouse.

21 Theodoric himself had given a solemn and voluntary promise of fidelity, which was understood both in Gaul and Spain.

> *Romae sum, te duce, amicus,*
> *Principe te, Miles.*

Sidon., *Panegyr. Avit.*, 511.

['At Rome, when you command, I am your friend; now that you are emperor, I am a soldier in your ranks.']

22 *Quaeque sinu pelagi iactat se Bracara dives.*

Auson., *de Claris Urbibus*, p. 245.

['Wealthy Braga, which flaunts itself in an inlet of the sea.']

From the design of the king of the Suevi, it is evident that the navigation from the ports of Gallicia to the Mediterranean was known and practised. The ships of Bracara, or Braga, cautiously steered along the coast, without daring to lose themselves in the Atlantic.

* *page 690* [overthrown]

23 The Suevic war is the most authentic part of the Chronicle of Idatius, who, as bishop of Iria Flavia, was himself a spectator and a sufferer. Jornandes (44, 675–87) has expatiated with pleasure on the Gothic victory.

24 In one of the porticoes or galleries belonging to Trajan's library, among the statues of famous writers and orators. Sidon. Apoll., ix, 16, 284. *Carm.*, viii, 350.

* *page 691* [father-in-law]

25 *Luxuriose agere volens a senatoribus proiectus est* ['In his desire to lead a riotous life, he was deposed by the senators'], is the concise expression of Gregory of Tours (ii, xi, in ii, 168). An old Chronicle (in ii, 649) mentions an indecent jest of Avitus, which seems more applicable to Rome than to Treves.

26 Sidonius (*Panegyr. Anthem.*, 362, etc.) praises the royal birth of Ricimer, the lawful heir, as he chooses to insinuate, both of the Gothic and Suevic kingdoms.

27 See the Chronicle of Idatius. Jornandes (44, 676) styles him, with some truth, *virum egregium, et pene tunc in Italia ad exercitum singularem* ['an exceptional man and almost unequalled in military action'].

28 *Parcens innocentiae Aviti* ['sparing the innocent Avitus'] is the compassionate but contemptuous language of Victor Tunnunensis (in *Chron. apud.* Scaliger Euseb.). In another place, he calls him, *vir totius simplicitatis* [a man of absolute simplicity]. This commendation is more humble, but it is more solid and sincere, than the praises of Sidonius.

29 He suffered, as it is supposed, in the persecution of Diocletian (Tillemont, *Mém. Ecclés.*, v, 279, 696). Gregory of Tours, his peculiar votary, has dedicated to the glory of Julian the Martyr an entire book (*de Gloria Martyrum*, ii, in *Max. Bibliot. Patrum*, xi, 861–71), in which he relates about fifty foolish miracles performed by his relics.

30 Gregory of Tours (ii, xi, 168) is concise, but correct, in the reign of his countryman. The words of Idatius, *caret imperio, caret et vita* ['he lost the empire and his life'] seem to imply that the death of Avitus was violent; but it must have been secret, since Evagrius (ii, 7) could suppose that he died of the plague.

31 After a modest appeal to the examples of his brethren, Virgil and Horace, Sidonius honestly confesses the debt, and promises payment.

> *Sic mihi diverso nuper sub Marte cadenti*
> *Iussisti placido victor ut essem animo.*
> *Serviat ergo tibi servati lingua poetae,*
> *Atque meae vitae laus tua sit pretium.*

Sidon. Apoll., Carm., iv, 308.

['I recently faltered under another military leader, but you, in your victory, bade me be of good cheer. So may the poet you saved serve you with his tongue, and may my praise of you be my ransom.']

See Dubos, *Hist. Critique*, i, 448, etc.

32 The words of Procopius deserve to be transcribed; οὗτος γὰρ ὁ Μαιορῖνος ξύμπαντας τοὺς πώποτε Ῥωμαίων βεβασιλευκότας ὑπεραίρων ἀρετῇ πάσῃ; and afterwards, ἀνὴρ τὰ μὲν εἰς τοὺς ὑπηκόους μέτριος γεγονώς, φοβερὸς δὲ τὰ ἐς τοὺς πολεμίους (*de Bell. Vandal.*, i, 7, 194): a concise but comprehensive definition of royal virtue.

33 The panegyric was pronounced at Lyons before the end of the year 458, while the emperor was still consul. It has more art than genius and more labour than art. The ornaments are false or trivial, the expression is feeble and prolix; and Sidonius wants the skill to exhibit the principal figure in a strong and distinct light. The private life of Majorian occupies about two hundred lines, 107–305.

34 She pressed his immediate death, and was scarcely satisfied with his disgrace. It should seem that Aetius, like Belisarius and Marlborough [commanders under

the emperor Justinian and Queen Anne, respectively], was governed by his wife; whose fervent piety, though it might work miracles (Gregor. Turon., ii, 7, 162), was not incompatible with base and sanguinary counsels.

35 The Alemanni had passed the Rhaetian Alps, and were defeated in the Campi Canini or Valley of Bellinzone, through which the Tesin flows, in its descent from Mount Adula to the Lago Maggiore (Cluver., *Italia Antiq.*, i, 100–1). This boasted victory over *nine hundred* Barbarians (*Panegyr. Majorian.*, 373, etc.) betrays the extreme weakness of Italy.

* *page 692*   [Roman senators]

36 *Imperatorem me factum, P. C., electionis vestrae arbitrio, et fortissimi exercitus ordinatione agnoscite* (*Novell. Majorian.*, iii, 34, *ad calcem Cod. Theodos.*). Sidonius proclaims the unanimous voice of the empire.

> *Postquam ordine vobis*
> *Ordo omnis regnum dederat; plebs, curia, miles,*
> *Et collega simul.*   [*Carm.*, 5] 386.

['All the constitutional orders of the state invested you with supreme power: the people, the Senate, the army, and your colleague (i.e. Ricimer) at one and the same time.']

This language is ancient and constitutional; and we may observe that the *clergy* were not yet considered as a distinct order of the state.

* *page 693*   [denunciations for treason]

37 Either *dilationes* [delays] or *delationes* would afford a tolerable reading; but there is much more sense and spirit in the latter, to which I have therefore given the preference.

38 *Ab externo hoste et a domestica clade liberavimus;* by the latter, Majorian must understand the tyranny of Avitus; whose death he consequently avowed as a meritorious act. On this occasion, Sidonius is fearful and obscure, he describes the twelve Caesars, the nations of Africa, etc., that he may escape the dangerous name of Avitus (305–69).

39 See the whole edict or epistle of Majorian to the senate (*Novell.*, iv, 34). Yet the expression, *regnum nostrum* [our kingdom, or rule], bears some taint of the age, and does not mix kindly with the word *respublica* [republic], which he frequently repeats.

40 See the laws of Majorian (they are only nine, but very long and various) at the end of the Theodosian Code, *Novell.*, iv, 32–37. Godefroy has not given any commentary on these additional pieces.

† *page 693*   [property taxes and additional taxes]

41 *Fessas provincialium varia atque multiplici tributorum exactione fortunas, et extraordinariis fiscalium solutionum oneribus attritas*, etc. *Novell. Majorian.*, iv, 34.

42 The learned Greaves (i, 329–31) has found, by a diligent enquiry, that *aurei* [the *aureus* was the standard Roman coin] of the Antonines weighed one hundred and eighteen, and those of the fifth century only sixty-eight, English grains. Majorian gives currency to all gold coin, excepting only the *Gallic solidus* [originally called and equivalent to the *aureus*], from its deficiency, not in the weight, but in the standard.

43 The whole edict (*Novell. Majorian.*, vi, 35) is curious. *Antiquarum aedium dissipatur speciosa constructio; et ut* [*earum*] *aliquid reparetur, magna diruuntur. Hinc iam occasio nascitur, ut etiam unusquisque privatum aedificium construens, per gratiam iudicum . . . praesumere de publicis locis necessaria, et transferre non dubitet*, etc. ['The

splendid architecture of the old buildings is dispersed; and great edifices are demolished in order to effect some repair. Hence whoever puts up a private building does not hesitate to appropriate the materials he needs from public buildings . . . with the permission of the magistrates.'] With equal zeal, but with less power, Petrarch, in the fourteenth century, repeated the same complaints (*Vie de Petrarque*, i, 326–27). If I prosecute this History, I shall not be unmindful of the decline and fall of the *city* of Rome; an interesting object, to which my plan was originally confined.

* *page 695*   [between old and young]

44 The emperor chides the lenity of Rogatian, consular of Tuscany, in a style of acrimonious reproof, which sounds almost like personal resentment (*Novell.*, ix, 47). The law of Majorian, which punished obstinate widows, was soon afterwards repealed by his successor Severus (*Novell. Sever.*, i, 37).

45 Sidon., *Panegyr. Majorian.*, 385–440.

* *page 696*   [the river Dnieper]

† *page 696*   [the river Don]

46 The review of the army, and passage of the Alps, contain the most tolerable passages of the *Panegyric* (470–552). M. de Buat (*Hist des Peuples*, etc., viii, 49–55) is a more satisfactory commentator than either Savaron or Sirmond.

47 τὰ μὲν ὅπλοις, τὰ δὲ λόγοις ['partly with arms, partly with words'], is the just and forcible distinction of Priscus (*Excerpt. Legat.*, p. 42) in a short fragment, which throws much light on the history of Majorian. Jornandes has suppressed the defeat and alliance of the Visigoths, which were solemnly proclaimed in Gallicia, and are marked in the Chronicle of Idatius.

48 Florus, ii, 2. He amuses himself with the poetical fancy that the trees had been transformed into ships; and indeed the whole transaction, as it is related in the first book of Polybius, deviates too much from the probable course of human events.

49
> Interea duplici texis dum littore classem
> Inferno superoque mari, cadit omnis in aequor
> Silva tibi, etc.   Sidon., *Panegyr. Majorian.*, 441–61.

['Meanwhile, as you build up your fleet on two shores on the Tuscan and Ionian seas, an entire forest is launched upon the waters, etc.'] The number of ships, which Priscus fixes at 300, is magnified by an indefinite comparison with the fleets of Agamemnon, Xerxes, and Augustus.

50 Procopius, *de Bell. Vandal.*, i, 8, 194. When Genseric conducted his unknown guest into the arsenal of Carthage, the arms clashed of their own accord. Majorian had tinged his yellow locks with a black colour.

51
> Spoliisque potitus
> Immensis, robur luxu iam perdidit omne,
> Quo valuit dum pauper erat.   *Panegyr. Majorian.*, 330.

['Having once gained the immense spoils, it lost through luxury all the strength with which it had prevailed for as long as it was poor.'] He afterwards applies to Genseric, unjustly as it should seem, the vices of his subjects.

52 He burnt the villages, and poisoned the springs (Priscus, p. 42). Dubos (*Hist. Critique*, i, 475) observes that the magazines [stores] which the Moors buried in the earth might escape his destructive search. Two or three hundred pits are sometimes dug in the same place, and each pit contains at least 400 bushels of corn. Shaw's *Travels*, p. 139.

53 Idatius, who was safe in Gallicia from the power of Ricimer, boldly and honestly declares, *Vandali, per proditores admoniti,* etc. ['The Vandals, having been warned by traitors, etc.']; he dissembles, however, the name of the traitor.

54 Procop., *de Bell. Vandal.*, i, 8, 194. The testimony of Idatius is fair and impartial; *Majorianum de Galliis Romam redeuntem et Romano imperio vel nomini res necessarias ordinantem, Richimer livore percitus, et invidorum consilio ultus, fraude interficit circumventum.* ['As Majorian was returning from Gaul to Rome and making arrangements required by Rome's empire or prestige, Ricimer, inspired by envy and avenging himself on the advice of jealous men, set upon and treacherously murdered him.'] Some read *Suevorum* [ie. on the advice of the Suevi], and I am unwilling to efface either of the words, as they express the different accomplices who united in the conspiracy of Majorian.

55 See the *Epigrams* of Ennodius, No. cxxxv, *inter* Sirmond. *Opera*, i, 1903. It is flat and obscure; but Ennodius was made bishop of Pavia fifty years after the death of Majorian, and his praise deserves credit and regard.

56 Sidonius gives a tedious account (i, xi, 25–31) of a supper at Arles, to which he was invited by Majorian, a short time before his death. He had no intention of praising a deceased emperor, but a casual disinterested remark, *Subrisit Augustus; ut erat, auctoritate servata, cum se communioni dedisset ioci plenus* ['The emperor smiled; such was his character that he maintained his authority even though he joined in the friendly discourse, full of good humour'], outweighs the six hundred lines of his venal panegyric.

57 Sidonius (*Paneg. Anth.*, 317) dismisses him to heaven.

> *Auxerat Augustus naturae lege Severus*
> *Divorum numerum*

['The emperor Severus naturally joined the ranks of the deities'].

And an old list of the emperors, composed about the time of Justinian, praises his piety and fixes his residence at Rome (Sirmond, *Not. ad* Sidon., pp. 111–12).
* *page 698*   [distinguish]

58 Tillemont, who is always scandalised by the virtues of Infidels, attributes this advantageous portrait of Marcellinus (which Suidas has preserved) to the partial zeal of some Pagan historian (*Hist. des Empereurs*, vi, 330).

59 Procopius, *de Bell. Vandal.*, i, 6, 191. In various circumstances of the life of Marcellinus, it is not easy to reconcile the Greek historian with the Latin Chronicles of the times.

60 I must apply to Aegidius the praises which Sidonius (*Panegyr. Majorian.*, 553) bestows on a nameless master-general, who commanded the rear guard of Majorian. Idatius, from public report, commends his Christian piety; and Priscus mentions (p. 42 [fr. 30]) his military virtues.

61 Greg. Turon., ii, 12, in ii, 168. The Père Daniel, whose ideas were superficial and modern, has started some objections against the story of Childeric (*Hist. de France*, i, Préface Historique, pp. lxxviii, etc.); but they have been fairly satisfied by Dubos (*Hist. Critique*, i, 460–510) and by two authors who disputed the prize of the Academy of Soissons (pp. 131–77, 310–39). With regard to the term of Childeric's exile, it is necessary either to prolong the life of Aegidius beyond the date assigned by the Chronicle of Idatius, or to correct the text of Gregory, by reading *quarto* anno, instead of *octavo* ['in the fourth year' instead of 'in the eighth'].

62 The naval war of Genseric is described by Priscus (*Excerpta Legation.*, p. 42;

Procopius, (de Bell. Vandal., i, 5, 189–90; and 22, 228); Victor Vitensis (de Persecut. Vandal., i, 17; and Ruin., pp. 467–81), and in the three panegyrics of Sidonius, whose chronological order is absurdly transposed in the editions both of Savaron and Sirmond. (Avit. Carm., vii, 441–51; Majorian. Carm., v, 327–50, 385–440; Anthem. Carm., ii, 348–86.) In one passage the poet seems inspired by his subject, and expresses a strong idea by a lively image [Carm., 2, 348, sqq.]:

> Hinc Vandalus hostis
> Urget; et in nostrum numerosa classe quotannis
> Militat excidium; conversoque ordine Fati
> Torrida Caucaseos infert mihi Byrsa furores.

['The hostile Vandal (Genseric) attacks from Carthage, and every year, brings destruction upon us with his numerous fleet; the natural order of things is reversed: from tropical Carthage he sends wild men from the Caucasus against me.']

* page 699   [the straits of Gibraltar]

63 The poet himself is compelled to acknowledge the distress of Ricimer [ii, 352]:

> Praeterea invictus Ricimer, quem publica fata
> Respiciunt, proprio solus vix Marte repellit
> Piratam per rura vagum.

['The undefeated Ricimer, on whom the fate of Rome depended, even with Mars on his side, was barely able on his own to drive the vagabond pirate from place to place.']

Italy addresses her complaint to the Tiber, and Rome, at the solicitation of the river-god, transports herself to Constantinople, renounces her ancient claims, and implores the friendship of Aurora, the goddess of the East. This fabulous machinery, which the genius of Claudian had used and abused, is the constant and miserable resource of the muse of Sidonius.

* page 700   [Volume 3 of the first edition of the History ended with Chapter 38.]

64 The original authors of the reigns of Marcian, Leo, and Zeno are reduced to some imperfect fragments, whose deficiencies must be supplied from the more recent compilations of Theophanes, Zonaras, and Cedrenus.

65 St Pulcheria died AD 453, four years before her nominal husband, and her festival is celebrated on the 10th of September by the modern Greeks; she bequeathed an immense patrimony to pious, or at least to ecclesiastical, uses. See Tillemont, Mémoires Ecclés., xv, 181–84.

66 See Procopius, de Bell. Vandal., i, 4, 185.

67 From this disability of Aspar to ascend the throne, it may be inferred that the stain of Heresy was perpetual and indelible, while that of Barbarism disappeared in the second generation.

68 Theophanes, p. 95. This appears to be the first origin of a ceremony which all the Christian princes of the world have since adopted, and from which the clergy have deduced the most formidable consequences.

69 Cedrenus (pp. 345–46), who was conversant with the writers of better days, has preserved the remarkable words of Aspar, βασιλεῦ, τὸν ταύτην τὴν ἁλουργίδα περιβεβλημένον οὐ χρὴ διαψεύδεσθαι.

70 The power of the Isaurians agitated the Eastern empire in the two succeeding reigns of Zeno and Anastasius; but it ended in the destruction of those Barbarians, who maintained their fierce independence about two hundred and thirty years.

71   *Tali tu civis ab urbe*
                    Procopio genitore micas; cui prisca propago
                    Augustis venit a proavis.

['You derive your splendour as a Roman citizen from your father, Procopius, whose ancestry goes back to imperial forbears.']
The poet (Sidon., *Panegyr. Anthem.*, 67–306) then proceeds to relate the private life and fortunes of the future emperor, with which he must have been very imperfectly acquainted.

72 Sidonius discovers, with tolerable ingenuity, that this disappointment added new lustre to the virtues of Anthemius (210, etc.), who declined one sceptre and reluctantly accepted another (22, etc.).

73 The poet again celebrates the unanimity of all orders of the state (15–22); and the Chronicle of Idatius mentions the forces which attended his march.

74 *Interveni autem nuptiis Patricii Ricimeris, cui filia perennis Augusti in spem publicae securitatis copulabatur.* ['I attended the wedding of the patrician Ricimer, to whom the emperor's daughter was joined in marriage, in the hope that this would enhance the security of the state.'] [*Epp.* i, 5, 10]. The journey of Sidonius from Lyons, and the festival of Rome, are described with some spirit (i, 5, 9–13; *Epist.* 9, 21.

75 Sidonius (i, 9, 23–4) very fairly states his motive, his labour, and his reward. *Hic ipse Panegyricus, si non iudicium, certe eventum, boni operis accepit.* ['This panegyric received, if not the estimation, at least the reward, of a fine work.'] He was made bishop of Clermont, AD 471. Tillemont, *Mém. Ecclés.*, xvi, 750.

76 The palace of Anthemius stood on the banks of the Propontis [the Sea of Marmara]. In the ninth century, Alexius, the son-in-law of the emperor Theophilus, obtained permission to purchase the ground; and ended his days in a monastery which he founded on that delightful spot. Ducange, *Constantinopolis Christiana*, pp. 117, 152.

77 *Papa Hilarus . . . apud beatum Petrum Apostolum, palam ne id fieret, clara voce constrinxit, in tantum ut non ea facienda cum interpositione iuramenti idem promitteret Imperator.* Gelasius, *Epistol. ad Andronicum, apud* Baron., AD 467, No. 2. The cardinal observes, with some complacency, that it was much easier to plant heretics at Constantinople than at Rome.

78 Damascius, in the life of the philosopher Isidore, *apud* Photius, p. 1049. Damascius, who lived under Justinian, composed another work, consisting of 570 preternatural [supernatural] stories of souls, demons, apparitions, the dotage of Platonic Paganism.

79 In the poetical works of Sidonius, which he afterwards condemned (ix, 16, 285), the fabulous deities are the principal actors. If Jerome was scourged by the angels for only reading Virgil, the bishop of Clermont, for such a vile imitation, deserved an additional whipping from the Muses.

80 Ovid (*Fast.*, ii, 267–452) has given an amusing description of the follies of antiquity, which still inspired so much respect that a grave magistrate, running naked through the streets, was not an object of astonishment or laughter.

 * *page 703* [According to mythology, he emigrated from Arcadia to Italy sixty years before the Trojan War.]

81 See Dionys. Halicarn., i, 25, 65, edit. Hudson. The Roman antiquaries, Donatus (ii, 18, 173–74) and Nardini (pp. 386–87), have laboured to ascertain the true situation of the Lupercal.

82 Baronius published, from the manuscripts of the Vatican, this epistle of pope
Gelasius (AD 496, No. 28–45), which is entitled *Adversus Andromachum
Senatorem, ceterosque Romanos, qui Lupercalia secundum morem pristinum colenda
constituebant.* ['Against the senator Andromachus, and the other Romans who
decided that the Lupercalia should be celebrated in accordance with ancient
custom.'] Gelasius always supposes that his adversaries are nominal Christians,
and, that he may not yield to them in absurd prejudice, he imputes to this
harmless festival all the calamities of the age.

83 *Itaque nos quibus totius mundi regimen commisit superna provisio . . . Pius et
triumphator semper Augustus filius noster Anthemius, licet Divina Maiestas et nostra
creatio pietati eius plenam Imperii commiserit potestatem,* etc. . . . ['Thus we, to whom
divine providence has entrusted dominion over the whole world . . . pious, ever
triumphant emperor, our son Anthemius, may the divine majesty and our
action entrust full imperial power to his piety etc. . . . '] Such is the dignified
style of Leo, whom Anthemius respectfully names *Dominus et Pater meus Princeps
sacratissimus Leo* [Lord and Father, most sacred Emperor, Leo]. See *Novell.
Anthem.*, ii, iii, 38, *ad calcem Cod. Theod.*

84 The expedition of Heraclius is clouded with difficulties (Tillemont, *Hist. des
Empereurs*, vi, 640), and it requires some dexterity to use the circumstances
afforded by Theophanes without injury to the more respectable evidence of
Procopius.

* *page 704* [Julius Caesar's opponent, who committed suicide at Utica when his
cause was defeated.]

85 The march of Cato from Berenice, in the province of Cyrene, was much longer
than that of Heraclius from Tripoli. He passed the deep sandy desert in thirty
days, and it was found necessary to provide, besides the ordinary supplies, a great
number of skins filled with water, and several *Psylli*, who were supposed to
possess the art of sucking the wounds which had been made by the serpents of
their native country. See Plutarch, *in Caton. Uticens.*, iv, 275 (ch. 56). Strabon.,
Geograph., xvii, 1193.

86 The principal sum is clearly expressed by Procopius (*de Bell. Vandal.*, i, 6, 191);
the smaller constituent parts, which Tillemont (*Hist. des Empereurs*, vi, 396) has
laboriously collected from the Byzantine writers, are less certain, and less
important. The historian Malchus laments the public misery (*Excerpt. ex Suida
in Corp. Hist. Byzant.*, p. 58), but he is surely unjust when he charges Leo with
hoarding the treasures which he extorted from the people.

† *page 704* [wife of the emperor Leo I]

87 This promontory is forty miles from Carthage (Procop., i, 6, 192) and twenty
leagues from Sicily (Shaw's *Travels*, p. 89). Scipio [Roman general, 236–183 BC]
landed further in the bay, at the fair promontory; see the animated description
of Livy, xxix, 26–27.

88 Theophanes (p. 100) affirms that many ships of the Vandals were sunk. The
assertion of Jornandes (*de Successione Regn.*) that Basiliscus attacked Carthage
must be understood in a very qualified sense.

89 Damascius, in *Vit. Isidor. apud* Phot., p. 1048. It will appear, by comparing the
three short chronicles of the times, that Marcellinus had fought near Carthage
and was killed in Sicily.

90 For the African war, see Procopius (*de Bell. Vandal.*, i, 6, 191–93); Theophanes
(pp. 99–101); Cedrenus (pp. 349–50); and Zonaras (ii, xiv, 50–51). Montesquieu

(*Considérations sur la Grandeur*, etc., xx, iii, 497) has made a judicious observation on the failure of these great naval armaments.

91 Jornandes is our best guide through the reigns of Theodoric II and Euric (*de Rebus Geticis*, 44–47, 675–81). Idatius ends too soon, and Isidore is too sparing of the information which he might have given on the affairs of Spain. The events that relate to Gaul are laboriously illustrated in the third book of the Abbé Dubos, *Hist. Critique*, i, 424–620.

92 See Mariana, *Hist. Hispan.*, i, v, 5, 162.

93 An imperfect, but original, picture of Gaul, more especially of Auvergne, is shown by Sidonius; who, as a senator, and afterwards as a bishop, was deeply interested in the fate of his country. See v [*leg.* vii] *epist.* i, 5, 9, etc.

94 Sidonius, iii, *epist.* 3, 65–68; Greg. Turon., ii, 24, in ii, 174; Jornandes, 45, 675. Perhaps Ecdicius was only the son-in-law of Avitus, his wife's son by another husband.

95 *Si nullae a republica vires, nulla praesidia, si nullae, quantum rumor est, Anthemii principis opes, statuit, te auctore, nobilitas seu patriam dimittere seu capillos* (Sidon., ii, *epist.* 1, 33). The last words ['whether to lose their country or their hair'] (Sirmond, *Not.*, p. 25) may likewise denote the clerical tonsure, which was indeed the choice of Sidonius himself.

96 The history of these Britons may be traced in Jornandes ([44 and] 45, 678); Sidonius (iii, *epist.* 9, 73–74); and Gregory of Tours (ii, 18, in ii, 170). Sidonius (who styles these mercenary troops *argutos, armatos, tumultuosos, virtute, numero, contubernio contumaces* ['quick, well-armed, busy, stubborn in their courage, numbers and comradeship']) addresses their general in a tone of friendship and familiarity.

97 See Sidonius, i, *epist.* 7, 15–20, with Sirmond's notes. This letter does honour to his heart, as well as to his understanding. The prose of Sidonius, however vitiated by a false and affected taste, is much superior to his insipid verses.

98 When the Capitol ceased to be a temple, it was appropriated to the use of the civil magistrate; and it is still the residence of the Roman senator. The jewellers, etc. might be allowed to expose their precious wares in the porticoes.

99 *Haec ad regem Gothorum charta videbatur emitti, pacem cum Graeco Imperatore dissuadens, Britannos super Ligerim sitos impugnari oportere demonstrans, cum Burgundionibus iure gentium Gallias dividi debere confirmans.*

 * *page 708* [an island in the river Tiber]

100 *Senatusconsultum Tiberianum* (Sirmond, *Not.*, p. 17); but that law allowed only ten days between the sentence and execution: the remaining twenty were added in the reign of Theodosius.

 * *page 709* [wicked, infamous]

 † *page 709* [Roman conspirator, killed in 63 BC]

101 *Catilina seculi nostri* ['the Catiline of our age']. Sidonius, ii, *epist.* 1, 33; v, *epist.* 13, 143; vii, *epist.* 7, 185. He execrates the crimes, and applauds the punishment, of Seronatus, perhaps with the indignation of a virtuous citizen, perhaps with the resentment of a personal enemy.

102 Ricimer, under the reign of Anthemius, defeated and slew in battle Beorgor, king of the Alani (Jornandes, 45, 678). His sister had married the king of the Burgundians, and he maintained an intimate connection with the Suevic colony established in Pannonia and Noricum.

103 *Galatam concitatum* [the impetuous Galatian]. Sirmond (in his notes to

Ennodius) applies this application to Anthemius himself. The emperor was probably born in the province of Galatia, whose inhabitants, the Gallo-Grecians, were supposed to unite the vices of a savage, and a corrupted, people.

104 Epiphanius was thirty years bishop of Pavia (AD 467–97; see Tillemont, *Mém. Ecclés.*, xvi, 788). His name and actions would have been unknown to posterity if Ennodius, one of his successors, had not written his life (Sirmond, *Opera*, i, 1647–92), in which he presents him as one of the greatest characters of the age.

105 Ennodius (pp. 1659–64) has related this embassy of Epiphanius; and his narrative, verbose and turgid as it must appear, illustrates some curious passages in the fall of the Western empire.

106 Priscus, *Excerpt. Legation.*, p. 74. Procopius, *de Bell. Vandal.*, i, 6, 191. Eudoxia and her daughter were restored after the death of Majorian. Perhaps the consulship of Olybrius (AD 464) was bestowed as a nuptial present.

107 The hostile appearance of Olybrius is fixed (notwithstanding the opinion of Pagi) by the duration of his reign. The secret connivance of Leo is acknowledged by Theophanes and the Paschal Chronicle. We are ignorant of his motives; but in this obscure period our ignorance extends to the most public and important facts.

108 Of the fourteen regions, or quarters, into which Rome was divided by Augustus, only *one*, the Janiculum lay on the Tuscan side of the Tiber. But, in the fifth century, the Vatican suburb formed a considerable city; and in the ecclesiastical distribution, which had been recently made by Simplicius, the reigning pope, *two* of the *seven* regions, or parishes, of Rome depended on the church of St Peter. See Nardini, *Roma Antica*, p. 67. It would require a tedious dissertation to mark the circumstances, in which I am inclined to depart from the topography of that learned Roman.

109 *Nuper Anthemii et Ricimeris civili furore subversa est.* Gelasius (in *Epist. ad Andromach. apud* Baron., AD 496, No. 42); Sigonius (i, xiv, *de Occidentali Imperio*, pp. 542–43); and Muratori (*Ann. d'Italia*, iv, 308–9), with the aid of a less imperfect Ms. of the *Historia Miscella*, have illustrated this dark and bloody transaction.

110 Such had been the *saeva ac deformis urbe tota facies* ['cruel and ugly spectacle throughout the city'], when Rome was assaulted and stormed by the troops of Vespasian (see Tacit. *Hist.*, iii, 82–83); and every cause of mischief had since acquired much additional energy. The revolution of ages may bring round the same calamities; but ages may revolve without producing a Tacitus to describe them.

111 See Ducange, *Familiae Byzantinae*, pp. 74–75. Areobindus, who appears to have married the niece of the emperor Justinian, was the eighth descendant of the elder Theodosius.

112 The last revolutions of the Western empire are faintly marked in Theophanes (p. 102); Jornandes (45, 679); the Chronicle of Marcellinus, and the fragments of an anonymous writer, published by Valesius at the end of Ammianus (pp. 716–17). If Photius had not been so wretchedly concise, we should derive much information from the contemporary histories of Malchus and Candidus. See his *Extracts*, pp. 172–79.

113 See Greg. Turon., ii, 28, in ii, 175; Dubos, *Hist. Critique*, ii, 613. By the murder, or death, of his two brothers, Gundobald acquired the sole possession of the kingdom of Burgundy, whose ruin was hastened by their discord.

114 *Julius Nepos armis pariter summus Augustus ac moribus.* Sidonius, v, 16, 146. Nepos had given to Ecdicius the title of Patrician, which Anthemius had promised, *decessoris Anthemii fidem absolvit* ['he carried out the promise of the late Anthemius']. See viii, 7, 224.

115 Epiphanius was sent ambassador from Nepos to the Visigoths for the purpose of ascertaining the *fines Imperii Italici* [boundaries of the Italian Empire] (Ennodius in Sirmond, i, 1665–69). His pathetic discourse concealed the disgraceful secret, which soon excited the just and bitter complaints of the bishop of Clermont [Sidonius].

116 Malchus, *apud* Phot., p. 172. Ennod., *Epigram.*, Bk lxxxii, in Sirmond, *Oper.*, ii, 1879. Some doubt may however be raised on the identity of the emperor and the archbishop.

117 Our knowledge of these mercenaries who subverted the Western empire, is derived from Procopius (*de Bell. Gothico*, i, i, 308). The popular opinion and the recent historians represent Odoacer in the false light of a *stranger* and a *king*, who invaded Italy with an army of foreigners, his native subjects.

118 *Orestes, qui eo tempore quando Attila ad Italiam venit se illi iunxit, et eius notarius factus fuerat* ['Orestes, who at the time when Attila entered Italy, joined him and became his secretary']. Anonym. Vales., p. 716. He is mistaken in the date; but we may credit his assertion that the secretary of Attila was the father of Augustulus.

 * *page 712*   [in Chapter 34]
 * *page 713*   [turned]

119 See Ennodius (in *Vit. Epiphan.*, Sirmond, i, 1669–70). He adds weight to the narrative of Procopius, though we may doubt whether the devil actually contrived the siege of Pavia to distress the bishop and his flock.

 † *page 713*   [Chapter 34]

120 Jornandes, 53–54, 692–95. M. de Buat (*Hist. des Peuples de l'Europe*, viii, 221–28) has clearly explained the origin and adventures of Odoacer. I am almost inclined to believe that he was the same who pillaged Angers and commanded a fleet of Saxon pirates on the ocean. Greg. Turon., ii, 18, in ii, 170.

121 *Vade ad Italiam, vade vilissimis nunc pellibus coopertus; sed multis cito plurima largiturus.* Anonym. Vales., p. 717. He quotes the life of St Severinus, which is extant, and contains much unknown and valuable history; it was composed by his disciple Eugippius (AD 511) thirty years after his death. See Tillemont, *Mém. Ecclés.*, xvi, 168–81.

122 Theophanes, who calls him a Goth, affirms that he was educated, nursed (τραφέντος), in Italy (p. 102); and, as this strong expression will not bear a literal interpretation, it must be explained by long service in the Imperial guards.

123 *Nomen regis Odoacer assumpsit, cum tamen neque purpura nec regalibus uteretur insignibus.* Cassiodor. in *Chron.*, AD 476. He seems to have assumed the abstract title of a king, without applying it to any particular nation or country.

124 Malchus, whose loss excites our regret, has preserved (in *Excerpt. Legat.*, 93) this extraordinary embassy from the senate to Zeno. The anonymous fragment (p. 717) and the extract from Candidus (*apud* Phot., p. 176) are likewise of some use.

125 The precise year in which the Western empire was extinguished is not positively ascertained. The vulgar era of AD 476 *appears* to have the sanction of authentic chronicles. But the two dates assigned by Jornandes (46, 680)

would delay that great event to the year 479; and, though M. de Buat has overlooked *his* evidence, he produces (viii, 261–88) many collateral circumstances in support of the same opinion.

126 See his medals in Ducange (*Fam. Byzantin.*, p. 81); Priscus (*Excerpt. Legat.*, p. 56); Maffei (*Osservazioni Letterarie*, ii, 314). We may allege a famous and similar case. The meanest subjects of the Roman empire assumed the *illustrious* name of *Patricius*, which, by the conversion of Ireland, has been communicated to a whole nation.

127 *Ingrediens autem Ravennam deposuit Augustulum de regno, cuius infantiam misertus concessit ei sanguinem; et quia pulcher erat, tamen donavit ei reditum sex millia solidos, et misit eum intra Campaniam cum parentibus suis libere vivere.* Anonym. Vales., p. 716. Jornandes says (46, 680), *in Lucullano Campaniae castello exilii poena damnavit.*

128 See the eloquent Declamation of Seneca (*epist.* lxxxvi). The philosopher might have recollected that all luxury is relative; and that the elder Scipio, whose manners were polished by study and conversation, was himself accused of that vice by his ruder contemporaries (Livy, xxix, 19).

  * *page 715* [Marius]

129 Sulla, in the language of a soldier, praised his *peritia castrametandi* [skill in designing a fortified place] (Plin., *Hist Natur.*, xviii, 7). Phaedrus, who makes its shady walks (*laeta viridia*) the scene of an insipid fable (ii, 5), has thus described the situation:

> *Caesar Tiberius quum petens Neapolim*
> *In Misenensem villam venisset suam*
> *Quae monte summo posita Luculli manu*
> *Prospectat Siculum et prospicit Tuscum mare.*

['The Emperor Tiberius, on his way to Naples, reached his villa at Misenum. Built by Lucullus on the top of the mountain, it overlooks the Sicilian and the Tuscan seas.']

130 From seven myriads and a half to two hundred and fifty myriads of drachmae. Yet even in the possession of Marius, it was a luxurious retirement. The Romans derided his indolence: they soon bewailed his activity. See Plutarch, *in Mario*, ii, 524 [c. 34].

131 Lucullus had other villas of equal, though various, magnificence, at Baiae, Naples, Tusculum, etc. He boasted that he changed his climate with the storks and cranes. Plutarch, in *Lucull.*, iii, 193 [39].

132 Severinus died in Noricum, AD 482. Six years afterwards, his body, which scattered miracles as it passed, was transported by his disciples into Italy. The devotion of a Neapolitan lady invited the saint to the Lucullan villa, in the place of Augustulus, who was probably no more. See Baronius (*Annal. Eccles.*, AD 496, Nos. 50–51) and Tillemont (*Mém. Ecclés.*, xvi, 178–81) from the original life by Eugippius. The narrative of the last migration of Severinus to Naples is likewise an authentic piece.

  * *page 716* [reserved for the consuls]

133 The consular *Fasti* [registers] may be found in Pagi or Muratori. The consuls named by Odoacer, or perhaps by the Roman senate, appear to have been acknowledged in the Eastern empire.

134 Sidonius Apollinaris (i, *epist.* 9, 22; edit. Sirmond) has compared the two leading senators of his time (AD 468), Gennadius Avienus and Caecina Basilius.

To the former he assigns the specious, to the latter the solid, virtues of public and private life. A Basilius junior, possibly his son, was consul in the year 480.

135 Epiphanius interceded for the people of Pavia; and the king first granted an indulgence of five years, and afterwards relieved them from the oppression of Pelagius, the Praetorian praefect (Ennodius, *in Vit. St. Epiphan.*, in Sirmond., *Oper.*, i, 1670, 1672).

* *page 717*   [transferring]

136 See Baronius, *Annal. Eccles.*, AD 483, No. 10–15. Sixteen years afterwards, the irregular proceedings of Basilius were condemned by pope Symmachus in a Roman synod.

137 The wars of Odoacer are concisely mentioned by Paul the Deacon (*de Gest. Langobard.*, i, 19, 757, edit. Grot.) and in the two Chronicles of Cassiodorus and Cuspinian. *The Life of St Severinus*, by Eugippius, which the Count de Buat (*Hist. des Peuples*, etc., viii, 1, 4, 8, 9) has diligently studied, illustrates the ruin of Noricum and the Bavarian antiquities.

138 Tacit., *Annal.*, iii, 53. The *Recherches sur l'Administration des Terres chez les Romains* (pp. 351–61) clearly state the progress of internal decay.

139 A famine which afflicted Italy at the time of the irruption of Odoacer, king of the Heruli, is eloquently described in prose and verse by a French poet (*Les Mois*, ii, 174, 206, edit. in 12mo). I am ignorant from whence he derives his information; but I am well assured that he relates some facts incompatible with the truth of history.

140 See the xxxixth epistle of St Ambrose, as it is quoted by Muratori, *sopra le Antichità Italiane*, i, xxi, 354.

141 *Aemilia, Tuscia, ceteraeque provinciae in quibus hominum prope nullus exsistit.* Gelasius, *Epist. ad Andromachum, ap.* Baronium, *Annal. Eccles.*, AD 496, No. 36.

142 *Verumque confitentibus, latifundia perdidere Italiam.* Pliny, *Hist. Natur.*, xviii, 7.

143 Such are the topics of consolation, or rather of patience, which Cicero (*ad Familiares*, ix, 17) suggests to his friend Papirius Paetus, under the military despotism of Caesar. The argument, however, of *vivere pulcherrimum duxi* ['I have shown how life may best be lived'], is more forcibly addressed to a Roman philosopher, who possessed the free alternative of life or death.

CHAPTER 37

Origin, progress, and effects of the monastic life –conversion of the
Barbarians to Christianity and Arianism – persecution of the
Vandals in Africa – extinction of Arianism among the Barbarians

The indissoluble connection of civil and ecclesiastical affairs has compelled and encouraged me to relate the progress, the persecutions, the
establishment, the divisions, the final triumph, and the gradual corruption
of Christianity. I have purposely delayed the consideration of two
religious events, interesting in the study of human nature, and important
in the decline and fall of the Roman empire: I. The institution of the
monastic life;[1] and, II. The conversion of the northern Barbarians.

I. Prosperity and peace introduced the distinction of the *vulgar** and the
Ascetic Christians.[2] The loose and imperfect practice of religion satisfied
the conscience of the multitude. The prince or magistrate, the soldier or
merchant, reconciled their fervent zeal, and implicit faith, with the
exercise of their profession, the pursuit of their interest, and the indulgence of their passions; but the Ascetics, who obeyed and abused the rigid
precepts of the gospel, were inspired by the savage enthusiasm which
represents man as a criminal and God as a tyrant. They seriously
renounced the business, and the pleasures, of the age; abjured the use of
wine, of flesh, and of marriage; chastised their body, mortified their
affections, and embraced a life of misery, as the price of eternal happiness.
In the reign of Constantine, the Ascetics fled from a profane and
degenerate world, to perpetual solitude, or religious society. Like the first
Christians of Jerusalem,[3] they resigned the use, or the property, of their
temporal possessions; established regular communities of the same sex,
and a similar disposition; and assumed the names of *Hermits*, *Monks*, and
Anachorets,[†] expressive of their lonely retreat in a natural or artificial
desert. They soon acquired the respect of the world, which they despised;
and the loudest applause was bestowed on this Divine Philosophy,[4] which
surpassed, without the aid of science or reason, the laborious virtues of the
Grecian schools. The monks might indeed contend with the Stoics in the
contempt of fortune, of pain, and of death; the Pythagorean silence and
submission were revived in their servile discipline; and they disdained, as
firmly as the Cynics themselves, all the forms and decencies of civil
society. But the votaries of this Divine Philosophy aspired to imitate a
purer and more perfect model. They trod in the footsteps of the prophets,
who had retired to the desert;[5] and they restored the devout and
contemplative life, which had been instituted by the Essenians, in

Palestine and Egypt. The philosophic eye of Pliny had surveyed with astonishment a solitary people, who dwelt among the palm-trees near the Dead Sea; who subsisted without money, who were propagated without women; and who derived from the disgust and repentance of mankind a perpetual supply of voluntary associates.[6]

Egypt, the fruitful parent of superstition, afforded the first example of the monastic life. Antony,[7] an illiterate[8] youth of the lower parts of Thebais, distributed his patrimony,[9] deserted his family and native home, and executed his *monastic* penance with original and intrepid fanaticism. After a long and painful novitiate among the tombs and in a ruined tower, he boldly advanced into the desert three days' journey to the eastward of the Nile; discovered a lonely spot, which possessed the advantages of shade and water; and fixed his last residence on Mount Colzim near the Red Sea, where an ancient monastery still preserves the name and memory of the saint.[10] The curious devotion of the Christians pursued him to the desert; and, when he was obliged to appear at Alexandria, in the face of mankind, he supported his fame with discretion and dignity. He enjoyed the friendship of Athanasius, whose doctrine he approved; and the Egyptian peasant respectfully declined a respectful invitation from the emperor Constantine. The venerable patriarch (for Antony attained the age of one hundred and five years) beheld the numerous progeny which had been formed by his example and his lessons. The prolific colonies of monks multiplied with rapid increase on the sands of Libya, upon the rocks of Thebais, and in the cities of the Nile. To the south of Alexandria, the mountain, and adjacent desert, of Nitria were peopled by 5000 anachorets; and the traveller may still investigate the ruins of fifty monasteries, which were planted in that barren soil by the disciples of Antony.[11] In the Upper Thebais, the vacant Island of Tabenne[12] was occupied by Pachomius, and fourteen hundred of his brethren. That holy abbot successively founded nine monasteries of men, and one of women; and the festival of Easter sometimes collected fifty thousand religious persons, who followed his *angelic* rule of discipline.[13] The stately and populous city of Oxyrinchus, the seat of Christian orthodoxy, had devoted the temples, the public edifices, and even the ramparts, to pious and charitable uses; and the bishop, who might preach in twelve churches, computed ten thousand females, and twenty thousand males, of the monastic profession.[14] The Egyptians, who gloried in this marvellous revolution, were disposed to hope, and to believe, that the number of the monks was equal to the remainder of the people;[15] and posterity might repeat the saying, which had formerly been applied to the sacred animals of the same country, that, in Egypt, it was less difficult to find a god than a man.

Athanasius introduced into Rome the knowledge and practice of the monastic life; and a school of this new philosophy was opened by the disciples of Antony, who accompanied their primate to the holy threshold of the Vatican. The strange and savage appearance of these Egyptians excited, at first, horror and contempt, and at length applause and zealous imitation. The senators, and more especially the matrons, transformed their palaces and villas into religious houses; and the narrow institution of *six* Vestals was eclipsed by the frequent monasteries, which were seated on the ruins of ancient temples, and in the midst of the Roman Forum.[16] Inflamed by the example of Antony, a Syrian youth, whose name was Hilarion,[17] fixed his dreary abode on a sandy beach, between the sea and a morass, about seven miles from Gaza. The austere penance, in which he persisted forty-eight years, diffused a similar enthusiasm; and the holy man was followed by a train of two or three thousand anachorets, whenever he visited the innumerable monasteries of Palestine. The fame of Basil[18] is immortal in the monastic history of the East. With a mind that had tasted the learning and eloquence of Athens, with an ambition scarcely to be satisfied by the archbishopric of Caesarea, Basil retired to a savage solitude in Pontus; and deigned, for a while, to give laws to the spiritual colonies which he profusely scattered along the coast of the Black Sea. In the West, Martin of Tours,[19] a soldier, an hermit, a bishop, and a saint, established the monasteries of Gaul; two thousand of his disciples followed him to the grave; and his eloquent historian challenges the deserts of Thebais to produce, in a more favourable climate, a champion of equal virtue. The progress of the monks was not less rapid or universal than that of Christianity itself. Every province, and at last every city, of the empire was filled with their increasing multitudes; and the bleak and barren isles, from Lerins to Lipari, that arise out of the Tuscan sea, were chosen by the anachorets, for the place of their voluntary exile. An easy and perpetual intercourse by sea and land connected the provinces of the Roman world; and the life of Hilarion displays the facility with which an indigent hermit of Palestine might traverse Egypt, embark for Sicily, escape to Epirus, and finally settle in the island of Cyprus.[20] The Latin Christians embraced the religious institutions of Rome. The pilgrims, who visited Jerusalem, eagerly copied, in the most distant climates of the earth, the faithful model of the monastic life. The disciples of Antony spread themselves beyond the tropic, over the Christian empire of Ethiopia.[21] The monastery of Banchor,[22] in Flintshire, which contained above two thousand brethren, dispersed a numerous colony among the Barbarians of Ireland;[23] and Iona, one of the Hebrides, which was planted by the Irish monks, diffused over the northern regions a doubtful ray of science and superstition.[24]

These unhappy exiles from social life were impelled by the dark and implacable genius of superstition. Their mutual resolution was supported by the example of millions, of either sex, of every age, and of every rank; and each proselyte, who entered the gates of a monastery, was persuaded that he trod the steep and thorny path of eternal happiness.[25] But the operation of these religious motives was variously determined by the temper and situation of mankind. Reason might subdue, or passion might suspend, their influence; but they acted most forcibly on the infirm minds of children and females; they were strengthened by secret remorse or accidental misfortune; and they might derive some aid from the temporal considerations of vanity or interest. It was naturally supposed that the pious and humble monks, who had renounced the world to accomplish the work of their salvation, were the best qualified for the spiritual government of the Christians. The reluctant hermit was torn from his cell, and seated, amidst the acclamations of the people, on the episcopal throne; the monasteries of Egypt, of Gaul, and of the East supplied a regular succession of saints and bishops; and ambition soon discovered the secret road which led to the possession of wealth and honours.[26] The popular monks, whose reputation was connected with the fame and success of the order, assiduously laboured to multiply the number of their fellow-captives. They insinuated themselves into noble and opulent families; and the specious arts of flattery and seduction were employed to secure those proselytes who might bestow wealth or dignity on the monastic profession. The indignant father bewailed the loss, perhaps, of an only son;[27] the credulous maid was betrayed by vanity to violate the laws of nature; and the matron aspired to imaginary perfection, by renouncing the virtues of domestic life. Paula yielded to the persuasive eloquence of Jerome;[28] and the profane title of mother-in-law of God[29] tempted that illustrious widow to consecrate the virginity of her daughter Eustochium. By the advice, and in the company, of her spiritual guide, Paula abandoned Rome and her infant son; retired to the holy village of Bethlem; founded an hospital and four monasteries; and acquired, by her alms and penance, an eminent and conspicuous station in the Catholic church. Such rare and illustrious penitents were celebrated as the glory and example of their age; but the monasteries were filled by a crowd of obscure and abject plebeians,[30] who gained in the cloister much more than they had sacrificed in the world. Peasants, slaves, and mechanics might escape from poverty and contempt to a safe and honourable profession, whose apparent hardships are mitigated by custom, by popular applause, and by the secret relaxation of discipline.[31] The subjects of Rome, whose persons and fortunes were made responsible for unequal and exorbitant tributes, retired from the oppression of the Imperial government; and the pusillanimous youth preferred the penance of a monastic, to the dangers of a military, life. The affrighted provincials, of every rank, who fled before the Barbarians, found shelter and subsistence; whole legions were buried in these religious sanctuaries; and the same cause, which relieved the distress of individuals, impaired the strength and fortitude of the empire.[32]

The monastic profession of the ancients[33] was an act of voluntary devotion. The inconstant fanatic was threatened with the eternal vengeance of the God whom he deserted; but the doors of the monastery were still open for repentance. Those monks, whose conscience was fortified by reason or passion, were at liberty to resume the character of men and citizens; and even the spouses of Christ might accept the legal embraces of an earthly lover.[34] The examples of scandal and the progress of superstition suggested the propriety of more forcible restraints. After a sufficient trial, the fidelity of the novice was secured by a solemn and perpetual vow; and his irrevocable engagement was ratified by the laws of the church and state. A guilty fugitive was pursued, arrested, and restored to his perpetual prison; and the interposition of the magistrate oppressed the freedom and merit which had alleviated, in some degree, the abject slavery of the monastic discipline.[35] The actions of a monk, his words and even his thoughts, were determined by an inflexible rule,[36] or a capricious superior; the slightest offences were corrected by disgrace or confinement, extraordinary fasts or bloody flagellation; and disobedience, murmur, or delay were ranked in the catalogue of the most heinous sins.[37] A blind submission to the commands of the abbot, however absurd, or even criminal, they might seem, was the ruling principle, the first virtue of the Egyptian monks; and their patience was frequently exercised by the most extravagant trials. They were directed to remove an enormous rock; assiduously to water a barren staff, that was planted in the ground, till, at the end of three years, it should vegetate and blossom like a tree; to walk into a fiery furnace; or to cast their infant into a deep pond: and several saints, or madmen, have been immortalised in monastic story by their thoughtless and fearless obedience.[38] The freedom of the mind, the source of every generous and rational sentiment, was destroyed by the habits of credulity and submission; and the monk, contracting the vices of a slave, devoutly followed the faith and passions of his ecclesiastical tyrant. The peace of the Eastern church was invaded by a swarm of fanatics, incapable of fear, or reason, or humanity; and the Imperial troops acknowledged, without shame, that they were much less apprehensive of an encounter with the fiercest Barbarians.[39]

Superstition has often framed and consecrated the fantastic garments of the monks;[40] but their apparent singularity sometimes proceeds from their uniform attachment to a simple and primitive model, which the revolutions of fashion have made ridiculous in the eyes of mankind. The father of the Benedictines expressly disclaims all idea of choice or merit, and soberly exhorts his disciples to adopt the coarse and convenient dress of the countries which they may inhabit.[41] The monastic habits of the ancients varied with the climate and their mode of life; and they assumed, with the same indifference, the sheepskin of the Egyptian peasants or the cloak of the Grecian philosophers. They allowed themselves the use of linen in Egypt, where it was a cheap and domestic manufacture; but in the West they rejected such an expensive article of foreign luxury.[42] It was the practice of the monks either to cut or shave their hair; they wrapped their heads in a cowl, to escape the sight of profane objects; their legs and feet were naked, except in the extreme cold of winter; and their slow and feeble steps were supported by a long staff. The aspect of a genuine anachoret was horrid and disgusting; every sensation that is offensive to man was thought acceptable to God; and the angelic rule of Tabenne condemned the salutary custom of bathing the limbs in water and of anointing them with oil.[43] The austere monks slept on the ground, on a hard mat or a rough blanket; and the same bundle of palm-leaves served them as a seat in the day and a pillow in the night. Their original cells were low narrow huts, built of the slightest materials; which formed, by the regular distribution of the streets, a large and populous village, enclosing within the common wall a church, an hospital, perhaps a library, some necessary offices, a garden, and a fountain or reservoir of fresh water. Thirty or forty brethren composed a family of separate discipline and diet; and the great monasteries of Egypt consisted of thirty or forty families.

Pleasure and guilt are synonymous terms in the language of the monks; and they had discovered, by experience, that rigid fasts and abstemious diet are the most effectual preservatives against the impure desires of the flesh.[44] The rules of abstinence, which they imposed, or practised, were not uniform or perpetual: the cheerful festival of the Pentecost was balanced by the extraordinary mortification of Lent; the fervour of new monasteries was insensibly relaxed; and the voracious appetite of the Gauls could not imitate the patient and temperate virtue of the Egyptians.[45] The disciples of Antony and Pachomius were satisfied with their daily pittance[46] of twelve ounces of bread, or rather biscuit,[47] which they divided into two frugal repasts, of the afternoon and of the evening. It was esteemed a merit, and almost a duty, to abstain from the boiled vegetables which were provided for the refectory; but the extraordinary bounty of the abbot sometimes indulged them with the luxury of cheese, fruit, salad, and the small dried fish of the Nile.[48] A more ample latitude of sea and river fish was gradually allowed or assumed; but the use of flesh was long confined to the sick or travellers; and, when it gradually prevailed in the less rigid monasteries of Europe, a singular distinction was introduced; as if birds, whether wild or domestic, had been less profane than the grosser animals of the field. Water was the pure and innocent beverage of the primitive monks; and the founder of the Benedictines regrets the daily portion of half a pint of wine, which had been extorted from him by the intemperance of the age.[49] Such an allowance might be easily supplied by the vineyards of Italy; and his victorious disciples, who passed the Alps, the Rhine, and the Baltic, required, in the place of wine, an adequate compensation of strong beer or cider.

The candidate who aspired to the virtue of evangelical poverty abjured, at his first entrance into a regular community, the idea, and even the name, of all separate or exclusive possession.[50] The brethren were supported by their manual labour; and the duty of labour was strenuously recommended as a penance, as an exercise, and as the most laudable means of securing their daily sustenance.[51] The garden and fields, which the industry of the monks had often rescued from the forest or the morass, were diligently cultivated by their hands. They performed, without reluctance, the menial offices of slaves and domestics; and the several trades that were necessary to provide their habits, their utensils, and their lodging, were exercised within the precincts of the great monasteries. The monastic studies have tended, for the most part, to darken, rather than to dispel, the cloud of superstition. Yet the curiosity or zeal of some learned solitaries has cultivated the ecclesiastical, and even the profane, sciences; and posterity must gratefully acknowledge that the monuments of Greek and Roman literature have been preserved and multiplied by their indefatigable pens.[52] But the more humble industry of the monks, especially in Egypt, was contented with the silent, sedentary, occupation of making wooden sandals or of twisting the leaves of the palm-trees into mats and baskets. The superfluous stock, which was not consumed in domestic use, supplied, by trade, the wants of the community; the boats of Tabenne, and the other monasteries of Thebais, descended the Nile as far as Alexandria; and, in a Christian market, the sanctity of the workmen might enhance the intrinsic value of the work.

But the necessity of manual labour was insensibly superseded. The novice was tempted to bestow his fortune on the saints, in whose society he was resolved to spend the remainder of his life; and the pernicious indulgence of the laws permitted him to receive, for their use, any future accessions of legacy or inheritance.[53] Melania contributed her plate, three hundred pounds weight of silver, and Paula contracted an immense debt, for the relief of their favourite monks; who kindly imparted the merits of their prayers and penance to a rich and liberal sinner.[54] Time continually increased, and accidents could seldom diminish, the estates of the popular monasteries, which spread over the adjacent country and cities; and, in the first century of their institution, the infidel Zosimus has maliciously observed that, for the benefit of the poor, the Christian monks had reduced a great part of mankind to a state of beggary.[55] As long as they maintained their original fervour, they approved themselves,* however, the faithful and benevolent stewards of the charity which was entrusted to their care. But their discipline was corrupted by prosperity: they gradually assumed the pride of wealth, and at last indulged the luxury of expense. Their public luxury might be excused by the magnificence of religious worship and the decent motive of erecting durable habitations for an immortal society. But every age of the church has accused the licentiousness of the degenerate monks; who no longer remembered the object of their institution, embraced the vain and sensual pleasures of the world which they had renounced,[56] and scandalously abused the riches which had been acquired by the austere virtues of their founders.[57] Their natural descent from such painful and dangerous virtue to the common vices of humanity will not, perhaps, excite much grief or indignation in the mind of a philosopher.

The lives of the primitive monks were consumed in penance and solitude, undisturbed by the various occupations which fill the time, and exercise the faculties, of reasonable, active, and social beings. Whenever they were permitted to step beyond the precincts of the monastery, two jealous companions were the mutual guards and spies of each other's actions; and, after their return, they were condemned to forget, or, at least, to suppress, whatever they had seen or heard in the world. Strangers, who professed the orthodox faith, were hospitably entertained in a separate apartment; but their dangerous conversation was restricted to some chosen elders of approved discretion and fidelity. Except in their presence, the monastic slave might not receive the visits of his friends or kindred; and it was deemed highly meritorious if he afflicted a tender sister or an aged parent by the obstinate refusal of a word or look.[58] The monks themselves passed their lives, without personal attachments, among a crowd, which had been formed by accident and was detained, in the same prison, by force or prejudice. Recluse fanatics have few ideas or sentiments to communicate; a special licence of the abbot regulated the time and duration of their familiar* visits; and, at their silent meals, they were enveloped in their cowls, inaccessible, and almost invisible, to each other.[59] Study is the resource of solitude; but education had not prepared and qualified for any liberal studies the mechanics and peasants, who filled the monastic communities. They might work; but the vanity of spiritual perfection was tempted to disdain the exercise of manual labour, and the industry must be faint and languid which is not excited by the sense of personal interest.

According to their faith and zeal, they might employ the day, which they passed in their cells, either in vocal or mental prayer; they assembled in the evening, and they were awakened in the night, for the public worship of the monastery. The precise moment was determined by the stars, which are seldom clouded in the serene sky of Egypt; and a rustic horn or trumpet, the signal of devotion, twice interrupted the vast silence of the desert.[60] Even sleep, the last refuge of the unhappy, was rigorously measured; the vacant hours of the monk heavily rolled along, without business or pleasure; and, before the close of each day, he had repeatedly accused the tedious progress of the Sun.[61] In this comfortless state, superstition still pursued and tormented her wretched votaries.[62] The repose which they had sought in the cloister was disturbed by tardy repentance, profane doubts, and guilty desires; and, while they considered each natural impulse as an unpardonable sin, they perpetually trembled on the edge of a flaming and bottomless abyss. From the painful struggles of disease and despair these unhappy victims were sometimes relieved by madness or death; and, in the sixth century, an hospital was founded at Jerusalem for a small portion of the austere penitents, who were deprived of their senses.[63] Their visions, before they attained this extreme and acknowledged term of frenzy, have afforded ample materials of supernatural history. It was their firm persuasion that the air which they breathed was peopled with invisible enemies; with innumerable daemons, who watched every occasion, and assumed every form, to terrify, and above all to tempt, their unguarded virtue. The imagination, and even the senses, were deceived by the illusions of distempered fanaticism; and the hermit, whose midnight prayer was oppressed by involuntary slumber, might easily confound the phantoms of horror or delight which had occupied his sleeping and his waking dreams.[64]

The monks were divided into two classes: the *Coenobites*, who lived under a common and regular discipline; and the *Anachorets*, who indulged their unsocial, independent fanaticism.[65] The most devout, or the most ambitious, of the spiritual brethren renounced the convent, as they had renounced the world. The fervent monasteries of Egypt, Palestine, and Syria were surrounded by a *Laura*,[66] a distant circle of solitary cells; and the extravagant penance of the Hermits was stimulated by applause and emulation.[67] They sunk under the painful weight of crosses and chains; and their emaciated limbs were confined by collars, bracelets, gauntlets, and greaves, of massy and rigid iron. All superfluous encumbrance of dress they contemptuously cast away; and some savage saints of both sexes have been admired, whose naked bodies were only covered by their long hair. They aspired to reduce themselves to the rude and miserable state in which the human brute is scarcely distinguished above his kindred animals; and a numerous sect of Anachorets derived their name from their humble practice of grazing in the fields of Mesopotamia with the common herd.[68] They often usurped the den of some wild beast whom they affected to resemble; they buried themselves in some gloomy cavern which art or nature had scooped out of the rock; and the marble quarries of Thebais are still inscribed with the monuments of their penance.[69] The most perfect hermits are supposed to have passed many days without food, many nights without sleep, and many years without speaking; and glorious was the *man* (I abuse that name) who contrived any cell, or seat, of a peculiar construction, which might expose him, in the most inconvenient posture, to the inclemency of the seasons.

Among these heroes of the monastic life, the name and genius of Simeon Stylites[70] have been immortalised by the singular invention of an aerial penance. At the age of thirteen, the young Syrian deserted the profession of a shepherd and threw himself into an austere monastery. After a long and painful novitiate, in which Simeon was repeatedly saved from pious suicide, he established his residence on a mountain about thirty or forty miles to the east of Antioch. Within the space of a *mandra*, or circle of stones, to which he had attached himself by a ponderous chain, he ascended a column, which was successively raised from the height of nine, to that of sixty, feet from the ground.[71] In this last and lofty station, the

Syrian Anachoret resisted the heat of thirty summers, and the cold of as many winters. Habit and exercise instructed him to maintain his dangerous situation without fear or giddiness, and successively to assume the different postures of devotion. He sometimes prayed in an erect attitude with his outstretched arms in the figure of a cross; but his most familiar practice was that of bending his meagre skeleton from the forehead to the feet; and a curious spectator, after numbering twelve hundred and forty-four repetitions, at length desisted from the endless account. The progress of an ulcer in his thigh[72] might shorten, but it could not disturb, this *celestial* life; and the patient Hermit expired without descending from his column. A prince who should capriciously inflict such tortures would be deemed a tyrant; but it would surpass the power of a tyrant to impose a long and miserable existence on the reluctant victims of his cruelty. This voluntary martyrdom must have gradually destroyed the sensibility both of the mind and body; nor can it be presumed that the fanatics, who torment themselves, are susceptible of any lively affection for the rest of mankind. A cruel unfeeling temper has distinguished the monks of every age and country: their stern indifference, which is seldom mollified by personal friendship, is inflamed by religious hatred; and their merciless zeal has strenuously administered the holy office of the Inquisition.

The monastic saints, who excite only the contempt and the pity of a philosopher, were respected, and almost adored, by the prince and people. Successive crowds of pilgrims from Gaul and India saluted the divine pillar of Simeon; the tribes of Saracens disputed in arms the honour of his benediction; the queens of Arabia and Persia gratefully confessed his supernatural virtue; and the angelic Hermit was consulted by the younger Theodosius, in the most important concerns of the church and state. His remains were transported from the mountain of Telenissa, by a solemn procession of the patriarch, the master-general of the East, six bishops, twenty-one counts or tribunes, and six thousand soldiers; and Antioch revered his bones, as her glorious ornament and impregnable defence. The fame of the apostles and martyrs was gradually eclipsed by these recent and popular Anachorets; the Christian world fell prostrate before their shrines; and the miracles ascribed to their relics exceeded, at least in number and duration, the spiritual exploits of their lives. But the golden legend of their lives[73] was embellished by the artful credulity of their interested* brethren; and a believing age was easily persuaded that the slightest caprice of an Egyptian or a Syrian monk had been sufficient to interrupt the eternal laws of the universe. The favourites of Heaven were accustomed to cure inveterate diseases with a touch, a word, or a distant message; and to expel the most obstinate daemons from the souls, or bodies, which they possessed. They familiarly accosted, or imperiously commanded, the lions and serpents of the desert; infused vegetation into a sapless trunk; suspended iron on the surface of the water; passed the Nile on the back of a crocodile, and refreshed themselves in a fiery furnace.

These extravagant tales, which display the fiction, without the genius, of poetry, have seriously affected the reason, the faith, and the morals of the Christians. Their credulity debased and vitiated the faculties of the mind; they corrupted the evidence of history; and superstition gradually extinguished the hostile light of philosophy and science. Every mode of religious worship which had been practised by the saints, every mysterious doctrine which they believed, was fortified by the sanction of divine revelation, and all the manly virtues were oppressed by the servile and pusillanimous reign of the monks. If it be possible to measure the interval between the philosophic writings of Cicero and the sacred legend of Theodoret, between the character of Cato and that of Simeon, we may appreciate the memorable revolution which was accomplished in the Roman empire within a period of five hundred years.

II. The progress of Christianity has been marked by two glorious and decisive victories: over the learned and luxurious citizens of the Roman empire; and over the warlike Barbarians of Scythia and Germany, who subverted the empire, and embraced the religion, of the Romans. The Goths were the foremost of these savage proselytes; and the nation was indebted for its conversion to a countryman, or, at least, to a subject, worthy to be ranked among the inventors of useful arts, who have deserved the remembrance and gratitude of posterity. A great number of Roman provincials had been led away into captivity by the Gothic bands who ravaged Asia in the time of Gallienus;* and of these captives, many were Christians, and several belonged to the ecclesiastical order. Those involuntary missionaries, dispersed as slaves in the villages of Dacia, successively laboured for the salvation of their masters. The seeds, which they planted, of the evangelic doctrine, were gradually propagated; and before the end of a century, the pious work was achieved by the labours of Ulphilas, whose ancestors had been transported beyond the Danube from a small town of Cappadocia.

Ulphilas, the bishop and apostle of the Goths,[74] acquired their love and reverence by his blameless life and indefatigable zeal; and they received, with implicit confidence, the doctrines of truth and virtue which he preached and practised. He executed the arduous task of translating the Scriptures into their native tongue, a dialect of the German or Teutonic language; but he prudently suppressed the four books of Kings, as they might tend to irritate the fierce and sanguinary spirit of the Barbarians. The rude, imperfect, idiom of soldiers and shepherds, so ill-qualified to communicate any spiritual ideas, was improved and modulated by his genius; and Ulphilas, before he could frame his version, was obliged to compose a new alphabet of twenty-four letters; four of which he invented, to express the peculiar sounds that were unknown to the Greek, and Latin, pronunciation.[75] But the prosperous state of the Gothic church was soon afflicted by war and intestine discord, and the chieftains were divided by religion as well as by interest. Fritigern, the friend of the Romans, became the proselyte of Ulphilas; while the haughty soul of Athanaric disdained the yoke of the empire, and of the Gospel.* The faith of the new converts was tried by the persecution which he excited. A waggon, bearing aloft the shapeless image of Thor, perhaps, or of Woden, was conducted in solemn procession through the streets of the camp; and the rebels, who refused to worship the God of their fathers, were immediately burned, with their tents and families. The character of Ulphilas recommended him to the esteem of the Eastern court, where he twice appeared as the minister of peace; he pleaded the cause of the distressed Goths, who implored the protection of Valens; and the name of *Moses* was applied to this spiritual guide, who conducted his people, through the deep waters of the Danube, to the Land of Promise.[76] The devout shepherds, who were attached to his person and tractable to his voice, acquiesced in their settlement, at the foot of the Maesian mountains, in a country of woodlands and pastures, which supported their flocks and herds and enabled them to purchase the corn and wine of the more plentiful provinces. These harmless barbarians multiplied in obscure peace and the profession of Christianity.[77]

Their fiercer brethren, the formidable Visigoths, universally adopted the religion of the Romans, with whom they maintained a perpetual intercourse, of war, of friendship, or of conquest. In their long and victorious march from the Danube to the Atlantic ocean, they converted their allies; they educated the rising generation; and the devotion which reigned in the camp of Alaric, or the court of Toulouse, might edify, or disgrace, the palaces of Rome and Constantinople.[78] During the same period, Christianity was embraced by almost all the Barbarians, who established their kingdoms on the ruins of the Western empire; the Burgundians in Gaul, the Suevi in Spain, the Vandals in Africa, the Ostrogoths in Pannonia, and the various bands of mercenaries that raised Odoacer to the throne of Italy. The Franks and the Saxons still persevered in the errors of Paganism; but the Franks obtained the monarchy of Gaul by their submission to the example of Clovis; and the Saxon conquerors of Britain were reclaimed from their savage superstition by the missionaries of Rome. These Barbarian proselytes displayed an ardent and successful zeal in the propagation of the faith. The Merovingian kings, and their successors, Charlemagne and the Othos, extended, by their laws and victories, the dominion of the cross. England produced the apostle of Germany;† and the evangelic light was gradually diffused from the neighbourhood of the Rhine to the nations of the Elbe, the Vistula, and the Baltic.[79]

The different motives which influenced the reason, or the passions, of the Barbarian converts cannot easily be ascertained. They were often capricious and accidental; a dream, an omen, the report of a miracle, the example of some priest or hero, the charms of a believing wife, and, above all, the fortunate event of a prayer or vow which, in a moment of danger, they had addressed to the God of the Christians.[80] The early prejudices of education were insensibly erased by the habits of frequent and familiar society; the moral precepts of the Gospel were protected by the extravagant virtues of the monks; and a spiritual theology was supported by the visible power of relics and the pomp of religious worship. But the rational and ingenious mode of persuasion which a Saxon bishop[81] suggested to a popular saint might sometimes be employed by the missionaries who laboured for the conversion of infidels. 'Admit,' says the sagacious disputant, 'whatever they are pleased to assert of the fabulous, and carnal, genealogy of their gods and goddesses, who are propagated from each other. From this principle deduce their imperfect nature, and human infirmities, the assurance they were *born*, and the probability that they will *die*. At what time, by what means, from what cause, were the eldest of the gods or goddesses produced? Do they still continue, or have they ceased, to propagate? If they have ceased, summon your antagonists to declare the reason of this strange alteration. If they still continue, the number of the gods must become infinite; and shall we not risk, by the indiscreet worship of some impotent deity, to excite the resentment of his jealous superior? The visible heavens and earth, the whole system of the universe, which may be conceived by the mind, is it created or eternal? If created, how, or where, could the gods themselves exist before the creation? If eternal, how could they assume the empire of an independent and pre-existing world? Urge these arguments with temper and moderation; insinuate, at seasonable intervals, the truth, and beauty, of the Christian revelation; and endeavour to make the unbelievers ashamed, without making them angry.' This metaphysical reasoning, too refined perhaps for the Barbarians of Germany, was fortified by the grosser weight of authority and popular consent. The advantage of temporal prosperity had deserted the Pagan cause, and passed over to the service of Christianity. The Romans themselves, the most powerful and enlightened nation of the globe, had renounced their ancient superstition; and, if the ruin of their empire seemed to accuse the efficacy of the new faith, the disgrace was already retrieved by the conversion of the victorious Goths. The valiant and fortunate Barbarians, who subdued the provinces of the West, successively received, and reflected, the same edifying example. Before the age of Charlemagne, the Christian nations of Europe might exult in the exclusive possession of the temperate climates, of the fertile lands, which produced corn, wine, and oil, while the savage idolaters, and their helpless idols, were confined to the extremities of the earth, the dark and frozen regions of the North.[82]

Christianity, which opened the gates of Heaven to the Barbarians, introduced an important change in their moral and political condition. They received, at the same time, the use of letters, so essential to a religion whose doctrines are contained in a sacred book; and, while they studied the divine truth, their minds were insensibly enlarged by the distant view of history, of nature, of the arts, and of society. The version of the Scriptures into their native tongue, which had facilitated their conversion, must excite, among their clergy, some curiosity to read the original text, to understand the sacred liturgy of the church, and to examine, in the writings of the fathers, the chain of ecclesiastical tradition. These spiritual gifts were preserved in the Greek and Latin languages, which concealed the inestimable monuments of ancient learning. The immortal productions of Virgil, Cicero, and Livy, which were accessible to the Christian Barbarians, maintained a silent intercourse between the reign of Augustus and the times of Clovis and Charlemagne. The emulation of mankind was encouraged by the remembrance of a more perfect state; and the flame of science was secretly kept alive, to warm and enlighten the mature age of the Western world. In the most corrupt state of Christianity, the Barbarians might learn justice from the law, and mercy from the gospel; and, if the knowledge of their duty was insufficient to guide their actions or to regulate their passions, they were sometimes restrained by conscience, and frequently punished by remorse. But the direct authority of religion was less effectual than the holy communion which united them with their Christian brethren in spiritual friendship. The influence of these sentiments contributed to secure their fidelity in the service, or the alliance, of the Romans, to alleviate the horrors of war, to moderate the insolence of conquest, and to preserve, in the downfall of the empire, a permanent respect for the name and institutions of Rome. In the days of Paganism, the priests of Gaul and Germany reigned over the people, and controlled the jurisdiction of the magistrates; and the zealous proselytes transferred an equal, or more ample, measure of devout obedience to the pontiffs of the Christian faith. The sacred character of the bishops was supported by their temporal possessions; they obtained an honourable seat in the legislative assemblies of soldiers and freemen; and it was their interest, as well as their duty, to mollify, by peaceful counsels, the fierce spirit of the Barbarians. The perpetual correspondence of the Latin clergy, the frequent pilgrimages to Rome and Jerusalem, and the growing authority of the Popes, cemented the union of the Christian republic; and gradually produced the similar manners, and common jurisprudence, which have distinguished, from the rest of mankind, the independent, and even hostile, nations of modern Europe.

But the operation of these causes was checked and retarded by the unfortunate accident which infused a deadly poison into the cup of Salvation. Whatever might be the early sentiments of Ulphilas, his connections with the empire and the church were formed during the reign of Arianism. The apostle of the Goths subscribed the creed of Rimini; professed with freedom, and perhaps with sincerity, that the Son was not equal or consubstantial to the Father;[83] communicated these errors to the clergy and people; and infected the Barbaric world with an heresy[84] which the great Theodosius proscribed and extinguished among the Romans. The temper and understanding of the new proselytes were not adapted to metaphysical subtleties; but they strenuously maintained what they had piously received, as the pure and genuine doctrines of Christianity. The advantage of preaching and expounding the Scriptures in the Teutonic language promoted the apostolic labours of Ulphilas and his successors; and they ordained a competent number of bishops and presbyters, for the instruction of the kindred tribes. The Ostrogoths, the Burgundians, the Suevi, and the Vandals, who had listened to the eloquence of the Latin clergy,[85] preferred the more intelligible lessons of their domestic teachers; and Arianism was adopted as the national faith of the warlike converts who were seated on the ruins of the Western empire. This irreconcilable difference of religion was a perpetual source of jealousy and hatred; and the reproach of *Barbarian* was embittered by the more odious epithet of *Heretic*. The heroes of the North, who had submitted, with some reluctance, to believe that all their ancestors were in hell,[86] were astonished and exasperated to learn that they themselves had only changed the mode of their eternal condemnation. Instead of the smooth applause which Christian kings are accustomed to expect from their loyal prelates, the orthodox bishops and their clergy were in a state of opposition to the Arian courts; and their indiscreet opposition frequently became criminal, and might sometimes be dangerous.[87] The pulpit, that safe and sacred organ of sedition, resounded with the names of Pharaoh and Holofernes;*[88] the public discontent was inflamed by the hope or promise of a glorious deliverance; and the seditious saints were tempted to promote the accomplishment of their own predictions. Notwithstanding these provocations, the Catholics of Gaul, Spain, and Italy enjoyed, under the reign of the Arians, the free and peaceful exercise of their religion. Their haughty masters respected the zeal of a numerous people, resolved to die at the foot of their altars; and the example of their devout constancy was admired and imitated by the Barbarians themselves. The conquerors evaded, however, the disgraceful reproach, or confession, of fear, by attributing their toleration to the liberal motives of reason and humanity; and, while they affected the language, they imperceptibly imbibed the spirit, of genuine Christianity.

The peace of the church was sometimes interrupted. The Catholics were indiscreet, the Barbarians were impatient; and the partial acts of severity or injustice which had been recommended by the Arian clergy were exaggerated by the orthodox writers. The guilt of persecution may be imputed to Euric, king of the Visigoths; who suspended the exercise of ecclesiastical, or, at least, of episcopal, functions, and punished the popular bishops of Aquitain with imprisonment, exile, and confiscation.[89] But the cruel and absurd enterprise of subduing the minds of a whole people was undertaken by the Vandals alone. Genseric himself, in his early youth, had renounced the orthodox communion; and the apostate could neither grant nor expect a sincere forgiveness. He was exasperated to find that the Africans who had fled before him in the field still presumed to dispute his will in synods and churches; and his ferocious mind was incapable of fear or of compassion. His Catholic subjects were oppressed by intolerant laws and arbitrary punishments. The language of Genseric was furious and formidable; the knowledge of his intentions might justify the most unfavourable interpretations of his actions; and the Arians were reproached with the frequent executions which stained the palace and the dominions of the tyrant. Arms and ambition were, however, the ruling passions of the monarch of the sea. But Hunneric, his inglorious son, who seemed to inherit only his vices, tormented the Catholics with the same unrelenting fury which had been fatal to his brother, his nephews, and the friends and favourites of his father, and even to the Arian patriarch, who was inhumanly burnt alive in the midst of Carthage. The religious war was preceded and prepared by an insidious truce; persecution was made the serious and important business of the Vandal court; and the loathsome disease, which hastened the death of Hunneric, revenged the injuries, without contributing to the deliverance, of the church. The throne of Africa was successively filled by the two nephews of Hunneric; by Gundamund, who reigned about twelve, and by Thrasimund, who governed the nation above twenty-seven, years. Their administration was hostile and oppressive to the orthodox party. Gundamund appeared to emulate, or even to surpass, the cruelty of his uncle; and, if at length he relented, if he recalled the bishops and restored the freedom of Athanasian worship, a premature death intercepted the benefits of his tardy clemency. His brother, Thrasimund, was the greatest and most accomplished of the Vandal kings, whom he excelled in beauty, prudence, and magnanimity of soul. But this magnanimous character was degraded by his intolerant zeal and deceitful clemency. Instead of threats and tortures, he employed the gentle but efficacious powers of seduction. Wealth, dignity, and the royal favour were the liberal rewards of apostasy; the Catholics, who had violated the laws, might purchase their pardon by the renunciation of their faith; and, whenever Thrasimund meditated any rigorous measure, he patiently waited till the indiscretion of his adversaries furnished him with a specious opportunity. Bigotry was his last sentiment in the hour of death; and he exacted from his successor a solemn oath that he would never tolerate the sectaries of Athanasius. But his successor, Hilderic, the gentle son of the savage Hunneric, preferred the duties of humanity and justice to the vain obligation of an impious oath; and his accession was gloriously marked by the restoration of peace and universal freedom. The throne of that virtuous, though feeble, monarch was usurped by his cousin Gelimer, a zealous Arian; but the Vandal kingdom, before he could enjoy or abuse his power, was subverted by the arms of Belisarius; and the orthodox party retaliated the injuries which they had endured.[90]

The passionate declamations of the Catholics, the sole historians of this persecution, cannot afford any distinct series of causes and events, any impartial view of characters or counsels; but the most remarkable circumstances, that deserve either credit or notice, may be referred to the following heads: I. In the original law, which is still extant,[91] Hunneric expressly declares, and the declaration appears to be correct, that he had faithfully transcribed the regulations and penalties of the Imperial edicts, against the heretical congregations, the clergy, and the people, who dissented from the established religion. If the rights of conscience had been understood, the Catholics must have condemned their past conduct, or acquiesced in their actual sufferings. But they still persisted to refuse the indulgence which they claimed. While they trembled under the lash of persecution, they praised the *laudable* severity of Hunneric himself, who burnt or banished great numbers of Manichaeans:[92] and they rejected, with horror, the ignominious compromise that the disciples of Arius and of Athanasius should enjoy a reciprocal and similar toleration in the territories of the Romans and in those of the Vandals.[93] II. The practice of a conference, which the Catholics had so frequently used to insult and punish their obstinate antagonists, was retorted against themselves.[94] At the command of Hunneric, four hundred and sixty-six orthodox bishops assembled at Carthage; but, when they were admitted into the hall of audience, they had the mortification of beholding the Arian Cyrila exalted on the patriarchal throne. The disputants were separated, after the mutual and ordinary reproaches of noise and silence, of delay and precipitation, of military force and of popular clamour. One martyr and one confessor were selected among the Catholic bishops; twenty-eight escaped by flight, and eighty-eight by conformity, forty-six were sent into Corsica to cut timber for the royal navy; and three hundred and two were banished to the different parts of Africa, exposed to the insults of their enemies, and carefully deprived of all the temporal and spiritual comforts of life.[95] The hardships of ten years' exile must have reduced their numbers; and, if they had complied with the law of Thrasimund, which prohibited any episcopal consecrations, the orthodox church of Africa must have expired with the lives of its actual members. They disobeyed; and their disobedience was punished by a second exile of two hundred and twenty bishops into Sardinia; where they languished fifteen years, till the accession of the gracious Hilderic.[96] The two islands were judiciously chosen by the malice of their Arian tyrants. Seneca, from his own experience, has deplored and exaggerated the miserable state of Corsica,[97] and the plenty of Sardinia was overbalanced by the unwholesome quality of the air.[98] III. The zeal of Genseric and his successors for the conversion of the Catholics must have rendered them still more jealous to guard the purity of the Vandal faith. Before the churches were finally shut, it was a crime to appear in a Barbarian dress; and those who presumed to neglect the royal mandate were rudely dragged backwards by their long hair.[99] The Palatine officers* who refused to profess the religion of their prince were ignominiously stripped of their honours and employments; banished to Sardinia and Sicily; or condemned to the servile labours of slaves and peasants in the fields of Utica. In the districts which had been peculiarly allotted to the Vandals, the exercise of the Catholic worship was more strictly prohibited; and severe penalties were denounced against the guilt both of the missionary and the proselyte. By these arts, the faith of the Barbarians was preserved, and their zeal was inflamed; they discharged, with devout fury, the office of spies, informers, or executioners; and, whenever their cavalry took the field, it was the favourite amusement of the march to defile the churches and to insult the clergy of the adverse faction.[100] IV. The citizens who had been educated in the luxury of the Roman province were delivered, with exquisite cruelty, to the Moors of the desert. A venerable train of bishops, presbyters, and deacons, with a faithful crowd of four thousand and ninety-six persons, whose guilt is not precisely ascertained, were torn from their native homes, by the command of Hunneric. During the night, they were confined, like a herd of cattle, amidst their own ordure; during the day, they pursued their march over the burning sands; and, if they fainted under the heat and fatigue, they were goaded or dragged along, till they expired in the hands of their tormentors.[101] These unhappy exiles, when they reached the Moorish huts, might excite the compassion of a people, whose native humanity was neither improved by reason nor corrupted by fanaticism; but, if they escaped the dangers, they were condemned to share the distress, of a savage life. V. It is incumbent on the authors of persecution previously to reflect, whether they are determined to support it in the last extreme. They excite the flame which they strive to extinguish; and it soon becomes necessary to chastise the contumacy, as well as the crime, of the offender. The fine, which he is unable or unwilling to discharge, exposes his person to the severity of the law; and his contempt of lighter penalties suggests the use and propriety of capital punishment. Through the veil of fiction and declamation, we may clearly perceive that the Catholics, more especially under the reign of Hunneric, endured the most cruel and ignominious treatment.[102] Respectable citizens, noble matrons, and consecrated virgins were stripped naked, and raised in the air by pulleys, with a weight suspended at their feet. In this painful attitude their naked bodies were torn with scourges, or burnt in the most tender parts with red-hot plates of iron. The amputation of the ears, the nose, the tongue, and the right hand was inflicted by the Arians; and, although the precise number cannot be defined, it is evident that many persons, among whom a bishop[103] and a proconsul[104] may be named, were entitled to the crown of martyrdom. The same honour has been ascribed to the memory of count Sebastian, who professed the Nicene creed with unshaken constancy; and Genseric might detest, as an heretic, the brave and ambitious fugitive whom he dreaded as a rival.[105] VI. A new mode of conversion, which might subdue the feeble, and alarm the timorous, was employed by the Arian ministers. They imposed, by fraud or violence, the rites of baptism; and punished the apostasy of the Catholics, if they disclaimed this odious and profane ceremony, which scandalously violated the freedom of the will and the unity of the sacrament.[106] The hostile sects had formerly allowed the validity of each other's baptism; and the innovation, so fiercely maintained by the Vandals, can be imputed only to the example and advice of the Donatists. VII. The Arian clergy surpassed, in religious cruelty, the king and his Vandals; but they were incapable of cultivating the spiritual vineyard which they were so desirous to possess. A patriarch[107] might seat himself on the throne of Carthage; some bishops, in the principal cities, might usurp the place of their rivals; but the smallness of their numbers and their ignorance of the Latin language[108] disqualified the Barbarians for the ecclesiastical ministry of a great church; and the Africans, after the loss of their orthodox pastors, were deprived of the public exercise of Christianity. VIII. The emperors were the natural protectors of the Homoousian doctrine; and the faithful people of Africa, both as Romans and as Catholics, preferred their lawful sovereignty to the usurpation of the Barbarous heretics. During an interval of peace and friendship, Hunneric restored the cathedral of Carthage, at the intercession of Zeno, who reigned in the East, and of Placidia, the daughter and relict* of emperors, and the sister of the queen of the Vandals.[109] But this decent regard was of short duration; and the haughty tyrant displayed his contempt for the religion of the Empire by studiously arranging the bloody images of persecution in all the principal streets through which the Roman ambassador must pass in his way to the palace.[110] An oath was required from the bishops, who were assembled at Carthage, that they would support the succession of his son Hilderic, and that they would renounce all foreign or *transmarine* correspondence. This engagement, consistent as it should seem with their moral and religious duties, was refused by the more sagacious members[111] of the assembly. Their refusal, faintly coloured by the pretence that it is unlawful for a Christian to swear, must provoke the suspicions of a jealous tyrant.

The Catholics, oppressed by royal and military force, were far superior to their adversaries in numbers and learning. With the same weapons which the Greek[112] and Latin fathers had already provided for the Arian controversy, they repeatedly silenced, or vanquished, the fierce and illiterate successors of Ulphilas. The consciousness of their own superiority might have raised them above the arts and passions of religious warfare. Yet, instead of assuming such honourable pride, the orthodox theologians were tempted, by the assurance of impunity, to compose fictions, which must be stigmatised with the epithets of fraud and forgery. They ascribed their own polemical works to the most venerable names of Christian antiquity; the characters of Athanasius and Augustine were awkwardly personated by Vigilius and his disciples;[113] and the famous creed which so clearly expounds the mysteries of the Trinity and the Incarnation is

deduced, with strong probability, from this African school.[114] Even the
scriptures themselves were profaned by their rash and sacrilegious hands.
The memorable text which asserts the unity of the Three who bear witness
in heaven[115] is condemned by the universal silence of the orthodox fathers,
ancient versions, and authentic manuscripts.[116] It was first alleged by the
Catholic bishops whom Hunneric summoned to the conference of
Carthage.[117] An allegorical interpretation, in the form, perhaps, of a
marginal note, invaded the text of the Latin Bibles, which were renewed
and corrected in a dark period of ten centuries.[118] After the invention of
printing,[119] the editors of the Greek Testament yielded to their own
prejudices, or those of the times;[120] and the pious fraud, which was
embraced with equal zeal at Rome and at Geneva, has been infinitely
multiplied in every country and every language of modern Europe.

The example of fraud must excite suspicion; and the specious miracles
by which the African Catholics have defended the truth and justice of
their cause may be ascribed, with more reason, to their own industry than
to the visible protection of Heaven. Yet the historian, who views this
religious conflict with an impartial eye, may condescend to mention *one*
preternatural event which will edify the devout and surprise the incredulous. Tipasa,[121] a maritime colony of Mauritania, sixteen miles to the east
of Caesarea, had been distinguished, in every age, by the orthodox zeal of
its inhabitants. They had braved the fury of the Donatists;[122] they resisted,
or eluded, the tyranny of the Arians. The town was deserted on the
approach of an heretical bishop: most of the inhabitants who could
procure ships passed over to the coast of Spain; and the unhappy remnant,
refusing all communion with the usurper, still presumed to hold their
pious, but illegal, assemblies. Their disobedience exasperated the cruelty
of Hunneric. A military count was dispatched from Carthage to Tipasa;
he collected the Catholics in the Forum, and, in the presence of the
whole province, deprived the guilty of their right hands and their
tongues. But the holy confessors continued to speak without tongues; and
this miracle is attested by Victor, an African bishop, who published an
history of the persecution within two years after the event.[123] 'If anyone,'
says Victor, 'should doubt of the truth, let him repair to Constantinople,
and listen to the clear and perfect language of Restitutus, the subdeacon,
one of these glorious sufferers, who is now lodged in the palace of the
emperor Zeno, and is respected by the devout empress.' At Constantinople we are astonished to find a cool, a learned, an unexceptionable
witness, without interest, and without passion. Aeneas of Gaza, a Platonic
philosopher, has accurately described his own observations on these
African sufferers. 'I saw them myself: I heard them speak: I diligently
enquired by what means such an articulate voice could be formed
without any organ of speech: I used my eyes to examine the report of my
ears: I opened their mouth, and saw that the whole tongue had been
completely torn away by the roots, an operation which the physicians

generally suppose to be mortal.'[124] The testimony of Aeneas of Gaza might be confirmed by the superfluous evidence of the emperor Justinian, in a perpetual edict; of count Marcellinus, in his Chronicle of the times; and of Pope Gregory I, who had resided at Constantinople, as the minister of the Roman pontiff.[125] They all lived within the compass of a century; and they all appeal to their personal knowledge, or the public notoriety, for the truth of a miracle which was repeated in several instances, displayed on the greatest theatre of the world, and submitted, during a series of years, to the calm examination of the senses. This supernatural gift of the African confessors, who spoke without tongues, will command the assent of those, and of those only, who already believe that their language was pure and orthodox. But the stubborn mind of an infidel is guarded by secret incurable suspicion; and the Arian, or Socinian, who has seriously rejected the doctrine of the Trinity, will not be shaken by the most plausible evidence of an Athanasian miracle.

The Vandals and the Ostrogoths persevered in the profession of Arianism till the final ruin of the kingdoms which they had founded in Africa and Italy. The Barbarians of Gaul submitted to the orthodox dominion of the Franks; and Spain was restored to the Catholic church by the voluntary conversion of the Visigoths.

This salutary revolution[126] was hastened by the example of a royal martyr, whom our calmer reason may style an ungrateful rebel. Leovigild, the Gothic monarch of Spain, deserved the respect of his enemies, and the love of his subjects: the Catholics enjoyed a free toleration, and his Arian synods attempted, without much success, to reconcile their scruples by abolishing the unpopular rite of a *second* baptism. His eldest son Hermenegild, who was invested by his father with the royal diadem, and the fair principality of Baetica, contracted an honourable and orthodox alliance with a Merovingian princess, the daughter of Sigibert, king of Austrasia, and of the famous Brunechild. The beauteous Ingundis, who was no more than thirteen years of age, was received, beloved, and persecuted in the Arian court of Toledo; and her religious constancy was alternately assaulted with blandishments and violence by Goisvintha, the Gothic queen, who abused the double claim of maternal authority.[127] Incensed by her resistance, Goisvintha seized the Catholic princess by her long hair, inhumanly dashed her against the ground, kicked her till she was covered with blood, and at last gave orders that she should be stripped, and thrown into a bason, or fish-pond.[128] Love and honour might excite Hermenegild to resent this injurious treatment of his bride; and he was gradually persuaded that Ingundis suffered for the cause of divine truth. Her tender complaints and the weighty arguments of Leander, archbishop of Seville, accomplished his conversion; and the heir of the Gothic monarchy was initiated in the Nicene faith by the solemn rites of confirmation.[129] The rash youth, inflamed by zeal, and perhaps by ambition, was tempted to violate the duties of a son, and a subject; and the

Catholics of Spain, although they could not complain of persecution, applauded his pious rebellion against an heretical father. The civil war was protracted by the long and obstinate sieges of Merida, Cordova, and Seville, which had strenuously espoused the party of Hermenegild. He invited the orthodox Barbarians, the Suevi, and the Franks, to the destruction of his native land; he solicited the dangerous aid of the Romans, who possessed Africa and a part of the Spanish coast; and his holy ambassador, the archbishop Leander, effectually negotiated in person with the Byzantine court. But the hopes of the Catholics were crushed by the active diligence of a monarch who commanded the troops and treasures of Spain; and the guilty Hermenegild, after his vain attempts to resist or to escape, was compelled to surrender himself into the hands of an incensed father. Leovigild was still mindful of that sacred character; and the rebel, despoiled of the regal ornaments, was still permitted, in a decent exile, to profess the Catholic religion. His repeated and unsuccessful treasons at length provoked the indignation of the Gothic king; and the sentence of death, which he pronounced with apparent reluctance, was privately executed in the tower of Seville. The inflexible constancy with which he refused to accept the Arian communion, as the price of his safety, may excuse the honours that have been paid to the memory of St Hermenegild. His wife and infant son were detained by the Romans in ignominious captivity; and this domestic misfortune tarnished the glories of Leovigild, and embittered the last moments of his life.

His son and successor, Recared, the first Catholic king of Spain, had imbibed the faith of his unfortunate brother, which he supported with more prudence and success. Instead of revolting against his father, Recared patiently expected the hour of his death. Instead of condemning his memory, he piously supposed that the dying monarch had abjured the errors of Arianism and recommended to his son the conversion of the Gothic nation. To accomplish that salutary end, Recared convened an assembly of the Arian clergy and nobles, declared himself a Catholic, and exhorted them to imitate the example of their prince. The laborious interpretation of doubtful texts, or the curious pursuit of metaphysical arguments, would have excited an endless controversy; and the monarch discreetly proposed to his illiterate audience two substantial and visible arguments, the testimony of Earth and of Heaven. The *Earth* had submitted to the Nicene synod: the Romans, the Barbarians, and the inhabitants of Spain, unanimously professed the same orthodox creed; and the Visigoths resisted, almost alone, the consent of the Christian world. A superstitious age was prepared to reverence, as the testimony of *Heaven*, the preternatural cures, which were performed by the skill or virtue of the Catholic clergy; the baptismal fonts of Osset in Baetica,[130] which were spontaneously replenished each year on the vigil of Easter;[131] and the miraculous shrine of St Martin of Tours, which had already converted the Suevic prince and people of Gallicia.[132] The Catholic king encountered some difficulties on this important change of the national religion. A conspiracy, secretly fomented by the queen-dowager, was formed against his life; and two counts excited a dangerous revolt in the Narbonnese Gaul. But Recared disarmed the conspirators, defeated the rebels, and executed severe justice; which the Arians, in their turn, might brand with the reproach of persecution. Eight bishops, whose names betray their Barbaric origin, abjured their errors; and all the books of Arian theology were reduced to ashes, with the house in which they had been purposely collected. The whole body of the Visigoths and Suevi were allured or driven into the pale of the Catholic communion; the faith, at least of the rising generation, was fervent and sincere; and the devout liberality of the Barbarians enriched the churches and monasteries of Spain. Seventy bishops, assembled in the council of Toledo, received the submission of their conquerors; and the zeal of the Spaniards improved the Nicene creed, by declaring the procession of the Holy Ghost from the Son, as well as from the Father: a weighty point of doctrine, which produced, long afterwards, the schism of the Greek and Latin Churches.[133] The royal proselyte immediately saluted and consulted pope Gregory, surnamed the Great, a learned and holy prelate, whose reign was distinguished by the conversion of heretics and infidels. The ambassadors of Recared respectfully offered on the threshold of the Vatican his rich presents of gold and gems; they accepted, as a lucrative exchange, the hairs of St John the Baptist, a cross which enclosed a small piece of the true wood, and a key that contained some particles of iron which had been scraped from the chains of St Peter.[134]

The same Gregory, the spiritual conqueror of Britain,* encouraged the pious Theodelinda, queen of the Lombards, to propagate the Nicene faith among the victorious savages, whose recent Christianity was polluted by the Arian heresy. Her devout labours still left room for the industry and success of future missionaries; and many cities of Italy were still disputed by hostile bishops. But the cause of Arianism was gradually suppressed by the weight of truth, of interest, and of example; and the controversy, which Egypt had derived from the Platonic school, was terminated, after a war of three hundred years, by the final conversion of the Lombards of Italy.[135]

The first missionaries who preached the gospel to the Barbarians appealed to the evidence of reason, and claimed the benefit of toleration.[136] But no sooner had they established their spiritual dominion than they exhorted the Christian kings to extirpate, without mercy, the remains of Roman or Barbaric superstition. The successors of Clovis inflicted one hundred lashes on the peasants who refused to destroy their idols; the crime of sacrificing to the daemons was punished by the Anglo-Saxon laws with the heavier penalties of imprisonment and confiscation; and even the wise Alfred adopted, as an indispensable duty, the extreme rigour of the Mosaic institutions.[137] But the punishment, and the crime, were gradually abolished among a Christian people; the theological disputes of the schools were suspended by propitious ignorance; and the intolerant spirit, which could find neither idolaters nor heretics, was reduced to the persecution of the Jews. That exiled nation had founded some synagogues in the cities of Gaul; but Spain, since the time of Hadrian, was filled with their numerous colonies.[138] The wealth which they accumulated by trade, and the management of the finances, invited the pious avarice of their masters; and they might be oppressed without danger, as they had lost the use, and even the remembrance, of arms. Sisebut, a Gothic king, who reigned in the beginning of the seventh century, proceeded at once to the last extremes of persecution.[139] Ninety thousand Jews were compelled to receive the sacrament of baptism; the fortunes of the obstinate infidels were confiscated, their bodies were tortured; and it seems doubtful whether they were permitted to abandon their native country. The excessive zeal of the Catholic king was moderated, even by the clergy of Spain, who solemnly pronounced an inconsistent sentence: *that* the sacraments should not be forcibly imposed; but *that* the Jews who had been baptised should be constrained, for the honour of the church, to persevere in the external practice of a religion which they disbelieved and detested. Their frequent relapses provoked one of the successors of Sisebut to banish the whole nation from his dominions; and a council of Toledo published a decree that every Gothic king should swear to maintain this salutary edict. But the tyrants were unwilling to dismiss the victims, whom they delighted to torture, or to deprive themselves of the industrious slaves, over whom they might exercise a lucrative oppression. The Jews still continued in Spain, under the weight of the civil and ecclesiastical laws, which in the same country have been faithfully transcribed in the Code of the Inquisition. The Gothic kings and bishops at length discovered that injuries will produce hatred and that hatred will find the opportunity of revenge. A nation, the secret or professed enemies of Christianity, still multiplied in servitude and distress; and the intrigues of the Jews promoted the rapid success of the Arabian conquerors.[140]

As soon as the Barbarians withdrew their powerful support, the unpopular heresy of Arius sunk into contempt and oblivion. But the Greeks still retained their subtle and loquacious disposition; the establishment of an obscure doctrine suggested new questions and new disputes; and it was always in the power of an ambitious prelate, or a fanatic monk, to violate the peace of the church, and, perhaps, of the empire. The historian of the empire may overlook those disputes which were confined to the obscurity of schools and synods. The Manichaeans, who laboured to reconcile the religions of Christ and of Zoroaster, had secretly introduced themselves into the provinces; but these foreign sectaries were involved in the common disgrace of the Gnostics, and the Imperial laws were executed by the public hatred. The rational opinions of the

Pelagians were propagated from Britain to Rome, Africa and Palestine, and silently expired in a superstitious age. But the East was distracted by the Nestorian and Eutychian controversies; which attempted to explain the mystery of the incarnation, and hastened the ruin of Christianity in her native land. These controversies were first agitated under the reign of the younger Theodosius; but their important consequences extend far beyond the limits of the present volume. The metaphysical chain of argument, the contests of ecclesiastical ambition, and their political influence on the decline of the Byzantine empire, may afford an interesting and instructive series of history, from the general councils of Ephesus and Chalcedon to the conquest of the East by the successors of Mahomet.

NOTES TO CHAPTER 37

1 The origin of the monastic institution has been laboriously discussed by Thomassin (*Discipline de l'Eglise*, i, 1419–26) and Helyot (*Hist. des Ordres Monastiques*, i, 1–66). These authors are very learned and tolerably honest, and their difference of opinion shows the subject in its full extent. Yet the cautious Protestant, who distrusts *any* popish guides, may consult the seventh book of Bingham's *Christian Antiquities*.

 * *page 733* [ordinary]

2 See Euseb., *Demonstrat. Evangel.*, (i, 20–21, edit. Graec. Rob. Stephani, Paris, 1545). In his *Ecclesiastical History*, published twelve years after the *Demonstration*, Eusebius (ii, 17) asserts the Christianity of the Therapeutae; but he appears ignorant that a similar institution was actually revived in Egypt.

3 Cassian (*Collat.*, xviii, 5) claims this origin for the institution of the *Coenobites* which gradually decayed till it was restored by Antony and his disciples.

 * *page 733* [anchorites]

4 ὠφελιμώτατον γάρ τι χρῆμα εἰς ἀνθρώπους ἐλθοῦσα Θεοῦ ἡ τοιαύτη φιλοσοφία. ['For our most useful possession is this divine philosophy, which has come to mankind.'] These are the expressive words of Sozomen, who copiously and agreeably describes (i, 12–14) the origin and progress of this monkish philosophy (see Suicer., *Thesaur. Eccles.*, ii, 1441). Some modern writers, Lipsius (iv, 448; *Manuduct. ad Philosoph. Stoic.*, iii, 13) and La Mothe le Vayer (tom. ix, *de la Vertu des Payens*, pp. 228–62), have compared the Carmelites to the Pythagoreans, and the Cynics to the Capucins.

5 The Carmelites derive their pedigree, in regular succession, from the prophet Elijah (see the *Theses of Beziers*, ad 1682, in Bayle's *Nouvelles de la République des Lettres, Oeuvres*, i, 82, etc. and the prolix irony of the *Ordres Monastiques*, an anonymous work, i, 1–433. Berlin, 1751). Rome and the inquisition of Spain silenced the profane criticism of the Jesuits of Flanders (Helyot, *Hist. des Ordres Monastiques*, i, 282–300), and the statue of Elijah, the Carmelite, has been erected in the church of St Peter (*Voyages* du P. Labat, iii, 87).

6 Pliny, *Hist. Natur.*, v, 15. *Gens sola, et in toto orbe praeter ceteras mira, sine ulla femina, omni venere abdicata, sine pecunia, socia palmarum. Ita per seculorum millia (incredibile dictu) gens aeterna est in qua nemo nascitur. Tam fecunda illis aliorum vitae*

penitentia est. He places them just beyond the noxious influence of the lake, and names Engaddi and Masada as the nearest towns. The Laura and monastery of St Sabas could not be far distant from this place. See Reland, *Palestin.*, i, 295; ii, 763, 874, 880, 890.

7 See Athanas., *Op.*, ii, 450–505 and the *Vit. Patrum* [ed. 1628], pp. 26–74, with Rosweyde's Annotations. The former is the Greek original; the latter a very ancient Latin version by Evagrius, the friend of St Jerome.

8 γράμματα μὲν μαθεῖν οὐκ ἠνέσχετο ['he refused to learn to read or write'], Athanas., tom. ii, in *Vit. St Anton.*, p. 452; and the assertion of his total ignorance has been received by many of the ancients and moderns. But Tillemont (*Mém. Ecclés.*, vii, 666) shows, by some probable arguments, that Antony could read and write in the Coptic, his native tongue, and that he was only a stranger to the *Greek letters*. The philosopher Synesius (p. 51) acknowledges that the natural genius of Antony did not require the aid of learning.

9 *Arurae autem erant ei trecentae uberes, et valde optimae.* ['He possessed three hundred *arurae* of very good fertile land.'] (*Vit. Patr.*, i, 36). If the *arura* be a square measure of an hundred Egyptian cubits (Rosweyde, *Onomasticon ad Vit. Patrum*, pp. 1014–15) and the Egyptian cubit of all ages be equal to twenty-two English inches (Greaves, i, 233), the arura will consist of about three-quarters of an English acre.

10 The description of the monastery is given by Jerome (i, 248–49, in *Vit. Hilarion*) and the P. Sicard (*Missions du Levant*, v, 122–200). Their accounts cannot always be reconciled: the father painted from his fancy, and the Jesuit from his experience.

11 Jerome, i, 146 [ep. 22], *ad Eustochium; Hist. Lausiac.*, ch. 7; in *Vit. Patrum*, p. 712. The P. Sicard (*Missions du Levant*, ii, 29–79) visited, and has described, this desert, which now contains four monasteries, and twenty or thirty monks. See D'Anville, *Description de l'Egypte*, p. 74.

12 Tabenne is a small island in the Nile, in the diocese of Tentyra or Dendera, between the modern town of Girge and the ruins of ancient Thebes (D'Anville, p. 194). M. de Tillemont doubts whether it was an isle, but I may conclude, from his own facts, that the primitive name was afterwards transferred to the great monastery of Bau or Pabau (*Mém. Ecclés.*, vii, 678, 688).

13 See in the *Codex Regularum* (published by Lucas Holstenius, Rome, 1661) a preface of St Jerom to his Latin version of the *Rule of Pachomius*, i, 61.

14 Rufin., ch. 5, in *Vit. Patrum*, p. 459. He calls it, *civitas ampla valde et populosa*, and reckons twelve churches. Strabo (xvii, 1166) and Ammianus (xxii, 16) have made honourable mention of Oxyrinchus, whose inhabitants adored a small fish in a magnificent temple.

15 *Quanti populi habentur in urbibus, tantae paene habentur in desertis multitudines monachorum.* Rufin., ch. 7, in *Vit. Patrum*, p. 461. He congratulates the fortunate change.

16 The introduction of the monastic life into Rome and Italy is occasionally mentioned by Jerome (i, 119–20, 199).

17 See the *Life of Hilarion*, by St Jerome (i, 241, 252). The stories of Paul, Hilarion, and Malchus, by the same author, are admirably told; and the only defect of these pleasing compositions is the want of truth and common sense.

18 His original retreat was in a small village on the banks of the Iris, not far from Neo-Caesarea. The ten or twelve years of his monastic life were disturbed by

long and frequent avocations. Some critics have disputed the authenticity of his Ascetic rules; but the external evidence is weighty, and they can only prove that it is the work of a real or affected enthusiast. See Tillemont, *Mém. Ecclés.*, ix, pp. 636–44. Helyot, *Hist. des Ordres Monastiques*, i, 175–81.

19 See his Life, and the three Dialogues by Sulpicius Severus, who asserts (*Dialog.* i, 16) that the booksellers of Rome were delighted with the quick and ready sale of his popular work.

20 When Hilarion sailed from Paraetonium to Cape Pachynus, he offered to pay his passage with a book of the Gospels. Posthumian, a Gallic monk, who had visited Egypt, found a merchant-ship bound from Alexandria to Marseilles, and performed the voyage in thirty days (Sulp. Sever., *Dialog.*, i, 1). Athanasius, who addressed his Life of St Antony to the foreign monks, was obliged to hasten the composition, that it might be ready for the sailing of the fleets (ii, 451).

21 See Jerome (i, 126); Assemanni, *Bibliot. Orient.*, iv, 92, 857–919; and Geddes, *Church History of Aethiopia*, pp. 29–31. The Abyssinian monks adhere very strictly to the primitive institution.

22 Camden's *Britannia*, i, 666–67.

23 All that learning can extract from the rubbish of the dark ages is copiously stated by Archbishop Usher, in his *Britannicarum Ecclesiarum Antiquitates*, xvi, 425–503.

24 This small though not barren spot, Iona, Hy, or Columbkill, only two miles in length, and one mile in breadth, has been distinguished, 1. By the monastery of St Columba, founded AD 566, whose abbot exercised an extraordinary jurisdiction over the bishops of Caledonia; 2. By a *classic* library, which afforded some hopes of an entire Livy; and, 3. By the tombs of sixty kings, Scots, Irish and Norwegians, who reposed in holy ground. See Usher (pp. 311, 360–70) and Buchanan (*Rer. Scot.*, ii, 15, edit. Ruddiman).

25 Chrysostom (in the first tome of the Benedictine edition) has consecrated three books to the praise and defence of the monastic life. He is encouraged, by the example of the ark, to presume that none but the elect (the monks) can possibly be saved (i, 55–56). Elsewhere indeed he becomes more merciful (iii, 83–84) and allows different degrees of glory, like the sun, moon, and stars. In his lively comparison of a king and a monk (iii, 116–21) he supposes (what is hardly fair) that the king will be more sparingly rewarded and more rigorously punished.

26 Thomassin (*Discipline de l'Eglise*, i, 1426–69) and Mabillon (*Oeuvres Posthumes*, ii, 115–58). The monks were gradually adopted as a part of the ecclesiastical hierarchy.

27 Dr Middleton (i, 110) liberally censures the conduct and writings of Chrysostom, one of the most eloquent and successful advocates for the monastic life.

28 Jerome's devout ladies form a very considerable portion of his works: the particular treatise which he styles the Epitaph of Paula (i, 169–92 [ep. 108]) is an elaborate and extravagant panegyric. The exordium is ridiculously turgid: 'If all the members of my body were changed into tongues, and if all my limbs resounded with a human voice, yet should I be incapable,' etc.

29 *Socrus Dei esse coepisti* (Jerome, i, 140, *ad Eustochium*). Rufinus (in *Hieronym. Op.*, iv, 223), who was justly scandalised, asks his adversary, From what Pagan poet he had stolen an expression so impious and absurd?

30 *Nunc autem veniunt plerumque ad hanc professionem servitutis Dei, et ex conditione servili, vel etiam liberati, vel propter hoc a Dominis liberati sive liberandi; et ex vita*

rusticana, et ex opificum exercitatione, et plebeio labore. Augustin., *de Oper. Monach.*, ch. 22, *ap.* Thomassin, *Discipline de l'Eglise*, iii, 1094. The Egyptian who blamed Arsenius owned that he led a more comfortable life as a monk than as a shepherd. See Tillemont, *Mém. Ecclés.*, xiv, 679.

31 A Dominican friar (*Voyages du P. Labat*, i, 10) who lodged at Cadiz in a convent of his brethren soon understood that their repose was never interrupted by nocturnal devotion; *quoiqu'on ne laisse pas de sonner pour l'édification du peuple* ['although they do not fail to ring the bells for the edification of the people'].

32 See a very sensible preface of Lucas Holstenius to the *Codex Regularum*. The emperors attempted to support the obligation of public and private duties; but the feeble dykes were swept away by the torrent of superstition; and Justinian surpassed the most sanguine wishes of the monks (Thomassin, i, 1782-99, and Bingham, vii, 3, 253).

33 The monastic institutions, particularly those of Egypt, about the year 400, are described by four curious and devout travellers: Rufinus (*Vit. Patrum*, ii, iii, 424-536); Posthumian (Sulp. Sever., *Dialog.* i); Palladius (*Hist. Lausiac.* in *Vit. Patrum*, pp. 709-863) and Cassian (see in tom. vii, *Bibliothec. Max. Patrum*, his four first books of Institutes, and the twenty-four Collations or Conferences).

34 The example of Malchus (Jerome, i, 256) and the design of Cassian and his friend (Collation xxiv, 1) are incontestable proofs of their freedom; which is elegantly described by Erasmus in his life of St Jerome. See Chardon, *Hist. des Sacremens*, vi, 279-300.

35 See the laws of Justinian (*Novel.*, cxxiii, No. 42) and of Lewis the Pious (in the *Historians of France*, vi, 427), and the actual jurisprudence of France, in Denissart (*Décisions*, etc., iv, 855, etc.).

36 The ancient *Codex Regularum*, collected by Benedict Anianinus, the reformer of the monks in the beginning of the ninth century, and published in the seventeenth by Lucas Holstenius, contains thirty different rules for men and women. Of these, seven were composed in Egypt, one in the East, one in Cappadocia, one in Italy, one in Africa, four in Spain, eight in Gaul, or France, and one in England.

37 The rule of Columbanus, so prevalent in the West, inflicts one hundred lashes for very slight offences (*Cod. Reg.*, ii, 174). Before the time of Charlemagne, the abbots indulged themselves in mutilating their monks, or putting out their eyes: a punishment much less cruel than the tremendous *vade in pace* (the subterraneous dungeon, or sepulchre) which was afterwards invented. See an admirable discourse of the learned Mabillon (*Oeuvres Posthumes*, ii, 321-36), who, on this occasion, seems to he inspired by the genius of humanity. For such an effort, I can forgive his defence of the holy tear of Vendôme (pp. 361-99).

38 Sulp. Sever., *Dialog.* i, 12-13, 532, etc. Cassian., *Institut.*, iv, 26-27. *Praecipua ibi virtus et prima est obedientia* ['the first and principal virtue there is obedience']. Among the *Verba seniorum* [the sayings of the elders] (in *Vit. Patrum*, v, 617) the fourteenth libel or discourse is on the subject of obedience, and the Jesuit Rosweyde, who published that huge volume for the use of convents, has collected all the scattered passages in his two copious indexes.

39 Dr Jortin (*Remarks on Ecclesiastical History*, iv, 161) has observed the scandalous valour of the Cappadocian monks, which was exemplified in the banishment of Chrysostom.

40 Cassian has simply, though copiously, described the monastic habit of Egypt

(*Institut.*, Bk i), to which Sozomen (iii, 14) attributes such allegorical meaning and virtue.

41 Regul. Benedict. No. 55, in *Cod. Regul.*, ii, 51.

42 See the Rule of Ferreolus, bishop of Ufez (No. 31, in *Cod. Regul.*, ii, 136), and of Isidore, bishop of Seville (No. 13, in *Cod. Regul.*, ii, 214).

43 Some partial indulgences were granted for the hands and feet. *Totum autem corpus nemo unguet nisi causa infirmitatis, nec lavabitur aqua nudo corpore, nisi languor perspicuus sit.* ['But no one anoints himself all over except in case of infirmity, or washes his naked body unless he is plainly suffering from lethargy.'] (*Regul. Pachom.*, xcii, i, 78.).

44 St Jerome, in strong, but indiscreet, language, expresses the most important use of fasting and abstinence: *Non quod Deus universitatis Creator et Dominus, intestinorum nostrorum rugitu, et inanitate ventris, pulmonisque ardore delectetur, sed quod aliter pudicitia tuta esse non possit.* ['Not because God, the Creator and Lord of the Universe, delights in our rumbling stomach, empty belly and pangs of hunger, but because our sense of shame cannot be safeguarded in any other way'.] (*Op.*, i, 137, *ad Eustochium*). See the twelfth and twenty-second Collations of Cassian, *de Castitate*, and *de Illusionibus Nocturnis*.

45 *Edacitas in Graecis gula est, in Gallis natura.* ['Gourmandising among the Greeks is a form of greed; among the Gauls it is their nature.'] (*Dialog.* i, 4, 521). Cassian fairly owns that the perfect model of abstinence cannot be imitated in Gaul, on account of the *aerum temperies*, and the *qualitas nostrae fragilitatis* ['the temperateness of the climate and our natural weakness'] (*Institut.*, iv, 11). Among the Western rules, that of Columbanus is the most austere; he had been educated amidst the poverty of Ireland, as rigid perhaps, and inflexible, as the abstemious virtue of Egypt. The Rule of Isidore of Seville is the mildest: on holidays he allows the use of flesh.

46 'Those who drink only water and have no nutritious liquor ought, at least, to have a pound and a half (*twenty-four ounces*) of bread every day.' *State of Prisons*, p. 40, by Mr Howard [published in 1777].

47 See Cassian, *Collat.*, ii, 19–21. The small loaves, or biscuit, of six ounces each, had obtained the name of *Paximacia* (Rosweyde, *Onomasticon*, p. 1045), Pachomius, however, allowed his monks some latitude in the quantity of their food; but he made them work in proportion as they ate (Pallad., in *Hist. Lausiac.*, ch. 38–39, in *Vit. Patrum*, viii, 736–37).

48 See the banquet to which Cassian (Collation viii, 1) was invited by Serenus, an Egyptian abbot.

49 See the Rule of St Benedict, No. 39–40 (in *Cod. Reg.*, ii, 41–42). *Licet legamus vinum omnino monachorum non esse, sed quia nostris temporibus id monachis persuaderi non potest* ['Although we read that wine forms part of the monks' diet, nevertheless because in our day the monks are not to be persuaded of it'], he allows them a Roman *hemina*, a measure which may be ascertained from Arbuthnot's Tables. [John Arbuthnot, 1667–1735, mathematician and physician, published Tables of Coins, Weights of Measures in 1727.]

50 Such expressions as *my* book, *my* cloak, *my* shoes (Cassian., *Institut.*, iv, 13) were not less severely prohibited among the Western monks (*Cod. Regul.*, ii, 174, 235, 288), and the Rule of Columbanus punished them with six lashes. The ironical author of the *Ordres Monastiques*, who laughs at the foolish nicety of modern convents, seems ignorant that the ancients were equally absurd.

51 Two great masters of ecclesiastical science, the P. Thomassin (*Discipline de l'Eglise*, iii, 1090–1139) and the P. Mabillon (*Etudes Monastiques*, i, 116–55), have seriously examined the manual labour of the monks, which the former considers as a *merit*, and the latter as a *duty*.

52 Mabillon (*Etudes Monastiques*, i, 47–55) has collected many curious facts to justify the literary labours of his predecessors, both in the East and West. Books were copied in the ancient monasteries of Egypt (Cassian., *Institut.*, iv, 12) and by the disciples of St Martin (Sulp. Sever, in *Vit. Martin.*, 7, 473). Cassiodorus has allowed an ample scope for the studies of the monks; and we shall not be scandalised, if their pen sometimes wandered from Chrysostom and Augustine to Homer and Virgil.

53 Thomassin (*Discipline de l'Eglise*, iii, 18, 145–46, 171–79) has examined the revolution of the civil, canon, and common, law. Modern France confirms the death which monks have inflicted on themselves, and justly deprives them of all right of inheritance.

54 See Jerome (i, 176, 183). The monk Pambo made a sublime answer to Melania, who wished to specify the value of her gift: 'Do you offer it to me or to God? If to God, HE who suspends the mountains in a balance need not be informed of the weight of your plate.' (Pallad., *Hist. Lausiac.*, ch. 10, in the *Vit. Patrum*, viii, 715.)

55 Τὸ πολὺ μέρος τῆς γῆς ᾠκειώσαντο, προφάσει τοῦ μεταδιδόναι πάντων πτωχοῖς πάντας (ὡς εἰπεῖν) πτωχοὺς καταστήσαντες. Zosim., v, 325. Yet the wealth of the Eastern monks was far surpassed by the princely greatness of the Benedictines.

* *page 739* [showed themselves]

56 The sixth general council (the Quinisext in Trullo, Canon xlvii, in Beveridge, i, 213) restrains women from passing the night in a male, or men in a female, monastery. The seventh general council (the second Nicene, Canon xx, in Beveridge, i, 325) prohibits the erection of double or promiscuous monasteries of both sexes; but it appears from Balsamon that the prohibition was not effectual. On the irregular pleasures and expenses of the clergy and *monks*, see Thomassin, iii, 1334–68.

57 I have somewhere heard or read the frank confession of a Benedictine abbot: 'My vow of poverty has given me an hundred thousand crowns a year; my vow of obedience has raised me to the rank of a sovereign prince'. – I forget the consequences of his vow of chastity.

58 Pior, an Egyptian monk, allowed his sister to see him: but he shut his eyes during the whole visit. See *Vit. Patrum*, iii, 504. Many such examples might be added.

* *page 740* [family]

59 The 7th, 8th, 29th, 30th, 31st, 34th, 57th, 60th, 86th, and 95th articles of the Rule of Pachomius impose most intolerable *laws* of silence and mortification.

60 The diurnal and nocturnal prayers of the monks are copiously discussed by Cassian in the third and fourth books of his *Institutions*; and he constantly prefers the liturgy, which an angel had dictated to the monasteries of Tabenne.

61 Cassian, from his own experience, describes the *acedia*, or listlessness of mind and body to which a monk was exposed, when he sighed to find himself alone. *Saepiusque egreditur et ingreditur cellam, et Solem velut ad occasum tardius properantem crebrius intuetur* (*Institut.*, x, 1).

62 The temptations and sufferings of Stagirius were communicated by that unfortunate youth to his friend St Chrysostom. See Middleton's *Works*, i, 107–10. Something similar introduces the life of every saint; and the famous Inigo,

or Ignatius, the founder of the Jesuits (*Vie d'Inigo de Guiposcoa*, i, 29–38), may serve as a memorable example.

63 Fleury, *Hist. Ecclésiastique*, vii, 46. I have read somewhere, in the *Vitae Patrum*, but I cannot recover the place, that *several*, I believe *many*, of the monks, who did not reveal their temptations to the abbot, became guilty of suicide.

64 See the seventh and eighth Collations of Cassian, who gravely examines why the daemons were grown less active and numerous since the time of St Antony. Rosweyde's copious index to the *Vitae Patrum* will point out a variety of infernal scenes. The devils were most formidable in a female shape.

65 For the distinction of the *Coenobites* and the *Hermits*, especially in Egypt, see Jerome (i, 45, *ad Rusticum*); the first Dialogue of Sulpicius Severus, Rufinus (ch. 22, in *Vit. Patrum*, ii, 478); Palladius (ch. 7, 69, in *Vit. Patrum*, viii, 712, 758); and, above all, the eighteenth and nineteenth Collations of Cassian. These writers, who compare the common and solitary life, reveal the abuse and danger of the latter.

66 Suicer., *Thesaur. Ecclesiast.*, ii, 205, 218. Thomassin (*Discipline de l'Eglise*, i, 1501–2) gives a good account of these cells. When Gerasimus founded his monastery, in the wilderness of Jordan, it was accompanied by a Laura of seventy cells.

67 Theodoret, in a large volume (the *Philotheus* in *Vit. Patrum*, ix, 793–863), has collected the lives and miracles of thirty Anachorets. Evagrius (i, 12) more briefly celebrates the monks and hermits of Palestine.

68 Sozomen, vi, 33. The great St Ephrem composed a panegyric on these βόσκοι, or grazing monks (Tillemont, *Mém. Ecclés.*, viii, 292).

69 The P. Sicard (*Missions du Levant*, ii, 217–33) examined the caverns of the Lower Thebais with wonder and devotion. The inscriptions are in the old Syriac character, which was used by the Christians of Abyssinia.

70 See Theodoret (in *Vit. Patrum*, ix, 848–54); Antony (in *Vit. Patrum*, i, 170–77); Cosmas (in Asseman., *Bibliot. Oriental.*, i, 239–53); Evagrius (i, 13–14); and Tillemont (*Mém. Ecclés.*, xv, 347–92).

71 The narrow circumference of two cubits, or three feet, which Evagrius assigns for the summit of the column, is inconsistent with reason, with facts, and with the rules of architecture. The people who saw it from below might be easily deceived.

72 I must not conceal a piece of ancient scandal concerning the origin of this ulcer. It has been reported that the Devil, assuming an angelic form, invited him to ascend, like Elijah, into a fiery chariot. The saint too hastily raised his foot, and Satan seized the moment of inflicting this chastisement on his vanity.

73 I know not how to select or specify the miracles contained in the *Vitae Patrum* of Rosweyde, as the number very much exceeds the thousand pages of that voluminous work. An elegant specimen may be found in the Dialogues of Sulpicius Severus, and his life of St Martin. He reveres the monks of Egypt; yet he insults them with the remark that *they* never raised the dead; whereas the bishop of Tours had restored *three* dead men to life.

* *page 742* [partisan]

* *page 743* [emperor, AD 260–68]

74 On the subject of Ulphilas, and the conversion of the Goths, see Sozomen, vi, 37; Socrates, iv, 33; Theodoret, iv, 37; Philostorg., ii, 5. The heresy of Philostorgius appears to have given him superior means of information.

75 A mutilated copy of the four gospels, in the Gothic version, was published AD 1665, and is esteemed the most ancient monument of the Teutonic language, though Wetstein attempts, by some frivolous conjectures, to deprive Ulphilas of the honour of the work. Two of the four additional letters express the *W* and our own *Th*. See Simon, *Hist. Critique du Nouveau Testament*, ii, 219–23; Mill, *Prolegom.*, p. 151, edit. Kuster; Wetstein, *Prolegom.*, i, 114.

 * *page 744* [Fritigern and Athanaric were Gothic chiefs at the time of the Emperor Valens, AD 364–78.]

76 Philostorgius erroneously places this passage under the reign of Constantine; but I am much inclined to believe that it preceded the great emigration.

77 We are obliged to Jornandes (*de Reb. Get.*, 51, 688) for a short and lively picture of these lesser Goths. *Gothi minores, populus immensus, cum suo Pontifice ipsoque primate Wulfila*. ['The lesser Goths, an immense tribe, together with their Pope and the primate Wulfila (i.e. Ulphilas) himself.'] The last words, if they are not mere tautology, imply some temporal jurisdiction.

78 *At non ita Gothi non ita Vandali; malis licet doctoribus instituti, meliores tamen etiam in hac parte quam nostri*. ['It is not so with the Goths and Vandals: even though they may have been brought up by bad teachers, nonetheless they are more devout than our fellow Romans.'] Salvian, *de Gubern. Dei*, vii, 243.

 † *page 744* [Winifrith, known also as St Boniface, in the 8th century]

79 Mosheim has slightly sketched the progress of Christianity in the North, from the fourth to the fourteenth century. The subject would afford materials for an ecclesiastical, and even philosophical, history.

80 To such a cause has Socrates (vii, 30) ascribed the conversion of the Burgundians, whose Christian piety is celebrated by Orosius (vii, 19).

81 See an original and curious epistle from Daniel, the first bishop of Winchester (Beda, *Hist. Eccles. Angloram*, v, 18, 203, edit. Smith), to St Boniface, who preached the Gospel among the Savages of Hesse and Thuringia. Epistol. Bonifacii, lxvii, in the *Maxima Bibliotheca Patrum*, xiii, 93.

82 The sword of Charlemagne added weight to the argument; but, when Daniel wrote this epistle (AD 723), the Mahometans, who reigned from India to Spain, might have retorted it against the Christians.

83 The opinions of Ulphilas and the Goths inclined to Semi-Arianism, since they would not say that the Son was a *creature*, though they held communion with those who maintained that heresy. Their apostle represented the whole controversy as a question of trifling moment, which had been raised by the passions of the clergy. Theodoret, iv, 37.

84 The Arianism of the Goths has been imputed to the emperor Valens: *Itaque iusto Dei iudicio ipsi eum vivum incenderunt, qui propter eum etiam mortui, vitio erroris arsuri sunt*. ['By the righteous judgment of God, he was burned alive by those who, on his account and because of their heresy, will suffer the flames after their death.'] Orosius, vii, 33, 554. This cruel sentence is confirmed by Tillemont (*Mém. Ecclés.*, vi, 604–10), who coolly observes, *un seul homme entraîna dans l'enfer un nombre infini de Septentrionaux*, etc. ['One man consigned to hell an infinite number of northern people.'] Salvian (*de Gubern. Dei*, v, 150–51) pities and excuses their involuntary error.

85 Orosius affirms, in the year 416 (7, 41, 580), that the churches of Christ (of the Catholics) were filled with Huns, Suevi, Vandals, Burgundians.

86 Radbod, king of the Frisons, was so much scandalised by this rash declaration

of a missionary that he drew back his foot after he had entered the baptismal font. See Fleury, *Hist. Ecclés.*, ix, 167.

87 The epistles of Sidonius, bishop of Clermont, under the Visigoths, and of Avitus, bishop of Vienna, under the Burgundians, explain, sometimes in dark hints, the general dispositions of the Catholics. The history of Clovis and Theodoric will suggest some particular facts.

* *page 747* [commander-in-chief of the armies of Nebuchadnezzar, King of the Assyrians]

88 Genseric confessed the resemblance by the severity with which he punished such indiscreet allusions. Victor Vitensis, 1, 7, p. 10.

89 Such are the contemporary complaints of Sidonius, bishop of Clermont (vii, 6, 182, etc. edit. Sirmond). Gregory of Tours, who quotes this Epistle (ii, 25, in ii, 174), extorts an unwarrantable assertion that, of the nine vacancies in Aquitain, some had been produced by episcopal *martyrdoms*.

90 The original monuments of the Vandal persecution are preserved in the five books of the History of Victor Vitensis (*de Persecutione Vandalica*), a bishop who was exiled by Hunneric; in the Life of St Fulgentius, who was distinguished in the persecution of Thrasimund (in *Biblioth. Max. Patrum*, ix, 4–16); and in the first book of the Vandalic War, by the impartial Procopius (7–8, 196–99). Dom. Ruinart, the last editor of Victor, has illustrated the whole subject with a copious and learned apparatus of notes and supplement (Paris, 1694).

91 Victor, iv, 2, 65. Hunneric refuses the name of Catholics to the *Homoousians*. [Arians. See Chapter 21.] He describes, as the *veri Divinae Maiestatis cultores* [the true worshippers of God], his own party, who professed the faith, confirmed by more than a thousand bishops, in the synods of Rimini and Seleucia.

92 Victor, ii, 1, 21–22, *Laudabilior . . . videbatur* ['It seemed to them more praiseworthy']. In the manuscripts which omit this word, the passage is unintelligible. See Ruinart, *Not.*, p. 164.

93 Victor, ii, 2, 22–23. The clergy of Carthage called these conditions, *periculosae* [dangerous]; and they seem, indeed, to have been proposed as a snare to entrap the Catholic bishops.

94 See the narrative of this conference and the treatment of the bishops in Victor, ii, 13–18, 35–42, and the whole fourth book, pp. 63–171. The third book, pp. 42–62, is entirely filled by their apology, or confession of faith.

95 See the list of the African bishops, in Victor, pp. 117–40; and Ruinart's notes, pp. 215–397. The schismatic name of *Donatus* frequently occurs, and they appear to have adopted (like our fanatics of the last age) the pious appellations of *Deodatus, Deogratias, Quidvultdeus, Habetdeum*, etc. [God-given, God-be-thanked, God's-will, Has-god, etc.].

96 Fulgent., *Vit.*, ch. 16–29. Thrasimund affected the praise of moderation and learning; and Fulgentius addressed three books of controversy to the Arian tyrant, whom he styles *piissime Rex* [most pious King] (*Biblioth. Maxim. Patrum*, ix, 41). Only sixty bishops are mentioned as exiles in the life of Fulgentius; they are increased to one hundred and twenty by Victor Tunnunensis, and Isidore; but the number of two hundred and twenty is specified in the *Historia Miscella* and a short authentic chronicle of the times. See Ruinart, pp. 570–71.

97 See the base and insipid epigrams of the Stoic, who could not support exile with more fortitude than Ovid. Corsica might not produce corn, wine, or oil; but it could not be destitute of grass, water, and even fire. [Seneca was exiled by

Nero, Ovid by Augustus.]

98 *Si ob gravitatem caeli interissent vile damnum.* ['If they died from the unwholesome climate, the loss was negligible.'] Tacit., *Annal.*, ii, 85. In this application, Thrasimund would have adopted the reading of some critics, *utile damnum* [the loss was advantageous].

99 See these preludes of a *general* persecution, in Victor, ii, 3–4, 7, and the two edicts of Hunneric, ii, 35; iv, 64.

* *page 749* [palace officials]

100 See Procopius, *de Bell. Vandal.*, i, 7, 197–98. A Moorish prince endeavoured to propitiate the God of the Christians by his diligence to erase the marks of the Vandal sacrilege.

101 See this story in Victor, ii, 8–12, 30–34. Victor describes the distress of these confessors as an eyewitness.

102 See the fifth book of Victor. His passionate complaints are confirmed by the sober testimony of Procopius and the public declaration of the emperor Justinian (*Cod.*, i, xxvii).

103 Victor, ii, 18, 41.

104 Victor, v, 4, 74–75. His name was Victorianus, and he was a wealthy citizen of Adrumetum, who enjoyed the confidence of the king; by whose favour he had obtained the office, or at least the title, of proconsul of Africa.

105 Victor, i, 6, 8–9. After relating the firm resistance and dexterous reply of count Sebastian, he adds, *quare alio generis argumento postea bellicosum virum occidit.* ['He (Genseric) therefore used another kind of argument and put the valiant man to death.']

106 Victor, v, 12–13. Tillemont, *Mém. Ecclés.*, vi, 609.

107 *Primate* was more properly the title of the bishop of Carthage; but the name of *patriarch* was given by the sects and nations to their principal ecclesiastic. See Thomassin, *Discipline de l'Eglise*, i, 155, 158.

108 The patriarch Cyrila himself publicly declared that he did not understand Latin (Victor, ii, 18, 42): *Nescio Latine*; and he might converse with tolerable ease, without being capable of disputing or preaching in that language. His Vandal clergy were still more ignorant; and small confidence could be placed in the Africans, who had conformed.

* *page 751* [widow]

109 Victor, ii, 1–2, 22.

110 Victor, v, 7, 77. He appeals to the ambassador himself, whose name was Uranius.

111 *Astutiores*, Victor, iv, 4, 70. He plainly intimates that their quotation of the Gospel, *Non iurabitis in toto* ['you shall not swear'], was only meant to elude the obligation of an inconvenient oath. The forty-six bishops who refused were banished to Corsica; the three hundred and two who swore were distributed through the provinces of Africa.

112 Fulgentius, bishop of Ruspae, in the Byzacene province, was of a senatorial family, and had received a liberal education. He could repeat all Homer and Menander before he was allowed to study Latin, his native tongue (*Vit. Fulgent.*, ch. 1). Many African bishops might understand Greek, and many Greek theologians were translated into Latin.

113 Compare the two prefaces to the Dialogue of Vigilius of Thapsus (pp. 118–19, edit. Chiflet). He might amuse his learned reader with an innocent fiction,

but the subject was too grave, and the Africans were too ignorant.

114 The P. Quesnel started this opinion, which has been favourably received. But the three following truths, however surprising they may seem, are *now* universally acknowledged (Gerard Vossius, vi, 516–22; Tillemont, *Mém. Ecclés.*, viii, 667–71). 1. St Athanasius is not the author of the creed which is so frequently read in our churches. 2. It does not appear to have existed within a century after his death. 3. It was originally composed in the Latin tongue, and, consequently, in the Western provinces. Gennadius, patriarch of Constantinople, was so much amazed by this extraordinary composition that he frankly pronounced it to be the work of a drunken man. Petav., *Dogmat. Theologica*, ii, vii, 8, 687.

115 John, i, 7. See Simon, *Hist. Critique du Nouveau Testament*, i, xviii, 203–18, and ii, ix, 99–121, and the elaborate Prolegomena and Annotations of Dr Mill and Wetstein to their editions of the Greek Testament. In 1689, the papist Simon strove to be free; in 1707, the protestant Mill wished to be a slave; in 1751, the Arminian Wetstein used the liberty of his times, and of his sect.

116 Of *all* the Mss. now extant, above fourscore in number, some of which are more than 1200 years old (Wetstein *ad loc.*). The *orthodox* copies of the Vatican, of the Complutensian editors, of Robert Stephens, are become invisible; and the *two* Mss. of Dublin and Berlin are unworthy to form an exception. See Emlyn's *Works*, ii, 227–55, 269–99; and M. de Missy's four ingenious letters, in viii, and ix, of the *Journal Britannique*.

117 Or, more properly, by the *four* bishops who composed and published the profession of faith in the name of their brethren. They style this text, *luce clarius* [clearer than light] (Victor Vitensis, *de Persecut. Vandal.*, iii, 11, 54). It is quoted soon afterwards by the African polemics, Vigilius and Fulgentius.

118 In the eleventh and twelfth centuries, the Bibles were corrected by Lanfranc, archbishop of Canterbury, and by Nicolas, a cardinal and librarian of the Roman church, *secundum orthodoxam fidem* [in accordance with the orthodox faith] (Wetstein, *Prolegom.*, pp. 84–85). Notwithstanding these corrections, the passage is still wanting in twenty-five Latin manuscripts (Wetstein *ad loc.*), the oldest and the fairest: two qualities seldom united, except in manuscripts.

119 The art which the Germans had invented was applied in Italy to the profane writers of Rome and Greece. The original Greek of the New Testament was published about the same time (AD 1514, 1516, 1520) by the industry of Erasmus and the munificence of cardinal Ximenes. The Complutensian Polyglot [Spanish edition of the Bible, published 1515–22] cost the cardinal 50,000 ducats. See Mattaire, *Annal. Typograph.*, ii, 2–8, 125–33; and Wetstein, *Prolegomena*, pp. 116–27.

120 The three witnesses have been established in our Greek Testaments by the prudence of Erasmus; the honest bigotry of the Complutensian editors; the typographical fraud, or error, of Robert Stephens in the placing a crotchet; and the deliberate falsehood, or strange misapprehension, of Theodore Beza.

121 Pliny, *Hist. Natural.*, v, 1. *Itinerar.* Wesseling, p. 15. Cellarius, *Geograph. Antiq.*, ii, ii, 127. This Tipasa (which must not be confounded with another in Numidia) was a town of some note, since Vespasian endowed it with the right of Latium.

122 Optatus Milevitanus, *de Schism. Donatist.*, ii, 38.

123 Victor Vitensis, v, 6, 76; Ruinart, pp. 483–87.

124 Aeneas Gazaeus *in Theophrasto*, in *Biblioth. Patrum.*, viii, 664–65. He was a Christian, and composed this Dialogue (the *Theophrastus*) on the immortality of the soul and the resurrection of the body, besides twenty-five Epistles, still extant. See Cave (*Hist. Litteraria*, p. 297) and Fabricius (*Bibl. Graec.*, i, 422).

125 Justinian, *Codex*, i, xxvii; Marcellin. in *Chron.* p. 45, in *Thesaur. Temporum* Scaliger; Procopius, *de Bell. Vandal.*, i, 7, 196; Gregor. Magnus, *Dialog.*, iii, 32. None of these witnesses have specified the number of the confessors, which is fixed at sixty in an old menology [a biographical calendar of saints' days] (*apud* Ruinart, p. 486). Two of them lost their speech by fornication, but the miracle is enhanced by the singular instance of a boy who had *never* spoken before his tongue was cut out.

126 See the two general historians of Spain, Mariana (*Hist. de Rebus Hispaniae*, i, v, 12–15, 182–94) and Ferreras (French translation, ii, 206–47). Mariana almost forgets that he is a Jesuit, to assume the style and spirit of a Roman classic. Ferreras, an industrious compiler, reviews his facts and rectifies his chronology.

127 Goisvintha successively married two kings of the Visigoths: Athanagild, to whom she bore Brunechild, the mother of Ingundis; and Leovigild, whose two sons, Hermenegild and Recared, were the issue of a former marriage.

128 *Iracundiae furore succensa, adprehensam per comam capitis puellam in terram conlidit, et diu calcibus verberatam, ac sanguine cruentatam, iussit exspoliari, et piscinae immergi.* Greg. Turon., v, 39, in ii, 255. Gregory is one of our best originals for this portion of history.

129 The Catholics who admitted the baptism of heretics repeated the rite, or, as it was afterwards styled, the sacrament, of confirmation, to which they ascribed many mystic and marvellous prerogatives, both visible and invisible. See Chardon, *Hist. des Sacrémens*, i, 405–552.

130 Osset, or Julia Constantia, was opposite to Seville, on the northern side of the Baetis (Pliny, *Hist. Natur.*, iii, 3); and the authentic reference of Gregory of Tours (*Hist. Francor.*, vi, 43, 288) deserves more credit than the name of Lusitania (*de Gloria Martyr.*, ch. 24) which has been eagerly embraced by the vain and superstitious Portuguese (Ferreras, *Hist. d'Espagne*, ii, 166).

131 This miracle was skilfully performed. An Arian king sealed the doors, and dug a deep trench round the church, without being able to intercept the Easter supply of baptismal water.

132 Ferreras (ii, 168–75, AD 550) has illustrated the difficulties which regard the time and circumstances of the conversion of the Suevi. They had been recently united by Leovigild to the Gothic monarchy of Spain.

133 This addition to the Nicene, or rather the Constantinopolitan, creed was first made in the eighth council of Toledo, AD 653; but it was expressive of the popular doctrine (Gerard Vossius, xi, 527, *de tribus Symbolis*).

134 See Gregor. Magn., vii, epist. 126, apud Baronium, *Annal. Eccles.*, AD 599, No. 25–6, ix, 122.

* *page 755* [Gregory sent St Augustine to Kent in ad 597.]

135 Paul Warnefrid (*de Gestis Langobard.*, iv, 44, 853, edit. Grot.) allows that Arianism still prevailed under the reign of Rotharis (AD 636–52). The pious Deacon does not attempt to mark the precise era of the national conversion which was accomplished, however, before the end of the seventh century.

136 *Quorum fidei et conversioni ita congratulatus esse rex perhibetur, ut nullum tamen*

cogeret ad Christianismum . . . Didicerat enim a doctoribus auctoribusque suae salutis, servitium Christi voluntarium non coactitium esse debere. ['Although he is said to have wished them well in their faith and conversion, nevertheless the King never compelled anyone to accept Christianity . . . For he had learned from the learned men who had brought about his own salvation that the service of Christ must be voluntary not compulsory.'] Bedae *Hist. Ecclesiastic.*, i, 26, 62, edit. Smith.

137 See the *Historians of France*, iv, 114; and Wilkins, *Leges Anglo-Saxonicae*, pp. 11, 31. *Siquis sacrificium immolaverit praeter Deo soli morte moriatur.* ['If anyone makes a sacrifice other than to God alone, let him be put to death.']

138 The Jews pretend that they were introduced into Spain by the fleets of Solomon and the arms of Nebuchadnezzar; that Hadrian transported forty thousand families of the tribe of Judah, and ten thousand of the tribe of Benjamin, etc. Basnage, *Hist. des Juifs*, vii, 9, 240–56.

139 Isidore, at that time archbishop of Seville, mentions, disapproves, and congratulates the zeal of Sisebut (*Chron. Goth.*, p. 728). Baronius (AD 614, No. 41) assigns the number on the evidence of Aimoin (iv, 22); but the evidence is weak, and I have not been able to verify the quotation (*Historians of France*, iii, 127).

140 Basnage (viii, 13, 388–400) faithfully represents the state of the Jews; but he might have added from the canons of the Spanish councils and the laws of the Visigoths many curious circumstances, essential to his subject, though they are foreign to mine.

CHAPTER 38 (Summary)

*Reign and conversion of Clovis – his victories over the Alemanni,
Burgundians, and Visigoths – establishment of the French
monarchy in Gaul – laws of the Barbarians – state of the
Romans – the Visigoths of Spain – conquest of Britain
by the Saxons – general observations on the fall of
the Roman empire in the West*

Gibbon describes the founding of the Frankish kingdom under Clovis at
the end of the fifth century. Clovis defeated Syagrius, the son of the
Roman general Aegidius mentioned in Chapter 36, and then forced into
submission the Alemanni, who had occupied both banks of the Rhine. In
AD 496, he was converted to Christianity and ruled as a Catholic king.
United with his kingdom in northern Gaul were the Armoricans, with
vestiges of Roman discipline in their bands of cavalry and infantry. Clovis
extended his power by defeating the Burgundians near Dijon in AD 500,
and subsequently defeated the Visigoths near Poitiers, adding Aquitaine
to his kingdom. Before his reign, codes of laws were in existence amongst
the different tribes, and Gibbon compares the penalties for murder, trial
procedures and rules for distributing land taken by conquest. Many who
lost their land were reduced to servitude, and there was much civil strife
under the rule of the sons of Clovis. In Spain, under the rule of the
Visigoths, the bishops maintained order through the Councils of Toledo.
Meanwhile, Roman Britain had fallen to the Saxons, Angles and Jutes, in
spite of the resistance of the legendary Arthur. Gibbon concludes Volume
III of the original edition with a discussion of the general causes of the
disappearance of the empire in the West. The Roman empire had been
divided, but the founding of Constantinople had helped to preserve it in
the East. Christianity had contributed to the undermining of the Roman
military spirit, but it had softened the manners of the barbarians. Gibbon
finally speculates on the unlikelihood of a similar eclipse of civilisation in
his own time.

CHAPTER 39 (Summary)

Zeno and Anastasius, emperors of the East — birth, education,
and first exploits of Theodoric the Ostrogoth — his invasion
and conquest of Italy — the Gothic kingdom of Italy —
state of the West — military and civil government —
the senator Boethius — last acts and death of Theodoric

The last three volumes of *The Decline and Fall* were published in 1788.
Gibbon begins Volume IV with an account of the career of Theodoric
the Ostrogoth. Theodoric was educated in Constantinople and, as an ally
of the emperor Anastasius, invaded Italy in AD 493. He defeated Odoacer
and ruled peacefully as king of Italy for thirty-three years, maintaining a
balance of power in western Europe through a series of family alliances.
In Italy, Theodoric preserved the Roman laws and administration without being a great legislator himself. He also preserved the monuments of
Rome, though he resided in Ravenna. The economy of Italy revived and
there was religious toleration even though Theodoric was an Arian. His
reign was distinguished by the statesmanship and learning of Boethius,
but the philosopher was unjustly accused of a conspiracy with the empire
in the East against the Goths. Boethius wrote his *Consolation of Philosophy*
while awaiting his execution in AD 524. Theodoric himself died in 526.

CHAPTER 40 (Summary)

Elevation of Justin the Elder — reign of Justinian — (1) the empress
Theodora — (2) factions of the Circus, and sedition of
Constantinople — (3) trade and manufacture of silk —
(4) finances and taxes — (5) edifices of Justinian — Church
of St Sophia — fortifications and frontiers of the Eastern empire —
(6) abolition of the schools of Athens, and the consulship of Rome

Gibbon relates the rise of Justinian, who became emperor in AD 527, in
succession to his uncle, Justin I. He married the actress, Theodora, who
became his firm support at times of crisis. Civil order was often threatened
by the factions of the blues and the greens at the circus games, culminat-
ing in the tumult called the 'Nika sedition' of AD 532, in which the
cathedral of St Sophia was burnt. Gibbon then describes the economy of

the empire under Justinian, including the silk trade and the importation of the silkworm to Constantinople in AD 552. Gibbon wonders what greater benefit there might have been if printing had been imported from China. Under Justinian, expenditure exceeded revenue, taxes were increased and monopolies damaged trade. Corrupt ministers, such as John of Cappadocia, were partly to blame. New buildings arose in Constantinople, including the magnificently rebuilt cathedral of St Sophia. The fortifications of Constantinople were extended and Justinian built forts and walls in Asia Minor to provide protection from the Persians. Gibbon reproaches Justinian, however, for suppressing the ancient schools of philosophy and eloquence in Athens and the ancient Roman office of consul.

CHAPTER 41 (Summary)

Conquests of Justinian in the West — character and first campaigns of Belisarius — he invades and subdues the Vandal kingdom of Africa — his triumph — the Gothic war — he recovers Sicily, Naples and Rome — siege of Rome by the Goths — their retreat and losses — surrender of Ravenna — glory of Belisarius — his domestic shame and misfortunes

Having bought peace with the Persians, Justinian turned his attention to the Vandals in Africa. Gibbon devotes Chapter 41 to an account of the remarkable successes of Belisarius in Africa and Italy. Belisarius was already an experienced warrior against the Persians. His army was carried in ships to Africa via Sicily and landed near Carthage in AD 533. He defeated the Vandals under Gelimar and Carthage was returned to the Roman empire. Belisarius then received the honours of a triumph in Constantinople. The Moors remained a threat to the Romans, but Solomon, the successor to Belisarius in Africa, defeated them in AD 539 and extended further the Roman boundaries. Justinian also restored Roman influence in Spain by allying with a warring faction of the Visigoths. Meanwhile, the Goths in Italy were afflicted with civil discord after Theodoric's death in AD 526, enabling Justinian eventually to intervene. Again, Belisarius was the commander, and Sicily quickly surrendered to his naval expedition. Rome capitulated without a battle in AD 536, but the Goths regathered their forces under Vitiges and Belisarius was besieged in Rome for more than a year. The emperor sent relief supplies and Vitiges was forced by Belisarius to retreat to Ravenna, in spite of Burgundian and Frankish support for the Goths. Justinian offered peace terms to Vitiges, but Belisarius exploited the situation to force the surrender of Vitiges in AD 539. Nevertheless, Vitiges was received by Justinian in Constantinople and given the rank of senator. Belisarius was honoured by the soldiers and the people. He had remained loyal to Justinian despite lack of support; in fame and merit he was without a rival, but his wife was unfaithful to him and his power and his wealth declined.

CHAPTER 42 (Summary)

State of the Barbaric world — establishment of the Lombards on the Danube — tribes and inroads of the Sclavonians — origin, empire, and embassies of the Turks — the flight of the Avars — Chosroes I or Nushirvan, king of Persia — his prosperous reign and wars with the Romans — the Colchian or Lazic war — the Ethiopians

The defeat of the Goths in Italy is shown to have led to inroads of more Germanic tribes from the North, and Justinian allied with the Lombards to resist other invaders from across the Danube. Constantinople was threatened by invasions of Sclavonians. The rise of the Turks in the far East, meanwhile, precipitated further barbarian migrations. An alliance of the Romans and the Turks was formed to oppose the powerful and ambitious Persian kingdom of Chosroes. At first, Justinian bought peace with Persia, but Chosroes invaded Syria in AD 540 and left Antioch in ruins. Belisarius was sent to prevent Chosroes from invading Palestine. Instead, the Persian king tried to gain control of the Black Sea but was resisted by the Colchians at the foot of mount Caucasus. Eventually, a fifty-year peace was negotiated by Justinian and Chosroes in AD 562.

CHAPTER 43 (Summary)

*Rebellions of Africa – restoration of the Gothic kingdom by
Totila – loss and recovery of Rome – final conquest of
Italy by Narses – extinction of the Ostrogoths – defeat
of the Franks and Alemanni – last victory, disgrace,
and death of Belisarius – death and character of
Justinian – comets, earthquakes, and plague*

Gibbon begins Chapter 43 with a description of the taxation policy of the empire, which provoked riots in Africa after Belisarius had departed. Carthage was pillaged and order was restored only when Belisarius returned. Imperial rule continued in Carthage for a century more, but Africa was desolated by Moorish inroads. Meanwhile, the Goths rebelled in Italy under Totila. He offered more security and prosperity than did the extortionate rule of Justinian. Again, Belisarius was sent to retrieve the situation; but he had insufficient supplies and found little support for the imperial cause. Totila besieged Rome in AD 546 and the Romans were reduced by famine to surrender. He would have destroyed its walls and buildings to prevent further sieges had Belisarius not intervened. Belisarius was recalled by Justinian in AD 548 but a further expedition under Narses the Eunuch was prepared. With the help of the Lombards, Narses defeated the Goths and recaptured Rome in AD 552. Most of the senators had been killed in the vicissitudes of war and the days of the Roman senate were effectively over. A wave of Franks and Alemanni now invaded Italy and they were finally defeated by Narses in AD 554. The Gothic kingdom of Italy had lasted sixty years, and Narses ruled as Exarch of Ravenna and representative of the emperor until AD 568. Meanwhile, Belisarius was needed once more as a warrior to repel a Bulgarian invasion, which threatened Constantinople in AD 559. Soon afterwards, he was implicated in a conspiracy against Justinian. His innocence was not acknowledged until shortly before his death in AD 565. In the same year, Justinian died: Gibbon refers to his accessibility, his justice, his abstemious diet, and his love of fame; but he did not lead his armies into battle, and Gibbon regards his fame as being eclipsed by that of Belisarius. He concludes the chapter with an account of the comets, earthquakes and plague that troubled Justinian's reign.

CHAPTER 44 (Summary)

*Idea of the Roman jurisprudence – the laws of the kings –
the twelve tables of the Decemvirs – the laws of the people –
the decrees of the Senate – the edicts of the magistrates
and emperors – authority of the civilians – Code, Pandects,
Novels, and Institutes of Justinian – (1) rights of persons –
(2) rights of things – (3) private injuries and actions –
(4) crimes and punishments*

Chapter 44 contains an account of the evolution of the Roman legal system from the early kings of Rome to the reformation of laws under Justinian. The tribunes of the people established the right of every Roman citizen to enact the laws which he was bound to obey, but Augustus replaced the popular assemblies with six hundred senators with legislative authority. A perpetual edict of Hadrian fixed the standard of civil jurisprudence, and thereafter the laws and orders of the emperors were codified by Constantine and Theodosius. Schools of jurisprudence developed from the time of Cicero. Justinian commissioned a scholar called Tribonian to produce twelve books or tables of laws, known as the Code of Justinian, for distribution throughout the empire. Seventeen lawyers under Tribonian then produced the Pandects and the Institutes, the digest and the elements of Roman law, which, together with the Code, formed from AD 533 the basis of civil jurisprudence in the courts and schools. (The Novels were new decrees.) Previous writings on the law were then neglected and tended to disappear. Gibbon examines the elements of Roman law under four heads: persons, including social rank and paternal and family ties; things or property, where Gibbon notes with approval that primogeniture did not feature; actions or contracts; and private wrongs, leading to a discussion of the principles of criminal law. There were nine capital offences under the earliest laws, but citizens were later exempt from capital punishment. Slaves were subject to private justice. Punishments, for example for adultery, became more severe under Constantine with the adoption of Christianity. Gibbon concludes that, in spite of the codification of the laws, the subjects of Justinian were oppressed by the multiplicity of their laws and the arbitrary will of the emperor.

CHAPTER 45 (Summary)

Reign of the younger Justin – embassy of the Avars – their
settlement on the Danube – conquest of Italy by the
Lombards – adoption and reign of Tiberius – of Maurice –
state of Italy under the Lombards and the Exarchs of Ravenna –
distress of Rome – character and pontificate of Gregory I

Gibbon relates the accession of Justinian's nephew, Justin II, as emperor in AD 565. He replaced Narses as Exarch of Ravenna, but was powerless to resist an invasion of Italy by the Lombards under Alboin. In AD 574 Justin, in failing health, associated his captain of the guards, Tiberius, with his rule, and died four years later. The reign of Tiberius held great promise, but he too was struck down by illness and chose Maurice, a victorious general against the Persians, as his successor. In Italy, the new emperor opposed the Lombards by purchasing the aid of the Franks, but the Lombard kingdom of Italy was established by Autharis, in spite of the survival of the Exarchate of Ravenna for a further two hundred years. Rome was reduced to a desolate state, depopulated by flood and famine and now the refuge of monks. Still regarded as part of the Empire, it was inspired to lead a new role by its bishop, known as Pope Gregory the Great, who reigned from AD 590 to 604. He maintained the discipline of the church in the West, and under his leadership the Arians of Italy and Spain were reconciled to the Catholic Church, and the Anglo-Saxons in Britain were baptised. He used the income from ecclesiastical estates to help the poor, and saved Rome from the pillage of the Lombards and the general neglect of the Empire.

CHAPTER 46 (Summary)

Revolutions of Persia after the death of Chosroes or Nushirvan – his son, Hormouz, a tyrant, is deposed – usurpation of Bahram – flight and restoration of Chosroes II – his gratitude to the Romans – the Chagan of the Avars – revolt of the army against Maurice – his death – tyranny of Phocas – elevation of Heraclius – the Persian war – Chosroes subdues Syria, Egypt and Asia Minor – siege of Constantinople by the Persians and Avars – Persian expeditions – victories and triumph of Heraclius

The peace treaty of Justinian and Chosroes, the king of the Persians, was frequently broken before the death of Chosroes in AD 579. Gibbon describes how his successor, Hormouz, was deposed by a rebellion and how the grandson of Chosroes, of the same name, sought refuge with the emperor Maurice, and was restored with imperial support to the Persian throne in AD 591. Meanwhile, the empire was threatened by the Avars on the Danube. The troops of Maurice eventually rebelled and elected a centurion called Phocas as emperor in AD 602. He indulged in the cruel extermination of the family of Maurice and was himself overthrown by Heraclius, the son of the Exarch of Africa, in AD 610. After the death of Maurice, Chosroes II of Persia had decided to attack the Empire. He invaded Syria and captured Antioch in AD 611 and Jerusalem in AD 614. He invaded Egypt in AD 616 and reached Tripoli in Libya, while another Persian army marched through Asia Minor and captured Chalcedon, opposite Constantinople on the Bosphorus. The first twelve years of the reign of Heraclius seemed to herald the dissolution of the empire. Chosroes negotiated an extortionate peace treaty, and Heraclius, while trying to collect the tribute for the Persians, decided instead on war. The church lent their treasure in aid and in three years from AD 622 Heraclius campaigned victoriously in Asia Minor as far as the Caspian Sea and Ispahan. In retaliation, Chosroes allied with the Avars, who unsuccessfully besieged Constantinople in AD 626. Heraclius allied with the Turks, and at Nineveh, the next year, the Persian army was destroyed. Chosroes was overthrown by his own people and his country was reduced to anarchy. Heraclius returned in triumph to Constantinople; yet, in the next eight years, he was to lose the recovered provinces of Syria and Palestine to the Arabs.

CHAPTER 47 (Summary)

Theological history of the doctrine of the incarnation – the human and divine nature of Christ – enmity of the Patriarchs of Alexandria and Constantinople – St Cyril and Nestorius – Third General Council of Ephesus – heresy of Eutyches – Fourth General Council of Chalcedon – civil and ecclesiastical discord – intolerance of Justinian – the three Chapters– the Monothelite controversy – state of the Oriental sects – (1) the Nestorians – (2) the Jacobites – (3) the Maronites – (4) the Armenians – (5) the Copts – (6) the Abyssinians

Chapter 47 begins with a review of the early theories of the incarnation of Christ and the different interpretations of his nature. Gibbon then describes the persecutions and rivalry of St Cyril of Alexandria and Nestorius, Patriarch of Constantinople, in the first half of the fifth century. The council of Ephesus, called by the emperor Theodosius II in AD 431, was a trial of strength involving physical violence. St Cyril's views on the incarnation were upheld and Nestorius eventually abdicated in AD 435, but it was not until the Council of Chalcedon in AD 451 that the doctrine of Christ in one person but with two natures was established. Its opponents in the East remained active and caused a religious war which threatened to overthrow the emperor Anastasius in AD 514. The emperor Justinian was a devout Catholic who was willing to enter into religious controversy. He persecuted unorthodox Christians and pagans, but later, under the influence of Theodora, alienated the church of Rome by attempting to reconcile the unorthodox in the East. At the instigation of the emperor Heraclius, there was an attempt at compromise through the doctrine of Christ with two natures but one will, but the Roman church withdrew its support. It was not until the end of the seventh century that the belief that two wills are harmonised in the person of Christ was generally accepted. Only the Syriac and Coptic churches of the East then remained separate, and Gibbon concludes the chapter with a review of those churches: the Nestorians in Persia, who sent missionaries to India and the far East; the Jacobites, named after the monk Jacobus Baradaeus; the Maronites, named after a Syrian hermit; the Armenians, who believe in the single, incorruptible nature of Christ; and the Coptic church of Egypt and Abyssinia which remained independent of Constantinople.

CHAPTER 48 (Summary)

Plan of the last two volumes – succession and characters of
the Greek emperors of Constantinople, from the time
of Heraclius to the Latin conquest

Gibbon outlines the subjects of the remaining two volumes of his history, and then rapidly reviews the reigns of the successors of Heraclius at Constantinople. The dynasty of Heraclius was followed in AD 717 by a line of Syrian emperors known as the Iconoclasts for their attempt to suppress image-worship in the church. Emperors rose and fell as a result of conspiracies in the army or in the palace until the emergence of the Macedonian dynasty of Basil I in AD 867. Gibbon recognises his superior merit, in leading his army in person and restoring the financial administration. During his reign, the laws of Justinian were translated into Greek. The Macedonian dynasty lasted until AD 1057, with little distinction except for some military successes against the Saracens, the Russians and Bulgarians. 'A ray of freedom, or at least of spirit' began to emerge with the accession of Alexius, the first of the Comneni dynasty, in AD 1081. For thirty-seven years, amidst the danger of invasions from the barbarians across the Danube, from the Turks, the Normans and the Latin Christians, he maintained the laws and the arts, though he was regarded as devious in the West. During the reign of his son, John II, the death sentence was abolished, the magnificence of the court was reduced and the maritime provinces of Asia prospered. His younger brother, Manuel I, ruled as a great military leader, and Gibbon narrates the military and amorous adventures of their cousin, Andronicus. In a civil war that followed the death of Manuel, Andronicus rose by violence to become emperor, but was himself killed by the mob in AD 1185. The discord of his successors allowed the Latins to capture Constantinople in AD 1204.

CHAPTER 49 (Summary)

*Introduction, worship, and persecution of images – revolt of Italy
and Rome – temporal dominion of the popes – conquest of Italy
by the Franks – establishment of images – character and
coronation of Charlemagne – restoration and decay of
the Roman empire in the West – independence
of Italy – constitution of the Germanic body*

Gibbon describes how the issue of image worship divided the churches of
the East and the West. There were no authentic likenesses of Christ
surviving from his earthly life, and the emperor Leo III and his successors
in the eighth century developed a policy of banning images in churches.
All worship of images was condemned by the synod of Constantinople in
AD 754, and their destruction led to rioting. The popes of Rome resisted
the policy, with popular support. The popes had become in effect the
temporal rulers of Rome, and when its independence was threatened by
the Lombards, they appealed for aid to the Frankish kingdom of Pepin
and his son, Charlemagne. Crowned emperor of the Romans in AD 800
after defeating the Lombards, Charlemagne effectively became the successor of the Exarchs, the former representatives of the emperors of the
East in Italy. Already, the fictitious donation of Rome to the papacy by
Constantine had been invented. Meanwhile, the issue of images had been
resolved with their restoration, although the struggle between the break-
ers and worshippers of images continued into the ninth century. Gibbon
then assesses the achievements of Charlemagne's reign and reviews the
extent of his empire from the Ebro to the Elbe. Though the empire soon
separated into the kingdoms of Germany, France and Italy, its fortunes
were revived under Otho I in the second half of the tenth century, when
the rule was established that the prince who was elected by his German
feudatories acquired the kingdom of Italy and was crowned emperor by
the pope. The Romans occasionally claimed their independence from the
German emperors, and by the twelfth century the league of Lombard
cities was becoming economically self-assertive. The power of the
emperors was also reduced in Germany through the growing independence of the dukes and bishops with the right of election. Gibbon contrasts
the powerless ostentation of the emperor Charles IV of Bohemia in AD
1356 with the might of the first Augustus, who had nevertheless maintained the private character of a Roman citizen.

CHAPTER 50

Description of Arabia and its inhabitants – birth, character, and
doctrine of Mahomet – he preaches at Mecca – flies to Medina –
propagates his religion by the sword – voluntary or reluctant
submission of the Arabs – his death and successors –
the claims and fortunes of Ali and his descendants

After pursuing, above six hundred years, the fleeting Caesars of Constantinople and Germany, I now descend, in the reign of Heraclius, on the eastern borders of the Greek monarchy. While the state was exhausted by the Persian war, and the church was distracted by the Nestorian and Monophysite sects, Mahomet, with the sword in one hand and the Koran in the other, erected his throne on the ruins of Christianity and of Rome. The genius of the Arabian prophet, the manners of his nation, and the spirit of his religion involve the causes of the decline and fall of the Eastern empire; and our eyes are curiously intent on one of the most memorable revolutions which have impressed a new and lasting character on the nations of the globe.[1]

In the vacant space between Persia, Syria, Egypt, and Ethiopia, the Arabian peninsula[2] may be conceived as a triangle of spacious but irregular dimensions. From the northern point of Beles[3] on the Euphrates, a line of fifteen hundred miles is terminated by the straits of Babelmandeb and the land of frankincense. About half this length may be allowed for the middle breadth from east to west, from Bassora to Suez, from the Persian Gulf to the Red Sea.[4] The sides of the triangle are gradually enlarged, and the southern basis presents a front of a thousand miles to the Indian ocean. The entire surface of the peninsula exceeds in a fourfold proportion that of Germany or France; but the far greater part has been justly stigmatised with the epithets of the *stony* and the *sandy*. Even the wilds of Tartary are decked by the hand of nature with lofty trees and luxuriant herbage; and the lonesome traveller derives a sort of comfort and society from the presence of vegetable life. But in the dreary waste of Arabia, a boundless level of sand is intersected by sharp and naked mountains, and the face of the desert, without shade or shelter, is scorched by the direct and intense rays of a tropical sun. Instead of refreshing breezes, the winds, particularly from the southwest, diffuse a noxious and even deadly vapour; the hillocks of sand which they alternately raise and scatter are compared to the billows of the ocean; and whole caravans, whole armies, have been lost and buried in the whirlwind. The common benefits of water are an object of desire and contest; and such is the scarcity of wood that some art is requisite to preserve and propagate the element of fire. Arabia is destitute of navigable rivers, which fertilise the soil and convey its produce to the adjacent regions; the torrents that fall from the hills are imbibed by the thirsty earth; the rare and hardy plants, the tamarind or the acacia, that strike their roots into the clefts of the rocks, are nourished by the dews of the night; a scanty supply of rain is collected in cisterns and aqueducts; the wells and springs are the secret treasure of the desert; and the pilgrim of Mecca,[5] after many a dry and sultry march, is disgusted by the taste of the waters, which have rolled over a bed of sulphur or salt. Such is the general and genuine picture of the climate of Arabia. The experience of evil enhances the value of any local or partial enjoyments. A shady grove, a green pasture, a stream of fresh water, are sufficient to attract a colony of sedentary Arabs to the fortunate spots which can afford food and refreshment to themselves and their cattle, and which encourage their industry in the cultivation of the palm tree and the vine. The high lands that border on the Indian ocean are distinguished by their superior plenty of wood and water; the air is more temperate, the fruits are more delicious, the animals and the human race more numerous; the fertility of the soil invites and rewards the toil of the husbandman; and the peculiar gifts of frankincense[6] and coffee have attracted, in different ages, the merchants of the world. If it be compared with the rest of the peninsula, this sequestered region may truly deserve the appellation of the *happy*; and the splendid colouring of fancy and fiction has been suggested by contrast and countenanced* by distance. It was for this earthly paradise that nature had reserved her choicest favours and her most curious workmanship; the incompatible blessings of luxury and innocence were ascribed to the natives; the soil was impregnated with gold[7] and gems, and both the land and sea were taught to exhale the odours of aromatic sweets. This division of the *sandy*, the *stony*, and the *happy*, so familiar to the Greeks and Latins, is unknown to the Arabians themselves; and it is singular enough that a country, whose language and inhabitants had ever been the same, should scarcely retain a vestige of its ancient geography. The maritime districts of *Bahrein* and *Oman* are opposite to the realm of Persia. The kingdom of *Yemen* displays the limits, or at least the situation, of Arabia Felix;† the name *Neged* is extended over the inland space; and the birth of Mahomet has illustrated the province of *Hejaz* along the coast of the Red Sea.[8]

The measure of population is regulated by the means of subsistence; and the inhabitants of this vast peninsula might be outnumbered by the subjects of a fertile and industrious province. Along the shores of the Persian gulf, of the ocean,‡ and even the Red Sea, the *Ichthyophagi*,[9] or fish-eaters, continued to wander in quest of their precarious food. In this primitive and abject state, which ill deserves the name of society, the human brute, without arts or laws, almost without sense or language, is poorly distinguished from the rest of the animal creation. Generations and ages might roll away in silent oblivion, and the helpless savage was

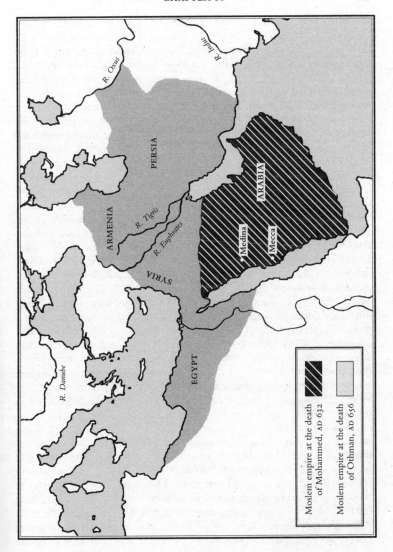

The growth of the Moslem empire AD 632–56

restrained from multiplying his race by the wants and pursuits which confined his existence to the narrow margin of the sea-coast. But in an early period of antiquity the great body of the Arabs had emerged from this scene of misery; and, as the naked wilderness could not maintain a people of hunters, they rose at once to the more secure and plentiful condition of the pastoral life. The same life is uniformly pursued by the roving tribes of the desert, and in the portrait of the modern *Bedoweens* we may trace the features of their ancestors,[10] who, in the age of Moses or Mahomet, dwelt under similar tents, and conducted their horses and camels and sheep to the same springs and the same pastures. Our toil is lessened, and our wealth is increased, by our dominion over the useful animals; and the Arabian shepherd had acquired the absolute possession of a faithful friend and a laborious slave.[11] Arabia, in the opinion of the naturalist, is the genuine and original country of the *horse*; the climate most propitious, not indeed to the size, but to the spirit and swiftness, of that generous* animal. The merit of the Barb,† the Spanish, and the English breed is derived from a mixture of Arabian blood;[12] the Bedoweens preserve, with superstitious care, the honours and the memory of the purest race; the males are sold at a high price, but the females are seldom alienated;‡ and the birth of a noble foal was esteemed, among the tribes, as a subject of joy and mutual congratulation. These horses are educated in the tents among the children of the Arabs, with a tender familiarity, which trains them in the habits of gentleness and attachment. They are accustomed only to walk and to gallop; their sensations are not blunted by the incessant abuse of the spur and the whip: their powers are reserved for the moments of flight and pursuit; but no sooner do they feel the touch of the hand or the stirrup than they dart away with the swiftness of the wind; and, if their friend be dismounted in the rapid career, they instantly stop till he has recovered his seat. In the sands of Africa and Arabia the *camel* is a sacred and precious gift. That strong and patient beast of burthen can perform, without eating or drinking, a journey of several days; and a reservoir of fresh water is preserved in a large bag, a fifth stomach of the animal, whose body is imprinted with the marks of servitude. The larger breed is capable of transporting a weight of a thousand pounds; and the dromedary, of a lighter and more active frame, outstrips the fleetest courser in the race. Alive or dead, almost every part of the camel is serviceable to man; her milk is plentiful and nutritious; the young and tender flesh has the taste of veal;[13] a valuable salt is extracted from the urine; the dung supplies the deficiency of fuel; and the long hair, which falls each year and is renewed, is coarsely manufactured into the garments, the furniture, and the tents, of the Bedoweens. In the rainy seasons they consume the rare and insufficient herbage of the desert; during the heats of summer and the scarcity of winter, they remove their encampments to the sea-coast, the hills of Yemen, or the neighbourhood of the Euphrates, and have often extorted the dangerous licence of visiting the banks of the Nile and the villages of Syria and Palestine. The life of a wandering Arab is a life of danger and distress; and, though sometimes, by rapine or exchange, he may appropriate the fruits of industry, a private citizen in Europe is in the possession of more solid and pleasing luxury than the proudest emir who marches in the field at the head of ten thousand horse.

Yet an essential difference may be found between the hordes of Scythia and the Arabian tribes, since many of the latter were collected into towns and employed in the labours of trade and agriculture. A part of their time and industry was still devoted to the management of their cattle; they mingled in, peace and war, with their brethren of the desert; and the Bedoweens derived from their useful intercourse some supply of their wants and some rudiments of art and knowledge. Among the forty-two cities of Arabia,[14] enumerated by Abulfeda, the most ancient and populous were situate in the *happy* Yemen; the towers of Saana[15] and the marvellous reservoir of Merab[16] were constructed by the kings of the Homerites;* but their profane lustre was eclipsed by the prophetic glories of MEDINA[17] and MECCA,[18] near the Red Sea, and at the distance from each other of two hundred and seventy miles. The last of these holy places was known to the Greeks under the name of Macoraba; and the termination of the word is expressive of its greatness, which has not indeed, in the most flourishing period, exceeded the size and populousness of Marseilles. Some latent motive, perhaps of superstition, must have impelled the founders, in the choice of a most unpromising situation. They erected their habitations of mud or stone in a plain about two miles long and one mile broad, at the foot of three barren mountains; the soil is a rock; the water even of the holy well of Zemzem is bitter or brackish; the pastures are remote from the city; and grapes are transported about seventy miles from the gardens of Tayef. The fame and spirit of the Koreishites, who reigned in Mecca, were conspicuous among the Arabian tribes; but their ungrateful soil refused the labours of agriculture, and their position was favourable to the enterprises of trade. By the seaport of Gedda, at the distance only of forty miles, they maintained an easy correspondence with Abyssinia; and that Christian kingdom afforded the first refuge to the disciples of Mahomet. The treasures of Africa were conveyed over the peninsula to Gerrha or Katif, in the province of Bahrein, a city built, as it is said, of rock-salt, by the Chaldaean exiles;[19] and from thence, with the native pearls of the Persian Gulf, they were floated on rafts to the mouth of the Euphrates. Mecca is placed almost at an equal distance, a month's journey, between Yemen on the right, and Syria on the left, hand. The former was the winter, the latter the summer, station of her caravans; and their seasonable arrival relieved the ships of India from the tedious and troublesome navigation of the Red Sea. In the markets of Saana and Merab, in the harbours of Oman and Aden, the camels of the Koreishites were laden with a precious cargo of aromatics;

a supply of corn and manufactures were purchased in the fairs of Bostra and Damascus; the lucrative exchange diffused plenty and riches in the streets of Mecca; and the noblest of her sons united the love of arms with the profession of merchandise.[20]

The perpetual independence of the Arabs has been the theme of praise among strangers and natives; and the arts of controversy transform this singular event into a prophecy and a miracle, in favour of the posterity of Ismael.*[21] Some exceptions, that can neither be dissembled nor eluded, render this mode of reasoning as indiscreet as it is superfluous: the kingdom of Yemen has been successively subdued by the Abyssinians, the Persians, the sultans of Egypt,[22] and the Turks;[23] the holy cities of Mecca and Medina have repeatedly bowed under a Scythian tyrant; and the Roman province of Arabia[24] embraced the peculiar wilderness in which Ismael and his sons must have pitched their tents in the face of their brethren. Yet these exceptions are temporary or local; the body of the nation has escaped the yoke of the most powerful monarchies; the arms of Sesostris[†] and Cyrus, of Pompey and Trajan, could never achieve the conquest of Arabia; the present sovereign of the Turks[25] may exercise a shadow of jurisdiction, but his pride is reduced to solicit the friendship of a people whom it is dangerous to provoke and fruitless to attack. The obvious causes of their freedom are inscribed on the character and country of the Arabs. Many ages before Mahomet,[26] their intrepid valour had been severely felt by their neighbours in offensive and defensive war. The patient and active virtues of a soldier are insensibly nursed in the habits and discipline of a pastoral life. The care of the sheep and camels is abandoned to the women of the tribe; but the martial youth under the banner of the emir is ever on horseback and in the field, to practise the exercise of the bow, the javelin, and the scymetar.[‡] The long memory of their independence is the firmest pledge of its perpetuity, and succeeding generations are animated to prove their descent and to maintain their inheritance. Their domestic feuds are suspended on the approach of a common enemy; and in their last hostilities against the Turks the caravan of Mecca was attacked and pillaged by fourscore thousand of the confederates. When they advance to battle, the hope of victory is in the front; in the rear, the assurance of a retreat. Their horses and camels, who in eight or ten days can perform a march of four or five hundred miles, disappear before the conqueror; the secret waters of the desert elude his search; and his victorious troops are consumed with thirst, hunger, and fatigue, in the pursuit of an invisible foe, who scorns his efforts, and safely reposes in the heart of the burning solitude. The arms and deserts of the Bedoweens are not only the safeguards of their own freedom, but the barriers also of the happy Arabia, whose inhabitants, remote from war, are enervated by the luxury of the soil and climate. The legions of Augustus melted away in disease and lassitude;[27] and it is only by a naval power that the reduction of Yemen has been successfully attempted. When

Mahomet erected his holy standard,[28] that kingdom was a province of the Persian empire; yet seven princes of the Homerites still reigned in the mountains; and the vicegerent of Chosroes* was tempted to forget his distant country and his unfortunate master. The historians of the age of Justinian represent the state of the independent Arabs, who were divided by interest or affection in the long quarrel of the East: the tribe of *Gassan* was allowed to encamp on the Syrian territory; the princes of *Hira* were permitted to form a city about forty miles to the southward of the ruins of Babylon. Their service in the field was speedy and vigorous; but their friendship was venal, their faith inconstant, their enmity capricious: it was an easier task to excite than to disarm these roving barbarians; and, in the familiar intercourse of war, they learned to see, and to despise, the splendid weakness both of Rome and of Persia. From Mecca to the Euphrates, the Arabian tribes[29] were confounded by the Greeks and Latins under the general appellation of Saracens,[30] a name which every Christian mouth has been taught to pronounce with terror and abhorrence.

The slaves of domestic tyranny may vainly exult in their national independence; but the Arab is personally free; and he enjoys, in some degree, the benefits of society, without forfeiting the prerogatives of nature. In every tribe, superstition, or gratitude, or fortune has exalted a particular family above the heads of their equals. The dignities of sheikh and emir invariably descend in this chosen race; but the order of succession is loose and precarious; and the most worthy or aged of the noble kinsmen are preferred to[†] the simple, though important, office of composing disputes by their advice and guiding valour by their example. Even a female of sense and spirit[‡] has been permitted to command the countrymen of Zenobia.[31] The momentary junction of several tribes produces an army; their more lasting union constitutes a nation; and the supreme chief, the emir of emirs, whose banner is displayed at their head, may deserve, in the eyes of strangers, the honours of the kingly name. If the Arabian princes abuse their power, they are quickly punished by the desertion of their subjects, who had been accustomed to a mild and parental jurisdiction. Their spirit is free, their steps are unconfined, the desert is open, and the tribes and families are held together by a mutual and voluntary compact. The softer natives of Yemen supported the pomp and majesty of a monarch; but, if he could not leave his palace without endangering his life,[32] the active powers of government must have been devolved on his nobles and magistrates. The cities of Mecca and Medina present, in the heart of Asia, the form, or rather the substance, of a commonwealth. The grandfather of Mahomet and his lineal ancestors appear in foreign and domestic transactions as the princes of their country; but they reigned, like Pericles at Athens, or the Medici at Florence, by the opinion of their wisdom and integrity; their influence was divided with their patrimony; and the sceptre was transferred from the uncles of the prophet to a younger branch of the tribe of Koreish. On solemn occasions they convened the assembly of the people; and, since mankind must be either compelled or persuaded to obey, the use and reputation of oratory among the ancient Arabs is the clearest evidence of public freedom.[33] But their simple freedom was of a very different cast from the nice and artificial machinery of the Greek and Roman republics, in which each member possessed an undivided share of the civil and political rights of the community. In the more simple state of the Arabs the nation is free, because each of her sons disdains a base submission to the will of a master. His breast is fortified with the austere virtues of courage, patience, and sobriety; the love of independence prompts him to exercise the habits of self-command; and the fear of dishonour guards him from the meaner apprehension of pain, of danger, and of death. The gravity and firmness of the mind is conspicuous in his outward demeanour; his speech is slow, weighty, and concise; he is seldom provoked to laughter; his only gesture is that of stroking his beard, the venerable symbol of manhood; and the sense of his own importance teaches him to accost his equals without levity and his superiors without awe.[34] The liberty of the Saracens survived their conquests; the first caliphs indulged the bold and familiar language of their subjects; they ascended the pulpit to persuade and edify the congregation; nor was it before the seat of empire was removed to the Tigris that the Abbassides adopted the proud and pompous ceremonial of the Persian and Byzantine courts.

In the study of nations and men, we may observe the causes that render them hostile or friendly to each other, that tend to narrow or enlarge, to mollify or exasperate, the social character. The separation of the Arabs from the rest of mankind has accustomed them to confound the ideas of stranger and enemy; and the poverty of the land has introduced a maxim of jurisprudence which they believe and practise to the present hour. They pretend that, in the division of the earth, the rich and fertile climates were assigned to the other branches of the human family: and that the posterity of the outlaw Ismael might recover, by fraud or force, the portion of inheritance of which he had been unjustly deprived. According to the remark of Pliny, the Arabian tribes are equally addicted to theft and merchandise; the caravans that traverse the desert are ransomed or pillaged; and their neighbours, since the remote times of Job and Sesostris,[35] have been the victims of their rapacious spirit. If a Bedoween discovers from afar a solitary traveller, he rides furiously against him, crying, with a loud voice, 'Undress thyself, thy aunt (*my wife*) is without a garment.' A ready submission entitles him to mercy; resistance will provoke the aggressor, and his own blood must expiate the blood which he presumes to shed in legitimate defence. A single robber or a few associates are branded with their genuine name; but the exploits of a numerous band assume the character of a lawful and honourable war. The temper of a people, thus armed against mankind, was doubly inflamed by the domestic licence of rapine, murder, and revenge. In the constitution of Europe, the right of peace and war is now confined to a small, and the actual exercise to a much smaller, list of respectable potentates; but each Arab, with impunity and renown, might point his javelin against the life of his countryman. The union of the nation consisted only in a vague resemblance of language and manners; and in each community the jurisdiction of the magistrate was mute and impotent. Of the time of ignorance which preceded Mahomet, seventeen hundred battles[36] are recorded by tradition; hostility was embittered with the rancour of civil faction; and the recital, in prose or verse, of an obsolete feud was sufficient to rekindle the same passions among the descendants of the hostile tribes. In private life, every man, at least every family, was the judge and avenger of its own cause. The nice sensibility of honour, which weighs the insult rather than the injury, sheds its deadly venom on the quarrels of the Arabs; the honour of their women, and of their *beards*, is most easily wounded; an indecent* action, a contemptuous word, can be expiated only by the blood of the offender; and such is their patient inveteracy that they expect whole months and years the opportunity of revenge. A fine or compensation for murder is familiar to the barbarians of every age; but in Arabia the kinsmen of the dead are at liberty to accept the atonement, or to exercise with their own hands the law of retaliation. The refined malice of the Arabs refuses even the head of the murderer, substitutes an innocent to the guilty person, and transfers the penalty to the best and most considerable of the race by whom they have been injured. If he falls by their hands, they are exposed in their turn to the danger of reprisals; the interest and principal of the bloody debt are accumulated; the individuals of either family lead a life of malice and suspicion, and fifty years may sometimes elapse before the account of vengeance be finally settled.[37] This sanguinary spirit, ignorant of pity or forgiveness, has been moderated, however, by the maxims of honour, which require in every private encounter some decent equality of age and strength, of numbers and weapons. An annual festival of two, perhaps of four, months was observed by the Arabs before the time of Mahomet, during which their swords were religiously sheathed, both in foreign and domestic hostility; and this partial truce is more strongly expressive of the habits of anarchy and warfare.[38]

But the spirit of rapine and revenge was attempered by the milder influence of trade and literature. The solitary peninsula is encompassed by the most civilised nations of the ancient world; the merchant is the friend of mankind; and the annual caravans imported the first seeds of knowledge and politeness into the cities and even the camps of the desert. Whatever may be the pedigree of the Arabs, their language is derived from the same original stock with the Hebrew, the Syriac, and the Chaldaean tongues; the independence of the tribes was marked by their peculiar dialects;[39] but each, after their own, allowed a just preference to the pure and perspicuous idiom of Mecca. In Arabia as well as in Greece, the perfection of language outstripped the refinement of manners; and her speech could diversify the fourscore names of honey, the two hundred of a serpent, the five hundred of a lion, the thousand of a sword, at a time when this copious dictionary was entrusted to the memory of an illiterate people. The monuments of the Homerites were inscribed with an obsolete and mysterious character; but the Cufic letters, the ground-work of the present alphabet, were invented on the banks of the Euphrates; and the recent invention was taught at Mecca by a stranger who settled in that city after the birth of Mahomet. The arts of grammar, of metre, and of rhetoric were unknown to the freeborn eloquence of the Arabians; but their penetration was sharp, their fancy luxuriant, their wit strong and sententious,[40] and their more elaborate compositions were addressed with energy and effect to the minds of their hearers. The genius and merit of a rising poet was celebrated by the applause of his own and the kindred tribes. A solemn banquet was prepared, and a chorus of women, striking their tymbals,* and displaying the pomp of their nuptials, sung in the presence of their sons and husbands the felicity of their native tribe; that a champion had now appeared to vindicate their rights; that a herald had raised his voice to immortalise their renown. The distant or hostile tribes resorted to an annual fair, which was abolished by the fanaticism of the first Moslems: a national assembly that must have contributed to refine and harmonise the barbarians. Thirty days were employed in the exchange, not only of corn and wine, but of eloquence and poetry. The prize was disputed by the generous emulation of the bards; the victorious performance was deposited in the archives of princes and emirs; and we may read in our own language the seven original poems which were inscribed in letters of gold and suspended in the temple of Mecca.[41] The Arabian poets were the historians and moralists of the age; and, if they sympathised with the prejudices, they inspired and crowned the virtues, of their countrymen. The indissoluble union of generosity and valour was the darling theme of their song; and, when they pointed their keenest satire against a despicable race, they affirmed, in the bitterness of reproach, that the men knew not how to give nor the women to deny.[42] The same hospitality which was practised by Abraham and celebrated by Homer is still renewed in the camps of the Arabs. The ferocious Bedoweens, the terror of the desert, embrace, without inquiry or hesitation, the stranger who dares to confide in their honour and to enter their tent. His treatment is kind and respectful; he shares the wealth or the poverty of his host; and, after a needful repose, he is dismissed on his way, with thanks, with blessings, and perhaps with gifts. The heart and hand are more largely expanded by the wants of a brother or a friend; but the heroic acts that could deserve the public applause must have surpassed the narrow measure of discretion and experience. A dispute had arisen, who, among the citizens of Mecca, was entitled to the prize of generosity;

and successive application was made to the three who were deemed most worthy of the trial. Abdallah, the son of Abbas, had undertaken a distant journey, and his foot was in the stirrup when he heard the voice of a suppliant, 'O son of the uncle of the apostle of God, I am a traveller, and in distress!' He instantly dismounted to present the pilgrim with his camel, her rich caparison, and a purse of four thousand pieces of gold, excepting only the sword, either for its intrinsic value or as the gift of an honoured kinsman. The servant of Kais informed the second suppliant that his master was asleep; but he immediately added, 'Here is a purse of seven thousand pieces of gold (it is all we have in the house), and here is an order that will entitle you to a camel and a slave.' The master, as soon as he awoke, praised and enfranchised his faithful steward, with a gentle reproof that by respecting his slumbers he had stinted his bounty. The third of these heroes, the blind Arabah, at the hour of prayer, was supporting his steps on the shoulders of two slaves. 'Alas!' he replied, 'my coffers are empty! but these you may sell; if you refuse, I renounce them.' At these words, pushing away the youths, he groped along the wall with his staff. The character of Hatem is the perfect model of Arabian virtue;[43] he was brave and liberal, an eloquent poet and a successful robber: forty camels were roasted at his hospitable feast; and at the prayer of a suppliant enemy he restored both the captives and the spoil. The freedom of his countrymen disdained the laws of justice; they proudly indulged the spontaneous impulse of pity and benevolence.

The religion of the Arabs,[44] as well as of the Indians, consisted in the worship of the sun, the moon, and the fixed stars; a primitive and specious mode of superstition. The bright luminaries of the sky display the visible image of a Deity: their number and distance convey to a philosophic, or even a vulgar, eye the idea of boundless space: the character of eternity is marked on these solid globes, that seem incapable of corruption or decay: the regularity of their motions may be ascribed to a principle of reason or instinct; and their real or imaginary influence encourages the vain belief that the earth and its inhabitants are the object of their peculiar care. The science of astronomy was cultivated at Babylon; but the school of the Arabs was a clear firmament and a naked plain. In their nocturnal marches, they steered by the guidance of the stars; their names, and order, and daily station were familiar to the curiosity and devotion of the Bedoween; and he was taught by experience to divide in twenty-eight parts the zodiac of the moon, and to bless the constellations who refreshed with salutary rains the thirst of the desert. The reign of the heavenly orbs could not be extended beyond the visible sphere; and some metaphysical powers were necessary to sustain the transmigration of souls and the resurrection of bodies; a camel was left to perish on the grave, that he might serve his master in another life; and the invocation of departed spirits implies that they were still endowed with consciousness and power. I am ignorant, and I am careless, of the blind mythology of the barbarians; of the local deities, of the stars, the air, and the earth, of their sex or titles, their attributes or subordination. Each tribe, each family, each independent warrior, created and changed the rites and the object of his fantastic worship; but the nation, in every age, has bowed to the religion, as well as to the language, of Mecca. The genuine antiquity of the Caaba ascends beyond the Christian era: in describing the coast of the Red Sea, the Greek historian Diodorus[45] has remarked, between the Thamudites and the Sabaeans, a famous temple, whose superior sanctity was revered by *all* the Arabians; the linen or silken veil, which is annually renewed by the Turkish emperor, was first offered by a pious king of the Homerites, who reigned seven hundred years before the time of Mahomet.[46] A tent or a cavern might suffice for the worship of the savages, but an edifice of stone and clay has been erected in its place; and the art and power of the monarchs of the East have been confined to the simplicity of the original model.[47] A spacious portico encloses the quadrangle of the Caaba, a square chapel, twenty-four cubits long, twenty-three broad, and twenty-seven high; a door and a window admit the light; the double roof is supported by three pillars of wood; a spout (now of gold) discharges the rainwater, and the well Zemzem is protected by a dome from accidental pollution. The tribe of Koreish, by fraud or force, had acquired the custody of the Caaba: the sacerdotal office devolved through four lineal descents to the grandfather of Mahomet; and the family of the Hashemites, from whence he sprung, was the most respectable and sacred in the eyes of their country.[48] The precincts of Mecca enjoyed the rights of sanctuary; and, in the last month of each year, the city and the temple were crowded with a long train of pilgrims, who presented their vows and offerings in the house of God. The same rites, which are now accomplished by the faithful Musulman, were invented and practised by the superstition of the idolaters. At an awful distance they cast away their garments; seven times, with hasty steps, they encircled the Caaba, and kissed the black stone; seven times they visited and adored the adjacent mountains; seven times they threw stones into the valley of Mina; and the pilgrimage was achieved, as at the present hour, by a sacrifice of sheep and camels, and the burial of their hair and nails in the consecrated ground. Each tribe either found or introduced in the Caaba their domestic worship; the temple was adorned, or defiled, with three hundred and sixty idols of men, eagles, lions, and antelopes; and most conspicuous was the statue of Hebal, of red agate, holding in his hand seven arrows, without heads or feathers, the instruments and symbols of profane divination. But this statue was a monument of Syrian arts; the devotion of the ruder ages was content with a pillar or a tablet; and the rocks of the desert were hewn into gods or altars, in imitation of the black stone[49] of Mecca, which is deeply tainted with the reproach of an idolatrous origin. From Japan to Peru, the use of sacrifice has universally prevailed; and the votary has expressed his gratitude, or fear, by destroying or consuming, in honour of the gods, the dearest and most precious of their gifts. The life of a man[50] is the most precious oblation to deprecate a public calamity: the altars of Phoenicia and Egypt, of Rome and Carthage, have been polluted with human gore; the cruel practice was long preserved among the Arabs; in the third century, a boy was annually sacrificed by the tribe of the Dumatians;[51] and a royal captive was piously slaughtered by the prince of the Saracens, the ally and soldier of the emperor Justinian.[52] A parent who drags his son to the altar exhibits the most painful and sublime effort of fanaticism; the deed, or the intention, was sanctified by the example of saints and heroes; and the father of Mahomet himself was devoted by a rash vow, and hardly* ransomed for the equivalent of an hundred camels. In the time of ignorance, the Arabs, like the Jews and Egyptians, abstained from the taste of swine's flesh;[53] they circumcised[54] their children at the age of puberty; the same customs, without the censure or the precept of the Koran, have been silently transmitted to their posterity and proselytes. It has been sagaciously conjectured that the artful legislator indulged the stubborn prejudices of his countrymen. It is more simple to believe that he adhered to the habits and opinions of his youth, without foreseeing that a practice congenial to the climate of Mecca might become useless or inconvenient on the banks of the Danube or the Volga.

Arabia was free; the adjacent kingdoms were shaken by the storms of conquest and tyranny, and the persecuted sects fled to the happy land where they might profess what they thought and practise what they professed. The religions of the Sabians and Magians, of the Jews and Christians, were disseminated from the Persian Gulf to the Red Sea. In a remote period of antiquity, Sabianism was diffused over Asia by the science of the Chaldeans[55] and the arms of the Assyrians. From the observations of two thousand years the priests and astronomers of Babylon[56] deduced the eternal laws of nature and providence. They adored the seven gods or angels who directed the course of the seven planets and shed their irresistible influence on the earth. The attributes of the seven planets, with the twelve signs of the zodiac and the twenty-four constellations of the northern and southern hemisphere, were represented by images and talismans; the seven days of the week were dedicated to their respective deities; the Sabians prayed thrice each day; and the temple of the moon at Haran was the term of their pilgrimage.[57] But the flexible genius of their faith was always ready either to teach or to learn; in the tradition of the creation, the deluge, and the patriarchs, they held a singular agreement with their Jewish captives; they appealed to the secret books of Adam, Seth, and Enoch; and a slight infusion of the gospel has transformed the last remnant of the Polytheists into the Christians of St John, in the territory of Bassora.[58] The altars of Babylon were overturned by the Magians; but the injuries of the Sabians were revenged by the sword of Alexander; Persia groaned above five hundred years under a foreign yoke; and the purest disciples of Zoroaster escaped from the contagion of idolatry, and breathed with their adversaries the freedom of the desert.[59] Seven hundred years before the death of Mahomet, the Jews were settled in Arabia; and a far greater multitude was expelled from the Holy Land in the wars of Titus and Hadrian. The industrious exiles aspired to liberty and power: they erected synagogues in the cities and castles in the wilderness, and their Gentile converts were confounded with the children of Israel, whom they resembled in the outward mark of circumcision. The Christian missionaries were still more active and successful: the Catholics asserted their universal reign; the sects whom they oppressed successively retired beyond the limits of the Roman empire; the Marcionites and the Manichaeans dispersed their *phantastic*** opinions and apocryphal gospels; the churches of Yemen, and the princes of Hira and Gassan, were instructed in a purer creed by the Jacobite and Nestorian bishops.[60] The liberty of choice was presented to the tribes: each Arab was free to elect or to compose his own private religion; and the rude superstition of his house was mingled with the sublime theology of saints and philosophers. A fundamental article of faith was inculcated by the consent of the learned strangers: the existence of one supreme God, who is exalted above the powers of heaven and earth, but who has often revealed himself to mankind by the ministry of his angels and prophets, and whose grace or justice has interrupted, by seasonable miracles, the order of nature. The most rational of the Arabs acknowledged his power, though they neglected his worship;[61] and it was habit rather than conviction that still attached them to the relics of idolatry. The Jews and Christians were the people of the *book*; the Bible was already translated into the Arabic language,[62] and the volume of the Old Testament was accepted by the concord of these implacable enemies. In the story of the Hebrew patriarchs, the Arabs were pleased to discover the fathers of their nation. They applauded the birth and promises of Ismael; revered the faith and virtue of Abraham; traced his pedigree and their own to the creation of the first man, and imbibed with equal credulity the prodigies of the holy text and the dreams and traditions of the Jewish rabbis.

The base and plebeian origin of Mahomet is an unskilful calumny of the Christians,[63] who exalt instead of degrading the merit of their adversary. His descent from Ismael was a national privilege or fable; but, if the first steps of the pedigree[64] are dark and doubtful, he could produce many generations of pure and genuine nobility: he sprung from the tribe of Koreish and the family of Hashem, the most illustrious of the Arabs, the princes of Mecca, and the hereditary guardians of the Caaba. The grandfather of Mahomet was Abdol Motalleb, the son of Hashem, a wealthy and generous citizen, who relieved the distress of famine with the supplies of commerce. Mecca, which had been fed by the liberality of the father, was saved by the courage of the son. The kingdom of Yemen was subject to the Christian princes of Abyssinia; their vassal Abrahah was provoked by an insult to avenge the honour of the cross; and the holy city was invested by a train of elephants and an army of Africans. A treaty was proposed; and in the first audience the grandfather of Mahomet demanded the restitution of his cattle. 'And why,' said Abrahah, 'do you not rather implore my clemency in favour of your temple, which I have threatened to destroy?' 'Because,' replied the intrepid chief, 'the cattle is my own; the Caaba belongs to the gods, and *they* will defend their house from injury and sacrilege.' The want of provisions, or the valour of the Koreish, compelled the Abyssinians to a disgraceful retreat; their discomfiture has been adorned with a miraculous flight of birds, who showered down stones on the heads of the infidels; and the deliverance was long commemorated by the era of the elephant.[65] The glory of Abdol Motalleb was crowned with domestic happiness, his life was prolonged to the age of one hundred and ten years, and he became the father of six daughters and thirteen sons. His best beloved Abdallah was the most beautiful and modest of the Arabian youth; and in the first night, when he consummated his marriage with Amina, of the noble race of the Zahrites, two hundred virgins are said to have expired of jealousy and despair. Mahomet, or more properly Mohammed, the only son of Abdallah and Amina, was born at Mecca, four years after the death of Justinian, and two months after the defeat of the Abyssinians,[66] whose victory would have introduced into the Caaba the religion of the Christians. In his early infancy, he was deprived of his father, his mother, and his grandfather; his uncles were strong and numerous; and, in the division of the inheritance, the orphan's share was reduced to five camels and an Ethiopian maid-servant. At home and abroad, in peace and war, Abu Taleb, the most respectable of his uncles, was the guide and guardian of his youth; in his twenty-fifth year, he entered into the service of Cadijah, a rich and noble widow of Mecca, who soon rewarded his fidelity with the gift of her hand and fortune. The marriage contract, in the simple style of antiquity, recites the mutual love of Mahomet and Cadijah; describes him as the most accomplished of the tribe of Koreish; and stipulates a dowry of twelve ounces of gold and twenty camels, which was supplied by the liberality of his uncle.[67] By this alliance, the son of Abdallah was restored to the station of his ancestors; and the judicious matron was content with his domestic virtues, till, in the fortieth year of his age,[68] he assumed the title of a prophet, and proclaimed the religion of the Koran.

According to the tradition of his companions, Mahomet[69] was distinguished by the beauty of his person, an outward gift which is seldom despised, except by those to whom it has been refused. Before he spoke, the orator engaged on his side the affections of a public or private audience. They applauded his commanding presence, his majestic aspect, his piercing eye, his gracious smile, his flowing beard, his countenance that painted every sensation of the soul, and his gestures that enforced each expression of the tongue. In the familiar offices of life he scrupulously adhered to the grave and ceremonious politeness of his country; his respectful attention to the rich and powerful was dignified by his condescension and affability to the poorest citizens of Mecca; the frankness of his manner concealed the artifice of his views; and the habits of courtesy were imputed to personal friendship or universal benevolence. His memory was capacious and retentive, his wit easy and social, his imagination sublime, his judgment clear, rapid, and decisive. He possessed the courage both of thought and action; and, although his designs might gradually expand with his success, the first idea which he entertained of his divine mission bears the stamp of an original and superior genius. The son of Abdallah was educated in the bosom of the noblest race, in the use of the purest dialect of Arabia; and the fluency of his speech was corrected and enhanced by the practice of discreet and seasonable silence. With these powers of eloquence, Mahomet was an illiterate barbarian; his youth had never been instructed in the arts of reading and writing;[70] the common ignorance exempted him from shame or reproach, but he was reduced to a narrow circle of existence, and deprived of those faithful mirrors which reflect to our mind the minds of sages and heroes. Yet the book of nature and of man was open to his view; and some fancy has been indulged in the political and philosophical observations which are ascribed to the Arabian *traveller*.[71] He compares the nations and the religions of the earth; discovers the weakness of the Persian and Roman monarchies; beholds, with pity and indignation, the degeneracy of the times; and resolves to unite, under one God and one king, the invincible spirit and primitive virtues of the Arabs. Our more accurate inquiry will suggest that, instead of visiting the courts, the camps, the temples of the East, the two journeys of Mahomet into Syria were confined to the fairs of Bostra and Damascus; that he was only thirteen years of age when he accompanied the caravan of his uncle; and that his duty compelled him to return as soon as he had disposed of the merchandise of Cadijah. In these hasty and superficial excursions, the eye of genius might discern some objects invisible to his grosser companions; some seeds of knowledge might be cast upon a fruitful soil; but his ignorance of the Syriac language must have checked his curiosity; and I cannot perceive, in the life or writings of Mahomet, that his prospect was far extended beyond the limits of the Arabian world. From every region of that solitary world, the pilgrims of Mecca were annually assembled by the calls of devotion and commerce: in the free concourse of multitudes, a simple citizen, in his native tongue, might study the political state and character of the tribes, the theory and practice of the Jews and Christians. Some useful strangers might be tempted, or forced, to implore the rights of hospitality; and the enemies of Mahomet have named the Jew, the Persian, and the Syrian monk, whom they accuse of lending their secret aid to the composition of the Koran.[72] Conversation enriches the understanding, but solitude is the school of genius; and the uniformity of a work denotes the hand of a single artist. From his earliest youth Mahomet was addicted to religious contemplation; each year, during the month of Ramadan, he withdrew from the world and from the arms of Cadijah; in the cave of Hera, three miles from Mecca,[73] he consulted the spirit of fraud or enthusiasm, whose abode is not in the heavens, but in the mind of the prophet. The faith which, under the name of *Islam*, he preached to his family and nation is compounded of an eternal truth, and a necessary fiction, That there is only one God, and that Mahomet is the Apostle of God.

It is the boast of the Jewish apologists that, while the learned nations of antiquity were deluded by the fables of polytheism, their simple ancestors of Palestine preserved the knowledge and worship of the true God. The moral attributes of Jehovah may not easily be reconciled with the standard of *human* virtue; his metaphysical qualities are darkly expressed; but each page of the Pentateuch and the Prophets is an evidence of his power; the unity of his name is inscribed on the first table of the law and his sanctuary was never defiled by any visible image of the invisible essence. After the ruin of the temple, the faith of the Hebrew exiles was purified, fixed, and enlightened, by the spiritual devotion of the synagogue; and the authority of Mahomet will not justify his perpetual reproach that the Jews of Mecca or Medina adored Ezra as the son of God.[74] But the children of Israel had ceased to be a people; and the religions of the world were guilty, at least in the eyes of the prophet, of giving sons, or daughters, or companions, to the supreme God. In the rude idolatry of the Arabs, the crime is manifest and audacious; the Sabians are poorly excused by the pre-eminence of the first planet or intelligence in their celestial hierarchy; and in the Magian system the conflict of the two principles betrays the imperfection of the conqueror. The Christians of the seventh century had insensibly relapsed into a semblance of paganism; their public and private vows were addressed to the relics and images that disgraced the temples of the East; the throne of the Almighty was darkened by a cloud of martyrs, and saints, and angels, the objects of popular veneration; and the Collyridian heretics, who flourished in the fruitful soil of Arabia, invested the Virgin Mary with the name and honours of a goddess.[75] The mysteries of the Trinity and Incarnation *appear* to contradict the principle of the divine unity. In their obvious sense they introduce three equal deities, and transform the man Jesus into the substance of the son of God;[76] an orthodox commentary will satisfy only a believing mind; intemperate curiosity and zeal had torn the veil of the sanctuary; and each of the Oriental sects was eager to confess that all, except themselves, deserved the reproach of idolatry and polytheism. The creed of Mahomet is free from suspicion or ambiguity; and the Koran is a glorious testimony to the unity of God. The prophet of Mecca rejected the worship of idols and men, of stars and planets, on the rational principle that whatever rises must set, that whatever is born must die, that whatever is corruptible must decay and perish.[77] In the author of the universe, his rational enthusiasm confessed and adored an infinite and eternal being, without form or place, without issue or similitude, present to our most secret thoughts, existing by the necessity of his own nature, and deriving from himself all moral and intellectual perfection. These sublime truths, thus announced in the language of the prophet,[78] are firmly held by his disciples, and defined with metaphysical precision by the interpreters of the Koran. A philosophic Atheist might subscribe the popular creed of the Mahometans:[79] a creed too sublime perhaps for our present faculties. What object remains for the fancy, or even the understanding, when we have abstracted from the unknown substance all ideas of time and space, of motion and matter, of sensation and reflection? The first principle of reason and revelation was confirmed by the voice of Mahomet; his proselytes, from India to Morocco, are distinguished by the name of *Unitarians*; and the danger of idolatry has been prevented by the interdiction of images. The doctrine of eternal decrees and absolute predestination is strictly embraced by the Mahometans; and they struggle with the common difficulties, *how* to reconcile the prescience of God with the freedom and responsibility of man; *how* to explain the permission of evil under the reign of infinite power and infinite goodness.

The God of nature has written his existence on all his works, and his law in the heart of man. To restore the knowledge of the one, and the practice of the other, has been the real or pretended aim of the prophets of every age; the liberality of Mahomet allowed to his predecessors the same credit which he claimed for himself; and the chain of inspiration was prolonged from the fall of Adam to the promulgation of the Koran.[80] During that period, some rays of prophetic light had been imparted to one hundred and twenty-four thousand of the elect, discriminated by their respective measure of virtue and grace; three hundred and thirteen apostles were sent with a special commission to recall their country from idolatry and vice; one hundred and four volumes have been indicated by the Holy Spirit; and six legislators of transcendent brightness have announced to mankind the six successive revelations of various rights, but of one immutable religion. The authority and station of Adam, Noah, Abraham, Moses, Christ, and Mahomet rise in just gradation above each other; but whosoever hates or rejects any one of the prophets is numbered with the infidels. The writings of the patriarchs were extant only in the apocryphal copies of the Greeks and Syrians;[81] the conduct of Adam had not entitled him to the gratitude or respect of his children; the seven precepts of Noah were observed by an inferior and imperfect class of the proselytes of the synagogues;[82] and the memory of Abraham was obscurely revered by the Sabians in his native land of Chaldaea; of the myriads of prophets, Moses and Christ alone lived and reigned; and the remnant of the inspired writings was comprised in the books of the Old and the New Testament. The miraculous story of Moses is consecrated and embellished in the Koran;[83] and the captive Jews enjoy the secret revenge of imposing their own belief on the nations whose recent creeds they deride. For the author of Christianity, the Mahometans are taught by the prophet to entertain a high and mysterious reverence.[84] 'Verily, Christ Jesus, the son of Mary, is the apostle of God, and his word, which he conveyed unto Mary, and a Spirit proceeding from him: honourable in this world, and in the world to come; and one of those who approach near to the presence of God.'[85] The wonders of the genuine and apocryphal gospels[86] are profusely heaped on his head; and the Latin church has not disdained to borrow from the Koran the immaculate conception[87] of his virgin mother. Yet Jesus was a mere mortal; and, at the day of judgment, his testimony will serve to condemn both the Jews, who reject him as a prophet, and the Christians, who adore him as the Son of God. The malice of his enemies aspersed his reputation and conspired against his life; but their intention only was guilty, a phantom or a criminal was substituted on the cross, and the innocent saint was translated to the seventh heaven.[88] During six hundred years the gospel was the way of truth and salvation; but the Christians insensibly forgot both the laws and the example of their founder; and Mahomet was instructed by the Gnostics to accuse the Church, as well as the synagogue, of corrupting the integrity of the sacred text.[89] The piety of Moses and of Christ rejoiced in the assurance of a future prophet, more illustrious than themselves; the evangelic promise of the *Paraclete*, or Holy Ghost, was prefigured in the name, and accomplished in the person, of Mahomet,[90] the greatest and the last of the apostles of God.

The communication of ideas requires a similitude of thought and language; the discourse of a philosopher would vibrate, without effect, on the ear of a peasant; yet how minute is the distance of *their* understandings, if it be compared with the contact of an infinite and a finite mind, with the word of God expressed by the tongue or the pen of a mortal? The inspiration of the Hebrew prophets, of the apostles and evangelists of Christ, might not be incompatible with the exercise of their reason and memory; and the diversity of their genius is strongly marked in the style and composition of the books of the Old and New Testament. But Mahomet was contented with a character more humble, yet more sublime, of a simple editor; the substance of the Koran,[91] according to himself or his disciples, is uncreated and eternal, subsisting in the essence of the Deity, and inscribed with a pen of light on the table of his everlasting decrees. A paper copy in a volume of silk and gems was brought down to the lowest heaven by the angel Gabriel, who, under the Jewish economy,* had indeed been dispatched on the most important errands; and this trusty messenger successively revealed the chapters and verses to the Arabian prophet. Instead of a perpetual and perfect measure of the divine will, the fragments of the Koran were produced at the discretion of Mahomet; each revelation is suited to the emergencies of his policy or passion; and all contradiction is removed by the saving maxim that any text of scripture is abrogated or modified by any subsequent passage. The word of God and of the apostle was diligently recorded by his disciples on palm-leaves and the shoulder-bones of mutton; and the pages, without order or connection, were cast into a domestic chest, in the custody of one of his wives. Two years after the death of Mahomet, the sacred volume was collected and published by his friend and successor Abubeker; the work was revised by the caliph Othman, in the thirtieth year of the Hegira; and the various editions of the Koran assert the same miraculous privilege of an uniform and incorruptible text. In the spirit of enthusiasm or vanity, the prophet rests the truth of his mission on the merit of his book, audaciously challenges both men and angels to imitate the beauties of a single page, and presumes to assert that God alone could dictate this incomparable performance.[92] This argument is most power-fully addressed to a devout Arabian, whose mind is attuned to faith and rapture, whose ear is delighted by the music of sounds, and whose ignorance is incapable of comparing the productions of human genius.[93] The harmony and copiousness of style will not reach, in a version,* the European infidel; he will peruse, with impatience, the endless incoherent rhapsody of fable, and precept, and declamation, which seldom excites a sentiment or an idea, which sometimes crawls in the dust and is some-times lost in the clouds. The divine attributes exalt the fancy of the Arabian missionary; but his loftiest strains must yield to the sublime simplicity of the book of Job, composed in a remote age, in the same country, and in the same language.[94] If the composition of the Koran exceed the faculties of a man, to what superior intelligence should we ascribe the Iliad of Homer or the Philippics of Demosthenes? In all religions, the life of the founder supplies the silence of his written revelation: the sayings of Mahomet were so many lessons of truth; his actions so many examples of virtue; and the public and private memorials were preserved by his wives and companions. At the end of two hundred years, the *Sonna*, or oral law, was fixed and consecrated by the labours of Al Bochari, who discriminated seven thousand two hundred and seventy-five genuine traditions, from a mass of three hundred thousand reports of a more doubtful or spurious character. Each day the pious author prayed in the temple of Mecca, and performed his ablutions with the water of Zemzem; the pages were successively deposited on the pulpit and the sepulchre of the apostle; and the work has been approved by the four orthodox sects of the Sonnites.[95]

The mission of the ancient prophets, of Moses and of Jesus, had been confirmed by many splendid prodigies; and Mahomet was repeatedly urged, by the inhabitants of Mecca and Medina, to produce a similar evidence of his divine legation: to call down from heaven the angel or the volume of his revelation, to create a garden in the desert, or to kindle a conflagration in the unbelieving city. As often as he is pressed by the demands of the Koreish, he involves himself in the obscure boast of vision and prophecy, appeals to the internal proofs of his doctrine, and shields himself behind the providence of God, who refuses those signs and wonders that would depreciate the merit of faith and aggravate the guilt of infidelity. But the modest or angry tone of his apologies betrays his weakness and vexation; and these passages of scandal establish, beyond suspicion, the integrity of the Koran.[96] The votaries of Mahomet are more assured than himself of his miraculous gifts, and their confidence and credulity increase as they are farther removed from the time and place of his spiritual exploits. They believe or affirm that trees went forth to meet him; that he was saluted by stones; that water gushed from his fingers; that he fed the hungry, cured the sick, and raised the dead; that a beam groaned to him; that a camel complained to him; that a shoulder of mutton informed him of its being poisoned; and that both animate and inanimate nature were equally subject to the apostle of God.[97] His dream of a nocturnal journey is seriously described as a real and corporeal transaction. A mysterious animal, the Borak, conveyed him from the temple of Mecca to that of Jerusalem; with his companion Gabriel, he successively ascended the seven heavens, and received and repaid the salutations of the patriarchs, the prophets, and the angels, in their respective mansions. Beyond the seventh heaven, Mahomet alone was permitted to proceed; he passed the veil of unity, approached within two bow-shots of the throne, and felt a cold that pierced him to the heart, when his shoulder was touched by the hand of God. After this familiar* though important conversation,† he again descended to Jerusalem, mounted the Borak, returned to Mecca, and performed in the tenth part of a night the journey of many thousand years.[98] According to another legend, the apostle confounded in a national assembly the malicious challenge of the Koreish. His resistless word split asunder the orb of the moon: the obedient planet stooped from her station in the sky, accomplished the seven revolutions round the Caaba, saluted Mahomet in the Arabian tongue, and, suddenly contracting her dimensions, entered at the collar, and issued forth through the sleeve, of his shirt.[99] The vulgar are amused with these marvellous tales; but the gravest of the Musulman doctors imitate the modesty of their master, and indulge a latitude of faith or interpretation.[100] They might speciously‡ allege that, in preaching the religion, it was needless to violate the harmony of nature; that a creed unclouded with mystery may be excused from miracles; and that the sword of Mahomet was not less potent than the rod of Moses.

The polytheist is oppressed and distracted by the variety of superstition: a thousand rites of Egyptian origin were interwoven with the essence of the Mosaic law; and the spirit of the Gospel had evaporated in the pageantry of the church. The prophet of Mecca was tempted by prejudice, or policy, or patriotism, to sanctify the rites of the Arabians and the custom of visiting the holy stone of the Caaba. But the precepts of Mahomet himself inculcate a more simple and rational piety: prayer, fasting, and alms are the religious duties of a Musulman; and he is encouraged to hope that prayer will carry him half way to God, fasting will bring him to the door of his palace, and alms will gain him admittance.[101] I. According to the tradition of the nocturnal journey, the apostle, in his personal conference with the Deity, was commanded to impose on his disciples the daily obligation of fifty prayers. By the advice of Moses, he applied for an alleviation of this intolerable burthen; the number was gradually reduced to five; without any dispensation of business or pleasure, or time or place: the devotion of the faithful is repeated at daybreak, at noon, in the afternoon, in the evening, and at the first watch of the night; and, in the present decay of religious fervour, our travellers are edified by the profound humility and attention of the Turks and Persians. Cleanliness is the key of prayer: the frequent lustration of the hands, the face, and the body, which was practised of old by the Arabs, is solemnly enjoined by the Koran; and a permission is formally granted to supply with sand the scarcity of water. The words and attitudes of supplication, as it is performed either sitting, or standing, or prostrate on the ground, are prescribed by custom or authority, but the prayer is poured forth in short and fervent ejaculations; the measure of zeal is not exhausted by a tedious liturgy; and each Musulman, for his own person, is invested with the character of a priest. Among the Theists, who reject the use of images, it has been found necessary to restrain the wanderings of the fancy by directing the eye and the thought towards a *kebla*, or visible point of the horizon. The prophet was at first inclined to gratify the Jews by the choice of Jerusalem; but he soon returned to a more natural partiality; and five times every day the eyes of the nations at Astracan, at Fez, at Delhi, are devoutly turned to the holy temple of Mecca. Yet every spot for the service of God is equally pure; the Mahometans indifferently pray in their chamber or in the street. As a distinction from the Jews and Christians, the Friday in each week is set apart for the useful institution of public worship; the people is assembled in the mosch; and the imam, some respectable elder, ascends the pulpit, to begin the prayer and pronounce the sermon. But the Mahometan religion is destitute of priesthood or sacrifice; and the independent spirit of fanaticism looks down with contempt on the ministers and the slaves of superstition. II. The voluntary[102] penance of the ascetics, the torment and glory of their lives, was odious to a prophet who censured in his companions a rash vow of abstaining from flesh, and women, and sleep, and firmly declared that he would suffer no monks in his religion.[103] Yet he instituted, in each year, a fast of thirty days; and strenuously recommended the observance, as a discipline which purifies the soul and subdues the body, as a salutary exercise of obedience to the will of God and his apostle. During the month of Ramadan, from the rising to the setting of the sun, the

Musulman abstains from eating, and drinking, and women, and baths, and perfumes; from all nourishment that can restore his strength, from all pleasure that can gratify his senses. In the revolution of the lunar year, the Ramadan coincides by turns with the winter cold and the summer heat; and the patient martyr, without assuaging his thirst with a drop of water, must expect the close of a tedious and sultry day. The interdiction of wine, peculiar to some orders of priests or hermits, is converted by Mahomet alone into a positive and general law;[104] and a considerable portion of the globe has abjured, at his command, the use of that salutary though dangerous liquor. These painful restraints are, doubtless, infringed by the libertine and eluded by the hypocrite; but the legislator, by whom they are enacted, cannot surely be accused of alluring his proselytes by the indulgence of their sensual appetites. III. The charity of the Mahometans descends to the animal creation; and the Koran repeatedly inculcates, not as a merit, but as a strict and indispensable duty, the relief of the indigent and unfortunate. Mahomet, perhaps, is the only lawgiver who has defined the precise measure of charity: the standard may vary with the degree and nature of property, as it consists either in money, in corn or cattle, in fruits or merchandise; but the Musulman does not accomplish the law, unless he bestows a *tenth* of his revenue; and, if his conscience accuses him of fraud or extortion, the tenth, under the idea of restitution, is enlarged to a *fifth*.[105] Benevolence is the foundation of justice, since we are forbid to injure those whom we are bound to assist. A prophet may reveal the secrets of heaven and of futurity; but in his moral precepts he can only repeat the lessons of our own hearts.

The two articles of belief and the four practical duties of Islam are guarded by rewards and punishments; and the faith of the Musulman is devoutly fixed on the event of the judgment and the last day. The prophet has not presumed to determine the moment of that awful catastrophe, though he darkly announces the signs, both in heaven and earth, which will precede the universal dissolution, when life shall be destroyed and the order of creation shall be confounded in the primitive chaos. At the blast of the trumpet, new worlds will start into being; angels, genii,* and men will arise from the dead, and the human soul will again be united to the body. The doctrine of the resurrection was first entertained by the Egyptians;[106] and their mummies were embalmed, their pyramids were constructed, to preserve the ancient mansion of the soul, during a period of three thousand years. But the attempt is partial and unavailing; and it is with a more philosophic spirit that Mahomet relies on the omnipotence of the Creator, whose word can reanimate the breathless clay, and collect the innumerable atoms that no longer retain their form or substance.[107] The intermediate state of the soul it is hard to decide; and those who most firmly believe her immaterial nature are at a loss to understand how she can think or act without the agency of the organs of sense.

The reunion of the soul and body will be followed by the final judgment of mankind; and, in his copy of the Magian picture, the prophet has too faithfully represented the forms of proceeding, and even the slow and successive operations, of an earthly tribunal. By his intolerant adversaries he is upbraided for extending, even to themselves, the hope of salvation, for asserting the blackest heresy that every man who believes in God, and accomplishes good works, may expect in the last day a favourable sentence. Such rational indifference is ill adapted to the character of a fanatic; nor is it probable that a messenger from heaven should depreciate the value and necessity of his own revelation. In the idiom of the Koran,[108] the belief of God is inseparable from that of Mahomet; the good works are those which he has enjoined; and the two qualifications imply the profession of Islam, to which all nations and all sects are equally invited. Their spiritual blindness, though excused by ignorance and crowned with virtue, will be scourged with everlasting torments; and the tears which Mahomet shed over the tomb of his mother, for whom he was forbidden to pray, display a striking contrast of humanity and enthusiasm.*[109] The doom of the infidels is common: the measure of their guilt and punishment is determined by the degree of evidence which they have rejected, by the magnitude of the errors which they have entertained; the eternal mansions of the Christians, the Jews, the Sabians, the Magians, and the idolaters, are sunk below each other in the abyss; and the lowest hell is reserved for the faithless hypocrites who have assumed the mask of religion. After the greater part of mankind has been condemned for their opinions, the true believers only will be judged by their actions. The good and evil of each Musulman will be accurately weighed in a real or allegorical balance, and a singular mode of compensation will be allowed for the payment of injuries: the aggressor will refund an equivalent of his own good actions, for the benefit of the person whom he has wronged; and, if he should be destitute of any moral property, the weight of his sins will be loaded with an adequate share of the demerits of the sufferer. According as the shares of guilt or virtue shall preponderate, the sentence will be pronounced, and all, without distinction, will pass over the sharp and perilous bridge of the abyss; but the innocent, treading in the footsteps of Mahomet, will gloriously enter the gates of paradise, while the guilty will fall into the first and mildest of the seven hells. The term of expiation will vary from nine hundred to seven thousand years; but the prophet has judiciously promised that *all* his disciples, whatever may be their sins, shall be saved, by their own faith and his intercession, from eternal damnation. It is not surprising that superstition should act most powerfully on the fears of her votaries, since the human fancy can paint with more energy the misery than the bliss of a future life. With the two simple elements of darkness and fire we create a sensation of pain, which may be aggravated to an infinite degree by the idea of endless duration. But the same idea operates with an opposite effect on the continuity of pleasure; and too much of our present enjoyments is obtained from the relief, or the comparison, of evil. It is natural enough that an Arabian prophet should dwell with rapture on the groves, the fountains, and the rivers of paradise; but, instead of inspiring the blessed inhabitants with a liberal taste for harmony and science, conversation and friendship, he idly celebrates the pearls and diamonds, the robes of silk, palaces of marble, dishes of gold, rich wines, artificial dainties, numerous attendants, and the whole train of sensual and costly luxury, which becomes insipid to the owner, even in the short period of this mortal life. Seventy-two *Houris*, or black-eyed girls of resplendent beauty, blooming youth, virgin purity, and exquisite sensibility, will be created for the use of the meanest believer; a moment of pleasure will be prolonged to a thousand years, and his faculties will be increased an hundredfold, to render him worthy of his felicity. Notwithstanding a vulgar prejudice, the gates of heaven will be open to both sexes; but Mahomet has not specified the male companions of the female elect, lest he should either alarm the jealousy of their former husbands or disturb their felicity by the suspicion of an everlasting marriage. This image of a carnal paradise has provoked the indignation, perhaps the envy, of the monks: they declaim against the impure religion of Mahomet; and his modest apologists are driven to the poor excuse of figures and allegories. But the sounder and more consistent party adhere, without shame, to the literal interpretation of the Koran; useless would be the resurrection of the body, unless it were restored to the possession and exercise of its worthiest faculties; and the union of sensual and intellectual enjoyment is requisite to complete the happiness of the double animal, the perfect man. Yet the joys of the Mahometan paradise will not be confined to the indulgence of luxury and appetite; and the prophet has expressly declared that all meaner happiness will be forgotten and despised by the saints and martyrs, who shall be admitted to the beatitude of the divine vision.[110]

The first and most arduous conquests of Mahomet[111] were those of his wife, his servant, his pupil, and his friend;[112] since he presented himself as a prophet to those who were most conversant with his infirmities as a man. Yet Cadijah believed the words, and cherished the glory, of her husband; the obsequious and affectionate Zeid was tempted by the prospect of freedom; the illustrious Ali, the son of Abu Taleb, embraced the sentiments of his cousin with the spirit of a youthful hero; and the wealth, the moderation, the veracity of Abubeker confirmed the religion of the prophet whom he was destined to succeed. By his persuasion, ten of the most respectable citizens of Mecca were introduced to the private lessons of Islam; they yielded to the voice of reason and enthusiasm; they repeated the fundamental creed: 'there is but one God, and Mahomet is the apostle of God'; and their faith, even in this life, was rewarded with riches and honours, with the command of armies and the government of kingdoms. Three years were silently employed in the conversion of fourteen proselytes, the first fruits of his mission; but in the fourth year he assumed the prophetic office, and, resolving to impart to his family the light of divine truth, he prepared a banquet, a lamb, as it is said, and a bowl of milk, for the entertainment of forty guests of the race of Hashem. 'Friends and kinsmen,' said Mahomet to the assembly, 'I offer you, and I alone can offer, the most precious of gifts, the treasures of this world and of the world to come. God has commanded me to call you to his service. Who among you will support my burthen? Who among you will be my companion and my vizir?'[113] No answer was returned, till the silence of astonishment, and doubt, and contempt was at length broken by the impatient courage of Ali, a youth in the fourteenth year of his age. 'O prophet, I am the man; whosoever rises against thee, I will dash out his teeth, tear out his eyes, break his legs, rip up his belly. O prophet, I will be thy vizir over them.' Mahomet accepted his offer with transport, and Abu Taleb was ironically exhorted to respect the superior dignity of his son. In a more serious tone, the father of Ali advised his nephew to relinquish his impracticable design. 'Spare your remonstrances,' replied the intrepid fanatic to his uncle and benefactor; 'if they should place the sun on my right hand and the moon on my left, they should not divert me from my course.' He persevered ten years in the exercise of his mission; and the religion which has overspread the East and the West advanced with a slow and painful progress within the walls of Mecca. Yet Mahomet enjoyed the satisfaction of beholding the increase of his infant congregation of Unitarians, who revered him as a prophet, and to whom he seasonably dispensed the spiritual nourishment of the Koran. The number of proselytes may be esteemed* by the absence of eighty-three men and eighteen women, who retired to Ethiopia in the seventh year of his mission; and his party was fortified by the timely conversion of his uncle Hamza, and of the fierce and inflexible Omar, who signalised in the cause of Islam the same zeal which he had exerted for its destruction. Nor was the charity of Mahomet confined to the tribe of Koreish or the precincts of Mecca: on solemn festivals, in the days of pilgrimage, he frequented the Caaba, accosted the strangers of every tribe, and urged, both in private converse and public discourse, the belief and worship of a sole Deity. Conscious of his reason and of his weakness, he asserted the liberty of conscience, and disclaimed the use of religious violence;[114] but he called the Arabs to repentance, and conjured them to remember the ancient idolaters of Ad and Thamud, whom the divine justice had swept away from the face of the earth.[115]

The people of Mecca was hardened in their unbelief by superstition and envy. The elders of the city, the uncles of the prophet, affected to despise the presumption of an orphan, the reformer of his country; the pious orations of Mahomet in the Caaba were answered by the clamours of Abu Taleb. 'Citizens and pilgrims, listen not to the tempter, hearken not to his impious novelties. Stand fast in the worship of Al Lâta and Al Uzzah.' Yet the son of Abdallah was ever dear to the aged chief; and he protected the fame and person of his nephew against the assaults of the Koreishites, who had long been jealous of the pre-eminence of the family of Hashem. Their malice was coloured with the pretence of religion; in the age of Job, the crime of impiety was punished by the Arabian magistrate;[116] and Mahomet was guilty of deserting and denying the national deities. But so loose was the policy of Mecca that the leaders of the Koreish, instead of accusing a criminal, were compelled to employ the measures of persuasion or violence. They repeatedly addressed Abu Taleb in the style of reproach and menace. 'Thy nephew reviles our religion; he accuses our wise forefathers of ignorance and folly; silence him quickly, lest he kindle tumult and discord in the city. If he persevere, we shall draw our swords against him and his adherents, and thou wilt be responsible for the blood of thy fellow-citizens.' The weight and moderation of Abu Taleb eluded the violence of religious faction: the most helpless or timid of the disciples retired to Ethiopia; and the prophet withdrew himself to various places of strength in the town and country. As he was still supported by his family, the rest of the tribe of Koreish engaged themselves to renounce all intercourse with the children of Hashem, neither to buy nor sell, neither to marry nor to give in marriage, but to pursue them with implacable enmity, till they should deliver the person of Mahomet to the justice of the gods. The decree was suspended* in the Caaba before the eyes of the nation; the messengers of the Koreish pursued the Musulman exiles in the heart of Africa; they besieged the prophet and his most faithful followers, intercepted their water, and inflamed their mutual animosity by the retaliation of injuries and insults. A doubtful truce restored the appearances of concord: till the death of Abu Taleb abandoned Mahomet to the power of his enemies, at the moment when he was deprived of his domestic comforts by the loss of his faithful and generous Cadijah. Abu Sophian, the chief of the branch of Ommiyah, succeeded to the principality of the republic of Mecca. A zealous votary of the idols, a mortal foe of the line of Hashem, he convened an assembly of the Koreishites and their allies, to decide the fate of the apostle. His imprisonment might provoke the despair of his enthusiasm; and the exile of an eloquent and popular fanatic would diffuse the mischief through the provinces of Arabia. His death was resolved; and they agreed that a sword from each tribe should be buried in his heart, to divide the guilt of his blood and baffle the vengeance of the Hashemites. An angel or a spy revealed their conspiracy; and flight was the only resource of Mahomet.[117] At the dead of night, accompanied by his friend Abubeker, he silently escaped from his house; the assassins watched at the door; but they were deceived by the figure of Ali, who reposed on the bed, and was covered with the green vestment, of the apostle. The Koreish respected the piety of the heroic youth; but some verses of Ali, which are still extant, exhibit an interesting picture of his anxiety, his tenderness, and his religious confidence. Three days Mahomet and his companion were concealed in the cave of Thor, at the distance of a league from Mecca; and in the close of each evening they received from the son and daughter of Abubeker a secret supply of intelligence and food. The diligence of the Koreish explored every haunt in the neighbourhood of the city; they arrived at the entrance of the cavern; but the providential deceit of a spider's web and a pigeon's nest is supposed to convince them that the place was solitary and inviolate. 'We are only two,' said the trembling Abubeker. 'There is a third,' replied the prophet; 'it is God himself.' No sooner was the pursuit abated than the two fugitives issued from the rock and mounted their camels; on the road to Medina, they were overtaken by the emissaries of the Koreish; they redeemed themselves with prayers and promises from their hands. In this eventful moment the lance of an Arab might have changed the history of the world. The flight of the prophet from Mecca to Medina has fixed the memorable era of the *Hegira*,[118] which, at the end of twelve centuries, still discriminates the lunar years of the Mahometan nations.[119]

The religion of the Koran might have perished in its cradle, had not Medina embraced with faith and reverence the holy outcasts of Mecca. Medina, or the *city*, known under the name of Yathreb before it was sanctified by the throne of the prophet, was divided between the tribes of the Charegites and the Awsites, whose hereditary feud was rekindled by the slightest provocations: two colonies of Jews, who boasted a sacerdotal race, were their humble allies, and without converting the Arabs, they introduced the taste of science and religion, which distinguished Medina as the city of the Book. Some of her noblest citizens, in a pilgrimage to the Caaba, were converted by the preaching of Mahomet; on their return, they diffused the belief of God and his prophet, and the new alliance was ratified by their deputies in two secret and nocturnal interviews on a hill in the suburbs of Mecca. In the first, ten Charegites and two Awsites, united in faith and love, protested,* in the name of their wives, their children, and their absent brethren, that they would for ever profess the creed, and observe the precepts, of the Koran. The second was a political association, the first vital spark of the empire of the Saracens.[120] Seventy-three men and two women of Medina held a solemn conference with Mahomet, his kinsmen, and his disciples; and pledged themselves to each other by a mutual oath of fidelity. They promised in the name of the city that, if he should be banished, they would receive him as a confederate, obey him as a leader, and defend him to the last extremity, like their wives and children. 'But, if you are recalled by your country,' they asked with a flattering anxiety, 'will you not abandon your new allies?' 'All things,' replied Mahomet with a smile, 'are now common between us; your blood is as my blood, your ruin as my ruin. We are bound to each other by the ties of honour and interest. I am your friend, and the enemy of your foes.' 'But, if we are killed in your service, what,' exclaimed the deputies of Medina, 'will be our reward?' 'Paradise', replied the prophet. 'Stretch forth thy hand.' He stretched it forth, and they reiterated the oath of allegiance and fidelity. Their treaty was ratified by the people, who unanimously embraced the profession of Islam; they rejoiced in the exile of the apostle, but they trembled for his safety, and impatiently expected his arrival. After a perilous and rapid journey along the seacoast, he halted at Koba, two miles from the city, and made his public entry into Medina, sixteen days after his flight from Mecca. Five hundred of the citizens advanced to meet him; he was hailed with acclamations of loyalty and devotion; Mahomet was mounted on a she-camel, an umbrella shaded his head, and a turban was unfurled before him to supply the deficiency of a standard. His bravest disciples, who had been scattered by the storm, assembled round his person; and the equal, though various, merit of the Moslems was distinguished by the names of *Mohagerians* and *Ansars*, the fugitives of Mecca, and the auxiliaries of Medina. To eradicate the seeds of jealousy, Mahomet judiciously coupled his principal followers with the rights and obligations of brethren; and, when Ali found himself without a peer, the prophet tenderly declared that *he* would be the companion and brother of the noble youth. The expedient was crowned with success; the holy fraternity was respected in peace and war, and the two parties vied with each other in a generous emulation of courage and fidelity. Once only the concord was slightly ruffled by an accidental quarrel: a patriot of Medina arraigned the insolence of the strangers, but the hint of their expulsion was heard with abhorrence, and his own son most eagerly offered to lay at the apostle's feet the head of his father.

From his establishment at Medina, Mahomet assumed the exercise of the regal and sacerdotal office; and it was impious to appeal from a judge whose decrees were inspired by the divine wisdom. A small portion of ground, the patrimony of two orphans, was acquired by gift or purchase;[121] on that chosen spot he built an house and a mosch, more venerable in their rude simplicity than the palaces and temples of the Assyrian caliphs. His seal of gold, or silver, was inscribed with the apostolic title; when he prayed and preached in the weekly assembly, he leaned against the trunk of a palm-tree; and it was long before he indulged himself in the use of a chair or pulpit of rough timber.[122] After a reign of six years, fifteen hundred Moslems, in arms and in the field, renewed their oath of allegiance; and their chief repeated the assurance of protection, till the death of the last member of the final dissolution of the party. It was in the same camp that the deputy of Mecca was astonished by the attention of the faithful to the words and looks of the prophet, by the eagerness with which they collected his spittle, an hair that dropped on the ground, the refuse water of his lustrations, as if they participated in some degree of the prophetic virtue. 'I have seen,' said he, 'the Chosroes of Persia and the Caesar of Rome, but never did I behold a king among his subjects like Mahomet among his companions.' The devout fervour of enthusiasm acts with more energy and truth than the cold and formal servility of courts.

In the state of nature every man has a right to defend, by force of arms, his person and his possessions; to repel, or even to prevent, the violence of his enemies, and to extend his hostilities to a reasonable measure of satisfaction and retaliation. In the free society of the Arabs, the duties of subject and citizen imposed a feeble restraint; and Mahomet, in the exercise of a peaceful and benevolent mission, had been despoiled and banished by the injustice of his countrymen. The choice of an independent people had exalted the fugitive of Mecca to the rank of a sovereign; and he was invested with the just prerogative of forming alliances and of waging offensive or defensive war. The imperfection of human rights was supplied and armed by the plenitude of divine power; the prophet of Medina assumed, in his new revelations, a fiercer and more sanguinary tone, which proves that his former moderation was the effect of weakness:[123] the means of persuasion had been tried, the season of forbearance was elapsed, and he was now commanded to propagate his religion by the sword, to destroy the monuments of idolatry, and, without regarding the sanctity of days or months, to pursue the unbelieving nations of the earth. The same bloody precepts, so repeatedly inculcated in the Koran, are ascribed by the author to the Pentateuch and the Gospel. But the mild tenor of the evangelic style may explain an ambiguous text, that Jesus did not bring peace on the earth, but a sword: his patient and humble virtues should not be confounded with the intolerant zeal of princes and bishops, who have disgraced the name of his disciples. In the prosecution of religious war, Mahomet might appeal with more propriety to the example of Moses, of the judges, and the kings of Israel. The military laws of the Hebrews are still more rigid than those of the Arabian legislator.[124] The Lord of Hosts marched in person before the Jews; if a city resisted their summons, the males, without distinction, were put to the sword; the seven nations of Canaan were devoted to destruction; and neither repentance nor conversion could shield them from the inevitable doom that no creature within their precincts should be left alive. The fair option of friendship, or submission, or battle, was proposed to the enemies of Mahomet. If they professed the creed of Islam, they were admitted to all the temporal and spiritual benefits of his primitive disciples, and marched under the same banner to extend the religion which they had embraced. The clemency of the prophet was decided by his interest, yet he seldom trampled on a prostrate enemy; and he seems to promise that, on the payment of a tribute, the least guilty of his unbelieving subjects might be indulged in their worship, or at least in their imperfect faith. In the first months of his reign, he practised the lessons of holy warfare, and displayed his white banner before the gates of Medina; the martial apostle fought in person at nine battles or sieges;[125] and fifty enterprises of war were achieved in ten years by himself or his lieutenants The Arab continued to unite the professions of a merchant and a robber; and his petty excursions, for the defence or the attack of a caravan, insensibly prepared his troops for the conquest of Arabia. The distribution of the spoil was regulated by a divine law;[126] the whole was faithfully collected in one common mass; a fifth of the gold and silver, the prisoners and cattle, the moveables and immoveables, was reserved by the prophet for pious and charitable uses; the remainder was shared in adequate portions by the soldiers who had obtained the victory or guarded the camp; the rewards of the slain devolved to their widows and orphans; and the increase of cavalry was encouraged by the allotment of a double share to the horse and to the man. From all sides the roving Arabs were allured to the standard of religion and plunder; the apostle sanctified the licence of embracing the female captives as their wives or concubines; and the enjoyment of wealth and beauty was a feeble type* of the joys of paradise prepared for the valiant martyrs of the faith. 'The sword,' says Mahomet, 'is the key of heaven and of hell: a drop of blood shed in the cause of God, a night spent in arms, is of more avail than two months of fasting or prayer: whosoever falls in battle, his sins are forgiven; at the day of judgment his wounds shall be resplendent as vermilion, and odoriferous as musk; and the loss of his limbs shall be supplied by the wings of angels and cherubim.' The intrepid souls of the Arabs were fired with enthusiasm; the picture of the invisible world was strongly painted on their imagination; and the death which they had always despised became an object of hope and desire. The Koran inculcates, in the most absolute sense, the tenets of faith and predestination, which would extinguish both industry and virtue, if the actions of man were governed by his speculative belief. Yet their influence in every age has exalted the courage of the Saracens and Turks. The first companions of Mahomet advanced to battle with a fearless confidence; there is no danger where there is no chance: they were ordained to perish in their beds; or they were safe and invulnerable amidst the darts of the enemy.[127]

Perhaps the Koreish would have been content with the flight of Mahomet, had they not been provoked and alarmed by the vengeance of an enemy who could intercept their Syrian trade as it passed and repassed through the territory of Medina. Abu Sophian himself, with only thirty or forty followers, conducted a wealthy caravan of a thousand camels; the fortune or dexterity of his march escaped the vigilance of Mahomet; but the chief of the Koreish was informed that the holy robbers were placed in ambush to await his return. He dispatched a messenger to his brethren of Mecca and they were roused by the fear of losing the merchandise and their provisions, unless they hastened to his relief with the military force of the city. The sacred band of Mahomet was formed of three hundred and thirteen Moslems, of whom seventy-seven were fugitives, and the rest auxiliaries; they mounted by turns a train of seventy camels (the camels of Yathreb were formidable in war); but such was the poverty of his first disciples that only two could appear on horseback in the field.[128] In the fertile and famous vale of Beder,[129] three stations from Medina, he was informed by his scouts of the caravan that approached on the one side; of the Koreish, one hundred horse, eight hundred and fifty foot, who advanced on the other. After a short debate, he sacrificed the prospect of wealth to the pursuit of glory and revenge; and a slight entrenchment was formed to cover his troops, and a stream of fresh water that glided through the valley. 'O God,' he exclaimed as the numbers of the Koreish descended from the hills, 'O God, if these are destroyed, by whom wilt thou be worshipped on the earth? – Courage, my children; close your ranks; discharge your arrows, and the day is your own.' At these words he placed himself, with Abubeker, on a throne or pulpit,[130] and instantly demanded the succour of Gabriel and three thousand angels. His eye was fixed on the field of battle; the Musulmans fainted* and were pressed; in that decisive moment the prophet started from his throne, mounted his horse, and cast a handful of sand into the air: 'Let their faces be covered with confusion.' Both armies heard the thunder of his voice; their fancy beheld the angelic warriors;[131] the Koreish trembled and fled; seventy of the bravest were slain; and seventy captives adorned the first victory of the faithful. The dead bodies of the Koreish were despoiled and insulted; two of the most obnoxious prisoners were punished with death; and the ransom of the others, four thousand drachms of silver, compensated in some degree the escape of the caravan. But it was in vain that the camels of Abu Sophian explored a new road through the desert and along the Euphrates; they were overtaken by the diligence of the Musulmans; and wealthy must have been the prize, if twenty thousand drachms could be set apart for the fifth† of the apostle. The resentment of the public and private loss stimulated Abu Sophian to collect a body of three thousand men, seven hundred of whom were armed with cuirasses, and two hundred were mounted on horseback; three thousand camels attended his march; and his wife Henda, with fifteen matrons of Mecca, incessantly sounded their timbrels‡ to animate the troops, and to magnify the greatness of Hobal, the most popular deity of the Caaba. The standard of God and Mahomet was upheld by nine hundred and fifty believers; the disproportion of numbers was not more alarming than in the field of Beder; and their presumption of victory prevailed against the divine and human sense of the apostle. The second battle was fought on mount Ohud, six miles to the north of Medina;[132] the Koreish advanced in the form of a crescent; and the right wing of cavalry was led by Caled, the fiercest and most successful of the Arabian warriors. The troops of Mahomet were skilfully posted on the declivity of the hill; and their rear was guarded by a detachment of fifty archers. The weight of their charge impelled and broke the centre of the idolaters; but in the pursuit they lost the advantage of their ground; the archers deserted their stations; the Musulmans were tempted by the spoil, disobeyed their general, and disordered their ranks. The intrepid Caled, wheeling his cavalry on their flank and rear, exclaimed with a loud voice, that Mahomet was slain. He was indeed wounded in the face with a javelin; two of his teeth were shattered with a stone; yet, in the midst of tumult and dismay, he reproached the infidels with the murder of a prophet; and blessed the friendly hand that staunched his blood and conveyed him to a place of safety. Seventy martyrs died for the sins of the people; they fell, said the apostle, in pairs, each brother embracing his lifeless companion;[133] their bodies were mangled by the inhuman females of Mecca; and the wife of Abu Sophian tasted the entrails of Hamza, the uncle of Mahomet. They might applaud their superstition and satiate their fury; but the Musulmans soon rallied in the field, and the Koreish wanted strength or courage to undertake the seige of Medina. It was attacked the ensuing year by an army of ten thousand enemies; and this third expedition is variously named from the *nations*, which marched under the banner of Abu Sophian, from the *ditch* which was drawn before the city, and a camp of three thousand Musulmans. The prudence of Mahomet declined a general engagement; the valour of Ali was signalised in single combat; and the war was protracted twenty days, till the final separation of the confederates. A tempest of wind, rain, and hail overturned their tents; their private quarrels were fomented by an insidious adversary; and the Koreish, deserted by their allies, no longer hoped to subvert the throne or to check the conquests of their invincible exile.[134]

The choice of Jerusalem for the first kebla* of prayer discovers the early propensity of Mahomet in favour of the Jews; and happy would it have been for their temporal interest, had they recognised, in the Arabian prophet, the hope of Israel and the promised Messiah. Their obstinacy converted his friendship into implacable hatred, with which he pursued that unfortunate people to the last moment of his life; and, in the double character of an apostle and a conqueror, his persecution was extended to both worlds.[135] The Kainoka dwelt at Medina, under the protection of the city: he seized the occasion of an accidental tumult, and summoned them to embrace his religion or contend with him in battle. 'Alas,' replied the trembling Jews, 'we are ignorant of the use of arms, but we persevere in the faith and worship of our fathers: why wilt thou reduce us to the necessity of a just defence?' The unequal conflict was terminated in fifteen days; and it was with extreme reluctance that Mahomet yielded to the importunity of his allies and consented to spare the lives of the captives. But their riches were confiscated; their arms became more effectual in the hands of the Musulmans; and a wretched colony of seven hundred exiles was driven with their wives and children to implore a refuge on the confines of Syria. The Nadhirites were more guilty, since they conspired in a friendly interview to assassinate the prophet. He besieged their castle three miles from Medina, but their resolute defence obtained an honourable capitulation; and the garrison, sounding their trumpets and beating their drums, was permitted to depart with the honours of war. The Jews had excited and joined the war of the Koreish: no sooner had the *nations* retired from the *ditch*, than Mahomet, without laying aside his armour, marched on the same day to extirpate the hostile race of the children of Koraidha. After a resistance of twenty-five days, they surrendered at discretion. They trusted to the intercession of their old allies of Medina; they could not be ignorant that fanaticism obliterates the feelings of humanity. A venerable elder, to whose judgment they appealed, pronounced the sentence of their death: seven hundred Jews were dragged in chains to the marketplace of the city; they descended alive into the grave prepared for their execution and burial; and the apostle beheld with an inflexible eye the slaughter of his helpless enemies. Their sheep and camels were inherited by the Musulmans; three hundred cuirasses, five hundred pikes, a thousand lances, composed the most useful portion of the spoil. Six days' journey to the north-east of Medina, the ancient and wealthy town of Chaibar was the seat of the Jewish power in Arabia; the territory, a fertile spot in the desert, was covered with plantations and cattle, and protected by eight castles, some of which were esteemed of impregnable strength. The forces of Mahomet consisted of two hundred horse and fourteen hundred foot: in the succession of eight regular and painful sieges, they were exposed to danger, and fatigue, and hunger; and the most undaunted chiefs despaired of the event. The apostle revived their faith and courage by the example of Ali, on whom he bestowed the surname of the Lion of God: perhaps we may believe that an Hebrew champion of gigantic stature was cloven to the chest by his irresistible scymetar; but we cannot praise the modesty of romance, which represents him as tearing from its hinges the gate of a fortress and wielding the ponderous buckler in his left hand.[136] After the reduction of the castles, the town of Chaibar submitted to the yoke. The chief of the tribe was tortured in the presence of Mahomet, to force a confession of his hidden treasure; the industry of the shepherds and husbandmen was rewarded with a precarious toleration; they were permitted, so long as it should please the conqueror, to improve their patrimony, in equal shares, for *his* emolument and their own. Under the reign of Omar, the Jews of Chaibar were transplanted to Syria; and the caliph alleged the injunction of his dying master, that one and the true religion should be professed in his native land of Arabia.[137]

Five times each day the eyes of Mahomet were turned towards Mecca,[138] and he was urged by the most sacred and powerful motives to revisit, as a conqueror, the city and the temple from whence he had been driven as an exile. The Caaba was present to his waking and sleeping fancy; an idle dream was translated into vision and prophecy; he unfurled the holy banner; and a rash promise of success too hastily dropped from the lips of the apostle. His march from Medina to Mecca displayed the peaceful and solemn pomp of a pilgrimage: seventy camels, chosen and bedecked for sacrifice, preceded the van; the sacred territory was respected, and the captives were dismissed without ransom to ploclaim his clemency and devotion. But no sooner did Mahomet descend into the plain, within a day's journey of the city, than he exclaimed, 'They have clothed themselves with the skins of tigers'; the numbers and resolution of the Koreish opposed his progress; and the roving Arabs of the desert might desert or betray a leader whom they had followed for the hopes of spoil. The intrepid fanatic sunk into a cool and cautious politician: he waived in the treaty his title of apostle of God, concluded with the Koreish and their allies a truce of ten years, engaged to restore the fugitives of Mecca who should embrace his religion, and stipulated only, for the ensuing year, the humble privilege of entering the city as a friend and of remaining three days to accomplish the rites of the pilgrimage. A cloud of shame and sorrow hung on the retreat of the Musulmans, and their disappointment might justly accuse the failure of a prophet who had so often appealed to the evidence of success. The faith and hope of the pilgrims were rekindled by the prospect of Mecca; their swords were sheathed; seven times in the footsteps of the apostle they encompassed the Caaba; the Koreish had retired to the hills, and Mahomet, after the customary sacrifice, evacuated the city on the fourth day. The people was edified by his devotion; the hostile chiefs were awed, or divided, or seduced; and both Caled and Amrou, the future conquerors of Syria and Egypt, most seasonably deserted the sinking cause of idolatry. The power of Mahomet was increased by the submission of the Arabian tribes: ten thousand soldiers were assembled for the conquest of Mecca, and the idolaters, the weaker party, were easily convicted of violating the truce. Enthusiasm and discipline impelled the march and preserved the secret, till the blaze of ten thousand fires proclaimed to the astonished Koreish the design, the approach, and the irresistible force of the enemy. The haughty Abu Sophian presented the keys of the city; admired the variety of arms and ensigns that passed before him in review; observed that the son of Abdallah had acquired a mighty kingdom; and confessed, under the scymetar of Omar, that he was the apostle of the true God. The return of Marius* and Sulla[†] was stained with the blood of the Romans; the revenge of Mahomet was stimulated by religious zeal, and his injured followers were eager to execute or to prevent[‡] the order of a massacre. Instead of indulging their passions and his own,[139] the victorious exile forgave the guilt, and united the factions, of Mecca. His troops in three divisions marched into the city; eight-and-twenty of the inhabitants were slain by the sword of Caled; eleven men and six women were proscribed by the sentence of Mahomet; but he blamed the cruelty of his lieutenant; and several of the most obnoxious victims were indebted for their lives to his clemency or contempt. The chiefs of the Koreish were prostrate at his feet. 'What mercy can you expect from the man whom you have wronged?' 'We confide in the generosity of our kinsman.' 'And you shall not confide in vain: Begone! you are safe, you are free.' The people of Mecca deserved[§] their pardon by the profession of Islam; and, after an exile of seven years, the fugitive missionary was enthroned as the prince and prophet of his native country.[140] But the three hundred and sixty idols of the Caaba were ignominiously broken; the house of God was purified and adorned; as an example to future times, the apostle again fulfilled the duties of a pilgrim; and a perpetual law was enacted that no unbeliever should dare to set his foot on the territory of the holy city.[141]

The conquest of Mecca determined the faith and obedience of the Arabian tribes;[142] who, according to the vicissitudes of fortune, had obeyed or disregarded the eloquence or the arms of the prophet. Indifference for rites and opinions still marks the character of the Bedoweens; and they might accept, as loosely as they hold, the doctrine of the Koran. Yet an obstinate remnant still adhered to the religion and liberty of their ancestors, and the war of Honain derived a proper appellation from the *idols*, whom Mahomet had vowed to destroy, and whom the confederates of Tayef had sworn to defend.[143] Four thousand Pagans advanced with secrecy and speed to surprise the conqueror; they pitied and despised the supine negligence of the Koreish, but they depended on the wishes, and perhaps the aid, of a people which had so lately renounced their gods and bowed beneath the yoke of their enemy. The banners of Medina and Mecca were displayed by the prophet; a crowd of Bedoweens increased the strength or numbers of the army, and twelve thousand Musulmans entertained a rash and sinful presumption of their invincible strength. They descended without precaution into the valley of Honain; the heights had been occupied by the archers and slingers of the confederates; their numbers were oppressed, their discipline was confounded, their courage was appalled, and the Koreish smiled at their impending destruction. The prophet, on his white mule, was encompassed by the enemies; he attempted to rush against their spears in search of a glorious death; ten of his faithful companions interposed their weapons and their breasts; three of these fell dead at his feet. 'O my brethren,' he repeatedly cried with sorrow and indignation, 'I am the son of Abdallah, I am the apostle of truth! O man, stand fast in the faith! O God, send down thy succour!' His uncle Abbas, who, like the heroes of Homer, excelled in the loudness of his voice, made the valley resound with the recital of the gifts and promises of God; the flying Moslems returned from all sides to the holy standard; and Mahomet observed with pleasure that the furnace was again rekindled; his conduct and example restored the battle, and he animated his victorious troops to inflict a merciless revenge on the authors of their shame. From the field of Honain he marched without delay to the siege of Tayef, sixty miles to the south-east of Mecca, a fortress of strength, whose fertile lands produce the fruits of Syria in the midst of the Arabian desert. A friendly tribe, instructed (I know not how) in the art of sieges, supplied him with a train of battering-rams and military engines, with a body of five hundred artificers.* But it was in vain that he offered freedom to the slaves of Tayef; that he violated his own laws by the extirpation of the fruit-trees; that the ground was opened by the miners;* that the breach was assaulted by the troops. After a siege of twenty days, the prophet sounded a retreat; but he retreated with a song of devout triumph, and affected to pray for the repentance and safety of the unbelieving city. The spoil of this fortunate expedition amounted to six thousand captives, twenty-four thousand camels, forty thousand sheep, and four thousand ounces of silver; a tribe who had fought at Honain, redeemed their prisoners by the sacrifice of their idols; but Mahomet compensated the loss by resigning to the soldiers his fifth of the plunder, and wished for their sake that he possessed as many head of cattle as there were trees in the province of Tehama. Instead of chastising the disaffection of the Koreish, he endeavoured to cut out their tongues (his own expression) and to secure their attachment by a superior measure of liberality: Abu Sophian alone was presented with three hundred camels and twenty ounces of silver; and Mecca was sincerely converted to the profitable religion of the Koran.

The *fugitives* and *auxiliaries* complained that they who had borne the burthen were neglected in the season of victory. 'Alas,' replied their artful leader, 'suffer me to conciliate these recent enemies, these doubtful proselytes, by the gift of some perishable goods. To your guard I entrust my life and fortunes. You are the companions of my exile, of my kingdom, of my paradise.' He was followed by the deputies of Tayef, who dreaded the repetition of a siege. 'Grant us, O apostle of God! a truce of three years, with the toleration of our ancient worship.' 'Not a month, not an hour.' 'Excuse us at least from the obligation of prayer.' 'Without prayer religion is of no avail.' They submitted in silence; their temples were demolished, and the same sentence of destruction was executed on all the idols of Arabia. His lieutenants, on the shores of the Red Sea, the Ocean, and the Gulf of Persia, were saluted by the acclamations of a faithful people; and the ambassadors who knelt before the throne of Medina were as numerous (says the Arabian proverb) as the dates that fall from the maturity of a palm-tree. The nation submitted to the God and the sceptre of Mahomet; the opprobrious name of tribute was abolished; the spontaneous or reluctant oblations of alms and tithes were applied to the service of religion; and one hundred and fourteen thousand Moslems accompanied the last pilgrimage of the apostle.[144]

When Heraclius returned in triumph from the Persian war, he entertained, at Emesa, one of the ambassadors of Mahomet, who invited the princes and nations of the earth to the profession of Islam. On this foundation the zeal of the Arabians has supposed the secret conversion of the Christian emperor; the vanity of the Greeks has feigned a personal visit to the prince of Medina, who accepted from the royal bounty a rich domain and a secure retreat in the province of Syria.[145] But the friendship of Heraclius and Mahomet was of short continuance: the new religion had inflamed rather than assuaged the rapacious spirit of the Saracens; and the murder of an envoy afforded a decent pretence for invading, with three thousand soldiers, the territory of Palestine that extends to the eastward of the Jordan. The holy banner was entrusted to Zeid; and such was the discipline or enthusiasm of the rising sect that the noblest chiefs served without reluctance under the slave of the prophet. On the event of his decease, Jaafar and Abdallah were successively substituted to the command; and, if the three should perish in the war, the troops were authorised to elect their general. The three leaders were slain in the battle of Muta,[146] the first military action which tried the valour of the Moslems against a foreign enemy. Zeid fell, like a soldier, in the foremost ranks; the death of Jaafar was heroic and memorable; he lost his right hand; he shifted the standard to his left; the left was severed from his body; he embraced the standard with his bleeding stumps, till he was transfixed to the ground with fifty honourable wounds. 'Advance,' cried Abdallah, who stepped into the vacant place, 'advance with confidence: either victory or paradise is our own.' The lance of a Roman decided the alternative; but the falling standard was rescued by Caled, the proselyte of Mecca: nine swords were broken on his hand; and his valour withstood and repulsed the superior numbers of the Christians. In the nocturnal council of the camp he was chosen to command: his skilful evolutions of the ensuing day secured either the victory or the retreat of the Saracens; and Caled is renowned among his brethren and his enemies by the glorious appellation of the *Sword of God*. In the pulpit, Mahomet described, with prophetic rapture, the crowns of the blessed martyrs; but in private he betrayed the feelings of human nature; he was surprised as he wept over the daughter of Zeid. 'What do I see?' said the astonished votary. 'You see,' replied the apostle, 'a friend who is deploring the loss of his most faithful friend.' After the conquest of Mecca the sovereign of Arabia affected to prevent the hostile preparations of Heraclius; and solemnly proclaimed war against the Romans, without attempting to disguise the hardships and dangers of the enterprise.[147] The Moslems were discouraged: they alleged the want of money, or horses, or provisions; the season of harvest, and the intolerable heat of the summer: 'Hell is much hotter,' said the indignant prophet. He disdained to compel their service; but on his return he admonished the most guilty by an excommunication of fifty days. Their desertion enhanced the merit of Abubeker, Othman, and the faithful companions who devoted their lives and fortunes; and Mahomet displayed his banner at the head of ten thousand horse and twenty thousand foot. Painful indeed was the distress of the march; lassitude and thirst were aggravated by the scorching and pestilential winds of the desert; ten men rode by turns on the same camel; and they were reduced to the shameful necessity of drinking the water from the belly of that useful animal. In the midway, ten days' journey from Medina and Damascus, they reposed near the grove and fountain of Tabuc. Beyond that place, Mahomet declined the prosecution of the war; he declared himself satisfied with the peaceful intentions, he was more probably daunted by the martial array, of the emperor of the East. But the active and intrepid Caled spread around the terror of his name; and the prophet received the submission of the tribes and cities from the Euphrates to Ailah at the head of the Red Sea. To his Christian subjects Mahomet readily granted the security of their persons, the freedom of their trade, the property of their goods, and the toleration of their worship.[148] The weakness of their Arabian brethren had restrained them from opposing his ambition; the disciples of Jesus were endeared to the enemy of the Jews; and it was the interest of a conqueror to propose a fair capitulation to the most powerful religion of the earth.

Till the age of sixty-three years, the strength of Mahomet was equal to the temporal and spiritual fatigues of his mission. His epileptic fits, an absurd calumny of the Greeks, would be an object of pity rather than abhorrence;[149] but he seriously believed that he was poisoned at Chaibar by the revenge of a Jewish female.[150] During four years, the health of the prophet declined; his infirmities increased; but his mortal disease was a fever of fourteen days, which deprived him by intervals of the use of reason. As soon as he was conscious of his danger, he edified his brethren by the humility of his virtue or penitence. 'If there be any man,' said the apostle from the pulpit, 'whom I have unjustly scourged, I submit my own back to the lash of retaliation. Have I aspersed the reputation of a Musulman? Let him proclaim *my* faults in the face of the congregation. Has anyone been despoiled of his goods? The little that I possess shall compensate the principal and the interest of the debt.' 'Yes,' replied a voice from the crowd, 'I am entitled to three drachms of silver.' Mahomet heard the complaint, satisfied the demand, and thanked his creditor for accusing him in this world rather than at the day of judgment. He beheld with temperate firmness the approach of death; enfranchised his slaves (seventeen men, as they are named, and eleven women); minutely directed the order of his funeral; and moderated the lamentations of his weeping friends, on whom he bestowed the benediction of peace. Till the third day before his death, he regularly performed the function of public prayer. The choice of Abubeker to supply his place appeared to mark that ancient and faithful friend as his successor in the sacerdotal and regal office; but he prudently declined the risk and envy of a more explicit nomination. At a moment when his faculties were visibly impaired, he called for pen and ink, to write, or more properly to dictate, a divine book, the sum and accomplishment of all his revelations: a dispute arose in the chamber whether he should be allowed to supersede the authority of the Koran; and the prophet was forced to reprove the indecent vehemence of his disciples. If the slightest credit may be afforded to the traditions of his wives and companions, he maintained in the bosom of his family, and to the last moments of his life, the dignity of an apostle and the faith of an enthusiast; described the visits of Gabriel, who bid an everlasting farewell to the earth, and expressed his lively confidence not only of the mercy, but of the favour, of the Supreme Being. In a familiar discourse he had mentioned his special prerogative, that the angel of death was not allowed to take his soul till he had respectfully asked the permission of the prophet. The request was granted; and Mahomet immediately fell into the agony of his dissolution: his head was reclined on the lap of Ayesha, the best beloved of all his wives; he fainted with the violence of pain; recovering his spirits, he raised his eyes towards the roof of the house, and, with a steady look, though a faltering voice, uttered the last broken, though articulate, words: 'O God! . . . pardon my sins . . . Yes, . . . I come, . . . among my fellow-citizens on high'; and thus peaceably expired on a carpet spread upon the floor. An expedition for the conquest of Syria was stopped by this mournful event; the army halted at the gates of Medina; the chiefs were assembled round their dying master. The city, more especially the house of the prophet, was a scene of clamorous sorrow, or silent despair: fanaticism alone could suggest a ray of hope and consolation. 'How can he be dead, our witness, our intercessor, our mediator with God? By God, he is not dead; like Moses and Jesus, he is wrapt in a holy trance, and speedily will he return to his faithful people.' The evidence of sense was disregarded; and Omar, unsheathing his scymetar, threatened to strike off the heads of the infidels who should dare to affirm that the prophet was no more. The tumult was appeased by the weight and moderation of Abubeker. 'Is it Mahomet,' said he to Omar and the multitude, 'or the God of Mahomet, whom you worship? The God of Mahomet liveth for ever, but the apostle was a mortal like ourselves, and, according to his own prediction, he has experienced the common fate of mortality.' He was piously interred by the hands of his nearest kinsman, on the same spot on which he expired;[151] Medina has been sanctified by the death and burial of Mahomet; and the innumerable pilgrims of Mecca often turn aside from the way, to bow in voluntary devotion[152] before the simple tomb of the prophet.[153]

At the conclusion of the life of Mahomet, it may perhaps be expected that I should balance his faults and virtues, that I should decide whether the title of enthusiast or impostor more properly belongs to that extraordinary man. Had I been intimately conversant with the son of Abdallah, the task would still be difficult, and the success uncertain: at the distance of twelve centuries, I darkly contemplate his shade through a cloud of religious incense; and, could I truly delineate the portrait of an hour, the fleeting resemblance would not equally apply to the solitary of mount Hera, to the preacher of Mecca, and to the conqueror of Arabia. The author of a mighty revolution appears to have been endowed with a pious and contemplative disposition: so soon as marriage had raised him above the pressure of want, he avoided the paths of ambition and avarice; and, till the age of forty, he lived with innocence, and would have died without a name. The unity of God is an idea most congenial to nature and reason; and a slight conversation with the Jews and Christians would teach him to despise and detest the idolatry of Mecca. It was the duty of a man and a citizen to impart the doctrine of salvation, to rescue his country from the dominion of sin and error. The energy of a mind incessantly bent on the same object would convert a general obligation into a particular call; the warm suggestings of the understanding or the fancy would be felt as the inspirations of heaven; the labour of thought would expire in rapture and vision; and the inward sensation, the invisible monitor, would be described with the form and attributes of an angel of God.[154] From enthusiasm to imposture the step is perilous and slippery; the daemon of Socrates[155] affords a memorable instance, how a wise man may deceive himself, how a good man may deceive others, how the conscience may slumber in a mixed and middle state between self-illusion and voluntary fraud. Charity may believe that the original motives of Mahomet were those of pure and genuine benevolence; but a human missionary is incapable of cherishing the obstinate unbelievers who reject his claims, despise his arguments, and persecute his life; he might forgive his personal adversaries, he may lawfully hate the enemies of God; the stern passions of pride and revenge were kindled in the bosom of Mahomet, and he sighed, like the prophet of Nineveh,* for the destruction of the rebels whom he had condemned. The injustice of Mecca and the choice of Medina transformed the citizen into a prince, the humble preacher into the leader of armies; but his sword was consecrated by the example of the saints; and the same God who afflicts a sinful world with pestilence and earthquakes might inspire for their conversion or chastisement the valour of his servants. In the exercise of political government, he was compelled to abate of the stern rigour of fanaticism, to comply in some measure with the prejudices and passions of his followers, and to employ even the vices of mankind as the instruments of their salvation. The use of fraud and perfidy, of cruelty and injustice, were often subservient to the propagation of the faith; and Mahomet commanded or approved the assassination of the Jews and idolaters who had escaped from the field of battle. By the repetition of such acts, the character of Mahomet must have been gradually stained; and the influence of such pernicious habits would be poorly compensated by the practice of the personal and social virtues which are necessary to maintain the reputation of a prophet among his sectaries and friends. Of his last years, ambition was the ruling passion; and a politician will suspect that he secretly smiled (the victorious impostor!) at the enthusiasm of his youth and the credulity of his proselytes.[156] A philosopher will observe that *their* credulity and *his* success would tend more strongly to fortify the assurance of his divine mission, that his interest and religion were inseparably connected, and that his conscience would be soothed by the persuasion that he alone was absolved by the Deity from the obligation of positive and moral laws. If he retained any vestige of his native innocence, the sins of Mahomet may be allowed as an evidence of his sincerity. In the support of truth, the arts of fraud and fiction may be deemed less criminal; and he would have started at the foulness of the means, had he not been satisfied of the importance and justice of the end. Even in a conqueror or a priest, I can surprise a word or action of unaffected humanity; and the decree of Mahomet that, in the sale of captives, the mothers should never be separated from their children may suspend or moderate the censure of the historian.[157]

The good sense of Mahomet[158] despised the pomp of royalty; the apostle of God submitted to the menial offices of the family; he kindled the fire, swept the floor, milked the ewes, and mended with his own hands his shoes and his woollen garment. Disdaining the penance and merit of a hermit, he observed, without effort or vanity, the abstemious diet of an Arab and a soldier. On solemn occasions, he feasted his companions with rustic and hospitable plenty; but in his domestic life many weeks would elapse without a fire being kindled on the hearth of the prophet. The interdiction of wine was confirmed by his example; his hunger was appeased with a sparing allowance of barley bread; he delighted in the taste of milk and honey; but his ordinary food consisted of dates and water. Perfumes and women were the two sensual enjoyments which his nature required and his religion did not forbid; and Mahomet affirmed that the fervour of his devotion was increased by these innocent pleasures. The heat of the climate inflames the Blood of the Arabs; and their libidinous complexion has been noticed by the writers of antiquity.[159] Their incontinence was regulated by the civil and religious laws of the Koran; their incestuous alliances were blamed; the boundless licence of polygamy was reduced to four legitimate wives or concubines; their rights both of bed and of dowry were equitably determined; the freedom of divorce was discouraged, adultery was condemned as a capital offence, and fornication, in either sex, was punished with an hundred stripes.[160] Such were the calm and rational precepts of the legislator; but in his private conduct Mahomet indulged the appetites of a man and abused the claims of a prophet. A special revelation dispensed him from the laws which he had imposed on his nation; the female sex, without reserve, was abandoned to his desires; and this singular prerogative excited the envy, rather than the scandal, the veneration, rather than the envy, of the devout Musulmans. If we remember the seven hundred wives and three hundred concubines of the wise Solomon, we shall applaud the modesty of the Arabian, who espoused no more than seventeen or fifteen wives; eleven are enumerated who occupied at Medina their separate apartments round the house of the apostle, and enjoyed in their turns the favour of his conjugal society. What is singular enough, they were all widows, excepting only Ayesha, the daughter of Abubeker. *She* was doubtless a virgin, since Mahomet consummated his nuptials (such is the premature ripeness of the climate) when she was only nine years of age. The youth, the beauty, the spirit of Ayesha gave her a superior ascendant; she was beloved and trusted by the prophet; and, after his death, the daughter of Abubeker was long revered as the mother of the faithful. Her behaviour had been ambiguous and indiscreet; in a nocturnal march, she was accidentally left behind; and in the morning Ayesha returned to the camp with a man. The temper of Mahomet was inclined to jealousy; but a divine revelation assured him of her innocence: he chastised her accusers, and published a law of domestic peace that no woman should be condemned unless four male witnesses had seen her in the act of adultery.[161] In his adventures with Zeineb, the wife of Zeid, and with Mary, an Egyptian captive, the amorous prophet forgot the interest of his reputation. At the house of Zeid, his freedman and adopted son, he beheld, in a loose undress, the beauty of Zeineb, and burst forth into an ejaculation of devotion and desire. The servile or grateful freedman understood the hint, and yielded, without hesitation, to the love of his benefactor. But, as the filial relation had excited some doubt and scandal, the angel Gabriel descended from heaven to ratify the deed, to annul the adoption, and gently to reprove the apostle for distrusting the indulgence of his God. One of his wives, Hafsa, the daughter of Omar, surprised him on her own bed in the embraces of his Egyptian captive: she promised secrecy and forgiveness; he swore that he would renounce the possession of Mary. Both parties forgot their engagements; and Gabriel again descended with a chapter of the Koran, to absolve him from his oath, and to exhort him freely to enjoy his captives and concubines without listening to the clamours of his wives. In a solitary retreat of thirty days, he laboured, alone with Mary, to fulfil the commands of the angel. When his love and revenge were satiated, he summoned to his presence his eleven wives, reproached their disobedience and indiscretion, and threatened them with a sentence of divorce both in this world and in the next: a dreadful sentence, since those who had ascended the bed of the prophet were for ever excluded from the hope of a second marriage. Perhaps the incontinence of Mahomet may be palliated by the tradition of his natural or preternatural gifts:[162] he united the manly virtue of thirty of the children of Adam; and the apostle might rival the thirteenth labour[163] of the Grecian Hercules.[164] A more serious and decent excuse may be drawn from his fidelity to Cadijah. During the twenty-four years of their marriage, her youthful husband abstained from the right of polygamy, and the pride or tenderness of the venerable matron was never insulted by the society of a rival. After her death he placed her in the rank of the four perfect women, with the sister of Moses, the mother of Jesus, and Fatima, the best beloved of his daughters. 'Was she not old?' said Ayesha, with the insolence of a blooming beauty; 'has not God given you a better in her place? 'No, by God,' said Mahomet, with an effusion of honest gratitude; 'there never can be a better! she believed in me, when men despised me; she relieved my wants, when I was poor and persecuted by the world.'[165]

In the largest indulgence of polygamy, the founder of a religion and empire might aspire to multiply the chances of a numerous posterity and a lineal succession. The hopes of Mahomet were fatally disappointed. The virgin Ayesha, and his ten widows of mature age and approved fertility, were barren in his potent embraces. The four sons of Cadijah died in their infancy. Mary, his Egyptian concubine, was endeared to him by the birth of Ibrahim. At the end of fifteen months the prophet wept over his grave; but he sustained with firmness the raillery of his enemies, and checked the adulation or credulity of the Moslems, by the assurance that an eclipse of the sun was not occasioned by the death of the infant. Cadijah had likewise given him four daughters, who were married to the most faithful of his disciples; the three eldest died before their father; but Fatima, who possessed his confidence and love, became the wife of her cousin Ali and the mother of an illustrious progeny. The merit and misfortunes of Ali and his descendants will lead me to anticipate, in this place, the series of the Saracen caliphs, a title which describes the commanders of the faithful as the vicars and successors of the apostle of God.[166]

The birth, the alliance, the character of Ali, which exalted him above the rest of his countrymen, might justify his claim to the vacant throne of Arabia. The son of Abu Taleb was, in his own right, the chief of the family of Hashem, and the hereditary prince or guardian of the city and temple of Mecca. The light of prophecy was extinct; but the husband of Fatima might expect the inheritance and blessing of her father; the Arabs had sometimes been patient of a female reign; and the two grandsons of the prophet had often been fondled in his lap and shown in his pulpit, as the hope of his age and the chief of the youth of paradise. The first of the true believers might aspire to march before them in this world and in the next; and, if some were of a graver and more rigid cast, the zeal and virtue of Ali were never outstripped by any recent proselyte. He united the qualifications of a poet, a soldier, and a saint; his wisdom still breathes in a collection of moral and religious sayings;[167] and every antagonist, in the combats of the tongue or of the sword, was subdued by his eloquence and valour. From the first hour of his mission to the last rites of his funeral, the apostle was never forsaken by a generous friend, whom he delighted to name his brother, his vicegerent, and the faithful Aaron of a second Moses. The son of Abu Taleb was afterwards reproached for neglecting to secure his interest by a solemn declaration of his right, which would have silenced all competition and sealed his succession by the decrees of heaven. But the unsuspecting hero confided in himself; the jealousy of empire, and perhaps the fear of opposition, might suspend the resolutions of Mahomet; and the bed of sickness was besieged by the artful Ayesha, the daughter of Abubeker and the enemy of Ali.

The silence and death of the prophet restored the liberty of the people; and his companions convened an assembly to deliberate on the choice of his successor. The hereditary claim and lofty spirit of Ali were offensive to an aristocracy of elders, desirous of bestowing and resuming the sceptre by a free and frequent election; the Koreish could never be reconciled to the proud pre-eminence of the line of Hashem; the ancient discord of the tribes was rekindled; the *fugitives* of Mecca and the *auxiliaries* of Medina asserted their respective merits; and the rash proposal of choosing two independent caliphs would have crushed, in their infancy, the religion and empire of the Saracens. The tumult was appeased by the disinterested resolution of Omar, who, suddenly renouncing his own pretensions, stretched forth his hand, and declared himself the first subject of the mild and venerable Abubeker. The urgency of the moment and the acquiescence of the people might excuse this illegal and precipitate measure; but Omar himself confessed from the pulpit that, if any Musulman should hereafter presume to anticipate the suffrage of his brethren, both the elector and the elected would be worthy of death.[168] After the simple inauguration of Abubeker, he was obeyed in Medina, Mecca, and the provinces of Arabia; the Hashemites alone declined the oath of fidelity; and their chief, in his own house, maintained, above six months, a sullen and independent reserve, without listening to the threats of Omar, who attempted to consume with fire the habitation of the daughter of the apostle. The death of Fatima and the decline of his party subdued the indignant spirit of Ali: he condescended to salute the commander of the faithful, accepted his excuse of the necessity of preventing their common enemies, and wisely rejected his courteous offer of abdicating the government of the Arabians. After a reign of two years, the aged caliph was summoned by the angel of death. In his testament, with the tacit approbation of the companions, he bequeathed the sceptre to the firm and intrepid virtue of Omar. 'I have no occasion,' said the modest candidate, 'for the place.' 'But the place has occasion for you,' replied Abubeker; who expired with a fervent prayer that the God of Mahomet would ratify his choice and direct the Musulmans in the way of concord and obedience. The prayer was not ineffectual, since Ali himself, in a life of privacy and prayer, professed to revere the superior worth and dignity of his rival; who comforted him for the loss of empire by the most flattering marks of confidence and esteem. In the twelfth year of his reign, Omar received a mortal wound from the hand of an assassin; he rejected with equal impartiality the names of his son and of Ali, refused to load his conscience with the sins of his successor, and devolved on six of the most respectable companions the arduous task of electing a commander of the faithful. On this occasion Ali was again blamed by his friends[169] for submitting his right to the judgment of men, for recognising their jurisdiction by accepting a place among the six electors. He might have obtained their suffrage, had he deigned to promise a strict and servile conformity, not only to the Koran and tradition, but likewise to the determinations of two *seniors*.[170] With these limitations, Othman, the secretary of Mahomet, accepted the government; nor was it till after the third caliph, twenty-four years after the death of the prophet, that Ali was invested, by the popular choice, with the regal and sacerdotal office. The manners of the Arabians retained their primitive simplicity, and the son of Abu Taleb despised the pomp and vanity of this world. At the hour of prayer, he repaired to the mosch of Medina, clothed in a thin cotton gown, a coarse turban on his head, his slippers in one hand, and his bow in the other, instead of a walking staff. The companions of the prophet and the chiefs of the tribes saluted their new sovereign, and gave him their right hands as a sign of fealty and allegiance.

The mischiefs that flow from the contests of ambition are usually confined to the times and countries in which they have been agitated. But the religious discord of the friends and enemies of Ali has been renewed in every age of the Hegira, and is still maintained in the immortal hatred of the Persians and Turks.[171] The former, who are branded with the appellation of *Shiites*, or sectaries, have enriched the Mahometan creed with a new article of faith; and, if Mahomet be the apostle, his companion Ali is the vicar, of God. In their private converse, in their public worship, they bitterly execrate the three usurpers who intercepted his indefeasible right to the dignity of Imam and Caliph; and the name of Omar expresses, in their tongue, the perfect accomplishment of wickedness and impiety.[172] The *Sonnites*,* who are supported by the general consent and orthodox tradition of the Musulmans, entertain a more impartial, or at least a more decent, opinion. They respect the memory of Abubeker, Omar, Othman, and Ali, the holy and legitimate successors of the prophet. But they assign the last and most humble place to the husband of Fatima, in the persuasion that the order of succession was determined by the degrees of sanctity.[173] An historian who balances the four caliphs with a hand unshaken by superstition will calmly pronounce that their manners were alike pure and exemplary; that their zeal was fervent, and probably sincere; and that, in the midst of riches and power, their lives were devoted to the practice of moral and religious duties. But the public virtues of Abubeker and Omar, the prudence of the first, the severity of the second, maintained the peace and prosperity of their reigns. The feeble temper and declining age of Othman were incapable of sustaining the weight of conquest and empire. He chose, and he was deceived; he trusted, and he was betrayed: the most deserving of the faithful became useless or hostile to his government, and his lavish bounty was productive only of ingratitude and discontent. The spirit of discord went forth in the provinces, their deputies assembled at Medina, and the Charegites, the desperate fanatics who disclaimed the yoke of subordination and reason, were confounded among the free-born Arabs, who demanded the redress of their wrongs and the punishment of their oppressors. From Cufa, from Bassora, from Egypt, from the tribes of the desert, they rose in arms, encamped about a league from Medina, and dispatched a haughty mandate to their sovereign, requiring him to execute justice or to descend from the throne. His repentance began to disarm and disperse the insurgents; but their fury was rekindled by the arts of his enemies, and the forgery of a perfidious secretary was contrived to blast his reputation and precipitate his fall. The caliph had lost the only guard of his predecessors, the esteem and confidence of the Moslems: during a siege of six weeks his water and provisions were intercepted, and the feeble gates of the palace were protected only by the scruples of the more timorous rebels. Forsaken by those who had abused his simplicity, the helpless and venerable caliph expected the approach of death; the brother of Ayesha marched at the head of the assassins; and Othman, with the Koran in his lap, was pierced with a multitude of wounds. A tumultuous anarchy of five days was appeased by the inauguration of Ali; his refusal would have provoked a general massacre. In this painful situation he supported the becoming pride of the chief of the Hashemites; declared that he had rather serve than reign; rebuked the presumption of the strangers; and required the formal, if not the voluntary, assent of the chiefs of the nation. He has never been accused of prompting the assassin of Omar; though Persia indiscreetly celebrates the festival of that holy martyr. The quarrel between Othman and his subjects was assuaged by the early mediation of Ali; and Hassan, the eldest of his sons, was insulted and wounded in the defence of the caliph. Yet it is doubtful whether the father of Hassan was strenuous and sincere in his opposition to the rebels; and it is certain that he enjoyed the benefit of their crime. The temptation was indeed of such magnitude as might stagger and corrupt the most obdurate virtue. The ambitious candidate no longer aspired to the barren sceptre of Arabia: the Saracens had been victorious in the East and West; and the wealthy kingdoms of Persia, Syria, and Egypt were the patrimony of the commander of the faithful.

A life of prayer and contemplation had not chilled the martial activity of Ali; but in a mature age, after a long experience of mankind, he still betrayed in his conduct the rashness and indiscretion of youth. In the first days of his reign, he neglected to secure, either by gifts or fetters, the doubtful allegiance of Telha and Zobeir, two of the most powerful of the Arabian chiefs. They escaped from Medina to Mecca, and from thence to Bassora; erected the standard of revolt; and usurped the government of Irak, or Assyria, which they had vainly solicited as the reward of their services. The mask of patriotism is allowed to cover the most glaring inconsistencies; and the enemies, perhaps the assassins, of Othman now demanded vengeance for his blood. They were accompanied in their flight by Ayesha, the widow of the prophet, who cherished, to the last hour of her life, an implacable hatred against the husband and the posterity of Fatima. The most reasonable Moslems were scandalised that the mother of the faithful should expose in a camp her person and character; but the superstitious crowd was confident that her presence would sanctify the justice, and assure the success, of their cause. At the head of twenty thousand of his loyal Arabs and nine thousand valiant auxiliaries of Cufa, the caliph encountered and defeated the superior numbers of the rebels under the walls of Bassora. Their leaders, Telha and Zobeir, were slain in the first battle that stained with civil blood the arms of the Moslems. After passing through the ranks to animate the troops, Ayesha had chosen her post amidst the dangers of the field. In the heat of the action, seventy men who held the bridle of her camel were successively killed or wounded; and the cage or litter in which she sat was stuck with javelins and darts like the quills of a porcupine. The venerable captive sustained with firmness the reproaches of the conqueror, and was speedily dismissed to her proper station, at the tomb of Mahomet, with the respect and tenderness that was still due to the widow of the apostle. After this victory, which was styled the Day of the Camel, Ali marched against a more formidable adversary: against Moawiyah, the son of Abu Sophian, who had assumed the title of caliph, and whose claim was supported by the forces of Syria and the interest of the house of the Ommiyah. From the passage of Thapsacus, the plain of Siffin[174] extends along the western bank of the Euphrates. On this spacious and level theatre, the two competitors waged a desultory war of one hundred and ten days. In the course of ninety actions or skirmishes, the loss of Ali was estimated at twenty-five, that of Moawiyah at forty-five, thousand soldiers; and the list of the slain was dignified by the names of five-and-twenty veterans who had fought at Beder under the standard of Mahomet. In this sanguinary contest, the lawful caliph displayed a superior character of valour and humanity. His troops were strictly enjoined to await the first onset of the enemy, to spare their flying brethren, and to respect the bodies of the dead and the chastity of the female captives. He generously proposed to save the blood of the Moslems by a single combat; but his trembling rival declined the challenge as a sentence of inevitable death. The ranks of the Syrians were broken by the charge of a hero who was mounted on a piebald horse, and wielded with irresistible force his ponderous and two-edged sword. As often as he smote a rebel, he shouted the Allah Acbar, 'God is victorious'; and in the tumult of a nocturnal battle he was heard to repeat four hundred times that tremendous exclamation. The prince of Damascus already meditated his flight, but the certain victory was snatched from the grasp of Ali by the disobedience and enthusiasm of his troops. Their conscience was awed by the solemn appeal to the books of the Koran which Moawiyah exposed on the foremost lances; and Ali was compelled to yield to a disgraceful truce and an insidious compromise. He retreated with sorrow and indignation to Cufa; his party was discouraged; the distant provinces of Persia, of Yemen, and of Egypt were subdued or seduced by his crafty rival; and the stroke of fanaticism which was aimed against the three chiefs of the nation was fatal only to the cousin of Mahomet. In the temple of Mecca, three Charegites or enthusiasts discoursed of the disorders of the church and state: they soon agreed that the deaths of Ali, of Moawiyah, and of his friend Amrou, the viceroy of Egypt, would restore the peace and unity of religion. Each of the assassins chose his victim, poisoned his dagger, devoted his life, and secretly repaired to the scene of action. Their resolution was equally desperate; but the first mistook the person of Amrou and stabbed the deputy who occupied his seat; the prince of Damascus was dangerously hurt by the second; the lawful caliph in the mosch of Cufa received a mortal wound from the hand of the third. He expired in the sixty-third year of his age, and mercifully recommended to his children that they would dispatch the murderer by a single stroke. The sepulchre of Ali[175] was concealed from the tyrants of the house of Ommiyah;[176] but, in the fourth age of the Hegira, a tomb, a temple, a city, arose near the ruins of Cufa.[177] Many thousands of the Shiites repose in holy ground at the feet of the vicar of God; and the desert is vivified by the numerous and annual visits of the Persians, who esteem their devotion not less meritorious than the pilgrimage of Mecca.

The persecutors of Mahomet usurped the inheritance of his children; and the champions of idolatry became the supreme heads of his religion and empire. The opposition of Abu Sophian had been fierce and obstinate; his conversion was tardy and reluctant; his new faith was fortified by necessity and interest; he served, he fought, perhaps he believed; and the sins of the time of ignorance were expiated by the recent merits of the family of Ommiyah. Moawiyah, the son of Abu Sophian and of the cruel Henda, was dignified in his early youth with the office or title of secretary of the prophet; the judgment of Omar entrusted him with the government of Syria; and he administered that important province about forty years either in a subordinate or a supreme rank. Without renouncing the fame of valour and liberality, he affected the reputation of humanity and moderation; a grateful people was attached to their benefactor; and the victorious Moslems were enriched with the spoils of Cyprus and Rhodes. The sacred duty of pursuing the assassins of Othman was the engine* and pretence of his ambition. The bloody shirt of the martyr was exposed in the mosch of Damascus; the emir deplored the fate of his injured kinsman; and sixty thousand Syrians were engaged in his service by an oath of fidelity and revenge. Amrou, the conquerer of Egypt, himself an army, was the first who saluted the new monarch, and divulged the dangerous secret that the Arabian caliphs might be created elsewhere than in the city of the prophet.[178] The policy of Moawiyah eluded the valour of his rival; and, after the death of Ali, he negotiated the abdication of his son Hassan, whose mind was either above or below the government of the world, and who retired without a sigh from the palace of Cufa to an humble cell near the tomb of his grandfather. The aspiring wishes of the caliph were finally crowned by the important change of an elective to an hereditary kingdom. Some murmurs of freedom or fanaticism attested the reluctance of the Arabs, and four citizens of Medina refused the oath of fidelity; but the designs of Moawiyah were conducted with vigour and address; and his son Yezid, a feeble and dissolute youth, was proclaimed as the commander of the faithful and the successor of the apostle of God.

A familiar story is related of the benevolence of one of the sons of Ali. In serving at table, a slave had inadvertently dropped a dish of scalding broth on his master; the heedless wretch fell prostrate, to deprecate his punishment, and repeated a verse of the Koran: 'Paradise is for those who command their anger:' – 'I am not angry:' – 'and for those who pardon offences:' – 'I pardon your offence:' – 'and for those who return good for evil:' – 'I give you your liberty, and four hundred pieces of silver.' With an equal measure of piety, Hosein, the younger brother of Hassan, inherited a remnant of his father's spirit, and served with honour against the Christians in the siege of Constantinople. The primogeniture of the line of Hashem and the holy character of grandson of the apostle had centred in his person, and he was at liberty to prosecute his claim against Yezid the tyrant of Damascus, whose vices he despised, and whose title he had never deigned to acknowledge. A list was secretly transmitted from Cufa to Medina of one hundred and forty thousand Moslems, who professed their attachment to his cause, and who were eager to draw their swords so soon as he should appear on the banks of the Euphrates. Against the advice of his wisest friends, he resolved to trust his person and family in the hands of a perfidious people. He traversed the desert of Arabia with a timorous retinue of women and children; but, as he approached the confines of Irak, he was alarmed by the solitary or hostile face of the country, and suspected either the defection or ruin of his party. His fears were just: Obeidollah, the governor of Cufa, had extinguished the first sparks of an insurrection; and Hosein, in the plain of Kerbela, was encompassed by a body of five thousand horse, who intercepted his communication with the city and the river. He might still have escaped to a fortress in the desert that had defied the power of Caesar and Chosroes,* and confided in the fidelity of the tribe of Tai, which would have armed ten thousand warriors in his defence. In a conference with the chief of the enemy, he proposed the option of three honourable conditions: that he should be allowed to return to Medina, or be stationed in a frontier garrison against the Turks, or safely conducted to the presence of Yezid. But the commands of the caliph, or his lieutenant, were stern and absolute; and Hosein was informed that he must either submit as a captive and a criminal to the commander of the faithful or expect the consequences of his rebellion. 'Do you think,' replied he, 'to terrify me with death?' And, during the short respite of a night, he prepared with calm and solemn resignation to encounter his fate. He checked the lamentations of his sister Fatima, who deplored the impending ruin of his house. 'Our trust,' said Hosein, 'is in God alone. All things, both in heaven and earth, must perish and return to their Creator. My brother, my father, my mother, were better than me; and every Musulman has an example in the prophet.' He pressed his friends to consult their safety by a timely flight: they unanimously refused to desert or survive their beloved master; and their courage was fortified by a fervent prayer and the assurance of paradise. On the morning of the fatal day, he mounted on horseback, with his sword in one hand and the Koran in the other; his generous band of martyrs consisted only of thirty-two horse and forty foot; but their flanks and rear were secured by the tent-ropes, and by a deep trench which they had filled with lighted faggots, according to the practice of the Arabs. The enemy advanced with reluctance; and one of their chiefs deserted, with thirty followers, to claim the partnership of inevitable death. In every close onset or single combat, the despair of the Fatimites was invincible; but the surrounding multitudes galled them from a distance with a cloud of arrows, and the horses and men were successively slain: a truce was allowed on both sides for the hour of prayer; and the battle at length expired by the death of the last of the companions of Hosein. Alone, weary and wounded, he seated himself at the door of his tent. As he tasted a drop of water, he was pierced in the mouth with a dart; and his son and nephew, two beautiful youths, were killed in his arms. He lifted his hands to heaven, they were full of blood, and he uttered a funeral prayer for the living and the dead. In a transport of despair his sister issued from the tent, and adjured the general of the Cufians that he would not suffer Hosein to be murdered before his eyes: a tear trickled down his venerable beard; and the boldest of his soldiers fell back on every side as the dying hero threw himself among them. The remorseless Shamer, a name detested by the faithful, reproached their cowardice; and the grandson of Mahomet was slain with three-and-thirty strokes of lances and swords. After they had trampled on his body, they carried his head to the castle of Cufa, and the inhuman Obeidollah struck him on the mouth with a cane: 'Alas!' exclaimed an aged Musulman, 'on these lips have I seen the lips of the apostle of God!' In a distant age and climate the tragic scene of the death of Hosein will awaken the sympathy of the coldest reader.[179] On the annual festival of his martyrdom, in the devout pilgrimage to his sepulchre, his Persian votaries abandon their souls to the religious frenzy of sorrow and indignation.[180]

When the sisters and children of Ali were brought in chains to the throne of Damascus, the caliph was advised to extirpate the enmity of a popular and hostile race, whom he had injured beyond the hope of reconciliation. But Yezid preferred the counsels of mercy; and the mourning family was honourably dismissed to mingle their tears with their kindred at Medina. The glory of martyrdom superseded the right of primogeniture; and the twelve Imams,[181] or pontiffs, of the Persian creed are Ali, Hassan, Hosein, and the lineal descendants of Hosein to the ninth generation. Without arms or treasures or subjects, they successively enjoyed the veneration of the people and provoked the jealousy of the reigning caliphs; their tombs at Mecca or Medina, on the banks of the Euphrates or in the province of Chorasan, are still visited by the devotion of their sect. Their names were often the pretence of sedition and civil war; but these royal saints despised the pomp of the world, submitted to the will of God and the injustice of man, and devoted their innocent lives to the study and practice of religion. The twelfth and last of the Imams, conspicuous by the title of *Mahadi* or the Guide, surpassed the solitude and sanctity of his predecessors. He concealed himself in a cavern near Bagdad; the time and place of his death are unknown; and his votaries pretend that he still lives and will appear before the day of judgment to overthrow the tyranny of Dejal or the Antichrist.[182] In the lapse of two or three centuries the posterity of Abbas, the uncle of Mahomet, had multiplied to the number of thirty-three thousand;[183] the race of Ali might be equally prolific; the meanest individual was above the first and greatest of princes; and the most eminent were supposed to excel the perfection of angels. But their adverse fortune and the wide extent of the Musulman empire allowed an ample scope for every bold and artful impostor who claimed affinity with the holy seed: the sceptre of the Almohades in Spain and Afric, of the Fatimites in Egypt and Syria,[184] of the Sultans of Yemen and of the Sophis of Persia,[185] has been consecrated by this vague and ambiguous title. Under their reigns it might be dangerous to dispute the legitimacy of their birth; and one of the Fatimite caliphs silenced an indiscreet question by drawing his scymetar: 'This,' said Moez, 'is my pedigree; and these,' casting an handful of gold to his soldiers, 'and these are my kindred and my children.' In the various conditions of princes, or doctors, or nobles, or merchants, or beggars, a swarm of the genuine or fictitious descendants of Mahomet and Ali is honoured with the appellation of sheiks, or sherifs, or emirs. In the Ottoman empire, they are distinguished by a green turban, receive a stipend from the treasury, are judged only by their chief, and, however debased by fortune or character, still assert the proud pre-eminence of their birth. A family of three hundred persons, the pure and orthodox branch of the caliph Hassan, is preserved without taint or suspicion in the holy cities of Mecca and Medina, and still retains, after the revolutions of twelve centuries, the custody of the temple and the sovereignty of their native land. The fame and merit of Mahomet would ennoble a plebeian race, and the ancient blood of the Koreish transcends the recent majesty of the kings of the earth.[186]

The talents of Mahomet are entitled to our applause, but his success has perhaps too strongly attracted our admiration. Are we surprised that a multitude of proselytes should embrace the doctrine and the passions of an eloquent fanatic? In the heresies of the church, the same seduction has been tried and repeated from the time of the apostles to that of the reformers. Does it seem incredible that a private citizen should grasp the sword and the sceptre, subdue his native country, and erect a monarchy by his victorious arms? In the moving picture of the dynasties of the East, an hundred fortunate usurpers have arisen from a baser origin, surmounted more formidable obstacles, and filled a larger scope of empire and conquest. Mahomet was alike instructed to preach and to fight, and the union of these opposite qualities, while it enhanced his merit, contributed to his success: the operation of force and persuasion, of enthusiasm and fear, continually acted on each other, till every barrier yielded to their irresistible power. His voice invited the Arabs to freedom and victory, to arms and rapine, to the indulgence of their darling passions in this world and the other; the restraints which he imposed were requisite to establish the credit of the prophet and to exercise the obedience of the people; and the only objection to his success was his rational creed of the unity and perfections of God. It is not the propagation but the permanency of his religion that deserves our wonder: the same pure and perfect impression which he engraved at Mecca and Medina is preserved, after the revolutions of twelve centuries, by the Indian, the African, and the Turkish proselytes of the Koran. If the Christian apostles, St Peter or St Paul, could return to the Vatican, they might possibly inquire the name of the Deity who is worshipped with such mysterious rites in that magnificent temple: at Oxford or Geneva, they would experience less surprise; but it might still be incumbent on them to peruse the catechism of the church, and to study the orthodox commentators on their own writings and the words of their Master. But the Turkish dome of St Sophia, with an increase of splendour and size, represents the humble tabernacle erected at Medina by the hands of Mahomet. The Mahometans have uniformly withstood the temptation of reducing the object of their faith and devotion to a level with the senses and imagination of man. 'I believe in one God, and Mahomet the apostle of God,' is the simple and invariable profession of Islam. The intellectual image of the Deity has never been degraded by any visible idol; the honours of the prophet have never transgressed the measure of human virtue; and his living precepts have restrained the gratitude of his disciples within the bounds of reason and religion. The votaries of Ali have indeed consecrated the memory of their hero, his wife, and his children; and some of the Persian doctors pretend that the divine essence was incarnate in the person of the Imams; but their superstition is universally condemned by the Sonnites; and their impiety has afforded a seasonable warning against the worship of saints and martyrs. The metaphysical questions on the attributes of God and the liberty of man have been agitated in the schools of the Mahometans as well as in those of the Christians; but among the former they have never engaged the passions of the people or disturbed the tranquillity of the state. The cause of this important difference may be found in the separation or union of the regal and sacerdotal characters. It was the interest of the caliphs, the successors of the prophet and commanders of the faithful, to repress and discourage all religious innovations: the order, the discipline, the temporal and spiritual ambition of the clergy are unknown to the Moslems; and the sages of the law are the guides of their conscience and the oracles of their faith. From the Atlantic to the Ganges, the Koran is acknowledged as the fundamental code, not only of theology but of civil and criminal jurisprudence; and the laws which regulate the actions and the property of mankind are guarded by the infallible and immutable sanction of the will of God. This religious servitude is attended with some practical disadvantage; the illiterate legislator had been often misled by his own prejudices and those of his country; and the institutions of the Arabian desert may be ill adapted to the wealth and numbers of Ispahan and Constantinople. On these occasions, the Cadhi* respectfully places on his head the holy volume, and substitutes a dexterous interpretation, more apposite to the principles of equity and the manners and policy of the times.

His beneficial or pernicious influence on the public happiness is the last consideration in the character of Mahomet. The most bitter or most bigoted of his Christian or Jewish foes will surely allow that he assumed a false commission to inculcate a salutary doctrine, less perfect only than their own. He piously supposed, as the basis of his religion, the truth and sanctity of *their* prior revelations, the virtues and miracles of their founders. The idols of Arabia were broken before the throne of God; the blood of human victims was expiated by prayer and fasting and alms, the laudable or innocent arts of devotion; and his rewards and punishments of a future life were painted by the images most congenial to an ignorant and carnal generation. Mahomet was perhaps incapable of dictating a moral and political system for the use of his countrymen; but he breathed among the faithful a spirit of charity and friendship, recommended the practice of the social virtues, and checked, by his laws and precepts, the thirst of revenge and the oppression of widows and orphans. The hostile tribes were united in faith and obedience, and the valour which had been idly spent in domestic quarrels was vigorously directed against a foreign enemy. Had the impulse been less powerful, Arabia, free at home and formidable abroad, might have flourished under a succession of her native monarchs. Her sovereignty was lost by the extent and rapidity of conquest. The colonies of the nation were scattered over the East and West, and their blood was mingled with the blood of their converts and captives. After the reign of three caliphs the throne was transported from Medina to the valley of Damascus and the banks of the Tigris; the holy cities were violated by impious war; Arabia was ruled by the rod of a subject, perhaps of a stranger; and the Bedoweens of the desert, awakening from their dream of dominion, resumed their old and solitary independence.[187]

1 As in this and the following chapter I shall display much Arabic learning, I must profess my total ignorance of the Oriental tongues, and my gratitude to the learned interpreters, who have transfused their science into the Latin, French and English languages. Their collections, versions, and histories, I shall occasionally notice.

2 The geographers of Arabia may be divided into three classes: 1. The *Greeks* and *Latins*, whose progressive knowledge may be traced in Agatharchides (*de Mari Rubro*, in Hudson, *Geograph. Minor.*, tom. i); Diodorus Siculus (i, ii, 159–67; iii, 211–16, edit. Wesseling); Strabo (xvi, 1112–14, from Eratosthenes; pp. 1122–32, from Artemidorus); Dionysius (*Periegesis*, 927–69); Pliny (*Hist. Natur.*, v, 12, vi, 32); and Ptolemy (*Descript. et tabulae Urbium*, in Hudson, tom. iii). 2. The *Arabic writers*, who have treated the subject with the zeal of patriotism or devotion: the extracts of Pocock (*Specimen Hist. Arabum*, pp. 125–28) from the Geography of the Sherif al Edrissi, render us still more dissatisfied with the version or abridgment (pp. 24–27, 44–56, 108, etc., 119, etc.) which the Maronites have published under the absurd title of *Geographia Nubiensis* [the Geography of Nubia] (Paris, 1619); but the Latin and French translators, Greaves (in Hudson, tom. iii) and Galland (*Voyage de la Palestine par la Roque*, pp. 265–346), have opened to us the *Arabia* of Abulfeda, the most copious and correct account of the peninsula, which may be enriched, however, from the *Bibliothèque Orientale* of d'Herbelot, p. 120, *et alibi passim*. 3. The *European travellers*; among whom Shaw (pp. 438–55) and Niebuhr (Description, 1773, *Voyages* tom. i, 1776) deserve an honourable distinction; Busching (*Géographie* par Berenger, viii, 416–510) has compiled with judgment; and d'Anville's Maps (*Orbis Veteribus Notus*, and 1ᵉ *Partie de l'Asie*) should lie before the reader, with his *Géographie Ancienne*, ii, 203–31.

3 Abulfed., *Descript. Arabiae*, p. 1; d'Anville, *l'Euphrate et le Tigre*, pp. 19–20. It was in this place, the paradise or garden of a satrap, that Xenophon and the Greeks first passed the Euphrates (*Anabasis*, i, 10, 29, edit. Wells).

4 Reland has proved, with much superfluous learning, 1. That our Red Sea (the Arabian Gulf) is no more than a part of the *Mare Rubrum*, the Ἐρυθρὰ θάλασσα [Red Sea] of the ancients, which was extended to the indefinite space of the Indian ocean. 2. That the synonymous words ἐρυθρός [red-brown], αἰθίοψ [Ethiopian], allude to the colour of the blacks or negroes (*Dissert. Miscell.*, i, 59–117).

5 In the thirty days, or stations, between Cairo and Mecca, there are fifteen destitute of good water. See the route of the Hadjees, in Shaw's *Travels*, p. 477.

6 The aromatics, especially the *thus* or frankincense, of Arabia occupy the xiith book of Pliny. Our great poet (*Paradise Lost*, Bk iv) introduces, in a simile, the spicy odours that are blown by the north-east wind from the Sabaean coast:

> Many a league,
> Pleas'd with the grateful scent, old Ocean smiles.

> (Pliny, *Hist. Natur.*, xii, 42.)

* *page 782* [lent plausibility]

7 Agatharchides affirms that lumps of pure gold were found, from the size of an olive to that of a nut; that iron was twice, and silver ten times, the value of gold

(de Mari Rubro, p. 60). These real or imaginary treasures are vanished; and no gold mines are at present known in Arabia (Niebuhr, Description, p. 124).

† page 782   ['happy' Arabia]

8 Consult, peruse, and study the Specimen Historiae Arabum of Pocock! (Oxon. 1650, in 4to). The thirty pages of text and version are extracted from the Dynasties of Gregory Abulpharagius, which Pocock afterwards translated (Oxon. 1663, in 4to); the three hundred and fifty-eight notes from a classic and original work on the Arabian antiquities.

* page 782   [the Indian Ocean]

9 Arrian remarks the Ichthyophagi of the coast of Hejaz (Periplus Maris Erythraei, p. 12), and beyond Aden (p. 15). It seems probable that the shores of the Red Sea (in the largest sense) were occupied by these savages in the time, perhaps, of Cyrus; but I can hardly believe that any cannibals were left among the savages in the reign of Justinian (Procop., de Bell. Persic., i, 19).

10 See the Specimen Historiae Arabum of Pocock, pp. 2, 5, 86, etc. The journey of M. d'Arvieux, in 1664, to the camp of the emir of Mount Carmel (Voyage de la Palestine, Amsterdam, 1718), exhibits a pleasing and original picture of the life of the Bedoweens, which may be illustrated from Niebuhr (Description de l'Arabie, pp. 327–44), and Volney (i, 343–85), the last and most judicious of our Syrian travellers.

11 Read (it is no unpleasing task) the incomparable articles of the Horse and the Camel, in the Natural History of M. de Buffon.

* page 784   [noble, thoroughbred]

† page 784   [from North Africa]

12 For the Arabian horses, see d'Arvieux (pp. 159–73) and Niebuhr (pp. 142–44). At the end of the thirteenth century, the horses of Neged were esteemed sure-footed, those of Yemen strong and serviceable, those of Hejaz most noble. The horses of Europe, the tenth and last class, were generally despised, as having too much body and too little spirit (d'Herbelot, Bibliot. Orient, p. 339); their strength was requisite to bear the weight of the knight and his armour.

‡ page 784   [sold]

13 Qui carnibus camelorum vesci solent odii tenaces sunt ['those who feed on camel's flesh are steadfast in hating'], was the opinion of an Arabian physician (Pocock, Specimen, p. 88). Mahomet himself, who was fond of milk, prefers the cow, and does not even mention the camel; but the diet of Mecca and Medina was already more luxurious (Gagnier, Vie de Mahomet, iii, 404).

14 Yet Marcian of Heraclea (in Periplo, p. 16, in tom. i, Hudson, Minor. Geograph.) reckons one hundred and sixty-four towns in Arabia Felix. The size of the towns might be small – the faith of the writer might be large.

15 It is compared by Abulfeda (in Hudson, iii, 54) to Damascus, and is still the residence of the Imam of Yemen (Voyages de Niebuhr, i, 331–42). Saana is twenty-four parasangs from Dafar (Abulfeda, p. 51), and sixty-eight from Aden (p. 53). [A parasang was an ancient Persian measure equal to about 3¼ miles.]

16 Pocock, Specimen, p. 57; Geograph. Nubiensis, p. 52. Meriaba, or Merab, six miles in circumference, was destroyed by the legions of Augustus (Pliny, Hist. Nat., vi, 32), and had not revived in the fourteenth century (Abulfed., Descript. Arab., p. 58).

* page 785   [people of the Yemen]

17 The name of city, Medina, was appropriated, κατ᾿ ἐξοχήν [above all], to Yatreb

(the Iatrippa of the Greeks), the seat of the prophet. The distances from Medina are reckoned by Abulfeda in stations, or days' journey of a caravan (p. 15), to Bahrein, xv; to Bassora, xviii; to Cufah, xx; to Damascus or Palestine, xx; to Cairo xxxi, to Mecca, x; from Mecca to Saana (p. 52), or Aden, xxx; to Cairo, xxxi days, or 412 hours (Shaw's *Travels*, p. 477); which, according to the estimate of d'Anville (*Mesures Itinéraires*, p. 99), allows about twenty-five English miles for a day's journey. From the land of frankincense (Hadramaut, in Yemen, between Aden and Cape Fartasch) to Gaza, in Syria, Pliny (*Hist. Nat.*, xii, 32) computes lxv mansions of camels. These measures may assist fancy and elucidate facts.

18 Our notions of Mecca must be drawn from the Arabians (d'Herbelot, *Bibliothèque Orientale*, pp. 368–71; Pocock, *Specimen*, pp. 125–28; Abulfeda, pp. 11–40). As no unbeliever is permitted to enter the city, our travellers are silent; and the short hints of Thévenot (*Voyages du Levant*, i, 490) are taken from the suspicious mouth of an African renegado. Some Persians counted 6000 houses (Chardin, iv, 167).

19 Strabo, xvi, 1110. See one of these salt houses near Bassora, in d'Herbelot, *Bibliot. Orient.*, p. 6.

20 *Mirum dictu ex innumeris populis pars aequa in commerciis aut in latrociniis degit* ['Strangely enough, of the enormous population, half lives by trade, half by robbery'] (Pliny, *Hist. Nat.*, vi, 32). See Sale's Koran, Surat cvi, 503; Pocock, *Specimen*, p. 2; d'Herbelot, *Bibliot. Orient.*, p. 361; Prideaux's *Life of Mahomet*, p. 5; Gagnier, *Vie de Mahomet*, i, 72, 120, 126, etc.

  * *page 786*   [son of Abraham]

21 A nameless doctor (*Universal Hist.*, vol. xx, octavo edition) has formally *demonstrated* the truth of Christianity by the independence of the Arabs. A critic, besides the exceptions of fact, might dispute the meaning of the text (Gen. xvi, 12), the extent of the application, and the foundation of the pedigree.

22 It was subdued, AD 1173, by a brother of the great Saladin, who founded a dynasty of Curds or Ayoubites (Guignes, *Hist. des Huns*, i, 425. D'Herbelot, p. 477).

23 By the lieutenant of Soliman I (AD 1538), and Selim II (1568). See Cantemir's *Hist. of the Othman empire*, pp. 201, 221. The Pasha, who resided at Saana, commanded twenty-one Beys, but no revenue was ever remitted to the Porte (Marsigli, *Stato Militare dell' Imperio Ottomanno*, p. 124), and the Turks were expelled about the year 1630 (Niebuhr, pp. 167–68).

24 Of the Roman province, under the name of Arabia and the third Palestine, the principal cities were Bostra and Petra, which dated their era from the year 105, when they were subdued by Palma, a lieutenant of Trajan (Dion. Cassius, Bk lxviii). Petra was the capital of the Nabathaeans; whose name is derived from the eldest of the sons of Ismael (Gen. xxv:12, etc. with the Commentaries of Jerome, Le Clerc, and Calmet). Justinian relinquished a palm country of ten days' journey to the south of Aelah (Procop., *de Bell. Persic.*, i, 19), and the Romans maintained a centurion and a custom-house (Arrian., *in Periplo Maris Erythraei*, p. 11, in Hudson, tom. i) at a place (λευκὴ κώμη, Pagus Albus, Hawara) in the territory of Medina (d'Anville, *Mémoire sur l'Egypte*, p. 243). These real possessions, and some naval inroads of Trajan (*Peripl.*, pp. 14–15), are magnified by history and medals into the Roman conquest of Arabia.

  † *page 786*   [king of Egypt, 1900 BC]

25 Niebuhr (*Description de l'Arabie*, pp. 302–03, 329–31) affords the most recent and authentic intelligence of the Turkish empire in Arabia.

26 Diodorus Siculus (ii, xix, 390–93, edit. Wesseling) has clearly exposed the freedom of the Nabathaean Arabs, who resisted the arms of Antigonus [general of Alexander the Great] and his son.

† *page 000* [scimitar]

27 Strabo, xvi, 1127–29; Pliny, *Hist. Natur.*, vi, 32. Aelius Gallus landed near Medina, and marched near a thousand miles into the part of Yemen between Mareb and the Ocean. The *non ante devictis Sabaeae regibus* [the hitherto unconquered kings of Sheba] (*Od.*, i, 29), and the *intacti Arabum thesauri* [the untouched treasures of the Arabs] (*Od.*, iii, 24), of Horace attest the virgin purity of Arabia.

28 See the imperfect history of Yemen in Pocock, *Specimen*, pp. 55–66, of Hira, pp. 66–74, of Gassan, pp. 75–78, as far as it could be known or preserved in the time of ignorance.

* *page 787* [King Chosroes II of Persia, AD 591–628, who was defeated by the emperor Heraclius, deposed and murdered.]

29 Τὰ Σαρακηνικὰ φῦλα, μυριάδες ταῦτα καὶ τὸ πλεῖστον αὐτῶν ἐρημονόμοι καὶ ἀδέσποτοι ['The Saracen tribes number tens of thousands, and most of them live wild and free'], are described by Menander (*Excerpt. Legation.*, p. 149), Procopius (*de Bell. Persic.*, i, 17, 19; ii, 10), and, in the most lively colours, by Ammianus Marcellinus (xiv, 4), who had spoken of them as early as the reign of Marcus [Aurelius].

30 The name which, used by Ptolemy and Pliny in a more confined, by Ammianus and Procopius in a larger, sense, has been derived, ridiculously from *Sarah*, the wife of Abraham, obscurely from the village of *Saraka* (μετὰ Ναβαταίους. Stephan., *de Urbibus*), more plausibly from the Arabic words which signify a *thievish* character, or *Oriental* situation (Hottinger, *Hist. Oriental.*, i, i, 7–8; Pocock, *Specimen*, pp. 33, 35; Asseman., *Bibliot. Orient.*, iv, 567). Yet the last and most popular of these etymologies is refuted by Ptolemy (*Arabia*, p. 2, 18, in Hudson, tom. iv), who expressly remarks the western and southern position of the Saracens, then an obscure tribe on the borders of Egypt. The appellation cannot therefore allude to any *national* character; and, since it was imposed by strangers, it must be found, not in Arabic, but in a foreign language.

† *page 787* [advanced to]

‡ *page 787* [the queen of Palmyra, whose defeat by the Emperor Aurelian is related in Chapter 11.]

31 *Saraceni . . . mulieres aiunt in eos regnare* ['The Saracens assert that women rule over them'] (*Expositio totius Mundi*, p. 3, in Hudson, tom. iii). The reign of Mavia is famous in ecclesiastical story. Pocock, *Specimen*, pp. 69, 83.

32 μὴ ἐξεῖναι ἐκ τῶν βασιλείων, is the report of Agatharchides (*de Mari Rubro*, pp. 63–64, in Hudson, tom. i); Diodorus Siculus (i, iii, 47, 215); and Strabo (xvi, 1124). But I much suspect that this is one of the popular tales or extraordinary accidents which the credulity of travellers so often transforms into a fact, a custom, and a law.

33 *Non gloriabantur antiquitus Arabes, nisi gladio, hospite, et eloquentia.* ['In ancient times, the Arabs boasted only of their warfare, their hospitality and their eloquence.'] (Sephadius, apud Pocock, *Specimen*, pp. 161–62). This gift of speech they shared only with the Persians; and the sententious Arabs would

probably have disdained the simple and sublime logic of Demosthenes.

34 I must remind the reader that d'Arvieux, d'Herbelot, and Niebuhr represent, in the most lively colours, the manners and government of the Arabs, which are illustrated by many incidental passages in the life of Mahomet.

35 Observe the first chapter of Job, and the long wall of 1500 stadia which Sesostris built from Pelusium to Heliopolis (Diodor. Sicul., i, i, 67). Under the name of *Hycsos*, the shepherd kings, they had formerly subdued Egypt (Marsham, *Canon. Chron.*, pp. 98–163, etc.).

36 Or, according to another account, 1200 (d'Herbelot, *Bibliothèque Orientale*, p. 75). The two historians who wrote of the *Ayam al Arab*, the battles of the Arabs, lived in the ninth and tenth century. The famous war of Dahes and Gabrah was occasioned by two horses, lasted forty years, and ended in a proverb (Pocock, *Specimen*, p. 48).

 * *page 789* [offensive]

37 The modern theory and practice of the Arabs in the revenge of murder are described by Niebuhr (*Description*, pp. 26–31). The harsher features of antiquity may be traced in the Koran, 2, 20; 17, 230, with Sale's Observations.

38 Procopius (*de Bell. Persic.*, i, 16) places the *two* holy months about the summer solstice. The Arabians consecrate *four* months of the year – the first, seventh, eleventh, and twelfth and pretend that in a long series of ages the truce was infringed only four or six times. (Sale's *Preliminary Discourse*, pp. 147–50, and Notes on the ninth chapter of the Koran, pp. 154, etc. Casiri, *Bibliot. Hispano-Arabica*, ii, 20–21.)

39 Arrian, in the second century, remarks (*in Periplo Maris Erythraei*, p. 12) the partial or total difference of the dialects of the Arabs. Their language and letters are copiously treated by Pocock (*Specimen*, pp. 150–54); Casiri (*Bibliot. Hispano-Arabica*, i, 1, 83, 292; ii, 25, etc.), and Niebuhr (*Description de l'Arabie*, pp. 72–86). I pass slightly; I am not fond of repeating words like a parrot.

40 A familiar tale in Voltaire's *Zadig* (*le Chien et le Cheval*) is related to prove the natural sagacity of the Arabs (d'Herbelot, *Bibliot. Orient.*, pp. 120–21; Gagnier, *Vie de Mahomet*, i, 37–46); but d'Arvieux, or rather La Roque (*Voyage de Palestine*, p. 92), denies the boasted superiority of the Bedoweens. The one hundred and sixty-nine sentences of Ali (translated by Ockley, London, 1718) afford a just and favourable specimen of Arabian wit.

 * *page 790* [drums]

41 Pocock (*Specimen*, pp. 158–61) and Casiri (*Bibliot. Hispano-Arabica*, i, 48, 84, etc., 119; ii, 17, etc.) speak of the Arabian poets before Mahomet; the seven poems of the Caaba have been published in English by Sir William Jones [orientalist, 1746–94]; but his honourable mission to India has deprived us of his own notes, far more interesting than the obscure and obsolete text.

42 Sale's *Preliminary Discourse*, pp. 29–30.

43 D'Herbelot, *Bibliot. Orient.*, p. 458; Gagnier, *Vie de Mahomet*, iii, 118. Caab and Hesnus (Pocock, *Specimen*, pp. 43, 46, 48) were likewise conspicuous for their liberality; and the latter is elegantly praised by an Arabian poet: *Videbis eum cum accesseris exultantem, ac si dares illi quod ab illo petis* ['You will see him rejoice when you approach him for something, and equally if you give him what you seek from him'].

44 Whatever can now be known of the idolatry of the ancient Arabians may be found in Pocock (*Specimen*, pp. 89–136, 163–64). His profound erudition is

more clearly and concisely interpreted by Sale (*Preliminary Discourse*, pp. 14–24); and Assemanni (*Bibliot. Orient.*, iv, 580–90) has added some valuable remarks.

45 ἱερὸν ἁγιώτατον ἵδρυται τιμώμενον ὑπὸ πάντων Ἀράβων περιττότερον (Diodor. Sicul., i, iii, 211). The character and position are so correctly apposite, that I am surprised how this curious passage should have been read without notice or application. Yet this famous temple had been overlooked by Agatharchides (*de Mari Rubro*, p. 58, in Hudson, tom. i), whom Diodorus copies in the rest of the description. Was the Sicilian more knowing than the Egyptian? Or was the Caaba built between the years of Rome 650 and 746, the dates of these respective histories? (Dodwell, in Dissert., *ad* tom. i, Hudson p. 72; Fabricius, *Bibliot. Graec.*, ii, 770.) [Diodorus, a Sicilian, wrote in the first century BC.]

46 Pocock, *Specimen*, pp. 60–61. From the death of Mahomet we ascend to 68, from his birth to 129, years before the Christian era. The veil or curtain, which is now of silk and gold, was no more than a piece of Egyptian linen (Abulfeda, *in Vit. Mohammed.*, 6, 14).

47 The original plan of the Caaba (which is servilely copied in Sale, the *Universal History*, etc.) was a Turkish draught, which Reland (*de Religione Mohammedica*, pp. 113–23) has corrected and explained from the best authorities. For the description and legend of the Caaba, consult Pocock (*Specimen*, pp. 115–22); the *Bibliothèque Orientale* of d'Herbelot (*Caaba, Hagiar, Zemzem*, etc.) and Sale (*Preliminary Discourse*, pp. 114–22).

48 Cosa, the fifth ancestor of Mahomet, must have usurped the Caaba, AD 440; but the story is differently told by Jannabi (Gagnier, *Vie de Mahomet*, i, 65–69) and by Abulfeda (*in Vit. Moham.*, 6, 13).

49 In the second century, Maximus of Tyre attributes to the Arabs the worship of a stone – Ἀράβιοι σέβουσι μὲν, ὅντινα δὲ οὐκ οἶδα, τὸ δὲ ἄγαλμα εἶδον λίθος ἦν τετράγωνος ['The Arabs do worship; whom I do not know, but the image which I have seen was a four-sided stone'] (*Dissert.* viii, i, 143, edit. Reiske); and the reproach is furiously re-echoed by the Christians (Clemens, *Alex. in Protreptico*, p. 40; Arnobius, *contra Gentes*, vi, 246). Yet these stones were no other than the βαίτυλα of Syria and Greece, so renowned in sacred and profane antiquity (Euseb., *Praep. Evangel.*, i, 37; Marsham, *Canon. Chron.*, pp. 54–56).

50 The two horrid subjects of ἀνδροθυσία and παιδοθυσία [human sacrifice and child sacrifice] are accurately discussed by the learned Sir John Marsham (*Canon. Chron.*, pp. 76–78, 301–04). Sanchoniatho derives the Phoenician sacrifices from the example of Chronus; but we are ignorant whether Chronus lived before or after Abraham, or indeed whether he lived at all.

51 κατ᾽ ἔτος ἕκαστον παῖδα ἔθυον, is the reproach of Porphyry; but he likewise imputes to the Romans the same barbarous custom, which, AUC 657, had been finally abolished. Dumaetha, *Daumat al Gendal*, is noticed by Ptolemy (*Tabul.*, p. 37; *Arabia*, pp. 9–29); and Abulfeda (p. 57); and may be found in d'Anville's maps, in the mid-desert between Chaibar and Tadmor.

52 Procopius (*de Bell. Persico*, i, 28); Evagrius (vi, 21); and Pocock (*Specimen*, pp. 72, 86) attest the human sacrifices of the Arabs in the vith century. The danger and escape of Abdallah is a tradition rather than a fact (Gagnier, *Vie de Mahomet*, i, 82–84).

* *page 793*   [with difficulty]

53 *Suillis carnibus abstinent*, says Solinus (*Polyhistor.*, ch. 33), who copies Pliny (viii, 68) in the strange supposition that hogs cannot live in Arabia. The Egyptians

were actuated by a natural and superstitious horror for that unclean beast (Marsham, *Canon.*, p. 205). The old Arabians likewise practised, *post coitum*, the rite of ablution (Herodot., i, 80), which is sanctified by the Mahometan law (Reland, p. 75, etc; Chardin, or rather the *Mollah* of Shaw Abbas, iv, 71, etc.)

54 The Mahometan doctors are not fond of the subject, yet they hold circumcision necessary to salvation, and even pretend that Mahomet was miraculously born without a foreskin (Pocock, *Specimen*, pp. 319–20; Sale's *Preliminary Discourse*, pp. 106–07).

55 Diodorus Siculus (i, ii, 142–45) has cast on their religion the curious, but superficial, glance of a Greek. Their astronomy would be far more valuable: they had looked through the telescope of reason, since they could doubt whether the sun were in the number of the planets or of the fixed stars.

56 Simplicius (who quotes Porphyry), *de Caelo*, ii, xlvi, 123, 18; *apud* Marsham, *Canon. Chron.*, p. 474, who doubts the fact, because it is adverse to his systems. The earliest date of the Chaldean observations is the year 2234 before Christ. After the conquest of Babylon by Alexander, they were communicated, at the request of Aristotle, to the astronomer Hipparchus. What a moment in the annals of science!

57 Pocock (*Specimen*, pp. 138–46); Hottinger (*Hist. Oriental.*, pp. 162–203); Hyde (*de Religione Vet. Persarum*, pp. 124, 128, etc.); d'Herbelot (*Sabi*, pp. 725–26); and Sale (*Preliminary Discourse*, pp. 14–15), rather excite than gratify our curiosity; and the last of these writers confounds Sabianism with the primitive religion of the Arabs.

58 D'Anville (*L'Euphrates et le Tigre*, pp. 130–47) will fix the position of these ambiguous Christians; Assemannus (*Bibliot. Oriental.*, iv, 607–14) may explain their tenets. But it is a slippery task to ascertain the creed of an ignorant people, afraid and ashamed to disclose their secret traditions.

59 The Magi were fixed in the province of Bahrein (Gagnier, *Vie de Mahomet*, iii, 114) and mingled with the old Arabians (Pocock, *Specimen*, pp. 146–50).

* *page 794*   [fanciful]

60 The state of the Jews and Christians in Arabia is described by Pocock from Sharestani, etc. (*Specimen*, pp. 60, 134, etc.); Hottinger (*Hist. Orient.*, pp. 212–38); d'Herbelot (*Bibliot. Orient.*, pp. 474–76); Basnage (*Hist. des Juifs*, vii, 185; viii, 280); and Sale (*Preliminary Discourse*, pp. 22, etc. 33, etc.).

61 In their offerings, it was a maxim to defraud God for the profit of the idol, not a more potent, but a more irritable patron (Pocock, *Specimen*, pp. 108–09).

62 Our versions now extant, whether Jewish or Christian, appear more recent than the Koran; but the existence of a prior translation may be fairly inferred: 1. From the perpetual practice of the synagogue, of expounding the Hebrew lesson by a paraphrase in the vulgar tongue of the country; 2. From the analogy of the Armenian, Persian, Aethiopic versions, expressly quoted by the fathers of the fifth century, who assert that the Scriptures were translated into *all* the Barbaric languages (Walton, *Prolegomena ad Biblia Polygot.*, pp. 34, 93–97; Simon, *Hist. Critique du V. et du N. Testament*, i, 180–81, 282–86, 293, 305–06; iv, 206).

63 *In eo conveniunt omnes, ut plebeio viliquegenere ortum*, etc. (Hottinger, *Hist. Orient.*, p. 136). Yet Theophanes, the most ancient of the Greeks and the father of many a lie, confesses that Mahomet was of the race of Ismael, ἐκ μιᾶς γενικωτάτης φυλῆς [from the same original stock] (*Chronograph.*, p. 277).

64 Abulfeda (*in Vit. Mohammed.*, ch. 1, 2) and Gagnier (*Vie de Mahomet*, pp. 25–97)

describe the popular and approved genealogy of the prophet. At Mecca, I would not dispute its authenticity: at Lausanne, I will venture to observe, 1. *That* from Ismael to Mahomet, a period of 2500 years, they reckon thirty, instead of seventy-five, generations; 2. *That* the modern Bedoweens are ignorant of their history and careless of their pedigree (*Voyage* d'Arvieux, pp. 100, 103).

65 The seed of this history, or fable, is contained in the cvth chapter of the Koran; and Gagnier (in *Praefat. ad Vit. Moham.*, pp. 18, etc.) has translated the historical narrative of Abulfeda, which may be illustrated from d'Herbelot (*Bibliot. Orientale*, p. 12) and Pocock (*Specimen*, p. 64). Prideaux (*Life of Mahomet*, p. 48) calls it a lie of the coinage of Mahomet; but Sale (Koran, pp. 501–03), who is half a Musulman, attacks the inconsistent faith of the Doctor for believing the miracles of the Delphic Apollo. Maracci (*Alcoran*, i, ii, 14; ii, 823) ascribes the miracle to the devil, and extorts from the Mahometans the confession that God would not have defended against the Christians the idols of the Caaba.

66 The safest eras of Abulfeda (*in Vit.*, i, 2), of Alexander, or the Greeks 882, of Bocht Naser, or Nabonasser, 1316, equally lead us to the year 569. The old Arabian calendar is too dark and uncertain to support the Benedictines (*Art de vérifier les Dates*, p. 15), who from the day of the month and week deduce a new mode of calculation, and remove the birth of Mahomet to the year of Christ 570, the 10th of November. Yet this date would agree with the year 882 of the Greeks, which is assigned by Elmacin (*Hist. Saracen.*, p. 5) and Abulpharagius (*Dynast.*, p. 101, and Errata, Pocock's version). While we refine our chronology, it is possible that the illiterate prophet was ignorant of his own age.

67 I copy the honourable testimony of Abu Taleb to his family and nephew. *Laus Dei, qui nos a stirpe Abrahami et semine Ismaelis constituit, et nobis regionem sacram dedit, et nos iudices hominibus statuit. Porro Mohammed filius Abdollahi nepotis mei* (nepos meus) *quocum ex aequo librabitur e Koraishidis quispiam cui non praeponderaturus est, bonitate et excellentia, et intellectu et gloria et acumine etsi opum inops fuerit (et certe opes umbra transiens sunt et depositum quod reddi debet), desiderio Chadijae filiae Chowailedi tenetur, et illa vicissim ipsius; quicquid autem dotis vice petieritis, ego in me suscipiam.* ['Praise be to God, who has created us from the stock of Abraham and the seed of Ishmael, and has given us a holy place, and has set us up as judges among men. Henceforth Mahomet, son of Abdallah, my nephew, is joined in love with Cadijah, daughter of Chowailed, and she with him. In goodness and excellence and intellect and glory and perception none among the Koreish will be found to excel him, even if he lacks worldly goods (and certainly riches are a fleeting shadow that must be returned); whatever you ask by way of dowry, I myself will undertake to pay.'] (Pocock, *Specimen*, e septima parte libri Ebn Hamduni.)

68 The private life of Mahomet, from his birth to his mission, is preserved by Abulfeda (*in Vit.*, ch. 3–7) and the Arabian writers of genuine or apocryphal note who are alleged by Hottinger (*Hist. Orient.*, p. 204–11); Maracci (i, 10–14); and Gagnier (*Vie de Mahomet*, i, 97–134).

69 Abulfeda, *in Vit.*, ch. 65–66; Gagnier, *Vie de Mahomet*, iii, 272–89; the best traditions of the person and conversation of the prophet are derived from Ayesha, Ali, and Abu Horaira (Gagnier, ii, 267; Ockley's *Hist. of the Saracens*, ii, 149), surnamed the father of a cat, who died in the year 59 of the Hegira [Mahomet's flight from Mecca to Medina in AD 622, from which the Mohammedan era is calculated].

70 Those who believe that Mahomet could read or write are incapable of reading what is written, with another pen, in the Surats, or chapters of the Koran, vii, xxix, xcvi. These texts, and the tradition of the Sonna, are admitted without doubt by Abulfeda (*in Vit.*, ch. vii); Gagnier (*Not. ad* Abulfed., p. 15); Pocock (*Specimen*, p. 151); Reland (*de Religione Mohammedica*, p. 236); and Sale (*Preliminary Discourse*, p. 42). Mr White, almost alone, denies the ignorance, to accuse the imposture, of the prophet. His arguments are far from satisfactory. Two short trading journeys to the fairs of Syria were surely not sufficient to infuse a science so rare among the citizens of Mecca; it was not in the cool deliberate act of a treaty that Mahomet would have dropped the mask; nor can any conclusion be drawn from the words of disease and delirium. The *lettered* youth, before he aspired to the prophetic character, must have often exercised, in private life, the arts of reading and writing; and his first converts, of his own family, would have been the first to detect and upbraid his scandalous hypocrisy. White's Sermons, pp. 203, 204, Notes, pp. xxxvi–xxxviii.

71 The Count de Boulainvilliers (*Vie de Mohammed*, pp. 202–28) leads his Arabian pupil, like the *Telemachus* of Fénélon, or the *Cyrus* of Ramsay. [Fénélon's *Télémaque* (1699) and the Chevalier de Ramsay's *Voyage de Cyrus* (1727) were fictitious accounts of the education of a prince.] His journey to the court of Persia is probably a fiction; nor can I trace the origin of his exclamation, *Les Grecs sont pourtant des hommes* ['The Greeks are nevertheless human beings']. The two Syrian journeys are expressed by almost all the Arabian writers, both Mahometans and Christians (Gagnier, *ad* Abulfed., p. 10).

72 I am not at leisure to pursue the fables or conjectures which name the strangers accused or suspected by the infidels of Mecca (Koran, 16, 223; 35, 297 with Sale's Remarks; Prideaux's *Life of Mahomet*, pp. 22–27; Gagnier, *Not. ad Abulfed.*, pp. 11, 74; Maracci, ii, 400). Even Prideaux has observed that the transaction must have been secret, and that the scene lay in the heart of Arabia.

73 Abulfeda, *in Vit.*, 7, 15; Gagnier, i, 133, 135. The situation of Mount Hera is remarked by Abulfeda (*Geograph. Arab.*, p. 4). Yet Mahomet had never read of the cave of Egeria *ubi nocturnae Numa constituebat amicae* ['where Numa had nocturnal assignments with his fair companion, viz. the Nymph Egeria'], of the Idaean Mount where Minos conversed with Jove, etc.

74 Koran, 9, 153. Al Beidawi and the other commentators quoted by Sale adhere to the charge; but I do not understand that it is coloured by the most obscure or absurd tradition of the Talmudists [commentators on the Jewish law].

75 Hottinger, *Hist. Orient.*, p. 225–28. The Collyridian heresy was carried from Thrace to Arabia by some women, and the name was borrowed from the κολλυρίς, or cake, which they offered to the goddess. This example, that of Beryllus, bishop of Bostra (Euseb., *Hist. Eccles.*, vi, 33), and several others, may excuse the reproach, *Arabia haereseon ferax* ['Arabia fertile in heresies'].

76 The three gods in the Koran (4, 81; 5, 92) are obviously directed against our Catholic mystery; but the Arabic commentators understand them of the Father, the Son, and the Virgin Mary, an heretical Trinity, maintained, as it is said, by some barbarians at the council of Nicaea (Eutych., *Annal.*, i, 440). But the existence of the *Marianites* is denied by the candid Beausobre (*Hist. de Manichéisme*, i, 532), and he derives the mistake from the word *Rouah*, the Holy Ghost, which, in some Oriental tongues, is of the feminine gender, and is figuratively styled the Mother of Christ in the gospel of the Nazarenes.

77 This train of thought is philosophically exemplified in the character of Abraham, who opposed in Chaldaea the first introduction of idolatry (Koran, 6, 106; d'Herbelot, *Bibliot. Orient.*, p. 13).

78 See the Koran, particularly the second (p. 30), the fifty-seventh (p. 437), the fifty-eighth (p. 441), chapters, which proclaim the omnipotence of the Creator.

79 The most orthodox creeds are translated by Pocock (*Specimen*, pp. 274, 284–92); Ockley (*Hist. of the Saracens*, ii, lxxxii–xcv); Reland (*de Religion. Moham.*, i, 7–13); and Chardin (*Voyages en Perse*, iv, 4–28). The great truth that God is without similitude, is foolishly criticised by Maracci (*Alcoran*, i, iii, 87–94), because he made man after his own image.

80 Reland, *de Relig. Moham.*, i, 17–47; Sale's *Preliminary Discourse*, pp. 73–76; *Voyages* de Chardin, iv, 28–37 and 37–47 for the Persian addition, 'Ali is the vicar of God!' Yet the precise number of prophets is not an article of faith.

81 For the Apocryphal books of Adam, see Fabricius, *Codex Pseudepigraphus V. T.*, pp. 27–29; of Seth, pp. 154–57; of Enoch, pp. 160–219. But the book of Enoch is consecrated, in some measure, by the quotation of the apostle St Jude; and a long legendary fragment is alleged by Syncellus and Scaliger.

82 The seven precepts of Noah are explained by Marsham (*Canon. Chronicus*, pp. 154–80), who adopts, on this occasion, the learning and credulity of Selden.

83 The articles of *Adam, Noah, Abraham, Moses*, etc. in the *Bibliothèque* of d'Herbelot, are gaily bedecked with the fanciful legends of the Mahometans, who have built on the groundwork of Scripture and the Talmud.

84 Koran, 7, 128, etc.; 10, 173, etc.; d'Herbelot, pp. 647, etc.

85 Koran, 3, 40; 4, 80; d'Herbelot, pp. 399, etc.

86 See the gospel of St Thomas, or of the Infancy, in the *Codex Apocryphus N. T.* of Fabricius, who collects the various testimonies concerning it (pp. 128–58). It was published in Greek by Cotelier, and in Arabic by Sike, who thinks our present copy more recent than Mahomet. Yet his quotations agree with the original about the speech of Christ in his cradle, his living birds of clay, etc. (Sike, 1, 168–69; 36, 198–99; 46, 206; Cotelier, 2, 160–61).

87 It is darkly hinted in the Koran (3, 39), and more clearly explained by the tradition of the Sonnites (Sale's Note, and Maracci, ii, 112). In the xiith century, the immaculate conception was condemned by St Bernard as a presumptuous novelty (Fra Paolo, *Istoria del Concilio di Trento*, Bk ii).

88 See the Koran, 3, 53 and 4, 156 of Maracci's edition. *Deus est praestantissimus dolose agentium* (an odd praise) . . . *nec crucifixerunt eum, sed obiecta est eis similitudo* ['God is most high among the deceivers . . . nor did they crucify him, but a substitute was given to them in his stead']: an expression that may suit with the system of the Docetes; but the commentators believe (Maracci, ii, 113–15, 173; Sale, pp. 42–43, 79) that another man, a friend or an enemy, was crucified in the likeness of Jesus: a fable which they had read in the gospel of St Barnabas, and which had been started as early as the time of Irenaeus [AD *c.*120–*c.*200] by some Ebionite heretics (Beausobre, *Hist. du Manichéisme*, ii, 25; Mosheim, *de Reb. Christ.*, p. 353).

89 This charge is obscurely urged in the Koran (3, 45), but neither Mahomet nor his followers are sufficiently versed in languages and criticism to give any weight or colour to their suspicions. Yet the Arians and Nestorians could relate some stories, and the illiterate prophet might listen to the bold assertions of the Manichaeans. See Beausobre, i, 291–305.

90 Among the prophecies of the Old and New Testament, which are perverted by the fraud or ignorance of the Musulmans, they apply to the prophet the promise of the *Paraclete*, or Comforter, which had been already usurped by the Montanists and Manichaeans (Beausobre, *Hist. Critique du Manichéisme*, i, 263, etc.); and the easy change of letters, περικλυτός [renowned] for παράκλητος [comforter], affords the etymology of the name of Mohammed (Maracci, i, i, 15–28).

91 For the Koran, see d'Herbelot, pp. 85–88; Maracci, tom. i *in Vit. Mohammed.*, pp. 32–45; Sale, *Preliminary Discourse*, pp. 56–70.

  * *page 799* [doctrine]

92 Koran, 17, 89. In Sale, pp. 235–36. In Maracci, p. 410.

93 Yet a sect of Arabians was persuaded that it might be equalled or surpassed by an human pen (Pocock, *Specimen*, pp. 221, etc.); and Maracci (the polemic is too hard for the translator) derides the rhyming affectation of the most applauded passage (i, ii, 69–75).

  * *page 800* [translation]

94 *Colloquia* (whether real or fabulous) *in media Arabia atque ab Arabibus habita* (Lowth, *de Poesi Hebraeorum Praelect.*, xxxii, xxxiii, xxxiv, with his German editor Michaelis, *Epimetron* iv). Yet Michaelis (pp. 671–73) has detected many Egyptian images, the elephantiasis, papyrus, Nile, crocodile, etc. The language is ambiguously styled *Arabico-Hebraea*. The resemblance of the sister dialects was much more visible in their childhood than in their mature age (Michaelis, p. 682; Schultens, in *Praefat. Job*).

95 Al Bochari died AH 224 [AH, in the year of the Hegira]. See d'Herbelot, pp. 208, 416, 827. Gagnier, *Not. ad* Abulfed., 19, 33.

96 See more remarkably, Koran, ch. 2, 6, 12, 13, 17. Prideaux (*Life of Mahomet*, pp. 18–19) has confounded the impostor. Maracci, with a more learned apparatus, has shown that the passages which deny his miracles are clear and positive (*Alcoran*, i, ii, 7–12), and those which seem to assert them are ambiguous and insufficient (pp. 12–22).

97 See the *Specimen Hist. Arabum*, the text of Abulpharagius, p. 17; the notes of Pocock, pp. 187–90; d'Herbelot, *Bibliothèque Orientale*, pp. 76–77; *Voyages* de Chardin, iv, 200–03. Maracci (*Alcoran*, i, 22–64) has most laboriously collected and confuted the miracles and prophecies of Mahomet, which according to some writers, amount to three thousand.

  * *page 801* [intimate]
  † *page 801* [encounter]

98 The nocturnal journey is circumstantially related by Abulfeda (*in Vit. Mohammed.*, 19, 33), who wishes to think it a vision; by Prideaux (pp. 31–40), who aggravates the absurdities; and by Gagnier (i, 252–343), who declares, from the zealous Al Jannabi, that to deny this journey is to disbelieve the Koran. Yet the Koran, without naming either heaven or Jerusalem or Mecca, has only dropped a mysterious hint: *Laus illi qui transtulit servum suum ab oratorio Haram ad oratorium remotissimum* ['Praise be upon him who bore his servant from the shrine of Haram to the remotest shrine'] (Koran, 17, 1, in Maracci, ii, 407; for Sale's version is more licentious). A slender basis for the aerial structure of tradition.

99 In the prophetic style, which uses the present or past for the future, Mahomet had said: *Appropinquavit hora et scissa est luna* ['The hour has come and the moon

is split asunder'] (Koran, 54, 1; in Maracci, ii, 688). This figure of rhetoric has been converted into a fact, which is said to be attested by the most respectable eye-witnesses (Maracci, ii, 690). The festival is still celebrated by the Persians (Chardin, iv, 201); and the legend is tediously spun out by Gagnier (*Vie de Mahomet*, i, 183–234) on the faith, as it should seem, of the credulous Al Jannabi. Yet a Mahometan doctor has arraigned the credit of the principal witness (*apud* Pocock, *Specimen*, p. 187); the best interpreters are content with the simple sense of the Koran (Al Beidawi, *apud* Hottinger, *Hist. Orient.*, ii, 302); and the silence of Abulfeda is worthy of a prince and a philosopher.

100 Abulpharagius, in *Specimen Hist. Arab.*, p. 17; and his scepticism is justified in the notes of Pocock, pp. 190–94, from the purest authorities.

‡ *page 801* [plausibly]

101 The most authentic account of these precepts, pilgrimage, prayer, fasting, alms, and ablutions is extracted from the Persian and Arabian theologians by Maracci (*Prodrom.*, iv, 9–24); Reland (in his excellent treatise *de Religione Mohammedica*, Utrecht, 1717, pp. 67–123); and Chardin (*Voyages en Perse*, iv, 47–195). Maracci is a partial accuser; but the jeweller, Chardin, had the eyes of a philosopher; and Reland, a judicious student, had travelled over the East in his closet at Utrecht. The xivth letter of Tournefort (*Voyage du Levant*, ii, 325–60, in octavo) describes what he had seen of the religion of the Turks.

102 Mahomet (Sale's Koran, 9, 153) reproaches the Christians with taking their priests and monks for their lords, besides God. Yet Maracci (*Prodromus*, iii, 69–70) excuses the worship, especially of the pope, and quotes, from the Koran itself, the case of Eblis, or Satan, who was cast from heaven for refusing to adore Adam.

103 Koran, 5, 94, and Sale's note, which refers to the authority of Jallaloddin and Al Beidawi. D'Herbelot declares that Mahomet condemned *la vie religieuse*; and that the first swarms of fakirs, dervises, etc. did not appear till after the year 300 of the Hegira (*Bibliot. Orient.*, pp. 292, 718).

104 See the double prohibition (Koran, 2, 25; 5, 94), the one in the style of a legislator, the other in that of a fanatic. The public and private motives of Mahomet are investigated by Prideaux (*Life of Mahomet*, pp. 62–64) and Sale (*Preliminary Discourse*, p. 124).

105 The jealousy of Maracci (*Prodromus*, iv, 33) prompts him to enumerate the more liberal alms of the Catholics of Rome. Fifteen great hospitals are open to many thousand patients and pilgrims, fifteen hundred maidens are annually portioned, fifty-six charity schools are founded for both sexes, one hundred and twenty confraternities relieve the wants of their brethren, etc. The benevolence of London is still more extensive; but I am afraid that much more is to be ascribed to the humanity than to the religion of the people.

* *page 803* [spirits]

106 See Herodotus (ii, 123) and our learned countryman Sir John Marsham (*Canon. Chronicus*, p. 46). The Ἅδης [Hades] of the same writer (pp. 254–74) is an elaborate sketch of the infernal regions, as they were painted by the fancy of the Egyptians and Greeks, of the poets and philosophers of antiquity.

107 The Koran (2, 259, etc.; of Sale, p. 32; of Maracci, p. 97) relates an ingenious miracle, which satisfied the curiosity, and confirmed the faith, of Abraham.

108 The candid Reland has demonstrated that Mahomet damns all unbelievers (*de Religion. Moham.*, pp. 128–42); that devils will not be finally saved (pp. 196–

99); that paradise will not *solely* consist of corporeal delights (pp. 199–205); and that women's souls are immortal (pp. 205–09).

109 Al Beidawi, *apud* Sale, Koran, 9, 164. The refusal to pray for an unbelieving kindred is justified, according to Mahomet, by the duty of a prophet, and the example of Abraham, who reprobated his own father as an enemy of God. Yet Abraham (he adds, 9, 116; Maracci, ii, 317) *fuit sane pius, mitis* [was certainly pious and gentle].

  * *page 804* [religious zeal]

110 For the day of judgment, hell, paradise, etc. consult the Koran (2, 25; 56, 78, etc.), with Maracci's virulent, but learned, refutation (in his notes, and in the *Prodromus*, iv, 78, 120, 122, etc.); d'Herbelot (*Bibliothèque Orientale*, pp. 368, 375); Reland (pp. 47–61); and Sale (pp. 76–173). The original ideas of the Magi are darkly and doubtfully explored by their apologist, Dr Hyde (*Hist. Religionis Persarum*, 33, 402–12, Oxon., 1760). In the article of Mahomet, Bayle has shown how indifferently wit and philosophy supply the absence of genuine information.

111 Before I enter on the history of the prophet, it is incumbent on me to produce my evidence. The Latin, French, and English versions of the Koran are preceded by historical discourses, and the three translators, Maracci (i, 10–32); Savary (i, 1–248); and Sale (*Preliminary Discourse*, pp. 33–56), had accurately studied the language and character of their author. Two professed lives of Mahomet have been composed by Dr Prideaux (*Life of Mahomet*, seventh edition, London, 1718, in octavo) and the Count de Boulainvilliers (*Vie de Mahomed*, Londres, 1730, in octavo), but the adverse wish of finding an impostor or an hero has too often corrupted the learning of the Doctor and the ingenuity of the Count. The article in d'Herbelot (*Bibliot. Orient.*, p. 598–603) is chiefly drawn from Novairi and Mircond, but the best and most authentic of our guides is M. Gagnier, a Frenchman by birth, and professor at Oxford of the Oriental tongues. In two elaborate works (Ismael Abulfeda, *de Vita et Rebus gestis Mohammedis*, etc., Latine vertit, Praefatione et Notis illustravit Johannes Gagnier, Oxon. 1723, in folio. *La Vie de Mahomet traduite et compilée de l'Alcoran, des Traditions authentiques de la Sonna et des meilleurs Auteurs Arabes*; Amsterdam, 1748, 3 vols. in 12mo) he has interpreted, illustrated, and supplied the Arabic text of Abulfeda and Al Jannabi: the first, an enlightened prince, who reigned at Hamah in Syria AD 1310–32 (see Gagnier, *Praefat. ad* Abulfed.); the second, a credulous doctor, who visited Mecca, AD 1566 (d'Herbelot, p. 397; Gagnier, iii, 209–10). These are my general vouchers, and the inquisitive reader may follow the order of time and the division of chapters. Yet I must observe that both Abulfeda and Al Jannabi are modern historians, and that they cannot appeal to any writers of the first century of the Hegira.

112 After the Greeks, Prideaux (p. 8) discloses the secret doubts of the wife of Mahomet. As if he had been a privy counsellor of the prophet, Boulainvilliers (pp. 272, etc.) unfolds the sublime and patriotic views of Cadijah and the first disciples.

113 *Vezirus, portitor, bajulus, onus ferens* [vizier, porter, carrier, load-bearer]; and this plebeian name was transferred by an apt metaphor to the pillars of the state (Gagnier, Not. *ad* Abulfed., p. 19). I endeavour to preserve the Arabian idiom, as far as I can feel it myself in a Latin or French translation.

* *page 806* [estimated]

114 The passages of the Koran in behalf of toleration are strong and numerous; 2, 257; 16, 129; 17, 54; 45, 15; 50, 39; 88, 21, etc., with the notes of Maracci and Sale. This character alone may generally decide the doubts of the learned, whether a chapter was revealed at Mecca or Medina.

115 See the Koran (*passim*, and especially 7, 123, 124, etc.) and the tradition of the Arabs (Pocock, *Specimen*, pp. 35–37). The caverns of the tribe of Thamud, fit for men of the ordinary stature, were shown in the midway between Medina and Damascus (Abulfed., *Arabiae Descript.*, pp. 43–44), and may be probably ascribed to the Troglodytes of the primitive world (Michaelis, *ad* Lowth, *de Poesi Hebraeor.*, pp. 131–34. *Recherches sur les Egyptiens*, ii, 48, etc.).

116 In the time of Job, the crime of impiety was punished by the Arabian magistrate (31, 26–28). I blush for a respectable prelate (*de Poesi Hebraeorum*, pp. 650–51, edit. Michaelis; and letter of a late professor in the university of Oxford, pp. 15–53), who justifies and applauds this patriarchal inquisition.

* *page 807* [posted]

117 D'Herbelot, *Bibliot. Orient.*, p. 445. He quotes a particular history of the flight of Mahomet.

118 The *Hegira* was instituted by Omar, the second caliph, in imitation of the era of the martyrs of the Christians (d'Herbelot, p. 444); and properly commenced sixty-eight days before the flight of Mahomet, with the first of Moharren or first day of that Arabian year, which coincides with Friday, July 16th, AD 622 (Abulfeda, *Vit. Moham.*, 22–23, 45–50, and Greaves's edition of Ullug Beg's *Epochae Arabum*, etc., 1, 8, 10, etc.).

119 Mahomet's life, from his mission to the Hegira, may be found in Abulfeda (pp. 14–45) and Gagnier (i, 134–251, 342–83). The legend from pp. 187–234 is vouched by Al Jannabi, and disdained by Abulfeda.

* *page 808* [declared]

120 The triple inauguration of Mahomet is described by Abulfeda (pp. 30, 33, 40, 86), and Gagnier (i, 342, etc.; 349, etc.; ii, 223, etc.).

121 Prideaux (*Life of Mahomet*, p. 44) reviles the wickedness of the impostor, who despoiled two poor orphans, the sons of a carpenter: a reproach which he drew from the *Disputatio contra Saracenos*, composed in Arabic before the year 1130; but the honest Gagnier (*ad* Abulfed., p. 53) has shown that they were deceived by the word *Al Nagjar*, which signifies, in this place, not an obscure trade, but a noble tribe of Arabs. The desolate state of the ground is described by Abulfeda; and his worthy interpreter has proved, from Al Bochari, the offer of a price; from Al Jannabi, the fair purchase; and from Ahmed Ben Joseph, the payment of the money by the generous Abubeker. On these grounds the prophet must be honourably acquitted.

122 Al Jannabi (*apud* Gagnier, ii, 246, 324) describes the seal and pulpit as two venerable relics of the apostle of God; and the portrait of his court is taken from Abulfeda (44, 85).

123 The viiith and ixth chapters of the Koran are the loudest and most vehement; and Maracci (*Prodromus*, iv, 59–64) has inveighed with more justice than discretion against the double-dealing of the impostor.

124 The xth and xxth chapters of Deuteronomy, with the practical comments of Joshua, David, etc., are read with more awe than satisfaction by the pious Christians of the present age. But the bishops, as well as the rabbis of former

times, have beat the drum-ecclesiastic with pleasure and success (Sale's *Preliminary Discourse*, pp. 142–43).

125 Abulfeda, *in Vit. Moham.*, p. 156. The private arsenal of the apostle consisted of nine swords, three lances, seven pikes or half-pikes, a quiver and three bows, seven cuirasses, three shields, and two helmets (Gagnier, iii, 328–34), with a large white standard, a black banner (p. 335), twenty horses (p. 322), etc. Two of his martial sayings are recorded by tradition (Gagnier, ii, 88, 337).

126 The whole subject *de jure belli Mohammedanorum* [of the Mohammedan law of war] is exhausted in a separate dissertation by the learned Reland (*Dissertationes Miscellaneae*, tom. iii, Dissertat. x, pp. 3–53).

  * *page 811* [image]

127 The doctrine of absolute predestination, on which few religions can reproach each other, is sternly exposed in the Koran (3, 52–53; 4, 70, etc., with the notes of Sale; and 17, 413, with those of Maracci). Reland (*de Relig. Mohamm.*, p. 61–64) and Sale (*Prelim. Discourse*, p. 103) represent the opinions of the doctors [scholars], and our modern travellers the confidence, the fading confidence, of the Turks.

128 Al Jannabi (*apud* Gagnier, ii, 9) allows him seventy or eighty horse; and on two other occasions, prior to the battle of Ohud, he enlists a body of thirty (p. 10), and of 500 (p. 66), troopers. Yet the Musulmans, in the field of Ohud, had no more than two horses, according to the better sense of Abulfeda (*in Vit. Mohamm.*, 31, 65). In the *Stony* province, the camels were numerous; but the horse appears to have been less common than in the *Happy* or the *Desert* Arabia.

129 Beder Houneene, twenty miles from Medina and forty from Mecca, is on the high road of the caravan of Egypt; and the pilgrims annually commemorate the prophet's victory by illuminations, rockets etc. Shaw's *Travels*, p. 477.

130 The place to which Mahomet retired during the action is styled by Gagnier (in Abulfeda, 27, 58; *Vie de Mahomet*, ii, 30, 33), *umbraculum, une loge de bois avec une porte* [an arbour (Latin), a wooden hut with a door (French)]. The same Arabic word is rendered by Reiske (*Annales Moslemici Abulfedae*, p. 23) by *solium, suggestus editior* [a throne, a raised daïs]; and the difference is of the utmost moment for the honour both of the interpreter and of the hero. I am sorry to observe the pride and acrimony with which Reiske chastises his fellow-labourer. *Saepe sic vertit, ut integrae paginae nequeant nisi una litura corrigi: Arabice non satis callebat et carebat judicio critico* ['His approach is often such that whole pages can only be corrected by emendation: he was not sufficiently knowledgeable in Arabic and he lacked critical judgment']. J. J. Reiske, *Prodidagmata ad Hagji Chalisae Tabulas*, p. 228, *ad calcem* Abulfedae Syriae Tabulae; Lipsiae, 1766, in 4to.

  * *page 812* [weakened]

131 The loose expressions of the Koran (3, 124–25; 8, 9) allow the commentators to fluctuate between the numbers of 1000, 3000, or 9000 angels; and the smallest of these might suffice for the slaughter of seventy of the Koreish (Maracci, *Alcoran.*, ii, 131). Yet the same scholiasts confess that this angelic band was not visible to any mortal eye (Maracci, p. 297). They refine on the words (ch. 8, 16), 'not thou, but God,' etc. (d'Herbelot, *Bibliot. Orientale*, pp. 600–01).

  † *page 812* [the part of his income given to charity]
  ‡ *page 812* [tambourines]

132 *Geograph. Nubiensis*, p. 47.

133 In the iiid chapter of the Koran (pp. 50–53, with Sale's Notes) the prophet alleges some poor excuses for the defeat of Ohud.

134 For the detail of the three Koreish wars, of Beder, of Ohud, and of the ditch, peruse Abulfeda (pp. 56–61, 64–69, 73–77); Gagnier (ii, 23–45, 70–96, 120–39), with the proper articles of d'Herbelot, and the abridgments of Elmacin (*Hist. Saracen.*, pp. 6–7) and Abulpharagius (*Dynast.*, p. 102).

  * *page 813* [the place which Mahomet faced when at prayer; subsequently Mecca]

135 The wars of Mahomet against the Jewish tribes of Kainoka, the Nadhirites, Koraidha, and Chaibar, are related by Abulfeda (pp. 61, 71, 77, 87, etc.) and Gagnier (ii, 61–5, 107–12, 139–48, 268–94).

136 Abu Rafe, the servant of Mahomet, is said to affirm that he himself, and seven other men, afterwards tried, without success, to move the same gate from the ground (Abulfeda, p. 90). Abu Rafe was an eye-witness, but who will be witness for Abu Rafe?

137 The banishment of the Jews is attested by Elmacin (*Hist. Saracen.*, p. 9) and the great Al Tabari (Gagnier, ii, 285). Yet Niebuhr (*Description de l'Arabie*, p. 324) believes that the Jewish religion, and Kareite sect, are still professed by the tribe of Chaibar; and that in the plunder of the caravans the disciples of Moses are the confederates of those of Mahomet.

138 The successive steps of the reduction of Mecca are related by Abulfeda (pp. 84–87, 97–100, 102–11); and Gagnier (ii, 209–45, 309–22; iii, 1–58); Elmacin (*Hist. Saracen.*, pp. 8–10); Abulpharagius (*Dynast.*, p. 103).

  * *page 815* [Roman general, 155–86 bc]
  † *page 815* [rival of Marius, 138–78 bc]
  ‡ *page 815* [anticipate]

139 After the conquest of Mecca, the Mahomet of Voltaire imagines and perpetrates the most horrid crimes. The poet confesses that he is not supported by the truth of history, and can only allege *que celui qui fait la guerre à sa patrie au nom de Dieu est capable de tout* ['that whoever makes war on his country in the name of God is capable of anything'] (*Oeuvres de* Voltaire, xv, 282). The maxim is neither charitable nor philosophic, and some reverence is surely due to the fame of heroes and the religion of nations. I am informed that a Turkish ambassador at Paris was much scandalised at the representation of this tragedy.

  § *page 815* [earned]

140 The Mahometan doctors still dispute whether Mecca was reduced by force or consent (Abulfeda, p. 107, *et* Gagnier *ad locum*); and this verbal controversy is of as much moment as our own about William the *Conqueror*.

141 In excluding the Christians from the peninsula of Arabia, the province of Hejaz, or the navigation of the Red Sea, Chardin (*Voyages en Perse*, iv, 166) and Reland (*Dissert. Miscell.*, iii, 51) are more rigid than the Musulmans themselves. The Christians are received without scruple into the ports of Mocha, and even of Gedda, and it is only the city and precincts of Mecca that are inaccessible to the profane (Niebuhr, *Description de l'Arabie*, pp. 308–09; *Voyage en Arabie*, i, 205, 248, etc.).

142 Abulfeda, pp. 112–15; Gagnier, iii, 67–88; D'Herbelot, *Mohammed*.

143 The siege of Tayef, division of the spoil, etc. are related by Abulfeda (pp. 117–23) and Gagnier (iii, 88–111). It is Al Jannabi who mentions the engines and engineers of the tribe of Daws. The fertile spot of Tayef was supposed to be a piece of the land of Syria detached and dropped in the general deluge.

* *page 816*   [soldiers trained in siege warfare]
* *page 817*   [sappers]

144 The last conquests and pilgrimage of Mahomet are contained In Abulfeda (pp. 121–33); Gagnier (iii, 119–219); Elmacin (pp. 10–11); Abulpharagius (p. 103). The ixth of the Hegira was styled the Year of Embassies (Gagnier, *Not. ad* Abulfed., p. 121).

145 Compare the bigoted Al Jannabi (*apud* Gagnier, ii, 232–55) with the no less bigoted Greeks; Theophanes (pp. 276–78); Zonaras (ii, xiv, 86); and Cedrenus (p. 421).

146 For the battle of Muta and its consequences, see Abulfeda (pp. 100–02); and Gagnier (ii, 327–43). Χάλεδος (says Theophanes) ὃν λέγουσι μάχαιραν τοῦ Θεοῦ. ['Caled . . . whom they call the sword of God.']

147 The expedition of Tabuc is recorded by our ordinary historians, Abulfeda (*Vit. Moham.*, pp. 123–27) and Gagnier (*Vie de Mahomet*, iii, 147–63); but we have the advantage of appealing to the original evidence of the Koran (9, 154, 165), with Sale's learned and rational notes.

148 The *Diploma securitatis Ailensibus* [charter of rights of the people of Ailah] is attested by Ahmed Ben Joseph, and the author *Libri Splendorum* (Gagnier, *Not. ad* Abulfed., p. 125); but Abulfeda himself, as well as Elmacin (*Hist. Saracen.*, p. 11), though he owns Mahomet's regard for the Christians (p. 13), only mentions peace and tribute. In the year 1630, Sionita published at Paris the text and version of Mahomet's patent in favour of the Christians; which was admitted and reprobated by the opposite taste of Salmasius and Grotius (Bayle, *MAHOMET*, Rem. AA). Hottinger doubts of its authenticity (*Hist. Orient.*, p. 237); Renaudot urges the consent of the Mahometans (*Hist. Patriarch. Alex.*, p. 169); but Mosheim (*Hist. Eccles.*, p. 244) shows the futility of their opinion, and inclines to believe it spurious. Yet Abulpharagius quotes the impostor's treaty with the Nestorian patriarch (Asseman., *Bibliot. Orient.*, ii, 418); but Abulpharagius was primate of the Jacobites.

149 The epilepsy, or falling-sickness, of Mahomet, is asserted by Theophanes Zonaras, and the rest of the Greeks; and is greedily swallowed by the gross bigotry of Hottinger (*Hist. Orient.*, pp. 10–11); Prideaux (*Life of Mahomet*, p. 12); and Maracci (tom. ii, *Alcoran*, pp. 762–63). The titles (*the wrapped up, the covered*) of two chapters of the Koran (73–74) can hardly be strained to such an interpretation; the silence, the ignorance of the Mahometan commentators is more conclusive than the most peremptory denial; and the charitable side is espoused by Ockley (*Hist. of the Saracens*, i, 301); Gagnier (*ad* Abulfed., p. 9; *Vie de Mahomet*, i, 118); and Sale (Koran, pp. 469–74).

150 This poison (more ignominious since it was offered as a test of his prophetic knowledge) is frankly confessed by his zealous votaries, Abulfeda (p. 92) and Al Jannabi (*apud* Gagnier, ii, 286–88).

151 The Greeks and Latins have invented and propagated the vulgar and ridiculous story that Mahomet's iron tomb is suspended in the air at *Mecca* (σῆμα μετεωριζόμενον, Laonicus Chalcocondyles *de Rebus Turcicis*, iii, 66), by the action of equal and potent loadstones (*Dictionnaire de Bayle, Mahomet*, Rem EE, FF). Without any philosophical inquiries, it may suffice that, 1. The prophet was not buried at Mecca; and 2. That his tomb at Medina, which has been visited by millions, is placed on the ground (Reland, *de Relig. Moham.*, ii, 19, 209–11; Gagnier, *Vie de Mahomet*, iii, 263–68).

152 Al Jannabi enumerates (*Vie de Mahomet*, iii, 372–91) the multifarious duties of a pilgrim who visits the tombs of the prophet and his companions; and the learned casuist decides that this act of devotion is nearest in obligation and merit to a divine precept. The doctors are divided, which, of Mecca and Medina, be the most excellent (pp. 391–94).

153 The last sickness, death, and burial of Mahomet are described by Abulfeda and Gagnier (*Vit. Moham.*, pp. 133–42; *Vie de Mahomet*, iii, 220–71). The most private and interesting circumstances were originally received from Ayesha, Ali, the sons of Abbas, etc.; and, as they dwelt at Medina and survived the prophet many years, they might repeat the pious tale to a second or third generation of pilgrims.

154 The Christians, rashly enough, have assigned to Mahomet a tame pigeon, that seemed to descend from heaven and whisper in his ear. As this pretended miracle is urged by Grotius (*de Veritate Religionis Christianae*), his Arabic translator, the learned Pocock, inquired of him the names of his authors; and Grotius confessed that it is unknown to the Mahometans themselves. Lest it should provoke their indignation and laughter, the pious *lie* is suppressed in the Arabic version; but it has maintained an edifying place in the numerous editions of the Latin text (Pocock, *Specimen Hist. Arabum*, pp. 186–87; Reland, *de Religion. Moham.*, ii, 39, 259–62).

155 Ἐμοὶ δὲ τοῦτό ἐστιν ἐκ παιδὸς ἀρξάμενον, φωνή τις γιγνομένη ἦ ὅταν γένηται ἀεὶ ἀποτρέπει με τούτου ὃ ἂν μέλλω πράττειν, προτρέπει δὲ οὔποτε. ['This is something which began in my childhood: I hear a voice, which whenever it calls, always dissuades me from whatever I am about to do, and never incites me to do it.'] (Plato, in *Apolog. Socrat.*, 19, 121–22, edit. Fischer). The familiar examples, which Socrates urges in his Dialogue with Theages (Platon. *Opera*, i, 128–29, edit. Hen. Stephan.), are beyond the reach of human foresight; and the divine inspiration (the δαιμόνιον) of the philosopher is clearly taught in the *Memorabilia* of Xenophon. The ideas of the most rational Platonists are expressed by Cicero (*de Divinat.*, i, 54), and in the fourteenth and fifteenth Dissertations of Maximus of Tyre (pp. 153–72, edit. Davis).

* *page 821* [Jonah]

156 In some passage of his voluminous writings, Voltaire compares the prophet, in his old age, to a fakir: *qui détache la chaîne de son cou pour en donner sur les oreilles à ses confrères* ['who removes the bonds from his neck in order to put them over the ears of his fellows'].

157 Gagnier relates, with the same impartial pen, this humane law of the prophet, and the murders of Caab, and Sophian, which he prompted and approved (*Vie de Mahomet*, ii, 69, 97, 208).

158 For the domestic life of Mahomet, consult Gagnier, and the corresponding chapters of Abulfeda, for his diet (iii, 285–88), his children (pp. 189, 289), his wives (pp. 290–303), his marriage with Zeineb (ii, 152–60), his amour with Mary (pp. 303–09), the false accusation of Ayesha (pp. 186–99). The most original evidence of the three last transactions is contained in the xxivth, xxxiiird and lxvith chapters of the Koran, with Sale's Commentary. Prideaux (*Life of Mahomet*, pp. 80–90) and Maracci (*Prodrom. Alcoran*, iv, 49–59) have maliciously exaggerated the frailties of Mahomet.

159 *Incredibile est quo ardore apud eos in Venerem uterque solvitur sexus* ['The passion for lovemaking of both sexes is incredible'] (Ammian. Marcellin., xiv, 4).

160 Sale (*Preliminary Discourse*, pp. 133–37) has recapitulated the laws of marriage, divorce, etc., and the curious reader of Selden's *Uxor Hebraica* will recognise many Jewish ordinances.

161 In a memorable case, the Caliph Omar decided that all presumptive evidence was of no avail; and that all the four witnesses must have actually seen *stylum in pyxide* [the pen in the inkwell] (Abulfedae, *Annales Moslemici*, p. 71, vers. Reiske).

162 *Sibi robur ad generationem, quantum triginta viri habent inesse jactaret; ita ut unica hora posset undecim feminis satisfacere, ut ex Arabum libris refert Stus Petrus Paschasius*, ch. 2. ['He boasted of having the potency of thirty men, so that in a single hour he could satisfy eleven women, as St Peter Paschasius relates from the books of the Arabs.'] (Maracci, *Prodromus Alcoran*, p. iv, p. 55. See likewise Observations de Belon, iii, 10, fol. 179, recto.) Al Jannabi (Gagnier, iii, 487) records his own testimony that he surpassed all men in conjugal vigour; and Abulfeda mentions the exclamation of Ali, who washed his body after his death, *O propheta, certe penis tuus caelum versus erectus est* ['O prophet, your penis is pointing up to heaven'] (*in Vit. Mohammed.*, p. 140).

163 I borrow the style of a father of the church, ἐναθλεύων Ἡρακλῆς τρισκαιδέκατον ἆθλον (Greg. Nazianzen, *Orat.*, iii, 108).

164 The common and most glorious legend includes, in a single night, the fifty victories of Hercules over the virgin daughters of Thestius (Diodor. Sicul., i, iv, 274; Pausanias, ix, 763; Statius, *Sylv.*, i, iii, 42). But Athenaeus allows seven nights (*Deipnosophist.*, xiii, 556) and Apollodorus fifty, for this arduous achievement of Hercules, who was then no more than eighteen years of age (*Bibliot.*, ii, 4, 111, *cum notis* Heyne, i, 332).

165 Abulfeda, *in Vit. Moham.*, pp. 12–13, 16–17, *cum notis* Gagnier.

166 This outline of the Arabian history is drawn from the *Bibliothèque Orientale* of d'Herbelot (under the names of *Aboubecre, Omar, Othman, Ali*, etc.), from the Annals of Abulfeda, Abulpharagius, and Elmacin (under the proper years of the *Hegira*), and especially from Ockley's *History of the Saracens* (i, 1–10, 115–22, 229, 249, 363–72, 378–91, and almost the whole of the second volume). Yet we should weigh with caution the traditions of the hostile sects, a stream which becomes still more muddy as it flows farther from the source. Sir John Chardin has too faithfully copied the fables and errors of the modern Persians (*Voyages*, ii, 235–50, etc.).

167 Ockley (at the end of his second volume) has given an English version of 169 sentences, which he ascribes, with some hesitation, to Ali, the son of Abu Taleb. His preface is coloured by the enthusiasm of a translator; yet these sentences delineate a characteristic, though dark, picture of human life.

168 Ockley (*Hist. of the Saracens*, i, i, 5–6), from an Arabian manuscript, represents Ayesha as adverse to the substitution of her father in the place of the apostle. This fact, so improbable in itself, is unnoticed by Abulfeda, Al Jannabi, and Al Bochari; the last of whom quotes the tradition of Ayesha herself (*Vit. Mohammed*, p. 136; *Vie de Mahomet*, iii, 236).

169 Particularly by his friend and cousin Abdallah, the son of Abbas, who died AD 687, with the title of grand doctor of the Moslems. In Abulfeda he recapitulated the important occasions in which Ali had neglected his salutary advice (p. 76, vers. Reiske); and concludes (p. 85), *O princeps fidelium, absque controversia tu quidem vere fortis es, at inops boni consilii et rerum gerendarum parum*

callens. ['O leader of the faithful, without doubt you are indeed a man of true strength, but wanting in good counsel and with too little understanding of the ways of the world.']

170 I suspect that the two seniors (Abulpharagius, p. 115; Ockley, i, 371) may signify not two actual counsellors, but his two predecessors, Abubeker and Omar.

171 The schism of the Persians is explained by all our travellers of the last century, especially in the iid and ivth volumes of their master, Chardin. Niebuhr, though of inferior merit, has the advantage of writing so late as the year 1764 (*Voyages en Arabie*, etc., ii, 208–33), since the ineffectual attempt of Nadir Shah to change the religion of the nation (see his *Persian History*, translated into French by Sir William Jones, ii, 5–6, 47–48, 144–55).

172 Omar is the name of the devil; his murderer is a saint. When the Persians shoot with the bow, they frequently cry, 'May this arrow go to the heart of Omar!' (*Voyages* de Chardin, ii, 239–40, 259, etc.).

  * *page 826*   [Sunni]

173 This gradation of merit is distinctly marked in a creed illustrated by Reland (*de Relig. Mohamm.*, i, 37), and a Sonnite argument inserted by Ockley (*Hist. of the Saracens*, ii, 230). The practice of cursing the memory of Ali was abolished, after forty years, by the Ommiades themselves (d'Herbelot, p. 690); and there are few among the Turks who presume to revile him as an infidel (*Voyages* de Chardin, iv, 46).

174 The plain of Siffin is determined by d'Anville (*L'Euphrate et le Tigre*, p. 29) to be the Campus Barbaricus of Procopius.

175 Abulfeda, a moderate Sonnite, relates the different opinions concerning the burial of Ali, but adopts the sepulchre of Cufa, *hodie fama numeroque religiose frequentantium celebratum* ['today honoured both by its reputation and by the number of its pilgrims']. This number is reckoned by Niebuhr to amount annually to 2000 of the dead, and 5000 of the living (ii, 208–09).

176 All the tyrants of Persia, from Adhad el Dowlat (AD 977, d'Herbelot, pp. 58–59, 95) to Nadir Shah (AD 1743, *Hist. de Nadir Shah*, ii, 155), have enriched the tomb of Ali with the spoils of the people. The dome is copper, with a bright and massy gilding, which glitters to the sun at the distance of many a mile.

177 The city of Meshed Ali, five or six miles from the ruins of Cufa, and one hundred and twenty to the south of Bagdad, is of the size and form of the modern Jerusalem. Meshed Hosein, larger and more populous, is at the distance of thirty miles.

  * *page 829*   [driving force]

178 I borrow, on this occasion, the strong sense and expression of Tacitus (*Hist.*, i, 4): *Evulgato imperii arcano posse imperatorem alibi quam Romae fieri.* ['The secret of empire was revealed that an emperor could be made elsewhere than at Rome.']

  * *page 830*   [Heraclius and Chosroes II, earlier in the century]

179 I have abridged the interesting narrative of Ockley (ii, 170–231). It is long and minute; but the pathetic, almost always, consists in the detail of little circumstances.

180 Niebuhr the Dane (*Voyages en Arabie*, etc., ii, 208, etc.) is perhaps the only European traveller who has dared to visit Meshed Ali and Meshed Hosein. The two sepulchres are in the hands of the Turks, who tolerate and tax the devotion

of the Persian heretics. The festival of the death of Hosein is amply described by Sir John Chardin, a traveller whom I have often praised.

181 The general article of *Imam*, in d'Herbelot's *Bibliothèque*, will indicate the succession; and the lives of the twelve are given under their respective names.

182 The name of *Antichrist* may seem ridiculous, but the Mahometans have liberally borrowed the fables of every religion (Sale's *Preliminary Discourse*, pp. 80, 82). In the royal stable of Ispahan, two horses were always kept saddled, one for the Mahadi himself, the other for his lieutenant, Jesus the son of Mary.

183 In the year of the Hegira 200 (AD 815). See d'Herbelot, p. 546.

184 D'Herbelot, p. 342. The enemies of the Fatimites disgraced them by a Jewish origin. Yet they accurately deduced their genealogy from Jaafar, the sixth Imam; and the impartial Abulfeda allows (*Annal. Moslem.*, p. 230) that they were owned by many, *qui absque controversia genuini sunt Alidarum, homines propaginum suae gentis exacte callentes* ['who, without doubt, are of the same stock as the race of Ali, men who have an accurate knowledge of the descendants of their people']. He quotes some lines from the celebrated *Sherif* or *Radhi, Egone humilitatem induam in terris hostium?* (I suspect him to be an Edrissite of Sicily) *cum in Aegypto sit Chalifa de gente Alii, quocum ego communem habeo patrem et vindicem.* ['Am I to assume an attitude of humility in the lands of the enemy . . . when the caliph of Egypt is of the race of Ali, with whom I share a common father and protector.']

185 The kings of Persia of the last dynasty are descended from Sheik Sefi, a saint of the fourteenth century, and through him from Moussa Cassem, the son of Hosein, the son of Ali (Olearius, p. 957; Chardin, iii, 288). But I cannot trace the intermediate degrees in any genuine or fabulous pedigree. If they were truly Fatimites, they might draw their origin from the princes of Mazanderan, who reigned in the ixth century (d'Herbelot, p. 96).

186 The present state of the family of Mahomet and Ali is most accurately described by Demetrius Cantemir (*Hist. of the Othman Empire*, p. 94), and Niebuhr (*Description de l'Arabie*, pp. 9–16, 317, etc.). It is much to be lamented that the Danish traveller was unable to purchase the chronicles of Arabia.

* *page 834*   [civil judge]

187 The writers of the *Modern Universal History* (vol. i and ii) have compiled, in 850 folio pages, the life of Mahomet and the annals of the caliphs. They enjoyed the advantage of reading, and sometimes correcting, the Arabic text; yet, notwithstanding their high-sounding boasts, I cannot find, after the conclusion of my work, that they have afforded me much (if any) additional information. The dull mass is not quickened by a spark of philosophy or taste; and the compilers indulge the criticism of acrimonious bigotry against Boulainvilliers, Sale, Gagnier, and all who have treated Mahomet with favour, or even justice. [The *Universal History* was published in London in seven volumes between 1736 and 1744.]

CHAPTER 51 (Summary)

The conquest of Persia, Syria, Egypt, Africa, and Spain, by the Arabs or Saracens – empire of the caliphs, or successors of Mahomet – state of the Christians, etc. under their government

Gibbon begins with a review of the frugality and zeal of the early caliphs, the successors of Mahomet. He attributes their conquests beyond Arabia, however, to the degeneracy of the Persian and Roman empires. By the early years of the eighth century, those conquests stretched from India to the Atlantic, and Gibbon narrates them under five headings:

1. Persia. The Moslems defeated the Persians and founded the cities of Basra and Cufa. They overthrew Yezdegerd, the last of the Sassanian kings of Persia, in AD 651 and spread their forces as far as the Indus and the Caspian Sea by AD 710.

2. Syria. Damascus fell to the Moslems by AD 635 and in the next three years Jerusalem, Aleppo and Antioch also fell. The emperor Heraclius withdrew his troops and the Moslems raided the islands of the Aegean Sea with impunity.

3. Egypt. Gibbon describes the career of Amrou, who, with the help of the Coptic Christians, captured Alexandria in AD 641. Gibbon does not believe the story that the library of the Ptolemies at Alexandria was burnt by the Moslems.

4. Africa. The Moslem conquest of North Africa was achieved by Akbah as far as Tangier by AD 683, but it was not until the beginning of the eighth century that the Moors were converted to Islam.

5. Spain. The first Moslem expedition to Spain under Tarik was in AD 710 and, in the following year, he defeated the Goths under King Roderic at Jerez. The whole country was quickly overrun, but the Christians were allowed to retain their churches and agriculture prospered.

Gibbon ends his longest chapter with a review of the decline of the Persian Magian religion and of Christianity in Africa and Spain. By AD 718, the caliphs of Arabia were 'the most potent and absolute monarchs of the globe'.

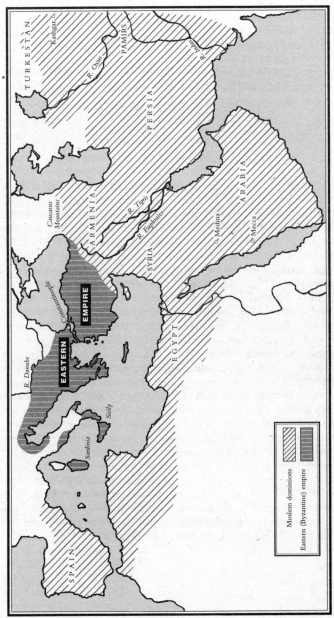

The Moslem empire, AD 750

CHAPTER 52 (Summary)

The two sieges of Constantinople by the Arabs – their invasion of France, and defeat by Charles Martel – civil war of the Ommiades and Abbassides – learning of the Arabs – luxury of the caliphs – naval enterprises on Crete, Sicily, and Rome – decay and division of the empire of the caliphs – defeats and victories of the Greek emperors

In Chapter 52, Gibbon turns his attention to the Moslem attempt to capture Constantinople. For seven years, the city was besieged, but its defences and the use of 'Greek fire' (probably fuelled with liquid bitumen) kept the Saracens at bay, and in AD 677 a truce of thirty years was agreed. A further siege in AD 716–18 was also resisted. The Moslem invasion of the Frankish kingdom was more successful, until Charles Martel turned the tide by defeating the Saracens between Tours and Poitiers in AD 732. By AD 755, they were driven back beyond the Pyrenees. Meanwhile, civil war among the descendants of Mahomet caused a split in the caliphate; three rival caliphs reigned in the tenth century at Baghdad, Kairouan in Tunisia and Cordova. As the energy of the early Moslems was sapped by luxury, scholarship revived. Greek volumes on science were translated and there was particular interest in philosophy, mathematics, astronomy and medicine, including anatomy, botany and chemistry. Gibbon regrets, however, that the Moslems did not read the language of the Latin and Greek classics – such knowledge might have inspired them to seek more liberty. At the end of the eighth century, Constantinople was paying tribute to the caliph Harun to preserve its independence, but Harun continued to threaten and captured Heraclea on the Black Sea in AD 806. Crete and Cyprus were lost to the Saracens during the ninth century. Even Rome was invaded in AD 846, but was saved by Pope Leo IV, who restored the city walls. The caliphs at Baghdad used Turks as mercenaries and their power was eroded by palace revolutions, a new wave of fanaticism known as the Carmathian movement, and the rise of independent dynasties. During the reigns of the Emperors Nicephorus II and John I Zimisces from AD 963 to 976, the Greeks were able to recapture Crete, Cilicia, Syria and Cyprus.

CHAPTER 53 (Summary)

*State of the Eastern empire in the tenth century – extent and
division – wealth and revenue – palace of Constantinople –
titles and offices – pride and power of the emperors –
tactics of the Greeks, Arabs and Franks – loss of the
Latin tongue – studies and solitude of the Greeks*

At the beginning of this Chapter, Gibbon reviews the Byzantine sources
for the history of the Eastern empire in the tenth century. The empire was
divided into twenty-nine 'themes' or military governments. Constantinople remained by far the greatest city, attracting fugitives from parts of
the empire that had fallen to the Moslems. Gibbon describes the state of
the Peloponnese, where there were still traces of Roman freedom and of
wealth from the manufacture of silk. Revenue from the empire poured
into Constantinople where the royal palace had grown into 'a vast and
irregular pile' of buildings. An elaborate court etiquette of ranks, offices,
dress and ceremonies had developed. Despotism had caused the suppression of the senate and the church was quiescent. Gibbon reviews the naval
and military strengths of the empire, contrasting the frequent defeats with
the enthusiasm of the Moslems, still inspired by their religion. Meanwhile, the third power in the western world, the Frankish empire of
Charlemagne, had become divided under his successors and was sunk into
feudal anarchy. After Justinian, Latin had declined in use at Constantinople and was claimed by the Franks as their language, although the Eastern
emperors maintained their Roman origin to the end. In the ninth century,
Greek studies had revived under the librarian Photius, but Gibbon regrets
that no new works were composed. 'The tragic, epic and lyric muses
were silent and inglorious.'

CHAPTER 54 (Summary)

*Origin and doctrine of the Paulicians – their persecution by the
Greek emperors – revolt in Armenia, etc. – transplantation
into Thrace – propagation in the West – the seeds,
character, and consequences of the Reformation*

Gibbon devotes a short chapter to the Paulicians, a Christian sect which
rejected the Old Testament and venerated the teachings of St Paul. They
flourished first in Asia Minor and were persecuted by the Greek emperors. Their suffering led to a revolt in Armenia in the ninth century which
was supported by the caliphate. Some of their adherents were settled in
Thrace as warriors, from where they spread into France and Italy. They
were noted for their opposition to idolatry and to Rome. In the thirteenth
century, when they were known as the Albigenses, from the name of the
French town of Albi where they had settled, they were subject to a
particularly fierce persecution. Gibbon sees them as the precursors of the
Reformation and ends the chapter with a review of the benefits which
have stemmed from that movement.

CHAPTER 55 (Summary)

*The Bulgarians – origin, migrations, and settlement of the
Hungarians – their inroads in the East and West –
the monarchy of Russia – geography and trade wars of the
Russians against the Greek empire – conversion of the Barbarians*

Gibbon narrates the Scythian invasions of the Byzantine empire in the
ninth, tenth and eleventh centuries, under the headings of Bulgarians,
Hungarians and Russians. The Bulgarians defeated and killed the emperor
Nicephorus in battle in AD 811. Subsequently, they were converted to
Christianity, aspired to form a rival empire to Constantinople under their
king, Simeon, but were divided and defeated in the eleventh century.
The Hungarians had originally come from Asia and had settled on the
Danube by the end of the ninth century. Their raids penetrated far into
the German empire of Charlemagne's successors, but they were defeated
in battle by the German emperors, Henry the Fowler in AD 934 and Otho
the Great in AD 955; thereafter they developed a more settled life under a
dynasty of kings lasting three hundred years. The Russians had been the

subjects of the Normans of Scandinavia in the ninth century. Novgorod and Kiev were early centres of commerce and Russian merchants traded from the Baltic to Constantinople. Wars interrupted trade, and four times in two hundred years the Russians attacked Constantinople by sea, being repelled each time. As allies of the Byzantine empire, they defeated the Bulgarians, but when they again threatened Constantinople they were defeated by the emperor John I in AD 972. At the end of the tenth century, the Russians were converted to Christianity, the result of 'active and patient' courage on the part of the missionaries from Greece and Germany, and the rudiments of arts and science spread throughout north and eastern Europe.

CHAPTER 56 (Summary)

The Saracens, Franks, and Greeks, in Italy – first adventures and settlement of the Normans – character and conquest of Robert Guiscard, Duke of Apulia – deliverance of Sicily by his brother Roger – victories of Robert over the emperors of the East and West – Roger, King of Sicily, invades Africa and Greece – the emperor Manuel Comnenus – wars of the Greeks and Normans – extinction of the Normans

Gibbon begins with an account of the recovery of southern Italy by the Greek empire from the Saracens and the Lombard princes at the end of the ninth century. Opponents of the Greeks invited Norman adventurers to help them, and when the Greeks tried to capture Sicily from the Saracens in AD 1038, the Normans seized Apulia. At this period the Latin Church made the final breach with the Greek Church by investing the Normans with the right of conquest in Apulia, Calabria and Sicily. In AD 1054, Robert Guiscard became their leader. Among the most noteworthy of his possessions were the medical school at Salerno and the trade and wealth of Amalfi. The conquest of Sicily was achieved in thirty years by his youngest brother, Roger. The island was restored to the Latin Church and the Moslems were allowed religious freedom. Robert Guiscard meanwhile invaded the Greek empire and defeated the emperor Alexius at Durazzo in AD 1081. He then returned to Italy to face the German emperor, Henry IV, who had allied with Alexius and was besieging Rome. The emperor retreated before the Normans but Rome suffered from fire and pillage. Robert died in AD 1085, after renewing his campaign against the Greeks. Gibbon then proceeds to narrate the career, in the first half of the twelfth century, of Roger II of Sicily, who united the Norman territories of southern Italy under his rule. He annexed Malta and forced much of the north African coast to pay tribute. Athens and Corinth were attacked by sea and, as a result, the silk industry was brought to Sicily and the crusader king, Louis VII of France, was rescued from his Greek captors. Under the emperor Manuel, AD 1143–1180, the Greeks renewed their claims to Italy and encouraged the cities to resist the German emperor Frederic Barbarossa, but the Pope Alexander III refused to be swayed. Meanwhile, the power of Norman Sicily had declined and in AD 1194 it was conquered by the son of Frederic Barbarossa, the emperor Henry VI.

CHAPTER 57

The Turks of the house of Seljuk – their revolt against Mahmud, conqueror of Hindostan – Togrul subdues Persia, and protects the caliphs – defeat and captivity of the emperor Romanus Diogenes by Alp Arslan – power and magnificence of Malek Shah – conquest of Asia Minor and Syria – state and oppression of Jerusalem – pilgrimages to the Holy Sepulchre

From the isle of Sicily the reader must transport himself beyond the Caspian Sea, to the original seat of the Turks or Turkmans, against whom the first crusade was principally directed. Their Scythian empire of the sixth century was long since dissolved; but the name was still famous among the Greeks and Orientals; and the fragments of the nation, each a powerful and independent people, were scattered over the desert from China to the Oxus and the Danube: the colony of Hungarians was admitted into the republic of Europe, and the thrones of Asia were occupied by slaves and soldiers of Turkish extraction. While Apulia and Sicily were subdued by the Norman lance, a swarm of these northern shepherds overspread the kingdoms of Persia: their princes of the race of Seljuk erected a splendid and solid empire from Samarcand to the confines of Greece and Egypt; and the Turks have maintained their dominion in Asia Minor till the victorious crescent has been planted on the dome of St Sophia.

One of the greatest of the Turkish princes was Mamood or Mahmud,[1] the Gaznevide, who reigned in the eastern provinces of Persia one thousand years after the birth of Christ. His father Sebectagi was the slave of the slave of the slave of the commander of the faithful.* But in this descent of servitude, the first degree was merely titular, since it was filled by the sovereign of Transoxiana and Chorasan, who still paid a nominal allegiance to the caliph of Bagdad. The second rank was that of a minister of state, a lieutenant of the Samanides,[2] who broke, by his revolt, the bonds of political slavery. But the third step was a state of real and domestic servitude in the family of that rebel; from which Sebectagi, by his courage and dexterity, ascended to the supreme command of the city and province of Gazna,[3] as the son-in-law and successor of his grateful master. The falling dynasty of the Samanides was at first protected, and at last overthrown, by their servants; and, in the public disorders, the fortune of Mahmud continually increased. For him, the title of *sultan*[4] was first invented; and his kingdom was enlarged from Transoxiana to the neighbourhood of Ispahan, from the shores of the Caspian to the mouth of the Indus. But the principal source of his fame and riches was the holy war which he waged against the Gentoos of Hindostan. In this foreign narrative I may not consume a page; and a volume would scarcely suffice to recapitulate the battles and sieges of his twelve expeditions. Never was the Musulman hero dismayed by the inclemency of the seasons, the height of the mountains, the breadth of the rivers, the barrenness of the desert, the multitudes of the enemy, or the formidable array of their elephants of war.[5] The sultan of Gazna surpassed the limits of the conquests of Alexander; after a march of three months, over the hills of Cashmir and Thibet, he reached the famous city of Kinnoge,[6] on the Upper Ganges; and, in a naval combat on one of the branches of the Indus, he fought and vanquished four thousand boats of the natives. Delhi, Lahor, and Multan were compelled to open their gates; the fertile kingdom of Guzarat attracted his ambition and tempted his stay; and his avarice indulged the fruitless project of discovering the golden and aromatic isles of the Southern Ocean. On the payment of a tribute, the *rajahs* preserved their dominions; the people, their lives and fortunes; but to the religion of Hindostan the zealous Musulman was cruel and inexorable; many hundred temples, or pagodas, were levelled with the ground; many thousand idols were demolished; and the servants of the prophet were stimulated and rewarded by the precious materials of which they were composed. The pagoda of Sumnat was situated on the promontory of Guzarat, in the neighbourhood of Diu, one of the last remaining possessions of the Portuguese.[7] It was endowed with the revenue of two thousand villages; two thousand Brahmins were consecrated to the service of the Deity, whom they washed each morning and evening in water from the distant Ganges: the subordinate ministers consisted of three hundred musicians, three hundred barbers, and five hundred dancing girls, conspicuous for their birth and beauty. Three sides of the temple were protected by the ocean, the narrow isthmus was fortified by a natural or artificial precipice; and the city and adjacent country were peopled by a nation of fanatics. They confessed the sins and the punishment of Kinnoge and Delhi; but, if the impious stranger should presume to approach *their* holy precincts, he would surely be overwhelmed by a blast of the divine vengeance. By this challenge the faith of Mahmud was animated to a personal trial of the strength of this Indian deity. Fifty thousand of his worshippers were pierced by the spear of the Moslems: the walls were scaled; the sanctuary was profaned; and the conqueror aimed a blow of his iron mace at the head of the idol. The trembling Brahmins are said to have offered ten millions sterling for his ransom; and it was urged by the wisest counsellors that the destruction of a stone image would not change the hearts of the Gentoos, and that such a sum might be dedicated to the relief of the true believers. 'Your reasons,' replied the Sultan, 'are specious* and strong; but never in the eyes of posterity shall Mahmud appear as a merchant of idols.' He repeated his blows, and a treasure of pearls and rubies, concealed in the belly of the statue, explained in some degree the devout prodigality of the Brahmins. The fragments of the idol were distributed to Gazna, Mecca, and Medina. Bagdad listened to the edifying tale; and Mahmud was saluted by the caliph with the title of guardian of the fortune and faith of Mahomet.

From the paths of blood, and such is the history of nations, I cannot refuse to turn aside to gather some flowers of science or virtue. The name of Mahmud the Gaznevide is still venerable in the East: his subjects enjoyed the blessings of prosperity and peace; his vices were concealed by the veil of religion; and two familiar examples will testify his justice and magnanimity. I. As he sat in the Divan,† an unhappy subject bowed before the throne to accuse the insolence of a Turkish soldier who had driven him from his house and bed. 'Suspend your clamours,' said Mahmud, 'inform me of his next visit and ourself in person will judge and punish the offender.' The sultan followed his guide, invested the house with his guards, and, extinguishing the torches, pronounced the death of the criminal, who had been seized in the act of rapine and adultery. After the execution of his sentence, the lights were rekindled, Mahmud fell prostrate in prayer, and, rising from the ground, demanded some homely fare, which he devoured with the voraciousness of hunger. The poor man, whose injury he had avenged, was unable to suppress his astonishment and curiosity; and the courteous monarch condescended to explain the motives of this singular behaviour. 'I had reason to suspect that none except one of my sons could dare to perpetrate such an outrage; and I extinguished the lights, that my justice might be blind and inexorable. My prayer was a thanksgiving on the discovery of the offender; and so painful was my anxiety that I had passed three days without food since the first moment of your complaint.' II. The Sultan of Gazna had declared war against the dynasty of the Bowides, the sovereigns of the western Persia; he was disarmed by an epistle of the sultana mother, and delayed his invasion till the manhood of her son.[8] 'During the life of my husband,' said the artful regent, 'I was ever apprehensive of your ambition; he was a prince and a soldier worthy of your arms. He is now no more; his

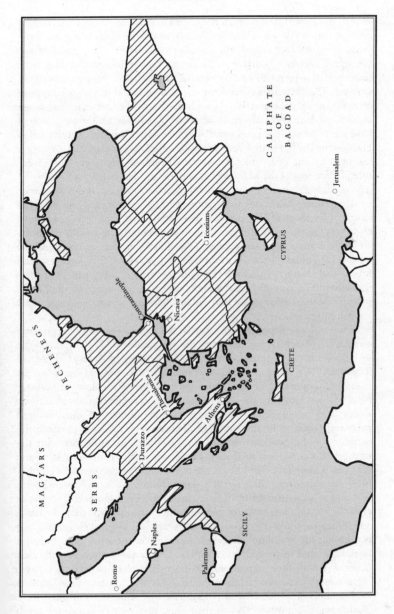

The Byzantine empire, AD *c.*1050

sceptre has passed to a woman and a child, and you *dare not* attack their infancy and weakness. How inglorious would be your conquest, how shameful your defeat! and yet the event of war is in the hand of the Almighty.' Avarice was the only defect that tarnished the illustrious character of Mahmud; and never has that passion been more richly satisfied. The Orientals exceed the measure of credibility in the account of millions of gold and silver, such as the avidity of man has never accumulated; in the magnitude of pearls, diamonds, and rubies, such as have never been produced by the workmanship of nature.[9] Yet the soil of Hindostan is impregnated with precious minerals; her trade, in every age, has attracted the gold and silver of the world; and her virgin spoils were rifled by the first of the Mahometan conquerors. His behaviour, in the last days of his life, evinces the vanity of these possessions, so laboriously won, so dangerously held, and so inevitably lost. He surveyed the vast and various chambers of the treasury of Gazna; burst into tears; and again closed the doors, without bestowing any portion of the wealth which he could no longer hope to preserve. The following day he reviewed the state of his military force: one hundred thousand foot, fifty-five thousand horse, and thirteen hundred elephants of battle.[10] He again wept the instability of human greatness; and his grief was embittered by the hostile progress of the Turkmans, whom he had introduced into the heart of his Persian kingdom.

In the modern depopulation of Asia, the regular operation of government and agriculture is confined to the neighbourhood of cities; and the distant country is abandoned to the pastoral tribes of Arabs, Curds, and *Turkmans*.[11] Of the last-mentioned people, two considerable branches extend on either side of the Caspian Sea: the western colony can muster forty thousand soldiers; the eastern, less obvious to the traveller, but more strong and populous, has increased to the number of one hundred thousand families. In the midst of civilised nations, they preserve the manners of the Scythian desert, remove their encampments with the change of seasons, and feed their cattle among the ruins of palaces and temples. Their flocks and herds are their only riches; their tents, either black or white, according to the colour of the banner, are covered with felt, and of a circular form; their winter apparel is a sheepskin; a robe of cloth or cotton their summer garment: the features of the men are harsh and ferocious; the countenance of their women is soft and pleasing. Their wandering life maintains the spirit and exercise of arms; they fight on horseback; and their courage is displayed in frequent contests with each other and with their neighbours. For the licence of pasture they pay a slight tribute to the sovereign of the land; but the domestic jurisdiction is in the hands of the chiefs and elders. The first emigration of the eastern Turkmans, the most ancient of their race, may be ascribed to the tenth century of the Christian era.[12] In the decline of the caliphs, and the weakness of their lieutenants, the barrier of the Jaxartes was often

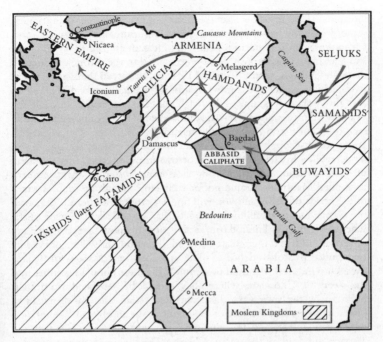

The coming of the Seljuks, AD *c.*970–1070

violated: in each invasion, after the victory or retreat of their countrymen, some wandering tribe, embracing the Mahometan faith, obtained a free encampment in the spacious plains and pleasant climate of Transoxiana and Carizme. The Turkish slaves who aspired to the throne encouraged these emigrations, which recruited their armies, awed their subjects and rivals, and protected the frontier against the wilder natives of Turkestan; and this policy was abused by Mahmud the Gaznevide beyond the example of former times. He was admonished of his error by a chief of the race of Seljuk, who dwelt in the territory of Bochara. The sultan had enquired what supply of men he could furnish for military service. 'If you send,' replied Ismael, 'one of these arrows into our camp, fifty thousand of your servants will mount on horseback.' 'And if that number,' continued Mahmud, 'should not be sufficient?' 'Send this second arrow to the horde of Balik, and you will find fifty thousand more.' 'But,' said the Gaznevide, dissembling his anxiety, 'if I should stand in need of the whole force of your kindred tribes?' 'Dispatch my bow,' was the last reply of Ismael, 'and, as it is circulated around, the summons will be obeyed by two hundred thousand horse.' The apprehension of such formidable friendship induced Mahmud to transport the most obnoxious tribes into the heart of Chorasan, where they would be separated from their brethren by the river Oxus, and enclosed on all sides by the walls of obedient cities. But the face of the country was an object of temptation rather than terror; and the vigour of government was relaxed by the absence and death of the sultan of Gazna. The shepherds were converted into robbers; the bands of robbers were collected into an army of conquerors; as far as Ispahan and the Tigris, Persia was afflicted by their predatory inroads; and the Turkmans were not ashamed or afraid to measure their courage and numbers with the proudest sovereigns of Asia. Massoud, the son and successor of Mahmud, had too long neglected the advice of his wisest Omrahs.* 'Your enemies,' they repeatedly urged, 'were in their origin a swarm of ants; they are now little snakes; and, unless they be instantly crushed, they will acquire the venom and magnitude of serpents.' After some alternatives of truce and hostility, after the repulse or partial success of his lieutenants, the sultan marched in person against the Turkmans, who attacked him on all sides with bar- barous shouts and irregular onset. 'Massoud,' says the Persian historian,[13] 'plunged singly to oppose the torrent of gleaming arms, exhibiting such acts of gigantic force and valour as never king had before displayed. A few of his friends, roused by his words and actions, and that innate honour which inspires the brave, seconded their lord so well that, wheresoever he turned his fatal sword, the enemies were mowed down or retreated before him. But now, when victory seemed to blow on his standard, misfortune was active behind it; for, when he looked round, he beheld almost his whole army, excepting that body he commanded in person, devouring the paths of flight.' The Gaznevide was abandoned by the cowardice or treachery of some generals of Turkish race; and this memorable day of Zendecan[14] founded in Persia the dynasty of the shepherd kings.[15]

The victorious Turkmans immediately proceeded to the election of a king; and, if the probable tale of a Latin historian[16] deserves any credit, they determined by lot the choice of their new master. A number of arrows were successively inscribed with the name of a tribe, a family, and a candidate; they were drawn from the bundle by the hand of a child; and the important prize was obtained by Togrul Beg, the son of Michael, the son of Seljuk, whose surname was immortalised in the greatness of his posterity. The sultan Mahmud, who valued himself on his skill in national genealogy, professed his ignorance of the family of Seljuk; yet the father of that race appears to have been a chief of power and renown.[17] For a daring intrusion into the harem of his prince, Seljuk was banished from Turkestan; with a numerous tribe of his friends and vassals, he passed the Jaxartes, encamped in the neighbourhood of Samarcand, embraced the religion of Mahomet, and acquired the crown of martyr-dom in a war against the infidels. His age, of an hundred and seven years, surpassed the life of his son, and Seljuk adopted the care of his two grandsons, Togrul and Jaafar; the eldest of whom, at the age of forty-five, was invested with the title of sultan, in the royal city of Nishabur. The blind determination of chance was justified by the virtues of the success-ful candidate. It would be superfluous to praise the valour of a Turk; and the ambition of Togrul[18] was equal to his valour. By his arms, the Gaznevides were expelled from the eastern kingdoms of Persia, and gradually driven to the banks of the Indus, in search of a softer and more wealthy conquest. In the West he annihilated the dynasty of the Bowides; and the sceptre of Irak passed from the Persian to the Turkish nation. The princes who had felt, or who feared, the Seljukian arrows, bowed their heads in the dust; by the conquest of Aderbijan, or Media, he approached the Roman confines; and the shepherd presumed to dispatch an ambassa-dor, or herald, to demand the tribute and obedience of the emperor of Constantinople.[19] In his own dominions, Togrul was the father of his soldiers and people; by a firm and equal administration Persia was relieved from the evils of anarchy; and the same hands which had been imbrued in blood became the guardians of justice and the public peace. The more rustic, perhaps the wisest, portion of the Turkmans[20] contin-ued to dwell in the tents of their ancestors; and, from the Oxus to the Euphrates, these military colonies were protected and propagated by their native princes. But the Turks of the court and city were refined by business and softened by pleasure; they imitated the dress, language, and manners of Persia; and the royal palaces of Nishabur and Rei displayed the order and magnificence of a great monarchy. The most deserving of the Arabians and Persians were promoted to the honours of the state; and the whole body of the Turkish nation embraced with fervour and sincerity the religion of Mahomet. The northern swarms of barbarians, who overspread both Europe and Asia, have been irreconcilably separated by the consequences of a similar conduct. Among the Moslems, as among the Christians, their vague and local traditions have yielded to the reason and authority of the prevailing system, to the fame of antiquity, and the consent of nations. But the triumph of the Koran is more pure and meritorious, as it was not assisted by any visible splendour of worship which might allure the Pagans by some resemblance of idolatry. The first of the Seljukian sultans was conspicuous by his zeal and faith: each day he repeated the five prayers which are enjoined to the true believers; of each week, the two first days were consecrated by an extraordinary fast; and in every city a mosch was completed, before Togrul presumed to lay the foundations of a palace.[21]

With the belief of the Koran, the son of Seljuk imbibed a lively reverence for the successor of the prophet. But that sublime character was still disputed by the caliphs of Bagdad and Egypt, and each of the rivals was solicitous to prove his title in the judgment of the strong, though illiterate, barbarians. Mahmud the Gaznevide had declared himself in favour of the line of Abbas;* and had treated with indignity the robe of honour which was presented by the Fatimite† ambassador. Yet the ungrateful Hashemite had changed with the change of fortune; he applauded the victory of Zendecan, and named the Seljukian sultan his temporal vicegerent over the Moslem world. As Togrul executed and enlarged this important trust, he was called to the deliverance of the caliph Cayem, and obeyed the holy summons, which gave a new kingdom to his arms.[22] In the palace of Bagdad, the commander of the faithful still slumbered, a venerable phantom. His servant or master, the prince of the Bowides, could no longer protect him from the insolence of meaner tyrants; and the Euphrates and Tigris were oppressed by the revolt of the Turkish and Arabian emirs. The presence of a conqueror was implored as a blessing; and the transient mischiefs of fire and sword were excused as the sharp but salutary remedies which alone could restore the health of the republic. At the head of an irresistible force, the sultan of Persia marched from Hamadan: the proud were crushed, the prostrate were spared; the prince of the Bowides disappeared; the heads of the most obstinate rebels were laid at the feet of Togrul; and he inflicted a lesson of obedience on the people of Mosul and Bagdad. After the chastisement of the guilty and the restoration of peace, the royal shepherd accepted the reward of his labours; and a solemn comedy represented the triumph of religious prejudice over barbarian power.[23] The Turkish sultan embarked on the Tigris, landed at the gate of Racca, and made his public entry on horseback. At the palace-gate he respectfully dismounted, and walked on foot, preceded by his emirs without arms. The caliph was seated behind his black veil; the black garment of the Abbassides was cast over his shoulders, and he held in his hand the staff of the apostle of God. The conqueror of the East kissed the ground, stood some time in a modest posture, and was led towards the throne by the vizir and an interpreter. After Togrul had seated himself on another throne, his commission was publicly read, which declared him the temporal lieutenant of the vicar of the prophet. He was successively invested with seven robes of honour, and presented with seven slaves, the natives of the seven climates of the Arabian empire. His mystic veil was perfumed with musk; two crowns were placed on his head; two scymetars were girded on his side, as the symbols of a double reign over the East and West. After this inauguration, the sultan was prevented from prostrating himself a second time; but he twice kissed the hand of the commander of the faithful, and his titles were proclaimed by the voice of heralds and the applause of the Moslems. In a second visit to Bagdad, the Seljukian prince again rescued the caliph from his enemies; and devoutly, on foot, led the bridle of his mule from the prison to the palace. Their alliance was cemented by the marriage of Togrul's sister with the successor of the prophet. Without reluctance he had introduced a Turkish virgin into his harem; but Cayem proudly refused his daughter to the sultan, disdained to mingle the blood of the Hashemites with the blood of a Scythian shepherd; and protracted the negotiation many months, till the gradual diminution of his revenue admonished him that he was still in the hands of a master. The royal nuptials were followed by the death of Togrul himself;[24] as he left no children, his nephew Alp Arslan succeeded to the title and prerogatives of sultan; and his name, after that of the caliph, was pronounced in the public prayers of the Moslems. Yet in this revolution the Abbassides acquired a larger measure of liberty and power. On the throne of Asia, the Turkish monarchs were less jealous of the domestic administration of Bagdad; and the commanders of the faithful were relieved from the ignominious vexations to which they had been exposed by the presence and poverty of the Persian dynasty.

Since the fall of the caliphs, the discord and degeneracy of the Saracens respected the Asiatic provinces of Rome; which, by the victories of Nicephorus,* Zimisces,† and Basil,‡ had been extended as far as Antioch and the eastern boundaries of Armenia. Twenty-five years after the death of Basil, his successors were suddenly assaulted by an unknown race of barbarians, who united the Scythian valour with the fanaticism of new proselytes and the art and riches of a powerful monarchy.[25] The myriads of Turkish horse overspread a frontier of six hundred miles from Taurus to Arzeroum, and the blood of one hundred and thirty thousand Christians was a grateful sacrifice to the Arabian prophet. Yet the arms of Togrul did not make any deep or lasting impression on the Greek empire. The torrent rolled away from the open country; the sultan retired without glory or success from the siege of an Armenian city; the obscure hostilities were continued or suspended with a vicissitude of events; and the bravery of the Macedonian legions renewed the fame of the conqueror of Asia.[26] The name of Alp Arslan, the valiant lion, is expressive of the popular idea of the perfection of man; and the successor of Togrul displayed the fierceness and generosity of the royal animal. He passed the Euphrates at the head of the Turkish cavalry, and entered Caesarea, the metropolis of Cappadocia, to which he had been attracted by the fame and wealth of the temple of St Basil. The solid structure resisted the destroyer; but he carried away the doors of the shrine incrusted with gold and pearls, and profaned the relics of the tutelar saint, whose mortal frailties were now covered by the venerable rust of antiquity. The final conquest of Armenia and Georgia was achieved by Alp Arslan. In Armenia, the title of a kingdom and the spirit of a nation were annihilated; the artificial fortifications were yielded by the mercenaries of Constantinople; by strangers without faith, veterans without pay or arms, and recruits without experience or discipline. The loss of this important frontier was the news of a day; and the Catholics were neither surprised nor displeased that a people so deeply infected with the Nestorian and Eutychian errors* had been delivered by Christ and his mother into the hands of the infidels.[27] The woods and valleys of mount Caucasus were more strenuously defended by the native Georgians[28] or Iberians: but the Turkish sultan and his son Malek were indefatigable in this holy war; their captives were compelled to promise a spiritual as well as temporal obedience; and, instead of their collars and bracelets, an iron horse-shoe, a badge of ignominy, was imposed on the infidels who still adhered to the worship of their fathers. The change, however, was not sincere or universal; and, through ages of servitude, the Georgians have maintained the succession of their princes and bishops. But a race of men, whom nature has cast in her most perfect mould, is degraded by poverty, ignorance, and vice; their profession, and still more their practice, of Christianity is an empty name; and, if they have emerged from heresy, it is only because they are too illiterate to remember a metaphysical creed.[29]

The false or genuine magnanimity of Mahmud the Gaznevide was not imitated by Alp Arslan; and he attacked, without scruple, the Greek empress Eudocia† and her children. His alarming progress compelled her to give herself and her sceptre to the hand of a soldier; and Romanus Diogenes was invested with the Imperial purple. His patriotism, and perhaps his pride, urged him from Constantinople within two months after his accession; and the next campaign‡ he most scandalously took the field during the holy festival of Easter. In the palace, Diogenes was no more than the husband of Eudocia; in the camp, he was the emperor of the Romans, and he sustained that character with feeble resources and invincible courage. By his spirit and success, the soldiers were taught to act, the subjects to hope, and the enemies to fear. The Turks had penetrated into the heart of Phrygia; but the sultan himself had resigned to his emirs the prosecution of the war; and their numerous detachments were scattered over Asia in the security of conquest. Laden with spoil and careless of discipline, they were separately surprised and defeated by the Greeks; the activity of the emperor seemed to multiply his presence; and, while they heard of his expedition to Antioch, the enemy felt his sword on the hills of Trebizond. In three laborious campaigns, the Turks were driven beyond the Euphrates; in the fourth and last, Romanus undertook the deliverance of Armenia. The desolation of the land obliged him to transport a supply of two months' provisions; and he marched forwards to the siege of Malazkerd,[30] an important fortress in the midway between the modern cities of Arzeroum and Van. His army amounted, at the least, to one hundred thousand men. The troops of Constantinople were reinforced by the disorderly multitudes of Phrygia and Cappadocia; but the real strength was composed of the subjects and allies of Europe, the legions of Macedonia, and the squadrons of Bulgaria; the Uzi, a Moldavian horde, who were themselves of the Turkish race;[31] and, above all, the mercenary and adventurous bands of French and Normans. Their lances were commanded by the valiant Ursel of Baliol, the kinsman or father of the Scottish kings,[32] and were allowed to excel in the exercise of arms, or, according to the Greek style, in the practice of the Pyrrhic dance.

On the report of this bold invasion, which threatened his hereditary dominions, Alp Arslan flew to the scene of action at the head of forty thousand horse.[33] His rapid and skilful evolutions distressed and dismayed the superior numbers of the Greeks; and in the defeat of Basilacius, one of their principal generals, he displayed the first example of his valour and clemency. The imprudence of the emperor had separated his forces after the reduction of Malazkerd. It was in vain that he attempted to recall the mercenary Franks: they refused to obey his summons; he disdained to await their return; the desertion of the Uzi filled his mind with anxiety and suspicion; and against the most salutary advice he rushed forward to speedy and decisive action. Had he listened to the fair proposals of the sultan, Romanus might have secured a retreat, perhaps a peace; but in these overtures he supposed the fear or weakness of the enemy, and his answer was conceived in the tone of insult and defiance. 'If the barbarian wishes for peace, let him evacuate the ground which he occupies for the encampment of the Romans, and surrender his city and palace of Rei as a pledge of his sincerity.' Alp Arslan smiled at the vanity of the demand, but he wept the death of so many faithful Moslems; and, after a devout prayer, proclaimed a free permission to all who were desirous of retiring from the field. With his own hands he tied up his horse's tail, exchanged his bow and arrow for a mace and scymetar, clothed himself in a white garment, perfumed his body with musk, and declared that, if he were vanquished, that spot should be the place of his burial.[34] The sultan himself had affected to cast away his missile weapons; but his hopes of victory were placed in the arrows of the Turkish cavalry, whose squadrons were loosely distributed in the form of a crescent. Instead of the successive lines and reserves of the Grecian tactics, Romanus led his army in a single and solid phalanx, and pressed with vigour and impatience the artful and yielding resistance of the barbarians. In this desultory and fruitless combat, he wasted the greater part of a summer's day, till prudence and fatigue compelled him to return to his camp. But a retreat is always perilous in the face of an active foe; and no sooner had the standard been turned to the rear than the phalanx was broken by the base cowardice, or the baser jealousy, of Andronicus, a rival prince, who disgraced his birth and the purple of the Caesars.[35] The Turkish squadrons poured a cloud of arrows on this moment of confusion and lassitude; and the horns of their formidable crescent were closed in the rear of the Greeks. In the destruction of the army and pillage of the camp, it would be needless to mention the number of the slain or captives. The Byzantine writers deplore the loss of an inestimable pearl: they forget to mention that, in this fatal day, the Asiatic provinces of Rome were irretrievably sacrificed.

As long as a hope survived, Romanus attempted to rally and save the relics of his army. When the centre, the Imperial station, was left naked on all sides, and encompassed by the victorious Turks, he still, with desperate courage, maintained the fight till the close of day, at the head of the brave and faithful subjects who adhered to his standard. They fell around him; his horse was slain; the emperor was wounded; yet he stood alone and intrepid, till he was oppressed and bound by the strength of multitudes. The glory of this illustrious prize was disputed by a slave and a soldier: a slave who had seen him on the throne of Constantinople, and a soldier whose extreme deformity had been excused on the promise of some signal service. Despoiled of his arms, his jewels, and his purple, Romanus spent a dreary and perilous night on the field of battle, amidst a disorderly crowd of the meaner barbarians. In the morning the royal captive was presented to Alp Arslan, who doubted of his fortune, till the identity of the person was ascertained by the report of his ambassadors, and by the more pathetic evidence of Basilacius, who embraced with tears the feet of his unhappy sovereign. The successor of Constantine, in a plebeian habit, was led into the Turkish divan, and commanded to kiss the ground before the lord of Asia. He reluctantly obeyed; and Alp Arslan, starting from his throne, is said to have planted his foot on the neck of the Roman emperor.[36] But the fact is doubtful; and, if, in this moment of insolence, the sultan complied with a national custom, the rest of his conduct has extorted the praise of his bigoted foes, and may afford a lesson to the most civilised ages. He instantly raised the royal captive from the ground; and, thrice clasping his hand with tender sympathy, assured him that his life and dignity should be inviolate in the hands of a prince who had learned to respect the majesty of his equals and the vicissitudes of fortune. From the divan Romanus was conducted to an adjacent tent, where he was served with pomp and reverence by the officers of the sultan, who, twice each day, seated him in the place of honour at his own table. In a free and familiar conversation of eight days, not a word, not a look, of insult escaped from the conqueror; but he severely censured the unworthy subjects who had deserted their valiant prince in the hour of danger, and gently admonished his antagonist of some errors which he had committed in the management of the war. In the preliminaries of negotiation, Alp Arslan asked him what treatment he expected to receive, and the calm indifference of the emperor displays the freedom of his mind. 'If you are cruel,' said he, 'you will take my life; if you listen to pride, you will drag me at your chariot wheels; if you consult your interest, you will accept a ransom, and restore me to my country.' – 'And what,' continued the sultan, 'would have been your own behaviour, had fortune smiled on your arms?' The reply of the Greek betrays a sentiment, which prudence, and even gratitude, should have taught him to suppress. 'Had I vanquished,' he fiercely said, 'I would have inflicted on thy body many a stripe.' The Turkish conqueror smiled at the insolence of his captive; observed that the Christian law inculcated the love of enemies and forgiveness of injuries; and nobly declared that he would not imitate an example which he condemned. After mature deliberation, Alp Arslan dictated the terms of liberty and peace, a ransom of a million, an annual tribute of three hundred and sixty thousand pieces of gold,[37] the marriage of the royal children, and the deliverance of all the Moslems who were in the power of the Greeks. Romanus, with a sigh, subscribed this treaty, so disgraceful to the majesty of the empire; he was immediately invested with a Turkish robe of honour; his nobles and patricians were restored to their sovereign; and the sultan, after a courteous embrace, dismissed him with rich presents and a military guard. No sooner did he reach the confines of the empire than he was informed that the palace and provinces had disclaimed their allegiance to a captive: a sum of two hundred thousand pieces was painfully collected; and the fallen monarch transmitted this part of his ransom, with a sad confession of his impotence and disgrace. The generosity, or perhaps the ambition, of the sultan prepared to espouse the cause of his ally; but his designs were prevented by the defeat, imprisonment, and death of Romanus Diogenes.[38]

In the treaty of peace it does not appear that Alp Arslan extorted any province or city from the captive emperor; and his revenge was satisfied with the trophies of his victory, and the spoils of Anatolia from Antioch to the Black Sea. The fairest part of Asia was subject to his laws; twelve hundred princes, or the sons of princes, stood before his throne; and two hundred thousand soldiers marched under his banners. The sultan disdained to pursue the fugitive Greeks; but he meditated the more glorious conquest of Turkestan, the original seat of the house of Seljuk. He moved from Bagdad to the banks of the Oxus; a bridge was thrown over the river; and twenty days were consumed in the passage of his troops. But the progress of the great king was retarded by the governor of Berzem; and Joseph the Carizmian presumed to defend his fortress against the powers of the East. When he was produced a captive in the royal tent, the sultan, instead of praising his valour, severely reproached his obstinate folly; and the insolent replies of the rebel provoked a sentence, that he should be fastened to four stakes and left to expire in that painful situation. At this command the desperate Carizmian, drawing a dagger, rushed headlong towards the throne: the guards raised their battle-axes; their zeal was checked by Alp Arslan, the most skilful archer of the age; he drew his bow, but his foot slipped, the arrow glanced aside, and he received in his breast the dagger of Joseph, who was instantly cut in pieces. The wound was mortal; and the Turkish prince bequeathed a dying admonition to the pride of kings. 'In my youth,' said Alp Arslan, 'I was advised by a sage to humble myself before God; to distrust my own strength; and never to despise the most contemptible foe. I have neglected these lessons; and my neglect has been deservedly punished. Yesterday, as from an eminence I beheld the numbers, the discipline, and the spirit of my armies, the earth seemed to tremble under my feet; and I said in my heart, surely thou art the king of the world, the greatest and most invincible of warriors. These armies are no longer mine; and, in the confidence of my personal strength, I now fall by the hand of an assassin.'[39] Alp Arslan possessed the virtues of a Turk and a Musulman; his voice and stature commanded the reverence of mankind; his face was shaded with long whiskers; and his ample turban was fashioned in the shape of a crown. The remains of the sultan were deposited in the tomb of the Seljukian dynasty; and the passenger might read and meditate this useful inscription:[40] 'O ye who have seen the glory of Alp Arslan exhalted to the heavens, repair to Maru, and you will behold it buried in the dust!' The annihilation of the inscription, and the tomb itself, more forcibly proclaims the instability of human greatness.

During the life of Alp Arslan, his eldest son had been acknowledged as the future sultan of the Turks. On his father's death, the inheritance was disputed by an uncle, a cousin, and a brother: they drew their scymetars, and assembled their followers; and the triple victory of Malek Shah[41] established his own reputation and the right of primogeniture. In every age, and more especially in Asia, the thirst of power has inspired the same passions and occasioned the same disorders; but, from the long series of civil war, it would not be easy to extract a sentiment more pure and magnanimous than is contained in a saying of the Turkish prince. On the eve of the battle, he performed his devotions at Thous, before the tomb of the Imam Riza. As the sultan rose from the ground, he asked his vizir Nizam, who had knelt beside him, what had been the object of his secret petition: 'That your arms may be crowned with victory', was the prudent and most probably the sincere answer of the minister. 'For my part,' replied the generous Malek, 'I implored the Lord of Hosts that he would take from me my life and crown, if my brother be more worthy than myself to reign over the Moslems.' The favourable judgment of heaven was ratified by the caliph; and for the first time the sacred title of Commander of the Faithful was communicated to a barbarian. But this barbarian, by his personal merit and the extent of his empire, was the greatest prince of his age. After the settlement of Persia and Syria, he marched at the head of innumerable armies to achieve the conquest of Turkestan, which had been undertaken by his father. In his passage of the Oxus, the boatmen, who had been employed in transporting some troops, complained that their payment was assigned on the revenues of Antioch. The sultan frowned at this preposterous choice, but he smiled at the artful flattery of his vizir. 'It was not to postpone their reward that I selected those remote places, but to leave a memorial to posterity that under your reign Antioch and the Oxus were subject to the same sovereign.' But this description of his limits was unjust and parsimonious: beyond the Oxus, he reduced to his obedience the cities of Bochara, Carizme, and Samarcand, and crushed each rebellious slave, or independent savage, who dared to resist. Malek passed the Sihon or Jaxartes, the last boundary of Persian civilisation: the lords of Turkestan yielded to his supremacy; his name was inserted on the coins, and in the prayers, of Cashgar, a Tartar kingdom on the extreme borders of China. From the Chinese frontier, he stretched his immediate jurisdiction or feudatory sway to the west and south, as far as the mountains of Georgia, the neighbourhood of Constantinople, the holy city of Jerusalem, and the spicy groves of Arabia Felix. Instead of resigning himself to the luxury of his harem, the shepherd king, both in peace and war, was in action and in the field. By the perpetual motion of the royal camp, each province was successively blessed with his presence; and he is said to have perambulated twelve times the wide extent of his dominions, which surpassed the *Asiatic* reign of Cyrus and the caliphs. Of these expeditions, the most pious and splendid was the pilgrimage of Mecca; the freedom and safety of the caravans were protected by his arms; the citizens and pilgrims were enriched by the profusion of his alms; and the desert was cheered by the places of relief and refreshment, which he instituted for the use of his brethren. Hunting was the pleasure, and even the passion, of the sultan, and his train consisted of forty-seven thousand horses; but, after the massacre of a Turkish chase, for each piece of game, he bestowed a piece of gold on the poor, a slight atonement, at the expense of the people, for the cost and mischief of the amusement of kings. In the peaceful prosperity of his reign, the cities of Asia were adorned with palaces and hospitals, with mosques and colleges; few departed from his divan without reward, and none without justice. The language and literature of Persia revived under the house of Seljuk;[42] and, if Malek emulated the liberality of a Turk less potent than himself,[43] his palace might resound with the song of an hundred poets. The sultan bestowed a more serious and learned care on the reformation of the calendar, which was effected by a general assembly of the astronomers of the East. By a law of the prophet, the Moslems are confined to the irregular course of the lunar months; in Persia, since the age of Zoroaster, the revolution of the sun has been known and celebrated as an annual festival,[44] but, after the fall of the Magian empire, the intercalation* had been neglected; the fractions of minutes and hours were multiplied into days; and the date of the Spring was removed from the sign of Aries to that of Pisces. The reign of Malek was illustrated by the *Gelalaean* era; and all errors, either past or future, were corrected by a computation of time, which surpasses the Julian, and approaches the accuracy of the Gregorian, style.[45]

In a period when Europe was plunged in the deepest barbarism, the light and splendour of Asia may be ascribed to the docility rather than the knowledge of the Turkish conquerors. An ample share of their wisdom and virtue is due to a Persian vizir, who ruled the empire under the reign of Alp Arslan and his son. Nizam, one of the most illustrious ministers of the East, was honoured by the caliph as an oracle of religion and science; he was trusted by the sultan as the faithful vicegerent of his power and justice. After an administration of thirty years, the fame of the vizir, his wealth, and even his services, were transformed into crimes. He was overthrown by the insidious arts of a woman and a rival; and his fall was hastened by a rash declaration that his cap and ink-horn, the badges of his office, were connected by the divine decree with the throne and diadem of the sultan. At the age of ninety-three years, the venerable statesman was dismissed by his master, accused by his enemies, and murdered by a fanatic: the last words of Nizam attested his innocence, and the remainder of Malek's life was short and inglorious. From Ispahan, the scene of this disgraceful transaction, the sultan moved to Bagdad, with the design of transplanting the caliph, and of fixing his own residence in the capital of the Moslem world. The feeble successor of Mahomet obtained a respite of ten days; and, before the expiration of the term, the barbarian was summoned by the angel of death. His ambassadors at Constantinople had asked in marriage a Roman princess; but the proposal was decently eluded; and the daughter of Alexius, who might herself have been the victim, expresses her abhorrence of this unnatural conjunction.[46] The daughter of the sultan was bestowed on the caliph Moctadi, with the imperious condition that, renouncing the society of his wives and concubines, he should for ever confine himself to this honourable alliance.

The greatness and unity of the Turkish empire expired in the person of Malek Shah. His vacant throne was disputed by his brother and his four sons; and, after a series of civil wars, the treaty which reconciled the surviving candidates confirmed a lasting separation in the *Persian* dynasty, the eldest and principal branch of the house of Seljuk. The three younger dynasties were those of *Kerman*, of *Syria*, and of *Roum*: the first of these commanded an extensive, though obscure,[47] dominion on the shores of the Indian Ocean;[48] the second expelled the Arabian princes of Aleppo and Damascus; and the third, our peculiar care, invaded the Roman provinces of Asia Minor. The generous policy of Malek contributed to their elevation; he allowed the princes of his blood, even those whom he had vanquished in the field, to seek new kingdoms worthy of their ambition; nor was he displeased that they should draw away the more ardent spirits who might have disturbed the tranquillity of his reign. As the supreme head of his family and nation, the great sultan of Persia commanded the obedience and tribute of his royal brethren; the throne of Kerman and Nicaea, of Aleppo and Damascus; the Atabeks, and emirs of Syria and Mesopotamia, erected their standards under the shadow of his sceptre;[49] and the hordes of Turkmans overspread the plains of the western Asia. After the death of Malek, the bands of union and subordination were relaxed and finally dissolved; the indulgence of the house of Seljuk invested their slaves with the inheritance of kingdoms; and, in the Oriental style, a crowd of princes arose from the dust of their feet.[50]

A prince of the royal line, Cutulmish, the son of Izrail, the son of Seljuk, had fallen in a battle against Alp Arslan; and the humane victor had dropped a tear over his grave. His five sons, strong in arms, ambitious of power, and eager for revenge, unsheathed their scymetars against the son of Alp Arslan. The two armies expected the signal, when the caliph, forgetful of the majesty which secluded him from vulgar eyes, interposed his venerable mediation. 'Instead of shedding the blood of your brethren, your brethren both in descent and faith, unite your forces in an holy war against the Greeks, the enemies of God and his apostle.' They listened to his voice; the sultan embraced his rebellious kinsmen; and the eldest, the valiant Soliman, accepted the royal standard, which gave him the free conquest and hereditary command of the provinces of the Roman empire, from Arzeroum to Constantinople and the unknown regions of the West.[51] Accompanied by his four brothers, he passed the Euphrates: the Turkish camp was soon seated in the neighbourhood of Kutaieh, in Phrygia; and his flying cavalry laid waste the country as far as the Hellespont and the Black Sea. Since the decline of the empire, the peninsula of Asia Minor had been exposed to the transient though destructive inroads of the Persians and Saracens; but the fruits of a lasting conquest were reserved for the Turkish sultan; and his arms were introduced by the Greeks, who aspired to reign on the ruins of their country. Since the captivity of Romanus, six years the feeble son of Eudocia had trembled under the weight of the Imperial crown,* till the provinces of the East and West were lost in the same month by a double rebellion: of either chief Nicephorus was the common name; but the surnames of Bryennius and Botoniates distinguish the European and Asiatic candidates. Their reasons, or rather their promises, were weighed in the divan; and, after some hesitation, Soliman declared himself in favour of Botoniates, opened a free passage to his troops in their march from Antioch to Nicaea, and joined the banner of the crescent to that of the cross. After his ally had ascended the throne of Constantinople, the sultan was hospitably entertained in the suburb of Chrysopolis or Scutari; and a body of two thousand Turks was transported into Europe, to whose dexterity and courage the new emperor was indebted for the defeat and captivity of his rival Bryennius. But the conquest of Europe was dearly purchased by the sacrifice of Asia: Constantinople was deprived of the obedience and revenue of the provinces beyond the Bosphorus and Hellespont; and the regular progress of the Turks, who fortified the passes of the rivers and mountains, left not a hope of their retreat or expulsion. Another candidate implored the aid of the sultan: Melissenus, in his purple robes and red buskins, attended the motions of the Turkish camp; and the desponding cities were tempted by the summons of a Roman prince, who immediately surrendered them into the hands of the barbarians. These acquisitions were confirmed by a treaty of peace with the emperor Alexius;* his fear of Robert[†] compelled him to seek the friendship of Soliman; and it was not till after the sultan's death that he extended as far as Nicomedia, about sixty miles from Constantinople, the eastern boundary of the Roman world. Trebizond alone, defended on either side by the sea and mountains, preserved at the extremity of the Euxine the ancient character of a Greek colony, and the future destiny of a Christian empire.

Since the first conquests of the caliphs, the establishment of the Turks in Anatolia, or Asia Minor, was the most deplorable loss which the church and empire had sustained. By the propagation of the Moslem faith, Soliman deserved the name of *Gazi*, a holy champion; and his new kingdom of the Romans, or of *Roum*, was added to the tables of Oriental geography. It is described as extending from the Euphrates to Constantinople, from the Black Sea to the confines of Syria; pregnant with mines of silver and iron, of alum and copper, fruitful in corn and wine, and productive of cattle and excellent horses.[52] The wealth of Lydia, the arts of the Greeks, the splendour of the Augustan age, existed only in books and ruins, which were equally obscure in the eyes of the Scythian conquerors. Yet, in the present decay, Anatolia still contains *some* wealthy and populous cities; and, under the Byzantine empire, they were far more flourishing in numbers, size, and opulence. By the choice of the sultan, Nicaea, the metropolis of Bithynia, was preferred for his palace and fortress: the seat of the Seljukian dynasty of Roum was planted one hundred miles from Constantinople; and the divinity of Christ was denied and derided in the same temple in which it had been pronounced by the first general synod of the Catholics. The unity of God and the mission of Mahomet were preached in the mosques; the Arabian learning was taught in the schools; the Cadhis judged according to the law of the Koran; the Turkish manners and language prevailed in the cities; and Turkman camps were scattered over the plains and mountains of Anatolia. On the hard conditions of tribute and servitude, the Greek Christians might enjoy the exercise of their religion; but their most holy churches were profaned; their priests and bishops were insulted;[53] they were compelled to suffer the triumph of the *pagans* and the apostasy of their brethren; many thousand children were marked by the knife of circumcision; and many thousand captives were devoted to the service or the pleasures of their masters.[54] After the loss of Asia, Antioch still maintained her primitive allegiance to Christ and Caesar; but the solitary province was separated from all Roman aid, and surrounded on all sides by the Mahometan powers. The despair of Philaretus the governor prepared the sacrifice of his religion and loyalty, had not his guilt been prevented by his son, who hastened to the Nicene palace, and offered to deliver this valuable prize into the hands of Soliman. The ambitious sultan mounted on horseback, and in twelve nights (for he reposed in the day) performed a march of six hundred miles. Antioch was oppressed by the speed and secrecy of his enterprise; and the dependent cities, as far as Laodicea and the confines of Aleppo,[55] obeyed the example of the metropolis. From Laodicea to the Thracian Bosphorus, or arm of St George, the conquests and reign of Soliman extended thirty days' journey in length, and in breadth about ten or fifteen, between the rocks of Lycia and the Black Sea.[56] The Turkish ignorance of navigation protected, for a while, the inglorious safety of the emperor; but no sooner had a fleet of two hundred ships been constructed by the hands of the captive Greeks, than Alexius trembled behind the walls of his capital. His plaintive epistles were dispersed over Europe, to excite the compassion of the Latins, and to paint the danger, the weakness, and the riches, of the city of Constantine.[57]

But the most interesting conquest of the Seljukian Turks was that of Jerusalem,[58] which soon became the theatre of nations. In their capitulation with Omar,* the inhabitants had stipulated the assurance of their religion and property; but the articles were interpreted by a master against whom it was dangerous to dispute; and in the four hundred years of the reign of the caliphs, the political climate of Jerusalem was exposed to the vicissitudes of storms and sunshine.[59] By the increase of proselytes and population, the Mahometans might excuse their usurpation of three-fourths of the city; but a peculiar quarter was reserved for the patriarch with his clergy and people; a tribute of two pieces of gold was the price of protection; and the sepulchre of Christ, with the church of the Resurrection, was still left in the hands of his votaries. Of these votaries, the most numerous and respectable portion were strangers to Jerusalem: the pilgrimages to the Holy Land had been stimulated, rather than suppressed, by the conquest of the Arabs; and the enthusiasm which had always prompted these perilous journeys was nourished by the congenial† passions of grief and indignation. A crowd of pilgrims from the East and West continued to visit the holy sepulchre and the adjacent sanctuaries, more especially at the festival of Easter; and the Greeks and Latins, the Nestorians and Jacobites, the Copts and Abyssinians, the Armenians and Georgians, maintained the chapels, the clergy, and the poor of their respective communions. The harmony of prayer in so many various tongues, the worship of so many nations in the common temple of their religion, might have afforded a spectacle of edification and peace; but the zeal of the Christian sects was embittered by hatred and revenge; and in the kingdom of a suffering Messiah, who had pardoned his enemies, they aspired to command and persecute their spiritual brethren. The pre-eminence was asserted by the spirit and numbers of the Franks; and the greatness of Charlemagne[60] protected both the Latin pilgrims, and the Catholics of the East. The poverty of Carthage, Alexandria, and Jerusalem was relieved by the alms of that pious emperor; and many monasteries of Palestine were founded or restored by his liberal devotion. Harun Alrashid,* the greatest of the Abbassides, esteemed in his Christian brother a similar supremacy of genius and power; their friendship was cemented by a frequent intercourse of gifts and embassies; and the caliph, without resigning the substantial dominion, presented the emperor with the keys of the holy sepulchre, and perhaps of the city of Jerusalem. In the decline of the Carlovingian monarchy, the republic of Amalphi promoted the interest of trade and religion in the East. Her vessels transported the Latin pilgrims to the coasts of Egypt and Palestine, and deserved, by their useful imports, the favour and alliance of the Fatimite caliphs:[61] an annual fair was instituted on mount Calvary; and the Italian merchants founded the convent and hospital of St John of Jerusalem, the cradle of the monastic and military order, which has since reigned in the isles of Rhodes and of Malta. Had the Christian pilgrims been content to revere the tomb of a prophet, the disciples of Mahomet, instead of blaming, would have imitated, their piety; but these rigid *Unitarians*† were scandalised by a worship which represents the birth, death, and resurrection, of a God; the Catholic images were branded with the name of idols; and the Moslems smiled with indignation[62] at the miraculous flame, which was kindled on the eve of Easter in the holy sepulchre.[63] This pious fraud, first devised in the ninth century,[64] was devoutly cherished by the Latin crusaders, and is annually repeated by the clergy of the Greek, Armenian, and Coptic sects,[65] who impose on the credulous spectators[66] for their own benefit and that of their tyrants. In every age, a principle of toleration has been fortified by a sense of interest; and the revenue of the prince and his emir was increased each year by the expense and tribute of so many thousand strangers.

The revolution which transferred the sceptre from the Abbassides to the Fatimites was a benefit, rather than an injury, to the Holy Land. A sovereign resident in Egypt was more sensible of the importance of Christian trade; and the emirs of Palestine were less remote from the justice and power of the throne. But the third of these Fatimite caliphs was the famous Hakem,‡[67] a frantic youth, who was delivered by his impiety and despotism from the fear either of God or man; and whose reign was a wild mixture of vice and folly. Regardless of the most ancient customs of Egypt, he imposed on the women an absolute confinement:

the restraint excited the clamours of both sexes; their clamours provoked his fury; a part of Old Cairo was delivered to the flames; and the guards and citizens were engaged many days in a bloody conflict. At first the caliph declared himself a zealous Musulman, the founder or benefactor of mosques and colleges: twelve hundred and ninety copies of the Koran were transcribed at his expense in letters of gold; and his edict extirpated the vineyards of the Upper Egypt. But his vanity was soon flattered by the hope of introducing a new religion; he aspired above the fame of a prophet, and styled himself the visible image of the Most High God, who, after nine apparitions on earth, was at length manifest in his royal person. At the name of Hakem, the lord of the living and the dead, every knee was bent in religious adoration: his mysteries were performed on a mountain near Cairo; sixteen thousand converts had signed his profession of faith; and at the present hour, a free and warlike people, the Druses of mount Libanus, are persuaded of the life and divinity of a madman and tyrant.[68] In his divine character, Hakem hated the Jews and Christians, as the servants of his rivals; while some remains of prejudice or prudence still pleaded in favour of the law of Mahomet. Both in Egypt and Palestine, his cruel and wanton persecution made some martyrs and many apostates: the common rights and special privileges of the sectaries were equally disregarded; and a general interdict was laid on the devotion of strangers and natives. The temple of the Christian world, the church of the Resurrection, was demolished to its foundations; the luminous prodigy* of Easter was interrupted, and much profane labour was exhausted to destroy the cave in the rock, which properly constitutes the holy sepulchre. At the report of this sacrilege, the nations of Europe were astonished and afflicted; but, instead of arming in the defence of the Holy Land, they contented themselves with burning or banishing the Jews, as the secret advisers of the impious barbarian.[69] Yet the calamities of Jerusalem were in some measure alleviated by the inconstancy or repentance of Hakem himself; and the royal mandate was sealed for the restitution of the churches, when the tyrant was assassinated by the emissaries of his sister. The succeeding caliphs resumed the maxims of religion and policy; a free toleration was again granted; with the pious aid of the emperor of Constantinople the holy sepulchre arose from its ruins; and, after a short abstinence, the pilgrims returned with an increase of appetite to the spiritual feast.[70] In the sea-voyage of Palestine, the dangers were frequent and the opportunities rare; but the conversion of Hungary opened a safe communication between Germany and Greece. The charity of St Stephen, the apostle of his kingdom, relieved and conducted his itinerant brethren;[71] and from Belgrade to Antioch they traversed fifteen hundred miles of a Christian empire. Among the Franks, the zeal of pilgrimage prevailed beyond the example of former times; and the roads were covered with multitudes of either sex and of every rank, who professed their contempt of life, so soon as they should have kissed the tomb of their Redeemer. Princes and prelates abandoned the care of their dominions; and the numbers of these pious caravans were a prelude to the armies which marched in the ensuing age under the banner of the cross. About thirty years before the first crusade, the archbishop of Mentz, with the bishops of Utrecht, Bamberg, and Ratisbon, undertook this laborious journey from the Rhine to the Jordan; and the multitude of their followers amounted to seven thousand persons. At Constantinople, they were hospitably entertained by the emperor; but the ostentation of their wealth provoked the assault of the wild Arabs; they drew their swords with scrupulous reluctance, and sustained a siege in the village of Capernaum, till they were rescued by the venal protection of the Fatimite emir. After visiting the holy places, they embarked for Italy, but only a remnant of two thousand arrived in safety in their native land. Ingulphus, a secretary of William the Conqueror, was a companion of this pilgrimage: he observes that they sallied from Normandy, thirty stout and well-appointed horsemen; but that they repassed the Alps, twenty miserable palmers,* with the staff in their hand, and the wallet at their back.[72]

After the defeat of the Romans, the tranquillity of the Fatimite caliphs was invaded by the Turks.[73] One of the lieutenants of Malek Shah, Atsiz the Carizmian, marched into Syria at the head of a powerful army, and reduced Damascus by famine and the sword. Hems, and the other cities of the province, acknowledged the caliph of Bagdad and the sultan of Persia; and the victorious emir advanced without resistance to the banks of the Nile; the Fatimite was preparing to fly into the heart of Africa; but the negroes of his guard and the inhabitants of Cairo made a desperate sally, and repulsed the Turk from the confines of Egypt. In his retreat, he indulged the licence of slaughter and rapine; the judge and notaries of Jerusalem were invited to his camp; and their execution was followed by the massacre of three thousand citizens. The cruelty or the defeat of Atsiz was soon punished by the sultan Toucush, the brother of Malek Shah, who, with a higher title and more formidable powers, asserted the dominion of Syria and Palestine. The house of Seljuk reigned about twenty years in Jerusalem;[74] but the hereditary command of the holy city and territory was entrusted or abandoned to the emir Ortok, the chief of a tribe of Turkmans, whose children, after their expulsion from Palestine, formed two dynasties on the borders of Armenia and Assyria.[75] The Oriental Christians and the Latin pilgrims deplored a revolution, which, instead of the regular government and old alliance of the caliphs, imposed on their necks the iron yoke of the strangers of the north.[76] In his court and camp the great sultan had adopted in some degree the arts and manners of Persia; but the body of the Turkish nation, and more especially the pastoral tribes, still breathed the fierceness of the desert. From Nicaea to Jerusalem, the western countries of Asia were a scene of foreign and domestic hostility; and the shepherds of Palestine, who held a precarious sway on a doubtful frontier, had neither leisure nor capacity to await the slow profits of commercial and religious freedom. The pilgrims, who, through innumerable perils, had reached the gates of Jerusalem, were the victims of private rapine or public oppression, and often sunk under the pressure of famine and disease, before they were permitted to salute the holy sepulchre. A spirit of native barbarism, or recent zeal, prompted the Turkmans to insult the clergy of every sect; the patriarch was dragged by the hair along the pavement and cast into a dungeon, to extort a ransom from the sympathy of his flock; and the divine worship in the church of the Resurrection was often disturbed by the savage rudeness of its masters. The pathetic tale excited the millions of the West to march under the standard of the Cross to the relief of the Holy Land; and yet how trifling is the sum of these accumulated evils, if compared with the single act of the sacrilege of Hakem, which had been so patiently endured by the Latin Christians! A slighter provocation inflamed the more irascible temper of their descendants: a new spirit had arisen of religious chivalry and papal dominion; a nerve was touched of exquisite feeling; and the sensation vibrated to the heart of Europe.

NOTES TO CHAPTER 57

1 I am indebted for his character and history to d'Herbelot (*Bibliothèque Orientale, Mahmud*, pp. 533–37); M. de Guignes (*Histoire des Huns*, iii, 155–73), and our countryman, Colonel Alexander Dow (i, 23–83). In the two first volumes of his *History of Hindostan*, he styles himself the translator of the Persian *Ferishta*, but in his florid text it is not easy to distinguish the version and the original.

* *page 862*   [Mahomet]

2 The dynasty of the Samanides continued 125 years, AD 874–999, under ten princes. See their succession and ruin, in the Tables of M. de Guignes (*Hist. des Huns*, i, 404–06). They were followed by the Gaznevides, AD 999–1183. (See i, 239–40). His division of nations often disturbs the series of time and place.

3 *Gaznah hortos non habet; est emporium et domicilium mercaturae Indicae* ['Gaznah has no gardens; it is an emporium and centre of Indian commerce']. Abulfeda, *Geograph.*, tab. xxiii, p. 349, Reiske; d'Herbelot, p. 364. It has not been visited by any modern traveller.

4 By the ambassador of the caliph of Bagdad, who employed an Arabian or Chaldaic word that signifies *lord* and *master* (d'Herbelot, p. 825). It is interpreted Αὐτοκράτωρ, Βασιλεὺς Βασιλέων ['sole ruler, king of kings'], by the Byzantine writers of the eleventh century; and the name (Σουλτανός, Soldanus) is familiarly employed in the Greek and Latin languages, after it had passed from the Gaznevides to the Seljukides, and other emirs of Asia and Egypt. Ducange (Dissertation xvi, *sur* Joinville, pp. 238–40, *Gloss. Graec. et Latin.*) labours to find the title of sultan in the ancient kingdom of Persia; but his proofs are mere shadows; a proper name in the Themes of Constantine (ii, 11), an anticipation of Zonaras, etc. and a medal of Kai Khosrou, not (as he believes) the Sassanide

of the vith, but the Seljukide of Iconium of the xiiith, century (de Guignes, *Hist. des Huns*, i, 246).

5 Ferishta (*apud* Dow, *Hist. of Hindostan*, i, 49) mentions the report of a *gun* in the Indian army. But, as I am slow in believing this premature (AD 1008) use of artillery, I must desire to scrutinise first the text and then the authority of Ferishta, who lived in the Mogul court in the last century.

6 Kinnoge or Canouge (the old Palimbothra) is marked in latitude 27° 3', longitude 80° 13'. See d'Anville (*Antiquité de l'Inde*, pp. 60–62), corrected by the local knowledge of Major Rennell (in his excellent Memoir on his map of Hindostan, pp. 37–43): 300 jewellers, 30,000 shops for the areca nut, 60,000 bands of musicians, etc. (Abulfed., *Geograph.*, tab. xv, p. 274; Dow, i, 16) will allow an ample deduction.

7 The idolators of Europe, says Ferishta (Dow, i, 66). Consult Abulfeda (p. 272) and Rennell's map of Hindostan.

* *page 864*   [attractive]

† *page 864*   [the court or council, where the sultan dispensed justice]

8 D'Herbelot, *Bibliothèque Orientale*, p. 527. Yet these letters, apophthegms, etc., are rarely the language of the heart, or the motives of public action.

9 For instance, a ruby of four hundred and fifty miskals (Dow, i, 53) or six pounds three ounces: the largest in the treasury of Delhi weighed seventeen miskals (*Voyages* de Tavernier, ii, 280). It is true that in the East all coloured stones are called rubies (p. 355), and that Tavernier saw three larger and more precious among the jewels *de notre grand roi, le plus puissant et plus magnifique de tous les Rois de la terre* ['of our great king, the most powerful and magnificent of all the kings of the earth'] (p. 376).

10 Dow, i, 65. The sovereign of Kinnoge is said to have possessed 2500 elephants (Abulfed., *Geograph.*, tab. xv, p. 274). From these Indian stories the reader may correct a note in my first volume (p. 226); or from that note he may correct these stories. [Gibbon is referring to footnote 49 of Chapter 8.]

11 See a just and natural picture of these pastoral manners, in the history of William, archbishop of Tyre (i, vii, in the *Gesta Dei per Francos*, pp. 633–34), and a valuable note by the editor of the *Histoire Généalogique des Tatars*, pp. 535–38.

12 The first emigrations of the Turkmans, and doubtful origin of the Seljukians, may be traced in the laborious *History of the Huns*, by M. de Guignes (tom. i, *Tables Chronologique*s, v; tom. iii, vii, ix and x); and the *Bibliothèque Orientale* of d'Herbelot (pp. 799–802, 897–901); Elmacin (*Hist. Saracen.*, pp. 331–33); and Abulpharagius (*Dynast.*, pp. 221–22).

* *page 868*   [grandees]

13 Dow, *Hist. of Hindostan*, i, 89, 95–98. I have copied this passage as a specimen of the Persian manner; but I suspect that by some odd fatality the style of Ferishta has been improved by that of Ossian.

14 The Zendekan of d'Herbelot (p. 1028), the Dindaka of Dow (i, 97), is probably the Dandanekan of Abulfeda (*Geograph.*, p. 345, Reiske), a small town of Chorasan, two days' journey from Marû, and renowned through the East for the production and manufacture of cotton.

15 The Byzantine historians (Cedrenus, ii, 766–67; Zonaras, ii, 255; Nicephorus Bryennius, p. 21) have confounded, in this revolution, the truth of time and place, of names and persons, of causes and events. The ignorance and errors of these Greeks (which I shall not stop to unravel) may inspire some distrust of the

story of Cyaxares and Cyrus, as it is told by their most eloquent predecessors.

16 Willerm. Tyr., i, 7, 633. The divination by arrows is ancient and famous in the East.

17 D'Herbelot, p. 801. Yet, after the fortune of his posterity, Seljuk became the thirty-fourth in lineal descent from the great Afrasiab, emperor of Touran (p. 800). The Tartar pedigree of the house of Zingis gave a different cast to flattery and fable; and the historian Mirkhond derives the Seljukides from Alankavah, the virgin mother (801, col. 2). If they be the same as the *Zalzuts* of Abulghazi Bahader Khan (*Hist. Généalogique*, p. 148), we quote in their favour the most weighty evidence of a Tartar prince himself, the descendant of Zingis, Alankavah, or Alancu, and Oguz Khan.

18 By a slight corruption, Togrul Beg is the Tangroli-pix of the Greeks. His reign and character are faithfully exhibited by d'Herbelot (*Bibliothèque Orientale*, pp. 1027–28) and de Guignes (*Hist. des Huns*, iii, 189–201).

19 Cedrenus, ii, 774–75; Zonaras, ii, 257. With their usual knowledge of Oriental affairs, they describe the ambassador as a *sherif*, who, like the syncellus of the patriarch, was the vicar and successor of the caliph.

20 From William of Tyre, I have borrowed this distinction of Turks and Turkmans, which at least is popular and convenient. The names are the same, and the addition of *man* is of the same import in the Persic and Teutonic idioms. Few critics will adopt the etymology of James de Vitry (*Hist. Hierosol.*, i, 11, 1061), of Turcomani, *quasi Turci et Comani*, a mixed people.

21 *Hist. Générale des Huns*, iii, 165–67. M. de Guignes quotes Abulmahasen, an historian of Egypt.

 * *page 870* [the caliphs at Bagdad]

 † *page 870* [the caliphs in Egypt]

22 Consult the *Bibliothèque Orientale*, in the articles of the *Abbassides*, *Caher*, and *Caiem*, and the Annals of Elmacin and Abulpharagius.

23 For this curious ceremony, I am indebted to M. de Guignes (iii, 197–98), and that learned author is obliged to Bondari, who composed in Arabic the history of the Seljukides (v, 365). I am ignorant of his age, country and character.

24 *Eodem anno* (AH 455) *obiit princeps Togrulbecus . . . rex fuit clemens, prudens, et peritus regnandi, cuius terror corda mortalium invaserat, ita ut obedirent ei reges atque ad ipsum scriberent.* ['That same year Togrul died . . . he was a merciful king, prudent, a wise ruler, who had inspired fear of himself in human hearts, so that kings obeyed him and corresponded with him.'] Elmacin, *Hist. Saracen.*, p. 342, vers. Erpenii.

 * *page 871* [emperor Nicephorus II, AD 963–69]

 † *page 871* [emperor John I Zimisces, AD 969–76]

 ‡ *page 871* [emperor Basil II, AD 976–1025]

25 For these wars of the Turks and Romans, see in general the Byzantine histories of Zonaras and Cedrenus, Scylitzes the continuator of Cedrenus, and Nicephorus Bryennius Caesar. The two first of these were monks, the two latter statesmen; yet such were the Greeks that the difference of style and character is scarcely discernible. For the Orientals, I draw as usual on the wealth of d'Herbelot (see titles of the first Seljukides) and the accuracy of de Guignes (*Hist. des Huns*, iii, x).

26 Ἐφέρετο γὰρ ἐν Τούρκοις λόγος, ὡς εἴη πεπρωμένον καταστραφῆναι τὸ Τούρκων γένος ἀπὸ τῆς τοιαύτης δυνάμεως, ὁποίαν ὁ Μακεδὼν Ἀλέξανδρος ἔχων κατεστρέψατο Πέρσας. ['For it was rumoured among the Turks that the Turkish nation was

destined to be destroyed by a power as great as that which Alexander of Macedon possessed when he destroyed the Persians.'] Cedrenus, ii, 791. The credulity of the vulgar is always probable; and the Turks had learned from the Arabs the history or legend of Escander Dulcarnein (d'Herbelot, pp. 317, etc.).

* *page 872*   [Their heresies are discussed by Gibbon in Chapter 47.]

27 Οἳ καὶ Ἰβηρίαν καὶ Μεσοποταμίαν καὶ Ἀρμενίαν οἰκοῦσιν καὶ οἳ τὴν Ἰουδαικὴν τοῦ Νεστορίου καὶ τῶν Ἀκεφάλων θρησκεύουσιν αἵρεσιν ['Those who live in Iberia (Georgia), Mesopotamia and Armenia, and who follow the Judaic heresy of Nestorians and the Schismatics'] (Scylitzes, *ad calcem* Cedreni, ii, 834, whose ambiguous construction shall not tempt me to suspect that he confounded the Nestorian and Monophysite heresies). He familiarly talks of the μῆνις, χόλος, ὀργή Θεοῦ ['wrath, anger, fury of God'], qualities, as I should apprehend, very foreign to the perfect Being; but his bigotry is forced to confess that they were soon afterwards discharged on the orthodox Romans.

28 Had the name of Georgians been known to the Greeks (Stritter, *Memoriae Byzant.*, tom. iv, *Iberica*), I should derive it from their agriculture, as the Σκύθαι γεωργοί [Scythian farmers] of Herodotus (iv, 18, 289, edit. Wesseling). But it appears only since the crusades, among the Latins (Jac. a Vitriaco, *Hist. Hierosol.*, 79, 1095) and Orientals (d'Herbelot, p. 407), and was devoutly borrowed from St George of Cappadocia.

29 Mosheim, *Institut. Hist. Eccles.*, p. 632. See in Chardin's *Travels* (i, 171–75) the manners and religion of this handsome but worthless nation. See the pedigree of their princes from Adam to the present century, in the Tables of M. de Guignes (i, 433–38).

† *page 872*   [widow of the emperor Constantine X, who ruled AD 1059–67]

‡ *page 872*   [in the following year]

30 This city is mentioned by Constantine Porphyrogenitus (*de Administrat. Imperii*, ii, 44, 119) and the Byzantines of the xith century, under the name of Mantzikierte, and by some is confounded with Theodosiopolis; but Delisle, in his notes and maps, has very properly fixed the situation. Abulfeda (*Geograph.*, tab. xviii, p. 310) describes Malasgerd as a small town, built with black stone, supplied with water, without trees, etc.

31 The Uzi of the Greeks (Stritter, *Memor. Byzant.*, iii, 923–48) are the Gozz of the Orientals (*Hist. des Huns*, ii, 522; iii, 133, etc.). They appear on the Danube and the Volga, in Armenia, Syria, and Chorasan, and the name seems to have been extended to the whole Turkman race.

32 Urselius (the Russelius of Zonaras) is distinguished by Jeffrey Malaterra (i, 33) among the Norman conquerors of Sicily, and with the surname of *Baliol*; and our own historians will tell how the Baliols came from Normandy to Durham, built Bernard's Castle on the Tees, married an heiress of Scotland, etc. Ducange (Not. *ad* Nicephor. Bryennium, ii, No. 4) has laboured the subject in honour of the president de Bailleul, whose father had exchanged the sword for the gown.

33 Elmacin (pp. 343–44) assigns this probable number, which is reduced by Abulpharagius to 15,000 (p. 227) and by d'Herbelot (p. 102) to 12,000 horse. But the same Elmacin gives 300,000 men to the emperor, of whom Abulpharagius says, *cum centum hominum millibus, multisque equis et magna pompa instructus*. ['He was arrayed with 100,000 men, many horses and great pomp.'] The Greeks abstain from any definition of numbers.

34 The Byzantine writers do not speak so distinctly of the presence of the sultan;

he committed his forces to an eunuch, had retired to a distance, etc. Is it ignorance, or jealousy, or truth?

35 He was the son of the Caesar John Ducas, brother of the emperor Constantine (Ducange, *Fam. Byzant.*, p. 165). Nicephorus Bryennius applauds his virtues, and extenuates his faults (i, 30, 38; ii, 53). Yet he owns his enmity to Romanus, οὐ πάνυ δὲ φιλίως ἔχων πρὸς βασιλέα ['not being very well disposed towards the emperor']. Scylitzes speaks more explicitly of his treason.

36 This circumstance, which we read and doubt in Scylitzes and Constantine Manasses, is more prudently omitted by Nicephorus and Zonaras.

37 The ransom and tribute are attested by reason and the Orientals. The other Greeks are modestly silent; but Nicephorus Bryennius dares to affirm that the terms were οὐκ ἀναξίας Ῥωμαίων ἀρχῆς ['not unworthy of the Roman empire'], and that the emperor would have preferred death to a shameful treaty.

38 The defeat and captivity of Romanus Diogenes may be found in John Scylitzes, *ad calcem* Cedreni, ii, 835–43; Zonaras, ii, 281–84; Nicephorus Bryennius, i, 25–32; Glycas, pp. 325–57; Constantine Manasses, p. 134; Elmacin, *Hist. Saracen.*, pp. 343–44; Abulpharag., *Dynast.*, p. 227; d'Herbelot, pp. 102–03; de Guignes, iii, 207–11. Besides my old acquaintance, Elmacin and Abulpharagius, the historian of the Huns has consulted Abulfeda, and his epitomiser, Benschounah, a Chronicle of the Caliphs, by Soyouthi, Abulmahasen of Egypt, and Novairi of Africa.

39 This interesting death is told by d'Herbelot (pp. 103–04) and M. de Guignes (iii, 212–13) from their Oriental writers; but neither of them have transfused the spirit of Elmacin (*Hist. Saracen.*, pp. 344–45).

40 A critique [critic] of high renown (the late Dr Johnson), who has severely scrutinised the epitaphs of Pope, might cavil in this sublime inscription at the words, 'repair to Maru', since the reader must already be at Maru before he could peruse the inscription.

41 The *Bibliothèque Orientale* has given the text of the reign of Malek (pp. 542–44, 654–55), and the *Histoire Générale des Huns* (iii, 214–24) has added the usual measure of repetition, emendation, and supplement. Without these two learned Frenchmen, I should be blind indeed in the Eastern world.

42 See an excellent discourse at the end of Sir William Jones's *History of Nadir Shah*, and the articles of the poets, Amak, Anvari, Raschadi, etc. in the *Bibliothèque Orientale*.

43 His name was Kheder Khan. Four bags were placed round his sopha, and as he listened to the song, he cast handfuls of gold and silver to the poets (d'Herbelot, p. 107). All this may be true; but I do not understand how he could reign in Transoxiana in the time of Malek Shah, and much less how Kheder could surpass him in power and pomp. I suspect that the beginning, not the end, of the xith century is the true era of his reign.

44 See Chardin, *Voyages en Perse*, ii, 235.

* *page 878* [the insertion of additional days in the calendar in order to harmonise the calendar with the solar year]

45 The Gelalaean era (Gelaleddin, Glory of the Faith, was one of the names or titles of Malek Shah) is fixed to the 15th of March, AH 471, AD 1079. Dr Hyde has produced the original testimonies of the Persians and Arabians (*de Religione veterum Persarum*, 16, 200–11).

46 She speaks of this Persian royalty as ἀπάσης κακοδαιμονέστερον πενίας ['more

wretched than any degree of poverty']. Anna Comnena was only nine years old at the end of the reign of Malek Shah (AD 1092), and, when she speaks of his assassination, she confounds the sultan with the vizir (*Alexias*, vi, 177–78).

47 So obscure that the industry of M. de Guignes could only copy (i, 244; iii, i, 269, etc.) the history, or rather list, of the Seljukides of Kerman, in *Bibliothèque Orientale*. They were extinguished before the end of the xiith century.

48 Tavernier, perhaps the only traveller who has visited Kerman, describes the capital as a great ruinous village, twenty-five days' journey from Ispahan, and twenty-seven from Ormus, in the midst of a fertile country (*Voyages en Turquie et en Perse*, pp. 107, 110).

49 It appears from Anna Comnena that the Turks of Asia Minor obeyed the signet and chiauss [envoy] of the great sultan (*Alexias*, vi, 170) and that the two sons of Soliman were detained in his court (p. 180).

50 This expression is quoted by Petit de la Croix (*Vie de Gengiscan*, p. 161) from some poet, most probably a Persian.

51 On the conquest of Asia Minor, M. de Guignes has derived no assistance from the Turkish or Arabian writers, who produce a naked list of the Seljukides of Roum. The Greeks are unwilling to expose their shame, and we must extort some hints from Scylitzes (pp. 860, 863); Nicephorus Bryennius (pp. 88, 91–92, etc. 103–04); and Anna Comnena (*Alexias*, pp. 91–92, etc. 168, etc.).

* *page 879*   [Michael VII Ducas, emperor 1071–78]

* *page 880*   [Alexius I Comnenus, emperor 1081–1118]

† *page 880*   [Robert Guiscard, the Norman Duke of Apulia]

52 Such is the description of Roum by Haiton the Armenian, whose Tartar history may be found in the collections of Ramusio and Bergeron (see Abulfeda, *Geograph. climat.*, xvii, pp 301–05).

53 *Dicit eos quendam abusione Sodomiticâ intervertisse episcopum* ['He says that they sodomised a bishop'] (Guibert. Abbat., *Hist. Hierosol.*, i, 468). It is odd enough that we should find a parallel passage of the same people in the present age. *Il n'est point d'horreur que ces Turcs n'ayent commis, et semblables aux soldats effrénés, qui dans le sac d'une ville non contens de disposer de tout à leur gré pretendent encore aux succès les moins désirables, quelques Sipahis ont porté leurs attentats sur la personne du vieux rabbi de la synagogue, et celle de l'Archévêque Grec.* ['There is no atrocity which these Turks failed to commit, and, like the soldiers who run wild when sacking a town, and, not content to lay hands on whatever takes their fancy, also lay claim to the least desirable triumphs, several sipahis [horsemen] committed indecent assaults on the persons of the old rabbi of the synagogue and of the Greek archbishop.'] (*Mémoires* du Baron de Tott, ii, 193).

54 The emperor, or abbot, describe the scenes of a Turkish camp as if they had been present. *Matres correptae in conspectu filiarum multipliciter repetitis diversorum coitibus vexabantur* (is that the true reading?), *cum filiae assistentes carmina praecinere saltando cogerentur. Mox eadem passio ad filias*, etc. ['Mothers were seized and subjected to multiple rape by different assailants, which their daughters were compelled to witness and to accompany with song and dance. Soon the same ordeal overtook the daughters, etc.']

55 See Antioch, and the death of Soliman, in Anna Comnena (*Alexias*, vi, 168–69), with the notes of Ducange.

56 William of Tyre (i, 9–10, 635) gives the most authentic and deplorable account

of these Turkish conquests.

57 In his epistle to the count of Flanders, Alexius seems to fall too low beneath his character and dignity; yet it is approved by Ducange (Not. *ad Alexiad.*, pp. 335, etc.) and paraphrased by the abbot Guibert, a contemporary historian. The Greek text no longer exists; and each translator and scribe might say with Guibert (p. 475), *verbis vestita meis* ['it is expressed in my words'], a privilege of most indefinite latitude.

58 Our best fund for the history of Jerusalem from Heraclius to the crusades is contained in two large and original passages of William, archbishop of Tyre (i, 1–10; xviii, 5–6), the principal author of the *Gesta Dei per Francos*. M. de Guignes has composed a very learned *Mémoire sur le Commerce des François dans le Levant avant les Croisades*, etc. (*Mém. de l'Académie des Inscriptions*, xxxvii, 467–500).

* *page 881* [Omar was the second caliph after Mahomet and in AD 637 crossed the desert to receive the surrender of Jerusalem.]

59 *Secundum Dominorum dispositionem plerumque lucida plerumque nubila recepit intervalla, et aegrotantis more temporum praesentium gravabatur aut respirabat qualitate* (i, 3, 630). The Latinity of William of Tyre is by no means contemptible; but in his account of 490 years, from the loss to the recovery of Jerusalem, he exceeds the true account by thirty years.

† *page 881* [related]

60 For the transactions of Charlemagne with the Holy Land, see Eginhard (*de Vita Caroli Magni*, 16, 79–82); Constantine Porphyrogenitus (*de Administratione Imperii*, ii, 26, 80); and Pagi (*Critica*, tom. iii, AD 800, No. 13–15).

* *page 882* [caliph AD 786–809]

61 The caliph granted his privileges, *Amalphitanis viris amicis et utilium introductoribus* ['to the friendly people of Amalfi, the bringers of useful goods'] (*Gesta Dei*, p. 934). The trade of Venice to Egypt and Palestine cannot produce so old a title unless we adopt the laughable translation of a Frenchman who mistook the two factions of the circus (Veneti et Prasini) for the Venetians and Parisians.

† *page 882* [believers in one God: here, the Moslems]

62 An Arabic chronicle of Jerusalem (apud Asseman., *Bibliot. Orient.*, i, 628; iv, 368) attests the unbelief of the caliph and the historian; yet Cantacuzene presumes to appeal to the Mahometans themselves for the truth of this perpetual miracle.

63 In his *Dissertations on Ecclesiastical History*, the learned Mosheim has separately discussed this pretended miracle (ii, 214–306), *de lumine sancti sepulchri*.

64 William of Malmsbury (iv, ii, 209) quotes the Itinerary of the monk Bernard, an eye-witness, who visited Jerusalem AD 870. The miracle is confirmed by another pilgrim some years older; and Mosheim ascribes the invention to the Franks soon after the decease of Charlemagne.

65 Our travellers, Sandys (p. 134), Thévenot (pp. 621–27), Maundrell (pp. 94–95), etc., describe this extravagant farce. The Catholics are puzzled to decide *when* the miracle ended and the trick began.

66 The Orientals themselves confess the fraud, and plead necessity and edification (*Mémoires* du Chevalier d'Arvieux, ii, 140; Joseph Abudacni, *Hist. Copt.*, ch. 20); but I will not attempt, with Mosheim, to explain the mode. Our travellers have failed with the blood of St Januarius at Naples [which is said to liquify].

‡ *page 882* [caliph from AD 996–1021]

67 See d'Herbelot (*Bibliot. Orientale*, p. 411); Renaudot (*Hist. Patriarch. Alex.*, pp. 390, 397, 400–01); Elmacin (*Hist. Saracen.*, p. 321–23); and Marei (pp. 384–86), an historian of Egypt, translated by Reiske from Arabic into German, and verbally interpreted to me by a friend.

68 The religion of the Druses is concealed by their ignorance and hypocrisy. Their secret doctrines are confined to the elect who profess a contemplative life, and the vulgar Druses, the most indifferent of men, occasionally conform to the worship of the Mahometans and Christians of their neighbourhood. The little that is, or deserves to be, known may be seen in the industrious Niebuhr (*Voyages*, ii, 354–57) and the second volume of the recent and instructive *Travels* of M. de Volney.

* *page 883* [the miraculous flame]

69 See Glaber, iii, 7, and the *Annals* of Baronius and Pagi, AD 1009.

70 *Per idem tempus ex universo orbe tam innumerabilis multitudo coepit confluere ad sepulchrum Salvatoris Hierosolymis, quantum nullus hominum prius sperare poterat. Ordo inferioris plebis . . . mediocres . . . reges et comites . . . praesules . . . mulieres multae nobiles cum pauperioribus . . . Pluribus enim erat mentis desiderium mori priusquam ad propria reverterentur* ['At the same time such an innumerable host from every corner of the earth began to congregate at the sepulchre of the Saviour at Jerusalem, as no human being could previously have hoped. The lower order of people . . . people of the middle rank . . . kings and counts . . . leaders . . . many noble woman and poor folk . . . For most of them wished to die (in the Holy Land) rather than return to their own lands.'] (Glaber, iv, 6; Bouquet, *Historians of France*, x, 50).

71 Glaber, iii, 1. Katona (*Hist. Critic. Regum Hungariae*, i, 304–11) examines whether St Stephen founded a monastery at Jerusalem.

* *page 884* [pilgrims]

72 Baronius (AD 1064, No. 43–56) has transcribed the greater part of the original narratives of Ingulphus, Marianus, and Lambertus.

73 See Elmacin (*Hist. Saracen.*, pp. 349–50) and Abulpharagius (*Dynast.*, p. 237, vers. Pocock). M. de Guignes (*Hist. des Huns*, iii, i, 215–16) adds the testimonies, or rather the names, of Abulfeda and Novairi.

74 From the expedition of Isar Atsiz (AH 469, AD 1076) to the expulsion of the Ortokides (AD 1096). Yet William of Tyre (i, 6, 633) asserts that Jerusalem was thirty-eight years in the hands of the Turks; and an Arabic chronicle, quoted by Pagi (iv, 202), supposes that the city was reduced by a Carizmian general to the obedience of the caliph of Bagdad, AH 463, AD 1070. These early dates are not very compatible with the general history of Asia; and I am sure that, as late as AD 1064, the regnum Babylonicum (of Cairo) still prevailed in Palestine (Baronius, AD 1064, No. 56).

75 De Guignes, *Hist. des Huns*, i, 249–52.

76 Willerm. Tyr., i, 8, 634, who strives hard to magnify the Christian grievances. The Turks exacted an *aureus* [gold piece] from each pilgrim! The *caphar* [a toll or duty imposed by the Turks on Christian merchants] of the Franks is now fourteen dollars; and Europe does not complain of this voluntary tax.

CHAPTER 58

*Origin and numbers of the first Crusade – characters of the
Latin princes – their march to Constantinople – policy of
the Greek emperor Alexius – conquest of Nicaea,
Antioch, and Jerusalem, by the Franks –
deliverance of the Holy Sepulchre – Godfrey of Bouillon, first
King of Jerusalem – institutions of the French or Latin kingdom*

About twenty years after the conquest of Jerusalem by the Turks, the holy
sepulchre was visited by an hermit of the name of Peter, a native of
Amiens, in the province of Picardy[1] in France. His resentment and
sympathy were excited by his own injuries and the oppression of the
Christian name; he mingled his tears with those of the patriarch, and
earnestly inquired if no hopes of relief could be entertained from the
Greek emperors of the East. The patriarch exposed the vices and
weakness of the successors of Constantine. 'I will rouse,' exclaimed the
hermit, 'the martial nations of Europe in your cause;' and Europe was
obedient to the call of the hermit. The astonished patriarch dismissed him
with epistles of credit and complaint; and no sooner did he land at Bari
than Peter hastened to kiss the feet of the Roman Pontiff. His stature was
small, his appearance contemptible; but his eye was keen and lively; and
he possessed that vehemence of speech which seldom fails to impart the
persuasion of the soul.[2] He was born of a gentleman's family (for we must
now adopt a modern idiom), and his military service was under the
neighbouring counts of Boulogne, the heroes of the first crusade. But he
soon relinquished the sword and the world; and, if it be true that his wife,
however noble, was aged and ugly, he might withdraw, with the less
reluctance, from her bed to a convent, and at length to an hermitage. In
this austere solitude, his body was emaciated, his fancy was inflamed;
whatever he wished, he believed; whatever he believed, he *saw* in dreams
and revelations. From Jerusalem the pilgrim returned an accomplished
fanatic; but, as he excelled in the popular madness of the times, Pope
Urban the Second received him as a prophet, applauded his glorious
design, promised to support it in a general council, and encouraged him
to proclaim the deliverance of the Holy Land. Invigorated by the
approbation of the Pontiff, his zealous missionary traversed, with speed
and success, the provinces of Italy and France. His diet was abstemious,
his prayers long and fervent, and the alms which he received with one
hand, he distributed with the other; his head was bare, his feet naked, his
meagre body was wrapt in a coarse garment; he bore and displayed a

weighty crucifix; and the ass on which he rode was sanctified in the public eye by the service of the man of God. He preached to innumerable crowds in the churches, the streets, and the highways: the hermit entered with equal confidence the palace and the cottage; and the people, for all was people, were impetuously moved by his call to repentance and arms. When he painted the sufferings of the natives and pilgrims of Palestine, every heart was melted to compassion; every breast glowed with indignation, when he challenged the warriors of the age to defend their brethren and rescue their Saviour: his ignorance of art and language was compensated by sighs, and tears, and ejaculations; and Peter supplied the deficiency of reason by loud and frequent appeals to Christ and his mother, to the saints and angels of paradise, with whom he had personally conversed. The most perfect orator of Athens might have envied the success of his eloquence: the rustic enthusiast inspired the passions which he felt, and Christendom expected with impatience the counsels and decrees of the supreme Pontiff.

The magnanimous spirit of Gregory the Seventh* had already embraced the design of arming Europe against Asia; the ardour of his zeal and ambition still breathes in his epistles. From either side of the Alps, fifty thousand Catholics had enlisted under the banner of St Peter;[3] and his successor reveals *his* intention of marching at their head against the impious sectaries of Mahomet. But the glory or reproach of executing, though not in person, this holy enterprise was reserved for Urban the Second,[4†] the most faithful of his disciples. He undertook the conquest of the East, whilst the larger portion of Rome was possessed and fortified by his rival, Guibert of Ravenna, who contended with Urban for the name and honours of the pontificate. He attempted to unite the powers of the West, at a time when the princes were separated from the church, and the people from their princes, by the excommunication which himself and his predecessors had thundered against the emperor and the king of France. Philip the First,[‡] of France, supported with patience the censures which he had provoked by his scandalous life and adulterous marriage. Henry the Fourth,[§] of Germany, asserted the right of investitures, the prerogative of confirming his bishops by the delivery of the ring and crosier. But the emperor's party was crushed in Italy by the arms of the Normans and the Countess Mathilda;** and the long quarrel had been recently envenomed by the revolt of his son Conrad, and the shame of his wife,[5] who, in the synods of Constance and Placentia, confessed the manifold prostitutions to which she had been exposed by an husband regardless of her honour and his own.[6] So popular was the cause of Urban, so weighty was his influence, that the council which he summoned at Placentia[7] was composed of two hundred bishops of Italy, France, Burgundy, Swabia, and Bavaria. Four thousand of the clergy, and thirty thousand of the laity, attended this important meeting; and, as the most spacious cathedral would have been inadequate to the multitude, the session of seven days was held in a plain adjacent to the city. The ambassadors of the Greek emperor, Alexius Comnenus, were introduced to plead the distress of their sovereign, and the danger of Constantinople, which was divided only by a narrow sea from the victorious Turks, the common enemy of the Christian name. In their suppliant address, they flattered the pride of the Latin princes; and, appealing at once to their policy and religion, exhorted them to repel the barbarians on the confines of Asia rather than to expect them in the heart of Europe. At the sad tale of the misery and perils of their Eastern brethren, the assembly burst into tears; the most eager champions declared their readiness to march; and the Greek ambassadors were dismissed with the assurance of a speedy and powerful succour. The relief of Constantinople was included in the larger and most distant project of the deliverance of Jerusalem; but the prudent Urban adjourned the final decision to a second synod, which he proposed to celebrate in some city of France in the autumn of the same year. The short delay would propagate the flame of enthusiasm; and his firmest hope was in a nation of soldiers,[8] still proud of the pre-eminence of their name, and ambitious to emulate their hero Charlemagne,[9] who, in the popular romance of Turpin,[10] had achieved the conquest of the Holy Land. A latent motive of affection or vanity might influence the choice of Urban. He was himself a native of France, a monk of Clugny,* and the first of his countrymen who ascended the throne of St Peter. The Pope had illustrated his family and province. Nor is there perhaps a more exquisite gratification than to revisit, in a conspicuous dignity, the humble and laborious scenes of our youth.

It may occasion some surprise that the Roman pontiff should erect, in the heart of France, the tribunal from whence he hurled his anathemas against the king; but our surprise will vanish, so soon as we form a just estimate of a king of France of the eleventh century.[11] Philip the First was the great-grandson of Hugh Capet, the founder of the present race, who, in the decline of Charlemagne's posterity, added the regal title to his patrimonial estates of Paris and Orleans. In this narrow compass he was possessed of wealth and jurisdiction; but, in the rest of France, Hugh and his first descendants were no more than the feudal lords of about sixty dukes and counts, of independent and hereditary power,[12] who disdained the control of laws and legal assemblies, and whose disregard of their sovereign was revenged by the disobedience of their inferior vassals. At Clermont, in the territories of the count of Auvergne,[13] the pope might brave with impunity the resentment of Philip; and the council which he convened in that city was not less numerous or respectable than the synod of Placentia.[14] Besides his court and council of Roman cardinals, he was supported by thirteen archbishops and two hundred and twenty-five bishops; the number of mitred prelates was computed at four hundred; and the fathers of the church were blessed by the saints, and enlightened by the doctors, of the age. From the adjacent kingdoms a martial train of lords and knights of power and renown attended the council,[15] in high expectation of its resolves; and such was the ardour of zeal and curiosity that the city was filled, and many thousands, in the month of November, erected their tents or huts in the open field. A session of eight days produced some useful or edifying canons for the reformation of manners; a severe censure was pronounced against the licence of private war; the Truce of God[16] was confirmed, a suspension of hostilities during four days of the week; women and priests were placed under the safeguard of the church; and a protection of three years was extended to husbandmen and merchants, the defenceless victims of military rapine. But a law, however venerable be the sanction, cannot suddenly transform the temper of the times; and the benevolent efforts of Urban deserve the less praise, since he laboured to appease some domestic quarrels that he might spread the flames of war from the Atlantic to the Euphrates. From the synod of Placentia the rumour of his great design had gone forth among the nations; the clergy, on their return, had preached in every diocese the merit and glory of the deliverance of the Holy Land; and, when the pope ascended a lofty scaffold in the marketplace of Clermont, his eloquence was addressed to a well-prepared and impatient audience. His topics were obvious, his exhortation was vehement, his success inevitable. The orator was interrupted by the shout of thousands, who with one voice, and in their rustic idiom, exclaimed aloud, 'God wills it, God wills it!'[17] 'It is indeed the will of God,' replied the pope; 'and let this memorable word, the inspiration surely of the Holy Spirit, be for ever adopted as your cry of battle, to animate the devotion and courage of the champions of Christ. His cross is the symbol of your salvation; wear it, a red, a bloody cross, as an external mark on your breasts or shoulders, as a pledge of your sacred and irrevocable engagement.' The proposal was joyfully accepted; great numbers both of the clergy and laity impressed on their garments the sign of the cross,[18] and solicited the pope to march at their head. This dangerous honour was declined by the more prudent successor of Gregory, who alleged the schism of the church, and the duties of his pastoral office, recommending to the faithful, who were disqualified by sex or profession, by age or infirmity, to aid, with their prayers and alms, the personal service of their robust brethren. The name and powers of his legate he devolved on Adhemar, bishop of Puy, the first who had received the cross at his hands. The foremost of the temporal chiefs was Raymond, count of Toulouse, whose ambassadors in the council excused the absence, and pledged the honour, of their master. After the confession and absolution of their sins, the champions of the cross were dismissed with a superfluous admonition to invite their countrymen and friends; and their departure for the Holy Land was fixed to the festival of the Assumption, the fifteenth of August, of the ensuing year.[19]

So familiar, and as it were so natural, to man is the practice of violence that our indulgence allows the slightest provocation, the most disputable

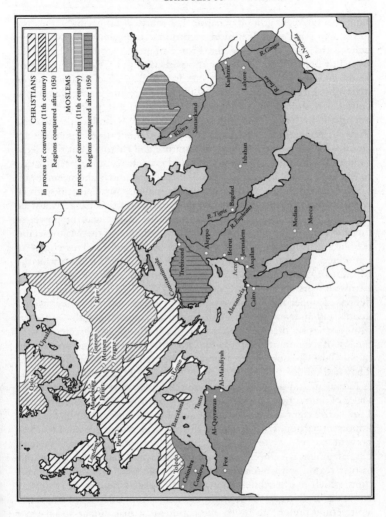

Islam and Christianity on the eve of the Crusades

right, as a sufficient ground of national hostility. But the name and nature of an *holy war* demands a more rigorous scrutiny; nor can we hastily believe that the servants of the Prince of Peace would unsheath the sword of destruction, unless the motives were pure, the quarrel legitimate, and the necessity inevitable. The policy of an action may be determined from the tardy lessons of experience; but, before we act, our conscience should be satisfied of the justice and propriety of our enterprise. In the age of the crusades, the Christians, both of the East and West, were persuaded of their lawfulness and merit; their arguments are clouded by the perpetual abuse of scripture and rhetoric; but they seem to insist on the right of natural and religious defence, their peculiar title to the Holy Land, and the impiety of their Pagan and Mahometan foes.[20] I. The right of a just defence may fairly include our civil and spiritual allies: it depends on the existence of danger; and that danger must be estimated by the twofold consideration of the malice and the power of our enemies. A pernicious tenet has been imputed to the Mahometans, the duty of *extirpating* all other religions by the sword. This charge of ignorance and bigotry is refuted by the Koran, by the history of the Musulman conquerors, and by their public and legal toleration of the Christian worship. But it cannot be denied that the Oriental churches are depressed under their iron yoke; that, in peace and war, they assert a divine and indefeasible claim of universal empire; and that, in their orthodox creed, the unbelieving nations are continually threatened with the loss of religion or liberty. In the eleventh century, the victorious arms of the Turks presented a real and urgent apprehension of these losses. They had subdued, in less than thirty years, the kingdoms of Asia, as far as Jerusalem and the Hellespont; and the Greek empire tottered on the verge of destruction. Besides an honest sympathy for their brethren, the Latins had a right and interest in the support of Constantinople, the most important barrier of the West; and the privilege of defence must reach to prevent, as well as to repel, an impending assault. But this salutary purpose might have been accomplished by a moderate succour; and our calmer reason must disclaim the innumerable hosts and remote operations which overwhelmed Asia and depopulated Europe. II. Palestine could add nothing to the strength or safety of the Latins; and fanaticism alone could pretend to justify the conquest of that distant and narrow province. The Christians affirmed that their inalienable title to the promised land had been sealed by the blood of their divine Saviour: it was their right and duty to rescue their inheritance from the unjust possessors, who profaned his sepulchre and oppressed the pilgrimage of his disciples. Vainly would it be alleged that the pre-eminence of Jerusalem and the sanctity of Palestine have been abolished with the Mosaic law; that the God of the Christians is not a local deity; and that the recovery of Bethlehem or Calvary, his cradle or his tomb, will not atone for the violation of the moral precepts of the gospel. Such

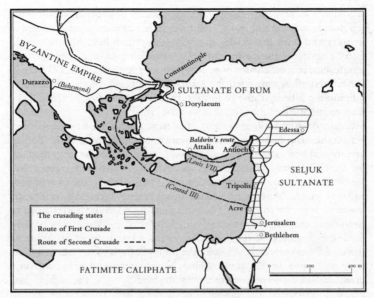

The First and Second Crusades

arguments glance aside from the leaden shield of superstition; and the religious mind will not easily relinquish its hold on the sacred ground of mystery and miracle. III. But the holy wars which have been waged in every climate of the globe, from Egypt to Livonia, and from Peru to Hindostan, require the support of some more general and flexible tenet. It has been often supposed, and sometimes affirmed, that a difference of religion is a worthy cause of hostility; that obstinate unbelievers may be slain or subdued by the champions of the cross; and that grace is the sole fountain of dominion as well as of mercy. Above four hundred years before the first crusade, the eastern and western provinces of the Roman empire had been acquired about the same time, and in the same manner, by the barbarians of Germany and Arabia. Time and treaties had legitimated the conquests of the *Christian* Franks; but, in the eyes of their subjects and neighbours, the Mahometan princes were still tyrants and usurpers, who, by the arms of war or rebellion, might be lawfully driven from their unlawful possession.[21]

As the manners of the Christians were relaxed, their discipline of penance[22] was enforced; and, with the multiplication of sins, the remedies were multiplied. In the primitive church, a voluntary and open confession prepared the work of atonement. In the middle ages, the bishops and priests interrogated the criminal; compelled him to account for his thoughts, words, and actions; and prescribed the terms of his reconciliation with God. But, as this discretionary power might alternately be abused by indulgence and tyranny, a rule of discipline was framed, to inform and regulate the spiritual judges. This mode of legislation was invented by the Greeks; their *penitentials*[23] were translated, or imitated, in the Latin church; and, in the time of Charlemagne, the clergy of every diocese were provided with a code, which they prudently concealed from the knowledge of the vulgar. In this dangerous estimate of crimes and punishments, each case was supposed, each difference was remarked, by the experience or penetration of the monks; some sins are enumerated which innocence could not have suspected, and others which reason cannot believe; and the more ordinary offences of fornication and adultery, of perjury and sacrilege, of rapine and murder, were expiated by a penance which, according to the various circumstances, was prolonged from forty days to seven years. During this term of mortification, the patient was healed, the criminal was absolved, by a salutary regimen of fasts and prayers; the disorder of his dress was expressive of grief and remorse; and he humbly abstained from all the business and pleasure of social life. But the rigid execution of these laws would have depopulated the palace, the camp, and the city; the barbarians of the West believed and trembled; but nature often rebelled against principle; and the magistrate laboured without effect to enforce the jurisdiction of the priest. A literal accomplishment of penance was indeed impracticable: the guilt of adultery was multipled by daily repetition; that of homicide might involve the massacre of a whole people; each act was separately numbered; and, in those times of anarchy and vice, a modest sinner might easily incur a debt of three hundred years. His insolvency was relieved by a commutation, or *indulgence*: a year of penance was appreciated at twenty-six *solidi*[24] of silver, about four pounds sterling, for the rich; at three solidi, or nine shillings, for the indigent: and these alms were soon appropriated to the use of the church, which derived, from the redemption of sins, an inexhaustible source of opulence and dominion. A debt of three hundred years, or twelve hundred pounds, was enough to impoverish a plentiful fortune; the scarcity of gold and silver was supplied by the alienation of land; and the princely donations of Pepin and Charlemagne are expressly given for the *remedy* of their soul. It is a maxim of the civil law, That whosoever cannot pay with his purse must pay with his body; and the practice of flagellation was adopted by the monks, a cheap, though painful, equivalent. By a fantastic arithmetic, a year of penance was taxed at three thousand lashes;[25] and such was the skill and patience of a famous hermit, St Dominic of the Iron Cuirass,[26] that in six days he could discharge an entire century, by a whipping of three hundred thousand stripes. His example was followed by many penitents of both sexes; and, as a vicarious sacrifice was accepted, a sturdy disciplinarian might expiate on his own back the sins of his benefactors.[27] These compensations of the purse and the person introduced, in the eleventh century, a more honourable mode of satisfaction. The merit of military service against the Saracens of Africa and Spain had been allowed by the predecessors of Urban the Second. In the council of Clermont, that Pope proclaimed a plenary indulgence to those who should enlist under the banner of the cross: the absolution of *all* their sins, and a full receipt for *all* that might be due of canonical penance.[28] The cold philosophy of modern times is incapable of feeling the impression that was made on a sinful and fanatic world. At the voice of their pastor, the robber, the incendiary, the homicide, arose by thousands to redeem their souls, by repeating on the infidels the same deeds which they had exercised against their Christian brethren; and the terms of atonement were eagerly embraced by offenders of every rank and denomination. None were pure; none were exempt from the guilt and penalty of sin; and those who were the least amenable to the justice of God and the church were the best entitled to the temporal and eternal recompense of their pious courage. If they fell, the spirit of the Latin clergy did not hesitate to adorn their tomb with the crown of martyrdom;[29] and, should they survive, they could expect without impatience the delay and increase of their heavenly reward. They offered their blood to the Son of God, who had laid down his life for their salvation: they took up the cross, and entered with confidence into the way of the Lord. His providence would watch over their safety; perhaps his visible and miraculous power would smooth the difficulties of their holy enterprise. The cloud and pillar of Jehovah had marched before the Israelites into the promised land. Might not the Christians more reasonably hope that the rivers would open for their passage; that the walls of the strongest cities would fall at the sound of their trumpets; and that the sun would be arrested in his mid-career, to allow them time for the destruction of the infidels?

Of the chiefs and soldiers who marched to the holy sepulchre, I will dare to affirm that *all* were prompted by the spirit of enthusiasm, the belief of merit, the hope of reward, and the assurance of divine aid. But I am equally persuaded that in *many* it was not the sole, that in *some* it was not the leading, principle of action. The use and abuse of religion are feeble to stem, they are strong and irresistible to impel, the stream of national manners. Against the private wars of the barbarians, their bloody tournaments, licentious loves, and judicial duels, the popes and synods might ineffectually thunder. It is a more easy task to provoke the metaphysical disputes of the Greeks, to drive into the cloister the victims of anarchy or despotism, to sanctify the patience of slaves and cowards, or to assume the merit of the humanity and benevolence of modern Christians. War and exercise were the reigning passions of the Franks or Latins; they were enjoined, as a penance, to gratify those passions, to visit distant lands, and to draw their swords against the nations of the East. Their victory, or even their attempt, would immortalise the names of the intrepid heroes of the cross; and the purest piety could not be insensible to the most splendid prospect of military glory. In the petty quarrels of Europe, they shed the blood of their friends and countrymen, for the acquisition perhaps of a castle or a village. They could march with alacrity against the distant and hostile nations who were devoted to their arms:* their fancy already grasped the golden sceptres of Asia; and the conquest of Apulia and Sicily by the Normans might exalt to royalty the hopes of the most private adventurer. Christendom, in her rudest state, must have yielded to the climate and cultivation of the Mahometan countries; and their natural and artificial wealth had been magnified by the tales of pilgrims and the gifts of an imperfect commerce. The vulgar, both the great and small, were taught to believe every wonder, of lands flowing with milk and honey, of mines and treasures, of gold and diamonds, of palaces of marble and jasper, and of odoriferous groves of cinnamon and frankincense. In this earthly paradise each warrior depended on his sword to carve a plenteous and honourable establishment, which he measured only by the extent of his wishes.[30] Their vassals and soldiers trusted their fortunes to God and their master: the spoils of a Turkish emir might enrich the meanest follower of the camp; and the flavour of the wines, the beauty of the Grecian women,[31] were temptations more adapted to the nature, than to the profession, of the champions of the cross. The love of freedom was a powerful incitement to the multitudes who were oppressed by feudal or ecclesiastical tyranny. Under this holy sign, the peasants and burghers, who were attached to the servitude of the glebe,† might escape from an haughty lord, and transplant themselves and their families to a land of liberty. The monk might release himself from the discipline of his convent; the debtor might suspend the accumulation of usury and the pursuit of his creditors; and outlaws and malefactors of every cast might continue to brave the laws and elude the punishment of their crimes.[32]

These motives were potent and numerous: when we have singly computed their weight on the mind of each individual, we must add the infinite series, the multiplying powers of example and fashion. The first proselytes became the warmest and most effectual missionaries of the cross: among their friends and countrymen they preached the duty, the merit, and the recompense of their holy vow; and the most reluctant hearers were insensibly drawn within the whirlpool of persuasion and authority. The martial youths were fired by the reproach or suspicion of cowardice; the opportunity of visiting with an army the sepulchre of Christ was embraced by the old and infirm, by women and children, who consulted rather their zeal than their strength; and those who in the evening had derided the folly of their companions were the most eager, the ensuing day, to tread in their footsteps. The ignorance, which magnified the hopes, diminished the perils, of the enterprise. Since the Turkish conquest, the paths of pilgrimage were obliterated; the chiefs themselves had an imperfect notion of the length of the way and the state of their enemies; and such was the stupidity of the people that, at the sight of the first city or castle beyond the limits of their knowledge, they were ready to ask, whether that was not the Jerusalem, the term and object of their labours. Yet the more prudent of the crusaders, who were not sure that they should be fed from heaven with a shower of quails or manna, provided themselves with those precious metals which, in every country, are the representatives of every commodity. To defray, according to their rank, the expenses of the road, princes alienated* their provinces, nobles their lands and castles, peasants their cattle and the instruments of husbandry. The value of property was depreciated by the eager competition of multitudes; while the price of arms and horses was raised to an exorbitant height, by the wants and impatience of the buyers.[33] Those who remained at home, with sense and money, were enriched by the epidemical disease: the sovereigns acquired at a cheap rate the domains of their vassals; and the ecclesiastical purchasers completed the payment by the assurance of their prayers. The cross, which was commonly sewed on the garment, in cloth or silk, was inscribed by some zealots on their skin; an hot iron, or indelible liquor, was applied to perpetuate the mark; and a crafty monk, who showed the miraculous impression on his breast, was repaid with the popular veneration and the richest benefices of Palestine.[34]

The fifteenth of August had been fixed in the council of Clermont for the departure of the pilgrims; but the day was anticipated by the thoughtless and needy crowd of plebeians; and I shall briefly dispatch the calamities which they inflicted and suffered, before I enter on the more serious and successful enterprise of the chiefs. Early in the spring, from the confines of France and Lorraine, about sixty thousand of the populace of both sexes flocked round the first missionary of the crusade, and pressed him with clamorous importunity to lead them to the holy sepulchre. The hermit, assuming the character, without the talents or authority, of a general, impelled or obeyed the forward impulse of his votaries along the banks of the Rhine and Danube. Their wants and numbers soon compelled them to separate, and his lieutenant, Walter the Pennyless, a valiant though needy soldier, conducted a vanguard of pilgrims, whose condition may be determined from the proportion of eight horsemen to fifteen thousand foot. The example and footsteps of Peter were closely pursued by another fanatic, the monk Godescal, whose sermons had swept away fifteen or twenty thousand peasants from the villages of Germany. Their rear was again pressed by an herd of two hundred thousand, the most stupid and savage refuse of the people, who mingled with their devotion a brutal licence of rapine, prostitution, and drunkenness. Some counts and gentlemen, at the head of three thousand horse, attended the motions of the multitude to partake in the spoil; but their genuine leaders (may we credit such folly?) were a goose and a goat, who were carried in the front, and to whom these worthy Christians ascribed an infusion of the divine Spirit.[35] Of these and of other bands of enthusiasts, the first and most easy warfare was against the Jews, the murderers of the Son of God. In the trading cities of the Moselle and the Rhine, their colonies were numerous and rich; and they enjoyed, under the protection of the emperor and the bishops, the free exercise of their religion.[36] At Verdun, Treves, Mentz, Spires, Worms, many thousands of that unhappy people were pillaged and massacred;[37] nor had they felt a more bloody stroke since the persecution of Hadrian.* A remnant was saved by the firmness of their bishops, who accepted a feigned and transient conversion; but the more obstinate Jews opposed their fanaticism to the fanaticism of the Christians, barricadoed their houses, and, precipitating themselves, their families, and their wealth, into the rivers or the flames, disappointed the malice, or at least the avarice, of their implacable foes.

Between the frontiers of Austria and the seat of the Byzantine monarchy, the crusaders were compelled to traverse an interval of six hundred miles, the wild and desolate countries of Hungary[38] and Bulgaria. The soil is fruitful, and intersected with rivers; but it was then covered with morasses and forests, which spread to a boundless extent, whenever man has ceased to exercise his dominion over the earth. Both nations had imbibed the rudiments of Christianity; the Hungarians were ruled by their native princes; the Bulgarians by a lieutenant of the Greek emperor; but on the slightest provocation, their ferocious nature was rekindled, and ample provocation was afforded by the disorders of the first pilgrims. Agriculture must have been unskilful and languid among a people, whose cities were built of reeds and timber, which were deserted in the summer

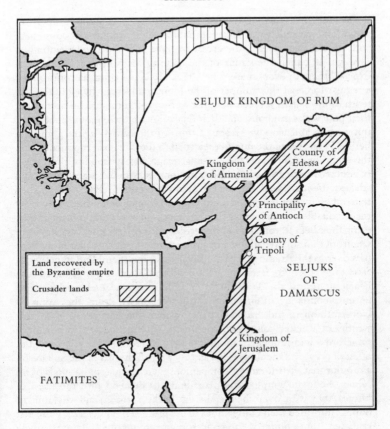

Results of the First Crusade AD *c.1100*

season for the tents of hunters and shepherds. A scanty supply of provisions was rudely demanded, forcibly seized, and greedily consumed; and, on the first quarrel, the crusaders gave a loose to indignation and revenge. But their ignorance of the country, of war, and of discipline exposed them to every snare. The Greek prefect of Bulgaria commanded a regular force; at the trumpet of the Hungarian king, the eighth or the tenth of his martial subjects bent their bows and mounted on horseback; their policy was insidious, and their retaliation on these pious robbers was unrelenting and bloody.[39] About a third of the naked fugitives, and the hermit Peter was of the number, escaped to the Thracian mountains; and the emperor, who respected the pilgrimage and succour of the Latins, conducted them by secure and easy journeys to Constantinople, and advised them to wait the arrival of their brethren. For a while they remembered their faults and losses; but no sooner were they revived by the hospitable entertainment than their venom was again inflamed; they stung their benefactor, and neither gardens nor palaces nor churches were safe from their depredations. For his own safety, Alexius allured them to pass over to the Asiatic side of the Bosphorus; but their blind impetuosity soon urged them to desert the station which he had assigned, and to rush headlong against the Turks, who occupied the road of Jerusalem. The hermit, conscious of his shame, had withdrawn from the camp to Constantinople; and his lieutenant, Walter the Pennyless, who was worthy of a better command, attempted, without success, to introduce some order and prudence among the herd of savages. They separated in quest of prey, and themselves fell an easy prey to the arts of the Sultan. By a rumour that their foremost companions were rioting in the spoils of his capital, Soliman tempted the main body to descend into the plain of Nicaea; they were overwhelmed by the Turkish arrows; and a pyramid of bones[40] informed their companions of the place of their defeat. Of the first crusaders, three hundred thousand had already perished, before a single city was rescued from the infidels, before their graver and more noble brethren had completed the preparations of their enterprise.[41]

None of the great sovereigns of Europe embarked their persons in the first crusade. The emperor Henry the Fourth was not disposed to obey the summons of the pope; Philip the First of France was occupied by his pleasures; William Rufus of England by a recent conquest; the kings of Spain were engaged in a domestic war against the Moors; and the northern monarchs of Scotland, Denmark,[42] Sweden, and Poland, were yet strangers to the passions and interests of the South. The religious ardour was more strongly felt by the princes of the second order, who held an important place in the feudal system. Their situation will naturally cast, under four distinct heads, the review of their names and characters; but I may escape some needless repetition by observing at once that courage and the exercise of arms are the common attribute of these Christian adventurers. I. The first rank both in war and council is justly due to Godfrey of Bouillon; and happy would it have been for the crusaders, if they had trusted themselves to the sole conduct of that accomplished hero, a worthy representative of Charlemagne, from whom he was descended in the female line. His father was of the noble race of the counts of Boulogne: Brabant, the lower province of Lorraine,[43] was the inheritance of his mother; and, by the emperor's bounty, he was himself invested with that ducal title, which has been improperly transferred to his lordship of Bouillon in the Ardennes.[44] In the service of Henry the Fourth he bore the great standard of the empire, and pierced with his lance the breast of Rodolph, the rebel king: Godfrey was the first who ascended the walls of Rome; and his sickness, his vow, perhaps his remorse for bearing arms against the pope, confirmed an early resolution of visiting the holy sepulchre, not as a pilgrim, but a deliverer. His valour was matured by prudence and moderation; his piety, though blind, was sincere; and, in the tumult of a camp, he practised the real and fictitious virtues of a convent. Superior to the private factions of the chiefs, he reserved his enmity for the enemies of Christ; and, though he gained a kingdom by the attempt, his pure and disinterested zeal was acknowledged by his rivals. Godfrey of Bouillon[45] was accompanied by his two brothers, by Eustace the elder, who had succeeded to the county of Boulogne, and by the younger, Baldwin, a character of more ambiguous virtue. The Duke of Lorraine was alike celebrated on either side of the Rhine; from birth and education, he was equally conversant with the French and Teutonic languages: the barons of France, Germany, and Lorraine assembled their vassals; and the confederate force that marched under his banner was composed of fourscore thousand foot and about ten thousand horse. II. In the parliament that was held at Paris, in the king's presence, about two months after the council of Clermont, Hugh, count of Vermandois, was the most conspicuous of the princes who assumed the cross. But the appellation of *the Great* was applied, not so much to his merit or possessions (though neither were contemptible), as to the royal birth of the brother of the king of France.[46] Robert, duke of Normandy, was the eldest son of William the Conqueror; but on his father's death he was deprived of the kingdom of England, by his own indolence and the activity of his brother Rufus. The worth of Robert was degraded by an excessive levity and easiness of temper; his cheerfulness seduced him to the indulgence of pleasure; his profuse liberality impoverished the prince and people; his indiscriminate clemency multiplied the number of offenders; and the amiable qualities of a private man became the essential defects of a sovereign. For the trifling sum of ten thousand marks he mortgaged Normandy during his absence to the English usurper;[47] but his engagement and behaviour in the holy war announced in Robert a reformation of manners, and restored him in some degree to the public esteem. Another Robert was count of Flanders, a royal province, which, in this century, gave three queens to the thrones of France, England, and

Denmark. He was surnamed the Sword and Lance of the Christians; but in the exploits of a soldier he sometimes forgot the duties of a general. Stephen, count of Chartres, of Blois, and of Troyes, was one of the richest princes of the age; and the number of his castles has been compared to the three hundred and sixty-five days of the year. His mind was improved by literature; and, in the council of the chiefs, the eloquent Stephen[48] was chosen to discharge the office of their president. These four were the principal leaders of the French, the Normans, and the pilgrims of the British isles; but the list of the barons, who were possessed of three or four towns, would exceed, says a contemporary, the catalogue of the Trojan war.[49] III. In the south of France, the command was assumed by Adhemar, bishop of Puy, the Pope's legate, and by Raymond, count of St Giles and Toulouse, who added the prouder titles of duke of Narbonne and marquis of Provence. The former was a respectable prelate, alike qualified for this world and the next. The latter was a veteran warrior, who had fought against the Saracens of Spain, and who consecrated his declining age, not only to the deliverance, but to the perpetual service, of the holy sepulchre. His experience and riches gave him a strong ascendant in the Christian camp, whose distress he was often able, and sometimes willing, to relieve. But it was easier for him to extort the praise of the infidels than to preserve the love of his subjects and associates. His eminent qualities were clouded by a temper, haughty, envious, and obstinate; and, though he resigned an ample patrimony for the cause of God, his piety, in the public opinion, was not exempt from avarice and ambition.[50] A mercantile rather than a martial spirit prevailed among his *provincials*,[51] a common name, which included the natives of Auvergne and Languedoc,[52] the vassals of the kingdom of Burgundy or Arles. From the adjacent frontier of Spain he drew a band of hardy adventurers; as he marched through Lombardy, a crowd of Italians flocked to his standard; and his united force consisted of one hundred thousand horse and foot. If Raymond was the first to enlist, and the last to depart, the delay may be excused by the greatness of his preparation and the promise of an everlasting farewell. IV. The name of Bohemond, the son of Robert Guiscard, was already famous by his double victory over the Greek emperor;* but his father's will had reduced him to the principality of Tarentum and the remembrance of his Eastern trophies, till he was awakened by the rumour and passage of the French pilgrims. It is in the person of this Norman chief that we may seek for the coolest policy and ambition, with a small allay of religious fanaticism. His conduct may justify a belief that he had secretly directed the design of the pope, which he affected to second with astonishment and zeal. At the siege of Amalphi, his example and discourse inflamed the passions of a confederate army; he instantly tore his garment, to supply crosses for the numerous candidates, and prepared to visit Constantinople and Asia at the head of ten thousand horse and twenty thousand foot. Several princes of the

Norman race accompanied this veteran general; and his cousin Tancred[53] was the partner, rather than the servant, of the war. In the accomplished character of Tancred we discover all the virtues of a perfect knight,[54] the true spirit of chivalry, which inspired the generous sentiments and social offices of man far better than the base philosophy, or the baser religion, of the times.

Between the age of Charlemagne and that of the crusades, a revolution had taken place among the Spaniards, the Normans, and the French, which was gradually extended to the rest of Europe. The service of the infantry was degraded to the plebeians; the cavalry formed the strength of the armies, and the honourable name of *miles*, or soldier, was confined to the gentlemen[55] who served on horseback and were invested with the character of knighthood. The dukes and counts, who had usurped the rights of sovereignty, divided the provinces among their faithful barons: the barons distributed among their vassals the fiefs or benefices of their jurisdiction; and these military tenants, the peers of each other and of their lord, composed the noble or equestrian order, which disdained to conceive the peasant or burgher as of the same species with themselves. The dignity of their birth was preserved by pure and equal alliances; their sons alone, who could produce four quarters or lines of ancestry, without spot or reproach, might legally pretend to the honour of knighthood; but a valiant plebeian was sometimes enriched and ennobled by the sword, and became the father of a new race. A single knight could impart, according to his judgment, the character which he received; and the warlike sovereigns of Europe derived more glory from this personal distinction than from the lustre of their diadem. This ceremony, of which some traces may be found in Tacitus and the woods of Germany,[56] was in its origin simple and profane; the candidate, after some previous trial, was invested with the sword and spurs; and his cheek or shoulder was touched with a slight blow, as an emblem of the last affront which it was lawful for him to endure. But superstition mingled in every public and private action of life; in the holy wars, it sanctified the profession of arms; and the order of chivalry was assimilated in its rights and privileges to the sacred orders of priesthood. The bath and white garment of the novice were an indecent copy of the regeneration of baptism; his sword, which he offered on the altar, was blessed by the ministers of religion; his solemn reception was preceded by fasts and vigils; and he was created a knight, in the name of God, of St George, and of St Michael the archangel. He swore to accomplish the duties of his profession; and education, example, and the public opinion were the inviolable guardians of his oath. As the champion of God and the ladies (I blush to unite such discordant names), he devoted himself to speak the truth; to maintain the right; to protect the distressed; to practise *courtesy*, a virtue less familiar to the ancients; to pursue the infidels; to despise the allurements of ease and safety; and to vindicate in every perilous adventure the honour of his character. The abuse of the same spirit provoked the illiterate knight to disdain the arts of industry and peace; to esteem himself the sole judge and avenger of his own injuries; and proudly to neglect the laws of civil society and military discipline. Yet the benefits of this institution, to refine the temper of barbarians, and to infuse some principles of faith, justice, and humanity, were strongly felt, and have been often observed. The asperity of national prejudice was softened; and the community of religion and arms spread a similar colour and generous emulation over the face of Christendom. Abroad in enterprise and pilgrimage, at home in martial exercise, the warriors of every country were perpetually associated; and impartial taste must prefer a Gothic tournament to the Olympic games of classic antiquity.[57] Instead of the naked spectacles which corrupted the manners of the Greeks and banished from the stadium the virgins and the matrons, the pompous decoration of the lists was crowned with the presence of chaste and highborn beauty, from whose hands the conqueror received the prize of his dexterity and courage. The skill and strength that were exerted in wrestling and boxing bear a distant and doubtful relation to the merit of a soldier; but the tournaments, as they were invented in France and eagerly adopted both in the East and West, presented a lively image of the business of the field. The single combats, the general skirmish, the defence of a pass or castle, were rehearsed as in actual service; and the contest, both in real and mimic war, was decided by the superior management of the horse and lance. The lance was the proper and peculiar weapon of the knight; his horse was of a large and heavy breed; but this charger, till he was roused by the approaching danger, was usually led by an attendant, and he quietly rode a pad* or palfrey of a more easy pace. His helmet and sword, his greaves and buckler, it would be superfluous to describe; but I may remark that at the period of the crusades the armour was less ponderous than in later times; and that, instead of a massy cuirass, his breast was defended by an hauberk or coat of mail. When their long lances were fixed in the rest, the warriors furiously spurred their horses against the foe; and the light cavalry of the Turks and Arabs could seldom stand against the direct and impetuous weight of their charge. Each knight was attended to the field by his faithful squire, a youth of equal birth and similar hopes; he was followed by his archers and men at arms, and four, or five, or six soldiers were computed as the furniture of a complete *lance*. In the expeditions to the neighbouring kingdoms or the Holy Land, the duties of the feudal tenure no longer subsisted; the voluntary service of the knights and their followers was either prompted by zeal or attachment, or purchased with rewards and promises; and the numbers of each squadron were measured by the power, the wealth, and the fame of each independent chieftain. They were distinguished by his banner, his armorial coat, and his cry of war; and the most ancient families of Europe must seek in these achievements the origin and proof of their nobility. In this rapid portrait of chivalry, I have been urged to anticipate on the story of the crusades, at once an effect, and a cause, of this memorable institution.[58]

Such were the troops, and such the leaders, who assumed the cross for the deliverance of the holy sepulchre. As soon as they were relieved by the absence of the plebeian multitude, they encouraged each other, by interviews and messages, to accomplish their vow and hasten their departure. Their wives and sisters were desirous of partaking the danger and merit of the pilgrimage; their portable treasures were conveyed in bars of silver and gold; and the princes and barons were attended by their equipage of hounds and hawks, to amuse their leisure and to supply their table. The difficulty of procuring subsistence for so many myriads of men and horses engaged them to separate their forces; their choice or situation determined the road; and it was agreed to meet in the neighbourhood of Constantinople, and from thence to begin their operations against the Turks. From the banks of the Meuse and the Moselle, Godfrey of Bouillon followed the direct way of Germany, Hungary, and Bulgaria; and, as long as he exercised the sole command, every step afforded some proof of his prudence and virtue. On the confines of Hungary he was stopped three weeks by a Christian people, to whom the name, or at least the abuse, of the cross was justly odious. The Hungarians still smarted with the wounds which they had received from the first pilgrims; in their turn they had abused the right of defence and retaliation; and they had reason to apprehend a severe revenge from an hero of the same nation, and who was engaged in the same cause. But, after weighing the motives and the events, the virtuous duke was content to pity the crimes and misfortunes of his worthless brethren; and his twelve deputies, the messengers of peace, requested in his name a free passage and an equal market. To remove their suspicions, Godfrey trusted himself, and afterwards his brother, to the faith of Carloman, king of Hungary, who treated them with a simple but hospitable entertainment: the treaty was sanctified by their common gospel; and a proclamation, under pain of death, restrained the animosity and licence of the Latin soldiers. From Austria to Belgrade, they traversed the plains of Hungary, without enduring or offering an injury; and the proximity of Carloman, who hovered on their flanks with his numerous cavalry, was a precaution not less useful for their safety than for his own. They reached the banks of the Save; and no sooner had they passed the river than the king of Hungary restored the hostages and saluted their departure with the fairest wishes for the success of their enterprise. With the same conduct and discipline, Godfrey pervaded the woods of Bulgaria and the frontiers of Thrace; and might congratulate himself that he had almost reached the first term of his pilgrimage without drawing his sword against a Christian adversary. After an easy and pleasant journey through Lombardy, from Turin to Aquileia, Raymond and his provincials marched forty days through the savage country of Dalmatia[59] and Sclavonia. The weather was a perpetual fog; the land was mountainous and desolate; the natives were either fugitive or hostile; loose in their religion and government, they refused to furnish provisions or guides; murdered the stragglers; and exercised by night and day the vigilance of the count, who derived more security from the punishment of some captive robbers than from his interview and treaty with the prince of Scodra.[60] His march between Durazzo and Constantinople was harassed, without being stopped, by the peasants and soldiers of the Greek emperor; and the same faint and ambiguous hostility was prepared for the remaining chiefs, who passed the Adriatic from the coast of Italy. Bohemond had arms and vessels, and foresight and discipline; and his name was not forgotten in the provinces of Epirus and Thessaly. Whatever obstacles he encountered were surmounted by his military conduct and the valour of Tancred; and, if the Norman prince affected to spare the Greeks, he gorged his soldiers with the full plunder of an heretical castle.[61] The nobles of France pressed forwards with the vain and thoughtless ardour of which their nation has been sometimes accused. From the Alps to Apulia, the march of Hugh the Great, of the two Roberts, and of Stephen of Chartres, through a wealthy country, and amidst the applauding Catholics, was a devout or triumphant progress: they kissed the feet of the Roman pontiff; and the golden standard of St Peter was delivered to the brother of the French monarch.[62] But in this visit of piety and pleasure they neglected to secure the season and the means of their embarkation: the winter was insensibly lost; their troops were scattered and corrupted in the towns of Italy. They separately accomplished their passage, regardless of safety or dignity: and within nine months from the feast of the Assumption, the day appointed by Urban, all the Latin princes had reached Constantinople. But the Count of Vermandois was produced as a captive; his foremost vessels were scattered by a tempest; and his person, against the law of nations, was detained by the lieutenants of Alexius. Yet the arrival of Hugh had been announced by four-and-twenty knights in golden armour, who commanded the emperor to revere the general of the Latin Christians, the brother of the King of kings.[63]

In some Oriental tale I have read the fable of a shepherd, who was ruined by the accomplishment of his own wishes: he had prayed for water; the Ganges was turned into his grounds; and his flock and cottage were swept away by the inundation. Such was the fortune, or at least the apprehension, of the Greek emperor, Alexius Comnenus, whose name has already appeared in this history,* and whose conduct is so differently represented by his daughter Anna[64] and by the Latin writers.[65] In the council of Placentia, his ambassadors had solicited a moderate succour, perhaps of ten thousand soldiers; but he was astonished by the approach of so many potent chiefs and fanatic nations. The emperor fluctuated between hope and fear, between timidity and courage; but in the crooked policy which he mistook for wisdom I cannot believe, I cannot discern, that he maliciously conspired against the life or honour of the French heroes. The promiscuous multitudes of Peter the Hermit were savage beasts, alike destitute of humanity and reason; nor was it possible for Alexius to prevent or deplore their destruction. The troops of Godfrey and his peers were less contemptible, but not less suspicious, to the Greek emperor. Their motives *might* be pure and pious; but he was equally alarmed by his knowledge of the ambitious Bohemond and his ignorance of the Transalpine chiefs: the courage of the French was blind and headstrong; they might be tempted by the luxury and wealth of Greece, and elated by the view and opinion of their invincible strength; and Jerusalem might be forgotten in the prospect of Constantinople. After a long march and painful abstinence, the troops of Godfrey encamped in the plains of Thrace; they heard with indignation that their brother, the count of Vermandois, was imprisoned by the Greeks; and their reluctant Duke was compelled to indulge them in some freedom of retaliation and rapine. They were appeased by the submission of Alexius; he promised to supply their camp; and, as they refused, in the midst of winter, to pass the Bosphorus, their quarters were assigned among the gardens and palaces on the shores of that narrow sea. But an incurable jealousy still rankled in the minds of the two nations, who despised each other as slaves and barbarians. Ignorance is the ground of suspicion, and suspicion was inflamed into daily provocations; prejudice is blind, hunger is deaf; and Alexius is accused of a design to starve or assault the Latins on a dangerous post, on all sides encompassed with the waters.[66] Godfrey sounded his trumpets, burst the net, overspread the plain, and insulted* the suburbs; but the gates of Constantinople were strongly fortified; the ramparts were lined with archers; and, after a doubtful conflict, both parties listened to the voice of peace and religion. The gifts and promises of the emperor insensibly soothed the fierce spirit of the western strangers; as a Christian warrior, he rekindled their zeal for the prosecution of their holy enterprise, which he engaged to second with his troops and treasures. On the return of spring, Godfrey was persuaded to occupy a pleasant and plentiful camp in Asia; and no sooner had he passed the Bosphorus, than the Greek vessels were suddenly recalled to the opposite shore. The same policy was repeated with the succeeding chiefs, who were swayed by the example, and weakened by the departure, of their foremost companions. By his skill and diligence, Alexius prevented the union of any two of the confederate armies at the same moment under the walls of Constantinople; and, before the feast of the Pentecost, not a Latin pilgrim was left on the coast of Europe.

The same arms which threatened Europe might deliver Asia and repel the Turks from the neighbouring shores of the Bosphorus and Hellespont. The fair provinces from Nicaea to Antioch were the recent patrimony of the Roman emperor; and his ancient and perpetual claim still embraced the kingdoms of Syria and Egypt. In his enthusiasm, Alexius indulged, or affected, the ambitious hope of leading his new allies to subvert the thrones of the East; but the calmer dictates of reason and temper dissuaded him from exposing his royal person to the faith of unknown and lawless barbarians. His prudence, or his pride, was content with extorting from the French princes an oath of homage and fidelity, and a solemn promise that they would either restore, or hold, their Asiatic conquests as the humble and loyal vassals of the Roman empire. Their independent spirit was fired at the mention of this foreign and voluntary servitude; they successively yielded to the dextrous application of gifts and flattery; and the first proselytes became the most eloquent and effectual missionaries to multiply the companions of their shame. The pride of Hugh of Vermandois was soothed by the honours of his captivity; and in the brother of the French king the example of submission was prevalent and weighty. In the mind of Godfrey of Bouillon, every human consideration was subordinate to the glory of God and the success of the crusade. He had firmly resisted the temptations of Bohemond and Raymond, who urged the attack and conquest of Constantinople. Alexius esteemed his virtues, deservedly named him the champion of the empire, and dignified his homage with the filial name and the rights of adoption.[67] The hateful Bohemond was received as a true and ancient ally; and, if the emperor reminded him of former hostilities, it was only to praise the valour that he had displayed, and the glory that he had acquired, in the fields of Durazzo and Larissa.* The son of Guiscard was lodged and entertained, and served with Imperial pomp: one day, as he passed through the gallery of the palace, a door was carelessly left open to expose a pile of gold and silver, of silk and gems, of curious and costly furniture, that was heaped in seeming disorder from the floor to the roof of the chamber. 'What conquests,' exclaimed the ambitious miser, 'might not be achieved by the possession of such a treasure!' 'It is your own,' replied a Greek attendant, who watched the motions of his soul; and Bohemond, after some hesitation, condescended to accept this magnificent present. The Norman was flattered by the assurance of an independent principality; and Alexius eluded, rather than denied, his daring demand of the office of great domestic, or general, of the East. The two Roberts, the son of the conqueror of England and the kinsman of three queens,[68] bowed in their turn before the Byzantine throne. A private letter of Stephen of Chartres attests his admiration of the emperor, the most excellent and liberal of men, who taught him to believe that he was a favourite, and promised to educate and establish his youngest son. In his southern province, the count of St Giles and Toulouse faintly recognised the supremacy of the king of France, a prince of a foreign nation and language. At the head of an hundred thousand men, he declared that he was the soldier and servant of Christ alone, and that the Greek might be satisfied with an equal treaty of alliance and friendship. His obstinate resistance enhanced the value and the price of his submission; and he shone, says the princess Anne, among the barbarians, as the sun amidst the stars of heaven. His disgust of the noise and insolence of the French, his suspicions of the designs of Bohemond, the emperor imparted to his faithful Raymond; and that aged statesman might clearly discern that, however false in friendship, he was sincere in his enmity.[69] The spirit of chivalry was last subdued in the person of Tancred; and none could deem themselves dishonoured by the imitation of that gallant knight. He disdained the gold and flattery of the Greek monarch; assaulted in his presence an insolent patrician; escaped to Asia in the habit of a private soldier; and yielded with a sigh to the authority of Bohemond and the interest of the Christian cause. The best and most ostensible reason was the impossibility of passing the sea and accomplishing their vow, without the licence and the vessels of Alexius; but they cherished a secret hope that, as soon as they trod the continent of Asia, their swords would obliterate their shame, and dissolve the engagement, which on his side might not be very faithfully performed. The ceremony of their homage was grateful to a people who had long since considered pride as the substitute of power. High on his throne, the emperor sat mute and immoveable: his majesty was adored by the Latin princes; and they submitted to kiss either his feet or his knees, an indignity which their own writers are ashamed to confess and unable to deny.[70]

Private or public interest suppressed the murmurs of the dukes and counts; but a French baron (he is supposed to be Robert of Paris[71]) presumed to ascend the throne, and to place himself by the side of Alexius. The sage reproof of Baldwin provoked him to exclaim, in his barbarous idiom, 'Who is this rustic, that keeps his seat, while so many valiant captains are standing round him?' The emperor maintained his silence, dissembled his indignation, and questioned his interpreter concerning the meaning of the words, which he partly suspected from the universal language of gesture and countenance. Before the departure of the pilgrims, he endeavoured to learn the name and condition of the audacious baron. 'I am a Frenchman,' replied Robert, 'of the purest and most ancient nobility of my country. All that I know is, that there is a church in my neighbourhood,[72] the resort of those who are desirous of approving their valour in single combat. Till an enemy appears, they address their prayers to God and his saints. That church I have frequently visited, but never have I found an antagonist who dared to accept my defiance.' Alexius dismissed the challenger with some prudent advice for his conduct in the Turkish warfare; and history repeats with pleasure this lively example of the manners of his age and country.

The conquest of Asia was undertaken and achieved by Alexander, with thirty-five thousand Macedonians and Greeks;[73] and his best hope was in the strength and discipline of his phalanx of infantry. The principal force of the crusaders consisted in their cavalry; and, when that force was mustered in the plains of Bithynia, the knights and their martial attendants on horseback amounted to one hundred thousand fighting men completely armed with the helmet and coat of mail. The value of these soldiers deserved a strict and authentic account; and the flower of European chivalry might furnish, in a first effort, this formidable body of heavy horse. A part of the infantry might be enrolled for the service of scouts, pioneers, and archers; but the promiscuous crowd were lost in their own disorder; and we depend not on the eyes or knowledge, but on the belief and fancy, of a chaplain of count Baldwin,[74] in the estimate of six hundred thousand pilgrims able to bear arms, besides the priests and monks, the women and children, of the Latin camp. The reader starts; and, before he is recovered from his surprise, I shall add, on the same testimony, that if all who took the cross had accomplished their vow, above SIX MILLIONS would have migrated from Europe to Asia. Under this oppression of faith, I derive some relief from a more sagacious and thinking writer,[75] who, after the same review of the cavalry, accuses the credulity of the priest of Chartres, and even doubts whether the *Cisalpine** regions (in the geography of a Frenchman) were sufficient to produce and pour forth such incredible multitudes. The coolest scepticism will remember that of these religious volunteers great numbers never beheld Constantinople and Nicaea. Of enthusiasm the influence is irregular and transient; many were detained at home by reason or cowardice, by poverty or weakness; and many were repulsed by the obstacles of the way, the more insuperable as they were unforeseen to these ignorant fanatics. The savage countries of Hungary and Bulgaria were whitened with their bones; their vanguard was cut in pieces by the Turkish sultan; and the loss of the first adventure, by the sword, or climate, or fatigue, has already been stated at three hundred thousand men. Yet the myriads that survived, that marched, that pressed forwards on the holy pilgrimage were a subject of astonishment to themselves and to the Greeks. The copious energy of her language sinks under the efforts of the princess Anne;[76] the images of locusts, of leaves and flowers, of the sands of the sea, or the stars of heaven, imperfectly represent what she had seen and heard; and the daughter of Alexius exclaims that Europe was loosened from its foundations and hurled against Asia. The ancient hosts of Darius and Xerxes[†] labour under the same doubt of a vague and indefinite magnitude; but I am inclined to believe that a larger number has never been contained within the lines of a single camp than at the siege of Nicaea, the first operation of the Latin princes. Their motives, their characters, and their arms have been already displayed. Of their troops, the most numerous portion were natives of France; the Low Countries, the banks of the Rhine, and Apulia, sent a powerful reinforcement; some bands of adventurers were drawn from Spain, Lombardy, and England;[77] and from the distant bogs and mountains of Ireland or Scotland[78] issued some naked and savage fanatics, ferocious at home, but unwarlike abroad. Had not superstition condemned the sacrilegious prudence of depriving the poorest or weakest Christian of the merit of the pilgrimage, the useless crowd, with mouths but without hands, might have been stationed in the Greek empire, till their companions had opened and secured the way of the Lord. A small remnant of the pilgrims, who passed the Bosphorus, was permitted to visit the holy sepulchre. Their northern constitution was scorched by the rays, and infected by the vapours, of a Syrian sun. They consumed, with heedless prodigality, their stores of water and provisions; their numbers exhausted the inland country; the sea was remote, the Greeks were unfriendly, and the Christians of every sect fled before the voracious and cruel rapine of their brethren. In the dire necessity of famine, they sometimes roasted and devoured the flesh of their infant or adult captives. Among the Turks and Saracens, the idolaters of Europe were rendered more odious by the name and reputation of cannibals; the spies who introduced themselves into the kitchen of Bohemond were shown several human bodies turning on the spit; and the artful Norman encouraged a report, which increased at the same time the abhorrence and the terror of the infidels.[79]

I have expatiated with pleasure on the first steps of the crusaders, as they paint the manners and character of Europe; but I shall abridge the tedious and uniform narrative of their blind achievements, which were performed by strength and are described by ignorance. From their first station in the neighbourhood of Nicomedia, they advanced in successive divisions, passed the contracted limit of the Greek empire, opened a road through the hills, and commenced, by the siege of his capital, their pious warfare against the Turkish sultan. His kingdom of Roum extended from the Hellespont to the confines of Syria and barred the pilgrimage of Jerusalem; his name was Kilidge-Arslan, or Soliman,[80] of the race of Seljuk, and son of the first conqueror; and, in the defence of a land which the Turks considered as their own, he deserved the praise of his enemies, by whom alone he is known to posterity. Yielding to the first impulse of the torrent, he deposited his family and treasure in Nicaea, retired to the mountains with fifty thousand horse, and twice descended to assault the camps or quarters of the Christian besiegers, which formed an imperfect circle of above six miles. The lofty and solid walls of Nicaea were covered by a deep ditch, and flanked by three hundred and seventy towers; and on the verge of Christendom the Moslems were trained in arms and inflamed by religion. Before this city, the French princes occupied their stations, and prosecuted their attacks without correspondence or subordination; emulation prompted their valour; but their valour was sullied by cruelty, and their emulation degenerated into envy and civil discord. In the siege of Nicaea the arts and engines of antiquity were employed by the Latins; the mine and the battering-ram, the tortoise, and the belfry or moveable turret, artificial fire, and the *catapult* and *balist*, the sling, and the crossbow for the casting of stones and darts.[81] In the space of seven weeks much labour and blood were expended, and some progress, especially by Count Raymond, was made on the side of the besiegers. But the Turks could protract their resistance and secure their escape, as long as they were masters of the lake Ascanius,[82] which stretches several miles to the westward of the city. The means of conquest were supplied by the prudence and industry of Alexius; a great number of boats was transported on sledges from the sea to the lake; they were filled with the most dextrous of his archers; the flight of the sultana was intercepted; Nicaea was invested by land and water; and a Greek emissary persuaded the inhabitants to accept his master's protection, and to save themselves, by a timely surrender, from the rage of the savages of Europe. In the moment of victory, or at least of hope, the crusaders, thirsting for blood and plunder, were awed by the Imperial banner that streamed from the citadel, and Alexius guarded with jealous vigilance this important conquest. The murmurs of the chiefs were stifled by honour or interest; and, after an halt of nine days, they directed their march towards Phrygia, under the guidance of a Greek general, whom they suspected of secret connivance with the sultan. The consort and the principal servants of Soliman had been honourably restored without ransom, and the emperor's generosity to the *miscreants*[83] was interpreted as treason to the Christian cause.

Soliman was rather provoked than dismayed by the loss of his capital; he admonished his subjects and allies of this strange invasion of the western barbarians; the Turkish emirs obeyed the call of loyalty or religion; the Turkman hordes encamped round his standard; and his whole force is loosely stated by the Christians at two hundred, or even three hundred and sixty, thousand horse. Yet he patiently waited till they had left behind them the sea and the Greek frontier, and, hovering on the flanks, observed their careless and confident progress in two columns, beyond the view of each other. Some miles before they could reach Dorylaeum in Phrygia, the left and least numerous division was surprised, and attacked, and almost oppressed, by the Turkish cavalry.[84] The heat of the weather, the clouds of arrows, and the barbarous onset overwhelmed the crusaders; they lost their order and confidence, and the fainting fight was sustained by the personal valour, rather than by the military conduct, of Bohemond, Tancred, and Robert of Normandy. They were revived by the welcome banners of duke Godfrey, who flew to their succour, with the count of Vermandois and sixty thousand horse, and was followed by Raymond of Toulouse, the bishop of Puy, and the remainder of the sacred army. Without a moment's pause they formed in new order, and advanced to a second battle. They were received with equal resolution; and, in their common disdain for the unwarlike people of Greece and Asia, it was confessed on both sides that the Turks and the Franks were the only nations entitled to the appellation of soldiers.[85] Their encounter was varied and balanced by the contrast of arms and discipline; of the direct charge, and wheeling evolutions; of the couched lance, and the brandished javelin; of a weighty broadsword, and a crooked sabre; of cumbrous armour, and thin flowing robes; and of the long Tartar bow, and the *arbalist* or crossbow, a deadly weapon, yet unknown to the Orientals.[86] As long as the horses were fresh and the quivers full, Soliman maintained the advantage of the day; and four thousand Christians were pierced by the Turkish arrows. In the evening, swiftness yielded to strength; on either side, the numbers were equal, or at least as great as any ground could hold or any generals could manage; but in turning the hills the last division of Raymond and his *provincials** was led, perhaps without design, on the rear of an exhausted enemy; and the long contest was determined. Besides a nameless and unaccounted multitude, three thousand *pagan* knights were slain in the battle and pursuit; the camp of Soliman was pillaged; and in the variety of precious spoil the curiosity of the Latins was amused with foreign arms and apparel, and the new aspect of dromedaries and camels. The importance of the victory was proved by the hasty retreat of the sultan: reserving ten thousand guards of the relics of his army, Soliman evacuated the kingdom of Roum, and hastened to implore the aid, and kindle the resentment, of his Eastern brethren. In a march of five hundred miles, the crusaders traversed the Lesser Asia, through a wasted land and deserted towns, without either finding a friend or an enemy. The geographer[87] may trace the position of Dorylaeum, Antioch of Pisidia, Iconium, Archelais, and Germanicia, and may compare those classic appellations with the modern names of Eskishehr the old city, Akshehr the white city, Cogni, Erekli, and Marash. As the pilgrims passed over a desert, where a draught of water is exchanged for silver, they were tormented by intolerable thirst; and on the banks of the first rivulet their haste and intemperance were still more pernicious to the disorderly throng. They climbed with toil and danger the steep and slippery sides of mount Taurus; many of the soldiers cast away their arms to secure their footsteps; and, had not terror preceded their van, the long and trembling file might have been driven down the precipice by an handful of resolute enemies. Two of their most respectable chiefs, the duke of Lorraine and the count of Toulouse, were carried in litters; Raymond was raised, as it is said, by miracle, from an hopeless malady; and Godfrey had been torn by a bear, as he pursued that rough and perilous chase in the mountains of Pisidia.

To improve the general consternation, the cousin[†] of Bohemond and the brother[‡] of Godfrey were detached from the main army, with their respective squadrons of five and of seven hundred knights. They overran, in a rapid career, the hills and seacoast of Cilicia, from Cogni to the Syrian gates; the Norman standard was first planted on the walls of Tarsus and Malmistra; but the proud injustice of Baldwin at length provoked the patient and generous Italian, and they turned their consecrated swords against each other in a private and profane quarrel. Honour was the motive, and fame the reward, of Tancred; but fortune smiled on the more selfish enterprise of his rival.[88] He was called to the assistance of a Greek or Armenian tyrant, who had been suffered under the Turkish yoke to reign over the Christians of Edessa. Baldwin accepted the character of his son and champion; but no sooner was he introduced into the city than he inflamed the people to the massacre of his father, occupied the throne and treasure, extended his conquests over the hills of Armenia and the plain of Mesopotamia, and founded the first principality of the Franks or Latins, which subsisted fifty-four years beyond the Euphrates.[89]

Before the Franks could enter Syria, the summer, and even the autumn, were completely wasted: the siege of Antioch, or the separation and repose of the army during the winter season, was strongly debated in their council; the love of arms and the holy sepulchre urged them to advance, and reason perhaps was on the side of resolution, since every hour of delay abates the fame and force of the invader and multiplies the resources of defensive war. The capital of Syria was protected by the river Orontes, and the *iron bridge* of nine arches derives its name from the massy gates of the two towers which are constructed at either end. They were opened by the sword of the duke of Normandy: his victory gave entrance to three hundred thousand crusaders, an account which may allow some scope for losses and desertion, but which clearly detects much exaggeration in the review of Nicaea. In the description of Antioch[90] it is not easy to define a middle term between her ancient magnificence, under the successors of Alexander and Augustus, and the modern aspect of Turkish desolation. The Tetrapolis, or four cities, if they retained their name and position, must have left a large vacuity in a circumference of twelve miles; and that measure, as well as the number of four hundred towers, are not perfectly consistent with the five gates, so often mentioned in the history of the siege. Yet Antioch must have still flourished as a great and populous capital. At the head of the Turkish emirs, Baghisian, a veteran chief, commanded in the place; his garrison was composed of six or seven thousand horse and fifteen or twenty thousand foot: one hundred thousand Moslems are said to have fallen by the sword, and their numbers were probably inferior to the Greeks, Armenians, and Syrians, who had been no more than fourteen years the slaves of the house of Seljuk. From the remains of a solid and stately wall it appears to have arisen to the height of threescore feet in the valleys; and wherever less art and labour had been applied, the ground was supposed to be defended by the river, the morass, and the mountains. Notwithstanding these fortifications, the city had been repeatedly taken by the Persians, the Arabs, the Greeks, and the Turks; so large a circuit must have yielded many pervious points of attack; and, in a siege that was formed about the middle of October, the vigour of the execution could alone justify the boldness of the attempt. Whatever strength and valour could perform in the field, was abundantly discharged by the champions of the cross: in the frequent occasions of sallies, of forage, of the attack and defence of convoys, they were often victorious; and we can only complain that their exploits are sometimes enlarged beyond the scale of probability and truth. The sword of Godfrey[91] divided a Turk from the shoulder to the haunch, and one half of the infidel fell to the ground, while the other was transported by his horse to the city gate. As Robert of Normandy rode against his antagonist, 'I devote thy head,' he piously exclaimed, 'to the demons of hell,' and that head was instantly cloven to the breast by the resistless stroke of his descending faulchion. But the reality or report of such gigantic prowess[92] must have taught the Moslems to keep within their walls, and against those walls of earth or stone the sword and the lance were unavailing weapons. In the slow and successive labours of a siege the crusaders were supine and ignorant, without skill to contrive, or money to purchase, or industry to use the artificial engines and implements of assault. In the conquest of Nicaea they had been powerfully assisted by the wealth and knowledge of the Greek emperor: his absence was poorly supplied by some Genoese and Pisan vessels that were attracted by religion or trade to the coast of Syria; the stores were scanty, the return precarious, and the communication difficult and dangerous. Indolence or weakness had prevented the Franks from investing the entire circuit; and the perpetual freedom of two gates relieved the wants, and recruited the garrison, of the city. At the end of seven months, after the ruin of their cavalry, and an enormous loss by famine, desertion, and fatigue, the progress of the crusaders was imperceptible, and their success remote, if the Latin Ulysses, the artful and ambitious Bohemond, had not employed the arms of cunning and deceit. The Christians of Antioch were numerous and discontented: Phirouz, a Syrian renegado, had acquired the favour of the emir and the command of three towers; and the merit of his repentance disguised to the Latins, and perhaps to himself, the foul design of perfidy and treason. A secret correspondence, for their mutual interest, was soon established between Phirouz and the prince of Tarento; and Bohemond declared in the council of the chiefs that he could deliver the city into their hands. But he claimed the sovereignty of Antioch as the reward of his service; and the proposal which had been rejected by the envy, was at length extorted from the distress, of his equals. The nocturnal surprise was executed by the French and Norman princes, who ascended in person the scaling-ladders that were thrown from the walls; their new proselyte, after the murder of his too scrupulous brother, embraced and introduced the servants of Christ: the army rushed through the gates; and the Moslems soon found that, although mercy was hopeless, resistance was impotent. But the citadel still refused to surrender; and the victors themselves were speedily encompassed and besieged by the innumerable forces of Kerboga, prince of Mosul, who, with twenty-eight Turkish emirs, advanced to the deliverance of Antioch. Five and twenty days the Christians spent on the verge of destruction; and the proud lieutenant of the caliph and the sultan left them only the choice of servitude or death.[93]

In this extremity they collected the relics of their strength, sallied from the town, and in a single memorable day annihilated or dispersed the host of Turks and Arabians, which they might safely report to have consisted of six hundred thousand men.[94] Their supernatural allies I shall proceed to consider: the human causes of the victory of Antioch were the fearless despair of the Franks; and the surprise, the discord, perhaps the errors, of their unskilful and presumptuous adversaries. The battle is described with as much disorder as it was fought; but we may observe the tent of Kerboga, a moveable and spacious palace, enriched with the luxury of Asia, and capable of holding above two thousand persons; we may distinguish his three thousand guards, who were cased, the horses as well as men, in complete steel.

In the eventful period of the siege and defence of Antioch, the crusaders were, alternately, exalted by victory or sunk in despair; either swelled with plenty or emaciated with hunger. A speculative reasoner might suppose that their faith had a strong and serious influence on their practice; and that the soldiers of the cross, the deliverers of the holy sepulchre, prepared themselves by a sober and virtuous life for the daily contemplation of martyrdom. Experience blows away this charitable illusion; and seldom does the history of profane war display such scenes of intemperance and prostitution as were exhibited under the walls of Antioch. The grove of Daphne no longer flourished; but the Syrian air was still impregnated with the same vices; the Christians were seduced by every temptation[95] that nature either prompts or reprobates; the authority of the chiefs was despised; and sermons and edicts were alike fruitless against those scandalous disorders, not less pernicious to military discipline than repugnant to evangelic purity. In the first days of the siege and the possession of Antioch, the Franks consumed with wanton and thoughtless prodigality the frugal subsistence of weeks and months; the desolate country no longer yielded a supply; and from that country they were at length excluded by the arms of the besieging Turks. Disease, the faithful companion of want, was envenomed by the rains of the winter, the summer heats, unwholesome food, and the close imprisonment of multitudes. The pictures of famine and pestilence are always the same, and always disgustful; and our imagination may suggest the nature of their sufferings and their resources. The remains of treasure or spoil were eagerly lavished in the purchase of the vilest nourishment; and dreadful must have been the calamities of the poor, since, after paying three marks of silver for a goat, and fifteen for a lean camel,[96] the count of Flanders was reduced to beg a dinner, and duke Godfrey to borrow an horse. Sixty thousand horses had been reviewed in the camp; before the end of the siege they were diminished to two thousand, and scarcely two hundred fit for service could be mustered on the day of battle. Weakness of body and terror of mind extinguished the ardent enthusiasm of the pilgrims; and every motive of honour and religion was subdued by the desire of life.[97]

Among the chiefs three heroes may be found without fear or reproach:
Godfrey of Bouillon was supported by his magnanimous piety;
Bohemond by ambition and interest; and Tancred declared, in the true
spirit of chivalry, that, as long as he was at the head of forty knights, he
would never relinquish the enterprise of Palestine. But the count of
Toulouse and Provence was suspected of a voluntary indisposition; the
duke of Normandy was recalled from the sea-shore by the censures of the
church; Hugh the Great, though he led the vanguard of the battle,
embraced an ambiguous opportunity of returning to France; and
Stephen, count of Chartres, basely deserted the standard which he bore,
and the council in which he presided. The soldiers were discouraged by
the flight of William, viscount of Melun, surnamed the *Carpenter*, from
the weighty strokes of his axe; and the saints were scandalised by the fall
of Peter the Hermit, who, after arming Europe against Asia, attempted to
escape from the penance of a necessary fast. Of the multitude of recreant
warriors, the names (says an historian) are blotted from the book of life;
and the opprobrious epithet of the rope-dancers was applied to the
deserters who dropt in the night from the walls of Antioch. The emperor
Alexius,[98] who seemed to advance to the succour of the Latins, was
dismayed by the assurance of their hopeless condition. They expected
their fate in silent despair: oaths and punishments were tried without
effect; and, to rouse the soldiers to the defence of the walls, it was found
necessary to set fire to their quarters.

For their salvation and victory, they were indebted to the same
fanaticism which had led them to the brink of ruin. In such a cause, and
in such an army, visions, prophecies, and miracles were frequent and
familiar. In the distress of Antioch, they were repeated with unusual
energy and success; St Ambrose had assured a pious ecclesiastic that two
years of trial must precede the season of deliverance and grace; the
deserters were stopped by the presence and approaches of Christ himself;
the dead had promised to arise and combat with their brethren; the Virgin
had obtained the pardon of their sins; and their confidence was revived by
a visible sign, the seasonable and splendid discovery of the HOLY LANCE.
The policy of their chiefs has on this occasion been admired and might
surely be excused; but a pious fraud is seldom produced by the cool
conspiracy of many persons; and a voluntary impostor might depend on
the support of the wise and the credulity of the people. Of the diocese of
Marseilles, there was a priest of low cunning and loose manners, and his
name was Peter Bartholemy. He presented himself at the door of the
council-chamber, to disclose an apparition of St Andrew, which had been
thrice reiterated in his sleep, with a dreadful menace if he presumed to
suppress the commands of Heaven. 'At Antioch,' said the apostle, 'in the
church of my brother St Peter, near the high altar, is concealed the steel
head of the lance that pierced the side of our Redeemer. In three days,
that instrument of eternal, and now of temporal, salvation will be

manifested to his disciples. Search, and ye shall find; bear it aloft in battle; and that mystic weapon shall penetrate the souls of the miscreants.' The pope's legate, the bishop of Puy, affected to listen with coldness and distrust; but the revelation was eagerly accepted by count Raymond, whom his faithful subject, in the name of the apostle, had chosen for the guardian of the holy lance. The experiment was resolved; and on the third day, after a due preparation of prayer and fasting, the priest of Marseilles introduced twelve trusty spectators, among whom were the count and his chaplain; and the church doors were barred against the impetuous multitude. The ground was opened in the appointed place; but the workmen, who relieved each other, dug to the depth of twelve feet without discovering the object of their search. In the evening, when count Raymond had withdrawn to his post, and the weary assistants began to murmur, Bartholemy, in his shirt and without his shoes, boldly descended into the pit; the darkness of the hour and of the place enabled him to secrete and deposit the head of a Saracen lance, and the first sound, the first gleam, of the steel was saluted with a devout rapture. The holy lance was drawn from its recess, wrapt in a veil of silk and gold, and exposed to the veneration of the crusaders; their anxious suspense burst forth in a general shout of joy and hope, and the desponding troops were again inflamed with the enthusiasm of valour. Whatever had been the arts, and whatever might be the sentiments of the chiefs, they skilfully improved this fortunate revolution by every aid that discipline and devotion could afford. The soldiers were dismissed to their quarters, with an injunction to fortify their minds and bodies for the approaching conflict, freely to bestow their last pittance on themselves and their horses, and to expect with the dawn of day the signal of victory. On the festival of St Peter and St Paul, the gates of Antioch were thrown open; a martial psalm, 'Let the Lord arise, and let his enemies be scattered!' was chanted by a procession of priests and monks; the battle array was marshalled in twelve divisions, in honour of the twelve apostles; and the holy lance, in the absence of Raymond, was entrusted to the hands of his chaplain. The influence of this relic or trophy was felt by the servants, and perhaps by the enemies, of Christ;[99] and its potent energy was heightened by an accident, a stratagem, or a rumour, of a miraculous complexion. Three knights, in white garments and resplendent arms, either issued, or seemed to issue, from the hills: the voice of Adhemar, the pope's legate, proclaimed them as the martyrs St George, St Theodore, and St Maurice; the tumult of battle allowed no time for doubt or scrutiny; and the welcome apparition dazzled the eyes or the imagination of a fanatic army. In the season of danger and triumph, the revelation of Bartholemy of Marseilles was unanimously asserted; but, as soon as the temporary service was accomplished, the personal dignity and liberal alms which the count of Toulouse derived from the custody of the holy lance provoked the envy, and awakened the reason, of his rivals. A Norman clerk presumed to sift, with a philosophic spirit, the truth of the legend, the circumstances of the discovery, and the character of the prophet; and the pious Bohemond ascribed their deliverance to the merits and intercession of Christ alone. For a while the Provincials defended their national palladium with clamours and arms; and new visions condemned to death and hell the profane sceptics who presumed to scrutinise the truth and merit of the discovery. The prevalence of incredulity compelled the author to submit his life and veracity to the judgment of God. A pile of faggots, four feet high and fourteen feet long, was erected in the midst of the camp; the flames burnt fiercely to the elevation of thirty cubits; and a narrow path of twelve inches was left for the perilous trial. The unfortunate priest of Marseilles traversed the fire with dexterity and speed: but his thighs and belly were scorched by the intense heat; he expired the next day, and the logic of believing minds will pay some regard to his dying protestations of innocence and truth. Some efforts were made by the Provincials to substitute a cross, a ring, or a tabernacle, in the place of the holy lance, which soon vanished in contempt and oblivion.[100] Yet the revelation of Antioch is gravely asserted by succeeding historians; and such is the progress of credulity that miracles, most doubtful on the spot and at the moment, will be received with implicit faith at a convenient distance of time and space.

The prudence or fortune of the Franks had delayed their invasion till the decline of the Turkish empire.[101] Under the manly government of the three first sultans, the kingdoms of Asia were united in peace and justice; and the innumerable armies which they led in person were equal in courage, and superior in discipline, to the barbarians of the West. But at the time of the crusade, the inheritance of Malek Shah was disputed by his four sons; their private ambition was insensible of the public danger; and, in the vicissitudes of their fortune, the royal vassals were ignorant, or regardless, of the true object of their allegiance. The twenty-eight emirs who marched with the standard of Kerboga were his rivals or enemies; their hasty levies were drawn from the towns and tents of Mesopotamia and Syria; and the Turkish veterans were employed or consumed in the civil wars beyond the Tigris. The caliph of Egypt embraced this opportunity of weakness and discord to recover his ancient possessions; and his sultan Aphdal besieged Jerusalem and Tyre, expelled the children of Ortok,* and restored in Palestine the civil and ecclesiastical authority of the Fatimites.[102] They heard with astonishment of the vast armies of Christians that had passed from Europe to Asia, and rejoiced in the sieges and battles which broke the power of the Turks, the adversaries of their sect and monarchy. But the same Christians were the enemies of the prophet; and from the overthrow of Nicaea and Antioch, the motive of their enterprise, which was gradually understood, would urge them forward to the banks of the Jordan, or perhaps of the Nile. An intercourse of epistles and embassies, which rose and fell with the events of war, was maintained between the throne of Cairo and the camp of the Latins; and their adverse pride was the result of ignorance and enthusiasm. The ministers of Egypt declared in an haughty, or insinuated in a milder, tone that their sovereign, the true and lawful commander of the faithful, had rescued Jerusalem from the Turkish yoke; and that the pilgrims, if they would divide their numbers and lay aside their arms, should find a safe and hospitable reception at the sepulchre of Jesus. In the belief of their lost condition, the caliph Mostali despised their arms and imprisoned their deputies: the conquest and victory of Antioch prompted him to solicit those formidable champions with gifts of horses and silk robes, of vases, and purses of gold and silver; and, in his estimate of their merit or power, the first place was assigned to Bohemond, and the second to Godfrey. In either fortune the answer of the crusaders was firm and uniform: they disdained to inquire into the private claims or possessions of the followers of Mahomet: whatsoever was his name or nation, the usurper of Jerusalem was their enemy; and, instead of prescribing the mode and terms of their pilgrimage, it was only by a timely surrender of the city and province, their sacred right, that he could deserve their alliance or deprecate their impending and irresistible attack.[103]

Yet this attack, when they were within the view and reach of their glorious prize, was suspended above ten months after the defeat of Kerboga. The zeal and courage of the crusaders were chilled in the moment of victory: and, instead of marching to improve the consternation, they hastily dispersed to enjoy the luxury, of Syria. The causes of this strange delay may be found in the want of strength and subordination. In the painful and various service of Antioch the cavalry was annihilated; many thousands of every rank had been lost by famine, sickness, and desertion; the same abuse of plenty had been productive of a third famine; and the alternative of intemperance and distress had generated a pestilence, which swept away above fifty thousand of the pilgrims. Few were able to command and none were willing to obey: the domestic feuds, which had been stifled by common fear, were again renewed in acts, or at least in sentiments, of hostility; the fortune of Baldwin and Bohemond excited the envy of their companions; the bravest knights were enlisted for the defence of their new principalities; and count Raymond exhausted his troops and treasures in an idle expedition into the heart of Syria. The winter was consumed in discord and disorder; a sense of honour and religion was rekindled in the spring; and the private soldiers, less susceptible of ambition and jealousy, awakened with angry clamours the indolence of their chiefs. In the month of May, the relics of this mighty host proceeded from Antioch to Laodicea: about forty thousand Latins, of whom no more than fifteen hundred horse and twenty thousand foot were capable of immediate service. Their easy march was continued between Mount Libanus and the seashore; their wants were liberally supplied by the coasting traders of Genoa and Pisa; and they drew large contributions from the emirs of Tripoli, Tyre, Sidon, Acre, and Caesarea, who granted a free passage and promised to follow the example of Jerusalem. From Caesarea they advanced into the midland country; their clerks* recognised the sacred geography of Lydda, Ramla, Emmaus, and Bethlem; and, as soon as they descried the holy city, the crusaders forgot their toils, and claimed their reward.[104]

Jerusalem has derived some reputation from the number and importance of her memorable sieges. It was not till after a long and obstinate contest that Babylon and Rome could prevail against the obstinacy of the people, the craggy ground that might supersede the necessity of fortifications, and the walls and towers that would have fortified the most accessible plain.[105] These obstacles were diminished in the age of the crusades. The bulwarks[†] had been completely destroyed, and imperfectly restored; the Jews, their nation and worship, were for ever banished; but nature is less changeable than man, and the site of Jerusalem, though somewhat softened and somewhat removed, was still strong against the assaults of an enemy. By the experience of a recent siege, and a three years' possession, the Saracens of Egypt had been taught to discern, and in some degree to remedy, the defects of a place which religion, as well as honour, forbade them to resign. Aladin or Iftikhar, the caliph's lieutenant, was entrusted with the defence; his policy strove to restrain the native Christians by the dread of their own ruin and that of the holy sepulchre; to animate the Moslems by the assurance of temporal and eternal rewards. His garrison is said to have consisted of forty thousand Turks and Arabians; and, if he could muster twenty thousand of the inhabitants, it must be confessed that the besieged were more numerous than the besieging army.[106] Had the diminished strength and numbers of the Latins allowed them to grasp the whole circumference of four thousand yards (about two English miles and a half),[107] to what useful purpose should they have descended into the valley of Ben Hinnom and torrent of Kedron,[108] or approached the precipices of the south and east, from whence they had nothing either to hope or fear? Their siege was more reasonably directed against the northern and western sides of the city. Godfrey of Bouillon erected his standard on the first swell of Mount Calvary; to the left, as far as St Stephen's gate, the line of attack was continued by Tancred and the two Roberts; and count Raymond established his quarters from the citadel to the foot of Mount Sion, which was no longer included within the precincts of the city. On the fifth day, the crusaders made a general assault, in the fanatic hope of battering down the walls without engines, and of scaling them without ladders. By the dint of brutal force they burst the first barrier, but they were driven back with shame and slaughter to the camp; the influence of vision and prophecy was deadened by the too frequent abuse of those pious stratagems; and time and labour were found to be the only means of victory. The time of the siege was indeed fulfilled in forty days, but they were forty days of calamity and anguish. A repetition of the old complaint of famine may be imputed in some degree to the voracious or disorderly appetite of the Franks; but the stony soil of Jerusalem is almost destitute of water; the scanty springs and hasty torrents were dry in the summer season; nor was the thirst of the besiegers relieved, as in the city, by the artificial supply of cisterns and aqueducts. The circumjacent country is equally destitute of trees for the uses of shade or building; but some large beams were discovered in a cave by the crusaders: a wood near Sichem, the enchanted grove of Tasso,[109] was cut down; the necessary timber was transported to the camp, by the vigour and dexterity of Tancred; and the engines were framed by some Genoese artists, who had fortunately landed in the harbour of Jaffa. Two moveable turrets were constructed at the expense, and in the stations, of the duke of Lorraine and the count of Toulouse, and rolled forwards with devout labour, not to the most accessible, but to the most neglected, parts of the fortification. Raymond's tower was reduced to ashes by the fire of the besieged; but his colleague was more vigilant and successful; the enemies were driven by his archers from the rampart; the drawbridge was let down; and on a Friday, at three in the afternoon, the day and hour of the Passion, Godfrey of Bouillon stood victorious on the walls of Jerusalem. His example was followed on every side by the emulation of valour; and, about four hundred and sixty years after the conquest of Omar, the holy city was rescued from the Mahometan yoke. In the pillage of public and private wealth, the adventurers had agreed to respect the exclusive property of the first occupant; and the spoils of the great mosque, seventy lamps and massy vases of gold and silver, rewarded the diligence, and displayed the generosity, of Tancred. A bloody sacrifice was offered by his mistaken votaries to the God of the Christians; resistance might provoke, but neither age nor sex could mollify, their implacable rage; they indulged themselves three days in a promiscuous massacre;[110] and the infection of the dead bodies produced an epidemic disease. After seventy thousand Moslems had been put to the sword, and the harmless Jews had been burnt in their synagogue, they could still reserve a multitude of captives whom interest or lassitude persuaded them to spare. Of these savage heroes of the cross, Tancred alone betrayed some sentiments of compassion; yet we may praise the more selfish lenity of Raymond, who granted a capitulation and safe-conduct to the garrison of the citadel.[111] The holy sepulchre was now free; and the bloody victors prepared to accomplish their vow. Bareheaded and barefoot, with contrite hearts, and in an humble posture, they ascended the hill of Calvary, amidst the loud anthems of the clergy; kissed the stone which had covered the Saviour of the world; and bedewed with tears of joy and penitence the monument of their redemption. This union of the fiercest and most tender passions has been variously considered by two philosophers: by the one,[112] as easy and natural; by the other,[113] as absurd and incredible. Perhaps it is too rigorously applied to the same persons and the same hour: the example of the virtuous Godfrey awakened the piety of his companions; while they cleansed their bodies, they purified their minds; nor shall I believe that the most ardent in slaughter and rapine were the foremost in the procession to the holy sepulchre.

Eight days after this memorable event, which Pope Urban did not live to hear, the Latin chiefs proceeded to the election of a king, to guard and govern their conquests in Palestine. Hugh the Great and Stephen of Chartres had retired with some loss of reputation, which they strove to regain by a second crusade and an honourable death. Baldwin was established at Edessa, and Bohemond at Antioch; and the two Roberts, the duke of Normandy[114] and the count of Flanders, preferred their fair inheritance in the West to a doubtful competition or a barren sceptre. The jealousy and ambition of Raymond were condemned by his own followers, and the free, the just, the unanimous voice of the army proclaimed Godfrey of Bouillon the first and most worthy of the champions of Christendom. His magnanimity accepted a trust as full of danger as of glory; but in a city where his Saviour had been crowned with thorns the devout pilgrim rejected the name and ensigns of royalty; and the founder of the kingdom of Jerusalem contented himself with the modest title of Defender and Baron of the Holy Sepulchre. His government of a single year,[115] too short for the public happiness, was interrupted in the first fortnight by a summons to the field, by the approach of the vizir or sultan of Egypt, who had been too slow to prevent, but who was impatient to avenge, the loss of Jerusalem. His total overthrow in the battle of Ascalon sealed the establishment of the Latins in Syria, and signalised the valour of the French princes, who, in this action, bade a long farewell to the holy wars. Some glory might be derived from the prodigious inequality of numbers, though I shall not count the myriads of horse and foot on the side of the Fatimites; but, except three thousand Ethiopians or Blacks, who were armed with flails or scourges of iron, the barbarians of the South fled on the first onset, and afforded a pleasing comparison between the active valour of the Turks and the sloth and effeminacy of the natives of Egypt. After suspending before the holy sepulchre the sword and standard of the sultan, the new king (he deserves the title) embraced his departing companions, and could retain only with the gallant Tancred three hundred knights and two thousand foot-soldiers for the defence of Palestine. His sovereignty was soon attacked by a new enemy, the only one against whom Godfrey was a coward. Adhemar, Bishop of Puy, who excelled both in council and action, had been swept away in the last plague of Antioch; the remaining ecclesiastics preserved only the pride and avarice of their character; and their seditious clamours had required that the choice of a bishop should precede that of a king. The revenue and jurisdiction of the lawful patriarch were usurped by the Latin clergy; the exclusion of the Greeks and Syrians was justified by the reproach of heresy or schism;[116] and, under the iron yoke of their deliverers, the Oriental Christians regretted the tolerating government of the Arabian caliphs. Daimbert, Archbishop of Pisa, had long been trained in the secret policy of Rome: he brought a fleet of his countrymen to the succour of the Holy Land, and was installed, without a competitor, the spiritual and temporal head of the church. The new patriarch[117] immediately grasped the sceptre which had been acquired by the toil and blood of the victorious pilgrims; and both Godfrey and Bohemond submitted to receive at his hands the investiture of their feudal possessions. Nor was this sufficient; Daimbert claimed the immediate property of Jerusalem and Jaffa: instead of a firm and generous refusal, the hero negotiated with the priest; a quarter of either city was ceded to the church; and the modest bishop was satisfied with an eventual reversion of the rest, on the death of Godfrey without children, or on the future acquisition of a new seat at Cairo or Damascus.

Without this indulgence, the conqueror would have almost been stripped of his infant kingdom, which consisted only of Jerusalem and Jaffa, with about twenty villages and towns of the adjacent country.[118] Within this narrow verge, the Mahometans were still lodged in some impregnable castles; and the husbandman, the trader, and the pilgrim were exposed to daily and domestic hostility. By the arms of Godfrey himself, and of the two Baldwins, his brother and cousin, who succeeded to the throne, the Latins breathed with more ease and safety; and at length they equalled, in the extent of their dominions, though not in the millions of their subjects, the ancient princes of Judah and Israel.[119] After the reduction of the maritime cities of Laodicea, Tripoli, Tyre, and Ascalon,[120] which were powerfully assisted by the fleets of Venice, Genoa, and Pisa, and even of Flanders and Norway,[121] the range of sea-coast from Scanderoon to the borders of Egypt was possessed by the Christian pilgrims. If the prince of Antioch disclaimed his supremacy, the counts of Edessa and Tripoli owned themselves the vassals of the king of Jerusalem: the Latins reigned beyond the Euphrates; and the four cities of Hems, Hamah, Damascus, and Aleppo were the only relics of the Mahometan conquests in Syria.[122] The laws and language, the manners and titles, of the French nation and Latin church, were introduced into these transmarine colonies. According to the feudal jurisprudence, the principal states and subordinate baronies descended in the line of male and female succession;[123] but the children of the first conquerers,[124] a motley and degenerate race, were dissolved by the luxury of the climate; the arrival of new crusaders from Europe was a doubtful hope and a casual event. The service of the feudal tenures[125] was performed by six hundred and sixty-six knights, who might expect the aid of two hundred more under the banner of the count of Tripoli; and each knight was attended to the field by four squires or archers on horseback.[126] Five thousand and seventy-five *serjeants*, most probably foot-soldiers, were supplied by the churches and the cities; and the whole legal militia of the kingdom could not exceed eleven thousand men, a slender defence against the surrounding myriads of Saracens and Turks.[127] But the firmest bulwark of Jerusalem was founded on the knights of the Hospital of St John,[128] and of the temple of Solomon;[129] on the strange association of a monastic and military life, which fanaticism might suggest, but which policy must approve. The flower of the nobility of Europe aspired to wear the cross, and to profess the vows, of these respectable orders; their spirit and discipline were immortal; and the speedy donation of twenty-eight thousand farms, or manors,[130] enabled them to support a regular force of cavalry and infantry for the defence of Palestine. The austerity of the convent soon evaporated in the exercise of arms; the world was scandalised by the pride, avarice, and corruption of these Christian soldiers; their claims of immunity and jurisdiction disturbed the harmony of the church and state; and the public peace was endangered by their jealous emulation. But in their most dissolute period, the knights of the Hospital and Temple maintained their fearless and fanatic character; they neglected to live, but they were prepared to die, in the service of Christ; and the spirit of chivalry, the parent and offspring of the crusades, has been transplanted by this institution from the holy sepulchre to the isle of Malta.[131]

The spirit of freedom, which pervades the feudal institutions, was felt in its strongest energy by the volunteers of the cross, who elected for their chief the most deserving of his peers. Amidst the slaves of Asia, unconscious of the lesson or example, a model of political liberty was introduced; and the laws of the French kingdom are derived from the purest source of equality and justice. Of such laws, the first and indispensable condition is the assent of those whose obedience they require, and for whose benefit they are designed. No sooner had Godfrey of Bouillon accepted the office of supreme magistrate than he solicited the public and private advice of the Latin pilgrims who were the best skilled in the statutes and customs of Europe. From these materials, with the counsel and approbation of the patriarch and barons, of the clergy and laity, Godfrey composed the *Assise of Jerusalem*,[132] a precious monument of feudal jurisprudence. The new code, attested by the seals of the king, the patriarch, and the viscount of Jerusalem, was deposited in the holy sepulchre, enriched with the improvements of succeeding times, and respectfully consulted as often as any doubtful question arose in the tribunals of Palestine. With the kingdom and city all was lost;[133] the fragments of the written law were preserved by jealous tradition,[134] and variable practice, till the middle of the thirteenth century; the code was restored by the pen of John d'Ibelin, count of Jaffa, one of the principal feudatories;[135] and the final revision was accomplished in the year thirteen hundred and sixty-nine, for the use of the Latin kingdom of Cyprus.[136]

The justice and freedom of the constitution were maintained by two tribunals of unequal dignity, which were instituted by Godfrey of Bouillon after the conquest of Jerusalem. The king, in person, presided in the upper court, the court of the barons. Of these the four most conspicuous were the prince of Galilee, the lord of Sidon and Caesarea, and the counts of Jaffa and Tripoli, who, perhaps with the constable and marshal,[137] were in a special manner the compeers and judges of each other. But all the nobles, who held their lands immediately of the crown, were entitled and bound to attend the king's court; and each baron exercised a similar jurisdiction in the subordinate assemblies of his own feudatories. The connection of lord and vassal was honourable and voluntary: reverence was due to the benefactor, protection to the dependent; but they mutually pledged their faith to each other, and the obligation on either side might be suspended by neglect or dissolved by injury. The cognisance of marriages and testaments was blended with religion and usurped by the clergy; but the civil and criminal causes of the nobles, the inheritance and tenure of their fiefs, formed the proper occupation of the supreme court. Each member was the judge and guardian both of public and private rights. It was his duty to assert with his tongue and sword the lawful claims of the lord; but, if an unjust superior presumed to violate the freedom or property of a vassal, the confederate peers stood forth to maintain his quarrel by word and deed. They boldly affirmed his innocence and his wrongs; demanded the restitution of his liberty or his lands; suspended, after a fruitless demand, their own service; rescued their brother from prison; and employed every weapon in his defence, without offering direct violence to the person of their lord, which was ever sacred in their eyes.[138] In their pleadings, replies, and rejoinders, the advocates of the court were subtle and copious; but the use of argument and evidence was often superseded by judicial combat; and the *Assise of Jerusalem* admits in many cases this barbarous institution, which has been slowly abolished by the laws and manners of Europe.

The trial by battle was established in all criminal cases which affected the life or limb or honour of any person; and in all civil transactions of or above the value of one mark of silver. It appears that in criminal cases the combat was the privilege of the accuser, who, except in a charge of treason, avenged his personal injury or the death of those persons whom he had a right to represent; but, wherever, from the nature of the charge, testimony could be obtained, it was necessary for him to produce witnesses of the fact. In civil cases, the combat was not allowed as the means of establishing the claim of the demandant; but he was obliged to produce witnesses who had, or assumed to have, knowledge of the fact. The combat was then the privilege of the defendant; because he charged the witness with an attempt by perjury to take away his right. He came, therefore, to be in the same situation as the appellant in criminal cases. It was not, then, as a mode of proof that the combat was received, nor as making negative evidence (according to the supposition of Montesquieu);[139] but in every case the right to offer battle was founded on the right to pursue by arms the redress of an injury; and the judicial combat was fought on the same principle, and with the same spirit, as a private duel. Champions were only allowed to women, and to men maimed or past the age of sixty. The consequence of a defeat was death to the person accused, or to the champion or witness, as well as to the accuser himself; but in civil cases the demandant was punished with infamy* and the loss of his suit, while his witness and champion suffered an ignominious death. In many cases, it was in the option of the judge to award or to refuse the combat; but two are specified in which it was the inevitable result of the challenge: if a faithful vassal gave the lie to his compeer, who unjustly claimed any portion of their lord's demesnes; or if an unsuccessful suitor presumed to impeach the judgment and veracity of the court. He might impeach them, but the terms were severe and perilous: in the same day he successively fought *all* the members of the tribunal, even those who had been absent; a single defeat was followed by death and infamy; and, where none could hope for victory, it is highly probable that none would adventure the trial. In the *Assise of Jerusalem*, the legal subtlety of the count of Jaffa is more laudably employed to elude, than to facilitate, the judicial combat, which he derives from a principle of honour rather than of superstition.[140]

Among the causes which enfranchised the plebeians from the yoke of feudal tyranny, the institution of cities and corporations is one of the most powerful; and, if those of Palestine are coeval with the first crusade, they may be ranked with the most ancient of the Latin world. Many of the pilgrims had escaped from their lords under the banner of the cross; and it was the policy of the French princes to tempt their stay by the assurance of the rights and privileges of freemen. It is expressly declared in the *Assise of Jerusalem* that, after instituting, for his knights and barons, the court of Peers, in which he presided himself, Godfrey of Bouillon established a second tribunal, in which his person was represented by his viscount. The jurisdiction of this inferior court extended over the burgesses of the kingdom; and it was composed of a select number of the most discreet and worthy citizens, who were sworn to judge, according to the laws, of the actions and fortunes of their equals.[141] In the conquest and settlement of new cities, the example of Jerusalem was imitated by the kings and their great vassals; and above thirty similar corporations were founded before the loss of the Holy Land. Another class of subjects, the Syrians,[142] or Oriental Christians, were oppressed by the zeal of the clergy, and protected by the toleration of the state. Godfrey listened to their reasonable prayer that they might be judged by their own national laws. A third court was instituted for their use, of limited and domestic jurisdiction; the sworn members were Syrians, in blood, language, and religion; but the office of the president (in Arabic, of the *rais*) was sometimes exercised by the viscount of the city. At an immeasurable distance below the *nobles*, the *burgesses*, and the *strangers*, the *Assise of Jerusalem* condescends to mention the *villains* and *slaves*, the peasants of the land and the captives of war, who were almost equally considered as the objects of property. The relief or protection of these unhappy men was not esteemed worthy of the care of the legislator; but he diligently provides for the recovery, though not indeed for the punishment, of the fugitives. Like hounds, or hawks, who had strayed from the lawful owner, they might be lost and claimed; the slave and falcon were of the same value; but three slaves, or twelve oxen, were accumulated to equal the price of the war-horse; and a sum of three hundred pieces of gold was fixed, in the age of chivalry, as the equivalent of the more noble animal.[143]

NOTES TO CHAPTER 58

1 Whimsical enough is the origin of the name of *Picards*, and from thence of *Picardie*, which does not date earlier than AD 1200. It was an academical joke, an epithet first applied to the quarrelsome humour of those students, in the university of Paris, who came from the frontier of France and Flanders (Valesii *Notitia Galliarum*, p. 447; Longuerue, *Description de la France*, p. 54).

2 William of Tyre (i, 11, 637, 638) thus describes the hermit: *Pusillus, persona contemptibilis, vivacis ingenii, et oculum habens perspicacem gratumque, et sponte fluens ei non deerat eloquium.* See Albert Aquensis, p. 185; Guibert, p. 482; Anna Comnena, in *Alexiad.*, x, 284, etc. with Ducange's notes, p. 349.

* *pages 894* [Pope, AD 1073–1085]

3 *Ultra quinquaginta millia, si me possunt in expeditione pro duce et pontifice habere, armata manu volunt in inimicos Dei insurgere, et ad sepulchrum Domini ipso ducente pervenire* (Gregor., vii, *epist.* ii, 31; in tom. xii, 322, *Concil.*).

† *pages 894* [Pope, AD 1088–1099]

4 See the original lives of Urban II by Pandulphus Pisanus and Bernardus Guido, in Muratori, *Rer. Ital. Script.*, iii, i, 352, 353.

‡ *pages 894* [reigned AD 1060–1108]

§ *pages 894* [reigned AD 1056–1106]

** *pages 894* [Countess of Tuscany who supported the papacy against the emperor. Died AD 1115.]

5 She is known by the different names of Praxes, Eupraecia, Eufrasia, and Adelais, and was the daughter of a Russian prince and the widow of a Margrave of Brandenburg. Struv., *Corpus Hist. Germanicae*, p. 340.

6 *Henricus odio eam coepit habere: ideo incarceravit eam, et concessit ut plerique vim ei inferrent; imo filium hortans ut eam subagitaret* ['Henry conceived a hatred for her, so much so that he had her locked up and allowed many men to take her by force; indeed he encouraged his son to lie with her']. (Dodechin, Continuat. Marian Scot. *apud* Baron. AD 1093, No. 4). In the synod of Constance, she is described by Bertholdus, *rerum inspector: quae se tantas et tam inauditas fornicationum spurcitias, et a tantis passam fuisse conquesta est*, etc. ['she complained that she was subjected to so many unheard of and filthy varieties of sexual abuse and at the hands of so many, etc.']. And again at Placentia: *satis misericorditer suscepit, eo quod ipsam tantas spurcitias non tam commississe quam invitam pertulisse pro certo cognoverit Papa cum sancta synodo.* ['So appalling were her experiences that the Pope and the holy synod accepted as a fact that she had not so much committed these filthy practices as submitted to them against her will.'] *Apud*

Baron., AD 1093, No. 4, AD 1094, No. 3. A rare subject for the infallible decision of a Pope and council ! These abominations are repugnant to every principle of human nature, which is not altered by a dispute about rings and crosiers. Yet it should seem that the wretched woman was tempted by the priests to relate or subscribe some infamous stories of herself and her husband.

7 See the narrative and acts of the synod of Placentia, *Concil.*, xii, 821, etc.

8 Guibert, himself a Frenchman, praises the piety and valour of the French nation, the author and example of the crusades: *Gens nobilis, prudens, bellicosa, dapsilis, et nitida.— Quos enim Britones, Anglos, Ligures, si bonis eos moribus videamus, non illico Francos homines appellemus?* (p. 478) ['A noble people, wise, warlike, rich and splendid. If we saw similar virtues among the Britons, the English or the Ligurians, would we not likewise call them Frenchmen?'] He owns, however, that the vivacity of the French degenerates into petulance among foreigners (p. 483), and vain loquaciousness (p. 502).

9 *Per viam quam iamdudum Carolus Magnus, mirificus rex Francorum, aptari fecit usque C. P.* (*Gesta Francorum*, p. 1; Robert. Monach., *Hist. Hieros.*, 1, 33, etc.).

10 John Tilpinus, or Turpinus, was Archbishop of Rheims, AD 773. After the year 1000, this romance was composed in his name by a monk of the borders of France and Spain; and such was the idea of ecclesiastical merit that he describes himself as a fighting and drinking priest! Yet the book of lies was pronounced authentic by Pope Calixtus II (AD 1122), and is respectfully quoted by the abbot Suger, in the great Chronicles of St Denys (Fabric., *Bibliot. Latin. medii Aevi*, edit. Mansi, tom. iv, 161).

* *pages 895* [Cluny]

11 See *Etat de la France*, by the Count de Boulainvilliers, i, 180–82, and the second volume of the *Observations sur l'Histoire de France*, by the Abbé de Mably.

12 In the provinces to the south of the Loire, the first *Capetians* were scarcely allowed a feudal supremacy. On all sides, Normandy, Bretagne, Aquitain, Burgundy, Lorraine, and Flanders contracted the name and limits of the *proper* France. See Hadrian. Vales., *Notitia Galliarum*.

13 These counts, a younger branch of the dukes of Aquitain, were at length despoiled of the greatest part of their country by Philip Augustus [King Philip II of France, AD 1180–1223]. The bishops of Clermont gradually became princes of the city. *Mélanges tirés d'une grande Bibliothèque*, xxxvi, 288, etc.

14 See the acts of the council of Clermont, *Concil.*, xii, 829, etc.

15 *Confluxerunt ad concilium e multis regionibus viri, potentes et honorati, innumeri quamvis cingulo laicalis militiae superbi* (Baldric, an eye-witness, pp. 86–88. Robert. Mon., pp. 31, 32. Will. Tyr., i, 14, 15, pp. 639–41. Guibert, pp. 478–80. Fulcher. Caront., p. 332).

16 The Truce of God (*Treva,* or *Treuga Dei*) was first invented in Aquitain, AD 1032; blamed by some bishops as an occasion of perjury, and rejected by the Normans as contrary to their privileges (Ducange, *Gloss. Latin.*, vi, pp. 682–85).

17 *Deus vult, Deus vult!* was the pure acclamation of the clergy who understood Latin (Robert. Mon., i, 32). By the illiterate laity, who spoke the *Provincial* [Provençal] or *Limousin* idiom, it was corrupted to *Deus lo volt,* or *Diex el volt.* See *Chron. Casinense*, iv, 11, 497, in Muratori, *Script. Rerum Ital.*, tom. iv, and Ducange (*Dissertat.*, xi, 207 sur Joinville, and *Gloss Lat.*, ii, 690), who, in his preface, produces a very difficult specimen of the dialect of Rovergue, AD 1100, very near, both in time and place, to the council of Clermont (pp. 15, 16).

18 Most commonly on their shoulders, in gold, or silk, or cloth, sewed on their garments. In the first crusade, all were red; in the third, the French alone preserved that colour, while green crosses were adopted by the Flemings, and white by the English (Ducange, ii, 651). Yet in England the red ever appears the favourite, and, as it were, the national, colour of our military ensigns and uniforms.

19 Bongarsius, who has published the original writers of the crusades, adopts, with much complacency, the fanatic title of Guibertus, *Gesta Dei per Francos* [God's work carried out by the Franks]; though some critics propose to read *Gesta Diaboli per Francos* [the Devil's work carried out by the Franks] (Hanoviae, 1611, two vols. in folio). I shall briefly enumerate, as they stand in this collection, the authors whom I have used for the first crusade. I *Gesta Francorum*; II Robertus Monachus; III Baldricus; IV Raimundus de Agiles; V Albertus Aquensis; VI Fulcherius Carnotensis; VII Guibertus; VIII Willielmus Tyriensis; Muratori has given us, IX Radulphus Cadomensis, *de Gestis Tancredi* (*Script. Rer. Ital.*, v, pp. 285–333); and x Bernardus Thesaurarius, *de Acquisitione Terrae Sanctae* (vii, 664–848). The last of these was unknown to a late French historian, who has given a large and critical list of the writers of the crusades (*Esprit des Croisades*, i, 13–141), and most of whose judgments my own experience will allow me to ratify. It was late before I could obtain a sight of the French historians collected by Duchesne. I Petri Tudebodi Sacerdotis Sivracensis, *Historia de Hierosolymitano Itinere* (iv, pp. 773–815) has been transfused into the first anonymous writer of Bongarsius. II *The Metrical History of the First Crusade*, in vii books (pp. 890–912), is of small value or account.

20 If the reader will turn to the first scene of the *First Part of Henry IV*, he will see in the text of Shakespeare the natural feelings of enthusiasm; and in the notes of Dr Johnson the workings of a bigoted though vigorous mind, greedy of every pretence to hate and persecute those who dissent from his creed. [These remarks were written after Johnson's death in 1784. Gibbon and Johnson knew each other as members of an exclusive literary club known as The Club.]

21 The Sixth Discourse of Fleury on Ecclesiastical History (pp. 223–61) contains an accurate and rational view of the causes and effects of the crusades.

22 The penance, indulgences, etc. of the middle ages are amply discussed by Muratori (*Antiquitat. Italiae medii Aevi*, v, lxviii, 709–68) and by M. Chais (*Lettres sur les Jubilés et les Indulgences*, ii, 21 and 22, pp. 478–556), with this difference, that the abuses of superstition are mildly, perhaps faintly, exposed by the learned Italian, and peevishly magnified by the Dutch minister.

23 Schmidt (*Histoire des Allemands*, ii, 211–20, 452–62) gives an abstract of the Penitential of Rhegino in the ixth, and of Burchard in the xth, century. In one year, five and thirty murders were perpetrated at Worms.

24 Till the xiith century, we may support the clear account of xii *denarii*, or pence, to the *solidus*, or shilling; and xx *solidi* to the pound weight of silver, about the pound sterling. Our money is diminished to a third, and the French to a fiftieth, of this primitive standard.

25 Each century of lashes was sanctified with the recital of a psalm; and the whole psalter, with the accompaniment of 15,000 stripes, was equivalent to five years.

26 The Life and Achievements of St Dominic Loricatus was composed by his friend and admirer, Peter Damianus. See Fleury, *Hist. Eccles.*, xiii, 96–104; Baronius, AD 1056, No. 7, who observes from Damianus, how fashionable, even among

ladies of quality (*sublimis generis*), this expiation (*purgatorii genus*) was grown.

27 At a quarter, or even half, a rial [real, a Spanish gold coin] a lash, Sancho Panza was a cheaper and possibly not a more dishonest workman. I remember, in Père Labat (*Voyages en Italie*, vii, 16–29), a very lively picture of the *dexterity* of one of these artists.

28 *Quicunque pro sola devotione, non pro honoris vel pecuniae adeptione, ad liberandam ecclesiam Dei Jerusalem profectus fuerit, iter illud pro omni poenitentia reputetur. Canon. Concil. Claromont.*, ii, p. 829. Guibert styles it, *novum salutis genus* ['a new kind of salvation'] (p. 471), and is almost philosophical on the subject.

29 Such at least was the belief of the crusaders, and such is the uniform style of the historians (*Esprit des Croisades*, iii, 477); but the prayers for the repose of their souls is inconsistent in orthodox theology with the merits of martyrdom.

* *pages 902* [the designated targets of their attacks]

30 The same hopes were displayed in the letters of the adventurers, *ad animandos qui in Francia resederant* ['in order to rouse up those who had remained in France']. Hugh de Reiteste could boast that his share amounted to one abbey and ten castles, of the yearly value of 1500 marks, and that he should acquire an hundred castles by the conquest of Aleppo (Guibert, pp. 554, 555).

31 In his genuine or fictitious letter to the Count of Flanders, Alexius mingles with the danger of the church, and the relics of saints, the *auri et argenti amor* [love of gold and silver] and *pulcherrimarum feminarum voluptas* [delights of possessing the most beautiful women], as if, says the indignant Guibert, the Greek women were handsomer than those of France. [See footnote 57 of Chapter 57.]

† *pages 902* [the land]

32 See the privileges of the *Crucesignati* [those who volunteered to go on crusade], freedom from debt, usury, injury, secular justice, etc. The pope was their perpetual guardian (Ducange, ii, 651, 652).

* *pages 903* [sold off]

33 Guibert (p. 481) paints in lively colours this general emotion. He was one of the few contemporaries who had genius enough to feel the astonishing scenes that were passing before their eyes. *Erat itaque videre miraculum caro omnes emere atque vili vendere*, etc.

34 Some instances of these *stigmata* are given in the *Esprit des Croisades* (iii, p. 169, etc.), from authors whom I have not seen.

35 *Fuit et aliud scelus detestabile in hac congregatione pedestris populi stulti et vesanae levitatis, . . . anserem quendam divino Spiritu asserebant afflatum, et capellam non minus eodem repletam, et has sibi duces secundae viae fecerant*, etc. (Albert. Aquensis, i, 31, 196). Had these peasants founded an empire they might have introduced, as in Egypt, the worship of animals, which their philosophic descendants would have glossed over with some specious and subtle allegory.

36 Benjamin of Tudela describes the state of his Jewish brethren from Cologne along the Rhine: they were rich, generous, learned, hospitable, and lived in the eager hope of the Messiah (*Voyage*, i, 243–45, par Baratier). In seventy years (he wrote about AD 1170) they had recovered from these massacres.

37 These massacres and depredations on the Jews, which were renewed at each crusade, are *coolly* related. It is true that St Bernard (*epist.* 363, i, 329) admonishes the Oriental Franks, *non sunt persequendi Judaei, non sunt trucidandi* ['the Jews are not to be persecuted or massacred']. The contrary doctrine had been preached by a *rival* monk.

938   THE DECLINE AND FALL OF THE ROMAN EMPIRE

* *pages 904* [AD 135]

38 See the contemporary description of Hungary in Otho of Frisingen, ii, 31, in Muratori, *Script. Rerum Italicarum*, vi, 665, 666.

39 The old Hungarians, without excepting Turotzius, are ill informed of the first crusade, which they involve in a single passage. Katona, like ourselves, can only quote the writers of France; but he compares with local science the ancient and modern geography. *Ante portam Cyperon*, is Sopron, or Poson; *Mallevilla*, Zemlin; *Fluvius Maroe*, Savus; *Lintax*, Leith; *Mesebroch*, or *Marseburg*, Ouar, or Moson; *Tollenburg*, Pragg (*de Regibus Hungariae*, iii, pp. 19–53).

40 Anna Comnena (*Alexias*, x, 287) describes this ὀστῶν κολωνός as a mountain, ὑψηλὸν καὶ βάθος καὶ πλάτος ἀξιολογώτατον ['quite remarkable for its height, depth and breadth']. In the siege of Nicaea, such were used by the Franks themselves as the materials of a wall.

41 To save time and space, I shall represent, in a short table, the particular references to the great events of the first crusade. [See facing page.]

42 The author of the *Esprit des Croisades* has doubted, and might have disbelieved, the crusade and tragic death of Prince Sueno, with 1500 or 15,000 Danes, who was cut off by Sultan Soliman in Cappadocia, but who still lives in the poem of Tasso (iv, 111–15) [Torquato Tasso, AD 1544–95, whose poem *Gerusalemme Liberate* (The Liberation of Jerusalem) was first published in 1581].

43 The fragments of the kingdoms of Lotharingia, or Lorraine, were broken into the two duchies, of the Moselle, and of the Meuse; the first has preserved its name, which in the latter has been changed into that of Brabant (Vales., *Notit. Gall.*, pp. 283–88).

44 See, in the description of France, by the Abbé de Longuerue, the articles of *Boulogne*, i, 54; *Brabant*, ii, 47, 48; *Bouillon*, p. 134. On his departure, Godfrey sold or pawned Bouillon to the church for 1300 marks.

45 See the family character of Godfrey in William of Tyre, ix, 5–8; his previous design in Guibert (p. 485); his sickness and vow in Bernard. Thesaur. (ch. 78).

46 Anna Comnena supposes that Hugh was proud of his nobility, riches, and power (x, 288); the two last articles appear more equivocal; but an εὐγένεια, which, seven hundred years ago, was famous in the palace of Constantinople, attests the ancient dignity of the Capetian family of France.

47 Will. Gemeticensis, vii, 7, 672, 673, in *Camden. Normanicis*. He pawned the duchy for one hundredth part of the present yearly revenue. Ten thousand marks may be equal to five hundred thousand livres, and Normandy annually yields fifty-seven millions to the king (Necker, *Administration des finances*, i, 287).

48 His original letter to his wife is inserted in the *Spicilegium* of Dom. Luc. d'Acheri, tom. iv and quoted in the *Esprit des Croisades*, i, 63.

49 *Unius enim, duum, trium, seu quatuor oppidorum dominos quis numeret? quorum tanta fuit copia, ut non vix totidem Troiana obsidio coegisse putetur.* (Ever the lively and interesting Guibert, p. 486.)

50 It is singular enough that Raymond of St Giles, a second character in the genuine history of the crusades, should shine as the first of heroes in the writings of the Greeks (Anna Comnen., *Alexiad.*, x, xi and the Arabians (*Longueruana*, p. 129).

51 *Omnes de Burgundia, et Alvernia, et Vasconia, et Gothi* (of Languedoc), *provinciales appellabantur, ceteri vero Francigenae, et hoc in exercitu; inter hostes autem Franci dicebantur.* Raymond de Agiles, p. 144.

52 The town of his birth, or first appanage, was consecrated to St Aegidius, whose name, as early as the first crusade, was corrupted by the French into St Gilles, or St Giles. It is situate in the Lower Languedoc, between Nismes and the Rhone, and still boasts a collegiate church of the foundation of Raymond (*Mélanges tirés d'une grande Bibliothèque*, xxxvii, p. 51).

* *pages 908* [narrated by Gibbon in Chapter 56]

53 The mother of Tancred was Emma, sister of the great Robert Guiscard; his father, the marquis Odo the Good. It is singular enough that the family and country of so illustrious a person should be unknown; but Muratori reasonably conjectures that he was an Italian, and perhaps of the race of the marquises of Montferrat in Piedmont (*Script.*, v, 281, 282).

54 To gratify the childish vanity of the house of Este, Tasso has inserted in his poem, and in the first crusade, a fabulous hero, the brave and amorous Rinaldo (x, 75; xvii, 66–94). He might borrow his name from a Rinaldo, with the *Aquila bianca Estense*, who vanquished, as the standard-bearer of the Roman church, the emperor Frederic I [known as Barbarossa, who ruled AD 1152–90] (*Storia Imperiale* di Ricobaldo, in Muratori, *Script. Ital.*, ix, 360; Ariosto, *Orlando Furioso*, iii, 30). But, 1) The distance of sixty years between the youth of the two Rinaldos destroys their identity. 2) The *Storia Imperiale* is a forgery of the Conte Boyardo, at the end of the xvth century (Muratori, pp. 281–89). 3) This Rinaldo and his exploits are not less chimerical than the hero of Tasso (Muratori, *Antichità Estense*, i, 350).

55 Of the words, *gentilis, gentilhomme, gentleman,* two etymologies are produced: 1) From the barbarians of the fifth century, the soldiers, and at length the conquerors, of the Roman empire, who were vain of their foreign nobility; and, 2) From the sense of the civilians [Roman lawyers], who consider *gentilis* as synonymous with *ingenuus* [freeborn]. Selden [English jurist, 1584–1654] inclines to the first, but the latter is more pure, as well as probable.

56 *Framea scutoque iuvenem ornant.* Tacitus, *Germania*, c. 13. ['They decorate the young man with a spear and shield.']

57 The athletic exercises, particularly the coestus and pancratium [boxing and all-in wrestling], were condemned by Lycurgus, Philopoemen, and Galen, a lawgiver, a general, and a physician. Against their authority and reasons, the reader may weigh the apology of Lucian, in the character of Solon. See West on the Olympic Games, in his Pindar, ii, 86–96, 245–48.

* *pages 910* [a slow-paced horse]

58 On the curious subject of knighthood, knights' service, nobility, arms, cry of war, banners, and tournaments, an ample fund of information may be sought in Selden (*Opera*, iii, 1; *Titles of Honour*, ii, 1, 3, 5, 8), Ducange (*Gloss. Latin.*, iv, 398–412, etc.), *Dissertations sur Joinville* (i, vi–xii, 127–42, 165–222), and M. de St Palaye (*Mémoires sur la Chevalerie*).

59 The *Familiae Dalmaticae* of Ducange are meagre and imperfect; the national historians are recent and fabulous, the Greeks remote and careless. In the year 1104, Coloman reduced the maritime country as far as Trau and Salona (Katona, *Hist. Crit.*, iii, 195–207).

60 Scodra appears in Livy as the capital and fortress of Gentius, king of the Illyrians, *arx munitissima* [a strongly-fortified citadel], afterwards a Roman colony (Cellarius, i, 393, 394). It is now called Iscodar, or Scutari (d'Anville, *Géographie Ancienne*, i, 164). The sanjiak (now a pasha) of Scutari, or Schendeire, was the

viiith under the Beglerbeg of Romania, and furnished 600 soldiers on a revenue of 78,787 rix dollars (Marsigli, *Stato Militare del Impero Ottomano*, p. 128).

61 *In Pelagonia castrum haereticum . . . spoliatum cum suis habitatoribus igne combussere. Nec id eis iniuria contigit: quia illorum detestabilis sermo et cancer serpebat, iamque circumiacentes regiones suo pravo dogmate foedaverat.* ['In Pelagonia they sacked a heretical castle and burned it down together with its inhabitants. Nor was there any injustice in this event; for the foul cancer of their language was spreading and had already polluted the surrounding area with their vicious dogma.'] (Robert. Mon., pp. 36, 37). After coolly relating the fact, the archbishop Baldric adds, as a phrase, *Omnes siquidem illi viatores, Iudaeos; haereticos, Saracenos aequaliter habent exosos; quos omnes appellant inimicos Dei.* ['The travellers hold equally in detestation Jews, heretics and Saracens, and call them all the enemy of God.'] (p. 92).

62 Ἀναλαβόμενος ἀπὸ Ῥώμης τὴν χρυσῆν τοῦ Ἁγίου Πέτρου σημαίαν (*Alexiad*, x, 288).

63 Ὁ Βασιλεὺς τῶν βασιλέων, καὶ ἀρχηγὸς τοῦ Φραγγικοῦ στρατεύματος ἅπαντος [King of kings, chief of all the French army] This Oriental pomp is extravagant in a count of Vermandois, but the patriot Ducange repeats with much complacency (Not. ad *Alexiad.*, p. 352, 353; *Dissert.* xxvii, sur Joinville, p. 315) the passages of Matthew Paris (AD 1254) and Froissard (iv, 201), which style the King of France *rex regum* and *chef de tous les rois Chrétiens.*

* *pages 912*   [His character and reign are reviewed in Chapter 48.]

64 Anna Comnena was born on the 1st of December, AD 1083, indiction vii. (*Alexiad*, vi, 166, 167). At thirteen, the time of the first crusade, she was nubile, and perhaps married to the younger Nicephorus Bryennius, whom she fondly styles τὸν ἐμὸν Καίσαρα ['my Caesar'] (x, 295, 296). Some moderns have *imagined* that her enmity to Bohemond was the fruit of disappointed love. In the transactions of Constantinople and Nicaea, her partial accounts (*Alex.*, x, xi, pp. 283–317) may be opposed to the partiality of the Latins; but in their subsequent exploits she is brief and ignorant.

65 In their views of the character and conduct of Alexius, Maimbourg has favoured the *Catholic* Franks, and Voltaire has been partial to the *schismatic* Greeks. The prejudice of a philosopher is less excusable than that of a Jesuit.

66 Between the Black Sea, the Bosphorus, and the river Barbyses, which is deep in summer, and runs fifteen miles through a flat meadow. Its communication with Europe and Constantinople is by the stone bridge of the *Blachernae*, which in successive ages was restored by Justinian and Basil (Gyllius, *de Bosphoro Thracio*, ii, 3; Ducange, *C. P. Christiana*, iv, 2, 179).

* *pages 913*   [invaded]

67 There were two sorts of adoption, the one by arms, the other by introducing the son between the shirt and skin of his father. Ducange (sur Joinville, xxii, p. 270) supposes Godfrey's adoption to have been of the latter sort.

* *pages 914*   [Norman battles against the Eastern empire, AD 1081 and 1082, in Albania and Thessaly (narrated in Chapter 56)]

68 After his return, Robert of Flanders became the *man* of the King of England, for a pension of 400 marks. See the first act in Rymer's *Foedera.*

69 *Sensit vetus regnandi, falsos in amore odia non fingere.* Tacit., vi, 44.

70 The proud historians of the crusades slide and stumble over this humiliating step. Yet, since the heroes knelt to salute the emperor as he sat motionless on his throne, it is clear that they must have kissed either his feet or knees. It is only

singular that Anna should not have amply supplied the silence or ambiguity of the Latins. The abasement of their princes would have added a fine chapter to the Ceremoniale Aulae Byzantinae.

71 He called himself Φράγγος καθαρὸς τῶν εὐγενῶν [a Frank of the purest nobility] (*Alexias*, x, p. 301). What a title of *noblesse* of the xith century, if any one could now prove his inheritance! Anna relates, with visible pleasure, that the swelling barbarian, Λατῖνος τετυφωμένος, was killed, or wounded, after fighting in the front in the battle of Dorylaeum (xi, 317). This circumstance may justify the suspicion of Ducange (Not., p. 362) that he was no other than Robert of Paris, of the district most peculiarly styled the Duchy or Island of France *(L'Isle de France)*.

72 With the same penetration, Ducange discovers his church to be that of St Drausus, or Drosin, of Soissons, *quem duello dimicaturi solent invocare: pugiles qui ad memoriam eius* (his tomb) *pernoctant invictos reddit, ut et de Burgundia et Italia tali necessitate confugiatur ad eum* ['whom those who are about to engage in battle are wont to invoke: warriors who pass a whole night at his tomb he sends away invincible, so that men with such a need have recourse to him from Burgundy and Italy'], Joan. Sariburiensis, epist. 139.

73 There is some diversity on the numbers of his army; but no authority can be compared with that of Ptolemy, who states it at five thousand horse and thirty thousand foot (See Usher's *Annales*, p. 152).

74 Fulcher. Carnotensis, p. 387. He enumerates nineteen nations of different names and languages (p. 389); but I do not clearly apprehend his difference between the *Franci* and *Galli, Itali* and *Apuli*. Elsewhere (p. 385) he contemptuously brands the deserters.

75 Guibert, p. 556. Yet even his gentle opposition implies an immense multitude. By Urban II, in the fervour of his zeal, it is only rated at 300,000 pilgrims (Epist. xvi; *Concil.*, xii, 731).

 * *pages 916* [on the French side of the Alps]

76 *Alexias*, x, 283. Her fastidious delicacy complains of their strange and inarticulate names; and indeed there is scarcely one that she has not contrived to disfigure with the proud ignorance, so dear and familiar to a polished people. I shall select only one example, *Sangeles*, for the count of St Giles.

 † *pages 916* [kings of Persia]

77 William of Malmesbury (who wrote about the year 1130) has inserted in his history (iv, 130–54) a narrative of the first crusade, but I wish that, instead of listening to the *tenue murmur* [faint murmur] which had passed the British ocean (p. 143), he had confined himself to the numbers, families, and adventures of his countrymen. I find in Dugdale that an English Norman, Stephen, Earl of Albemarle and Holdernesse, led the rearguard with Duke Robert, at the battle of Antioch (*Baronage*, i, 61).

78 *Videres Scotorum apud se ferocium alias imbellium cuneos* (Guibert, p. 471); the *crus intectum* [bare legs] and *hispida chlamys* [sodden cloak], may suit the Highlanders; but the *finibus uliginosis* [marshy frontier] may rather apply to the Irish bogs. William of Malmesbury expressly mentions the Welsh and Scots, etc. (iv, 133), who quitted, the former *venationem saltuum* [hunting groves], the latter *familiaritatem pulicum* [the close proximity of fleas].

79 This cannibal hunger, sometimes real, more frequently an artifice or a lie, may be found in Anna Comnena (*Alexias*, x, 288), Guibert (p. 546), Radulph.

Cadom. (ch. 97). The stratagem is related by the author of the *Gesta Francorum*, the monk Robert, Baldric, and Raymond des Agiles, in the siege and famine of Antioch.

80 His Musulman appellation of Soliman is used by the Latins, and his character is highly embellished by Tasso. His Turkish name of Kilidge-Arslan (AH 485–500, AD 1092–1106; see de Guignes's Tables, i, 245) is employed by the Orientals, and with some corruption by the Greeks, but little more than his name can be found in the Mahometan writers, who are dry and sulky on the subject of the first crusade (de Guignes, iii, ii, 10–30). [Gibbon's account is not quite correct. Soliman died in AD 1086. His son of the same name succeeded in AD 1092 and died in AD 1106.]

81 On the fortifications, engines, and sieges of the middle ages, see Muratori (*Antiquitat. Italiae*, ii, xxvi, 452–524). The *belfredus*, from whence our belfry, was the moveable tower of the ancients (Ducange, i, 608).

82 I cannot forbear remarking the resemblance between the siege and lake of Nicaea, with the operations of Hernan Cortez before Mexico. See Dr Robertson, *Hist. of America*, Bk v [William Robertson (1721–93), the celebrated Scottish historian].

83 *Mécréant*, a word invented by the French crusaders, and confined in that language to its primitive sense. It should seem that the zeal of our ancestors boiled higher, and that they branded every unbeliever as a rascal. A similar prejudice still lurks in the minds of many who think themselves Christians.

84 Baronius has produced a very doubtful letter to his brother Roger (AD 1098, No. 15). The enemies consisted of Medes, Persians, Chaldeans; be it so. The first attack was, *cum nostro incommodo* [to our detriment]; true and tender. But why Godfrey of Bouillon and Hugh *brothers*? Tancred is styled *filius* [son]; of whom? certainly not of Roger, nor of Bohemond. [See footnote 53 of this chapter.]

85 *Veruntamen dicunt se esse de Francorum generatione; et quia nullus homo naturaliter debet esse miles nisi Franci et Turci* (*Gesta Francorum*, p. 7) The same community of blood and valour is attested by Archbishop Baldric (p. 99).

86 *Balista, Balestra, Arbalestre.* See Muratori, *Antiq.*, ii, 517–24. Ducange, *Gloss. Latin.*, i, 531, 532. In the time of Anna Comnena this weapon, which she describes under the name of *tzangra*, was unknown in the East (x, 291). By an humane inconsistency, the pope strove to prohibit it in Christian wars.

* *pages 919*   [See note 51.]

87 The curious reader may compare the classic learning of Cellarius and the geographical science of D'Anville. William of Tyre is the only historian of the crusades who has any knowledge of antiquity; and M. Otter trod almost in the footsteps of the Franks from Constantinople to Antioch (*Voyage en Turquie et en Perse*, i, 35–88).

† *pages 919*   [Tancred]

‡ *pages 919*   [Baldwin]

88 This detached conquest of Edessa is best represented by Fulcherius Carnotensis, or of Chartres (in the collections of Bongarsius, Duchesne, and Martenne), the valiant chaplain of Count Baldwin (*Esprit des Croisades*, i, 13–14). In the disputes of that prince with Tancred, his partiality is encountered by the partiality of Radulphus Cadomensis, the soldier and historian of the gallant marquis.

89 See de Guignes, *Hist. des Huns*, i, 456.

90 For Antioch, see Pococke (*Description of the East*, ii, i, 188–93), Otter (*Voyage*

en Turquie, etc., i, 81, etc.), the Turkish geographer (in Otter's notes), the *Index Geographicus* of Schultens (*ad calcem Bohadin. Vit. Saladin.*), and Abulfeda (*Tabula Syriae*, p. 115–116, vers. Reiske).

91 *Ensem elevat, eumque a sinistra parte scapularum tanta virtute intorsit, ut quod pectus medium disiunxit spinam et vitalia interrupit; et sic lubricus ensis super crus dextrum integer exivit; sicque caput integrum cum dextra parte corporis immersit gurgite, partemque quae equo praesidebat remisit civitati* (Robert Mon. p. 50). *Cuius ense traiectus, Turcus duo factus est Turci, ut inferior alter in urbem equitaret, alter arcitenens in flumine nataret* (Radulph. Cadom., 53, 304). Yet he justifies the deed by the *stupendis viribus* [astonishing strength] of Godfrey; and William of Tyre covers it by *obstupuit populus facti novitate . . . mirabilis* ['the people were struck dumb by the strangeness of this extraordinary event'] (v, 6, 701). Yet it must not have appeared incredible to the knights of that age.

92 See the exploits of Robert, Raymond, and the modest Tancred, who imposed silence on his squire (Radulph. Cadom., ch. 53).

93 After mentioning the distress and humble petition of the Franks, Abulpharagius adds the haughty reply of Codbuka, or Kerboga; *Non evasuri estis nisi per gladium* ['You shall not escape except by the sword'] (*Dynast.*, p. 242).

94 In describing the host of Kerboga, most of the Latin historians, the author of the *Gesta* (p. 17), Robert Monachus (p. 56), Baldric (p. 111), Fulcherius Carnotensis (p. 392), Guibert (p. 512), William of Tyre (vi, iii, 714), Bernard Thesaurarius (39, 695), are content with the vague expressions of *infinita multitudo, immensum agmen, innumerae copiae*, or *gentes* [an infinite multitude, an immense army, innumerable forces . . . hordes], which correspond with the μετὰ ἀναριθμήτων χιλιάδων [with innumerable thousands] of Anna Comnena (*Alexias*, xi, 318–20). The numbers of the Turks are fixed by Albert Aquensis at 200,000 (iv, x, 242), and by Radulphus Cadomensis at 400,000 horse (lxxii, 309).

95 See the tragic and scandalous fate of an archdeacon of royal birth, who was slain by the Turks as he reposed in an orchard, playing at dice with a Syrian concubine.

96 The value of an ox rose from five solidi (fifteen shillings) at Christmas to two marks (four pounds), and afterwards much higher: a kid or lamb, from one shilling to eighteen of our present money: in the second famine, a loaf of bread, or the head of an animal, sold for a piece of gold. More examples might be produced; but it is the ordinary, not the extraordinary, prices that deserve the notice of the philosopher.

97 *Alii multi quorum nomina non tenemus; quia, deleta de libro vitae, praesenti operi non sunt inserenda* ['There were many others whose names we do not possess; stricken from the book of life, they are not to be included in this work'] (Will. Tyr., vi, v, 715). Guibert (pp. 518–23) attempts to excuse Hugh the Great, and even Stephen of Chartres.

98 See the progress of the crusade, the retreat of Alexius, the victory of Antioch, and the conquest of Jerusalem, in the *Alexiad*, xi, 317–27. Anna was so prone to exaggeration that she magnifies the exploits of the Latins.

99 The Mahometan Aboulmahasen (*apud* de Guignes, ii, 95) is more correct in his account of the holy lance than the Christians, Anna Comnena and Abulpharagius: the Greek princess confounds it with a nail of the cross (xi, 326); the Jacobite primate, with St Peter's staff (p. 242).

100 The two antagonists who express the most intimate knowledge and the strongest conviction of the *miracle*, and of the *fraud*, are Raymond des Agiles and Radulphus Cadomensis, the one attached to the Count of Toulouse, the other to the Norman prince. Fulcherius Carnotensis presumes to say, *Audite fraudem et non fraudem*! and afterwards, *Invenit lanceam, fallaciter occultatam forsitan*. ['Hear of a fraud which is not a fraud . . . He found the lance which perhaps was deceitfully hidden.'] The rest of the herd are loud and strenuous.

101 See M. de Guignes (ii, ii, 223, etc.); and the articles of *Barkiarok, Mohammed, Sangiar*, in d'Herbelot.

* *pages 925*   [the emir to whom Jerusalem was entrusted in ad 1076]

102 The emir, or sultan, Aphdal recovered Jerusalem and Tyre, AH 489 [AD 1096] (Renaudot, *Hist. Patriarch. Alexandrin.*, p. 478; de Guignes, i, 249, from Abulfeda and Ben Schounah). *Jerusalem ante adventum vestrum recuperavimus, Turcos eiecimus*, say the Fatimite ambassadors ['We retook Jerusalem, we expelled the Turks before your arrival'].

103 See the transactions between the caliphs of Egypt and the crusaders, in William of Tyre (iv, 24; vi, 19) and Albert Aquensis (iii, 59), who are more sensible of their importance than the contemporary writers.

* *pages 927*   [clergymen]

104 The greatest part of the march of the Franks is traced, and most accurately traced, in Maundrell's Journey from Aleppo to Jerusalem (pp. 1–67): *un des meilleurs morceaux, sans contredit, qu'on ait dans ce genre* ['unquestionably one of the best pieces of writing of its kind'] (d'Anville, *Mémoire sur Jérusalem*, p. 27).

105 See the masterly description of Tacitus (*Hist.*, v, 11, 12, 13), who supposes that the Jewish lawgivers had provided for a perpetual state of hostility against the rest of mankind.

† *pages 927*   [ramparts]

106 The lively scepticism of Voltaire is balanced with sense and erudition by the French author of the *Esprit des Croisades* (iv, 386–88), who observes that, according to the Arabians, the inhabitants of Jerusalem must have exceeded 200,000; that in the siege of Titus, Josephus collects 1,300,000 Jews; that they are stated by Tacitus himself at 600,000, and that the largest defalcation that his *accepimus* can justify will still leave them more numerous than the Roman army.

107 Maundrell, who diligently perambulated the walls, found a circuit of 4630 paces, or 4167 English yards (pp. 109, 110); from an authentic plan, d'Anville concludes a measure nearly similar, of 1960 French *toises* (pp. 23–29), in his scarce and valuable tract. For the topography of Jerusalem, see Reland (*Palestina*, ii, 832–60).

108 Jerusalem was possessed only of the torrent of Kedron, dry in summer, and of the little spring or brook of Siloe (Reland, i, 294, 300). Both strangers and natives complained of the want of water, which, in time of war, was studiously aggravated. Within the city, Tacitus mentions a perennial fountain, an aqueduct, and cisterns for rainwater. The aqueduct was conveyed from the rivulet Tekoe, or Etham, which is likewise mentioned by Bohadin (in *Vit. Saladin.*, p. 238).

109 *Gierusalemme Liberata*, canto xiii. It is pleasant enough to observe how Tasso has copied and embellished the minutest details of the siege.

110 Besides the Latins, who are not ashamed of the massacre, see Elmacin (*Hist. Saracen.*, p. 363), Abulpharagius (*Dynast.*, p. 243), and M. de Guignes (ii, ii, 99), from Aboulmahasen.

111 The old tower Psephina, in the middle ages Neblosa, was named Castellum Pisanum, from the patriarch Daimbert [archbishop of Pisa]. It is still the citadel, the residence of the Turkish aga, and commands a prospect of the Dead Sea, Judea, and Arabia (d'Anville, pp. 19–23). It was likewise called the Tower of David, πύργος παμμεγεθέστατος [the immense tower].

112 Hume, in his *History of England*, i, 311, 312, octavo edition.

113 Voltaire, in his *Essai sur l'Histoire Générale*, ii, 54, 345, 346.

114 The English ascribe to Robert of Normandy, and the Provincials to Raymond of Toulouse, the glory of refusing the crown; but the honest voice of tradition has preserved the memory of the ambition and revenge (Villehardouin, No. 136) of the count of St Giles. He died at the siege of Tripoli, which was possessed by his descendants.

115 See the election, the battle of Ascalon, etc. in William of Tyre, ix, 1–12, and the conclusion of the Latin historians of the first crusade.

116 Renaudot, *Hist. Patriarch. Alex.*, p. 479.

117 See the claims of the patriarch Daimbert, in William of Tyre (ix, 15–18; x, 4, 7, 9), who asserts with marvellous candour the independence of the conquerors and kings of Jerusalem.

118 Willem. Tyr., x, 19. The *Historia Hierosolymitana* of Jacobus a Vitriaco (i, 21–50) and the *Secreta Fidelium Crucis* of Marinus Sanutus (iii, 1) describe the state and conquests of the Latin kingdom of Jerusalem.

119 An actual muster, not including the tribes of Levi and Benjamin, gave David an army of 1,300,000, or 1,574,000 fighting men; which, with the addition of women, children, and slaves, may imply a population of thirteen millions, in a country sixty leagues in length and thirty broad. The honest and rational Le Clerc (Comment. on 2 Samuel xxiv and 1 Chronicles xxi) *aestuat angusto in limite* [finds himself on the horns of a dilemma], and mutters his suspicion of a false transcript – a dangerous suspicion!

120 These sieges are related, each in its proper place, in the great history of William of Tyre, from the ixth to the xviiith book, and more briefly told by Bernardus Thesaurarius (*de Acquisitione Terrae Sanctae*, 89–98, 732–40). Some domestic facts are celebrated in the Chronicles of Pisa, Genoa, and Venice, in the vith, ixth, and xiith tomes of Muratori.

121 *Quidam populus de insulis occidentis egressus, et maxime de ea parte quae Norvegia dicitur* ['a certain people from the islands of the west and particularly that part which is called Norway']. William of Tyre (xi, 14, 804) marks their course *per Britannicum mare et Calpen* ['through the English Channel and Gibraltar'] to the siege of Sidon.

122 Benelathir, *apud* de Guignes, *Hist. des Huns*, ii, ii, 150, 151, AD 1127. He must speak of the inland country.

123 Sanut very sensibly descants on the mischiefs of female succession in a land *hostibus circumdata, ubi cuncta virilia et virtuosa esse deberent* ['surrounded by enemies, where masculinity and courage were everywhere necessary']. Yet, at the summons, and with the approbation, of her feudal lord, a noble damsel was obliged to choose a husband and champion (*Assises de Jérusalem*, ch. 242, etc.). See in M. de Guignes (i, 441–71) the accurate and useful tables of these dynasties, which are chiefly drawn from the *Lignages d'Outremer*.

124 They were called by derision *Poullains, Pullani* [colts, yearlings], and their name is never pronounced without contempt (Ducange, *Gloss. Latin.*, v, 535;

and *Observations* sur Joinville, pp. 84, 85; Jacob. a Vitriaco, *Hist. Hierosol.*, i, 67, 72; and Sanut, iii, viii, 2, 182). *Illustrium virorum qui ad Terrae Sanctae . . . liberationem in ipsa manserunt degeneres filii . . . in deliciis enutriti, molles et effeminati*, etc. ['The degenerate sons of the illustrious liberators of the Holy Land who remained there . . . were reared in luxury, soft and effeminate, etc.']

125 This authentic detail is extracted from the *Assises de Jérusalem* (chs 324, 326–31). Sanut (iii, viii, i, 174) reckons only 518 knights and 5775 followers.

126 The sum-total, and the division, ascertain the service of the three great baronies at 100 knights each; and the text of the *Assises*, which extends the number to 500, can only be justified by this supposition.

127 Yet on great emergencies (says Sanut) the barons brought a voluntary aid; *decentem comitivam militum iuxta statum suum* ['a company of soldiers appropriate to their status'].

128 William of Tyre (xviii, 3, 4, 5) relates the ignoble origin and early insolence of the Hospitalers, who soon deserted their humble patron, St John the Eleemosynary, for the more august character of St John the Baptist. (See the ineffectual struggles of Pagi, *Critica*, AD 1099, No. 14–18.) They assumed the profession of arms about the year 1120; the Hospital was *mater*, the Temple *filia*; the Teutonic order was founded AD 1190, at the siege of Acre (Mosheim, *Institut.*, 389, 390).

129 See St Bernard, *de Laude Novae Militiae Templi*, composed AD 1132–36; in *Opp.*, i, ii, 547–63, edit. Mabillon. Venet. 1750. Such an encomium, which is thrown away on the dead Templars, would be highly valued by the historians of Malta.

130 Matthew Paris, *Hist. Major*, p. 544. He assigns to the Hospitalers 19,000, to the Templars 9000 *maneria*, a word of much higher import (as Ducange has rightly observed) in the English than in the French idiom. *Manor* is a lordship, *manoir* a dwelling.

131 In the three first books of the *Histoire des Chevaliers de Malthe*, par l'Abbé de Vertot, the reader may amuse himself with a fair, and sometimes flattering, picture of the order, while it was employed for the defence of Palestine. The subsequent books pursue their emigrations to Rhodes and Malta.

132 The *Assises de Jérusalem*, in old Law-French, were printed with Beaumanoir's *Coutumes de Beauvoisis* (Bourges and Paris, 1690, in folio), and illustrated by Gaspard Thaumas de la Thaumassière, with a comment and glossary. An Italian version had been published in 1535, at Venice, for the use of the kingdom of Cyprus.

133 *A la terre perdue, tout fut perdu*, is the vigorous expression of the *Assise* (ch. 281). Yet Jerusalem capitulated with Saladin: the queen and the principal Christians departed in peace; and a code so precious and so portable could not provoke the avarice of the conquerors. I have sometimes suspected the existence of this original copy of the Holy Sepulchre, which might be invented to sanctify and authenticate the traditionary customs of the French in Palestine.

134 A noble lawyer, Raoul de Tabarie, denied the prayer of King Amauri (AD 1195–1205), that he would commit his knowledge to writing; and frankly declared, *que de ce qu'il savoit ne feroit-il ja nul borjois son pareill, ne nul sage homme lettré* ['that no burgher would ever be his equal in knowledge, nor even an educated man'] (ch. 281).

135 The compiler of this work, Jean d'Ibelin, was Count of Jaffa and Ascalon, Lord

of Baruth (Berytus) and Rames, and died AD 1266 (Sanut, iii, xii, 5, 8). The family of Ibelin, which descended from a younger brother of a count of Chartres in France, long flourished in Palestine and Cyprus (see the *Lignages de de-ça Mer*, or *d'Outremer*, ch. 6, at the end of the *Assises de Jérusalem*, an original book, which records the pedigrees of the French adventurers).

136 By sixteen commissioners chosen in the states of the island, the work was finished the 3rd of November, 1369, sealed with four seals, and deposited in the cathedral of Nicosia (see the preface to the *Assises*).

137 The cautious John d'Ibelin argues, rather than affirms, that Tripoli is the fourth barony, and expresses some doubt concerning the right or pretension of the constable and marshal (ch. 323).

138 *Entre seignor et homme ne n'a que la foi; . . . mais tant que l'homme doit à son seignor reverence en toutes choses* (ch. 206). *Tous les hommes dudit royaume sont par la dite Assise tenus les uns as autres . . . et en celle manière que le seignor mette main ou face mettre au cors ou au fié d'aucun d'yaus sans esgard et sans connoissance de court, que tous les autres doivent venir devant le seignor*, etc. (212). The form of their remonstrances is conceived with the noble simplicity of freedom.

139 See *l'Esprit des Loix*, xxviii. In the forty years since its publication, no work has been more read and criticised, and the spirit of inquiry which it has excited is not the least of our obligations to the author.

* *pages 933* [loss of civil rights]

140 For the intelligence of this obscure and obsolete jurisprudence (chs 80–111), I am deeply indebted to the friendship of a learned lord, who, with an accurate and discerning eye, has surveyed the philosophic history of law. By his studies, posterity might be enriched; the merit of the orator and the judge can be *felt* only by his contemporaries. [The reference is to Lord Loughborough (1733–1805).]

141 Louis le Gros, who is considered as the father of this institution in France, did not begin his reign till nine years (AD 1108) after Godfrey of Bouillon (*Assises*, 2, 324). For its origin and effects, see the judicious remarks of Dr Robertson (*History of Charles V*, i, 30–36, 251–65, quarto edition).

142 Every reader conversant with the historians of the crusades, will understand by the *peuple des Suriens*, the Oriental Christians, Melchites, Jacobites, or Nestorians, who had all adopted the use of the Arabic language (v, 151).

143 See the *Assises de Jérusalem* (310–12). These laws were enacted as late as the year 1358, in the kingdom of Cyprus. In the same century, in the reign of Edward I, I understand, from a late publication (of his Book of Account), that the price of a war-horse was not less exorbitant in England.

CHAPTER 59

*Preservation of the Greek empire – numbers, passage, and event,
of the second and third Crusades – St Bernard – reign of Saladin
in Egypt and Syria – his conquest of Jerusalem – naval crusades –
Richard I of England – Pope Innocent III; and the fourth
and fifth Crusades – the emperor Frederic II – Louis IX
of France; and the two last Crusades – expulsion of
the Latins or Franks by the Mamalukes*

In a style less grave than that of history, I should perhaps compare the emperor Alexius[1] to the jackal, who is said to follow the steps, and to devour the leavings, of the lion. Whatever had been his fears and toils in the passage of the first crusade, they were amply recompensed by the subsequent benefits which he derived from the exploits of the Franks. His dexterity and vigilance secured their first conquest of Nicaea; and from this threatening station the Turks were compelled to evacuate the neighbourhood of Constantinople. While the crusaders, with blind valour, advanced into the midland countries of Asia, the crafty Greek improved the favourable occasion when the emirs of the sea-coast were recalled to the standard of the Sultan. The Turks were driven from the isles of Rhodes and Chios: the cities of Ephesus and Smyrna, of Sardes, Philadelphia, and Laodicea, were restored to the empire, which Alexius enlarged from the Hellespont to the banks of the Maeander and the rocky shores of Pamphylia. The churches resumed their splendour; the towns were rebuilt and fortified; and the desert country was peopled with colonies of Christians, who were gently removed from the more distant and dangerous frontier. In these paternal cares, we may forgive Alexius, if he forgot the deliverance of the holy sepulchre; but, by the Latins, he was stigmatised with the foul reproach of treason and desertion. They had sworn fidelity and obedience to his throne; but *he* had promised to assist their enterprise in person, or, at least, with his troops and treasures; his base retreat dissolved their obligations; and the sword, which had been the instrument of their victory, was the pledge and title of their just independence. It does not appear that the emperor attempted to revive his obsolete claims over the kingdom of Jerusalem;[2] but the borders of Cilicia and Syria were more recent in his possession, and more accessible to his arms. The great army of the crusaders was annihilated or dispersed; the principality of Antioch was left without a head, by the surprise and captivity of Bohemond:* his ransom had oppressed him with a heavy debt; and his Norman followers were insufficient to repel the hostilities of the Greeks and Turks. In this distress, Bohemond embraced a magnanimous resolution, of leaving the defence of Antioch to his kinsman, the faithful Tancred, of arming the West against the Byzantine empire, and of executing the design which he inherited from the lessons and example of his father Guiscard. His embarkation was clandestine; and, if we may credit a tale of the Princess Anne,* he passed the hostile sea closely secreted in a coffin.³ But his reception in France was dignified by the public applause and his marriage with the king's daughter; his return was glorious, since the bravest spirits of the age enlisted under his veteran command; and he repassed the Adriatic at the head of five thousand horse and forty thousand foot, assembled from the most remote climates of Europe.⁴ The strength of Durazzo and prudence of Alexius, the progress of famine and approach of winter, eluded his ambitious hopes; and the venal confederates were seduced from his standard. A treaty of peace⁵ suspended the fears of the Greeks; and they were finally delivered by the death of an adversary whom neither oaths could bind nor dangers could appal nor prosperity could satiate. His children succeeded to the principality of Antioch; but the boundaries were strictly defined, the homage was clearly stipulated, and the cities of Tarsus and Malmistra were restored to the Byzantine emperors. Of the coast of Anatolia, they possessed the entire circuit from Trebizond to the Syrian gates. The Seljukian dynasty of Roum⁶ was separated on all sides from the sea and their Musulman brethren; the power of the sultans was shaken by the victories, and even the defeats, of the Franks; and after the loss of Nicaea they removed their throne to Cogni or Iconium, an obscure and inland town above three hundred miles from Constantinople.⁷ Instead of trembling for their capital, the Comnenian princes waged an offensive war against the Turks, and the first crusade prevented the fall of the declining empire.

In the twelfth century, three great emigrations marched by land from the West to the relief of Palestine. The soldiers and pilgrims of Lombardy, France, and Germany were excited by the example and success of the first crusade.⁸ Forty-eight years after the deliverance of the holy sepulchre, the emperor and the French king, Conrad the Third and Louis the Seventh, undertook the second crusade to support the falling fortunes of the Latins.⁹ A grand division of the third crusade was led by the emperor Frederic Barbarossa,¹⁰ who sympathised with his brothers of France and England in the common loss of Jerusalem. These three expeditions may be compared in their resemblance of the greatness of numbers, their passage through the Greek empire, and the nature and event of their Turkish warfare; and a brief parallel may save the repetition of a tedious narrative. However splendid it may seem, a regular story of the crusades would exhibit a perpetual return of the same causes and effects; and the frequent attempts for the defence and recovery of the Holy Land would appear so many faint and unsuccessful copies of the original.

I. Of the swarms that so closely trod in the footsteps of the first pilgrims, the chiefs were equal in rank, though unequal in fame and merit, to Godfrey of Bouillon and his fellow-adventurers. At their head were displayed the banners of the dukes of Burgundy, Bavaria, and Aquitain: the first a descendant of Hugh Capet, the second a father of the Brunswick line; the archbishop of Milan, a temporal prince, transported, for the benefit of the Turks, the treasures and ornaments of his church and palace; and the veteran crusaders, Hugh the Great and Stephen of Chartres, returned to consummate their unfinished vow. The huge and disorderly bodies of their followers moved forwards in two columns; and, if the first consisted of two hundred and sixty thousand persons, the second might possibly amount to sixty thousand horse and one hundred thousand foot.[11] The armies of the second crusade might have claimed the conquest of Asia: the nobles of France and Germany were animated by the presence of their sovereigns; and both the rank and personal characters of Conrad and Louis gave a dignity to their cause and a discipline to their force, which might be vainly expected from the feudatory chiefs. The cavalry of the emperor, and that of the king, was each composed of seventy thousand knights and their immediate attendants in the field,[12] and, if the light-armed troops, the peasant infantry, the women and children, the priests and monks, be rigorously excluded, the full account will scarcely be satisfied with four hundred thousand souls. The West, from Rome to Britain, was called into action; the kings of Poland and Bohemia obeyed the summons of Conrad; and it is affirmed by the Greeks and Latins that, in the passage of a strait or river, the Byzantine agents, after a tale of nine hundred thousand, desisted from the endless and formidable computation.[13] In the third crusade, as the French and English preferred the navigation of the Mediterranean, the host of Frederic Barbarossa was less numerous. Fifteen thousand knights, and as many squires, were the flower of the German chivalry; sixty thousand horse and one hundred thousand foot were mustered by the emperor in the plains of Hungary; and after such repetitions we shall no longer be startled at the six hundred thousand pilgrims which credulity has ascribed to this last emigration.[14] Such extravagant reckonings prove only the astonishment of contemporaries; but their astonishment most strongly bears testimony to the existence of an enormous though indefinite multitude. The Greeks might applaud their superior knowledge of the arts and stratagems of war, but they confessed the strength and courage of the French cavalry and the infantry of the Germans;[15] and the strangers are described as an iron race, of gigantic stature, who darted fire from their eyes, and spilt blood like water on the ground. Under the banners of Conrad, a troop of females rode in the attitude and armour of men; and the chief of these Amazons, from her gilt spurs and buskins, obtained the epithet of the Golden-footed Dame.

II. The numbers and character of the strangers was an object of terror to the effeminate Greeks, and the sentiment of fear is nearly allied to that of hatred. This aversion was suspended or softened by the apprehension of the Turkish power; and the invectives of the Latins will not bias our more candid belief that the emperor Alexius dissembled their insolence, eluded their hostilities, counselled their rashness, and opened to their ardour the road of pilgrimage and conquest. But, when the Turks had been driven from Nicaea and the sea-coast, when the Byzantine princes no longer dreaded the distant sultans of Cogni, they felt with purer indignation the free and frequent passage of the western barbarians, who violated the majesty, and endangered the safety, of the empire. The second and third crusades were undertaken under the reign of Manuel Comnenus and Isaac Angelus. Of the former, the passions were always impetuous and often malevolent; and the natural union of a cowardly and a mischievous temper was exemplified in the latter, who, without merit or mercy, could punish a tyrant and occupy his throne. It was secretly, and perhaps tacitly, resolved by the prince and people to destroy, or at least to discourage, the pilgrims by every species of injury and oppression; and their want of prudence and discipline continually afforded the pretence or the opportunity. The Western monarchs had stipulated a safe passage and fair market in the country of their Christian brethren; the treaty had been ratified by oaths and hostages; and the poorest soldier of Frederic's army was furnished with three marks of silver to defray his expenses on the road. But every engagement was violated by treachery and injustice; and the complaints of the Latins are attested by the honest confession of a Greek historian, who has dared to prefer truth to his country.[16] Instead of an hospitable reception, the gates of the cities, both in Europe and Asia, were closely barred against the crusaders; and the scanty pittance of food was let down in baskets from the walls. Experience or foresight might excuse this timid jealousy; but the common duties of humanity prohibited the mixture of chalk, or other poisonous ingredients, in the bread; and, should Manuel be acquitted of any foul connivance, he is guilty of coining base money for the purpose of trading with the pilgrims. In every step of their march they were stopped or misled: the governors had private orders to fortify the passes, and break down the bridges against them; the stragglers were pillaged and murdered; the soldiers and horses were pierced in the woods by arrows from an invisible hand; the sick were burnt in their beds; and the dead bodies were hung on gibbets along the highways. These injuries exasperated the champions of the cross, who were not endowed with evangelical patience; and the Byzantine princes, who had provoked the unequal conflict, promoted the embarkation and march of these formidable guests. On the verge of the Turkish frontiers, Barbarossa spared the guilty Philadelphia,[17] rewarded the hospitable Laodicea, and deplored the hard necessity that had stained his sword with any drops of Christian blood. In their intercourse with the monarchs of

Germany and France, the pride of the Greeks was exposed to an anxious trial. They might boast that on the first interview the seat of Louis was a low stool beside the throne of Manuel;[18] but no sooner had the French king transported his army beyond the Bosphorus than he refused the offer of a second conference, unless his brother would meet him on equal terms, either on the sea or land. With Conrad and Frederic the ceremonial was still nicer and more difficult: like the successors of Constantine, they styled themselves Emperors of the Romans,[19] and firmly maintained the purity of their title and dignity. The first of these representatives of Charlemagne would only converse with Manuel on horseback in the open field; the second, by passing the Hellespont rather than the Bosphorus, declined the view of Constantinople and its sovereign. An emperor who had been crowned at Rome was reduced in the Greek epistles to the humble appellation of *Rex*, or prince of the Alemanni;* and the vain and feeble Angelus affected to be ignorant of the name of one of the greatest men and monarchs of the age. While they viewed with hatred and suspicion the Latin pilgrims, the Greek emperors maintained a strict, though secret, alliance with the Turks and Saracens. Isaac Angelus complained that by his friendship for the great Saladin he had incurred the enmity of the Franks; and a mosque was founded at Constantinople for the public exercise of the religion of Mahomet.[20]

III. The swarms that followed the first crusade were destroyed in Anatolia by famine, pestilence, and the Turkish arrows: and the princes only escaped with some squadrons of horse to accomplish their lamentable pilgrimage. A just opinion may be formed of their knowledge and humanity: of their knowledge, from the design of subduing Persia and Chorasan in their way to Jerusalem; of their humanity, from the massacre of the Christian people, a friendly city, who came out to meet them with palms and crosses in their hands. The arms of Conrad and Louis were less cruel and imprudent; but the event of the second crusade was still more ruinous to Christendom; and the Greek Manuel is accused by his own subjects of giving seasonable intelligence to the sultan, and treacherous guides to the Latin princes. Instead of crushing the common foe, by a double attack at the same time but on different sides, the Germans were urged by emulation, and the French were retarded by jealousy. Louis had scarcely passed the Bosphorus when he was met by the returning emperor, who had lost the greatest part of his army in glorious, but unsuccessful, action on the banks of the Maeander. The contrast of the pomp of his rival hastened the retreat of Conrad: the desertion of his independent vassals reduced him to his hereditary troops; and he borrowed some Greek vessels to execute by sea the pilgrimage of Palestine. Without studying the lessons of experience or the nature of war, the king of France advanced through the same country to a similar fate. The vanguard, which bore the royal banner and the oriflamme of St Denys,[21] had doubled their march with rash and inconsiderate speed; and the rear, which the king commanded in person, no longer found their companions in the evening camp. In darkness and disorder, they were encompassed, assaulted, and overwhelmed by the innumerable host of Turks, who, in the art of war, were superior to the Christians of the twelfth century. Louis, who climbed a tree in the general discomfiture, was saved by his own valour and the ignorance of his adversaries; and with the dawn of day he escaped alive, but almost alone, to the camp of the vanguard. But, instead of pursuing his expedition by land, he was rejoiced to shelter the relics of his army in the friendly seaport of Satalia. From thence he embarked for Antioch; but so penurious was the supply of Greek vessels that they could only afford room for his knights and nobles; and the plebeian crowd of infantry was left to perish at the foot of the Pamphylian hills. The emperor and the king embraced and wept at Jerusalem; their martial trains, the remnant of mighty armies, were joined to the Christian powers of Syria, and a fruitless siege of Damascus was the final effort of the second crusade. Conrad and Louis embarked for Europe with the personal fame of piety and courage; but the Orientals had braved these potent monarchs of the Franks, with whose names and military forces they had been so often threatened.[22] Perhaps they had still more to fear from the veteran genius of Frederic the First, who in his youth had served in Asia under his uncle Conrad. Forty campaigns in Germany and Italy had taught Barbarossa to command; and his soldiers, even the princes of the empire, were accustomed under his reign to obey. As soon as he lost sight of Philadelphia and Laodicea, the last cities of the Greek frontier, he plunged into the salt and barren desert, a land (says the historian) of horror and tribulation.[23] During twenty days, every step of his fainting and sickly march was besieged by the innumerable hordes of Turkmans,[24] whose numbers and fury seemed after each defeat to multiply and inflame. The emperor continued to struggle and to suffer; and such was the measure of his calamities that, when he reached the gates of Iconium, no more than one thousand knights were able to serve on horseback. By a sudden and resolute assault, he defeated the guards, and stormed the capital, of the sultan,[25] who humbly sued for pardon and peace. The road was now open, and Frederic advanced in a career of triumph, till he was unfortunately drowned in a petty torrent of Cilicia.[26] The remainder of his Germans was consumed by sickness and desertion, and the emperor's son expired with the greatest part of his Swabian vassals at the siege of Acre. Among the Latin heroes, Godfrey of Bouillon and Frederic Barbarossa alone could achieve the passage of the Lesser Asia; yet even their success was a warning, and in the last and most experienced ages of the crusades every nation preferred the sea to the toils and perils of an inland expedition.[27]

The enthusiasm of the first crusade is a natural and simple event, while hope was fresh, danger untried, and enterprise congenial to the spirit of the times. But the obstinate perseverance of Europe may indeed excite our pity and admiration; that no instruction should have been drawn from constant and adverse experience; that the same confidence should have repeatedly grown from the same failures; that six succeeding generations should have rushed headlong down the precipice that was open before them; and that men of every condition should have staked their public and private fortunes on the desperate adventure of possessing or recovering a tombstone two thousand miles from their country. In a period of two centuries after the council of Clermont, each spring and summer produced a new emigration of pilgrim warriors for the defence of the Holy Land; but the seven great armaments or crusades were excited by some impending or recent calamity: the nations were moved by the authority of their pontiffs, and the example of their kings: their zeal was kindled, and their reason was silenced, by the voice of their holy orators; and among these Bernard,[28] the monk or the saint, may claim the most honourable place. About eight years before the first conquest of Jerusalem, he was born of a noble family in Burgundy; at the age of three and twenty, he buried himself in the monastery of Citeaux, then in the primitive fervour of the institution; at the end of two years he led forth her third colony, or daughter, to the valley of Clairvaux[29] in Champagne; and was content, till the hour of his death, with the humble station of abbot of his own community. A philosophic age has abolished, with too liberal and indiscriminate disdain, the honours of these spiritual heroes. The meanest amongst them are distinguished by some energies of the mind; they were at least superior to their votaries and disciples, and in the race of superstition they attained the prize for which such numbers contended. In speech, in writing, in action, Bernard stood high above his rivals and contemporaries; his compositions are not devoid of wit and eloquence; and he seems to have preserved as much reason and humanity as may be reconciled with the character of a saint. In a secular life he would have shared the seventh part of a private inheritance; by a vow of poverty and penance, by closing his eyes against the visible world,[30] by the refusal of all ecclesiastical dignities, the abbot of Clairvaux became the oracle of Europe and the founder of one hundred and sixty convents. Princes and pontiffs trembled at the freedom of his apostolical censure; France, England, and Milan consulted and obeyed his judgment in a schism of the church; the debt was repaid by the gratitude of Innocent the Second; and his successor Eugenius the Third was the friend and disciple of the holy Bernard. It was in the proclamation of the second crusade that he shone as the missionary and prophet of God, who called the nations to the defence of his holy sepulchre.[31] At the parliament of Vézelay he spoke before the king; and Louis the Seventh, with his nobles, received their crosses from his hand. The abbot of Clairvaux then marched to the less easy conquest of the emperor Conrad: a phlegmatic people, ignorant of his language, was transported by the pathetic vehemence of his tone and gestures; and his progress from Constance to Cologne was the triumph of eloquence and zeal. Bernard applauds his own success in the depopulation of Europe; affirms that cities and castles were emptied of their inhabitants; and computes that only one man was left behind for the consolation of seven widows.[32] The blind fanatics were desirous of electing him for their general; but the example of the hermit Peter was before his eyes; and, while he assured the crusaders of the divine favour, he prudently declined a military command, in which failure and victory would have been almost equally disgraceful to his character.[33] Yet, after the calamitous event, the abbot of Clairvaux was loudly accused as a false prophet, the author of the public and private mourning; his enemies exulted, his friends blushed, and his apology was slow and unsatisfactory. He justifies his obedience to the commands of the pope; expatiates on the mysterious ways of Providence; imputes the misfortunes of the pilgrims to their own sins; and modestly insinuates that his mission had been approved by signs and wonders.[34] Had the fact been certain, the argument would be decisive; and his faithful disciples, who enumerate twenty or thirty miracles in a day, appeal to the public assemblies of France and Germany, in which they were performed.[35] At the present hour such prodigies will not obtain credit beyond the precincts of Clairvaux; but in the preternatural cures of the blind, the lame, or the sick, who were presented to the man of God, it is impossible for us to ascertain the separate shares of accident, of fancy, of imposture, and of fiction.

Omnipotence itself cannot escape the murmurs of its discordant votaries; since the same dispensation which was applauded as a deliverance in Europe was deplored, and perhaps arraigned, as a calamity in Asia. After the loss of Jerusalem the Syrian fugitives diffused their consternation and sorrow: Bagdad mourned in the dust; the Cadhi Zeineddin of Damascus tore his beard in the caliph's presence; and the whole divan shed tears at his melancholy tale.[36] But the commanders of the faithful could only weep; they were themselves captives in the hands of the Turks; some temporal power was restored to the last age of the Abbassides; but their humble ambition was confined to Bagdad and the adjacent province. Their tyrants, the Seljukian sultans, had followed the common law of the Asiatic dynasties, the unceasing round of valour, greatness, discord, degeneracy, and decay: their spirit and power were unequal to the defence of religion; and, in his distant realm of Persia, the Christians were strangers to the name and the arms of Sangiar, the last hero of his race.[37] While the sultans were involved in the silken web of the harem, the pious task was undertaken by their slaves, the Atabeks,[38] a Turkish name, which, like the Byzantine patricians, may be translated by Father of the Prince. Ascansar, a valiant Turk, had been the favourite of Malek Shah, from whom he received the privilege of standing on the right hand of the throne; but, in the civil wars that ensued on the monarch's death, he lost his head and the government of Aleppo. His domestic emirs persevered in their attachment to his son Zenghi, who proved his first arms against the Franks in the defeat of Antioch; thirty campaigns in the service of the caliph and sultan established his military fame; and he was invested with the command of Mosul, as the only champion that could avenge the cause of the prophet. The public hope was not disappointed: after a siege of twenty-five days, he stormed the city of Edessa, and recovered from the Franks their conquests beyond the Euphrates:[39] the martial tribes of Curdistan were subdued by the independent sovereign of Mosul and Aleppo: his soldiers were taught to behold the camp as their only country; they trusted to his liberality for their rewards; and their absent families were protected by the vigilance of Zenghi. At the head of these veterans, his son Noureddin gradually united the Mahometan powers; added the kingdom of Damascus to that of Aleppo, and waged a long and successful war against the Christians of Syria: he spread his ample reign from the Tigris to the Nile, and the Abbassides rewarded their faithful servant with all the titles and prerogatives of royalty. The Latins themselves were compelled to own the wisdom and courage, and even the justice and piety, of this implacable adversary.[40] In his life and government, the holy warrior revived the zeal and simplicity of the first caliphs. Gold and silk were banished from his palace; the use of wine from his dominions; the public revenue was scrupulously applied to the public service; and the frugal household of Noureddin was maintained from the legitimate share of the spoil, which he vested in the purchase of a private estate. His favourite sultana sighed for some female object of expense: 'Alas,' replied the king, 'I fear God, and am no more than the treasurer of the Moslems. Their property I cannot alienate, but I still possess three shops in the city of Hems: these you may take, and these alone can I bestow.' His chamber of justice was the terror of the great and the refuge of the poor. Some years after the sultan's death, an oppressed subject called aloud in the streets of Damascus, 'O Noureddin, Noureddin, where art thou now? Arise, arise, to pity and protect us!' A tumult was apprehended, and a living tyrant blushed and trembled at the name of a departed monarch.

By the arms of the Turks and Franks, the Fatimites had been deprived of Syria. In Egypt the decay of their character and influence was still more essential. Yet they were still revered as the descendants and successors of the prophet; they maintained their visible state in the palace of Cairo; and their person was seldom violated by the profane eyes of subjects or strangers. The Latin ambassadors[41] have described their own introduction through a series of gloomy passages, and glittering porticoes; the scene was enlivened by the warbling of birds and the murmur of fountains; it was enriched by a display of rich furniture and rare animals; of the Imperial treasures, something was shown, and much was supposed; and the long order of unfolding doors was guarded by black soldiers and domestic eunuchs. The sanctuary of the presence-chamber was veiled with a curtain; and the vizir, who conducted the ambassadors, laid aside his scymetar, and prostrated himself three times on the ground; the veil was then removed; and they beheld the commander of the faithful, who signified his pleasure to the first slave of the throne. But this slave was his master; the vizirs or sultans had usurped the supreme administration of Egypt; the claims of the rival candidates were decided by arms; and the name of the most worthy, of the strongest, was inserted in the royal patent of command. The factions of Dargham and Shawer alternately expelled each other from the capital and country; and the weaker side implored the dangerous protection of the Sultan of Damascus, or the king of Jerusalem, the perpetual enemies of the sect and monarchy of the Fatimites. By his arms and religion the Turk was most formidable; but the Frank, in an easy direct march, could advance from Gaza to the Nile; while the intermediate situation of his realm compelled the troops of Noureddin to wheel round the skirts of Arabia, a long and painful circuit, which exposed them to thirst, fatigue, and the burning winds of the desert. The secret zeal and ambition of the Turkish prince aspired to reign in Egypt under the name of the Abbassides; but the restoration of the suppliant Shawer was the ostensible motive of the first expedition; and the success was entrusted to the emir Shiracouh, a valiant and veteran commander. Dargham was oppressed and slain; but the ingratitude, the jealousy, the just apprehensions, of his more fortunate rival, soon provoked him to invite the king of Jerusalem to deliver Egypt from his insolent benefactors. To this union, the forces of Shiracouh were unequal; he relinquished the premature conquest; and the evacuation of Belbeis, or Pelusium, was the condition of his safe retreat. As the Turks defiled before the enemy, and their general closed the rear, with a vigilant eye, and a battle-axe in his hand, a Frank presumed to ask him if he were not afraid of an attack? 'It is doubtless in your power to begin the attack,' replied the intrepid emir, 'but rest assured that not one of my soldiers will go to paradise till he has sent an infidel to hell.' His report of the riches of the land, the effeminacy of the natives, and the disorders of the government, revived the hopes of Noureddin; the caliph of Bagdad applauded the pious design; and Shiracouh descended into Egypt a second time with twelve thousand Turks and eleven thousand Arabs. Yet his forces were still inferior to the confederate armies of the Franks and Saracens; and I can discern an unusual degree of military art in his passage of the Nile, his retreat into Thebais, his masterly evolutions in the battle of Babain, the surprise of Alexandria, and his marches and countermarches in the flats and valley of Egypt, from the tropic to the sea. His conduct was seconded by the courage of his troops, and on the eve of action a Mamaluke[42] exclaimed, 'If we cannot wrest Egypt from the Christian dogs, why do we not renounce the honours and rewards of the sultan, and retire to labour with the peasants, or to spin with the females of the harem?' Yet after all his efforts in the field,[43] after the obstinate defence of Alexandria[44] by his nephew Saladin, an honourable capitulation and retreat concluded the second enterprise of Shiracouh; and Noureddin reserved his abilities for a third and more propitious occasion. It was soon offered by the ambition and avarice of Amalric, or Amaury, king of Jerusalem,* who had imbibed the pernicious maxim that no faith should be kept with the enemies of God. A religious warrior, the great master of the hospital, encouraged him to proceed; the emperor of Constantinople either gave, or promised, a fleet to act with the armies of Syria; and the perfidious Christian, unsatisfied with spoil and subsidy, aspired to the conquest of Egypt. In this emergency the Moslems turned their eyes towards the sultan of Damascus; the vizir, whom danger encompassed on all sides, yielded to their unanimous wishes, and Noureddin seemed to be tempted by the fair offer of one third of the revenue of the kingdom. The Franks were already at the gates of Cairo; but the suburbs, the old city, were burnt on their approach; they were deceived by an insidious negotiation; and their vessels were unable to surmount the barriers of the Nile. They prudently declined a contest with the Turks in the midst of an hostile country; and Amaury retired into Palestine, with the shame and reproach that always adhere to unsuccessful injustice. After this deliverance, Shiracouh was invested with a robe of honour, which he soon stained with the blood of the unfortunate Shawer. For a while, the Turkish emirs condescended to hold the office of vizir; but this foreign conquest precipitated the fall of the Fatimites themselves; and the bloodless change was accomplished by a message and a word. The caliphs had been degraded by their own weakness and the tyranny of the vizirs: their subjects blushed, when the descendant and successor of the prophet presented his naked hand to the rude grip of a Latin ambassador; they wept when he sent the hair of his women, a sad emblem of their grief and terror, to excite the pity of the sultan of Damascus. By the command of Noureddin, and the sentence of the doctors,† the holy names of Abubeker, Omar, and Othman were solemnly restored; the caliph Mosthadi, of Bagdad, was acknowledged in the public prayers as the true commander of the faithful; and the green livery of the sons of Ali was exchanged for the black colour of the Abbassides. The last of his race, the caliph Adhed, who survived only ten days, expired in happy ignorance of his fate; his treasures secured the loyalty of the soldiers, and silenced the murmurs of the sectaries; and in all subsequent revolutions Egypt has never departed from the orthodox tradition of the Moslems.[45]

The hilly country beyond the Tigris is occupied by the pastoral tribes of the Curds;[46] a people hardy, strong, savage, impatient of the yoke, addicted to rapine, and tenacious of the government of their national chiefs. The resemblance of name, situation, and manners seem to identify them with the Carduchians of the Greeks;[47] and they still defend against the Ottoman Porte the antique freedom which they asserted against the successors of Cyrus.‡ Poverty and ambition prompted them to embrace the profession of mercenary soldiers: the service of his father and uncle prepared the reign of the great Saladin;[48] and the son of Job or Ayub, a simple Curd, magnanimously smiled at his pedigree, which flattery deduced from the Arabian caliphs.[49] So unconscious was Noureddin of the impending ruin of his house that he constrained the reluctant youth to follow his uncle Shiracouh into Egypt; his military character was established by the defence of Alexandria; and, if we may believe the Latins, he solicited and obtained from the Christian general the *profane* honours of knighthood.[50] On the death of Shiracouh, the office of grand vizir was bestowed on Saladin, as the youngest and least powerful of the emirs; but with the advice of his father, whom he invited to Cairo, his genius obtained the ascendant over his equals, and attached the army to his person and interest. While Noureddin lived, these ambitious Curds were the most humble of his slaves; and the indiscreet murmurs of the divan were silenced by the prudent Ayub, who loudly protested that at the command of the sultan he himself would lead his son in chains to the foot of the throne. 'Such language,' he added in private, 'was prudent and proper in an assembly of your rivals; but we are now above fear and obedience; and the threats of Noureddin shall not extort the tribute of a sugar-cane.' His seasonable death relieved them from the odious and doubtful conflict: his son, a minor of eleven years of age, was left for a while to the emirs of Damascus; and the new lord of Egypt was decorated by the caliph with every title[51] that could sanctify his usurpation in the eyes of the people. Nor was Saladin long content with the possession of Egypt; he despoiled the Christians of Jerusalem, and the Atabeks of Damascus, Aleppo, and Diarbekir; Mecca and Medina acknowledged him for their temporal protector; his brother subdued the distant regions of Yemen, or the Happy Arabia; and at the hour of his death his empire was spread from the African Tripoli to the Tigris, and from the Indian ocean to the mountains of Armenia. In the judgment of his character, the reproaches of treason and ingratitude strike forcibly on *our* minds, impressed as they are with the principle and experience of law and loyalty. But his ambition may in some measure be excused by the revolutions of Asia,[52] which had erased every notion of legitimate succession; by the recent example of the Atabeks themselves; by his reverence to the son of his benefactor; his humane and generous behaviour to the collateral branches; by *their* incapacity and *his* merits; by the approbation of the caliph, the sole source of all legitimate power; and, above all, by the wishes and interest of the people, whose happiness is the first object of government. In *his* virtues, and in those of his patron, they admired the singular union of the hero and the saint; for both Noureddin and Saladin are ranked among the Mahometan saints; and the constant meditation of the holy wars appears to have shed a serious and sober colour over their lives and actions. The youth of the latter[53] was addicted to wine and women; but his aspiring spirit soon renounced the temptations of pleasure for the graver follies of fame and dominion. The garment of Saladin was of coarse woollen; water was his only drink; and, while he emulated the temperance, he surpassed the chastity, of his Arabian prophet. Both in faith and practice he was a rigid Musulman; he ever deplored that the defence of religion had not allowed him to accomplish the pilgrimage of Mecca; but at the stated hours, five times each day, the sultan devoutly prayed with his brethren; the involuntary omission of fasting was scrupulously repaid; and his perusal of the Koran on horseback, between the approaching armies, may be quoted as a proof, however ostentatious, of piety and courage.[54] The superstitious doctrine of the sect of Shafei was the only study that he deigned to encourage; the poets were safe in his contempt; but all profane science was the object of his aversion; and a philosopher, who had vented some speculative novelties, was seized and strangled by the command of the royal saint. The justice of his divan was accessible to the meanest suppliant against himself and his ministers; and it was only for a kingdom that Saladin would deviate from the rule of equity. While the descendants of Seljuk and Zenghi held his stirrup, and smoothed his garments, he was affable and patient with the meanest of his servants. So boundless was his liberality, that he distributed twelve thousand horses at the siege of Acre; and, at the time of his death, no more than forty-seven drams of silver, and one piece of gold coin, were found in the treasury; yet in a martial reign, the tributes* were diminished, and the wealthy citizens enjoyed, without fear or danger, the fruits of their industry. Egypt, Syria, and Arabia, were adorned by the royal foundations of hospitals, colleges, and mosques; and Cairo was fortified with a wall and citadel; but his works were consecrated to public use;[55] nor did the sultan indulge himself in a garden or palace of private luxury. In a fanatic age, himself a fanatic, the genuine virtues of Saladin commanded the esteem of the Christians; the emperor of Germany gloried in his friendship;[56] the Greek emperor solicited his alliance;[57] and the conquest of Jerusalem diffused, and perhaps magnified, his fame both in the East and West.

During its short existence, the kingdom of Jerusalem[58] was supported by the discord of the Turks and Saracens; and both the Fatimite caliphs and the sultans of Damascus were tempted to sacrifice the cause of their religion to the meaner considerations of private and present advantage. But the powers of Egypt, Syria, and Arabia were now united by an hero, whom nature and fortune had armed against the Christians. All without now bore the most threatening aspect; and all was feeble and hollow in the internal state of Jerusalem. After the two first Baldwins, the brother and cousin of Godfrey of Bouillon, the sceptre devolved by female succession to Melisenda, daughter of the second Baldwin, and her husband Fulk, count of Anjou, the father, by a former marriage, of our English Plantagenets. Their two sons, Baldwin the Third, and Amaury, waged a strenuous and not unsuccessful war against the infidels; but the son of Amaury, Baldwin the Fourth, was deprived by the leprosy, a gift of the crusades, of the faculties both of mind and body. His sister, Sybilla, the mother of Baldwin the Fifth, was his natural heiress. After the suspicious death of her child, she crowned her second husband, Guy of Lusignan, a prince of a handsome person, but of such base renown that his brother Jeffrey was heard to exclaim, 'Since they have made *him* a king, surely they would have made *me* a god!' The choice was generally blamed; and the most powerful vassal, Raymond, count of Tripoli, who had been excluded from the succession and regency, entertained an implacable hatred against the king, and exposed his honour and conscience to the temptations of the sultan. Such were the guardians of the holy city: a leper, a child, a woman, a coward, and a traitor; yet its fate was delayed twelve years by some supplies from Europe, by the valour of the military orders, and by the distant or domestic avocations* of their great enemy. At length, on every side the sinking state was encircled and pressed by an hostile line; and the truce was violated by the Franks, whose existence it protected. A soldier of fortune, Reginald of Chatillon, had seized a fortress on the edge of the desert, from whence he pillaged the caravans, insulted Mahomet, and threatened the cities of Mecca and Medina. Saladin condescended to complain; rejoiced in the denial of justice; and, at the head of fourscore thousand horse and foot, invaded the Holy Land. The choice of Tiberias for his first siege was suggested by the count of Tripoli, to whom it belonged; and the king of Jerusalem was persuaded to drain his garrisons, and to arm his people, for the relief of that important place.[59] By the advice of the perfidious Raymond, the Christians were betrayed into a camp destitute of water; he fled on the first onset, with the curses of both nations;[60] Lusignan was overthrown, with the loss of thirty thousand men; and the wood of the true cross, a dire misfortune! was left in the power of the infidels. The royal captive was conducted to the tent of Saladin; and, as he fainted with thirst and terror, the generous victor presented him with a cup of sherbet cooled in snow, without suffering his companion, Reginald of Chatillon, to partake of this pledge of hospitality and pardon. 'The person and dignity of a king,' said the sultan, 'are sacred; but this impious robber must instantly acknowledge the prophet, whom he has blasphemed, or meet the death which he has so often deserved.' On the proud or conscientious refusal of the Christian warrior, Saladin struck him on the head with his scymetar, and Reginald was dispatched by the guards.[61] The trembling Lusignan was sent to Damascus to an honourable prison, and speedy ransom; but the victory was stained by the execution of two hundred and thirty knights of the hospital, the intrepid champions and martyrs of their faith. The kingdom was left without a head; and of the two grand masters of the military orders, the one was slain, and the other was made a prisoner. From all the cities, both of the sea-coast and the inland country, the garrisons had been drawn away for this fatal field. Tyre and Tripoli alone could escape the rapid inroad of

Saladin; and three months after the battle of Tiberias he appeared in arms before the gates of Jerusalem.[62]

He might expect that the siege of a city so venerable on earth and in heaven, so interesting to Europe and Asia, would rekindle the last sparks of enthusiasm; and that, of sixty thousand Christians, every man would be a soldier, and every soldier a candidate for martyrdom. But queen Sybilla trembled for herself and her captive husband; and the barons and knights, who had escaped from the sword and the chains of the Turks, displayed the same factious and selfish spirit in the public ruin. The most numerous portion of the inhabitants were composed of the Greek and Oriental Christians, whom experience had taught to prefer the Mahometan before the Latin yoke;[63] and the holy sepulchre attracted a base and needy crowd, without arms or courage, who subsisted only on the charity of the pilgrims. Some feeble and hasty efforts were made for the defence of Jerusalem; but in the space of fourteen days a victorious army drove back the sallies of the besieged, planted their engines, opened the wall to the breadth of fifteen cubits, applied their scaling ladders, and erected on the breach twelve banners of the prophet and the sultan. It was in vain that a barefoot procession of the queen, the women, and the monks implored the Son of God to save his tomb and his inheritance from impious violation. Their sole hope was in the mercy of the conqueror, and to their first suppliant deputation that mercy was sternly denied. 'He had sworn to avenge the patience and long-suffering of the Moslems; the hour of forgiveness was elapsed, and the moment was now arrived to expiate in blood, the innocent blood which had been spilt by Godfrey and the first crusaders.' But a desperate and successful struggle of the Franks admonished the sultan that his triumph was not yet secure; he listened with reverence to a solemn adjuration in the name of the common Father of mankind; and a sentiment of human sympathy mollified the rigour of fanaticism and conquest. He consented to accept the city, and to spare the inhabitants. The Greek and Oriental Christians were permitted to live under his dominion; but it was stipulated, that in forty days all the Franks and Latins should evacuate Jerusalem, and be safely conducted to the seaports of Syria and Egypt; that ten pieces of gold should be paid for each man, five for each woman, and one for every child; and that those who were unable to purchase their freedom should be detained in perpetual slavery. Of some writers it is a favourite and invidious theme to compare the humanity of Saladin with the massacre of the first crusade. The difference would be merely personal; but we should not forget that the Christians had offered to capitulate, and that the Mahometans of Jerusalem sustained the last extremities of an assault and storm. Justice is indeed due to the fidelity with which the Turkish conqueror fulfilled the conditions of the treaty; and he may be deservedly praised for the glance of pity which he cast on the misery of the vanquished. Instead of a rigorous exaction of his debt, he accepted a sum of thirty thousand byzants,* for the ransom of seven thousand poor; two or three thousand more were dismissed by his gratuitous clemency; and the number of slaves was reduced to eleven or fourteen thousand persons. In his interview with the queen, his words, and even his tears, suggested the kindest consolations; his liberal alms were distributed among those who had been made orphans or widows by the fortune of war; and, while the knights of the hospital were in arms against him, he allowed their more pious brethren to continue, during the term of a year, the care and service of the sick. In these acts of mercy, the virtue of Saladin deserves our admiration and love: he was above the necessity of dissimulation; and his stern fanaticism would have prompted him to dissemble, rather than to affect, this profane compassion for the enemies of the Koran. After Jerusalem had been delivered from the presence of the strangers, the sultan made his triumphant entry, his banners waving in the wind, and to the harmony of martial music. The great mosque of Omar, which had been converted into a church, was again consecrated to one God and his prophet Mahomet; the walls and pavement were purified with rose-water; and a pulpit, the labour of Noureddin, was erected in the sanctuary. But, when the golden cross that glittered on the dome was cast down, and dragged through the streets, the Christians of every sect uttered a lamentable groan, which was answered by the joyful shouts of the Moslems. In four ivory chests the patriarch had collected the crosses, the images, the vases, and the relics of the holy place: they were seized by the conqueror, who was desirous of presenting the caliph with the trophies of Christian idolatry. He was persuaded, however, to entrust them to the patriarch and prince of Antioch; and the pious pledge was redeemed by Richard of England, at the expense of fifty-two thousand byzants of gold.[64]

The nations might fear and hope the immediate and final expulsion of the Latins from Syria; which was yet delayed above a century after the death of Saladin.[65] In the career of victory, he was first checked by the resistance of Tyre; the troops and garrisons, which had capitulated, were imprudently conducted to the same port: their numbers were adequate to the defence of the place; and the arrival of Conrad of Montferrat inspired the disorderly crowd with confidence and union. His father, a venerable pilgrim, had been made prisoner in the battle of Tiberias; but that disaster was unknown in Italy and Greece, when the son was urged by ambition and piety to visit the inheritance of his royal nephew, the infant Baldwin. The view of the Turkish banners warned him from the hostile coast of Jaffa; and Conrad was unanimously hailed as the prince and champion of Tyre, which was already besieged by the conqueror of Jerusalem. The firmness of his zeal, and perhaps his knowledge of a generous foe, enabled him to brave the threats of the sultan, and to declare that, should his aged parent be exposed before the walls, he himself would discharge the first arrow, and glory in his descent from a Christian martyr.[66] The Egyptian fleet was allowed to enter the harbour of Tyre; but the chain was suddenly drawn, and five galleys were either sunk or taken; a thousand Turks were slain in a sally; and Saladin, after burning his engines, concluded a glorious campaign by a disgraceful retreat to Damascus. He was soon assailed by a more formidable tempest. The pathetic narratives, and even the pictures, that represented in lively colours the servitude and profanation of Jerusalem, awakened the torpid sensibility of Europe; the emperor, Frederic Barbarossa, and the kings of France and England assumed the cross; and the tardy magnitude of their armaments was anticipated by the maritime states of the Mediterranean and the Ocean. The skilful and provident Italians first embarked in the ships of Genoa, Pisa, and Venice. They were speedily followed by the most eager pilgrims of France, Normandy, and the Western Isles. The powerful succour of Flanders, Frise, and Denmark filled near an hundred vessels; and the northern warriors were distinguished in the field by a lofty stature and a ponderous battle-axe.[67] Their increasing multitudes could no longer be confined within the walls of Tyre, or remain obedient to the voice of Conrad. They pitied the misfortunes, and revered the dignity, of Lusignan, who was released from prison, perhaps to divide the army of the Franks. He proposed the recovery of Ptolemais, or Acre, thirty miles to the south of Tyre; and the place was first invested by two thousand horse and thirty thousand foot under his nominal command. I shall not expatiate on the story of this memorable siege, which lasted near two years, and consumed, in a narrow space, the forces of Europe and Asia. Never did the flame of enthusiasm burn with fiercer and more destructive rage, nor could the true believers, a common appellation, who consecrated their own martyrs, refuse some applause to the mistaken zeal and courage of their adversaries. At the sound of the holy trumpet, the Moslems of Egypt, Syria, Arabia, and the Oriental provinces assembled under the servant of the prophet:[68] his camp was pitched and removed within a few miles of Acre; and he laboured, night and day, for the relief of his brethren and the annoyance of the Franks. Nine battles, not unworthy of the name, were fought in the neighbourhood of Mount Carmel, with such vicissitude of fortune that in one attack the sultan forced his way into the city; that in one sally the Christians penetrated to the royal tent. By the means of divers and pigeons a regular correspondence was maintained with the besieged; and, as often as the sea was left open, the exhausted garrison was withdrawn, and a fresh supply was poured into the place. The Latin camp was thinned by famine, the sword, and the climate; but the tents of the dead were replenished with new pilgrims, who exaggerated the strength and speed of their approaching countrymen. The vulgar was astonished by the report that the pope himself, with an innumerable crusade, was advanced as far as Constantinople. The march of the emperor filled the East with more serious alarms; the obstacles which he encountered in Asia, and perhaps in Greece, were raised by the policy of Saladin; his joy on the death of Barbarossa was measured by his esteem; and the Christians were rather dismayed than encouraged at the sight of the duke of Swabia and his wayworn remnant of five thousand Germans. At length, in the spring of the second year, the royal fleets of France and England cast anchor in the bay of Acre, and the siege was more vigorously prosecuted by the youthful emulation of the two kings, Philip Augustus and Richard Plantagenet.* After every re-source had been tried, and every hope was exhausted, the defenders of Acre submitted to their fate; a capitulation was granted, but their lives and liberties were taxed at the hard conditions of a ransom of two hundred thousand pieces of gold, the deliverance of one hundred nobles and fifteen hundred inferior captives, and the restoration of the wood of the holy cross. Some doubts in the agreement, and some delay in the execution, rekindled the fury of the Franks, and three thousand Moslems, almost in the sultan's view, were beheaded by the command of the sanguinary Richard.[69] By the conquest of Acre the Latin powers acquired a strong town and a convenient harbour; but the advantage was most dearly purchased. The minister and historian of Saladin computes, from the report of the enemy, that their numbers, at different periods, amounted to five or six hundred thousand; that more than one hundred thousand Christians were slain; that a far greater number was lost by disease or shipwreck; and that a small portion of this mighty host could return in safety to their native countries.[70]

Philip Augustus and Richard the First are the only kings of France and England who have fought under the same banners; but the holy service in which they were enlisted was incessantly disturbed by their national jealousy; and the two factions which they protected in Palestine were more averse to each other than to the common enemy. In the eyes of the Orientals the French monarch was superior in dignity and power: and, in the emperor's absence, the Latins revered him as their temporal chief.[71] His exploits were not adequate to his fame. Philip was brave, but the statesman predominated in his character; he was soon weary of sacrificing his health and interest on a barren coast; the surrender of Acre became the signal of his departure: nor could he justify this unpopular desertion by leaving the duke of Burgundy, with five hundred knights and ten thousand foot, for the service of the Holy Land. The King of England, though inferior in dignity, surpassed his rival in wealth and military renown;[72] and, if heroism be confined to brutal and ferocious valour, Richard Plantagenet will stand high among the heroes of the age. The memory of *Coeur de Lion*, of the lion-hearted prince, was long dear and glorious to his English subjects; and, at the distance of sixty years, it was celebrated in proverbial sayings by the grandsons of the Turks and Saracens against whom he had fought: his tremendous name was em-ployed by the Syrian mothers to silence their infants; and, if an horse suddenly started from the way, his rider was wont to exclaim, 'Dost thou think King Richard is in that bush?'[73] His cruelty to the Mahometans was the effect of temper and zeal; but I cannot believe that a soldier, so free and fearless in the use of his lance, would have descended to whet a dagger against his valiant brother, Conrad of Montferrat, who was slain at Tyre by some secret assassins.[74] After the surrender of Acre and the departure of Philip, the king of England led the crusaders to the recovery of the sea-coast; and the cities of Caesarea and Jaffa were added to the fragments of the kingdom of Lusignan. A march of one hundred miles from Acre to Ascalon was a great and perpetual battle of eleven days. In the disorder of his troops, Saladin remained on the field with seventeen guards, without lowering his standard or suspending the sound of his brazen kettledrum: he again rallied and renewed the charge; and his preachers or heralds called aloud on the *Unitarians* manfully to stand up against the Christian idolaters. But the progress of these idolaters was irresistible; and it was only by demolishing the walls and buildings of Ascalon that the sultan could prevent them from occupying an important fortress on the confines of Egypt. During a severe winter the armies slept; but in the spring the Franks advanced within a day's march of Jerusalem, under the leading standard of the English king; and his active spirit intercepted a convoy, or caravan, of seven thousand camels. Saladin[75] had fixed his station in the holy city; but the city was struck with consternation and discord: he fasted; he prayed; he preached; he offered to share the dangers of the siege; but his Mamalukes, who remembered the fate of their companions at Acre, pressed the sultan with loyal or seditious clamours to preserve *his* person and *their* courage for the future defence of the religion and empire.[76] The Moslems were delivered by the sudden or, as they deemed, the miraculous retreat of the Christians;[77] and the laurels of Richard were blasted by the prudence or envy of his companions. The hero, ascending an hill, and veiling his face, exclaimed with an indignant voice, 'Those who are unwilling to rescue, are unworthy to view, the sepulchre of Christ!' After his return to Acre, on the news that Jaffa was surprised by the sultan, he sailed with some merchant vessels, and leaped foremost on the beach; the castle was relieved by his presence; and sixty thousand Turks and Saracens fled before his arms. The discovery of his weakness provoked them to return in the morning; and they found him carelessly encamped before the gates with only seventeen knights and three hundred archers. Without counting their numbers, he sustained their charge; and we learn from the evidence of his enemies, that the king of England, grasping his lance, rode furiously along their front, from the right to the left wing, without meeting an adversary who dared to encounter, his career.[78] Am I writing the history of Orlando or Amadis?*

During these hostilities a languid and tedious negotiation[79] between the Franks and the Moslems was started, and continued, and broken, and again resumed, and again broken. Some acts of royal courtesy, the gift of snow and fruit, the exchange of Norway hawks and Arabian horses, softened the asperity of religious war: from the vicissitude of success, the

Results of the Third Crusade AD *c.*1190

monarchs might learn to suspect that Heaven was neutral in the quarrel; nor, after the trial of each other, could either hope for a decisive victory.[80] The health both of Richard and Saladin appeared to be in a declining state; and they respectively suffered the evils of distant and domestic warfare: Plantagenet was impatient to punish a perfidious rival who had invaded Normandy in his absence; and the indefatigable sultan was subdued by the cries of the people, who was the victim, and of the soldiers, who were the instruments, of his martial zeal. The first demands of the king of England were the restitution of Jerusalem, Palestine, and the true cross; and he firmly declared that himself and his brother-pilgrims would end their lives in the pious labour, rather than return to Europe with ignominy and remorse. But the conscience of Saladin refused, without some weighty compensation, to restore the idols, or promote the idolatry, of the Christians: he asserted, with equal firmness, his religious and civil claim to the sovereignty of Palestine; descanted on the importance and sanctity of Jerusalem; and rejected all terms of the establishment, or partition, of the Latins. The marriage which Richard proposed, of his sister with the sultan's brother, was defeated by the difference of faith; the princess abhorred the embraces of a Turk; and Adel, or Saphadin, would not easily renounce a plurality of wives. A personal interview was declined by Saladin, who alleged their mutual ignorance of each other's language; and the negotiation was managed with much art and delay by their interpreters and envoys. The final agreement was equally disapproved by the zealots of both parties, by the Roman pontiff, and the caliph of Bagdad. It was stipulated that Jerusalem and the holy sepulchre should be open, without tribute or vexation, to the pilgrimage of the Latin Christians; that, after the demolition of Ascalon, they should inclusively possess the sea-coast from Jaffa to Tyre; that the count of Tripoli and the prince of Antioch should be comprised in the truce; and that, during three years and three months, all hostilities should cease. The principal chiefs of the two armies swore to the observance of the treaty; but the monarchs were satisfied with giving their word and their right hand; and the royal Majesty was excused from an oath, which always implies some suspicion of falsehood and dishonour. Richard embarked for Europe, to seek a long captivity and a premature grave; and the space of a few months concluded the life and glories of Saladin. The Orientals describe his edifying death, which happened at Damascus; but they seem ignorant of the equal distribution of his alms among the three religions,[81] or of the display of a shroud, instead of a standard, to admonish the East of the instability of human greatness. The unity of empire was dissolved by his death; his sons were oppressed by the stronger arm of their uncle Saphadin; the hostile interests of the Sultans of Egypt, Damascus, and Aleppo[82] were again revived; and the Franks or Latins stood, and breathed, and hoped, in their fortresses along the Syrian coast.

The noblest monument of a conqueror's fame, and of the terror which he inspired, is the Saladine tenth, a general tax, which was imposed on the laity, and even the clergy, of the Latin church, for the service of the holy war. The practice was too lucrative to expire with the occasion; and this tribute became the foundation of all the tithes and tenths on ecclesiastical benefices which have been granted by the Roman pontiffs to Catholic sovereigns, or reserved for the immediate use of the apostolic see.[83] This pecuniary emolument must have tended to increase the interest of the Popes in the recovery of Palestine; after the death of Saladin they preached the crusade by their epistles, their legates, and their missionaries; and the accomplishment of the pious work might have been expected from the zeal and talents of Innocent the Third.[84] Under that young and ambitious priest the successors of St Peter attained the full meridian of their greatness; and in a reign of eighteen years he exercised a despotic command over the emperors and kings, whom he raised and deposed; over the nations, whom an interdict of months or years deprived, for the offence of their rulers, of the exercise of Christian worship. In the council of the Lateran he acted as the ecclesiastical, almost as the temporal, sovereign of the East and West. It was at the feet of his legate that John of England surrendered his crown; and Innocent may boast of the two most signal triumphs over sense and humanity, the establishment of transubstantiation* and the origin of the inquisition. At his voice, two crusades, the fourth and the fifth, were undertaken; but, except a king of Hungary, the princes of the second order were at the head of the pilgrims; the forces were inadequate to the design; nor did the effects correspond with the hopes and wishes of the pope and the people. The fourth crusade was diverted from Syria to Constantinople; and the conquest of the Greek or Roman empire by the Latins will form the proper and important subject of the next chapter. In the fifth,[85] two hundred thousand Franks were landed at the eastern mouth of the Nile. They reasonably hoped that Palestine must be subdued in Egypt, the seat and storehouse of the sultan; and, after a siege of sixteen months, the Moslems deplored the loss of Damietta. But the Christian army was ruined by the pride and insolence of the legate Pelagius, who, in the Pope's name, assumed the character of general; the sickly Franks were encompassed by the waters of the Nile and the Oriental forces; and it was by the evacuation of Damietta that they obtained a safe retreat, some concessions for the pilgrims, and the tardy restitution of the doubtful relic of the true cross. The failure may in some measure be ascribed to the abuse and multiplication of the crusades, which were preached at the same time against the pagans of Livonia, the Moors of Spain, the Albigeois of France, and the kings of Sicily of the Imperial family.[86] In these meritorious services the volunteers might acquire at home the same spiritual indulgence and a larger measure of temporal rewards; and even the popes, in their zeal against a domestic enemy, were sometimes tempted to forget the distress of their Syrian brethren. From the last age of the crusades they derived the occasional command of an army and revenue; and some deep reasoners have suspected that the whole enterprise, from the first synod of Placentia, was contrived and executed by the policy of Rome. The suspicion is not founded either in nature or in fact. The successors of St Peter appear to have followed, rather than guided, the impulse of manners and prejudice; without much foresight of the seasons or cultivation of the soil, they gathered the ripe and spontaneous fruits of the superstition of the times. They gathered these fruits without toil or personal danger: in the council of the Lateran, Innocent the Third declared an ambiguous resolution of animating the crusaders by his example; but the pilot of the sacred vessel could not abandon the helm; nor was Palestine ever blessed with the presence of a Roman pontiff.[87]

The persons, the families, and estates of the pilgrims were under the immediate protection of the popes; and these spiritual patrons soon claimed the prerogative of directing their operations and enforcing, by commands and censures, the accomplishment of their vow. Frederic the Second,[88] the grandson of Barbarossa, was successively the pupil, the enemy, and the victim of the church. At the age of twenty-one years, and in obedience to his guardian Innocent the Third, he assumed the cross; the same promise was repeated at his royal and imperial coronations; and his marriage with the heiress of Jerusalem* for ever bound him to defend the kingdom of his son Conrad. But, as Frederic advanced in age and authority, he repented of the rash engagements of his youth; his liberal sense and knowledge taught him to despise the phantoms of superstition and the crowns of Asia; he no longer entertained the same reverence for the successors of Innocent; and his ambition was occupied by the restoration of the Italian monarchy from Sicily to the Alps. But the success of this project would have reduced the popes to their primitive simplicity; and, after the delays and excuses of twelve years, they urged the emperor, with entreaties and threats, to fix the time and place of his departure for Palestine. In the harbours of Sicily and Apulia, he prepared a fleet of one hundred galleys, and of one hundred vessels, that were framed to transport and land two thousand five hundred knights, with their horses and attendants; his vassals of Naples and Germany formed a powerful army; and the number of English crusaders was magnified to sixty thousand by the report of fame. But the inevitable or affected slowness of these mighty preparations consumed the strength and provisions of the more indigent pilgrims; the multitude was thinned by sickness and desertion, and the sultry summer of Calabria anticipated the mischiefs of a Syrian campaign. At length the emperor hoisted sail at Brundusium, with a fleet and army of forty thousand men; but he kept the sea no more than three days; and his hasty retreat, which was ascribed by his friends to a grievous indisposition, was accused by his enemies as a voluntary and obstinate disobedience. For suspending his vow Frederic was excommunicated by Gregory the Ninth; for presuming, the next year, to accomplish his vow, he was again excommunicated by the same pope.[89] While he served under the banner of the cross, a crusade was preached against him in Italy; and after his return he was compelled to ask pardon for the injuries which he had suffered. The clergy and military orders of Palestine were previously instructed to renounce his communion and dispute his commands; and in his own kingdom the emperor was forced to consent that the orders of the camp should be issued in the name of God and of the Christian republic. Frederic entered Jerusalem in triumph; and with his own hands (for no priest would perform the office) he took the crown from the altar of the holy sepulchre. But the patriarch cast an interdict on the church which his presence had profaned; and the knights of the hospital and temple informed the sultan how easily he might be surprised and slain in his unguarded visit to the river Jordan. In such a state of fanaticism and faction, victory was hopeless and defence was difficult; but the conclusion of an advantageous peace may be imputed to the discord of the Mahometans, and their personal esteem for the character of Frederic. The enemy of the church is accused of maintaining with the miscreants an intercourse of hospitality and friendship, unworthy of a Christian; of despising the barrenness of the land; and of indulging a profane thought that, if Jehovah had seen the kingdom of Naples, he never would have selected Palestine for the inheritance of his chosen people. Yet Frederic obtained from the sultan the restitution of Jerusalem, of Bethlem and Nazareth, of Tyre and Sidon; the Latins were allowed to inhabit and fortify the city; an equal code of civil and religious freedom was ratified for the sectaries of Jesus, and those of Mahomet; and, while the former worshipped at the holy sepulchre, the latter might pray and preach in the mosque of the temple,[90] from whence the prophet undertook his nocturnal journey to heaven. The clergy deplored this scandalous toleration; and the weaker Moslems were gradually expelled; but every rational object of the crusades was accomplished without bloodshed; the churches were restored, the monasteries were replenished; and, in the space of fifteen years, the Latins of Jerusalem exceeded the number of six thousand. This peace and prosperity, for which they were ungrateful to their benefactor, was terminated by the irruption of the strange and savage hordes of Carizmians.[91] Flying from the arms of the Moguls, those shepherds of the Caspian rolled headlong on Syria; and the union of the Franks with the sultans of Aleppo, Hems, and Damascus was insufficient to stem the violence of the torrent. Whatever stood against them was cut off by the sword or dragged into captivity; the military orders were almost exterminated in a single battle; and in the pillage of the city, in the profanation of the holy sepulchre, the Latins confess and regret the modesty and discipline of the Turks and Saracens.

Of the seven crusades, the two last were undertaken by Louis the Ninth, king of France, who lost his liberty in Egypt, and his life on the coast of Africa. Twenty-eight years after his death, he was canonised at

Rome; and sixty-five miracles were readily found, and solemnly attested, to justify the claim of the royal saint.[92] The voice of history renders a more honourable testimony, that he united the virtues of a king, an hero, and a man; that his martial spirit was tempered by the love of private and public justice; and that Louis was the father of his people, the friend of his neighbours, and the terror of the infidels. Superstition alone, in all the extent of her baleful influence,[93] corrupted his understanding and his heart; his devotion stooped to admire and imitate the begging friars of Francis and Dominic; he pursued with blind and cruel zeal the enemies of the faith; and the best of kings twice descended from his throne to seek the adventures of a spiritual knight-errant. A monkish historian would have been content to applaud the most despicable part of his character; but the noble and gallant Joinville,[94] who shared the friendship and captivity of Louis, has traced with the pencil of nature the free portrait of his virtues, as well as of his failings. From this intimate knowledge we may learn to suspect the political views of depressing their great vassals, which are so often imputed to the royal authors of the crusades. Above all the princes of the middle age, Louis the Ninth successfully laboured to restore the prerogatives of the crown; but it was at home, and not in the East, that he acquired for himself and his posterity; his vow was the result of enthusiasm and sickness; and, if he were the promoter, he was likewise the victim, of this holy madness. For the invasion of Egypt, France was exhausted of her troops and treasures; he covered the sea of Cyprus with eighteen hundred sails; the most modest enumeration amounts to fifty thousand men; and, if we might trust his own confession, as it is reported by Oriental vanity, he disembarked nine thousand five hundred horse, and one hundred and thirty thousand foot, who performed their pilgrimage under the shadow of his power.[95]

In complete armour, the oriflamme* waving before him, Louis leaped foremost on the beach; and the strong city of Damietta, which had cost his predecessors a siege of sixteen months, was abandoned on the first assault by the trembling Moslems. But Damietta was the first and last of his conquests; and in the fifth and sixth crusades the same causes, almost on the same ground, were productive of similar calamities.[96] After a ruinous delay, which introduced into the camp the seeds of an epidemical disease, the Franks advanced from the sea-coast towards the capital of Egypt, and strove to surmount the unseasonable inundation of the Nile, which opposed their progress. Under the eye of their intrepid monarch, the barons and knights of France displayed their invincible contempt of danger and discipline: his brother, the count of Artois, stormed with inconsiderate† valour the town of Massoura; and the carrier-pigeons announced to the inhabitants of Cairo, that all was lost. But a soldier, who afterwards usurped the sceptre, rallied the flying troops; the main body of Christians was far behind their vanguard; and Artois was overpowered and slain. A shower of Greek fire was incessantly poured on the invaders;

the Nile was commanded by the Egyptian galleys, the open country by the Arabs; all provisions were intercepted; each day aggravated the sickness and famine; and about the same time a retreat was found to be necessary and impracticable. The Oriental writers confess that Louis might have escaped, if he would have deserted his subjects: he was made prisoner, with the greatest part of his nobles; all who could not redeem their lives by service or ransom were inhumanly massacred; and the walls of Cairo were decorated with a circle of Christian heads.[97] The king of France was loaded with chains; but the generous victor, a great-grandson of the brother of Saladin, sent a robe of honour to his royal captive; and his deliverance, with that of his soldiers, was obtained by the restitution of Damietta[98] and the payment of four hundred thousand pieces of gold. In a soft and luxurious climate, the degenerate children of the companions of Noureddin and Saladin were incapable of resisting the flower of European chivalry; they triumphed by the arms of their slaves or Mamalukes, the hardy natives of Tartary, who at a tender age had been purchased of the Syrian merchants, and were educated in the camp and palace of the sultan. But Egypt soon afforded a new example of the danger of praetorian bands; and the rage of these ferocious animals, who had been let loose on the strangers, was provoked to devour their benefactor. In the pride of conquest, Touran Shah, the last of his race, was murdered by his Mamalukes; and the most daring of the assassins entered the chamber of the captive king, with drawn scymetars, and their hands imbrued in the blood of their sultan. The firmness of Louis commanded their respect;[99] their avarice prevailed over cruelty and zeal; the treaty was accomplished; and the king of France, with the relics of his army, was permitted to embark for Palestine. He wasted four years within the walls of Acre, unable to visit Jerusalem, and unwilling to return without glory to his native country.

The memory of his defeat excited Louis, after sixteen years of wisdom and repose, to undertake the seventh and last of the crusades. His finances were restored, his kingdom was enlarged; a new generation of warriors had arisen, and he embarked with fresh confidence at the head of six thousand horse and thirty thousand foot. The loss of Antioch had provoked the enterprise; a wild hope of baptising the King of Tunis tempted him to steer for the African coast; and the report of an immense treasure reconciled his troops to the delay of their voyage to the Holy Land. Instead of a proselyte he found a siege; the French panted and died on the burning sands; St Louis expired in his tent; and no sooner had he closed his eyes than his son and successor gave the signal of the retreat.[100] 'It is thus,' says a lively writer, 'that a Christian king died near the ruins of Carthage, waging war against the sectaries of Mahomet, in a land to which Dido had introduced the deities of Syria.'[101]

A more unjust and absurd constitution cannot be devised than that which condemns the natives of a country to perpetual servitude, under the arbitrary dominion of strangers and slaves. Yet such has been the state of Egypt above five hundred years. The most illustrious sultans of the Baharite and Borgite dynasties[102] were themselves promoted from the Tartar and Circassian bands; and the four-and-twenty beys or military chiefs, have ever been succeeded not by their sons but by their servants. They produce the great charter of their liberties, the treaty of Selim the First with the republic;[103] and the Othman emperor still accepts from Egypt a slight acknowledgment of tribute and subjection. With some breathing intervals of peace and order, the two dynasties are marked as a period of rapine and bloodshed;[104] but their throne, however shaken, reposed on the two pillars of discipline and valour; their sway extended over Egypt, Nubia, Arabia, and Syria; their Mamalukes were multiplied from eight hundred to twenty-five thousand horse; and their numbers were increased by a provincial militia of one hundred and seven thousand foot, and the occasional aid of sixty-six thousand Arabs.[105] Princes of such power and spirit could not long endure on their coast an hostile and independent nation; and, if the ruin of the Franks was postponed about forty years, they were indebted to the cares of an unsettled reign, to the invasion of the Mogols, and to the occasional aid of some warlike pilgrims. Among these, the English reader will observe the name of our first Edward, who assumed the cross in the lifetime of his father Henry. At the head of a thousand soldiers, the future conqueror of Wales and Scotland delivered Acre from a siege; marched as far as Nazareth with an army of nine thousand men; emulated the fame of his uncle Richard; extorted, by his valour, a ten years' truce; and escaped, with a dangerous wound, from the dagger of a fanatic *assassin*.[106] Antioch,[107] whose situation had been less exposed to the calamities of the holy war, was finally occupied and ruined by Bondocdar, or Bibars, sultan of Egypt and Syria; the Latin principality was extinguished; and the first seat of the Christian name was dispeopled by the slaughter of seventeen, and the captivity of one hundred thousand, of her inhabitants. The maritime towns of Laodicea, Gabala, Tripoli, Berytus, Sidon, Tyre, and Jaffa, and the stronger castles of the Hospitalers and Templars, successively fell; and the whole existence of the Franks was confined to the city and colony of St John of Acre, which is sometimes described by the more classic title of Ptolemais.

After the loss of Jerusalem, Acre,[108] which is distant about seventy miles, became the metropolis of the Latin Christians, and was adorned with strong and stately buildings, with aqueducts, an artificial port, and a double wall. The population was increased by the incessant streams of pilgrims and fugitives; in the pauses of hostility the trade of the East and West was attracted to this convenient station; and the market could offer the produce of every clime and the interpreters of every tongue. But in this conflux of nations every vice was propagated and practised; of all the disciples of Jesus and Mahomet, the male and female inhabitants of Acre were esteemed the most corrupt; nor could the abuse of religion be corrected by the discipline of law. The city had many sovereigns, and no government. The kings of Jerusalem and Cyprus, of the house of Lusignan, the princes of Antioch, the counts of Tripoli and Sidon, the great masters of the Hospital, the Temple, and the Teutonic order, the republics of Venice, Genoa, and Pisa, the pope's legate, the kings of France and England, assumed an independent command; seventeen tribunals exercised the power of life and death; every criminal was protected in the adjacent quarter; and the perpetual jealousy of the nations often burst forth in acts of violence and blood. Some adventurers, who disgraced the ensign of the cross, compensated their want of pay by the plunder of the Mahometan villages; nineteen Syrian merchants, who traded under the public faith,* were despoiled and hanged by the Christians; and the denial of satisfaction justified the arms of the sultan Khalil. He marched against Acre, at the head of sixty thousand horse and one hundred and forty thousand foot; his train of artillery (if I may use the word) was numerous and weighty; the separate timbers of a single engine were transported in one hundred waggons; and the royal historian, Abulfeda, who served with the troops of Hamah, was himself a spectator of the holy war. Whatever might be the vices of the Franks, their courage was rekindled by enthusiasm and despair; but they were torn by the discord of seventeen chiefs, and overwhelmed on all sides by the power of the sultan. After a siege of thirty-three days, the double wall was forced by the Moslems; the principal tower yielded to their engines; the Mamalukes made a general assault; the city was stormed; and death or slavery was the lot of sixty thousand Christians. The convent, or rather fortress, of the Templars resisted three days longer; but the great master was pierced with an arrow; and, of five hundred knights, only ten were left alive, less happy than the victims of the sword, if they lived to suffer on a scaffold in the unjust and cruel proscription of the whole order. The king of Jerusalem, the patriarch and the great master of the Hospital effected their retreat to the shore; but the sea was rough, the vessels were insufficient; and great numbers of the fugitives were drowned before they could reach the isle of Cyprus, which might comfort Lusignan for the loss of Palestine. By the command of the sultan, the churches and fortifications of the Latin cities were demolished; a motive of avarice or fear still opened the holy sepulchre to some devout and defenceless pilgrims; and a mournful and solitary silence prevailed along the coast which had so long resounded with the world's debate.[109]

1 Anna Comnena relates her father's conquests in Asia Minor, *Alexiad*, xi, 321–25; xiv, 419; his Cilician war against Tancred and Bohemond, pp. 328–42; the war of Epirus, with tedious prolixity, xii, xiii, 345–406; the death of Bohemond, xiv, 419.

2 The kings of Jerusalem submitted, however, to a nominal dependence; and in the dates of their inscriptions (one is still legible in the church of Bethlem) they respectfully placed before their own name that of the reigning emperor (Ducange, *Dissertations* sur Joinville, xxvii, 319).

* *page 948* [He was taken prisoner by the Turks in AD 1100.]

* *page 949* [Anna Comnena]

3 Anna Comnena adds that, to complete the imitation, he was shut up with a dead cock; and condescends to wonder how the barbarian could endure the confinement and putrefaction. This absurd tale is unknown to the Latins.

4 ἀπὸ Θούλης [from Thule], in the *Byzantine Geography*, must mean England; yet we are more credibly informed that our Henry I would not suffer him to levy any troops in his kingdom (Ducange, Not. *ad Alexiad*, p. 41).

5 The copy of the treaty (*Alexiad*, xiii, 406–16) is an original and curious piece, which would require, and might afford, a good map of the principality of Antioch.

6 See in the learned work of M. de Guignes (ii, ii) the history of the Seljukians of Iconium, Aleppo, and Damascus, as far as it may be collected from the Greeks, Latins and Arabians. The last are ignorant or regardless of the affairs of *Roum*.

7 Iconium is mentioned as a station by Xenophon, and by Strabo with the ambiguous title of Κωμόπολις (Cellarius, ii, 121) [κωμόπολις = 'village-city']. Yet St Paul found in that place a multitude (πλῆθος) of Jews and Gentiles. Under the corrupt name of *Kunijah*, it is described as a great city, with a river and gardens, three leagues from the mountains, and decorated (I know not why) with Plato's tomb (Abulfeda, *tabul.* xvii, 303, vers. Reiske; and the *Index Geographicus* of Schultens from Ibn Said).

8 For this supplement to the first crusade, see Anna Comnena (*Alexias*, xi, 331, etc.) and the viiith book of Albert Aquensis.

9 For the second crusade of Conrad III and Louis VII see William of Tyre (xvi, 18–29), Otho of Frisingen (i, 34–45, 59, 60), Matthew Paris (*Hist. Major*, p. 68), Struvius (*Corpus Hist. Germanicae*, pp. 372, 373), *Scriptores Rerum Francicarum* a Duchesne, iv; Nicetas, *in Vit. Manuel.*, i, 4, 5, 6, pp. 41–48.

10 For the third crusade, of Frederic Barbarossa, see Nicetas, *in Isaac. Angel.*, i, 3–8, 257–66; Struv. (*Corpus Hist. Germ.*, p. 414), and two historians, who probably were spectators, Tagino (in *Scriptor. Freher.*, i, 406–16, edit. Struv.) and the Anonymus *de Expeditione Asiatica Fred. I* (in *Canisii Antiq. Lection.*, iii, ii, 498–526, edit. Basnage).

11 Anne, who states these later swarms at 40,000 horse, and 100,000 foot, calls them Normans, and places at their head two brothers of Flanders. The Greeks were strangely ignorant of the names, families, and possessions of the Latin princes.

12 William of Tyre, and Matthew Paris, reckon 70,000 *loricati* [clad in chain-mail] in each of the armies.

13 The imperfect enumeration is mentioned by Cinnamus (ἐννενήκοντα μυριάδες) [900,000], and confirmed by Odo de Diogilo *apud* Ducange ad Cinnamum, with the more precise sum of 900,556. Why must therefore the version and comment suppose the modest and insufficient reckoning of 90,000? Does not Godfrey of Viterbo (*Pantheon*, p. xix, in Muratori, vii, 462) exclaim –

> *numerum si poscere quaeras* –
> *Millia millena milites agmen erat ?*

['Should you ask the number, the army consisted of one million soldiers.']

14 This extravagant account is given by Albert of Stade (*apud* Struvium, p. 414; my calculation is borrowed from Godfrey of Viterbo, Arnold of Lubeck, *apud eundem*, and Bernard Thesaur. (169, 804). The original writers are silent. The Mahometans gave him 200,000 or 260,000 men (Bohadin, *in Vit. Saladin.*, p. 110).

15 I must observe that, in the second and third crusades, the subjects of Conrad and Frederic are styled by the Greeks and Orientals *Alamanni*. The Lechi and Tzechi of Cinnamus are the Poles and Bohemians; and it is for the French that he reserves the ancient appellation of Germans. He likewise names the Βρίττιοι, or Βριταννοί [British].

16 Nicetas was a child at the second crusade, but in the third he commanded against the Franks the important post of Philippopolis. Cinnamus is infected with national prejudice and pride.

17 The conduct of the Philadelphians is blamed by Nicetas, while the anonymous German accuses the rudeness of his countrymen (*culpa nostra*) ['we were at fault']. History would be pleasant, if we were embarrassed only by such contradictions. It is likewise from Nicetas that we learn the pious and humane sorrow of Frederic.

18 χθαμαλὴ ἕδρα, which Cinnamus translates into Latin by the word σελλίον. Ducange works very hard to save his king and country from such ignominy (*sur* Joinville, *dissertat.* xxvii, 317–20). Louis afterwards insisted on a meeting *in mari ex aequo* ['at sea, on equal terms'], not *ex equo* [on horseback], according to the laughable readings of some manuscripts.

19 *Ego Romanorum imperator sum, ille Romaniorum* ['I am Emperor of the Romans, he is Emperor of the Romanians'] (Anonym. Canis. p. 512). The public and historical style of the Greeks was Ῥήξ . . . *princeps*. Yet Cinnamus owns, that Ἰμπεράτωρ ['imperator', emperor] is synonymous to Βασιλεύς ['king'].

* *page 952*   [the Germans]

20 In the epistles of Innocent III (xiii, 184) and the History of Bohadin (pp. 129, 130), see the views of a pope and a cadhi [Islamic judge] on this *singular* toleration.

21 As counts of Vexin, the kings of France were the vassals and advocates of the monastery of St Denys. The saint's peculiar banner, which they received from the abbot, was of a square form and a red or *flaming* colour. The *oriflamme* appeared at the head of the French armies from the xiith to the xvth century (Ducange *sur* Joinville, *dissertat.* xviii, 244–53).

22 The original French histories of the second crusade are the *Gesta Ludovici VII* published in the ivth volume of Duchesne's collection. The same volume contains many original letters of the king, of Suger his minister, etc., the best documents of authentic history.

23 *Terram horroris et salsuginis, terram siccam, sterilem, inamoenam.* Anonym. Canis., p. 517. The emphatic language of a sufferer.

24 *Gens innumera, sylvestris, indomita, praedones sine ductore* ['an innumerable people of the woods, unconquered, a leaderless race of bandits']. The sultan of Cogni might sincerely rejoice in their defeat. Anonym. Canis., pp. 517–18.

25 See in the anonymous writer in the collection of Canisius, Tagino, and Bohadin (*Vit. Saladin.*, 119, 120, ch. 70), the ambiguous conduct of Kilidge Arslan, sultan of Cogni, who hated and feared both Saladin and Frederic.

26 The desire of comparing two great men has tempted many writers to drown Frederic in the river Cydnus, in which Alexander so imprudently bathed (Q. Curt., iii, 4, 5). But, from the march of the emperor, I rather judge that his Saleph is the Calycadnus, a stream of less fame, but of a longer course.

27 Marinus Sanutus, AD 1321, lays it down as a precept, *quod stolus ecclesiae per terram nullatenus est ducenda* ['that the ecclesiastical stole is not to be taken by land']. He resolves, by the divine aid, the objection, or rather exception, of the first crusade (*Secreta Fidelium Crucis*, ii, ii,. i, 37).

28 The most authentic information of St Bernard must be drawn from his own writings, published in a correct edition by Père Mabillon, and reprinted at Venice, 1750, in six volumes in folio. Whatever friendship could recollect, or superstition could add, is contained in the two lives, by his disciples, in the vith volume: whatever learning and criticism could ascertain, may be found in the prefaces of the Benedictine editor.

29 Clairvaux, surnamed the Valley of Absynth, is situate among the woods near Bar-sur-Aube in Champagne. St Bernard would blush at the pomp of the church and monastery; he would ask for the library, and I know not whether he would be much edified by a tun of 800 muids (914½ hogsheads) which almost rivals that of Heidelberg (*Mélanges Tirés d'une Grande Bibliothèque*, xlvi, 15–20).

30 The disciples of the saint (*Vit. 1ma*, iii, 2, 1232; *Vit. 2da*, 16, 45, 1383) record a marvellous example of his pious apathy. *Iuxta lacum etiam Lausannensem totius diei itinere pergens, penitus non attendit, aut se videre non vidit. Cum enim vespere facto de eodem lacu socii colloquerentur, interrogabat eos ubi lacus ille esset; et mirati sunt universi.* ['For though he made a whole day's journey alongside Lake Lausanne, he paid no attention to it at all, or was not conscious of seeing it. For when, that evening, his fellows were speaking of the lake, he asked them where the lake was; at which they were all astonished.'] To admire or despise St Bernard as he ought, the reader, like myself, should have before the windows of his library the beauties of that incomparable landscape.

31 Otho Frising., i, 4. Bernard, Epist. 363, *ad Francos Orientales*, Opp., i, 328. *Vit. 1ma*, iii, 4, vi, 1235.

32 *Mandastis et obedivi . . . multiplicati sunt super numerum; vacuantur urbes et castella; et pene iam non inveniunt quem apprehendant septem mulieres unum virum; adeo ubique viduae vivis remanent viris.* Bernard, Epist. p. 247. We must be careful not to construe *pene* as a substantive. [*Pene* or *paene* is an adverb meaning 'scarcely'. If *pene* is mistaken for a noun, the sentence reads 'and seven women cannot find one man to hold by the penis'.]

33 *Quis ego sum ut disponam acies, ut egrediar ante facies armatorum, aut quid tam remotum a professione mea, si vires, si peritia*, etc. ['Who am I to arrange lines of battle, to stand in front of men-at-arms, or what could be further from my profession, even if my strength, skill, etc.'], 256, i, 259. He speaks with contempt of the hermit Peter, *vir quidam* [a certain man], epist. 363.

34 *Sic dicunt forsitan isti unde scimus quod a Domino sermo egressus sit? Quae signa tu facis,*

ut credamus tibi? Non est quod ad ista ipse respondeam; parcendum verecundiae meae; responde tu pro me, et pro te ipso, secundum quae vidisti et audisti, et secundum quod te inspiraverit Deus. ['But perhaps they will say: how do we know that your words come from God? What signs do you produce, that we should believe you? It is not for me to reply to these questions. My modesty should be spared. Do you reply for me and for yourself, according to what you have seen and heard, and to how God has inspired you.'] *Consolat.*, ii, 1; *Opp.*, ii, 421–23.

35 See the testimonies in *Vita 1ma*, iv, 5, 6; *Opp.*, vi, 1258–61, vi, 1–17, 1287–1314.

36 Abulmahasen *apud* de Guignes, *Hist. des Huns*, ii, p. ii, 99.

37 See his *article* in the *Bibliothèque Orientale* of d'Herbelot and de Guignes, ii, i, 230–61. Such was his valour that he was styled the second Alexander; and such the extravagant love of his subjects that they prayed for the sultan a year after his decease. Yet Sangiar might have been made prisoner by the Franks, as well as by the Uzes. He reigned near fifty years (AD 1103–52), and was a munificent patron of Persian poetry.

38 See the Chronology of the Atabeks of Irak and Syria, in de Guignes, i, 254; and the reigns of Zenghi and Noureddin in the same writer (ii, ii, 147–221), who uses the Arabic text of Benelathir, Ben Schouna, and Abulfeda; the *Bibliothèque Orientale*, under the articles *Atabeks* and *Noureddin*; and the Dynasties of Abulpharagius, pp. 250–67, vers. Pocock.

39 William of Tyre (xvi, 4, 5, 7) describes the loss of Edessa and the death of Zenghi. The corruption of his name into *Sanguin*, afforded the Latins a comfortable allusion to his *sanguinary* character and end, *fit sanguine sanguinolentus*.

40 *Noradinus* (says William of Tyre, xx, 33) *maximus nominis et fidei Christianae persecutor; princeps tamen iustus, vafer, providus, et secundum gentis suae traditiones religiosus.* To this Catholic witness we may add the primate of the Jacobites (Abulpharag., p. 267), *quo non alter erat inter reges vitae ratione magis laudabili, aut quae pluribus iustitiae experimentis abundaret* ['there was no other king whose life was based on such admirable principles, or was so full of proofs of his justice']. The true praise of kings is after their death and from the mouth of their enemies.

41 From the ambassador, William of Tyre (xix, 17, 18) describes the palace of Cairo. In the caliph's treasure were found a pearl as large as a pigeon's egg, a ruby weighing seventeen Egyptian drams, an emerald a palm and a half in length, and many vases of crystal and porcelain of China (Renaudot, p. 536).

42 *Mamluc*, plur. *Mamalic*, is defined by Pocock (*Prolegom. ad* Abulpharag., i, 7) and d'Herbelot (p. 545), *servum emptitium, seu qui pretio numerato in domini possessionem cedit* ['a slave acquired by purchase, or who comes into his master's possession at a particular price']. They frequently occur in the wars of Saladin (Bohadin, p. 236, etc.); and it was only the *Bahartie* Mamalukes that were first introduced into Egypt by his descendants.

43 Jacobus a Vitriaco (p. 1116) gives the king of Jerusalem no more than 374 knights. Both the Franks and the Moslems report the superior numbers of the enemy, a difference which may be solved by counting or omitting the unwarlike Egyptians.

44 It was the Alexandria of the Arabs, a middle term in extent and riches between the period of the Greeks and Romans, and that of the Turks (Savary, *Lettres sur l'Egypte*, i, 25, 26).

* *page 958*   [Amalric I, reigned AD 1163–74]

† *page 958*   [scholars]

45 For this great revolution of Egypt, see William of Tyre (xix, 5–7, 12–31; xx, 5–12); Bohadin (in *Vit. Saladin.*, pp. 30–34); Abulfeda (in *Excerpt.* Schultens, pp. 1–12); d'Herbelot (Bibliot. Orient. *Adhed, Fathemah*, but very incorrect); Renaudot (*Hist. Patriarch. Alex.*, pp. 522–25, 532–77); Vertot (*Hist. des Chevaliers de Malthe*, i, 141–163, in 4to); and M. de Guignes (ii, ii, 185–215).

46 For the Curds, see de Guignes, i, 416, 417, the *Index Geographicus* of Schultens, and Tavernier, *Voyages*, i, 308, 309. The Ayoubites descended from the tribe of the Rawadiaei, one of the noblest; but, as *they* were infected with the heresy of the Metempsychosis [theory of transmigration of souls], the orthodox sultans insinuated that their descent was only on the mother's side, and that their ancestor was a stranger who settled among the Curds.

47 See the ivth book of the *Anabasis* of Xenophon. The ten thousand suffered more from the arrows of the free Carduchians than from the splendid weakness of the Great King [Artaxerxes of Persia].

‡ *page 958*   [the Persians]

48 We are indebted to the Professor Schultens (Lugd. Bat., 1755, 1732, in folio) for the richest and most authentic materials, a life of Saladin by his friend and minister the cadhi Bohadin, and copious extracts from the history of his kinsman, the Prince Abulfeda of Hamah. To these we may add the article of *Salaheddin* in the *Bibliothèque Orientale*, and all that may be gleaned from the dynasties of Abulpharagius.

49 Since Abulfeda was himself an Ayoubite, he may share the praise for imitating at least tacitly the modesty of the founder.

50 *Hist. Hierosol.* in the *Gesta Dei per Francos*, p. 1152. A similar example may be found in Joinville (p. 42, edition du Louvre); but the pious St Louis refused to dignify infidels with the order of Christian knighthood (Ducange, *Observations*, p. 70).

51 In these Arabic titles, *religionis* [of religion] must always be understood; *Noureddin, lumen r.* [the light of r(eligion)]; *Ezzodin, decus* [glory]; *Amadoddin, columen* [safety]; our hero's proper name was Joseph, and he was styled *Salahoddin, salus* [salvation]; *Al Malichus Al Nasirus, rex defensor* [king and defender]; *Abu Medaffir, pater victoriae* [father of victory]. Schultens, *Praefat.*

52 Abulfeda, who descended from a brother of Saladin, observes, from many examples, that the founders of dynasties took the guilt for themselves, and left the reward to their innocent collaterals (*Excerpt.* p. 10).

53 See his life and character in Renaudot, pp. 537–48.

54 His civil and religious virtues are celebrated in the first chapter of Bohadin (pp. 4–30), himself an eye-witness and an honest bigot.

* *page 960*   taxes]

55 In many works, particularly Joseph's well in the castle of Cairo, the sultan and the patriarch have been confounded by the ignorance of natives and travellers.

56 Anonym. Canisii, iii, ii, 504.

57 Bohadin, pp. 129, 130.

58 For the Latin kingdom of Jerusalem, see William of Tyre, from the ixth to the xxiid book. Jacob. a Vitriaco, *Hist. Hierosolym.*, Bk. i, and Sanutus, *Secreta Fidelium Crucis*, iii, vi–ix.

* *page 961*   [distractions]

59 *Templarii ut apes bombabant et Hospitalarii ut venti stridebant, et barones se exitio offerebant, et Turcopuli* (the Christian light troops) *semet ipsi in ignem injiciebant* (Ispahani, *de Expugnatione Kudsitica*, p. 18, *apud* Schultens) ['The Templars buzzed like bees and the Hospitalers howled like the wind, and the barons offered themselves for destruction, and even the Turcopuli . . . threw themselves into the fire']: a specimen of Arabian eloquence somewhat different from the style of Xenophon!

60 The Latins affirm, the Arabians insinuate, the treason of Raymond; but, had he really embraced their religion, he would have been a saint and a hero in the eyes of the latter.

61 Reaud, Reginald, or Arnold de Châtillon, is celebrated by the Latins in his life and death; but the circumstances of the latter are more distinctly related by Bohadin and Abulfeda; and Joinville (*Hist. de St Louis*, p. 70) alludes to the practice of Saladin, of never putting to death a prisoner who had tasted his bread and salt. Some of the companions of Arnold had been slaughtered, and almost sacrificed, in an alley of Mecca, *ubi sacrificia mactantur* ['where the sacrificial animals are slaughtered'] (Abulfeda, p. 32).

62 Vertot, who well describes the loss of the kingdom and city (*Hist. des Chevaliers de Malthe*, i, ii, 226–78), inserts two original epistles of a knight-templar.

63 Renaudot, *Hist. Patriarch. Alex.*, p. 545.

* *page 963* [gold coins]

64 For the conquest of Jerusalem, Bohadin (pp. 67–75) and Abulfeda (pp. 40–43) are our Moslem witnesses. Of the Christian, Bernard Thesaurarius (*c.*151–67) is the most copious and authentic; see likewise Matthew Paris (pp. 120–24).

65 The sieges of Tyre and Acre are most copiously described by Bernard Thesaurarius (*de Acquisitione Terrae Sanctae*, chs 167–79), the author of the *Historia Hierosolymitana* (pp. 1150–72, in Bongarsius), Abulfeda (pp. 43–50), and Bohadin (pp. 75–179).

66 I have followed a moderate and probable representation of the fact; by Vertot, who adopts without reluctance a romantic tale, the old marquis is actually exposed to the darts of the besieged.

67 *Northmanni et Gothi, et ceteri populi insularum quae inter occidentem et septemtrionem sitae sunt, gentes bellicosae, corporis proceri, mortis intrepidae, bipennibus armatae, navibus rotundis quae Ysnachiae* [=esnecca, νάχχα] *dicuntur advectae*.

68 The historian of Jerusalem (p. 1108) adds the nations of the East from the Tigris to India, and the swarthy tribes of Moors and Getulians, so that Asia and Africa fought against Europe.

* *page 965* [Richard I of England, AD 1189–99]

69 Bohadin, p. 180; and this massacre is neither denied nor blamed by the Christian historians. *Alacriter iussa complentes* ['carrying out their orders eagerly'] (the English soldiers), says Galfridus, a Vinesauf (iv, iv, 346), who fixes at 2700 the number of victims; who are multiplied to 5000 by Roger Hoveden (pp. 697, 698). The humanity or avarice of Philip Augustus was persuaded to ransom his prisoners (Jacob. a Vitriaco, i, 98, 1122).

70 Bohadin, p. 14. He quotes the judgment of Balianus and the prince of Sidon, and adds, *Ex illo mundo quasi hominum paucissimi redierunt*. Among the Christians who died before St John d'Acre, I find the English names of De Ferrers, Earl of Derby (Dugdale, *Baronage*, i, 260), Mowbray (idem, p. 124), de Mandevil, de Fiennes, St John, Scrope, Pigot, Talbot, etc.

71 *Magnus hic apud eos, interque reges eorum tum virtute, tum majestate eminens . . . summus rerum arbiter* (Bohadin, p. 159). He does not seem to have known the names either of Philip or Richard.

72 *Rex Angliae praestrenuus . . . rege Gallorum minor apud eos censebatur ratione regni atque dignitatis; sed tum divitiis florentior, tum bellica virtute multo erat celebrior* (Bohadin, p. 161). A stranger might admire those riches; the national historians will tell with what lawless and wasteful oppression they were collected.

73 Joinville, p. 17. *Cuides-tu que ce soit le roi Richart?*

74 Yet he was guilty in the opinion of the Moslems, who attest the confession of the assassins that they were sent by the king of England (Bohadin, p. 225); and his only defence is an absurd and palpable forgery (*Hist. de l'Académie des Inscriptions*, xvi, 155–63), a pretended letter from the prince of the assassins, the Sheich, or old man of the mountain, who justified Richard, by assuming to himself the guilt or merit of the murder.

75 See the distress and pious firmness of Saladin, as they are described by Bohadin (pp. 7–9; 235–27), who himself harangued the defenders of Jerusalem. Their fears were not unknown to the enemy (Jacob. a Vitriaco, i, 100, 1123; Vinisauf, v, 50, 399).

76 Yet unless the sultan, or an Ayoubite prince, remained in Jerusalem, *nec Curdi Turcis, nec Turci essent obtemperaturi Curdis* ['the Curds would not have obeyed the Turks, nor the Turks the Curds'] (Bohadin, p. 236). He draws aside a corner of the political curtain.

77 Bohadin (p. 237), and even Jeffrey de Vinisauf (vi, 1–8, 403–9), ascribe the retreat to Richard himself; and Jacobus a Vitriaco observes that, in his impatience to depart, *in alterum virum mutatus est* [he became another man] (p. 1123). Yet Joinville, a French knight, accuses the envy of Hugh, duke of Burgundy (p. 116), without supposing, like Matthew Paris, that he was bribed by Saladin.

78 The expeditions to Ascalon, Jerusalem, and Jaffa are related by Bohadin (pp. 184–249) and Abulfeda (pp. 51, 52). The author of the *Itinerary*, or the monk of St Albans, cannot exaggerate the Cadhi's account of the prowess of Richard (Vinisauf, vi, 14–24, 412–21; [Matthew Paris] *Hist. Major*, pp. 137–43); and on the whole of this war there is a marvellous agreement between the Christian and Mahometan writers, who mutually praise the virtues of their enemies.

* *page 966* [Orlando: the hero of Ariosto's epic poem *Orlando Furioso* (1516); Amadis de Gaulle: hero of a medieval courtly tale]

79 See the progress of negotiation and hostility in Bohadin (pp. 207–60), who was himself an actor in the treaty. Richard declared his intention of returning with new armies to the conquest of the Holy Land; and Saladin answered the menace with a civil compliment (Vinisauf, vi, 28, 423).

80 The most copious and original account of this holy war is Galfridi a Vinisauf, *Itinerarium Regis Anglorum Richardi et aliorum in Terram Hierosolymorum*, in six books, published in the iid volume of Gale's *Scriptores Hist. Anglicanae* (p. 247–429). Roger Hoveden and Matthew Paris afford likewise many valuable materials; and the former describes with accuracy the discipline and navigation of the English fleet.

81 Even Vertot (i, 251) adopts the foolish notion of the indifference of Saladin, who professed the Koran with his last breath.

82 See the succession of the Ayoubites, in Abulpharagius (*Dynast.*, p. 227, etc.), and the tables of M. de Guignes, *l'Art de Vérifier les Dates*, and the *Bibliothèque Orientale*.

83 Thomassin (*Discipline de l'Eglise*, iii, 311–74) has copiously treated of the origin, abuses, and restrictions of these tenths. A theory was started, but not pursued, that they were rightfully due to the pope, a *tenth* of the Levites' tenth to the high-priest (Selden on Tithes. See his *Works*, iii, ii, 1083).

84 See the *Gesta Innocentii III* in Muratori, *Script. Rer. Ital.* (iii, 486–568).

  * *page 969* [the doctrine that the bread and wine partaken of during mass literally become the body and blood of Christ]

85 See the vth crusade, and the siege of Damietta, in Jacobus a Vitriaco (iii, 1125–49, in the *Gesta Dei* of Bongarsius), an eye-witness; Bernard Thesaurarius (in *Script. Muratori*, vii, 825–46, 190–207), a contemporary; and Sanutus (*Secreta Fidel. Crucis*, iii, xi, 4–9), a diligent compiler; and of the Arabians, Abulpharagius (*Dynast.*, p. 294), and the Extracts at the end of Joinville (pp. 533, 537, 540, 547, etc.).

86 To those who took the cross against Mainfroy, the pope (AD 1255) granted *plenissimam peccatorum remissionem. Fideles mirabantur quod tantum eis promitteret pro sanguine Christianorum effundendo quantum pro cruore infidelium aliquando* ['complete remission of sins. The faithful marvelled that he promised them as much for shedding Christian blood as he once promised for that of the infidels'] (Matthew Paris, p. 785). A high flight for the reason of the xiiith century!

87 This simple idea is agreeable to the good sense of Mosheim (*Institut. Hist. Eccles.*, p. 332) and the fine philosophy of Hume (*Hist. of England*, i, 330).

88 The original materials for the crusade of Frederic II may be drawn from Richard de St Germano (in Muratori, *Script. Rerum Ital.*, vii, 1002–13), and Matthew Paris (pp. 286, 291, 300, 302, 304). The most rational moderns are Fleury (*Hist. Ecclés.*, tom. xvi), Vertot (*Chevaliers de Malthe*, i, iii), Giannone (*Istoria Civile di Napoli*, ii, xvi), and Muratori (*Annali d'Italia*, tom. x).

  * *page 970* [Yolande, daughter of John of Brienne, who was king of Jerusalem AD 1210–25]

89 Poor Muratori knows what to think, but knows not what to say, *Chinò qui il capo* ['Here I bow my head (in shame)'], etc., p. 322.

90 The clergy artfully confounded the mosque, or church of the temple, with the holy sepulchre; and their wilful error has deceived both Vertot and Muratori.

91 The irruption of the Carizmians, or Corasmins, is related by Matthew Paris (pp. 546, 547) and by Joinville, Nangis, and the Arabians (pp. 111, 112, 191, 192, 528, 530).

92 Read, if you can, the life and miracles of St Louis, by the confessor of Queen Margaret (pp. 291–523; Joinville, du Louvre).

93 He believed all that Mother-church taught (Joinville, p. 10), but he cautioned Joinville against disputing with infidels. *L'omme lay*, said he in his old language, *quand il ot medire de la loy Chrestienne, ne doit pas deffendre la loy Chrestienne ne mais que de l'espée, de quoi il doit donner parmi le ventre dedens, tant comme elle y peut entrer* ['The layman, when he hears the Christian faith defamed, should never defend it except with the sword, which he should plunge into the stomach as far as it will go'] (p. 12).

94 I have two editions of Joinville: the one (Paris 1688) most valuable for the *Observations* of Ducange; the other (Paris, au Louvre, 1761) most precious for the pure and authentic text. a manuscript of which has been recently discovered.

  The last editor proves that the history of St Louis was finished ad 1309, without explaining or even admiring the age of the author, which must have exceeded ninety years (Preface, p. xi; *Observations* de Ducange, p. 17).

95 Joinville, p. 32; *Arabic Extracts*, p. 549.

* *page 972* [red banner of St Denis]

96 The last editors have enriched their Joinville with large and curious extracts from the Arabic historians, Macrizi, Abulfeda, etc. See likewise Abulpharagius (*Dynast.*, p. 322–25), who calls him by the corrupt name of *Redefrans*. Matthew Paris (pp. 683, 684) has described the rival folly of the French and English who fought and fell at Massoura.

† *page 972* [reckless]

97 Savary, in his agreeable *Lettres sur l'Egypt*, has given a description of Damietta (i, xxiii, 274–90) and a narrative of the expedition of St Louis (xxv, 306).

98 For the ransom of St Louis, a million of byzants was asked and granted; but the sultan's generosity reduced that sum to 800,000 byzants, which are valued by Joinville at 400,000 French livres of his own time, and expressed by Matthew Paris by 100,000 marks of silver (Ducange, *Dissertation* xx, *sur* Joinville).

99 The idea of the emirs to choose Louis for their sultan is seriously attested by Joinville (pp. 77, 78), and does not appear to me so absurd as to M. de Voltaire (*Hist. Générale*, ii, 386, 387). The Mamalukes themselves were strangers, rebels and equals; they had felt his valour, they hoped his conversion: and such a motion, which was not seconded, might be made perhaps by a secret Christian in their tumultuous assembly.

100 See the expedition in the *Annals of St Louis*, by William de Nangis, pp. 270–87, and the *Arabic Extracts*, pp. 545, 555 of the Louvre edition of Joinville.

101 Voltaire, *Hist. Générale*, ii, 391.

102 The chronology of the two dynasties of Mamalukes, the Baharites, Turks or Tartars of Kipzak, and the Borgites, Circassians, is given by Pocock (*Prolegom. ad* Abulpharag., pp. 6–31) and de Guignes (i, 264–70); their history from Abulfeda, Macrizi, etc., to the beginning of the 15th century, by the same M. de Guignes (iv, 110–328).

103 Savary, *Lettres sur l'Egypt*, ii, lettre xv, 189–208. I much question the authenticity of this copy; yet it is true that Sultan Selim concluded a treaty with the Circassians or Mamalukes of Egypt, and left them in possession of arms, riches, and power. See a new *Abrégé de l'Histoire Ottomane*, composed in Egypt, and translated by M. Digeon (i, 55–58, Paris 1781), a curious, authentic, and national history.

104 *Si totum quo regnum occuparunt tempus respicias, presertim quod fini propius, reperies illud bellis, pugnis, iniuriis, ac rapinis refertum* (Al Jannabi *apud* Pocock p. 31). The reign of Mohammed (AD 1311–41) affords an happy exception (de Guignes, iv, 208–10).

105 They are now reduced to 8500; but the expense of each Mamaluke may be rated at 100 louis, and Egypt groans under the avarice and insolence of these strangers (*Voyages* de Volney, i,. 89–187).

106 See Carte's *History of England*, ii, 165–75, and his original authors, Thomas Wikes and Walter Hemingford (iii, 34, 35) in Gale's *Collections* (ii, 97, 589–92). They are both ignorant of the Princess Eleanor's piety in sucking the poisoned wound, and saving her husband at the risk of her own life.

107 Sanutus, *Secret. Fidelium Crucis*, iii, xii, 9, and de Guignes, *Hist. des Huns*, iv, 143, from the Arabic historians.

108 The state of Acre is represented in all the chronicles of the times, and most
accurately in John Villani, vii, 144, in Muratori, *Scriptores Rerum Italicarum*, xiii,
337, 338.

* *page 975*   [in reliance on the terms of the truces agreed between crusaders and
Moslems]

109 See the final expulsion of the Franks, in Sanutus, iii, xii, 11–22; Abulfeda,
Macrizi, etc., in de Guignes, iv, 162, 164; and Vertot, i, iii, 407–28.

CHAPTER 60 (Summary)

*Schism of the Greeks and Latins – state of Constantinople –
revolt of the Bulgarians – Isaac Angelus dethroned by
his brother Alexius – origin of the fourth Crusade –
alliance of the French and Venetians with the son of Isaac –
their naval expedition to Constantinople – the two sieges,
and final conquest of the city by the Latins*

In this Chapter, Gibbon sees the schism between the Greek and Latin Churches as precipitating the decline and fall of the Roman Empire in the East. The dispute reached a climax in AD 1054 when the Latin Pope excommunicated the Greek Patriarch. The events of the first three crusades were a further cause of animosity between the Churches. The most regular contact, however, between Italy and Constantinople was through the merchants of Venice, Genoa and Pisa. National hostilities caused a massacre of Latin residents at Constantinople in AD 1183 during the reign of the Emperor Andronicus. His successor, Isaac II, 'slept on the throne and was awakened only by the sound of pleasure'. The Bulgarians asserted their independence from Constantinople and declared their allegiance to Rome. Isaac was deposed and replaced by his brother, Alexius, in AD 1195. Meanwhile the fourth Crusade was preached by Pope Innocent III. Six ambassadors from France negotiated a treaty with Enrico Dandalo, the Doge of Venice, to convey the crusaders by sea. Their first assault was on Zara on the Dalmatian coast, for the benefit of the Venetians. The crusaders were then persuaded by the son of the deposed Emperor Isaac to support the restoration of his father, with the promise of ending the schism between the Greek and Latin Churches. They sailed without opposition to Constantinople. After a siege of eleven days, the usurper Alexius fled and Isaac II and his son were jointly crowned as emperors. However, the crusaders plundered the Greek churches, the emperors lost the support of both Latins and Greeks and were overthrown by a Greek usurper called Mourzoufle. Constantinople was subjected to a second siege and capture by the Latins. The riches of the city were systematically pillaged, statues of brass were melted down and libraries destroyed.

CHAPTER 61 (Summary)

*Partition of the empire by the French and Venetians – five Latin
emperors of the houses of Flanders and Courtenay – their
wars against the Bulgarians and Greeks – weakness and
poverty of the Latin empire – recovery of Constantinople
by the Greeks – general consequences of the Crusades –
digression on the family of Courtenay*

Gibbon relates the election, by the French and Venetian representatives,
of Baldwin, Count of Flanders, as Latin emperor of the East. The
Venetian received a large share of the Greek territories, but the unity of
the Latin empire was severely undermined by the divisions of their feudal
system. Their Greek subjects rebelled and, with the aid of the Bulgarians,
defeated Baldwin in AD 1205. He died in captivity and was succeeded by
his brother, Henry, who ruled for ten years and attempted to reconcile
the Greeks. On his death, his brother-in-law, Peter of Courtenay,
became emperor; but he died in captivity in Epirus on his way from
France to Constantinople. The fall of the Latin empire was delayed by the
intervention and military successes of John of Brienne, titular King of
Jerusalem, but after his death in AD 1237, Baldwin II could raise income to
stave off defeat only by pawning holy relics. Finally, in AD 1261, the Latin
empire was recovered by the Greeks under Michael Palaeologus. In a
general review of the Crusades, Gibbon argues that the Latins learnt little
from their contact with the Greeks or the Arabs, but that the dissipation
of their strength in the Near East helped to free 'the most numerous and
useful part' of their community in the West. He concludes with a note on
the history of the Courtenay family in Edessa, France and England.

CHAPTER 62 (Summary)

The Greek emperors of Nicaea and Constantinople – elevation and reign of Michael Palaeologus – his false union with the Pope and the Latin Church – hostile designs of Charles of Anjou – revolt of Sicily – war of the Catalans in Asia and Greece – revolutions and present state of Athens

Chapter 62 begins with an account of how the Greeks in exile had established a new nation state, centred on Nicaea in Asia Minor, under the Lascaris family. Michael Palaeologus had risen to power after the death of Theodore Lascaris II in AD 1258 and on the fall of Constantinople he was crowned emperor. His authority was undermined by his excommunication by the Patriarch for blinding the heir to the Lascaris, and he failed in his attempt to reconcile the Eastern and Western Churches. His main opponent in the West was Charles of Anjou, who won the Kingdom of the Two Sicilies in AD 1266. Michael gave financial assistance to Peter of Arragon when a rebellion occurred in Palermo ('The Sicilian Vespers' of AD 1282), and Charles was defeated by the Catalans. In the next generation, Catalan mercenaries went to Constantinople to fight the Turks but they brought devastation to most parts of the Greek Empire. Gibbon ends the chapter with a survey of Athens up to his own times, remarking that 'the Athenians walk with supine indifference among the glorious ruins of antiquity.'

CHAPTER 63 (Summary)

Civil wars, and ruin of the Greek empire – reigns of Andronicus, the elder and younger, and John Palaeologus – regency, revolt, reign, and abdication of John Cantacuzene – establishment of a Genoese colony at Pera or Galata – their wars with the empire and city of Constantinople

Gibbon describes the civil wars which afflicted the Greek empire under the successors of Michael Palaeologus, until John Cantacuzene entered Constantinople in AD 1347 and ruled as regent for the minor, John Palaeologus; but feuds and theological disputes continued to weaken the empire. There was rivalry between the Genoese and Venetian merchants, and when the Greeks supported the Venetians against the Genoese in AD 1352, they were defeated in a naval battle under the walls of Constantinople and forced to grant a monopoly of trade to the Genoese.

CHAPTER 64 (Summary)

Conquests of Zingis Khan and the Moguls from China to Poland – escape of Constantinople and the Greeks – origin of the Ottoman Turks in Bithynia – reigns and victories of Othman, Orchan, Amurath I, and Bajazet I – foundation and progress of the Turkish monarchy in Asia and Europe – danger of Constantinople and the Greek empire

Gibbon reviews the origins of the Moguls and Tartars, who founded the Ottoman race. He attributes their military discipline, laws and religious tolerance to their first emperor, Zingis (Genghis Khan, AD 1206–27). Under his four successors, they subdued most of Asia and a large portion of Eastern Europe, adopting the civilisation of China in the East and the religion of Mahomet in the West. Divisions between their leaders saved Constantinople, and their decline facilitated the rise of the Turkish or Ottoman Empire in Asia Minor in the early fourteenth century. The Greeks lost all their possessions across the Bosphorus, but in their civil wars sometimes allied with the Turks. In the late fourteenth century, the Turks gained possession of most of the Balkans, defeating the Hungarians at the battle of Nicopolis in AD 1396. Only the conquests of Tamerlane, discussed in the next chapter, distracted the Turks from taking Constantinople.

CHAPTER 65 (Summary)

*Elevation of Timour or Tamerlane to the throne of Samarcand –
his conquests in Persia, Georgia, Tartary, Russia, India,
Syria, and Anatolia – his Turkish war – defeat and
captivity of Bajazet – death of Timour – civil war of the
sons of Bajazet – restoration of the Turkish monarchy
by Mahomet I – siege of Constantinople by Amurath II*

Gibbon traces the origins of Timour or Tamerlane near Samarcand and
then reviews his conquests in Persia, Siberia, Russia and India, before
describing his campaign against the Ottoman empire. At the battle of
Angora, in AD 1402, Tamerlane decisively beat the Sultan Bajazet and
overran his empire in Asia Minor. Three years later, Tamerlane died on
his way to conquer China. Gibbon sees more violence than prosperity
resulting from his rule, the Mogul of India being the most successful of
his descendants. The Ottoman empire was divided between the sons of
Bajazet, but Constantinople gained little from their civil wars. It was
besieged by the Sultan Amurath II in AD 1422 but saved by a revolt
within the Ottoman Empire. Yet the superior discipline of the Turks
made their ultimate victory inevitable, especially when the use of
gunpowder became generally known.

CHAPTER 66 (Summary)

*Application of the Eastern emperors to the popes – visits to the
West, of John I, Manuel, and John II Palaeologus – union of the
Greek and Latin Churches, promoted by the Council of Basel,
and concluded at Ferrara and Florence – state of literature at
Constantinople – its revival in Italy by the Greek fugitives –
curiosity and emulation of the Latins*

Gibbon describes the diplomatic approaches by the Greek emperors to the
papacy for help against the Turks. The emperor John Palaeologus I
(known also as John V) in AD 1355 negotiated a secret treaty with Pope
Innocent VI. He visited Pope Urban V at Rome in AD 1369, and his son,
the emperor Manuel II, also visited the West, including France and
England in AD 1400–02. Relations between the Churches improved when

the Turks threatened Constantinople again after the death of Tamerlane. In AD 1438, the emperor John Palaeologus II (John VIII) sailed to Venice and met the Pope Eugenius IV at Ferrara and Florence. The Pope was denounced by the Council of Basel, but an act of union between the Churches was negotiated and the Council was dissolved. Gibbon concludes the chapter with an account of how the Greek language had been preserved by the court and the church of Constantinople. Petrarch (AD 1304–74) is seen as 'the first harbinger of day', who studied the Greek language in the West, but it was not until the emperor Manuel dispatched envoys to Italy at the end of the fourteenth century that the rediscovery of Greek classical writers was secured. In the middle of the fifteenth century, Pope Nicholas V collected Greek manuscripts, as did Cosimo di Medici.

CHAPTER 67 (Summary)

Schism of the Greeks and the Latins – reign and character of Amurath II – crusade of Ladislaus, King of Hungary – his defeat and death – John Huniades – Scanderbeg – Constantine Palaeologus, last emperor of the East

Gibbon relates how the ecclesiastical act of union was widely repudiated when the emperor and his prelates returned to Constantinople. The Pope, Eugenius IV, however, formed a league against the Turks, with Ladislaus, King of Poland and Hungary, at its head. At first, Ladislaus was successful, but at the battle of Varna, in AD 1444, he was defeated and killed. His commander, John Huniades, continued to resist the Turks and successfully defended Belgrade in AD 1456. Another champion of the Christian cause was Scanderbeg, Prince of Albania, who campaigned against the Turks for twenty-three years. Meanwhile, Constantine, the last of the Greek emperors, succeeded to the throne of the Caesars in AD 1448.

CHAPTER 68

Reign and character of Mahomet II – siege, assault and final conquest of Constantinople by the Turks – death of Constantine Palaeologus – servitude of the Greeks – extinction of the Roman empire in the East – consternation of Europe – conquests and death of Mahomet II

The siege of Constantinople by the Turks attracts our first attention to the person and character of the great destroyer. Mahomet the Second[1] was the son of the second Amurath; and, though his mother has been decorated with the titles of Christian and princess, she is more probably confounded with the numerous concubines who peopled from every climate the harem of the sultan. His first education and sentiments were those of a devout Musulman; and, as often as he conversed with an infidel, he purified his hands and face by the legal rites of ablution. Age and empire appear to have relaxed this narrow bigotry; his aspiring genius disdained to acknowledge a power above his own; and in his looser hours he presumed (it is said) to brand the prophet of Mecca as a robber and impostor. Yet the Sultan persevered in a decent reverence for the doctrine and discipline of the Koran;[2] his private indiscretion must have been sacred from the vulgar ear; and we should suspect the credulity of strangers and sectaries, so prone to believe that a mind which is hardened against truth must be armed with superior contempt for absurdity and error. Under the tuition of the most skilful masters, Mahomet advanced with an early and rapid progress in the paths of knowledge; and, besides his native tongue, it is affirmed that he spoke or understood five languages,[3] the Arabic, the Persian, the Chaldaean or Hebrew, the Latin, and the Greek. The Persian might, indeed, contribute to his amusement, and the Arabic to his edification; and such studies are familiar to the Oriental youth. In the intercourse of the Greeks and Turks, a conqueror might wish to converse with the people over whom he was ambitious to reign; his own praises in Latin poetry[4] or prose[5] might find a passage to the royal ear; but what use or merit could recommend to the statesman or the scholar the uncouth dialect of his Hebrew slaves? The history and geography of the world were familiar to his memory; the lives of the heroes of the East, perhaps of the West,[6] excited his emulation; his skill in astrology is excused by the folly of the times, and supposes some rudiments of mathematical science; and a profane taste for the arts is betrayed in his liberal invitation and reward of the painters of Italy.[7] But the influence of religion and learning were employed without effect on his savage and licentious nature. I will not transcribe, nor do I firmly believe, the stories of his fourteen pages, whose bellies were ripped open in search of a stolen melon; or of the beauteous slave, whose head he severed from her body, to convince the Janizaries that their master was not the votary of love. His sobriety is attested by the silence of the Turkish annals, which accuse three, and three only, of the Ottoman line of the vice of drunkenness.[8] But it cannot be denied that his passions were at once furious and inexorable; that in the palace, as in the field, a torrent of blood was spilt on the slightest provocation; and that the noblest of the captive youth were often dishonoured by his unnatural lust. In the Albanian war, he studied the lessons, and soon surpassed the example, of his father; and the conquest of two empires, twelve kingdoms, and two hundred cities, a vain and flattering account, is ascribed to his invincible sword. He was doubtless a soldier, and possibly a general; Constantinople has sealed his glory; but, if we compare the means, the obstacles, and the achievements, Mahomet the Second must blush to sustain a parallel with Alexander or Timour.* Under his command, the Ottoman forces were always more numerous than their enemies; yet their progress was bounded by the Euphrates and the Adriatic; and his arms were checked by Huniades† and Scanderbeg,‡ by the Rhodian knights,§ and by the Persian king.

In the reign of Amurath, he twice tasted of royalty, and twice descended from the throne; his tender age was incapable of opposing his father's restoration, but never could he forgive the vizirs who had recommended that salutary measure. His nuptials were celebrated with the daughter of a Turkman emir; and, after a festival of two months, he departed from Hadrianople with his bride to reside in the government of Magnesia. Before the end of six weeks, he was recalled by a sudden message from the divan, which announced the decease of Amurath and the mutinous spirit of the Janizaries. His speed and vigour commanded their obedience; he passed the Hellespont with a chosen guard; and, at a distance of a mile from Hadrianople, the vizirs and emirs, the imams and cadhis, the soldiers and the people, fell prostrate before the new sultan. They affected to weep, they affected to rejoice; he ascended the throne at the age of twenty-one years, and removed the cause of sedition by the death, the inevitable death, of his infant brothers.[9] The ambassadors of Europe and Asia soon appeared to congratulate his accession, and solicit his friendship; and to all he spoke the language of moderation and peace. The confidence of the Greek emperor was revived by the solemn oaths and fair assurances with which he sealed the ratification of the treaty; and a rich domain on the banks of the Strymon was assigned for the annual payment of three hundred thousand aspers, the pension of an Ottoman prince who was detained at his request in the Byzantine court. Yet the neighbours of Mahomet might tremble at the severity with which a youthful monarch reformed the pomp of his father's household; the expenses of luxury were applied to those of ambition, and an useless train of seven thousand falconers was either dismissed from his service or enlisted in his troops. In the first summer of his reign, he visited with an army the Asiatic provinces; but, after humbling the pride, Mahomet accepted the submission, of the Caramanian, that he might not be diverted by the smallest obstacle from the execution of his great design.[10]

The Mahometan, and more especially the Turkish, casuists have pronounced that no promise can bind the faithful against the interest and duty of their religion; and that the sultan may abrogate his own treaties and those of his predecessors. The justice and magnanimity of Amurath had scorned this immoral privilege; but his son, though the proudest of men, could stoop from ambition to the basest arts of dissimulation and deceit. Peace was on his lips, while war was in his heart: he incessantly sighed for the possession of Constantinople; and the Greeks, by their own indiscretion, afforded the first pretence of the fatal rupture.[11] Instead of labouring to be forgotten, their ambassadors pursued his camp, to demand the payment and even the increase of their annual stipend: the divan was importuned by their complaints, and the vizir, a secret friend of the Christians, was constrained to deliver the sense of his brethren. 'Ye foolish and miserable Romans,' said Calil, 'we know your devices, and ye are ignorant of your own danger! The scrupulous Amurath is no more; his throne is occupied by a young conqueror, whom no laws can bind and no obstacles can resist; and, if you escape from his hands, give praise to the divine clemency, which yet delays the chastisement of your sins. Why do ye seek to affright us by vain and indirect menaces? Release the fugitive Orchan, crown him sultan of Romania; call the Hungarians from beyond the Danube; arm against us the nations of the West; and be assured that you will only provoke and precipitate your ruin.' But, if the fears of the ambassadors were alarmed by the stern language of the vizir, they were soothed by the courteous audience and friendly speeches of the Ottoman prince; and Mahomet assured them that on his return to Hadrianople he would redress the grievances, and consult the true interests, of the Greeks. No sooner had he repassed the Hellespont than he issued a mandate to suppress their pension and to expel their officers from the banks of the Strymon: in this measure he betrayed an hostile mind; and the second order announced, and in some degree commenced, the siege of Constantinople. In the narrow pass of the Bosphorus, an Asiatic fortress had formerly been raised by his grandfather: in the opposite situation, on the European side, he resolved to erect a more formidable castle; and a thousand masons were commanded to assemble in the spring, on a spot named Asomaton, about five miles from the Greek metropolis.[12] Persuasion is the resource of the feeble; and the feeble can seldom persuade: the ambassadors of the emperor attempted, without success, to divert Mahomet from the execution of his design. They represented, that his grandfather had solicited the permission of Manuel to build a castle on his

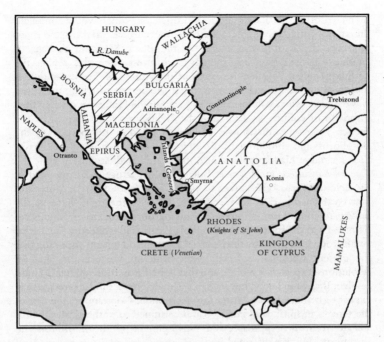

The Ottoman empire before AD *1453*

own territories; but that this double fortification, which would command the strait, could only tend to violate the alliance of the nations, to intercept the Latins who traded in the Black Sea, and perhaps to annihilate the subsistence of the city. 'I form no enterprise,' replied the perfidious sultan, 'against the city; but the empire of Constantinople is measured by her walls. Have you forgot the distress to which my father was reduced, when you formed a league with the Hungarians; when they invaded our country by land, and the Hellespont was occupied by the French galleys? Amurath was compelled to force the passage of the Bosphorus; and your strength was not equal to your malevolence. I was then a child at Hadrianople; the Moslems trembled; and for a while the *Gabours*[13] insulted our disgrace. But, when my father had triumphed in the field of Warna,* he vowed to erect a fort on the western shore, and that vow it is my duty to accomplish. Have ye the right, have ye the power, to control my actions on my own ground? For that ground *is* my own: as far as the shores of the Bosphorus, Asia is inhabited by the Turks, and Europe is deserted by the Romans. Return, and inform your king that the present Ottoman is far different from his predecessors; that *his* resolutions surpass *their* wishes; and that *he* performs more than *they* could resolve. Return in safety; but the next who delivers a similar message may expect to be flayed alive.' After this declaration, Constantine, the first of the Greeks in spirit as in rank,[14] had determined to unsheath the sword, and to resist the approach and establishment of the Turks on the Bosphorus. He was disarmed by the advice of his civil and ecclesiastical ministers, who recommended a system less generous, and even less prudent, than his own, to approve† their patience and long-suffering, to brand the Ottoman with the name and guilt of an aggressor, and to depend on chance and time for their own safety and the destruction of a fort which could not be long maintained in the neighbourhood of a great and populous city. Amidst hope and fear, the fears of the wise and the hopes of the credulous, the winter rolled away; the proper business of each man, and each hour, was postponed; and the Greeks shut their eyes against the impending danger, till the arrival of the spring and the sultan decided the assurance of their ruin.

Of a master who never forgives, the orders are seldom disobeyed. On the twenty-sixth of March, the appointed spot of Asomaton was covered with an active swarm of Turkish artificers; and the materials by sea and land were diligently transported from Europe and Asia.[15] The lime had been burnt in Cataphrygia; the timber was cut down in the woods of Heraclea and Nicomedia; and the stones were dug from the Anatolian quarries. Each of the thousand masons was assisted by two workmen; and a measure of two cubits was marked for their daily task. The fortress[16] was built in a triangular form; each angle was flanked by a strong and massy tower; one on the declivity of the hill, two along the seashore; a thickness of twenty-two feet was assigned for the walls, thirty for the towers; and the whole building was covered with a solid platform of lead. Mahomet himself pressed and directed the work with indefatigable ardour; his three vizirs claimed the honour of finishing their respective towers; the zeal of the cadhis emulated that of the Janizaries; the meanest labour was ennobled by the service of God and the sultan; and the diligence of the multitude was quickened by the eye of a despot, whose smile was the hope of fortune, and whose frown was the messenger of death. The Greek emperor beheld with terror the irresistible progress of the work; and vainly strove, by flattery and gifts, to assuage an implacable foe, who sought, and secretly fomented, the slightest occasion of a quarrel. Such occasions must soon and inevitably be found. The ruins of stately churches, and even the marble columns which had been consecrated to St Michael the archangel, were employed without scruple by the profane and rapacious Moslems; and some Christians, who presumed to oppose the removal, received from their hands the crown of martyrdom. Constantine had solicited a Turkish guard to protect the fields and harvests of his subjects: the guard was fixed; but their first order was to allow free pasture to the mules and horses of the camp, and to defend their brethren if they should be molested by the natives. The retinue of an Ottoman chief had left their horses to pass the night among the ripe corn: the damage was felt; the insult was resented; and several of both nations were slain in a tumultuous conflict. Mahomet listened with joy to the complaint; and a detachment was commanded to exterminate the guilty village: the guilty had fled; but forty innocent and unsuspecting reapers were massacred by the soldiers. Till this provocation, Constantinople had been open to the visits of commerce and curiosity: on the first alarm, the gates were shut; but the emperor, still anxious for peace, released on the third day his Turkish captives,[17] and expressed, in a last message, the firm resignation of a Christian and a soldier. 'Since neither oaths, nor treaty, nor submission, can secure peace, pursue,' said he to Mahomet, 'your impious warfare. My trust is in God alone: if it should please him to mollify your heart, I shall rejoice in the happy change; if he delivers the city into your hands, I submit without a murmur to his holy will. But, until the Judge of the earth shall pronounce between us, it is my duty to live and die in the defence of my people.' The sultan's answer was hostile and decisive; his fortifications were completed; and before his departure for Hadrianople he stationed a vigilant Aga and four hundred Janizaries to levy a tribute of the ships of every nation that should pass within the reach of their cannon. A Venetian vessel, refusing obedience to the new lords of the Bosphorus, was sunk with a single bullet. The master and thirty sailors escaped in the boat; but they were dragged in chains to the *Porte*; the chief was impaled; his companions were beheaded; and the historian Ducas[18] beheld, at Demotica, their bodies exposed to the wild beasts. The siege of Constantinople was deferred till the ensuing spring; but an Ottoman army marched into the Morea to divert the force of the brothers of

Constantine. At this era of calamity, one of these princes, the despot Thomas, was blessed or afflicted with the birth of a son, 'the last heir,' says the plaintive Phranza, 'of the last spark of the Roman empire.'[19]

The Greeks and the Turks passed an anxious and sleepless winter: the former were kept awake by their fears, the latter by their hopes; both by the preparations of defence and attack; and the two emperors, who had the most to lose or to gain, were the most deeply affected by the national sentiment. In Mahomet, that sentiment was inflamed by the ardour of his youth and temper: he amused his leisure with building at Hadrianople[20] the lofty palace of Jehan Numa (the watchtower of the world); but his serious thoughts were irrevocably bent on the conquest of the city of Caesar. At the dead of night, about the second watch, he started from his bed, and commanded the instant attendance of his prime vizir. The message, the hour, the prince, and his own situation alarmed the guilty conscience of Calil Basha, who had possessed the confidence, and advised the restoration,* of Amurath. On the accession of the son, the vizir was confirmed in his office and the appearances of favour; but the veteran statesman was not insensible that he trod on a thin and slippery ice, which might break under his footsteps and plunge him in the abyss. His friendship for the Christians, which might be innocent under the late reign, had stigmatised him with the name of Gabour Ortachi, or foster brother of the infidels;[21] and his avarice entertained a venal and treasonable correspondence, which was detected and punished after the conclusion of the war. On receiving the royal mandate, he embraced, perhaps for the last time, his wife and children; filled up a cup with pieces of gold, hastened to the palace, adored the sultan, and offered, according to the Oriental custom, the slight tribute of his duty and gratitude.[22] 'It is not my wish,' said Mahomet, 'to resume my gifts, but rather to heap and multiply them on thy head. In my turn, I ask a present far more valuable and important – Constantinople.' As soon as the vizir had recovered from his surprise, 'The same God,' said he, 'who has already given thee so large a portion of the Roman empire, will not deny the remnant, and the capital. His providence and thy power assure thy success; and myself, with the rest of thy faithful slaves, will sacrifice our lives and fortunes.' 'Lala'[23] (or preceptor), continued the sultan, 'do you see this pillow? All the night, in my agitation, I have pulled it on one side and the other; I have risen from my bed, again have I lain down; yet sleep has not visited these weary eyes. Beware of the gold and silver of the Romans; in arms we are superior; and with the aid of God, and the prayers of the prophet, we shall speedily become masters of Constantinople.' To sound the disposition of his soldiers, he often wandered through the streets alone and in disguise; and it was fatal to discover the sultan, when he wished to escape from the vulgar eye. His hours were spent in delineating the plan of the hostile city; in debating with his generals and engineers, on what spot he should erect his batteries; on which side he should assault the walls; where he should

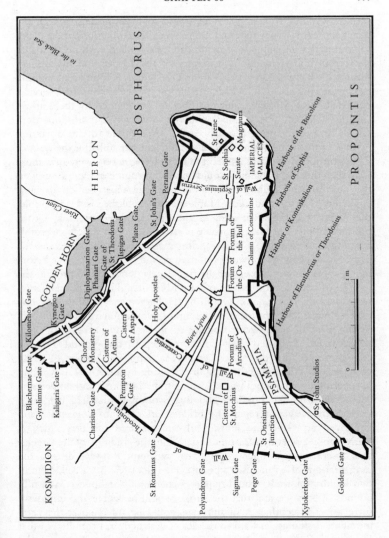

Constantinople

spring his mines; to what place he should apply his scaling-ladders; and the exercises of the day repeated and proved the lucubrations of the night.

Among the implements of destruction, he studied with peculiar care the recent and tremendous discovery of the Latins; and his artillery surpassed whatever had yet appeared in the world. A founder of cannon, a Dane or Hungarian, who had been almost starved in the Greek service, deserted to the Moslems, and was liberally entertained by the Turkish sultan. Mahomet was satisfied with the answer to his first question, which he eagerly pressed on the artist. 'Am I able to cast a cannon capable of throwing a stone or ball of sufficient size to batter the walls of Constantinople? I am not ignorant of their strength, but, were they more solid than those of Babylon, I could oppose an engine of superior power; the position and management of that engine must be left to your engineers.' On this assurance, a foundry was established in Hadrianople: the metal was prepared; and, at the end of three months, Urban produced a piece of brass ordnance of stupendous and almost incredible magnitude; a measure of twelve palms is assigned to the bore; and the stone bullet weighed above six hundred pounds.[24] A vacant place before the new palace was chosen for the first experiment; but, to prevent the sudden and mischievous effects of astonishment and fear, a proclamation was issued that the cannon would be discharged the ensuing day. The explosion was felt or heard in the circuit of an hundred furlongs: the ball, by the force of gunpowder, was driven above a mile; and on the spot where it fell, it buried itself a fathom deep in the ground. For the conveyance of this destructive engine, a frame or carriage of thirty waggons was linked together and drawn along by a team of sixty oxen; two hundred men on both sides were stationed to poise and support the rolling weight; two hundred and fifty workmen marched before to smooth the way and repair the bridges; and near two months were employed in a laborious journey of one hundred and fifty miles. A lively[25] philosopher derides, on this occasion, the credulity of the Greeks, and observes, with much reason, that we should always distrust the exaggerations of a vanquished people. He calculates that a ball, even of two hundred pounds, would require a charge of one hundred and fifty pounds of powder; and that the stroke would be feeble and impotent, since not a fifteenth part of the mass could be inflamed at the same moment. A stranger as I am to the act of destruction, I can discern that the modern improvements of artillery prefer the number of pieces to the weight of metal; the quickness of the fire to the sound, or even the consequence, of a single explosion. Yet I dare not reject the positive and unanimous evidence of contemporary writers; nor can it seem improbable that the first artists, in their rude and ambitious efforts, should have transgressed the standard of moderation. A Turkish cannon, more enormous than that of Mahomet, still guards the entrance of the Dardanelles; and, if the use be inconvenient, it has been found on a late trial that the effect was far from contemptible. A stone bullet of *eleven* hundred pounds weight was once discharged with three hundred and thirty pounds of powder; at the distance of six hundred yards, it shivered into three rocky fragments, traversed the strait, and, leaving the waters in a foam, again rose and bounded against the opposite hill.[26]

While Mahomet threatened the capital of the East, the Greek emperor implored with fervent prayers the assistance of earth and heaven. But the invisible powers were deaf to his supplications; and Christendom beheld with indifference the fall of Constantinople, while she derived at least some promise of supply from the jealous and temporal policy of the sultan of Egypt. Some states were too weak, and others too remote; by some the danger was considered as imaginary, by others as inevitable: the Western princes were involved in their endless and domestic quarrels; and the Roman pontiff was exasperated by the falsehood or obstinacy of the Greeks. Instead of employing in their favour the arms and treasures of Italy, Nicholas the Fifth had foretold their approaching ruin; and his honour was engaged in the accomplishment of his prophecy. Perhaps he was softened by the last extremity of their distress; but his compassion was tardy; his efforts were faint and unavailing; and Constantinople had fallen, before the squadrons of Genoa and Venice could sail from their harbours.[27] Even the princes of the Morea and of the Greek islands affected a cold neutrality: the Genoese colony of Galata negotiated a private treaty; and the sultan indulged them in the delusive hope that by his clemency they might survive the ruin of the empire. A plebeian crowd, and some Byzantine nobles, basely withdrew from the danger of their country; and the avarice of the rich denied the emperor, and reserved for the Turks, the secret treasures which might have raised in their defence whole armies of mercenaries.[28] The indigent and solitary prince prepared, however, to sustain his formidable adversary; but, if his courage were equal to the peril, his strength was inadequate to the contest. In the beginning of the spring, the Turkish vanguard swept the towns and villages as far as the gates of Constantinople: submission was spared and protected; whatever presumed to resist was exterminated with fire and sword. The Greek places on the Black Sea, Mesembria, Acheloum, and Bizon, surrendered on the first summons; Selybria alone deserved the honours of a siege or blockade; and the bold inhabitants, while they were invested by land, launched their boats, pillaged the opposite coast of Cyzicus, and sold their captives in the public market. But on the approach of Mahomet himself all was silent and prostrate; he first halted at the distance of five miles; and from thence advancing in battle-array planted before the gate of St Romanus the Imperial standard; and, on the sixth day of April, formed the memorable siege of Constantinople.

The troops of Asia and Europe extended on the right and left from the Propontis to the harbour; the Janizaries in the front were stationed before the sultan's tent; the Ottoman line was covered by a deep entrenchment;

and a subordinate army enclosed the suburb of Galata, and watched the doubtful faith of the Genoese. The inquisitive Philelphus, who resided in Greece about thirty years before the siege, is confident that all the Turkish forces, of any name or value, could not exceed the number of sixty thousand horse and twenty thousand foot; and he upbraids the pusillanimity of the nations who had tamely yielded to a handful of barbarians. Such, indeed, might be the regular establishment of the *Capiculi*,[29] the troops of the Porte who marched with the prince and were paid from his royal treasury. But the bashaws, in their respective governments, maintained or levied a provincial militia; many lands were held by a military tenure; many volunteers were attracted by the hope of spoil; and the sound of the holy trumpet invited a swarm of hungry and fearless fanatics, who might contribute at least to multiply the terrors, and in a first attack to blunt the swords, of the Christians. The whole mass of the Turkish powers is magnified by Ducas, Chalcocondyles, and Leonard of Chios, to the amount of three or four hundred thousand men; but Phranza was a less remote and more accurate judge; and his precise definition of two hundred and fifty-eight thousand does not exceed the measure of experience and probability.[30] The navy of the besiegers was less formidable: the Propontis was overspread with three hundred and twenty sail; but of these no more than eighteen could be rated as galleys of war; and the far greater part must be degraded to the condition of storeships and transports, which poured into the camp fresh supplies of men, ammunition, and provisions. In her last decay, Constantinople was still peopled with more than an hundred thousand inhabitants; but these numbers are found in the accounts, not of war, but of captivity; and they mostly consisted of mechanics, of priests, of women, and of men devoid of that spirit which even women have sometimes exerted for the common safety. I can suppose, I could almost excuse, the reluctance of subjects to serve on a distant frontier, at the will of a tyrant; but the man who dares not expose his life in the defence of his children and his property has lost in society the first and most active energies of nature. By the emperor's command, a particular inquiry had been made through the streets and houses, how many of the citizens, or even of the monks, were able and willing to bear arms for their country. The lists were entrusted to Phranza;[31] and, after a diligent addition, he informed his master, with grief and surprise, that the national defence was reduced to four thousand nine hundred and seventy *Romans*. Between Constantine and his faithful minister, this comfortless secret was preserved; and a sufficient proportion of shields, crossbows, and muskets was distributed from the arsenal to the city bands. They derived some accession from a body of two thousand strangers, under the command of John Justiniani, a noble Genoese; a liberal donative was advanced to these auxiliaries; and a princely recompense, the isle of Lemnos, was promised to the valour and victory of their chief. A strong chain was drawn across the mouth of the harbour; it was supported by some Greek and Italian vessels of war and merchandise; and the ships of every Christian nation, that successively arrived from Candia and the Black Sea, were detained for the public service. Against the powers of the Ottoman empire, a city of the extent of thirteen, perhaps of sixteen, miles was defended by a scanty garrison of seven or eight thousand soldiers. Europe and Asia were open to the besiegers; but the strength and provisions of the Greeks must sustain a daily decrease; nor could they indulge the expectation of any foreign succour or supply.

The primitive Romans would have drawn their swords in the resolution of death or conquest. The primitive Christians might have embraced each other, and awaited in patience and charity the stroke of martyrdom. But the Greeks of Constantinople were animated only by the spirit of religion, and that spirit was productive only of animosity and discord. Before his death,* the emperor John Palaeologus had renounced the unpopular measure of an union with the Latins; nor was the idea revived, till the distress of his brother Constantine imposed a last trial of flattery and dissimulation.[32] With the demand of temporal aid, his ambassadors were instructed to mingle the assurance of spiritual obedience; his neglect of the church was excused by the urgent cares of the state; and his orthodox wishes solicited the presence of a Roman legate. The Vatican had been too often deluded; yet the signs of repentance could not decently be overlooked; a legate was more easily granted than an army; and, about six months before the final destruction, the cardinal Isidore of Russia appeared in that character with a retinue of priests and soldiers. The emperor saluted him as a friend and father; respectfully listened to his public and private sermons; and with the most obsequious of the clergy and laymen subscribed the act of union, as it had been ratified in the council of Florence.† On the twelfth of December, the two nations, in the church of St Sophia, joined in the communion of sacrifice and prayer; and the names of the two pontiffs were solemnly commemorated: the names of Nicholas the Fifth, the vicar of Christ, and of the patriarch Gregory, who had been driven into exile by a rebellious people.

But the dress and language of the Latin priest who officiated at the altar were an object of scandal; and it was observed with horror that he consecrated a cake or wafer of *unleavened* bread and poured cold water into the cup of the sacrament. A national historian acknowledges with a blush that none of his countrymen, not the emperor himself, were sincere in this occasional conformity.[33] Their hasty and unconditional submission was palliated by a promise of future revisal; but the best or the worst of their excuses was the confession of their own perjury. When they were pressed by the reproaches of their honest brethren, 'Have patience,' they whispered, 'have patience till God shall have delivered the city from the great dragon who seeks to devour us. You shall then perceive whether we are truly reconciled with the Azymites.'‡ But patience is not the attribute of zeal; nor can the arts of a court be adapted to the freedom and violence of popular enthusiasm. From the dome of St Sophia, the inhabitants of either sex and of every degree rushed in crowds to the cell of the monk Gennadius,[34] to consult the oracle of the church. The holy man was invisible; entranced, as it should seem, in deep meditation or divine rapture; but he had exposed on the door of his cell a speaking tablet; and they successively withdrew, after reading these tremendous words: 'O miserable Romans! why will ye abandon the truth? And why, instead of confiding in God, will ye put your trust in the Italians? In losing your faith, you will lose your city. Have mercy on me, O Lord! I protest, in thy presence, that I am innocent of the crime. O miserable Romans! consider, pause, and repent. At the same moment that you renounce the religion of your fathers, by embracing impiety, you submit to a foreign servitude.' According to the advice of Gennadius, the religious virgins, as pure as angels and as proud as daemons, rejected the act of union and abjured all communion with the present and future associates of the Latins; and their example was applauded and imitated by the greatest part of the clergy and people. From the monastery, the devout Greeks dispersed themselves in the tavern; drank confusion to the slaves of the pope; emptied their glasses in honour of the image of the holy Virgin; and besought her to defend against Mahomet the city which she had formerly saved from Chosroes and the Chagan.* In the double intoxication of zeal and wine, they valiantly exclaimed, 'What occasion have we for succour, or union, or Latins? Far from us be the worship of the Azymites!' During the winter that preceded the Turkish conquest, the nation was distracted by this epidemical frenzy; and the season of Lent, the approach of Easter, instead of breathing charity and love, served only to fortify the obstinacy and influence of the zealots. The confessors scrutinised and alarmed the conscience of their votaries, and a rigorous penance was imposed on those who had received the communion from a priest who had given an express or tacit consent to the union. His service at the altar propagated the infection to the mute and simple spectators of the ceremony; they forfeited, by the impure spectacle, the virtue of their sacerdotal character; nor was it lawful, even in danger of sudden death, to invoke the assistance of their prayers or absolution. No sooner had the church of St Sophia been polluted by the Latin sacrifice than it was deserted as a Jewish synagogue, or an heathen temple, by the clergy and people; and a vast and gloomy silence prevailed in that venerable dome, which had so often smoked with a cloud of incense, blazed with innumerable lights, and resounded with the voice of prayer and thanksgiving. The Latins were the most odious of heretics and infidels; and the first minister of the empire, the great duke, was heard to declare that he had rather behold, in Constantinople, the turban of Mahomet than the pope's tiara or a cardinal's hat.[35] A sentiment so unworthy of Christians and patriots was familiar and fatal to the Greeks: the emperor was deprived of the affection and support of his subjects; and their native cowardice was sanctified by resignation to the divine decree or the visionary hope of a miraculous deliverance.

Of the triangle which composes the figure of Constantinople, the two sides along the sea were made inaccessible to an enemy: the Propontis by nature, and the harbour by art. Between the two waters, the basis of the triangle, the land-side was protected by a double wall and a deep ditch of the depth of one hundred feet. Against this line of fortification, which Phranza, an eyewitness, prolongs to the measure of six miles,[36] the Ottomans directed their principal attack; and the emperor, after distributing the service and command of the most perilous stations, undertook the defence of the external wall. In the first days of the siege, the Greek soldiers descended into the ditch, or sallied into the field; but they soon discovered that, in the proportion of their numbers, one Christian was of more value than twenty Turks; and, after these bold preludes, they were prudently content to maintain the rampart with their missile weapons. Nor should this prudence be accused of pusillanimity. The nation was indeed pusillanimous and base; but the last Constantine deserves the name of an hero; his noble band of volunteers was inspired with Roman virtue; and the foreign auxiliaries supported the honour of the Western chivalry. The incessant volleys of lances and arrows were accompanied with the smoke, the sound, and the fire of their musketry and cannon. Their small arms discharged at the same time either five or even ten balls of lead of the size of a walnut; and, according to the closeness of the ranks and the force of the powder, several breastplates and bodies were transpierced by the same shot. But the Turkish approaches were soon sunk in trenches or covered with ruins. Each day added to the science of the Christians; but their inadequate stock of gunpowder was wasted in the operations of each day. Their ordnance was not powerful either in size or number; and, if they possessed some heavy cannon, they feared to plant them on the walls, lest the aged structure should be shaken and overthrown by the explosion.[37] The same destructive secret had been revealed to the Moslems; by whom it was employed with the superior energy of zeal, riches, and despotism. The great cannon of Mahomet has been separately noticed: an important and visible object in the history of the times; but that enormous engine was flanked by two fellows almost of equal magnitude;[38] the long order of the Turkish artillery was pointed against the walls; fourteen batteries thundered at once on the most accessible places; and of one of these it is ambiguously expressed that it was mounted with one hundred and thirty guns, or that it discharged one hundred and thirty bullets. Yet, in the power and activity of the sultan, we may discern the infancy of the new science. Under a master who counted the moments, the great cannon could be loaded and fired no more than seven times in one day.[39] The heated metal unfortunately burst; several workmen were destroyed; and the skill of an artist was admired, who bethought himself of preventing the danger and the accident, by pouring oil, after each explosion, into the mouth of the cannon.

The first random shots were productive of more sound than effect; and it was by the advice of a Christian that the engineers were taught to level their aim against the two opposite sides of the salient angles of a bastion. However imperfect, the weight and repetition of the fire made some impression on the walls; and the Turks, pushing their approaches to the edge of the ditch, attempted to fill the enormous chasm and to build a road to the assault.[40] Innumerable fascines* and hogsheads and trunks of trees were heaped on each other; and such was the impetuosity of the throng that the foremost and the weakest were pushed headlong down the precipice and instantly buried under the accumulated mass. To fill the ditch was the toil of the besiegers; to clear away the rubbish was the safety of the besieged; and, after a long and bloody conflict, the web that had been woven in the day was still unravelled in the night. The next resource of Mahomet was the practice of mines; but the soil was rocky; in every attempt he was stopped and undermined by the Christian engineers; nor had the art been yet invented of replenishing those subterraneous passages with gunpowder and blowing whole towers and cities into the air.[41] A circumstance that distinguishes the siege of Constantinople is the reunion of the ancient and modern artillery. The cannon were intermingled with the mechanical engines for casting stones and darts; the bullet and the battering-ram were directed against the same walls; nor had the discovery of gunpowder superseded the use of the liquid and inextinguishable fire. A wooden turret of the largest size was advanced on rollers; this portable magazine of ammunition and fascines was protected by a threefold covering of bulls' hides; incessant volleys were securely discharged from the loop holes; in the front, three doors were contrived for the alternate sally and retreat of the soldiers and workmen. They ascended by a staircase to the upper platform, and, as high as the level of that platform, a scaling ladder could be raised by pulleys to form a bridge and grapple with the adverse rampart. By these various arts of annoyance, some as new as they were pernicious to the Greeks, the tower of St Romanus was at length overturned; after a severe struggle, the Turks were repulsed from the breach and interrupted by darkness; but they trusted that with the return of light they should renew the attack with fresh vigour and decisive success. Of this pause of action, this interval of hope, each moment was improved by the activity of the emperor and Justiniani,[†] who passed the night on the spot, and urged the labours which involved the safety of the church and city. At the dawn of day, the impatient sultan perceived, with astonishment and grief, that his wooden turret had been reduced to ashes: the ditch was cleared and restored; and the tower of St Romanus was again strong and entire. He deplored the failure of his design; and uttered a profane exclamation that the word of the thirty-seven thousand prophets should not have compelled him to believe that such a work, in so short a time, should have been accomplished by the infidels.

The generosity of the Christian princes was cold and tardy; but, in the first apprehension of a siege, Constantine had negotiated, in the isles of the Archipelago, the Morea, and Sicily, the most indispensable supplies. As early as the beginning of April, five[42] great ships, equipped for merchandise and war, would have sailed from the harbour of Chios, had not the wind blown obstinately from the north.[43] One of these ships bore the Imperial flag;* the remaining four belonged to the Genoese; and they were laden with wheat and barley, with wine, oil, and vegetables, and, above all, with soldiers and mariners, for the service of the capital. After a tedious delay, a gentle breeze, and, on the second day, a strong gale from the south, carried them through the Hellespont and the Propontis; but the city was already invested by sea and land; and the Turkish fleet, at the entrance of the Bosphorus, was stretched from shore to shore, in the form of a crescent, to intercept, or at least to repel, these bold auxiliaries. The reader who has present to his mind the geographical picture of Constantinople, will conceive and admire the greatness of the spectacle. The five Christian ships continued to advance with joyful shouts, and a full press both of sails and oars, against an hostile fleet of three hundred vessels; and the rampart, the camp, the coasts of Europe and Asia, were lined with innumerable spectators, who anxiously awaited the event of this momentous succour. At the first view, that event could not appear doubtful: the superiority of the Moslems was beyond all measure or account; and, in a calm, their numbers and valour must inevitably have prevailed. But their hasty and imperfect navy had been created, not by the genius of the people, but by the will of the sultan. In the height of their prosperity, the Turks have acknowledged that, if God had given them the earth, he had left the sea to the infidels;[44] and a series of defeats, a rapid progress of decay, has established the truth of their modest confession. Except eighteen galleys of some force, the rest of their fleet consisted of open boats, rudely constructed and awkwardly managed, crowded with troops and destitute of cannon; and, since courage arises in a great measure from the consciousness of strength, the bravest of the Janizaries might tremble on a new element. In the Christian squadron, five stout and lofty ships were guided by skilful pilots, and manned with the veterans of Italy and Greece, long practised in the arts and perils of the sea. Their weight was directed to sink or scatter the weak obstacles that impeded their passage; their artillery swept the waters; their liquid fire was poured on the heads of the adversaries who, with the design of boarding, presumed to approach them; and the winds and waves are always on the side of the ablest navigators. In this conflict, the Imperial vessel, which had been almost overpowered, was rescued by the Genoese; but the Turks, in a distant and closer attack, were twice repulsed with considerable loss. Mahomet himself sat on horseback on the beach, to encourage their valour by his voice and presence, by the promise of reward, and by fear more potent than the fear of the enemy. The passions of his soul, and even the gestures of his body,[45] seemed to imitate the actions of the combatants; and, as if he had been the lord of nature, he spurred his horse with a fearless and impotent effort into the sea. His loud reproaches, and the clamours of the camp, urged the Ottomans to a third attack, more fatal and bloody than the two former; and I must repeat, though I cannot credit, the evidence of Phranza, who affirms, from their own mouth, that they lost above twelve thousand men in the slaughter of the day. They fled in disorder to the shores of Europe and Asia, while the Christian squadron, triumphant and unhurt, steered along the Bosphorus and securely anchored within the chain of the harbour. In the confidence of victory, they boasted that the whole Turkish power must have yielded to their arms; but the admiral, or captain-bashaw, found some consolation for a painful wound in his eye, by representing that accident as the cause of his defeat. Baltha Ogli was a renegade of the race of the Bulgarian princes; his military character was tainted with the unpopular vice of avarice; and, under the despotism of the prince or people, misfortune is a sufficient evidence of guilt. His rank and services were annihilated by the displeasure of Mahomet. In the royal presence, the captain-bashaw was extended on the ground by four slaves, and received one hundred strokes with a golden rod;[46] his death had been pronounced; and he adored* the clemency of the sultan, who was satisfied with the milder punishment of confiscation and exile. The introduction of this supply revived the hopes of the Greeks, and accused the supineness of their Western allies. Amidst the deserts of Anatolia and the rocks of Palestine, the millions of the crusades had buried themselves in a voluntary and inevitable grave; but the situation of the Imperial city was strong against her enemies, and accessible to her friends; and a rational and moderate armament of the maritime states might have saved the relics of the Roman name and maintained a Christian fortress in the heart of the Ottoman empire. Yet this was the sole and feeble attempt for the deliverance of Constantinople; the more distant powers were insensible of its danger; and the ambassador of Hungary, or at least of Huniades, resided in the Turkish camp, to remove the fears, and to direct the operations, of the sultan.[47]

It was difficult for the Greeks to penetrate the secret of the divan; yet the Greeks are persuaded that a resistance, so obstinate and surprising, had fatigued the perseverance of Mahomet. He began to meditate a retreat, and the siege would have been speedily raised, if the ambition and jealousy of the second vizir had not opposed the perfidious advice of Calil Bashaw, who still maintained a secret correspondence with the Byzantine court. The reduction of the city appeared to be hopeless, unless a double attack could be made from the harbour as well as from the land; but the harbour was inaccessible: an impenetrable chain was now defended by eight large ships, more than twenty of a smaller size, with several galleys and sloops; and, instead of forcing this barrier, the Turks might apprehend a naval sally and a second encounter in the open sea. In this perplexity, the genius of Mahomet conceived and executed a plan of a bold and marvellous cast, of transporting by land his lighter vessels and military stores from the Bosphorus into the higher part of the harbour. The distance is about ten miles; the ground is uneven, and was overspread with thickets; and, as the road must be opened behind the suburb of Galata, their free passage or total destruction must depend on the option of the Genoese. But these selfish merchants were ambitious of the favour of being the last devoured; and the deficiency of art was supplied by the strength of obedient myriads. A level way was covered with a broad platform of strong and solid planks; and to render them more slippery and smooth, they were anointed with the fat of sheep and oxen. Fourscore light galleys and brigantines of fifty and thirty oars were disembarked on the Bosphorus shore; arranged successively on rollers; and drawn forwards by the power of men and pulleys. Two guides or pilots were stationed at the helm and the prow of each vessel; the sails were unfurled to the winds; and the labour was cheered by song and acclamation. In the course of a single night, this Turkish fleet painfully climbed the hill, steered over the plain, and was launched from the declivity into the shallow waters of the harbour, far above the molestation of the deeper vessels of the Greeks. The real importance of this operation was magnified by the consternation and confidence which it inspired; but the notorious, unquestionable fact was displayed before the eyes, and is recorded by the pens, of the two nations.[48] A similar stratagem had been repeatedly practised by the ancients;[49] the Ottoman galleys (I must again repeat) should be considered as large boats; and, if we compare the magnitude and the distance, the obstacles and the means, the boasted miracle[50] has perhaps been equalled by the industry of our own times.[51] As soon as Mahomet had occupied the upper harbour with a fleet and army, he constructed, in the narrowest part, a bridge, or rather mole, of fifty cubits in breadth and one hundred in length; it was formed of casks and hogsheads, joined with rafters linked with iron, and covered with a solid floor. On this floating battery he planted one of his largest cannon, while the fourscore galleys, with troops and scaling-ladders, approached the most accessible side, which had formerly been stormed by the Latin conquerors.* The indolence of the Christians has been accused for not destroying these unfinished works; but their fire, by a superior fire, was controlled and silenced; nor were they wanting in a nocturnal attempt to burn the vessels as well as the bridge of the sultan. His vigilance prevented their approach; their foremost galliots† were sunk or taken; forty youths, the bravest of Italy and Greece, were inhumanly massacred at his command; nor could the emperor's grief be assuaged by the just though cruel retaliation of exposing from the walls the heads of two hundred and sixty Musulman captives. After a siege of forty days, the fate of Constantinople could no longer be averted. The diminutive garrison was exhausted by a double attack; the fortifications, which had stood for ages against hostile violence, were dismantled on all sides by the Ottoman cannon; many breaches were opened; and near the gate of St Romanus four towers had been levelled with the ground. For the payment of his feeble and mutinous troops, Constantine was compelled to despoil the churches, with the promise of a fourfold restitution; and his sacrilege offered a new reproach to the enemies of the union. A spirit of discord impaired the remnant of the Christian strength; the Genoese and Venetian auxiliaries asserted the pre-eminence of their respective service; and Justiniani and the Great Duke, whose ambition was not extinguished by the common danger, accused each other of treachery and cowardice.

During the siege of Constantinople, the words of peace and capitulation had been sometimes pronounced; and several embassies had passed between the camp and the city.[52] The Greek emperor was humbled by adversity; and would have yielded to any terms compatible with religion and royalty. The Turkish sultan was desirous of sparing the blood of his soldiers; still more desirous of securing for his own use the Byzantine treasures; and he accomplished a sacred duty in presenting to the *Gabours** the choice of circumcision, of tribute, or of death. The avarice of Mahomet might have been satisfied with an annual sum of one hundred thousand ducats; but his ambition grasped the capital of the East; to the prince he offered a rich equivalent, to the people a free toleration or a safe departure; but, after some fruitless treaty, he declared his resolution of finding either a throne or a grave under the walls of Constantinople. A sense of honour and the fear of universal reproach forbade Palaeologus to resign the city into the hands of the Ottomans; and he determined to abide the last extremities of war. Several days were employed by the sultan in the preparations of the assault; and a respite was granted by his favourite science of astrology, which had fixed on the twenty-ninth of May as the fortunate and fatal hour. On the evening of the twenty-seventh, he issued his final orders; assembled in his presence the military chiefs; and dispersed his heralds through the camp to proclaim the duty and the motives of the perilous enterprise. Fear is the first principle of a despotic government; and his menaces were expressed in the Oriental style, that the fugitives and deserters, had they the wings of a bird,[53] should not escape from his inexorable justice. The greatest part of his bashaws and Janizaries were the offspring of Christian parents; but the glories of the Turkish name were perpetuated by successive adoption; and, in the gradual change of individuals, the spirit of a legion, a regiment, or an *oda* is kept alive by imitation and discipline. In this holy warfare, the Moslems were exhorted to purify their minds with prayer, their bodies with seven ablutions; and to abstain from food till the close of the ensuing day. A crowd of dervishes visited the tents, to instil the desire of martyrdom, and the assurance of spending an immortal youth amidst the rivers and gardens of paradise and in the embraces of the black-eyed virgins. Yet Mahomet principally trusted to the efficacy of temporal and visible rewards. A double pay was promised to the victorious troops: 'The city and the buildings,' said Mahomet, 'are mine; but I resign to your valour the captives and the spoil, the treasures of gold and beauty; be rich and be happy. Many are the provinces of my empire: the intrepid soldier who first ascends the walls of Constantinople shall be rewarded with the government of the fairest and most wealthy; and my gratitude shall accumulate his honours and fortunes above the measure of his own hopes.' Such various and potent motives diffused among the Turks a general ardour, regardless of life and impatient for action; the camp re-echoed with the Moslem shouts of 'God is God, there is but one God, and Mahomet is the apostle of God';[54] and the sea and land, from Galata to the seven towers, were illuminated by the blaze of their nocturnal fires.

Far different was the state of the Christians; who, with loud and impotent complaints, deplored* the guilt, or the punishment, of their sins. The celestial image of the Virgin had been exposed in solemn procession; but their divine patroness was deaf to their entreaties: they accused the obstinacy of the emperor for refusing a timely surrender; anticipated the horrors of their fate; and sighed for the repose and security of Turkish servitude. The noblest of the Greeks, and the bravest of the allies, were summoned to the palace, to prepare them, on the evening of the twenty-eighth, for the duties and dangers of the general assault. The last speech of Palaeologus was the funeral oration of the Roman Empire:[55] he promised, he conjured, and he vainly attempted to infuse the hope which was extinguished in his own mind. In this world all was comfortless and gloomy; and neither the gospel nor the church have proposed any conspicuous recompense to the heroes who fall in the service of their country. But the example of their prince and the confinement of a siege had armed these warriors with the courage of despair; and the pathetic scene is described by the feelings of the historian Phranza, who was himself present at this mournful assembly. They wept, they embraced; regardless of their families and fortunes, they devoted their lives; and each commander, departing to his station, maintained all night a vigilant and anxious watch on the rampart. The emperor, and some faithful companions, entered the dome of St Sophia, which in a few hours was to be converted into a mosque; and devoutly received, with tears and prayers, the sacrament of the holy communion. He reposed some moments in the palace, which resounded with cries and lamentations; solicited the pardon of all whom he might have injured;[56] and mounted on horseback to visit the guards and explore the motions of the enemy. The distress and fall of the last Constantine are more glorious than the long prosperity of the Byzantine Caesars.

In the confusion of darkness an assailant may sometimes succeed; but, in this great and general attack, the military judgment and astrological knowledge of Mahomet advised him to expect the morning, the memorable twenty-ninth of May, in the fourteen hundred and fifty-third year of the Christian era. The preceding night had been strenuously employed: the troops, the cannon, and the fascines were advanced to the edge of the ditch, which, in many parts, presented a smooth and level passage to the breach; and his fourscore galleys almost touched, with the prows and their scaling-ladders, the less defensible walls of the harbour. Under pain of death, silence was enjoined; but the physical laws of motion and sound are not obedient to discipline or fear; each individual might suppress his voice and measure his footsteps; but the march and labour of thousands must inevitably produce a strange confusion of dissonant clamours, which reached the ears of the watchmen of the towers. At daybreak, without the customary signal of the morning-gun, the Turks assaulted the city by sea and land; and the similitude of a twined or twisted thread has been applied to the closeness and continuity of their line of attack.[57] The foremost ranks consisted of the refuse of the host, a voluntary crowd, who fought without order or command; of the feebleness of age or childhood, of peasants and vagrants, and of all who had joined the camp in the blind hope of plunder and martyrdom. The common impulse drove them onwards to the wall; the most audacious to climb were instantly precipitated; and not a dart, not a bullet of the Christians was idly wasted on the accumulated throng. But their strength and ammunition were exhausted in this laborious defence; the ditch was filled with the bodies of the slain; they supported the footsteps of their companions; and of this devoted* vanguard the death was more serviceable than the life. Under their respective bashaws and sanjaks, the troops of Anatolia and Romania were successively led to the charge: their progress was various and doubtful; but, after a conflict of two hours, the Greeks still maintained and improved their advantage; and the voice of the emperor was heard, encouraging his soldiers to achieve, by a last effort, the deliverance of their country. In that fatal moment, the Janizaries arose, fresh, vigorous, and invincible. The sultan himself on horseback, with an iron mace in his hand, was the spectator and judge of their valour; he was surrounded by ten thousand of his domestic troops, whom he reserved for the decisive occasion; and the tide of battle was directed and impelled by his voice and eye. His numerous ministers of justice were posted behind the line, to urge, to restrain, and to punish; and, if danger was in the front, shame and inevitable death were in the rear of the fugitives. The cries of fear and of pain were drowned in the martial music of drums, trumpets, and attaballs;† and experience has proved that the mechanical operation of sounds, by quickening the circulation of the blood and spirits, will act on the human machine more forcibly than the eloquence of reason and honour. From the lines, the galleys, and the bridge, the Ottoman artillery thundered on all sides; and the camp and city, the Greeks and the Turks, were involved in a cloud of smoke, which could only be dispelled by the final deliverance or destruction of the Roman empire. The signal combats of the heroes of history or fable amuse our fancy and engage our affections; the skilful evolutions of war may inform the mind, and improve a necessary though pernicious science. But, in the uniform and odious pictures of a general assault, all is blood, and horror, and confusion; nor shall I strive, at the distance of three centuries and a thousand miles, to delineate a scene of which there could be no spectators, and of which the actors themselves were incapable of forming any just or adequate idea.

The immediate loss of Constantinople may be ascribed to the bullet, or arrow, which pierced the gauntlet of John Justiniani. The sight of his blood, and the exquisite pain, appalled the courage of the chief, whose arms and counsel were the firmest rampart of the city. As he withdrew from his station in quest of a surgeon, his flight was perceived and stopped by the indefatigable emperor. 'Your wound,' exclaimed Palaeologus, 'is slight; the danger is pressing; your presence is necessary; and whither will you retire?' 'I will retire?' said the trembling Genoese, 'by the same road which God has opened to the Turks;' and at these words he hastily passed through one of the breaches of the inner wall. By this pusillanimous act, he stained the honours of a military life; and the few days which he survived in Galata, or the isle of Chios, was embittered by his own and the public reproach.[58] His example was imitated by the greatest part of the Latin auxiliaries, and the defence began to slacken when the attack was pressed with redoubled vigour. The number of the Ottomans was fifty, perhaps an hundred, times superior to that of the Christians; the double walls were reduced by the cannon to an heap of ruins; in a circuit of several miles, some places must be found more easy of access or more feebly guarded; and, if the besiegers could penetrate in a single point, the whole city was irrecoverably lost. The first who deserved the sultan's reward was Hassan, the Janizary, of gigantic stature and strength. With his scymetar in one hand and his buckler* in the other, he ascended the outward fortification; of the thirty Janizaries, who were emulous of his valour, eighteen perished in the bold adventure. Hassan and his twelve companions had reached the summit: the giant was precipitated from the rampart; he rose on one knee, and was again oppressed by a shower of darts and stones. But his success had proved that the achievement was possible: the walls and towers were instantly covered with a swarm of Turks; and the Greeks, now driven from the vantage ground, were overwhelmed by increasing multitudes. Amidst these multitudes, the emperor,[59] who accomplished all the duties of a general and a soldier, was long seen, and finally lost. The nobles who fought round his person sustained, till their last breath, the honourable names of Palaeologus and Cantacuzene: his mournful exclamation was heard, 'Cannot there be found a Christian to cut off my head?'[60] and his last fear was that of falling alive into the hands of the infidels.[61] The prudent despair of Constantine cast away the purple;* amidst the tumult, he fell by an unknown hand, and his body was buried under a mountain of the slain. After his death, resistance and order were no more; the Greeks fled towards the city; and many were pressed and stifled in the narrow pass of the gate of St Romanus. The victorious Turks rushed through the breaches of the inner wall; and, as they advanced into the streets, they were soon joined by their brethren, who had forced the gate Phenar on the side of the harbour.[62] In the first heat of the pursuit, about two thousand Christians were put to the sword; but avarice soon prevailed over cruelty; and the victors acknowledged that they should immediately have given quarter, if the valour of the emperor and his chosen bands had not prepared them for a similar opposition in every part of the capital. It was thus, after a siege of fifty-three days, that Constantinople, which had defied the power of Chosroes, the Chagan, and the caliphs, was irretrievably subdued by the arms of Mahomet the Second. Her empire only had been subverted by the Latins; her religion was trampled in the dust by the Moslem conquerors.[63]

The tidings of misfortune fly with a rapid wing; yet such was the extent of Constantinople that the more distant quarters might prolong, some moments, the happy ignorance of their ruin.[64] But in the general consternation, in the feelings of selfish or social anxiety, in the tumult and thunder of the assault, a *sleepless* night and morning must have elapsed; nor can I believe that many Grecian ladies were awakened by the Janizaries from a sound and tranquil slumber. On the assurance of the public calamity, the houses and convents were instantly deserted; and the trembling inhabitants flocked together in the streets, like an herd of timid animals, as if accumulated weakness could be productive of strength, or in the vain hope that amid the crowd each individual might be safe and invisible. From every part of the capital, they flowed into the church of St Sophia: in the space of an hour, the sanctuary, the choir, the nave, the upper and lower galleries, were filled with the multitudes of fathers and husbands, of women and children, of priests, monks, and religious virgins; the doors were barred on the inside, and they sought protection from the sacred dome which they had so lately abhorred as a profane and polluted edifice.† Their confidence was founded on the prophecy of an enthusiast or impostor, that one day the Turks would enter Constantinople, and pursue the Romans as far as the column of Constantine in the square before St Sophia; but that this would be the term of their calamities; that an angel would descend from heaven, with a sword in his hand, and would deliver the empire, with that celestial weapon, to a poor man seated at the foot of the column. 'Take this sword,' would he say, 'and avenge the people of the Lord.' At these animating words, the Turks would instantly fly, and the victorious Romans would drive them from the West, and from all Anatolia, as far as the frontiers of Persia. It is on this occasion that Ducas, with some fancy and much truth, upbraids the discord and obstinacy of the Greeks. 'Had that angel appeared,' exclaims the historian, 'had he offered to exterminate your foes if you would consent to the union of the church, even then, in that fatal moment, you would have rejected your safety or have deceived your God.'[65]

While they expected the descent of the tardy angel, the doors were broken with axes; and, as the Turks encountered no resistance, their bloodless hands were employed in selecting and securing the multitude of their prisoners. Youth, beauty, and the appearance of wealth attracted their choice; and the right of property was decided among themselves by a prior seizure, by personal strength, and by the authority of command. In the space of an hour, the male captives were bound with cords, the females with their veils and girdles. The senators were linked with their slaves; the prelates with the porters of the church; and young men of a plebeian class with noble maids, whose faces had been invisible to the sun and their nearest kindred. In this common captivity, the ranks of society were confounded; the ties of nature were cut asunder; and the inexorable soldier was careless of the father's groans, the tears of the mother, and the lamentations of the children. The loudest in their wailings were the nuns, who were torn from the altar with naked bosoms, outstretched hands, and dishevelled hair; and we should piously believe that few could be tempted to prefer the vigils of the harem to those of the monastery. Of these unfortunate Greeks, of these domestic animals, whole strings were rudely driven through the streets; and, as the conquerors were eager to return for more prey, their trembling pace was quickened with menaces and blows. At the same hour, a similar rapine was exercised in all the churches and monasteries, in all the palaces and habitations of the capital; nor could any palace, however sacred or sequestered, protect the persons or the property of the Greeks. Above sixty thousand of this devoted people were transported from the city to the camp and fleet; exchanged or sold according to the caprice or interest of their masters, and dispersed in remote servitude through the provinces of the Ottoman empire. Among these we may notice some remarkable characters. The historian Phranza, first chamberlain and principal secretary, was involved with his family in the common lot. After suffering four months the hardships of slavery, he recovered his freedom; in the ensuing winter he ventured to Hadrianople, and ransomed his wife from the *mir bashi*, or master of horse; but his two children, in the flower of youth and beauty, had been seized for the use of Mahomet himself. The daughter of Phranza died in the seraglio, perhaps a virgin; his son, in the fifteenth year of his age, preferred death to infamy, and was stabbed by the hand of the royal lover.[66] A deed thus inhuman cannot surely be expiated by the taste and liberality with which he released a Grecian matron and her two daughters, on receiving a Latin ode from Philelphus, who had chosen a wife in that noble family.[67] The pride or cruelty of Mahomet would have been most sensibly gratified by the capture of a Roman legate; but the dexterity of Cardinal Isidore eluded the search, and he escaped from Galata in a plebeian habit.[68]

The chain and entrance of the outward harbour was still occupied by the Italian ships of merchandise and war. They had signalised their valour in the siege; they embraced the moment of retreat, while the Turkish mariners were dissipated in the pillage of the city. When they hoisted sail, the beach was covered with a suppliant and lamentable crowd; but the means of transportation were scanty; the Venetians and Genoese selected their countrymen; and, notwithstanding the fairest promises of the sultan, the inhabitants of Galata evacuated their houses and embarked with their most precious effects.

In the fall and the sack of great cities, an historian is condemned to repeat the tale of uniform calamity; the same effects must be produced by the same passions; and, when those passions may be indulged without control, small, alas! is the difference between civilised and savage man. Amidst the vague exclamations of bigotry and hatred, the Turks are not accused of a wanton or immoderate effusion of Christian blood; but, according to their maxims (the maxims of antiquity), the lives of the vanquished were forfeited; and the legitimate reward of the conqueror was derived from the service, the sale, or the ransom, of his captives of both sexes.[69] The wealth of Constantinople had been granted by the sultan to his victorious troops; and the rapine of an hour is more productive than the industry of years. But, as no regular division was attempted of the spoil, the respective shares were not determined by merit; and the rewards of valour were stolen away by the followers of the camp, who had declined the toil and danger of the battle. The narrative of their depredations could not afford either amusement or instruction; the total amount, in the last poverty of the empire, has been valued at four millions of ducats;[70] and of this sum a small part was the property of the Venetians, the Genoese, the Florentines, and the merchants of Ancona. Of these foreigners, the stock was improved in quick and perpetual circulation; but the riches of the Greeks were displayed in the idle ostentation of palaces and wardrobes, or deeply buried in treasures of ingots and old coin, lest it should be demanded at their hands for the defence of their country. The profanation and plunder of the monasteries and churches excited the most tragic complaints. The dome of St Sophia itself, the earthly heaven, the second firmament, the vehicle of the cherubim, the throne of the glory of God,[71] was despoiled of the oblations of ages; and the gold and silver, the pearls and jewels, the vases and sacerdotal ornaments, were most wickedly converted to the service of mankind. After the divine images had been stripped of all that could be valuable to a profane eye, the canvas, or the wood, was torn, or broken, or burnt, or trod under foot, or applied, in the stables or the kitchen, to the vilest uses. The example of sacrilege was imitated, however, from the Latin conquerors of Constantinople; and the treatment which Christ, the Virgin, and the saints had sustained from the guilty Catholic might be inflicted by the zealous Musulman on the monuments of idolatry.

Perhaps, instead of joining the public clamour, a philosopher will observe that in the decline of the arts the workmanship could not be more valuable than the work, and that a fresh supply of visions and miracles would speedily be renewed by the craft of the priest and the credulity of the people. He will more seriously deplore the loss of the Byzantine libraries, which they destroyed or scattered in the general confusion: one hundred and twenty thousand manuscripts are said to have disappeared;[72] ten volumes might be purchased for a single ducat; and the same ignominious price, too high perhaps for a shelf of theology, included the whole works of Aristotle and Homer, the noblest productions of the science and literature of ancient Greece. We may reflect with pleasure that an inestimable portion of our classic treasures was safely deposited in Italy; and that the mechanics of a German town had invented an art which derides the havoc of time and barbarism.

From the first hour[73] of the memorable twenty-ninth of May, disorder and rapine prevailed in Constantinople till the eighth hour of the same day; when the sultan himself passed in triumph through the gate of St Romanus. He was attended by his vizirs, bashaws, and guards, each of whom (says a Byzantine historian) was robust as Hercules, dexterous as Apollo, and equal in battle to any ten of the race of ordinary mortals. The conqueror[74] gazed with satisfaction and wonder on the strange though splendid appearance of the domes and palaces, so dissimilar from the style of Oriental architecture. In the hippodrome, or *atmeidan*, his eye was attracted by the twisted columns of the three serpents; and, as a trial of his strength, he shattered with his iron mace or battle-axe the underjaw of one of these monsters,[75] which in the eye of the Turks were the idols or talismans of the city. At the principal door of St Sophia, he alighted from his horse and entered the dome; and such was his jealous regard for that monument of his glory that, on observing a zealous Musulman in the act of breaking the marble pavement, he admonished him with his scymetar that, if the spoil and captives were granted to the soldiers, the public and private buildings had been reserved for the prince. By his command the metropolis of the Eastern church was transformed into a mosque: the rich and portable instruments of superstition had been removed; the crosses were thrown down; and the walls, which were covered with images and mosaics, were washed and purified and restored to a state of naked simplicity. On the same day, or on the ensuing Friday, the *muezin* or crier ascended the most lofty turret, and proclaimed the *ezan*, or public invitation, in the name of God and his prophet; the imam preached; and Mahomet the Second performed the *namaz* of prayer and thanksgiving on the great altar, where the Christian mysteries had so lately been celebrated before the last of the Caesars.[76] From St Sophia he proceeded to the august but desolate mansion of an hundred successors of the great Constantine; but which, in a few hours, had been stripped of the pomp of royalty. A melancholy reflection on the vicissitudes of human greatness forced itself on his mind; and he repeated an elegant distich of Persian poetry, 'The spider has wove his web in the imperial palace; and the owl hath sung her watch-song on the towers of Afrasiab.'[77]

Yet his mind was not satisfied, nor did the victory seem complete, till he was informed of the fate of Constantine; whether he had escaped, or been made prisoner, or had fallen in the battle. Two Janizaries claimed the honour and reward of his death: the body, under a heap of slain, was discovered by the golden eagles embroidered on his shoes; the Greeks acknowledged with tears the head of their late emperor; and, after exposing the bloody trophy,[78] Mahomet bestowed on his rival the honours of a decent funeral. After his decease, Lucas Notaras, great duke,[79] and first minister of the empire, was the most important prisoner. When he offered his person and his treasures at the foot of the throne, 'And why,' said the indignant sultan, 'did you not employ these treasures in the defence of your prince and country?' 'They were yours,' answered the slave; 'God had reserved them for your hands.' 'If he reserved them for me,' replied the despot, 'how have you presumed to withhold them so long by a fruitless and fatal resistance?' The great duke alleged the obstinacy of the strangers, and some secret encouragement from the Turkish vizir; and from this perilous interview he was at length dismissed with the assurance of pardon and protection. Mahomet condescended to visit his wife, a venerable princess, oppressed with sickness and grief; and his consolation for her misfortunes was in the most tender strain of humanity and filial reverence. A similar clemency was extended to the principal officers of state, of whom several were ransomed at his expense; and during some days he declared himself the friend and father of the vanquished people. But the scene was soon changed; and before his departure the hippodrome streamed with the blood of his noblest captives. His perfidious cruelty is execrated by the Christians. They adorn with the colours of heroic martyrdom the execution of the great duke and his two sons; and his death is ascribed to the generous refusal of delivering his children to the tyrant's lust. Yet a Byzantine historian has dropped an unguarded word of conspiracy, deliverance, and Italian succour: such treason may be glorious; but the rebel who bravely ventures has justly forfeited his life; nor should we blame a conqueror for destroying the enemies whom he can no longer trust. On the eighteenth of June, the victorious sultan returned to Hadrianople; and smiled at the base and hollow embassies of the Christian princes, who viewed their approaching ruin in the fall of the Eastern empire.

Constantinople had been left naked and desolate, without a prince or a people. But she could not be despoiled of the incomparable situation which marks her for the metropolis of a great empire; and the genius of the place will ever triumph over the accidents of time and fortune. Boursa and Hadrianople, the ancient seats of the Ottomans, sunk into provincial towns; and Mahomet the Second established his own residence, and that of his successors, on the same commanding spot which had been chosen by Constantine.[80] The fortifications of Galata, which might afford a shelter to the Latins, were prudently destroyed; but the damage of the Turkish cannon was soon repaired; and before the month of August great quantities of lime had been burnt for the restoration of the walls of the capital. As the entire property of the soil and buildings, whether public or private, or profane or sacred, was now transferred to the conqueror, he first separated a space of eight furlongs from the point of the triangle for the establishment of his seraglio, or palace. It is here, in the bosom of luxury, that the *Grand Signor* (as he has been emphatically named by the Italians) appears to reign over Europe and Asia; but his person on the shores of the Bosphorus may not always be secure from the insults of an hostile navy. In the new character of a mosque, the cathedral of St Sophia was endowed with an ample revenue, crowned with lofty minarets, and surrounded with groves and fountains, for the devotion and refreshment of the Moslems. The same model was imitated in the *jami*, or royal mosques; and the first of these was built by Mahomet himself, on the ruins of the church of the Holy Apostles and the tombs of the Greek emperors. On the third day after the conquest, the grave of Abu Ayub, or Job,* who had fallen in the first siege of the Arabs, was revealed in a vision; and it is before the sepulchre of the martyr that the new sultans are girded with the sword of empire.[81] Constantinople no longer appertains to the Roman historian; nor shall I enumerate the civil and religious edifices that were profaned or erected by its Turkish masters: the population was speedily renewed; and before the end of September five thousand families of Anatolia and Romania had obeyed the royal mandate, which enjoined them, under pain of death, to occupy their new habitations in the capital. The throne of Mahomet was guarded by the numbers and fidelity of his Moslem subjects; but his rational policy aspired to collect the remnant of the Greeks; and they returned in crowds, as soon as they were assured of their lives, their liberties, and the free exercise of their religion. In the election and investiture of a patriarch, the ceremonial of the Byzantine court was revived and imitated. With a mixture of satisfaction and horror, they beheld the sultan on his throne, who delivered into the hands of Gennadius the crosier, or pastoral staff, the symbol of his ecclesiastical office; who conducted the patriarch to the gate of the seraglio, presented him with an horse richly caparisoned, and directed the vizirs and bashaws to lead him to the palace which had been allotted for his residence.[82] The churches of Constantinople were shared between the two religions: their limits were marked; and, till it was infringed by Selim, the grandson of Mahomet, the Greeks[83] enjoyed above sixty years the benefit of this equal partition. Encouraged by the ministers of the divan, who wished to elude the fanaticism of the sultan, the Christian advocates presumed to allege that this division had been an act, not of generosity but of justice; not a concession, but a compact; and that, if one half of the city had been taken by storm, the other moiety had surrendered on the faith of a sacred capitulation. The original grant had indeed been consumed by fire; but the loss was supplied by the testimony of three aged Janizaries who remembered the transaction; and their venal oaths are of more weight in the opinion of Cantemir than the positive and unanimous consent of the history of the times.[84]

The remaining fragments of the Greek kingdom in Europe and Asia I shall abandon to the Turkish arms; but the final extinction of the two last dynasties[85] which have reigned in Constantinople should terminate the decline and fall of the Roman empire in the East. The despots of the Morea, Demetrius and Thomas,[86] the two surviving brothers of the name of Palaeologus, were astonished by the death of the emperor Constantine and the ruin of the monarchy. Hopeless of defence, they prepared, with the noble Greeks who adhered to their fortune, to seek a refuge in Italy, beyond the reach of the Ottoman thunder. Their first apprehensions were dispelled by the victorious sultan, who contented himself with a tribute of twelve thousand ducats; and, while his ambition explored the continent and the islands in search of prey, he indulged the Morea in a respite of seven years. But this respite was a period of grief, discord, and misery. The *hexamilion*, the rampart of the Isthmus, so often raised and so often subverted, could not long be defended by three hundred Italian archers: the keys of Corinth were seized by the Turks; they returned from their summer excursions with a train of captives and spoil; and the complaints of the injured Greeks were heard with indifference and disdain. The Albanians, a vagrant tribe of shepherds and robbers, filled the peninsula with rapine and murder; the two despots implored the dangerous and humiliating aid of a neighbouring bashaw; and, when he had quelled the revolt, his lessons inculcated the rule of their future conduct. Neither the ties of blood, nor the oaths which they repeatedly pledged in the communion and before the altar, nor the stronger pressure of necessity, could reconcile or suspend their domestic quarrels. They ravaged each other's patrimony with fire and sword; the alms and succours of the West were consumed in civil hostility; and their power was only exerted in savage and arbitrary executions, The distress and revenge of the weaker rival invoked their supreme lord; and, in the season of maturity and revenge, Mahomet declared himself the friend of Demetrius, and marched into the Morea with an irresistible force. When he had taken possession of Sparta, 'You are too weak,' said the sultan, 'to control this turbulent province. I will take your daughter to my bed; and you shall pass the remainder of your life in security and honour.' Demetrius sighed, and obeyed; surrendered his daughter and his castles; followed to Hadrianople his sovereign and son; andreceived, for his own mainte-nance, and that of his followers, a city in Thrace, and the adjacent isles of Imbros, Lemnos, and Samothrace. He was joined the next year by a companion of misfortune, the last of the Comnenian race, who, after the taking of Constantinople by the Latins, had founded a new empire on the coast of the Black Sea.[87] In the progress of his Anatolian conquests, Mahomet invested, with a fleet and army, the capital of David, who presumed to style himself Emperor of Trebizond;[88] and the negotiation was comprised in a short and peremptory question, 'Will you secure your life and treasures by resigning your kingdom? Or had you rather forfeit your kingdom, your treasures, and your life?' The feeble Comnenus was subdued by his own fears, and the example of a Musulman neighbour, the prince of Sinope,[89] who, on a similar summons, had yielded a fortified city with four hundred cannon and ten or twelve thousand soldiers. The capitulation of Trebizond was faithfully performed; and the emperor, with his family, was transported to a castle in Romania; but on a slight suspicion of corresponding with the Persian king, David and the whole Comnenian race were sacrificed to the jealousy or avarice of the conqueror. Nor could the name of father long protect the unfortunate Demetrius from exile and confiscation: his abject submission moved the pity and contempt of the sultan; his followers were transplanted to Constantinople; and his poverty was alleviated by a pension of fifty thousand aspers, till a monastic habit and a tardy death released Palaeologus from an earthly master. It is not easy to pronounce whether the servitude of Demetrius or the exile of his brother Thomas[90] be the most inglorious. On the conquest of the Morea, the despot escaped to Corfu, and from thence to Italy, with some naked adherents; his name, his sufferings, and the head of the apostle St Andrew entitled him to the hospitality of the Vatican; and his misery was prolonged by a pension of six thousand ducats from the pope and cardinals. His two sons, Andrew and Manuel, were educated in Italy; but the eldest, contemptible to his enemies and burdensome to his friends, was degraded by the baseness of his life and marriage. A title was his sole inheritance; and that inheritance he successively sold to the kings of France and Arragon.[91] During this transient prosperity, Charles the Eighth was ambitious of joining the empire of the East with the kingdom of Naples: in a public festival, he assumed the appellation and the purple of *Augustus*: the Greeks rejoiced, and the Ottoman already trembled, at the approach of the French chivalry.[92] Manuel Palaeologus, the second son, was tempted to revisit his native country: his return might be grateful, and could not be dangerous, to the Porte; he was maintained at Constantinople in safety and ease; and an honourable train of Christians and Moslems attended him to the grave. If there be some animals of so generous a nature that they refuse to propagate in a domestic state, the last of the Imperial race must be ascribed to an inferior kind: he accepted from the sultan's liberality two beautiful females; and his surviving son was lost in the habit and religion of a Turkish slave.

The importance of Constantinople was felt and magnified in its loss: the pontificate of Nicholas the Fifth, however peaceful and prosperous, was dishonoured by the fall of the Eastern empire; and the grief and terror of the Latins revived, or seemed to revive, the old enthusiasm of the crusades. In one of the most distant countries of the West, Philip, duke of Burgundy, entertained, at Lisle in Flanders, an assembly of his nobles; and the pompous pageants of the feast were skilfully adapted to their fancy and feelings.[93] In the midst of the banquet, a gigantic Saracen entered the hall, leading a fictitious elephant with a castle on his back; a matron in a mourning robe, the symbol of religion, was seen to issue from the castle; she deplored her oppression and accused the slowness of her champions; the principal herald of the golden fleece advanced, bearing on his fist a live pheasant, which, according to the rites of chivalry, he presented to the duke. At this extraordinary summons, Philip, a wise and aged prince, engaged his person and powers in the holy war against the Turks; his example was imitated by the barons and knights of the assembly; they swore to God, the Virgin, the ladies, and the *pheasant*; and their particular vows were not less extravagant than the general sanction of their oath. But the performance was made to depend on some future and foreign contingency; and, during twelve years, till the last hour of his life, the duke of Burgundy might be scrupulously, and perhaps sincerely, on the eve of his departure. Had every breast glowed with the same ardour; had the union of the Christians corresponded with their bravery; had every country, from Sweden[94] to Naples, supplied a just proportion of cavalry and infantry, of men and money, it is indeed probable that Constantinople would have been delivered, and that the Turks might have been chased beyond the Hellespont or the Euphrates. But the secretary of the emperor, who composed every epistle and attended every meeting, Aeneas Sylvius,[95] a statesman and orator, describes from his own experience the repugnant state and spirit of Christendom. 'It is a body,' says he, 'without an head; a republic without laws or magistrates. The pope and the emperor may shine as lofty titles, as splendid images; but *they* are unable to command, and none are willing to obey; every state has a separate prince, and every prince has a separate interest. What eloquence could unite so many discordant and hostile powers under the same standard? Could they be assembled in arms, who would dare to assume the office of general? What order could be maintained? – what military discipline? Who would undertake to feed such an enormous multitude? Who would understand their various languages, or direct their stranger and incompatible manners? What mortal could reconcile the English with the French, Genoa with Arragon, the Germans with the natives of Hungary and Bohemia? If a small number enlisted in the holy war, they must be overthrown by the infidels; if many, by their own weight and confusion.' Yet the same Aeneas, when he was raised to the papal throne, under the name of Pius the Second, devoted his life to the prosecution of the Turkish war. In the council of Mantua,* he excited some sparks of a false or feeble enthusiasm; but, when the pontiff appeared at Ancona,† to embark in person with the troops, engagements vanished in excuses; a precise day was adjourned to an indefinite term; and his effective army consisted of some German pilgrims, whom he was obliged to disband with indulgences and alms. Regardless of futurity, his successors and the powers of Italy were involved in the schemes of present and domestic ambition; and the distance or proximity of each object determined, in their eyes, its apparent magnitude. A more enlarged view of their interest would have taught them to maintain a defensive and naval war against the common enemy; and the support of Scanderbeg and his brave Albanians might have prevented the subsequent invasion of the kingdom of Naples. The siege and sack of Otranto by the Turks diffused a general consternation; and Pope Sixtus was preparing to fly beyond the Alps, when the storm was instantly dispelled by the death of Mahomet the Second, in the fifty-first year of his age.[96] His lofty genius aspired to the conquest of Italy: he was possessed of a strong city and a capacious harbour; and the same reign might have been decorated with the trophies of the New and the Ancient Rome.[97]

NOTES TO CHAPTER 68

1 For the character of Mahomet II it is dangerous to trust either the Turks or the Christians. The most moderate picture appears to be drawn by Phranza (i, 33), whose resentment had cooled in age and solitude; see likewise Spondanus (AD 1451, No. 11), and the continuator of Fleury (xxii, 552), the *Elogia* of Paulus Jovius (iii, 164–66), and the *Dictionnaire* de Bayle (iii, 272–79).

2 Cantemir (p. 115), and the mosques which he founded, attest his public regard for religion. Mahomet freely disputed with the patriarch Gennadius on the two religions (Spond., AD 1453, No. 22).

3 *Quinque linguas praeter suam noverat; Graecam, Latinam, Chaldaicam, Persicam.* The Latin translator of Phranza has dropped the Arabic, which the Koran must recommend to every Musulman.

4 Philelphus, by a Latin ode, requested and obtained the liberty of his wife's mother and sisters from the conqueror of Constantinople. It was delivered into the sultan's hands by the envoys of the duke of Milan. Philelphus himself was suspected of a design of retiring to Constantinople; yet the orator often sounded the trumpet of holy war (see his Life by M. Lancelot in the *Mémoires de l'Académie des Inscriptions*, x, 718, 724, etc.).

5 Robert Valturio published at Verona, in 1483, his twelve books, *de Re Militari*, in which he first mentions the use of bombs. By his patron Sigismond Malatesta, prince of Rimini, it had been addressed with a Latin epistle to Mahomet II.

6 According to Phranza, he assiduously studied the lives and actions of Alexander, Augustus, Constantine and Theodosius. I have read somewhere that Plutarch's Lives were translated by his orders into the Turkish language. If the sultan himself understood Greek, it must have been for the benefit of his subjects. Yet these Lives are a school of freedom as well as of valour.

7 The famous Gentile Bellino [AD c.1429–1507], whom he had invited from Venice, was dismissed with a chain and collar of gold, and a purse of 3000 ducats. With Voltaire I laugh at the foolish story of a slave purposely beheaded, to instruct the painter in the action of the muscles.

8 These Imperial drunkards were Soliman I, Selim II, and Amurath IV (Cantemir, p. 61). The sophis of Persia can produce a more regular succession; and in the last age our European travellers were the witnesses and the companions of their revels.

* pages 993   [Tamerlane the Great (AD 1336–1405), the Mongol chief]

† pages 993   [John Huniades, the Hungarian leader who successfully defended Belgrade against Mahomet II in AD 1456]

‡ pages 993   [Prince of Albania (AD c.1404–1467)]

§ pages 993   [The order of the Knights of St John fixed their abode in Rhodes.]

9 Calapin, one of these royal infants, was saved from his cruel brother, and baptised at Rome under the name of Callistus Othomannus. The emperor Frederic III presented him with an estate in Austria, where he ended his life; and Cuspinian, who in his youth conversed with the aged prince at Vienna, applauds his piety and wisdom (de Caesaribus, pp. 672, 673).

10 See the accession of Mahomet II in Ducas (ch. 33), Phranza (i, 33; ii, 2), Chalcocondyles (vii, 199), and Cantemir (p. 96).

11 Before I enter on the siege of Constantinople, I shall observe that, except the short hints of Cantemir and Leunclavius, I have not been able to obtain any Turkish account of this conquest; such an account as we possess of the siege of Rhodes by Soliman II (Mémoires de l'Académie des Inscriptions, xxvi, 723–69). I must therefore depend on the Greeks, whose prejudices, in some degree, are subdued by their distress. Our standard texts are those of Ducas (chs 34–42), Phranza (iii, 7–20), Chalcocondyles (viii, 201–14), and Leonardus Chiensis (Historia C. P. a Turco expugnatae, Norimberghae, 1544, in 4to, 20 leaves). The last of these narratives is the earliest in date, since it was composed in the isle of Chios the 16th of August, 1453, only seventy-nine days after the loss of the city, and in the first confusion of ideas and passions. Some hints may be added from an epistle of Cardinal Isidore (in Farragine Rerum Turcicarum, ad calcem Chalcocondyl. Clauseri, Basel, 1556) to Pope Nicholas V, and a tract of Theodosius Zygomala, which he addressed, in the year 1581, to Martin Crusius (Turco-Graecia, i, 74–98, Basel, 1584). The various facts and materials are briefly though critically reviewed by Spondanus (AD 1453, No. 1–27). The hearsay-relations of Monstrelet and the distant Latins, I shall take leave to disregard.

12 The situation of the fortress, and the topography of the Bosphorus, are best learned from Peter Gyllius (de Bosphoro Thracio, ii, 13), Leunclavius (Pandect., p. 445), and Tournefort (Voyage dans le Levant, ii, lettre xv, 443, 444); but I must regret the map or plan which Tournefort sent to the French minister of the marine. The reader may turn back to Chap. 17 of this history.

13 The opprobrious name which the Turks bestow on the Infidels is expressed Καβουρ by Ducas, and Giaour by Leunclavius and the moderns. The former term is derived by Ducange (Gloss. Graec., i, 530) from καβουρον, in vulgar Greek a tortoise, as denoting a retrograde motion from the faith. But, alas! Gabour is no more than Gheber, which was transferred from the Persian to the Turkish language, from the worshippers of fire to those of the crucifix (d' Herbelot, Bibliot. Orient. p. 375).

* *pages 996*   [in ad 1444 against Ladislaus, the King of Poland and Hungary]

14 Phranza does justice to his master's sense and courage: *Calliditatem hominis non ignorans Imperator prior arma movere constituit* ['well knowing the man's cunning, the Emperor resolved to take up arms first'], and stigmatises the folly of the *cum sacri tum profani proceres*, which he had heard, *amentes spe vana pasci* ['the leaders both ecclesiastical and lay . . . in their madness fed on empty hopes']. Ducas was not a privy counsellor.

† *pages 996*   [show]

15 Instead of this clear and consistent account, the *Turkish Annals* (Cantemir, p. 97) revived the foolish tale of the ox's hide, and Dido's stratagem in the foundation of Carthage. These annals (unless we are swayed by an antichristian prejudice) are far less valuable than the Greek historians.

16 In the dimensions of this fortress, the old castle of Europe, Phranza does not exactly agree with Chalcocondyles, whose description has been verified on the spot by his editor Leunclavius.

17 Among these were some pages of Mahomet, so conscious of his inexorable rigour that they begged to lose their heads in the city unless they could return before sunset.

18 Ducas, ch. 35; Phranza (iii, 3), who had sailed in his vessel, commemorates the Venetian pilot as a martyr.

19 *Auctum est Palaeologorum genus, et Imperii successor, parvaeque Romanorum scintillae heres natus, Andreas*, etc. (Phranza, iii, 7). The strong expression was inspired by his feelings.

20 Cantemir, pp. 97, 98. The sultan was either doubtful of his conquest or ignorant of the superior merits of Constantinople. A city or a kingdom may sometimes be ruined by the Imperial fortune of their sovereign.

* *pages 998*   [after his abdication in ad 1442]

21 Σύντροφος, by the president Cousin, is translated *père nourricier* [foster father], most correctly indeed from the Latin version; but in his haste he has overlooked the note by which Ismael Boillaud (ad Ducam, ch. 35) acknowledges and rectifies his own error.

22 The Oriental custom of never appearing without gifts before a sovereign or a superior is of high antiquity, and seems analogous with the idea of sacrifice, still more ancient and universal. See the examples of such Persian gifts, Aelian, *Hist. Var.*, i, 31–33.

23 The *Lala* of the Turks (Cantemir, p. 34) and the *Tata* of the Greeks (Ducas, ch. 35) are derived from the natural language of children; and it may be observed that all such primitive words which denote their parents are the simple repetition of one syllable, composed of a labial or dental consonant and an open vowel (des Brosses, *Méchanisme des Langues*, i, 231–47).

24 The Attic talent weighed about sixty minae, or avoirdupois pounds (see Hooper on Ancient Weights, Measures, etc.); but among the modern Greeks that classic appellation was extended to a weight of one hundred or one hundred and twenty-five pounds (Ducange, τάλαντον). Leonardus Chiensis measured the ball or stone of the *second* cannon: *Lapidem, qui palmis undecim ex meis ambibat in gyro* ['a stone measuring eleven palms across'].

25 See Voltaire (*Hist. Générale*, xci, 294, 295). He was ambitious of universal monarchy; and the poet frequently aspires to the name and style of an astronomer, a chemist, etc.

26 The Baron de Tott (iii, 85–89), who fortified the Dardanelles against the Russians, describes in a lively, and even comic, strain his own prowess and the consternation of the Turks. But that adventurous traveller does not possess the art of gaining our confidence.

27 *Non audivit, indignum ducens* ['He (the Pope) paid no attention, not thinking it worth his while'], says the honest Antoninus; but, as the Roman court was afterwards grieved and ashamed, we find the more courtly expression of Platina, *in animo fuisse pontifici iuvare Graecos* ['the Pope had intended to help the Greeks'], and the positive assertion of Aeneas Sylvius, *structam classem*, etc. ['a fleet was assembled, etc.'], (Spond. AD 1453, No. 3).

28 Antonin. in Prooem. – *Epist. Cardinal. Isidor. apud Spondanum*; and Dr Johnson, in the tragedy of *Irene* [1737], has happily seized this characteristic circumstance –

> The groaning Greeks dig up the golden caverns,
> The accumulated wealth of hoarding ages;
> That wealth which, granted to their weeping prince,
> Had rang'd embattled nations at their gates.

29 The palatine troops are styled *Capiculi*, the provincials, *Seratculi*; and most of the names and institutions of the Turkish militia existed before the *Canon Nameh* of Soliman II, from which, and his own experience, Count Marsigli has composed his *Military State of the Ottoman empire*.

30 The observation of Philelphus is approved by Cuspinian in the year 1508 (*de Caesaribus*, in Epilog. *de Militia Turcica*, p. 697). Marsigli proves that the effective armies of the Turks are much less numerous than they appear. In the army that besieged Constantinople, Leonardus Chiensis reckons no more than 15,000 Janizaries.

31 *Ego eidem* (Imp.) *tabellas extribui non absque dolore et maestitia, mansitque apud nos duos aliis occultus numerus* (Phranza, iii, 3). With some indulgence for national prejudices, we cannot desire a more authentic witness, not only of public facts, but of private counsels.

* *pages 1003* [in AD 1448]

32 In Spondanus, the narrative of the union is not only partial but imperfect. The bishop of Pamiers died in 1642, and the history of Ducas, which represents these scenes (chs 36, 37) with such truth and spirit, was not printed till the year 1649.

† *pages 1003* [in AD 1438]

33 Phranza, one of the conforming Greeks, acknowledges that the measure was adopted only *propter spem auxilii* ['in the hope of assistance']; he affirms with pleasure that those who refused to perform their devotions in St Sophia, *extra culpam et in pace essent* ['were without blame and were untroubled'] (iii, 20).

‡ *pages 1003* [users of unleavened bread for the host, i.e. Roman Catholics]

34 His primitive and secular name was George Scholarius, which he changed for that of Gennadius, either when he became a monk or a patriarch. His defence, at Florence, of the same union which he so furiously attacked at Constantinople, has tempted Leo Allatius (*Diatrib. de Georgiis*, in Fabric., *Bibliot. Graec.*, x, 760–86) to divide him into two men; but Renaudot (pp. 343–83) has restored the identity of his person, and the duplicity of his character.

* *pages 1004* [Chosroes II of Persia, and the Chagan or king of the Avars, who had threatened Constantinople in AD 626]

35 φακιόλιον, καλύπτρα may be fairly translated a cardinal's hat. The difference of the Greek and Latin habits embittered the schism.

36 We are obliged to reduce the Greek miles to the smallest measure which is preserved in the wersts of Russia, of 547 French *toises*, and of 104⅖ to a degree. The six miles of Phranza do not exceed four English miles (d'Anville, *Mésures Itinéraires*, pp. 61, 123, etc.).

37 *At in dies doctiores nostri facti paravere contra hostes machinamenta, quae tamen avare dabantur. Pulvis erat nitri modica, exigua; tela modica; bombardae, si aderant incommoditate loci, primum hostes offendere maceriebus alveisque tectos non poterant. Nam siquae magnae erant, ne murus concuteretur noster, quiescebant.* This passage of Leonardus Chiensis is curious and important.

38 According to Chalcocondyles and Phranza, the great cannon burst: an accident which, according to Ducas, was prevented by the artist's skill. It is evident that they do not speak of the same gun.

39 Near an hundred years after the siege of Constantinople, the French and English fleets in the Channel were proud of firing 300 shot in an engagement of two hours (*Mémoires* de Martin du Bellay, Bk x in the *Collection Générale*, xxi, 239).

40 I have selected some curious facts, without striving to emulate the bloody and obstinate eloquence of the Abbé de Vertot, in his prolix descriptions of the sieges of Rhodes, Malta, etc. But that agreeable historian had a turn for romance, and, as he wrote to please the Order, he has adopted the same spirit of enthusiasm and chivalry.

 * *pages 1006* [bundles of sticks]

41 The first theory of mines with gunpowder appears in 1480, in a manuscript of George of Sienna (Tiraboschi, vi, i, 324). They were first practised at Sarzanella, in 1487; but the honour and improvement in 1503 is ascribed to Peter of Navarre, who used them with success in the wars of Italy (*Hist. de la Ligue de Cambray*, ii, 93–97).

 † *pages 1006* [the Genoese leader]

42 It is singular that the Greeks should not agree in the number of these illustrious vessels; the *five* of Ducas, the *four* of Phranza and Leonardus, and the *two* of Chalcocondyles, must be extended to the smaller, or confined to the larger, size. Voltaire, in giving one of these ships to Frederic III, confounds the emperors of the East and West.

43 In bold defiance, or rather in gross ignorance, of language and geography, the President Cousin detains them at Chios with a south, and wafts them to Constantinople with a north, wind.

 * *pages 1007* [of the Holy Roman (German) Empire]

44 The perpetual decay and weakness of the Turkish navy may be observed in Rycaut (*State of the Ottoman Empire*, pp. 372–78), Thévenot (*Voyages*, i, 229–42), and Tott (*Mémoires*, tom. iii); the last of whom is always solicitous to amuse and amaze his reader.

45 I must confess that I have before my eyes the living picture which Thucydides (vii, 71) has drawn of the passions and gestures of the Athenians in a naval engagement in the great harbour of Syracuse.

46 According to the exaggeration or corrupt text of Ducas (ch. 38), this golden bar was of the enormous and incredible weight of 500 *librae*, or pounds. Bouillaud's reading of 500 drachms, or five pounds, is sufficient to exercise the arm of Mahomet and bruise the back of his admiral.

* *pages 1008*   [glorified]

47 Ducas, who confesses himself ill informed of the affairs of Hungary, assigns a motive of superstition, a fatal belief that Constantinople would be the term of the Turkish conquests. See Phranza (iii, 20) and Spondanus.

48 The unanimous testimony of the four Greeks is confirmed by Cantemir (p. 96) from the Turkish annals; but I could wish to contract the distance of *ten* miles and to prolong the term of *one* night.

49 Phranza relates two examples of a similar transportation over the six miles of the isthmus of Corinth: the one fabulous, of Augustus after the battle of Actium; the other true, of Nicetas, a Greek general, in the xth century. To these he might have added a bold enterprise of Hannibal, to introduce his vessels into the harbour of Tarentum (Polybius, viii, 749, edit. Gronov).

50 A Greek of Candia, who had served the Venetians in a similar undertaking (Spond., AD 1438, No. 37), might possibly be the adviser and agent of Mahomet.

51 I particularly allude to our own embarkations on the lakes of Canada, in the years 1776 and 1777, so great in the labour, so fruitless in the event. [Gibbon refers to the War of American Independence.]

* *pages 1009*   [in AD 1204]

† *pages 1009*   [small galleys]

52 Chalcocondyles and Ducas differ in the time and circumstances of the negotiation; and, as it was neither glorious nor salutary, the faithful Phranza spares his prince even the thought of a surrender.

* *pages 1010*   [See note 13.]

53 These wings (Chalcocondyles, viii, 208) are no more than an Oriental figure; but, in the tragedy of *Irene* [by Samuel Johnson], Mahomet's passion soars above sense and reason:

> Should the fierce North, upon his frozen wings,
> Bear him aloft above the wondering clouds,
> And seat him in the Pleiads' golden chariot –
> Thence should my fury drag him down to tortures.

Besides the extravagance of the rant, I must observe, 1. That the operation of the winds must be confined to the *lower* region of the air. 2. That the name, etymology, and fable of the Pleiads are purely Greek (Scholiast ad Homer, 18, 686; Eudocia in Ionia, p. 399; Apollodor., iii, 10; Heine, p. 229, note 682), and had no affinity with the astronomy of the East (Hyde ad Ulugbeg, *Tabul. in Syntagma Dissert.*, i, 40, 42; Goguet, *Origine des Arts*, etc., vi, 73–78; Gebelin, *Hist. du Calendrier*, p. 73), which Mahomet had studied. 3. The golden chariot does not exist either in science or fiction, but I much fear that Dr Johnson has confounded the Pleiads with the great bear or waggon, the zodiac with a northern constellation:

> Ἄρκτον θ᾽ ἣν καὶ ἅμαξαν ἐπίκλησιν καλέουσι
> ['the Bear, which they also call the Waggon', *Iliad*, 18, 487].

54 Phranza quarrels with these Moslem acclamations, not for the name of God, but for that of the Prophet: the pious zeal of Voltaire is excessive, and even ridiculous.

* *pages 1011*   [bewailed]

55 I am afraid that this discourse was composed by Phranza himself; and it smells so grossly of the sermon and the convent that I almost doubt whether it was

pronounced by Constantine. Leonardus assigns him another speech, in which he addresses himself more respectfully to the Latin auxiliaries.

56 This abasement, which devotion has sometimes extorted from dying princes, is an improvement of the gospel doctrine of the forgiveness of injuries; it is more easy to forgive 490 times than once to ask pardon of an inferior.

57 Besides the 10,000 guards, and the sailors and the marines, Ducas numbers in this general assault 250,000 Turks, both horse and foot.

* *pages 1012*   [doomed]

† *pages 1012*   [kettledrums]

58 In the severe censure of the flight of Justiniani, Phranza expresses his own feelings and those of the public. For some private reasons, he is treated with more lenity and respect by Ducas; but the words of Leonardus Chiensis express his strong and recent indignation, *gloriae salutis suique oblitus* ['forgetful of honour, of the (public) safety, and of himself']. In the whole series of their Eastern policy, his countrymen, the Genoese, were always suspected, and often guilty.

* *pages 1013*   [round shield]

59 Ducas kills him with two blows of Turkish soldiers; Chalcocondyles wounds him in the shoulder, and then tramples him in the gate. The grief of Phranza carrying him among the enemy escapes from the precise image of his death; but we may, without flattery, apply these noble lines of Dryden –

> As to Sebastian, let them search the field;
> And, where they find a mountain of the slain,
> Send one to climb, and looking down beneath,
> There they will find him at his manly length,
> With his face up to heaven, in that red monument
> Which his good sword had digg'd.

60 Spondanus (AD 1453, No. 10), who has hopes of his salvation, wishes to absolve this demand from the guilt of suicide.

61 Leonardus Chiensis very properly observes that the Turks, had they known the emperor, would have laboured to save and secure a captive so acceptable to the sultan.

* *pages 1014*   [the imperial mantle]

62 Cantemir, p. 96. The Christian ships in the mouth of the harbour had flanked and retarded this naval attack.

63 Chalcocondyles most absurdly supposes that Constantinople was sacked by the Asiatics in revenge for the ancient calamities of Troy; and the grammarians of the xvth century are happy to melt down the uncouth appellation of Turks into the more classical name of *Teucri* [Trojans].

64 When Cyrus surprised Babylon during the celebration of a festival, so vast was the city, and so careless were the inhabitants, that much time elapsed before the distant quarters knew that they were captives. Herodotus (i, 191), and Usher (*Annal.*, p. 78), who has quoted from the prophet Jeremiah a passage of similar import.

† *pages 1014*   [See pages 1038–39.]

65 This lively description is extracted from Ducas (ch. 39), who two years afterwards was sent ambassador from the prince of Lesbos to the sultan (ch. 44). Till Lesbos was subdued in 1463 (Phranza, iii, 27), that island must have been full of the fugitives of Constantinople, who delighted to repeat, perhaps to adorn, the tale of their misery.

66 See Phranza, iii, 20, 21. His expressions are positive: *Ameras sua manu iugulavit . . . volebat enim eo turpiter et nefarie abuti. Me miserum et infelicem.* ['The Emir slew him with his own hand . . . having sought to subject him to shameful and wicked abuse. Wretched and unhappy that I am.'] Yet he could only learn from report the bloody or impure scenes that were acted in the dark recesses of the seraglio.

67 See Tiraboschi (vi, i, 290), and Lancelot (*Mém. de l'Académie des Inscriptions*, x, 718). I should be curious to learn how he could praise the public enemy, whom he so often reviles as the most corrupt and inhuman of tyrants.

68 The Commentaries of Pius II suppose that he craftily placed his cardinal's hat on the head of a corpse, which was cut off and exposed in triumph, while the legate himself was bought and delivered, as a captive of no value. The great Belgic Chronicle adorns his escape with new adventures, which he suppressed (says Spondanus, AD 1453, No. 15) in his own letters, lest he should lose the merit and reward of suffering for Christ.

69 Busbequius expatiates with pleasure and applause on the rights of war and the use of slavery among the ancients and the Turks (*de Legat. Turcica*, iii, 161).

70 This sum is specified in a marginal note of Leunclavius (Chalcocondyles, viii, 211), but in the distribution to Venice, Genoa, Florence, and Ancona, of 50, 20, 20, and 15,000 ducats, I suspect that a figure has been dropped. Even with the restitution, the foreign property would scarcely exceed one-fourth.

71 See the enthusiastic praises and lamentations of Phranza (iii, 17).

72 See Ducas (ch. 43), and an epistle, 15th July, 1453, from Laurus Quirinus to Pope Nicholas V (Hody, *de Graecis*, p. 192, from a manuscript in the Cotton Library).

73 The Julian calendar, which reckons the days and hours from midnight, was used at Constantinople. But Ducas seems to understand the natural hours from sunrise.

74 See the *Turkish Annals*, p. 329, and the *Pandects* of Leunclavius, p. 448.

75 I have had occasion [in Chapter 17] to mention this curious relic of Grecian antiquity.

76 We are obliged to Cantemir (p. 102) for the Turkish account of the conversion of St Sophia, so bitterly deplored by Phranza and Ducas. It is amusing enough to observe in what opposite lights the same object appears to a Musulman and a Christian eye.

77 This distich, which Cantemir gives in the original, derives new beauties from the application. It was thus that Scipio [Roman general, 232–183 BC] repeated, in the sack of Carthage, the famous prophecy of Homer. The same generous feeling carried the mind of the conqueror to the past or the future.

78 I cannot believe, with Ducas (see Spondanus, AD 1453, No. 13), that Mahomet sent round Persia, Arabia, etc., the head of the Greek emperor; he would surely content himself with a trophy less inhuman.

79 Phranza was the personal enemy of the great duke; nor could time, or death, or his own retreat to a monastery, extort a feeling of sympathy or forgiveness. Ducas is inclined to praise and pity the martyr; Chalcocondyles is neuter, but we are indebted to him for the hint of the Greek conspiracy.

80 For the restitution of Constantinople and the Turkish foundations, see Cantemir (pp. 102–09), Ducas (ch. 42), with Thévenot, Tournefort, and the rest of our modern travellers. From a gigantic picture of the greatness, population, etc., of Constantinople and the Ottoman empire (*Abrégé de*

l'Histoire Ottomane, i, 16–21), we may learn that in the year 1586 the Moslems were less numerous in the capital than the Christians or even the Jews.

* *pages 1019* [companion of Mahomet who fell during the first siege of Constantinople by the Arabs in AD 668–75]

81 The *Turbé*, or sepulchral monument of Abu Ayub, is described and engraved in the *Tableau Général de l'Empire Ottoman* (Paris, 1787, in large folio), a work of less use, perhaps, than magnificence (i, 305, 306).

82 Phranza (iii, 19) relates the ceremony, which has possibly been adorned in the Greek reports to each other, and to the Latins. The fact is confirmed by Emanuel Malaxus, who wrote, in vulgar Greek, the history of the Patriarchs after the taking of Constantinople, inserted in the *Turco-Graecia* of Crusius (v, 106–84). But the most patient reader will not believe that Mahomet adopted the Catholic form, *Sancta Trinitas quae mihi donavit imperium te in patriarcham novae Romae deligit* ['The Holy Trinity, which gave me my throne, has chosen you as patriarch of the new Rome'].

83 From the *Turco-Graecia* of Crusius, etc. Spondanus (AD 1453, No. 21; 1458, No. 16) describes the slavery and domestic quarrels of the Greek Church. The patriarch who succeeded Gennadius threw himself in despair into a well.

84 Cantemir (pp. 101–05) insists on the unanimous consent of the Turkish historians, ancient as well as modern, and argues that they would not have violated the truth to diminish their national glory, since it is esteemed more honourable to take a city by force than by composition. But 1. I doubt this consent, since he quotes no particular historian, and the Turkish Annals of Leunclavius affirm, without exception, that Mahomet took Constantinople *per vim* [by force] (p. 329). 2. The same argument may be turned in favour of the Greeks of the times, who would not have forgotten this honourable and salutary treaty. Voltaire, as usual, prefers the Turks to the Christians.

85 For the genealogy and fall of the Comneni of Trebizond, see Ducange (*Fam. Byzant.* p. 195); for the last Palaeologi, the same accurate antiquarian (pp. 244, 247, 248). The Palaeologi of Montferrat were not extinct till the next century; but they had forgotten their Greek origin and kindred.

86 In the worthless story of the disputes and misfortunes of the two brothers, Phranza (iii, 21–30) is too partial on the side of Thomas, Ducas (ch. 44, 45) is too brief, and Chalcocondyles (Bks viii, ix, x) too diffuse and digressive.

87 See the loss or conquest of Trebizond in Chalcocondyles (ix, 263–66), Ducas (ch. 45), Phranza (iii, 27), and Cantemir (p. 107).

88 Though Tournefort (iii, lettre xvii, 179) speaks of Trebizond as *mal peuplée* [thinly populated], Peyssonel, the latest and most accurate observer, can find 100,000 inhabitants (*Commerce de la Mer Noire*, ii, 72, and for the province, pp. 53–90). Its prosperity and trade are perpetually disturbed by the factious quarrels of two *odas* [regiments] of Janizaries, in one of which 30,000 Lazi are commonly enrolled (*Mémoires* de Tott, iii, 16, 17).

89 Ismael Beg, prince of Sinope or Sinople, was possessed (chiefly from his copper mines) of a revenue of 200,000 ducats (Chalcocond., ix, 258, 259). Peyssonel (*Commerce de la Mer Noire*, ii, 100) ascribes to the modern city 60,000 inhabitants This account seems enormous; yet it is by trading with a people that we become acquainted with their wealth and numbers.

90 Spondanus (from Gobelin, *Comment. Pii II*, Bk v) relates the arrival and reception of the despot Thomas at Rome (AD 1461, No. 3).

91 By an act dated AD 1494, 6th Sept., and lately transmitted from the archives of the Capitol to the royal library of Paris, the despot Andrew Palaeologus, reserving the Morea, and stipulating some private advantages, conveys to Charles VIII, King of France, the empires of Constantinople and Trebizond (Spondanus, AD 1495, No. 2). M. de Foncemagne (*Mém. de l'Académie des Inscriptions*, xvii, 539–78) has bestowed a dissertation on this national title, of which he had obtained a copy from Rome.

92 See Philippe de Comines (vii, 14), who reckons with pleasure the number of Greeks who were prepared to rise, sixty miles of an easy navigation, eighteen days' journey from Valona to Constantinople, etc. On this occasion the Turkish empire was saved by the policy of Venice.

93 See the original feast in Olivier de la Marche (*Mémoires*, i, 29, 30), with the abstract and observations of M. de St Palaye (*Mémoires sur la Chevalerie*, i, iii, 182–85). The peacock and the pheasant were distinguished as royal birds.

94 It was found by an actual enumeration that Sweden, Gothland, and Finland contained 1,800,000 fighting men, and consequently were far more populous than at present.

95 In the year 1454, Spondanus has given, from Aeneas Sylvius, a view of the state of Europe, enriched with his own observations. That valuable annalist, and the Italian Muratori, will continue the series of events from the year 1453 to 1481, the end of Mahomet's life, and of this chapter.

* *pages 1022* [in AD 1459]

† *pages 1022* [in AD 1464]

96 Besides the two annalists, the reader may consult Giannone (*Istoria Civile*, iii, 449–55) for the Turkish invasion of the kingdom of Naples. For the reign and conquests of Mahomet II I have occasionally used the *Memorie Istoriche de' Monarchi Ottomanni* di Giovanni Sagredo (Venezia, 1677, in 4to). In peace and war, the Turks have ever engaged the attention of the republic of Venice. All her dispatches and archives were open to a procurator of St Mark, and Sagredo is not contemptible either in sense or style. Yet he too bitterly hates the infidels; he is ignorant of their language and manners; and his narrative, which allows only seventy pages to Mahomet II (pp. 69–140), becomes more copious and authentic as he approaches the years 1640 and 1644, the term of the historic labours of John Sagredo.

97 As I am now taking an everlasting farewell of the Greek empire, I shall briefly mention the great collection of Byzantine writers, whose names and testimonies have been successively repeated in this work. The Greek presses of Aldus and the Italians were confined to the classics of a better age; and the first rude editions of Procopius, Agathias, Cedrenus, Zonaras, etc., were published by the learned diligence of the Germans. The whole Byzantine series (36 volumes in folio) has gradually issued (AD 1648, etc.) from the royal press of the Louvre, with some collateral aid from Rome and Leipsic; but the Venetian edition (AD 1729), though cheaper and more copious, is not less inferior in correctness than in magnificence to that of Paris. The merits of the French editors are various; but the value of Anna Comnena, Cinnamus, Villehardouin, etc., is enhanced by the historical notes of Charles du Fresne du Cange. His supplemental works, the *Greek Glossary*, the *Constantinopolis Christiana*, the *Familiae Byzantinae*, diffuse a steady light over the darkness of the Lower Empire.

CHAPTER 69 (Summary)

*State of Rome from the twelfth century — temporal dominion of
the popes — seditions of the city — political heresy of Arnold of
Brescia — restoration of the republic — the senators — pride
of the Romans — their wars — they are deprived of the election
and presence of the popes, who retire to Avignon — the Jubilee —
noble families of Rome — feud of the Colonna and Ursini*

Gibbon returns to the subject of Rome in Chapter 69 to review its history
under the papacy. The popes were often vulnerable to popular risings
because of their wealth and were often involved in political rivalries. In
the twelfth century, Arnold of Brescia preached that the Church should
confine itself to spiritual concerns and the laws of the republic should be
restored to Rome. The Roman senate was revived in AD 1144 and issued
its own currency, but its power was eclipsed by the appointment of
officials from other states to be chief magistrates, the most notable
example being Brancaleone of Bologna, who in the period 1252–58
maintained law and order in the city. The senate appealed to the German
emperors to restore the republic of Rome, but it was a false sense of
history that inspired them and they lacked military force and discipline. In
the twelfth century, one cause of disorder was removed when the right to
elect the popes was confined to the college of cardinals. In the next
century, the popes withdrew from riots in Rome to reside elsewhere in
Italy, and from AD 1308 Avignon became their residence for seventy
years. In Rome, the institution of Holy Years in 1300 and 1350 helped to
maintain the flow of pilgrims to the apostolic churches of St Peter and St
Paul. Gibbon ends the chapter with an account of the leading families of
Rome, giving special attention to the rival houses of Colonna and Ursini.

CHAPTER 70 (Summary)

Character and coronation of Petrarch — restoration of the freedom and government of Rome by the tribune Rienzi — his virtues and vices, his expulsion and death — return of the popes from Avignon — great schism of the West — reunion of the Latin Church — last struggles of Roman liberty — statutes of Rome — final settlement of the ecclesiastical state

Gibbon begins Chapter 70 with a critical assessment of Petrarch's writings and then relates his 'coronation' as poet laureate in Rome in AD 1341. Petrarch was a friend of Rienzi, the son of an innkeeper and a washer-woman, who was inspired by the Roman classical writers to preach the reform of Rome. In 1347, Rienzi appealed to the populace and assumed the government of Rome as tribune. He was careful to associate the Church with his rule, but his extravagant conduct quickly eroded his power. The nobles rebelled and were defeated, but Rienzi was forced to abdicate by the Church and an alienated populace. Further risings occurred and in 1354 Rienzi was restored to power with the aid of the papacy in Avignon. After four months, he was killed in another rising. Petrarch's hopes for the future of Rome now centred on the return of the papacy. Pope Gregory VII returned to Rome in 1377, but on his death the following year, the cardinals were divided and two popes were elected, Urban VI, who resided at Rome, and Clement VII, at Avignon. The schism of the West lasted for forty years until the Council of Constance in 1419, when Otho Colonna was elected pope as Martin V and established himself at Rome. Civil government was placed under a first magistrate, and laws, codified as the Statutes of Rome in the sixteenth century, maintained the form of a republic under the absolute powers of the papacy. Stephen Porcaro made the last attempt to restore the ancient republic in 1453 and was executed. By the end of the century, the papacy was secure, with a military force to prevent civil disorder. In his concluding remarks, Gibbon regrets the lack of freedom and the temporal power of the papacy, but his wish is 'to depart in charity with all mankind; nor am I willing, in these last moments, to offend even the pope and clergy of Rome.' In the last footnote to the chapter, he pays tribute to Muratori, 'my guide and master in the history of Italy'.

CHAPTER 71

Prospect of the ruins of Rome in the fifteenth century – four causes of decay and destruction – example of the Coliseum – renovation of the city – conclusion of the whole work

In the last days of Pope Eugenius the Fourth, two of his servants, the learned Poggius[1] and a friend, ascended the Capitoline Hill; reposed themselves among the ruins of columns and temples; and viewed from that commanding spot, the wide and various prospect of desolation.[2] The place and the object gave ample scope for moralising on the vicissitudes of fortune, which spares neither man nor the proudest of his works, which buries empires and cities in a common grave; and it was agreed that in proportion to her former greatness the fall of Rome was the more awful and deplorable. 'Her primaeval state, such as she might appear in a remote age, when Evander entertained the stranger of Troy,[3] has been delineated by the fancy of Virgil. This Tarpeian rock was then a savage and solitary thicket: in the time of the poet, it was crowned with the golden roofs of a temple: the temple is overthrown, the gold has been pillaged, the wheel of fortune has accomplished her revolution, and the sacred ground is again disfigured with thorns and brambles. The hill of the Capitol, on which we sit, was formerly the head of the Roman empire, the citadel of the earth, the terror of kings; illustrated by the footsteps of so many triumphs, enriched with the spoils and tributes of so many nations. This spectacle of the world, how is it fallen! how changed! how defaced! The path of victory is obliterated by vines, and the benches of the senators are concealed by a dunghill. Cast your eyes on the Palatine hill, and seek, among the shapeless and enormous fragments, the marble theatre, the obelisks, the colossal statues, the porticoes of Nero's palace: survey the other hills of the city, the vacant space is interrupted only by ruins and gardens. The forum of the Roman people, where they assembled to enact their laws and elect their magistrates, is now enclosed for the cultivation of pot-herbs or thrown open for the reception of swine and buffaloes. The public and private edifices, that were founded for eternity, lie prostrate, naked, and broken, like the limbs of a mighty giant; and the ruin is the more visible, from the stupendous relics that have survived the injuries of time and fortune.'[4]

These relics are minutely described by Poggius, one of the first who raised his eyes from the monuments of legendary, to those of classic, superstition.[5] 1. Besides a bridge, an arch, a sepulchre, and the pyramid of Cestius, he could discern, of the age of the republic, a double row of vaults in the salt-office of the Capitol, which were inscribed with the name and munificence of Catulus. 2. Eleven temples were visible in some degree, from the perfect form of the Pantheon, to the three arches and a marble column of the temple of Peace, which Vespasian erected after the civil wars and the Jewish triumph. 3. Of the number, which he rashly defines, of seven *thermae*, or public baths, none were sufficiently entire to represent the use and distribution of the several parts; but those of Diocletian and Antoninus Caracalla still retained the titles of the founders, and astonished the curious spectator, who, in observing their solidity and extent, the variety of marbles, the size and multitude of the columns, compared the labour and expense with the use and importance. Of the baths of Constantine, of Alexander,* Domitian, or rather of Titus, some vestige might yet be found. 4. The triumphal arches of Titus, Severus,† and Constantine were entire, both the structure and the inscriptions; a falling fragment was honoured with the name of Trajan; and two arches, then extant in the Flaminian Way, have been ascribed to the baser memory of Faustina and Gallienus. 5. After the wonder of the Coliseum, Poggius might have overlooked a small amphitheatre of brick, most probably for the use of the praetorian camp. The theatres of Marcellus and Pompey were occupied, in a great measure, by public and private buildings; and in the Circus, Agonalis and Maximus, little more than the situation and the form could be investigated. 6. The columns of Trajan and Antonine‡ were still erect; but the Egyptian obelisks were broken or buried. A people of gods and heroes, the workmanship of art, was reduced to one equestrian figure of gilt brass, and to five marble statues, of which the most conspicuous were the two horses of Phidias and Praxiteles.§ 7. The two mausoleums or sepulchres of Augustus and Hadrian could not totally be lost; but the former was only visible as a mound of earth; and the latter, the castle of St Angelo, had acquired the name and appearance of a modern fortress. With the addition of some separate and nameless columns, such were the remains of the ancient city; for the marks of a more recent structure might be detected in the walls, which formed a circumference of ten miles, included three hundred and seventy-nine turrets, and opened into the country by thirteen gates.

This melancholy picture was drawn above nine hundred years after the fall of the Western empire, and even of the Gothic kingdom of Italy. A long period of distress and anarchy, in which empire, and arts, and riches had migrated from the banks of the Tiber, was incapable of restoring or adorning the city; and, as all that is human must retrograde if it do not advance, every successive age must have hastened the ruin of the works of antiquity. To measure the progress of decay, and to ascertain, at each era, the state of each edifice, would be an endless and a useless labour; and I shall content myself with two observations, which will introduce a short inquiry into the general causes and effects. 1. Two hundred years before the eloquent complaint of Poggius, an anonymous writer composed a description of Rome.[6] His ignorance may repeat the same objects under strange and fabulous names. Yet this barbarous topographer had eyes and ears: he could observe the visible remains; he could listen to the tradition of the people; and he distinctly enumerates seven theatres, eleven baths, twelve arches, and eighteen palaces, of which many had disappeared before the time of Poggius. It is apparent that many stately monuments of antiquity survived till a late period,[7] and that the principles of destruction acted with vigorous and increasing energy in the thirteenth and fourteenth centuries. 2. The same reflection must be applied to the three last ages;* and we should vainly seek the Septizonium† of Severus,[8] which is celebrated by Petrarch and the antiquarians of the sixteenth century. While the Roman edifices were still entire, the first blows, however weighty and impetuous, were resisted by the solidity of the mass and the harmony of the parts; but the slightest touch would precipitate the fragments of arches and columns that already nodded to their fall.

After a diligent inquiry, I can discern four principal causes of the ruin of Rome, which continued to operate in a period of more than a thousand years. I. The injuries of time and nature. II. The hostile attacks of the barbarians and Christians. III. The use and abuse of the materials. And, IV. The domestic quarrels of the Romans.

I. The art of man is able to construct monuments far more permanent than the narrow span of his own existence; yet these monuments, like himself, are perishable and frail; and, in the boundless annals of time, his life and his labours must equally be measured as a fleeting moment. Of a simple and solid edifice, it is not easy, however, to circumscribe the duration. As the wonders of ancient days, the pyramids[9] attracted the curiosity of the ancients: an hundred generations, the leaves of autumn,[10] have dropped into the grave; and, after the fall of the Pharaohs and Ptolemies, the Caesars and Caliphs, the same pyramids stand erect and unshaken above the floods of the Nile. A complex figure of various and minute parts is more accessible to injury and decay; and the silent lapse of time is often accelerated by hurricanes and earthquakes, by fires and inundations. The air and earth have doubtless been shaken; and the lofty turrets of Rome have tottered from their foundations; but the seven hills do not appear to be placed on the great cavities of the globe; nor has the city, in any age, been exposed to the convulsions of nature which, in the climate of Antioch, Lisbon, or Lima‡ have crumbled in a few moments the works of ages into dust. Fire is the most powerful agent of life and death: the rapid mischief may be kindled and propagated by the industry or negligence of mankind; and every period of the Roman annals is marked by the repetition of similar calamities. A memorable conflagration, the guilt or misfortune of Nero's reign, continued, though with unequal fury, either six or nine days.[11] Innumerable buildings, crowded in close and crooked streets, supplied perpetual fuel for the flames; and, when they ceased, four only of the fourteen regions were left entire; three were totally destroyed, and seven were deformed by the relics of smoking and lacerated edifices.[12]

In the full meridian of empire, the metropolis arose with fresh beauty from her ashes; yet the memory of the old deplored their irreparable losses, the arts of Greece, the trophies of victory, the monuments of primitive or fabulous antiquity. In the days of distress and anarchy, every wound is mortal, every fall irretrievable; nor can the damage be restored either by the public care of government or the activity of private interest. Yet two causes may be alleged, which render the calamity of fire more destructive to a flourishing than a decayed city. 1. The more combustible materials of brick, timber, and metals are first melted or consumed; but the flames may play without injury or effect on the naked walls and massy arches that have been despoiled of their ornaments. 2. It is among the common and plebeian habitations that a mischievous spark is most easily blown to a conflagration; but, as soon as they are devoured, the greater edifices which have resisted or escaped are left as so many islands in a state of solitude and safety. From her situation, Rome is exposed to the danger of frequent inundations. Without excepting the Tiber, the rivers that descend from either side of the Apennine have a short and irregular course; a shallow stream in the summer heats; an impetuous torrent, when it is swelled in the spring or winter by the fall of rain and the melting of the snows. When the current is repelled from the sea by adverse winds, when the ordinary bed is inadequate to the weight of waters, they rise above the banks, and overspread, without limits or control, the plains and cities of the adjacent country. Soon after the triumph of the first Punic war, the Tiber was increased by unusual rains; and the inundation, surpassing all former measure of time and place, destroyed all the buildings that were situate below the hills of Rome. According to the variety of ground, the same mischief was produced by different means; and the edifices were either swept away by the sudden impulse, or dissolved and undermined by the long continuance, of the flood.[13] Under the reign of Augustus, the same calamity was renewed: the lawless river overturned the palaces and temples on its banks;[14] and, after the labours of the emperor in cleansing and widening the bed that was encumbered with ruins,[15] the vigilance of his successors was exercised by similar dangers and designs. The project of diverting into new channels the Tiber itself, or some of the dependent streams, was long opposed by superstition and local interests;[16] nor did the use compensate the toil and cost of the tardy and imperfect execution. The servitude of rivers is the noblest and most important victory which man has obtained over the licentiousness of nature;[17] and, if such were the ravages of the Tiber under a firm and active government, what could oppose, or who can enumerate, the injuries of the city after the fall of the Western empire? A remedy was at length produced by the evil itself: the accumulation of rubbish and the earth that had been washed down from the hills is supposed to have elevated the plain of Rome fourteen or fifteen feet, perhaps, above the ancient level;[18] and the modern city is less accessible to the attacks of the river.[19]

II. The crowd of writers of every nation, who impute the destruction of the Roman monuments to the Goths and the Christians, have neglected to inquire how far they were animated by an hostile principle and how far they possessed the means and the leisure to satiate their enmity. In the preceding volumes of this History, I have described the triumph of barbarism and religion; and I can only resume, in a few words, their real or imaginary connection with the ruin of ancient Rome. Our fancy may create, or adopt, a pleasing romance, that the Goths and Vandals sallied from Scandinavia, ardent to avenge the flight of Odin,[20] to break the chains, and to chastise the oppressors, of mankind; that they wished to burn the records of classic literature and to found their national architecture on the broken members of the Tuscan and Corinthian orders. But, in simple truth, the northern conquerors were neither sufficiently savage nor sufficiently refined to entertain such aspiring ideas of destruction and revenge. The shepherds of Scythia and Germany had been educated in the armies of the empire, whose discipline they acquired, and whose weakness they invaded; with the familiar use of the Latin tongue, they had learned to reverence the name and titles of Rome; and, though incapable of emulating, they were more inclined to admire than to abolish, the arts and studies of a brighter period. In the transient possession of a rich and unresisting capital, the soldiers of Alaric and Genseric were stimulated by the passions of a victorious army; amidst the wanton indulgence of lust or cruelty, portable wealth was the object of their search; nor could they derive either pride or pleasure from the unprofitable reflection that they had battered to the ground the works of the consuls and Caesars. Their moments were indeed precious: the Goths evacuated Rome on the sixth,[21] the Vandals on the fifteenth, day;[22] and, though it be far more difficult to build than to destroy, their hasty assault would have made a slight impression on the solid piles of antiquity. We may remember that both Alaric and Genseric affected to spare the buildings of the city; that they subsisted in strength and beauty under the auspicious government of Theodoric;[23] and that the momentary resentment of Totila[24] was disarmed by his own temper and the advice of his friends and enemies. From these innocent barbarians the reproach may be transferred to the Catholics of Rome. The statues, altars, and houses of the daemons were an abomination in their eyes; and in the absolute command of the city they might labour with zeal and perseverance to erase the idolatry of their ancestors. The demolition of the temples of the East[25] affords to *them* an example of conduct, and to *us* an argument of belief; and it is probable that a portion of guilt or merit may be imputed with justice to the Roman proselytes. Yet their abhorrence was confined to the monuments of heathen superstition; and the civil structures that were dedicated to the business or pleasure of society might be preserved without injury or scandal. The change of religion was accomplished, not by a popular tumult, but by the decrees of the emperor, of the senate, and of time. Of the Christian hierarchy, the bishops of Rome were commonly the most prudent and least fanatic; nor can any positive charge be opposed to the meritorious act of saving and converting the majestic structure of the Pantheon.[26]

III. The value of any object that supplies the wants or pleasures of mankind is compounded of its substance and its form, of the materials and the manufacture. Its price must depend on the number of persons by whom it may be acquired and used; on the extent of the market; and consequently on the ease or difficulty of remote exportation, according to the nature of the commodity, its local situation, and the temporary circumstances of the world. The barbarian conquerors of Rome usurped in a moment the toil and treasure of successive ages; but, except the luxuries of immediate consumption, they must view without desire all that could not be removed from the city in the Gothic waggons or the fleet of the Vandals.[27] Gold and silver were the first objects of their avarice; as in every country, and in the smallest compass, they represent the most ample command of the industry and possessions of mankind. A vase or a statue of those precious metals might tempt the vanity of some barbarian chief; but the grosser multitude, regardless of the form, was tenacious only of the substance; and the melted ingots might be readily divided and stamped into the current coin of the empire. The less active or less fortunate robbers were reduced to the baser plunder of brass, lead, iron, and copper; whatever had escaped the Goths and Vandals was pillaged by the Greek tyrants; and the emperor Constans,* in his rapacious visit, stripped the bronze tiles from the roof of the Pantheon.[28] The edifices of Rome might be considered as a vast and various mine: the first labour of extracting the materials was already performed; the metals were purified and cast; the marbles were hewn and polished; and, after foreign and domestic rapine had been satiated, the remains of the city, could a purchaser have been found, were still venal. The monuments of antiquity had been left naked of their precious ornaments, but the Romans would demolish with their own hands the arches and walls, if the hope of profit could surpass the cost of the labour and exportation. If Charlemagne had fixed in Italy the seat of the Western empire, his genius would have aspired to restore, rather than to violate, the works of the Caesars; but policy confined the French monarch to the forests of Germany; his taste could be gratified only by destruction; and the new palace of Aix la Chapelle was decorated with the marbles of Ravenna[29] and Rome.[30] Five hundred years after Charlemagne, a king of Sicily, Robert,† the wisest and most liberal sovereign of the age, was supplied with the same materials by the easy navigation of the Tiber and the sea; and Petrarch‡ sighs an indignant complaint that the ancient capital of the world should adorn, from her own bowels, the slothful luxury of Naples.[31] But these examples of plunder or purchase were rare in the darker ages; and the Romans, alone and unenvied, might have applied to their private or public use the remaining structures of antiquity, if in their present form and situation they had not been useless in a great measure to the city and its inhabitants. The walls still described the old circumference, but the city had descended from the seven hills into the Campus Martius; and some of the noblest monuments which had braved the injuries of time were left in a desert, far remote from the habitations of mankind. The palaces of the senators were no longer adapted to the manners or fortunes of their indigent successors; the use of baths[32] and porticoes was forgotten; in the sixth century, the games of the theatre, amphitheatre, and circus had been interrupted; some temples were devoted to the prevailing worship; but the Christian churches preferred the holy figure of the cross; and fashion or reason had distributed, after a peculiar model, the cells and offices of the cloister. Under the ecclesiastical reign, the number of these pious foundations was enormously multiplied; and the city was crowded with forty monasteries of men, twenty of women, and sixty chapters and colleges of canons and priests,[33] who aggravated, instead of relieving, the depopulation of the tenth century. But, if the forms of ancient architecture were disregarded by a people insensible of their use and beauty, the plentiful materials were applied to every call of necessity or superstition, till the fairest columns of the Ionic and Corinthian orders, the richest marbles of Paros and Numidia, were degraded, perhaps, to the support of a convent or a stable. The daily havoc which is perpetrated by the Turks in the cities of Greece and Asia may afford a melancholy example; and, in the gradual destruction of the monuments of Rome, Sixtus the Fifth* may alone be excused for employing the stones of the Septizonium in the glorious edifice of St Peter's.[34] A fragment, a ruin, howsoever mangled or profaned, may be viewed with pleasure and regret; but the greater part of the marble was deprived of substance, as well as of place and proportion; it was burnt to lime for the purpose of cement. Since the arrival of Poggius, the temple of Concord[35] and many capital structures had vanished from his eyes; and an epigram of the same age expresses a just and pious fear that the continuance of this practice would finally annihilate all the monuments of antiquity.[36] The smallness of their numbers was the sole check on the demands and depredations of the Romans. The imagination of Petrarch might create the presence of a mighty people;[37] and I hesitate to believe that even in the fourteenth century they could be reduced to a contemptible list of thirty-three thousand inhabitants. From that period to the reign of Leo the Tenth,† if they multiplied to the amount of eighty-five thousand,[38] the increase of citizens was in some degree pernicious to the ancient city.

IV. I have reserved for the last and most potent and forcible cause of destruction, the domestic hostilities of the Romans themselves. Under the dominion of the Greek and French emperors, the peace of the city was disturbed by accidental though frequent seditions: it is from the decline of the latter, from the beginning of the tenth century, that we may date the licentiousness of private war, which violated with impunity the laws of the Code and the Gospel, without respecting the majesty of the absent sovereign or the presence and person of the vicar of Christ. In a dark period of five hundred years, Rome was perpetually afflicted by the sanguinary quarrels of the nobles and the people, the Guelphs and Ghibelines, the Colonna and Ursini; and, if much has escaped the knowledge, and much is unworthy of the notice, of history, I have exposed in the two preceding chapters the causes and effects of the public disorders. At such a time, when every quarrel was decided by the sword and none could trust their lives or properties to the impotence of law, the powerful citizens were armed for safety or offence against the domestic enemies whom they feared or hated. Except Venice alone, the same dangers and designs were common to all the free republics of Italy; and the nobles usurped the prerogative of fortifying their houses, and erecting strong towers[39] that were capable of resisting a sudden attack. The cities were filled with these hostile edifices; and the example of Lucca, which contained three hundred towers, her law, which confined their height to the measure of fourscore feet, may be extended, with suitable latitude, to the more opulent and populous states. The first step of the senator Brancaleone* in the establishment of peace and justice was to demolish (as we have already seen)† one hundred and forty of the towers of Rome; and in the last days of anarchy and discord, as late as the reign of Martin the Fifth,‡ forty-four still stood in one of the thirteen or fourteen regions of the city. To this mischievous purpose, the remains of antiquity were most readily adapted: the temples and arches afforded a broad and solid basis for the new structures of brick and stone; and we can name the modern turrets that were raised on the triumphal monuments of Julius Caesar, Titus, and the Antonines.[40] With some slight alterations, a theatre, an amphitheatre, a mausoleum, was transformed into a strong and spacious citadel. I need not repeat that the mole of Hadrian has assumed the title and form of the castle of St Angelo;[41] the Septizonium of Severus was capable of standing against a royal army;[42] the sepulchre of Metella has sunk under its outworks;[43] the theatres of Pompey and Marcellus were occupied by the Savelli[44] and Ursini families; and the rough fortress has been gradually softened to the splendour and elegance of an Italian palace. Even the churches were encompassed with arms and bulwarks, and the military engines on the roof of St Peter's were the terror of the Vatican and the scandal of the Christian world. Whatever is fortified will be attacked; and whatever is attacked may be destroyed. Could the Romans have wrested from the popes the castle of St Angelo, they had resolved, by a public decree, to annihilate that monument of servitude. Every building of defence was exposed to a siege; and in every siege the arts and engines of destruction were laboriously employed. After the death of Nicholas the

Fourth,* Rome, without a sovereign or a senate, was abandoned six months to the fury of civil war. 'The houses,' says a cardinal and poet of the times,[45] 'were crushed by the weight and velocity of enormous stones;[46] the walls were perforated by the strokes of the battering-ram; the towers were involved in fire and smoke; and the assailants were stimulated by rapine and revenge.' The work was consummated by the tyranny of the laws; and the factions of Italy alternately exercised a blind and thoughtless vengeance on their adversaries, whose houses and castles they rased to the ground.[47] In comparing the *days* of foreign, with the *ages* of domestic, hostility, we must pronounce that the latter have been far more ruinous to the city; and our opinion is confirmed by the evidence of Petrarch. 'Behold,' says the laureate, 'the relics of Rome, the image of her pristine greatness! Neither time nor the barbarian can boast the merit of this stupendous destruction: it was perpetrated by her own citizens, by the most illustrious of her sons; and your ancestors (he writes to a noble Annibaldi) have done with the battering-ram, what the Punic hero could not accomplish with the sword.'[48] The influence of the two last principles of decay must, in some degree, be multiplied by each other; since the houses and towers, which were subverted by civil war, required a new and perpetual supply from the monuments of antiquity.

These general observations may be separately applied to the amphitheatre of Titus, which has obtained the name of the Coliseum,[49] either from its magnitude or from Nero's colossal statue: an edifice, had it been left to time and nature, which might, perhaps, have claimed an eternal duration. The curious antiquaries, who have computed the numbers and seats, are disposed to believe that, above the upper row of stone steps, the amphitheatre was encircled and elevated with several stages of wooden galleries, which were repeatedly consumed by fire and restored by the emperors. Whatever was precious, or portable, or profane, the statues of gods and heroes, and the costly ornaments of sculpture, which were cast in brass, or overspread with leaves of silver and gold, became the first prey of conquest or fanaticism, of the avarice of the barbarians or the Christians. In the massy stones of the Coliseum many holes are discerned; and the two most probable conjectures represent the various accidents of its decay. These stones were connected by solid links of brass or iron, nor had the eye of rapine overlooked the value of the baser metals:[50] the vacant space was converted into a fair or market; the artisans of the Coliseum are mentioned in an ancient survey; and the chasms were perforated or enlarged, to receive the poles that supported the shops or tents of the mechanic trades.[51] Reduced to its naked majesty, the Flavian amphitheatre was contemplated with awe and admiration by the pilgrims of the North; and their rude enthusiasm broke forth in a sublime proverbial expression, which is recorded in the eighth century, in the fragments of the venerable Bede: 'As long as the Coliseum stands, Rome shall stand; when the Coliseum falls, Rome will fall; when Rome falls, the world will fall'.[52] In the modern system of war, a situation commanded by three hills would not be chosen for a fortress; but the strength of the walls and arches could resist the engines of assault; a numerous garrison might be lodged in the enclosure; and, while one faction occupied the Vatican and the Capitol, the other was entrenched in the Lateran and the Coliseum.[53]

The abolition at Rome of the ancient games must be understood with some latitude; and the carnival sports of the Testacean Mount and the Circus Agonalis[54] were regulated by the law[55] or custom of the city. The senator presided with dignity and pomp to adjudge and distribute the prizes, the gold ring, or the *pallium*,[56] as it was styled, of cloth or silk. A tribute on the Jews supplied the annual expense;[57] and the races, on foot, on horseback, or in chariots, were ennobled by a tilt and tournament of seventy-two of the Roman youth. In the year one thousand three hundred and thirty two, a bull-feast, after the fashion of the Moors and Spaniards, was celebrated in the Coliseum itself; and the living manners are painted in a diary of the times.[58] A convenient order of benches was restored; and a general proclamation, as far as Rimini and Ravenna, invited the nobles to exercise their skill and courage in this perilous adventure. The Roman ladies were marshalled in three squadrons, and seated in three balconies, which on this day, the third of September, were lined with scarlet cloth. The fair Jacova di Rovere led the matrons from beyond the Tiber, a pure and native race, who still represent the features and character of antiquity. The remainder of the city was divided, as usual, between the Colonna and Ursini; the two factions were proud of the number and beauty of their female bands: the charms of Savella Ursini are mentioned with praise; and the Colonna regretted the absence of the youngest of their house, who had sprained her ankle in the garden of Nero's tower. The lots of the champions were drawn by an old and respectable citizen; and they descended into the *arena* or pit, to encounter the wild bulls on foot, as it should seem, with a single spear. Amidst the crowd, our annalist has selected the names, colours, and devices, of twenty of the most conspicuous knights. Several of the names are the most illustrious of Rome and the ecclesiastical state; Malatesta, Polenta, della Valle, Cafarello, Savelli, Capoccio, Conti, Annibaldi, Altieri, Corsi; the colours were adapted to their taste and situation; the devices are expressive of hope or despair, and breathe the spirit of gallantry and arms. 'I am alone like the youngest of the Horatii,' the confidence of an intrepid stranger; 'I live disconsolate,' a weeping widower; 'I burn under the ashes,' a discreet lover; 'I adore Lavinia, or Lucretia,' the ambiguous declaration of a modern passion; 'My faith is as pure,' the motto of a white livery; 'Who is stronger than myself?' of a lion's hide; 'If I am drowned in blood, what a pleasant death!' the wish of ferocious courage. The pride or prudence of the Ursini restrained them from the field, which was occupied by three of their hereditary rivals, whose inscriptions denoted the lofty greatness of the Colonna name: 'Though sad, I am strong';

'Strong as I am great'; 'If I fall,' addressing himself to the spectators, 'you fall with me' – intimating (says the contemporary writer) that, while the other families were the subjects of the Vatican, they alone were the supporters of the Capitol. The combats of the amphitheatre were dangerous and bloody. Every champion successively encountered a wild bull; and the victory may be ascribed to the quadrupeds, since no more than eleven were left on the field, with the loss of nine wounded, and eighteen killed, on the side of their adversaries. Some of the noblest families might mourn, but the pomp of the funerals, in the churches of St John Lateran and St Maria Maggiore, afforded a second holiday to the people. Doubtless it was not in such conflicts that the blood of the Romans should have been shed; yet, in blaming their rashness, we are compelled to applaud their gallantry; and the noble volunteers, who display their magnificence and risk their lives under the balconies of the fair, excite a more generous sympathy than the thousands of captives and malefactors who were reluctantly dragged to the scene of slaughter.[59]

This use of the amphitheatre was a rare, perhaps a singular, festival: the demand for the materials was a daily and continual want, which the citizens could gratify without restraint or remorse. In the fourteenth century, a scandalous act of concord secured to both factions the privilege of extracting stones from the free and common quarry of the Coliseum;[60] and Poggius laments that the greater part of these stones had been burnt to lime by the folly of the Romans.[61] To check this abuse, and to prevent the nocturnal crimes that might be perpetrated in the vast and gloomy recess, Eugenius the Fourth* surrounded it with a wall; and, by a charter long extant, granted both the ground and edifice to the monks of an adjacent convent.[62] After his death, the wall was overthrown in a tumult of the people; and, had they themselves respected the noblest monument of their fathers, they might have justified the resolve that it should never be degraded to private property. The inside was damaged; but, in the middle of the sixteenth century, an era of taste and learning, the exterior circumference of one thousand six hundred and twelve feet was still entire and inviolate; a triple elevation of fourscore arches, which rose to the height of one hundred and eight feet. Of the present ruin the nephews of Paul the Third† are the guilty agents; and every traveller who views the Farnese palace may curse the sacrilege and luxury of these upstart princes.[63] A similar reproach is applied to the Barberini; and the repetition of injury might be dreaded from every reign, till the Coliseum was placed under the safeguard of religion by the most liberal of the pontiffs, Benedict the Fourteenth,‡ who consecrated a spot which persecution and fable had stained with the blood of so many Christian martyrs.[64]

When Petrarch first gratified his eyes with a view of those monuments whose scattered fragments so far surpass the most eloquent descriptions, he was astonished at the supine indifference[65] of the Romans themselves;[66] he was humbled rather than elated by the discovery that, except his friend

Rienzi and one of the Colonna, a stranger of the Rhône was more conversant with these antiquities than the nobles and natives of the metropolis.[67] The ignorance and credulity of the Romans are elaborately displayed in the old survey of the city, which was composed about the beginning of the thirteenth century; and, without dwelling on the manifold errors of name and place, the legend of the Capitol[68] may provoke a smile of contempt and indignation. 'The Capitol,' says the anonymous writer, 'is so named as being the head of the world; where the consuls and senators formerly resided for the government of the city and the globe. The strong and lofty walls were covered with glass and gold, and crowned with a roof of the richest and most curious carving. Below the citadel stood a palace, of gold for the greatest part, decorated with precious stones, and whose value might be estimated at one third of the world itself. The statues of all the provinces were arranged in order, each with a small bell suspended from its neck; and such was the contrivance of art or magic[69] that, if the province rebelled against Rome, the statue turned round to that quarter of the heavens, the bell rang, the prophet of the Capitol reported the prodigy, and the senate was admonished of the impending danger.' A second example of less importance, though of equal absurdity, may be drawn from the two marble horses, led by two naked youths, which have since been transported from the baths of Constantine to the Quirinal Hill. The groundless application of the names of Phidias and Praxiteles may perhaps be excused; but these Grecian sculptors should not have been removed above four hundred years from the age of Pericles to that of Tiberius; they should not have been transformed into two philosophers or magicians, whose nakedness was the symbol of truth and knowledge, who revealed to the emperor his most secret actions, and, after refusing all pecuniary recompense, solicited the honour of leaving this eternal monument of themselves.[70] Thus awake to the power of magic, the Romans were insensible to the beauties of art: no more than five statues were visible to the eyes of Poggius; and, of the multitudes which chance or design had buried under the ruins, the resurrection was fortunately delayed till a safer and more enlightened age.[71] The Nile, which now adorns the Vatican, had been explored by some labourers in digging a vineyard near the temple, or convent, of the Minerva; but the impatient proprietor, who was tormented by some visits of curiosity, restored the unprofitable marble to its former grave.[72] The discovery of a statue of Pompey, ten feet in length, was the occasion of a lawsuit. It had been found under a partition-wall: the equitable judge had pronounced that the head should be separated from the body, to satisfy the claims of the contiguous owners; and the sentence would have been executed, if the intercession of a cardinal and the liberality of a pope had not rescued the Roman hero from the hands of his barbarous countrymen.[73]

But the clouds of barbarism were gradually dispelled; and the peaceful authority of Martin the Fifth* and his successors restored the ornaments of the city as well as the order of the ecclesiastical state. The improvements of Rome, since the fifteenth century, have not been the spontaneous produce of freedom and industry. The first and most natural root of a great city is the labour and populousness of the adjacent country, which supplies the materials of subsistence, of manufactures, and of foreign trade. But the greater part of the Campagna of Rome is reduced to a dreary and desolate wilderness; the overgrown estates of the princes and the clergy are cultivated by the lazy hands of indigent and hopeless vassals; and the scanty harvests are confined or exported for the benefit of a monopoly. A second and more artificial cause of the growth of a metropolis is the residence of a monarch, the expense of a luxurious court, and the tributes of dependent provinces. Those provinces and tributes had been lost in the fall of the empire; and, if some streams of the silver of Peru and the gold of Brazil have been attracted by the Vatican, the revenues of the cardinals, the fees of office, the oblations of pilgrims and clients, and the remnant of ecclesiastical taxes afford a poor and precarious supply, which maintains, however, the idleness of the court and city. The population of Rome, far below the measure of the great capitals of Europe, does not exceed one hundred and seventy thousand inhabitants;[74] and, within the spacious enclosure of the walls, the largest portion of the seven hills is overspread with vineyards and ruins. The beauty and splendour of the modern city may be ascribed to the abuses of the government, to the influence of superstition. Each reign (the exceptions are rare) has been marked by the rapid elevation of a new family, enriched by the childless pontiff at the expense of the church and country. The palaces of these fortunate nephews are the most costly monuments of elegance and servitude; the perfect arts of architecture, painting, and sculpture have been prostituted in their service; and their galleries and gardens are decorated with the most precious works of antiquity, which taste or vanity has prompted them to collect. The ecclesiastical revenues were more decently employed by the popes themselves in the pomp of the Catholic worship; but it is superfluous to enumerate their pious foundation of altars, chapels, and churches, since these lesser stars are eclipsed by the sun of the Vatican, by the dome of St Peter, the most glorious structure that ever has been applied to the use of religion. The fame of Julius the Second, Leo the Tenth, and Sixtus the Fifth is accompanied by the superior merit of Bramante and Fontana, of Raphael and Michael-Angelo; and the same munificence which had been displayed in palaces and temples was directed with equal zeal to revive and emulate the labours of antiquity. Prostrate obelisks were raised from the ground and erected in the most conspicuous places; of the eleven aqueducts of the Caesars and Consuls, three were restored; the artificial rivers were conducted over a long series of old or of new arches, to discharge into marble basins a flood of salubrious and refreshing waters; and the spectator, impatient to ascend the steps of St Peter's, is detained by a column of Egyptian granite, which rises between two lofty and perpetual fountains to the height of one hundred and twenty feet. The map, the description, the monuments of ancient Rome have been elucidated by the diligence of the antiquarian and the student;[75] and the footsteps of heroes, the relics, not of superstition, but of empire, are devoutly visited by a new race of pilgrims from the remote, and once savage, countries of the North.

Of these pilgrims, and of every reader, the attention will be excited by an History of the Decline and Fall of the Roman Empire: the greatest, perhaps, and most awful scene in the history of mankind. The various causes and progressive effects are connected with many of the events most interesting in human annals: the artful policy of the Caesars, who long maintained the name and image of a free republic; the disorder of military despotism; the rise, establishment, and sects of Christianity; the foundation of Constantinople; the division of the monarchy; the invasion and settlements of the Barbarians of Germany and Scythia; the institutions of the civil law; the character and religion of Mahomet; the temporal sovereignty of the popes; the restoration and decay of the Western empire of Charlemagne; the crusades of the Latins in the East; the conquests of the Saracens and Turks; the ruin of the Greek empire; the state and revolutions of Rome in the middle age. The historian may applaud the importance and variety of his subject; but, while he is conscious of his own imperfections, he must often accuse the deficiency of his materials. It was among the ruins of the Capitol that I first conceived the idea of a work which has amused and exercised near twenty years of my life, and which, however inadequate to my own wishes, I finally deliver to the curiosity and candour of the public.

LAUSANNE, *27 June 1787*

NOTES TO CHAPTER 71

1 I have already (notes on ch. 65) mentioned the age [AD 1380–1459], character, and writings of Poggius; and particularly noticed the date of this elegant moral lecture on the varieties of fortune.

2 *Consedimus in ipsis Tarpeiae arcis ruinis, pone ingens portae cujusdam, ut puto, templi, marmoreum limen, plurimasque passim confractas columnas, unde magna ex parte prospectus urbis patet* (p. 5).

3 *Aeneid*, viii, 97–369. This ancient picture, so artfully introduced and so exquisitely finished, must have been highly interesting to an inhabitant of Rome; and our early studies allow us to sympathise in the feelings of a Roman.

4 *Capitolium adeo. . . immutatum ut vineae in senatorum subsellia successerint, stercorum ac purgamentorum receptaculum factum. Respice ad Palatinum montem . . . vasta rudera*

. . . ceteros colles perlustra omnia vacua aedificiis, ruinis vineisque oppleta conspicies (Poggius, *de Varietat. Fortunae*, p. 21).

5 See Poggius, pp. 8–22.

* *pages 1036* [Alexander Severus]

† *pages 1036* [Septimius Severus]

‡ *pages 1036* [Marcus Aurelius]

§ *pages 1036* [Greek sculptors of the 5th and 4th centuries BC]

6 *Liber de Mirabilibus Romae*, ex Registro Nicolai Cardinalis de Arragonia, in Bibliotheca St Isidori Armario IV, No. 69. This treatise, with some short but pertinent notes, has been published by Montfaucon (*Diarium Italicum*, pp. 283–301), who thus delivers his own critical opinion: *Scriptor xiiimi circiter saeculi, ut ibidem notatur, antiquariae rei imperitus, et, ut ab illo aevo, nugis et anilibus fabellis refertus: sed quia monumenta quae iis temporibus Romae supererant pro modulo recenset, non parum inde lucis mutuabitur qui Romanis antiquitatibus indagandis operam navabit.* ['A writer in around the thirteenth century, as is noted there; unskilled in history, and as was typical of those times, full of nonsense and foolish tales; but, since he gives an adequate account of the surviving monuments of Rome, he who assists in tracing the antiquities of Rome will obtain no little enlightenment from it.'] (p. 283).

7 The Père Mabillon (*Analecta*, iv, 502) has published an anonymous pilgrim of the ixth century, who, in his visit round the churches and holy places of Rome, touches on several buildings, especially porticoes, which had disappeared before the xiiith century.

* *pages 1037* [centuries]

† *pages 1037* [palace]

8 On the Septizonium, see the *Mémoires sur Pétrarque* (i, 325), Donatus (p. 338), and Nardini (pp. 117, 414).

9 The age of the pyramids is remote and unknown, since Diodorus Siculus (i, i, 44, 72) is unable to decide whether they were constructed 1000 or 3400 years before the clxxxth Olympiad. Sir John Marshman's contracted scale of the Egyptian dynasties would fix them about 2000 years before Christ (*Canon. Chronicus*, p. 47).

10 See the speech of Glaucus in the *Iliad* (VI, 146). This natural but melancholy image is familiar to Homer.

‡ *pages 1037* [Lima was destroyed by an earthquake in 1746, Lisbon in 1755.]

11 The learning and criticism of M. des Vignoles (*Histoire Critique de la République des Lettres*, viii, 74–118; ix, 172–87) dates the fire of Rome from AD 64, 19 July, and the subsequent persecution of the Christians from 15 November of the same year.

12 *Quippe in regiones quatuordecim Roma dividitur, quarum quatuor integrae manebant, tres solo tenus deiectae; septem reliquis pauca tectorum vestigia supererant, lacera et semiusta.* Among the old relics that were irreparably lost, Tacitus enumerates the temple of the Moon of Servius Tullius; the fane and altar consecrated by Evander *praesenti Herculi*; the temple of Jupiter Stator, a vow of Romulus; the palace of Numa; the temple of Vesta, *cum Penatibus populi Romani* ['together with images of the tutelar deities of the Roman people']. He then deplores the *opes tot victoriis quaesitae et Graecarum artium decora . . . multa quae seniores meminerant, quae reparari nequibant* ['wealth gained in so many victories, the splendid examples of Greek art . . . the many objects remembered by the older people which could not be restored'] (*Annal.*, xv, 40, 41).

13 AUC 507, *repentina subversio ipsius Romae praevenit triumphum Romanorum . . . diversae ignium aquarumque clades paene absumpsere urbem. Nam Tiberis insolitis auctus imbribus et ultra opinionem, vel diurnitate vel magnitudine redundans, omnia Romae aedificia in plano posita delevit. Diversae qualitates locorum ad unam convenere perniciem: quoniam et quae segnior inundatio tenuit madefacta dissolvit, et quae cursus torrentis invenit impulsa deiecit* (Orosius, *Hist.*, iv, 11, 244, edit. Havercamp). Yet we may observe that it is the plan and study of the Christian apologist to magnify the calamities of the pagan world.

14   *Vidimus flavum Tiberim retortis*
                                      Litore Etrusco violenter undis
                                      Ire deiectum monumenta Regis
                                          Templaque Vestae.   (Horat., *Carm.*, i. 2)

If the palace of Numa and temple of Vesta were thrown down in Horace's time, what was consumed of those buildings by Nero's fire could hardly deserve the epithets of *vetustissima* or *incorrupta* ['very old' or 'undamaged'].

15 *Ad coercendas inundationes alveum Tiberis laxavit ac repurgavit, completum olim ruderibus, et aedificiorum prolapsionibus coarctatum* (Suetonius, *in Augusto*, ch. 30).

16 Tacitus (*Annal.*, i, 79) reports the petitions of the different towns of Italy to the senate against the measure; and we may applaud the progress of reason. On a similar occasion local interests would undoubtedly be consulted; but an English House of Commons would reject with contempt the arguments of superstition, 'that nature had assigned to the rivers their proper course,' etc.

17 See the *Epoques de la Nature* of the eloquent and philosophic Buffon. His picture of Guyana in South America is that of a new and savage land, in which the waters are abandoned to themselves, without being regulated by human industry (pp. 212, 561, quarto edition).

18 In his *Travels in Italy*, Mr Addison (his works, ii, 98, Baskerville's edition) has observed this curious and unquestionable fact.

19 Yet, in modern times, the Tiber has sometimes damaged the city; and in the years 1530, 1557, 1598, the *Annals* of Muratori record three mischievous and memorable inundations, xiv, 268, 429; xv, 99, etc.

20 I take this opportunity of declaring that in the course of twelve years I have forgotten, or renounced, the flight of Odin from Azov to Sweden, which I never very seriously believed [Chapter 10]. The Goths are apparently Germans; but all beyond Caesar and Tacitus is darkness or fable in the antiquities of Germany.

21 [Chapter 31]

22 [Chapter 36]

23 [Chapter 39]

24 [Chapter 43]

25 [Chapter 28]

26 *Eodem tempore petiit a Phocate principe templum, quod appellant Pantheon, in quo fecit ecclesiam Sanctae Mariae semper Virginis, et omnium martyrum; in qua ecclesia princeps multa bona obtulit.* ['At that time he (the Pope) obtained from the Emperor Phocas the temple known as the Pantheon, which he converted into the Church of St Mary the Virgin and All the Martyrs; to which church the Emperor made many offerings.'] (Anastasius *vel potius Liber Pontificalis in Bonifacio IV*, in Muratori, *Script. Rerum Italicarum*, iii, i, 135). According to the anonymous writer in Montfaucon, the Pantheon had been vowed by Agrippa to Cybele and Neptune, and was dedicated by Boniface IV on the kalends of

November [AD 609] to the Virgin, *quae est mater omnium sanctorum* (pp. 297 298).

27 Flaminius Vacca (*apud* Montfaucon, pp. 155, 156; his Memoir is likewise printed, p. 21, at the end of the *Roma Antica* of Nardini), and several Romans, *doctrina graves* ['very learned men'], were persuaded that the Goths buried their treasures at Rome and bequeathed the secret marks *filiis nepotibusque* ['to their sons and grandsons']. He relates some anecdotes to prove that, in his own time, these places were visited and rifled by the Transalpine pilgrims, the heirs of the Gothic conquerors.

* *pages 1040*   [Constans II, emperor AD 641–68]

28 *Omnia quae erant in aere ad ornatum civitatis deposuit: sed et ecclesiam B. Mariae ad martyres quae de tegulis aereis cooperta discooperuit* (Anast., *in Vitalian.*, p. 141). The base and sacrilegious Greek had not even the poor pretence of plundering an heathen temple; the Pantheon was already a Catholic church.

29 For the spoils of Ravenna (*musiva atque marmora*) [mosaics and marbles] see the original grant of Pope Hadrian I to Charlemagne (*Codex Carolin.*, epist. lxvii; in Muratori, *Script Ital.*, iii, ii, 223).

30 I shall quote the authentic testimony of the Saxon poet (AD 887–99), *de Rebus gestis Caroli Magni*, v, 437–40, in the *Historians of France*, v, 180:

> Ad quae marmoreas praestabat Roma columnas,
> Quasdam praecipuas pulchra Ravenna dedit.
> De tam longinqua poterit regione vetustas
> Illius ornatum Francia ferre tibi.

['The marble columns of Rome and fair Ravenna, ancient decorative monuments from far distant parts, France will convey to your court.']

And I shall add, from the Chronicle of Sigebert (*Historians of France*, v, 378), *extruxit etiam Aquisgrani basilicam plurimae pulchritudinis, ad cuius structuram a Roma et Ravenna columnas et marmora devehi fecit.* ['He built a most splendid palace at Aix-la-Chapelle, for the construction of which he had columns and marbles transported from Rome and Ravenna.']

† *pages 1040*   [Robert of Anjou, King of Naples, AD 1309–43]

‡ *pages 1040*   [Italian poet, AD 1304–74]

31 I cannot refuse to transcribe a long passage of Petrarch (*Opp.*, pp. 536, 537, in *Epistola hortatoria ad Nicolaum Laurentium*), it is so strong and full to the point: *Nec pudor aut pietas continuit quominus impii spoliata Dei templa, occupatas arces, opes publicas, regiones urbis, atque honores magistratuum inter se divisos; (habeant?) qua una in re, turbulenti ac seditiosi homines et totius reliquae vitae consiliis et rationibus discordes, inhumani foederis stupenda societate convenirent, in pontes et moenia atque immeritos lapides desaevirent. Denique post vi vel senio collapsa palatia, quae quondam ingentes tenuerunt viri, post diruptos arcus triumphales (unde maiores horum forsitan corruerunt), de ipsius vetustatis ac propriae impietatis fragminibus vilem quaestum turpi mercimonio captare non puduit. Itaque nunc, heu dolor! heu scelus indignum! de vestris marmoreis columnis, de liminibus templorum (ad quae nuper ex orbe toto concursus devotissimus fiebat), de imaginibus sepulchrorum sub quibus patrum vestrorum venerabilis civis (cinis?) erat, ut reliquas sileam, desidiosa Neapolis adornatur. Sic paullatim ruinae ipsae deficiunt.* ['Neither shame nor piety has restrained wicked men from looting the temples, seizing the citadels, and dividing among themselves the public treasures, the districts of the city of Rome and the honours of the magistrates. These turbulent and rebellious men, who disagree on everything else in life, are astonishingly united in their barbaric agreement

on this one thing, to pillage the bridges, walls and innocent stones. Then once the palaces have collapsed (whether by force or decay), which great men once occupied, and the triumphal arches (whence many of them perhaps emerged *en masse*) – they have not scrupled to indulge in a sordid trade in these monuments of antiquity and of their own wickedness. And so today, alas, how painful, criminal and disgraceful! – slothful Naples is adorned with your marble columns, with the thresholds of the temples (where lately a most devout crowd of people used to assemble), with the tombstones beneath which lay the venerable ashes of your forefathers, to say no more. Thus the ruins themselves are gradually disappearing.'] Yet king Robert was the friend of Petrarch.

32 Yet Charlemagne washed and swam at Aix-la-Chapelle with an hundred of his courtiers (Eginhart, 22, 108, 109); and Muratori describes, as late as the year 814, the public baths which were built at Spoleto in Italy (*Annali*, vi, 416).

33 See the *Annals of Italy*, AD 988. For this and the preceding fact, Muratori himself is indebted to the Benedictine history of Père Mabillon.

* *pages 1041* [Pope, AD 1585–90]

34 *Vita di Sisto Quinto, da* Gregorio Leti, iii, 50.

35 *Porticus aedis Concordiae, quam cum primum ad urbem accessi vidi fere integram opere marmoreo admodum specioso: Romani postmodum ad calcem aedem totam et porticus partem disiectis columnis sunt demoliti* (p. 12). The temple of Concord was therefore *not* destroyed by a sedition in the xiiith century, as I have read in a manuscript treatise *del' Governo civile de Roma*, lent me formerly at Rome, and ascribed (I believe falsely) to the celebrated Gravina. Poggius likewise affirms that the sepulchre of Caecilia Metella was burnt for lime (pp. 19, 20).

36 Composed by Aeneas Sylvius, afterwards Pope Pius II, and published by Mabillon from a manuscript of the Queen of Sweden (*Musaeum Italicum*, i, 97):

> Oblectat me, Roma, tuas spectare ruinas:
>   Ex cuius lapsu gloria prisca patet.
> Sed tuus hic populus muris defossa vetustis
>   Calcis in obsequium marmora dura coquit.
> Impia tercentum si sic gens egerit annos,
>   Nullum hinc indicium nobilitatis erit.

['It delights me, Rome, to gaze upon your ruins: from your fall the glory of old is displayed. But now your people digs out the hard marble from the ancient walls and bakes it in the service of lime. If this impious race continues thus another three hundred years, no vestige of nobility will remain.']

37 *Vagabamur pariter in illa urbe tam magna; quae, cum propter spatium vacua videretur, populum habet immensum* (*Opp.*, p. 605; *Epist. Familiares*, ii, 14).

† *pages 1041* [Pope, AD 1513–31]

38 These states of the population of Rome, at different periods, are derived from an ingenious treatise of the physician Lancisi, *de Romani Coeli Qualitatibus* (p. 122).

39 All the facts that relate to the towers at Rome, and in other free cities of Italy, may be found in the laborious and entertaining compilation of Muratori, *Antiquitates Italiae medii Aevi*, xxvi (ii, 493–96, of the Latin, i, 446, of the Italian, work).

* *pages 1042* [Chief magistrate of Rome from 1252 to 1258]

† *pages 1042* [in Chapter 69]

‡ *pages 1042* [Pope, AD 1418–31]

40 As for instance, *Templum Jani nunc dicitur, turris Centii Frangapanis; et sane Jano*

impositae turris lateritiae conspicua hodieque vestigia supersunt ['The temple of Janus is now called the tower of Cencio Frangipani, and indeed, traces of the temple can be clearly seen today in the brickwork built over it'] (Montfaucon, *Diarium Italicum*, p. 186). The anonymous writer (p. 285) enumerates, *arcus Titi, turris Cartularia; arcus Julii Caesaris et Senatorum, turres de Bratis; arcus Antonini, turris de Cosectis*, etc. ['the arch of Titus – the tower of the Cartulari; the arch of Julius Caesar and the senators – the di Brati tower; the arch of Antoninus, the di Cosecti tower, etc.'].

41 *Hadriani molem . . . magna ex parte Romanorum iniuria . . . disturbavit: quod certe funditus evertissent, si eorum manibus pervia, absumptis grandibus saxis, reliqua moles exstitisset* (Poggius, *de Varietate Fortunae*, p. 12).

42 Against the emperor Henry IV [emperor, AD 1056–1106] (Muratori, *Annali d'Italia*, ix, 147) .

43 I must copy an important passage of Montfaucon: *Turris ingens rotunda . . . Caeciliae Metellae . . . sepulchrum erat, cuius muri tam solidi, ut spatium perquam minimum intus vacuum supersit: et Torre di Bove dicitur, a boum capitibus muro inscriptis. Huic sequiori aevo, tempore intestinorum bellorum, ceu urbecula adiuncta fuit, cuius moenia et turres etiamnum visuntur, ita ut sepulchrum Metellae quasi arx oppiduli fuerit. Ferventibus in urbe partibus, cum Ursini atque Columnenses mutuis cladibus perniciem inferrent civitati, in utriusve partis ditionem cederet magni momenti erat.* ['The large round tower . . . was the tomb of Caecilia Metella. Its walls are so solid that very little space remains within them. It is called *Torre di Bove* [Ox-tower] from the heads of oxen which have been drawn on the wall. In the next century, a period of civil wars, a sort of miniature city was added to it, whose walls and towers can still be seen; so that the tomb of Metella was, so to speak, the citadel of this little town. The civil war, which raged in the city, when the Ursini and the Colonna brought ruin to the state by the defeats or surrenders which they inflicted on one another, was a period of great significance.'] (p. 142).

44 See the testimonies of Donatus, Nardini, and Montfaucon. In the Savelli palace, the remains of the theatre of Marcellus are still great and conspicuous.

* *pages 1043*   [in AD 1292]

45 James, cardinal of St George *ad velum aureum* [of the golden veil], in his metrical life of Pope Celestin V, (Muratori, *Script Ital.* i, iii, 621; i, 1, 132, etc.).

> *Hoc dixisse sat est, Romam caruisse Senatu*
> *Mensibus exactis heu sex ; belloque vocatum (vocatos)*
> *In scelus, in socios fraternaque vulnera patres;*
> *Tormentis iecisse viros immania saxa;*
> *Perfodisse domus trabibus, fecisse ruinas*
> *Ignibus; incensas turres, obscuraque fumo*
> *Lumina vicino, quo sit spoliata supellex.*

46 Muratori (*Dissertazione sopra le Antiquità Italiane*, i, 427–31) finds that stone bullets, of two or three hundred pounds weight, were not uncommon; and they are sometimes computed at xii or xviii *cantari* of Genoa, each *cantaro* weighing 150 pounds.

47 The vith law of the Visconti prohibits this common and mischievous practice ; and strictly enjoins that the houses of banished citizens should be preserved *pro communi utilitate* [for the common good]. (Gualvaneus de la Flamma, in Muratori, *Script. Rerum Italicarum*, xii, 1041).

48 Petrarch thus addresses his friend, who, with shame and tears, had shown him

the *moenia, lacerae specimen miserabile Romae* ['the walls, the wretched proof of Rome's desolation'] and declared his own intention of restoring them (*Carmina Latina*, Bk ii, epist. *Paulo Annibalensi*, xii, 97, 98):

> *Nec te parva manet servatis fama ruinis*
> *Quanta quod integrae fuit olim gloria Romae*
> *Reliquiae testantur adhuc; quas longior aetas*
> *Frangere non valuit; non vis aut ira cruenti*
> *Hostis, ab egregiis franguntur civibus, heu! heu!*
> *. . . quod ille nequivit* (Hannibal)
> *Perficit hic aries.*

49 The fourth part of the *Verona illustrata* of the Marquis Maffei, professedly treats of amphitheatres, particularly those of Rome and Verona, of their dimensions, wooden galleries, etc. It is from magnitude that he derives the name of *Colosseum*, or *Coliseum*: since the same appellation was applied to the amphitheatre of Capua, without the aid of a colossal statue; since that of Nero was erected in the court (*in atrio*) of his palace, and not in the Coliseum (iv, 15–19; i, 4).

50 Joseph Maria Suarés, a learned bishop, and the author of an history of Praeneste, has composed a separate dissertation on the seven or eight probable causes of these holes, which has been since reprinted in the *Roman Thesaurus* of Sallengre. Montfaucon (*Diarium*, p. 233) pronounces the rapine of the barbarians to be the *unam germanamque causam foraminum* ['the one true reason for the holes'].

51 Donatus, *Roma Vetus et Nova*, p. 285.

52 *Quamdiu stabit Colyseus, stabit et Roma; quando cadet Colyseus, cadet Roma; quando cadet Roma, cadet et mundus* (Beda *in Excerptis seu Collectaneis, apud* Ducange *Glossar. med. et infimae Latinitatis*, ii, 407, edit. Basil). This saying must be ascribed to the Anglo-Saxon pilgrims who visited Rome before the year 735, the era of Bede's death; for I do not believe that our venerable monk ever passed the sea.

53 I cannot recover, in Muratori's original Lives of the Popes (*Script. Rerum Italicarum*, iii, i), the passage that attests this hostile partition, which must be applied to the end of the xith or the beginning of the xiith century.

54 Although the structure of the Circus Agonalis be destroyed, it still retains its form and name (Agona, Nagona, Navona): and the interior space affords a sufficient level for the purpose of racing. But the Monte Testaceo, that strange pile of broken pottery, seems only adapted for the annual practice of hurling from top to bottom some waggonloads of live hogs for the diversion of the populace (*Statuta Urbis Romae*, p. 186).

55 See the *Statuta Urbis Romae*, iii, 87, 88, 89, pp. 185, 186. I have already given an idea of this municipal code [in Chapter 70]. The races of Nagona and Monte Testaceo are likewise mentioned in the Diary of Peter Antonius, from 1404 to 1417 (Muratori, *Script. Rerum Italicarum*, xxiv, 1124).

56 The *Pallium*, which Menage so foolishly derives from *Palmarium*, is an extension of the idea and the words from the robe or cloak to the materials, and from thence to their application as a prize (Muratori, dissert. xxxiii).

57 For these expenses, the Jews of Rome paid each year 1130 florins, of which the odd thirty represented the pieces of silver for which Judas had betrayed his master to their ancestors. There was a foot-race of Jewish as well as of Christian youths (*Statuta Urbis*, ibidem).

58 This extraordinary bull-feast in the Coliseum is described, from tradition rather

than memory, by Ludovico Buonconte Monaldesco, in the most ancient fragments of Roman annals (Muratori, *Script. Rerum Italicarum*, xii, 535, 536); and, however fanciful they may seem, they are deeply marked with the colours of truth and nature.

59 Muratori has given a separate dissertation (the xxixth) to the games of the Italians in the middle ages.

60 In a concise but instructive memoir, the Abbé Barthélemy (*Mémoires de l'Académie des Inscriptions*, xxviii, p. 585) has mentioned this agreement of the factions of the xivth century *de Tiburtino faciendo* in the Coliseum, from an original act in the archives of Rome.

61 *Coliseum . . . ob stultitiam Romanorum maiori ex parte ad calcem deletum*, says the indignant Poggius (p. 17): but his expression, too strong for the present age, must be very tenderly applied to the xvth century.

* *pages 1045* [Pope, AD 1431–47]

62 Of the Olivetan monks. Montfaucon (p. 142) affirms this fact from the memorials of Flaminius Vacca (No. 72). They still hoped, on some future occasion, to revive and vindicate their grant.

† *pages 1045* [Pope, AD 1534–49]

63 After measuring the *priscus amphitheatri gyrus* [the original circumference of the amphitheatre], Montfaucon (p. 142) only adds that it was entire under Paul III; *tacendo clamat* [his silence is eloquent]. Muratori (*Annali d'Italia*, xiv, 371) more freely reports the guilt of the Farnese Pope and the indignation of the Roman people. Against the nephews of Urban VIII I have no other evidence than the vulgar saying, *Quod non fecerunt Barbari, fecere Barbarini* ['The Barbarini did what the barbarians failed to do'], which was perhaps suggested by the resemblance of the words.

‡ *pages 1045* [Pope, AD 1740–58]

64 As an antiquarian and a priest, Montfaucon thus deprecates the ruin of the Coliseum; *Quod si non suopte merito atque pulchritudine dignum fuisset quod improbas arceret manus, indigna res utique in locum tot martyrum cruore sacrum tantopere saevitum esse.*

65 Yet the Statutes of Rome (iii, 81, p. 182) impose a fine of 500 *aurei* on whosoever shall demolish any ancient edifice, *ne ruinis civitas deformetur, et ut antiqua aedificia decorem urbis perpetuo representent* ['so that the city shall not be deformed by ruins, and so that the ancient buildings shall commemorate the city in perpetuity'].

66 In his first visit to Rome (AD 1337; see *Mémoires sur Pétrarque*, i, 322, etc.), Petrarch is struck mute *miraculo rerum tantarum, et stuporis mole obrutus. . . . Praesentia vero, mirum dictu, nihil imminuit: vere maior fuit Roma maioresque sunt reliquiae quam rebar. Iam non orbem ab hac urbe domitum, sed tam sero domitum, miror* (*Opp.*, p. 605; *Familiares*, ii, 14; Joanni Columnae).

67 He excepts and praises the *rare* knowledge of John Colonna. *Qui enim hodie magis ignari rerum Romanarum, quam Romani cives? Invitus dico, nusquam minus Roma cognoscitur quam Romae.*

68 After the description of the Capitol, he adds, *statuae erant quot sunt mundi provinciae; et habebat quaelibet tintinnabulum ad collum. Et erant ita per magicam artem dispositae, ut quando aliqua regio Romano Imperio rebellis erat, statim imago illius provinciae vertebat se contra illam; unde tintinnabulum resonabat quod pendebat ad collum; tuncque vates Capitolii qui erant custodes senatui*, etc. He mentions an

example of the Saxons and Suevi, who, after they had been subdued by Agrippa, again rebelled; *tintinnabulum sonuit; sacerdos qui erat in speculo in hebdomada senatoribus nuntiavit* ['the bell rang, the priest who was on guard that week informed the senators']; Agrippa marched back and reduced the — Persians (Anonym., in Montfaucon, pp. 297, 298).

69 The same writer affirms that Virgil *captus a Romanis invisibiliter exiit ivitque Neapolim* ['having been captured by the Romans made an invisible escape and went to Naples']. A Roman magician, in the xith century, is introduced by William of Malmesbury (*de Gestis Regum Anglorum*, ii, 86); and in the time of Flaminius Vacca (No. 81, 103) it was the vulgar belief that the strangers (the *Goths*) invoked the daemons for the discovery of hidden treasures.

70 Anonym., p. 289. Montfaucon (p. 191) justly observes that, if Alexander be represented, these statues cannot be the work of Phidias (Olympiad lxxxiii), or Praxiteles (Olympiad civ), who lived before that conqueror (Pliny, *Hist. Natur.*, xxxiv, 19).

71 William of Malmesbury (ii, 86, 87) relates a marvellous discovery (AD 1046) of Pallas, the son of Evander, who had been slain by Turnus: the perpetual light in his sepulchre, a Latin epitaph, the corpse, yet entire, of a young giant, the enormous wound in his breast (*pectus perforat ingens*), etc. If this fable rests on the slightest foundation, we may pity the bodies, as well as the statues, that were exposed to the air in a barbarous age.

72 *Prope porticum Minervae, statua est recubantis, cuius caput integra effigie tantae magnitudinis, ut signa omnia excedat. Quidam ad plantandas arbores scrobes faciens detexit. Ad hoc visendum cum plures in dies magis concurrerent, strepitum adeuntium fastidiumque pertaesus, horti patronus congesta humo texit* (Poggius, *de Varietate Fortunae*, p. 12).

73 See the Memorials of Flaminius Vacca, No. 57, pp. 11, 12, at the end of the *Roma Antica* of Nardini (1704, in 4to).

* *pages 1046* [Pope, AD 1417–31]

74 In the year 1709, the inhabitants of Rome (without including eight or ten thousand Jews) amounted to 138,568 souls (Labat, *Voyages en Espagne et en Italie*, iii, 217,218). In 1740 they had increased to 146,080; and in 1765, I left them, without the Jews, 161,899. I am ignorant whether they have since continued in a progressive state.

75 The Père Montfaucon distributes his own observations into twenty days, he should have styled them weeks, or months, of his visits to the different parts of the city (*Diarium Italicum*, chs 8–20, pp. 104–301). That learned Benedictine reviews the topographers of ancient Rome; the first efforts of Blondus, Fulvius, Martianus and Faunus, the superior labours of Pyrrhus Ligorius, had his learning been equal to his labours; the writings of Onuphrius Panvinius, *qui omnes obscuravit* ['who eclipsed all others'], and the recent but imperfect books of Donatus and Nardini. Yet Montfaucon still sighs for a more complete plan and description of the old city, which must be attained by the three following methods: 1. The measurement of the space and intervals of the ruins. 2. The study of inscriptions and the places where they were found. 3. The investigation of all the acts, charters, diaries of the middle ages, which name any spot or building of Rome. The laborious work, such as Montfaucon desired, must be promoted by princely or public munificence; but the great modern plan of Nolli (AD 1748) would furnish a solid and accurate basis for the ancient topography of Rome.